Complex Digital Hardware Design

This book is about how to design the most complex types of digital circuit boards used inside servers, routers, and other equipment, from high-level system architecture down to the low-level signal integrity concepts. It explains common structures and subsystems that can be expanded into new designs in different markets.

The book is targeted to all levels of hardware engineers. There are shorter, lower-level introductions to every topic, while the book also takes the reader all the way to the most complex and most advanced topics of digital circuit design, layout design, analysis, and hardware architecture.

Istvan Nagy received a Master's degree in electrical engineering (MSC) from the Budapest University of Technology and Economics, Faculty of Electrical Engineering and Informatics, in Budapest, Hungary, in 2006. He has worked in several countries and industries, including on high-end data center networking equipment design in Silicon Valley as well as aerospace and industrial computing board design in Europe and Florida.

Complex Digital Hardware Design

Istvan Nagy

CRC Press is an imprint of the
Taylor & Francis Group, an **informa** business

Designed cover image: Meta Big Basin base board routing in the PCB layout from The Open Compute Project, the screenshot from the layout design is used for illustration under the Open Compute Project Hardware License (Permissive) Version 1.0 (The Open Compute ProjectHL-P) signed by Facebook, Inc. (Meta Platforms, Inc.).

First edition published 2024
by CRC Press
2385 NW Executive Center Drive, Suite 320, Boca Raton FL 33431

and by CRC Press
4 Park Square, Milton Park, Abingdon, Oxon, OX14 4RN

CRC Press is an imprint of Taylor & Francis Group, LLC

© 2024 Istvan Nagy

Reasonable efforts have been made to publish reliable data and information, but the author and publisher cannot assume responsibility for the validity of all materials or the consequences of their use. The authors and publishers have attempted to trace the copyright holders of all material reproduced in this publication and apologize to copyright holders if permission to publish in this form has not been obtained. If any copyright material has not been acknowledged please write and let us know so we may rectify in any future reprint.

Except as permitted under U.S. Copyright Law, no part of this book may be reprinted, reproduced, transmitted, or utilized in any form by any electronic, mechanical, or other means, now known or hereafter invented, including photocopying, microfilming, and recording, or in any information storage or retrieval system, without written permission from the publishers.

For permission to photocopy or use material electronically from this work, access www.copyright.com or contact the Copyright Clearance Center, Inc. (CCC), 222 Rosewood Drive, Danvers, MA 01923, 978-750-8400. For works that are not available on CCC please contact mpkbookspermissions@tandf.co.uk

Trademark notice: Product or corporate names may be trademarks or registered trademarks and are used only for identification and explanation without intent to infringe.

ISBN: 9781032702087 (hbk)
ISBN: 9781032702100 (pbk)
ISBN: 9781032702094 (ebk)

DOI: 10.1201/9781032702094

Typeset in Times New Roman
by Deanta Global Publishing Services, Chennai, India

Access the Support Material: www.routledge.com/9781032702087

Contents

About the Author

I have been working as a hardware design engineer for 18 years, after a 13-year student hobby electronics design "career". I worked in several different countries and industries, including industrial computers, military/aerospace boards, telecom, and leading-edge data center network equipment design in Silicon Valley. This allowed me not only to write about one specific type of product, but also to provide a wide-angle view that is applicable to many different designs the readers might be working on. Now I am sharing with you what I have learned and some of my own findings and ideas, too. Many of my designs were large multi-ASIC boards like line cards or appliance base boards. They utilized all the main large devices on the market, typically combinations of different types of processing chips. For example, having a processor, several FPGAs, and network ASICs on the same board were common.

Over the years I have received a lot of advice from Istvan Novak, as well as the community of the Si-List, about understanding the more ambiguous SI problems. The companies I worked at and the world-class hardware teams they had provided me with opportunities to work on increasingly complex and leading-edge design projects with uncommon technologies and high-performance devices.

1 Introduction

The purpose of this book is to show all aspects of a hardware design engineer's job in the more high-end digital board segments. This individual is sometimes called a hardware engineer, hardware design engineer, electrical engineer, electronics design engineer, CCA, or PCA engineer. The book is focused mainly on low-level detailed circuit implementation, but it also discusses high-level aspects like systems and manufacturing. This book is about advanced hardware design, so it is assumed that the reader has an EE degree and has already designed some lower-complexity digital circuit boards. There are short introductions to all topics, but the focus is on more advanced material.

This book includes a large amount of signal integrity topics, about half of the book's volume, and it focuses on how to apply them in a corporate design project by the designer. The rest of the topics are about hardware architecture and various engineering activities that are loosely affected by signal integrity in various ways. Complex hardware is always high speed, and it includes a large number of high-speed signals at high density. High-density, high-speed design is different from basic high-speed design with few high-speed signals. The large number of them at close proximity creates the need for advanced SI/PI mitigation solutions, which we study in this book. For example, a digital chip that has 400 instead of 4 signals running at 56Gig dissipates 400Watts, requires very high-end VRM and power plane designs, and requires a fanout pattern that takes up a very small board area for each controlled impedance via structure. Complexity also has emergent properties. Complex hardware has structures and functional circuits that do not exist in simple circuit boards. Complex boards are not simply more of the same that we see in simpler boards. For example, a microcontroller board would not need a second processor for system management. A laptop motherboard would not need several FPGAs.

The approach here is to present the intersection of signal integrity, layout constraints, firmware, and functional hardware architecture—specifically, how decisions in one domain affect the decisions that have to be made in the other domains. There is someone in the project team who has to understand all those things as one in full context, and this individual is the hardware design engineer, the target audience. This work is a bit like management, especially at large companies, and it requires making arrangements with multiple other departments daily, while also doing detailed hands-on work. Several good books on signal integrity are available, but they were written for full-time signal integrity engineers by full-time signal integrity engineers, and they focus on analysis. A hardware design engineer has several other responsibilities too, while still required to deliver SI excellence. A few books are available on hardware architecture, but they are written mainly from the marketing and user point of view and are not about how to design the underlying detailed circuits for them or why they chose those elements for the block diagram. This book seeks to improve understanding of both areas by talking about the combination of SI-driven detailed design and multi-level hardware architecture design.

Complex hardware is basically a circuit board with over 1,000 components on it and with chips that have over 600 pins, usually multiple large devices with thousands of pins each. The largest boards might have 10,000 to 20,000 components, including multiple large ASIC chips and FPGAs. Having 4k…8k are actually very common in data center network hardware and other equipment that regular consumers will never see in real life, while they all use them unknowingly every day when streaming videos or accessing media websites or smartphone apps. Hardware engineering is unlike other sciences—hardware engineers have to build new products out of several existing products. These existing products are silicon devices, other components made by third-party vendors and using board manufacturing technologies developed and marketed by service suppliers. Most of

DOI: 10.1201/9781032702094-1

this high-end data center equipment is designed in Silicon Valley (California), China, and Taiwan as well as in a few locales in Texas, Oregon, and Massachusetts. Still complex and high-speed but not the leading edge (mil/aero, telecom and consumer, with 1000...2000 components) equipment is designed at several other places, while these jobs are far from being available in every city, state, or country.

No one starts their career with a large multi-ASIC board design. That comes a few years later. Every designer has to start small, with a two-layer board with a few small chips or transistors on it, hopefully during the student years or as junior engineers. Students might have to pay for their own PCBs and components, but it is worth it. We can order them online. They then take a slightly more challenging project next with a small microcontroller or CPLD, and then again slightly more complex, maybe an ARM CPU with some memory and other chips. Students should take the initiative and decide what they want to design, do it in their free time, and pay for it with their own money. Do not wait for the professor to tell you to design it. While working as junior engineers, we have to lobby our managers to give us some cool design projects. This book does not explain these very first designs; rather, it picks up at that stage when the reader has already done a few smaller to medium-sized projects. This is because complex hardware design is a separate discipline from basic electronics, and it builds on top of it.

In the hardware industry detailed design files and drawings are considered secrets, so the only design examples used in the book are from made-up partial designs, from open-source projects, and from some of my old hobby projects. As a learning exercise, we can analyze how some of the open-source systems are built and designed and what parts and parameters go into it by reading the specifications or by reviewing their schematic and PCB layout files. This book mainly shows block diagrams and a few specific details, but the reader can find the actual schematic and layout files for reviewing the complete designs on the Internet. Any commercial design owned by different companies details cannot be shared here. Instead, specific design feature concepts are discussed, one detail at a time, or publicly available design files or on made-up partial designs. Several made-up single-issue examples are also used to demonstrate the effect of a certain parameter. Component information is provided only as long as it is also available in public datasheets, although newer under-NDA components are very similar to them, they would be designed into boards almost the same way. For most of the images and demonstrations free software tools were used, simply for the convenience of book publishing, although in the text there is discussion based on commercial software also. In real engineering we utilize various expensive commercial software, and our design files never get published as open source.

This book will refer to several standards, but explanations will be given only as much as necessary to understand hardware features or design activities. We will not be just listing the contents of each standard document for the sake of being precise or academic. Most standards have to be purchased to obtain the actual numbers, so they are omitted here. A big portion of most standards focus on how the chip designers have to implement a feature, and that is outside of the scope of this book.

In this book we use the "slang" ASIC for any large high-bandwidth digital chip, including CPUs, GPUs, FPGAs, and actual ASICs, to simplify the text. Designing boards for these four types is very similar, and most chapters are applicable to all of them. Another convention in the book is the many references to "speed" in Gbps, that is for each signal net, it does not refer to the total bandwidth of a multi-lane port, as the difficulty level for our work depends on the speed of each signal.

Most of the concepts and solutions described in this book are very common in the high-tech hardware industry—at least dozens of companies and hundreds of engineers practice them every day. Thus, they can be considered industry-wide best practices or de facto standards. Some of the ideas in the book are unique; however, they have been developed to make our work easier or more effective. For example, special diagrams made for helping the designer with pin mapping or with error checking. The data center networking industry has taken the lead in hardware technology and high-speed design in recent decades, and brand-new solutions and inventions have become common practice, having trickled down to the computing hardware industry a few years later (like the use of 56Gig SERDES), then, a few more years later, trickling down into other industries with a much larger number of companies, for example consumer and industrial electronics, medical devices, and aerospace. Thousands of engineers around the world are now starting to implement in their designs some of the things that we did 10 years ago in Silicon Valley. The design complexity in these downstream industries is not growing that much, but the processing performance and the high-speed interface implementations are.

The language and explanations here are more similar to two engineers talking at the water cooler or at a whiteboard rather than a university lecture. But we still have to involve some scientific topics like S-parameter analysis, and there are plenty of equations and flow charts also.

This book does not just provide data from expert to expert. This is also not a user manual or a datasheet or project spec. It is not just basic "information". Hardware engineering requires a kind of thinking different from most other engineering fields. We obsess for days over details that someone might dismiss as obvious. For example, "provide correct data to the simulator" . . . okay, but how do I know it is correct? Most of the time in hardware engineering we have to make decisions based on severely limited information, and this is different from simply deducting one parameter from two other parameters. A lot of design work requires reverse thinking, trying to guess what we need to do put in the design to arrive to a certain outcome or what error can cause a certain outcome. We also have to see everything through statistical (not actual) behavior and through risk management concerns. We often reiterate things everyone in the team knows for clarity, because we need super level clarity and precision for hardware engineering. Even common circuits behave differently in different boards. Expert designers know it when they see it, others stare at it without seeing it. We also use common tools in uncommon ways, and we use many lesser known tools. Many explanations in this book seem preachy or lengthy; it employs low-level philosophy to help bridge that gap. In hardware teams we get bogged down arguing these things all the time before a design or test action can be properly taken or interpreted. So it is a big part of our work—perhaps not in simple hardware projects but in complex projects for sure.

A lot of design effort goes into risk management. That is reducing the risk of getting completely nonfunctional and unfixable prototypes, and the risk of shipping unreliable production boards. This is done through various analysis tasks (spreadsheets, diagrams, and simulation) and by design fortification (like putting zero ohm resistors in the schematic and using proper power sequencing) that might seem excessive to inexperienced people. The causes of dysfunctional or unreliable hardware are often very convoluted, one will fully understand them only through experience. This is why most of these techniques are (high-tech) industry-wide best practices, followed by competent people, so most engineers do not have to create bad designs to learn from them. On the other hand, these are not basic fully documented practices such as those found in older professions (chemistry, machinery), so we cannot assume that all engineers and all companies just know it all. This book is intended to help readers learn about them so they can become more common outside of the data center industry.

Other sources of knowledge we can follow are the conferences relevant to hardware solutions. The most important conference is the DesignCon, followed by others like EdiCon, OCP Summit, and the Hot Chips Conference.

BOOK ORGANIZATION

The learning content of this book is organized in seventeen chapters.

Chapter 2 is titled "Digital Circuits". First we discuss digital signaling standards, then move onto slightly more complex standards involving signal terminations and continue in discussing basic bit-level and bus-addressing I/O protocol standards. This chapter also discusses a few key interface blocks used by many larger chips, like JTAG ports, parallel bus interfaces, and SERDES IPs.

Finally additional I/O features are discussed like debouncing, ESD protection, data corruption, and security.

Chapter 3 is titled "Major Interfaces". It continues the line of complexity where the previous chapter left off by discussing complex protocol standards like Ethernet, PCI-Express, and other modern SERDES-based high-performance interfaces.

Chapter 4 is titled "Power Supply Circuits". It describes power supply or voltage regulator module (VRM) designs from the point of view of the digital hardware designer. We digital designers mostly focus on digital circuits, but one type of analog circuit—the power supply circuit—is always present in our designs. Some aspects of these VRMs require the digital designer to handle, like power sequencing, and any features that affect or are dependent on our load ASIC chips. It is important to understand how we digital engineers work together with analog power supply engineers to ensure that the analog control loops of each VRM are fine tuned to work on our digital board.

Chapter 5 is simply titled "Components". This chapter starts out with explaining the design aspects of adding small parts into our complex circuits by describing not really the small components themselves but rather how they fit into our complex designs. After this, other slightly more complex components, the programmable active parts are introduced in several categories, like peripheral controllers, retimers, analog to digital converters, clocking chips, and bridge chips. Different connector types and mechanical parts are also discussed. This chapter ends with a discussion of the different memory chips and modules that we use.

Chapter 6 is titled "Main Chips". It is a continuation of the previous chapter, but focuses on the three main categories of the main large chips, the processors, FPGAs (Field Programmable Gate Arrays), and the ASICs (application Specific Integrated Circuits). Each has several subcategories that are introduced, together with category-specific design considerations.

Chapter 7 is titled "Hardware Architecture". It is all about how we put all these elements we learned about in all the previous chapters into complex design concepts, mainly at the block diagram level. This chapter also discusses how the different system signals of the large and small chips are connected together to create different subsystems. These are the data plane, control plane, management plane, glue logic, and power and clocking subsystems. Once we are able to create system architectures, we often divide them into multi-board systems, as described later on in this chapter. Finally, three complex board architecture examples are presented.

Chapter 8 is titled "System and Chassis". It describes the created hardware architectures from a more practical outside view or mechanical view, as they form a complete product or a system. This chapter also introduces typical systems from different industry segments and their design and internal architectural considerations, with several examples from industry, science, and aerospace, to the different types of high-end data center hardware products. These include servers, switches, and appliances.

Chapter 9 is titled "Hardware-Firmware Integration". It discusses how firmware teams develop their firmware and software that run on our hardware systems, and how we hardware engineers have to participate in teamwork with them. This includes data we have to prepare for them, and what we can expect from them. Some of the firmware is created for the sole purpose of testing out our new prototype hardware designs.

Chapter 10 is titled "Timing Analysis". It describes the complex topic of timing analysis that we sometimes have to perform on the non-SERDES types of parallel or serial interfaces. The purpose of this work is to generate trace length constraints for the layout design as well as to verify the reliability of the design.

Chapter 11 is titled "Signal Integrity". It discusses signal integrity from the point of view of the designer, not the full-time analyst. The hardware designer has to understand SI concepts, when or where to apply them, and how to interpret the results of any analysis. This chapter starts with considering scattering-parameters from stolen from RF analog engineering, then describes SI concepts that can ruin our designs, and explains what simulations really do and how to use them. It closes with the different fields of SERDES link analysis.

Chapter 12 is titled "PCB Materials and Stackups". It is related to signal integrity but focuses on how the PCB materials affect it. This chapter also explains trace impedance control, insertion loss control, various material effects, and how to design our own PCB layer stackup.

Chapter 13 is titled Power Integrity. It talks about power integrity that deals with the high-frequency behavior of the voltage rails that feed our ASIC chips. We learn about the elements and several design and analysis methods. An important part of the design is the decoupling capacitor selection, which is described through several different methods.

Chapter 14 is titled "Initial Design". This refers to all the engineering work that is being done in a project up to the point just before starting the PCB layout design. The various documents we have to produce, the analysis we have to perform, the way we select components and blocks for our block diagrams, and a little bit about how schematics of complex hardware differ from schematics of simple board designs are all explained here. Analysis is not just SI/PI or circuit simulation. We carry out a lot of analysis with a calculator and with spreadsheets and drawings or diagrams like floorplans before we are ready to settle down with the final hardware architecture and detailed schematics.

Chapter 15 is a long and important chapter titled "PCB Layout Design". This was not meant for layout only engineers and not as a layout tool training. It is more about how the hardware design engineer has to oversee and instruct the layout engineer's work on a daily basis; about what high-speed structures we want to see in the PCB. We have to understand the layout design and fabrication elements as well as the high frequency behavior of all of them. The design tool features that were developed to make the first computers and the more modern equipment accelerate and sometimes limit our ability to tame the high-frequency behavior. Complex high-speed hardware designs heavily rely on the high-speed or high-frequency behavior of the PCB layout and our methodologies employed to control them through constraints and layout instructions/reviews. We will read about how to design the different hardware portions, like decoupling networks, VRM subcircuits, SERDES link traces and vias, power planes, and memory interfaces.

Chapter 16 is titled "Prototyping". Once we have completed the hardware and layout design, our board gets manufactured, and we have to spend time in what is called the bring-up process. This is a combination of testing and measuring as well as debugging and inventing weird solutions to counteract our own design mistakes. Several interesting tools have been developed to help us with this process, for example live system boundary scan, command line Linux tools, and VRM test equipment.

Chapter 17 is titled "Measurements". It describes the measurements that we take in prototyping, during design verification testing (DVT), or sometimes in production debugging. In this book we focus on the measurement types that are more relevant to our complex high-speed hardware. These are limited oscilloscope measurements on live signals, passive PCB signal trace VNA (Vector Network analyzer) measurements, and power delivery system impedance measurements with a power-VNA and on-chip eye capture.

Chapter 18 is titled "Manufacturing". It discusses the larger scale manufacturing of our debugged and fixed designs. This is often also applicable to making the prototypes. We still have to do debugging and testing in manufacturing, which is described in this chapter. Other activities related to manufacturing, such as dealing with returned boards and analyzing them for design improvement as well as statistical reliability analysis and design considerations, are reviewed.

2 Digital Circuits

We studied basic digital circuits at university, but, in practical hardware design, there are more considerations required for designing these. These can be supporting circuits to the main chips or they can be part of the glue logic, the management subsystem, or even participate in high-bandwidth interfaces as minor functions like level translation. We also need to understand in detail the portions of the main chips that interact with other chips. Designing in any digital chip is done through interfacing their digital circuits to other chips.

2.1 I/O STANDARDS

An I/O standard is a set of standard parameters that are defined in a standard specification document that allows different chip and board vendors to build devices that can communicate with third-party devices reliably. The main difference between different I/O standards at the physical level is their voltage thresholds for logic low and logic high data value, and the termination schemes used. These I/O standards are innovations created for the purpose of achieving higher speed transmission than the previous I/O standards had, with little added cost.

We use two types of digital signals, the traditional "single-ended" signals and the "differential pairs". Memory interfaces have been pushing single-ended signaling above 5GHz, while all other types of interfaces switched over to differential above 150MHz. Single-ended is simply one single net carrying a voltage relative to the ground plane, with input logic voltage level thresholds also defined relative to the ground. Examples of I/O standards in the single-ended type are the most common CMOS with various different voltage options, the older TTL, and some newer SSTL types. Differential pairs (diffpairs in short) are made up of a single-ended signal with another single-ended signal that has the opposite value at all times, one versus zero or vice versa. Once the diffpair signals arrive to the chip input pins from the PCB trace, they are not compared against the ground level; rather, they are compared to each other. Usually, we use net names like XXX_P for the positive "leg" of the pair, and XXX_N for the negative leg. If the voltage on _P is larger than the voltage on _N then it is a logic high (one) level, otherwise a low (zero) level. The actual voltage on them relative to the ground is not too important, but it is normally either slightly below or above a "DC bias" voltage. On the PCB layout the two legs are routed together at once, with constant spacing between them maintained by the design tool, and with length matching enforced by constraints (explained later).

Most standards have an upper limit on toggling speed, or a speed versus bus length combination limit due to their terminations not being impedance matched to the trace impedance, and their timing architecture running out of time. Single-ended standards simply have absolute voltage level requirements, differential standards have differential, and common mode (bias) voltage level requirements. Some interfaces are AC-coupled, with a capacitor in series. They work only if the low frequency content is eliminated from the data stream by applying some type of encoding, and the line never stops toggling for more than a few bit periods. If AC-coupling is used then the bias (matching between transmitter and receiver) requirement is eliminated. Typically, 100 to 220nF ceramic capacitors are sufficient. The outputs have thresholds (guarantees), and the inputs also have thresholds (requirements), arranged in a way that the worst level output signal with worst-case PCB signal degradation will still meet the minimum input level requirements with a margin. This can be seen in Figure 2.1.

Differential signaling was invented to improve signal recovery from noisy and lossy channels. Common mode interference is less harmful to received differential signals, and we can

DOI: 10.1201/9781032702094-2

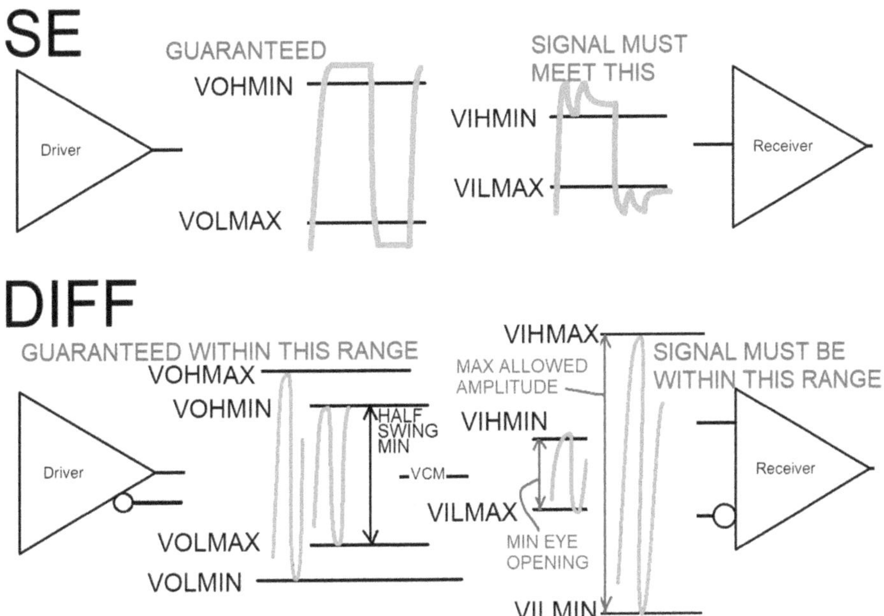

FIGURE 2.1 Signal logic levels in general.

recover data even after the single-ended amplitude has degraded 5–10 times. Differential signals are often displayed on an eye diagram, where the inside is the vertical eye opening (minimum requirement) and the outside is the amplitude (must be less than this to avoid stressing the circuits and improve signal to noise ratio). A single-ended signal would have an input eye height requirement as much as H>V_{IHMIN}-V_{ILMAX}, basically about 0.3*VDD, while differential signals have a much smaller requirement, basically as much as the input differential amplifier minimum input voltage H>Noise+Vout/Gain, about 0.05*VDD. Single-ended inputs that use a centered reference voltage threshold instead of fixed logic H/L thresholds, like the SSTLII standard, also have a small input eye height requirement, similar to differential inputs. The voltage thresholds are different in every I/O standard, as we can see in Table 2.1. The voltage level difference between the input and the output thresholds is the allowance for noises. These noises include crosstalk, reflection, insertion loss, and EMI interference. Usually we have 0.1 to 0.3*VDD, or at least 100mV gap available. Some devices (seen on their datasheets) violate the standard thresholds, so when using them we need to do a compatibility analysis (spreadsheet), checking whether we have at least 100mV gap at the low level, and a few hundred at the high level, between the transmitting and the receiving chip.

Voltage bias is part of many differential I/O standards. This pulls the signal line towards a certain voltage, which might be the same as VDD, GND, VDD/2, or any arbitrarily generated voltage level (VTT). AC-coupling is used when the transmitter and receiver chips have different and un-documented bias voltage levels. If the transmitter and receiver have (or might have) different bias voltage, then we have to use AC-coupling to prevent the two bias circuits from fighting each other (back-drive) while distorting and clipping the signal. If one chip's datasheet does not mention the bias voltage level, then we have to assume it is a different level than our other chip has, and we have to AC couple them. If the two devices are powered up at different times, for example if they are on different boards, then AC-coupling can prevent the biasing circuit from being damaged by the unpowered device shorting the signal lines to ground. We also have to check the chip's datasheet or reference design schematic for any clues about unusual cases of AC-coupling.

TABLE 2.1

Signal Logic Level Table

Name	Type	VOL min	VOL max	VOH min	VOH max	VO swing min	VIL min	VIL max	VIH min	VIH max	VI swing min	BIAS
5V CMOS	SE	0	0.5	4.44	VDD	7.88	-0.7	0.3*VDD	0.7*VDD	VDD+0.7	4	n/a
5V TTL	SE	0	0.4	2.4	VDD	4	-0.7	0.8	2	VDD+0.7	2.4	n/a
3.3V CMOS	SE	0	0.5	2.4	VDD	3.8	-0.7	0.8	2	VDD+0.7	2.4	n/a
3.3V TTL	SE	0	0.4	2.4	VDD	4	-0.7	0.8	2	VDD+0.7	2.4	n/a
1.8V CMOS	SE	0	0.45	VCC-0.45	VDD	1.8	-0.7	0.35*VDD	0.65*VDD	VDD+0.7	0.54	n/a
1.5V CMOS	SE	0	0.44	VCC-0.4	VDD	1.22	-0.7	0.35*VDD	0.65*VDD	VDD+0.7	0.45	n/a
SSTL	SE-Vr	0			VDD		0	0.5*VDD	0.5*VDD	VDD+0.7	0.1	0.5*VDD
LVPECL	Diff		1.68	2.275	VDD	0.8…1.2	0	1.825	2.135	<VDD	0.31	2
LVDS	Diff		1.252	1.249	VDD	0.25…0.45	0	1.252	1.249	<VDD	0.2	1.2
HSTL-1V5	Diff		0.4	VDD-0.4	VDD	1.4	0	VREF-0.2	VREF+0.2	<VDD	0.4	0.75
CML	Diff		VDD-0.4	VDD	VDD	0.8	0	n/a	n/a	VDD	0.4	VDD-0.2
HCSL	Diff		0	0.7	VDD	1.4	0	n/a	0.5	<VDD	0.25	n/a

2.1.1 Terminations and Reflections

Single-ended I/O standards are usually used at a slow enough data rate so that they do not need termination resistors, except if the traces are very long or the bus is really fast. Even signals that are much slower than 100MHz will still suffer from reflections since the long traces create a slow time constant for the reflection arrival (ringing) that can very well be within the ballpark of the bit time. This is when the traces become transmission lines. Low toggle rate (low-speed) signals might also have very fast rise times if the chip uses similar buffers on its high-speed and low-speed signal outputs. The reflections are naturally mitigated if the signal rise time is so slow that it does not finish rising by the time the reflected waves arrive. This creates a basic rule that terminations and trace impedance control are required if rise_time < 2* FT, where FT is the flight time of any signal through a specific length of PCB trace or cable, calculated as FT = TraceLength* SQRT(DK) / 11.8, in nanosecond and inch. The "propagation delay" is the rise time plus the flight time. For example, a 10MHz bus has 100ns bit time, but on a 5ft cable arrangement we can have reflections arriving at 2N*10ns, that is 20, 40, 60ns timestamps. We cannot use much more than 60ns rise time as it would eliminate the whole bit time. These cases require trace impedance control and some kind of termination at input pins of active devices, even on 3.3V CMOS and 5V TTL signals that are usually not terminated. They are designed to operate with low currents that would create unrecognizable logic levels when using trace impedance matched regular terminations. Terminations pull a lot of current, depending on I/O voltage. This is why these types of interfaces use AC termination, series termination, or sometimes very low I/O voltage to get within the range of the I/O buffer current drive capability. The designer has to calculate or better simulate the DC current that the termination would pull to see whether it is within the capability of the chip's output buffer.

Terminations and trace impedance starts to matter above 10MHz usually, in the same time trace impedance cannot be maintained to be flat and frequency independent below about 10MHz. It is fortunate that at the frequencies we need it, we are able to use impedance matched terminations and traces. Below 10MHz there is still a trace impedance, but it varies much with frequency, so only sine waves could have matched impedance, not wide band digital signals.

Some signals that toggle slowly in the few MHz or few mHz range are usually considered "slow signals" that do not require termination and impedance control, except if they are driven by chips that also drive very fast (like DDR3) signals on the same pin type. In that case they will have fast rise times and trigger the equation above. So below 10MHz we have to check what kind of buffer drives them. If they do need termination then we have to calculate the impedance for them at the frequency of their rise time (f=0.35/t_r), or at the 5th harmonic of their half baud rate, not at their data rate. For clock signals it is either the knee frequency or the 5th harmonic of their clock frequency. SERDES signals are analyzed at the half baud rate, called the Nyquist frequency. Signals driven by power/system management glue logic, microcontrollers, open drain buses, logic gates, and EEPROMs have slow enough rise times to use them without impedance control and matched termination. Instead of calculating the equation for every signal to determine the termination need below 10 to 200MHz data rate, we use categories and interface or device types. Another clue is if the buffer is incapable of driving enough current into a matched termination, then it also does not need impedance-controlled traces. Above 1.5V VIO the currents are unattainable for most chips. At 1.8V it would be 24mA, at 3.3V it would be 217mA.

Differential I/O standards always use terminations, especially differential clocks. Some chips have built-in input termination resistors (on-die termination, ODT), others do not; unfortunately, in many cases it is not clearly documented in the datasheet. What we can do is to add some DNP termination resistors at the receiver input. This is especially a problem for reference clock inputs. The high-speed data lines above 2Gbps always have impedance matched integrated terminations, so adding extra DNP resistors on board would distort the signal through stubs and parasitic capacitance.

Sometimes a resistor in the schematic is a bias resistor to create current on the output driver and drop voltage on it, not a termination resistor. But if its value matches the line impedance, then it also acts as termination, as is common with CML and its 50 Ohm pull up. HCSL and LVPECL outputs require biasing resistor pull-downs, at 49.9 Ohm and 130 to 200 Ohm, depending on the buffer's supply voltage. The resistor might be integrated in the device—in that case we do not need it on the board. The datasheets should help in selecting the resistor value. Sometimes an input termination is between the signal and a VTT voltage generated by the receiver chip, or they require an asymmetrical Thevenin termination that biases the input to the required VTT level, while receiving an AC-coupled signal.

Termination location can be series at source/TX, or parallel at source, or parallel at far end (at load/RX, or at the end of a multi-drop bus line). Parallel termination resistor can connect a signal line to ground, to VDD, to VTT (termination voltage, usually VDD/2), or to the complement signal in a differential pair (differential termination). If we terminate to VTT then a voltage regulator is needed to produce the VTT voltage rail, usually a fast-acting source/sink-capable LDO or a small switching buck regulator. We also create a small power shape for the VTT voltage, called the "termination island", usually on a surface layer so the many termination resistors can connect directly to it. We also need to provide decoupling to the termination island, around one 0402 100nF capacitor per 3 to 5 signals.

Parallel termination can also be a "Thevenin" type, when a 2*Z0 value resistor is connected from the signal to ground, and another one to VDD. This helps pulling the signal towards the middle. It will be more symmetrical, so it will spend equal time below the low threshold and above the high threshold, in case of symmetrical standards like LVCMOS1V8. The Thevenin termination also helps with reducing the output drive current capability requirement. For example, if we have a 1.5V CMOS system and want to do impedance matched end-termination with a 50 Ohm resistor to GND, then the output buffer will have to drive 28mA at high level and 0mA at low level. High-speed buffers with 28mA drive capability are almost non-existent. But if we use Thevenin termination of 100 Ohm up to the 1.5V rail and 100 Ohm to GND, with the same 50 Ohm impedance, now our buffer has to be able to drive only half as much, 14mA. More precisely +14mA when logic high, and -14mA when logic low. We can find many FPGAs that can do that, up to 16mA, or a few even to 24mA. The resistor value can be matched to Z0, or larger or smaller or asymmetrical to help with a signal that is already asymmetrical vertically. The upper resistor needs a return current path provided to the ground planes, so a decoupling capacitor needs to be placed at the Thevenin termination resistors, between VDD and GND. Alternatively to the Thevenin scheme we could use a single resistor terminated to VTT that is driven by a VRM at VDD/2 voltage. During a steady state this will consume less power than a Thevenin does with two resistors, as the Thevenin upper and lower resistors constantly draw current from the VDD power supply. All mentioned options of termination placement topologies can be seen in Figure 2.2. Figure 2.3 shows the waveforms produced by different termination schemes.

Termination resistor options on digital signals:

a) No terminations at all
b) Trace impedance (Z0) matched termination at both source (series) and far end (parallel)
c) Source series termination only, with impedance match

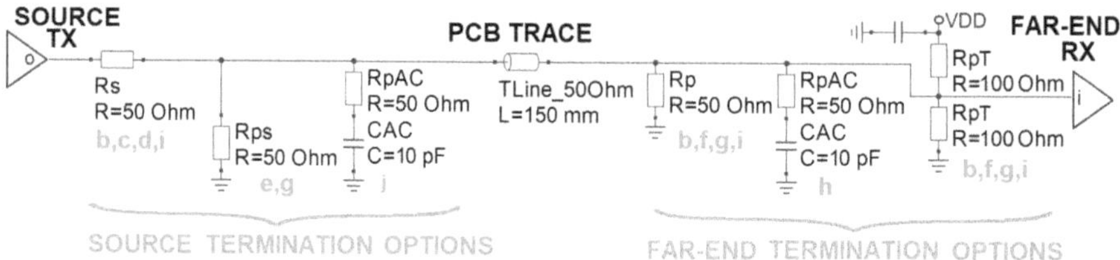

FIGURE 2.2 Termination options.

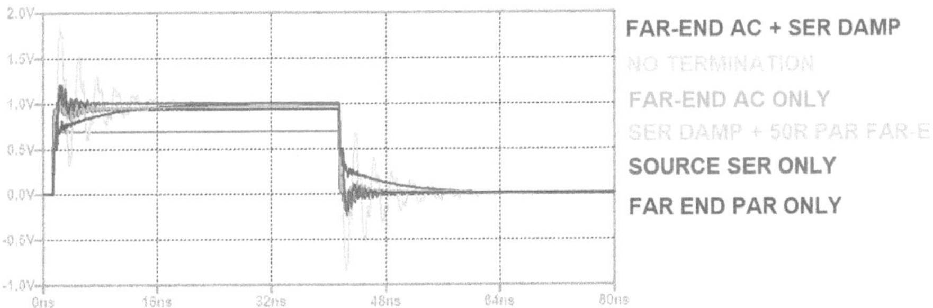

FIGURE 2.3 Mid-bus waveforms with different terminations, on a 12MHz 1V CMOS signal with an 18" long bus, LTspice simulations.

d) Source series termination only, but with Rs<<Z0
e) Source parallel termination only, with impedance match
f) Parallel at far end only, with impedance match
g) Parallel termination at source and load, with impedance match
h) Parallel AC termination at far end only, it is impedance-matched
i) Unmatched parallel termination at far end only, with Rp ~ 0.7 to 4*Z0
j) Parallel AC termination at source

Method a, the most basic option, is "No terminations at all". We can omit having any terminations only if the round-trip flight time is (much) less than the rise time, and it is much less than the bit time (just waiting out the ringing, but silicon chips might still be stressed (MTBF reduction) by overshoot and undershoot). $2*FT < t_{RISE} < t_{BIT}$

Method b is Trace impedance (Z0) matched termination at both source (series) and far end (parallel). Let us call it "full termination". This eliminates all ringing and reflections from mismatch, but there might be small reflections from discontinuities. Inputs can switch at the incident wave without having to wait for the reflections to complete the final voltage level. The logic high single-ended level will be half the VDD, formed by the voltage divider of the series TX and parallel RX termination resistors. It is only usable in differential I/O standards where the amplitude can degrade but the signal is still recovered by a difference amplifier. Half VDD signal level on CMOS is not detectable as a logic high level.

Method c is Source series termination only, with impedance match. With this scheme there will be one reflection from the far end, but that will be the last one. A device at the far end will see a little ringing, but mid-bus devices will see a two-step waveform, for them the signal setup time will be longer, as much as the roundtrip flight time instead of the length-based one-way flight time. If the capacitive load is high, it slows down the signals so much that they cannot reach proper logic levels at a given data rate. The RC delay has to be less than the round-trip delay, and the round-trip delay has to be less than half a bit time—ideally a lot less to meet setup timing too. It needs to be simulated. $R*C \ll 2*FT \ll 0.5* t_{BIT}$

Method d is Source series termination only, but with Rs<<Z0, typically 5 to 33 Ohm. This is called a damping resistor. With this scheme there will be reflections from both ends, multiple times, called ringing, with overshoot and undershoot. A device at the far end will see a little ringing, but mid-bus devices will see a two-step waveform, a big step and a small step. The RC (damping resistor with bus capacitance) delay has to be comparable to the round-trip flight time but less than half a bit time—ideally a lot less to meet setup timing too. $2*FT < R*C \ll 0.5*t_{BIT}$. Overshoot peak voltage at the far end can be as high as Vpk=2*VDD*(Z0/(Z0+Zsrc)), while at the mid-bus point it is somewhat lower but it has a plateau there. The height of the plateau is VPL=VDD*(Z0/(Z0+Zsrc)) on rising edge and VPL=VDD-VDD*(Z0/(Z0+Zsrc)) on falling edge. Needs to be simulated. Any source series termination slows down the rise time and limits the data rate. Sometimes we use it without trace impedance control, "hoping" that the trace impedance will be within 30 and 80 Ohms.

Method e is Source parallel termination only, with impedance match. With this scheme there will be one reflection from the far end, but that will be the last one, and the voltage levels are not reduced through voltage divider effect. A new transition should not start until the reflection returns to the source; this limits the speed. It requires strong output drive and low voltage signaling. Any mid-bus devices will see a two-step waveform, for them the signal setup time will be longer, as much as the round-trip delay. It is not useful for multi-drop buses, only for point-to-point topology.

Method f is Parallel termination at the far end only, with impedance match. It prevents reflections from the far end, so all devices on a multi-drop bus can act on the incident wave; there will not be a reflected wave, perfect waveforms. It requires the output drivers to have very high current capability, up to 60mA+ on 3.3V CMOS, that is not available with most chips, but 1 to 1.8V CMOS requires only up to 17 to 24mA in Thevenin mode that is available on some devices. It is mostly used on differential types with much smaller voltage levels. A 0.8Vpp differential driver would have to provide only 8mA into a 100 Ohm differential termination resistor.

Method g is Parallel termination at both the source and the load, with impedance match. This eliminates all ringing and reflections from mismatch and from discontinuities. This eliminates the voltage divider effect (distorted voltage levels) and allows high current drive and fast edge rates into capacitive load at a higher rate, and it consumes a lot of power. This is common at many gigabits per second rates. Typical SERDERS transceivers use calibrated on-die single-ended 50 Ohm (or Z0 matched) parallel terminations to internal BIAS voltage inside the far end RX circuit, and 50 Ohm pullup/bias resistors (current-mode driver that acts as termination too) to VDD inside the source TX circuit. This eliminates all reflections caused by termination values, but at high data rates there will be reflections from PCB discontinuities. Because of the bias VTT termination scheme, the signals must be AC-coupled. The internal termination resistor is automatically calibrated at power on to a 1% resistor that is connected to the ASIC calibration pin.

Method h is Parallel AC-termination at the far end only. It is an impedance-matched (39 to 60 Ohm) resistor with a capacitor (10pF to 10nF) in series. It reduces power consumption while still tries to match impedance, eliminating the multi-drop bus signal plateau. This only activates during the transitions and overshoots, and it should not affect the final logic levels. For this to work we need the capacitor to charge in less than half a bit time, but retain charge for the first period of ringing, which is dependent on trace flight time. These two requirements start to contradict above certain data rate or bus length. It needs to be simulated, but we can also use a formula: $2*FT < R*C << t_{BIT}$ Often they calculate the capacitor value C=2*FT/R in ns and nF, with R=Z0, and max data rate is: $f_{MAX}=1/(10*2*FT)$

Method i is Unmatched parallel termination at the far end only, with Rp ~ 0.7...4*Z0. This reduces overshoot amplitude, and overall ringing fade away time, while consuming less current from the output driver. We cannot consume more than the maximum output current listed in the datasheet. It is usable on LVCMOS; the output current is within grasp of a programmable FPGA I/O pin driver. The overshoot amplitude is very high, unless we combine it with a small value 5...15 Ohm source series termination.

Method j is Parallel AC termination at the source only, it is an impedance-matched (39 to 60 Ohm) resistor with a capacitor (10pF to 10nF) in series. It eliminates the second reflection at the source. It can be used in combination with far end termination types, instead of using both ends with matched parallel termination, this one requires less output drive current. The same speed limitations apply as the AC far end only option. $2*FT < R*C << t_{BIT}$

If the signal rise time is longer than the PCB trace (or cable) round-trip delay, then termination is usually not needed. This typically happens on short buses combined with low data rates below 50MHz, or long buses with very low data rates like 5–10MHz. Otherwise, unterminated lines have reflections, and they appear as plateaus and ringing after the signal transition (edge). Even if the line is matched-terminated, the parasitic RLC parameters will still cause some weaker plateaus to appear, so simulations and adjustments are necessary. The ringing first period that is the largest amplitude lasts for 4*FT. So, the pulse width (half clock period, or one bit of data) has to be at least 2 to 10 times that, meaning the pulse width has to be 8 to 40 times the flight time for these schemes to work, except the full termination. For example, if the ringing period is comparable to the signal period, then we cannot damp it without damping the signal also. This applies to source series terminations with impedance-match or small value damping, as well as to parallel RC terminations. We need to run an SI simulation with estimated trace segment lengths and IBIS models, to see if any of these three cases would work in a given design, while tuning passive part parameters, or even chip drive strength if available. The goal is to maintain acceptable logic levels, monotone edges, acceptable setup time, and not too much overshoot (<0.1*VDD). Typically, less than 0.1*VDD overshoot can be ignored ("absolute maximum ratings" in a datasheet), but the acceptable limit might be even lower on space applications (satellites, space probes, spacecraft). Even these slow signals require signal integrity simulations because we use the less perfect terminations schemes. As parallel 50 Ohms cannot be used on them; the voltage is too high and current too low for parallel termination. If it cannot be made to work on a given design with component value changes, then the trace length has to be reduced, the data rate has to be lowered, or the I/O buffer type and termination scheme have to be changed to parallel far end type with differential signaling. For the non-ideal types of terminations, like damping, and AC parallel far end termination, there is a limit to their usability, their frequency, and their trace length, depending on the situation. This is demonstrated in Figure 2.4.

There are several topologies used on different I/O standards, including point-to-point, balanced tree or balanced Tee, daisy-chain, fly-by, multi-drop, or multi-point, as shown in Figure 2.5. It depends on how many devices are on the bus as to how the signal propagates to one device versus to another device through definable transmission line segments, one after another or all at once, at what point the signal is terminated. Some can be used as unidirectional only, others can be used as bi-directional when the driver/receiver role swaps as part of the communications protocol.

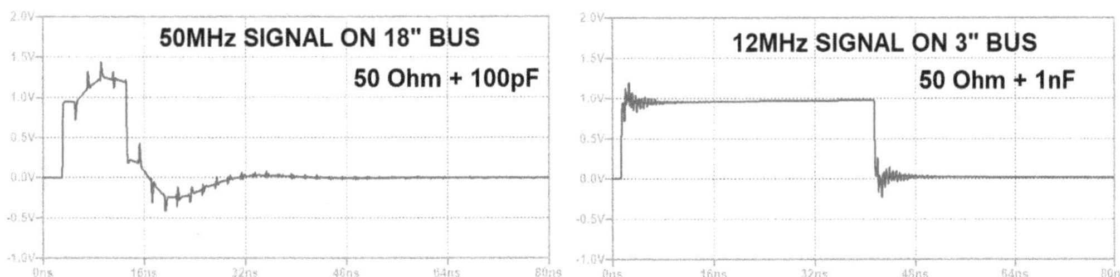

FIGURE 2.4 AC-termination effect depending on signal speed and bus length, mid-bus waveforms in Ltspice.

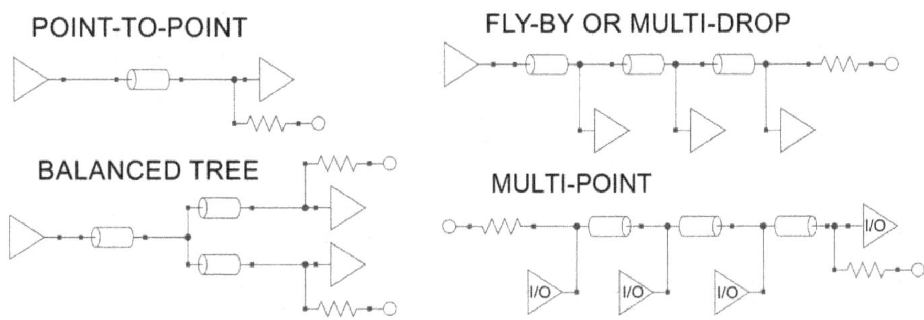

FIGURE 2.5 Bus topologies.

Multi-drop or multi-point buses, where one device is driving data onto the bus and multiple devices are listening to it along the line, have to be designed in a way that all devices can see a good signal waveform. A daisy-chain interface would mean that the output of one device is connected to the input of another device and its output to the following device. Basically, multi-drop or multi-point is a parallel connection in the schematic, while daisy-chain is serial. Sometimes people call a multi-point bus a daisy chain if they are routed on the board layout device to device without branches or splits. There are many common CMOS implementations, like PCI, SPI, VME, and LPC buses. CMOS was originally not designed for terminations, with its high voltage and low current outputs, so we can only attach weak types of terminations like damping, or parallel AC. Unless we use low voltage CMOS, at 1.8V we need 24mA drive, at 1.5V a 16mA driver might be suitable to drive impedance matched parallel terminations. Unterminated CMOS buses can cause the mid-bus devices to see a two-step waveform with a plateau due to round-trip delay, basically the signal lingering near the logic level threshold for a long time. We can see this plateau on a LTSPICE simulation in Figure 2.6. It might also cause metastability in the mid-bus devices. We have to keep the plateau away from the logic thresholds, and short to improve setup timing, by experimenting with source series and far end AC termination component values and bus length (system design) in an SI simulation. For timing analysis, the flight time seen by mid-bus devices is not based on direct routing distance, but it is based on round-trip reflected-wave delay, up to twice as much as far end devices see, unless we terminate it well. If our design is not multi-drop/point, rather point-to-point, like reference clocks, then the plateau issues can be ignored. For example, if there is only one receiver, then the plateau seen half-way on the trace will not cause any issues to the only far end receiver.

Multi-drop buses have only one driver and many receivers. On a multi-point bus any device can drive the bus, they are all bi-directional. In this case we need impedance matched parallel termination at both ends of the line if running too fast or the bus is too long. It is also necessary to route the bus as a single linear trace, without branches, so we have only two ends to terminate.

What Termination Types Should We Use

- Above about 150MHz on short buses, and above 40MHz on long buses, only parallel far end termination works, but it works only with high-current low-voltage I/O buffers.
- Source series termination with far end parallel termination is suitable only for differential singling, not for CMOS, due to the voltage divider effect.
- The "no-termination" setup can be used if the signal rise time is slow, and the trace flight time is short. $2*FT < t_{RISE}$
- We can use different combinations of these schemes, for example, source AC parallel, and far end parallel Thevenin all in the same time, or source damping with AC parallel at far

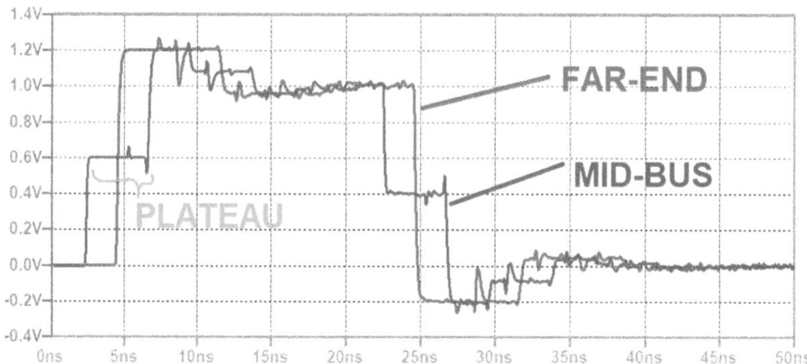

FIGURE 2.6 CMOS Multi-drop bus example, LTspice simulation.

end. The complex effect of these has to be simulated in a pre-layout SI simulation with IBIS models.

- Max data bus frequency for parallel far end termination is infinite, for matched source terminations it is $0.5/(R_S*C_{BUS}) > f < 1/(2*FT)$, for all other types the theoretical maximum is $f < 1/(5*2*FT)$, and it needs to be simulated in each case with IBIS models. For clocks (pulse width is half clock cycle) and multi-drop buses (plateau created by end reflection) the max bus frequency is half that, $f < 1/(10*2*FT)$. So, the max speed depends on bus length. If they are in a synchronous or asynchronous timing arrangement, then the round-trip access delay also limits the setup timing (longer setup time, less setup margin) and the bus frequency. See Chapter 10, "Timing Analysis".

Pullups

Open drain bi-directional buses like I2C and MDIO require a pullup resistor to pull the signal to logic high level, while the active devices will pull it to logic low level when logic low is required. The pullup resistor value has to be low enough so the signal rises fast enough (in less than half bit time), but not too low that the chip cannot pull it low enough below the output low max threshold. Bus capacitance slows down these buses, as we usually route them to many devices over long traces. The more capacitance, the lower resistor value needed. These resistor values are much higher than a termination resistor (line impedance) would be, so they do not act as terminations. When we have more than eight devices, then we usually create separate buses for them, for example, through a programmable I2C multiplexer or an analog mux.

Complex I/O Standards

We also have complex "I/O standards", which are a set of parameters together, including combinations of termination schemes, voltages, net topologies, biasing, and drive circuit designs. Table 2.2 and Figure 2.7 show a few of these complex standards and their termination options. In many cases

TABLE 2.2
Differential I/O Standards and Voltages

Standard	Drive	Termination	Vcm	Vdiff
LVDS	Push-pull	Far-end parallel 100R diff	1.25	0.7
LVPECL	Pull-up	Far-end parallel 50R SE to VTT	2	1.4
HCSL	Pull-down	Source damping + source parallel 50R	0.3	1.4
CML	Pull-down	Far-end parallel 50R SE to VTT	-	1.4

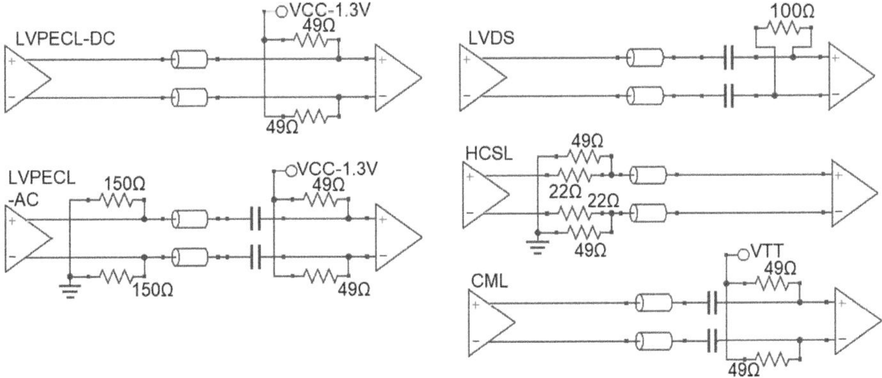

FIGURE 2.7 Differential I/O standards and terminations.

when a VTT rail is not available, we use asymmetrical Thevenin terminations, which also pull the signal line towards the right bias level. Damping resistors are also often included. Biasing resistors at inputs and outputs are not shown on the diagram; they depend on the chips, but often they follow common schemes. The chip datasheets should be able to give exact instructions on both biasing and termination resistors. CMOS and TTL standards do not include any terminations schemes, but we can add to them in custom solutions. Differential type I/O standard specifications, on the other hand, do include exact termination schemes. Some of them support both DC-coupling and AC-coupling (with series capacitor, usually 100nF). AC-coupling is preferred, as some of the ASIC inputs have undocumented bias voltage level and unusual circuits that would interfere with the output driver's biasing circuits. AC-coupling is usable only on signals that toggle constantly, like clock signals and encoded SERDES signals. Some chips have integrated terminations and biasing resistors while others require onboard resistors—we have to check their datasheets and appnotes for guidance.

High-speed SERDES links above 1GHz usually use some type of current-mode driver and AC-coupling. Starting at 25Gbps some ASIC chips have integrated AC-coupling capacitors, which eliminates the onboard AC-capacitor structure and improves signal integrity. SERDES link signal quality is usually assessed on eye diagrams, which are a waveform wrapped on itself many times, to show the different voltage levels and rising waveforms we get on different bits, depending on preceding bits, due to inter-symbol interference and reflections that have longer time constants than the bit time. Signals below 1Gbps onboard traces (not on long cables) can be assessed on simple waveforms on basic oscilloscopes.

2.1.2 PAM4 versus NRZ Signaling

Starting at 56Gbps/lane baud rate, most standards started using PAM4 signaling instead of the decades old traditional NRZ. NRZ means Non-Return to Zero, PAM4 means Pulse Amplitude Modulation 4-level. In NRZ we simply transmit a logic high voltage for "1" and a logic low voltage for "0". NRZ refers to being in contrast to an old RZ standard where every bit time's second half was zero. In PAM4 we can have one of four voltage levels in any given bit period, and the level is decoded into two bits of data. Four levels are four combinations for the on-chip digital data—in two bits of data we can have four combinations, such as 00, 01, 10, 11. Figure 2.8 shows both the typical NRZ and the PAM4 eye diagrams. Baud rate is the same as data rate for NRZ signaling, while baud rate is half the data rate for PAM4 signaling, since two bits are transmitted in each bit period. For example, 56G-PAM4 has 56G data rate and 28Gig baud rate, and we check the loss budget around half baud rate at 13GHz. Since PAM4 has about 1/3 the original voltage swing to settle the data, it is more noise sensitive than NRZ. This is why some standards only allow a 30dB loss budget for PAM4, while they allow 35dB for NRZ.

2.1.3 Level Translation

Sometimes we need to transmit data between two chips that use different I/O standards or different voltage levels. Then we have to employ level translation. In some cases (like glue logic signals) a simple resistor or two will do, at other times (buses) a level translating chip is needed. A single transistor inverts the signal. Some translators are dual VCC chips, others are single VCC clipping FET bus switches. There are level translator chips with 1 to 16 channels, their datasheets mention the supported voltage ranges on their A and B sides. They also specify which port must be the lower voltage port. For open drain buses like I2C there are special I2C level translator chips available, with two signals supported, one for SDA and one for SCL. Some translators are unidirectional, but they are controllable through a direction (DIR) pin; other translators are bi-directional in real time—having a pin for OE (output enable) is common.

Some chips are tolerant to higher voltages on their inputs, so they do not need a voltage level translation logic in between. For example, devices that are "5V Tolerant" (or 5VT), but run from

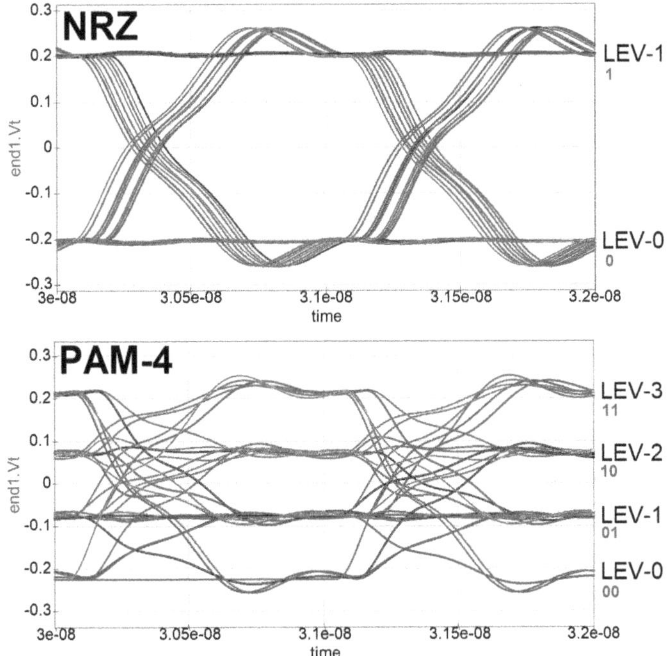

FIGURE 2.8 PAM4 versus NRZ eye diagrams in QUCS.

a 3.3V voltage rail, can receive a 5V signal on their input with neither damage to the device nor a distortion to the 5V signal.

When we try to convert between differential signals, it is important to know exactly the VCC and Vbias of both ends, but that is often not clearly documented in the datasheets. Then we have to use AC-coupling, instead of risking it, so after that only the differential swing and amplitude will have to be translated and the termination taken care of. Even if it is the same standard, but the VCC or Vbias are unknown, for example because the receiving device (ASIC chip clock input) has many voltage rails and we do not know which one is used for the clock input. Sometimes neither voltage rail is used; rather, they generate another rail internally.

A few cases of level translations are provided in the drawing in Figure 2.9, but we should always consult the datasheets for unusual termination requirements. If the VCC is different from 3.3V, then some of the termination resistors require values different from those shown on the drawing.

2.1.4 Protocols

So far in this chapter we have explained how different I/O standards were created to shape waveforms and ensure that one bit of data will be transmitted in a way that it can be recognized at the receiver. Signal levels, terminations, and routing topologies are defined in different ways, implementing different signal integrity innovations. There are also standards that are at one level higher abstraction, also called I/O standards confusingly, but they are really protocol standards. They are responsible for standardizing the bit timing and data launch and capture so devices from different vendors can share multi-bit data structures with each other. Usually an I/O protocol standard, or interface standard, is defined together with a signal-level I/O standard as a complete set of definitions. For example, the SPI bus is used together with the LVCMOS3V3 standard. The purpose of protocol standards is to ensure more complex information transmission, for example a multi-bit data and address association. In a simple case it just means 0x12345678 has to be stored in a register at address 0x9005. Some of the bus protocols allow more than two devices to exist on the same bus.

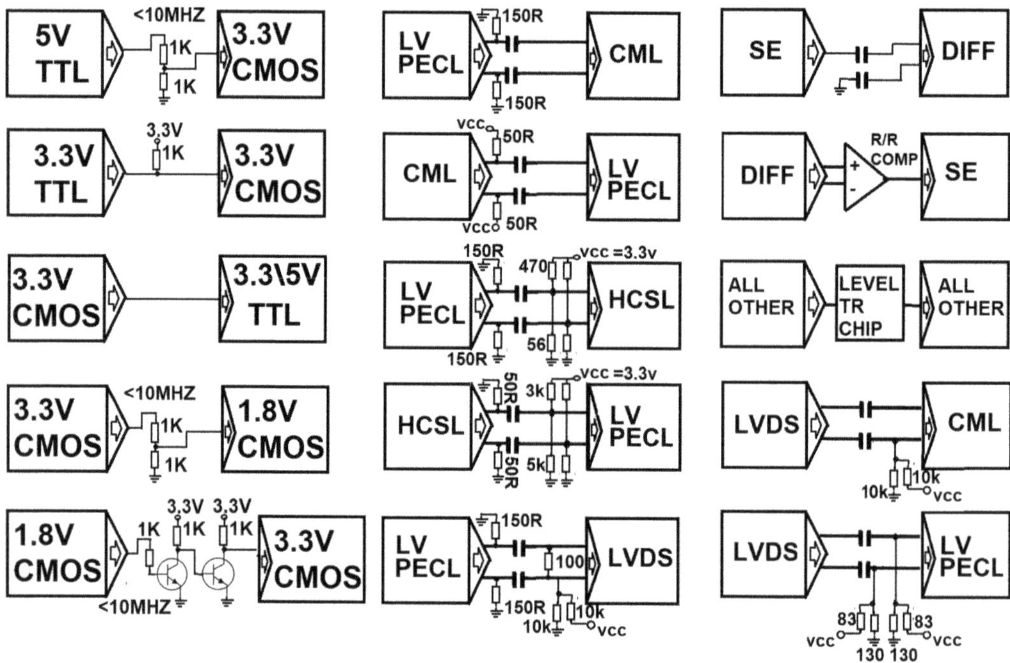

FIGURE 2.9 Basic Uni-directional level translation with passive parts.

For these cases, "addressing" was invented. Usually there is one master device that is able to talk to any one of several peripheral devices. One sequence of the master accessing one peripheral is a bus transaction. The bus transaction targets one certain device.

The master communicates the data, but before that it has to tell all devices what address it talks to. The address can be encoded in a serial stream or it can be on a bus as separate signals. Address is a binary number, where a specific combination like "01100101" refers to one specific device, often displayed in decimal or hexadecimal format. There are three types of interfaces: point to point with no addressing, with the use of chip select signals, and with a complete device address. Some interfaces are simply point to point, the data arriving is meant for whoever is seeing it, usually a single device at the other end, for example UART or SATA. The next level up is having a separate chip select signal for each slave device to tell who should respond. More complex interfaces are for when they send a data packet or bus transaction. They include the full device address, so other devices that might be listening on the shared bus and are not being talked to can ignore it. In the case of PCIe there are two device addresses, one for the system address space and one for the low level logic called destination ID. Each device knows what its own device address is, either through resistor strapping or through being written into a register during system initialization through a process called "enumeration" performed by the BIOS or the bootloader software. Strapping is done by the hardware designer, connecting the address strapping pins of the slave device to pull up or down resistors differently for each device. The strapping pins do not get connected to the bus. Usually, the upper address bits are device part number specific; the lower few bits are derived from the strapping pins. The designer has to calculate the complete address (from the datasheet) of each device and document it. PCIe and PCIe use enumeration, and I2C uses resistor strapping. Some SPI buses rely on the chip select; others also have strapping-based addressing.

Parallel buses use bus transactions with distinct timing and protocol phases like putting the address out, releasing the buffers so the other device can drive it (turnaround), data launch, and acknowledgment or handshaking. There can be multiple devices connecting to the same PCB traces. Serial interfaces use data packets, which are a complete set of bits and bytes with data and address portions, transaction type, and status indicators. Packets can be routed through packet switching ASICs by decoding the address fields before passing them through the right port. Instead of every device in the world directly connecting to every other device, the devices are connected to switches so as to save on resources.

There are two types of interfaces based on where the data go inside the receiving device. The simplest type just sends the data that the receiver chip has to decide where to put, for example, UART, Ethernet, and simple I2C or SPI implementations. They send a byte or a "packet" or perform a "bus transaction". The more complex and more common type of interface is where the data is sent with the intent to put the data into a certain location within the receiver's address space. This type uses slave devices that are handled through a register set. All communications are register reads or register writes. The transaction or packet contains the register address where the data have to be written to or read from. Most interface standards are like this, for example, PCI, PCIe, PMBUS, advanced implementations of SPI, parallel peripheral buses used on microcontrollers, and many others.

"Plug and play" is a feature available on certain interface standards. This allows a host processor to detect if something is plugged into a port or slot, determine what was plugged in, and then load the appropriate operating system driver software for it. These interfaces use slave devices that are handled through a register set. It works by having some of the registers standardized, and it contains a vendor identification code (Vendor ID) and a device identification code (Device ID). Based on this code, any modern updated operating system can identify the appropriate driver software to load, which allows application software to use the device (peripheral chip) through basic software I/O. Protocol standards that support VID/DID and Plug and Play are PCI, PCIe, USB, CXL, and a few others. In the case of PCIe, it is called "enumeration", and it is done by the BIOS firmware. Other simpler interfaces (LPC, I2C, SPI) require the firmware/software (BIOS, bootloader, or OS driver) to be hardcoded with the access location of the device, like port and address, and to know what kind of devices is there. Programmable devices that are handled through a register set will be mapped into an address range by the OS. The address range depends on what other devices are in the system, as they are determined after the power-on event. Non-transparent peer-to-peer (not master-slave) interfaces like Ethernet can be partially plug and play by a router detecting a device coming online, assigning an IP address to it, but not loading any driver or having any access to internal registers to control it. Other interfaces support detecting a plug-in card's manufacturer and model or other parameters for practical purposes other than loading an OS driver. This is typically done by accessing an EEPROM that is mounted on the plug-in module card over a side-band I2C bus. For example, DIMM memory modules, display monitors, or optical transceiver modules are made this way.

There are even more complex I/O (protocol) standards that define system management parameters and error correction, multi-lane data-splitting, with multiple layers of protocol, in some cases addressing throughout a complex chip hierarchy, sometimes through the whole world. For example, PCI-express that has three hardware layers, or various types of Ethernet interfaces that have seven hardware/software layers. Some of the layers are just basic wave forming; others are for establishing a "channel" or managing FIFO buffer levels while compensating for slight reference clock frequency differences or lane-to-lane propagation delay differences (Skew). Other chapters in this book describe common and complex protocol standards like PCIe, Ethernet, CXL, and others.

Digital pins/signals are used either as system signals or as buses/interfaces. The interfaces transmit multi-bit data chunks many times during operation, while system signals change state only once or twice during operation and indicate a device state. System signals (control or status) might be, for example, reset, interrupt, or configuration done indicators. One signal carries information, for example, if a door is closed or opened or whether another board is powered up or powered down. Most of the time they are used with glue logic FPGAs driven by VHDL/Verilog hardware state machines or management controllers. Most digital I/O pins are used to transmit data from one chip to one or more other chips. Every time they transmit a chunk (a byte, a Dword, a packet) of data, it is a "transaction". Parallel I/O completes a transaction in one or a few clock cycles; serial I/O transmits one bit after another until all bits are transmitted, to finish the one transaction. These interfaces perform transactions after transactions when needed.

A GPIO (general purpose input output) controller is a peripheral IP core built into many processors and chipsets. It is basically for implementing custom software-driven slow control and status signals (software-driven I/O). One GPIO controller is associated with several chip pins. Each pin can be set independently as an input or an output. There are at least three registers associated with the controller: The input register to read the input pin, the output register to determine output states (0 or 1), and a direction control register to set each pin to be either in input or in output mode. When a pin is set for input direction, its output driver circuit is tri-stated or disabled. Usually we access one pin using a read-modify-write software operation to make sure only one pin will change state and the others will remain as is. Each register bit refers to a specific pin. Software writes into it to change the output state. It is useful for controlling VRMs, doors, other device initialization, detecting other device status, communication flags to start/stop software routines or to signal the completion of a software task. Small microcontrollers are often used mainly through GPIOs, while X86 chipsets use a few GPIOs for low-level BIOS-related functions. Most system signals on large devices have dedicated unidirectional pins, but in some cases we use software-driven GPIO pins to connect the device to system signals if it makes sense for the particular case. We cannot just have the main reset signal to go into a GPIO input pin, but we can drive peripheral device resets out from a GPIO output on our main device. We might implement slow buses like JTAG at extremely low speeds like 1kHz—in that case we call it a "bit banging" operation.

2.1.4.1 Basic Interface Protocols

Basic low-speed interfaces that were introduced in computers decades ago are still in use in modern complex hardware, mainly in their system and power management subsystems. They can be implemented with minimal resources, without high-speed layout constraints and without high-powered chips. Some interfaces are parallel, meaning the whole data unit is transmitted in one clock cycle at once. Others are serial interfaces, where one bit is transmitted at a time in a sequence of several bits until the whole data unit (8-bit byte, 16-bit word, or 32bit Dword) gets transmitted. The interface controller block inside the chip converts a parallel bus into a serial one and vice versa.

SPI, I2C, and other buses can have additional protocols on top of the basic standard bit-serializing protocols, depending on the peripheral chip architecture, for example, how many bytes are in a transaction and what each byte is used for. Simple devices might just send a data byte, more complex devices might have a register address and a data byte in a 2byte to 4byte sequence. Even more complex devices might have device address (slave address), register address (command code), and then data bytes. Devices can support 1-byte data, 2-byte data, or 4-byte data fields. The device address is recognized by a peripheral if it matches the strapping pin state of the device. Strapping pins with pull-ups/downs are not connected to the bus; they only inform a device what its own address is. Usually, one to three address bits can be strapped, the rest are fixed and device specific (listed in the datasheet).

The I2C (Inter-Integrated Circuit) bus is a synchronous two-wire open-drain bidirectional interface operating at 100kHz or 400kHz. The two signals are the clock SCL and the data SDA. The basic protocol allows the transmission of one or more bytes of (serialized) data at a time, initiated by the I2C master device. Read transactions send an address byte, then expect a data byte(s) in return and an acknowledge bit, while writes send an address byte and one or more data bytes. Slave devices have address strapping pins to tell them what I2C address they have to respond to. The main limitation is the bus capacitance that slows down the rise time of the open drain signals if too many devices and too long traces are in a system. Usually we keep up to eight devices on one bus, and run it only at 100kHz; above that, we need to add more separate buses, otherwise devices might hang. At 400kHz it could run with one slave device. Often we need power domain isolation (with an analog multiplexer) or level translation with a bidirectional I2C level translator chip like the TCA9406 from Texas Instruments. The I2C bus is commonly used on complex boards for control plane register access to sensors, EEPROM memories, and small/simple programmable devices. The new I3C standard is a compatible improvement over I2C with more functionality (CRC, interrupts, dynamic addresses, arbitration) and higher speeds up to 12Mbps. High-end servers and DDR5 memory modules have started using I3C.

The I2C clock stretching protocol is the same as I2C, but slave and master devices support extending the response time by the slave holding the clock line low until it is able to gather the read response data. If an I2C slave uses clock stretching, then the master has to support it too. One sign that a master does not support it is if its clock pin in output only and 3state instead of open drain. The data line is always open drain on basic I2C.

SMBUS is meant to be used in low power standby subsystems, using larger value pullup resistors. Otherwise it is a data format protocol on top of the I2C bus standard. It allows register addressing within devices. The transactions are now longer—in a transaction the master sends slave address and register address (called command code). Then the data bytes or words (2 bytes) will be transmitted by the master (write) or the slave (read).

PMBUS is another protocol on top of SMBUS that is on top of I2C. PMBUS defines standard register addresses, commands, and register bit fields. This is used in some smart VRM controllers for device programming and telemetry. Figure 2.10 shows both the PMBUS protocol and the I2C waveform/protocol.

UART is a two-wire asynchronous peer-to-peer bus—one signal is for transmit, one for receive—at baud rates of 1 to 115kbps. Signaling is usually 3.3V CMOS. It does not have any complex protocol; rather, it just transmits one byte of data point to point without any addressing.

RS232 is a voltage level signaling standard on top of the UART protocol, replacing the CMOS signaling with a +/-5V signal. The RS232 transceiver chips have built-in step-up/inverting voltage regulators in the form of charge pumps. Normally we use this to control an embedded computer in a prototype during development or factory test. A computer or laptop is connected to the DUT using RS232 serial (COM) port. The laptop has to run a "hyper terminal" type application, like "putty", that displays the processor's console input and output information in text form. RS232 COM ports define seven signals (RX, TX and " signals), but we usually just use two, the RX and the TX. For external I/O a standard 9-pin DIN connector or an RJ45 connector is used.

SPI is a synchronous bus with unidirectional data lines (master-in-slave-out MISO and master-out-slave-in MOSI) and master supplied clock and chip select. SPI buses are used at 1 to 50MHz clock rates. At any rate we can have hold timing violations, and at 10 to 50MHz we can have setup violations also. A very short bus can run with one very fast device at 100MHz. This is why it is always worth using layout trace length constraints and/or doing timing analysis. It is typically used to access Flash memories or small peripheral chips, or to configure retimer chips. SPI devices are

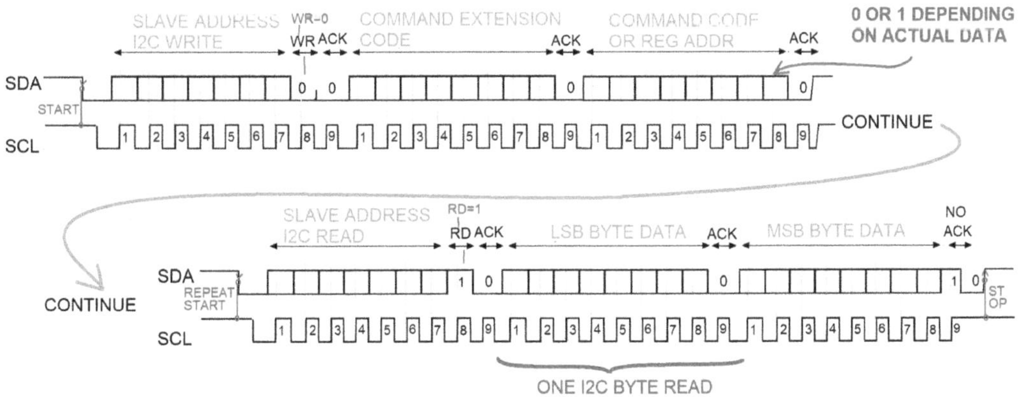

FIGURE 2.10 One PMBUS read-word transaction using 6 I2C byte transfers.

issued commands by the master, and different vendors' devices have slightly different command set support. Always check with the master device (FPGA, CPU) datasheet about what vendor and part number chips are supported. SPI bus transaction sequences can have different complexity depending on the peripheral chip—only data bytes, data bytes with register address, or data register, and device address bytes.

QSPI is an enhanced mode that some flash memory chips support when the MISO and MOSI become bi-directional, and there are two additional data lines; this increases the bandwidth four times. Usually a device starts up in 1x SPI legacy mode, then it can switch over to QSPI mode while keeping the same clock frequency.

LPC bus is a simplified version of the PCI bus with many fewer signals, typically used on X86 chipsets to access legacy devices like Super-IO controllers, port-80 decoders, or glue logic FPGAs.

Shift register interfaces can be customized for transmitting many signals over a reduced set of traces or cables. They are either serial to parallel or parallel to serial converters. We can create basic protocols using shift registers that are implemented either with discrete chips or with FPGA logic. A shift register would need a clock, a read data, a write data, and a frame signal to identify specific bit position in a serial stream. The parallel side is simply 8 to 32 data signals and a clock signal. We can implement an embedded-frame shift register interface on an FPGA to eliminate the need for a frame signal. This requires a bit-level protocol like "000000000 dddddddd1 dddddddd1 dddddddd1 11", where "d" means data bit, that an FPGA can use to extract the frame (start position). The only time nine zeroes are in one sequence is detected as the frame. This is a common clock synchronous interface, or a clock forwarding interface if we have separate read and write clocks. If there is a separate read clock for increasing the speed above 20MHz, it would need a FIFO for clock domain crossing inside the host controller and a clock loopback inside the peripheral. The round-trip delay causes the read clock at the host input to become a separate clock domain, hence the need for a FIFO. The parallel data bits can be any GPIO signals or an oversampled slow interface, or it can be a complete addressable parallel bus, in that case a system bus can be teleported into another device. If both the frame and the clock are embedded in the data stream. We call this a SERDES, in which case it requires a SERDES transceiver tile with complex protocol logic, as it is used on PCI-express and other standards.

Components that go with these interfaces are I2C multiplexers, I2C GPIO expanders, I2C accelerators, analog multiplexers (rail to rail types only), level translators, buffers, and RS232 transceivers. For more details on these components, see Chapter 5, "Components".

2.1.4.2 SPI/ISP

ISP means In-System Programming. Flash-based devices can be programmed in-system or offline before SMT assembly. Flash-FPGAs and microcontrollers are usually programmed over JTAG ports in system, while Flash memories can be programmed through either JTAG (TopJTAG Flash programmer, Corelis, or Xjtag) or through an SPI host/dongle. Many flash memory chips we use for ASIC device startup configuration have an SPI bus interface. The DediProg SF100, or the TotalPhase Aardvark with Flash Center Software can talk to the SPI-flash memory chip in-circuit and program it. We could also use a built-in embedded host processor to program it through GPIO bit bang. The way SPI bus works is that the local master (CPU, FPGA, ASIC) always drives the clock and MOSI lines and never tristates them, so we could not tap on the SPI lines with a dongle without bus contention. For this reason, we have to detach the local host ASIC from the SPI bus for the duration of the dongle programming. We can use an analog multiplexer, or, if the ASIC datasheet explicitly states that while in reset it tristates its SPI output pins, then simply device reset control can be used. When we plug in the dongle, its VCC or GND pins can be used through a header pin to drive glue logic that changes the board operating mode. These two schemes are demonstrated in Figure 2.11.

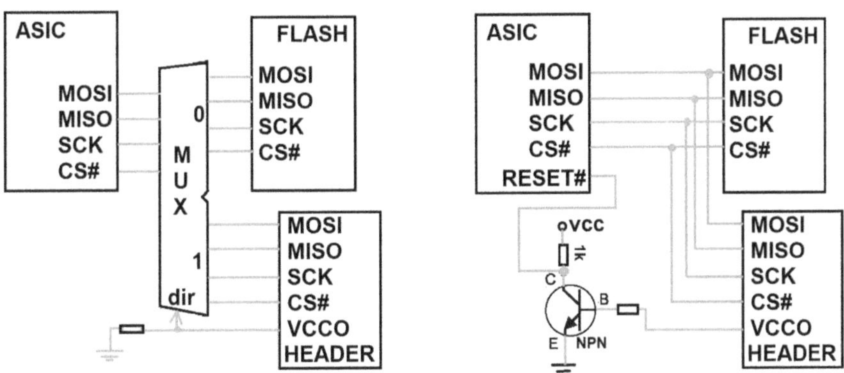

FIGURE 2.11 SPI ISP using a multiplexer and using reset control.

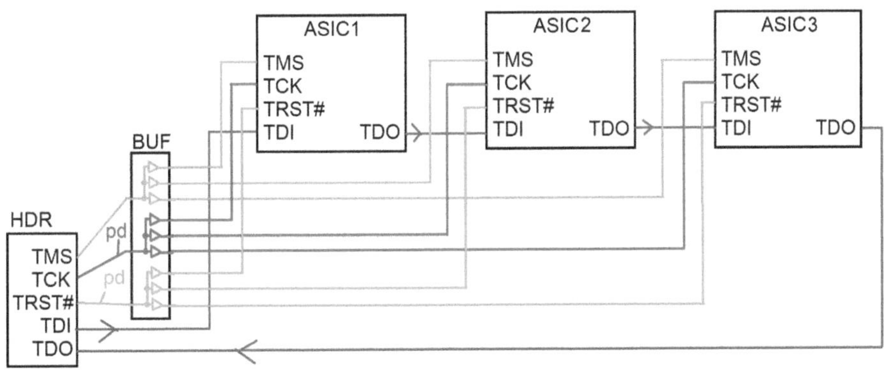

FIGURE 2.12 Typical Jtag chain.

2.2 JTAG

In the last few decades almost all complex digital chips have been built with an IEEE1149 standard JTAG interface. This interface allows several useful operations to be performed. A host computer and a test software running on it can communicate with the JTAG TAP (test access port) controller inside the DUT's ASIC chip via the 5-6 wire serial JTAG bus. Typically, a computer's USB port is cabled to a JTAG dongle adapter, which has the logic to create a JTAG bus master interface. The JTAG bus is usually implemented as a shift register chain, multiple ASICs are connected one after another, the connector's TDI signal is routed to the input of the first device, the output of the first device is routed to the input of the second device, and the output of the last device is routed to the JTAG connector. The control signals go to all devices in parallel, as we can see in Figure 2.12. A JTAG master can check what devices are in the chain by reading the IDCODEs that usually identify a part number or something recognizable. This is a common clock synchronous bus that usually goes all around the board, which can mean long traces on large boards. This typically results in a limited maximum 1 to 20MHz clock frequency, above which the data transfer fails. Buffering chips can help a little bit. JTAG software needs to know certain information about the devices on the bus, which is described in BSDL files. It usually matches the IDCODE found in devices with BSDL files found in a folder on the test computer. BSDL files are provided by ASIC vendors, but in the case of FPGAs the files have to be generated by the FPGA team so as to reflect the FPGA project pinout and signal directions (called post-configuration BSDL files). Sometimes the BSDL file contains generic names, so we may also need an FPGA pinout file to be imported. Some devices require the device reset or other signals to be toggled in a sequence with the JTAG signals to enable the JTAG port in the ASIC. In the case of processors, the code execution can be halted or stepped through a JTAG adapter+software package, called a JTAG debugger. Each FPGA and processor vendor has its own USB/JTAG dongle that has its own defined pinout and header type. We can purchase one from the vendor or from distributors.

The JTAG ports have several standard modes:

- Device programming, chip vendor specific.
- Device debugging (eye capture, program stepping), chip vendor specific.
- EXTEST mode that detaches the internal logic from the IO pins and allows the JTAG port to control all pins. In this mode the JTAG software can drive test vectors to the device's pins, and it can check on another device's pins (that are connected through a PCB trace) as to whether the correct signal level has arrived through the board. If not, then the PCB was not manufactured correctly, and there is an open or short circuit. Many production facilities have this test—they call it ICT or Boundary Scan Test. Equipment and test vector development software for production tests are available from vendors like Corelis and XJTAG. EXTEST mode can also be used for programming a flash memory chip that is attached to the JTAG capable ASIC's I/O pins.
- INTEST mode that detaches the internal logic from the IO pins and allows the JTAG port to control the internal logic, emulating a PCB to the chip.
- SAMPLE/PRELOAD mode where the ASIC chip operates normally, but the JTAG test software can sense/probe any pins logic states. They can be displayed on a computer screen as a logic analyzer real-time timing diagram. Independent software companies like TopJTag and UniversalScan offer test software at a low price. The UrJTAG command line tool is open source.
- IEEE 1149.6 AC-JTAG does boundary scan testing but through AC-coupled interfaces. At the output pin instead of setting the output to 0 or 1, we pulse it, then at the receiver instead of looking for 0 or 1 we detect a pulse. It is used with EXTEST mode on chips that support AC-JTAG.

If we have multiple devices on the same JTAG chain, and we have to program one or more of them, then we have to create chain programming files in the chip-vendor-specific developer application. This will ensure that the right device will be programmed. Most tools are able to generate a STAPL file (JESD-71 standard), that can be used by custom or third-party software.

If we put multiple devices on the same JTAG chain, then those devices are probably on different power domains. That means we can access any of the devices only when the power rails of all devices are turned on. The complication is that when one of the devices on the chain contains the power controller (power sequencing), then that device cannot be programmed because during programming it will cut power to the other devices on the chain and the chain breaks. Another issue can arise when on brand-new unprogrammed boards the power sequence is not working because the first device is unprogrammed, so the other devices prevent the first device from being programmed. Thus, we have to add a multiplexing circuit that detaches the unpowered part of the chain while we are programming the power control FPGA. The multiplexer would be controlled by a jumper or dip-switch or other simple logic. This can be seen in Figure 2.13. In many cases we need to connect a vendor specific JTAG debugger to one device (with a header direct connected to the JTAG signals of the device), and its software tool might not tolerate other vendors' devices on the same JTAG chain. This also requires bus multiplexing and isolation—either each chip vendor or each device has to be separable from the main chain. The main chain with all devices would be used for factory boundary scan testing, although most high-end testers support several independent JTAG chains to be controlled by the application at the same time. In the end the designer has to evaluate the combining versus separating needs and implement glue logic with multiplexers, buffers, or programmable logic if needed.

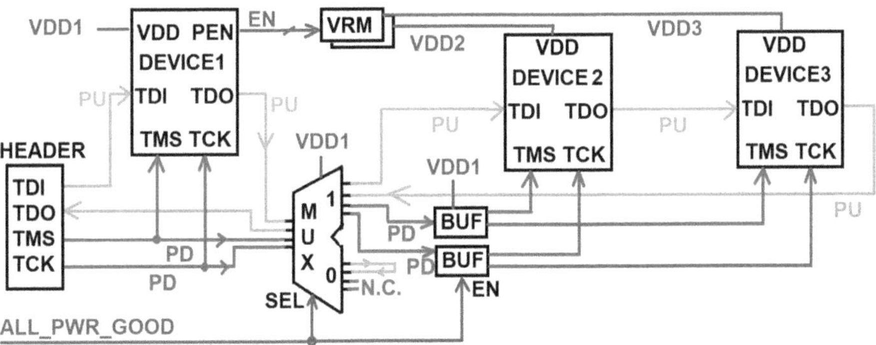

FIGURE 2.13 Switchable Jtag chain example, with one always-on device.

On complex digital boards, we often have a considerable amount of glue logic implemented using discrete logic chips (buffers and multiplexers). They are used for device isolation for debugging and early programming, power domain isolation for device protection, level translation, and buffering. JTAG buses typically run at 5 to 20MHz but can experience signal integrity issues on large boards, especially without buffering. Typically, shared signals (TMS, TCK, TRST) have multiple copies of them generated using buffers, so each has a point-to-point topology, instead of implementing them as a single net multi-drop bus. The TDI and TDO are in a daisy-chain topology where the output of one device is connected to the input of another device and its output to the following device. There are quad CMOS buffer chips available on the market in the SN75 and SN54 families, that we can use by connecting all four inputs to the programming header's TMS signal and have the four outputs separately routed to four ASICs' TMS input pins. We can use analog multiplexers to select a signal path or we can use buffers with enable pins for the same purpose. Some of this logic has to be switchable or configurable using a jumper, a dip switch, some glue logic, or a processor GPIO signal. One common trick is to use a pin on the programming header to control multiplexers, so that when a JTAG dongle is plugged in, it shorts that header pin through its ground dongle pin, otherwise pulled up on the board. We can also control the multiplexer select from a power sequencer all power good signal.

2.3 EXTERNAL PARALLEL INTERFACE

Modern high-performance processors and FPGAs/ASICs utilize point-to-point differential SERDES interfaces for data plane and control plane, like PCI-Express, DMI, or CCIX. But hardware designers often have to deal with the management subsystem, or some DSP glue logic design that implements a more traditional low speed parallel interface, to connect memory chips and peripheral controllers to a processor. Many Microcontrollers, DSPs, and FPGAs have a parallel single-ended 3.3V CMOS master bus interface that can support both synchronous (clocked) and asynchronous (strobe/handshaking-based) devices to be attached to the same bus. These can be RAM or Flash memories, custom functions implemented on FPGAs, or I/O controllers like SJA1000 CAN bus controller chip from NXP. Depending on what device the CPU is talking to, the maximum bus speed is 10 to 133MHz; it can be determined from timing analysis. Different devices on the same bus can be talked to by the CPU at different rates. The sync and async devices share the address and data signals, but they may have separate control signals. Texas Instruments (TI) calls it EMIF (external memory interface), Analog Devices calls is EBIU (external bus interface unit). A typical feature is the chip select (CS#) signal to notify one peripheral device that it is communicated to; that is asserted when the bus access goes into a certain address range, basically an address range is decoded inside the processor. We can implement further chip select signals using a small FPGA or CPLD that decodes the bus address. We can also isolate and separate the bus between devices using an FPGA, acting as a bus bridge. Separating the local bus into two segments, one close to the processor and one on the other side of the FPGA, allows the close segment to run faster without having to wait for slow devices on the other segment. The FPGA bus bridging function can be activated by a chip select coming from the processor or by the FPGA decoding and detecting pass through address ranges and generating downstream chip selects. The host interface internally is always synchronous, but externally the async devices will not receive any clock signal and rely on rising and falling edges of the strobe signals, like read strobe (RD# or OE#), write strobe (WR#), or address latch enable (ALE#). Figure 2.14 shows a generic microcontroller external interface wired up with one synchronous SDRAM memory chip, an FPGA, and an asynchronous peripheral chip. Some devices require the address and data to be sent to them on the same wires multiplexed, and the address latch enable signal tells them at what stage the signal represents address and when it represents data. The implementations of these vary a lot between different processors, for example, the signal active edges or the timing and protocols, so we need to study the datasheets of the processor and the peripheral chips before designing a board with them.

2.3.1 Synchronous Mode

In synchronous mode the processor talks to synchronous devices like SDRAMs, FIFOs, and FPGAs. The transactions involve address, data, I/O clock, chip select, write and read enable, and SDRAM-specific control signals. Every signal will be sampled at the rising edge of the clock by the receiving device. Some of the signals are shared between synchronous and asynchronous devices, like the ones with the most numerous pins, the data, and address buses. Usually, the clock is provided by the processor to the memory/peripheral chips. If we have to feed clock to more than one device, then we need a clock fanout buffer, specifically a "zero delay clock buffer", that eliminates the input to output phase difference by using a PLL to prevent any static timing issues. As we can see in Figure 2.15, chip select #2 is asserted twice, first for a read access to a synchronous peripheral, then for a write access to the same peripheral. We can see the first transaction starts with the chip select, the read signal, and the address launched after the same clock rising edge by the CPU, which the device samples at the next clock rising edge, then after some access latency it launches the read data onto the bus, which the CPU samples at the next clock rising edge, then takes away the CS/RD/ADDR signals to end the transaction.

2.3.2 Asynchronous Mode

Asynchronous devices do not rely on clock; instead, they sample data on the rising edge of the read and write strobes, and they launch data on the falling edge of the strobes. The strobes are programmed to be as long as the devices need based on their datasheet. The bit timing is described in detail in Chapter 10, "Timing Analysis".

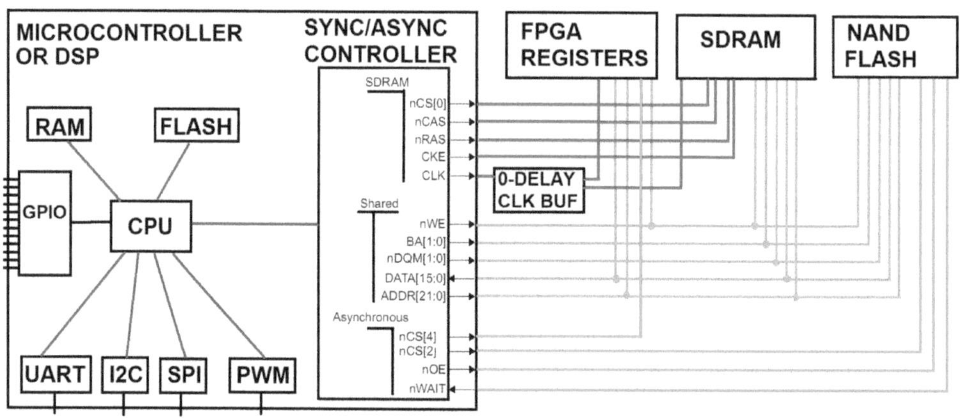

FIGURE 2.14 General microcontroller external memory interface (sketch).

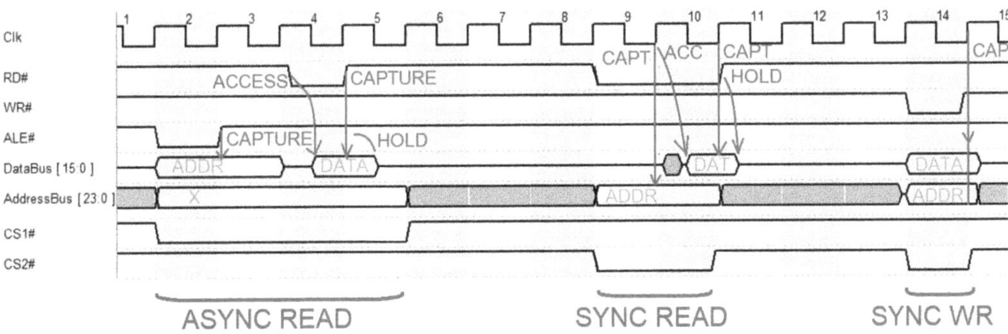

FIGURE 2.15 Bus access protocol and handshaking on a timing diagram.

We can see on the same timing diagram the very first transaction goes to an asynchronous peripheral, when the CPU asserts the CS1# chip select signal and the ALE# signal low and also puts the address out on the data bus; later it de-asserts the ALE to let the peripheral chip sample the address, then a little bit later removes the address and tri-states the bus. Later it asserts the read strobe that causes the peripheral to fetch the data internally and put it to the bus, then the CPU de-asserts the read strobe and samples the data in the same time, which causes the peripheral to stop driving the data onto the bus; later the CPU de-asserts the chip select to end the transaction. We can see the separate address bus is not used in this transaction because the peripheral device does not have address pins; rather, it needs the address multiplexed on the data bus.

2.3.3 Wait States

Some peripheral devices can tell the bus master (processor) to wait for the response because the peripheral is taking time to gather the data internally, by asserting a wait signal, or withholding a ready (RDY#) signal high until the data is available and launched on the bus. Modern buses like PCIe handle it by a "delayed read request", where a read request is sent in a short time interval, the target records it but also aborts it, so then the CPU has to re-try another transfer (delayed read completion) sometime later when it will receive the response data. In between the request and completion transactions the processor can execute code or talk to other devices. A posted write on PCIe does something similar with write transactions; it does not wait for the peripheral to store the data from its I/O flip-flop into its core registers, which can take place after the bus transaction. In most cases the processor with a traditional local peripheral bus is programmed to wait a certain amount of time, so there is no wait signal handshaking on the board.

2.3.4 Multi-Master Arbitration

When an external master device, like another processor or FPGA, wants to talk to some of the external peripherals, it has to request control access to the bus. This is done through the arbitration signals. When the external master wants access, it asserts the bus request signal (BR#). If the main processor is not using the bus, it will grant request through the BG# signal and tri-states its own bus pins. When the external master is done, it de-asserts the BR# signal. If the main processor wants the control back, but the external master is still using it, the main processor asserts the BGH# signal. This description assumes that the bus arbiter is built into the main processor.

2.4 SERDES IP

SERDES means serializer and de-serializer. They are used for transmitting data at multiple Gigabits per second over electrical differential pairs. They are also called multi-gigabit serial transceivers, or just transceivers. It is a silicon hard IP core with analog and digital circuits, built into many modern

ASIC chips. The purpose of it is to communicate with exactly one other device (point-to-point) through two differential pairs transmitting serialized and encoded data. One differential pair is used in each direction of a point-to-point bus. Higher bandwidth SERDES interfaces have multiple SERDES lanes—one lane consists of a transmit and a receive diffpair.

2.4.1 SERDES Signals

The SERDES signals are more complex than basic I/O signals generated through basic FPGA I/O pins. They are similar to shift register serial interfaces, but not only is the bit position identifying frame signal (as code) embedded into the data stream, but also the I/O clock, at the expense of increased chip complexity. This eliminates the static timing–related speed limits. Basically, it is an embedded frame embedded clock interface. One differential pair is used in each direction of a point-to-point bus, RX (receive) and TX (transmit). The RX pins of one device are connected to the TX pins of the other device. They are serialized, and packetized, include signal integrity mitigation circuits, link management, and clock compensation circuits. While I2C involves 8 or 16bits of digital data for a transaction, SERDES interfaces send packets in the range of 100 to 10k bytes. Their communication protocols are not just single level like in PMBUS; rather, they are a layered structure. Ethernet has four or seven layers depending on which documentation we are looking at; PCI-Express has three layers of silicon hardware protocol logic. Each layer has its packet format, with lower layers (closer to the wire) having smaller, more basic packages. To reduce the static timing design burden, the SERDES interfaces use something called "embedded clock", which means the clock is recovered from the data stream by the receiver, is kept going with a PLL, and is used to capture the data bits. This is called the Clock-Data-Recovery (CDR) circuit. SERDES links are always point to point, never multi-drop.

The signals are differential CML types and are always AC coupled. The capacitor value is typically 100nF, but for 128b130b encoded (contains more low frequency content than 8b10b) "slow" 8Gbps PCIe links it is 220nF. For 25Gig and faster interfaces, many ASICs implement integrated on-die AC-coupling capacitors inside the receiver to eliminate the discontinuity and board area requirement of the soldered-on capacitors. The designer has to verify whether this feature exists with both link partner ASICs datasheets. If the on-die cap feature does not exist, then we have to put the capacitors into the design. In the layout design we place the caps near the transmitter for PCI links (or the transmitter's board) but near the receiver for Ethernet links. If we design a multi-board system, then often we place the caps near the board-to-board connector.

In schematic drawings we just take care of the differential signal names, AC-caps, and reference clocks. In layout there are several layout rules and features that we have to use for SERDES signals, especially at or above 8Gbps, which are described in Chapter 15, "PCB Layout Design", and the analysis of these SERDES links is the main focus of Chapter 11, "Signal Integrity".

Many SERDES-based standards like PCIe and XAUI are multi-lane interfaces. The number of lanes is called the link width, denoted as x1 for a single-lane bus and x8 for an eight-lane bus. One lane is one TX diffpair and one RX diffpair. TX and RX are names relative to one of the pin names of the ASIC chips, while both link partners have TX and RX pins. The TX pins of one ASIC are connected to the RX pins of the other ASIC. A port is the set of pins on one ASIC, the link is the set of signal connections between the two ASICs. The data is split into as many chunks as the number of lanes, periodically, and sent over the separate differential pairs (lanes), then reassembled into a continuous parallel data stream inside the receiver ASIC. There are chip design features to handle the signal integrity aspects of the multi-lane transmission, such as each lane having FIFOs and a protocol to align the pointers of every FIFO to produce the parallel output in-sync to all other lanes. These FIFOs handle the board trace length related to lane-to-lane skew. This de-skew logic allows the board designer to have several bit-time long skew, not having to tightly match the PCB traces of the lanes and not having to fill them with length tuning meander structures. The protocol is handled through protocol logic state machines, partially hard silicon logic, partially soft-IP on FPGAs (hard IP on all other chips). During link training the transmitter inserts lane alignment symbols into the data stream on every lane, the receiver detects their positions in each lane's FIFOs and then sets the FIFO pointers such that each FIFO will produce the symbol at the same time.

There are design-bug resistant features implemented in some transceivers, sometimes automatically detecting the issue and the circuit swaps signals while in other cases they have to be programmed into device firmware. A peripheral ASIC cannot be programmed over the upstream interface if the link does not work, so they should have an EEPROM attached that can be programmed over JTAG. These can be like polarity swapping of the differential pair P/N pins, and lane reversal where the lane numbers get reversed (0123->3210). Speed, link width (number of lanes), and the choice of which lane will be lane-0 can be negotiated between two ASICs automatically. For example, if we intentionally connected ASIC2 that only has a x2 port (2 lanes) to ASIC1 that has a x8 port, they will end up establishing a link at x2 or x1 width.

Link training and auto-negotiation (auto-neg) are also higher level features used on SERDES-based interfaces. They allow both ASICs to detect if there is a link partner, get the CDRs and PLLs locked onto the stream, and set byte and lane alignment; then discover the other ASIC's speed and link width capability, any auto swapping needs, the channel SI quality; then set their own transceiver parameters to the lowest common denominator settings that works for both ASICs, and they set their equalizers for a setting that produces a good eye or BER. Link training is handled by a state machine that takes control over the data path with sending control characters only until the link is operational, then allows data to pass through. If we want to distinguish link training from auto-neg, then the latter is more for settling on the speed and link width, while link training is more for equalizer settings, but the two terms are often used interchangeably. In some devices the firmware engineers can disable link training and instead force hardcoded equalizer settings by writing into some control registers. On rare occasions the link training would end up with bad settings that can make the link unreliable, especially in the presence of excessive reflections on short channels. In those cases we can force basic flat settings for the RX-DFE and TX-FFE that would effectively neutralize their effect. We can call it a forced or disabled mode. In PCI-express they call this low-swing mode. In backplane Ethernet it is the Base-R mode instead of the Base-KR mode.

It is expected that some of the data bits received will be incorrect due to signal integrity effects. Most SERDES-based high-level standards include bit error detection using CRC (cyclic redundancy check) at different layers of the protocol stack. When a receiver detects a bit error in an incoming packet, it will not generate a local bus transaction; rather, it will send a re-try request packet back to its link partner, requesting to re-send the packet, and hoping to receive it correctly next time. The issue is the packet had to be sent twice, and re-try packet had to be sent, so that one packet with the bad data will be processed on the parallel bus on-chip with significantly increased latency, compared to the good packets. This causes indeterministic latency, but it is still good enough for most hardware systems. All modern computers still function this way. If we try to construct a control system with microsecond timing resolution, then it could become a problem. For these cases ASICs and interface standards that utilize forward error correction in the physical layer would be better.

2.4.2 Tile Architecture

In ASIC chip designs the many SERDES lanes are organized into SERDES tiles, or transceiver tiles, each tile having 4 to 16 lanes. A specific SERDES tile or core design has its own name, like the "Warp Core" on one of the older Broadcom ASICs or "GTM tile" on an AMD (Xilinx) FPGA. Each product generation with different speed capability has a different name of their SERDES tile. The main device datasheet shows which tile or core design is included in the particular FPGA or ASIC device. Each SERDES lane has a transmit signal path, a receive signal path, and a PLL. A tile has lanes, and clocking resources, as we can see in Figure 2.16. Additional features are contained with the SERDES tiles, for example, on-die eye capture and AC-JTAG.

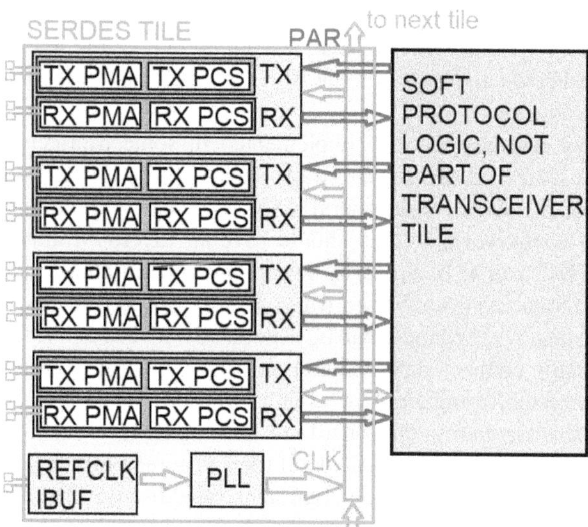

FIGURE 2.16 General block diagram of a SERDES tile.

Some devices provide an external reference clock input pin on each tile, plus internal on-chip clock inputs to the tile, while others only have on-chip internal refclock inputs. Often we want to provide one external reference clock to a few tiles that is distributed to each involved tile (within a group) using on-chip routing resources. Outside of the tiles, or between nearby tiles (same area on the silicon die), there are short clock routing resources. Short is the key because when a reference clock is routed across a whole span of a silicon die, it will pick up a lot of jitter, making the 10G+ operation impossible. Usually, a few nearby tiles can share one reference clock signal, so we end up with two to eight external reference clock signals having to be routed to one ASIC from a clock generator circuit. The reference clock signals are in the range of 100 to 322MHz, and the PLL circuits (phase locked loop inside each tile) create the line rate clock from it that matches the I/O speed. For example, a 25Gbps NRZ interface needs a 25GHz clock, but we cannot reliably route a 25GHz clock signal on-board, even on chip, so the lower frequency 100 to 322MHz clock signal has to be distributed instead. The PLLs in each lane have limitations in what line rate frequencies they can create. The PLL divider ratios can be found on ASIC datasheets, so the reference clock frequency can be calculated from the line rate and the PLL divider ratio. Often, they just tell us what frequency to use for a given common standard like PCI4.0. There are usually a few possible combinations, but the refclock frequency usually ends up a fractional number like 156.25MHz used on many 10.3125Gbps (aka 10Gig) Ethernet applications.

Internal loopback test options are also provided, connecting the PCS output of the TX path with the PCS input of the RX path, detaching the PMA blocks. What it does is it allows developers to test out protocol logic without anything connected to the external I/O. In an external loopback test we have to connect a cable or loopback plug between the RX and the TX of the same lane, then send a PRBS test pattern, and at the RX side compare the incoming data with the locally generated pattern. A remote loopback is when a device just sends back everything it received, so the other device can count error bits while testing out the physical link. Or we can send data packets (if the protocol allows sending un-addressed communication) and count the good bits received. PRBS means "pseudo-random binary sequence" that stresses the eye, or creates a worst-case eye diagram when doing on-die eye capture. Transceivers can be put into a PRBS mode where they detach the user data path and send PRBS test pattern code instead. The receiver is capable of calculating the same pattern and therefore comparing the incoming stream against the calculated one for determining each bit for correctness versus error. This allows counting bit errors, calculating bit error rate, or displaying BERT-scan style eye diagrams.

With higher bandwidth protocols, the complexity of the SERDES cores increases. The PMA block now supports both regular NRZ signaling as well as PAM4. In the case of PAM4, there will be a 2-bit output of the shift register that is used to encode a voltage level, one of four levels. The receiver might use a fast analog to digital converter instead of a comparator. The PCS block also has additional functions. For example, after the symbol encoding, they have trans-coding into a different symbol size and other data flow conversion operations. They implement Forward error-correction (FEC) that recovers bad bits without having to re-send them, that results in the bit error ratio and latency improvement. From very noisy received signals at 1E-3 BER they can produce a data stream having 1E-15 BER. FEC can also be seen as an improvement in insertion loss requirement by 5 to 10dB.

2.4.3 Transmit Signal Path

The transmit path is grouped into two sections: the PCS block that deals with parallel data bus and code-related logic and the PMA that is related to serialization. The core logic interface is a parallel bus, usually 32 to 128bit wide, but it might be divided between multiple lanes. The parallel PCS logic is usually 8 to 10bit wide, converted down by the FIFO to narrower but higher frequency. The shift register that is doing the final serialization further speeds up the signal ten times to the line rate. A PRBS generator can be connected to the signal path instead of the core logic bus for the purpose of PRBS testing and eye capture. The block diagram of the TX path can be seen in Figure 2.17.

Transmitters also contain circuits and logic for out-of-band signaling (OOB). The purpose of the OOB is to detect whether something is connected at the other end of the line by sending slow test signals from the TX pins to the board traces that pull current differently depending on the existence of termination resistors (an ASIC with its RX SERDES would have such). It is basically plug and play, or device presence detection.

An important part of the SERDES PCS is the encoder. An 8b10b encoder converts the 8bit data into a 10bit data "symbol", where 1/4th of the code combinations carries user data and the others are reserved for control characters. The encoding also helps with maintaining a DC balance for the clock/data recovery circuit and the AC-coupling to work. A few of these 10-bit codes can be easily recognized or detected, so they can be used for link maintenance control messaging that is not passed through the receiver's core logic bus. This adds a 20% overhead for the communication link. To reduce that overhead, 64b66b encoding has been invented that takes 64bit user data and converts it to a 66bit code, used for example on 10 to 100Gig Ethernet. Similarly, a 128b130b encoding scheme is used on PCIe3.0, while 8b10b is used on PCIe2.0.

Usually an ASIC that sends the data and the one receiving the data are running on separate clock oscillators that can never have exactly the same frequency. This would cause the receiving

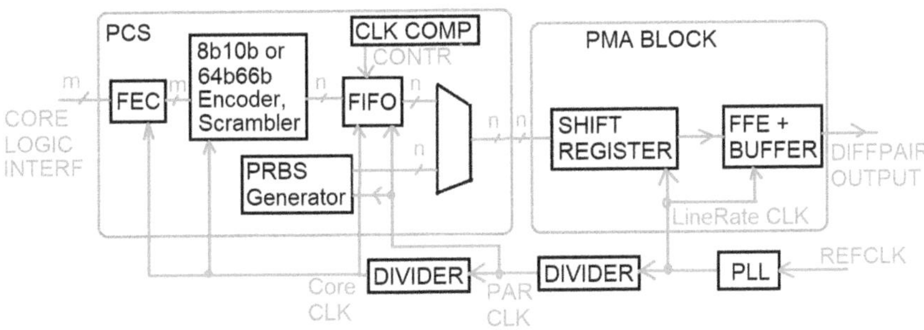

FIGURE 2.17 SERDES TX block diagram.

ASIC to receive more or less data than it expects, maybe hundreds of thousands of extra bits every second. As a workaround, "clock compensation" was invented. The TX PCS inserts clock compensation characters at regular intervals into the TX FIFO, then the receiver detects these characters (as encoded user data will never have these special characters in them) and decides to skip writing them into the RX FIFO or to write extra ones to prevent FIFO underrun or overrun. We want the FIFO pointer to float somewhere in the middle of the range, otherwise data transmission would be blocked by it.

Forward Error Correction (FEC) became commonly used with 56Gig transceivers, which helps eliminate small amounts of bit errors so the physical channel bit error rate requirement or the insertion loss budget can be relaxed.

The transmit buffer implements feed-forward equalization (FFE), shown in Figure 2.18. This means that instead of just driving the data stream to the output lines, it drives a sum of the data stream and the delayed version of the data stream. Each delayed version is referred to as a "tap". The tap values can be determined through link training automatically or hard coded by software (if we determined the best settings in the lab after trial/error). The tap values are stored in a PHY control register. Delay is done using a D-flip-flop that achieves exactly one clock period delay. The purpose of this is to fortify the signal such that it will come out more detectable at the other end. Due to inter-symbol interference (ISI) it is harder to detect a logic-high bit after a long sequence of logic lows, but that can be improved if that new logic high is driven stronger (larger amplitude). The most basic implementation of a TX-FFE is a pre-emphasis or de-emphasis, basically a 1-tap FFE. When the FFE is turned off, and all bits are driven equally, we call it a "low swing mode", which is the preferred mode for very short links. FFE and RX-DFE are mainly used to fight ISI and insertion loss on long links.

2.4.4 Receive Signal Path

The full path of a generic SERDES receive path can be seen in Figure 2.19. The signal comes into the chip from the board through the analog front end, which includes calibrated termination resistors and biasing circuits. An external calibration resistor connected between the calibration pin of the ASIC and ground on the board allows the startup state machine to calibrate the

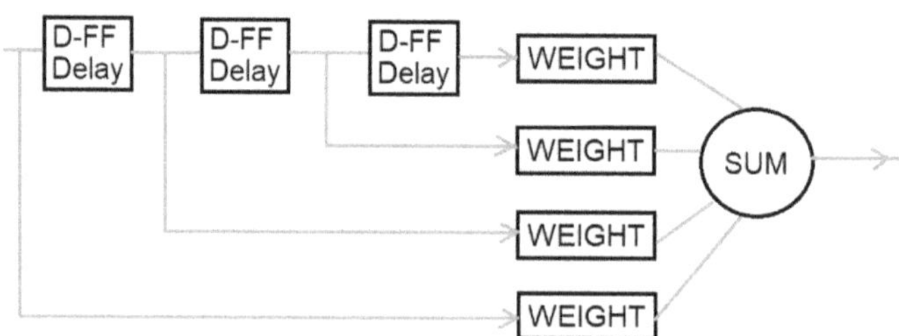

FIGURE 2.18 TX FFE concept.

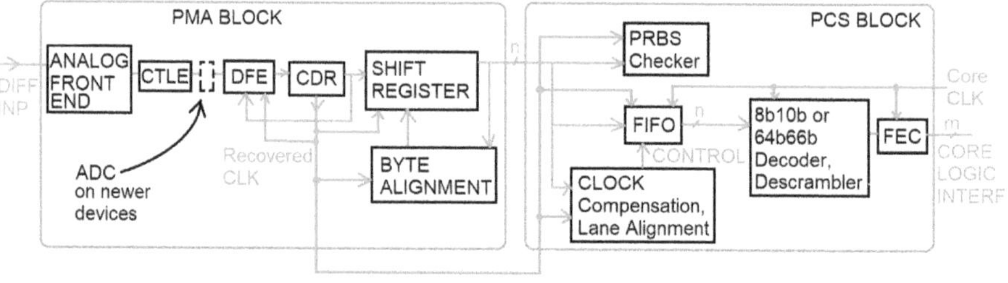

FIGURE 2.19 SERDES RX block diagram.

SERDES terminations to an accurate value. After the analog front end the received signal is routed through the continuous time linear equalizer (CTLE) that is a simple analog filter that has a frequency response that boosts higher frequencies to compensate for losses, basically the inverse of the insertion loss profile of a long channel. Often the CTLE is combined with a programmable gain amplifier. After this, the signal is passed through a digital equalizer, the decision feedback equalizer (DFE) block, seen in Figure 2.20, that further compensates for board-channel signal integrity effects, including losses and reflections. Then the signal is passed to the clock data recovery (CDR) block, which recovers the clock from the data stream and samples the data with the recovered clock at the ideal timing position. The data stream at the output of the CDR is fed back into the DFE and forwarded into the shift register to convert from line rate serial to a slower parallel bus. The shift register needs to know where one byte (or longer symbol) ends and where the next one starts. This is set up by the byte/symbol alignment (byte steering) logic during link training by looking for special 8b10b (or 64b66b or 128b130b) characters that are easily recognizable in an encoded stream. These characters can easily be seen where they start in a stream, so the logic steers the shift register alignment until the symbol start is at the shift register start position, then it remains there during run time. After link training the data is continuous, even in cases of no user data to be transmitted some IDLE characters (10 to 130bit) must be transmitted to fill unused bit times to keep the byte alignment and the CDR lock alive as long as the device is powered up. The receive FIFO has multiple purposes; clock domain crossing support from the line rate clock to the core clock domain, lane-to-lane de-skew and refclock frequency compensation. The clock domain crossing is a less than one clock period phase difference between two clock domains of similar frequency. During link training the receiver state machine must detect how much skew there is between each lane, as a lane-to-lane de-skew or "channel bonding" feature. This is also done by looking for special 8b10b or 64b66b code characters in the stream, then the state machine will add an offset to the FIFO indexing of each lane's FIFOs until all of them spit out the same alignment character in the same clock cycle. The clock compensation logic described earlier takes out the "skip" control characters from the FIFO to prevent overflow or underflow as a result of slightly different clock frequencies used by the two ASICs. The FIFO might be wider on the core side to allow the core logic to operate at a lower frequency and lower power. The symbol character decoder (8b10b…) simply re-creates the original data stream. By the time the signal arrives here, all the 8b10b control characters have already served their purpose and can be thrown away. The PRBS checker calculates the proper PRBS sequence and compares the incoming stream with the calculated one to detect bit errors; this is turned on only during a PRBS test mode.

Some of the lower speed older SERDES designs did not contain a digital DFE equalizer, only a CTLE. Some of the newer SERDES receivers are ADC (analog to digital converter) based. That means that the signal is sampled by the ADC with the recovered clock, but the DFE will not have an analog summation circuit but rather a digital one. On the block diagram there will be an ADC block between the CTLE and the DFE. Often, they refer to the fully digital DFE as a "DSP". Some

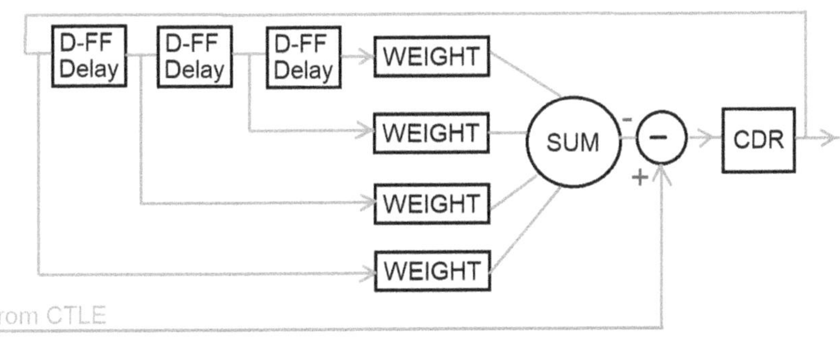

FIGURE 2.20 RX DFE concept.

ADC-based PAM4 transceivers might not support a die eye diagram scan, only a simplified statistical diagram; check with the transceiver user guides for FPGAs or the datasheets for processors and ASICs.

2.5 BUTTON OR SWITCH DEBOUNCING

Pushbuttons and user-operated switches have their output bouncing up and down before making full contact. Slow analog signals have a 1us or slower rise time, while fast rise time noise sits on the top of it, as we can see in Figure 2.21. Both cases result in digital input pins to register a state transition multiple times. There are two solutions: the first is to use an analog hysteresis comparator, the other is to use debouncing logic in an FPGA or debouncing code in a processor software. The comparator is not preferred as it is an extra component for purchasing and board space. The output digital waveform toggles several times during the threshold crossing, within a few nanoseconds or microseconds, that can violate hold timing of internal logic, or can confuse state machines thinking the switch was turned off and take action like shutting down the system. The debouncing solution is simple. The logic is to have a state machine—if it detects an input transition, it transitions into a waiting state where it waits for the debounce time (let us say 100us), then checks if the signal is still in the new state. If it is, then it transitions into a stable state and asserts its output. The input signal should only feed the debounce state machine directly, otherwise any downstream logic becomes unreliable through metastability. This creates a need to insert a state machine for every slow signal input into the code. This also causes a small delay in signal detection, but that is acceptable in most cases.

2.6 ESD

The silicon chips on the board have to be protected from electrostatic discharge (ESD) caused by the user connecting an external cable. So ESD protection devices are usually added to I/O lines that are entering or exiting the system through external connectors. They usually contain fast acting Zener diodes that will conduct any high voltage spike into the ground or into the power rail, as seen in Figure 2.22. The chosen protection device has to be able to not impede the data transmission, especially on high-speed buses like HDMI. There are devices for all types of external interfaces

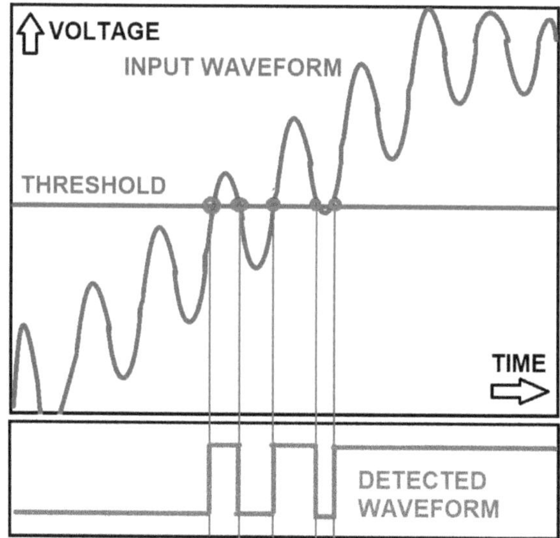

FIGURE 2.21 Input debouncing issue.

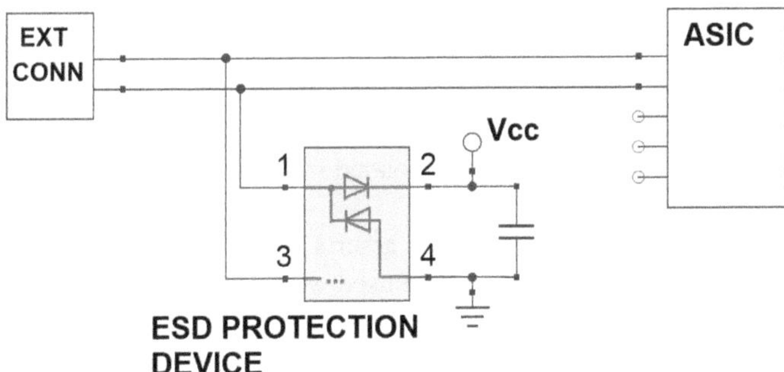

FIGURE 2.22 Basic ESD protection used on low-speed external I/O.

up to a few Gigabits per second—their datasheets list what they can be used on. Most SERDES interfaces do not use ESD protection diode components as they would create stubs and degrade the signal integrity beyond repair.

2.7 DATA CORRUPTION

Errors or data corruption in digital systems can happen during data transmission and during data storage. Errors during transmission, mainly caused by signal integrity issues or EMI interference, can be mitigated by error detection and error correction. Detection means a data packet contains a CRC (Cyclic Redundancy Check) portion that is checked after receiving the packet, and if the CRC calculated from the payload data and the received CRC do not match then the chip will request the data to be re-sent to it. Error correction means once the error bit(s) are detected they can be corrected without having to re-send the packet. There are limits to it, as only one to a few bits can be detected or reconstituted in a given packet. ECC (Error Correction Code) and FEC (Forward Error Correction in SERDES physical layer) encodings can help with correcting bit errors at the line rate. They can improve the bit error ratio by 1E12, which has a similar effect as to improving the insertion loss by 5 to 10dB (coding gain).

Data corruption in storage can happen due to ionizing radiation called SEU (Single Event Upset), affecting RAM and register cells and due to retention errors and data-aging in flash cells (10–20 years max) or through wearing out of the flash cell (cells become unreliable after a certain number of write cycles). We can store data in a redundant configuration using SATA RAID controllers and using two or more SSDs mirroring the same redundant data. DDRx memory subsystems are sometimes made with an additional 9th byte lane, called ECC, for Single-bit Error Correction and Double-bit Error Detection, that helps with both transmission and storage errors.

2.7.1 SEU

Single Even Upset (SEU) is a physical effect when ionizing radiation enters a piece of equipment and causes its register cells (or RAM cells or state machine flip-flops) to change state when they are supposed to retain their state by design. Flash memories are much less susceptible to this. There is ionizing radiation everywhere—just the amount is different in different places— and the dosage depends on time of exposure. It is a statistical phenomenon that increases with altitude and exposure time and with unit quantity per deployment. SEU is an important consideration in two main cases: In aerospace applications, where the equipment is on an airplane or spacecraft above the dense Earth atmosphere, it is exposed to much higher doses of radiation that ground equipment is exposed to. The other application is ground-based equipment with large-scale deployment, like data centers, where the large number of units (10k–100k) within one single facility produces similar failure rates per facility as the aerospace case produces per aircraft—not per unit. Products can be tested with neutron radiation at research nuclear reactors.

Hardware design can implement certain SEU mitigation features:

- Data packets can be re-sent; bad packets can be detected by CRC or even corrected by FEC or ECC.
- Data plane ASICs have to be able to be reloaded (reset, reconfigure) without critical loss of control or data.
- Some FPGAs have a CRC output pin that asserts when a SEU event is detected in the config SRAM cells in run time. This can be used with a management processor to re-load them.
- Resending packets already sent but through an alternate redundant route.
- Use discrete logic without register cells for critical signals.
- Use devices with resistor strapping instead of register programmability, for example, VRMs and clock chips.
- For the most critical subsystems, like glue logic and management, use flash-based devices. Flash-based FPGAs like the Microchip Igloo, ProASIC3, and RTG4 control their FPGA fabric from flash cells directly, as opposed to traditional FPGAs that control the fabric from SRAM cells that are loaded from an external flash chip at startup. Flash-based micro-controllers execute code directly from on-chip flash memory without copying the code to RAM.

2.8 SECURITY

Some types of electronic devices are designed with features that prevent unauthorized access, copy, or alteration of stored data or they prevent unauthorized use of devices. Some information is not intended to be public, even if it travels through public places. Some equipment is not made to allow anyone to operate it for their own purpose. There are several types of hardware-supported security features in complex designs:

- Secure configuration of FPGAs helps to prevent loading unauthorized FPGA code images into equipment that would circumvent its original intended use. The protection works by storing an encrypted image file in the boot flash chip, which is decrypted by the FPGA during the configuration load cycle using a key that is burned into the FPGAs ROM register.
- Encrypted Ethernet transfer via MACSEC: If both ends of a communication link contain ASICs that support MACSEC, then the data sent through the open Internet is un-decodable by wiretapping. It also helps in stopping threats like DDOS or unauthorized access.
- Trusted Platform Module is usually a small TPM chip or microcontroller soldered onto an X86 motherboard. It stores, checks, and generates cryptographic keys.
- Network packet inspection and rejection for threats using off-loading certain data traffic to security ASICs or FPGAs that will then do deep packet inspection for harmful payload content.

3 Major Interfaces

This chapter discusses the most common data transfer connections or interfaces between chips, boards, and chassis. They all utilize complex protocols.

3.1 ETHERNET

Ethernet is used in every computer and complex hardware board or system, mostly for connectivity external to a chassis, but sometimes internal. The Internet is the connection of all local Ethernet networks through the Internet backbone links in cities, countries, and globally. Ethernet is defined by the IEEE802.3 standard, and its several speed and "media" types (like optical, coax, backplane, etc.) related amendment documents (802.3XY). These can be purchased from the Institute of Electrical and Electronics Engineers (IEEE).

3.1.1 Protocol

Ethernet interfaces have a layered structure, as shown in Figure 3.1. The lower layers are implemented with cables, board designs, and chip designs. Switch and router ASICs also implement some of the higher layers in silicon. The Ethernet MAC or controller chips usually have a PCI-Express connection to a processor, so the processor can access the registers inside the MAC through memory mapped simple read/write transactions, as dictated by the software. The interface between the MAC and the PHY chip is the MII or C2C interface. There are several standards for that (see later chapters). Sometimes the MAC and the PHY are integrated on the same chip. We call these Ethernet controllers or NIC (network interface controller) chips. Ethernet switch chips also implement a MAC and a PHY, usually many ports on a single ASIC chip, plus additional hardware-based packet forwarding logic on some ASICs. Each MAC or port has a 6-byte MAC address, which is unique in the world, that is assigned at the time the board is manufactured and that is programmed into an EEPROM. The chips load the EEPROM content into their registers during startup. The IP address identifies a computer or an Ethernet port on a computer. It is usually assigned dynamically in run time or at startup. It is used for routing data to one computer through the whole Internet or by a router in a closed network.

PHY chips implement the lowest layer of the Ethernet protocol, namely the physical layer, which can be further divided into sublayers. The lowest one directly connected to the (external) line is the PMD (Physical Medium Dependent sublayer), including I/O buffer circuits and semi-analog circuits. The one above it is the PMA (Physical Medium Attachment sublayer) that handles serialization, clock/data recovery, and FIFO-based clock domain isolation. The top one is the PCS (Physical Coding sublayer) layer that handles encoding, MII/C2C-link packet handling, and de-skew.

Switching is when Ethernet packets are passed from one port to another by switch appliances, based on a knowledge built up inside the switch about which port leads towards a device having a particular MAC address. It is also called Layer-2 or L2 switch. Routing is when packets are directed based on IP address, similar to what the switch does but on Layer-3 (L3). Routing is more complicated, as the ASICs have to be able to decode more complex higher layer abstraction of the packets, and they have to maintain a larger set of routing information. Switches handle tens of servers in a data center at once, while routers usually handle hundreds of servers as their traffic is aggregated to a smaller number of cables by switches. On the Internet as a whole there are more switches than routers. Some of the larger and more modern switches (spine switches) have the capability of L3 routing as well.

DOI: 10.1201/9781032702094-3

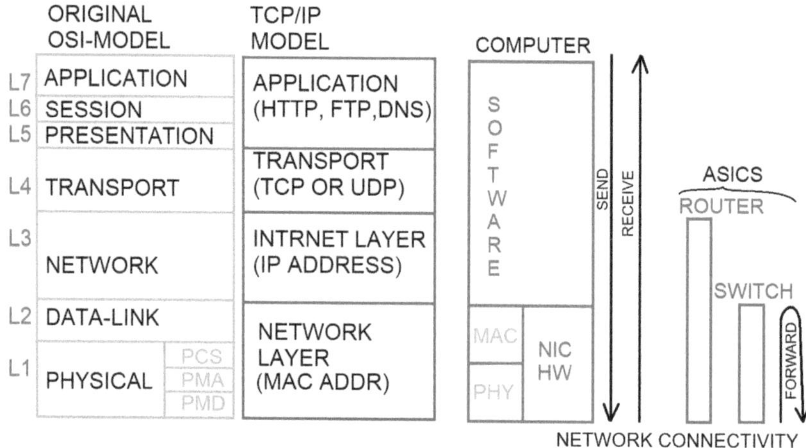

FIGURE 3.1 Layered Ethernet model.

3.1.2 External and Backplane Ports

Table 3.1 lists the most commonly used Ethernet port types. All the "-KR" types are differential pairs with DFE equalization used on-board or over a backplane. The "-KR4" is like KR but with four lanes, the number like 100G* denotes total bandwidth, not signaling rate. All the "-Base-T" and "Base-TX" types are meant for external ports to the chassis, but sometimes we also use them internally. They utilize RJ45 connectors, transformers, and twisted pair cables of two or four differential pairs. The transformer might be built into the connector, we call it a "MagJack". RJ45 connectors have a metal housing, and eight contacts for four diffpairs. 10/100Meg versions utilize only four pins, or one receive and one transmit diffpair. XAUI is a MAC to PHY interface, but sometimes it is used over a backplane instead of KR. The "Base-SR" and "Base-LR" are optical port types. The "Base-CR" types are twinax copper cables for 1 to 3m length within a data center rack, which plugs into the same cage socket as the LR and SR do.

3.1.3 MAC-PHY Interfaces

Ethernet ports of computers are organized as:

Host← →MAC← →PHY← →Port← →Ethernet connectivity (line)

For every Ethernet chip there is a host side (towards the CPU) and a line side towards the external cabling. Any set of these blocks can be implemented on a single chip. The host can be a processor or FPGA, or some data-moving logic in case of a switch ASIC. The MAC-Host interface is usually PCIe, or an on-chip interface. MAC means media access controller, PHY means physical layer device. If the MAC and the PHY are on separate chips, then we have two interfaces between them, a data plane interface and a control plane slow interface for configuring registers in the PHY. The data plane interface is called the media independent interface or MII, sometimes the C2C or short chip-to-chip link.

3.1.3.1 The Data Plane Interface

There are several different MII/C2C interfaces, depending on the external port speed and type, as we can see in Table 3.2. The ones above 1Gbps are concerned with return loss and insertion loss, and the standards constrain them. These are usually not equipped with the link training DFE capabilities of a KR backplane link, so a much lower amount of loss budget is available. It is about

TABLE 3.1
External Ethernet Port Types

Name	Parameters
100BASE-TX	1 lane Tx, 1 lane RX. 125Mbit/s baud rate, NRZI, 125Mbps bw per dir
1000Base-T	2 lane TX, 2 lane RX. 125Mbit/s baud rate, PAM5, 500Mbps bw per dir
1000Base-TX	1 lane TX, 1 lane RX. 250Mbit/s baud rate, PAM5, 500Mbps bw per dir
1000Base-KX	1 lane TX, 1 lane RX. 1000Mbit/s baud rate, NRZ, 1000Mbps bw per dir, for 1Gig on-board or backplane interface.
1000Base-X	1 lane TX, 1 lane RX. 1000Mbit/s baud rate, NRZ, 1000Mbps bw per dir, similar to KX, but used with optics, without link training.
2.5GBase-T	2 lane TX, 2 lane RX. 200Mbit/s baud rate, PAM16, 1250Mbps bw per dir
10GBase-T	2 lane TX, 2 lane RX. 800Mbit/s baud rate, PAM16, 5000Mbps bw per dir
25GBase-T	2 lane TX, 2 lane RX. 2000Mbit/s baud rate, PAM16, 12500Mbps bw per dir
10GBase-BX4 (XAUI)	4 lane TX, 4 lane RX. 3125Mbit/s baud rate, NRZ, 10Gbps bw per dir
10GBase-KR	1 lane TX, 1 lane RX. 10Gbit/s baud rate, NRZ, 10Gbps bw per dir, for 10Gig on-board or backplane interface, with automatic DFE equalizer link training. The SERDES channel is described in IEEE802.3ap-annex69B
10GBase-R	1 lane TX, 1 lane RX. 10Gbit/s baud rate, NRZ, 10Gbps bw per dir, same as KR, but without DFE link training, can use simpler or lower power chips, on shorter links.
10GBase-CR	1 lane TX, 1 lane RX. 10Gbit/s baud rate, NRZ, 10Gbps bw per dir, same as KR, but meant to be used in SFP optical cages hosting passive "copper" cables with twinax cabling and no active transceiver in the SFP.
25GBase-KR	1 lane TX, 1 lane RX. 25Gbit/s baud rate, NRZ, 25Gbps bw per dir, for on-board links or backplanes. The SERDES SI channel is the same as it was described in IEEE802.3bj-Section93.9 for the four-lane 4x25G
40GBase-KR4	4 lane TX, 4 lane RX. 10Gbit/s baud rate, NRZ, 40Gbps bw per dir, for on-board links or backplanes.
56GBase-KR	1 lane TX, 1 lane RX. 28Gbit/s baud rate, PAM4, 56Gbps bw per dir. The SERDES SI channel is in IEEE802.3cd-Section137
100GBase-KR	1 lane TX, 1 lane RX. 112Gbit/s baud rate, PAM4, 112Gbps bw per dir, for on-board links or backplanes.
100GBase-KR4	4 lane TX, 4 lane RX. 25Gbit/s baud rate, NRZ, 100Gbps bw per dir, for on-board links or backplanes. The SERDES SI channel is described in IEEE802.3bj-Section93.9
200GBase-KR4	4 lane TX, 4 lane RX. 56Gbit/s baud rate, PAM4, 200Gbps bw per dir, for on-board links or backplanes. The SERDES SI channel is described in IEEE802.3cd-Section137
400GBase-KR	4 lane TX, 4 lane RX. 112Gbit/s baud rate, PAM4, 200Gbps bw per dir, for on-board links or backplanes.

half or third of what a backplane link allows, the exact numbers are listed in the relevant standard documents/amendments.

3.1.3.2 The Control Plane Interface

The control plane interface is usually a MDIO (Management Data Input/Output) link with a clock (MDC) and a data (MDIO) line, running up to several Megahertz. In some cases, it may be an I2C bus. Either way they need pullups. There are two variants of the MDIO interface defined in the IEEE802.3 Ethernet standards, the "Clause-22", which is used for 1Gig PHY chips, and the Clause-45, which is used for 10Gig or faster devices. The pullup value has to be very low usually, but consult the PHY datasheet or reference design schematics. The MDIO interface can be hosted/mastered by the MAC or switch ASIC, or by the local host processor. The PHY register

TABLE 3.2
Mac-PHY Interface Data Plane Portion Types

Name	Parameters
MII	Original media-independent interface, it is an 4bit parallel CMOS bus with system signals, a 25MHz clock, a set of RX signals and a set of TX. It is a clock forwarding interface, see the chapter on timing analysis.
RMII	Reduced media-independent interface, with 2bit parallel bus and different clocking than MII.
GMII	Gigabit media-independent interface, similar to MII, with 8bit wide data, and 125MHz clock.
RGMII	Reduced gigabit media-independent interface, similar to GMII, but with 4bit bus, and multiplexed system signals.
SGMII	Serial gigabit media-independent interface, this is serialized, at 625MHz with double data rate, with differential signaling, one lane of TX and RX data, with TX and RX clocks. This supports PHYs with external 1Gig SFP (1000Base-X) interfaces.
HSGMII	High serial gigabit media-independent interface, same as SGMII, but supports 2.5Gig SFP.
QSGMII	Quad serial gigabit media-independent interface, it carries data for 4 external 1Gig Ethernet ports, for quad-port PHY chips, using one lane (one RX diffpair and one TX diffpair) of 5…10Gbit/s SERDES link. This allows a MAC to only dedicate 4 pins for 4 ports of 1000Base-T, that requires 4x8=16 pins on the PHY. Basically, it is like a fanout or port expansion interface.
XGMII	10-gigabit media-independent interface, to support 10Gbit external ports, it is a parallel 32bit interface, 2 sets like the MII has with clock forwarding, running at 156MHz double data rate.
XAUI	10 Gigabit Attachment Unit Interface with 4 lanes of regular SERDES at 3.1Gbps per lane.
XLAUI	40 Gigabit Attachment Unit Interface with 4 lanes of regular SERDES at 10Gbps per lane. The IEEE802.3ba-annex83A describes the SERDES SI channel. Also applicable to single-lane 10Gig types.
CAUI-4	100 Gigabit Attachment Unit Interface with 4 lanes of regular SERDES at 25Gbps per lane. The IEEE802.3bm-annex83D describes the SERDES SI channel. Also applicable to single-lane 25Gig types.
400GAUI-8-C2C	400 Gigabit Attachment Unit Interface with 8 lanes of regular SERDES at 53Gbps PAM4 per lane. The IEEE802.3bs-annex120D describes the SERDES SI channel.
800GAUI-8-C2C	800 Gigabit Attachment Unit Interface with 8 lanes of regular SERDES at 106Gbps PAM4 per lane.

configuration is usually decided by the software on the host processor anyway or by the embedded ARM processor inside a single switch ASIC in a simple switch.

3.1.4 Optical Ethernet Ports

Pluggable optical transceiver modules that convert onboard electrical SERDES signals to fiber optics (light) signals are the main types of external Ethernet ports above 1Gbps. The most common optical port types are listed in Table 3.3. The management or control plane link is I2C, with each module responding to the same address that is A0. Since all ports have the same address, they all need a separate I2C bus. The I2C can be mastered by a switch chip in low-end consumer switches, or it can be mastered by the host processor in the chassis for high end. We can direct connect an optical port to a switch ASIC only if the ASIC's datasheet explicitly mentions the electrical interface standard (like XLAUI, SFI), otherwise we need a PHY or gearbox chip to be designed-in between them. Figure 3.2 shows a made-up board block diagram that contains several types of external, optical, onboard, and MAC-PHY interfaces and how they are usually used.

The insertion and return loss requirements for chip to optical module links should be obtained from the SFF, OSFP, and QSFP-DD standards. They vary between 6 and 13dB. If no exact standard is found, a similar one at the same speed can be used or one with a different speed but with the limit lines scaled to the right baud rate.

TABLE 3.3
Common Optical Pluggable Module Types

Name	Parameters
SFP	1Gbit/s over single lane (one RX and one TX diffpair), the applicable standard is INF-8074. The electrical interface between the pluggable module and the PHY is 1000Base-X, that is a single lane 1Gbps NRZ.
SFP+	10Gbit/s over single lane, the applicable standard is SFF-8083. The electrical interface between the pluggable module and the PHY is SFI that is a single lane of 10Gbps NRZ, the SERDES channel is described in SFF-8418.
SFP28	28Gbit/s over single lane. For the SERDES channel sometimes usually we just scale the SFF-8418 10Gig channel specs along the frequency axis.
QSFP+	40Gbit/s over 4 lanes of 10Gbit/s each, the applicable standard is SFF-8436. The electrical interface between the pluggable module and the PHY is XLPPI that is 4 lanes of 10Gbps NRZ. SFF-8418 or IEEE802.3ba-annex86A can be used for the SERDES channel.
QSFP28 or QSFP100	100Gbit/s over 4 lanes of 28Gbit/s each, the applicable standard is SFF-8665. The electrical interface between the pluggable module and the PHY is CPPI that is 4 lanes of 25Gbps NRZ. In the IEEE802.3bm-annex83E the SERDES channel is called CAUI4-C2M.
QSFP-DD	400Gbit/s over 8 lanes of 53Gbit/s PAM4 each, QSFP-DD.com . The electrical interface between the pluggable module and the PHY is 400GAUI-8-C2M that is 8 lanes of 53Gig PAM4, from the IEEE802.3bs-annex120C.
OSFP	400Gbit/s over 8 lanes of 53Gbit/s PAM4 each, the applicable standard is osfpmsa.org . The electrical interface between the pluggable module and the PHY is 400GAUI-8-C2M that is 8 lanes of 53Gig PAM4, just like the above.
OSFP800G	800Gbit/s over 8 lanes of 106Gbit/s PAM4 each, the applicable standard is osfpmsa.org . The electrical interface between the pluggable module and the PHY is 800GAUI-8-C2M that is 8 lanes of 106Gig PAM4, from IEEE802.3df

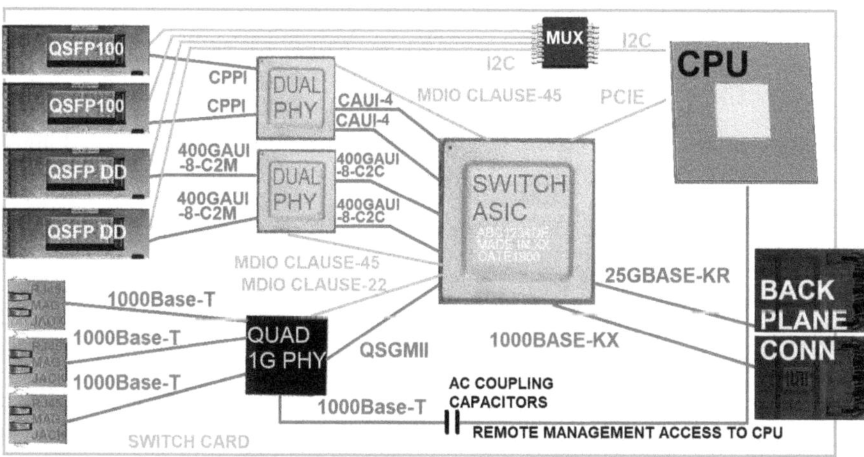

FIGURE 3.2 General use of on-board Ethernet electrical interfaces (sketch).

The fiber optics side of the pluggable optical transceiver modules can follow different standards even within the same module type. An example of the optical side standards is the 100GBase-SR4 used in QSFP100 modules, which is a short reach 100m cable with four multimode fibers per direction, and with eight optical couplers in the MTP optical connector. Another example is the 100GBase-LR4, which is a long reach 10km cable with thin single mode fibers, with a single TX and a single RX fiber, while four laser beams are wavelength division multiplexed onto a single fiber, WDM). At a minimum, any optical fiber connection contains one transmit and one receiver fiber.

3.1.5 Base-T Type Ethernet Coupling

Ethernet port types like 1000Base-T or 10GBase-T are meant to be transformer (magnetic) coupled and isolated. This helps with long cables and ESD protection, as well as impedance transformation to the twisted pair's 75 Ohms versus onboard 50 Ohm single ended. There are single/dual/quad/octal Ethernet magnetics modules available. Each port has four diffpairs, named MDI[0:3], each pair needs a transformer. No, this is not the MDIO interface. When we say, for example, dual magnetics, it means two sets of four transformers, a total of eight. These are not generic transformers, rather they are Ethernet transformers or Ethernet magnetics modules. They are available for Gigabit or 100Meg options. A popular way of providing an external 1Gig Ethernet port is through "Magjacks", which are RJ45 connectors with magnetics (four per port) built in.

There are different types of Ethernet magnetics on the market, depending on how many windings are in them. A few types are shown in Figure 3.3. Which type to use depends on the PHY chips, and it can be found out from the chip datasheet or reference design. These magnetics have transformers with center taps and sometimes common mode chokes also. The center tap is usually connected directly to VCC, or to GND through a decoupling cap on the PHY side, while on the line side the center tap is connected to a 75 Ohm AC termination. Base-T has a 75 Ohm line impedance, while the PHY-side interface is usually 100 Ohm differential. There are four diffpairs in one Base-T interface, while Base-TX interfaces are supported through two pairs.

1Gig Base-T Ethernet can be AC coupled between chips; transformers are only needed to external interfaces and off-board interfaces to comply with IEEE specifications. When AC coupling, check the reference designs of each chip, and see if the RJ45 transformer center tap pin is connected to VDD or GND. If connected to power, then they need an inductive pullup on that side of the AC cap where this chip resides, as seen in Figure 3.4. If we have to use transformers, then center taps have to be connected to GND or power/VDD based on the same check above, depending on the chip's reference design.

3.2 PCI AND PCIe

Both standards were defined by the organization called Peripheral Component Interconnect Special Interest Group (PCI-SIG). The modern PCI-Express bus (PCIe) is based on the PCI bus

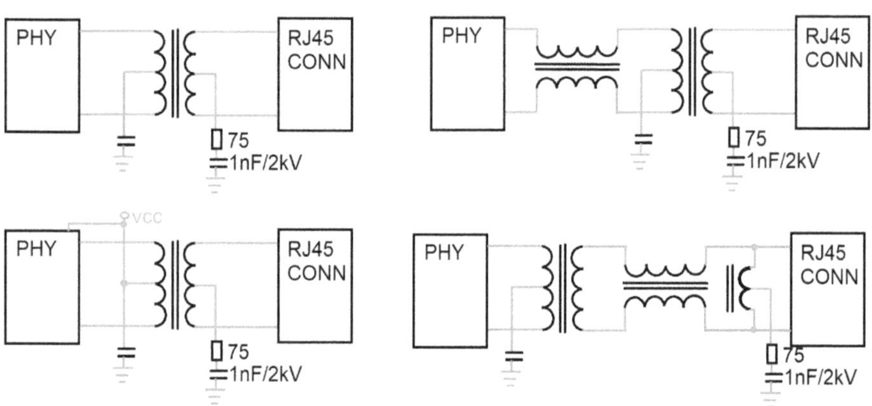

FIGURE 3.3 Example of Base-T magnetic modules.

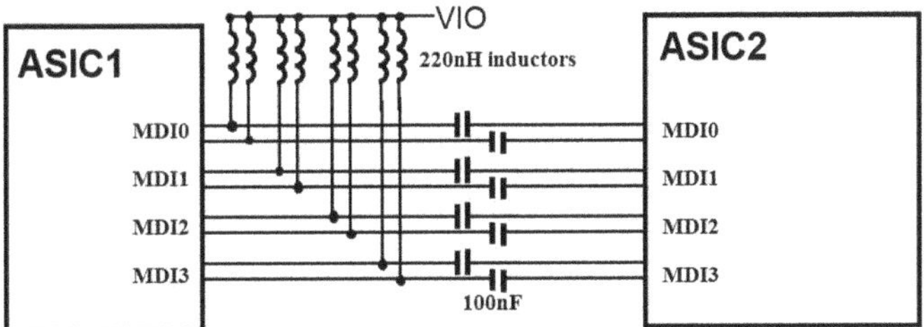

FIGURE 3.4 AC coupled 1000Base-T Ethernet. The chip on the left is VDD-based, the chip on the right is GND-based.

(Peripheral Component Interconnect) that was common years ago. These days the PCI bus exists only in some aerospace boards that have to support legacy add-in cards for upgrading old equipment. The PCI bus once served as the backbone of the X86 chipset as its main system bus. The PCI protocol level operation was made to be the standard way X86 computers discover peripherals and initialize a system. New computers and the new PCIe standard retained full compatibility with PCI at the protocol and software level, even though the physical layer signals are nothing alike. Both buses require complex chips for expansion to large complex systems, aka adding more peripheral devices to a computer system, instead of just attaching one or two devices directly to the processor. Consumer electronics almost never need expansion, while complex hardware designs do.

3.2.1 The PCI Bus

It is defined in the PCI Local Bus Specification; version 3.0 is the last one released. Even if we never plan to use PCI buses in our designs, it is worth understanding how the logical/protocol layer of the PCI bus works, as the device trees, device discovery, and system initialization methods are inherited by the PCIe bus and all computers still work this way.

3.2.1.1 Physical Layer

At the physical layer the PCI bus is a common clock synchronous parallel bus, using 3.3V CMOS single-ended signals. They can run at 33MHz or at 66MHz. The data bus width can be 32bit or 64bit wide. There is an address/data AD[31:0] bus that can carry address or data, and there is a 4bit command/byte-enable CBE[3:0] bus that helps the devices know what kind of information is on the AD bus. There are several protocol signals like target ready TRDY#, initiator ready IRDY#, STOP#, FRAME#, INT[A:D]#, DEVSEL#, and IDSEL. The full protocol will not be explained here; there are separate books on the topic.

Since it takes several clock cycles to fetch data from the inside of a PCI device, a read transaction will have to be a "split transaction", meaning the host will read twice, first as a "delayed read request". Then the device fetches the data from the core logic into the I/O registers, then the initiator issues the second read to the same address, then the device will immediately launch the data to the bus in the "read completion" transaction. Writing data into devices is simpler. It is called "posted write" when the data is written into the device's I/O register, than the device moves it into its core logic later without the host having to wait for it. This split transaction concept is also used on PCIe and many other SERDES interfaces.

There is a separate clock signal routed to each device, with the trace length of every clock signal to be matched in length, to ensure balanced setup/hold timing margins for all directions and transaction types. If the clock is provided by the host, then it goes into a clock buffer chip, and even the host will receive a copy of the buffered clocks, called the feedback clock, for the purpose of trace length matching.

Every PCI bus has four interrupt signals, INT[A:D]#, each device has its interrupt output wired to one of these four. Different devices use a different one, but since we only have four, there will be multiple devices reporting on the same line, which has to be resolved by software drivers. The X86 chipset interrupt controller has dedicated PCI INT[A:D]# pins on chip. Motherboard BIOS has to be hardcoded with the information about which device or card slot has which interrupt pin hooked up.

3.2.1.2 Logical Layer and Software

When a computer is powered on, the BIOS software will start running, and it will initialize all devices in the system. Many devices are PCI-based devices, so they will be initialized as follows: The motherboard designer shorts each device's IDSEL pin to one of the AD bus lines in the schematic. During the PCI device discovery, also known as "PCI enumeration", the CPU BIOS writes into the control register of the PCI master port inside the processor, and it will assert one of the AD lines, which causes one of the devices to receive a signal on its IDSEL, the one device that had its IDSEL shorted to that AD line. This establishes a communication channel. Then the BIOS will read the base address register (BAR) as well as other registers in the device's "PCI configuration header register structure". From this the BIOS can determine the device manufacturer (from vendor ID field) and device ID as well as how much memory-mapped space the device requires. The BIOS finds a suitable address range in the system memory map, and its start position will be written into the BAR of the device, then the address range enable bit and interrupt enable bit will be set. Then the BIOS will assert another AD line that is shorted to another device's IDSEL and so on until all possible devices are discovered and initialized.

The processor or a bus bridge chip is the "PCI initiator" device, all the peripheral devices are called "PCI Target". The master or main processor is always capable of being an initiator, called the host-initiator, but some peripheral chips can also initiate transactions and, like smart peripherals, they become a peripheral-initiator.

A PCI bus allows up to eight devices, including the local master. To add more devices to a system we have to create an additional bus by using a PCI-to-PCI bridge chip, as seen in Figure 3.5. This way there will be up to eight devices on the original bus and up to eight on the secondary bus of the bridge.

3.2.1.3 PCI-X

PCI-X is not PCI-Express. It is an extension to the PCI bus specification to allow faster operation, at 100MHz or 133MHz. There are additional signals like M66EN and PCIXCAP defined to detect the max speed capability of the slowest device on the bus. At 133MHz we can basically have a 2"–3" long point to point bus with one host and one target device, at 100MHz we can have two target devices and a host.

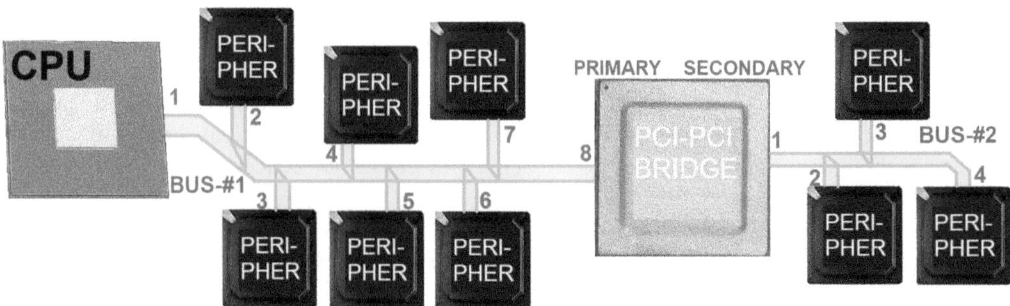

FIGURE 3.5 PCI buses with a bridge.

3.2.2 PCI Express

PCIe is a SERDES-based interface using a complex packet protocol. The signaling and logical level architecture is defined in the "PCI Express Base Specifications". It has several versions, which are related to the "generation" or speed level, for example, PCIe-v1.0 defines the Gen-1 at 2.5Gbps speed, and each generation doubles the speed and adds features to the previous generation. Several other specifications are also released, for example, the "PCI Express Card Electromechanical Specification" (CEM) that defines connector form factors, pinouts, and some of the signal trace lengths. Loss budgets can be found in both the Base and the CEM specs. The CEM focuses on system board and add-in-card data. The m.2 specs are similar to the CEM, but they are specifically for the m.2 form factor SSD/Wifi cards.

In PCIe there are three device classes, a root complex (RC) that is only one device in one system, an endpoint (basically peripheral or target devices), and the bridging or switching devices that pass data through. The RC is usually a processor, in PCI it is called a host-initiator.

3.2.2.1 The Layered Architecture

Once the devices are initialized, the PCIe hardware (board and silicon) are fully transparent to software. When any user software is trying to write a byte of data to the address that is within a device's memory region, then the CPU silicon state machines, PCIe switch silicon and device silicon will route that memory write automatically through PCIe bus transactions and all layers and devices. Each device implements the three layers on each port, as seen in Figure 3.6.

The highest layer is the transaction layer. This is the one that disassembles the arrived transaction layer packets or TLPs to find out what address or data is required when creating a local on-chip bus transaction. It also arranges bus transactions on the on-chip parallel bus to the core logic.

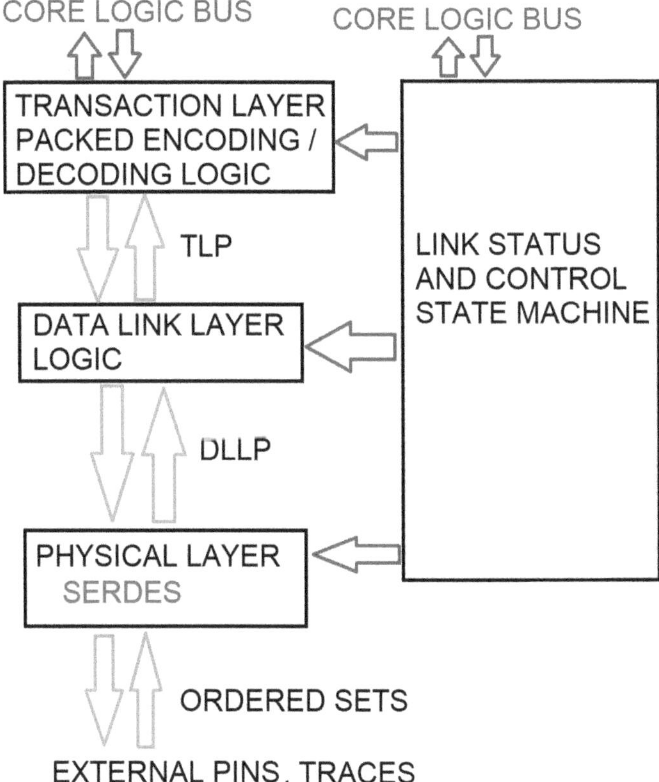

FIGURE 3.6 PCIe protocol layers.

A TLP contains a header (12 bytes) and payload data. Using PCIe is more efficient when the payload size is much larger than the header size, for example, writing 1kByte data instead of 1Byte of data. All devices have a limit to their max payload size, and the root complex or operating system should know what that is and not send oversized packets to avoid system crash. The header has bit fields like packet type (read request, completion, write request, interrupt, etc.), payload size, byte enable, requester or completer ID, memory address, status (successful or abort or unsupported request), tags, and flags with various parameters. Packets are routed based on ID that identifies every PCIe device in the system. A read request comes from a device with Requester ID=XYZ, then the endpoint device has to store that ID and put it into the completion packet header so it will be routed in complex systems back to the same master capable device that sent the original delayed read request. The endpoint will put its own Completer ID into the packet, so the requester knows who sent the data back.

The middle layer is the data link layer, which breaks down the TLPs into DLLPs (data link layer packets) as well as creates and receives non-payload DLLPs for automated link maintenance messaging like FIFO level flow control. This ensures that a device will not be sent more data than it can handle.

The physical layer is basically the SERDES tiles of the chip. It breaks down the TLLPs into "Ordered Sets", which are sets of four 8b10b characters or 128b130b symbols on Gen3. Some ordered sets are used to carry user data, others are used for basic low-level link operation. For example, keeping the CDR running when there is no data transfer by using IDLE characters or initializing a link with exchanging TS1 and TS2 ordered sets. On a smart oscilloscope with PCIe software we can observe whether there are any TS1 ordered sets going during link training or whether they keep repeating them, which means it keeps trying to train the link but it fails.

Interrupts are also available on PCIe links, but instead of discrete interrupt signals, we use encoded messages to send interrupts. There are two types supported. The "virtual wire interrupt" mimics the PCI INT[A:D] signals, one message can assert one of these four, or de-assert one. The virtual wire is a set of two register bits on-chip, one on each end of the link, and a packet sent updates one based on the state of the other one. The other type is the MSI or message signaled interrupt, which requires a more complicated OS interrupt driver to handle.

PCIe switch chips are used for port expansion with full bandwidth allowance to any device, as long as the others do not need full bandwidth at the same time. In most cases, the CPU initiates access to one endpoint device, so the other devices do not have a need for bandwidth in the meantime—except if we have a system with several DMA-capable devices (direct memory access, transfers initiated by the DMA controller inside of the endpoint ASIC instead of the CPU). A simple system design without PCIe switches would allow connecting everything up to a host processor in many cases, but it would limit the bandwidth of each individual endpoint device by having a narrow link to each, splitting (bifurcating) the processor's port to several separate ports. To be more precise it would limit the processor's ability to talk to any device at full bandwidth. It is unlikely that the CPU is blasting multiple devices in the same time at full bandwidth, so the arrangement on the left side of Figure 3.7 wastes resources and will lead to a massive bottleneck. Adding a PCIe switch allows the processor to use full bandwidth talking to any device. Another common use case of PCIe switches is when even bifurcation does not give enough number or ports, but we have too many devices. In some large chassis systems, we might need to have to connect dozens of cards and multiple devices on each card. There is no CPU with 20 to 100 independent PCIe ports available on it. In a complex chassis we might have two levels of PCIe switches, one big switch on the CPU card and one on each add-in card. Some endpoint devices, like some GPUs, do not work well through multiple switches and bridges.

3.2.2.2 High-Speed Signal Interface

PCIe is a multi-gigabit serial differential SERDES interface. It uses low voltage differential signaling. The signals are all differential pairs, one set of diffpairs in each direction. The signals are often

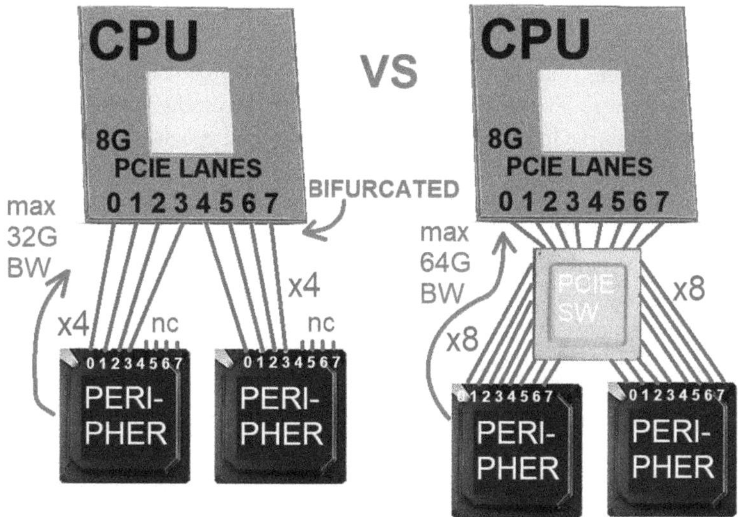

FIGURE 3.7 Using PCIe switches to allow full bandwidth on any device.

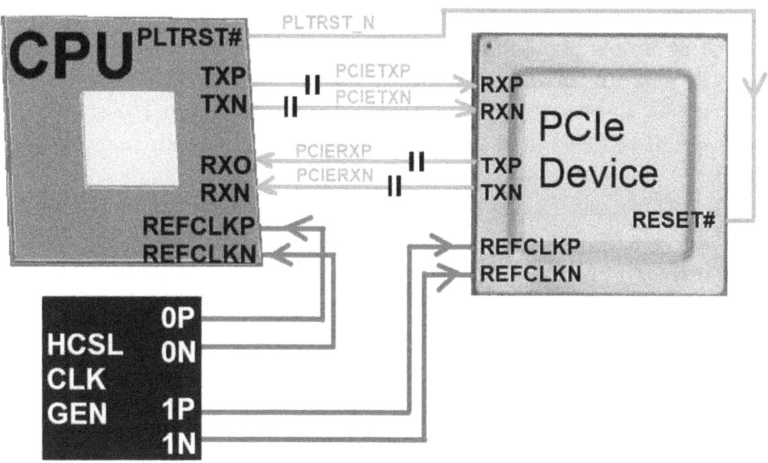

FIGURE 3.8 Basic 1-lane PCIe circuit.

called TX and RX signals, but the schematic signal names are usually named after the pin names of the host device. Every device has RX and TX pins. The TX pins of one device are connected to the RX pins of the other device through PCB traces and AC-coupling capacitors. The reference clock and the reset are also considered part of a PCI express design. All this can be seen on a simple example schematic in Figure 3.8.

A "link" is the connection between two devices. A "port" is the set of pins that are used for one link. A "lane" is a set of one RX and one TX diffpair. A link can be multi-lane with 1 to 16 lanes per link, to multiply the total bandwidth, usually marked as x1to x16, pronounced "by 16". If a port can be "bifurcated" then it splits into two or more separate ports, then the port is labeled as 2xx8 that means two ports of x8 width each. The one main host device in each system is the Root Complex. There are no more PCIe devices upstream from the RC, only downstream from it.

Various PCIe standards define insertion loss and return loss limits, as described in Chapter 11, "Signal Integrity". The PCIe specifications are released as several versions or generations. Gen-1 is in the PCIe v1.0 specs and are able to run at 2.5Gbps/lane, each generation doubles the bandwidth. Starting with Gen-6, the new PAM4 signaling scheme was introduced at 64Gbps/lane speed. Gen1-2 used 8b10b encoding, then later generations started using 128b130b encoding to reduce overhead. With 8b10b we were able to use 100nF AC-caps, but with the longer sequence we need to use larger capacitors at 220nF. On the PCB layout we place the capacitors near the TX pin or near the connector if there is one. With multi-board systems only the local chip's output signal (TX pin) needs an AC cap, the other signal will have the capacitor on the other board. In case of KR Ethernet the cap is more usually placed at the RX input pins. The traces are typically 85 Ohm differential controlled-impedance. The clock signals are also differential, 100MHz HCSL standard and routed at 100 Ohm. The clock may or may not need AC-cap or termination, check the chip datasheet and reference design.

Some devices support auto lane reversal, but usually we just use resistor strapping to tell one of the devices to reverse the lane numbers from 0 …7 to 7…0.

3.2.2.3 Link Training

After the system and the devices power up, all the devices will try to see if something is connected to all of their PCIe ports, and if yes then they will try to establish a link, using the link training process. This is handled by the link training and status state machine, or LTSSM, explained in Figure 3.9. If the devices do not link up on a prototype, then one of the two devices might be dysfunctional, but we need to know for certain. The state output of the LTSSM can be monitored on some devices, so if it recycles between state 0 and N, then there is an issue. If it steps up and stays at the L0 active state then it means the link is good, and both devices are alive and functional. Additionally, we can monitor the PCIe data stream with an oscilloscope, up to about 8Gbps, which has software to decode TS1 ordered sets, to observe a completing versus a recycling LTSSM. We might need to strap the devices to Gen1 or Gen2 to be able to accurately measure with an oscilloscope (soldered on active diff probe).

The first step is the "Electrical Load Detect", where a slow pulse is sent out on the TX output to see if it is reflected back (termination and device present) or not. This is the "detect" phase. If it is successful, then the "polling" stage starts, where both devices (link partners) will start sending TS1 ordered sets (eight symbol codes) on all lanes. This facilitates detecting how many lanes are

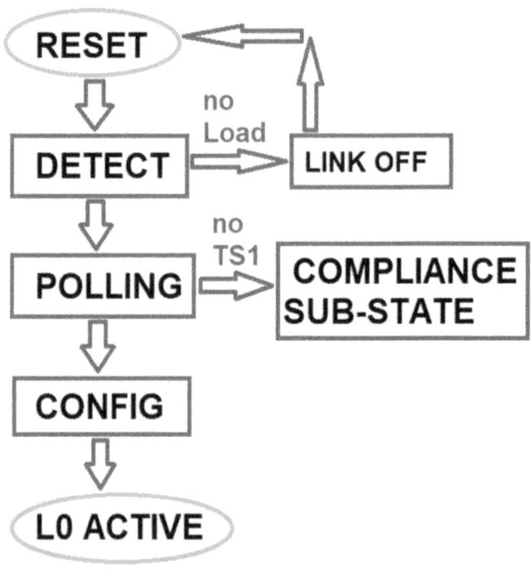

FIGURE 3.9 PCIe LTSSM.

connected, which lane has what lane number on which device, and the maximum speed capability of each device. The next stage after all data is collected is the "config" state, where the parameters are finalized and set. Both devices will set on the lowest common denominator for a safe and reliable continuous operation. After that the LTSSM enters the L0 state, which is the normal operation, where it stays until the user powers the system off. When data is being sent then there is data on the line, otherwise just IDLE ordered sets are sent infinitely. The line does not stay at a logic zero or something, waiting for a new transaction, like a CMOS bus would.

Compliance substate is entered by any PCIe device if its TX output has detected an electrical load termination but did not receive any TS1 ordered sets on its RX pins. This can occur when no real device or not working device is connected to it, but an oscilloscope is connected to the TX output. In this mode we can observe if the chip is well enough to drive a good quality PCIe compliant signal to its output.

3.2.2.4 Clocking

The two devices on the two ends of the PCIe link have a clocking relationship with each other. There are two methods for PCIe clocking: the regular constant frequency clock and the spread spectrum (SSC) clocking. SSC spreads the EMI radiation in the spectrum by varying the frequency periodically up and down to help pass EMI validation tests.

PCIe devices also support different clocking modes by another aspect; the synchronous clocking where both devices receive their reference clock signals from the same clock generator or buffer, and the independent clocking where the two devices use their own oscillators. Independent clocking can be used only if both of these are true: (1) SSC is turned off (in the BIOS), and (2) the two clock signals are no more than 300ppm deviate from each other. If we use 30ppm oscillators, then the two PCIe devices will be at 30+30=60ppm, which is within the 300ppm limit. With SSC on, the clocks would go 5000ppm apart. If we connect two boards with PCIe, there might not be a PCIe clock connection defined between them, so independent clocking must be used (each board with local clock generator), so SSC must be turned off for both ends.

3.2.3 Configuration

All chips that are PCI/PCIe capable have a configuration header, which is a standardized register set. This is used to provide device status to software as well as to initialize and set up each device. The header contains a vendor ID and a device ID, and other things. Vendor IDs are assigned to companies by PCI-SIG, if a company pays them an annual fee. The operating system can find the right device driver software for a device, based on VID and DID, if the driver software is installed. PCI/PCIe devices are all memory mapped, and their address location within the CPU's memory space is defined by a base address and a window size. The base address is assigned by the BIOS during system startup, but the BIOS needs to know how much space is required. The size information is discovered by a clever mechanism. The base address register (BAR) has its upper bits non-writeable all-zero, so when the BIOS writes a pattern into it and reads it back, it will be able to tell the required size. Then the BIOS writes back the base address into the BAR, so the device will know what address to respond to. Devices usually have control/status registers, and data buffers (on-chip or off-chip memory) mapped into their own memory window that all together is mapped into the memory region that is assigned to the device within the CPU's whole memory address space, as we can see in Figure 3.10. CPUs access all peripherals as memory mapped (or I/O range mapped) devices. The header also contains information about the speed/width capability of the device, and there are register bits to enable interrupts and independent clocking. If the device is a bridge, then it has a Type-1 config header that also contains information about the downstream bus.

The configuration space registers of the devices (endpoints and switch/bridge chips) are accessed by the CPU through "configuration access", which goes through the root complex's or

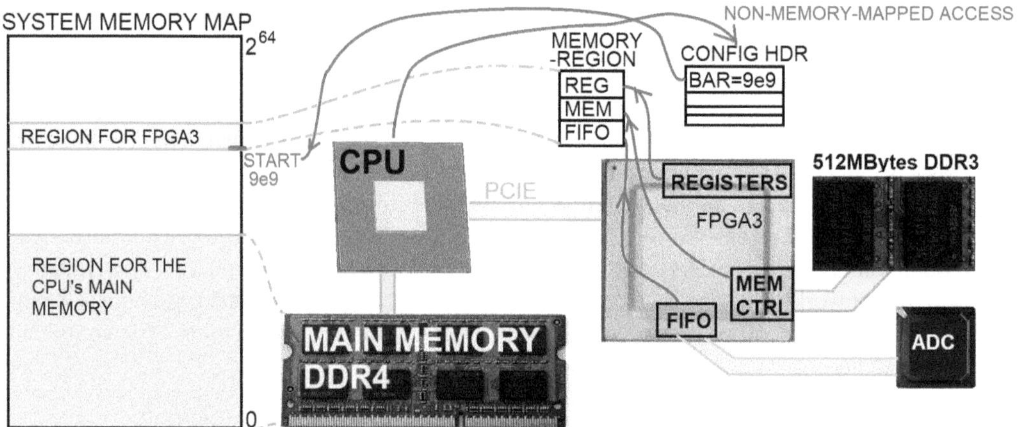

FIGURE 3.10 Memory mapping and device addressing in PCI/PCIe.

host controller's PCI(e) control register. The data plane communication to the endpoint device internal buffers goes through the memory region that is assigned to the device. In PCI systems the BIOS selects one device for configuration access by asserting its IDSEL signal, in PCIe it is done by port number basis. In PCI we can have up to eight devices on a bus, in PCIe we can have only one per bus/link. The system accounts for how many buses are discovered, and every device is listed (in a PCI scan) by bus number, device number, and function number for those devices that are divided into "functions". The only time we see multiple PCIe devices on the same bus number in the PCI scan command response, if we are looking at a PCIe-switch chip's internal virtual PCI-to-PCI bridge blocks sitting on the internal virtual PCI-bus. It is not a real bus, but it appears so for the software. One PCIe switch appears as multiple devices with the same device ID, as many as the number of ports, plus any internal function like a DMA controller block.

During prototyping we may want to access any of the registers of our FPGA/ASIC device for basic manual read and write access. If we run Windows-7 or older on the prototype then we can use the "RW-Everything" free program for that, but newer versions disable all PCIe devices (clears their BAR) that have no signed device drivers installed. It is unlikely to start a proto bringup with already existing fully debugged device drivers, especially for devices with custom register sets like FPGA blocks. For a hard ASIC a driver might exist before we start the project. On Linux we would use a custom memory-space driver with command line read and write commands, obtained either from the Internet or written by our software engineering team.

3.3 COMMON HB INTERFACES

The most common high-bandwidth or high-speed serial interfaces are the ones used inside consumer computers, but they are also used in high-end equipment. These are the PCIe and Ethernet, the HDMI video display output, the SATA storage device interface, and the USB 3.0 external attachment port.

3.3.1 SATA

SATA (Serial Advanced Technology Attachment) is an interface specifically designed for attaching a boot storage device to an X86 chipset used on modern computers. For the hardware designer, the SATA interface is a point-to-point command-based interface with two signals, an RX and a TX high-speed SERDES differential pair. Usually, an add-in card or cabled drive unit is connected through SATA to a motherboard. They specify AC-coupling capacitors on both boards/units on both signals. The speed is either 1.5Gbps, 3Gbps, or 6Gbps. At the logical level SATA is a storage-command protocol interface. It is suitable neither for memory mapped access to peripherals nor for peer-to-peer communications like Ethernet. It is simply for telling storage devices how to retrieve stored data blocks through a command-based protocol.

3.3.2 USB 3.0

The Universal Serial Bus (USB) is an interface meant to be used for connecting low performance devices to a computer through removable external cables. These devices are well known by every computer user, like USB stick flash drives, USB cameras, or JTAG programming cables. Sometimes we use USB chips on the motherboard, for example, USB hubs for port multiplication, or creating even lower speed buses that do not naturally come out of an X86 chipset, like UART, I2C, or SPI through bridge chips.

The original versions use a single differential pair with bidirectional signaling, at 480Mbps speed on USB 2.0, and 12Mbps for USB 1.1. USB ports can be expanded using USB hub chips. The three types of devices are the host, device, and hub. All USB devices and hubs can be checked (dead or alive test) during board bring-up using the LSUSB command in Linux. The standard trace and cable impedance for USB is 90 Ohm differential. USB peripheral devices have a pullup on the D_P or D_M line to let the host detect what speed the USB device supports and to detect a hot plug event. An integrated USB device designed on the motherboard does not need speed and hot plug detection resistors. There are standard USB connectors that everyone knows, and every few years they come out with a new USB connector standard. USB hosts provide power (VBUS pin) at the port connectors to the devices at 5V, 0.5A for USB1.0/2.0, and 1A for USB3.0. Power is usually switched by a USB power switch chip, which can be enabled by a GPIO signal controlled by BIOS, has overcurrent protection, and requires a 100 to 220uF capacitor on the VBUS line. The port circuits for a 2.0 host-side port can be seen in Figure 3.11.

USB3.0 preserved the USB2.0 signals and speeds on the single bidirectional diffpair, but also added two extra diffpairs, one for SERDES RX and one for SRDES TX at 5Gbit/sec speed. It also had to define new connectors with accommodation for the extra pins for the extra signals. USB Type-C is a common connector type these days. USB3.0 is sometimes also available in the same shape/size Type-A connector as it was defined for USB1.0/2.0, but with the extra pins in an area formerly blank. The Type-A female connector can be found on host computers, the Type-A male on cables and storage stick devices. Type-B is used on the other end of the cable. Type-C can be on either end. Modern X86 BIOS has drivers for USB1/2/3 device detection, and all operating systems support basic drivers for basic USB devices like hubs and storage stick drives.

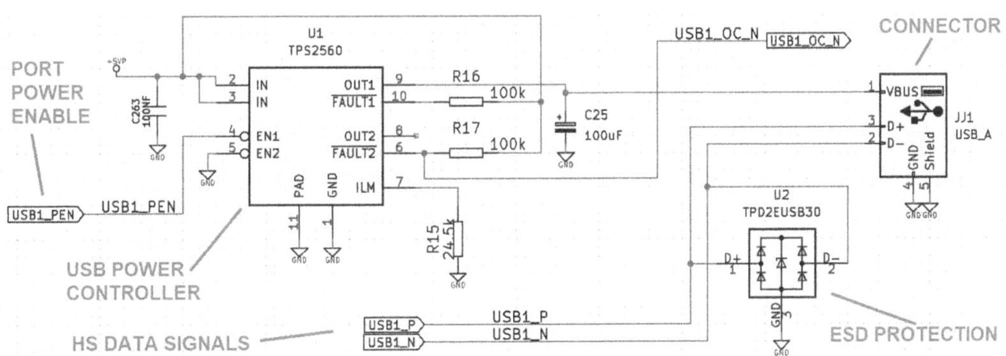

FIGURE 3.11 USB2.0 Type-A host side port circuits in KiCad.

3.3.3 Computer Video

Video interfaces are unidirectional, basically sending data from a computer to a display, or from a camera to a computer. HDMI became the dominant video standard for external connectors, after a long fight with VGA, DVI, Display Port, and LVDS. In military/aerospace, the ARINC818 serial digital video standard was adopted, with single-lane SERDES over coax cable or optical fiber. All other equipment if they have a video output connector (many do not) then it is usually HDMI. What is common between all video interfaces is they separately transmit three color signals, as images are decomposed to pixels, and pixels are decomposed to three color components. The color can be red/green/blue, or it can be a more complex YCbCr system, using either analog or digital signaling. They also transmit digital synchronization signals, like an I/O clock for LVDS/HDMI/DVI or a horizontal and a vertical sync pulse for analog VGA ports. They usually also have an I2C bus for helping a computer detect what type of display is plugged in, where the display will contain an EEPROM or microcontroller that has information about the display brand, model number and supported resolutions, and refresh rates. For high-end embedded hardware only a text-based console is used over a serial RS232 port, no graphical interfaces are implemented like in consumer electronics. The old composite-video TV signals and component video signals are no longer used, where pixel, color, and synchronization signals were multiplexed together into a very complex single analog waveform.

A multi-lane LVDS interface is used inside devices between a motherboard and a higher resolution graphics (pixel-matrix) LCD panel—one LVDS differential pair for each color, plus an additional pair for I/O clock/frame. Smaller LCD panels often utilize a parallel CMOS interface, with eight wires for each color, plus horizontal and vertical synchronization signals. LCD panels require a continuous stream of data in a specific format, usually through a flex/flat cable and a power input. There are several device-specific interface protocols. These panels are used in laptops, small devices, kiosks, and hand-held electronics. Touch screen panels are transparent thin panels sitting on top of the LCD surface, with a few-pin connector, routed to a touch controller chip on the main board. Data center and aerospace hardware usually do not have any kind of display.

The High-Definition Multimedia Interface (HDMI) is a unidirectional interface. It can utilize over 10Gbps speeds on long cables. It contains four differential pairs (called TMDS signals) and an I2C interface. Out of the four diffpairs three contain video data, one diffpair for each of three colors encoded with 8b10b, and one diffpair transmits a clock/frame signal for the clock forwarding timing scheme and bit alignment. Audio and horizontal/vertical synchronization pulses are also encoded in the color channels. This is not a generic SERDES interface as it is not an embedded clock interface. DVI is another interface standard, it uses the same signals as HDMI but with a different connector. DisplayPort (DP) is a third type of digital display interface, with 4-lane SERDES circuits having embedded clock, pre-emphasis, link training, and encoding. The host computer can receive information from the DP-compliant display about the received signal quality during link training through the AUX channel differential digital interface.

3.3.4 JESD204x

The JESD204A, B, C standards were created by JEDEC, for A/D converter to FPGA attachment, mainly at the Giga samples per second range, used in RF/DSP and software defined radio applications in the telecommunications, military, and aerospace industries. Version A was specified up to 3.125Gbps, version B to 12.5Gbps, and version C to 32Gbps. It uses SERDES transceivers, which can handle FIFO-based lane-to-lane de-skew just like PCIe or Ethernet. It requires a common clock source (synchronous clocking, no frequency compensation). It contains additional timing signals like SYNC. The packet structure is very simple, compared to PCIe, as it does not require device addressing. They introduced the channel operating margin (JCOM), similarly to the Ethernet COM. There are several timing-related elements of the standard, like subclasses that depend on the RF application and the use of a SYSREF clock (synchronization and deterministic latency) in addition to the "device clock" that is the ADC sample clock and transceiver line rate clock in one. The FPGA might run from a lower rate reference clock, if the clocking chip produces a lower rate for the JESD than it does for the analog sampling but is still frequency locked.

3.3.5 Data Center Chassis-to-Chassis Interconnects

Common interfaces between separate chassis in the same or nearby racks or between boards over a backplane, are like Fiber Channel, Fiber Channel Over Ethernet (FCoE), InfiniBand, SAS, external PCIe (with hot-plugging) over cable. Most copper (non-optical) cabling has a limit of 3 meters or 10 feet. FCoE is simply making server-to-storage connectivity using generic Ethernet ports and switches to allow physical separation of web servers from storage servers. FCoE encapsulates Fiber Channel storage access into Ethernet packets. Nvidia (acquired Mellanox) has InfiniBand switch chips for creating complex topologies with IB.

Aurora, an AMD (Xilinx) IP, is only defined as the physical and data-link layer interface. The user (who designs the chip or FPGA logic) has to implement the higher layer protocol in any way convenient to fit to unique cases.

3.4 HIGH PERFORMANCE COMPUTING LINKS

There are special interface standards used between the processors of a multi-head server, between elements of the chipsets (DMI used between CPU and South Bridge), or between accelerator ASICs. These interfaces are many-lane SERDES links. Multiple processors on the same motherboard or in the same chassis can work together through "shared memory multi-processing", and all processors can access all memory modules of all other processors. This is a "coherent" interface, meaning that the bus interface logic inside each CPU ensures that all processors in the system see the same view of memory. This would be an issue when a processor relies on data in its local cache memory instead of its external RAM. To resolve this, the cache coherent interface, when fetching data from the RAM to give it to the other processor, ensures the newer cached data is stored into the local RAM first. It "snoops" memory accesses, to keep an account to which data might have been taken out of the RAM and modified by a processor. The physical layer is (almost) identical to PCIe or 10G Ethernet KR, but their protocol layers are reduced to serve simple device-pair operations, buffer copy or shared memory access, and cache buffer snoop. Intel used QPI and UPI between their Xeon processors, AMD used Hyper Transport (now Infinity Fabric) and Nvidia used the NVLINK. Some newer devices started to support more than one standard option on the same pins. AI accelerator ASICs might support PCIe, CXL, or CCIX.

General purpose standards were released that can be used by any chip company, such as the Compute Express Link (CXL), Interlaken, RapidIO, InfiniBand, and Cache Coherent Interconnect for Accelerators (CCIX). Interlaken is used for one-on-one links, without addressing, switching, or routing. Mainly for connecting accelerator or off-loading secondary ASICs to the main ASICs on the board. Clock compensation is partially supported, but most implementations require exact clock match at 0ppm, even if the clock frequency is not equal for the two link partner ASICs, using a fractional-PLL clock buffer. InfiniBand and RapidIO are used with switching and addressing, for ASIC-to-ASIC direct links on the same board or over a backplane, or chassis-to-chassis links. Components like the 80HCPS1432 RapidIO switch helps with connecting multiple devices together. Ampere Altra ARM processors used CCIX for their multi-processing interconnect. CXL is more optimized for multi-host accesses to devices and shared memory, sharing resources, as well as device-to-device horizontal DMA accesses, while CCIX and UPI are more for cache coherent multi-processing.

In High Performance Computing a large amount of data needs to be loaded and stored (or DMA'ed) quickly, without having a top-down hierarchy or resource bottleneck that PCIe has, more in a peer-to-peer or multi-host fashion. DMA means direct memory access, where a smart peripheral, not the main CPU, initiates large bulk data transfers between itself and the system memory. This also allows a mesh topology where two devices can talk to each other at full bandwidth, while another two devices do the same also at full bandwidth. Inter-CPU links can be implemented on large motherboards that host multiple server CPUs, or they can be routed over a backplane, when a whole multi-slot chassis becomes one single computer with one memory space, or cabled between separate chassis. Figure 3.12 shows different topology options for Intel Xeon CPU-based multi-processing over the UPI interface. Typically, every processor has dedicated DIMM memory slots, although the content is accessible over UPI by any other CPU. Several CPUs can have PCIe slots, but only one will have a chipset (PCH) connected to it. The chipset has the main console I/O, power management, and SSD boot drives attached.

CXL can connect multiple hosts (CPUs/FPGAs/ASICs) with multiple devices through a CXL switch (like the XC50256 developed by Xconn Technologies) at a very high bandwidth. With CXL an ASIC can access regions of the memory buffers that are attached to other CXL-connected ASICs within the same system. New devices start supporting both CXL and PCIe on the same pins, since the physical layer is the same, and this allows hardware designers more flexibility in their hardware architecture. They call these ports "Flex Bus". Sometimes it is advertised as an alternate protocol that runs on standard PCIe ports through auto-negotiation. CXL 2.0 is at 32Gbits/sec, CXL3.0 is at 64Gbits/sec just like PCIe6.0.

Coherent memory sharing and memory pooling in CXL systems means multiple host ASICs can access a shared CXL memory buffer device. One such device is, for example, the Astera Labs Leo CXL Memory controller ASIC that has DRAM memory behind it (creating a "G-FAM" unit). CXL allows coherency only to the GFAM units, not to each CPU's own DRAM modules, while CCIX and UPI do coherency to them also. The shared CXL memory can also be the memory buffer of an AI ASIC, or an Ethernet NIC ASIC being accessed by multiple CPUs. When a host is trying to access a region in the shared memory that is cached by another host, then the CXL switch notifies the other host to write out the data back from its cache into the shared memory, then the transaction requested by the first host can be completed. This is how coherency is maintained, but only to device memory, not to host memory.

Multi-computing systems can be created with shared accelerator and memory resources through CXL switches, like we can see in Figure 3.13. MLD is an acronym describing Multi-Logical Devices,

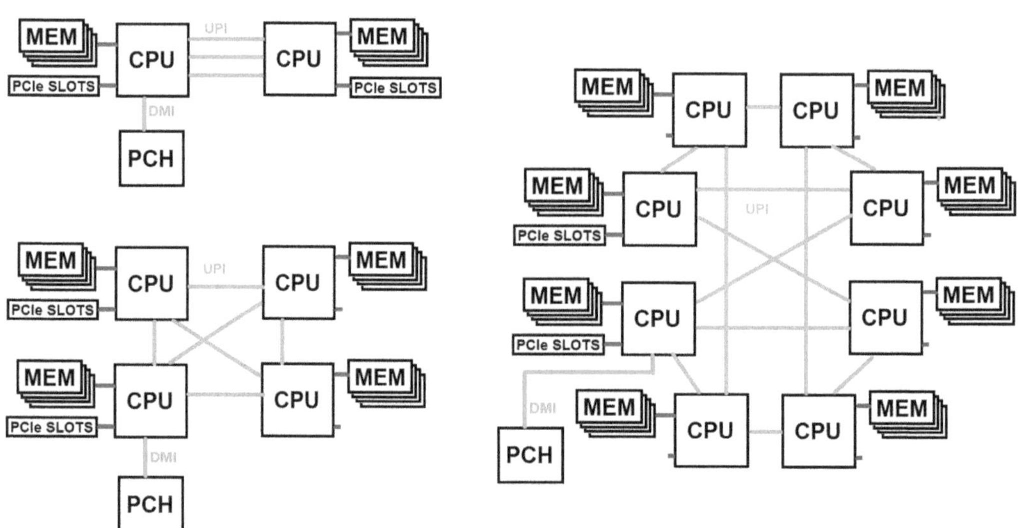

FIGURE 3.12 Multi-socket server UPI bus connection options with Intel Scalable Xeon processors.

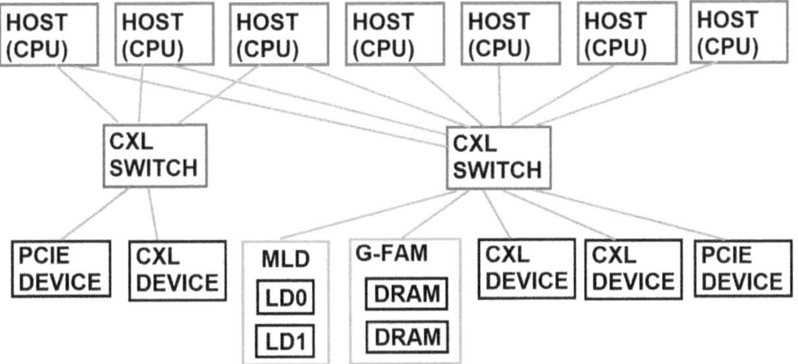

FIGURE 3.13 A possible CXL fabric system.

which are one device that appear as multiple resources (LD's or logical devices) at the software access level. A mesh backplane fabric system can be created by using CXL switches, where the cards plugged into a chassis each have a CXL switch at their backplane interface. If using two layers of CXL switches, in a similar fashion to the data center Ethernet switching leaf/spine architecture, then large supercomputers can be built. Larger mesh can be created with one layer of switch chips and partial mesh connections, using two-hop switching. Growing multi-node systems can be done through scale-up or scale-out concepts. In scale-out we distribute shared resources between the nodes, instead of having to go through a central resource or switch. Scale-out can be expanded more easily by adding nodes with resources. It also results in a need of horizontal node-to-node traffic, which can be well handled through the leaf-spine switching architecture, instead of the multi-level tree/star architecture. This is done in modern data centers for connecting servers through Ethernet switches, but the concept could also be applicable to multi-ASIC chassis systems, for example, through the use of peer-to-peer interface protocols (like CXL instead of PCIe) using switch ASICs that support high horizontal bandwidth and by adding more intelligence into each node.

4 Power Supply Circuits

Hardware is made of active devices that are supported by passive devices, but that are also supplied power by power supply circuits. In this chapter we discuss the components, circuits and the design and analysis methods required for them. Digital boards rarely have AC/DC, AC/AC, or DC/AC conversion, only DC/DC conversion from a higher to a lower voltage (step-down or buck converter). Any voltage regulator or DC/DC converter on the digital boards is a Voltage Regulator Module (VRM). The more complex and high-performance digital boards usually contain many VRM circuits, about 20% of the board area or component count. They are also not only analog circuits, but they have a few digital pins and partake in the digital power management subsystem. They have modes and parameters that are selected by the digital designer.

4.1 GLOBAL POWER CIRCUITS

Global power simply means it is devices and voltage rails that feed multiple boards or multiple devices on a single board, as opposed to point-of-load (POL) power that feeds one voltage rail of one ASIC.

4.1.1 Chassis Input Power

Chassis power supplies are usually in removable elongated metal boxes. They have their own small fan built in, and a many pin power/signal connector to connect to our motherboard. They are purchased by system companies, instead of being designed in-house. They typically provide a main 12V and a 3.3V or 5V standby (always on) voltage rail, and they have a power-on signal input that our digital board controls based on power buttons or glue logic state machines. They also have an I2C interface for telemetry. These chassis PSU modules typically have a 110V or 240V AC or DC input, and they are able to provide up to a few kilowatts of power (depending the outlet's limits). Most power supply modules are hot-swappable and removable; they have an ejector switch that allows sliding them out that click when we insert one into the chassis. Typical chassis designs provide some level of redundancy by providing more PSU modules that it needs. The PSUs have to have a current sharing feature, so when more than one PSU is inserted, they all provide an equal portion of the load current. Redundancy is described with numbers and a plus sign, where the number before the plus sign shows how many PSU modules are needed minimum for operation, the number after the plus sign is the extras. For example, "2+1" means our chassis needs 2 PSUs to be able to run, and one extra is provided for redundancy. If one of the three PSUs fail, the remaining two can still supply power to the system reliably, but the administrator has to replace the broken one soon, before another one would fail, as the chassis is running in non-redundant mode until the replacement. PSU redundancy is often handled through load current sharing. PSUs have a signal pin that is for current sharing control to help the modules adjust their output for achieving an equal current share. Other systems like ATCA allow each board to switch over from one source to another using a PIM module.

Within the chassis the power has to be delivered to the digital boards. This can be done through backplane/mezzanine connectors (maybe <500W/board), cables, bus bars for higher powered systems, or the PSU modules can be plugged into the digital board directly for "appliance" type products. Bus bars are mechanical parts, plated long copper bars that can be plugged into special electrical connectors.

DOI: 10.1201/9781032702094-4

4.1.2 Board Input Power

In mobile computers like laptops, smartphones there is a power controller circuit that handles the main (3 to 21V) battery connection, its charging, the motherboard load. It typically has two big MOSFETs to control which way the energy is flowing in or out of the battery. One such device is a BQ25672 chip.

Boards that are plugged into a chassis, especially if they are meant to be plugged in or removed while the system is running, need a "hot-swap controller", or HSC. This hot swap controller ensures that the board will not draw too much power during the plugging event by keeping a series MOSFET turned off, then turning it or ramping it up slowly in 1to 100ms. The devices on the board, but especially the decoupling capacitors, will start pulling in-rush-current or even spark if we did not have a hot swap controller (HSC) with soft start. Sometimes they are called eFUSE. We put a large sum of decoupling capacitors at the output of the hot-swap controller's MOSFET, but no more than 100nF at its input, otherwise it would cause backplane voltage drop during card insertion.

Some power switch circuits and VRMs are unstable or have a leakage when the load drops below a few milli Amps. So we put a minimum load circuit to the output, that is, a few 0402 resistors in series with each other between the output rail and ground. They share the power dissipation, each at half its 65mW rating. R=(V/N)^2/0.03

Each complex digital board contains glue logic and management circuits that control the power enable signals to the main data plane voltage regulators. The glue/management logic is usually implemented with low power flash-based FPGAs and microcontrollers, which are supplied by a small amount of power from a standby rail. The standby rail is always on, at least they are turned on immediately after insertion by themselves, not controlled by anything, while all other rails are controlled by the glue logic that is always on due to being on the standby domain. Non-removable cards, like those inside an appliance chassis, might not have any hot-swap controllers, but if they do then their purpose is just power sequencing. Figure 4.1 shows a typical removable card power scheme with hot-swap controllers.

Telecom boards like ATCA blades have to operate from 48V and from two redundant independent power sources (without current sharing through the backplane). For this they have a power input module (PIM) that selects one of the two inputs to feed to the output. The 48V being too high for any POL VRM controllers, we need an intermediate bus converter, a 48V to 12V converter module. They come in standard sizes, like half-brick, quarter-brick (2.3x1.45"), or eighth-brick. Some of them are isolated, others are non-isolated.

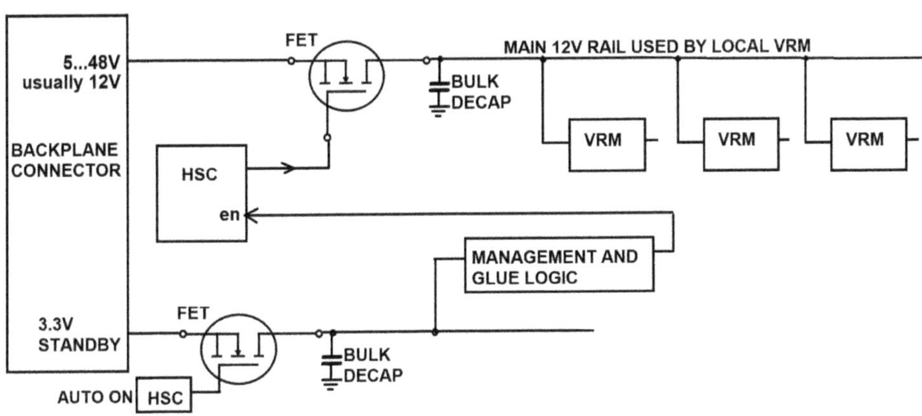

FIGURE 4.1 Board hot-swap control.

4.2 VOLTAGE REGULATOR MODULES (VRM)

4.2.1 VRM Architectures

Mostly we talk about the point-of-load (POL) power converters in this chapter, which provide power to one voltage rail of one ASIC. Several separate POLs are placed right next to the ASIC and they provide separate very low impedance power sources. Each board design also has a few global VRMs, for example, for the main glue logic 3.3V and the standby 3.3V. Technically there are several VRM topologies, depending on the input/output voltage relationship. If the input voltage is higher than the output, we call it a step-down (or buck) regulator. If it is the other way around, then it is a step-up (boost) regulator. If the input can vary above and below output, then it is a buck-boost converter. Digital boards very rarely contain anything other than buck converters. All of these topologies have a MOSFET power switch and a diode as active components. In recent decade all converters produced have been something called a "synchronous rectifier", which replaces the diode with a second MOSFET, and we get a "half-bridge" circuit with an upper and a lower MOSFET. This significantly reduces the power loss, as diodes dissipate power at P=V*I or 0.7V times the output current, while the lower MOSFET that replaces the diode has only a few milli Volts drop on it. The two MOSFETs are replaced in modern converters with a power stage chip that contain the 2 MOSFETs, some digital gate drive circuits, and thermal and current sensing analog circuits. Several of the common topologies of buck converters are shown on Figure 4.2.

On complex digital boards we have several Step-Down (buck) DC/DC controllers, or Voltage Regulator Modules (VRM). In some cases, there are more than 50 different ones on a single board. Typically, these complex boards have 3.3V and 12V, sometimes 24V or 48V coming in, sometimes through hot-swap controllers or eFUSE power switch chips. If it is larger than 12V then usually there is a large "bus converter module" that creates 12V from 48V, like the ones used on the ATCA form factor. After that most ASIC/FPGA/CPU chip power rails are created by "Point of Load" (POL) step-down converters operating from 12V or from 3.3V. Typical voltages we use at the load are between 0.6 and 3.3V. They are physically placed right next to their load ASIC on the PCB. ASIC core voltages that are the highest current rails are typically around 0.8 to 1.2V. Each ASIC has a core rail, a PLL (clocking) rail, several SERDES rails, and I/O buffer (for bus interfaces and system signal buffers) power rails.

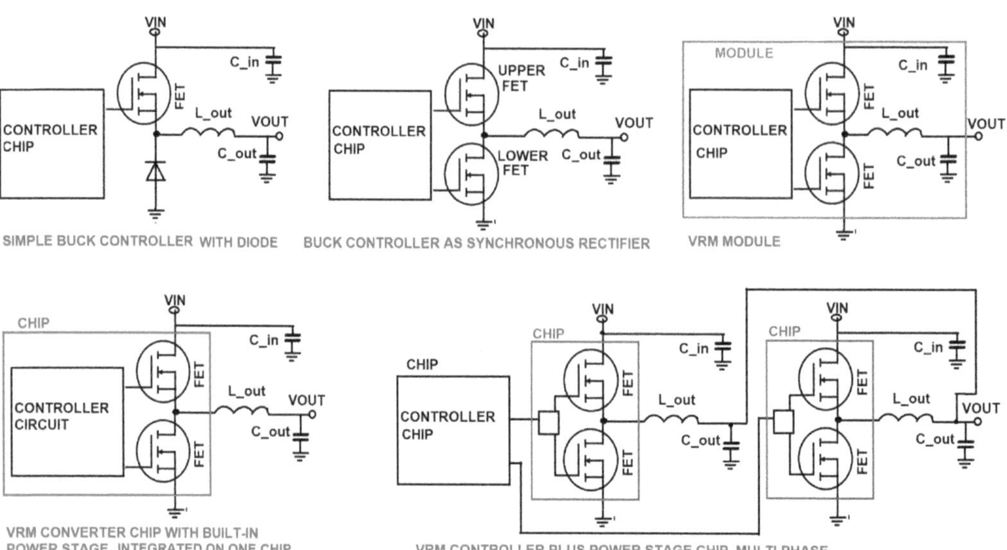

FIGURE 4.2 Buck VRM topologies.

The two main types of VRM are the switching controllers and the linear converters (usually for <300mA and sensitive PLL rails). Linear converters dissipate a lot of power, their efficiency is much lower than that of the switching regulators. They have a pass-through transistor on-chip that is controlled by a control loop to provide enough exact series resistance to drop the right amount of voltage on itself, the drop-out voltage being the input voltage minus the desired output voltage. If it was a resistor, then the output voltage would change when the load current changes, but being a transistor with a control circuit, it will maintain its voltage. The most common type of linear regulators is the low drop-out (LDO) regulators, which allow us to use them when the difference between the input and the output voltage is very small. They are used in special circumstances, like clocking or PLL circuit supply, that require a very low noise voltage rail. These are not switching regulators—they produce no switching ripple noise, only step load response noise. Most LDOs we use on complex digital boards are in the small packages, for example SO-8 or QFN-16. QFN packages that have a solder-down center pad can dissipate 0.3 to 1.5W, while SO-8 can dissipate 0.2 to 0.4W. The LDO's dissipated power has to be calculated and ensured to remain below the package thermal limit as:

$$P=(Vin-Vout)*Iout$$

The switching converters typically dissipate around 15% (that is 85% efficiency) as much as the output power, while linear regulators can dissipate 20% to 300% (that is 30% to 80% efficiency).

The switching VRM can be a "controller" plus "power stage chips" (or MOSFETs) or they can be "converters" with integrated controller and power stages in one single chip, used for lower current rails.

Multi-phase VRM circuits can be built with up to 16 power stage chips and a controller chip. Power stage chips have several vendor-specific analog and digital control signals, and they may need proper power sequencing of their input power. Some power stage chips require a 12V and a 3.3V/5V input power to be sequenced, and the designer also has to consider the power to the controller versus the power stage chips to be sequenced. If the sequence is not provided correctly, then it can cause intermittent startup failures, or even thermal blowup.

VRM's can be designed onto the board (chip-down), or we can use modules. The modules contain all the parts of the converter in a single package, usually a very small board with solder pins. The chip-down VRM solution requires the designer to place and route all parts on the board, the controller, switch MOSFETs, output inductor, input and output capacitors, and strapping and compensation parts. Chip down type designs are cheaper, and they can be tuned to work more reliably in a given situation. Almost all good quality high-end hardware designs use the chip-down solution for all point-of-load rails, mainly for its improved power integrity. Modules have extra parasitic inductance between the source and the load, and they cannot be tuned for a particular design's transient response. Modules are more commonly used where the extra inductance is not an issue, for example, for low current rails (<3A) or higher voltage (3.3V, 12V) global rails instead of POL. Modules are usually also taller.

A "smart VRM" is one that can be controlled and monitored through PMBUS, the output voltage might be programmed through PMBUS write command instead of resistor strapping (stored in flash or OTP memory), and it provides full telemetry (reading output voltage, temperature, and current with good <2% accuracy). They also log and save fault sources, but only into RAM registers, that get erased by a power cycle. There are two type of smart VRMs, the type with resistor strapping for voltage and overcurrent settings and PMBUS monitoring and the type with voltage/current programming. This second type must have a very low default "boot voltage" or its enable pin must be held low (not sequenced) before and during the first factory programming to avoid damaging any digital load ASICs.

The layout of switching regulators has to be designed in such a way as to use power shapes for the power nets and use only traces for the control signals. The power shapes have to be short and wide;

the placement has to be in such a way as to enable the short and wide power shapes. See Chapter 15, "PCB Layout Design". The pin to shape connection has to be direct so as to eliminate parasitic inductances.

Some point-of-load VRMs are constructed as single-phase, some are multi-phase (2 to 16), like the one seen in Figure 4.3. The multi-phase versions use all/most phases to produce the same voltage, to the same net or voltage rail, but with a certain degree of phase delay. For example, N-phase converters turn on each power stage at 360/N degree phase delay, relative to the previous power stage. Each phase has its own power stage chip, output inductor, and input and output capacitors. They all share one controller chip with one control loop. The power stage chips provide information in the form of analog signals to the controller, about current sensing and temperature. Figure 4.4 shows the typical connections of a single power stage in schematic view, from a multi-phase design. The other phases and the controller are not shown. The power stages also take care of the "dead band" timing, making sure the upper and lower MOSFETs will never be conducting in the same time, and the time they are both off will be small enough so as not to cause voltage spikes. Modern power stage chips are rated to more than 60A output current, but that is in extreme ideal conditions and low temperature. In a data center or embedded environment and with only board GND plane cooling (no heatsinks), 30 to 35A is a safe limit we can design for them, so a 360A ASIC core rail would require a 12 phases VRM. Utilizing half of the maximum current capability seems like a good reliable practice when using modern power stage chips and VRM converters. The old low current (1-5A) switchers can be used up to their maximum.

VRMs are used on digital boards not by themselves, but several of them are found on the same board. On the most complex digital boards we can have more than 70 of them. VRMs are sensitive to disturbances created by other VRMs and load ASICs. This is why we have to make them stable and working on the digital boards, not only on the chip vendor's eval board. This is also one of the reasons for powering up the boards in a power sequence. Only one VRM is turned on at a time, and only when it has finished the startup and stable do we allow turning on the next one. VRMs can disturb each other, especially when turning on. They are more sensitive while turning on, and they generate more disturbances while turning on. During the turn-on the control loops are not as stable as they will be in a fully started-up state. These disturbances can be spread through a shared input rail (usually the main 12V), or if we are feeding one VRM from another VRM then the downstream device appears as a negative impedance that can affect the upstream VRM's control loop stability. The load ASIC creates a load transient even that can make VRMs unstable, this is why we test them

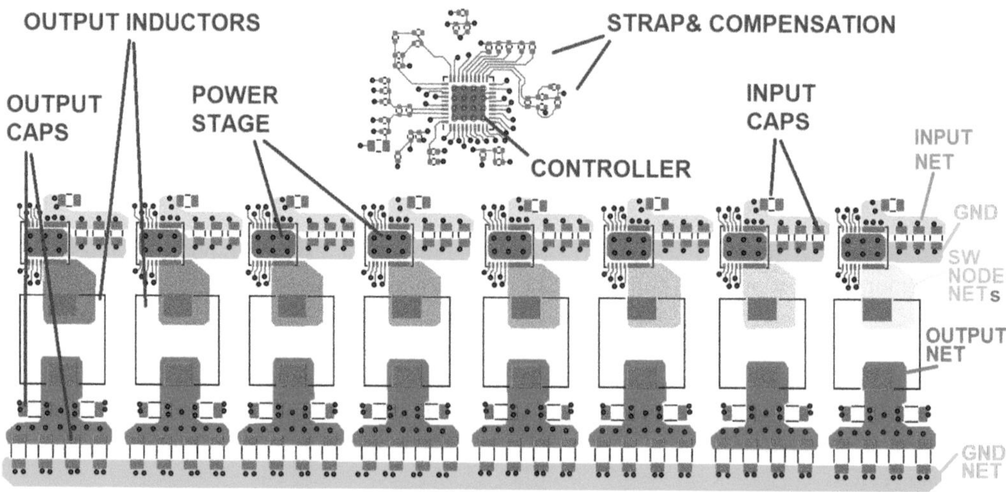

FIGURE 4.3 An 8-phase VRM layout example in KiCAD.

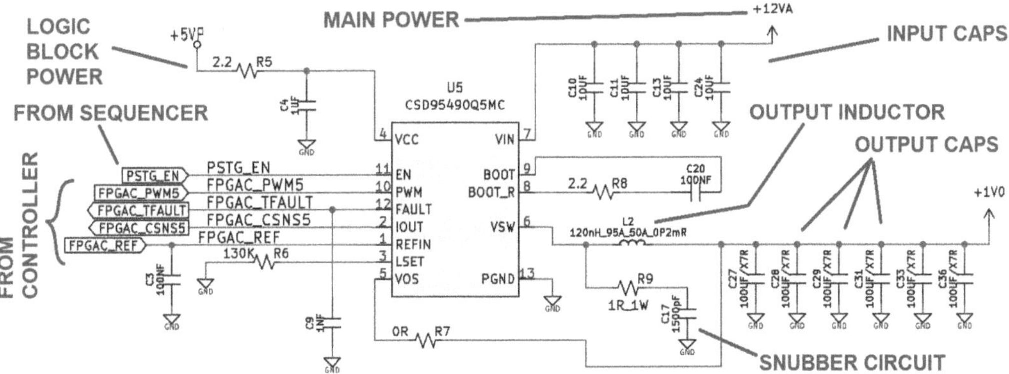

FIGURE 4.4 Schematic connections of a power stage chip in KiCad.

on the digital boards for load transient response. The slew rate and step size matters, but so too does the repetition rate. We might have an ASIC that receives data packets or executes commands periodically, causing the load current to go up and down at a certain frequency, in the range from 1Hz to 10kHz. We need to test for that too. The conclusion is that we do not just design VRMs to be stable; rather, we have to design them to be stable on the specific custom digital board and to not cause instability to other VRMs. A board with all VRMs together with all loads is one design. We cannot swap active VRM parts out without having to re-validate the whole board, typically in a functional burn-in test (running software or data traffic) or DVT. The disturbance created by a new VRM might be different or it might be more sensitive to disturbances already in the design created by other VRMs. The turn-on time varies from device to device, so the exact timing of the whole board power sequence depends on every VRM together. This means the main ASICs might become unstable if one of the delays in the sequence is different than before. It might fail to boot intermittently, or an IPMC might time out and shut down the board. A single-VRM change means it is a system design change. Not only the new VRM needs re-testing, but so do all others together too.

4.2.2 Basic Buck VRM Operation

At the switching period timing level, the MOSFETs turn on and off, the inductor current linearly increases and decreases, and the output voltage increases and decreases (ripple), as seen in Figure 4.5. The output stage is controlled through a CMOS pulse width modulation (PWM) digital signal, the PWM duty cycle percentage determines the nominal output voltage, a voltage ripple is added on top of that. The duty cycle is the on-time divided by the total cycle time period. The output voltage of a buck converter will be the input voltage multiplied by the duty cycle. Above a certain level of load current the output voltage could be maintained ideally by a fixed duty cycle. Below that load current threshold, the duty cycle has to be decreased by the controller circuit, otherwise the output voltage will increase until it reaches the input voltage level. Even above the threshold, the output voltage is not stable simply by a constant duty cycle because the load current changes, called a load transient (load step or load dump). During a load step the output voltage will dip, but the control loop increases the duty cycle a certain amount temporarily to prevent this. Similarly at a load dump event the PWM duty cycle has to be temporarily decreased to avoid a voltage spike. All this is done by the control loop that is built into every VRM controller or converter. There are several different control methods and control loop designs, as described in the next chapters.

Two sets of circuit parameters have to be calculated for the VRMs, tailored for each voltage/current, tolerance, and capacitive load conditions. One set is the power stage components based on the micro-level switching waveforms; the other set is the "feedback loop compensation" component values for the macro-level control loop timing behavior. Usually there are chip vendor– provided

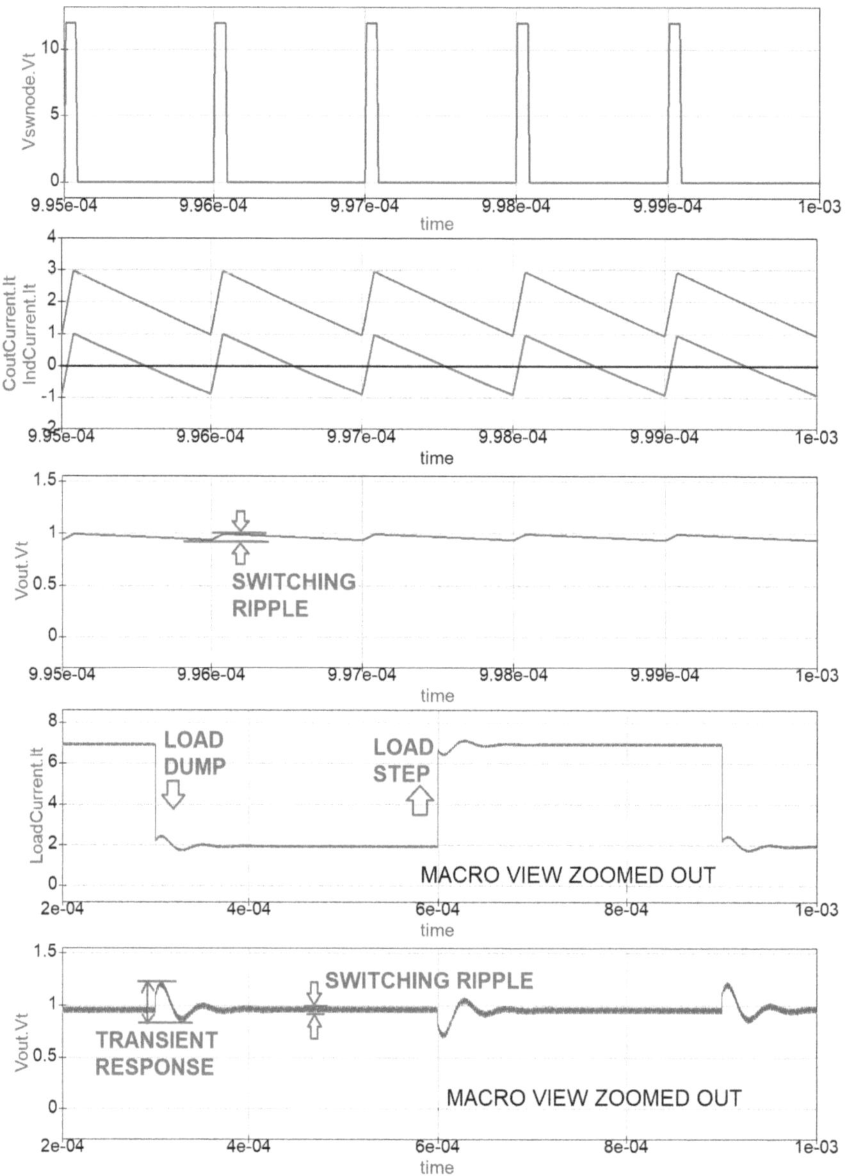

FIGURE 4.5 Synchronous rectifier Buck VRM power stage waveforms simulated in QUCS.

calculators and software or web tools for calculating all parameters. There are basic equations (like these below) and general calculators for calculating the inductor and capacitor values, but we should rely on chip vendor tools if available as they are more accurate, and they consider the unique control schemes of each VRM chip. The equations listed here are just for guidance and sanity check. If we calculate them ourselves, then we can use simplified equations, with 10% to 50% error, then make up for it by overdesigning it by 50%. The overdesign can be built into the equations.

The VRMs feed the ASICs on the board. The output voltage tolerance requirement comes from the ASIC datasheets, but, if not provided, then we can use 3% up to 2.5V rails, 5% between 2.5V and 6V, and 10% for 12V or higher rails. High-powered ASICs usually have a 1% tolerance requirement on their low voltage (<1.5V) rails, including DC error, load step response, and ripple. In calculations the 3% tolerance is a number like "0.03". In order to meet 1% on the low voltage high-current rails, the VRMs are optimized for load transient response by using smaller inductor values, so the inductor ripple current may be as high as 70% of the maximum output current. It helps if the device supports FCCM mode. These VRMs also need to be tested for output impedance, which will be a very low value in order to meet the 1% requirement, and the VRM control loop tuning is the way to achieve it. They also need to use remote sense lines, so the DC voltage drop of the PCB power planes layers can also be removed from the delivered voltage inaccuracy. This also makes it impossible to share a low-voltage VRM between separate digital ASICs because there is only one sense line for one VRM controller and the power delivery plane would be too long with too much drop.

Switch nodes sometimes experience high frequency ringing, at 20 to 200MHz, which can cause interference to other circuits on the board or inside the chassis. We sometimes mitigate it by adding a "snubber circuit", that is a dissipative series-RC circuit from the switch node to the ground. It can be designed by experimentation on a prototype, but using larger package sizes like 0603 or 0805 to dissipate the ringing energy.

Usually, the output ripple is our biggest concern, caused by a combination of three factors: not enough output capacitance or too high output cap ESR. The load step response caused by control loop performance is added on the top of the ripple. Sometimes we just call the combination of switching ripple and load step response as ripple, as it is seen on an oscilloscope. If the control loop response produces too large voltage spikes, the loop has to be tuned with altering its passive component values, or reprogramming the VRM parameters (if it is a smart VRM). All the components have to be selected in a way that they will not be overstressed by voltage, current, or heat dissipation.

Power stage component selection:

- Output inductor
  - Inductance. Often, we choose the ripple current to be k=0.1to 0.8 times of the maximum output current, then calculate inductance L= (Vout*(1-(Vout/Vin))) /(fsw*k*Ioutmax). For faster load transient response on ASIC core rails, we use smaller inductors with larger ripple current.
  - Saturation current rating, output current plus ripple current plus 20%.
  - RMS current rating, same as maximum output current + 20%
  - Physical size, usually we can afford 7x7 or 10x10mm board space for inductors on core rails, or 3x3mm or 4x4 on smaller 3 to 6A rails.
- Output capacitor bank
  - Capacitance C > Ioutmax / (frequency * Tolerance * Vout)
  - ESR < Tolerance * Vout / RippleCurrent
  - RMS current rating, same as the inductor ripple current.
  - Voltage, Vout +100%
  - Type of cap, ceramic versus polarized, depends on the controller chip. Many polarized caps have very low RMS current rating, while ceramic cap datasheets do not list it but usually are rated to high currents.
  - If using multiple capacitors, then we can use N times smaller capacitance and N times higher ESR. The current does not split evenly so all have to support maximum RMS current.
- Input capacitor bank
  - Capacitance, C > (Iout*Vout/Vin) / (fsw*0.003*Vin)
  - Voltage, Vin +100%.
  - RMS current rating, same as output current.
- MOSFETs
  - Both MOSFETs current and voltage rating, output current +50%, input voltage +100%.
  - Upper MOSFET for low enough total gate charge Qg < Idrive / fsw
  - Lower MOSFET for R_{DS_ON} < 1W / (Iout^2).

- Im most cases we use power stage chips these days, we just check their voltage and current rating and compatibility with the controller chip.
- Controller or power stage
  - Minimum on time. The chips have a minimum on time specification. We have to calculate our regular on time, then the chip has to be able to support much less than that. $T_{ON} < 0.2^* \text{ Vout} / (\text{Vin}^*\text{fsw})$

When the output current is more than half the inductor ripple current, then the inductor current never drops to zero, meaning it is in continuous conduction mode (CCM). If the load current is less than half the ripple then for some amount of time the inductor current will be zero—this is called discontinuous conduction mode (DCM). In forced CCM (FCCM) mode the inductor current can become negative for parts of the cycle, so it remains in CCM even at light load. Basically, the inductor charges and discharges the capacitor. FCCM provides better control for achieving good load transient response between light load and full load conditions, and chips that have this feature are a better deal.

4.2.3 Strapping and Settings

The most basic setting that every VRM has is the output voltage setting. This can be set by the designer through choosing the two voltage feedback resistor divider values as:

$$\text{Vout= Vref/(Rbottom/(Rbottom+Rtop)}$$

On some devices we need to select a single strapping resistor value from a table, while on smart VRMs this can be programmed into the internal flash memory over PMBUS. The control loop works in a way to maintain the voltage on the feedback pin equal to the internal reference voltage (usually 0.4 to 0.8V). The voltage divider divides the output voltage to the level of the reference voltage. The output voltage is directly connected to the top resistor with some simple VRM chips, or the resistor divider is connected internally to the VRM at the output of the difference amplifier that buffers the sense lines. Some high-power VRMs support remote voltage sensing, where instead of relying on the voltage at the VRM output, the controller measures the voltage inside the load digital ASIC through the remote sensing differential connection line. The ASIC package has pins to allow this sense connection for measuring the voltage between the VCC net and GND net on the die. Both schemes can be seen in Figure 4.6.

Other parameters can also be set through strapping resistors or through PMBUS programming (if the chip has PMBUS and flash memory), like soft start time, current limit, switching frequency,

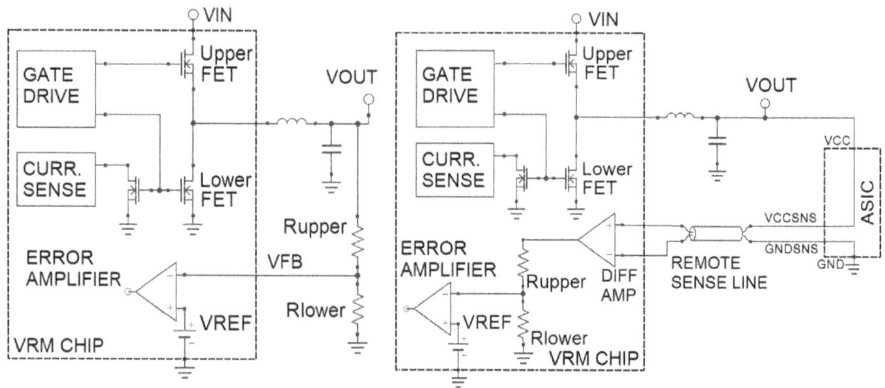

FIGURE 4.6 Buck VRM output voltage feedback divider, left traditional, right with remote sensing.

control loop mode, PMBUS slave address, and multi-phase and multi-output configurations. The datasheets usually provide tables or equations for selecting the resistor values.

The control loop compensation (frequency response alteration/tuning) parameters can be set using resistor and capacitor value selection if the chip has an analog compensation or through PMBUS if it has a digital compensation scheme. The components are usually placed near the voltage feedback divider resistors, on the feedback amplifier output, or to any arbitrary pins defined by the VRM chip datasheet. The values for these can be calculated through chip vendor– provided calculation tools, by an in-house power supply engineer, or by a VRM chip company field application engineer.

4.2.4 VRM Chip Features

In this chapter we list the common features found in modern VRM controllers. Usually, the digital hardware engineer chooses these features, while the VRM engineers focus on control loop stability and power stage analog design. We do not use every feature for every design. Most of them are created for using the VRMs in a complex board or to improve power integrity in demanding applications.

The most common VRM features include:

- Enable pin and PowerGood pin
- Differential Remote Voltage Sense inputs
- Under Voltage Lockout (UVLO)
- Current limit (ILIM), that can be set by a strapping resistor or programming.
- Output current sensing
- Tracking
- PMBUS for programming and telemetry
- Voltage Margining
- Output discharge
- Voltage identification interface (VID parallel, or SVID serial)
- Load Line
- Multi-phase and multi-output controllers
- Forced continuous conduction mode (FCCM)
- Pulse skipping

Enable and PowerGood pins are used to turn on a VRM only when we want it to turn on and to monitor if it is on or off. Its purpose is to allow power sequencing of our boards, so only one rail will be turned on at a time, which will eliminate startup system instability. The PowerGood output is generated by some internal logic inside the VRM chip, which shows that the output voltage is within regulation limits and there was no overcurrent fault. These are digital CMOS signals, usually 3.3V level. If sequencing is not needed then we can pull the enable input up by a voltage divider between Vin and ground. Some enable pins are internally pulled up to 12V. We have to find that in the datasheet, so we might have to add some circuits to protect the power sequencer chip output from being pulled to 12V. Normally we pull the enable pins low to prevent the signal from floating when the sequencer is not alive (not programmed yet, or not booted yet) and pull the PowerGood up to 3.3V standby as they are usually open drain.

Differential Remote Voltage Sense is used on high current (20A or more) VRMs. It allows the control loop to regulate the voltage at the center of the digital ASIC chip instead of at the VRM's output capacitor. This is useful when we expect significant voltage drop (droop) through the PCB power planes, and we want to eliminate the DC droop that the ASIC sees. The VRM will have to regulate its output to Vnom+Vdroop. As the load current changes, Vdroop also changes, so the voltage at the output cap will not be held constant, that is, by design. The physical implementation of voltage sensing is through a differential pair routed from the controller to the center of the ASIC and connected to VDD and GND there. Some ASICs have voltage sense pins, which makes this sense line to VDD/GND rail connection in the silicon die, so we can control the droop through the board and the package. Other ASICs do not have the sense pins, so for them we just use voltage sense resistors, which are zero ohm 0402 resistors placed under the ASIC or on the opposite side of the ASIC. On designs where the ASIC does have the sense connections, we still need the zero-ohm (or 100 Ohm) resistors, but de-populate them, and use them only on the "power boards" that are made for testing with ASIC not soldered on. We call these the catch resistors. Usually the feedback voltage divider is internal to the VRM controller chip and programmable when remote sense is used.

Current limit (ILIM), which can be set by a strapping resistor or programming, has multiple purposes, like detecting shorts, or a signal to help speeding up the control loop response. If the output load current reaches the limit, then the VRM controller shuts down, and it either re-tries to turn on or remains in the off state until the enable pin is toggled. When a VRM is being tested only on an eval board, we can set an ILIM to be 20% above the maximum expected load current. A VRM in a complex digital board will get scared by other VRMs (downstream VRMs or VRMs with shared 12V input plane) and loads, which can cause noise in the current sense circuits, and can experience intermittent shutdowns at startup or run time. The noises might be generated on an external sense signal, inside the package, or at the fanout via connections. To avoid this we can set ILIM to be two to three times the maximum load. That is the difference between complex digital boards and eval boards, based on experience on digital board behavior. Current limiting is most useful for detecting solder shorts on new production boards. It does not happen that a processor suddenly draws 1% higher current and we have to shut it down. Well-designed power sequencer glue logic will see the VRM's PowerGood signal de-asserting and keep the board powered down afterwards. This prevents damage, so the board can be repaired in the factory. Current limit is more like a fire alarm and not like a guide rail for everyday use.

Output current sensing used to be done using a sense resistors in series with the output inductor, but in recent devices it is done using a current mirror arrangements attached to the lower MOSFET on die inside the power stage chip. This current sensing circuit is used for three different purposes: telemetry, current limit, and current mode controller's current loop.

The soft start feature allows the VRM to slowly and linearly ramp up the output voltage. This eliminates overstressing of decoupling capacitors and global board power circuits that they would experience through an in-rush current. Typically, LDOs can be turned on in 0.1to 1ms, 0.5to 20A switching rails in 1ms, larger loads at 1to 20ms (most commonly 4ms). Without soft start the VRMs would turn on within 1to 100us with several times the nominal load current, which could cause any of the power circuits to fail with overcurrent and a voltage dip and shut down with fault.

Tracking is a feature that allows one VRM to track another VRM's output. For example, if we have a 1.8V VRM that tracks the output of a 3.3V rail, then the 1.8V rail will have identical voltage on it as the 3.3V rail has until they both reach about 1.8V, at which point the 1.8V rail will remain in regulation at nominal 1.8V while the 3.3V rail keeps rising until it reaches 3.3V and remains in regulation.

PMBUS is a communication bus with a power management protocol and a standard register set. Many VRMs have this, they are the "smart" VRMs. Usually, PMBUS is used for device programming (voltage or compensation set), telemetry (voltage, current, temperature) read-out, and fault information read-out. Fault logging can tell if the VRM has unexpectedly shut down, whether the cause was low input voltage, overcurrent, high temperature, or other causes. Note that most VRMs do not retain telemetry or fault data after their input power is turned off.

Voltage margining is when the local host or management controller instructs the VRM to intentionally increase or decrease the output voltage by a few percent, to stress out board circuits and load ASICs. It can be done if the controller circuit supports it. It is used typically in design validation and in production testing, to see if the main digital ASIC devices have any additional margins and are not hanging by a thread as to reliability. We check whether their internal processing cores and external interfaces remain functional without errors or crash when their rail voltages are offset.

Margining is a feature of the VRM circuit, but its purpose is to test the digital ASICs, not to test the VRM itself. Margining is built into smart VRMs—they can be instructed to go into margining mode over PMBUS commands. Basic or analog VRMs can be given margining capability by attaching a passive margining filter between a power management controller chip's PWM (Pulse Width Modulated square wave) signal and the VRM's voltage feedback input. A T-filter with R-C-R parts converts the PWM signal into a voltage offset, which is added to the feedback voltage. The filter has to be designed in a way to avoid interfering with the VRM's control loop when margining is turned off. The filter resistors have to be ten times higher value than the upper one in the feedback divider, and the capacitor has to be so small that the RC resonant frequency remains above the VRM control loop's cutoff frequency. This can be achieved only by using a very high PWM frequency. High frequency might cause duty cycle resolution issues. The part values also limit the margining range (in case of 0% or 100% duty cycle or short), which is good for not killing the load ASICs, but it has to allow our desired range, usually 1% to 5%. All these parameters need to be calculated.

Output discharge is a feature available on a few VRM chips. When the enable pin is low, the power stage actively shorts the output voltage rail to ground. The benefit of this is to provide a clean rail start, instead of allowing a voltage to creep up through leakage to a plateau half-way even before the VRM is enabled. This feature also helps with power-down sequencing to prevent the rail from slowly (like in seconds) decaying and, instead, firmly turning fully off to zero output voltage. It basically discharges large amounts of decoupling capacitors that might reside on the rail.

VID is a parallel digital input that can control the output voltage dynamically without much overshoot. The purpose is ASIC power dissipation management. SVID is the same but with a serial line on one or two pins. X86 processors require a vendor compatible SVID interface, as well as other specific control signals, described in the processor datasheets and IMVPx.y and VRMx.y specifications.

The "Load Line" is a feature used on X86 laptop processors. It is basically a virtual series resistance at the output of the VRM, without an actual resistance that would dissipate power. The goal of this concept is to reduce the rail voltage when the load current is high, to allow bigger load dump overshoot, and to increase the rail voltage at light load to allow bigger load step spike. There is a linear relationship between the current and the voltage, and it is produced by the control circuits. The Load Line resistance RLL is normally equal to the target impedance of the PDN design. This has not become very popular with other ASIC vendors. X86 processors require a compatible VRM that supports Load Line, SVID, and other CPU control interface signals.

Multi-phase and multi-output controllers can drive more than one power stage. Many of these VRM chips allow the user to select how many output voltages (usually limited to two or three) are needed, and how many phases will be assigned to each output. Forced continuous conduction mode (FCCM) allows the designer to use smaller value output inductors, with ripple currents 70% of the maximum current, to achieve faster load transient response while avoiding discontinuous conduction mode operation. Pulse skipping allows high efficiency under light load conditions, which is useful for battery-powered systems. Under Voltage Lockout (UVLO) is a feature that prevents the VRM from being turned on when the input voltage is too low.

4.2.5 VRM Control Loop Types

Besides the common output stage design, there is a control loop circuit inside every VRM controller or converter. Several methods have been devised to achieve the control, that is, reducing the transient response peaks by applying more or less power than the steady state power from the input source.

The Voltage-mode PWM is the most traditional method. If the output voltage decreases, then the output of the error amplifier increases, which increases the PWM duty cycle that increases the output voltage. This interaction path is speeded up or slowed down in certain frequency ranges by the compensation. Figure 4.7 shows both the voltage and the current mode control schemes.

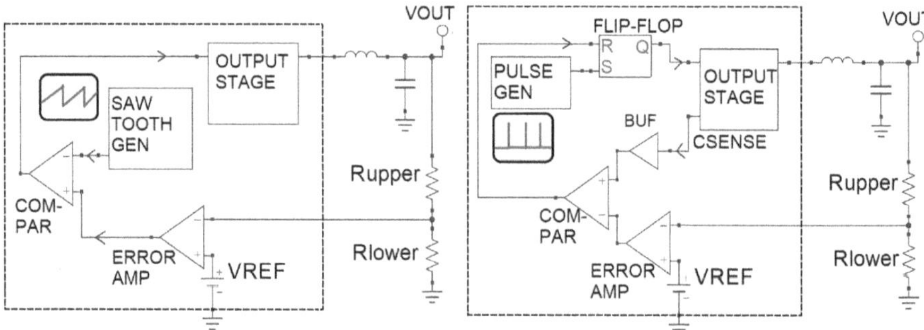

FIGURE 4.7 PWM control modes: voltage mode on the left, current mode on the right.

The Current-mode PWM has two control loops, a voltage loop that works like the voltage mode PWM and a current loop that detects the cause of the voltage drop, being the load current step, and increases the duty cycle. Detecting the cause of the voltage drop allows faster response in not having to wait for the effect to fully taking place. Faster response provides better voltage stability and better load transient response, with smaller fluctuation. If the VRM employs cycle-by-cycle current sensing instead of average current sensing, then the load transient response can be very fast.

Hysteretic controllers simply turn on the upper MOSFET when the output voltage drops below the hysteresis level, and they turn off when it goes above. It does not have PWM circuit. The error amplifier has a hysteresis setting, so it will not produce high-frequency oscillation. The control loop response is very fast, it regulates in every single switching period, but the switching frequency varies in a very wide range, which can cause interference. It provides good light-load efficiency for battery-operated devices.

Hysteretic Constant On-Time (COT) controllers have a constant on time but controlled off time. They work similar to the hysteretic, but after the output stage is turned on, it will turn off after a fixed set time. The goal of this is to keep the switching frequency in a smaller range.

Pulse Frequency Modulation (PFM):is similar to hysteretic, but instead of just turning on the upper MOSFET until the voltage threshold is reached, it keeps switching with fixed duty cycle until the voltage is reached and then completely off. Basically, it fires bursts at the load, then goes quiet until the next burst. It also provides good light-load efficiency.

VRM chip vendors have also invented custom control loop schemes. Some VRM chips switch between PFM and PWM modes depending on light/heavy load conditions. Digital control loops digitize the voltage sense, and they handle the control loop in the sampled digital time domain. This allows complex and innovative control loops that are not publicized. Even non-linear algorithmic control loops are available.

4.2.6 Feedback Loop Compensation

Each VRM controller contains a "control loop" that can be analyzed in the frequency domain using a Bode plot, or in the time domain using a load step (transient) response. Both can be done in simulation and in measurement. The Bode plot can be tested using a low frequency VNA like the Omicron Lab Bode-100, a Liquid Instruments Moku-Lab, or some newer oscilloscopes that have a frequency response analyzer feature. We also need an injection transformer to be connected between the VNA (vector network analyzer) and the DUT (device under test). The load step testing, to measure the transient response, can be done using electronic load instruments or small solder-on modules like the Intel's Mini Slammer or the Load Slammer devices. They toggle the load current between two user selectable levels, typically between 20% and 80% of the maximum load current. The simulation or measurement is typically done by a power supply engineer or by a VRM chip vendor FAE (field applications engineer), but in some cases the hardware design engineer can perform it. The hardware design engineer has to make sure it will be measurable by providing a 0 to 10 Ohm Bode-resistor in series with the sense input where the tester can inject the test signal and to make sure one proto board will be manufactured with the main ASIC load devices de-populated (called the "power board").

A Bode plot shows the control loop frequency response in the format of gain and phase curves, namely, two diagrams. The control loop is a closed loop when it operates, but for analysis we display the open loop response. Closed loop means the output change is fed back into the controller that adjusts the output, as an infinite analog loop. Open loop is a view of the design; it is not an open-loop design, where the chain of effects is cut, so we can analyze one cycle of the effect.

The control loop of a VRM is a linear system with built-in amplification and "compensation". The compensation is made of either passive resistor/capacitor networks (analog filter) or in the case of a digitally controlled VRM some kind of a FIR filter or non-linear algorithm. The compensation alters the frequency response of the control loop and increases amplification at certain frequencies while decreasing it at other frequencies. There are different strategies of choosing the alterations with the common goal of reducing the transient response voltage spikes on the VRM's output. This is achieved through meeting intermediate goals, such as requirements on loop bandwidth, phase margin, and gain margin. The control loop includes the output stage power components (inductor, output cap), the output voltage divider with any filter parts attached to it, the error amplifier, and any passive networks attached to that. Figure 4.8 shows a circuit model made for simulating voltage-mode VRM control loops, with the resulting Bode plot.

Control loop design is a wide field of science. It deals with "poles", "zeroes", phase margins, gain margins, and loop bandwidth. A pole or a zero is any first-order frequency-dependent filter-like (LR or RC) subcircuit that causes the control loop's gain curve and phase curve to change direction. They are represented with their frequency point and their complex-plane plot point.

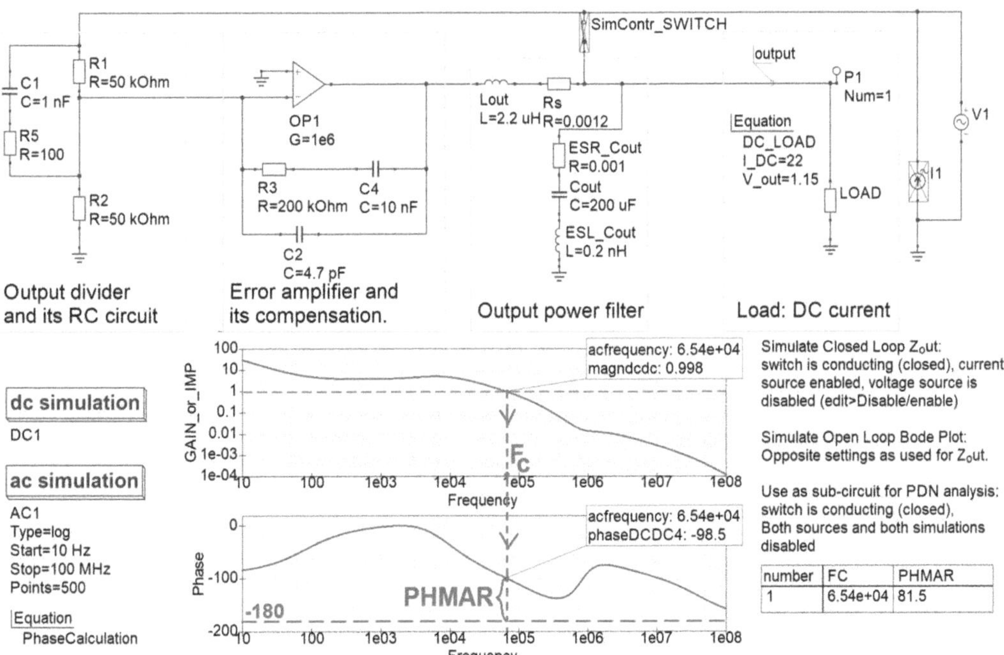

FIGURE 4.8 Feedback loop model and Bode plot simulation in QUCS.

We can add a zero to eliminate the effect of a pole, which is often the main design activity. Some poles and zeroes are consequential of the power and control circuits, others are artificially added by the designer. Many digital DSP-based VRM controllers might have a proprietary non-linear algorithm that is unlikely for the system company to tune, in that case we really need the FAEs to be involved.

4.2.6.1 Typical Goals for Bode Plot Optimization

Phase Margin (distance between the phase and the -180-degree line at the frequency where the gain curve reaches 0dB or "1") to be larger than 60 degrees, or 45 degrees in case of using ceramic output caps. A larger phase margin causes a smaller transient response peak, as seen in Figure 4.9. If it is below the limit then it is unstable.

The loop bandwidth or cut-off frequency (Fc, the frequency where the gain curve reaches 0dB or "1") should be as high as possible before compromising the phase margin. Typically, Fc would be around 1/5th of the switching frequency, but hysteretic converters can have Fc near/at the switching frequency. A larger bandwidth causes a smaller transient response peak. Given all these explanations, it will probably not be possible for us to tune the control loops ourselves, so either we work with a power supply engineer (in-house or FAE) who does it for us or we should read a book or two about the topic. But it should help to understand what we are asking our VRM expert colleagues to do.

4.2.7 VRM Analysis

VRM circuits need to be simulated for stability and output ripple before a prototype is built. This is typically done in the tools provided by the VRM chip vendors. These tools usually automatically provide component values that result in an optimal and stable design. This might be done by the hardware design engineer, the power supply engineer, or the VRM company FAE (field application engineer). In some cases, the VRM circuits are simulated in a circuit simulator like LTspice or Tina-TI if the chip vendor has provided SPICE model files. This is done in a new complex hardware design project only if we need additional debugging of non-trivial cases. We can build a simulation model in LTspice, QUCS, or Keysight ADS, with assumptions about the control loop, or by looking at the block diagrams and schematics in the VRM chip datasheet. It will only model a small signal analog control loop in an AC simulation, not a fully functioning VRM switcher. Switching circuits cannot be modeled in an AC simulation because they turn on and off like digital circuits; instead, we could use something called an "average model", that is, an RLC circuit, if available. It is possible to run a transient simulation in time domain that will include hundreds of switching cycles, and the control loop will be observed only through the load transient response.

We need to take measurements of the VRM performance on prototype boards. To do this we need our manufacturer to make one board with the digital ASICs removed but with all glue logic

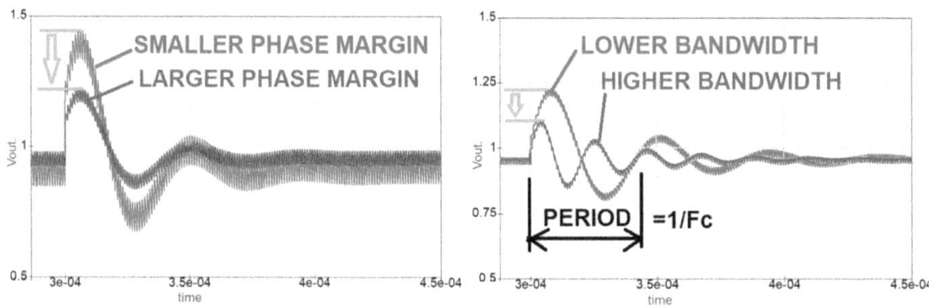

FIGURE 4.9 Load transient response dependence on Bode plot.

and power circuits still present. We call this a "power board". We will have to solder wires to it, the output voltage and ground will need thick wires for load testing, and the voltage ripple measurement and PDN impedance measurement will need soldered-on micro coax cables. On prototype digital boards we measure all VRMs for ripple noise using a regular oscilloscope, an active probe, or even better a soldered-on micro-coax cable. This is the cable typically used for connecting WIFI antennas with an SMA and a U.FL (cut it off) connector. We also need to do other measurements of the prototypes, like Bode plot measurements with a low frequency VNA like the Omicron-Lab Bode-100 and others, and load transient response measurements with an oscilloscope (while providing excitation with a programmable load like the Chroma 6300 or the LoadSlammer modules. The Bode plot is not only measured, but it also gives clues to the power supply engineer as to what changes to be made to improve the Bode plot, actually rework the boards to change passive part values (or re-program), then re-measure, and also re-measure the ripple noise and the load transient response. The previous subchapter described Bode plot measurements and load transient response measurements.

VRMs also need to be modeled for PDN analysis. The VRM is a part of the Power Distribution Network (PDN), which has an impedance profile, as described in Chapter 13, "Power Integrity". We can measure a VRM eval board with a low frequency VNA, then save the results into an S-parameter file that is usable in PDN simulation. It usually requires some post-processing to remove noise and evalboard artifacts. In some cases, the chip vendors provide a SPICE circuit model, which can be converted into an S-parameter model by running an S-parameter circuit simulation.

We also have to measure the whole PDN, including the VRM on the prototype digital boards with the VNA, and we might require the power supply engineer to re-tune the VRMs to provide low impedance at low frequencies. More detail are provided in Chapter 13, "Power Integrity" and Chapter 17, "Measurements".

Some effects in VRMs cannot be simulated; rather, we have to rely on experience in prototype testing of past projects. These are related to how multiple VRMs and digital circuits have to work together on the same high-density complex board rather than a VRM circuit working by itself in isolation. The effects are related to noises coupling into nearby circuits and from nearby circuits into the VRM being analyzed. A VRM can generate interference through its input pins into the input power rail, through its fanout vias into nearby circuits, and from the switch node it can generate high-frequency (100MHz) EMI noise. A VRM can suffer from interference created by other circuits like digital chips (load transient, periodic load toggles at certain toggle rates) and other VRMs. This can come into the VRM through sense lines, compensation circuit traces, power planes, and fanouts. The mitigation of these would be prototyping (DUT behavior) experience-based, rather than datasheet, simulation, or precise measurement-based. Examples are setting current limit much higher than the model would dictate, adding snubber circuits, improving the power plane connection fanouts, or using better input decoupling.

Too much ripple noise or load transient spikes causing digital chips to intermittently fail also belongs to the interference category, but it is the only one that can be precisely measured or scientifically analyzed. In that case we can analyze the ripple voltage but not the failure mode of the digital ASIC. We can make an assumption as to the digital ASIC failure mode only by looking at its datasheet that lists the maximum allowed power supply noise. No scientific proof can be provided by a board/system design company's hardware engineer as to why the ASIC fails when there is too much noise; rather, all we can do is to say the noise requirement is X, the measured noise is Y, then Y>X is the likely cause of the failure. We cannot say that one of the 100 million flip-flops changed its output and caused the PCIe TLP state machine to enter the wrong state. With hard ASICs it is impossible and with an FPGA project it may or may not be possible, but that is not a typical project goal, it is more a matter for a PhD thesis. Project members have to make decisions based on specs and high-level observation of hardware behavior. This is not super scientific, but it is typical hardware engineering. Hardware is complex at many levels, a lot of it is inside different proprietary black boxes interacting with other black boxes that prevents us from doing a true scientific analysis. The datasheets do not reveal all internal circuits of the components, only the "need to know" parts. Sometimes VRM specialists and FAEs will suggest component values that work in a model but that do not work on a complex digital board prototype. In those cases the hardware designer has to make a component choice that results in a stable hardware design.

5 Components

All electronic hardware is made of circuit boards and mechanical parts. All circuit boards are made of components, and connections are provided by the PCB (Printed Circuit Board). These components are third-party products that we build into our product. In this chapter we do not focus on "defining" the components; rather, we describe how they are used on complex high-speed hardware designs. We concentrate on how board designers make use of them, not on how the component factory makes them.

Every component has a datasheet document provided by the manufacturer. Passive components usually have very short datasheets, with footprint dimensions and main parameters—silicon chips or integrated circuits, ICs have more detailed datasheets. Those provide a feature list, pinout table with explanation of what each pin is used for, an absolute/maximum ratings table (to understand what kills a chip), a longer parameter table for normal operating conditions, applications circuit, strapping tables, and functional descriptions of each module and pin on the chip. In the normal operating conditions table, we find numbers like maximum output drive current capability, pin delay, and logic low threshold. Some of these numbers or parameters might not mean what we think they mean at first look, so we have to consider them with caution. Sometimes they are under certain conditions that we do not have in our board, other times they just use a word to mean something other than we thought it meant. This requires studying the datasheets and spending sufficient time considering them. If a specific detail is still not clear after reading them multiple times, because it was written too ambiguously, then we may contact the chip company's technical support website or our region's assigned FAE (field applications engineer from the chip company) directly. When we are designing a processor into our circuit board, we have to read all functional and circuit related portions, sometimes hundreds of pages and sometimes multiple documents. Sometimes we have to refer back to the same section multiple times to understand it in context. The more complex components (main ASICs, bridge and switch chips) sometimes also have other documents, such as product briefs (short feature lists), hardware manuals, programming manuals with register sets, application notes, design guides, and reference design schematics.

The part number of a device is usually very complex. The datasheets help us assembling them from several features/options, in a part number decoding or "ordering information" section. For example, XXXXC is for a commercial temperature range variant, XXXXI is for the wider industrial temperature range variant. Some devices come in different sizes (like FPGA resources), a different capacity (like flash chips at 32GB, 64GB, 128GB), or a different package (SSOP versus QFN), and all these options are reflected in the exact orderable part number.

On every chip package there is a pin-1 marking, or on grid packages like BGA (ball grid array) a pin-A1 marking, for assembly and probing orientation. Our schematic design or the BOM should always contain the exact part number to help in purchasing the exact part—either a manufacturer's part number or a unique number in our company database that refers to one or more unique manufacturer's part numbers. Components can be through-hole technology (THT) soldered, through-hole press-fit, or surface mount technology (SMT or SMD). The THT soldered has cost and reliability issues associated with them, so most newer designs are completely free of them, and they use only SMT and THT-press-fit parts. Press-fit is usually used for connectors, for a solder-less assembly, using a fixture and a lot of mechanical force.

Programmable integrated circuits or chips have several different types of pins that the hardware designer has to connect up in the schematic. There are many ground pins to be connected to the ground net and all the ground planes in the stackup. There are power pins, often several separate power rails each with several pins, to be supplied by VRMs. Some power pins only need decoupling

DOI: 10.1201/9781032702094-5

and no source attached. There are I/O pins that will be connected to signals going to other chips and connectors. There are control and status pins that allow the chip to change its behavior or report its internal status, like reset or configuration done. There are analog pins like calibration resistor attachments, thermal sensor diode connections, and voltage sense feedback to VRMs. There are also strapping or configuration pins, reserved pins that are used by the chip company, and NC pins that are to be left unconnected (although some NC pins have very specific strapping requirements, sometimes found only in reference designs). In some cases there are very unique use pins that are described in the datasheet. Voltage regulator chips that we use have additional analog pins. We have to read the pin list in the datasheet very carefully, anything not clear has to be double-checked with reference designs or other parts of the datasheet.

5.1 RESISTORS

In the context of complex hardware design, it is not so important to understand the difference between thick film and thin film resistor construction; rather, it is essential to understand the difference between calibration resistors and pull-up resistors, for example. In complex hardware schematics we use resistors in different ways and often in more creative ways than are found in simple circuit boards. They can serve different purposes.

Resistor use cases in complex digital boards:

- VRM and analog circuit parameter setting, compensation resistors, usually at 1% tolerance.
- Zero Ohm and DNP (do not populate) design insurance resistors. During prototyping we can remove a zero Ohm resistor with a solder iron, replace it with a higher value, or populate an originally DNP resistor footprint to alter the circuit behavior or re-route signals to a different path. We can connect two signal or voltage sources to the same destination through 0402 series resistors—one resistor will be 0R the other DNP or vice versa. The way to mark "DNP" status of a component varies by company and design tool. We make sure that the BOM and the Pick&Place program will exclude them. We can put both a pull-up and a pull-down resistor into the design, while one of the two will be DNP. We can route signals to one path or a different path through 0R/DNP choices that can be easily altered without a layout design re-spin.
- Pull: a resistor between a digital signal and GND (pull down) or VDD (pull up). PU is usually 3 to 10 times larger resistor value than PD. On 3.3V signals a 10k PU and 1k PD are typical, on lower voltage smaller values, like 2.7k PU on 1.8V I/O are typical. Their main purpose is to ensure a safe logic level when the driving chip is not ready yet during power on, or not programmed yet, or provide a constant level if we do not want to actively control it. Open-drain signals work only if they have a pull up. The resistor value should be more than high enough to drop sufficient voltage at given bias/drive current, but it should also be low enough to allow open drain signals to rise fast. Vcc/Imax << R << t_rise/10pF
- Strapping inputs of ASICs tell the ASIC what mode we want it to be operating in, by pulling them low (GND) or high (VDD) through a resistor. For example, PCIE switch chips might have a pin to set the maximum speed the device should negotiate to, either 8Gbps, 5Gbps, or 2.5Gbps, depending on whether the pin is pulled low, high, or disconnected. Often we provide both a pull up and a pull down on the same pin, and one of them is DNP, so during prototyping we can swap them. An FPGA or microcontroller might have a few strapping pins, and a large switch ASIC might have dozens.
- Impedance matched transmission line termination, series, or parallel.
- Biasing (DC level, or driver current) resistors on certain I/O standards like LVPECL.
- Calibration resistors, from ASIC pin to GND, to set certain ASIC internal circuits to a precise operating state or to allow them to calibrate to a known precise value. For example, calibrating all internal on-die terminations (memory interfaces and SERDES transceivers) to a fixed

1% accurate resistor. Silicon resistors are much more inaccurate than 1% passive resistors. The PCB trace between the ASIC and the resistor might need to be impedance controlled.
- Open drain circuit pullup to allow the signal to rise high, while devices only drive them low. The value to be low enough to work against the trace capacitance, but not too low to prevent a proper logic low level.
- To set LED current through a series resistor. R=(VCC-VF)/10mA
- Pre-charge resistors on backplane signals: pull the signal line to half VDD at the early stage of a hot-swap insertion.

Large complex boards typically rely on 0402 SMT package size resistors that match with the common 1mm pitch BGA grid also and are easy to rework under microscope. We use only large footprint resistors for current sense resistors in power circuits. Hand-held devices often use smaller resistors like 0201 or 01005. For analog strapping pins and analog circuits, we have to use 1% or 0.1% tolerance resistors. There are a few calculations that we have to take care of for resistors, such as making sure the resistor's power dissipation (P=V*I) is much lower (by 40%) than the power rating (e.g., 0.065W for 0402 package size).

5.2 CAPACITORS

We use capacitors for power rail decoupling, high-speed signal AC-coupling, VRM input/output capacitance, or analog circuit parameter setting. In slang lingo we often call them "caps". Most of the engineering work we do when dealing with caps on complex hardware is to assess their limitations in the context of our design. The most demanding are the VRM capacitors. Their ESR (Equivalent Series Resistance) is important in most cases (10A rails and above), and if their RMS current rating is exceeded on tantalum/polymer variants then they can blow up after days/months. On ceramic capacitors the current rating is usually unknown, but they are always able to handle the current going through them on regular VRM applications.

Most capacitors on the board are chosen (during schematic design) by a few sets of basic parameters, package size, capacitance and voltage. The higher demand applications like VRM input/output caps and decoupling have additional requirements, such as ESR and RMS current, so those capacitors in the schematic have to be chosen by part number. Typically, polarized capacitors are defined by part numbers, as their ESR and RMS current rating varies a lot—either manufacturer part number or a company part number that refers to a short list of approved manufacturer part numbers that all meet the ESR and RMS current requirement, validated by component engineering. We need to check the ESR of a specific part number, not just a device family. Often they are not provided, but usually ceramic caps have a much lower ESR. Other caps have their ESR vary by orders of magnitude between different models.

The capacitor's real parameters are poorer in a real board than the datasheet best numbers, which is caused by the circuit environment, and this is called "derating". The decline is stronger when we are closer to the ratings limits. With higher voltage the capacitance decreases. The nominal capacitance is measured at less than 20% of the voltage limit/rating. This means the capacitance is reduced at higher voltages. We need to choose capacitors that are rated to a higher voltage (be far from the limit to avoid steep decline) than what we will be using it at, and have more capacitance (to compensate for the decline) than we need. With higher temperature the capacitance decreases. This means we need to use larger capacitors than the minimum required, and operate them farther below their maximum temperature rating. With higher temperature the maximum voltage rating limit decreases. This means we need to choose capacitors that are rated to a much higher voltage than what we will be using it at. Over time the capacitance value decreases, which means we need to use larger capacitors than the minimum required. All these effects combined create derating curves from component vendors and derating guidelines from design companies. Typically, we use capacitors with a higher capacitance (50%), a larger voltage rating (double), and a larger temperature rating (30%) than we need.

The two main types of capacitors are ceramic and polarized electrolytic. We use polarized SMT capacitors up to 7443 package size, or ceramic capacitors (lower ESR, higher current) that come in X5R or X7R material varieties. These ceramic capacitor X name codes refer to temperature range and derating. X7R has better derating (15% capacitance decline up to 125C) curves than X5R (15% up to 85C), but it is not always available in a small enough package size, so then we might have to use X5R for high capacitance density. For example, on a dense board we can only "afford" 0603 capacitors in terms of space for the small 3A VRMs, and in 0603 we might find 22uF X5R and 10uF X7R, then we usually choose the X5R with 22uF. There are several other types of ceramic capacitors used by RF analog designers. Ceramic capacitors are available up to 47uF.

The polarized "electrolytic" capacitors provide a much larger capacitance and voltage, and they come in different varieties. When we need large bulk capacitance, like 330uF or 2200uF, we use these. If we use them as VRM output capacitors (not ASIC decoupling) then a lot of ripple current will flow through them constantly, which causes excessive heating and blowup. So for these applications we need to look for capacitor part numbers that have a published RMS current rating. For polarized caps the 7443-package size is most common, with different height varieties from 1.5 to 4.3mm height. OS-CON cylinder-shaped SMT capacitors are used on boards with not too tight height restrictions, when values above 330uF or larger voltages are required. The capacitor size is proportional to the capacitance multiplied by the voltage rating. A 10uF/20V capacitor might be the same size or volume as a 20uF/10V capacitor, but a 100uF/2.5V capacitor is about ten times smaller than a 100uF/25V capacitor. Smaller package sizes also come with smaller capacitance, and those compete with the extremely low ESR ceramic capacitors that win. The typical appearance of different capacitor types can be seen in Figure 5.1. Table 5.1 lists common package sizes.

Capacitor types:

- Ceramic (best ESR and current rating)
  - X5R, with the best capacitance density among ceramics, but worse temperature derating.
  - X7R, with better temperature derating.
  - Other types, available in very small capacitance values, some with very high stability, used in RF and analog applications (like VRM compensation).
- Polarized Electrolytic (highest capacitance density)
  - Aluminum, largest capacitance, usually in a cylinder shape and very tall. Typical SMT cylindrical aluminum capacitors are called OS-CON. Mainly used for 330uF or larger on higher voltage rails on larger complex digital boards.
  - Tantalum, Higher density than aluminum electrolytic capacitors, usually in rectangular 7443 packages.
  - Polymer (Tantalum-Polymer) Similar density as tantalum, but lower ESR. Some notable ones:
    - Kemet KO-Cap, organic polymer, ESR ~ 4 mΩ.
    - Panasonic POSCAP, ESR ~ 5 mΩ.

FIGURE 5.1 Capacitor images.

TABLE 5.1
Common SMT Sizes for Passive Parts

Component Type	Size code (in)	Size mm
Res, Cap, Ferrite	2512	6.3 x 3.2
	1210	3.2 x 2.5
	1206	3.0 x 1.5
	0805	2.0 x 1.3
	0603	1.5 x 0.8
	0402	1.0 x 0.5
	0201	0.6 x 0.3
	1005	0.4 x 0.2
Tant/Poly cap	Size A, 3216-18	3.2 x 1.6 x 1.6
	Size B, 3528-21	3.5 x 2.8 x 1.9
	Size C, 6032-28	6.0 x 3.2 x 2.2
	Size D, 7343-31	7.3 x 4.3 x 2.8
	Size E, 7343-43	7.3 x 4.3 x 4.1

FIGURE 5.2 High power-density inductors for core VRMs.

5.3 INDUCTORS

On complex digital boards we typically use shielded rectangle SMT inductors in voltage regulators, usually in a low-profile (<5mm tall) package. Due to density constraints, anything larger than a 7x7mm or 10x10mm footprint is not preferred even for 30A/phase core rails (0.1 to 0.3uH). On lower cost server boards, we can find 12x13mm and 10mm tall inductors too. The two main vendors are Vishay and Wurth Electronics—they definitely have high-density small parts that we need, but other vendors might also supply inductors if their specs match up. Inductors are in vendor-specific package sizes, not standard SMT like 0603. Some high-performance inductors that are used in ASIC core rails can be seen in Figure 5.2.

A special type is the ferrite bead inductors. They are small SMT parts used for series power filtering near ASIC power pins. They are defined by their impedance at 100MHz, their DCR (direct current resistance) and maximum current rating. Usually, we would use a bead that has 100 to 330 Ohm@100MHz impedance, while trying to keep the DCR below an Ohm.

5.4 LEDs

LEDs (Light Emitting Diodes) are used for quick user feedback of simple system states. Remember, "red LED bad". It means red LEDs are used for signaling abnormal system behavior or error, green

LEDs are used to signal "all good" feedback while amber is more for activity or port speed. RJ45 Ethernet port LED colors are loosely defined by the industry, each system company might define them in their own way that we should follow. We often use 3-pin SMT LEDs that provide light horizontally at the board edge. They usually have a hole on the front panel there. Vertical emitting LEDs are useful for board debugging and manufacturing checks, and are found on the front panel with plastic light pipes. The LEDs are usually not driven directly by digital chips but rather through a transistor. Sometimes we need many LEDs at the front panel. In these cases we can use an LED matrix, which is arranged through hole LEDs in a plastic mechanical holder. We also have LEDs in mid-board that are used only for proto and production debugging. The user will not see them in the fully assembled chassis. We could put down one LED for each power domain power good indication (driven by sequencer), BIOS boot completion, FPGA configuration done, and PCIe port link up indication (every port of a PCIe switch chip) to help us with testing and debugging. A few extra LEDs could be designed-in, which can be defined and re-purposed later to indicate internal block readiness in the FPGA, for example, self-test passed. They can flip on solid to show something is complete, or they can blink at every data packet—this behavior would be defined in FPGA code. The LED's role could be defined by FPGA logic or CPU software code, and it can be changed during the bring-up process to indicate different things. For example a CPU boot loader might normally complete 100 tasks, but if it hangs then we can add a line of code that turns the LED on when taks-34 is completed, then change it to taks-35 to find the one holding up the boot process. A resistor in series with the LED is required; the value depends on the LED's forward voltage (Vf). We cannot use high Vf LEDs like green or blue from low voltage circuits. Red LEDs have a Vf~1.3V, blue 3.3V, green 2.5V, and yellow 2.1V.

$$R = (VDD-Vf)/10mA$$

5.5 TRANSISTOR CIRCUITS

On complex digital boards we use transistors for three main purposes:

- Power switching, by a SO-8 power MOSFET, that is driven by a hot swap controller chip or a bipolar transistor. The bipolar transistors are in SOT-23 or SC-70 packages usually.
- Level Translation of one signal. One transistor inverts the signal, so usually two are used.
- Inversion, for example, LED control with active high versus low.

The resistor values are calculated to drop the whole input voltage on them when the transistor is ON or conducting. When a bipolar transistor is ON, it can drive a certain amount of current through itself, which is about 100 times (hfe=100, base to collector current gain) as much as its input base current, but we overdrive these transistors in digital mode so it will be about 20 times. The base current is set by the base resistor as Ib=VRb/Rb. MOSFETs are voltage controlled, if the Gate-Source voltage is above the threshold, then the source-drain channel is fully conducting. We (digital hardware designers) use the transistors in switching mode, where they are overdriven to provide a solid digital level. This means that the resistor at the collector is chosen to drop the whole input voltage on it even at five times lower current than we have. Figure 5.3 shows the mentioned three main uses of transistors on digital boards.

A basic calculation would for the level translator example can be seen below:

1) Let's say we want to provide up to 0.1mA output current.
2) At 0.1mA output current, Rc2 should not drop too much voltage (less than 0.2V) on itself, while T2 is off. Rc2 =< V/I = 0.2V/0.1mA = 2kOhm.
3) When T2 is on, it has to draw enough current to drop the whole Vcc=3.3V on Rc2, so Ic2 > V/R = 3.3/2kOhm = 1.65mA.

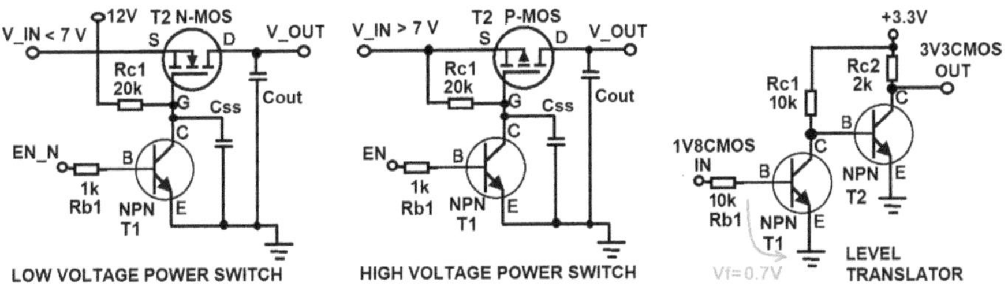

FIGURE 5.3 Typical transistor circuits for digital boards.

4) When T1 is off, Rcl has to be able to provide enough base current to fully turn on T2. T2 is turned on by Ib2=Ic2/100, but to provide reliable logic levels we need to overdrive T2 with 5x current, so Ib2 > Ic2/(100/5) = 1.65mA/20 = 82.5uA. So we need an Rcl resistor that provides 82.5uA, Rcl < (3.3V-0.7V)/82.5uA = 31.5kOhm. We can choose 10kOhm standard value for Rcl that meets the equation.
5) When T1 is on, it has to draw enough current to drop the whole Vcc=3.3V on Rcl, so Icl > V/R = 3.3V/10kOhm = 0.33mA.
6) To provide 0.33mA Icl when T1 is on, we need Ibl to be Ibl>Icl/100, but to provide reliable logic levels we use 5x overdrive, so Ibl > Icl/(100/5) = 0.33mA/20 = 16.5uA.
7) Rbl needs to be chosen to provide 16.5uA Ibl when the input is high at 1.8V CMOS levels, that is 0.65*1.8V=1.17V worst case. So Rbl < V/I = (1.17V-0.7V)/16.5uA = 28kOhm. We can choose the 10kOhm standard value for Rbl that meets the equation.

5.6 SMALL LOGIC ICs

Even on high-end complex hardware we still use some basic logic chips that have been available for decades, as glue logic, although in smaller package options. Their number on a board can be reduced by better glue logic design that integrates more functions on a small FPGA. Every silicon chip "die" comes in a "package" encapsulated by the chip vendor, and we solder the packaged chip to the PCB. The package can be metal and plastic parts molded together or a thin and fine-line PCB "substrate" with solder balls on the bottom, called a Ball Grid Array (BGA). These small chips come in small packages, like the ones shown in Figure 5.4.

Example of logic chips

- CMOS buffers simply strengthen the signals. They are used to drive longer traces or multiple devices at speed of 20-50MHz. JTAG chain implementations, off-board buses often use these.
- Special buffers are available for special I/O interface standards like LVDS, HDMI, or DisplayPort video interfaces.
- Inverters are used if we need the signal inverted from active high control to active low device input. Typically, we use single inverters in SC-70 5pin packages.
- Level translators are used when two devices or two boards use a different IO standard, for example, 1.8V CMOS versus 3.3V CMOS. Some level translators are "dual supply", some are single supply clipping bus multiplexers. Some are bidirectional, others are unidirectional with a direction control pin.
- I2C multiplexers are used to connect more than 8 I2C devices to one host processor. These devices are analog multiplexers with multiple down-stream ports and a built-in I2C device that controls the analog multiplexer. The host writes to the MUX local address, tells it to enable which port, then the host can access all devices that are downstream from the

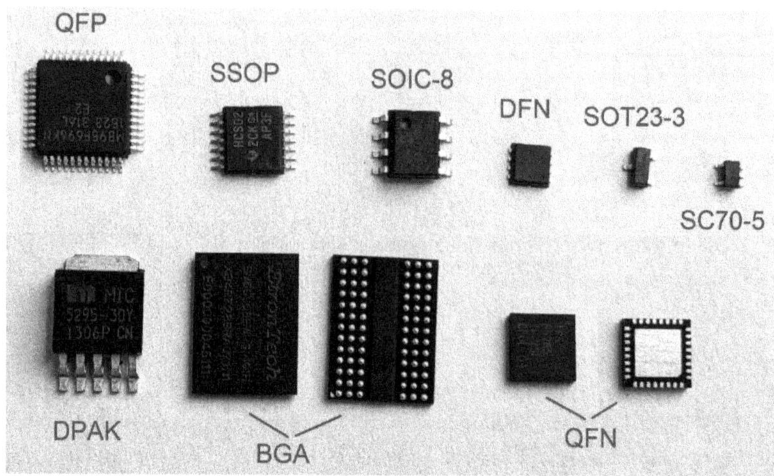

FIGURE 5.4 Small chip packaging types.

selected port. Typically on a very complex board we might have 50 I2C devices, which we have to organize into seven buses, so seven ports of a MUX chip are utilized. When we have 32 optical ports (SFP, QSFP…) each of those ports has a pluggable transceiver module, but all of them respond to the same address 0xA0, there is no way to strap different addresses to them. In this case we need a separate MUX port and bus to each transceiver port, 32 buses. That is only possible by using two levels of MUX chips, the top-level MUX creates eight buses, each bus will have a MUX on it to create eight ports each.

- I2C GPIO expanders are programmable small chips that provide 8 or 16 programmable GPIO ports, which can be controlled by the host processor over I2C bus. A GPIO is a pin that can be programmed to work as an input or an output, as a control or status signal.
- I2C accelerators can help when we have too long traces or too many devices that slow down the signal rise time, to accelerate low to high transitions, by tapping on the I2C bus.
- Analog multiplexers (MUX) are used to select signal routing to one device or another device from an always connected chip. The multiplexer must be a "rail-to-rail" type to allow proper CMOS signal levels to pass through. These are very common in SPI, I2C, and JTAG buses, under 100MHz. There are special signal multiplexers for multi-gigabit operation. The MUX has to be powered before the other devices so often we power them from a standby rail.
- Analog comparators are sometimes used to generate a PowerGood signal when a voltage rail is above a user defined threshold.
- USB power controller chips. USB ports are provided with a power pin, which sometimes has to be disabled by a host controller or when the attached devices pull too much load current. There are modern USB charge controller chips used in cell phones that are not used in complex data center or aerospace hardware.
- Fan controller chips, usually I2C-based programmable chips. They generate a PWM (pulse width modulation) signal that can be used for controlling the speed or airflow intensity of chassis fans. With higher PWM ratio we get higher airflow, which cools the ASICs in the system to a lower temperature through their heatsinks. They also have a tachometer input, which is a pulse rate counter for the TACH signal coming back from the fan and reports the rotation rate in a register. This requires the use of 4-wire DC fans.
- Thermal sensor chips. They are I2C slave devices, often with a built-in temperature sensor and also with remote sense capability. They require a diode to be connected to their remote sense pins. Many ASICs contain such a diode meant for on-die core temperature sensing;

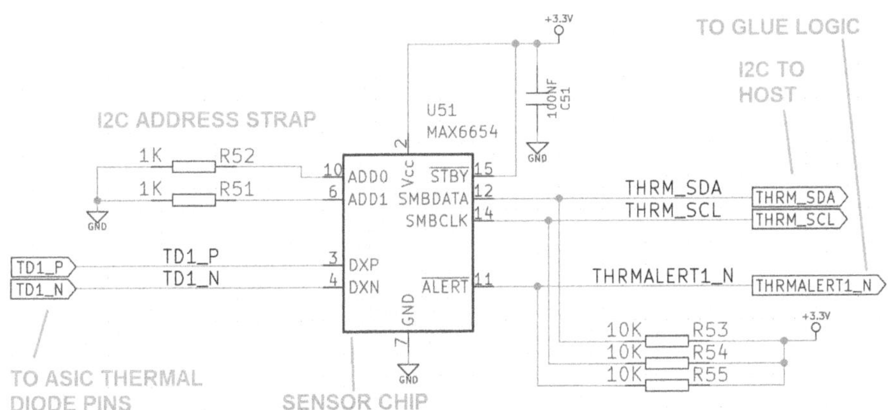

FIGURE 5.5 Thermal sensor circuit with on-die and local diodes in KiCad.

they provide two pins on the ASIC package for that. These can be connected to the sensor chip's remote sense pins using differential routing with no impedance control. Figure 5.5 shows an example circuit.

5.7 SUPER I/O CHIPS

Super I/O or SIO chips have the sole purpose of providing basic slow legacy computer interfaces like UARTs and PS/2 keyboard controllers to a computer motherboard. They are attached to the X86 chipset through the LPC bus. They are less common now than they were 10 to 20 years ago, but they are still available from Microchip (formerly SMSC) and Nuvoton. Usually these are unnecessarily large package chips, with few exceptions. On most embedded hardware we usually use an FPGA to implement this function as it takes up less space and is better on the procurement risk. The LPC bus is used because sometimes we want the BIOS to assign resources and memory-mapped (or I/O mapped) address ranges to our added ports. If that is not required, for example, if we use the ports only after the operating system was installed and already booted (and we do not need it to install the OS), then we can use other interfaces for attaching UART and PS/2 port controllers, for example, bridge chips that have an USB or PCIe upstream port, or we can implement them on FPGAs.

5.8 CLOCKING CHIPS

Reference clock signals are needed for every digital chip. Often multiple clocks at different frequencies, or even multiple copies of the same frequency are needed by the same ASIC. They provide the schedule mechanism for the millions of flip-flops inside the chips. A reference clock is not an I/O clock. An I/O clock is provided by a bridge chip or processor to the peripheral or memory devices for sampling board-level data signals (non-SERDES bus), while reference clocks are provided by clocking chips to the main ASICs. An ASIC might convert its reference clock into an I/O clock and provide it to peripheral devices through PCB traces. Memory controller and SERDES reference clocks are usually differential types, LVPECL, CML, LVDS, or HCSL, in the range of 100 to 600MHz. High-speed A/D converters sometimes use a line rate reference clock in the Gigahertz range.

Refclocks can be provided to ASICs by:

- Crystal circuit. The oscillator analog circuits are built into the digital chip, it just needs a crystal component with some passives to be connected to two pins (XIN, XOUT) of the digital chip. In digital designs we use crystals that have their "fundamental" frequency at the value we need, not the third order one. Crystal circuits that are high impedance are exposed to board surface, and they can stop working in the presence of moisture. This way mil/aero boards should avoid using basic crystals, but they should use oscillators instead. Crystals directly connecting to an ASIC are very rare. They are typically used for time-keeping on an X86 chipset or as a main source of a clocking chip. The ASIC needs to have a crystal driver analog circuit in it, which most digital chips do not have. The board-level circuit of a crystal oscillator can be seen in Figure 5.6. Modern crystals are available in 5x3 or3x2mm SMT packages with four pins, two of which are grounding pins.

- Oscillator. There are 4-pin and 6-pin oscillators available that are crystals or mems resonators with crystal driver analog circuits in one package with usually metallic casing. Standard sizes are 5x7, 3x5, and 2x3mm. There are oscillators with various I/O standards like LVPECL, CMOS1.8, and so on.
- Oscillator and a fanout buffer chip. If we need multiple clock signals of the same type and frequency, we connect a fanout buffer chip to the output of the oscillator on the board. An example to this can be seen in Figure 5.7. For PCIe, there are standardized (by intel) 4-output DB400 and 8-output DB800 chips available from multiple vendors.
- Programmable clocking chips if we need multiple clock signals of the same type and frequency, or different types and different frequencies.

We can build a clocking scheme using 4-pin or 6-pin oscillators that drive fanout buffer chips for all frequencies that are needed on a board, or we can use programmable clock chips that provide all the needed frequencies from one source. Programmable clock chips examples are the Skyworks (formerly Silicon Labs product line) Si5391D 12-output SERDES clock, the Analog Devices HMC7044 JESD204 ADC clock, the Renesas 8A34011 line card clock, or the Texas Instruments LMK03806 14-output SERDES clock. There are different ways of programming these clocking chips. Some devices can be purchased with a customized part number already pre-programmed by the chip vendor, others can be programmed over I2C during board manufacturing, while some devices need loading the configuration every time after power on. Many programmable clocks offer only one time programmability (OTP), but some allow power-on loading from an external EEPROM chip.

For FPGA and ASIC devices we often need multiple different frequency clock signals that are not integer multiples of each other. Then we have to use a clock chip with at least two to four separate PLLs and with fractional divider (FOD) functionality that can generate any frequency within a few PPM to the nominal value, well within the tolerance of the ASIC's frequency requirement. For many common reference clock frequencies, to achieve that exact value, FOD is required, even if just one signal is needed. For Interlaken interfaces that have no clock compensation in the SERDES

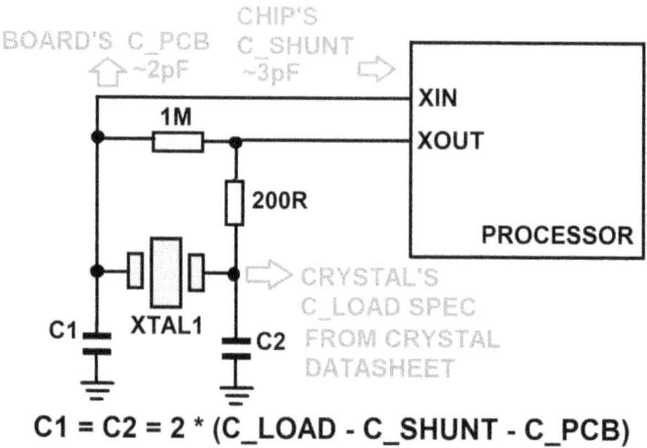

FIGURE 5.6 Crystal circuit.

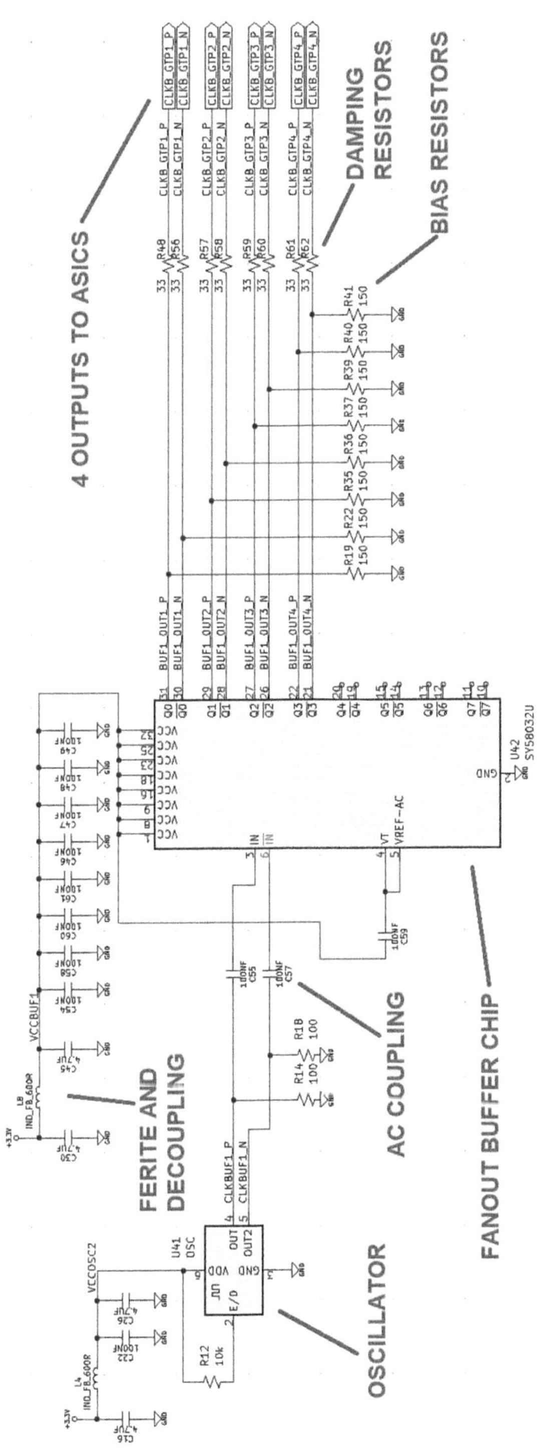

FIGURE 5.7 Simple OSC+BUF clocking for LVPECL in KiCad.

core, we need to provide two different frequency clocks that are at an exact ratio to each other to prevent buffer overrun—one for a peripheral device and one for its host device. X86 chipsets can be supplied from Intel-defined CK505 (or newer) standard clock chips that are available from multiple chip vendors.

Clock crystals and oscillators have important parameters like accuracy in PPM and temperature rating. Most I/O standards (like Ethernet, PCIe, USB) specify how accurate clocks are required, for example, 30ppm or 100ppm. The accuracy will not be reduced by the PLL clock chip, it is mainly driven by the crystal, unless we set a wrong frequency in the PLL divider, or we fail to use fractional divider capable clock chips.

The clocking solution has to meet the jitter requirements of the ASIC chip's datasheet. Clock generators have a jitter rating, and clock fanout buffers have an additive jitter specification. For example, if a certain ASIC requires 250 femtosecond or less jitter, then a clock generator at 150fs with a 50fs buffer will meet that at a total 150+50=200fs jitter. To verify it on a prototype board, we have to solder on two micro coax cables (one for P, one for N) at the removed receiver ASIC and route the clock to a splitter/combiner, then to a signal analyzer using good quality coax cables to display the jitter in terms of "phase noise RMS jitter".

Clock oscillators and clocking chips usually require the designer to put termination and biasing resistors on the board at the outputs. We can see examples of both on the diagram. We need to check in the clock chip datasheet or reference design schematics to see the exact resistor values and configurations that are required. Some ASICs require termination or AC-coupling at their reference clock inputs. This can be discovered also from the ASIC reference design or datasheet.

Clock chips and oscillators need to be powered from very low noise power rails. Usually, a clock chip has its own LDO power source or a filtered rail. If it is filtered, then there will be a ferrite bead in series with the source and decoupling capacitors before and after the ferrite bead.

5.9 PHY AND GEARBOX CHIPS

A PHY chip converts an internal "media independent interface" (MII or C2C) type Ethernet link, like SGMII, into an external (line) type Ethernet signal, like 1000Base-T. They are between the Ethernet MAC and the external port. Some Ethernet controller (MAC) chips do not have the high-powered transceivers required for creating an external Ethernet port, so a PHY does the conversion and implements the lower layers of the Ethernet protocol. Some PHY chips have two or four external ports, and they connect to the MAC through a single multiplexed QSGMII interface. PHY chips have to be configured and monitored (control/status register access) by the host (MAC) through an MDIO interface. Some of the Ethernet switch ASICs do not contain certain types of external Ethernet supports, while they support other types. For example, they may support 10G SFI, but not 10GBase-T, so a 10G SFI-to-Base-T PHY chip is required to add support for Base-T to our system. Many X86 chipsets are equipped with Ethernet MACs but no built-in PHYs for Base-T support, so Ethernet PHY chips are also manufactured to go with their processors/chipsets. Sometimes we include PHY chips in a design that does not need a PHY because some PHY chips have additional complex features like encryption, network security, or time synchronization. There are Ethernet chips that contain both a MAC and a PHY—they are called NIC (Network Interface Controller chips or Ethernet Controller chips), and they typically have a PCIe upstream interface to the host processor. They are meant to be used on network interface cards, but they often get integrated on the motherboard. For every Ethernet chip there is a host side (towards the CPU) and a line side (towards the external cabling).

Gearbox (GB) chips are similar to PHYs, but they convert an N-lane internal SERDES interface into an M-lane external SERDES interface, where $M<N$ and the baud rate per lane is larger on the external interface. For example, it may have 10 lanes of 10Gig SFI between the GB and MAC, that it converts to 4 lanes of 25Gig SFI to go between the GB and the QSFP100 optical cage connector. Gearbox chips usually show up when a new higher speed Ethernet port and optical

modules become available, but the main switch chips and FPGAs do not support the lane speed yet. This way the system/board designers can advertise that their product has support for the latest technology.

5.10 RETIMER CHIPS

These chips serve one purpose, that is, signal integrity improvements of SERDES links. The high-speed channel signal degradation might be too much by the time the signal arrives at the receiver chip, so we have to revive the signals just before they diminish into noise by inserting a re-driver or a retimer chip into the path. In most cases it is half way in the path. If it is placed near one end or the other, then it is not effective. Re-drivers are mainly analog comparator type circuits with filters that can reverse the effects of inter-symbol interference (ISI) caused by insertion loss and open up the eye so it can survive several more inches of travel. Retimer chips include a full receiver and transmitter (SERDES) digital circuit on each side. They have two sides or ports. They also include some protocol logic to support link training and speed negotiation. They are protocol specific. There are devices for Ethernet variants, PCI-express, SATA, and other standards. Retimers can reverse the effects of not only insertion loss, but also any eye diagram degradations caused by reflection, jitter, and crosstalk.

When we insert a retimer into a SERDES link, it creates two separate links. Retimer chips have to be involved in the link training process and actively communicate and negotiate with the immediate link partner chips. This way they are more complex, and they dissipate more heat also. A re-driver maintains the same single logical link/channel. In link training with a re-driver the two main devices (CPU, FPGA, ASIC) negotiate with each other, while with retimers they both negotiate with the retimer chip instead of with each other. In terms of signal integrity analysis, the channel is cut into two independent shorter channels by a retimer chip that have to meet the channel specs (PCI-SIG, IEEE, OIF…) separately and simulated separately. With re-drivers it is more complicated to simulate, as it is true that the channel is separated into two independent channels for meeting the insertion loss specs, but it remains one single channel for meeting the crosstalk and return loss (reflections) specs. For this a pass-through device model would be required while simulating the whole one channel.

Multi-lane SERDES links have special requirements. To correctly perform its link training duties, each retimer chip has to handle all lanes of a bus, we cannot split them. This is not required when we use re-drivers. Retimer chips are protocol locked, they are not simple analog components. All lanes of a port are required to be on the same retimer chip for any protocol to work, and the retimer chip has to support that particular protocol, like Ethernet or PCIe. This is demonstrated in Figure 5.8, with two cases of design configurations.

Most retimer chips allow the system developer to manually alter the transceiver equalization parameters. The new parameters have to be loaded into them over SPI or I2C after power on, or auto-loaded from an attached EEPROM that needs to be programmed once. Most retimers also support on die eye capture that we can read out through its configuration interface (I2C or SPI)—this helps with making the best use of the retimer function by allowing us to measure and adjust during prototyping in the lab. The retimer chip company usually provides an application for eye scan. If this is only a Windows GUI, then we have to design our hardware with a I2C/SPI/JTAG header so a vendor dongle can be connected and used with the GUI. If it is a Linux text-eye display, then we can have the retimer's config interface wired exclusively to the host processor that runs our Linux, where we will run the eye scan from command line. This is an important feature when selecting the retimer chip. If they do not provide eye scan, they may provide a bit error count that should show a low number (<10) after running for a few minutes.

Some interfaces might not support retimers due to custom low-level protocols, or the host ASICs disable a feature when retimers are used. For example, forward error correction (FEC). Some retimers support FEC while others do not. FEC-based interfaces require a retimer that supports FEC as

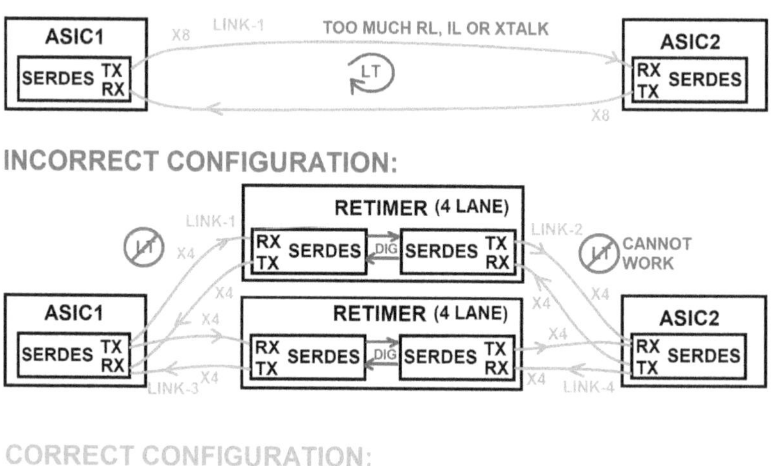

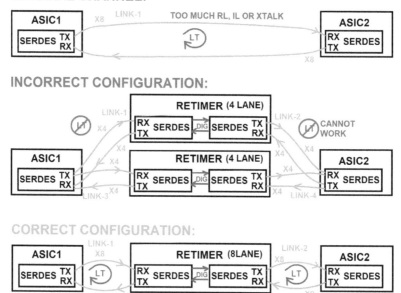

FIGURE 5.8 Retimer use correctly (enabling link training) and incorrectly on a multi-lane link.

a feature listed in their datasheet. Proprietary interfaces might have custom implementation of FEC that third party retimers might not support.

Larger retimers chips with 112G SERDES support are available (now in 2023) from Broadcom and Credo, slightly lower speed devices from Texas Instruments. PCIe retimers are available from Renesas (IDT) and Texas Instruments.

5.11 PERIPHERAL CONTROLLERS

Processors and chipsets have several integrated I/O interfaces, but our board design requirement might include additional interface types. This is achieved by attaching a peripheral controller chip to the processor or chipset through an internal expansion bus, such as PCIe or USB.

High-performance interfaces are usually added through a PCIe-to-XYZ bridge chip. XYZ might be RapidIO or InfiniBand. Sometimes for convenience we use PCIe for slow bus bridging like PCIe-to-UART, for example, the XR17V358 from MaxLinear. For an X86 CPU to communicate with a DSP through its external parallel interface or the host port interface (both parallel buses), we would use an old chip like the PCI2040 from TI (until it is finally obsolete) or we have to create a bridge using an FPGA and custom logic code. The last PCI to VME (form factor used in legacy aerospace systems) bus bridge chip was the Tundra/Marvell Universe II chip. Nowadays designers use an FPGA VME IP instead. The TI XIO2221 is a PCIe to FireWire bridge.

5.11.1 Ethernet NIC

There are Ethernet controller chips, also called NIC or Network Interface Controllers. They have a PCIe host interface, and create an Ethernet port (or 1 to 4 ports) downstream. A NIC chip consists of a MAC and a PHY function on a single chip. The Ethernet ports will have their own MAC addresses, which have to be assigned by manufacturing. They have to generate a unique MAC address for each port on each production (and proto) unit. Anything connecting to the Internet has to have a MAC address that is unique in the whole world. There are many different types of Ethernet ports defined by various IEEE standards. The chip datasheet will tell which ones are implemented by the chip. The Intel XL710 is/was a popular 40Gbit Ethernet NIC chip used to allow a local host processor to inject Ethernet traffic into the switching data plane subsystem, or as a main Ethernet port of a server node in a data center.

The schematic in Figure 5.9 shows a simple Intel I210 1Gbit Ethernet controller with a PCIe upstream interface, a MagJack connector, and a configuration EEPROM for the MAC address storage. Higher bandwidth Ethernet chips like the BCM57504 and the XL710 have many more pins and supporting components—their circuit would not fit on a book page, but otherwise they have similar features.

5.11.2 SATA/SAS Controller Chips

When we want to attach SATA or SAS storage drives to a processor that does not have these SATA or SAS ports, then we need to use a SATA Controller chip, which has a PCIe host interface. Marvell and Broadcom are the main vendors.

5.11.3 USB Chips

Often when we need to create additional USB ports in our system we use USB HUB chips, like the ones offered by Microchip (acquired SMSC). A hub creates four downstream ports from a single port provided by a host processor. All operating systems contain default drivers for them.

We can create SPI, I2C, Ethernet, or UART ports using a USB bridge chips, such as the ones offered by Microchip, Maxim, MaxLinear, Realtek, and Infineon/Cypress Semiconductors, for example, the USB-to-UART bridge chip, the famous FT232 chip originally created by FTDI. This helps in attaching devices that require a low-speed host port for configuration. Simple devices like VRM controllers, clock chips, glue logic FPGAs, and BMC controllers can be accessed through these slow buses. More complex devices like retimer or gearbox chips also have a low-speed configuration interface.

Silicon Motion and others offer USB graphics adapter chips that can add a graphics display output to a console-only embedded processor if we manage the software drivers for it. There are also USB peripheral controllers like touch pads and keyboards.

5.12 PCIe BRIDGING AND SWITCHING

PCI and PCIe are internal expansion buses normally used inside a chassis. Processors and FPGAs might have PCI host or PCIe root complex ports, but sometimes they are not sufficient to attach all the many and different types of devices we want to attach in a very complex system. In this case we use PCI or PCIe bridging or switching chips. Remember that PCI is a parallel bus, while PCI-Express (PCIe) is a SERDES interface, but both provide system-memory-mapped data transfers requested by a single host in the system or by intelligent peripherals. PCI and PCIe buses rely on bridge and switch chips to attach more devices (FPGA, ASIC) to a host controller (CPU, FPGA). These bridge/switch chips are plug-and-play devices, first configured from pin strapping or an EEPROM, then the standard BIOS firmware initializes them (through enumeration) and then they are fully functional. The devices connected to these bridge/switch chips are categorized as either Initiator versus Target on PCI-bus, or Root Complex versus Endpoint on PCI-Express. Ports are upstream (to the host that enumerates everyone else) or downstream. Later in this chapter we discuss the different bridge and switch devices and their various port types and modes. Figure 5.10 shows a made-up system with examples of all types described.

5.12.1 PCI-to-PCI Bridges (P2PB)

The parallel PCI bus (and its enhanced faster PCI-X version) has a limit of eight devices per bus segment. For more than eight devices a PCI-to-PCI bridge chip has to be added to the design. For

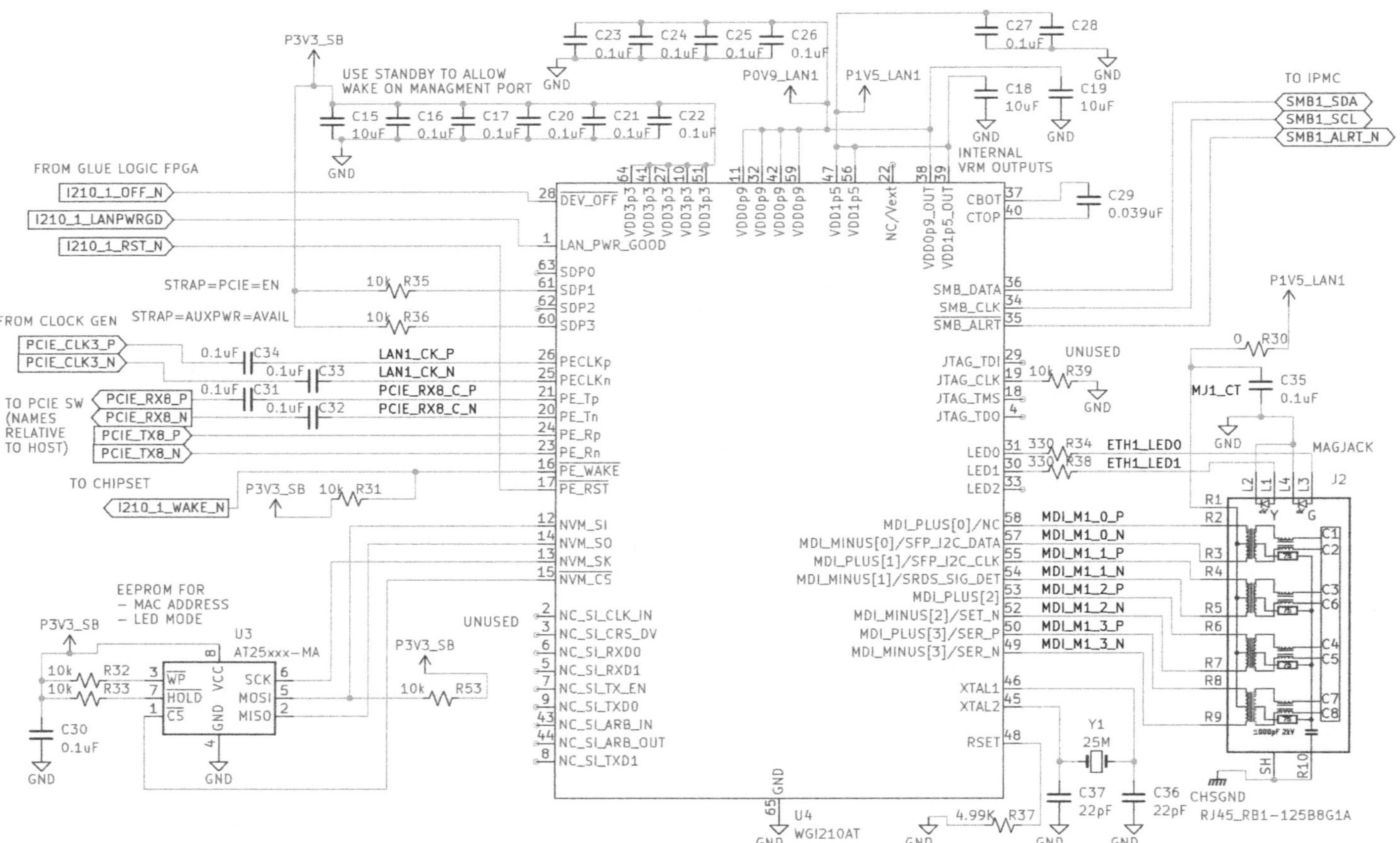

FIGURE 5.9 Schematics connections of an I210 Gigabit Ethernet controller chip in KiCAD.

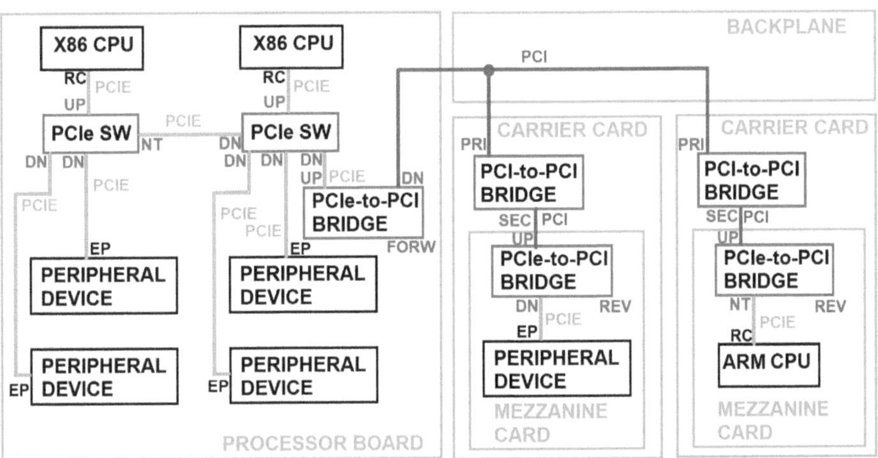

FIGURE 5.10 Theoretical system with all types of PCI/PCIe devices and modes.

example, the PLX/Broadcom PCI6254 device or a Texas Instruments PCI2050B was used for this purpose for decades. They are or soon will be discontinued, so we will likely use an FPGA-based implementation instead. These bridges have a primary port and a secondary port and a set of PCI and glue logic signals on each side. A reset coming in on one side might propagate out on the other side depending on device mode. In non-transparent mode a reset might generate an interrupt on the other side instead. The direction of the reset, REQ/GNT and clock pins depends on the mode selection.

These devices support the transparent mode, where the devices on the two sides of the bridge see the same addresses in the system. Some devices also support something called non-transparent mode (NT-mode), where the bridge device translates the address so the two sides do not see the same address ranges for the same objects/devices/memory buffers. Also, the bridge terminates BIOS-driven PCI enumeration at non-transparent ports, the remaining bus with all of its devices appearing as a single target (endpoint) device, to allow two processors initializing/enumerating their own devices separately. The other side has a config header and BAR created for the downstream port in NT-mode, like a target device, and it is initialized by the other processor. This is useful when we want to attach two host processors to one or more endpoint devices, and we want to DMA (direct memory access) data into the system memory from the device into each host processor. Then which host the DMA transfer will go to depends on the address range. Also, the two processors can DMA data to each other if they have a built-in DMA engine. DMA means direct memory address—it is basically a complex state machine that copies data from one address to another without the main processor having to handle each transfer. In all cases an endpoint device is assigned an address range within the processors address space through the Base Address Register or BAR. All memory read and memory write transactions from the host processor into this address range are directed into the endpoint device. Any access into an address outside of this range, originating from an intelligent endpoint, is routed upstream to access the rest of the memory mapped devices and the system memory of the host processor. Any bridge/switch devices get an address region to pass transactions to all their downstream target/endpoint devices. Bridge/switch type devices have a Tpe-1 PCI configuration header containing information about secondary bus and address region (pass through) base and limit registers, while regular endpoint/target devices have a Type-0 header without secondary bus fields.

5.12.2 PCIe-to-PCI Bridges (PE2PB)

They inherited many of the functionality of PCI-to-PCI bridge chips. Parallel PCI buses no longer exist in most CPUs and chipsets, but some aerospace form factors still use it for designing those we have to create PCI buses from the PCIe buses that are available on modern processors using PCIe-to-PCI bridge chips, for example, the Pericom (acquired by Diodes Inc) PI7C9X130 chip, the TI XIO2001 or the Broadcom/PLX PEX8112 (might be obsolete by now). These PCIe-to-PCI bridge chips have two operating modes, the forward bridge mode, where the PCIe connects to the upstream host, and the reverse bridge mode, where the PCI interface connects to the host and provides PCIe connectivity to devices.

These devices are useful on Compact-PCI form factor boards (PCI backplane), where a card might be plugged into a host slot or a peripheral slot and the bridge will be initialized in one mode or the other (rev/forward) depending on slot ID (SYS_CON signal). We can also use them to support PMC (PCI Mezzanine Card) form factor modules with a PCIe-only host processor. They are not used in modern consumer or even data center electronics; however, military, aerospace, and scientific research still makes use of old equipment that sometimes is upgraded with new cards to increase performance.

5.12.3 PCIe Switches (PESW)

PCI-to-PCI(e) bridges only have two ports, but PCIe switches can have many. On PCIe Root Complex ports of host controllers (the main processor) usually we can attach only one device—except if they allow "bifurcation", aka splitting a port into two to eight separate ones, as set up by BIOS. To attach more than one device, and to allow any device to utilize the full host port bandwidth, we have to use a PCIe Switch chip, which creates multiple downstream ports from one upstream port. Some devices support multiple upstream ports through NT-ports that allow multi-host systems to access the same resources. These devices are in use in many embedded, military/aerospace, and data center equipment. Usually in multi-board systems the host card might have a PCIe SW to support many other cards connecting over a backplane, or the downstream cards might have one if they have multiple devices on-board with one port coming in from the host CPU card. At the physical level, each PCIe bus is one point-to-point link. At the logical level, each bus contains only one host and one endpoint device. Also, at the logical level each port on a PCIe switch appears as a virtual PCI-to-PCI bridge, which creates a new bus number downstream to it. On a Linux PCI scan (lspci), we can see devices listed with bus number and device number. We see as many switch devices in the scan as the number of ports on the switch physical chip.

Several of these devices also have a programmable DMA (direct memory access) controller for moving a large amount of data without wasting the host processor's time on load/store transactions. Some devices support hot plug controllers, which facilitates using an external accelerator appliance chassis connecting to a server chassis using PCIe cables. All of these devices support On-Die Eye capture.

Several device families are available now:

- Broadcom (acquired PLX), 0 to 6 NT ports.
    - PEX86xx, PCIe gen2, 5Gbps, 4 to 96 lanes.
    - PEX87xx, PCIe gen3, 8Gbps, 12 to 96 lanes.
    - PEX97xx, PCIe gen3, 8Gbps, with ExpressFabric protocol.
    - PEX88xxx, PCIe gen4, 16Gbps, 26 to 98 lanes.
    - PEX89xxx, PCIe gen5, 32Gbps, 24 to 144 lanes.
- Microchip (Switchtec) PMxxxxx part numbers, 24 to 100 lanes.
    - PFX, Basic PCIe, Gen3,4,5 devices, 0 to 48 NT ports.
    - PSX, user-programmable, Gen3,4 devices, 0 to 48 NT ports.
    - PAX, data center fabric, Gen4 devices, no NT ports.
- Renesas (acquired IDT) 89Hxxxxx part numbers, 12 to 64 lanes, Gen3.
- Diodes Inc (acquired Pericom) PI7C9X series devices with fewer ports.

5.12.4 Configuring the Devices

All device modes, like transparent and non-transparent, reverse-bridge, forward-bridge, and universal mode, are set on the bridge/switch device using strapping pins. The pins are configurable through resistor strapping to function in different modes. For bridge chips the whole chip is in transparent or NT mode, while for switch devices one port at a time can be selected for a mode because each port on a switch is a virtual bridge. There is a "universal mode" for the bridge chips, where transparent/NT mode selection is dependent on which slot (host or peripheral) a card is plugged into. The host card and any basic peripherals will have transparent mode, the intelligent peripheral cards will have NT. These devices have many strapping pins for configuring them, so after power on they come up in the right mode and work plug-and-play with the BIOS firmware. Other strapping settings, specifically for PCIe switches, are like limiting the port speed, selecting the upstream port among many ports, and setting port configuration, (how many ports, how wide each). Some of the configuration is loaded from an attached SPI or I2C EEPROM device that has to be programmed during board manufacturing or during prototype bring-up using a console app running on the host processor. These are things like status LED mapping or transceiver settings overrides.

The bridge devices have several situation-specific strapping pins, and they are usually driven by a glue logic CPLD (or small FPGA) and have a different state depending on which slot a card is plugged into (reading a slot ID) or what is connected to the bridge on either side. The Glue logic CPLD also handles the resets as they are inputs or outputs depending on situation also. PCI clock routing and directionality are usually handled through analog multiplexers that are controlled by the CPLD. The bridge chip either operates from a clock received from the backplane or it operates from the local on-board oscillator chip that also provides clocks to other cards through the backplane. Clock trace delays play a part in I/O timing margins since these clocks are I/O clocks, not reference clocks. Any fast 66MHz bus signals do not go through the CPLD either as it would also ruin the timing margins.

The switch devices just need static strapping, which can be provided using resistors. All of their clocks are reference clocks—the delays do not matter to them—and they are HCSL differential format, usually AC-coupled. They can have SSC (spread spectrum clocking) enabled, but then all devices, the CPU, and the switch all must receive their clock signal from the same source through a fanout buffer called synchronous clocking. We cannot always guarantee that SSC will be disabled, so it is best practice to provide a synchronous clocking scheme. In many backplane applications a reference clock is not provided. Each board has its own clocking source, so we must ensure that SSC is disabled by the CPU, and all devices support the independent clocking scheme. The strapping and glue logic signals of the common PE2PB and PESW devices are illustrated in Figure 5.11. P2PB devices are no longer used in new designs.

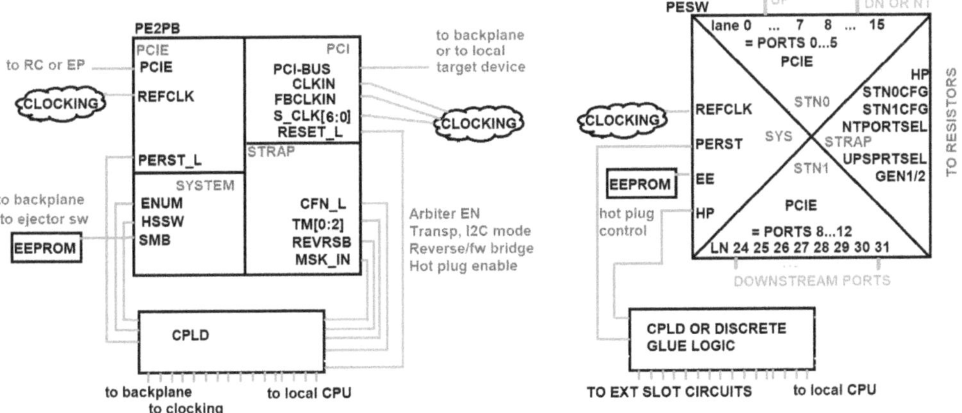

FIGURE 5.11 Simplified PCI/PCIe device configurations.

Each target/endpoint device, switch, or bridge chip has a maximum burst size (PCI) or packet payload size (PCIe). The host/RC port has to be set to never start a transaction larger than this, otherwise the transactions will fail with errors. The BIOS will set this parameter into the host/RC registers, but the OS might override it. In that case it has to be manually set lower in Linux boot scripts or in driver code. Using the hot swap feature of bridges and switches will require a special OS driver.

5.12.5 Switch Devices for Other Protocols

There are switch chips similar to the PCIe switches, but they are used on different protocol standards, like CXL, InfiniBand, RapidIO, CCIX, or NVLINK. Their structure, their pin types, their clocking, hot-plugging control, and their features are similar to the PCIe switch devices. Several interface standards are peer to peer, and all ports are non-transparent. More about how these interfaces work can be found in Chapter 3, "Major Interfaces". Ethernet switch chips are described in Chapter 6, "Main Chips" (it also discusses ASICs). They range from small 4-port-1Gig/port to larger 512-port-112Gig/port ASICs.

5.13 HIGH-SPEED ADCs

Some complex digital boards are used to process RF signals through something called software-defined radio concept. They have an RF front end with some amplifiers and buffers that feed into a high-speed (>1GSPS sample rate) analog to digital converter (ADC, A/D Converter). Just like ADCs, the digital to analog converters (DACs) are also used on some designs to complete the signal path. GHz-range ADCs are usually medium-complexity and power-hungry devices with their own heatsinks. The captured signal is transmitted into an FPGA or DSP through a high-speed digital data bus. This can be LVDS double data rate up to few hundred megahertz, or regular SERDES transceivers (JESD204x standard) at many Gigabits per seconds on multiple lanes. The JESD204x devices use a SYSREF clock (synchronization and deterministic latency) in addition to the "device clock", which is the ADC sample clock and transceiver line rate clock in one. This is not a low frequency "reference clock" like in PCIe; rather, it is a several GHz signal that either matches the data rate or is used in an internal small step PLL to create the JESD data rate from it (0.5 to 5x F_clk), depending on the operating mode of the device. The FPGA SERDES reference clock might have to be at a lower frequency but exact (not ppm) frequency locked to the ADC device clock. These are generated by clocking chips made for supporting the JESD204 requirements.

The main vendors are TI, Analog Devices, and Teledyne e2v. Example devices are the ADC12DJ5200 ADC chip from Texas Instruments and the AD9213 from Analog Devices. A generic block diagram can be seen in Figure 5.12. It shows the ADC chip itself, clocking, and the

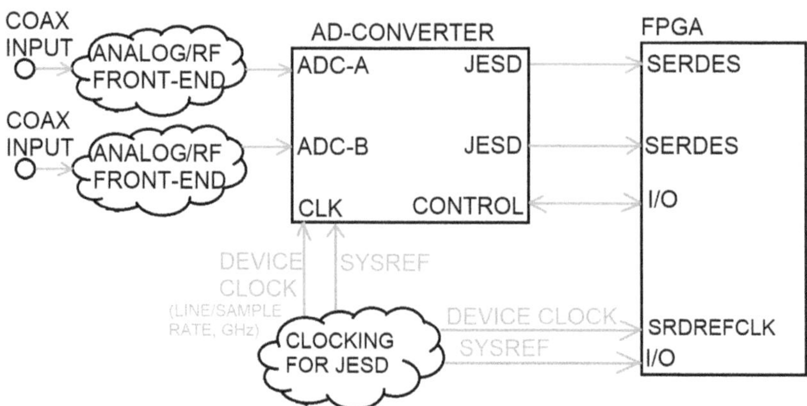

FIGURE 5.12 A generic view of a JESD204-based ADC.

analog front end. The analog/RF portion usually contains low noise amplifiers, ADC input driver amplifiers, programmable-gain amplifiers (PGA), filters, and biasing circuits. The FPGA usually controls the ADC over a slow serial interface as well as various control signals. Some of the analog circuits are also controlled through FPGA I/O pins, for example, driving a parallel code to set a PGA gain value. Some ADCs are combined with common RF circuits into RF front-end chips or mixed-signal front ends, for example, the AD9081 from Analog Devices. They sometimes also have digital filtering (DSP) capabilities.

5.14 BASIC CONNECTORS

For connecting cables to boards or boards to boards we use connectors. On complex hardware designs we use basic low-speed connectors for power delivery, fan cables, device programming, LEDs, or other purposes. They contain up to ~100MHz (1000Base-T Ethernet is actually with 125MHz baud rate) low speed buses. Usually these are straight (up) or right-angled (sideways) dual-row pin headers with 1/20" or 1/10" pitch. Sometimes we use a 1mm, 1/40", or 0.5mm pitch header with an adapter board or adapter cable. Often we want to provide access to multiple JTAG and I2C ports from our debug headers that result in 20 to 40 pins, which we can only justify on very high-density boards if we use a very small pitch connector. When the connector header is 1/10" pitch dual row and has a big plastic frame around it with a key cutout, it is called an IDC header. The keying prevents users from plugging them in the wrong 180 degree orientation. It is very convenient to use IDC headers as they are keyed, and their footprint preserves all the board space that the cable connector will need, so we can avoid designing it in and later being unable to plug anything in due to nearby tall components. Some connectors, in terms of manufacturing technology, are available in SMT format (gull-wing or BGA), others are through-hole (soldered or press-fit). In modern times larger backplane connectors are almost always press-fit, while small headers are usually SMT gull-wing.

Every board has power and I/O connectors. Power can come into a board through a board-to-board (from a backplane or host card or from a PSU module) or a wire-to-board connector. If it comes from a backplane, then usually it is a connector different from the one used for the signals, or it has different/larger contact blades inside a combined connector. Keying is an important feature of wire-to-board connectors so as to prevent incorrect orientation that can damage the board. Card-edge connectors are used as cost savings in certain applications, where only one side needs an actual connector part, the other side is the edge of the PCB that is milled to a specific shape. The board edge area has large contact surfaces that have a "hard-gold" surface finish that is thicker than the nickel-gold (NiAu) used on solder pads.

Rugged circular connectors (MIL-DTL-38999, MIL-DTL-26482 and other standardized types) are used on the chassis of military/aerospace applications for all external I/O connections. They are shock and dust proof; they allow the cable connector to be secured to the chassis using large threaded nuts. Most of them are not made for high-speed signals above 100MHz. Very few 10Gbps capable military-grade connectors are available as of 2022, but a few optical multi-fiber (ARINC 801 standard) ones are available.

5.15 HIGH-SPEED CONNECTORS

For our high-speed signals (>50MHz) we need to use high-speed capable connectors that are designed with good ground return, shielding, differential signaling, and impedance control. The datasheet should tell what speed they are rated at. There are two types: the external I/O and the internal board-to-board connectors. The external types are always standard connectors with metal shielding, the internal types are usually dependent on the system design company, except for standard form factors like VPX or ATCA.

The internal high-speed connectors usually have to carry more signals, as many as 32 to 128 diffpairs in a single connector, and we use multiple instances to provide all the bandwidth we need. The lower pin count options are dual row, but anything above 64 pins is usually made with a grid pinout. Normally front cards (or line replaceable units) have right-angle connectors that mate with a backplane's vertical connector or with a same-plane rear card or with an orthogonal fabric card. When we plug in daughter cards on top of another card in parallel, we use mezzanine or stacking connectors.

We have to select the connector model based on the signaling speed we are using; the part datasheet should list its speed rating. If it is not listed, then it is likely a very low speed connector that might only work at 1Gbps even when used with retimer chips. Some connectors allow free form pinout selection, where even the ground pin assignments are up to the user—they just have a uniform grid of pins. These connectors are good up to a few Gbps only. At 3Gbps or above exact differential pairs are defined inside the connector design and the ground shielding is created to form diffpair or twinax differential transmission and shielding. Depending on how extensive the ground shielding is, the ratio between the number of ground and signal pins has a strong effect on the speed capability and SERDES channel quality in terms of S-parameters. If the column spacing is large enough, then it allows an extra column of ground vias between the pin columns, which is commonly used at the 56Gbps singling rate.

Many backplane connectors contain "wafers" that are thin PCBs with microstrip differential pair traces; they terminate into metal mechanical pins on one end (press-fit into the PCB) and card edge gold finger type contacts at the other end. A mated right-angle connector has two parts: a right-angle part (on the front card) and a straight part (backplane part). The right-angled part contains the wafer and the longer part of the in-connector signal path. Other connectors are mechanically engineered plastic-metal structures without wafer PCBs. An example of a mating backplane connector set can be seen in Figure 5.13. Vertical mezzanine connectors are usually twin-axial mechanical (metal and plastic parts) rather than wafer-based. Some of the high-speed backplane connectors require a fan-out sideways, resulting in a need for a part placement gap between backplane connectors.

With any board-to-board connector we have to make sure we design the two boards to have matching pinouts and that the pinouts line up with the ASIC pinouts. Some connectors have row or column shift, or the rows and columns are transposed in the pinout of the mating connector. Thus, we have to account for that too while designing our schematic. For example, B1 on one side is C1 on the other side, or B5 on one side is F2 on the other side. We could easily orient one side by 180 degrees by mistake and make the system prototype useless. To avoid pin mapping mistakes, a pin orientation diagram could be made for the system and the boards involved that shows the connector part orientation and corner pin locations. This diagram can be used for guiding the mechanical, layout, and schematic design. An example is in Figure 5.14.

FIGURE 5.13 ExaMAX 56Gig Backplane connectors from Samtec.

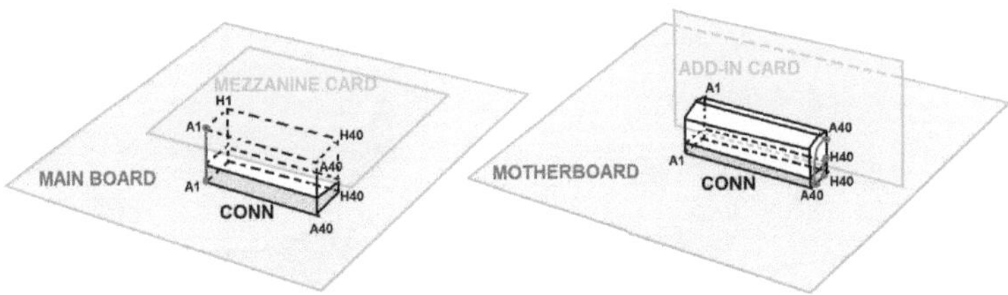

FIGURE 5.14 Pin orientation diagrams for a system.

5.16 OPTICAL CAGE CONNECTORS

High-bandwidth data connections external to the chassis are usually made using fiber optic links. Short reach SR optics with multimode optical fibers are used within a data center, a building, or a vehicle (aircraft, ship). Long reach LR optics with thinner single mode optical fibers are used to connect one building or city with another. These fiber optic cables are plugged into "pluggable fiber optic transceiver modules" that are plugged into the chassis front panel's optical cage connectors to form one port. Most of these cage connectors are standardized by SFF, and the standard documents (SFF-XXXX) are hosted on snia.org. The newer ones are on separate websites, such as QSFP-DD and OSFP. For example, SFF-8083 is the main standard for the 10Gbps SFP+, while SFF-8418 describers the SI requirements, and other SFF documents describing other details of it like mechanical or management. They define the mechanical dimensions, electrical connector pinouts, and high-speed board design constraints (insertion loss limits). The connectors actually have two separately assembled parts. An SMT connector soldered down in reflow that has the signal contacts, and a metal cage over it assembled using press-fit. The same connectors can also be used to insert something called "passive copper cables" that have a pluggable connector module (in the shape of an optical transceiver module but with no active components inside) and a group of twinax (differential) electrical cables inside a single plastic jacket cable bundle. Active copper cables have basically retimers or re-drivers inside the pluggable module. Copper cables are used up to 3 to 10ft length. Figure 5.15 shows several optical transceivers, cables, and connector cages used for 10Gig SFP+ and 40Gig QSFP+.

Each pluggable transceiver has either an EEPROM or a microcontroller in it, accessed over an I2C bus, so the host system (where it is plugged into) can read the module descriptor data. Even copper cables come with a transceiver casing but without an actual transceiver circuit that contains the EERPROM. These data can be used simply for logging, to notify the user what exact type and brand module was plugged into, or to set the ASIC transceivers to the correct mode and speed. The host to this I2C bus can be the switch ASIC or the local host processor. Low-end consumer switches connect the I2C bus to the switch ASIC that usually contains a small ARM processor core on the switch ASIC die, while high-end high-bandwidth data center systems with many optical ports configure the ASICs to try to not control or monitor their disconnected I2C ports; rather, the management processor (often X86) will communicate with the optical ports, both the EEPROM read and the control/status signals handling. This way a large switch or appliance that may contain multiple switch ASICs can centrally manage all ports. When a module is plugged in, the embedded processor's software can detect the event through the port status signals (GPIO), then read the EEPROM to determine the module type and manufacturer, and then it can set the ASICs port to the appropriate speed. Every module responds at the same address, at A0, so the host has to provide separate I2C buses to each connector.

Each standard has its own system signals, called low speed electrical interface, that we typically connect to an FPGA or GPIO controller. QSFP-DD signals: The ModSelL pin of the module can be used for I2C device select if we connect all modules to the same I2C bus. A ResetL can reset the module, LPMode/TxDis signals can turn off transmission or tell the module to limit power

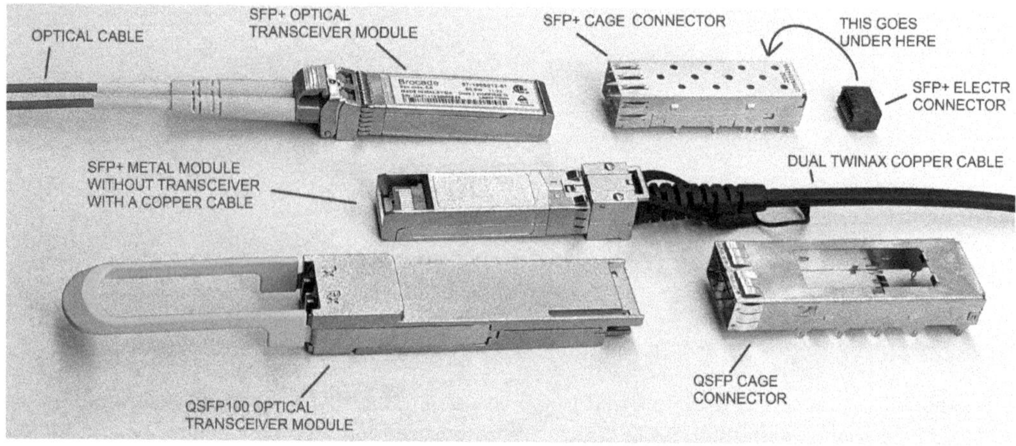

FIGURE 5.15 Optical transceivers, cables. and connectors.

consumption, the ModPrsL tells the host when a module is inserted, IntL/RxLOSL an interrupt from the module to the local host processor. SFP+ has a similar set of signals, but they are not exactly the same. It has TX_Fault interrupt to host, TX_Disable, RS0 and RS1 speed select, MOD_ABS is the same as ModPrsL on QSFP, RX_Los similarly to RX_LosL on QSFP,

A few common pluggable optical module standards:

- SFP: 1Gbit/s over single lane (one RX and one TX diffpair), INF-8074
- SFP+: 10Gbit/s over single lane, SFF-8418, SFF-8083
- zSFP+: same as SFP+ but with 25G-NRZ and 56G-PAM4, FC-PI-6, SFF-8402
- QSFP+: 40Gbit/s over 4 lanes of 10Gbit/s each, SFF-8436
- QSFP100: 100Gbit/s over 4 lanes of 28Gbit/s each, SFF-8665
- QSFP-DD: 400Gbit/s over 8 lanes of 53Gbit/s PAM4 each, or 800Gbit/s over 8 lanes of 106Gbit/s, see QSFP-DD.com
- OSFP: 400Gbit/s over 8 lanes of 53Gbit/s PAM4 each, or 800Gbit/s over 8 lanes of 106Gbit/s, osfpmsa.org

5.17 MECHANICAL PARTS

Complex and high-performance digital boards always require mechanical parts for cooling the hot ASICs and for securing the boards in place. Sometimes board-wide stiffener frames or holding plates (sleds) are screwed onto the board, for the purpose of preventing large boards from flexing and vibrating.

Bus bars are thick and long copper pieces, fixed shape, and they are used instead of multi-thread flexible wires. They are much thicker than wires and can carry much more DC current, usually used for delivering 12V power to large powerful (>500W) digital boards. The bus bar mates with electrical spring-contact connectors that are regular mass-produced parts. The bus bar is custom designed for a particular chassis, usually plated solid copper.

We put mounting holes into the design, which are not purchasable parts, just layout symbols for drilling and copper pads, for the purpose of securing boards to chassis or mechanical parts to the board. Some companies place mounting holes into the design from a schematic library, others from a footprint library. Mounting holes in the design are electrically connected to ground (directly) or chassis ground (through a ferrite bead if the design has a chassis ground). The number, size, and exact location of the mounting holes are negotiated between the hardware engineer and the mechanical engineer. Every board design has one or more mechanical engineer(s) assigned to it.

Every main ASIC needs an individual heatsink or an attachment surface on the main heat frame. For each ASIC there has to be two, four, six, or eight mounting holes, that are placed on the board in a way that it is symmetrical to the ASIC die center to even out the pressure over the ASIC package or die surface. Holes that are used to secure the board into the chassis are used to prevent the board from moving or flexing. They are usually placed at the corners, along the edges, or in the middle. Their position might be determined intuitively, based on the chassis metals design, or through a mechanical-resonance analysis. Often mounting holes are placed next to removable parts and connectors. Board designs have to comply with chassis mechanical and heatsink requirements, and the mechanical design has to comply with the devices and their locations on the board.

Fans are used in high-end equipment as chassis fans to blow or suck a constant airflow through the whole chassis, helping all passive heatsinks in the chassis. Usually the back side of a long chassis is covered with fans end to end, while others (like ATCA) have two large fans at the top or bottom of the chassis. Air baffles are sometimes used to guide the air pushed by the system fan towards the heatsinks. Air baffles are flat pieces secured to the board or chassis, made of sheet metal, high-temperature plastic or some type of industrial (aramid or other type) paper. In many systems the fans are mounted inside a fan module subassembly that contains finger guard sheet metal, a handle, an ejector, and a small PCB that hosts the right-angle connector with which the fan module will connect to a fan controller board. Mechanical engineering has to design these modules.

Alignment pins are used on some backplane-based form factors, like VPX, that helps to pull the card to the right position just before insertion, so the connectors will align to make correct contact. On the backplane it is a screw-mounted very thick metal pin, on the front card it is a metal part with a large hole that exactly fits the pin. So while plugging a card in, first the card is guided into the plastic guide rails, then the guide pin aligns the board further, then an ejector engages to help work against the connector's massive insertion force, and then finally the connector mates.

5.17.1 Heatsinks

Heatsinks, together with system fans, are used to cool individual or a group of main ASICs. Usually each ASIC has its own heatsink, due to mechanical flatness, plane, and height differences between even identical ASICs. Any digital device over 2 to 3W needs a heatsink. Heatsinks usually require two to eight mounting holes around the ASIC for securing it to the board. There are glue-on heatsinks that do not require mounting holes, but they might fall off after running hot for extended time and the glue wears out. Small heatsinks are usually with two mounting holes and use "push-pins" or spring-hooks instead of screws, typically up to few Watts BGA chips might use them. Any larger ASIC will need four mounting holes at the ASIC corners, and perhaps additional ones if the heatsink extends several inches away. Often the screws are part of the heatsink, and they screw into nuts assembled on the board or they screw into the board/module metal frame.

Most high-performance heatsinks used in data center equipment for 50Watt or higher power ASICs are called "stamped fin" or "zipper fin", and they have a high-density set of thin metal fins and a thick solid base. Below 20 to 50 Watts we often use more solid heatsinks with thicker fins that are cheaper to manufacture, like forged, extruded, or bonded types. The most reliable small heatsinks have metal or plastic "push pins" to lock into the board. Glued-only heatsinks can fall off. One example for both categories can be seen in Figure 5.16. Many larger heatsink designs have embedded heat pipes, or 2D flat "vapor chambers", to improve horizontal heat transfer through the flat base. Vapor chambers cover the whole bottom contact side of the heatsink, while heat pipes extend linearly on two sides. Both heat pipes and vapor chambers conduct heat horizontally much better than solid metal does. This is necessary to spread the heat from the small 1" ASIC core to the whole heatsink area and all its fins. Heatsinks have fins that are sheet metal pieces perpendicular to the base and ASIC top surface. Solid-base, embedded heat pipe, and vapor chamber–based heatsinks are usually custom designed by the heatsink vendors (for an NRE cost), although a few can be purchased off the shelf.

FIGURE 5.16 Typical heatsinks used in high-end hardware (push pin on the left, stamped-fin on the right).

There is a thermal interface material or TIM between the silicon chip and the heatsink. Usually we use a thermal paste, which has to be spread evenly and in a super thin layer to make it effective with low thermal resistance. Some designs use a thermal pad or gap pad, which is a solid sheet cut to size but much thicker than a paste spread would be. These are usable with lower power devices.

When larger heatsinks are attached to an ASIC and screwed to a board with four to eight screws and a lot of force, we put a custom-designed stiffener part on the bottom side of the board to prevent the board from bending between the chip and the mounting screws. It is called a backing plate, back plate, or bracket. This is usually a stainless-steel sheet-metal part with an X-shape or rectangle-shape, but it has a big cutout for the decoupling capacitor area. It also requires a complex shaped component and route keep-out area.

Aerospace hardware usually uses a heat frame for a whole board on both sides, attached to all hot devices using gap pads. The top frame can be screwed into the bottom frame, making it unnecessary to use individual heatsink backing plates. Consumer electronics might use “fan sinks” that are heatsinks with their own fans.

Thermal simulations are usually run by thermal or mechanical engineering, on the board or system, to determine the heatsink requirements. On data center hardware the heatsinks are usually pushed to the limits, so the exercise is to achieve a few more degrees lowering of the ASIC core temperature. Given fan speeds and air velocity, ambient temperature (the top end of the advertised range), the boards’ shapes, air baffles, and all heat sources (ASIC cores, and the board itself with QFNs) with heatsinks, they determine the ASIC core temperature. The ASIC vendor datasheet tells the maximum core or junction temperature that it can be running without having to issue a thermal shutdown.

Complex digital boards usually have several ground planes that can conduct some heat away and spread it across a board so the board acts as a heatsink. This is not very useful for 100W+ ASICs, but it is very useful for small QFN components that dissipate up to 1 to 2W completely through the PCB, for example, Ethernet NIC chips, smaller retimers, and VRM power stage chips. The QFN type packages have a large solder pad underneath, a thermal pad that is called bottom-terminated packages. On the board design we usually place several through drilled vias under this pad, in VIPPO format (to avoid the solder from being sucked away) to conduct heat from the thermal pad into the ground planes.

Water cooling has existed for a long time, but it is still not very common. Instead of big heatsinks inside the chassis, they have a small thermal interface brick that is attached to the ASIC. It has two water pipes going through it to the outside of the chassis into some larger heatsink with a fan.

Thermal design is based on a simple equation:

$$T_{junction} = T_{ambient} + R_{TH} / P_{diss}$$

Where R_{TH} is the thermal resistance of the whole cooling system, including the chip, package, and heatsink with airflow. The ASIC chip junction temperature is simulated in a thermal simulation, done by a thermal or mechanical engineering department. This has to be below the datasheet T_{jMAX} even when the ambient temperature is at the product's maximum.

5.18 FLYOVER CABLES

Sometimes our digital board just cannot deliver a good signal quality (too much loss or interference) to a far end of a board. In these cases we might use "flyover cables". Coax and Twinax cables provide much better signal integrity than PCB traces can. We can beat the reach limits caused by insertion loss budgets, but they have to be handled in the mechanical design, in the form of cable management arrangements. The cables have to be secured in position so they do not shake around components and do not suddenly start blocking or diverting airflow. The cables are in bundles to support many-pin connectors, for example, for a x8 PCIe link. Each cable in the bundle is a twin-axial shielded cable carrying one differential pair with impedance control. They are routed from one board-to-cable connector to an external I/O connector or internal backplane connector. The main limitation is the number of cable bundles we try to put into a box. Some types of systems only need a few long SERDES connections, some need over a thousand diffpairs, others are anywhere in between. About a dozen cable bundles can be managed within one smaller chassis.

Typically, flyover cables are used between a proximity of a main ASIC to a distant external (front panel or backplane) connector, as we can see in Figure 5.17. This allows having an ASIC placed on one end of a large board, while still accessing external I/O connectors placed at the other end of the board. The flyover cable can be built into an optical cage connector on one end (e.g., Samtec's Flyover-QSFP) and have a wire-to-board header on the other end. Or it can be between two board headers. RF analog applications use thin single-ended coaxial cables, while digital designs use twinax cables for diffpairs. There can also be optical cables inside a box. In some cases, there might be a small optical transceiver on board right next to the ASIC, and an optical signal/fiber cable is routed to the front panel to an optical coupler connector.

5.19 MEMORY

Main chips (processors, FPGAs, ASICs) use memory for storing data. Some types of memories might be integrated on the same chip with the main chip, but in many cases they are on separate chips, simply due to size or technology differences. Then the typical engineering problem is how to provide massive bandwidth between the processing chip and the memory chip. Some memory types are volatile—basically all modern RAM memories—they only need to store data temporarily until the next power down, but they might have to get overwritten millions of times in each run. The data

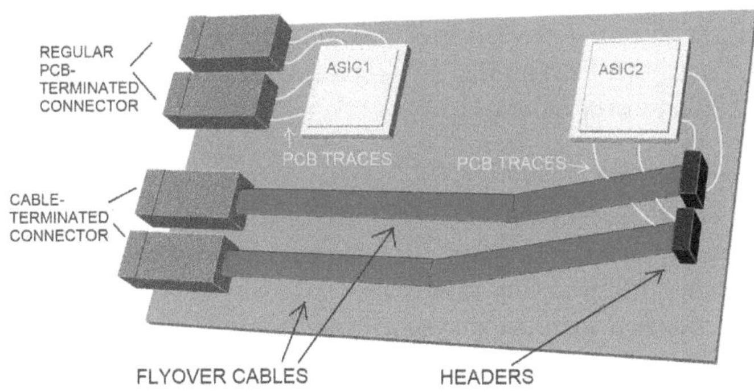

FIGURE 5.17 The typical use-case of flyover cables.

as a byte (8bit) is accessed through "Addressing". The binary code on the address bus signals or the address phase of a serial transaction defines which byte inside the memory cell matrix is being accessed. The non-volatile memory types store configuration, bootable code, or user data that has to be preserved throughout all future power cycles. Newer memory technologies usually build on the previous generations for performance enhancement and features, for example, DDR4 inherited a lot from DDR3, DDR2, DDR1, SDRAM, and even SRAM.

5.19.1 Non-volatile Memories

They are used for storing compiled software code or user data. Some NV memories contain a whole file system, while smaller ones might just contain a few bytes of data like a MAC address of an Ethernet controller chip. Most of them require programming when the board is manufactured. During this process an image file stored on a test computer is written into the NV-memory chip. Some can be programmed from a local host processor, from an attached device's JTAG port (proprietary or standard boundary scan), or off-line at the distributor company before purchased and they get soldered on the boards. In the latter case a small marking is placed on the chip like a colored dot.

5.19.1.1 EEPROM

EEPROMs are basic non-volatile memories. They typically have kilobytes or a few megabytes of storage capacity. They are very easy to handle through their typical SPI or I2C interfaces. We usually use them for storing chip configuration of ASICs, PCIe switches, and clock chips. Removable boards like QSFP optical modules often have an EEPROM on them that stores information about what are the module's part number and parameters. So when a removable board or module is plugged into a system, a management controller can read the module information and identify what was plugged in and how it should be set up.

EEPROM and flash memory chips have to be erased before we can write into them. The erasure sets all cells into a "1", and writing into them means basically flipping them to zero or not. The erase cycle is not done at individual address locations; rather, it is done in large blocks. This can take tens of milliseconds. The blocks are kilobyte or tens of kilobytes in size.

5.19.1.2 Flash

Flash memories are similar to EEPROMs, but they have a much larger capacity, up to several Gigabytes per chip. To access the large amount of data, higher bandwidth interfaces are required, for example, the ONFI (Open NAND Flash Interface) standard parallel interface that can be 8bit wide and run at 100MHz, or the QSPI interface. There are several types of flash memory chips on the market. The NOR flash is more reliable but it has larger cell size and higher cost per bit. NAND flash chips have smaller cell size, so they became the most common in consumer electronics, especially at larger Gbyte sizes. NAND flash has further subtypes: The SLC NAND, which has less chip area utilization but has the highest endurance of more than 100k write cycles. The TLC and the MLC utilize a bigger portion of the cell structure and achieve higher capacity at the expense of reduced endurance to 3k to 10k. Pseudo-SLC NAND is a mode of operation for TLC NAND where they reduce the utilization to gain endurance.

5.19.1.3 FRAM

FRAM (Ferro-Electric RAM) memory chips work like flash memory chips or EEPROMs, except that they do not require an "erase" operation, they can be overwritten as is, and they can be overwritten an infinite number of times. Compared to a Flash chip that can take only a few thousand writes to the same cell. The benefit of the missing erasure requirement is that we do not have to wait for 10 to 20ms for it to be ready to be written. This is useful in devices that want to save data when the power goes out. A flash device will have to have special power holdup circuits, together with the processor that is writing into it. It is useful in fault logging, and for saving state when a user turns a device off. Another benefit of FRAM chips is the ability to be overwritten more than few thousand times, for example, if we want to do continuous logging into a storage device, for example, to save state every few seconds, while using the equipment for years without having to throw it away due to wearout.

5.19.1.4 SSD

Solid State Drives (SSDs) are non-volatile flash memory modules used for computer main storage with a SERDES interface. They have a set of flash chips with a controller chip—like a more intelligent version of a flash memory chip. They usually utilize TLC-NAND or pseudo-SLC NAND flash chips. The main form factors are small PCB modules (e.g., m.2) and the multi-chip modules (MCM) in a solderable BGA package.

Flash chips and modules are available with several upstream host interface types. Basic flash chips have ONFI parallel bus, asynchronous parallel bus, and SPI or QSPI interfaces. The flash devices with PCIe or SATA interfaces are the SSDs, suitable for X86 computer attachment and OS boot. BGA SSD devices are available from Silicon Motion, Swissbit, and Apacer. The flash chips with SDIO (same as micro SD cards) interface are called eMMC. USB flash storage is implemented on-board using a USB-flash controller chip (e.g., Silicon Motion SM325 or SM3265) and a basic parallel flash chip. All types of flash chips are suitable for OS boot on ARM processor-based designs, including basic flash and the SSD/eMMC.

The m.2 form factor standard created by PCI-SIG defines several small card form factors as well as chip form factors for SSD storage drives. The cards are 22mm wide and 30 to 110mm long, the BGA chips are 22x16mm in size. They have a data interface (SATA or PCIe), a reset, reference clocks, and several glue logic signals described in their datasheets and in the m.2 spec document (can be purchased from PCI-SIG). For this particular standard there are separate tables for carrier card (platform) and add-in card (adapter) pinouts, differing only in the RX/TX pin mapping, designating the RX/TX chip-pin names from a given card. M.2 cards come with keying, which is a cutout on the card edge connector that prevents plugging it into an incompatible system. For example, SATA cards into a PCIe socket.

5.19.2 Volatile Memories

5.19.2.1 SRAM

The most basic volatile memory is the Static Random Access Memory. These days we have SRAMs inside FPGAs, microcontrollers, and ASICs. Inside the chip there are RAM memory cells in a matrix. The main chip address bus is broken down to a column address and a row address. An S-ram cell is a flip-flop; it stores state as a positive feedback loop of transistors.

When they are inside FPGAs, we call them "block RAMs"; inside processors, they are either called just code or data RAM or on larger processors they are the "cache memory". Cache memory is not used as individual storage; rather, it contains copies of data from the larger main memory and is managed by the processor's internal logic, which is not discussed here.

5.19.2.2 SDRAM

Synchronous Dynamic RAM are volatile memories that were commonly used as computer main memory in the late 20th century. Today only some DSP and microcontroller-based board designs utilize them. The dynamic in the name means it stores the data only temporarily, using a capacitor. SRAMs preserve data as long as the system is powered up, but DRAMs (SDRAMs) have an expiry date on all data stored in them, in about 20ms time. This is why DRAMs utilize refresh (or auto refresh) to re-vigorate the data before it expires. All this hassle was accepted by the computer hardware industry, because DRAMs can store a lot more data on the same chip area than SRAMs can. SDRAMs do not just have a simple address bus, they have an address/command/control bus that allows accessing data; controlling refresh cycles; read, write, row, and column address select (for multiplexing them over less address bits), bank select; and auto pre-charge. SDRAM memories are like programmable peripherals, compared to simple SRAMs. Since commands have to be loaded into them, they have an access latency of several clock cycles. SDRAMs have a common clock synchronous bus interface that is limited in speed to about 133MHz due to the roundtrip delay, even with -short traces.

5.19.2.3 HBM

HBM is a new volatile memory type. It has a much higher bandwidth than any DDRx types, but they can be used only as in-package memory, not as on-board memory. A few HBM dies are placed next to the ASIC die within the same BGA package. For the hardware board designer that means the ASICs are in larger packages than before, but we do not have to implement memory-down in the schematic or layout.

5.19.2.4 QDR SRAM

The QDR volatile memory is SRAM-based, so it has lower latency and faster access than DRAMs have, which might be helpful for some FPGA-based applications. Since they are SRAMs, they do not require extra time for refresh, pre-charge, and command buffering. The I/O interface is a quad data rate (QDR) bus, similar to DDR memory, but the data bus puts out four sets of data every clock cycle.

5.19.2.5 GDDR

Graphics DDR (GDDR) memory is similar to DDR, but it is meant to be used only in memory-down configurations, and it usually runs faster than standard DDR. Graphics processors and ASICs often require external memory in the form of GDDR. Just like DDR, it has versions. For example, GDDR6 can be used up to 18GT/s with its single-ended data bus, but only with short traces in a memory-down configuration, not as DIMM modules. Their buses are point to point, no tree or fly-by topologies are allowed at those higher speeds.

5.19.3 DDRx SDRAM Types

The DDR interface is double data rate; it transfers data at both the rising and the falling edge of the strobe signal. DDRx memories have a point-to-point data bus with source-synchronous (strobe-based) I/O timing and a multi-drop address bus with unidirectional synchronous (free running clock) I/O timing. These I/O timing architectures are described in Chapter 10, "Timing Analysis". DDRx memories are based on the SDRAM design—they have the same kind of address-control-command bus (ACC-bus) with few additional signal definitions.

A main device like a processor can have two to twelve separate channels or controllers, aka completely independent memory interfaces, but their bandwidth adds up. A "rank" is a complete set of DRAM chips that handle the full width of the memory channel. The purpose of having two ranks on each channel is to allow a larger size total system memory, given the largest density chips available on the market. Each rank is selected for transfer by the chip select signal. The "density" measures how many total bits are on one silicon die, like 8Gbit/die. Each memory chip also has a "width", either 4, 8, or 16bit wide. The same density is available with different widths. For a 64bit channel, we can use eight x8 chips or four x16 chips. The smaller the width at given density, the larger the memory size. The chosen chip width and the number of channels and ranks available on a processor determines the maximum total system memory size that is achievable in a system, in Gigabytes or Terabytes.

The memory channel implementation on a board can be "memory-down", or DIMM socket-based. DIMM means dual in-line memory module, which is a small PCB module plugged into a card edge connector on the motherboard. Server motherboards often connect the same memory channel's data bus to two DIMM sockets, acting as two ranks, so it is no longer point to point. In that case the data bus net topology is a multi-drop bus, where any of the three devices (CPU, DIMM1, DIMM2) can drive the bus. The controller tells any one memory module to enable or disable their terminations through a signal called ODT. This is not a fully matched termination, as the net split would require a trace width change for trace impedance match, but it would need to change the width when another device is driving the bus, which is an impossibility. In that case we are managing the reflected waves, not eliminating them. We can have two ranks on a channel in different ways. We can have two DIMM sockets with single-rank cards inserted, we can have one socket with a dual-rank card inserted, or we can have to sets of chips as memory-down on the motherboard.

DIMM memory cards have an EEPROM on them with data about the type of chips on the module. It is called Serial Presence Detect (SPD). The processor's BIOS reads it during boot up over SMBUS. Memory-down implementations must have the SPD data hard-coded into the BIOS source code, and the code that loads SPD over I2C must be commented out (disabled).

The standards that describe DDR memory chip level operation are the JESD79-x from JEDEC where x is the DDRx version. DIMM memory card design standards are described in the JESD21C documents, with each separate chapter being for a certain DIMM type. Each time is defined by the speed, chip width, and number of ranks on a DIMM. For each DDRx generation, there are a few different form factors like UDIMM or SODIMM. Within each generation and form factor combination there are several different "configurations" based on the number of ranks, the chip data bus width (x4, x8, x16), and ECC support (72bit versus 64bit). Table 5.2 describes the main generational changes in DDRx generations.

5.19.3.1 DDRx Signals and Hardware Design

There is an address/control/command (ACC) bus with unidirectional single ended signals that are latched by the DRAM chips at the rising edge of the differential clock signal. It is a multi-drop bus that can be implemented with different topologies on the PCB. The ACC signals have to be routed together and matched on a Pin-Pair basis. A pin on the processor and a pin on one DRAM chip is a Pin-Pair, all Pin-Pairs to the same DRAM chip are one matched group—the same pins on the processor and pins on another DRAM chip for separate Pin-Pairs and another matched group. The DDR1/DDR2 balanced-tree topology required all DRAM chips to receive the ACC bus signals in the same time (as flight time), while the DDR3 to 5 fly-by topology requires the ACC signals to arrive at each DRAM chip at separate times to ease the routing and to reduce simultaneous switching noise on the power rail. These ACC bus topologies are illustrated in Figure 5.18. A tree topology cannot be terminated perfectly, but a fly-by topology has only two ends that can be easily terminated. The ACC bus is usually routed at 40 Ohm impedance, but with FPGA implementations we can use 50 Ohm. DDR5 renamed some of the signals—instead of ACC bus (group of signals like A[0:14], BA[2:0], CKE, CS#, RAS, CAS, WE...), now they call it CA bus (CA[13:0]) and CS# (chip select).

The bi-directional (read and write) data bus consists of lanes, one memory channel might have up to nine lanes, one memory chip might have one, two, or four lanes. Each lane or byte lane consists of eight single-ended data signals (DQ), a data strobe diffpair (DQS), and a data mask single-ended signal (DM). They are point to point, source-synchronous, and need to be matched to reduce the signal arrival skew in order to maximize the DQS-to-DQ setup and hold margins. The DQ and DM signals are sampled at both the rising and the falling edge of DQS, or both crossings of the differential DQS_P/DQS_N. DQ signals are usually routed at 60 or 50 Ohm, DQS at 80 to 120 Ohm. An example 32-bit memory channel consisting of two x16 DDR3 chips can be seen in Figure 5.19.

We do not just connect the internal bus of a CPU to the DDRx memories. The CPU or other main chip has a DDRx controller IP that manages several control and command signals of one channel. Any one memory controller channel of the main chip might be connected to one to four ranks of memory. Most designs have several memory chips on one rank/channel to make up the complete 16

TABLE 5.2
DDRx Memory Features

Parameter	DDR1	DDR2	DDR3	DDR4	DDR5
Data Rate MT/s	200…400	400…800	800…1600	1600…3200	4800…7200
VIO	2.5	1.8	1.5 or 1.35	1.2	1.1
ACC Topology	Tree	Tree	Fly-by	Fly-by	Fly-by
Data Bus Termination	Motherboard	On-die	On-die	On-die	On-die
ACC Term	Motherboard	Motherboard	DIMM	DIMM	On-die
Main New Features from previous generation	Double data rate	Data bus on-die termination, differential DQS	Fly-by ACC bus, Read leveling, write leveling, ZQ termination calibration	BER contour eye diagrams, VREFDQ calibration, pseudo-open-drain I/O, CRC for data, parity for ACC bus, Data bus inversion	TX and RX Equalization, Split to two 40bit sub-channels, VRM on DIMM, Simulate with AMI models

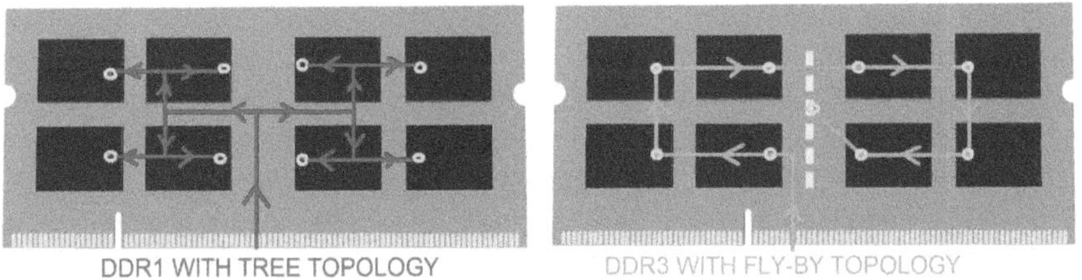

FIGURE 5.18 ACC bus topologies (sketch).

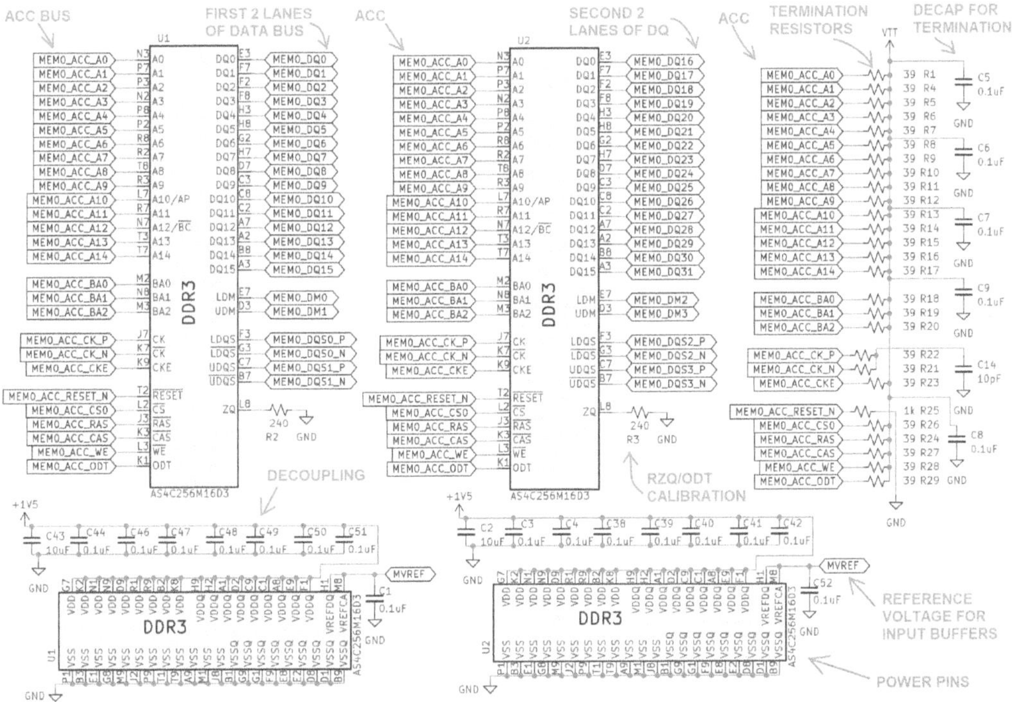

FIGURE 5.19 An example of 32bit memory-down channel schematic in KiCAD.

to 72bit width of the data bus, while a single chip having only 4/8/16bits. Each chip receives a shared full ACC bus. The ACC bus contains address, control, and command. The number of address bits depends on the chip density (Gbit size). Each rank needs a separate set of control signals (CS chip select, CKE clock enable, and ODT termination control) and clock routed to them, while the address and command (RAS, CAS, WE) signals are shared between ranks. Within a rank, all ACC signals are shared between the several DRAM memory chips in a parallel bus connection in the schematics and in a tree or fly-by topology in the layout. A dual-rank DIMM socket has two sets of control and clock signals wired to it on the motherboard. We can make use of having two chip select signals on one channel not only for selecting one rank or another, but also for designs that utilize address mirroring, like DDR4 dual-rank DIMMs or DDR4 clam-shell memory-down. In this case the DRAM chips on the top side of the board will use one chip select line, while the chips on the bottom side will use the other chip select line.

The memory chips internally are organized into a matrix like the pixels on a TV screen—actually, several matrices, called banks. The memory controller does not put out its own bus address to the memory. Sometimes it translates a section of the system memory address range into a range starting from zero for the memory. A 2^N size range of memory would be addressed on N bits, but the controller does not provide an N-bit wide basic address bus. Instead, it breaks it down into ranks (each with its own chip select), then banks (bank select code signals), then the remaining lower address is chopped into two pieces and sent out one piece after the other on the same PCB traces. This is called the row and column address, referencing to the matrix mentioned above. The lowest 1 to 3 address bits are not sent out; rather, they are decoded into the individual data mask (DM) signals to select which bytes to transfer within a whole data bus.

All data and ACC signals are terminated, some with on-chip, some with on-board terminations, depending on DDR-x generation. Far-end and source-series terminations are used with impedance matching to the trace impedance. On-board termination means a resistor from the signal line to the VTT voltage rail. On-chip termination is a Thevenin type between VDD and GND. The reset is not terminated, only pulled low. It is sometimes called on-die termination (ODT) or digitally controlled impedance (DCI). ODT/DCI is turned on or off based on which device sends and which receives the data. On the bi-directional data bus the controller (CPU/FPGA) enables parallel ODT in itself during reads and in the DRAM chips during writes. Dual rank channel configurations on servers can enable the termination in the unused DIMM when it is not participating in the transaction. The address bus is unidirectional fly-by, and it needs fixed end termination. This is achieved by connecting 30 to 39 Ohm termination resistors to a VTT plane on the motherboard for DDR1 to 2, on the DIMM for DDR3 to 4, and on-die enabled on the last DRAM in the chain for DDR5. The clock uses a differential termination resistor with center tap 3.3pF capacitor to ground at the end of the chain. Termination resistors are decoupled to ground. Trace routing impedance is usually 60 Ohm for data bus (sometimes 50), 40 Ohm for ACC bus (sometimes 45 or 50), 85 Ohm differential for strobes, and 60 Ohm differential for clocks. The values vary based on the design, even between different DIMM versions, determined through SI simulation. The motherboard section trace impedance is sometimes dictated by the ASIC/CPU design guide. The on-die termination resistor value is selectable by the memory controller firmware (BIOS), for both the end-termination and the driver, and it has to match the trace impedance closely. The hardware engineer needs to tell the firmware engineer what ODT values are required on a specific design. The allowed values can be looked up in the IBIS model setup, but usually the value of the 240 Ohm RZQ resistor is divided by a whole number like RZQ/7. The ODT impedance of each pin is calibrated one by one using a single shared resistor connected to the RZQ pin.

DDRx memory interfaces use several voltage rails. The main VIO consumes most of the power, and the voltage gets lower by the technology generation, 2.5V to 1.1V. On server motherboards it is a multi-phase buck converter. There is a VTT rail for termination resistors, which is at the VIO/2 level, usually generated by a fast LDO capable of sourcing and sinking a few Amps. There is a reference voltage needed for the chip input buffers as a decision threshold, it only consumes a few milli Amps. It is at the VIO/2 level for DDR1 to 3 and controllable for DDR4 to 5. DDR5 memories also require an additional higher voltage rail.

The JESD21C standards that were meant to help designing DIMM cards can also be used for memory-down to determine the exact topology and termination requirements for each signal group, clocks, ACC, and data. We just need to get the document that describes a DIMM design that is most similar to our memory-down plans to be able to implement a memory-down design, where the memory chips are on the motherboard, instead of residing on a DIMM module.

5.19.3.2 ODT

On die termination or ODT was invented for turning the parallel end termination on or off, depending on data bus direction of reads versus writes. Both the DRAM chips and the controller (CPU or FPGA) devices control their output drive ODT and input end-termination ODT dynamically. The ODT signal on the board allows the controller to turn the termination on or off inside the memory chips.

5.19.3.3 ZQ Calibration

Introduced with DDR3, ZQ calibration allows DDR3 memory chips and controllers to calibrate their ODT resistance to an external 1% accurate resistor after power on. This way the termination resistance will also be within 1%. The silicon resistors, implemented as transistors, do not have very accurate factory-defined resistance, but with some circuits they can be tuned every time the device is powered up. They might require periodic re-calibration as the temperature changes.

5.19.3.4 Read Leveling

This is a calibration process facilitated by BIOS software (or bootloader) code and enabled by DRAM chip and controller chip features, first implemented on DDR3. It allows the automatic measurement of the horizontal read data eye boundaries so at the end the software can set the DQS programmable delay half-way inside that measured data valid window to maximize setup and hold margins. The DQS is delayed by the controller by 90 degrees for both read and write transactions. For writes the on-board DQ and DQS are already 90 degree shifted, but for reads the on-board signals are aligned and the 90 degree shift will be added to the DQS by the controller after the read DQS signal has already reached the controller's I/O buffer. This 90 degrees number might not be optimal, so the read leveling adjusts it to the optimized delay value that results in the most optimal read data capture. It compensates for trace skew as well as buffer and termination asymmetries.

The process starts with a read leveling command that re-directs the data flow into the multi-purpose register in the DRAM chip, where we store a known code data. The controller keeps reading this register back while constantly incrementally increasing the DQS delay in small steps. At two delay values the returned data will flip its value—these are the two boundaries of the data valid window. After the two boundaries are found, the controller sets the final DQS delay half-way between for optimum setup/hold timing margin balance.

5.19.3.5 Write Leveling

This is a calibration process facilitated by the BIOS or bootloader code of a processor and enabled by DRAM chip and controller chip features, first implemented on DDR3. The fly-by topology causes the clock and DQS to have a large skew between them. The write leveling calibration adjusts each lane's DQ/DQS delay to allow a DQS/CK match at arrival at the DRAM chips. The controller sends a command to the DRAM chips, then the DRAM chip will start sampling the clock with the DQS edges, and the sampled signal is returned to the controller on the DQ0 line. The controller keeps adjusting the DQS delay in small steps and samples the clock in each step, seeking the delay-position where the sampled signal changes state, which determines the two edges of the timing window, then the controller sets the delay half-way as final delay value.

5.19.3.6 Eye Masks on DDR3 versus DDR4

DDRx memory interfaces use the SSTLx I/O standards, which technically have only a single voltage threshold level provided by a reference voltage generator (Vref) for deciding between high and low logic levels at their inputs. Due to the high-speed nature, this level splits to two or four voltage levels, which we have to use in our simulations, to obtain accurate timing measurements. The chips themselves are still using the single Vref threshold.

DDR1 to 3 memory devices define the AC and DC, high and low voltage thresholds for measuring timing. For example, when the DQ signal changes from low to high, we measure on the waveform how much time it takes to reach the AC high for setup timing and how much it takes to reach DC low for hold timing analysis. See Chapter 10, "Timing Analysis".

The DDR4 specs removed the AC and DC thresholds requirements that we used on DDR3, so now only one high and one low remain. We can use rectangle eye masks and BER contours for these. The input receiver compliance eye mask will need to be fitted into the 1e-16 BER contour. We can still use speed-adjusted and VDD-adjusted AC and DC thresholds for design robustness check,

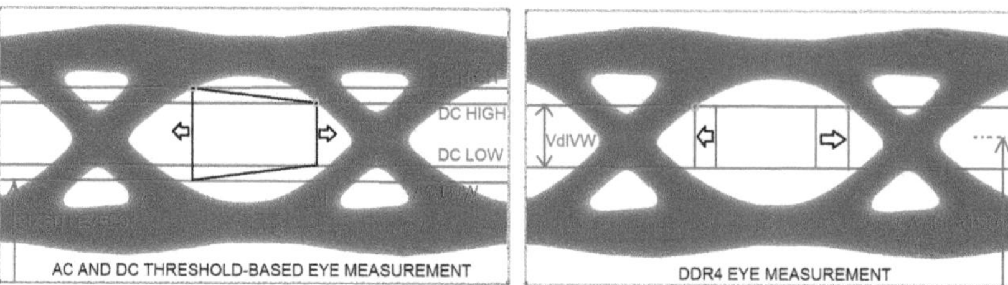

FIGURE 5.20 DDR3 and DDR4 eye measurements (sketch).

but we have to calculate the thresholds for that and set up a custom simulation with equations in ADS. Figure 5.20 shows the differences between the DDR3 and the DDR4 methods used for eye measurements.

In DDR4 the VTT and Vref are adjusted through a "DQ Vref Training" process (VREFDQ calibration) to the vertical center line of the eye, which usually settles around 0.7*VDD. In simulation we can generate an eye, then measure the ideal VTT, then re-simulate with the new VTT value to get eye width opening (fixed eye mask height VdIVW from the JESD79-4), which can be used in timing analysis. The minimum eye width depends on timing and speed grade.

5.19.3.7 The Memory Chip Market

DRAM and flash memory chips are on a commodity market, unlike other chips that are on long (years or decades) life cycles. Commodity devices are manufactured for one to two years. The chip vendors generate many part numbers, but only a few of those are actually manufactured in mass quantities—we can call them temporary favorites. They are the ones with the shortest lead time and lowest price. To determine which ones are the favorites at any given time requires market research with the main distributors. We have to design our boards to accommodate future replacement chips that will likely have larger capacity and hopefully are footprint compatible. DRAM chip footprints are controlled by standards, but the package outline varies a lot. So we need to leave space around the DRAM chip to fit larger packages or create a footprint drawing that accommodates two to three common package outlines/sizes.

6 Main Chips

Hardware board designs are centered around the main chips that perform the main data processing task. In most chapters in this book, we refer to processors, network ASICs, AI, and other types of ASICs and FPGAs as just "ASIC" or "main chip" to avoid having to include a string like "CPU/ASIC/FPGA" into every other sentence. The main chips or ASICs are typically high-powered devices. They come in 1000+ BGA or socketed LGA packages with either a metal heat spreader lid or exposed bare-die packaging. They are usually 23 to 80mm in size. The actual silicon chip on the BGA package is called the silicon "die". For multi-die packages a stiffener window was invented to prevent the heatsink installers from cornering (chipping) the die chips. A package might be multi-die if the manufacturer puts the main ASIC silicon chip die together with HBM memory silicon chip dies or a CPU die with the south bridge die into one BGA package. Some of these common packages used for main chips can be seen in Figure 6.1. Network switching and AI processing ASICs are the largest chips on the market, together with server processors. They usually come in ~5000 pin BGA or LGA packages. They dissipate 10 to 500W of power, while the rest of the main devices are in the range of 10 to 60W. These main chips require large amounts of PCB trace routing for connectivity and several multi-phase VRM devices to power them. They are cooled through heatsinks or heat frames. Most but not all of these devices have their datasheets available only under NDA (Non-Disclosure Agreement) and secure account access, and some of them have a minimum production volume requirement (tens of thousands of units) before the chip company will sign an NDA with a board/system company. Many chip companies give code names to their main chips, for example "Kaby Lake H" Processor or "Trident 2" ASIC, that we use in documents and block diagrams, but we use exact part numbers from the datasheets part numbering section in schematics and BOM. The chip vendors usually have a "roadmap" presentation available, showing all the main chips they plan to release in the next two years and showing code names instead of part numbers.

These large devices usually have pins for SERDES links, DRAM memory interface signals, boot flash memory signals, other interfaces, narrow control plane buses, several reference clock inputs, and slow glue logic (system) signals. The glue logic signals include strapping pins, power and thermal control signals routed to a glue logic small-FPGA or management controller, resets, and many device-specific unique signals. Some devices have several reset inputs and outputs by functional block or power domain. The reference clocks come from high-performance clock generators on our board. The clock inputs used for SERDES interfaces have very tight jitter requirements (in the ASIC datasheet) in the hundreds of femtoseconds range; we have to verify with the clock chip datasheets whether they can deliver that.

Each main chip needs its own set of point-of-load VRMs to reduce DC voltage drop and noise pollution. Only a main 3.3V is shared between ASICs and a 12V between the VRMs. They have multiple power supply pin groups at different voltages, running from separate point-of-load VRMs, that appear as separate power rails. Usually there is one pin group for the core power, one to four rails for the SERDES power, several different power rails for different interfaces, I/O banks at different voltages and functions, and PLL internal clocking power rails. Large chips are made of several internal IP cores, and each might have their own power pins on the package. Often one ASIC has several power pin groups with the same voltage level requirement, but we use separate VRMs for them anyway. They are not separate for all the five to 20 different-named pin groups, but we end up with two to four separate VRMs with the same voltage. Pin groups can share the same rail and VRM, if they are all digital blocks, meaning non-SERDES and non-PLL rails. A SERDES power pin group does not share a rail with core and digital-only parts of the chip to prevent noise coupling that can disturb the sensitive SERDES operation. If we have a dozen SERDES cores, they can

DOI: 10.1201/9781032702094-6

FIGURE 6.1 Main chip packaging types.

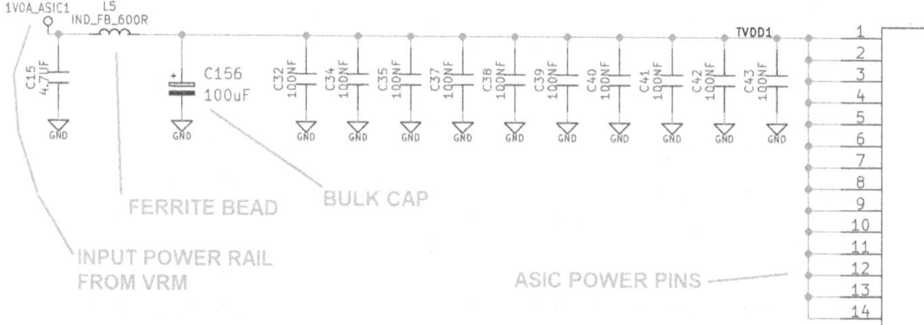

FIGURE 6.2 Power filtering and decoupling in schematics, sketch in KiCad.

share the same VRM, but they may or may not have their own ferrite bead filters to separate noises from each other. Sometimes we provide two to three separate VRMs and separate power nets for the power pins of the same SERDES core, as they often have separate RX, TX, and other internal subblock power pins. The PLL rails definitely, and sometimes also the SERDES power rails, have to be filtered through ferrite beads. Sometimes the SERDES power pins split into groups that each need a separate ferrite filter, as shown in Figure 6.2. This is simply a series ferrite bead part with sufficiently low DCR (depending on load current and voltage drop), and 100 to 330Ohm@100MHz impedance. The source side of the ferrite needs a small capacitor, the load side of the ferrite needs a large bulk capacitor and the regular decoupling caps, one for each pin. PLL rails are most often supplied by a separate LDO to provide ripple-free power, so the PLL can achieve a low-jitter operation for the SERDES links to transmit low-jitter signals. For all other rails, in most cases we use VRM chip-down designs instead of the convenient VRM modules, as modules would have too much inductance in series and there is no way to tune their control loops to our load conditions. The power pin fanout vias will need decoupling capacitors on the other side of the board, one cap per via, plus bulk capacitors around the package.

The chip "design-in" process is similar for all large main devices. Since they have so many pins, the schematic symbol splits to over a dozen separate rectangle symbols, and they will be placed throughout several schematic pages. When we are designing a main chip into our board schematic, we have to take care of several categories of pin connections and supporting devices. We connect the power rails with appropriate VRMs, ferrite power filters if needed, reference voltage sources, VRM remote sense lines, and the decoupling capacitors (bulk and ceramic). We also have to make the connections for the system signal pins (resets, interrupts, power management) to glue logic devices, clock signals from/to clocking chips, strapping (device mode select) and calibration resistors, and thermal diode pins to sensors. We have to hook up the I/O interface pins, including low-speed buses (I2C, SPI, MDIO, UART), any flash or EEPROM memory chips, external DRAM memory interfaces (if needed), and SERDES interfaces.

Most of the strapping input pins allow the board to tell the chip what interfaces to expect on the board or tell the chip how to behave. Sometimes we have strapping output pins that allow the chip to tell the board which chip version is soldered on so the board glue logic can set voltages or other things accordingly. Often we add both a pullup and a DNP pulldown resistor on the same strapping pin, or vice versa, so if we chose the wrong strapping option, we can revert it on the prototype board with a nice re-work. Typical strapping pins for Ethernet switch ASICs are I2C bus master or slave mode selection, I2C slave address, external vs internal processor to be used, external CPU slave interface selection, MDIO "IEEE802.3 clause" mode selection, EEPROM loading enable, PCIE endpoint port enable, test modes, PLL bypass, EEPROM type, PCIE speed limit, external memory buffer present or not. Typical straps for X86 CPUs are reserved mandatory straps, processor type output (core i3 vs i7), display type, PCIe lane reversal, PCIe bifurcation, PCIe link training delay. Typical straps for X86 chipsets are DMI-bus settings (AC-versus-DC coupling, termination, or mode depending on what CPU is attached), custom straps for BIOS on GPIO pins like memory down die size or board revision. Typical straps for ARM processors are boot flash port selection, boot flash size selection, console port selection, memory type code. Typical straps for FPGAs are configuration mode selection, config port VIO selection, I/O pullups enable.

The main large chips always have more documentation than just a datasheet. They have reference design schematics, which we have to follow detail by detail when designing our schematic, except for details and features that we definitely want to do differently and for which the datasheet allows it. Often there is a design guide document with supporting part selection and layout guidelines that might also contain a few details that are left out of the datasheet. Many vendors these days provide a schematic design checklist also, which they require us to fill out and comply with (often impossible due to our design being different from the reference design); otherwise, they will hesitate providing actual design support through their FAEs (field application engineer). We need an FAE to help us resolve ambiguous parts of the documentation in most projects, in person or by email, and we need to set up an online account with the chip vendor for file download. Often there are other documents written for separate features of the main chip, and, of course, we need to download various other documents too (like simulation models, test tools, BSDL JTAG files, and pin delay tables).

6.1 PROCESSORS

Processors, or central processing units (CPUs), are the chips that linearly execute a list of instructions from compiled software code—one instruction at a time, but multiple instructions can be in a pipeline in the same time at different stages of execution. Instructions are the low-level assembly or binary code that we get when the software is compiled from its easily readable high-level language that the software engineers use, like C/C++/Java. Most instructions are concerned with loading or storing data from RAM or peripherals to a CPU register (accumulator), then doing calculations on the data with the arithmetic/logic unit (ALU). CPUs have an instruction/code (to be executed) memory and a data memory (to be processed). The actual memory chips on-board might contain both, in that case the memory map is partitioned between code and data. Other devices like FPGAs and ASICs are used more in parallel (multiple streams in the same time) or continuous processing of data streams. Processors are easily programmable and can perform very versatile sets of tasks. Most modern processors (except microcontrollers and some DSPs) are made with multiple processor cores that share the same address space and I/O ports, and they see the same memory map. Even small low power processors are common with two to four CPU cores, laptop processors with two to 16 cores, server processors with four to 128 cores.

There are two types of CPUs, based on their instruction set type. The RISC (reduced instruction set, like ARM or PIC) and the CISC (complex instruction set, like X86). The instruction set is a list of basic operations a processor can perform. For example, arithmetic (C=A+B), logic (C=A&B),

load or store data from main memory into the main operand register (called Accumulator), or jump code execution to a different address in the code memory. The code that is being executed tells the CPU what to do with the data that are the operands of the instructions. Some types of processors have physically separate memory modules for data and code, for example, many microcontrollers have a directly executable flash memory for code and an on-chip RAM for data. Others copy all the code from a storage device (USB stick, SSD drive, flash chip) into the same off-chip RAM as the data resides in but that is partitioned into code and data regions by the software. Most modern processors, with the exception of small microcontrollers, have a "cache" memory, which is basically an on-chip SRAM that is accessible by the core without having to go through the bandwidth and latency bottleneck of using external memory interfaces. The cache contains copies of parts of the main memory. The cache size is usually very limited. It might be 1000 times smaller than the external RAM. Sometimes the processor needs to access the same small data structures or code pieces multiple times, so the cache handling logic loads data from the external RAM into the cache, then re-routes the processor core's subsequent memory accesses to go to the cache instead of the main RAM for the given address range corresponding to this data structure. This saves a lot of time and increases the apparent speed of the CPU.

6.1.1 Microcontrollers

Microcontrollers are sometimes referred to as uC, μC, or MCU. Simple devices like alarm systems and thermostats are based on microcontrollers. System-on-chip (SOC) is a phrase often used for microcontrollers and other smaller processors that do not require external peripherals, clocking chips, or memories to be connected to them on a board design. All their peripheral blocks are integrated on the same silicon die, together with data and code memory. On complex hardware we use micro controllers in the management subsystem. They typically monitor voltage, talk to temperature sensors and ejector switches, and generate interrupts or order boards to power up or down. Microcontrollers are typically very low power (0.01W to 1W), and they are fully integrated with their peripherals on a single chip, system memory, and boot flash memory into one single chip. The typical uC peripherals are UARTs, I2C, and SPI bus interfaces, low-speed A/D converters for voltage monitoring, timers for periodic interrupt generation, and watchdog timers for system hang recovery. They typically come in small BGA, QFN, or QFP packages, 5x5 to 25x25mm in size. The smaller microcontrollers run a simple code written in C or assembly language, without bootloader or any operating system. Many small PIC microcontrollers simply execute a less than 100-line assembly code, handling two relays, an LED and a door sensor. Popular small microcontroller families have a 16 or 32-bit ARM processor core or an 8-bit 8051 core, licensed and made by various chip companies, and there is the PIC family by Microchip. Larger MCUs typically have a parallel single-ended CMOS master bus interface, or local peripheral bus interface, that can support both synchronous (clocked) and asynchronous devices to be attached to the same bus in parallel, while the devices respond only when their chip select signal is activated. Many DSPs also support this type of interface—TI calls it EMIF (external memory interface), or EBIU in the Analog Devices terminology.

Specialized microcontrollers are available for X86 motherboards to control the power management of the main processor with the controller running on standby-domain power. Laptop motherboard versions are very simple single-chip solutions; server motherboards use chips with ~500 pins and external memory. These are called BMC (board management controller) or server management controllers. Other types of hardware might just use generic microcontrollers, sometimes called IPMI controller or IPMC.

Boot is the process of executing the first lines of code starting from a reset vector address, checking available memory, initializing DRAM controllers, copying data from flash to RAM, initializing peripherals (writing into their registers), and jumping execution to the RAM where the code was copied to. If the chip does not have internal flash, then the reset vector is routed to one of the external interfaces. To determine which one, the hard silicon logic checks the strapping pins that are set (pulled up/down) by the hardware designer. Simple microcontrollers like PIC or 8051 types just execute code from flash, without any operating system, and they do not have a lot of initialization to do, maybe writing to control registers of a serial port and a timer. Then the application code executes in an infinite loop that waits for user inputs or sensor inputs to be serviced by subroutines. For more complex microcontrollers, we run an operating system too. In that case the software that is first loaded from flash memory is called the bootloader. It initializes peripherals, detects and initializes any DRAM memory, then loads the operating system image, then hands over code execution to it. The OS will run multiple drivers and applications in a time share.

The simplest microcontroller boards contain VRMs, various I/O connectors, and their circuits as well as GPIO[driven machine-drive (train doors, water pumps) or control circuits using opto-couplers, relays, or MOSFETs. Sometimes A/D converters and D/A converters are connected to the uC over an SPI or I2C bus. These A/D converters are mainly for measurements or sensing, at a kilohertz sample rate. The fastest signal on-board might be a 1MHz SPI bus and the processor's clock crystal signal. The uC itself is often in a 16 to 144 pin non-BGA package. These allow low-cost assembly at any contractor; some boards can even be home-made. These boards usually have component count around 30 to 400, a one- to four-layer stackup, no high-speed signals on-board, larger 10 to 15mil via holes and HASL surface finish. The next level up is microcontrollers that require an external memory chip, in many cases the uC is provided in a 100 to 500 pin BGA package, and needs just one- or two-DRAM chips on board. Usually ARM core-based devices. That creates the need for some basic high-speed design constraints for the board designer. These can be total etch length control, length matching on point-to-point nets and the use of stitching vias/capacitors. The interfaces are also higher speed—they might have USB, Ethernet, or LVDS-video for an LCD panel. The signals can be as fast as a few hundred Megahertz. In some cases, audio or video converter chips, 100Meg Ethernet PHY chips, and larger flash memory chips are also found on the board designs with them. In rare cases we find a small FPGA or a CPLD helping with the GPIO-type control interface logic or with peripheral chip select decoding. These board designs can have component counts between 200 and 600, have stackups in a range from four to 10 layers, where some of the signals are ground referenced, others power plane referenced, and with even allowing dual-stripline layers. The BGAs are restricting the design via sizes and surface finish selections. When these microcontrollers are in a management subsystem of a complex data center board, then the stackup layer count and the via sizes are determined by the main data center ASICs on the design. This means we will be using a higher layer count and smaller vias, which will just make it overkill for the microcontroller circuits, but it is available for free as it is already needed on the board by the other devices.

6.1.2 ARM Processors

All ARM processors manufactured by different chip vendors are based on the ARM processor IP cores that are developed by the company ARM, which is based in Cambridge, England. ARM's various customers design their system-on-chip solutions, which is the ARM processor core with various peripheral and other IP cores combined on one chip. There are ARM processors available for different purposes and performance levels, from the low-power microcontrollers up to the high-power data center server processors. Most of the higher-end microcontrollers have an ARM core, but ARM processor cores are also used in media devices, in large ASIC on-die management functions, as management processors on large data center boards, and even as server or network processors computing high-bandwidth data plane data traffic. There are ARM processors in every cell phone, tablet, and other consumer electronics devices that have a display, even in smart devices like home automation. The ARM processor core is a RISC type engine, meaning reduced instruction set, as opposed to the X86 complex instruction set processors. They achieve better power efficiency.

Many switch ASICs have built-in ARM processors for initializing themselves without the need for an external CPU chip or board. Their firmware is provided by the chip vendor and stored in an on-board flash chip, but it can be customized. Some of these ASICs allow the option to turn off the ARM processor and let the chip be initialized by an external processor over PCIe. Some FPGAs come with ARM hard-IP cores inside of them for mixed HW-SW processing. In complex hardware designs, we sometimes use the lower power ARM processors for system management or initialization functions, for example, the NXP Semiconductors (acquired Freescale Semiconductors) IMX devices, the Texas Instruments Sitara and Jacinto "applications processors", or the Broadcom StrataGX BCM5871X series "communications processors". Figure 6.3 shows a mezzanine processor module with an IMX6, made by Bluechip Technology, that can be plugged onto a larger digital board to provide management functionality. If we want to run a low power processor with a console-Linux, a Microchip (acquired Atmel) SAM9 processor would do, although it is without PCIe so they cannot initialize any large ASICs. Also note that most large ASICs have software drivers that run only on X86 processors and Linux, but our fully custom FPGA design could be initialized by any code running on an ARM processor. In complex embedded or data center hardware we prefer to have certain types of interfaces available (like PCI-express, SATA), and have a larger 1mm (or 0.8mm) pitch BGA package that can be designed in with the same PCB technology as the main ASICs and FPGAs demand on the same board. Typical data plane ASICs demand the 1mm pitch BGA to allow our large number of SERDES links to be designed-in with controlled impedance differential via structures. These boards are usually without microvias, so having to add microvia technology just for the management processor will be too costly for a minor function. The ARM processors used on hand-held devices usually come with 0.4 to 0.6mm pitch BGA packages that demand microvias, so they are not usable here. Many small ARM processors come with a "companion chip" that provides all the voltage rails as well as some minimal glue logic.

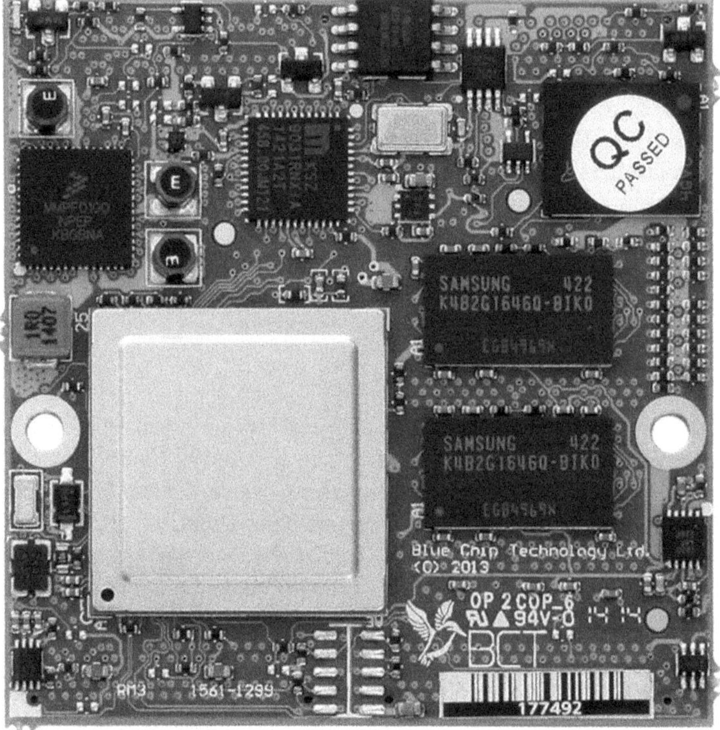

FIGURE 6.3 RM3, an ARM processor module with an NXP (Freescale) IMX6 processor and DDR3 memory, photograph provided by Blue Chip Technology Ltd.

6.1.2.1 ARM Servers

ARM processors are more common in low-power hand-held consumer devices, but with 128 cores on a single chip. Dissipating much more than 100W, they are comparable in performance to Xeon and EPIC X86 server processors. There are ARM server processors on the market manufactured by multiple vendors. They support 4 to 12 independent DDR4/5 memory controller channels, and 16 to 128 lanes of the fastest PCI-express ports, just like the X86 servers. Example devices are the Ampere Altra Max, Marvell's (acquired Cavium) ThunderX2, and Octeon. ARM server CPU vendors are more likely to adopt open standard interfaces for multi-processing communication, like CXL or CCIX, than X86 CPU vendors do. They might be available in solderable BGA, or socketed LGA packages, with 5000+ pins. The Ampere Altra processor comes in a 77mm 4926-pin LGA package, to be placed in a socket similar to those used with many X86 server processors. The AmpereOne is even larger and more powerful.

ARM server processors do not require an additional chip for I/O functions (south bridge or chipset), like X86 CPUs do, and they are more integrated single-chip solutions.

6.1.2.2 Specialty ARM Processors

The Marvell Octeon CN98XX processor is advertised as an "infrastructure processor" to be integrated into communications equipment. It has 20 lanes of built-in 25Gig Ethernet SERDES, while also maintaining server-like interfaces (6ch DDR4, PCIe) to be used for real-time data traffic processing. It is also sometimes called as a "network processor". It is meant for mobile base station equipment, firewall appliances, and really anything that needs software-driven CPU-type processing of wide bandwidth continuous data streams. With up to 32 CPU cores, while processing 0.5Tbit/s Ethernet traffic, they dissipate 45 to 120W of power.

6.1.2.3 ARM Software

ARM processors first load a bootloader firmware from an SPI flash chip, which does basic chip initialization, similarly to the BIOS firmware used on X86 systems. The bootloader then loads the operating system from a larger storage media. For smaller ARM systems the OS might be stored in the same flash chip where the bootloader is stored. For servers it is a PCIe SSD card on the motherboard's m.2 socket, or a SATA SSD attached through a PCIe/SATA/SAS controller chip or card. The bootloader used on smaller ARM processors is called "uboot". The bootloaders used on some ARM server CPUs are more advanced, and called "ARM Trusted Firmware" (ATF) and "UEFI". For operating system choice several different versions of ARM-based Linux distributions are available.

Many modern processors are actually multiprocessors on a single chip, each CPU type being multi-core, and loading their own firmware/software. The Texas Instruments AM69A98 device contains eight ARM A72 CPU cores as the main or system domain processor. It also contains DSP processors with MMUL cores as compute accelerators. The device also contains four ARM R5F processor cores as the "MCU" device-management function and a security processor called SMS. The main and the system domains have their own boot strapping pins, reset signals, and power rails. The startup process starts with all power domains sequenced up, clocks running, and then released from POR reset. Any glue logic FPGA must be powered before this so it can drive any strap pullups and reset signals. Then the SMS starts executing code contained in its internal ROM memory, then the MCU starts its own ROM code, which reads the MCU straps and loads its user bootloader software from flash into the internal RAM and execute it from there. This can be a ~Gbit size OSPI, QSPI, SPI, parallel NAND flash. After this the system domain boots similarly, but with additional different boot modes made available through the separate system boot mode straps. The system CPU can boot from the same flash chip or from additional sources like eMMC, PCIe-NVME SSD storage, or over a USB port. It boots another bootloader (Uboot) that initializes the DRAM, then it loads a Linux OS image into RAM and lets the Linux run. The DSPs can be loaded and re-loaded in run-time from application software. Both the CPU subsystems have their

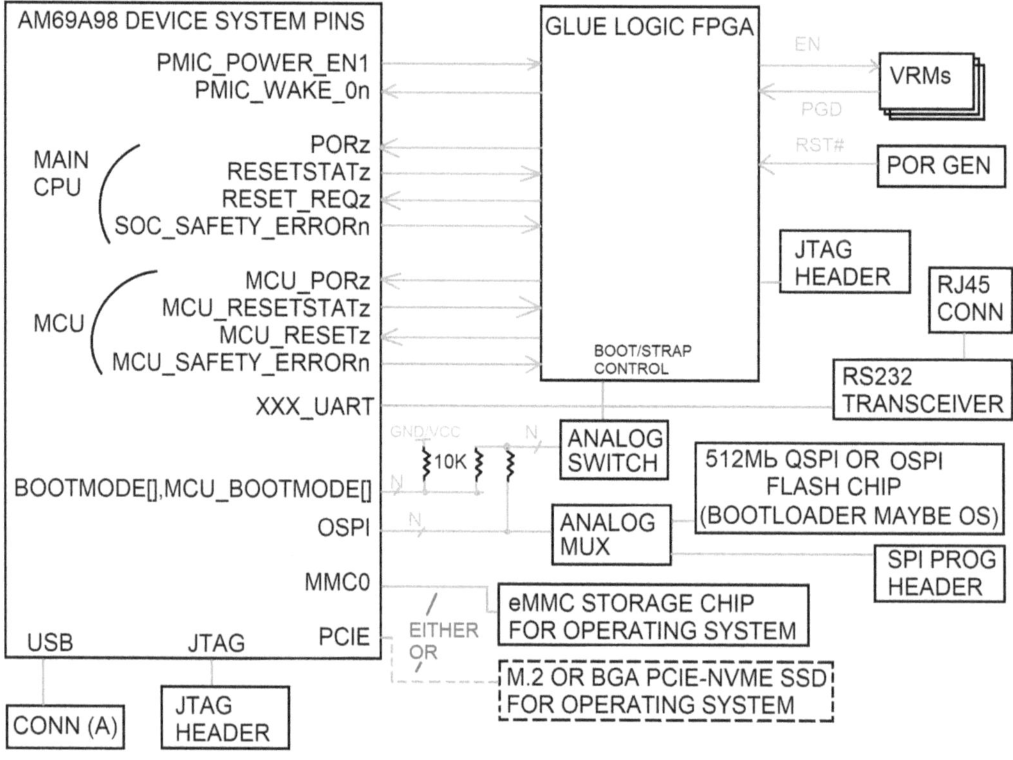

FIGURE 6.4 Texas Instruments AM69 Jacinto processor boot and initialization block diagram.

own set of reset signals, POR and warm, inputs and outputs. The chip can go into a sleep mode through PMIC signals, but that is the only self-power control logic for this device. At least one boot flash device needs to be connected (QSPI or OSPI) to store the various boot loaders of the various CPU cores and perhaps the operating system too, but often a second one is also present with a much larger capacity for a full-size OS. A USB and a JTAG port are used to load firmware into the board and a serial console to control it or set it up. An example system and boot logic sketch can be seen in Figure 6.4.

6.1.3 DSPs

Digital Signal Processors or DSPs are used for processing digitized waveforms. This is a compute-accelerator task for the data plane, not a host processor function. They have interfaces that are convenient for attachment of analog to digital or digital to analog converters through FPGAs. The ADCs might feed data into the FPGA continuously, which is stored there until the DSP comes and takes the data when not busy executing other code. Waveform buffers implemented on FPGAs are accessed by the DSPs through the external parallel interface or through PCIe. DSPs often have a "host port interface" (HPI) that is similar to an external parallel interface, but the DSP is the slave on it. Through this DSPs can also be loaded with new code or data by an ARM/X86 host processor, and the processed data (sampled waveforms) can be taken from the DSP's internal memory by the host processor. On newer DSPs both the external parallel and the HPI are replaced with PCIe, so they may have both a PCIe endpoint and a root complex port. They also have other SERDES type interfaces, like Serial RapidIO and Ethernet for intelligent-to-intelligent data transfer (instead of master-slave), among DSPs and host ARM/X86 processors.

6.1.3.1 The Multiply-Accumulate (MAC) Unit

DSPs have the MAC unit that makes a certain type of data computation run faster than it would on a general purpose CPU. This should not be confused with Ethernet MAC controllers. MAC is a mathematical process of multiplying a series of numbers with a fixed number, then adding the results of every multiplication towards the final result. This can be seen in Figure 6.5. MAC units are useful in digital signal processing applications, where waveforms have to be filtered through digital filters. These filters are called FIR (finite impulse response) filters and IIR (infinite IR) filters. A digital filter is a set of numbers, also called a vector in linear algebra. The input and output data streams are also vectors, representing quantized or sampled (with an A/D converter) waveforms. Without MAC units, using regular processor ALU units (arithmetic logic unit), digital filter processing will require several load/store instructions between each multiplication, which will take much longer time to complete. With sped-up MAC processing, a 100MHz DSP can easily perform complex audio waveform processing tasks, dissipating only a Watt or two.

6.1.3.2 DSP Devices

Digital Signal Processors (DSPs) are processors or CPUs that have a MAC unit built into them, accessible from the basic CPU instruction set. Some DSPs also have interfaces that are friendly towards the typical circuits that handle the signal streams, like A/D and D/A converters; others are fully reliant on FPGAs. Often DSPs are designed into boards together with FPGAs, which format the data input/output streams for the DSP (the FPGA is between the DSP and an ADC), provide captured data buffering and host access to the DSP's memory, and handle the DSP's firmware loading as well. Sometimes the DSP is a master device controlling the FPGAs behavior, in other designs

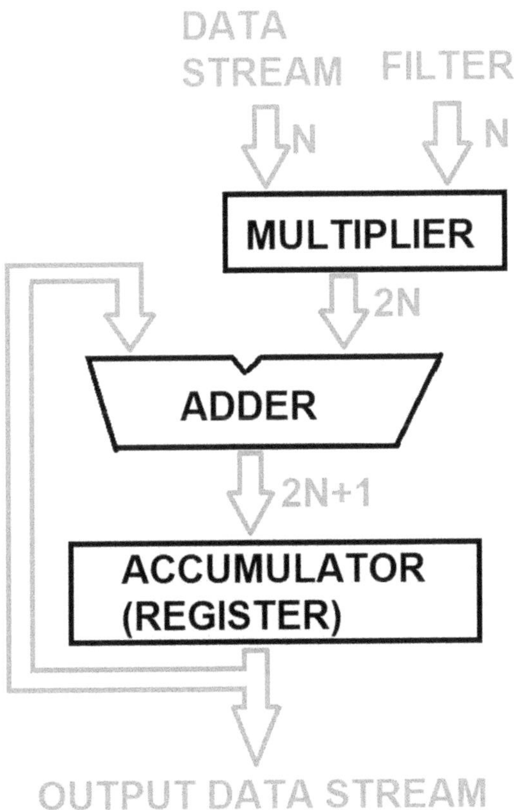

FIGURE 6.5 MAC unit data flow diagram.

the user (the host processor's automated firmware) can control the DSPs firmware and data loading through FPGA logic. The "DSP I/O bridge" is a common FPGA code project, fully customized, and it is very different in every board design. DSPs usually have similar boot modes and integrated peripherals as microcontrollers have, but they also have higher bandwidth streaming type interfaces for processing video or waveform data. DSPs can also run regular software, even operating systems, that helps with utilizing one single processor for both control and data plane tasks within the same system. There are chips on the market where a DSP processor and an ARM processor are on the same chip, for example, the OMAP, DaVinci, Jacinto, and KeyStone product lines from TI.

The main vendors providing DSP chips are Texas Instruments and Analog Devices. There are small DSP chips inside optical transceiver modules also, but they are not programmable, are rather specialized, and are minimized to perform one specific tasks. DSP processors are flexible and programmable, although there are different device families for different signal processing tasks. TI has three main DSP families, the C2000 (now they call them micro controllers), the C5000 (usually for audio), and the C6000 series, which is the more powerful family used for Video, data acquisition, and RF signal processing (Software Defined Radio SDR). C6000 DSPs usually have external DDRx memory and PCIe interfaces, which are common on X86 computer processors also, but DSPs have narrower ports. DSPs typically dissipate up to a few Watts and come in a less than 1000 pin BGA package. Analog Devices has several DSP families with marketing names such as ADSP-21xx, Blackfin, SHARC, and TigerSharc.

6.1.4 PowerPC

The PPC processor core was created in 1991 by the Apple–IBM–Motorola alliance. In recent years IBM, NXP Semiconductors (acquired Freescale Semiconductors) are the main manufactures of PPC processors, but several other companies also make them, like Samsung, BAE Systems, Teledyne e2v, and Sony. The RAD750 processor made by BAE Systems is a radiation-hardened CPU used in satellites, even Mars rovers. PPC processors compete with X86 processors, but their main advantage is the much lower power consumption, while still handling complex tasks, running complex operating systems, and supporting high-bandwidth interfaces (comparable to laptop-class X86 CPUs). Some of the PPC motherboards look like server motherboards; they are mainly used for bulk data processing, like databases. An example of a PPC server CPU is the IBM Power E1080 servers with Power10 processors, up to 16 CPUs, and 256 DIMM memory slots. Power10, the latest version of PPC core, is advertised to have AI acceleration on chip (inferencing). A special PowerPC processor made by NXP Semiconductors (formerly Freescale) is the QorIQ Qonverge Platform, which combines the PowerPC core with up to six DSPs and several baseband accelerator cores to be used in mobile or telecom base stations.

6.1.5 Soft Processors

There are several soft processor IP cores available to be synthesized on FPGAs or ASICs (by ASIC vendors). They are basically Verilog or VHDL code, which can be synthesized onto FPGAs or ASIC chip designs. They will run regular software. The proprietary MicroBlaze processor is available when using AMD (Xilinx) FPGAs, Intel's NIOS when using Intel/Altera FPGAs. NIOS used to be an Altera proprietary processor architecture, but recently Intel replaced it with RISC-V in the Quartus developer tools under the name Nios-V. The "RISC V" (pronounced "risk five") is an open-source processor specification created by the University of California Berkeley that can be coded/implemented by anyone, and it will be software compatible with other implementations. There is no official CPU-IP core source code release; rather, third-party companies offer their RISC-V implementations for a fee, not for free. A truly free and open source implementation called biRISC-V is available on GitHub as source code. Multiple vendors offer compilers, operating systems, and other tools to work with the RISC V processor; some of those are for free. There are hard-silicon implementations of the RISC-V, like the Renesas RZ/Five with 1GHz core clock speed. On FPGA soft core implementations, the processor core speeds are much more limited than hard silicon implementations, usually to 100 to 200MHz.

6.1.6 X86 CPUs and Chipsets

X86 processors are the standard architecture in all personal computers and most servers. The PCB that contains the processor is often called a "motherboard", even though we do not use that name for ASIC-based and FPGA-based boards. The Microsoft Windows and various Linux operating systems work on X86 processors with graphical user interface, using displays, keyboards, and mouse, but these processors can also be used in embedded applications with only a serial or network (telnet) console, called a "headless machine". Most embedded and server designs are headless, unlike consumer computers that are always used with a display. A personal computer is expected to be "driven" by the user for the duration of its use, while embedded and server computers perform automated tasks, and most are providing service access over the Ethernet network. A display would be part of both the control and the data plane, a console is only control plane. Modern X86 processors are "64-bit" architectures, which means they are capable of addressing a larger than 4GBytes memory space. 2^32=4GB was a limitation of the older 32-bit CPUs.

The Atom (low-power consumer), Core-I3/5/7 (laptop, desktop), and Xeon (high-performance server) processors are Intel's current product lines. Some of the Atom-type processors are sold under the Pentium and Celeron names, which used to be the names of the main Intel processors before the Core series. The Athlon (desktop), Ryzen (workstation, laptop), and EPYC (Server) are AMD's main product lines. All of these vendors provide processors to different markets with different levels of support. The consumer market receives several new processor models every year; they remain in production for one to two years only. They also have an "embedded program", where they release a few of their consumer processor models in a longer availability lifetime. We use these for aerospace/scientific/industrial designs and for embedded processor subsystems that we design-in as a portion of a larger board with ASICs/FPGAs. There is also a "communications infrastructure" program, where few processor models are available for a lifecycle of 10 years.

The detailed documentation of these processors can be downloaded from secure vendor websites, if we have an NDA signed with the chip vendor and access is granted to the specific documents. Sometimes two "datasheets" exist, both a public datasheet downloadable from the main website and a more detailed one under a different name that has all the key information for motherboard designers in it from the secured site. Newer processors might just have the detailed one on the secure site. There are usually several other documents that are needed for a successful motherboard design, such as design guides, appnotes, and a dozen other documents. All these have to be read by the hardware designer before starting the detailed motherboard design. For every new processor/chipset combination there is a motherboard design guide, which gives lots of details, including net topologies, layout constraints, and impedance requirements for each signal group. Even basic signals that we would consider slow glue logic signals are defined with impedance and routing topology. Any glue logic signal driven by a processor that is made with a <60nm or similar fine silicon technology can have very fast edges on all signals. Following all of the design guide instructions helps with reliable operation and a successful prototype bringup. Processor vendors sometimes also provide incremental training annually at their headquarters.

A processor model can be referred to by its short product number like "Xeon D-1702", by their product family code name like "Ice Lake-D", or by an exact part number that is a many digit alphanumeric string that we put into our schematic and BOM. There is usually a code name for a processor generation as well as for the narrower processor type. Processor and ASIC vendors usually provide engineering sample (ES) versions of their chips before they are officially released to allow board/system companies to develop their products and build prototypes and to be ready with working demo units or pre-production boards by the time of the chip release.

We can design boards with X86 processors for the sake of making universal processor boards or standalone computers, but in complex hardware we often design either a small processor board to act as a removable management card in a big chassis or we can design-in the X86 subsystem on a small portion of a larger board where the main data plane function is implemented using multiple large ASICs or FPGAs. The X86 processor will initialize and manage the data plane ASICs/FPGAs through the control plane, so the X86 CPU is part of the control plane infrastructure logic. A subsystem X86 design will utilize a 6 to 60W processor, and only one or two memory channels, while only taking up 10% to 30% of the total board space. Server motherboards are by themselves very complex boards, with two or more server CPUs in the range of 100W to 300W each, six to 16 channels of memory for each CPU, and several PCIe expansion connectors (for I/O and accelerator cards). The more memory channels available and populated, the more total bandwidth the CPU has to system memory access, and the maximum memory size is also larger. On server motherboards the CPU is the main data plane processing chip, for both the control plane and the data plane, and they can have add-in cards with smaller ASICs for computing acceleration of special tasks. Servers often contain two CPUs, but they can contain up to eight, using multiple boards and a backplane. Multi-processing boards have CPU-to-CPU interconnects using wide SERDES links in peer-to-peer or mesh configurations. Servers are usually cost-driven, due to large number of units deployed in the same data center, so they use cheaper PCB materials and less layers in the stackup than embedded CPU subsystems do, they also end up with a larger size and lower density than aerospace or telecom boards are.

6.1.6.1 Chipset Architectures and Buses

X86 processors rarely have any peripheral controller IPs integrated on their main silicon die. Instead, the CPU vendor releases new CPUs with new "chipsets". A chipset is one or two complex BGA chips that contain several different I/O interface controllers as well as system power management state machines to complement the CPU chip. New CPUs are released together with the new chipsets by the same vendor. Until around 2010 the chipset consisted of a "north bridge" and a "south bridge" chip. Since then, the north bridge has been integrated with the CPU on the same silicon die, while the south bridge remained, and has been renamed "Platform Controller Hub" (PCH). It is a single chip, but we still call it chipset. Intel used to call the north bridge "Memory Controller Hub" (MCH) and the south bridge "I/O Controller Hub" (ICH). In recent years a few fully integrated "platforms" were released, like the Xeon-D-1700, with the PCH and the CPU integrated in one single package, although many other processors still maintain the separate CPU plus PCH architecture. Figure 6.6 shows a few common chipset block diagrams and how they have evolved over the years. In 2023 most CPUs still require a chipset, but a few integrated devices are also available. Bare CPU code execution cores rely on "peripherals" to perform motherboard and I/O communication functions. X86 processors communicate with most external peripheral chips or cards through a PCIe interface. All external and on-chip (inside the chipset) peripherals appear as virtual PCI-bus devices to the processor, which all get "enumerated" by the BIOS during boot-up. Even though parallel PCI buses are not available on the chipsets anymore, the X86 architecture retained the legacy PCI bus high-level protocols.

The interface between the main elements of the chipset, like CPU to the chipset, are proprietary standards. Intel uses the "DMI" interface and several arbitrary glue logic signals (like PECI) described in their datasheets. The DMI works similarly to PCIe as a memory-mapped SERDES interface but with additional functions like virtual wire transactions used to convey interrupt and other legacy X86 signals. AMD used to use the Hyper Transport interface between the chipset elements, which was a clock-forwarding bus up to a few GHz, but now they use Infinity Fabric and CXL that are true SERDES links. In the old days there was a "front side bus" or FSB between the processor and north bridge that was a double data rate single-ended parallel bus.

The Management Engine (ME) is a microcontroller inside the Intel chipsets that acts as a security guard, which prevents boot if anything is out of the ordinary. This can help against hacking.

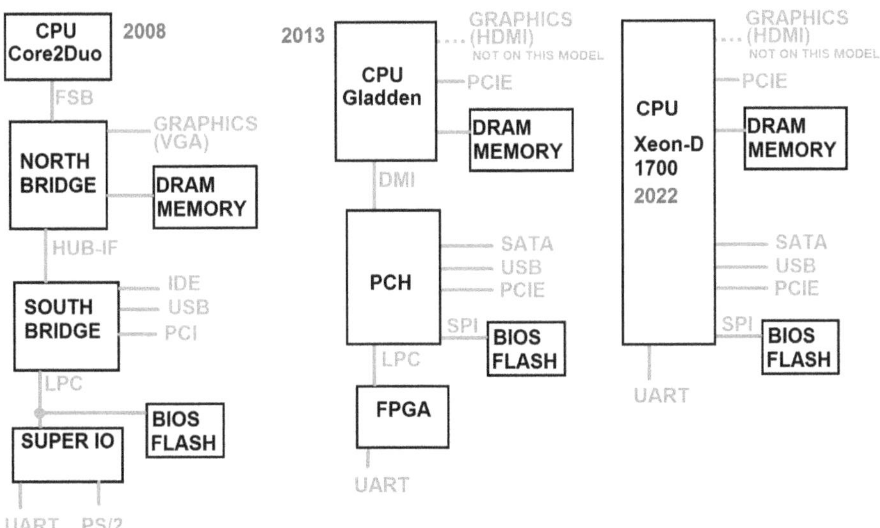

FIGURE 6.6 X86 motherboard architectures evolving towards more integration.

There are several standard chips invented for X86 motherboards, for example, the "Embedded Controller", which is a microcontroller that receives ACPI power management signals from the south bridge or PCH and handles the system power circuits. It is common on consumer and sever designs, but on embedded X86 boards we usually use a custom FPGA glue logic design instead, it is easier to adjust it to unique embedded circumstances. Several of the supporting chips are standardized, for example, the clocking chips for certain chipset generations are labeled with the CKxxx label (like CK510) that provides all the clocks to the PCH and the CPU. A typical X86 chipset needs several 100MHz refclocks, a 48MHz USB clock, a 14MHz for some chipset functions, 33MHz, and a separate 32kHz crystal for the real-time clock/calendar (RTC) function. Some PCH chipsets contain a clock source to the CPU and peripherals too. The CPU core VRM has to support the CPU power interface bus signals and protocols and the power control mechanism. These are standardized by the CPU vendors, with several versions of the standards. So we have to choose a VRM chip for our motherboard design that supports it.

X86 chipsets usually have an LPC bus interface for Super I/O (SIO) or FPGA attachment. The SIO chips were used on motherboards to provide serial port and PS/2 keyboard/mouse interfaces. Embedded hardware designers started implementing SIO functions on small FPGAs, which replaced the SIO chips, to allow supply-chain independence from the since obsolete SIO devices. Some X86 chipsets have serial ports, but usually just one, so we can still use an FPGA to create as many serial UART or RS232 ports as we need in an embedded system. We can also use PCIe/UART bridge chips for that purpose. Consumer computers no longer use serial ports, but embedded computers do use them as their main serial text console interface. The chipset also has slower interfaces like I2C master for DIMM memory SPD readout, I2C slave for receiving IPMI control, SPI for BIOS boot flash, several interrupt signals, GPIO, and glue logic pins. They have a real-time clock/calendar that runs on a 32kHz crystal and a coin cell battery, even when the system is powered off or unplugged.

X86 systems always have 64bit or 72bit memory channels, often two to 16 channels for each processor. A simple embedded design might just implement a single channel. Consumer and server designs usually utilize removable DIMM memory modules, but embedded designs more often prefer memory-down, as those are more resistant to shock and vibration and take up less chassis volume. In memory-down instead of sockets and memory cards, we solder the memory chips into the motherboard. X86 processors need several gigabytes of bootable non-volatile memory storage, these days we use SSD modules (various m.2 form factors) or soldered-down SSD BGA chips with SATA or PCIe interface.

A console is needed for engineers and technicians to access and configure the X86 subsystem. On consumer electronics it is always with high-end graphics (HDMI or LCD) output and USB keyboard+mouse, but in embedded systems we access the processors over RS232 serial port or over Ethernet. The standard connectivity of every embedded computer is a few USB ports, one RS232 console port over an RJ45 connector (use with a "roll-over" serial cable), and one 1000Base-T 1Gbit Ethernet port for management. The chipsets usually include at least one 1Gig Ethernet MAC to be used with an external PHY chip, made by the CPU/chipset vendor. If the embedded processor supports more than just management or control plane functions, then it also usually has one or two higher bandwidth Ethernet ports and a few wide PCIe ports. Embedded processors are usually interacting with the data plane ASICs/FPGAs over several PCIe links, so a PCIe switch is commonly included in the X86 subsystem to provide more ports/lanes to access our multiple ASICs. Some of the servers are fitted with a 10Gbit, 40Gbit, or 100Gbit optical Ethernet port for external data plane access. Most embedded and high-end X86-based board designs do not require any audio ports. Smaller industrial designs might do, in which case an audio codec chip is connected to the chipset over an I2S or similar CMOS synchronous serial interface.

Server computers usually have two or more processors, in which case one processor has all the connections described here, the other processors just have their own memory modules and a high-bandwidth connection (UPI or Infinity Fabric) to the main booting CPU. See the section about major interfaces for these multi-processing links.

6.1.6.2 Addressing

X86 processors have three address domains: The memory domain, the I/O domain (64k addresses, to talk to legacy peripherals), and MSR addressing (accessing internal CPU registers). Modern CPUs retained compatibility with very old X86 CPUs that had more basic addressing schemes. The memory and the I/O addresses can be routed to any of the main bus interfaces. The memory address domain is the most important one. It is a map of various independent objects, like the system DRAM memory, all the PCIe devices (register sets) and integrated peripherals inside the X86 chipset. Each device address window is subdivided by the devices themselves into register sets and buffer memories. The MS-DOS operating system commonly used in the 1980s by consumers, and it is still used in prototype debugging and has several functions defined in a small memory window, which all maps into a modern computer's much larger memory space. This included a text-based video memory, the BIOS code, add-in card BIOS extension ROM contents, and other standard peripherals like the interrupt controller. Since it is very small, modern computers reserve this 1Mbyte space for compatibility with old software and continuity of architecture. Simple interfaces like SPI, and even the DRAM controller, can be re-mapped into the system address space, so the address on the bus is different from the address the CPU sees. PCI(e) devices are told what address they have to respond to during enumeration, and they are told to respond to the same address, which is also programmed into the PCIe root complex registers. There are several bus logic blocs downstream from the CPU core; each directs all arriving transactions (from their upstream port) to different downstream ports based on the address range registers programmed to each port. This way any read or write accesses from the CPU will be routed to different interfaces, be it the DRAM, PCIe, SPI, or other. All this is demonstrated in Figure 6.7.

CPU address types:

- Logical or virtual address, that is seen by one user application.
- Linear address, what the CPU core silicon sees, the hole system memory-space.
- Physical address, separate on every bus, but main buses like PCIe contain the address within the system memory map.

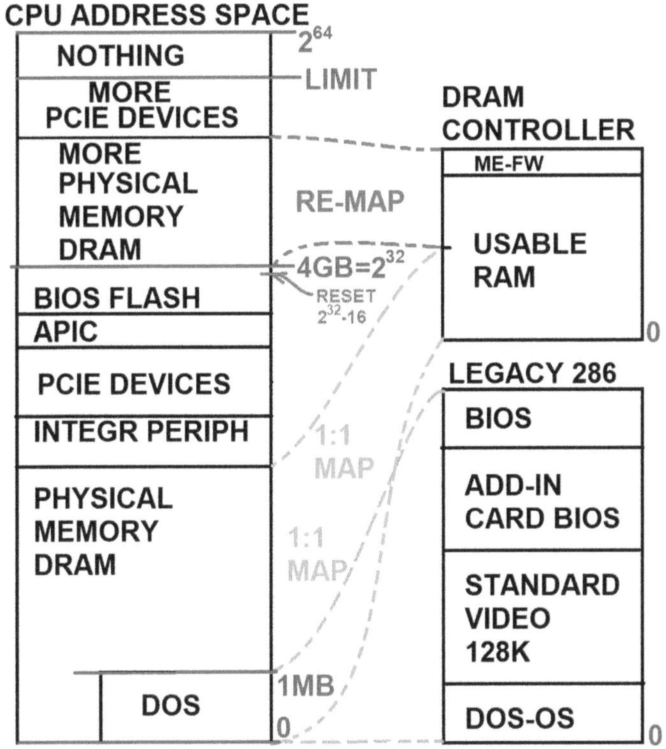

FIGURE 6.7 Modern X86 computer system memory address map.

CPU addressing modes:

- Real Mode, 8086 legacy mode up to 1Mbyte, processors default to this mode after reset, later the BIOS and OS switch over to more modern modes. Every application accesses objects within the system memory map through segment registers. Base+offset address is calculated by the CPU core, and uses the base address of the currently running application.
- Protected Mode (Segmented) with paging (hard drive load/store virtual memory). Similar to the real mode, but the segment registers are used for indexing a segment table. This was used on 32bit processors and 32bit operating systems. It is also very complicated, but since they are no longer common the detailed operation here is omitted.
- Flat 64bit, any application can access any item in the system memory map that is larger than 4GBytes. With 32-bit address logic any processor could address only up to 4GBytes of system memory space. That is solved by the introduction of 64bit CPUs. No segment registers or segment tables used. Modern X86 processors are all IA-64, AMD64, or 64bit devices and use this addressing method in normal operation.

6.1.6.3 Interrupts

Interrupts are used to stop normal software execution, and they jump to a predefined interrupt software routine to service an urgent hardware event. For example, data has arrived or a card was plugged in. The CPU has a few interrupt input pins. They used to be actual package pins, but in recent years they are encoded virtual signals over DMI bus packets. The chipset contains a programmable interrupt controller (APIC), which takes in many interrupt sources, and asserts its one output to the CPU (virtual signal). The CPU/software can read from the status registers of the APIC to find out which input caused the main IRQ line assertion. NMI is the non-maskable interrupt, compared to the IRQ that is maskable. Masking interrupts means software can write to a register and tell it to not let a specific source through, while with NMI it cannot do that. SMI is the system management interrupt, caused by power management events like sleep button signals. MSI is message signaled interrupt; it can be generated by PCIe devices, which causes an MSI message to be written into the system memory's MSI area, which write access is snooped by the CPU's bus interface and creates a real interrupt to the CPU. Instead of an APIC device in the PCH, the MSI uses a region in the system DRAM memory. The SERIRQ bus is a standard serial shift register style bus to provide many interrupt sources to an X86 chipset over a single pin plus the LPC clock. It runs at 33MHz. It was originally created for Super I/O chips, but we can also drive it with custom FPGA logic. X86 chipsets also have a few extra legacy interrupt pins that were meant to be driven by a SIO chip, like the RI# and the RCIN. Figure 6.8 shows all these types of interrupts in an X86 computer. The red lines are actual physical signal traces on the motherboard, the blue ones are logical or virtual signals, basically bits in data packets or registers, or on-chip signals.

6.1.6.4 CPU Boot-Up and Software Architecture

X86 CPUs have a two-stage boot process, first they load the BIOS (basic input/output system) from an SPI flash chip, then an OS (operating system) from a storage (SATA, PCIe, or USB) module. When the computer is powered up, it will be in reset, then it will come out of reset and starts executing code at the reset vector address, that is 0xFFFFFFF0, or 16 bytes below the 4 GB range limit. Earlier processors had their vector a lower addresses. At this address range location, the chipset bus interface logic has the SPI boot flash interface mapped. The SPI flash chip is attached to the chipset. The SPI flash can be programmed with an SPI dongle, or pre-programmed before assembly. So, the BIOS code in the SPI flash will start executing. The SPI flash contains the BIOS firmware code, as well as "soft strapping". Soft strapping is like a small binary file that is like an already programmed register set, with the register bits having a purpose of controlling chipset operation, an alternative to pin strapping that can be modified without design re-spin, for example, defining video outputs and the number of memory channels. The BIOS or the hardware engineer has to create a

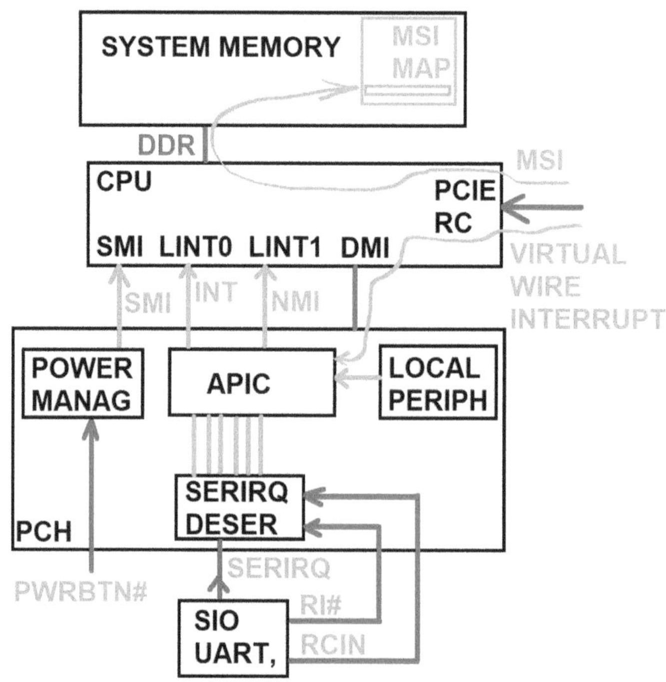

FIGURE 6.8 X86 interrupt signaling.

flash programming image. It contains the compiled BIOS code, several soft straps that describe the motherboard schematic hookup and intended uses, and in Intel's case a management engine (ME) firmware image also. The chipset state machines load the soft strapping, then they load the ME code, then load the BIOS code to execute directly from flash. The first portion of the BIOS code loads the rest of the BIOS code into cache memory, initializes the DRAM memory, enumerates the PCIe device structure, and initializes all devices and builds a final memory map. After this the BIOS looks for bootable operating system images over the SATA interface, as well as any PCIe or USB device that has a device ID implying a storage device, then starts loading the operating system from the selected one in the boot order list. The operating system loads from storage into DRAM, further initializes the system, the graphics controller (if the system uses one), finds driver software for PCIe devices based on their vendor and device IDs. The OS require a user to log in to control the system, but on many embedded systems there is automated software loaded after boot automatically that will perform the main application without any user control.

The BIOS firmware code has to be customized for every single new motherboard. The hardware engineer has to create a spreadsheet with all interfaces, strapping pins, and GPIO pins listed as how they were connected on the reference board versus on the new design. Any deviation requires code change implemented by the BIOS engineer. The BIOS code base is purchased from a BIOS vendor, and the BIOS chipset driver code from the CPU vendor, then it has to be merged and customized. The free and open-source BIOS base code "Coreboot" is often lagging six to 12 months from the mainstream BIOS codes and might have unresolved bugs in it. For a product for a competitive market, the open source delay is usually not acceptable, so the commercial versions are preferred. If a memory down design is used, then the SPD EEPROM loading function has to be disabled and SPD values hardcoded in the BIOS code.

Sometimes software or firmware engineers, while developing the BIOS code customization, need to halt or step the processor code execution or read out a register value using a JTAG dongle and a "debugger" application. Intel calls their JTAG port "XDP". They define the header pinout, which might be large, but it might be worth designing it in for development purposes. The XDP header contains far more than just JTAG signals. Some signals are in the 100MHz range and require trace length-controlled routing. Or we can choose to implement a reduced header instead, with limited functionality on high-density boards.

6.1.6.5 CPU Power and Thermal Control

X86 processors control their own core voltage level through a VID (voltage identification) or SVID (serial VID) bus routed to the core VRM. During the power on sequence, the core rail powers up to a VBOOT level, then as the processor executes more code, it will drive out the proper VID code, then the VRM will settle the voltage to the VID-defined level without glitches. The main signals between a modern processor and a VRM are the data, clock, and an alert signal. Older processors had a parallel VID bus and several other glue logic signals too. If a processor silicon also contains a GPU, then it might also have a VID bus for the graphics core VRM, not only for the CPU core VRM. Some processors have different variants that require a different I/O or SERDES voltage, so they have one or two single-ended low-voltage CMOS outputs that tell the board glue logic what voltage is required. 1.05V to 1.2V are commonly used by X86 processors for VIO of glue logic signals, and we need level translation when connecting them to other devices, except some of the signals going to the south bridge chipset. That CMOS signal can be decoded in a glue logic FPGA, then driven to a transistor circuit or analog multiplexer that alters the VRM strapping or feedback resistors and therefore its output voltage.

All X86 motherboards have a few standard thermal management signals. The PROCHOT# signal tells if the CPU core has reached 100C Tjmax to signify that the fans have to be driven to maximum speed and that the processor has reduced its core clock frequency and VID voltage. The THERMTRIP# signal asserts above Tjmax at around 125C to tell the board glue logic that it must shut down all VRMs immediately to prevent fire damage. We connect these to our glue logic FPGA.

The PECI is a one-wire interface between the CPU and the chipset to allow the south bridge or BMC (board management controller) to read out the CPU core on-die temperature sensors. Several "error" signals are also generated by the processors, like the CATERR#, that glue logic or a BMC can monitor to shut down the system if it was asserted.

X86 CPU vendors sometimes provide a software tool, which we can use to drive the CPU to perform computations that result in dissipating heat at 75% of the peak heat level that it can produce—75% is what they call thermal design power (TDP). With this, we can do thermal chamber testing of our board/system to see how efficient our cooling solution is by measuring the CPU core temperature in the process. During the test we usually measure the core temp with the on-die sensing feature. We also attach thermocouples through a hole drilled into the heatsinks to touch the CPU die.

The chipset contains the power management logic that tells the glue logic FPGA or BMC to turn all VRMs on or off through the SLP_Sx# signals, and the chipset itself gets turned on or off by the glue logic asserting the PWRBTN# (power button) signal. SLP_S3# is the main power domain enable signal, while SLP_S4# might be used to control the DRAM power to support sleep states on some designs. When high, they enable all rails of a certain power domain. The power button signal is driven by a button in laptop and desktop computers, but it is driven by glue logic in all other types of computers. If we do not want the chipset to control our system power, then we can trick the chipset by supplying fake power management signals to it from a glue-logic FPGA, IPMC, or BMC. This is useful, for example, in larger systems with multiple ASICs. An X86 motherboard is always in one of several power states, and the state is registered or determined by the logic inside the chipset, but it can be controlled by a glue-logic FPGA or an IPMI/BMC controller at a higher level. The chipset receives several power domain PowerGood signals from the glue logic, which our glue logic design has to prepare with the correct timing (see datasheet) relative to the VRMs turn on sequence. The chipset can receive a SYSRESET# signal from a reset button, from a glue logic FPGA, or from an IPMI/BMC controller. The main reset signal going to peripheral devices is the platform reset (PLTRST#), driven by the chipset, that can be individually gated to different devices, using custom glue logic. The power management logic inside the X86 chipset is powered by two power rails, the standby rail generated from the 12V or the main battery input and the coin cell battery (RTC rail). The 3V coin cell battery maintains the real-time clock (RTC) and calendar function and a few sticky registers called "CMOS" registers that remember some BIOS settings. It is typically implemented using a battery holder soldered down the motherboard, with a CR2032 or similar size battery lasting three to 10 years. The RTC also keeps ticking and counting regardless of whether the main power input is on or off. The standby rail that is always on as long as the laptop's battery is charged or the main AC input is plugged in powers the state machines that handle the SLP_Sx#, PWRBTN#, and reset signals. Both the standby and the RTC domain logic has their own reset input signals, which are generated through RC passive timing circuits from the voltage rails to provide a deterministic initial state for their state machines. These are the RSMRST# for the standby domain and RTCRST# for the RTC domain. For example, a desktop PC will start in the standby state after the AC cord is plugged in, so it will always require a power button press to fully start up. In embedded systems we might not want to have a thermally sensitive and large coin cell battery, in which case the RTC and standby rails might be shorted together in the design and the operating system has to expect to wake up with the same calendar day and hour every time. The standby reset (RSMRST#) might be driven by the glue logic or management processor in embedded systems, if the IPMC is the real power master and it is able to turn the standby rail to the X86 chipset completely off. X86 chipsets when they are in a sleep state (not standby) can be awakened by standby-domain peripherals on the motherboard, using the WAKEUP# signal. The chipsets contain several other power management signals that the glue logic must handle; they slightly vary over chipset generations.

The chipset handles a subset of the CPU's glue logic and power management signals, but a larger portion is handled by the board glue logic that is custom designed by the hardware design engineer, often with an FPGA or a BMC (board management controller or server management processor). The chipset has several strapping signals that informs the chipset about the designer's boot memory and I/O port mode selection. The tricky thing about X86 motherboard design is the dozens of non-standard signals that all have to go somewhere on the motherboard, some level translated, others pulled up or down, or require non-trivial circuits, and they have to not cause the BIOS to fail completing the boot process. If the BIOS expects something that is not there, it hangs. Most glue logic signals on X86 motherboards are related to power and thermal management. X86 processors and chipsets require a lot of glue logic parts to work, which includes level translators, transistors, FPGA or CPLD logic, or instead of a custom FPGA often a BMC microcontroller chip is used. ASPEED is one of the main vendors for BMC chips, while for FPGA we usually use a smaller flash-based device from Microchip (acquired Actel/Microsemi), or the Intel Max series (acquired Altera). These devices initialize themselves fast, and have many 3.3V CMOS I/O pins, usually we need 100…400 such pins.

6.1.6.6 Example CPU: Intel Gladden

The Intel Xeon-E3-1125C-V2 processor family, codenamed Gladden, within the Sandy Bridge CPU-core architecture was a two-chip solution available as a communications infrastructure processor from 2012 to 2022. The CPU came in a BGA package with a 1mm uniform grid, making it suitable for embedded applications where data plane ASICs with similar 1mm pitch BGAs are designed on the same board. The companion of this CPU is the Cave Creek PCH chipset (DH8900CC Intel Communications Chipset 89xx), connecting to the CPU over a DMI SERDES link and a PCIe link for its Ethernet controller block. This PCH is really two separate chips in one, a PCH and a quad Ethernet controller. Both the CPU and the chipset has several variants, or SKUs, with varying levels of power dissipation and core clock frequency, so before detailed design the exact part numbers need to be selected. Figure 6.9 shows the I/O block diagram of a typical computer block with the

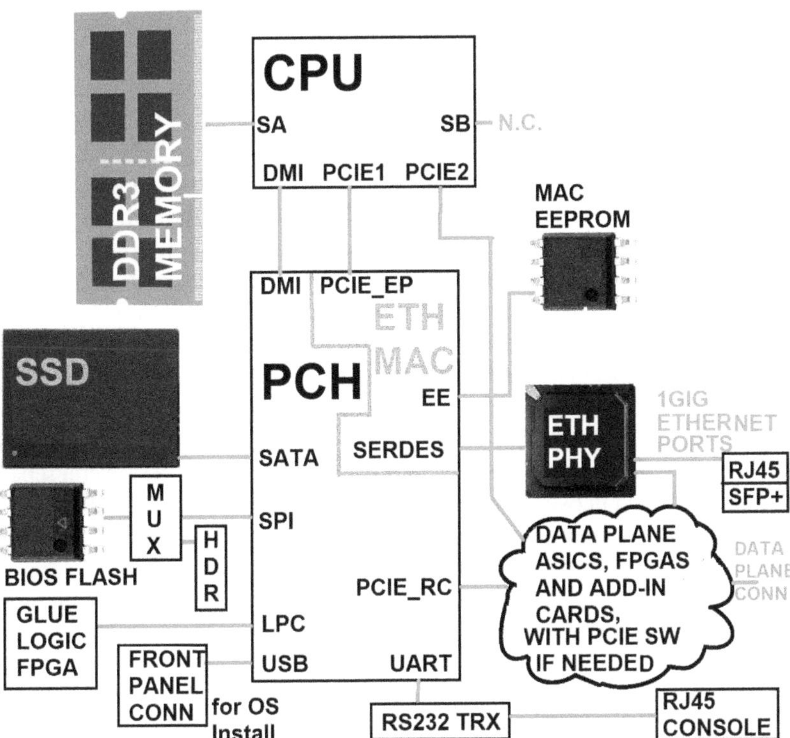

FIGURE 6.9 I/O block diagram of an embedded Gladden CPU subsystem.

Gladden CPU and the Cave Creek chipset. It would usually have a single channel memory-down block connected, a solid-state drive (SSD) chip for OS boot, an EEPROM for storing the MAC address of the Ethernet port, a serial port for main console, an SPI flash with a multiplexer for BIOS boot, and an USB port for installing the OS.

The Gladden CPU has two DDR3 memory channels with 72bit ECC support, PCIe signals, an intel-enhanced XDP JTAG port (for CPU code stepping), and a x4 DMI bus to the PCH. The CPU receives a single clock signal called BCLK that is a 100MHz differential pair from a standard CK420 clock chip. The CPU talks to its core VRM over an SVID bus, and it provides three logic output signals to let the glue logic set the I/O and SERDES rail voltages according to the CPU version. The CPU receives power good signals and several other glue logic signals from the PCH. The main CPU reset input is driven from the chipset's platform reset (PLTRST#) output, which is level translated to 1.05V. The CPU provides several thermal warning signals that are connected to the glue logic as well as to the chipset. The CPU's signal pins are low voltage at 1.05V, so if they are connected to the FPGA then they need level translating circuits (often just two transistors). Some of the signals between the CPU and PCH do need level translation, others do not, so we have to check the datasheets and reference schematics to determine. Many of the signals require pullups and pulldowns. The CPU has the CFG[17:0] main strapping signals, for the hardware designer to tell the CPU about the motherboard configuration, like what ports do we want to use in what modes and options, and to set the PCIe root complex port bifurcation. The CPU receives several voltages, the core VRM has to be an IMVP7-compliant device that generates the varying and live-controlled core voltage with a three-phase output stage. The 1.05V rail is called VIO and is common for Intel processors. It also receives 1.8V for the PLL, a 1.5V for the DDR3 memory interface, and a VCCSA rail that can vary depending on CPU variant. There are remote sense pins for all high current rails; they require catch resistors and termination resistors.

The PCH chipset handles a subset of the CPU's glue logic and power management signals, but the remaining portion is handled by the board glue logic FPGA. The chipset's I/O interfaces include the upstream DMI to the CPU, a PCIE_EP interface to the processor to provide for the quad Ethernet controller, some narrow ports of PCIE root complex for peripherals, SATA for an operating system SSD boot device, and a "SERDES" port for the Ethernet port to external PHY chip or SFP+ optical cage. The PCH also has slower interfaces like I2C master, I2C slave for IPMI control, SPI for BIOS boot flash, another SPI for the Ethernet controller's MAC address storage, LPC bus and several interrupt and glue logic signals for Super-I/O attachment. The PCH contains the power management logic that tells the glue logic FPGA or BMC to turn all VRMs on or off through the SLP_Sx# signals. The chipset itself gets turned on or off by the FPGA glue logic or a user (through a button) asserting the PWRBTN# (power button) signal. The PCH provides PowerGood signals to the CPU, while the FPGA/BMC provides similar PowerGood signals to the PCH, based on the VRM power on sequence timing. The PCH can receive a SYSRESET# signal from a reset button, a glue logic FPGA, or an IPMI controller. The PCH reset output the PLTRST# signal is the main reset output to all devices on the board, which can be individually gated to different devices using custom glue logic in the FPGA. The PCH maintains a 32kHz crystal clock for the battery-powered real-time clock, and receives a few faster clocks at 14 to 100MHz from the CK420 clock chip. The PCH requires several separate voltage rails, between 1 and 3.3V, and in two domains, the standby domain and the main S0 fully-on domain. The PCH has several dual-purpose signals used as strapping or GPIO and a few dedicated strapping signal that informs the chipset about the designer's boot memory device selection.

All the power management glue logic signals of the Gladden / Cave Creek chipset in typical embedded implementations can be seen in Figure 6.10. The FPGA logic implementation has to be determined based on the CPU and chipset datasheet descriptions of those signals.

6.1.6.7 X86 Server Processors and Chipsets

Server processors differ from the other type of X86 processors and chipsets. The most obvious thing is the performance and the power dissipation, but the motherboard design complexity and the way

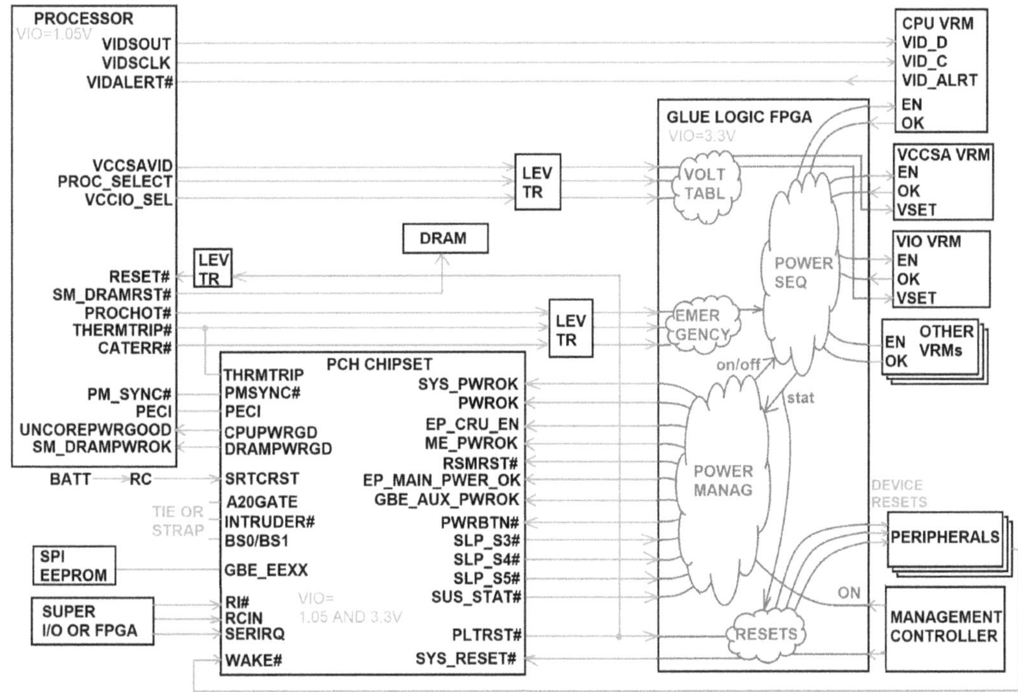

FIGURE 6.10 Gladden CPU and Cave Creek PCH power management glue logic signals.

system management subsystem is designed also differ. Servers CPUs like the Intel Xeon Scalable Processors or the AMD EPYC devices usually have more cores (16 to 56 cores versus 2 to 8 in non-server) and more power dissipation (60 to 400W versus 6 to 40W). They support more memory channels (4 to 12 versus 1 to 2) and a larger total memory size (Terabytes versus 8 to 64GBytes). They support x4 memory chips by providing one DQS signal for every four (not eight) data signal. Most of the time server processors are used on server motherboard designs that are cost driven, so they use lower component density and layer count. Server CPUs come in 3000 to 5000-pad LGA packages meant to be put into sockets, while smaller CPUs vary with 1000 to 2000-ball BGA or LGA packages. The socket itself is soldered down as a BGA part, but it has spring contacts to touch the gold-plated LGA pads. Similarly, the server chipsets come in larger BGA packages, with ~1300 vs ~700 pins on the mobile/embedded ones. Server motherboards have 4000 to 5000 components, while embedded boards with lower power X86 CPUs and consumer motherboards have ~1200 to 2000 parts. Any integrated ASICs or data plane devices on embedded designs would add to this part count. Servers usually do not have chip-down integrated ASICs, with the exception of an Ethernet controller, they have many add-in card sockets instead.

The management subsystem is based on a board management controller (BMC) or a server management processor on each motherboard, which is a low-power ARM microcontroller with its own external DDR and flash memory. Server BMC chips are also used for remote firmware and operating system upgrade of the server CPUs, while the EC on consumer and embedded boards are mainly used for power and hot-swap management. The server BMC can read/write the X86 BIOS boot flash by controlling an analog multiplexer used for SPI bus routing. It can also read the CPU temperature through the PECI slow serial interface. The server BMC can communicate with the server's software through UART or USB interfaces. Servers have more sources of thermal warning signals, not just the CPUs but all the DIMMs and larger VRMs can report, which are detected by the management controller. The whole thermal management scheme is more complicated, supporting shutdown, fan control, and CPU or memory performance throttle. Throttling is when the

CPU speed or memory access rate is reduced to allow cooling of the system, initiated by a throttle control signal. For example, the PROCHOT# signal is not just point to point between the CPU and the glue logic FPGA or CPLD, but also goes to the management processor. Several signals are combined into a complex web of interactions, the bi-directional capability (report output versus throttle input) is taken advantage of, as we can see on the general scheme shown in Figure 6.11. This is usually expanded with more detail, like actual pin numbers, in diagrams made for projects. The THERMTRIP#, I2C and SPI buses, resets, error reporting, memory hot warnings, NVDIMM, error reporting (CATERR#, FIVR_FAULT, ERROR0#), and other signals also split into separate complex diagrams and are wired to all of the BMC/chipset/CPLD devices when comparing the earlier described embedded computer block versus the server motherboard design. Figure 6.12 shows the concept of how DIMM memory or their VRM's overheating detection logic can throttle the server processor. Throttling means the CPU drops core frequency or memory access rate to reduce the temperature of itself and connected devices.

The server chipsets also have more glue logic signals and glue logic–related chipset pins than laptop or embedded processor have. For example, the "power capping" subsystem measures power load currents and interacts with the thermal throttling logic to keep the server's power consumption

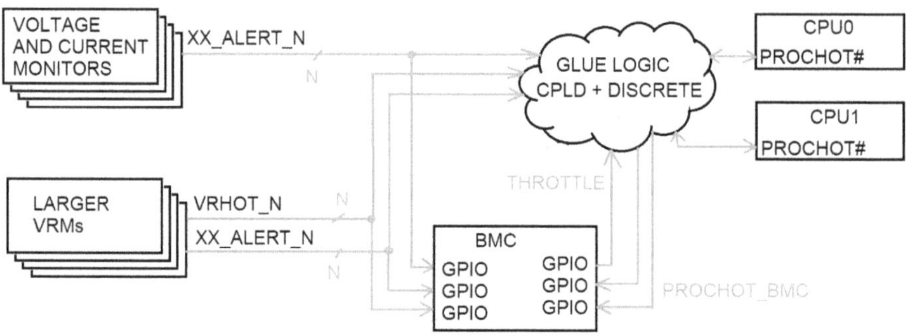

FIGURE 6.11 Typical PROCHOT logic on servers.

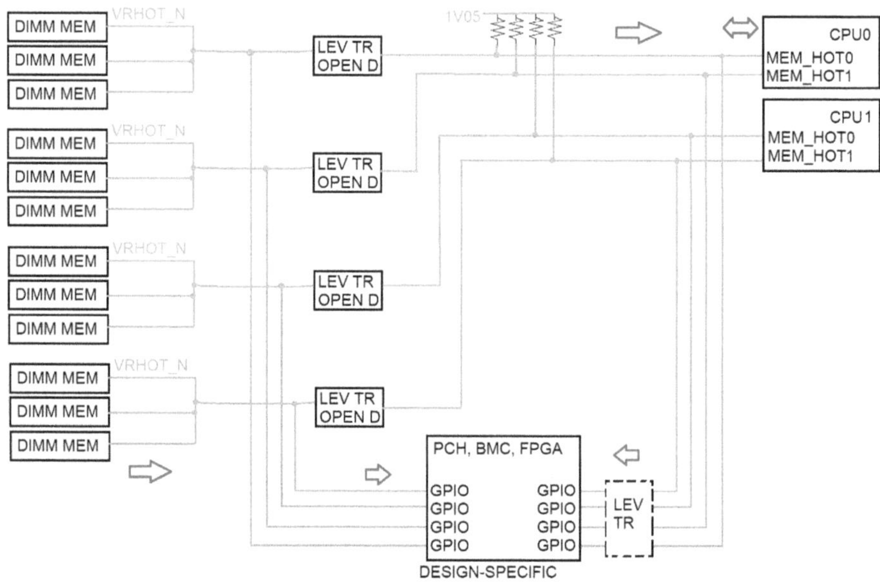

FIGURE 6.12 Typical memory thermal throttling logic on servers.

below a limit. These will not all be demonstrated here; rather, the motherboard designer has to study the detailed (real) datasheet, the design guide, and the reference design schematics of the particular chipset version. The design goal is to implement what we see in the reference design but deviate just enough to implement the unique features our marketing department asks for, any personal debug hooks, our system management scheme, and any components to be replaced with those that fit better with our procurement and design re-use strategies.

Server processors have a multi-computing interface that non-servers do not have, which is to connect two to eight CPUs in a point-to-point or mesh configuration together in a cache coherent manner so each CPU can see the DIMM memory content of the DRAMs attached to the other CPUs.

Server CPUs and server chipsets have a larger number of interfaces also. For example, a mobile processor might have 16 lanes of PCIe-Gen3, a server CPU might have 80 lanes of PCIe-Gen5. Servers usually route all the PCIe lanes to standard add-in card sockets, while embedded CPUs route it to backplane connectors, PCIE switch chips, and on-board FPGAs/ASICs directly. Server chipsets have a larger number of SMBUS and I2C ports to access devices like smart VRMs, current monitors, many thermal sensors, and EEPROMs as well as all the many add-in card slots through multiplexers. PCIe slots have PCIs SERDES signals, reset, power, and I2C connections. Some of these I2C ports are called SMLINK. These buses are also intercepted by the management processor in a dual master fashion.

On server CPUs the power management subsystem's SVID buses control multiple VRMs, not only the core rail. One SVID bus can have more than one VRM attached to it. The VRM power stages are usually driven to their limits, for example, a 70A chip would be used up to ~30A on an embedded or network design, but up to 50 to 60A on a server, that necessitates adding heatsinks on top of them. Up to 30A the power pad could cool the power stage chip to the motherboard's ground planes. So the power stages used in servers might be different part numbers and might have exposed thermal contacts on their top side too. Intel recommends that motherboard designs (they call it "platform") to be tested for CPU and memory-DIMM power delivery issues using modules called "VR Test Tool" made by Intel that can be attached to the motherboard.

6.2 FPGAS

FPGAs (field programmable gate arrays) are blank slate devices where the code designers can determine what chip logic functionality to implement. Some FPGAs are small, used for glue logic and control plane functions, some are large and used for data plane processing at high bandwidth, comparable to large ASICs and server processors. For raw power processing with versatile operations, a CPU is more suitable; for standard interface switching, ASICs are more suitable; for custom specialized processing, FPGAs are more suitable.

6.2.1 FPGA Basics

FPGAs internally are made of logic and routing resources (wires and switches), arranged in a matrix grid shape, as we can see in Figure 6.13. Both the routing and the logic can be configured to implement any digital logic design from a source code transformed automatically by the compilation tools. The configuration as a data file is usually stored inside the FPGA or in a flash memory chip attached to the FPGA. Any logic design can be described in Verilog or VHDL coding language (source code), called the RTL code, that can be synthesized into standard logic elements, then later the exact instances of the logic elements on the chip will be assigned to the logic in the synthesized code, then the routing resources will be configured to route the signals between the logic resources. The main logic resources inside the FPGA matrix are the configurable logic blocks (CLBs) that contain multiplexers, gates, and flip-flops. There are several other types of resources too, like the input output blocks (IOBs) that contain an I/O flip flop and a few logic circuits that have to be physically close to the external pins to meet board level I/O timing. Most FPGAs contain thousands of CLBs,

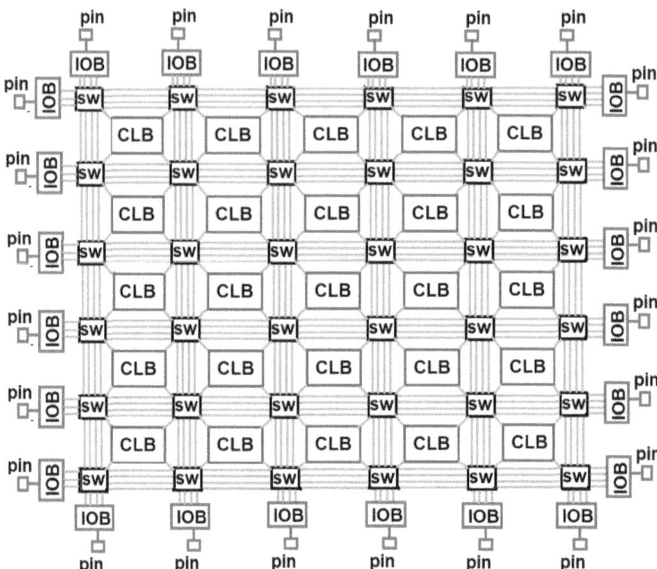

FIGURE 6.13 FPGA basic fabric architecture.

and the same number of IOBs as the number of external pins. There are balanced-skew internal clock networks to feed the CLBs and IOB flip-flops that can be driven by PLLs or external input pins. There are memory blocks and DSP blocks inside the devices too. High-performance FPGAs contain both general purpose I/O pins and SERDES transceiver tiles also. The CPLD devices, with a very low amount of logic resources, were in use for many years, but recently they have been replaced by small FPGAs; thus. the CPLD's own matrix logic architecture is not explained here.

FPGA device size is measured in terms of logic elements/cells or logic gates, as listed in datasheets and selection guides. One cell is about 50 gates for conversion. We can also measure them by the number of CLB flip-flops. When we estimate a logic design from IP core datasheets, we get an estimate in logic cells or gates, so we have to select an FPGA device that has 50% to 100% more than that—there has to be a portion left empty for routing flexibility and future code updates. We have to consider a "migration path", which means that we should pick a device density+package combination that allows a drop-in replacement in the design with a larger density device in the same package, as an insurance policy in case our design ends up not fitting in the smaller and cheaper device.

FPGA devices have these groups of pins that we have to connect in our schematic:

- General I/O pins, organized into IO banks.
- Global clock input pins, a subset of the general I/O pins set.
- Reference voltage and calibration resistor pins, which are parts of the I/O banks.
- SERDES transceiver pins, including TX, RX, refclock, and calibration resistors.
- Dedicated pins for configuration interface (SPI or other format) and control/status like CONF_DONE and INIT#. Some config pins are dual purpose with general I/O bank pins, especially for wide parallel options.
- Strapping pins for config mode selection.
- Dedicated JTAG pins.
- Power rails: core, transceiver, VIO for each IO bank, PLL, VAUX and config interface, remote sense for VRM, GND.
- Thermal diode pins for external temperature sensor measuring die temperature.

6.2.1.1 The Configuration Cycle

SRAM-based FPGAs need to load their own configuration from an external flash memory chip after power on. Flash-based devices do not have to do that, they are ready at power on. Most modern larger sized FPGAs are SRAM-based and are typically configured from QSPI Flash memories, but other methods are still supported like parallel configuration and host-processor slave configuration. The flash FPGAs and the flash memory chips require device programming on the prototype as well as in the production floor. An example parallel flash configuration circuit is shown in Figure 6.14.

The switch routing paths, the CLB multiplexer, and flip-flop input and output connections are configured by the content of the configuration file (bit file). All these configurable elements hold their configuration in RAM-like cells that are volatile, which disappears after a power cycle. Flash-based FPGAs (for example Microchip Igloo) have flash cells instead of RAM cells, so they do not have to be loaded at every power on event, they need only to be programmed once. This way they are ready immediately when its power rails are up, which is an advantage for system and power management applications that can take control of a board or system without hundreds of milliseconds of dead time. The Intel (Altera) Max-10 has built-in flash storage, but it still has to load it into its own SRAM cells, so it requires a config cycle, although it is faster than loading from an external flash. Flash FPGAs are typically used for board glue logic, which requires a much smaller number of resources than data plane FPGAs do, so they can be much smaller and lower power devices, supplied from a small amount of power on a standby voltage rail. They typically consume a few hundred milliwatts, but they need to have many 3.3V CMOS capable I/O pins (100 to 400) that larger FPGAs do not have. Most glue logic is 3.3V, with a few exceptions down to 1V. Most glue logic interacts with power circuits, device resets, device strapping, and status of the larger main chips.

SRAM-based FPGAs have strapping pins to select the configuration mode, usually set using pull up/down resistors or driven by a smaller glue logic FPGA. The selectable modes are SPI/QSPI flash, byte parallel flash, serial Platform Flash, slave parallel, or slave serial mode. Most often, we use SPI or QSPI flash chips, sometimes parallel AMD (Xilinx) Platform Flash chips, and the FPGA acts as the flash bus master. Parallel flash provides shorter config times, but it takes up more FPGA pins and board area. The configuration guides from the FPGA vendors list the flash chip part numbers that are supported. They also list the size of the bit file that is required for each FPGA device, and the flash has to be able to store as much, sometimes twice as much for redundancy. In some cases, compressed bit streams can be used, which can be stored in smaller flash devices—the datasheets should tell if there is support for that. We can also configure FPGAs by a local master like a microcontroller or a management or control plane processor/card in a slave serial or slave parallel mode. The processor can load the configuration into the data plane FPGA from a securely stored file in the X86 subsystem. For lab testing we can configure the FPGAs over JTAG. When we program a config flash chip, we can connect to the FPGA over JTAG, then the GUI will load a small FPGA image that is a flash programmer image, then it will load the flash image through it to program the attached flash chip.

The flash-loading cycle can take up to one second, depending on the configuration method used. For example, an QSPI (4bit parallel) flash chip configures faster than a SPI (fully serial), but a byte parallel flash can be even faster. These multi-wire SPI devices (QSPI and OSPI) start in 1-wire mode, start loading the config image, then if the config file says the device should be 4-wire then the FPGA config logic will switch the mode over and continue in the 4/8 wire modes. Similarly, the parallel flash config clock can also be controlled from a config image file—the device starts slow and can speed up. If the FPGA is a PCIe endpoint peripheral in a system, then the glue logic must hold the main processor in reset until the FPGA configuration is done, otherwise the BIOS will miss it and fail to enumerate the device. PCIe devices must be ready within 100ms from system reset. If we are designing an add-in card, then it has no control over the CPU reset, so the card must configure the FPGA within less than 100ms, so it has to use the fastest configuration methods that are available.

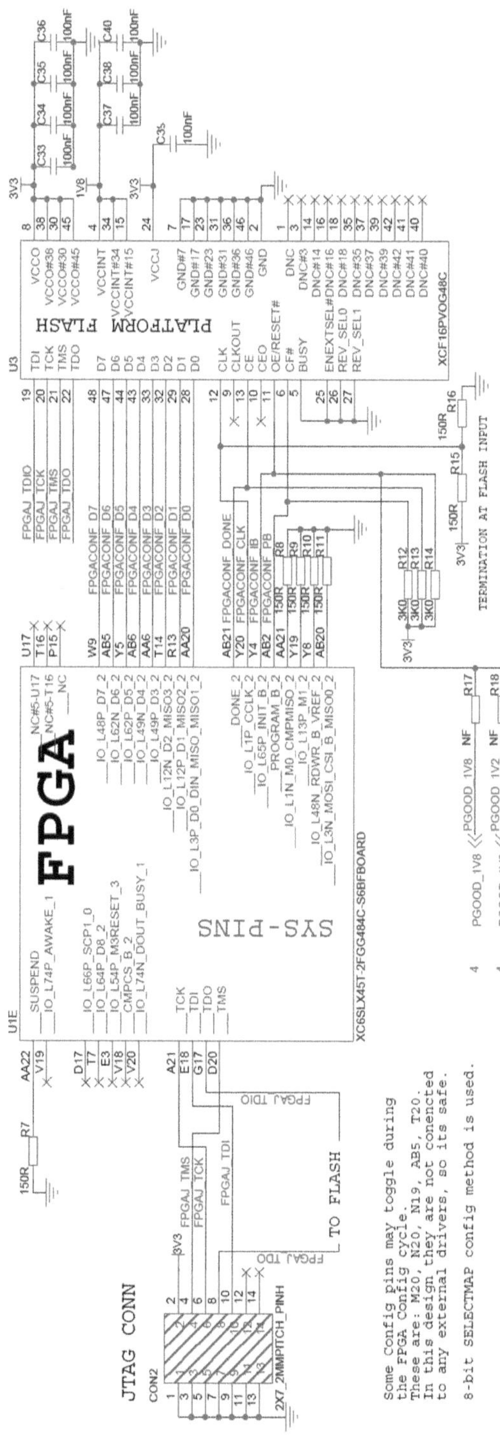

FIGURE 6.14 AMD (Xilinx) Spartan-6 configuration circuits with parallel Platform Flash.

Another interesting scheme was developed called CvP or configuration via protocol, when the FPGA loads a small logic configuration from flash after power on that contains a PCIe interface and not much more, then the real application code is loaded later by the local processor over PCIe into the device. This swap-out is called "partial reconfiguration". This way the real configuration data do not have to reside on the board in a flash chip; rather, they can be stored in the embedded processor's SDD drive securely. It also allows FPGAs to swap out their application when needed during run time. CvP can also be used for remote device re-programming or firmware upgrade, in that case, the initial image has to be a fully functional one.

Some AMD (Xilinx) FPGAs also implement hardware security, for example, configuration encryption. What it does is store an encoded image in the flash chip that cannot be reverse engineered. It is loaded into the FPGA, then the FPGA decrypts the image using the decryption key that was programmed inside the FPGA's ROM security key register during board manufacturing test.

AMD (Xilinx) FPGAs (and similarly Altera/Intel) have a few configuration-related signals that can be controlled or monitored by glue logic, to control or detect when the FPGA is operational. PROGRAM_B or PROG_B is an input to the FPGA; it starts configuration upon a low to high transition. Our glue logic can hold it low until all VRMs are fully up or until all our service logic is initialized. The INIT_B signal when used as an FPGA output, it signals that the internal initialization is in progress, then completed (goes high). The DONE or CONF_DONE output from the FPGA tells our glue logic that it is finished, and we can start the reset-de-assertion and OS boot sequences. Similarly, some devices have a CVP_CONF_DONE pin to be used when also using CvP. Any user logic reset input signals to the FPGA need to be held low until after the configuration was done to initialize the user logic registers to known states. There is also the config data interface with clock, data, and control signals. On FPGAs that contain CPUs too (ZYNQ, Versal, Agilex) it is a single boot flash interface for both FPGA fabric and CPU software code.

6.2.2 FPGA Families

The main FPGA vendors are AMD (acquired Xilinx), Intel (acquired Altera), Microchip (acquired Microsemi, earlier Actel), Lattice, and Achronix. These companies have several FPGA device families, they have new generations every few years marked with a number or tag, like Igloo-2, Stratix-10, or Virtex Ultrascale+. Each device family is a package deal of a certain range of logic resource amount and number and speed of SERDES transceiver lanes.

FPGAs come in all shapes and sizes. The larger and more expensive devices are used for data plane user data processing, while the very small FPGAs are used for power and system management and glue logic. Medium-size devices are used for control plane or lower performance data plane applications. We used to use devices called "CPLDs" with simplified internal fabric, but these days even the smallest of the modern devices are true FPGAs with distributed logic resources and routing elements in a matrix arrangement. The Microchip (acquired Actel/Microsemi) ProASIC and Igloo families and the Intel (acquired Altera) Max10 devices are popular for glue logic purposes. Microchip FPGA devices are flash-based, which means they do not need to perform a power-on configuration loading cycle, this way they are ready to perform immediately when the power is applied without delay. Although we still need to apply a power-on reset to our logic design for 1 to 10ms, but even during this our signals can have (constant) states defined by user code. This is very attractive for glue logic and system management applications. Small glue logic FPGAs come in 100 to 500 pin QFN and BGA packages. They are very low power and do not need a heatsink.

Larger FPGAs are meant for high-performance data plane processing, compute acceleration, network packet flow-through processing, and digitized communications RF waveform processing (software defined radio).

A list of FPGA families currently on the market:

- AMD (acquired Xilinx).
  - Spartan series, the smallest devices with very few low-speed transceivers, or no transceivers.
  - Artix series, one step up from Spartan.
  - Kintex, one step up from Artix.
  - Virtex, the largest FPGA devices with the fastest and largest lane count of transceivers.
  - ZYNQ is similar to Kintex, but with integrated ARM processors. The CPU is in charge, it boots first, then loads the FPGA fabric.
  - Versal is similar to ZYNQ, but with larger FPGA fabric and with AI acceleration hard IPs and 112G transceivers. The AI cores are meant to be controlled by the ARM processor.
- Intel (acquired Altera).
  - Max is the smallest and lowest power device for glue logic purposes, with no transceivers. Regular SRAM-based FPGA but with a bult-in config flash.
  - Cyclone, one step up from Max, with few slower transceivers.
  - Arria, one step up from Cyclone.
  - Stratix, the largest FPGA devices with the fastest and largest lane count of transceivers.
  - Agilex, large FPGAs for data center with 112Gbps transceivers and ARM CPUs.
- Microchip (acquired Microsemi, Actel).
  - RTG4, the radiation-hardened flash-based FPGA.
  - ProASIC, the older flash-based FPGA.
  - Igloo, most common flash-based FPGA for embedded glue logic applications.
  - Fusion, with built-in ADC.
  - PolarFire, mid-range processing FPGA.
- Achronix.
  - Speedster7t with 112Gbps transceivers.
- Lattice: Several families geared towards glue logic and low-power portable design.

6.2.3 FPGA Resources

FPGAs have several different "resources" inside of them that can be utilized by logic design. Smaller low-power FPGAs have less types of resources, as glue logic designs use only the basic CLB matrix and one or two global clocks. High-bandwidth data plane FPGAs utilize most or all of the available resource types. Sometimes there are separate manual documents for each resource type within the same FPGA device. Some of the more basic types of resources (like CLBs) are "inferred" by the synthesizer program, others have to be explicitly instantiated by the FPGA engineer in the code. Before selecting FPGA devices, we (the cross-functional team) need to know what type and how much of these resources will be needed in the design. The board hardware engineer controls the exact part number, so very clear communication and agreement with the FPGA team is required for the proper device selection. Board hardware designers have to deal with the IO banks and types, transceiver tiles, and clock capable pins in the board schematic design. Other resources like IO logic inside the IOBs and block RAMs are the responsibility of the FPGA engineers to utilize at the low level. Even if an area is the responsibility of the board hardware or the FPGA engineer, they have to work with their counterpart on exactly defining all of these. Before the design starts, the cross-functional team has to estimate the internal logic resource type usage to be able to fill out the power estimator spreadsheet because the rail currents and the power dissipation are an important board hardware design parameter.

Typical document titles from AMD (Xilinx):

- xx series FPGAs Memory Resources User Guide, describes how the block RAMs can be utilized.
- xx series FPGAs CLB User Guide, describes the core logic that is automatically configured by the synthesizer.
- xx series FPGAs SelectIO Resources User Guide, describes the IOB logic resources and IO pins and buffers.
- xx series FPGAs Clocking User Guide, describes the global and regional clock networks and how they can be utilized in a design, and shows the on-die location map of the regional clocks.
- xx series FPGAs Configuration User Guide, describes the different configuration modes, the supported flash devices, with pin and schematic connections.
- xx series FPGAs DSP slice User Guide.
- xx series FPGAs GTx Transceivers User Guide, describes how we can set up the transceivers for different protocols, and clocking schemes. The FPGA datasheet tells which type is on our selected device, GTP, GTH, …
- xx series FPGAs Packaging and Pinout Product Specification shows all density/package combination of devices, their IO bank locations on the package, the exact pinouts, IO buffer types, and mechanical package drawings. We also need to download pinout spreadsheet files.
- xx FPGAs Datasheet DC and AC switching characteristics—this will list the maximum achievable speeds and drive strengths on the different I/O protocols and transceiver pins (depending on speed grade and package type) and any transceiver speed limitations based on package type.
- xx FPGAs Datasheet Overview, the basics, listing features.
- xx series FPGAs Product selection Guide, it helps us select a device for density, package size, IO count and transceiver lane count.
- xx series FPGAs Integrated block for PCIe User Guide, the PCI-express endpoint hard IP and how to connect it to the user logic.
- xx series FPGAs Memory Controller User Guide, hard or soft memory controller, and how to connect it to user logic.
- xx Device Technical Reference Manual is a very long document explaining the operation and structure of hard-processor-based devices.

6.2.3.1 Global Clocks (GCKs)

On-chip FPGA logic designs are always implemented as common clock synchronous systems. The logic implementation while utilizing the CLB resources (multiplexers and flip-flops) require the same clock signal to be delivered to each CLB flip-flop at the same time. They can be delivered in the same time (aka low skew) if the clock is implemented on the silicon die as a tree topology, driven by a strong buffer circuit. So a global clock (design object) is the traces that reach every flip-flop on the die, with the buffer circuit that drives it. FPGA documentation often refers to it as a clock buffer, but really it is a buffer and an extensive tree-shaped trace structure. The compilation tools will assign (infer) a global clock network to a signal if it is used by many flip-flops (high fanout). Regional or I/O clock networks have to be manually assigned in VHDL code for timing critical I/O interface logic. One FPGA has a limited number of global clocks, but a good design would not use too many different clock domains. Other signals like resets can also be assigned to global clock networks. A global clock network can be driven by a PLL or by any internally generated signal, but often we drive them from global clock (GCK) input pins, which are a small subset of the regular bank I/O pins that have dedicated routing resources to the global clock buffer inputs.

6.2.3.2 Regional Clocks

Regional clocks work similarly to global clock networks, they have buffers, they have regional clock capable chip input pins, but they span only a small portion of the chip. The I/O clock networks only reach IOBs and adjacent CLBs, but not most of the core logic. The advantage of this is to be able to use low-jitter high-frequency clocks at even lower skew than the GCKs have, which are not slowed down by having to span the whole chip surface. They are typically used by small blocks of logic or by circuits in the IOBs, for example, high-performance I/O interfaces like DDRx memory. Some of the hard IP cores like the Spartan-6 PCIe endpoint block also rely on I/O or regional clocks for their core logic interface. Sometimes they are inferred by the synthesizer, at other times we have to put a macro or "primitive" into our code to use one and a placement constraint in the constraint file to associate an exact instance on the silicon die to the instance in our code. The naming convention is automatic—we have to find the instances in a GUI assignment editor so we can create the constraint with that instead of typing it into a text file from scratch. The clocking manuals list all the names of every instance (for example BUFIO2_X4Y20 on an AMD (Xilinx) Spartan-6 device) that can help us familiarize with it before using the editor. This can be seen in Figure 6.15 copied from the Xilinx Sparatan-6 clocking manual. All the PLLs and DCMs are centrally located. The global clocks are listed as BUFGMUX_X*Y*, the I/O clocks are labeled as BUFIO2_X*Y*, the global capable pins are listed as GCK*. The diagram also shows which I/O clock or BUFIO2 is located in which half of which I/O bank. Another diagram or table would list which pins belong to which BUFIO2 region. These buffers have a few inputs and outputs, with phase delays and signal types—make sure to look

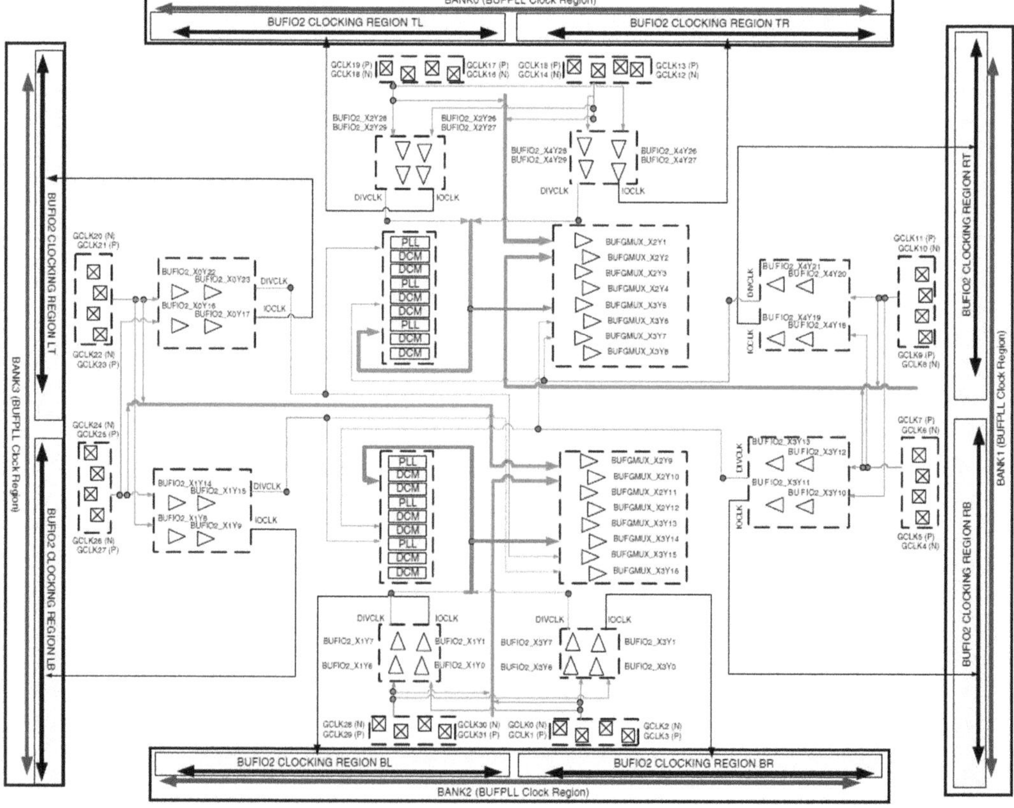

FIGURE 6.15 Device clocking resources, from Spartan-6 FPGA Clocking Resources User Guide, copyright June 2015, courtesy of AMD.

up the manual for finding out which ones we need in our application, if instantiating them in the code, instead of relying on the synthesizer to infer them.

6.2.3.3 PLLs, DCMs, and CMTs

Phase-locked loops (PLLs), digital clock managers (DCM), and clock management tiles (CMTs) can be used at the input of a clock network's buffer to create a different frequency (multiplication or scaling down) or to create a phase delay such that the clock network trace ends will be in phase with the input clock signal. PLLs can create a zero-phase-delay clock network, which is useful when we want a common clock synchronous system to be free of buffer delay to maximize the clock frequency or to minimize chip's input/output setup and hold requirements for a parallel external interface. In clock signals every period is the same. It is very predictable, so zero-phase-delay is created by taking the input signal that was already delayed by t_pd, and delaying it by an additional tDEL=tCLK-tpd, so the total delay is an exact clock cycle, which looks identical the clock without any delay. The I/O clock on a common clock or clock forwarding interface has to be routed to many flip-flops, which can be done only with a clock tree that has a very long delay, which can be eliminated using a PLL. Some AD and DA converter chips require a delayed clock to compensate for board level trace delay, which can be implemented by FPGA PLLs. PLLs can also create a -tX negative delay by delaying the clock by as much as tCLK-tX. PLLs only work if the clock is free-running, and it never goes idle between bus transactions, as they have to lock to the input clock, which can take thousands of clock cycles. Figure 6.16 shows how a PLL can be used to provide a clock signal to our interface logic with zero phase delay.

6.2.3.4 Block RAM Memory

A few kilobytes of RAM memory can be found in each these embedded block RAMs that are distributed throughout the FPGA die. They can be combined to larger sizes, and they can be used as simple RAM, dual port RAM, or FIFO. Many applications need data buffering between interface logic and core logic, sometimes with clock domain isolation. Soft processors need internal RAM. We can configure them to the mode and size we need using a core generator GUI (IP catalog), then the resulting VHDL code file can be added to our project and instantiated in our design code as a submodule.

6.2.3.5 DSP Slices

Many signal processing applications rely on multiply accumulate (MAC) units like the DSP processors have. High-end FPGAs contain hundreds of these MAC slices that they call DSP slices, which can be freely utilized in core logic design. FPGAs can implement many parallel pipelined signal processing paths to process more signal streams than DSP processor chips can with their single MAC unit.

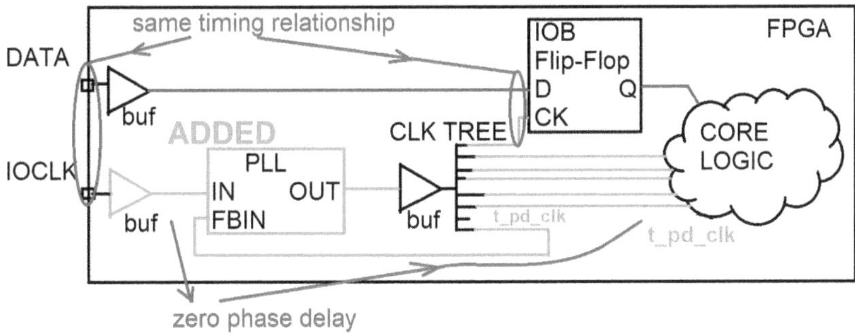

FIGURE 6.16 I/O clocking timing correction with a PLL.

6.2.3.6 Hard IPs

Many FPGAs contain hard IP cores for complex interfaces, for example, PCI-Express, CXL, CCIX, DDRx memory interfaces, sometimes hard processors (ARM or power PC). They can be configured for the mode and size (lane count) we need using the development tool GUI and instantiate them in our VHDL code. If it is to work with an external memory device, then we have to look up the IP core manual to find out what part numbers of devices are supported. Some of the hard IPs have fixed device pinout requirement, they cannot be freely assigned to any pins, the correct pinout should be listed in one of the documents.

6.2.3.7 I/O Logic

All the I/O pins (excluding SERDES pins) of an FPGA are grouped into I/O banks. All pins of the same bank have to use the same I/O voltage, and different banks can have different voltages. Different I/O standards can be assigned to pins within a bank, as long as they are defined by the same VIO voltage. Each bank has VIO pins that have to be supplied by the chosen I/O voltage from an on-board VRM. Device datasheets describe IO bank types within the same device, and the limitations of each type, like maximum I/O voltage, maximum drive current and support for ODT. The IO resources guides show tables of which bank (by bank number) is which type. ODT is the On-Die Termination, or digitally controlled impedance (DCI) that can be enabled or disabled on the fly by the interface logic IP, if we selected one of the I/O standards that relies on it. The design engineers have to ensure to assign the signal name within IO banks that have support for the buffer types and parameters we need for a particular bus or signal. This has to be verified through several documents, like the datasheet (bank types and limitations) and the IO users guide (for bank number to bank type table and bank to package pin area mapping diagram). Most FPGAs support both single-ended and differential signaling, where the negative pin has to be associated with the positive pin in the pin editor. A buffer has three pins towards the core logic and one pin on the package. The internal pins are input, output and output_enable, all three have to be hooked up in our logic code design as unidirectional signals. Bi-directional signals only exist on boards, none are inside FPGA silicon, they stop at the pin. The maximum data rate on these basic IO pins varies by device family between 100MHz and 1GHz, much lower than the SERDES transceivers that can go 3 to 100Gbps, also depending on device family. The SERDES interfaces are not implemented on the general IO banks—they have separate package pin groups.

The IOBs of medium- to high-performance FPGAs contain a lot of logic that help implementing high-performance I/O interfaces. This logic has to be in close proximity to the external pins to achieve high performance and good reliability with short delay and low skew. The most basic one is the IOB flip-flop. The IOB FF has a short delay path from the external pin to terminate the timing path of the external signal, reducing the input and output setup and hold times of the FPGA chip to a minimum. The automatic synthesis might not utilize the IOB FFs, which can result in long setup/hold times, but usually there is a setting we need to enable to "pack IOB FFs". To support DDR memory interfaces, there are also double data rate or DDR flip-flops, which are similar to a regular IOB D-flip-flop but capture or launch data at two clock edges instead of one. The ISERDES and OSERDES primitives are small cascadable shift registers found inside IOBs that help with more serialized interfaces, like LVDS display panel ports. These are not the main multi-gigabit SERDES transceiver tiles, despite the similar name. Those have CDR and DFE circuits to work with embedded clock protocols, while IOB logic does not have these and need I/O clock signals on the PCB. Many of these FFs, DDR FFs, and shift registers can be clocked by regional clocks that only span near a portion of the IOB area of the chip to help with reducing jitter and skew and improve the maximum data rate. Basic interfaces can be generated using a core generator GUI; it will pick up the right I/O logic and regional clock resources and generate VHDL/Verilog code with these instantiated and configured. The IO buffers support single-ended and differential, Vref-based and regular I/O buffers, selectable in the pin editor. On die termination, pull-up resistor and delay DLLs can also be enabled in IOBs, although some of the banks do not support some of these features.

When we are using one of the advanced I/O technologies, then some of the nearby pins become analog pins. For example, they may require us to connect a calibration resistor to allow ODT (DCI) calibration after power up, or they may require a reference voltage source at half the VIO rail's voltage level. The pin assignment of these is fixed, within each I/O bank, the datasheets should show their location.

6.2.3.8 SERDES Transceiver Tiles

FPGAs have two types of I/O pins: The regular I/O banks where a configurable buffer is located at each pin, and the SERDES tiles where an embedded-frame embedded-clock shift register transceivers are located. Several analog circuits and physical-layer protocol logic are provided. The SERDES can usually also run 5 to 100 times faster data rates compared to the regular I/O bank pins.

SERDES or transceiver tiles provide a few lanes of multi-gigabit serialized I/O. One FPGA may have multiple tiles to a total number of lanes listed in the product selection guide. These tiles are described in the chapter about Basic Digital Circuits and SERDES IP. They contain dedicated clocking, clock-data-recovery (for embedded clock protocols), serializers, equalizers, PCS (encoding), and PMA logic as needed by complex interface protocols like PCI-Express and Ethernet. The SERDES tiles will likely utilize special regional clocks at the core logic (user) interface. In many cases (especially on older and cheaper FPGAs) the clock region assignment is rigid, and the user has to specify which instance will be assigned, using a placement constraint. Different FPGA families contain different SERDES tile types, each type has a name like GTP or GTM and a maximum speed rating. Datasheet tables might further limit their speed on certain package types.

6.2.3.9 Hard Processor IPs

AMD (Xilinx) ZYNQ and Versal devices and the Intel Agilex devices include ARM processor hard IP cores. But these devices are actually not FPGAs with optional processor cores; rather, they are processors with an optional FPGA fabric (programmable logic block, PL) that the processor will initialize and may reload in run time. The FPGA fabric is only a flexible peripheral, not the main controller, and we cannot control the processor subsystem with soft FPGA logic. With AMD (Xilinx) devices it is a clear hierarchy: The processor boots first, then the PL is loaded by the processor. Intel's Agilex device is a bit more flexible than AMD—the developer can choose whether the FPGA fabric or the hard ARM processor user software should be loaded first, through config file soft straps defined after compilation. The CPU ROM code runs first, but we do not have to customize that one.

The CPU subsystem, or should it be called CPU master-system, has its own I/O banks. Even the configuration signals (now called boot signals) are moved to the CPU I/O bank's multipurpose pins. This includes boot source strapping, boot flash interface signals, other strapping and CPU interfaces (console, I2C...). The description of these pins can be found in the Device Technical Reference Manual or the reference schematic, not in the Packaging and Pinout Spec with the traditional pinout. ARM processors require certain external connections, like DRAM chips, serial console, and USB other interfaces. These devices also contain additional management and security processors, which are less powerful and concerned with system initialization and they need a firmware too.

The processor needs to load custom software, including the bootloader(s) and the operating system (ARM Linux). After the device has powered up the ARM processor executes a fixed ROM software code that reads the boot mode strapping pins. It then reads the boot header structure from the boot flash memory chip. After this it loads several user-compiled code images like a management processor software, the first stage boot loader software (FSBL created and configured by the tools), ARM trusted firmware (Versal only), the FPGA config file, the second stage boot loader (open-source U-Boot) software, and the operating system software (open-source Linux). The FSBL initializes the memory interfaces, so it has to be configured to match the custom board design, and it must succeed with the memory initialization to ensure allowing the rest to boot. Any subsequent software will be loaded into the external DRAM and executed from there. All this is contained in the same flash memory chip, attached to the processor I/O bank pins. In most cases the software, including the OS is small enough to fit in a few gigabytes QSPI flash chip. We need to have a serial console for commanding the Linux, and a method of copying files to the system during development, over USB, Ethernet, or micro-SD card. These interfaces will likely only be used in development and manufacturing, but not by the end users. JTAG programming of Gbit size flash memories can take tens of minutes.

With Intel Agilex the FPGA fabric image loading can be done before any custom software and loaded by the ROM code. Older device families like the AMD (Xilinx) Virtex-5 with its PowerPC hard processor core did not have a software-driven configuration scheme, it configured like a regular FPGA, and the processor block only connected to external devices through user-defined soft FPGA logic. For them a simpler sequence was followed: power on, load FPGA config, CPU reset by user logic, load bootloader and load OS. Basically, the FPGA fabric controlled the CPU boot, unlike what the new devices have where the CPU controls the FPGA config cycle. The same is true for soft processor IP cores, they are also subordinate to soft logic.

The development flow requires software engineering up front, at least the FSBL has to be customized to match our board design (like DRAM parameters) before the prototype would arrive. In many cases the U-Boot and the OS also needs to be fully working before we could start testing the FPGA fabric logic design.

The board design and the prototype bring-up sequence is more similar to the methodology used for processor boards than the one used for traditional FPGA boards. On processor boards we have to connect interfaces and devices to pins based on where the software expects them, instead of using any random suitable assignment based on a datasheet. The board bring-up involves debugging the software for boot-hang issues, caused by the software expecting different connections or memory part numbers than our custom prototype has. The only clue for what the software might expect is the device evaluation board schematics, just like it is for X86 processors and ARM microcontrollers. Theoretically it is possible to fully customize the software, but these bootloaders and OS drivers are so complex, having been developed for years, that, in practice, all we (the software engineering department) can do is to make a few small changes. Processor board designs are not started from scratch; rather, they are based on an eval board, and each deviation item from it has to be accounted for in a spreadsheet. The project schedule also has to account for the processor-related and hardware-software debugging activities described above.

6.2.4 FPGA Pinout Planning

We need to come up with an FPGA pinout that meets several requirements, like schematic design convenience, board rout-ability (match the floorplan, low layer usage, good return path), and silicon I/O timing performance. Slow-signal glue logic FPGA designs usually follow only the schematic-based aspects. Memory interfaces are very sensitive to the silicon I/O timing. All other types of designs focus on the PCB design aspects for pin assignments. Schematic convenience is best seen in the board schematic drawing, like functional signal groupings assigned in the same drawing area and adjacent pins in a visual sequence on the schematic symbol. Board rout-ability is best seen in the device pin assignment editor in the package view of the FPGA GUI, to avoid signal crossings, reduce crosstalk, and plan our fanout layer usage into pin rows or columns. The hardware engineer has to insert the FPGA I/O bank diagram into the board floorplan to determine which signal groups should be assigned to which I/O bank for routing without crossings. This is also how we can review prototype ASIC pin assignments for the ASIC team, although there we also control the ground pin placement. The I/O performance is best seen on the pin assignment GUI but in the silicon die view by assigning functional signal groups (byte lanes, buses) to have adjacent die pads without skipping or interleaving with other interfaces. It is also important to align them within the boundaries of I/O clock network regions, so it does not have to span across.

We have to check the pinout of the actual device part number in terms of bank numbers, pin types, and pin names in the pinout document. For AMD (Xilinx) it is the "[device family name] Packaging and Pinouts Product Specification" document. Each density/package option has its own pinout (device diagrams) and mechanical drawing (to verify if the device diagram was mirrored). We have to make sure we are looking at the drawing from the direction of the board top side, not the die top side, because flip chip BGAs are upside down in the BGA package. Some vendors provide die view images instead of top-down images.

In the first step of the pinout work we assign I/O banks and transceiver tiles to buses in a board-floorplan in a graphical editor. See the chapter about initial design and floor planning. We can find the relevant I/O bank device diagram in the FPGA documentation, take a screenshot, then paste it into an image editor like MS Paint. It is likely found in the Packaging and Pinout Product Specification. We also have to check which bank supports which buffer type, or which bank is which bank type, in various tables or diagrams. Different bank types have different feature sets and capability (max voltage, termination, drive strength). In the MS Paint basic graphical editor, we can mark up the screenshot (from the document) with lines, rectangles, and text, about which buses we want in each I/O bank or SERDES tile. An example of this marked up screenshot can be seen in Figure 6.17. Then finally we can paste this marked up diagram into our hardware spec and into the board floorplan to see if the pins are on the correct sides of the FPGA device to avoid crossing buses and long traces. Crossing costs extra layers in the stackup, as we cannot change layers mid-route with SERDES lanes for SI, with memory signals the added via length messing up the skew, with other buses the large number of signals would require hundreds of signal and ground vias taking up board space and destroy localization causing crosstalk.

In the second step of the pinout job, we assign exact pin numbers to every individual signal. It might be done in the board schematic first, followed by the FPGA pin editor, or the other way around, depending on project arrangements and high-speed features. The FPGA code has to be synthesized first, otherwise the GUI will not allow us to use the pin assignment editor, but we can have dummy logic and a full top level VHDL/Verilog file. Make sure the clocks are used as clock, which forces the checker to check clock rout-ability on the chip. Some companies' component

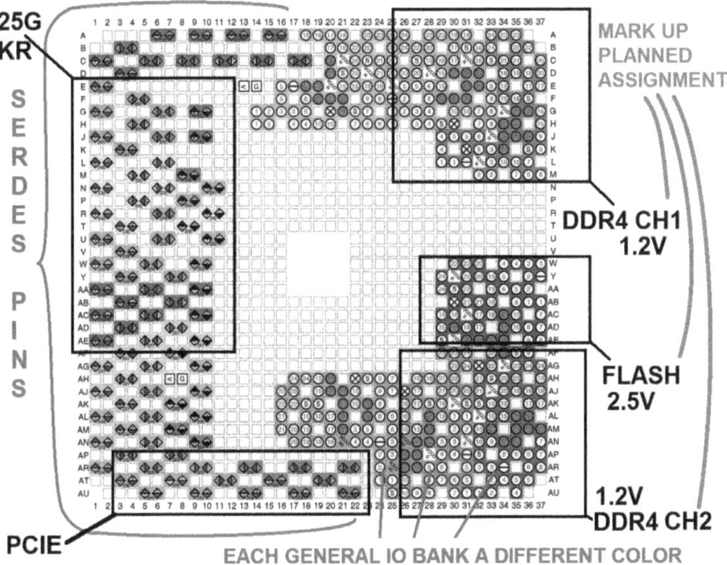

FIGURE 6.17 I/O Bank assignment in progress for a made-up project in a graphical editor using a screenshot of a XCVU23P device package I/O Bank Diagram. Original image from UltraScale and UltraScale+ FPGAs Packaging and Pinouts Product Specification, copyright April 2022, courtesy of AMD.

libraries allow for creating custom schematic symbols for each FPGA project, which allows us to meet all SI, timing and board routing needs first but still end up with a nice readable board schematic. Custom schematic symbols are usually created by first converting the pin constraints text file into an Excel spreadsheet manually in a text editor, then importing that into the schematic library tool. We have to manually format the spreadsheet from the FPGA tool's format to the schematic tool's format, in terms of columns, assign sub-symbol numbers, and finally merge it with the ground/power portion of the pin list from a device pinout file from the FPGA vendor. For memory interfaces and other high-speed parallel buses, we need to pack pins of the same byte lane in close proximity as seen on the die pad view (they are located around the perimeter of the die, not in a grid) to improve static timing (chip-level skew), and to keep them within the same I/O clock region, which cannot be done in the schematic or the package view. After the bank assignment is determined, in some cases we might have to do a combined method for the detailed pinout, assigning the hard-IP-related pins in the schematic first, while the high-speed general I/O signals in the GUI (package view and die view), the low-speed signals either in the schematic or the GUI.

There is a board route ability aspect of the exact pinout also; it is not only needed for the bank assignment from the floorplan. This comes up with wide buses like memory interfaces or large backplane connectors. Signal crossings on the board are costly in terms of extra layers and work hours. The hardware engineer can define the bit ordering in a diagram, and the FPGA engineer (or the hardware engineer) can assign pins accordingly in the GUI. This file will contain the assignment of top level VHDL/Verilog ports to device pin numbers, I/O standards, drive strength, and other details. It might also contain hard macro locations, such as which of the two PCIe cores our RTL block has to be placed into. For larger interfaces like a 72bit DDR4 memory we need to define which I/O bank and which corner of which bank should be used for which byte lane and the address bus. Further, within each group we need to indicate the bit ordering, such as 0 to 7 left to right or right to left. The partial or full floorplan would show first the DIMM or chip memory (photo) and the FPGA device diagram side by side. We would mark up the signal names on the memory, then as a straight projection also on the FPGA side. The memory signal names and their relative positions can be looked up in JESD21C standards and reference design files. We can create diagrams to help us see which signal goes near which pin, like the one in Figure 6.18. In AMD (Xilinx) Vivado we can create a pin planning project and import a constraint file. We can find an example constraint file and edit it by adding our own signals into it in Excel or text editor. Then in Vivado we can drag and drop signals from the signal list view onto the package view diagram's pin locations. Basically, while keeping our diagram and the GUI side by side, we can manually place the pins to match the drawing.

The detailed pinout must be validated by a full compilation before board fab-out, ideally before the board schematic is done. During the compilation we might find that some signals cannot really be assigned to the pins that we wanted, or they cannot have the termination type we wanted, or the I/O logic has no available regional clock network nearby. They will come up during compilation and the FPGA engineer will have to swap pins/banks to get it compiled, then we also have to update the board schematic and layout with the pinout change. This has to be a full compilation ending with a bitstream file, not just a synthesis. We have to check all the warnings and errors in the synthesis and implementation (map, place, and route) logs. There might be warnings about a typo in a constraint, but when that is fixed and the constraint is finally enforced, we might see a resource conflict that needs to be resolved with design or pinout change. Some errors are masking other errors, so we cannot dismiss them with a plan to fix them later.

During the PCB layout design, the layout engineer might request pin swapping to resolve trace routing issues. In that case we have to swap pins in the pin editor and check whether the new pinout still meets the FPGA speed requirements. If not, then respond with a compromise pinout proposal. We cannot swap between I/O banks. We should keep memory lane pins in an arrangement that results in routing one lane on one layer to avoid having vias with different lengths.

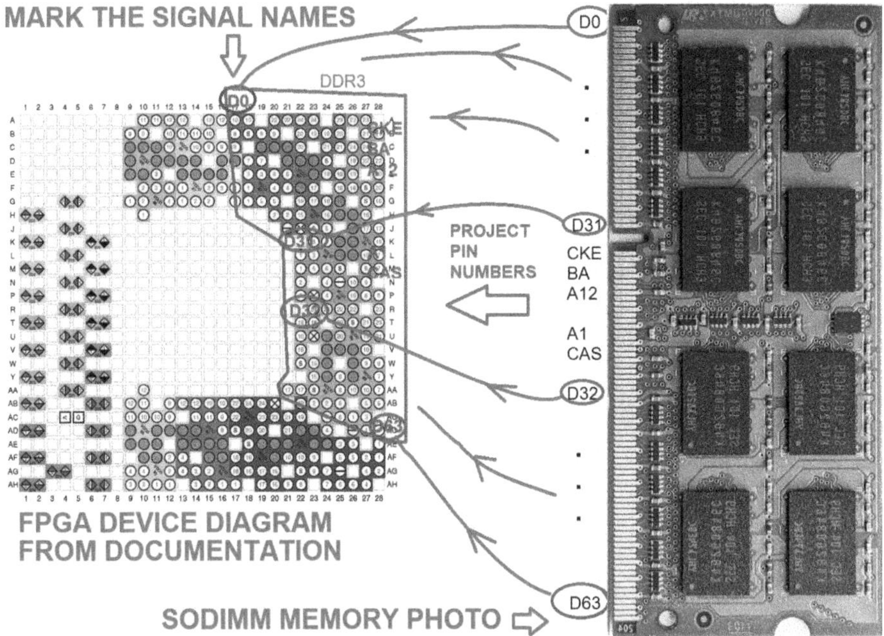

FIGURE 6.18 Example memory interface pin ordering diagram for a made-up project in a graphical editor using a screenshot of a XCAU25P device package I/O Bank Diagram. Original image from UltraScale and UltraScale+ FPGAs Packaging and Pinouts Product Specification, copyright April 2022, courtesy of AMD.

Pinout Rules:

- The device we choose has to have more I/O pins than we think we need, maybe 10% to 60% more. We will likely have to add signals to it during the design.
- Signals of different VCC I/O voltage need to be in different I/O banks. The VCCIO pins need to be connected in schematic to the correct voltage rail, depending on I/O standard in the bank.
- The configuration interface uses dedicated pins but might also use pins from I/O banks. In that case it forces us to use the required VIO power rail in that bank, which might cross our plans of using certain types of signals in that bank.
- FPGA devices have one or more different I/O bank types. Different types have different capabilities, like maximum output buffer drive current, maximum I/O voltage, and IO resources (on die termination, reference voltage) availability. Device documents list the available I/O banks types, and tables show which bank number is which type. The number of available I/O pins of the type we need has to be larger than what we need. For AMD (Xilinx), we have to check the driver type capabilities in the "SelectIO Resources" user guide document, the number of I/Os in the device selection guides. Some FPGAs do not have many or any 3.3V capable I/O banks, while 3.3V is needed on most glue logic signals and low-speed buses like I2C.
- Fast interfaces like DDRx require skew-timing-driven pin assignment. All signals of the same byte lane must be on adjacent die pads and within the same I/O clock region to minimize skew between the signals in the group.
- If not all SERDES links are used, then assign the ones that avoid crossing, and the ones that would have the shortest route on the board (floor plan). Use the inner rows, as some devices have incomplete G-S-S-G pin pattern for outer row signal pins for which we cannot maintain proper via and pin impedance.

- Board-level reference clocks are needed from a clock generator, not from on-chip PLLs, due to jitter concerns. Each memory interface channel may or may not need a reference clock, the board design should provide a direct external differential reference clock to each channel to an input pin that is capable of driving local and global I/O clock networks. Each SERDES interface needs one differential reference clock with very low jitter to the dedicated TRX refclock pins. One core ref clock is needed to a "global clock input" capable pin.
- Some buses can be assigned only to certain banks or pins, if they rely on a hard IP (like PCIe, DDR4 controllers) that is at a fixed location on the silicon die near certain pins.

6.2.5 Development Flow

The code development, IP core generation or customization, simulation, and compilation are done in the vendor-provided GUI or in a Linux command line toolset. AMD (Xilinx) used to provide the ISE Webpack, but it has been discontinued and the Vivado toolset has been created. Microchip (Microsemi, Actel) uses the Libero tools, Intel (Altera) has the Quartus tools. The development flow is complex, even after the code writing is done, we have to execute several compilation steps, debug the code and constraints based on error messages from each step, running simulations, and add logic analyzer setups and generate files. This is demonstrated in Figure 6.19.

The code for small glue logic FPGAs is sometimes developed by the board hardware design engineer and at other times by an FPGA engineer. The code for control plane and data plane FPGAs is mostly developed by full-time FPGA teams. The board hardware engineer has to work with the

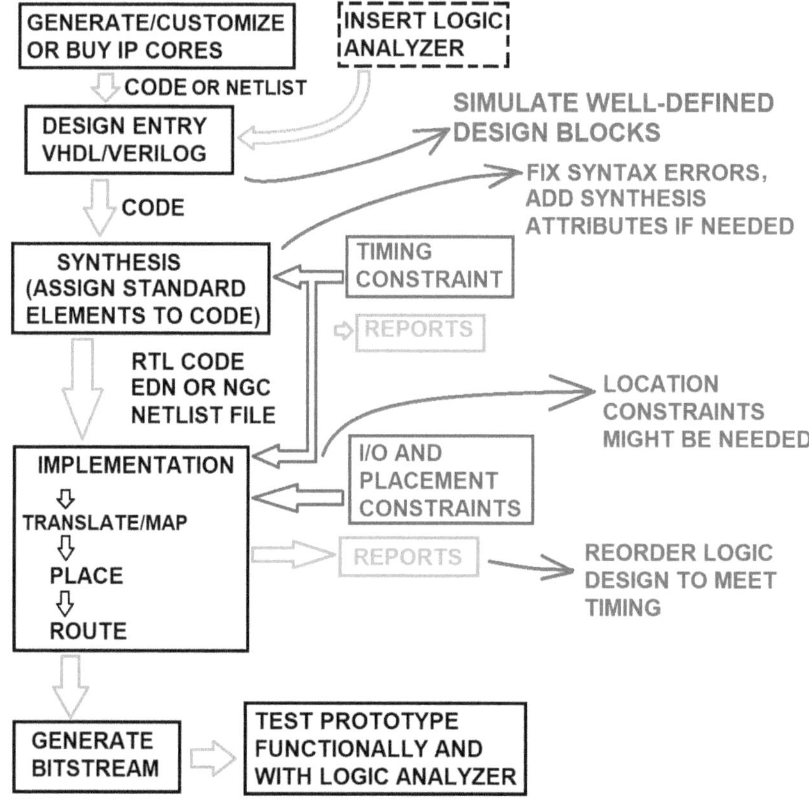

FIGURE 6.19 FPGA design and compilation flow.

FPGA team in defining the major blocks, interfaces, clocking scheme, and pinout. At the beginning of the FPGA project, we have to determine the main functional block diagram of the chip-level logic design and the IP cores we need to write or re-use. An IP is a well-defined functional block, called intellectual property. Every external interface requires a bus controller IP, plus some of the internal functions also require IP blocks. We have to determine the hardware-software partitioning of the FPGA logic, as some features can be implemented on a soft or hard processor, but they can also be implemented in VHDL/Verilog code, depending on project schedule, device cost, and available skillset. Some of the data plane designs require large buffering, so we need to determine the needed external memory interfaces. The number of memory channels, the width of each channel, and the memory chip density in Gbits, speed and type (DDR3, DDR4, QDR…) need to be determined. How many and how wide external memory channels we can have comes down to the pinout analysis, checking the number of suitable I/O banks and their pin counts. The maximum speed achievable using the same FPGA device on a 72bit interface is usually lower than on a 32bit or 16bit interface. We have to choose external components like DRAM and flash chips that work with the interface cores, seen from the core config wizard GUI. When all interfaces and core blocks are known, we have to determine how many and what type of external clocks will need to be provided to the FPGA by board-level clocking circuits. The next step is to estimate the required logic resources, the required I/O pins of different types (with current drive capability, DCI/ODT and voltage), and transceiver lanes and speeds. From that we can select a device part number and fill out the power estimator spreadsheet that helps us select the supporting VRMs.

The I/O pin assignment, the clocking, and the device-size-fit have to be validated before the board schematics or layout design is finished. While writing the FPGA code, we might find that we need additional signals from the board, so we have to update the pinout file and the board schematic. Sometimes we have to move signals to different pins to allow the use of internal hard macro resources or to improve static timing. These are the main reasons why we need a full compilation done before the board fab-out files can be released for manufacturing. These changes cannot be done after the board has been made or it is half-way through the manufacturing process. This is why a skeleton code compilation is a mandatory gating item for the board fab release. A skeleton code has all the pins of the final full FPGA logic design, has some of its hard IPs, clocks and I/O logic in place, but not necessarily have all the fully simulated complete core logic in it. Up to this point it is cross-functional teamwork, after this the FPGA team has to work out the details. During prototype bring-up it becomes cross-functional work again. In the case of glue logic FPGAs, we need the full code in place before board fab-out, not just a skeleton code.

The detailed logic design starts with generating and customizing cores, including basic I/O interfaces as well as generating wrapper code for hard IPs. A wrapper code instantiates a full IP core, sets many of its ports to user choice values, and only the functional ports are routed to the wrapper's top level port list. Once all the generated cores, wrappers, and new code files are put together, the compilation and simulation start. In simulation some of the new code can be tested as to whether they will work in assumed conditions, but a prototype testing and debugging will be needed later. For prototype testing the FPGA engineer might have to put logic analyzer (AMD/Xilinx ChipScope Pro, Microchip Identify, Intel SignalTap) hooks into the design, which can extract information over JTAG.

The compilation is not simple, the tools will produce many error messages that require the FPGA designer to alter the code or write placement and timing constraint files to eliminate errors, warnings, and timing violations. Most tools use the standard SDC format for timing constraints, while others use their own format, like the old Xilinx ISE used the UCF file format for it—now they use XDC. Area and primitive (like clock network/buffer instance) placement constraints usually go into the same vendor specific constraint file that contains the pinout in text format. They are not always used. The pinout constraints define which top level port is assigned to which device package pin, as well as other parameters for each pin like I/O standard (LVDS/CMOS/SSTL), output drive, terminations, and pullups. The graphical pin assignment editor GUI writes into the text constraint file. Most timing constraints are concerned with clock nets, meaning all signals launched by flip-flops that are clocked by the defined clock signal will get setup and hold timing analysis performed automatically, or concerned with I/O buffer delay limits. Chip-level (core logic) designs are always the "common clock synchronous" type. There are manuals on constraint file syntax, while many constraints can be created in a GUI or table editor. It might take a month to fix a design to a point that it will finally compile without errors. An altered version of the design can be tested out on an FPGA evaluation board, which has a different pinout and possibly different set of interfaces. This necessitates the FPGA team to maintain two similar FPGA designs.

The compilation has several distinct phases. The code we write is called the RTL (register transfer level code in VHDL or in Verilog language). The code we write can contain basic logic equations and flip-flops directly defined, but most of the time we write "behavioral" code, which looks similar to C programming, but it does not generate a linear step by step execution; rather, it generates a set of parallel digital logic circuits. In synthesis the RTL code is transformed into a set of low-level logic equations and hard macro types (like CLB flip-flops, multiplexers, or DRAM controller IPs). In the implementation phase these hard macro types get assigned to actual hard macro instances of the chosen device, the routing element switch configurations get set, and the I/O bank types get verified with the pinout constraints. During the synthesis we might get errors or warnings about syntax, bad synchronous description, missing assignments, missing signals from sensitivity list. These have to be fixed in the code and re-synthesized. Some of the issues, especially the ones related to clocks, require the designer to write a few "synthesis attributes" into the VHDL code, which forces the synthesizer to make the right decision about inferring or not inferring clock networks or certain buffer types to high-fanout signals. As we are moving forward with implementation phase, which consists of "Translate", "Map", "Placement", and "Routing" stages, we might get more obscure errors. Some of them can be resolved by adjusting the settings for each of these stages, for example "allow impossible" or "keep hierarchy". Placement errors on clocks and I/O logic can be resolved by defining exact locations/instances for clock networks/buffers, and I/O logic elements in placement constraint files. For example, if only one clock network is available for the internal parallel bus of a hard IP block (seen in the IP or clocking user guide), and the placer places another clock net to it, then later when it needs to place the IP's parallel clock, there will be no suitable location/instance left, unless we specify to place that one at the designated location, so it cannot place another one there. Sometimes we get errors about input clock pins if we assigned them to non-clock capable input pin numbers. In this case we have to change the pinout in both the constraint file and the board schematic.

If we get timing violations, then we have to re-order some of the logic. For example, we have to break up long decoding chains by inserting registers (flip-flops) and decoding a portion in one clock cycle and storing it in a register/variable, then the remaining portion on the next clock cycle into a new register/variable, aka register balancing and pipelining. Sometimes we need to create an area constraint to help meeting the timing, at other times we need to delete a constraint that is too restrictive. We need to try to parallelize some of the decoding, for example using "case" instead of "if then else", as seen in the next section. Sometimes we get un-routed net error, if the net has to go to too many loads, but if we manually assign a clock buffer to it that could resolve the issue. If we need to use regional clocks for high performance, then we have to instantiate them in the code as well as define their locations on the die using a placement constraint.

At the end we have to review all reports, especially the timing analysis reports for any violation (none can remain), the resource utilization report (all resources must be well under 100%), and any other reports for errors or warnings. Many of the errors and warnings are non-issues, we can manually ignore them one by one, or we can find a setting to suppress certain types of them. Typically, in a list of 300 warnings there might be four4 that are legitimate, but we have to find these needles in the haystack by reading the reports fully.

Weird stuff might occur during compilation. For example, the tools un-assign some of our signals from the pins, then they assign a constant low output drive or automatically assign them to different pin numbers. This can happen for two reasons: the first is the signal is unused in our design so the synthesizer eliminates the signal, at the next step it assigns the constant low to unused pins. This can wreck a prototype board, but it can be avoided by going to the compilation settings and disable the option for "assign output low to unused pins" or by connecting the signal to a readable register bit or debug shift register. The other cause might be that the tools have some bugs, then what we can do is to go to the pin assignment editor after compilation and verify that our original pinout is still intact. Sometimes the simple external interface we designed uses a CLB flip-flop for capturing the on-board signal, causing bad setup or hold timing on the board level interface. What we can do is to find the setting on "pack IOB flip-flops" and enable it or place macros of IOB flip flops into the code.

6.2.5.1 Logic Design

It is important to learn about logic design techniques, such as they are described in several books like *Advanced FPGA Design* from Steve Kilts, that discuss reliability and speed-related phenomenon caused by code structures, like throughput, parallelism, flattening, register balancing, path reordering, I/O registers, resets, clock domain crossing (double flopping, FIFOs, or handshaking), combinatorial loops, inferred latches, edge detection, and meta stability. A few of these are discussed below.

FPGAs contain our custom logic design, that is a combination of flip-flops, multiplexers, logic gates, and their connections described in several VHDL or Verilog source code files. One of the source code files is designated as the top level file, its ports are all assigned to the FPGA device pins in the pin constraints file. All other source files are instantiated into the top level file or into any file that is instantiated into the top level file in a hierarchical fashion. All files have ports to connect upwards in the hierarchy. They may have blocs referring to other source files down in the hierarchy defined and instantiated. Internal "signals" are defined in each source file, which are just connections within a block, or if they are given values in clocked statements then they become registers (flip-flops). Hard IP cores are instantiated like source files, except a source file does not exist for them. Most of the time they are instantiated in a wrapper source file, generated by the core configurator GUI, then we instantiate that into our code like all other source files.

We cannot just write anything into our code, we have to keep in mind what exactly they will be synthesized into. Some structures are unreliable or unstable when loaded into a prototype, even if they seem okay in an RTL simulation; others force us to lower our clock frequency to meet static timing, while they are mostly avoidable by using properly designed coding structures. For this reason, FPGA design is different from C-programming or software engineering because we have to keep in mind the generated circuits that is electrical engineering. We are not designing an abstract code; we are designing a limited circuit.

Metastability occurs when a signal that is not clocked by the same clock as the FPGA core logic input interface is clocked with arrives to a pin. What happens is the signal might change state when the clock changes state, violating its timing, and some of the capture flip-flop's downstream circuits will receive the old value of the input signal and some will receive the new value, which creates invalid data inside the FPGA. It can get even worse as it might ripple through several register stages, causing invalid unstable changing data deep inside our synchronous core logic. What we can do to mitigate is called "double-flopping", so the input signal is captured and clocked by a flip-flop without routing it to any combinatorial logic circuit, then routing the first flip-flop's output to a second flip-flop, and only interpreting the outputs of the second flip-flop. This usually avoids metastability; however, if we want to detect an edge on the double flopped signal it might still cause metastability in some devices. For this issue we can use a state machine with delays to detect an edge on the double flopped signal.

Metastability can also occur when a signal passes from a clock domain to another, for example, a logic that runs at 48MHz passes a signal to another block that is running at 25MHz. We can use the double-flopping for control/status signals, FIFO memories for parallel buses, or we can use handshaking protocols. Handshaking still requires double-flopping, but it allows both sides to know when the data is ready or taken. The first side asserts the READY signal, the other side detects it, waits for it to stabilize, then captures it, then reports back with another signal like TAKEN, then the first side detects that and concludes the transaction.

When our combinatorial (lots of long equations) logic incurs too much delay, it will cause setup timing violations at a given clock frequency or it will limit the maximum achievable clock frequency. We can shorten these paths and get rid of timing violations by using "flattening" or "register balancing" in our code. Flattening replaces the "if/elsif/elsif/else" priority encoder structures with "case" structures, which propagate a solution faster. Register balancing simply inserts a register into a long logic equation/path by forcing to create an intermediate variable as a register and compute the final variable in the next clock cycle from the output of the register. This adds one lock cycle latency, but we can run our clock faster for all computations and paths.

Another important thing while writing code is for board-level interfaces to capture the input signal "as is" with the IOB flip flop to reduce buffer delays, instead of capturing the result of a logic equation or an "if/else" selector into the flip-flop. If we capture the result of a combination, then it can be done only with a CLB flip-flop, then even the synthesizer cannot pack it into IOB flip-flops, which is bad for I/O timing. The two code options below show the basic versus the registered I/O code in action. This produces results in two clock cycles, but with better I/O pin static timing.

a) Basic high-level code without consideration for I/O registers:

```
if (STRB='1') then x <= PIN1 & DECODE & ENABLE; end if;
```

b) Taking care of capturing the board level signal first, then processing it at the next clock cycle:

```
x_iobff <= PIN1;
if (STRB='1') then x <= x_iobff & DECODE & ENABLE; end if;
```

6.2.5.2 Simulate and Test

We can simulate any well definable functional blocks, but not any glue logic that would interact with board circuits. The RTL level simulation is most useful, as it can be done in a reasonable timeframe, but it will not contain any timing- or metastability-related effects. We can also a run post-place and route simulation that contain those effects statistically, but it still might not be an accurate representation of a prototype. The Post-P&R simulation would take many times longer to run, in most cases prohibitively so. For simulations we set up test bench files that include input excitation waveforms. In some tools it can be defined in a timing diagram editor, but a Verilog or VHDL code definition is more common and more precise. We can generate a test bench file (VHDL syntax text file) in a GUI as a wrapper on top of our top-level file, then edit it in a text editor for the stimulus part. The stimulus is the sequential list of value assignments to input signals with delay steps in the test bench code. The simulator will display all input (Stimulus) signals and all output signals of our design block in a timing diagram. Many functional simulations require simulating thousands or millions of clock cycles.

Sometimes simulation is not accurate or feasible, so we have to wait until we get the prototype to test the functionality. We can test the functionality as it is intended to operate and observe at several points how it works. For example, we send a control data packet or command over an interface to the FPGA, and we observe if it performs a task that it is supposed to. We can also do eye capture on SERDES transceiver input pins to check signal integrity, or do loopback tests on external ports to verify basic partial functionality. If none of these result in a fully working system, then we start "instrumenting" the design by inserting a logic analyzer core into the code, set it up to capture internal signals that we want to observe, similar as to how we would have in a simulation. Then we need to recompile the design with the logic analyzer core included, then run the prototype system with the logic analyzer GUI monitored on our laptop over a JTAG cable. To look at different signals, we have to edit the instrumentation and recompile then re-test, possibly several times. The logic analyzer consumes a lot of FPGA resources, especially memory blocks, depending on how many signals and how deep (length of time) buffering of the waveforms we want. The core runs on the same clock as our design runs on, it samples signals by that clock. The logic analyzer core resource usage has to be considered for FPGA selection. As we add logic and increase utilization, the original design timing constraints might get harder to meet. AMD (Xilinx) has the Chip Scope Pro for logic analyzer, the iBert for eye capture. Microchip has the Actel Identify for logic analyzer. Intel/Altera has the Signal Tap Logic Analyzer and the Transceiver Toolkit for eye capture.

6.3 ASICS

ASIC stands for Application Specific Integrated Circuit. Basically, the cheaper version of hard silicon, which is as fast as hard silicon, faster, and has lower power than FPGAs. In this book we use the "slang" ASIC for any large high bandwidth digital chip, including actual ASICs, CPUs, GPUs, or FPGAs. This chapter is about the chips that are actual ASICs, not CPUs or FPGAs. CPUs and FPGAs are well known in low to medium complexity and consumer hardware, but high-end data center network switch/router blades and accelerator designs are also very reliant on ASICs.

An interesting activity is the ASIC BGA package pinout design, if we work in the board hardware team at a company that designs their own ASICs for their own boards and systems. When the ASIC team is ready to fab-out their chip, they provide a spreadsheet showing their proposed pinout diagram. Hardware and SI engineers can sometimes review and propose changes to that. The two main aspects we look for is sufficient number of ground pins and their relative location to signal pins (via impedance and crosstalk) and the distribution of signals in a way to minimize PCB routing layer count. For SERDES pins we will look for via fencing, for memory interfaces we will look for distributing ground pins and grouping signals of each lane in a way that we can route them on the same layer straight to match a memory device pinout.

6.3.1 Ethernet Switch ASICs

The long-distance communication between computing chassis is done through IEEE standardized Ethernet (and in extension the Internet) networks. Long here means longer than a few inches of PCB trace, more like feet or yards. The Ethernet network data get aggregated from multiple nodes to single/few connections at certain points of the network through switches and routers. Instead of thousands of servers all being wired to each other, they are all wired to switches that route data packets from any of their ports to any other port. Users access servers over the Internet, but servers also have to access each other for locating data or specialized processing.

6.3.1.1 ASIC Internal Features

Modern Ethernet switches implement higher level (layer-3 IP-address based routing) and more intelligent functions that 10 years ago only existed in routers. In switches we rely on complex switch ASICs. Both switches and routers perform more than just forwarding data packets from one port to another. They are programmable and configurable; a lot of software engineering goes into them. The line between Layer 3 Ethernet switches and traditional Layer 3 routers is blurring, and switch ASIC-based large chassis switches are replacing traditional router equipment.

Switch ASICs have a long list of networking and software-related features that systems and software engineers deal with. It is common to require more software engineering resources for a new switch design project than the hardware engineering resource needed for designing the switch board. After chassis startup the host processor has to load the configuration for all of these features, and manage them during run-time. These high-end switch ASICs can detect and monitor what is being forwarded, where they come from, and where they are going. This is called telemetry; it is aggregated by the host processor in the chassis, that can be remotely accessed by an administrator. The ASICs collect information about port-level and chip-level variables like utilization, as well as application (web, video, database) and individual user data. Some of this is computed as statistical data, for example download volume per server. Some of the data is automatically acted upon by the switch, for example access/policy enforcement, server load balancing and network security. The ASICs direct all traffic according to the pre-defined rules, isolate virtual networks and handle user access. Part of this functionality might not be integrated into the main switch ASICs; in that case we need to connect off-loading ASICs or FPGAs to the main switch ASIC on our switch board design, if the feature is required.

All switch ASICs with 10G or faster ports support on-die eye capture, which is retrieved for display over the configuration interface, that is usually a PCI-express, I2C, or SPI bus connected to a local host processor. The vendor SDK software/driver kit will allow extracting eye diagrams under console-style Linux as a text-based eye diagram. This is very important when designing data center switch boards that have hundreds of 10 to 112 SERDES links inaccessible for probing in any other way.

6.3.1.2 Device Port Architecture

External ports of switches/routers at 10Gbps speed or above are usually cage type connectors for high-bandwidth 10 to 800Gbps plug in optical transceiver modules, and the front panel is usually fully packed with as many ports as possible. We also have internal ports, usually between switch ASICs and FPGAs, on the same board or over a backplane or fabric card. These links consist of PCB traces with internal board-to-board connectors.

There are three different types of Ethernet switch chassis and the ASICs that go with them. The smallest <10 port ASICs are used in embedded environments to connect a few devices within a chassis or a large board, or used by consumers in their homes. There are small switch chassis based on a single ASIC that are used for top of the rack (TOR) switching in lower bandwidth environments. These switches usually have many one to 10 Gbit downstream ports and two to four higher bandwidth upstream ports (40 to 400Gbit). The last category is the data center switch chassis, larger TOR or modular spine switch chassis. These chassis usually have large expensive boards hosting one or several high bandwidth ASICs. These ASICs usually have many identical very-high bandwidth ports, for example, 32 ports of 400Gig speed. ASICs made for large scale-out multi-chip systems might have two types of ports, the external line or network interface ports and the internal facing fabric ports.

The smaller switch ASICs usually have one to four ports of 10 to 25Gbps and a dozen or so 1Gig ports. In some cases, we just need to connect a few cards using a switch chip. In large data center boards, it is common to see large switch ASICs that handle the data plane traffic through hundreds of lanes of 10 to 112Gig SERDES links, while the same boards also have a much smaller switch ASIC to handle the management subsystem traffic through a few 1Gig ports. If we want to connect a low-speed intelligent host device to a higher speed network, then we have to use a small Ethernet switch chip and connect only two ports of it. If we want to dual-host a single Ethernet port in a server rack, we can use a small Ethernet Switch ASIC or a dual-host PCIe NIC chip.

Modern large data center switch ASICs are highly integrated. They support hundreds of lanes/ports on a single ASIC, using the fastest SERDES technology in the world. In fact, data center switch ASICs are the first devices to implement the new fastest Ethernet I/O standard varieties, and fastest SERDES IPs, before any other devices (processors, FPGAs) and other industries (computing, industrial, military/aerospace, consumer). The largest switch ASICs are typically used with high bandwidth chassis/systems like multiple server nodes each having single 100Gbit port connections, connecting AI/GPU appliances to multiple servers or in spine switches handling a high-bandwidth horizontal mesh connectivity in a data center. Typically, all ports are used as high-bandwidth 100 to 800Gig (in 2023), so the architecture of these chips is more homogeneous. They have many identical SERDES cores using most of the package pins, and some control plane interfaces (I2C, MDIO,

LED-serializer, PCIe, SPI-flash) and strapping pins. If we want to hook up a few low-speed Ethernet ports to them, then we need external PHY or gearbox chips on our board, or an additional small switch ASIC on-board with fast upstream and slow downstream ports. Some external port standards may not be supported by these ASICs, even though they use the same speed SERDES. We can make sure of it from reading the datasheet, and then we include any PHY or gearbox ASICs in the board design if necessary.

6.3.1.3 Switch ASIC Vendors

For several years Broadcom led this transition towards more integrated, more intelligent switching in the data center, with their Trident and Tomahawk ASICs (StrataXGS product line) and their scalable Jericho and Ramon ASICs (StrataDNX product line). These high-end switch ASICs usually come in 2000 to 5000 pin BGA or LGA packages. A single Tomahawk 5 ASIC can be used to build a 64-port 800G/port top-of-the-rack (TOR) switch with 112Gig PAM4 signaling. The Trident family is more configurable with more features than the Tomahawk, but at a lower total bandwidth at the same generation. There are also switch ASIC families from Broadcom with lower and much lower bandwidth. They are usually referred to by their part number, for example, the BCM56170 ("Hurricane3") chip with 0.3Tbps total bandwidth.

There are other vendors also in the high-end data center network switching market. The Marvell (acquired Innovium) Teralynx8 ASIC with 25Tbps throughput, the Nvidia (acquired Mellanox) Spectrum-4 with 50 Tb/s throughput compete with the Broadcom Tomahawk 4 and 5 devices. The Intel (acquired Barefoot) Tofino ASIC is even more highly programmable, offering 12Tb/s throughput.

These vendors usually have a device generation or naming convention like XYZ2 and later XYZ3 to mark the fact that it is a newer generation with larger port speed and throughput but used the same kind of way as the previous generation. The product family code name is used when discussing architecture, but the actual part number goes into the schematic, such as BCM56982. Some of the router system vendors are/were making some of their own network ASIC chips, which are not available for third-party board/system companies to purchase.

All of these vendors also offer scaled-down-sized devices for less demanding applications, with less ports and slower port speeds. For example, instead of 512x112Gig SERDES, some variants "only" have 64x56Gig SERDES. Microchip offers several smaller switch devices with VSCxxxx part numbers, the product line was acquired from Vitesse Semiconductors. They are in the 8 to 200Gbit/device range.

6.3.1.4 Data Center Board/Chassis Topologies

A long time ago data center switching was mainly based on distributing the main external Internet connection to the many servers in a star like topology. Modern switches in data centers now also support horizontal traffic between servers through the leaf-spine architecture and having full-mesh connections in the middle of the hierarchy. This has created a need for very high port count and very high bandwidth spine switches in the data center, which are medium to large chassis with multiple very high bandwidth ASICs. A typical ASIC used in these in 2023 can handle 1 to 50Tbps, and the whole spine switch might be as big as a refrigerator and handle over 300Tbps of data through many line cards. Switch chassis that are built with multiple ASICs are also made of multiple boards. The boards on the front of the chassis are called the line cards, the ones in the back are the fabric or switch cards. We cannot fit dozens of ASICs each dissipating hundreds of Watts on a single board design, hence the need for multiple boards.

If we need more ports than a single device can provide, then multiple switch ASICs on multiple boards can be combined inside a chassis. In large multi-ASIC systems, we can use multiple identical Tomahawk or Trident ASICs or we can split the device roles into two different ASIC device categories, the line and the fabric ASICs to improve power consumption and latency. The line ASIC will interface with external cable ports having full Ethernet compatibility, while the internal connections between them can be switched by the fabric ASICs. So the line ASICs will have two types of ports, line interface ports (network interface or NIF) and fabric interface ports, while the fabric switch ASICs will have only fabric ports. An example of line ASICs is the Broadcom Jericho series, and an example of fabric ASICs is the Broadcom Ramon series. They talk to each other through the Broadcom proprietary fabric interface.

Those switch ASICs that are meant to be used alone to handle all the switching needs of a particular chassis (no topology), only have regular Ethernet ports, they do not break down to fabric and line ports. The higher bandwidth regular switch ASICs have just one type of port with the identical high-speed SERDES lanes, while smaller size switch ASICs have a few different types of ports based on speed capability. We can implement many port multi-ASIC Ethernet switch designs with different topologies, as we can see in Figure 6.20. The main difference between them is whether they can provide non-blocking full bandwidth path between any external port pairs in the system and the level of scalability. The simple mesh topology does not allow full bandwidth communication from all ports on the left ASIC to all ports on the right ASIC since half the fabric ports go elsewhere. If we try to build a larger switch with the star topology, but still want to provide full bandwidth from the left to the right node ASIC, then we will find that we will need a host ASIC with at least as high bandwidth as all the node ASICs combined. With anything less than that, we will note some port group to port group traffic as having a bottleneck, making the switch a blocking switch instead of the commonly desired non-blocking switch. So the star topology does not scale well unless we have multiple star point host devices. In that case the star/host devices become the fabric ASICs and the nodes become the line ASICs. This is helpful for building devices that can handle a massive amount of traffic in scale-out arrangements inside the switch chassis. These topology studies are true for any decentralized interface type, not only Ethernet, but also CXL, CCIX, NVLINK (GPUs), InfiniBand, or Aurora.

6.3.1.5 Switch Management and Control Plane

In a switch board/chassis there must be a host/management processor also. This processor might be integrated inside the switch ASIC silicon die, designed onto the switch board, or on a separate management CPU card. At a minimum, the software running on a host processor has to set up every port of the switch ASIC to the speed/mode to match the particular hardware design during system initialization. During run-time the management processor's software also has to monitor the traffic, utilization, counters, and other internal features. They also have to detect cable plug events and the types of the optical modules that were plugged in through I2C EEPROM reads and control/status signals.

Low-end switch ASICs that are used in consumer switches or as a minor subsystem on a complex board usually manage the small switch ASIC by a small ARM processor core that is integrated on the same silicon die with the switch ASIC. They also have a serial console for factory configuration

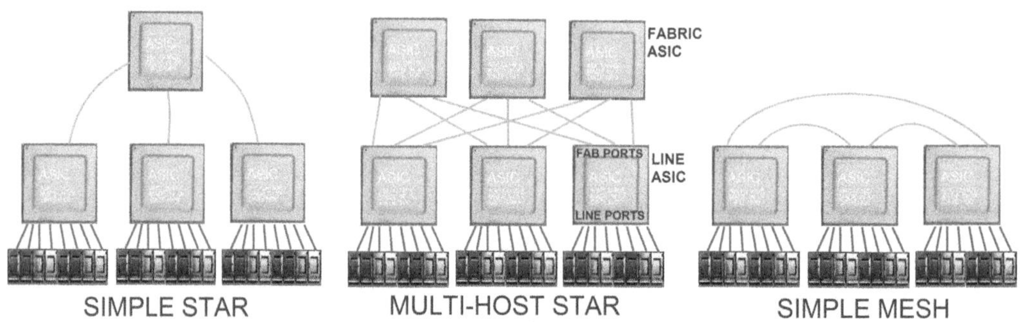

FIGURE 6.20 Switch multi-ASIC topologies.

and prototype debugging and a flash memory chip next to them on the board for storing the CPU configuration. They might have a DRAM chip also to support the on-die ARM processor. Larger data center switches and appliances usually utilize a management X86 processor, either designed down to the switch board or contained on a separate management card. That X86 processor would initialize and handle the switch ASICs through a narrow PCIe link or, in case of small switch ASICs, an I2C or SPI port.

The switch ASICs also have control plane master interfaces to handle PHY chips through MDIO or to handle optical modules through I2C. Although these can be taken over by the host processor subsystem.

6.3.1.6 Typical Board Design and Interfacing

For board hardware design, the data center switch ASICs are basically the most power-hungry and most SERDES-heavy chips in the world. While a laptop processor might have 18 lanes of 6-8Gig SERDES and 25W power, these network ASICs have ~500 lanes of 112Gig SERDES and 500W power. That requires more sophisticated board design techniques to manage both the massive routing amount without compromising signal integrity and the delivery of more power than all the lights in a house under a 2x2" delicate device without much voltage drop.

For schematic design we have to connect all pin types and groups of the ASIC to something. We need to hook up the many Ethernet SERDES links for the data plane, the PCIe signals for control plane, as well as the reference clocks, power pins, and glue logic pins. The glue logic pins include strapping pins, resets, boot mode selectors, EEPROM attachment signals, clock synchronization interfaces, MDIO to talk to any PHY chips, interrupts to the host CPU, hot swapping disconnect, power management signals, and the on-chip processor's signals (UART, memory, flash). We have to account for every single signal on the datasheet's pin list. For any pin that is not clear to us we may investigate for minutes or hours, look up in different documents, or even call the field application engineer.

We need to talk about LEDs. The users need to see whether a newly attached Ethernet cable connection is working after they have just plugged in another cable or transceiver module into a front panel port of the switch. Typically, one or two LEDs per port is provided for that to carry information about link up/down, activity (data passing through), and speed (like 100Gig or 40Gig depending on what is plugged in). This will be three LEDs, but can be encoded into one or two with bicolor or tricolor LEDs. For example, link up is a static indication, while activity is blinking, so it can be combined as off means no link; on means link up but no traffic, blinking means up and currently has traffic. Smaller Ethernet PHY or NIC chips might have individual LED control output pins for each port, but larger switch ASICs could not reserve that many pins on the package, so they utilize a LED serializer, a shift register style interface. This will take up two pins on the ASIC, but need to be routed into our glue logic FPGA to de-serialize it and generate individual LED control output signals. Then each FPGA pin will drive one LED through a series current-set (10mA probably) resistor. Each LED will be at the front panel, either as a right angle SMD LED on the bottom side under the connector, built into the connector (common with RJ45), use a LED matrix component, or use a vertical LED away from the board edge with a plastic light pipe to route the light to the front panel.

6.3.1.7 Example Switch ASIC: Broadcom's Tomahawk 3

At the time of writing this book in 2023, the Tomahawk 4 and 5 have already been released, but we have public datasheets available only up to Tomahawk 3. We cannot publish NDA material in this book, so the below description is about Tomahawk 3 that is similar in architecture and board design challenges to TH4 and TH5. The BCM5698x TH3 supports 256 lanes of 56Gig SERDES in a BGA4344 package. The last digit of the part number tells which device (size) it is within the family, like BCM56980 or BCM56982 that defines the number of cores/lanes available if decoded in a table in the datasheet. The largest member of the Tomahawk3 family features of 32 integrated 56G-PAM4 BlackhawkCore SERDES cores. Each of the BlackhawkCores can act as a single port

8-lane 400Gig Ethernet port (used with QSFP-DD or OSFP), or multiple one to four lane ports (10 to 200Gig). At some point every company in Silicon Valley is/was designing Tomahawk-based boards and systems, it was/is so popular. It is a device family with different size devices, but the largest bandwidth in the industry.

The ASIC architecture delivers complete L2 (MAC address) and L3 (IP address) switching, routing, as well as load balancing capabilities. We can attach long-reach (LR) and short-reach (SR) pluggable optical modules without external PHY chips. The chip provides debugging and validation features like SERDES error counters, on-die eye capture extracted through the host PCIe interface and Linux console by a host processor, and visibility into all on-chip packet drops and other events through status registers. It contains ARM processor cores so the ASIC can initialize and manage itself, but it can also be managed from a separate host processor over PCIe if the ARM CPU is disabled through strapping. Actually, it is easier to develop our control plane software on a generic CPU/card that talks to the ASIC over PCIe, than having to do that on an integrated custom on-die ARM processor. It dissipates ~300W of power, and requires a 300 Amp 10-phase core VRM.

6.3.1.8 Example Switch ASIC: Microchip VSC7558 (Sparx-5)

This is a chip family with different throughput sizes, but all of them were optimized to provide connectivity of low bandwidth (1Gbit) devices into a high-bandwidth upstream port pair. The largest device VSC7558 has 200Gbps total throughput. It has 20 SERDES lanes capable of 10Gbps, 8 SERDES capable of 25Gbps, but overall, 33 lanes of SERDES at least 2.5Gbps each. The device supports 64 1Gig ports on 33 lanes of SERDES through multiplexing by requiring the board designer to utilize external quad PHY chips (1x QSGMII on the 10G SERDES ports to create four 1000Base-T external ports). The device also supports several low-speed interfaces, like 1000BASE-X, KX, FX, SGMII. The way the chip is organized at the physical layer is with using 13 pieces of "SerDes5G", 12 pieces of "SerDes10G" and 8 pieces of "SerDes25G" transceiver blocks. The pins are named S0 to S32_RX/TXP/N. The Data Link Layer (MAC) is organized as different number of 2.5G/5G/10G/25G MACs that are multiplexed to the pins.

The architecture supports high-level features like IPv4/IPv6 Layer 3 routing, 4k VLANs, security features, IP Tunnels, and TCAM-based pattern matching. It contains two ARM processor cores with external DRAM interface so the ASIC can initialize and manage itself, but it can also be managed from a separate host processor over PCIe or SPI. A possible application block diagram can be seen in Figure 6.21. It also contains the ASIC's simplified block diagram, with just enough information for making board design decisions. This utilizes 1Gig and 10Gig direct backplane ports, transformer-coupled 1Gig front panel ports through the 10Gig QSGMII SERDES and QSFP100 upstream external optical ports. They come in a 0.8mm pitch 888-pin BGA package.

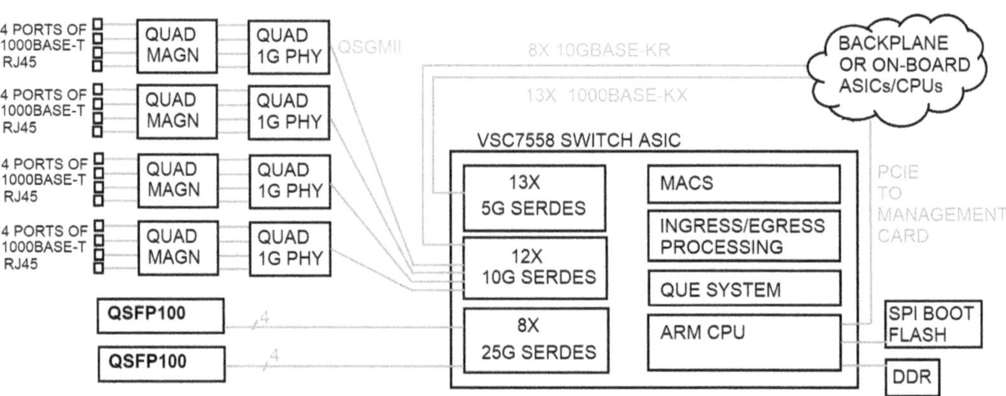

FIGURE 6.21 A possible application of the VSC7558 chip from Microchip.

6.3.2 GPUs

Graphics Processing Units (GPUs) maintain a screen image buffer, generate a continuous video output signal from the image, and insert objects into the image buffer from the CPU's main memory or from on-chip computation (rendering). They were originally created to enhance computer gaming visual experience. Now they make GPUs that have the same processing logic cells but that do not even have a video output because it was discovered that several computationally heavy tasks can be performed by GPUs with better price/power ratio than with the main CPUs. It is called compute acceleration—an alternative use of an existing technology. Now they make variants of GPU chips and boards without video output interfaces and call them general purpose GPUs (GPGPUs). They are basically large BGA chips with a wide PCIe or NVLINK interface upstream to the host processor, with fast GDDR memory chips on the board or HBM memory dies in the package. Usually, GPU and GPGPU chips are not available for purchase by small companies. The vendors prefer to sell cards with the chips on them—often not even cards but only complete chassis are sold.

In similar fashion to AI appliances, there are also GPU accelerator appliances. These usually contain eight GPGPUs, each on separate mezzanine cards plugged on top of a large base board, and with some switching logic to allow all of them to communicate with each other and with the host processor (connected over external cables to the server chassis). The switch chip and the interface used with Nvidia GPGPUs is called an NVLINK, and it is sometimes handled by NVSwitch devices. The GPU-GPU connectivity allows the scaling of computing asks from a single chip's data size capability to several (usually eight) chip's combined capability.

There are also regular form factor PCIe cards with one single GPGPU on each card, that can be plugged into third party servers. Server makers have been making motherboard designs optimized to accommodate several of these GPGPU cards in a single chassis, maximizing their number per server.

Regular GPUs are still in use for graphics applications, in personal computers, self-driving cars and aerospace hardware. A typical GPU chip comes in a 1000…5000 pins BGA package, with up to ~100W power dissipation, usually have GDDR memory chips integrated around them on the board, but newer ones have HBM memory on the package.

6.3.3 AI ASICs

Today's artificial intelligence (sometimes called machine learning [ML] and neural networks [NN]) is really a processing circuit for certain types of computing tasks, mainly for pattern matching and recognition, and they can be "trained" instead of simply programmed to do these tasks. At low-level implementation they use clusters of AI compute blocks, each block performs a matrix-by-matrix, or matrix-by-vector, or vector-by-vector multiplication task within a few clock cycles. Figure 6.22 shows the matrix-by-matrix multiplication concept. Simpler implementations (like the AMD/Xilinx Versal Gen 1) can only do vector by vector multiplication, while later generations can do matrix by matrix. Matrices (matrix) and vectors are defined in mathematics or linear algebra classes at universities. This is somewhat similar to the ALU units of regular processors or the MAC units of DSPs but multi-dimensional and fully parallelized. This shows the evolution of the core computing logic. There are dedicated AI ASICs that contain many AI compute blocks as well as data mover infrastructure logic. There are also traditional devices with additional AI cores, like FPGAs and processors.

The two main phases of the use of AI hardware are training and inference. During training the developers are feeding many example data or image patterns to the machine. During inference, in end-user normal use, the machine recognizes real-time patterns if they are similar-enough to what it received during training. Matrix multiplication can be used for inference. If the stored matrix and the live feed data matrix are similar, it will produce a certain output; if dissimilar it will produce a

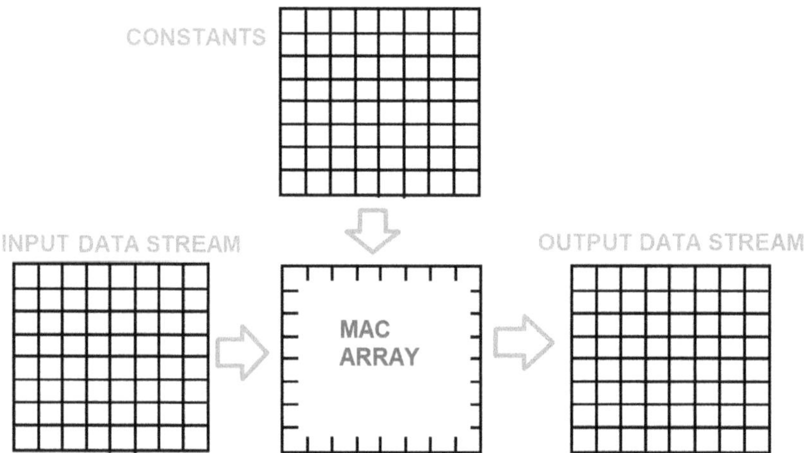

FIGURE 6.22 Concept of matrix multiplicator core for AI ASICs.

different output, a different level of error signal. This is how AI ASICs can "recognize" patterns, by measuring the error signal.

Usually there are dozens of Matrix-Multiplicator units (MMUL) on one ASIC silicon, each have to be fed data repeatedly with a high bandwidth data stream. The ASIC's data mover infrastructure logic, and modern buses like CXL, facilitate that process. An 8x8 input matrix can be loaded in a single clock cycle on a 64bit wide parallel on-die bus, or in eight clock cycles on an 8bit wide parallel bus. These must exist as separate buses for both input matrices and the output matrix, of each AI core, to utilize the full bandwidth of the MMUL cores. In an example, if we have 10 x 10 or 100 AI cores, each loaded with 64bits times two in one clock cycle. That means 64*2*10*10=12800 bits per clock cycle. Let's assume the ASIC is running at 200MHz core clock, then it means 2.5 Tbps of data have to be loaded into it. This can only be fed into the chip using at least 40 lanes of 64Gbps PCIe Gen6. The data moving logic includes the 300 sets of 64bit buses (2 in 1 out of each core), and a DMA engine that obtains the data from the processor's main memory (or from a shared CXL memory device) and distributes it to the 100 AI cores, then takes the results back into the memory on schedule. If we load each core in eight clock cycles instead of one, then the bandwidth is lower at 0.5Tbps, and we need less traces (300 sets of 8bit buses) routed on the silicon, Let's say we are now running the core logic at 320MHz clock speed, but we only need a PCIe Gen6 port with 8-lanes. If we do not have separate buses for each MMUL core, and loading them one by one, using single clock cycle 64bit wide bus transactions at 1GHz, then the bandwidth drops to 64Gbps, through a x8 Gen3 PCIe link. The issue with that is each MMUL core is only in use 1% of the time, then it makes sense to have just one core instead of 100.

The market for AI ASICs has been changing a lot with new startups and multiple corporate acquisitions. Many large data-center operators and Internet service companies have been developing their own board and system hardware, a few also started to build their own AI ASICs. Large processor chip vendors also have entered into the AI ASIC market. Most of these devices are not available for third-party board design companies; rather, the chip maker also builds the complete systems. The AMD (Xilinx) Versal device family are composite devices with FPGA fabric, ARM processor cores, and AI processing cores, together with several high-performance hard IP cores like DSP engines and SERDES transceivers. Versal has several subfamilies, optimized for different types of applications, like the AI Edge, AI Core, HBM, Premium, Net, and Prime series. Figure 6.23 shows the general block diagram of a Versal device. In recent years the Hot Chips Conference (held in Silicon Valley) has been dominated by AI ASIC chips and related technologies, even though the conference has a decades long history, originally focusing on CPUs and GPUs.

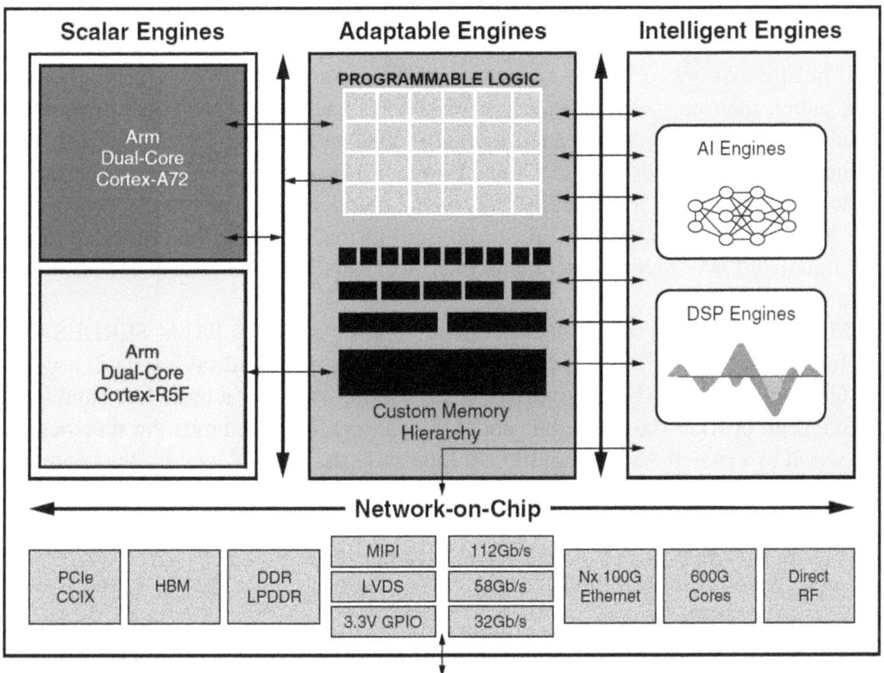

FIGURE 6.23 AMD (Xilinx) Xilinx Versal ACAP functional diagram, from the "Versal: The First Adaptive Compute Acceleration Platform (ACAP)" white paper, copyright September 2020, courtesy of AMD.

Current AI ASICs have very different unique implementations, but they can be compared with certain well-defined machine learning tasks. This is why they created a benchmarking standard called MLPerf.

6.3.4 Accelerator ASICs

There can be accelerator ASICs to be made for any complex task. The common theme is to process data using parallel logic, just like on FPGAs but faster and with lower power dissipation. The same logic implemented on an ASIC chip costs an order of magnitude less and can dissipate several times a less amount of power. Some known applications are network security, data packet inspection and switching, waveform processing for 5G communications, database lookup, encryption, and file compression. Often system/chassis vendors or data center operator companies develop these accelerator ASICs for their own internal use. We cannot purchase the chips online, but if we work there, then we could design them into new boards, and even get involved in the package pinout definition.

6.3.5 Search and TCAM ASICs

Sometimes data patterns have to be found in larger bulk data streams, like security threat signatures, IP addresses. These can be done on processors, FPGAs, but the most (cost and power) efficient way of implementing the pattern search is using search ASICs. The simpler versions are called TCAMs (ternary content-addressable memory), more advanced ones have marketing names like Neuron Search Processors (from Cavium/Marvell) or Knowledge-Based Processors (like the Broadcom BCM16K device). Search processors look for data patterns among many data entries, and, once found, they retrieve all other associated data within the same entry. For example, searching for all packets that come from a certain IP address, they are identified and then action taken based on related policy, like block it, log the events related to it, or redirect it.

The data have to be fed to the search ASICs by a main data plane ASIC or FPGA over a wide bandwidth interface like KR Ethernet, Interlaken, CXL, or vendor-specific SERDES link. They are mostly used in Ethernet network type applications. Their use is not obvious from a board design perspective; rather, their use is specified by ASIC or FPGA architects and software/systems engineering. Basically, they are attached to a more general ASIC or FPGA on the same board. The board design for them is simple, just provide clock and power and hook up the data plane interface and the control plane (config) interface to the main ASIC on the board design. The FPGA or software design is complex, it has to feed data to the ASIC at the right format and take the processed data. These devices are initialized over their control plane interface, usually an I2C bus or for some devices it can be PCIe.

The BCM16K device has a search interface with 32 lanes of 56Gig PAM4 SERDES lanes (can operate as Interlaken or as Broadcom fabric interface) for giving and taking data, it comes in a 1292-pin BGA package. It can be configured by a host processor over a basic low bandwidth PCIe interface, and it can provide statistical data about the packets processed over the statistics interface that can be wired to a switch ASIC or an FPGA. Internally the main blocks are the context and the result buffers and the key processing unit.

7 Hardware Architecture

Hardware architecture is about the functionality and structure of digital boards and systems, including chips and boards. Simple designs are based on a single main device. More complex hardware has multiple programmable devices that rely on each other through communication or I/O interfaces, usually but not always in a hierarchical structure.

7.1 BUILDING BLOCKS

Just like in movies, there are main roles and supporting roles among components in hardware. All the complex digital boards (hardware) use the same few categories of elements, as can be seen on the generic block diagram in Figure 7.1. On any block diagram a line represents a whole bus or interface with all its signals, while low level or unrelated details are not shown. Typically, there are one or more data processing main devices (red boxes on the generic diagram). There are also dedicated support circuits for each main device (green boxes). Support circuits can be (volatile and non-volatile) memory chips, point-of-load VRM circuits, clocking chips, buffers, or PHY chips. The support circuit requirements of the main chips and their parameters are defined by the main chip datasheets, design guides, and reference design schematics. The designer has to select suitable devices (features, price, availability) and design in their circuits. Some of the main devices have high-speed I/O connections to external or backplane connectors, but most main chips have connections to one or more of the other main chips on the same board. There are also global circuits (brown boxes) that are used for power and system management of the whole board. On most real product block diagrams, the VRMs and the global power circuits do not show up; rather, they have their own block diagrams, and these are discussed later in this chapter. The same component can be part of several different block diagrams, while different subsets of its interfaces are shown on each. They are shown here together to give a general sense of what is on a board in the component point of view, not the user functionality point of view. So on real projects we make several separate block diagrams for the separate subsystems and design "planes". If they are combined into one, then we just call it "the block diagram", or if the data signals show up without the power and clocks, then we call it the "main block diagram" or "I/O block diagram". A main block diagram can be made for one board or for a multi-board system.

After trying to implement the marketing requirements and the main ASIC's needs (from the ASIC's documentation) in the block diagram, these blocks will emerge. They are dependent on the exact product. Instead of detailing everything in specific examples, as there are infinite possible combinations, this chapter explains how different subsystems are constructed in different generic cases.

Some designs are based around one main device, some are based around multiple. Each main device has its own supporting smaller devices. Sometimes one main chip cannot handle the whole processing load so multiple instances are running in parallel. For example, a single-processor laptop motherboard versus a four-head server or a smaller switch card with one switch ASIC versus a larger switch card with a few identical switch ASICs handling more traffic. They can process pieces of the same one large task (like in supercomputers) or if we have thousands of smaller tasks then each chip handles a few hundred tasks. Some boards and systems contain two or three different types of large main devices, any type might have multiple instances. Often different main chips have different functions, like communications versus processing. One type of device might be used for loading and storing data, another type might be used for processing or inspecting the data. For example, a server processor used to receive requests from users' smart phones over the Internet for

DOI: 10.1201/9781032702094-7

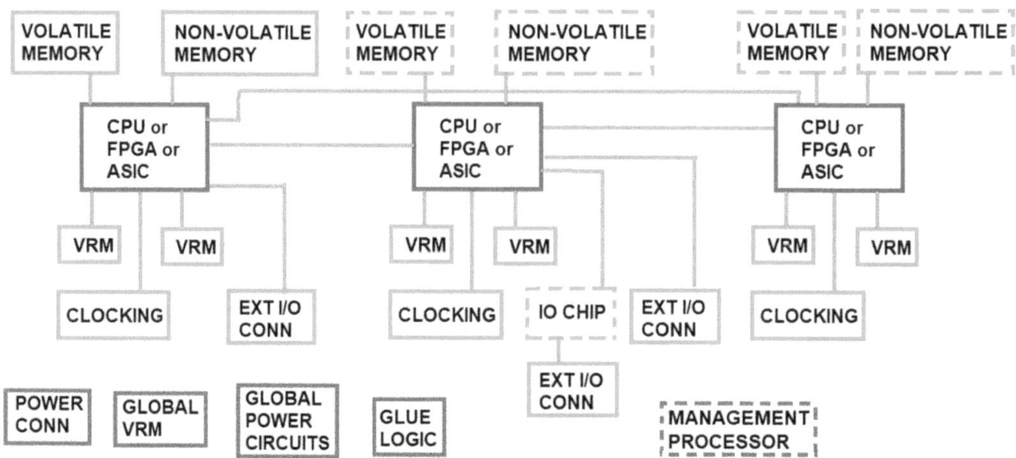

FIGURE 7.1 Generic complex hardware architecture block diagram.

speech translation, and it outsources the translation workload coming from 1000 users to the four FPGAs in the system. Sometimes we need to perform two different types of processing tasks, and one type is best done with a software driven CPU, another is best done with a specialized hard ASIC. A single-device system can initialize itself. When we have multiple large devices, then the system design gets more complex than any single-device hardware. For example, we need high-bandwidth SERDES links between the main devices to be able to share and off load the workload, and we need a management subsystem that monitors the health and manages the power states of the board(s). If more devices are needed than what we can fit in one large board, then multiple boards in the same chassis are needed. The same is true for multiple chassis that are interconnected to each other through network equipment like switches and router chassis, using cables, forming a data center. This is how we end up with multi-ASIC complex hardware designs, with complex glue logic, that are not common in consumer electronics but that are found in data center, military/aerospace, scientific instrumentation, and in telecommunications infrastructure equipment. This book focuses on the engineering done on these product types.

There is usually volatile (RAM) memory dedicated for each main chip for temporary storage. CPUs use RAM memory for application data (data, control, and management plane) as well as for executable code storage. Some data sets are stored for a short time, others for the whole duration between power up and power down. It is called system memory. FPGAs and ASICs only use larger RAM for very short-term application data storage. It is called buffer memory. They also contain a small amount of internal SRAM register cells for configuration. A data-moving logic utilizing SERDES links moves the data to the FPGA/ASIC and into its buffer RAM just before processing, and moves the result out soon after. The main chips contain some on-chip SRAM storage, but in most cases their size is insufficient. Very high bandwidth HBM memory silicon dies might be included in the main chip package as a multi-chip module, but, in most other cases, the board designer has to attach external memory. This off-chip memory is either memory-down (chips) or modules in sockets in the form of DRAM (DDR, GDDR) or QDR SRAM. GDDR is faster than DDR, uses point-to-point signaling in memory-down, and are used with GPUs and ASICs. The required total memory size and bandwidth is determined by software and systems engineering. To meet these parameters, the hardware designers have to choose memory chips or modules, number of ranks, chip count, their width, density and I/O data rate, within the confines of the main chip's I/O capability. The main chip's datasheet determines the maximum number of memory channels for our board, their width and speed, the width of the address bus, and the number of ranks. This is divided into modules and/or chips by us. For example, if an ASIC supports two channels at 64bit width each, then we can use eight chips of x8 wide, or four chips of x16, on each of the channels. If the largest memory chip (DRAM) on the market (with given address bus width) is X Gbits (density), then the x8 solution would lead to a total memory buffer size of 8*X, or the x16 solution would allow 4*X Gbits total. If we have two chip select signals instead of one then we can have twice that total size using a dual-rank configuration, with two memory chips on each byte lane of the data bus. The smaller number of chips the better for the layout design, the more chips the larger the total size we can achieve. In the case of FPGAs, it is more flexible. If our chip requires X Gbps of total bandwidth, the fastest chip we can use supports Y GHz speed, then we have to use W=X/Y bits of total width, divided into N number of 16bit, 32bit, or 64bit channels. There is also non-volatile (flash) memory attached to most main chips, for permanent code or configuration storage, that are programmed during board manufacturing. Their content is copied into RAM during the boot or initialization process right after power on.

There are other medium-sized chips in our designs that are not the main data processing devices but that are larger than just the support circuits of each main device. These can be PCIe switches, smaller Ethernet switch ASICs, Ethernet or storage (SAS, FC, SATA) controller chips, high-speed A/D converters, PHY, or gearbox chips. Most X86 processors come with a "chipset", sometimes called PCH or south bridge, which is also a large chip next to the CPU on the board. They have their own support circuits and heatsinks, but they facilitate only the data movement directed by the main chips in the design.

The communication links and components of the hardware architecture can be categorized into design "planes". The control plane is the set of parts and interfaces that are responsible for configuring the main ASICs after power on and for managing the operations and hardware events in run-time. The data plane is the set of parts and interfaces that process and forward the user application or payload data. There can be an additional design plane that controls the power management to the CP and DP logic, called the management plane, or the system management subsystem, usually implemented with management processors (BMC, IPMC), small FPGAs, or separate management CPU cards. The CP-DP-MP design plane distinction can be seen in Figure 7.2. Some people use the phrase "power plane" to describe the voltage regulators on the board and PSU modules in the system, together with the power sequencing control logic—not to be confused with power plane layers in a PCB layout. Others might include the power sequencing in the management plane, and the voltage regulators are just the support circuits of the main DP/CP/MP components, like the clock chips and memory

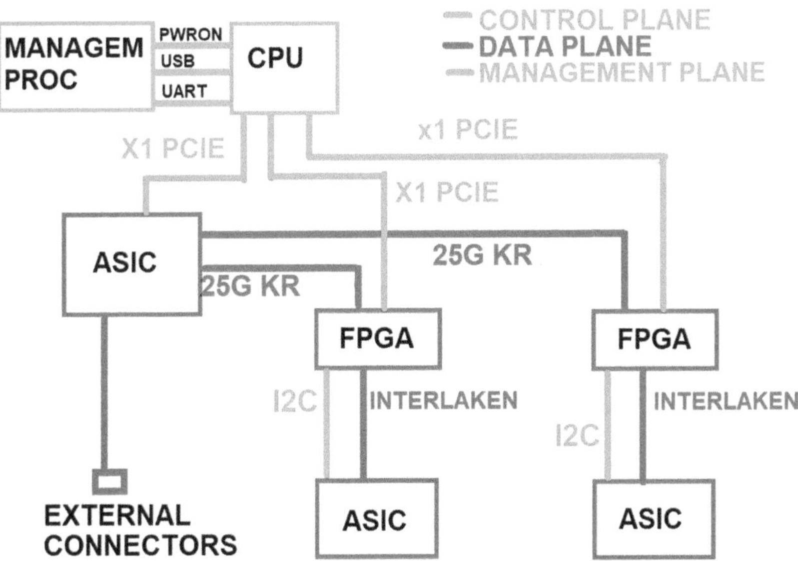

FIGURE 7.2 Difference between design planes.

devices. Simpler board designs will have one detailed block diagram drawn with all parts and all interfaces, but if our hardware architecture is made of distinct planes, then separate block diagrams for each plane will be more useful. All-in-one block diagrams are hardly readable for these very complex hardware, and they will not tell the story of how our board or system is supposed to work.

The topologies of the control and data planes are product specific. The data plane block diagram is usually specified by systems, ASIC or firmware engineering, management, marketing, or sometimes by the hardware engineer. It implements the actual product's main user features. HW engineers do feasibility checks and provide feedback on that, based on board resources and chip limitations. The control and management plane block diagrams are more under the control of hardware engineering, as it does not deal with user features and requires hardware expertise. Some topologies can be recognized as "star" when one central (host) device controls (or feeds with data) all other devices (nodes). Some interfaces require a central resource like a CPU that enumerates all devices or a switch on the top of a rack. The "dual-star" topology is the same but redundant, while the "mesh" topology is with node devices having an identical role and ability to act as hosts. Figure 7.3 shows these three different topologies side by side. The redundancy in dual star allows us to replace a host card while the system is running, and only pay for it as temporary bandwidth reduction instead of a system down. Similarly, a dual-dual-star (four hosts) or a multi-star (fabric) system can be built. If the system is designed to allow each host to have full bandwidth, then the bandwidth is not reduced at time of failure, just the redundancy is lost until the host card is replaced. The mesh topology requires the nodes to be able to initiate transactions or send packages in a peer-to-peer fashion and have actual separate physical connections between every device pair that works on Ethernet, UPI, CCIX, CXL, PCIe-p2p, or Aurora. Peer-to-peer communications can also go through a switch (that supports it), so the physical (board) topology remains a star (switch is the host), but the logical topology becomes a mesh inside the switch (without a CPU having to initiate every transaction). If the data do not care about which node it goes to, then the hosts have to run "load balancing" algorithms to ensure an even distribution of data or processing workload to the nodes, so no node will become a bottleneck in the system, for example, if the server has eight GPU cards, or a TOR switch talks to eight servers in a rack.

Most interface protocol types are suitable to carry both control plane and data plane communications. On the same system usually the data plane relies on high bandwidth many-lane SERDES links, while the control plane is lower speed SERDES with a single lane or use very low speed interfaces like I2C or SPI bus. For example, the DP might be on 10 lanes of 25Gig KR Ethernet, while the DP is on a single lane of 5Gig PCIe. Or a retimer chip carrying 800Gbps of Ethernet DP data might be configured over a 100kHz I2C bus.

A big part of the control plane, management plane, or glue logic, depending on product type, is the I2C subsystem. Usually, complex hardware boards have several to several dozen I2C devices that need to be accessed from a single I2C master port on the host processor. In most cases we can have different I2C devices from different chip vendors on the same I2C bus, except when it does not work. It is a good practice to segregate the different kind of devices made by different chip vendors to separate I2C buses so as to de-risk the project. If we have multiple devices that respond to the same fixed address, each needs a separate bus. We create additional I2C buses using programmable

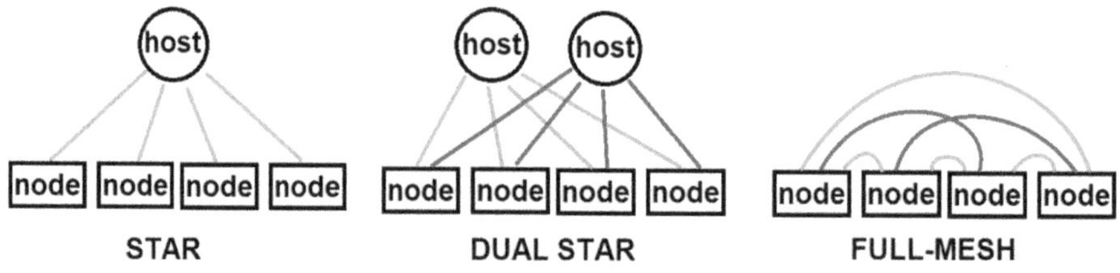

FIGURE 7.3 In-chassis or on-board communication topologies.

I2C multiplexer chips, which split one host port into eight downstream ports. They can even be cascaded to create up to 64 separate buses. These chips are told which downstream port to enable by writing into the multiplexer chip's control register at its own device address. The devices on different buses can have different protocols, like basic I2C, SMBUS, or PMBUS. The devices are typically temperature or voltage or current sensor chips, smart VRMs, the ID ports on the optical SFP/QSFP transceivers (all at the same address A0), glue logic FPGA registers, clocking chips, management ports of bridge or ASIC chips, retimer chips, or other smaller support chips. Some ports will require an I2C level translator as some devices do not support 3.3V. All separate I2C schematic nets will require a weak pullup, and the main bus requires a strong pullup. Often we make a separate block diagram for this and a device access table with device addresses and multiplexer port numbers. An example made-up I2C subsystem can be seen in Figure 7.4.

Similarly, to the I2C subsystem, many hardware designs have a PCIe subsystem that may be part of the data plane or control plane. PCIe is usually used with more complex devices than the ones connected by the I2C subsystem. PCIe has a similar need for port multiplication, but instead of multiplexers it uses PCIe switch chips. These PCIe switch chips can be cascaded like the I2C multiplexer chips can be to create a complex network of PCIe access from a host processor to several complex ASICs or FPGAs, for moving moderate to high amounts of data and to perform a full Linux driver-based initialization. In the case of multi-board systems, very often the card hosting the host processor might have a PCIe switch to provide individual backplane links, and the peripheral cards might also have a smaller PCIe switch to provide a single backplane uplink to multiple on-board downstream devices. An example made-up PCIe subsystem can be seen in Figure 7.5.

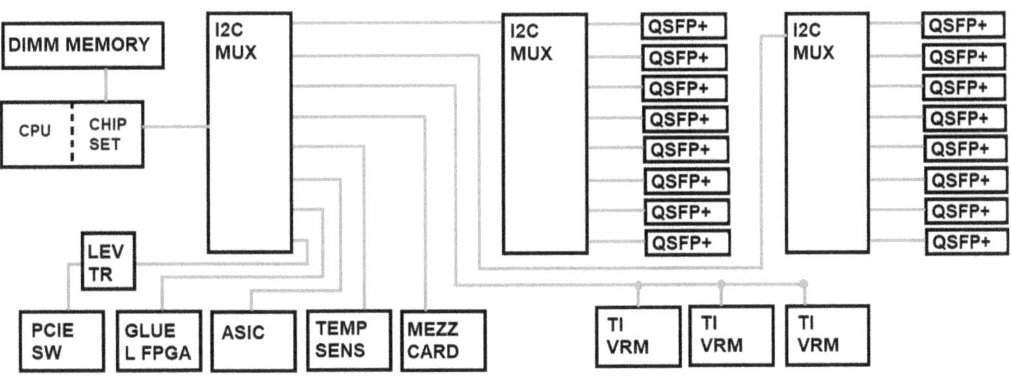

FIGURE 7.4 An example made-up I2C subsystem.

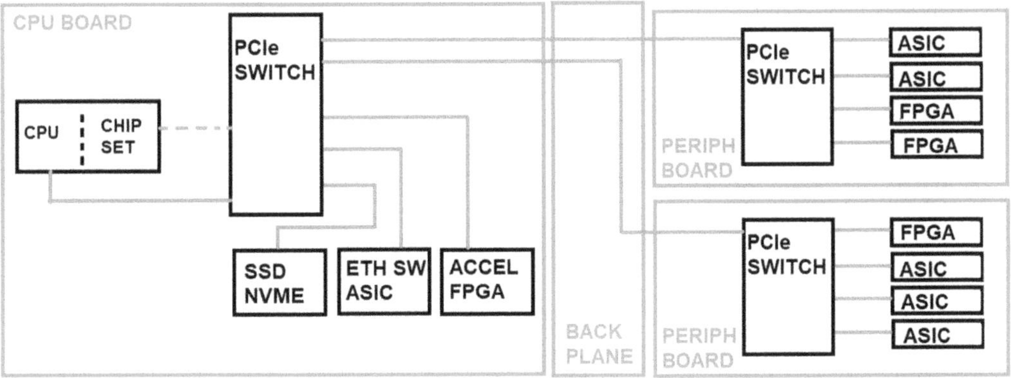

FIGURE 7.5 An example made-up PCIe subsystem.

Again similarly, many multi-board chassis systems have one or two internal Ethernet subsystems that use Ethernet switch ASICs instead of PCIe switch chips. Many designs have both. If the Ethernet is used for the data plane then the switch ASIC is a high-bandwidth and high-performance device utilizing the fastest SERDES types. If it is used for control plane or management plane purposes, then usually one-gigabit speed links are used, with small few-port 1GE switch ASICs. This is called the management Ethernet, or in some cases "base channel". Ethernet switch ASICs can also be cascaded, often done so at the board-backplane boundary, but mostly for control plane designs. In an in-chassis Ethernet network it is common that several devices initiate transfers, not just one host device. Ethernet and PCIe subsystems may include any number of protocol-compliant retimer chips if needed for SI improvement purposes. An example made-up Internal Ethernet subsystem can be seen in Figure 7.6. Most large systems do have all three types, one or more I2C subsystems, a PCIe subsystem, a data plane Ethernet, and a management Ethernet subsystem separately. The head of the I2C and PCIe subsystems is an on-board processor or a processor board. The head of the internal Ethernet network is either a CPU or a CPU card or a switch card. The topology shown on these diagrams is a star for simplicity, but it could be dual star or mesh. For example, the main CPU and the BMC could have shared custody over the I2C peripherals, by one of them controlling an analog multiplexer, or two switch cards could be used in a redundant manner. We can, and should, create separate subsystem block diagrams based on interface type (like I2C, PCIe, Ethernet, clocking, power management), based on design planes (data, control, management) and based on function. The function will be design-specific, for example, showing how one accelerator ASIC gets its data to be processed and its initialization and monitoring through multiple interfaces and switching chips, omitting unrelated details. Switch chips here mean protocol-processing switch, not analog switch or analog multiplexer. These switch chips reduce the maximum bandwidth at which each end point device can stream at simultaneously. This is why really high-performance systems try to provide some of their data plane connections without them, by having many-lane interfaces on the board connectors and on the host devices. For example, server processors can have a total 32 to 100 lanes of PCIe, allowing several accelerator ASICs to be hooked up to the CPU directly. Backplane connectors always have a limited number of pins, but using larger connectors, different board form factors or more connectors can allow extra bandwidth through a backplane or mezzanine connection.

The main user control access (control plane) to these complex boards and systems is usually through an RJ45 serial port (also known as COM port or RS232) or a 1Gbit management Ethernet port (telnet protocol) that provides text-based console access to control the system or inquire status. An engineer or technician would need to control it in the R&D lab, in manufacturing, or in the field if something went wrong. Very rarely there is an HDMI graphical display and a USB port

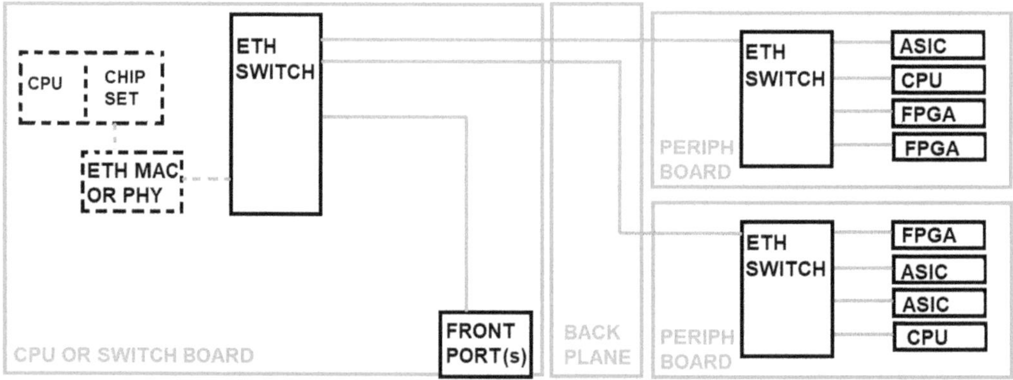

FIGURE 7.6 An example of a made-up internal Ethernet subsystem.

mouse and keyboard like it is with consumer computers. So testing high-end data center equipment is through typing lots of Linux commands into a console terminal like Putty. The serial console is usually accessible through an 8-pin RJ45 connector without transformer, using an RJ45 Serial Console Cable, also called a "Rollover cable". To the user it looks similar to a 1000Base-T Ethernet connector, except there are no LEDs in the corner. We also need an external I/O port for copying files to the system during development, which can be done over USB sticks, 1Gig Ethernet, or a micro-SD-card.

7.2 COMPUTERS

Everything is a computer—even a switch, and even a car is a computer. It is not that a car has a computer; rather, the car's computer has a car as a peripheral. The engine, the wheels, are the radio are peripherals to the car's computer. For complex hardware boards and systems, either their data plane or their control plane acts as a computer. It has a processor (or two or eight) that boots up and initializes all the peripheral devices. Data plane ASICs look like a peripheral to the control plane computer. For example, a storage controller ASIC is obviously a peripheral to this "computer", but even an Ethernet router ASIC or an AI ASIC is a peripheral, at least as far as the system initialization process is concerned. Sometimes the computers that are not laptop or desktop PCs or servers are called "embedded computers".

A peripheral is a chip that is told exactly what to do by a processor on the board/chassis. They are handled (control and feed data) over an interface and a register set. An intelligent peripheral is also told what to do, but only at a high level, not bit by bit, and it autonomously processes data. It is just told by the CPU which data to process. For example, in a Compact-PCI chassis there might be one main CPU card and several more CPU cards that are told what to do. In multi-device designs usually, there is a CPU and all other large devices are technically peripherals to the main CPU, but the other devices do more than just act as intelligent peripherals. They need only startup initialization and occasional intervention from the main CPU, but most of the time they obtain the data they need and know what to do with it. For example, a large switch ASIC is a peripheral to the control plane CPU card, as the CPU initializes it over PCIe, but the ASIC has its own external optical port connections to send and receive the main data plane data without the CPU having to ever see the user data itself. This is how control and data plane separates in really complex hardware. We might have a chassis with 24 slots, with complex chips on all slot cards, but they all have to get initialized at startup, monitored for health, and managed for hot-swapping or policy change (by user input) during run-time, so all of those cards in the chassis together are one single computer. The computer core or computer card in complex hardware systems is most commonly an X86 processor, sometimes ARM (if it has PCIe) that runs standard Linux and BIOS, with automated scripts without a user. A user or administrator only occasionally logs in over a text console for maintenance.

Of course, there are hardware designs, boards, and chassis that are only computers without automated data plane peripherals that would process data without the main CPU's intervention, for example, laptops, workstations, servers, or COMs (computer on module). For them there is no clear data plane versus control plane distinction. Most hardware design engineers who work on high-end boards design more of the other type where data plane ASICs do the main user application workload. For example, we might have a 25W X86 processor, with four large FPGAs on the same board, while the FPGAs get data plane streaming in and out directly through the external port connectors of the chassis and never pass through the CPU. On server motherboards the control and data plane are handled by the main CPUs, the accelerator and network cards are for data plane only, and usually there is a medium-size ARM processor for the management plane. That management processor might be there only for basic power management on some designs, or it might be able to upgrade the operating system or BIOS and it can take instructions over a low speed 1Gig Ethernet port, leaving nothing but data plane and partial control plane functions (like PCIe init of the AI ASICs) for the big server processors. Processors can be used in CP-only applications like a chassis manager card in a big Ethernet router, as a CP+DP function like a server or consumer computer, or as a DP-only function like an ATCA payload blade that processes communications packet data.

What is the core logic of a computer? Simply a processor (CPU) connected with volatile memory (RAM) and non-volatile memory (typically NAND Flash and/or SSD) and supporting circuitry (power, glue logic, and clocking). We can see a block diagram in Figure 7.7 showing this concept. On a complex digital board, there might be multiple devices (CPUs, ASICs, FPGAs, GPUs) that have some of these things connected to them. But during system initialization one dedicated processor will initialize all the others. Some computers are the main thing in the chassis, like in a rack server, the peripheral ASICs are plugged into the motherboard through PCIe cards. In other designs like medium to larger Ethernet switches the computer is a small area on the switch board or a separate smaller form factor card in the chassis.

7.2.1 System Buses

The main system buses in computers to attach peripherals to the processors used to be PCI and LPC, but today it is PCIe, and leaning towards CXL. The interface between an X86 CPU and its chipset (used to be north bridge and south bridge, now just one PCH chip) is a point-to-point SERDES interface called DMI (Intel) or Hyper Transport or now Infinity Fabric (AMD). It used to be a parallel bus called front-side-bus (FSB). Before even that (in the last century) the system bus of a CPU was a PCI bus to which we could also attach peripheral chips. Many DSPs and microcontrollers still have a parallel system bus interface available to attach peripheral devices, like CAN-controllers, flash memories, or waveform buffers implemented inside FPGAs. They are called external peripheral interface, external parallel interface, or external bus interface unit.

7.2.2 System Initialization

All the digital peripheral chips (and data plane ASICs and FPGAs) have many internal control registers and internal peripherals that have to be loaded with design-specific and architecture-specific content to tell them how to operate. They have to operate differently on different board designs. This

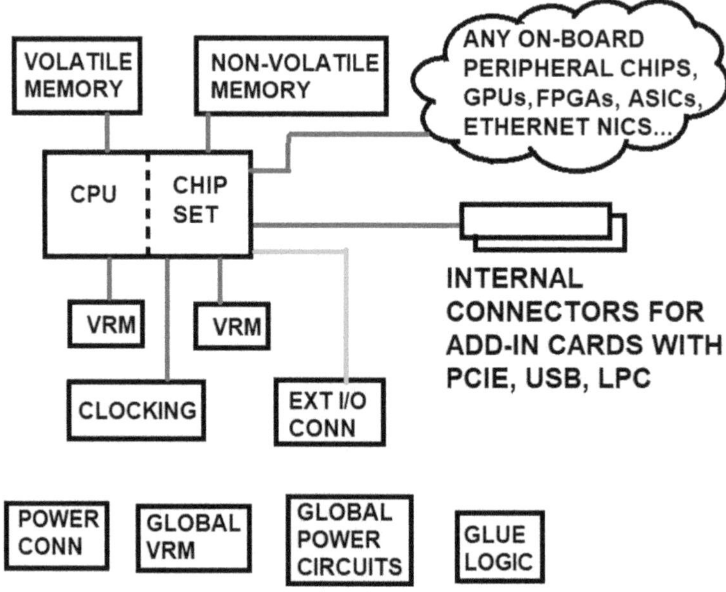

FIGURE 7.7 Basic computer architecture.

is computed, stored, and loaded by the main CPU over the control plane interfaces. At the very first step after system power on, the main CPU comes out of reset, starts loading its own code, starts executing it, initializes its own internal peripherals, then starts initializing other devices attached to it, as instructed by the software (BIOS, OS, device-drivers, bootloader, applications). Peripheral devices are found by the processor during PCIe enumeration or their bus/address location is hard-coded in software based on the custom hardware design, as communicated from hardware engineering to software engineering. Most computers are based on the PCI/PCIe bus architecture, which defines how peripherals are communicated with and how they are detected and initialized. In PCI/PCIe the BIOS discovers all devices in the system through a process called "enumeration", then assigns a memory-space address region to each device. The operating system and the device driver software as part of the OS, and later relies on these assigned address regions to access the devices and program their remaining non-standard registers. More details on this are found in Chapter 6, "Main Chips" in the Processors section, and in Chapter 3, "Major Interfaces" in the PCIe section. FPGAs initialize by themselves in some designs, but that is just the loading of the configuration file; after that, the actual volatile control registers have to be loaded with design or application specific control bits, including the standard PCIe header. This is how they are a peripheral to the "computer", even though a big part of their initialization was done by themselves. In some designs the main FPGA loading is also done by the local host CPU through some glue logic, called slave configuration, or if done over PCIe then it is called "configuration via protocol" (CVP).

7.2.3 Registers

Every digital chip (from small I2C multiplexers to custom glue logic FPGA codes to large ASICs) has registers that are accessible from an upstream interface by the local host processor. A register is a set of flip-flops or RAM cells in the width of the data bus that show status information at certain bit positions or control internal functions. Each bit can be set to zero or one. These are accessed at initialization and also during normal operation. Devices that contain these registers are called programmable devices. Most digital chips are such. A complete set of all registers in one device is usually described in a datasheet or in a programmer's manual as a register map. Which register is being accessed is determined by the address field in the bus transaction. Usually there are several registers, a glue logic FPGA/CPLD might just have 1 to 10 registers, a large ASIC might have thousands. The size of the registers is fixed by the device chip design or the interface type. For example, in one particular device that has a 32bit wide data bus all registers are 32bit wide, containing 32 individual bit fields. Some of these bit fields have individual meaning (like enable/disable a feature), others are grouped together (4bits to set an interface speed from a table). Depending on device and I/O standard the registers can be 8/16/32/64 bit wide, in one device all the same width. For PCIe interface it is usually 32 or 64 bits, for I2C it is 8 or 16 bits wide. Some of these registers are control registers (read/write), others are status registers (read only). The control registers have bit fields that set device operating parameters, or individual port parameters. For example, enable/disable interrupt generation to the host CPU or to enable/disable FEC error correction on port-25. Each bit also has a default value (reset value) that they are set to automatically after power on or reset, then the host software can overwrite them later. The default values are safe and non-operational, like all ports disabled. Status registers show operating parameters of the whole device (like PCIe endpoint base address) or a particular port (like port-12 has received 236867 error bits, or port-13 link is up). An example view of control and status registers and bit fields can be seen in Figure 7.8, from the open-source FPGA IP core project called OP2P.

Sometimes the registers are accessible through a slow I2C interface as well as a PCIe endpoint interface on the same device for debugging purposes or custom system initialization purposes. For example, the IPMI management microcontroller might want to write into the PCIe switch over I2C to set something up, before letting the main CPU to start booting and accessing the device through the PCIe port and start enumerating it right away. Or a TCAM chip needs to be set up over I2C for

offset	Register Name	Description
18h	op2p_rdreq_localaddress	Put the local buffer address of the data to be transferred into this register. (read request command)
1Ch	op2p_rdreq_destinationaddress	Put the remote buffer address of the data to be transferred into this register. (read request command)
20h	op2p_rdreq_sourceid	Put the device ID of the location hosting the data to be transferred into this register. (read request command)
24h	op2p_rdreq_destinationid	Put the device ID of this device into this register. (read request command)
28h	op2p_rdreq_bytecount	Put the number of bytes to be transferred into this register. (read request command)
2Ch	op2p_rdcompl_localaddress	If a read is completed, this FIFO will show the address where the data has been stored.
4Ch	op2p_link_status	Tells if the link is alive, and also which lanes bit description 0 CHANNEL_UP 2:1 LANE_UP 28:3 0 - unused 29 fc_haltlinkpartner 30 fc_halted_bylinkpartner 31 HARD_ERROR
50h	op2p_port_reset	We can initiate a soft reset to this OP2P port by register write bit-0: set 1 to hold reset, set 0 to release from reset. After startup the port is not in reset.

FIGURE 7.8 Example register and bit description from the open-source OP2P project.

the correct Interlaken mode on its high-speed interface before the ASIC or FPGA can start talking to it through the Interlaken SERDES link. All these registers as well as any state machines will be reset to default values by the reset signal input to the chip, which is the main purpose of having reset signals on the boards. A state machine is a chip-level logic feature that implements a flow chart type behavioral functionality. Typically, it controls something, or processes data.

7.3 DATA PLANE

The data plane is sometimes called "payload". The data plane is the set of components, signals, and circuits that take care of the main function of the board, which is processing or inspecting user data. Sometimes the same interface, such as a x16 PCIe link, is used for both data plane and control plane. Data plane chips are usually the large BGA chips (up to 8000 pins, up to 500W) connected with many-lane SERDES interconnects. For example, 10 lanes of 25G KR or 192 lanes of 56G Ethernet on one chip. One data plane ASIC in 2023 might be able to process 0.1 to 50 Tbit/s of data bandwidth. Control plane to the same chip (if not used for data plane also) is usually a x1 to x8 PCIe link, or an I2C bus with 30x to 10000x less bandwidth. Typical data plane main device functions are programmable peripherals, data processing (calculate new data sets), transforming (conversion, image manipulation), or data switching (forwarding packets from one port towards another port (Ethernet, PCIe, CXL, RapidIO, or other).

Some of the data processing might not be done by the main data plane device; rather, it is copied into a specialized chip's memory to be processed there, aka "accelerated". This can have a much better performance versus power dissipation or price ratio (as much as 1000x). These are the accelerator ASICs; they are attached to the main device over very high bandwidth SERDES links. A CPU can be accelerated by one or more FPGAs, AI ASICs, or GPUs. An FPGA or ASIC (custom or switching) can be accelerated by one or more ASIC or FPGA chips attached to each main FPGA/ASIC. Sometimes the data that are traveling between an external port and the main device might need additional processing on the way, or the task is "off-loaded" to an in-line specialized ASIC chip. Off-loading is not a standard term, it is introduced here for the sake of categorization. Some might call the off-loading also as acceleration. The main types of off-loading are data format conversion, compression, encryption, or inspection (finding things). For both acceleration and off-loading usually not all data and traffic types get processed by the extra ASIC chips; rather, only certain type types, the rest would bypass. In the case of acceleration, the main device decides the bypassing, in case of off-loading the specialized ASIC does.

Accelerators produce new data from the provided original data outside of the main host CPU. Figure 7.9 shows the generic concept of a server CPU loading some data into GPGPU cards, then taking the new data and sending it where it belongs to the user over Ethernet. We can use chip-down accelerator ASICs on the main board or use add-in cards or separate appliance chassis. An appliance is a chassis that has multiple accelerator ASICs, plus data switching chips using Ethernet, PCIe, CXL, or NVLINK, aggregated to inter-chassis cabling. The chip can be an AI ASIC (artificial intelligence), custom in-house designed ASIC, FPGA, or GPGPU (general purpose GPU). Any computer-intensive task can be accelerated, like AI inference, file compression, encryption, 5G cell phone base

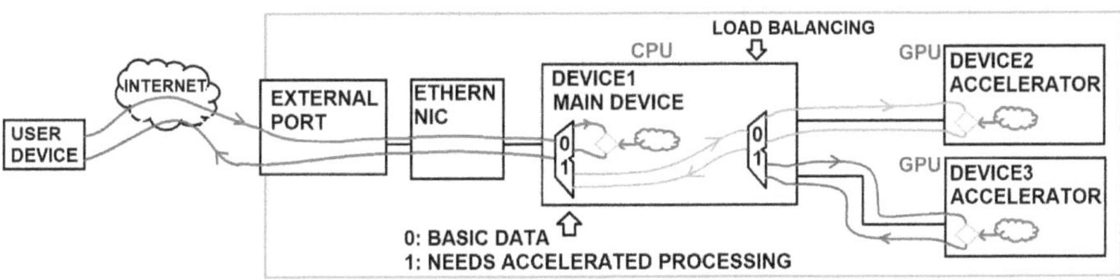

FIGURE 7.9 Server with accelerator cards.

station waveform, and protocols processing. For example, a live language translation task from a phone app might be transferred to a data center, to a server, and to an AI appliance that will recognize language and sentences, return the translated data that the processor sends back over the Internet to the phone app. Ethernet switching ASICs might utilize an accelerator ASIC to perform "telemetry", like counting data amount to each user for billing purposes or measuring data type statistics. Another common accelerator ASIC type is the TCAM and the search processor. Some newer Ethernet switch ASICs have integrated TCAM blocs, so they no longer need to externally accelerate this particular function, but custom FPGA-based designs can still use them. Accelerator ASICs usually have a wide bandwidth data plane interface to an upstream host and perhaps an additional low bandwidth (PCIe or I2C) interface to the same host for control plane. Some accelerator ASICs have local memory buffers also, in the form of DDR5, GDDR5, QDR, or HBM (on-package) memory.

An accelerator ASIC will take the data and produce completely new data, while the "off-loading ASIC" forwards the constantly flowing original data while inspecting it for what is in it or modifies it (for example encryption). Both accelerators and off-loading functions can be implemented on ASIC chips (by the chip company) or on FPGAs (by the board/system company). Off-loading is used more frequently on Ethernet links, which is otherwise used for forwarding data from one place to another. These off-loading ASICs are attached to general purpose ASICs or FPGAs. A basic diagram shows Device2 acting as an in-line off-loading ASIC in Figure 7.10. It might be used to detect data, control or block data, or modify the data flowing through. The use might be network security, format conversion, compression, or encryption. A high-speed A/D converter can be considered an off-loading device from the point of view of the main FPGA that first processes the digitized waveforms in an RF radio application. These data offloading schemes are designed by systems, software, and FPGA engineering, and the hardware designer has to implement the platform for it in the board design. Off-loading ASICs, just like the accelerators, usually have a wide bandwidth data plane interface to the main ASIC and a low bandwidth (PCIe or I2C) interface to the host processor for debugging and configuration.

In some systems the data plane ASICs move high bandwidth data in and out of a chassis by themselves, while in other systems they need to be given/taken data streams by a main switch ASIC or a high-performance host processor. This way we can have a chassis with multiple data plane ASICs and one or more "data mover" ASICs. In some cases, they all might be designed on the same one large and very complex PCB. A 20-inch deep (maximum size on a common fabricator panel size) and rack wide (16" to 18") board can host a half dozen hundred-Watt ASICs. In many cases it would be implemented on multiple cards plugged into a backplane or accelerator cards plugged into a server motherboard—one card hosting one main ASIC. Data moving can be done by a CPU loading and storing data (directed by software), by a DMA engine built into a switch ASIC, or by an Ethernet switch ASICs routing/switching/forwarding the data endlessly.

The health of the network has to be monitored from a large number of switching equipment into a centralized administrator accessible point, which is called telemetry. For this to work the network ASICs have to collect real time information. These are port utilization, buffer occupancy,

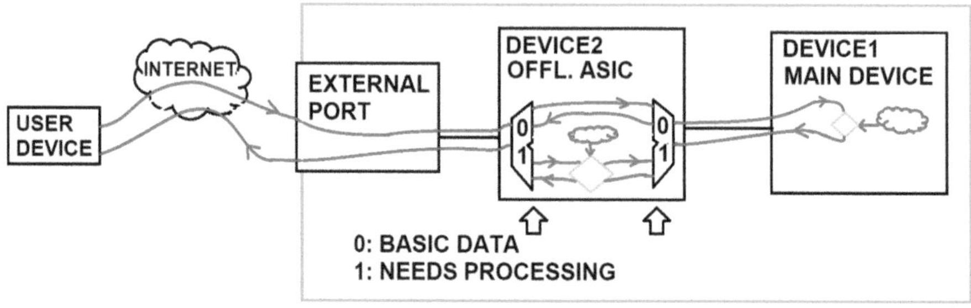

FIGURE 7.10 Generalized in-line processing with off-loading.

packet drop amount, latency, network jitter, and usage by application/location. Some of this data is represented as individual data points, others as statistics, which is accessible by a control plane or a management processor. If it is not integrated in the main switch ASIC chip, then there is the need to accelerate this function by another device on the switch board. If it is integrated, then it is nice to know about it, but not very important to the board hardware designer, but if it requires an extra chip that is a big hardware architecture item. This book is for board hardware designers. This whole topic of accelerators and off-loading are discussed here from the point of view of having to put extra chips and interfaces into our board designs. We also have to account for their management and initialization circuits, fitting those in with the whole board's init sequence. These ASICs also have a bandwidth that needs to be known, so we can calculate how many devices are needed in the system and how many ports or lanes of SERDES will they take up on the other devices to connect them. If they need external memory buffering then we need to know how much memory size and speed we need to design onto the board with them. Either from datasheet, from talking to the chip vendors, or from the in-house FPGA or ASIC team.

7.4 CONTROL PLANE

Control Plane is the set of components, signals, and circuits that take care of the initialization of the data plane components and interfaces, monitoring their health and operation readiness, in some cases collecting telemetry (temperature, voltage), altering their behavior on user command or scripts and logging fault details. This is usually done using a local X86 or ARM host processor, with additional components like lower power and smaller/medium-size FPGAs, PCI-Express switches, bridge chips, low speed Ethernet NICs, Ethernet switches, and PHYs and discrete logic chips. This might be integrated on the main board with the data plane ASICs or on a separate card in the chassis. In many chassis products there is a "management card" that works both as the control plane and as the management plane host. The telemetry is the collection of system health-related variables like rail voltages, currents, and temperature from any sensor or device on the board in regular time intervals. Smart VRMs or sequencer chips can collect voltage data that are readable over an I2C bus. In some cases, the control plane handles it, in other cases the management plane does it if the architecture has separated them. In some systems there is no clear distinction between the control and management planes if the system designers choose to use a single processor to handle both the large device initialization and the small device telemetry.

The Ethernet links used in the CP (if there is no separate management plane) are much slower compared to the data plane network speed—we call it "Management Ethernet" or sometimes "Base Channel". For example, the data plane might consist of 1000 lanes of 56Gig lines, while the control plane might only use a 5Gig PCIe x1 with a 1Gig Ethernet link. Most larger data plane ASICs have a PCI-Express endpoint interface, which requires enumeration, then initialization when the OS driver loads large number of register configurations into the chip. Some chips might get their configuration over slow (I2C, SPI, or MDIO) interfaces. Sometimes ASICs and FPGAs contain a small (ARM) integrated processor on chip that serves as the control plane function.

7.5 GLUE LOGIC

Glue logic circuits are needed on every complex digital board, in the CP, DP, MP portions (planes) of the design, to make all the main and support devices work together. This is the part that is the hardest to describe. It consists of digital and analog circuits that support, control, and monitor the low level (power up, stay powered, start booting) operation of all other parts of the board and system. This is not an isolated block; it interacts with everything. It allows all other parts of a board to work. Most of it is typically implemented on small low-power flash-based FPGAs or CPLDs, using VHDL or Verilog code, like simple logic equations, synchronous processes, state machines, and low speed interfaces (I2C, SPI). Some glue logic is implemented using simple discrete chips like

I2C multiplexers, CMOS buffers, level translators, EEPROMs, or thermal sensor chips. Most of the glue logic is powered from a standby power rail, which is powered up by itself even when the rest of the board is not powered up yet. It has a very low power consumption, overall 0.1 to 1W. This way it can control the power rails of those other circuits, and it is able to prepare control signal states to be ready before those other devices are ready to take them. Sometimes we also involve power sequencing chips and micro controllers in the glue logic subsystem, at other times these functions are implemented on the small FPGA. The glue logic is fully tailored to the particular board design. Its VHDL/Verilog code is an integral part of the board schematics, it cannot be treated a black box module like control plane FPGAs can be. This I why most companies expect the board designers to write it. Most of it (except the I/O interfaces and bigger state machines) cannot be simulated in a meaningful way since the surrounding board's digital and analog circuits cannot be simulated with it. It would, for example, require a complete server processor with its core temperature, system fans, heatsinks, air baffles being part of a simulation model, and that is impossible. So the design debug is done at the board and system prototype bring-up in the lab. There have been efforts to standardize a glue logic chip, as a one size fits all solution, but it fit nothing at all. We can re-use some glue logic code but expect 30% to 80% of changes when tailoring it to another board design.

In a glue logic FPGA code, there are several types of logic implementations. The simplest is the logic equation, for example, this power domain gating of a reset signal in VHDL below.

```
FPGARESET_N <= PLTRST_N AND FPGAC_POWERGOOD;
```

For a bit more complicated controls we use if/else statements, and they have to be put into a code frame called "process" to compile. The example below waits for a glitch or toggle event on the PGOOD input, then it asserts its output and remains high forever, so we can later check if there ever was a glitch or not. It holds or latches the output because the statement has no "else" clause.

```
process (RESET, PGOOD)
begin
if (RESET='1') then
       GLITCH_CATCH <= '0';
elsif PGOOD='0'
       GLITCH_CATCH <= '1';
end if;
end process;
```

Time-relevant and sequence-related glue logic signal controls can be implemented with a microcontroller chip running firmware or with a "state machine" inside an FPGA. A state machine is a flow-diagram implemented in a VHDL code. It runs on a clock and evaluates outputs only at the rising edge of the clock. State machines are used for power sequencing, reset generation, switch debouncing, or even as I/O bus interface logic. Some of them might be a 1000 lines long. An example can be seen below. It is a delay block that produces a PowerGood signal to an X86 chipset, with a 100 clock cycle delay after the chipset core voltage rail VRM PowerGood has asserted.

```
process (CLOCK, RESET, P1V0_PWRGD)
begin
if (RESET='0') then
       x_state <= "00";
       CHIPSET_PWRGD <= '0';
       x_counter <= "00000000";
else
if (CLOCK'event and CLOCK = '1') then
 case ( x_state ) is
       when "00" => --state 0
              CHIPSET_PWRGD <= '0';
              x_counter <= "00000000";
```

```
            if (P1V0_PWRGD ='1') then x_state <= "01";
      when "01" => --state 1
            if (x_counter="01100100") then CHIPSET_PWRGD <= '1';
            else x_counter <= x_counter + 1;
            end if;
            if (P1V0_PWRGD ='0') then x_state <= "00"; end if;
      when others => --error state
            x_state <= "00"; --go to state 0
 end case;
end if;
end if;
end process;
```

The next level up in complexity of features is using IP cores or blocks that are connected together with internal parallel synchronous buses. We can create a block diagram of the glue logic FPGA, like in Figure 7.11, but it will only show the larger blocks and communication interfaces, it will not show any low-level glue logic functions, neither will it show how the blocks interact with actual board signals.

Typical functions of board glue logic:

- System and board level power management.
- Power Sequencing of VRMs and power switches on board.
- Power domain gating of all control signals with power good signals.
- Reset overrides and forwarding/combining. Multiple sources can order a board or device to be put into reset, for example, the main host processor, the IPMI management processor, VRM power good, thermal shutdown.
- Hot-swap insertion control and status reporting.
- Thermal shutdown ordering the power sequencer.
- Fan control.
- Monitoring voltage rails and providing status to host.
- Status LED de-serialization from network ASICs.

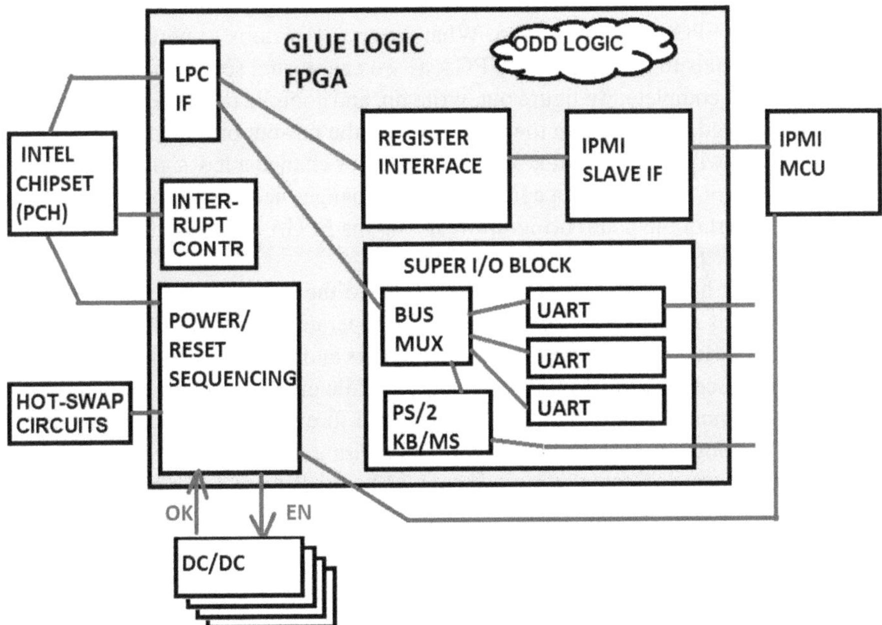

FIGURE 7.11 Typical glue logic FPGA block diagram main blocks.

- Backplane status/control, board mode setup, backplane bridge chip mode control.
- Helping parallel buses to expand and attach devices through address decoding and multiplexing.
- Data gathering and concentration in registers through low-speed buses.
- Initializing devices like larger FPGA, CPUs, DSPs, ASICs.
- Button and switch debouncing.
- Any ASIC control signal creation or scheduling.
- ASIC boot strap (strapping pin) control, instead of strapping resistors. This can be easily changed in the VHDL/Verilog code during prototyping.
- Register set accessible to host through I2C, LPC, or PCIe bus. Providing status and fault reporting and control access to any of the functions.
- Fault logging and reporting, in registers (erased by power cycle) or in external EEPROM/FRAM chips (black box function).
- X86 chipset power management interface (like THERMTRIP, PWRBTN, SLP_S3…).
- Payload FPGA configuration support and status monitoring (CONF_DONE…).
- Slow bus (JTAG, I2C, SPI) buffers and multiplexing.
- Logic level translation.
- Sensor polling and taking action if values out of range.
- GPIOs for controlling device modes or behavior.
- Shift registers for teleporting many signals from one FPGA to another.

Different hardware designers choose a different portion of the above list to be implemented on a single low-power FPGA or CPLD, between 0% and 90%, while the remaining portion is implemented with discrete or simple devices if needed. The higher the percentage, the lower the prototyping and project schedule risk because any bugs on FPGA-code-based glue logic can be fixed by code change and reprogramming on the same day, instead of board rework/re-spin.

The main and most important uses of the glue logic are board and system level power management, power sequencing, and reset logic. The glue logic FPGA is not the same type of device as the data plane FPGAs, those are much larger and more powerful devices. We cannot combine them into one device, as the glue logic has to run from a small amount of standby power and has to participate in managing the larger FPGA's configuration. What we typically do is to hook up as many of the on-board glue logic signals to the glue logic FPGA as we can during schematic design, then while waiting for the layout to complete, we figure out, write up, and compile the FPGA code to make sure everything was accounted for and fits in the device before the fab-out of the board. During writing the glue logic code, we will likely find that we need to add or change a few signals on the board, so it will affect the schematic and the layout a little. So these changes need to be applied before fab-out. Then during the first part of the board bring-up we debug the FPGA code and the board signals and circuits, together as one. This cannot be separated.

Glue logic is usually hard to think through compared to the data and control plane structures, so designing glue logic is more prone to error. Glue logic operation is a multi-dimensional complex function on every board. It is an interaction between all parts and all devices, all at once. Some parts of the glue logic can be seen as a clear tree/star topology, while others are more like a random mesh-like structure-less diagram where everything is connected to everything and affected in multiple ways. A lot of the glue logic is a cause-and-effect chain with a dozen or more steps. We can see a demonstration of this confusing complexity in Figure 7.12, which gives the impression that this traditional block diagram is not the right way to describe low-level glue logic. Usually when we create a glue logic block diagram for our project documentation, it only contains major blocks, but not any individual logic functions producing a single signal. Many single-signal (non-bus) logic equations are also parts of the glue logic FPGA. There can be 10 to 100 of those. Instead of making a single block diagram for the whole glue logic FPGA, we need to provide descriptions and diagrams to individual functions separately. Functional flow charts can help with designing and analyzing low-level

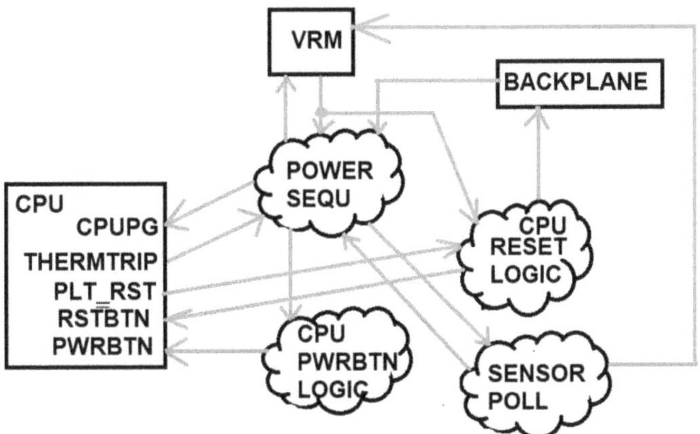

FIGURE 7.12 Confusing complexity of individual glue logic signals as schematic.

functions within the glue logic much better than schematic-like block diagrams could. Later in this chapter we will see several examples of flow charts. A schematic or block diagram only show where all the signals are going, but they do not show when they assert, while flow charts clearly show when the signals change state relative to other signals. The key is the "state", which is why we use state machines in the design that only assert a certain signal if other signals were asserted in a certain sequence previously. For example, we can explain all the alarm and warning signals as to how they affect the power and reset on one flow-chart diagram, then on a separate diagram we can show how the management controller's signals interact with starting/stopping the power sequencer. Flow charts show the temporal sequence of events, basically when a certain signal is supposed to affect another, not just that a signal might affect another sometimes (block diagram and schematic). A lot of heuristic thinking goes into glue logic design, not much systematizing, and a lot of prototype debugging. We use many small state machines, clocked processes, and asynchronous latching processes as well as, in few cases, just bare logic equations.

7.5.1 The Use of IP Cores

Sometimes in the glue logic FPGAs, and in the larger FPGAs too, we can re-use blocks of code that implement a well-defined function, like an SMBUS interface, a UART core, or a SPI-EEPROM controller. It only makes sense to use IP cores for the blocks that also show up on the main block diagram, like communication interfaces, or a general power sequencer. We can see an example in Figure 7.13. Some of these can be our own previous designs or they might be from a library within our company, purchased from an IP vendor, or from a free online source like OpenCores.org or GitHub.com.

When we use communication cores, then usually we also have to create a standard internal bus structure inside the FPGA, for example AMBA, Wishbone (open source), or AXI (AMD/Xilinx). These are common clock synchronous parallel buses. While board-level designs can have multiple devices connected to the same bus signal nets, the chip-level designs can use only point-to-point signals. This creates the need for bus multiplexing modules to be placed in the block diagram, which decodes addresses and multiplexes the transaction into one interface-port or another. It has a separate port for each device.

7.5.2 Power Management

Power management is about controlling the turn on/off events of the voltage regulator and power switch devices. This is controlled by the board glue logic, usually a small FPGA, and a management processor or microcontroller (sometimes an IPMI standard implementation).

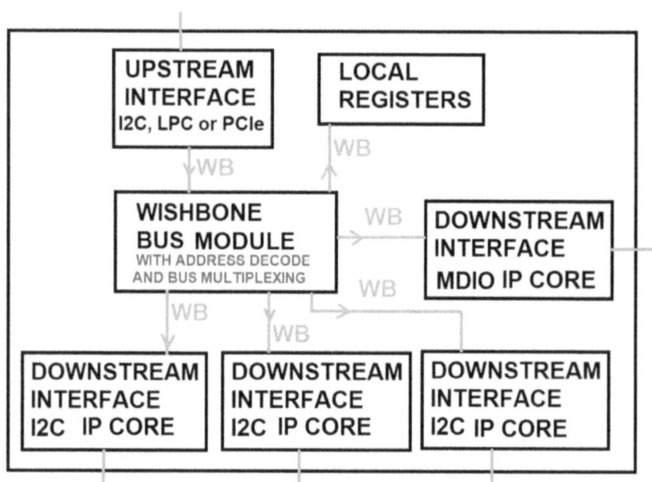

FIGURE 7.13 IP cores in small FPGA design.

7.5.2.1 System Power Management

In a system or chassis, there are multiple cards. Usually, the cards can be turned on or off individually by the main management card (chassis manager, shelf manager, supervisor). The mechanism for this has a sequence of events. First, the management card sends a command over the backplane I2C bus to one card, where the on-board IPMI microcontroller receives the command and instructs the glue logic to start the power on sequence. When the sequence is done it reports back through an IPMI status register, that the management card processor polls over I2C. When the status shows it is done, then the management card sends the power on command to the next card, and so on. The card power control commands are sent for different purposes, for example for power sequencing the chassis, hot swap insertion or ejection of a card, or fault handling. Power sequencing the system helps reducing the load step from the main power supply module, that helps preserving power circuit stability (avoid unexpected shutdown failure) and rail voltage within tolerance. In hot-swapping the card is not turned on immediately at insertion, but only after the management card detected what was plugged in and took precaution to prepare the system for adding a new module. The card also has to be turned off before it is ejected from the system, to avoid sparking. Either the user shuts the card down from software, a fault is detected and management protocol dictates to shut it down, or the ejection process started by the user opening the ejector handle (that contains a switch that sends an interrupt through the on-board IPMI microcontroller) at which point the software has less than one second to shut it down.

Each card in a system supposed to have a management controller or IPMI uC (IPMC) that sends status (reported in registers, for polling) and receives commands for power up/down or reset from the management card over the backplane, either as discrete signals or more commonly through I2C transactions. The management card reads (polls) or writes registers inside the on-board IPMC. Reporting to the management card can be through a backplane interrupt signal, but if it is not part of the design then the management card polls the IPMCs of each card frequently to get informed by card events. The IPMC tells the power sequencing FPGA when to sequence up or down, mixed with any local X86 chipset acting as a local power manager master. With X86 chipsets at power on, the IPMC tells the glue logic to turn on, it tells the X86 chipset through the power button signal, the chipset signals back through the SLP_S3# signal, then the glue logic sequences all VRMs up through their power enable and power good signals, then the glue logic tells the X86 chipset and the IPMC that all power is good. There can be two power manager masters on one board, one (the X86 CPU) thinks it is the main master, the other (IPMC) pretends to be a user pressing buttons.

7.5.2.2 Board Power Management

Boards and systems usually have a standby power domain that is always on and it is not dependent on any user interaction to turn it on, and also have a main power domain for the main ASICs. The VRMs in the main power domain are controlled by the glue logic chips (FPGAs, microcontrollers or power sequencer chips) that are powered by the standby power domain. On very large multi-ASIC boards large blocks of circuits can be a power domain, for example, one ASIC with its supporting circuits can be one domain. Within systems there are boards, often the boards are turned on or off by the management card, telling all other cards when to turn on or off through I2C commands sent to each board's IPMC.

The board startup begins with the standby domain power being applied when the AC cord is plugged in, the glue logic initializes itself with its fast POR reset circuit, then either waits for a user touching a power button or starts up the board by default, meaning it will turn on all VRMs in sequence. Most of the complex hardware in data center or aerospace products are "automated", not expected to interact with a user through buttons, so they start up when the power cable is plugged in.

There are "power domains" that are sets of circuits, devices, and VRMs that stay powered up in the same time, with a single power sequence. There are also "power states", which are temporary arrangements, defining which power domains are on and which ones are off. Boards with X86 processors can implement the ACPI (Advanced Configuration and Power Interface) power management architecture, as the X86 chipsets work with this in their most default setting. ACPI defines several power states, including the G3 (mechanical Off) when the power cord and/or battery is unplugged, the S5 (standby) state when the power cord and/or battery is plugged in and only the standby circuits are on, the S0 fully on state, and the S3 (suspend to RAM) state when only the system DDRx memory is powered to allow a quicker boot than a full S5-to-S0 boot-up. These states work with power domains. In an ACPI computer motherboard there is a standby power domain that powers the glue logic power sequencers, as well as the standby section of the X86 chipset. In the standby power state, only this standby domain is powered. There is a main "CPU" domain, and there is a memory domain for powering the DDRx RAM chips and associated circuits. In an X86 board startup with the standby domain power being applied, the glue logic initializes itself with its fast reset, the chipset standby portion initializes with RSMRST# driven by an RC circuit or by the glue logic. Then it either waits for a user (or management controllerwith glue logic) asserting the power button signal or starts up the board by default, then it will drive the SLP_S3# signal high from the chipset to the glue logic. Then the glue logic sequences all VRMs up. When it is fully on and running, the user has the option to put the board/system into an S3 sleep state from software GUI or console. Then the system will turn off all main rails by driving SLP_S3# low, except the standby and the DDRx memory rails. From sleep the board can be awakened (Wakeup event) through either the user pressing a power button, a peripheral asserting a motherboard WAKE# signal to the chipset, or someone sending "wake on LAN" Ethernet packets over the network to the motherboard's Ethernet controller's MAC address. At that point the chipset will drive SLP_S3# high again to let the glue logic know to sequence all VRMs back on again. The signals of the X86 power management scheme are demonstrated in Figure 7.14 and the state transitions in Figure 7.15. Color coding on the block diagram shows which device, power rail group, and control signal is in which power domain. Red is standby, green is the S3 domain used in normal operation and in sleep (suspend to RAM), and blue is general main (S0) domain.

The X86 chipset has a power button input pin that is driven by an actual button on basic consumer motherboards, but on complex hardware it is usually driven by the glue logic as it pulses it to imitate a human button press event, to let the chipset know it has to turn on and start booting. The X86 chipset is supposed to be in control of board power states, but on complex hardware boards the board glue logic is added as a higher layer of control on top of that. If a multi-ASIC board also contains an on-board X86 control plane processor, then the X86 CPU has to control the power to the whole board, or it has to think that it controls it while being subordinate to the glue logic and the IPMC. It is simply done by the FPGA glue logic handling all the chipset power management

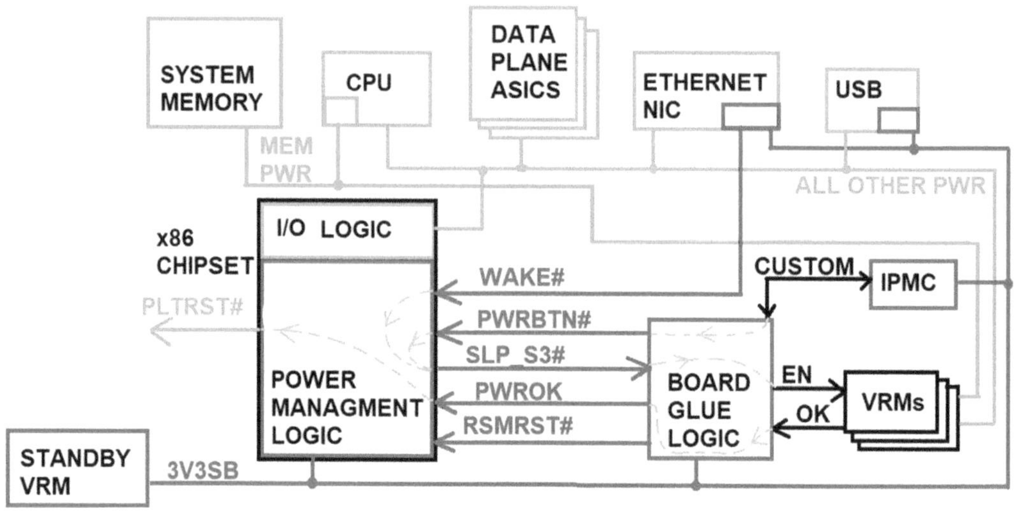

FIGURE 7.14 X86 power management logic block diagram with ACPI.

signals using simple state machines. General ASICs and FPGAs do not need to know the whole board power state, but X86 CPUs do as they were designed to be in control. The chipset and CPU has additional power management signals not mentioned here, for example, chipset PowerGood and a few others.

A non-X86 board power state transition sequence is a subset of the X86 sequence, basically simpler. There is no S3 sleep state, no wakeup events, no fake buttons, and there is no need to babysit a chipset through dozens of glue logic signals. The signals of the non-X86 power management scheme are demonstrated in Figure 7.16 and the state transitions in Figure 7.17.

7.5.2.3 Power Domain Crossing

On a complex digital board, we have multiple different power domains. As a minimum there is a standby and a main or payload domain. On some designs there is a standby, a control plane, a data plane, and a memory domain, or multiple data plane domains. During the system startup, or during sleep states, for a while some power domains are turned on while others are in the off state. During this time, we have the power domain crossing issue that has to be handled by design. Power domain crossing is when a signal is driven by a device that is in one power domain, but the receiver device is in another power domain. Devices can be informed about the states of other power domains through VRM PowerGood signals. In most designs we do not have all combinations of domains on or off ever present, only a subset. For example, the design guarantees through power sequencing that device 1 will never be on when device 2 is off, but device 2 can be on regardless whether device 1 is on or off.

Protection diodes are built into all digital chips that clip the I/O pin voltage to be no higher than VIO+0.7V. When a device is turned off through its POL VRMs being off, it diode shorts all I/O signals to the 0V VCC, basically to ground. So any signal that is driven into a pin of an unpowered device is driven into the ground and might damage the output buffer of the powered device. Any third-party device listening to that signal will see an erroneous low level.

In cases where the driver device is powered up but the receiver device is not, the driver device should drive its output signal low or tristate it, or the receiver device needs protection from the signal. If we drive a signal high (like a clock is high-low-high-low toggling) into an unpowered device, it will stress and potentially damage that device. It will also force a current into the power rail of that device through its I/O pin protection diode that is built into the circuits of most digital chips. That current will cause the unpowered device's I/O voltage rail to have a voltage on it between its nominal value and zero (a plateau), and the IO pin will act as a power pin that it was not designed for,

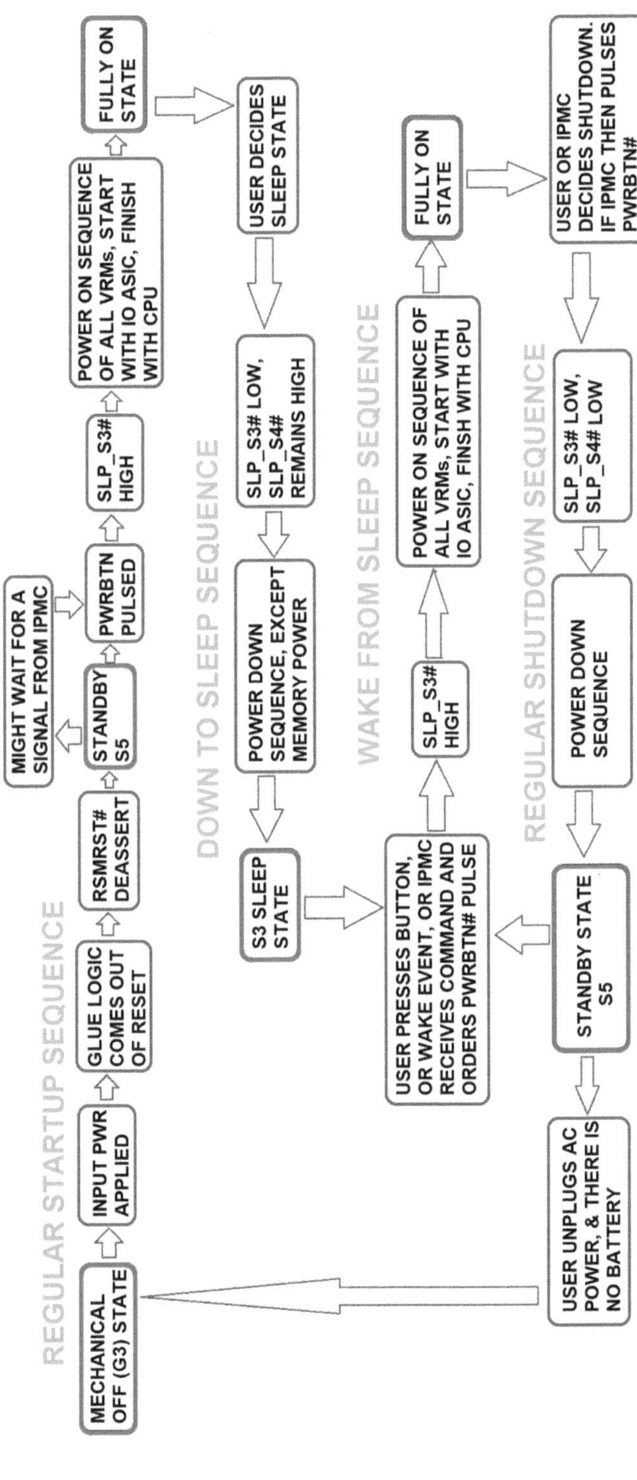

FIGURE 7.15 X86 board power sequence flow chart.

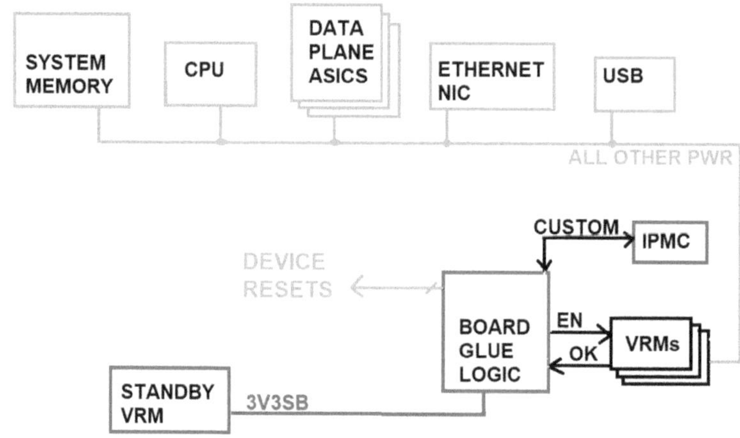

FIGURE 7.16 Non-X86 power management logic block diagram.

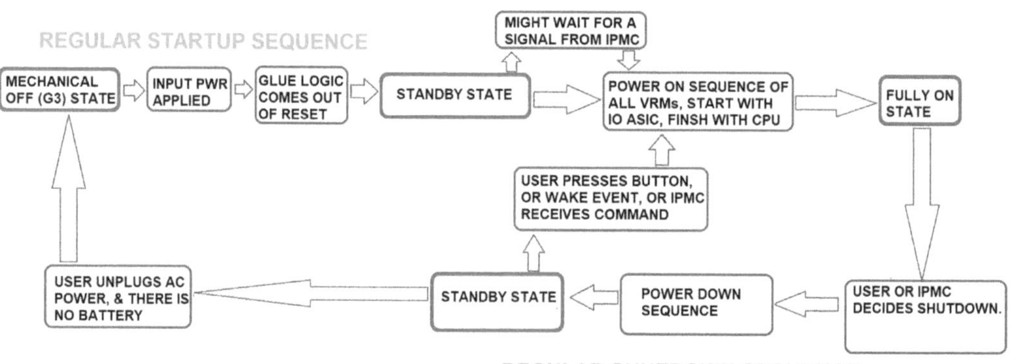

FIGURE 7.17 Non-X86 board power sequence flow chart.

likely damaging it. The damage might be immediate or it might kill the chip after being used for a few months by the customer. We can apply some AND-gated glue logic that overrides the outgoing signal state, to force it low, when the PowerGood signal of the other device is low.

In cases where the driver device is not powered but the receiver is powered, the receiver has to ignore the input signal. In this case the signal will be near zero volts or at logic low value. If it is a critical error indication active low signal, like a thermal alert, it would mean the other device is experiencing a critical failure, but that would be a false detection because the other device is turned off and there are no over temperature or other errors happening inside it. So for inputs coming from unpowered devices, we need some glue logic (discrete logic gates or multiplexers, or some code in the glue logic FPGA) that drives the signal to the safe or un-asserted state. When to apply the logic override can be determined from PowerGood signals of the VRMs. We need to OR-gate active low signals, AND-gate active high signals. If the VRM supplying the core rail to ASIC2 is off, its PowerGood signal is low, then our glue logic should alter the incoming signal to be un-asserted. The logic gates should be powered from the standby rail or from the rail that is powered on the same time ASIC1 is powered on. In real board designs most of these signals are between the glue logic FPGA and each data plane ASIC, so the handling logic would be some code in the glue logic FPGA, using a gating equation with PowerGood signals. In cases where the domain crossing signal is between two data plane ASICs, then we might want to route it through the glue logic FPGA or use discrete logic chips on board. Or there can be some software handshaking, all driving their outputs low and ignoring inputs, until they are both alive and then flip the input and output modes.

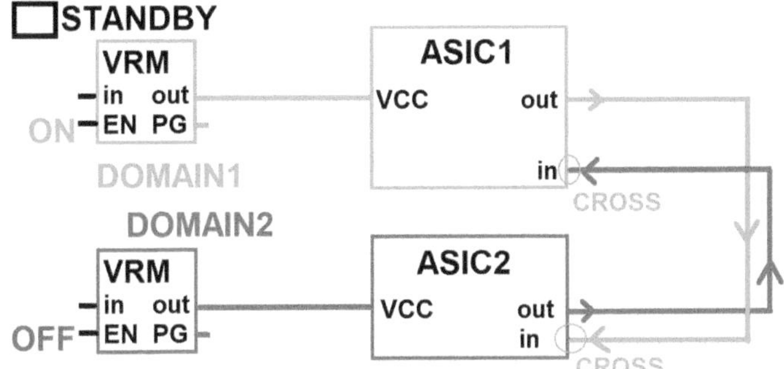

FIGURE 7.18 Power domain crossing without any mitigation.

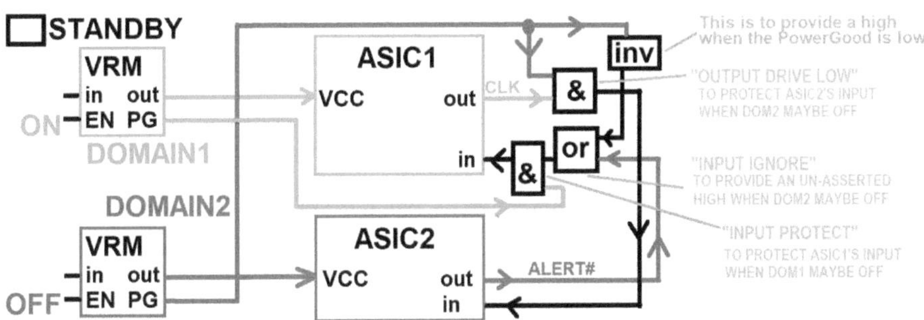

FIGURE 7.19 Power domain crossing mitigation with glue logic.

We can create diagrams where power domains are color coded. The device outline and the signals driven by the device would be one color, devices and signals driven by them in another domain would be another color. We can see if we have a problem when different colors meet at a pin. This can be seen in Figure 7.18. Then we can apply glue logic to the crossing and re-draw the diagram. We can mark the glue logic and the handled signal in black, so we can ignore any color-versus-black meeting at pins. Also, it makes sense to power the glue logic from the standby power domain, so it will be ready before the payload ASICs are ready and not produce transitioning waveforms while devices are powering up. Defaulting a signal to high-level using discrete OR-gate chips that run on standby will create an additional power domain crossing, but an extra AND-gate using the receiver device's PowerGood signal can handle that. So there are three cases that need handling: the "input ignore", the "input protect", and the "output drive low". The input ignore case and the output drive low case can be handled inside the chip without discrete parts if it is an FPGA (VHDL/Verilog) or a CPU (software). The input protect case needs discrete logic only if the driver is not a CPU or a FPGA that could have applied the output drive low policy. Discrete logic in practice would mean a single-gate in a SC-70 package or an analog multiplexer (detaches the signal) chip. We will detect the crossings with the diagram at the input pins, but the mitigation glue logic should be applied at the most convenient end, or at both ends for safety—except if one device is the glue logic and power manager FPGA because then the burden is only on that one device, it will never need input protection. Both the input and the output power domain handling logic are demonstrated with examples in Figure 7.19.

7.5.3 Power Sequencing

Power sequence means that when power is applied to a board, as when we want to turn the system on, the different voltage rails are turned on one by one, not all at once. This is to eliminate instability that would cause the system to shut down before even reaching a fully operational state. The instability could be caused by VRMs falsely detecting overcurrent due to their input rail's voltage fluctuation. Complex ASIC chips require many voltage rails, and they also require them to be turned on in a pre-defined (in the datasheet) order—this is the ASIC's power sequencing requirement. If we do not provide the correct sequence to each ASIC, then they will fail to initialize correctly some low percentage of the time, they will likely have intermittent startup failures. We also have to provide a power down sequence, in the exact reverse order, to prevent damaging any ASICs. In some cases, an ASIC might exhibit intermittent startup failures if it was previously shut down with an incorrect power-down sequence. Sometimes the sequence definition in the datasheet might be ambiguous, we might misunderstand it, then we end up having to change it on the prototype. We should not design our board power tree in a way that does not allow these kinds of changes. The easiest way to achieve that is by using only VRMs that run from 12V, not from intermediate voltages, and not share 3.3V rails between ASICs.

The "forward sequence" in power on is when the higher voltage rails are turned on earlier, and finish with the lowest voltage rail. The sequence goes by decreasing rail voltages forward, for example 3.3V → 2.5V → 1.8V → 1.5V → 1V. The "reverse sequence" is the opposite. ASIC device datasheets explain the rail order that the device needs; we have to recognize which type it is. Ideally, every rail on every device will be generated by a separate point-of-load VRM. This way we can provide any order of power on sequence, and we can change it on the prototype without board design re-spin when the ASIC does not work reliably. Using point-of-load VRMs is also necessary to reduce the DC voltage drop from source to destination to meet the tight voltage tolerance requirement. Point-of-load means the VRM is placed right next to the ASIC on the PCB and not shared between different ASICs.

We, the board hardware designers, have to combine the sequencing requirements of all ASICs on our board into one big power-on sequence, and design the board glue logic to implement it. Figure 7.20 shows an example on a made-up board based on a single X86 processor, a PCIe switch, and a data plane FPGA. The whole board sequence might not follow a strict rail voltage order-based sequence; rather, we start with the global rails, then we turn on all rails that belong to one ASIC in a voltage-order, then we turn on all rails that belong to another ASIC in a voltage-order until all ASIC subsystems are on.

Often we have one or two shared rails between devices, usually a global 3.3V rail. If any device requires a reverse sequence, then that device needs a MOSFET power switch on the shared rail to create a new 3.3V rail with a new net name, so we can delay the turn-on event of that rail to that one ASIC device only, while the rest of the devices are on a forward power-on sequence using the main 3.3V VRM output directly.

Depending on board complexity, we can have five different power sequencing schemes, as illustrated in Figure 7.21. Options-a/b/c are implemented without any sequencing chip, option-d uses an FPGA, while option-e uses a power sequencing chip like the UCD901xx series or the LTM2987 device. The simplest one, on option-a on the diagram, is when we supply the lower voltage rails from the higher voltage ones, with all enable pins tied to their inputs. It is used only on very basic boards. The next one, on option-b, is when we connect the PowerGood or PowerOK output of one VRM to the enable input of the next VRM, and so on, creating a chain. The first VRM in the chain might just have its enable pin tied to a reset generator or a pullup resistor. This cannot be modified on a prototype, so if we find our sequence wrong, it can be fixed only by a board re-spin. The next level up on option-c is to use voltage monitor ICs instead of PowerGood signals. Some VRMs do not have PowerGood outputs, and sometimes even if they do, we might still want to have a custom threshold to decide if the rail is in a sufficiently good state. If our ASIC has an X% voltage input tolerance, then our analog sensing circuits (ADC, monitor, comparator) should be set to a wider 2*X% to 5*X% tolerance for the PowerGood generation (threshold) because they are usually picking up phantom noises that can cause false alarms. Options d and e with digital sequencers are common on more complex boards with component count above ~600. They use

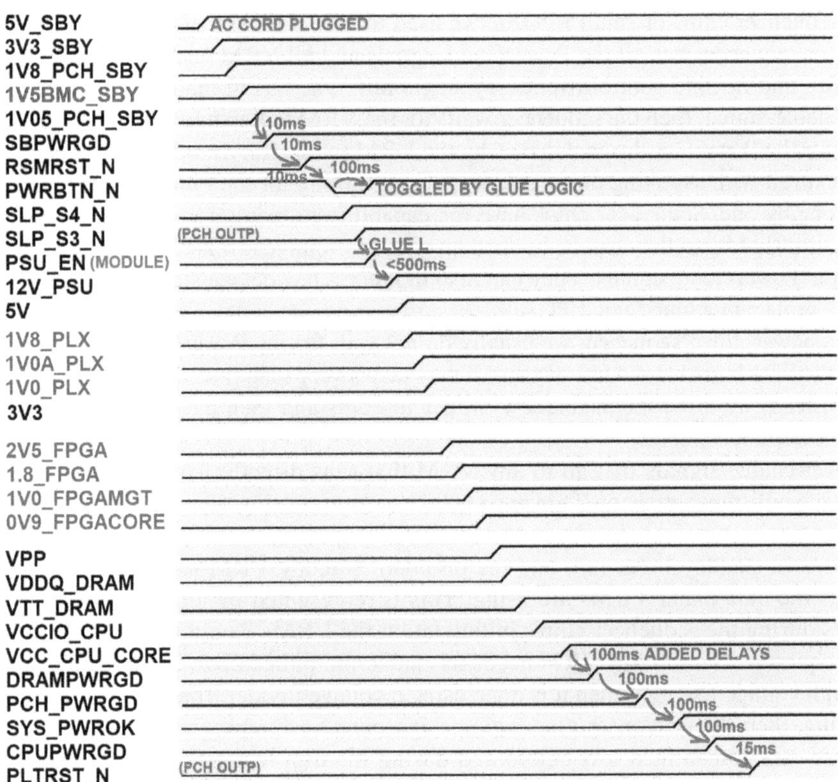

FIGURE 7.20 Example of a power-on sequence of a made-up motherboard concept.

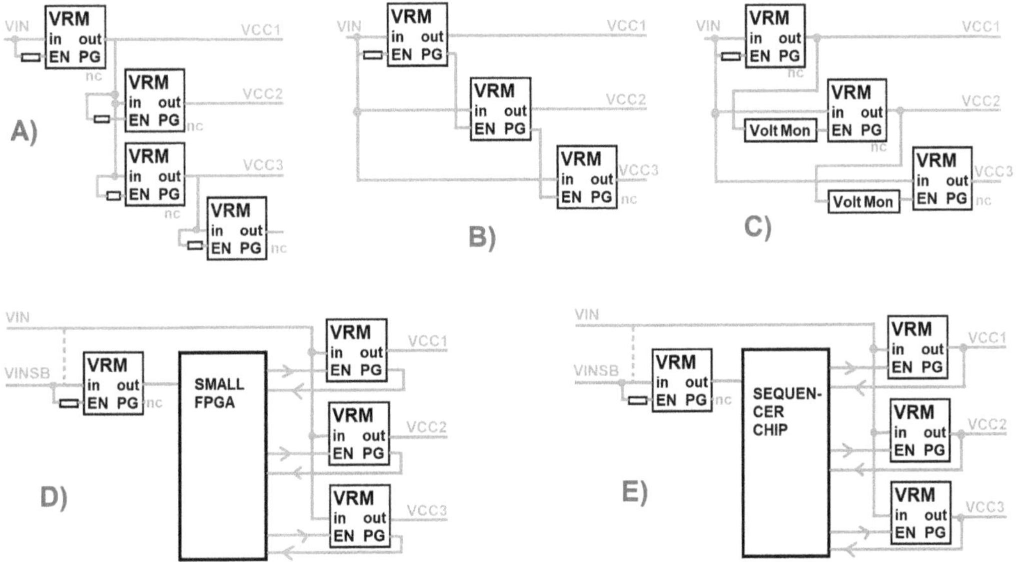

FIGURE 7.21 Power sequencing schemes.

dedicated sequencer chips or small FPGAs (we used to use CPLDs) that run from a standby rail. The FPGA or sequencer has all the PowerGood signals and all VRM enable signals connected to it, having full and flexible control over every single rail. One rail is enabled when the sequencer asserts its enable-signal, then the sequencer waits for the VRM to finish turning on, that is detected by waiting for the PowerGood signal driven by the VRM to assert. After that the sequencer moves on to the next rail with asserting the enable-signal and waiting for the PowerGood signal, for each rail/VRM one by one. Sequencer chips have the capability to monitor voltages with custom programmable thresholds, so they can be hooked up with the voltage rail itself (with voltage dividers) instead of the PowerGood signals. They can also monitor a few device status pins and control the reset signal, replacing a glue logic FPGA.

During a power-down sequence, we usually do not wait for the PowerGood to go low after we just driven the VRMs enable pin low because it may take a very long time due to decoupling capacitance. So instead, we drive the enable low, wait 1 to 20ms and then move onto the next rail and ignore the PowerGood signals.

The power-enable signals that go to any VRM that runs directly from the main (12V) input need to have a pull-down resistor. This prevents them from turning on when the sequencer is not programmed yet on new board units in the factory. The pull-down also helps on designs where there is no main standby input rail, and the on-board standby VRM runs from the same main input rail as the data plane VRMs are using. This is represented by a dotted line in the figure. These cases during the sequencer chip's initialization the VRMs would get enabled accidentally without a sequence. The standby VRM needs its enable-pin pulled up to its input, and if the input is a very high voltage like 12V then it is done using a voltage divider. If any smart VRMs require programming, then the sequencer glue logic design must have a programming mode where all VRM enables are forced held low before and during the first factory programming. This is to prevent damage to load ASICs. Except if the VRM uses its enable input as an internal reset, we really need to study the datasheet to see what options we have. We have to provide a DIP switch or a jumper, driving a signal into the FPGA, to put a board into a programming mode or a debug mode.

When using an FPGA-based sequencer, we have to consider some glue logic design aspects. The sequencer turns one voltage rail (VRM module) on at a time, using their enable signal, then wait for their PowerGood signal to be asserted by the VRM, then the FPGA moves on to the next rail, and repeat until all rails are on. The whole thing starts when a master state machine, X86 chipset or IPMI controller, gives a green light to start up the board. The voltage rails are numbered, so the sequencer can simply increment the rail number at each step with a counter.

On prototype boards it is very common that one voltage regulator fails to turn on or fails to remain on, which wrecks the sequence, so the downstream rails will never be turned on. In some cases, the VRM control loop (Bode plot) is unstable, causing the VRM output to shut down momentarily after several hours of run-time. VRM failures are caused by a dysfunctional VRM circuit, which is very common on first-round prototypes. The root cause of the dysfunction can be soldering quality, insufficient decoupling, too low current limit set, non-ideal component values (output inductor), or unstable feedback loop compensation (res/cap values or programmed). We need to know which rail failed, so the power sequencer should capture a failed rail number that we could read out over JTAG or I2C from the sequencer. In some cases, it is stored in a basic register, then the board input power must remain on until we are done reading it. In other cases, the failed rail number would be stored in a non-volatile memory chip or in a system management processor log file (the host CPU has read the register before power down and saved the data into a file). Any rail failures can be detected through PowerGood signals toggling or voltage rail sensing (<1kHz sample rate). Either the sequencer does the fault detection too, or a separate management controller does. In case of voltage sensing, smart VRM voltages can be read out of them over PMBUS (with chip vendor dongle and GUI), non-smart VRM voltages can be read through an A/D converter that is built into the management controller or the sequencer. Smart VRMs also capture the cause of failure, but must be read out over PMBUS before the input power cycle happens.

Fault handling is part of the sequencer. During the power-up sequence if one rail doesn't assert its PowerGood signal within a set timeout duration (typically 1sec) after it was enabled then it considered a fault. A timeout is generated by a counter counting up but reset by an arriving PowerGood. When the system is already fully powered on (run time), and one rail PowerGood goes down momentarily or permanently, is also considered a fault. If a thermal alert signal is asserted then it requires an emergency shutdown of all rails. In all these cases the sequencer has to go to a fault state, and depending on the code it will exhibit one of the three failure mode behaviors. At the time of the failure, by designer's choice the sequencer can shut all the rails down and stay off to prevent damage (until input power cycle), leave the sequence in a partially up state (debug mode), or restart the sequence (re-sequence) from the beginning to auto-recover the system. The choice can be made in the VHDL code, chip vendor GUI or with a jumper (or DIP-switch) if we have designed-in one. Keeping the sequencer in the partially-up state allows a person in the lab to observe what failed without register access. We can use a "debug mode" jumper or DIP-switch to tell the FPGA to use this failure mode. During prototyping the hardware engineer needs to identify which VRM was the culprit, so the VRM engineer can focus on the right one to be de-bugged. They also need the VRM to be constantly enabled while debugging it. In production we can also have one rail failing, but it is most likely a part/soldering problem to be repaired by factory technicians. In normal operation (shipping product) it would shut down all rails or re-sequence. These two modes only tell us about a failed rail number if smart flash/FRAM memory logging was part of the sequencer design. Choosing the re-sequence option also helps detecting power failures during system testing (console log shows reboot); this avoids being misled into debugging phantom digital ASIC or software issues.

The flow-chart of how an FPGA-based power sequencer state machine might work in normal operation (not in debug mode), can be seen in Figure 7.22. We can see there are stable states like the ready, the fully on and the failed state. The sequencer stays in these states, until an external masters orders it to transition to another stable state, by asserting a control signal or reset, marked in purple in the diagram. While transitioning between stable states, the sequencer stays in temporary states where it counts rail numbers and turns them on or off in the actual sequence.

Power sequencers must have an important feature, the "emergency shutdown", that is initiated when catastrophic events are detected, for example when the ASIC core temperature has reached a limit that could cause it to malfunction, be damaged or the unit to catch fire. This is detected through thermal diode sensors that assert a TEMP_ALERT# or PROCHOT# or similar signal, that causes the sequencer to turn everything off, without a sequence down or any waiting and it stays off. If any VRM glitches or turns off by itself due to a circuit stability failure during run-time, then the sequencer also has to enter the emergency shutdown mode. In case of a device fault depending on the end product, either the whole board shuts down, or only an isolated portion shuts down causing system degradation while retaining some limited availability. In most data center, industrial or consumer electronic equipment it is probably better to shut down everything on the board and halt the usage until it is serviced. On an airplane a full card shutdown can cause loss of life and assets, as the electronics might be required to serve until safe landing. This case we either design a chassis with lots of small cards managed by two management cards, or the one complex board has to be designed in a compartmentalized way in terms of power management. For example, each main ASIC and its supporting circuits having one compartment. Each compartment would have its own power sequencer state machine, then all sections combined into one whole board power sequence at startup but not at a failure condition, by a main state machine. To retain some availability, there would be redundant data plane circuits, like two Ethernet NICs instead of one.

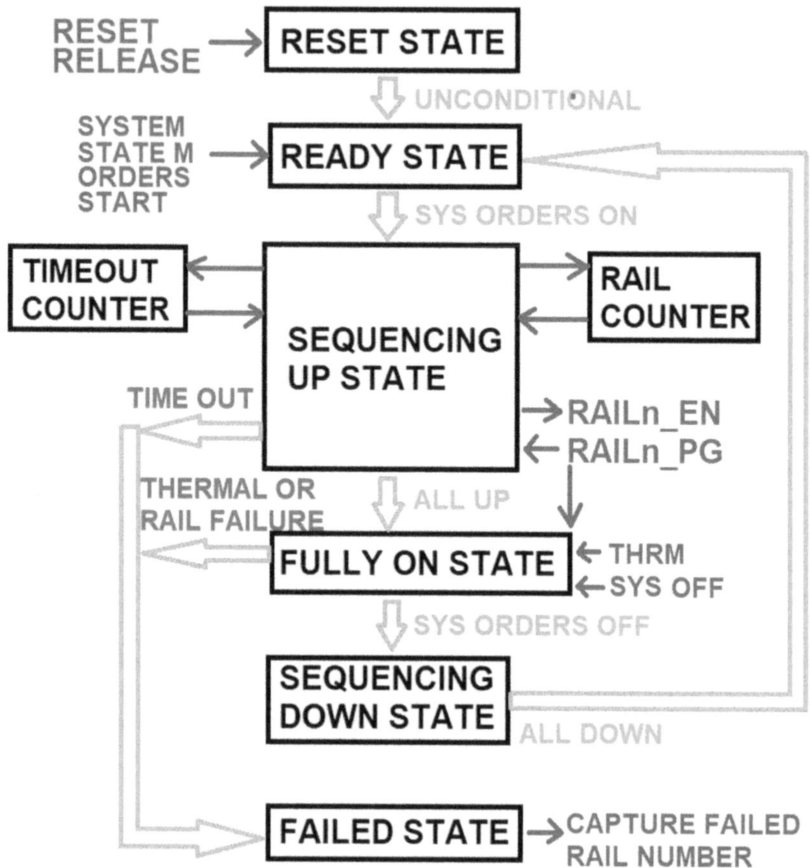

FIGURE 7.22 Flow chart of a typical power sequencer.

Power sequencers often control or monitor signals that are not VRM signals (Power Enable and PowerGood). For example, clock generator chips have clock enable inputs and PLL_LOCKED outputs, X86 chipsets have POWER_BUTTON and CHIPSET_PWRGD inputs, while FPGAs have PROGRAM inputs and CONFIG_DONE outputs. These can be treated as voltage rails and part of the overall power sequence. Some devices will also require a fixed delay state machine inside the FPGA to delay the signal provided to the device, and delay the next step in the sequence according to delay requirements from the chipset datasheet. Some of them are output only, that case the sequencer PowerGood input is simply the enable output looped back in VHDL code—or input only and the RAIL_X_ENA output is going nowhere.

In a made-up X86 motherboard design example let's say, rail 15 that is the 1.0V core VRM for the chipset gets enabled, then the after it is up the PowerGood 15 comes back high, then the sequencer steps to rail 16 that is a delay state machine (code). The delay STM input is asserted high, 100ms later its output goes high (PowerGood 16 for the sequencer), then it steps to rail 17. That is a CHIPSET_PWRGD glue logic signal that is asserted high by the sequencer as a fake rail and routed back through the code as PowerGood 17, then steps forwards to rail number 18 that is the CPU_VIO VRM to be turned on, once it is up it signals back through PowerGood-18, then the sequencer steps to rail 19.

Instead of FPGA logic, we can also use power sequencing chips like the UCD9xxx family from Texas Instruments or the ADM1266 from Analog Devices. They have to be configured over PMBUS using a chip vendor dongle and a GUI as well as an image file. They also support a few GPIO pins, for example, for an IPMI controller to start the sequence or to issue reset signals to ASICs.

7.5.4 Resets

Every digital chip that contains flip-flops, registers, or state machines needs to be initialized into a known default state before the chip can begin normal operation after a power-on event. For example, state machines, to be forced to state zero, enable registers to be initialized into a disabled state, counters to a zero count waiting for software to enable them. This way no functions will be randomly enabled, nor will state machines start at random states after power on. They are usually active low signals. When a reset signal is active all registers and flip-flops are held in default state, when the reset signal is high devices can function normally following the clock signal. At power on the reset signals are held low, then they are held low more until they are ready to be released, then they are driven high and remain high until the device is turned off or a user reset is issued. Device datasheets show the reset-default values of every register bit in their programmable control-register set.

Most complex devices can initialize their millions of flip-flops within 1 to 15ms, that is why an X86 processor soft reset is about 15ms. A small FPGA glue logic code with less than a hundred flip-flops can be initialized in 1ms or less. Glue logic circuits generate reset signals to other devices that are typically 3.3V or 1.8V CMOS level, and they are routed to every digital chip on the board. Even the glue logic FPGA needs its own reset, generated from a standby rail PowerGood signal with a few millisecond delay circuit.

Types of resets, based on what generates them under what conditions:

- Power-on reset (POR) signals are held low until the power-on sequence is complete, then continue to be held low for a pre-defined amount of time (1 to 100ms), then released (driven high) and stay high during normal operation. Often generated by small 5 or 6 pin reset generator chips.
- Manual reset comes from a reset button that the user can press and cause an already running system to re-initialize, used for error recovery. In complex hardware we often drive manual reset button pins of processors from glue logic or a management controller.
- Brown-out reset is usually handled by the same circuits as the POR. A brown-out even occurs when a system is already running, but there is a partial power failure, with the voltage rail dropping below the tolerance threshold.
- Warm reset is initiated by software in order to get back into a default state and re-start normal operation. It involves a reset signal going low then high again.
- Hot reset is a message sent over a PCIe bus to an endpoint peripheral device to reset that device.
- Cold reset is when the system was off and is now turning it on, then issues a POR.
- Power cycle reset is when we turn off all rails to a board, then turn them back on again, like in a cold reset. It can be automatically done under a software command issued to the chipset. Power management controllers that are running the whole time control the payload power down. Some registers might not reinitialize properly from a warm reset, but a power cycle would clear all that, and it also reloads any FPGAs.
- Hard reset is driven by hardware components.
- Soft reset is driven by software and or user commanding the software from the console or GUI, writing into a reset register, for example, in an X86 chipset.
- CMOS reset is when we short (with a jumper or dip switch) the coin cell battery rail that feeds the real-time clock inside an X86 chipset to clear the BIOS and calendar date settings. The RTCRST signal is also automatically de-asserted a few milliseconds after a battery was inserted into the socket on the motherboard.

On complex hardware boards we have some extensive glue logic that handles reset and power to the payload (data plane and control plane) devices. But the reset to the glue logic itself has to come from an analog reset generator chip (sometimes called voltage monitor chip or uP supervisor chip), like the ADM705 from analog devices. As the core voltage of the glue logic FPGA starts rising, it reaches a certain threshold, then the chip starts counting a pre-set delay time, usually 0.2 to 20ms, and after that it releases the reset output.

All payload or ASIC device resets are directly handled by the board glue logic, usually a small FPGA, and a management processor or microcontroller. The main host processor has a reset output signal, which the glue logic redistributes with unique gating logic to all other devices. They also monitor power rails, either directly or through the power sequencer ready state, to make sure resets will never be released high to unpowered devices and as a reset timing reference. Any payload FPGA devices that need to load their configuration have a CONF_DONE signal indicating whether they have completed their config cycle, which is another timing reference in the system startup/reset timing sequence. In general, there are reset sources and rest destinations. The reset pins on some devices (like bridge chips or backplane connectors) can be either output or input based on which slot the card is plugged into. Every medium to large complexity device has a reset input pin, and processors and bridge chips provide a reset output pin also. Signals are driven into backplanes towards other cards from a main processor card. IPMI subsystems can issue or override resets too if they receive reset commands over an I2C bus from a management card in the chassis. All these sources and destinations go through the glue logic, ideally through a small flash-based FPGA or CPLD. All these possible interactions are demonstrated on a generic block diagram in Figure 7.23, which shows a superset of the most common complex boards.

Reset output signals are usually generated from multiple sources through logic equations. For example, a reset to a device is generated from the CPU reset output, VRM power good (power domain gating protection), FPGA state machine states, and IPMI soft reset override. PLTRST# is usually the main reset output signal's name in X86 chipsets. In VHDL code it looks like:

DEV1RST_N

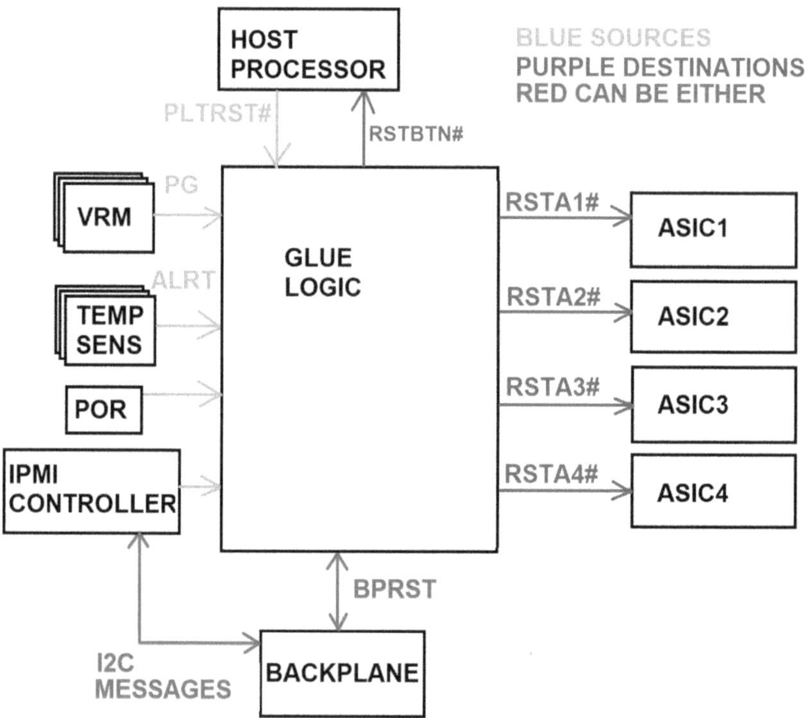

FIGURE 7.23 General view of resets on any board (superset).

7.5.4.1 Backplane Reset

Cards that plug into backplanes can be designed to be one of three types: host cards, peripheral cards, and universal cards. The reset connections of the first two types are obvious, the reset signal is unidirectional, an output from the host card into the backplane, and an input to the Ppripheral card from the backplane. For universal cards we need to implement additional glue logic that can detect the card slot type, whether it be a host slot or a peripheral slot, using a backplane strapping pin usually called SYSCON or "system controller". When the card is in a host slot, and sees SYSCON=1, the glue logic will route the bridge reset output or the processor PLTRST output to the backplane. When the card is in a peripheral slot, and sees SYSCON=0, it disconnects those lines and instead routes the backplane reset pin into the processor's manual reset input and the backplane bridge device input. Routing slow signals can be done using analog multiplexers or by FPGA glue logic. In Compact-PCI systems there is a bridge device connecting the data plane processor to the backplane traces, and these bridge devices support primary and secondary side reset input and output signals. Depending on exact device datasheet, it still requires some glue logic that routes these signals to the right destinations or sources. PCIe switches have only one reset input pin, which is to be supplied by a glue logic, sourcing it from the backplane when in a peripheral slot and from the local processor when in a host slot. The switch chips also need to set the port going to the backplane into transparent mode when in the host slot and into NT or non-transparent mode when in a peripheral slot for a universal card. A peripheral-only card does not need this logic; rather, it simply connects its upstream port to the backplane connector. We use universal cards for multi-processor systems, when one board design and one release part number can be used for both the main host CPU card and the peripheral CPU node cards. These card modes and their signal routings are visualized in Figure 7.24.

7.5.4.2 Software-Reset

X86 chipsets and Linux commands (serial console prompt) offer different software-initiated reset types: power cycle reset, warm reset, shutdown. The Linux commands basically write into the standard X86 reset register at address 0xCF9. What the software writes into the register depends on what "switches" were used in the command and which Linux distribution is used. For example, "reboot" is for warm reboot with reset signal toggling, "shutdown -P -r" for cold reboot, while "shutdown -P" is for power off and stay off. Either way there is a write transaction into the Reset Control Register to set the mode, then another write transaction to execute it. A warm reboot means the PLTRST# signal gets asserted low for a few milliseconds, then high so the system reboots. A cold reboot means the SLP_S3# and the PLTRST# signals get driven low for a few seconds to power every VRM and ASIC down temporarily, then driven high again so the power rails sequence back up again. In a shutdown both the SLP_Sx# and the PLTRST# get de-asserted and remain low, until the user presses a power button or unplugs and re-plugs the main power input cable. These are controlled by the X86 chipset's built-in power management state machine that runs in the standby power domain. During a power cycle reset the standby rail remains on. On a typical processor board glue logic, the chipset's SLP_S3# output going high is used to authorize sequencing up all the control/data plane voltage rails, and if it goes low that initiates a system power down sequence. FPGA glue logic relies on this SLP_S3# signal as a main command for the power sequencer.

In ARM processor-based systems the reset register might be different, but it has somewhat similar functionality. There is no SLP_S3# and PLTRST#, and the CPU is usually unable to control board power cycles. ASICs, FPGAs, and GPUs do not run software, so they do not have software resets.

In some architectures a reset is sent in a message encoded in a communication bus instead of a board-level CMOS reset signal. For example, PCIe devices can be reset by a device driver software, using a "hot reset" message sent over PCIe to them. This has no board design aspects. In many backplane/chassis systems reset and power up/down are communicated over I2C bus, instead of having dedicated CMOS signals. This is common with IPMI system management. They cannot be

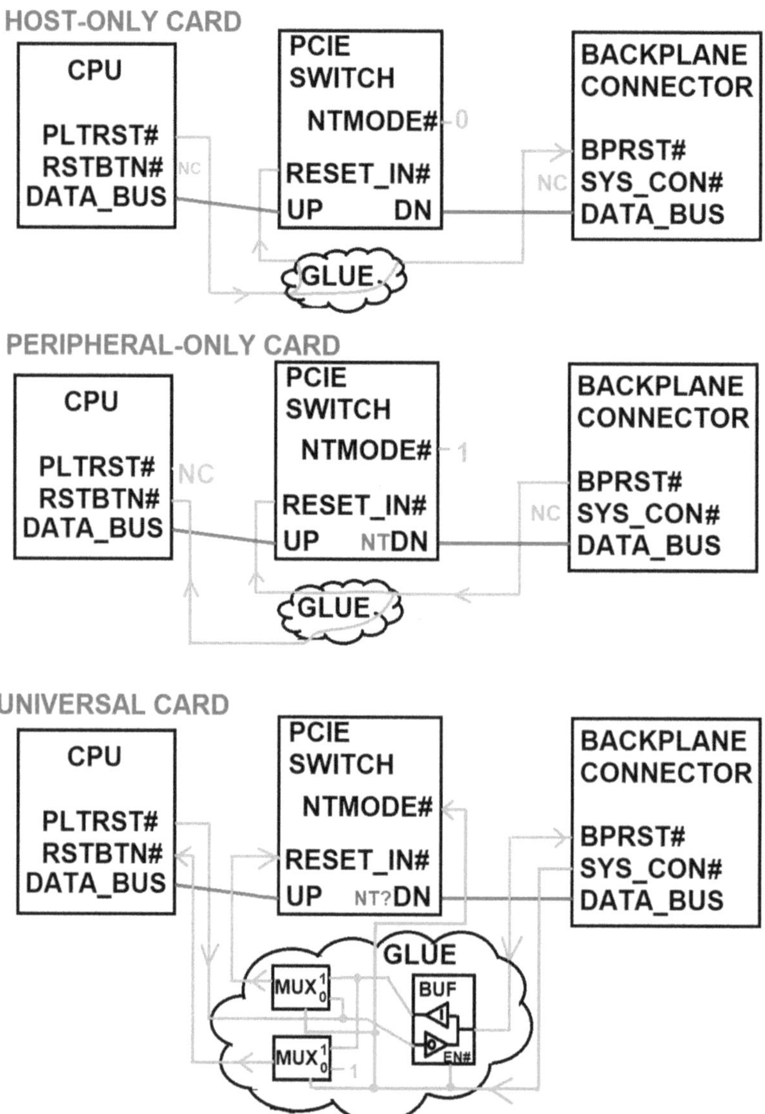

FIGURE 7.24 Simplified backplane reset diagram with a PCIe switch chip as the main backplane bridge, three different card types.

observed easily with a multimeter or oscilloscope but by looking into the internal signals and states of the glue logic FPGAs or IPMI microcontroller firmware. An I2C snooper dongle might help us see these commands.

7.5.5 Interrupts

Main management or data plane processors need to know when certain events happen so they can take immediate action. There are two ways of doing this: one is through interrupts and the other one is through polling. Polling means the processor's software checks the state of several GPIO signals periodically, and if one is at a state that requires action, then the processor will jump to a subroutine that is written to take care of pre-defined actions.

Interrupts include a single signal that breaks the processor's code execution and makes it to jump to an interrupt routine code to take immediate action to handle hardware events. These events can be a card was plugged in, a data packet arrived, or an analog signal sample was captured. Processors have silicon circuits that will make the processor execution to jump to the code area of the interrupt handler software. The location of that is part of the software architecture and operating systems. The physical format of interrupt signals can be individual CMOS signals (referred to as IRQ signals), they can be serialized on a SERIRQ bus (synchronous to the LPC bus at 33MHz), or they can be encoded into a packet or message on a communication bus like PCIe, DMI, UPI, or CXL. Interrupts signals can be level triggered or edge/event triggered. The level-triggered signal has to be de-asserted by the logic or device that asserted it before the processor gets into a repeating endless interrupt routine as it would keep seeing an active interrupt as long as it is logic low (active low). An edge-triggered interrupt input means an assertion (falling edge on a CMOS signal or an arriving interrupt packet) will generate exactly one interrupt code jump inside the processor, and it can generate another one only if the source de-asserts the signal first and then asserts it again.

Poling uses processor time as a resource constantly, so we only use it when it does not degrade the performance of the software or we do not need faster reaction. Polling has a slower reaction time, in the tens of milliseconds range, while interrupts can be serviced within a microsecond.

X86 processors take several types of interrupts, but the main categories are the regular IRQ and the NMI (non-maskable interrupt). NMI is used to prevent bad software from sabotaging hardware functions. Modern X86 processors are based on the old PCI bus at the logical level, meaning that devices are discovered and initialized/enumerated (base address register written) by the BIOS firmware in a standard way. The PCI bus standard has defined four interrupt signals, INTA#, INTB#, INTC#, and INTD#. All devices in the old computers had their interrupt output connected to one of these four signals. Now we no longer have PCI buses, but INT[A:D] lives on in the form of module ports of the interrupt controller block inside the chipset silicon and in the form of PCIe "virtual wire" interrupt packets. PCIe supports two types of interrupts: the virtual wire and the MSI (message signaled interrupt). The virtual wire basically asserts a chipset internal INT[A:D] signal through a PCIe packet bit field. Chapter 6, "Main Chips", dealing with main chips and X86 processors, gives more details and a diagram about all interrupt types. ARM and other processor types just have simple interrupt signals and basic delivery schemes.

7.6 SYSTEM MANAGEMENT

The system management subsystem, or management plane, usually consists of a small processor, microcontroller or flash-FPGA on each removable front card (LRUs, line replaceable units) or payload board, and a central management card (with an X86 processor running console-Linux) in the chassis. Some systems do not have a dedicated management processor card; rather, there is a main host processor card that performs both data plane and management plane functions. This is more common in aerospace systems. Modular telecom and data center chassis usually have a management-only small processor card, called a management card, supervisor, or shelf manager. Their main function is to handle hot-swapping of data plane cards, chassis-fan control, and sensor telemetry for sensors on all cards. Some chassis have one such management card, other chassis have two with their connectivity in a dual-star redundant fashion. In the case of server motherboards, there is no management card in the chassis; rather, another computer in the data center manages all motherboards over the 1Gig Management Ethernet network. Inside a modular chassis the management subsystems of the data plane boards communicate with the management card through reliable low speed buses like 1Gig Ethernet or I2C. Some systems do not contain a microcontroller on every data plane board; rather, the main chassis manager computer board controls them directly through CMOS glue logic signals. On data plane cards that do have a local management microcontroller to receive commands from the management card, this subsystem includes a lot of the glue logic so as to be able to collect sensor information and control the board power sequencing and resets.

Some companies make systems with standardized system management subsystems, like IPMI or the OpenRMC. These are standard interfaces and functional blocks with released specification documents, and system design companies design their products to comply to these specs. IPMI microcontrollers are single-chip small microcontrollers with less than 150 pins and a few milliwatts of power consumption. These standards have to be implemented exactly if we intend to plug third-party cards into our chassis or plug our board into a third-party chassis. If not, then we can do a partial implementation or a fully custom management plane design. The main management controller on each data plane card is usually a small microcontroller with or without small FPGAs.

The IPMI microcontroller on each payload card in a chassis is called the IPMC. The IPMI master, the management card, is usually redundant, having two cards in one chassis and two backplane I2C IPMI buses. The local management controller chip (IPMC) on the payload cards is responsible for monitoring local sensors (temperature, voltage, current, payload FPGA config status, local processor boot status), and for controlling each card power up/down, hot swapping, firmware loading, and chassis fan speed. The IPMC provides sensor reading to the main management card in the form of telemetry, every few seconds or more. The management card can save this data into log files on a storage drive and use it for real time fan control. The IPMC also makes decisions about immediate actions if the sensors are out of range. The acceptable range of each sensor is hardcoded in the firmware. The rail voltages are monitored, looking for any single glitch that would require a board shutdown or power cycle (preventing the use of corrupted data). The temperatures are monitored for any device violating its own maximum junction temperature, prompting a board shutdown.

Many X86 server motherboards contain a baseboard management controller (BMC), which is a small single-chip microcontroller, or a little bit higher performance "server management processor" that has its own on-board attached peripherals like DDR4 memory-down. An example of the device is the ASPEED AST2500 device. These are more capable than typical IPMI microcontrollers. They can upgrade the BIOS firmware and the operating system over the Ethernet, while the data center's system administrator is controlling it remotely.

For chassis fan speed control, controllable four-wire chassis fan modules are needed. They have 12V power and ground, a TACH (tachometer) signal (speed sensing through a revolution or RPM counter), and a PWM signal (pulse width modulation). The processor board will have a power switch to turn the fans on or off and transistors for level translating the PWM and TACH signals between the 12V fan power domain and the controller logic 3.3V domain. We know how much the maximum RPM the fan can produce from its datasheet, so the software-based control loop increases or decreases the PWM duty cycle until the desired RPM is detected. To count the tach pulses and reporting an RPM value in a register, as well as producing a PWM signal from a number written into a register, we need to design in either an I2C-controllable fan controller chip or some glue logic FPGA. The goal of the fan control, which is a software algorithm running on the management card, is to ensure that the hottest ASIC in the chassis will still be below its defined junction temperature limit. This is done by measuring all ASIC core and all board temperatures by each board's local IPMC and reporting all this telemetry data to the main management card through I2C registers that run the algorithm. It has to maintain a database of each sensor's parameters, meaning their maximum allowed values, so each reading can be compared against the table. To calculate thermal margins, find the one with the smallest margin at the moment and keep it larger than zero through fan speed. ASIC core temperatures are monitored through thermal sensor chips that have an analog (diffpair) connection to the thermal diodes residing on the ASIC die. They also have an I2C bus connection to the IPMC, which has another I2C over the backplane to the management card. Figure 7.25 shows the system-level connections involved in thermal control. Figure 7.26 shows the thermal sensing circuits that feed into the system-level thermal control on each payload or digital board. The blue lines are used on non-X86 boards; the red lines are used on X86 boards. There are complex boards that contain both. The internal diode inside the thermal sensor chips shows the temperature of the sensor chip itself and, therefore, the board area temperature. Sometimes the BMC or IPMC functionality is implemented as hard logic in the CPLD or FPGA. In that case, all the system signals

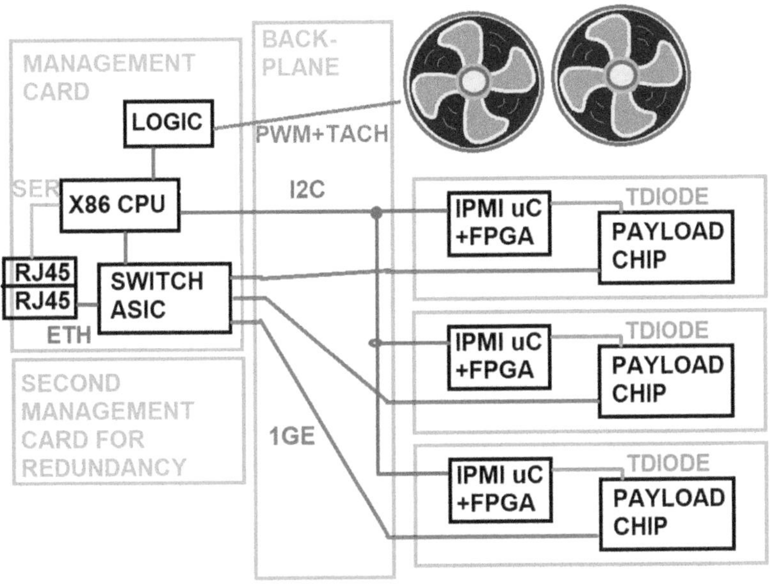

FIGURE 7.25 IPMI subsystem in a generalized chassis/system.

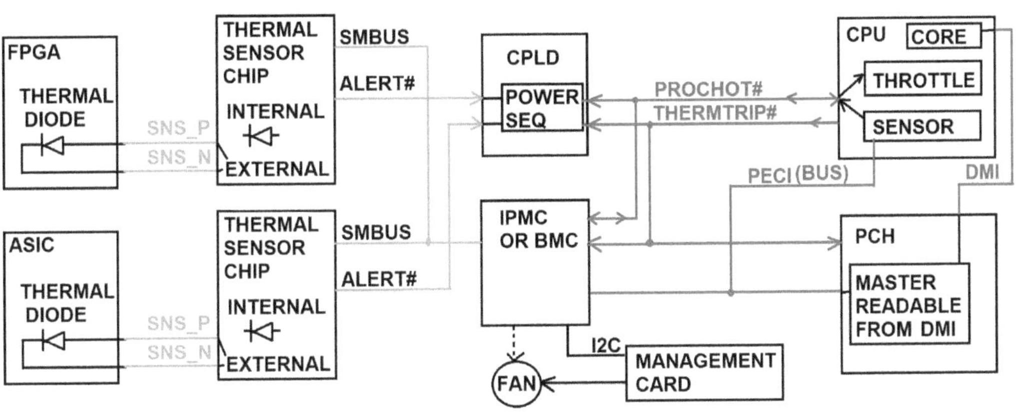

FIGURE 7.26 Thermal sensing subsystem on a board in general (blue is non-x86, red is x86).

are routed to it. Some systems have the control plane and the management plane implemented on the same processor card. In that case, the BMC/IPMC is not present, the sensor I2C signals and the alert signals (through GPIO) are routed to the host processor. More details can be found in Chapter 9, "Hardware-Firmware Integration".

7.6.1 Hot Swapping and Hot Plugging

In a modular system that supports hot swapping we can insert or remove cards from a chassis/backplane while the system is running. For hot-swap removal the user tries to eject the card with the help of the ejector handle, which also has a micro switch built into it, that produces an ejector signal that is routed to the board's IPMI management controller, which notifies the chassis manager card through an interrupt or polling. As a result, the chassis manager stops communications to any bus the card is attached to until after the card is out so as to prevent data corruption and removes the devices of the card from the operating system's device list. The management card also turns the power off to any payload electronics through the IPMI controller chip on the board. During hot-swap insertion the reverse takes place—the microcontroller gets powered first through standby rails from long connector pins, it sends an interrupt to (or gets detected through polling by) the management card, which stops any buses that might get corrupted. The IPMI controller gets notified of the full insertion from the ejector handle's switch (through the IPMC), then it allows the payload electronics to be turned on, then the chassis manager enumerates any devices on the card into the operating system's devices list. This works with any type of bus, including PCI, PCIe, and CXL. The hardware requirement for hot swapping is having an IPMI-like management controller on board, have bus interface chips to support hot swapping on their pins, have ejector handles with ejector switches, have a system-level protocol for interrupts or polling to communicate insertion or removal and power up/down control, have a hot-swap power switch circuit on each card, and have software to have the ability to pause bus transactions if needed to enumerate devices in a running system on demand, cards to have an ESD-strip to eliminate ESD pulses during insertion/removal, and analog multiplexers or bus switches to isolate/detach signals from the backplane for the duration of the insertion/removal process. Glue logic signals (ejector switch, interrupt, reset, power enable) are sometimes actual CMOS signal on a backplane; at other times, they are encoded into communication messages over I2C or PCIe. Interrupts are important in detecting hot-swap events, but polling can be suitable too. A user takes at least one second to complete an insertion or removal, so a less than 1s polling interval would be suitable. Figure 7.27 shows CMOS glue logic signals for hot-swap support in a compact PCI system.

Hot plugging is related to attaching or removing external cables to a connector on the chassis front panel. These ports usually have a power switch chip next to them on the board to enable power to the cable, and they also have hot-plug detection signals communicating with the bridge or interface controller chips. When a cable is plugged in, the "detect" signals change state, which interrupts the host processor (directly or through the bridge and PCIe interrupt messages), so the hot-plug driver running on it can request the operating system to enumerate (assign resources, port numbers, memory regions) any new devices that have just been attached. When a cable is unplugged the detect

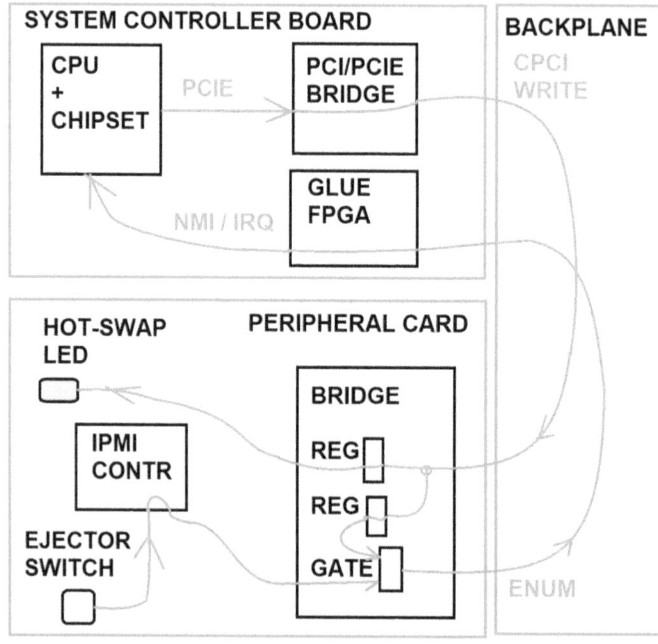

FIGURE 7.27 Old compact PCI system hot-swapping logic.

signal changes state, and interrupt is generated, the driver asks the OS to remove related devices from the list. Everyone is familiar with USB devices and their ease of use. USB uses pull resistors on the data lines instead of dedicated pins for detection. AI appliances are usually connected to servers through PCIe cables, and they require hot plugging also.

7.7 POWER SUBSYSTEM

The power subsystem is the set of power-related support circuits to data plane, control plane, and management plane devices, or global to the whole board. It consists mainly of the VRMs and hot-swapping circuits. For some people it may also contain the power sequencing FPGAs, power sequencing and monitor chips, any signals related to PMBUS telemetry and power handshaking logic. More commonly those would be categorized under the power management subsystem or power management glue logic. It might contain a portion of the chipset or processor that is meant to control system power. The control portion is called "power management", and the analog portion is called "power delivery". Some of this overlaps with the glue logic, which is not really a separate subsystem, and with the management plane. It is a matter of abstraction. Any programmable or telemetry capable VRM devices, and their communication channels and PMBUS hosts, are also part of the power management subsystem, but not the power subsystem. These are "smart VRMs". VRM telemetry is when a local host processor or management controller can read out voltage, current, and temperature information as well as fault details in case a VRM has failed and shut down. A VRM fault might be about what caused the failure, like output overcurrent or input or output voltage fault. The smart VRM devices also need to be programmed through the power management subsystem during production and prototype bringup. During prototyping we first try to control the devices from chip vendor–provided PMBUS dongles, but we will have to eventually test out the production programming path through the management subsystem. The management subsystem must not force the I2C clock; rather, three-state it while not accessing anything to allow the dongle to have full control. Otherwise, we need a multiplexer. It is good practice to separate the PMBUS into separate buses based on chip vendors. For example, the TI VRMs would be on one PMBUS and the Renesas VRMs on another bus. We can use I2C multiplexers to split a bus, or we can have multiple dedicated I2C host controller ports in the IPMC.

We make several power-related diagrams. The power subsystem requires a power tree (or power map) diagram and a power consumption spreadsheet. The power management subsystem requires a power management control glue logic block diagram and a PMBUS diagram for smart VRMs. The glue logic diagram was discussed in an earlier section. The PMBUS diagram is discussed here because when we select VRMs we consider their power and their smart capabilities at the same time.

A power tree, or power map, shows all VRMs, voltages, and currents. It also shows what load devices are fed by each voltage rail, and it shows if any VRM is fed by another VRM's output rail. We must avoid the power tree conflicting with power-sequencing requirements. For example, we cannot have a downstream VRM having to turn on before the upstream VRM. An example is shown in Figure 7.28. In this example we have one ASIC, two FPGAs, and some smaller circuits. Each of the three main data plane devices are displayed with 3 to 10 voltage rail inputs, which are fed by point of load VRMs. In reality, an ASIC might have 10 to 25 voltage rail pin groups, but in the schematic we will connect several of them to the same voltage source.

A power consumption spreadsheet lists each rail and several parameters of each rail. These are the voltage, current (typ/max), ripple, and tolerance, VRM part number, and programming address (and bus number) if applicable. It also calculates to total board power and rail power for multi load global rails. It has to show what load devices are on which rail, based on ASIC input pins. Each switching VRM is assumed to consume 15% additional power to the amount it delivers at its output. Each load device datasheet will define the maximum current that a power pin group can consume for a short time and the typical current averaged over milliseconds or more. The peak currents of

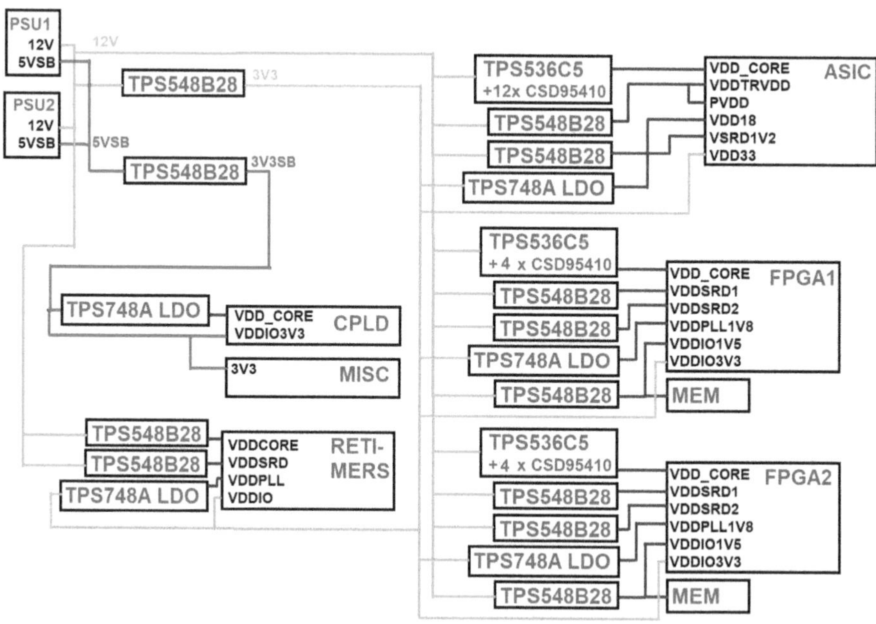

FIGURE 7.28 Example of a made-up board power tree.

	A	B	C	D	E	F	G	H	I	J
1	**Load chip/rail**	**Net Name**	**Voltage**	**Max Current**	**Typ Current**	**Sourced from**	**VRM chip PN**	**Typ Power + VRM loss**	**PMBUS number**	**PMBUS address**
2	Hotswapped 12V	VCC12V	12	n/a	n/a	n/a	LM9061-Q1	n/a	0	0x31
3	General 3V3	VCC3V3	3.3	3	1.4091	VCC12V	TPS1234	5.3475	1	0x10
4	ASIC1 Core	VCCA1_C	0.95	133	133	VCC12V	TPS53667	145.3025	1	0x61
5	ASIC1 serdes RX	VCCA1_SRX	1.2	25	22	VCC12V	TPS546D24A	30.36	2	0x11
6	ASIC1 serdes RX	VCCA1_STX	1.2	18	16	VCC12V	TPS546D24A	22.08	2	0x12
7	ASIC1 PLL	VCCA1_PLL	1.8	2	1	VCC12V	TPS543820E	2.07	n/a	n/a
8	ASIC1 VIO	VCCA1_VIO	3.3	1	0.5	VCC3V3	direct	1.65	n/a	n/a
9	ASIC2 Core	VCCA2_C	0.95	133	133	VCC12V	TPS53667	145.3025	1	0x63
10	ASIC2 serdes RX	VCCA2_SRX	1.2	25	22	VCC12V	TPS546D24A	30.36	2	0x13
11	ASIC2 serdes RX	VCCA2_STX	1.2	18	16	VCC12V	TPS546D24A	22.08	2	0x14
12	ASIC2 PLL	VCCA2_PLL	1.8	2	1	VCC12V	TPS543820E	2.07	n/a	n/a
13	ASIC2 VIO	VCCA2_VIO	3.3	1	0.5	VCC3V3	direct	1.65	n/a	n/a
14	FPGA core	VCORE_FP	1.5	0.5	0.4	VCC3V3	TPS543820E	0.69	n/a	n/a
15	FPGA VIO	VIO_FP	3.3	0.3	0.2	VCC3V3	direct	0.66	n/a	n/a
16	**Total Power**		12					404.9725	W	
17	**3.3V all loads**		3.3					4.65	W	

FIGURE 7.29 Example of a power budget spreadsheet made for demonstration.

different rails do not occur at the same time. The VRM has to be capable of delivering the maximum current, but for board power input and thermal design we use "average" current. An example is shown in Figure 7.29.

A PMBUS map shows all the smart VRM access, with bus number and device addresses. This helps software engineering visualize what power devices need programming. An example is shown in Figure 7.30. On most designs the non-smart VRM outputs are not measured by any device, so we

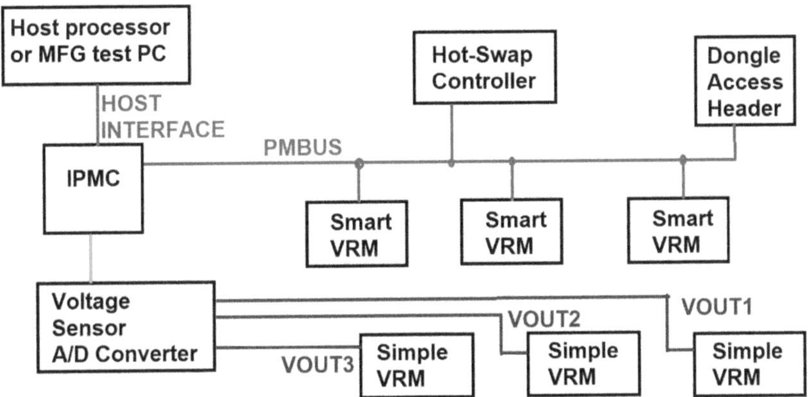

FIGURE 7.30 Typical PMBUS smart VRM map and voltage sensing.

have only PowerGood information. IPMI-based and BMC-based designs do have the voltage sensing for system health monitoring purposes but not for sequencing. Custom designs and standalone systems that do not have to be plugged into third-party chassis can have any combination of these features.

While drawing the power tree and power budget spreadsheets, we have to find out for each ASIC or main chip what voltage rails they need and how much typical and maximum current they need on each. The chip datasheets should help in providing that data. For FPGAs we have to use power estimator templates (Excel sheets) provided by the chip vendor, or generate power and current data from a compilation that is available only if we have compiled the full code before the board design starts. In the power estimator spreadsheet, we have to select the quantity of all logic resources such that utilization will get to 90%, on a migration-up device part number (pin compatible largest device), the right number and speed I/O and SERDES pins in use, temperature near the maximum, process parameter to worst case, select at least as many clock networks and PLLs as we will likely use. This should provide information about rail currents for VRM selection and power dissipation that the heatsinks and fans will need to handle.

The next step is to select VRM chip devices to each power rail of each main chip, based on the power tree and voltage/current requirements. Then the part numbers into the diagram are added. A VRM is selected based on a rail's max current +20% rounded up to a suitable device. For example, if we need 5.7A max, then with 20% it is 6.84A, if we have 6A and 8A regulators available then 6.84 rounds up to 8A, so choose the 8A device and decode its full part number from the datasheet. Some ASICs use the same voltage level for different input power rail pins—whether we can combine them or not depends on datasheet and reference design. We never combine one ASIC's rails with another ASIC's rails; instead, we provide a set of dedicated point of load regulators to each voltage of each ASIC—except a main 3.3V rail across the board. Some devices need their own 3.3V for satisfying their reverse power-sequencing requirement, which we can create with a MOSFET power switch from the global 3.3V rail.

Sometimes 1.8V rails within a few inch distance can be combined if they are used for basic low speed I/O pins. But in most cases, they cannot be combined. A PLL ASIC-pin needs its own dedicated VRM, usually an LDO with low noise requirement but with low current demand. Up to 0.5 to 1A we can use LDOs without creating a burning sun on the board, as LDOs have a very low efficiency compared to switchers. Typically, the core rail, the RX SERDES rail, and the TX SERDES rail being all near 1.0V, they still cannot be combined due to noise immunity requirements. They would spread noise to each other. For core rails we typically use multi-phase VRMs. The VRM power stage chip datasheets are stretching the truth a little bit because they claim 60–80A per rail capabilities, which might be true in very special and unusual circumstances. A 70A power stage chip can be used up to 30–35A on a typical high-density embedded board without power-stage chip heatsinks, so we need to divide our core rail's maximum current requirement by 35A, round up, and that is the number of phases we need. Server motherboards are lower density than aerospace, telecom or networking boards, so servers can afford the space for VRM power stage heatsinks, while the other types of systems can cool them only through the board up to 1 to 2W each.

VRM devices are selected not only for their voltage and current ratings, but also for their features. On some designs we prefer software programmable VRMs (smart VRMs); on other designs we prefer resistor strapable VRMs. In some cases, such as space applications, we prefer radiation hardened devices with no software registers for SEU immunity, while on some other designs we require full support PMBUS telemetry with lots of registers, which helps with design bug tracing during development. Chapter 4, "Power Supply Circuits" explains all the VRM features we consider.

7.8 CLOCKING SCHEME

The core logic and interface blocks of digital chips are running on continuously running reference clock signals that are provided on the board design. These are different from I/O clocks used on parallel buses for their static timing closure. The core logic runs on a reference clock, the different high-speed interface cores like the memory, and SERDES transceivers also require separate clocks. Figure 7.31 demonstrates this. The lesson from this diagram is that the board-level logic and the FPGA chip-level logic (utilization of on-chip clocking resources) has to be designed as one, so the hardware design engineer and the FPGA engineer have to work out the clocking scheme together before finishing the board schematic. In the event that we are using ASICs instead of FPGAs, the scheme is decided by the ASIC company and communicated through the ASIC datasheet and or the chip reference design schematic.

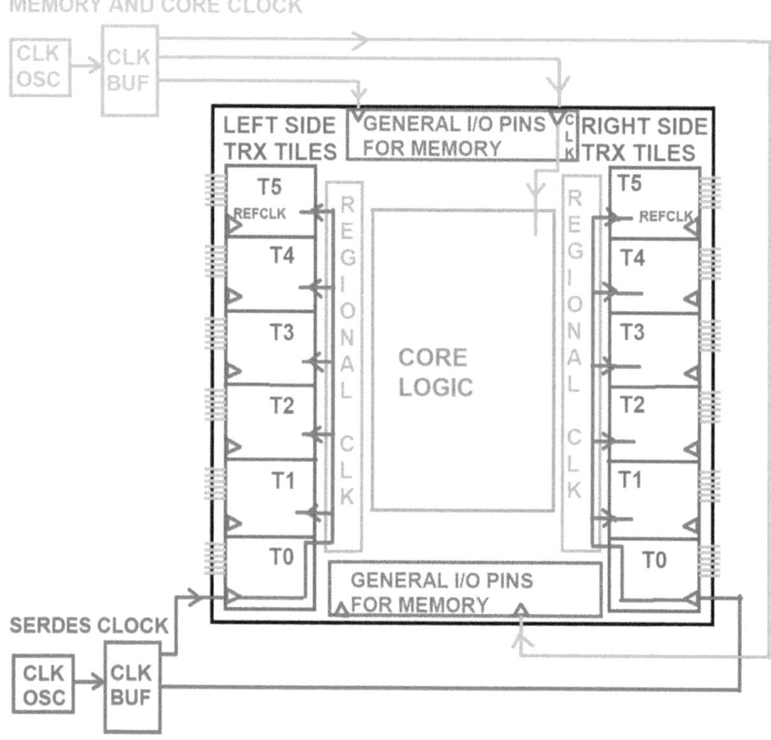

FIGURE 7.31 Typical ASIC or FPGA clocking scheme (sketch).

The different refclock inputs of the same ASIC have different I/O standards and frequency and jitter requirements. Memory and SERDES clocks are usually differential types, LVPECL, CML, LVDS, or HCSL. Core and basic I/O clocks are sometimes single ended. We have to choose depending on the ASIC datasheet. Large ASICs/CPUs/FPGAs have multiple SERDES transceiver blocks or tiles (or Cores), each with 4 to 16 lanes. They often require a separate reference clock for each group of SERDES tiles, where the group size might be arbitrary. If we use multiple clocks of the same type to the same device, then they have to originate from the same single oscillator source, otherwise the few PPM spread might derail the clock domain crossing buffers inside the chip. FPGAs provide the flexibility to run each tile on a separate reference clock signal provided by the board design, although they also contain on-chip regional clock routing resources to be able to run multiple tiles from a single clock, with limitations. For example, the left side of the FPGA die can run on one reference clock, the right side of the FPGA needs another one, assuming all SERDES lanes are implementing the same kind of interface in multi-lane fashion. The regional clocks have limits on larger ASICs, so 1/4th or 1/6th of the ASIC's SERDES tiles can run on a single reference clock (distributed to few tiles on chip). Some clock routes on the chip can be considered long, picking up too much jitter for a SERDES, so they are to be avoided by using separate off-chip clocks in the board design, often four to six copies of the same kind of clock signal. This can be provided by using a clock oscillator chip that feeds a clock fanout buffer chip. Fanout buffers create multiple copies from one input clock, usually in a 1:4 or 1:8 ratio.

SERDES reference clocks have a tight jitter specification, usually less than 1ps in the "phase noise" or "phase jitter" RMS type. Other types of jitter might be a lot higher than this. 25Gbps PAM4 and 56G-NRZ usually need <0.3ps, 10Gig SERDES usually can run from a clock with 0.7ps RMS or better phase noise. For any board design we have to check the ASIC datasheet for maximum allowed phase noise jitter on the reference clock input, then find a clocking solution that is a little bit better than that. The oscillator has a maximum worst-case output jitter specification, while clock fanout buffers have a jitter addition specification in their datasheet. The total jitter (RMS, phase noise) arriving at the ASIC's reference clock input pin is the jitter of the oscillator plus the jitter of the buffer. This has to be less than the ASIC's jitter specifications. Oscillators that do not specify phase noise jitter are not suitable—they usually have much higher than 1ps.

Network ASICs typically have two to eight transceiver reference clocks at 156.25MHz or similar standard frequency, a few core reference clocks at 25MHz, one to four (or none) memory reference clocks, and optional IEEE1588 (clock synchronization over Ethernet) clocks (input or output). X86 chipsets require multiple reference clocks for their different interfaces, so we can usually use standard clock chips (like CK505 type), that are manufactured by multiple different clock chip companies. These standard clock chips provide all the clocks that the X86 chipset needs.

Some chips have on-die termination at the clock inputs, others do not. The ones that do not will need an on-board termination resistor. If the datasheet is not clear then we should put a not populated (DNP) resistor, then we can measure the waveform on the proto board and decide to solder on a resistor or not. Note that measuring clock signals at the ASIC input will show a little plateau or non-monotony, which is only an artifact of probing an inch away from the silicon die since the BGA packages have a package trace length. Packages are basically small fine line PCBs. But no need to worry, the silicon die will not see that plateau. Some ASIC clock inputs are programmable—the on-die termination (ODT) can be enabled or disabled and the biasing parameters can be adjusted. Whether it is enabled or disabled depends on the firmware/software. This necessitates that we have some control over the firmware. Even during the boot process, we cannot have the ASIC crash before it has fully booted up due to unterminated reference clocks. It might not be the main processor firmware, but an ASIC configuration flash chip image or it can be an X86 BIOS or an OS driver. We can probe the clock with an active probe and a 1GHz analog-bandwidth scope, and if it looks very bad, then likely the ODT is not enabled. Sometimes the firmware turns it on or off during boot. That can be an issue, and firmware code change is needed. If we designed in a resistor to the board, assuming the chip has the ODT disabled, but then the chip turns it on and off, it will mess up the clock and crash the ASIC. In that case the firmware code has to be cleaned up. In some cases, we enter into a project that the firmware should not need adjusting for our user-features, but we end up in a situation like this and then we have to get the firmware code from the vendor or detailed register bit information. The register might be un-documented, and if we just guess that it exists, then we have to get confirmation and details (address, bit fields) from the ASIC vendor so we can adjust the firmware to control it—or just hack it until it works with nice waveforms.

We can build a clocking scheme using several different four or six pin oscillators that drive fanout buffer chips, one oscillator plus buffer combination for each frequency that are needed on a board, or we can use programmable (fractional divider) clock chips that provide all the needed frequencies from one source. We can cascade fanout buffers to generate enough number of clocks at the expense of a little added jitter. Most clock chips do not have fractional dividers—some have one, others have several. It is common that we need several different clock frequencies that are not divisible by each other. In that case we need a fractional divider and a PLL for each frequency within the clock generator device. It is better to use these devices rather than finding out during prototyping that we cannot program the frequencies that we wanted.

During the initial design we have to create a clocking subsystem block diagram that satisfies all data plane and control plane device needs. For example, the one in Figure 7.32 is a typical solution on networking cards. Switch ASICs usually require multiple copies of the same SERDES reference clock, and a few core clocks. FPGAs require fewer SERDES clocks, but they might need clocks for memory interfaces and other design-specific internal soft logic. Processors and chipsets usually require 100MHz differential clocks for different purposes, and 14MHz, 25, 33, 48MHz clocks for legacy interfaces, and a 32.768kHz crystal for the real-time calendar/clock. The clock tree also has to show or resolve any power domain crossing issues by controlling the clock enable inputs of the generators or buffers from the power management glue logic.

There are two main schemes used on digital boards for delivering reference clocks to SERDES transceivers of different devices. The first one is Synchronous Clocking, when one single oscillator

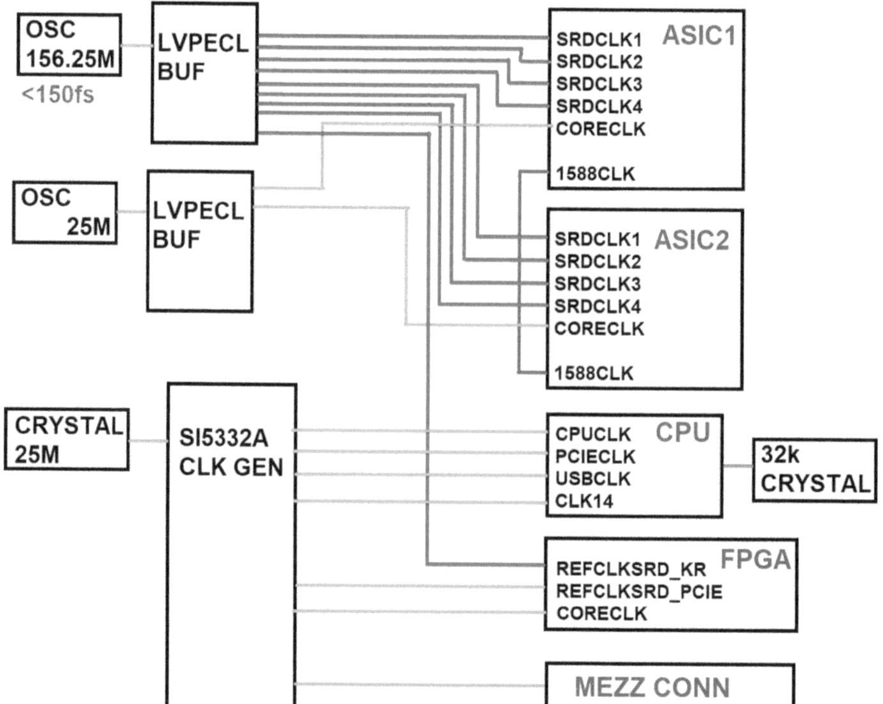

FIGURE 7.32 Example of a made-up board clocking subsystem.

is the source for both the RX and the TX ASICs at the two ends of the interface. The other option is Independent Clocking, when two different oscillators are the sources for each device but the sources are within a specified tolerance, like 100ppm to each other. The interface standards that are capable of running on independent clocks contain a mechanism for "clock compensation" using elastic FIFOs on-chip inside the transceiver IP and inserting SKIP characters into the data stream. Some interfaces require a single source synchronous scheme, even if the two devices are running on different reference clock frequencies. For example, an Interlaken interface requires a 156.25 MHz clock on the FPGA side but 100MHz on the TCAM ASIC side. The Interlaken implementation being simplistic, it does not contain elastic FIFOs for clock compensation. This can be solved only by using a programmable fractional divider clock chip that produces both frequencies with no PPM differences.

Spread spectrum clocking (SSC) is a feature of clock sources that modulate the clock frequency by 5000ppm to help the units pass an EMI certification test by spreading the clock's energy in a wider bandwidth. The downside is that it requires synchronous clocking when SSC is enabled, or we have to find a way to disable it. It is a common feature of PCIe buses.

7.8.1 Time Synchronization

Time synchronization between boards and chassis within the same deployment are sometimes needed by the user application layer. One deployment might be one data center, one aircraft, or one cellular base station. Sometimes a reference clock is distributed within a system that is not for time stamp synchronization but rather for software defined radio purposes. When devices talk to each other they both need to know "the time", to tell how long ago the signal/packet that has just arrived was sent or when it was sent or to act on events in sync. There are two main methods for this: the IEEE1588 standard (Precision Time Protocol or PTP) used in Ethernet-connected hardware (like network switch gear and data centers), and the "1PPS+ToD" used in telecom and aerospace. There can be devices that convert from one format to the other. Usually, one ASIC device in a chassis receives information from the outside of the system from a GPS receiver and generates a time synchronization signal that is distributed to other devices within the same system. It usually involves custom circuits, slow CMOS signals, and sometimes intermingling with the reference clocking tree of the board design. Both IEEE1588 and 1PPS distribute micro-second-accurate time signals, but in different ways. The IEEE1588 encodes it into Ethernet packets as timestamps, while the "1PPS+ToD" is a set of slow CMOS hardware signals using dedicated traces or cables. Between chassis the IEEE1588 is more common, between the chassis and a GPS receiver the 1PPS is used; if inside the chassis between ASICs, either can be used. The accuracy of time depends on the implementation, propagation delay, usually Nano seconds to hundreds of microseconds.

In the "1PPS+ToD" technology a one pulse per second 1PPS slow clock signal is generated by a GPS receiver, transmitted into all devices inside a chassis in the form of a square wave signal over a coaxial cable, plus a 10 to 100MHz square wave clock signal. ToD is basically a data stream or packet sent over any type of slow serial interface, about hours, minutes and seconds. It may be an asynchronous UART or a synchronous interface. So this interface might be a set of one, two, or three signals. GPS systems operate on knowing the precise time using an atomic clock, so GPS receivers can measure distance by knowing when a signal was sent from which satellite that has known positions. Using this GPS signal for timekeeping is a repurposing of an existing technology. Broadcom offers the BroadSync interface on their ASICs, which is similar to the "1PPS+ToD" but proprietary.

Some switch/NIC/PHY ASICs can insert or extract timing from Ethernet packets to/from the CMOS interface. In any deployment one device in one chassis is the IEEE588 GrandMaster, which converts the 1PPS signal coming from a GPS receiver and inserts it into every Ethernet packet passing through it. In a simple system all other ASICs in the deployment get their clocks from Ethernet packets. In some cases, one ASIC in a slave chassis converts this packet into a 1PPS signal for all other ASICs in the same chassis, or just lets them all get their time from the Ethernet packets. In the chassis hosting the GrandMaster ASIC, all other ASICs might receive the original GPS-provided 1PPS or the packetized clock/time.

7.8.2 RTC

A real time clock circuit is not about time synchronization; it is about simple time keeping and calendar, as in seconds, hours, days, years. It typically runs from a coin cell battery backup, so it counts the time even while the rest of the board/system is powered down. It is built into all X86 chipsets, and it features extremely low power consumption, the battery lasting for years. This is how laptops know what day/time it is. Externally for a board designer it is a coin cell battery and a 32kHz crystal connected to the chipset pins, but there are RTC chips also available to connect to embedded processors over I2C. The RTC gets its reset when the coin cell battery gets inserted through an RC (a resistor and a capacitor) delay circuit.

7.9 MULTI-BOARD ARCHITECTURES AND BACKPLANES

When the main block diagram of our hardware architecture contains too many main devices, then we have two choices. We can either design a very large board (up to 18" x 20") that sits at the bottom of a large and deep "appliance" chassis or we can split the block diagram into multiple boards. We can split it in different ways. We can split it in two halves and use mezzanine connectors between the two boards. We can also split it in an asymmetrical way such that the main star-point host device (CPU or switch ASIC) will go on a host board and have several smaller add-in cards plugged into it, which is typical in servers. We can also split the main block diagram into 3 to 24 separate identical-sized standard form factor cards and have a backplane board or a fabric card connecting them. A backplane is a large many-layered PCB with many connectors on it. Several identical-sized front cards are plugged into a backplane through right-angle many-pin connectors. A fabric card is similar, but instead of right angle connections, we use orthogonal connections, and the fabric cards can have lots of active circuits on them. The main data plane, control plane, and management buses between the main devices will be routed through the connectors and backplane traces. With any split, the global power, management, and glue logic blocks have to be implemented or replicated on every single board separately (except on backplanes), and they may talk to each other through a management bus over the backplane. Splitting to multiple cards improves overall manufacturing yield for the whole system. For example, with a 1E4 component count and a 2E-5 solder defect rate, a single-board design would have 1E4*2E-5=20% of the boards having solder defects and needing debug/repair or throw away. If we split the architecture to five similarly sized boards, then only 0.2E4*2E-5=4% of the boards will have defects. If we can split in a way to have some of the boards identical, then it can cut down on design time/cost (only design once) and manufacturing cost (larger quantity of fewer designs). Single-board systems can be large and flat but allow multiple ASICs with very tall heatsinks. Multi-board systems can be more compact (in volume), with replaceable cards that allow salvaging most of a failed unit at the cost of the extra connectors and multiple global circuit instances. Global circuits are mainly for power management and system management.

The main engineering work needed while dividing the architecture into multiple boards is to distribute the component count evenly into smaller boards without having to push too many signals overall and too many critical signals through the B2B (board-to-board) connectors. Additional work goes into ensuring that the division will follow some kind of a symmetry, identical repetition, or pattern to reduce our required design labor. This is heuristic. The third main area of analysis and concept design work is to ensure that the divided configuration is such that it will not prevent us from meeting all signal integrity requirements of any inter-board high-speed signals. Further aspects that the divided system has to ensure are easy system management, field replaceability, low-loss power distribution, serviceability, reduced internal cabling, unblocked airflow, and the even distribution of heat sources in the airflow/chassis cross-section. All of these require feasibility studies and detailed concepts for multiple division options.

The number of parts that fit on one board is driven by component density and board size. Typically, 30 to 90 components per square inch can fit. If it is less than 30 then we might throw money away, if it is more than 90 then we are compromising signal and power integrity. 50 is an ideal density, but still a bit hard to design it. The low end is with I/O-heavy designs that need board space for extra traces. If a design with 5000 components has 20 SERDES links versus 1000 SERDES links, the required density to achieve the same compactness and signal integrity will be different. Some devices are available in different sizes, mostly defined by their package pin count. We can estimate the number of components our board will contain by the pin counts of the main devices. For FPGAs it will be 0.7 comps/pin, for large network ASICs it will be 0.5 comps/pin, for embedded ARM processors 1 comp/pin, for secondary ASICs (like PHY chips, SSDs, and PCIe switches) it is about 0.8 comp/pin. A laptop-type X86 processor and chipset without special peripherals will pull about 1500 components. I/O connector interfaces all together 0.25comp/pin. Any special circuits will be counted separately. Global-supporting glue logic, power, and management circuits usually take up about 10% (1.1x) of the total board component count. From the number and type of main devices on the main block diagram, their individual subsystem part count estimates, and the chosen board size we can verify if they will fit. For example, a card with an embedded X86 CPU, 200 connector pins, and two 1500-pin FPGAs, the total count would be about (1500+2*1500*0.7+200*0.25)*1.1=4015 components. The board density is simply the component count divided by the board area. If we have a 12" x 11" board size, then we would get 4015/(12*11)=30.4 comps/sqin, that seems easily doable. In system design, when we divide the architecture into separate boards, we have to verify that the resulting individual boards are all within the 30 to 90 components per square inch range. If not, then we might have to move functions from one board to another or change the board size form factor, give up features, or downsize.

I/O-heavy designs with big bundles of hundreds of diffpairs have a lot more routing than most other boards do. For wide SERDES buses that require clear routing channels for signal integrity, we need some additional board area. The area of the routing channel can be calculated from N number of diffpairs on M layers, S pair-to-pair spacing for crosstalk, L average routing length estimate from a floorplan, and the width of each diffpair W (intra pair gap plus 2x trace width). Then we can calculate an effective board density, by using the original board area reduced by the routing channel area. This should be between 40 and 90 components per square inch. Basic routes do not have to be separately calculated, the original range included those.

RouteArea = L * N * (W + S) / M.

We also have to consider high-speed I/O for distributing blocks to different boards by checking loss budgets on all links, especially the backplane SERDES links. Sometimes the signal count also increases or decreases on the backplane connectors when we move one block to another board. The pin counts on backplane connectors are usually a limited resource. When moving blocks, in each iteration of the sketch architecture we have to verify the density, floorplan, power budgets, loss budgets, and connector signal counts. If any of the checks fail, it means we have to keep changing the architecture.

In case of a backplane, the cards that plug in are the front boards. They are plugged in or out at the front of the chassis. The chassis will have slide rails and the front cards will have ejector handles (built-in lever arms) to facilitate moving the front boards. Some systems allow cards to be inserted or extracted while the system is running, facilitated by management logic and isolation circuits on the front cards. Backplanes with their vertical connectors connect to front boards containing right-angle connectors. The backplanes are usually covered by connectors and have many layers to facilitate slot-to-slot connectivity. Usually there are no active components on backplanes, most of the time only connectors are assembled on them, but they have a very large number of signal traces. Backplanes provide connectivity between front boards. They are routed according to the topology of the data plane, control plane, and management subsystem architecture topology.

Backplane connector pinouts can be standardized or custom designed for a specific chassis. If we want our product to be compatible with third-party (made by other companies) cards and chassis, then standard is the way to go. There are data plane, control plane, management, power management, and power delivery signals. There are also a few common glue logic signal pins. For example, "SYS_CON", which is used on Compact-PCI and VPX and is connected to ground or not connected (NC) on the backplane, it tells the front card (that has a pull up) whether it is plugged into a system controller slot or peripheral slot. The previous section about resets explained how that works. Universal cards can be plugged into either, and they will act differently in the system controller slot versus in peripheral slots. Another common glue logic signal is the geographical address, which tells a front card which slot number it is plugged into, so it can set its own I2C slave address that it will respond to or adjust the port configuration of the switch/bridge ASIC chip that is used for backplane interfacing. Usually there is a reset signal from a main CPU card or from a management card, but sometimes the reset is encoded over I2C transactions. It is an output on one card and an input to all other cards.

Backplanes are usually passive, with no active (powered) silicon devices. In many cases they do not contain even passive components other than press-fit connectors. Backplanes usually have many more layers in their stackup than front cards have. They are very thick and sometimes they warp, but that is handled with mechanical fixtures tying them into a straight state.

Using orthogonal connectors to connect front cards to a connectivity board at the back of the chassis is an alternative to using backplanes. These boards are called fabric cards. Backplanes are usually lacking any active components, especially powerful ASICs, and the signals pass through two connectors and require routing under dense pin fields of the connectors needed for other slots. Fabric cards eliminate the issues of backplanes, such as the dense connector pin field pass through routes in the middle section of the card and the number of connectors a SERDES signal having to pass through is reduced from two to just one, improving return loss and crosstalk. They also open up the opportunity to place switching (Ethernet, PCIe, CCIX, CXL, InfiniBand) ASICs, retimer chips, or any kind of host device in the big open area. Signals going to a fabric card ASIC only pass through one connector, then a new signal from the ASIC will pass through the second connector. The different connector models have an upper-speed capability listed in their datasheet, that we have to check. With multiple fabric cards we can have redundancy and increased bandwidth also, while each line card will be connected to each fabric card. If the chassis is used for data center switches or routers, then the front cards (with external "line" interfaces) will be called the line cards. The line cards can be vertical and the fabric cards horizontal or the other way around.

Power has to be distributed from the main PSU modules to each card in the chassis up to a few hundred Watts per card. They can be distributed using power planes in a backplane PCB. We can have separate signal backplane and a power backplane with different stackups or we can use solid bus bars instead of a power backplane.

Pin mapping through backplane connectors might be complex. For example, the connector footprint on the front card might have NxM pins, while the mating part on the backplane might have (N+P)xM pins, and there is a table for pin number mapping. Orthogonal connectors might have number to alphabet mapping in a mapping table. These are all grid type connectors, with rows and columns, the pin numbers are marked as alphanumerical just like BGA components, for example "B15"N23", showing which row and which column the pin is in. During schematic design we have to be very precise about pin number to signal connections.

7.10 DESIGN EXAMPLES

This section demonstrates a few different main block diagrams of actual products, similar to the generic diagram but more specific and they reflect designs made for specific purposes.

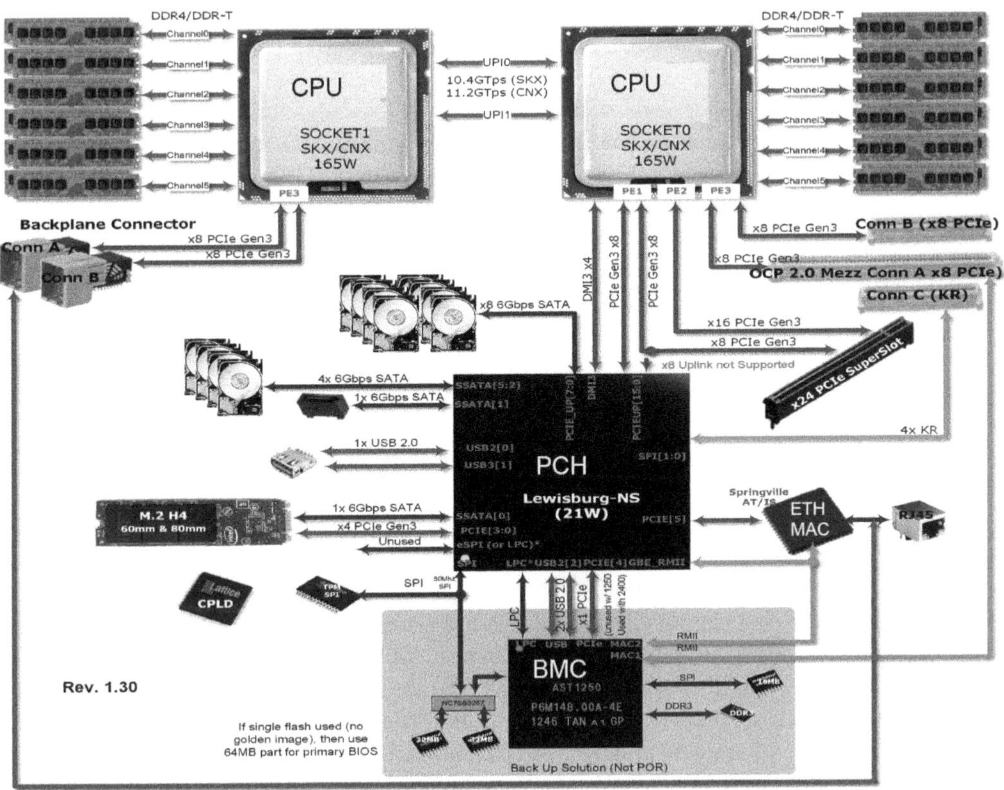

FIGURE 7.33 Main block diagram of the Tioga Pass server motherboard from the Open Compute Project, the image from the design schematics is used for illustration under the Open Web Foundation Final Specification Agreement ("OWFa 1.0") signed by Quanta Computer, Inc.

7.10.1 The Tioga Pass Node Server Motherboard

The first example in Figure 7.33 is a dual-processor Intel Xeon server motherboard called Tioga Pass project from the Open Compute Project (OCP) and Meta. This kind of design is very common—an advanced version of the personal computer that most people know. It is a dual-processor server that is used in large numbers in data centers. We can see that it has sockets for two Intel Xeon processors, and each CPU has multiple DIMM memory slots. The two CPUs are connected through a high-bandwidth UPI link to allow cache coherent multi-processing. The board has network connectivity, a Lewisburg-NS PCH south bridge chipset, a BMC management processor, a glue logic CPLD, an m.2 storage socket for operating system boot, and several PCIe expansion slots. Servers often have multiple PCIe sockets that can be populated with I/O cards for external interfacing ports or with accelerator cards. It has backplane connectors with PCIe links. The CPUs and the PCH are mainly used as control/data plane devices, while the BMC is used for the management plane together with the glue logic CPLD. The main block diagram does not explain what the CPLD does, and the clocking and power schemes are not displayed on it. This is because those functions are displayed on separate block diagrams to reduce clutter on the main diagram due to the overall board complexity. The official design package on the OCP website contains the full design information.

It is not seen on the diagram here, but from the design package we know that the Lattice CPLD handles the glue logic signals related to power management and power sequencing, system status LEDs, LPC-bus POST code display, device/slot resets, and X86 CPU/chipset glue logic signals. But it is really an extension to the BMC. The AST1250 baseboard management controller (BMC) has its own single-chip DDR3 memory down, a flash chip, and it is connected to everything on the board. It has an LPC slave interface hooked up to the intel chipset, has its GPIOs connected to the X86 power/thermal management glue logic signals, DIMM glue logic signals, fan control signals, and rail-voltage sensor analog inputs. The motherboard contains many I2C buses connecting to many devices like voltage and thermal sensors, internal/external PCIe slots, PSUs, and the PCH chipset. Some I2C buses are mastered by the chipset, some by the BMC, and some by both. The BMC connects to the CPU's external 1Gig Ethernet connection to receive remote management commands that it will convert to chipset control actions like reboot. It communicates with the Intel processor over UART, USB, PCIe, and 1Gig Ethernet. It can over-write the Intel chipset's BIOS flash through multiplexers.

7.10.2 The Minipack-2 SMB Switch Card

The second example in Figure 7.34 is a high-bandwidth data center switch card called the Minipack-2 SMB switch card. The Minipack-2 is a medium-sized data center spine switch. The chassis contains one switch card in the middle that connects to a management processor card and eight external network interface line cards. The line cards have the external optical port connectors and PHY chips. The switch card's architecture is actually a more common data center design; it contains features that support automated data handling. This is different from a well-known PC motherboard where everything serves basic user interface functions. The need for the main switch ASIC is obvious—it handles the high-bandwidth data plane traffic that is the main function of the switch chassis. On the other hand, the need for the CPLDs and FPGAs and other things is not so obvious. The need for them emerges from the specific project details. In this design the purpose of the IOB FPGA is to control the optical modules on the line cards over a custom synchronous serial interface, through another FPGA on each line card. The line cards' FPGAs have direct pin connections to the control and status signals of each optical port. These are a high number of low-speed 3.3V signals. The IOB FPGA itself is controlled by both the CPU card over PCIe and by the management card over USB. The PCIe switch simply splits the CPU's PCIe uplink between several downstream devices, including the main ASIC on the switch card and other devices on the line cards. The smaller out-of-band switch ASIC is designed-in to allow both the main CPU and the management CPU to be accessed from the external 1Gig management Ethernet port. The AST2620 management processor (BMC) takes remote management commands over the Ethernet network in the data center. It also handles the I2C identification interfaces of each optical module on the line cards through programmable I2C multiplexers. The BMC, the OOB Ethernet switch, and the CPLD are in the management plane and board glue logic. The Tomahawk 4 ASIC clearly serves the data plane, and the PCIE switch and IOB FPGA serve the control plane functions of the board. The clocking scheme is not part of the main block diagram as it operates semi independently while connecting to all main logic devices, so it has its own separate block diagram, which is not shown here.

7.10.3 The VXS DSP FMC Carrier Card

A VXS (VME with an extra high-speed connector) form-factor card was designed by CERN (European Organization for Nuclear Research) for scientific instrumentation purposes in their particle accelerators. The design files are available at the Open Hardware Repository (ohwr.org) website. This card contains two Xilinx Virtex-5 FPGAs, an Analog Devices SHARC DSP, and it can host two FMC cards that usually contain RF analog circuits and A/D or D/A converters. The block diagram can be seen in Figure 7.35. FPGA board block diagrams often show the internal blocks inside the FPGA, since those are application specific. The main FPGA handles the VME bus interfacing and loading and storing data to the DSP. The second FPGA handles signal processing for digitized waveform streams coming from/to the FMC cards. Both FPGAs have external fast SRAM

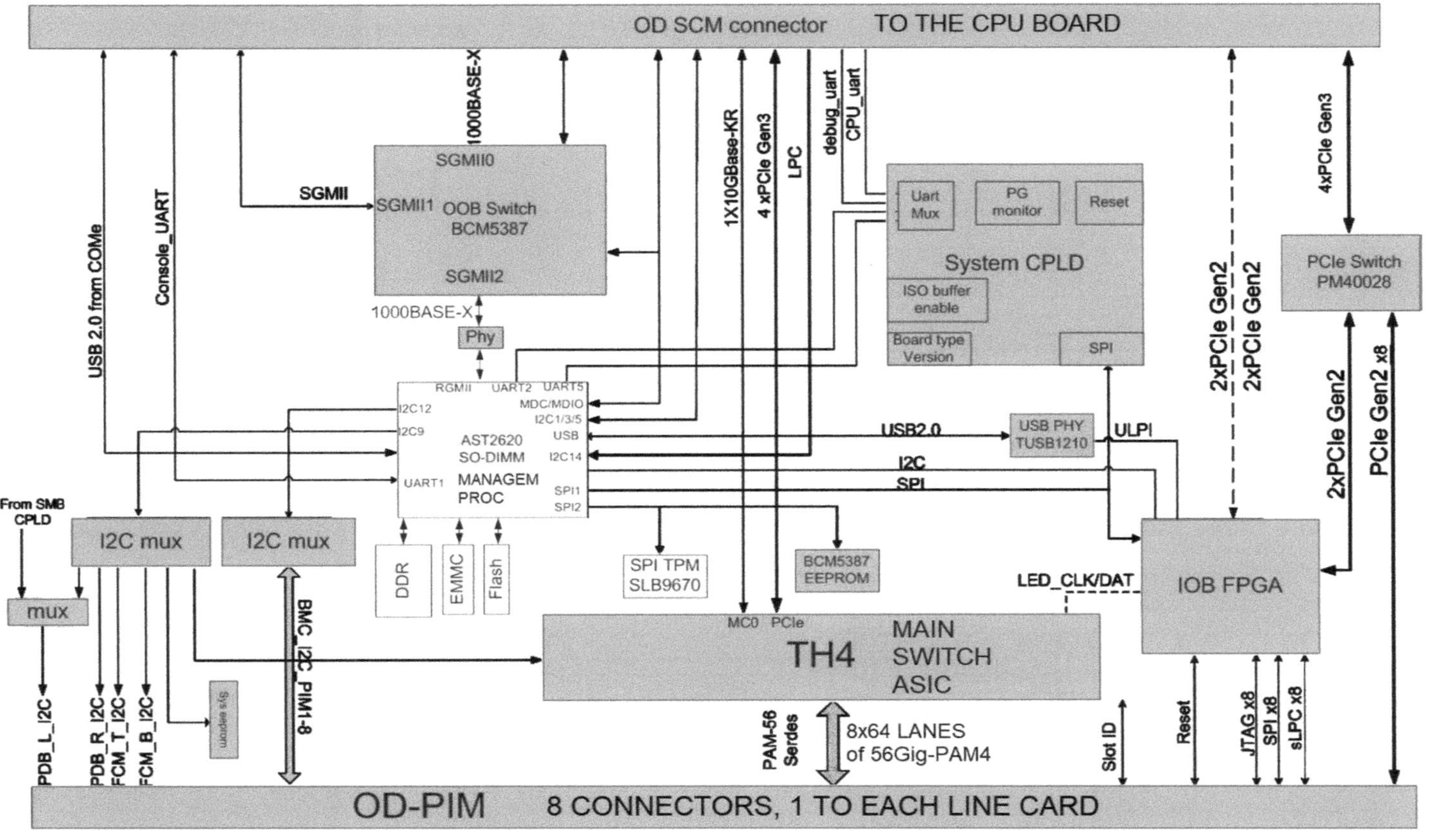

FIGURE 7.34 Main block diagram of the Minipack 2 SMB switch card from the Open Compute Project, the image from the design schematics is used for illustration under the Open Compute Project Hardware License (Permissive) Version 1.0 (Open Compute ProjectHL-P) signed by Meta Platforms, Inc.

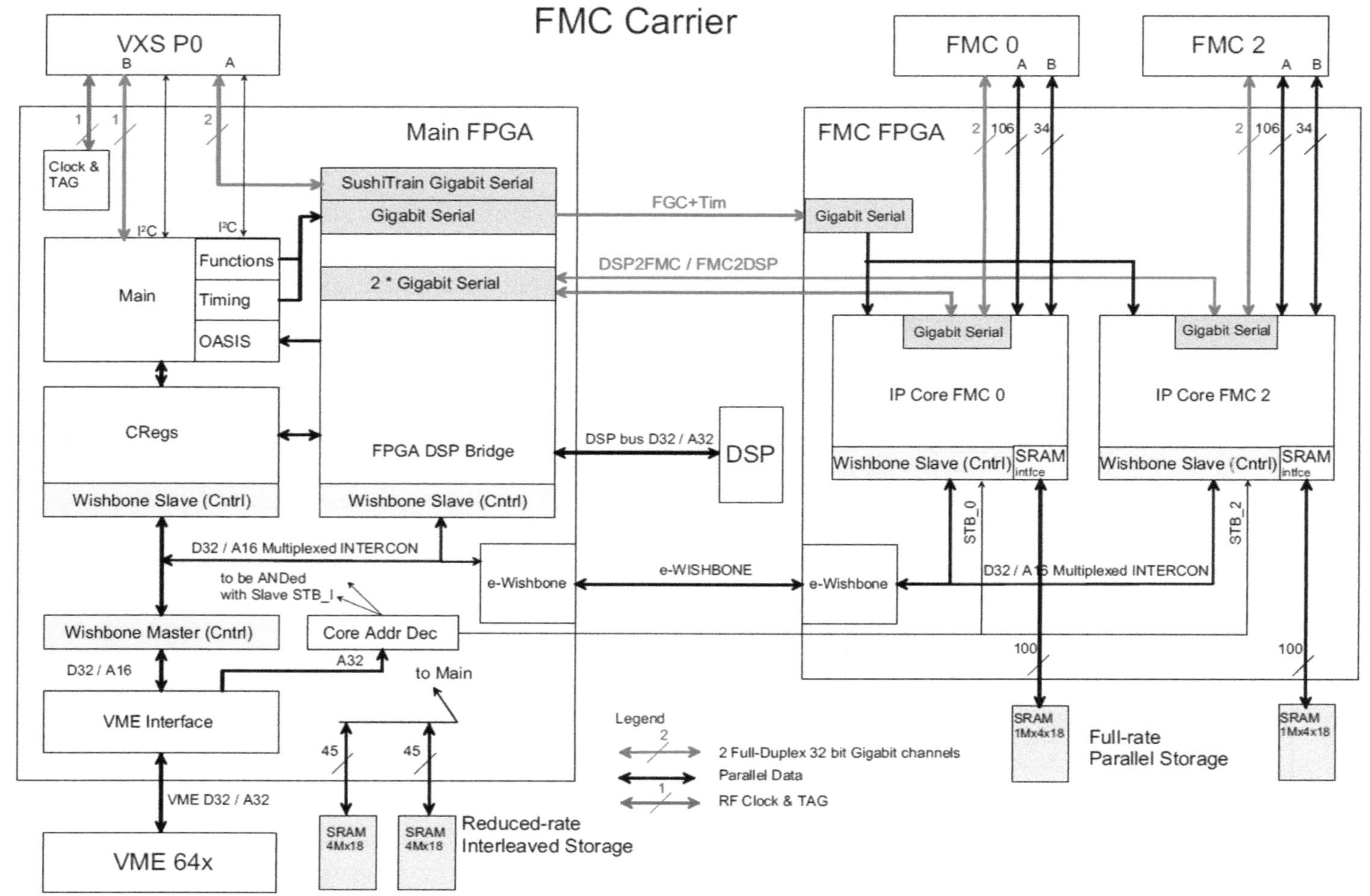

FIGURE 7.35 VXS DSP FMC carrier card from CERN and ohwr.org (Copyright CERN 2022, licensed under CC-BY-SA).

buffer chips attached. One of the FMC cards and one of the FPGAs also have access to a rear transition card over the high-speed VXS connector. The DSP can be used for signal processing tasks. It has internal code and data SRAM memories that can be loaded with executable code and data to be processed, then the post-processed data can be read out from it by the FPGA. The DSP's code execution and data moving are fully controlled through the main FPGA through the DSP's external port, DPI and DAI interfaces, and system signals. The card being an FMC carrier and having one of the FPGAs reconfigurable, this allows the card to be used in different science experiments and applications.

The data plane includes the communication links between the FMC sites, the FPGAs, the rear VXS connector, the VME bus, and the DSP. The VME bus allows a processor card to initiate data transfers from/to the card through the main FPGA. This way the VME bus can act as both the data plane and the control plane interface. The power management control signals seem to come from the backplane.

8 Systems and Chassis

A chassis is what hosts the system. It is a sheet metal box with PCBs and other things inside it. The system is the working arrangement of everything inside the chassis, including boards (hardware), mechanical design, software, and FPGA logic. It is usually designed by a cross-functional team that is led by system engineering or management or by hardware engineering. The functionality is actually done in software, and the hardware design provides the platform for it. The cross-functional team consists of hardware design engineers (electrical), mechanical, power supply, software, FPGA logic and systems engineering, and program management.

Different industries with different processing and communication needs usually have settled on different sizes and types of systems and chassis. Many systems can be mounted into 19" (or 21") wide data center racks.

8.1 FORM FACTORS

A "form factor" is a pre-defined board shape/size definition together with board-to-board connector part number and location, pinout tables, and hardware and software mechanisms for system management, defined in standards (specification documents). It can be an international standard specification adopted by many companies or it can be custom designed and used by one company only. The standard form factors vary between industries, for example, VPX is common in aerospace, while ATCA is more common in telecom. The most famous form factor organizations are VITA, PICMG, PCI-SIG, and OCP. Multi-board systems are placed inside a custom-designed chassis. A chassis usually contains the boards with heatsinks mounted on spacers or slide rails, a solid frame, sheet metal exterior, front panel with connector apertures, removable power supply modules, fan modules, air baffles, and in some cases also bus bars for power delivery and internal cabling. Some chassis have multiple standard-sized cards plugged in parallel; other chassis might include one or two fix-mounted large base boards with few daughter cards.

Typically, complex boards are used together with other complex boards within a chassis. Usually they are connected together through board-to-board connectors like backplane connectors (perpendicular to the backplane's surface), orthogonal connectors (both boards are connecting at the edge), mezzanine connectors (two boards have parallel planes), and rear connectors (same plane), as we can see in Figure 8.1. Sometimes complex active boards containing ASICs are connected together, in other cases the complex boards with the ASICs connect to a passive backplane acting as an interconnect to other complex boards that are also plugged into the same backplane. In the context of some standard form factors, the SERDES interface link widths on the connectors use a certain naming convention. For example, a "fat pipe" is an x4-lane interface, or 8 diffpairs total. An "ultra-thin pipe" is a x1 link, a "double-fat pipe" is a x8 link.

The main role of a complex digital board or chassis is either some type of computing or data communications handling (interfacing, switching, networking). Either of the processing or the communications boards/chassis have different typical implementations within different industries. For example, servers made for telecom look somewhat different from servers made for data centers. The same goes for switches and routers. They have somewhat different features, external interfaces, and form factors.

Some chassis form factors allow cards to be easily replaced, even replaced while the rest of the chassis is running, this is called hot swapping. The cards that are removable at the front side of the chassis can be called modules (in aerospace) and blades and line cards (in networking) or line replaceable units (LRUs). Many LRU cards and blades come with mechanical parts assembled to

DOI: 10.1201/9781032702094-8

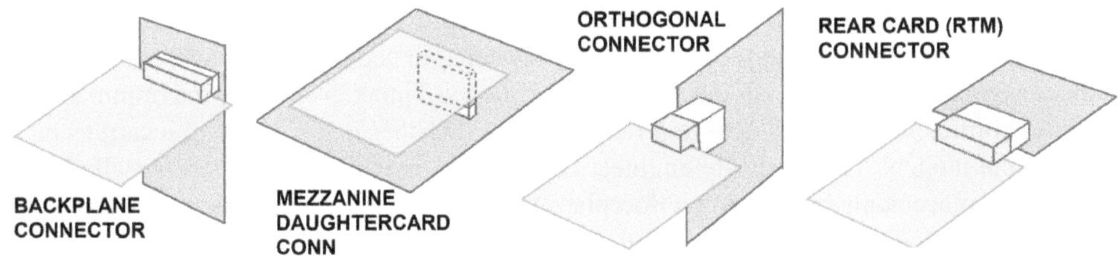

FIGURE 8.1 Multi-board connectivity options within a chassis (sketch).

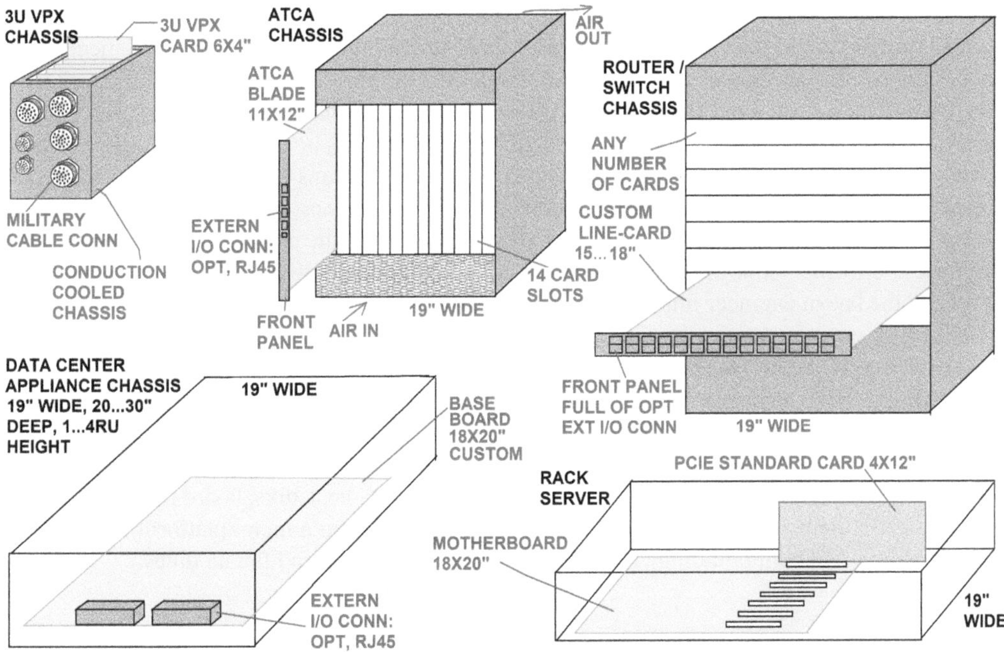

FIGURE 8.2 Example board and chassis form factors (sketch).

them as one unit. The removable cards usually connect to a base board or backplane using several many-pin high-speed I/O connectors, which take a large amount of force to insert or extract the card, so usually ejector handles are part of the design. Multiple backplane connectors having so many pins combined require a significant insertion and ejection force. An ejector handle hooks into an aperture on the chassis frame and acts like a lever that exerts a large force at one end by exerting only a small force over a greater distance at the other end. It also locks the card in. The cards are inserted and slid through a slide rail that allows movement in one direction only, and that direction will be stopped by the backplane and the ejector to hold the card in place for normal operation. The removable cards are normally mechanical subassemblies, or modules, with smaller mezzanine cards on top, heatsinks, stiffener frames, ejector handles, and other mechanical parts secured to the PCB. Figure 8.2 shows a few examples of board and chassis form factors and some support cards, which are easily removable by the user even during normal operation while others are fixed.

8.1.1 Working with Mechanical Engineering

We work with the mechanical engineers throughout the whole project. At the concept phase we try to work out how many boards and what size we need in a system. They tell us what we can do, we tell them what we would like to do. The system concept for the project proposal is complete only if the mechanical engineer agrees to it. For the system concept a thermal analysis is done by mechanical engineering to ensure all the ASICs remain below Tjmax even at the maximum ambient temperature. For this we might have to re-arrange the board shapes and sizes, chip locations on the floorplan, or fan models. The hardware engineers have to check if the system concept allows suitable component placements by creating a floorplan. We also have to check if the trace lengths will not be too long by doing a loss budget calculation based on the floorplan. So the SERDES links, the PCB floorplan, the cooling, the mechanical arrangement, the feature set (how many ASICs, how many ports, at what speed), manufacturability, and testability are all designed together to satisfy all requirements in the same time. The solution space of the system is the intersection of the solution spaces of each discipline.

We might have to involve other objects in the chassis besides boards, such as power supply units, bus bars, spacers, air baffles, a front panel, and internal cabling. Usually, the mechanical engineers design or select the heatsinks at the board level, or if they are big or interact with the chassis (through heat pipes) then at the chassis level. At the board level the hardware engineers negotiate or co-design several things with the mechanical engineer. For example, board size and shape, heatsink size and shape, mounting hole (board and heatsink mount) locations and sizes, connector types and exact locations, areas with different component height restrictions, and also bus bars and PSU modules if they directly connect into the board's connectors. Then the mechanical engineer creates a mechanical drawing about the agreed positions as a line drawing, which the hardware engineer reviews and the layout engineer imports into the board file to guide the layout placement. The locations and edges are exact, not suggestions. If we cannot fit it, then we have to re-negotiate. At the end of the layout design the layout engineer exports a line or 3D drawing, (DXF, EMN, STEP, or other file format), which the mechanical engineer checks if it still complies with the original mechanical concept or whether any part of the PCB interferes with any mechanical design features. Mechanical engineers design several components for complex hardware, but sometimes they use off-the-shelf parts. The custom parts are the chassis itself made of sheet metal, heatsinks, board frames, stiffener frames, sleds (in appliance chassis we can slide out the internals on a metal platform), light pipes (for external port LED light guiding), handles, board-securing parts, and fan modules.

8.1.2 Thermal

All electronics produce heat while turned on, which has to be continuously extracted; otherwise, the devices overheat, then malfunction or shut down or get damaged. Usually, the main ASICs produce most of the heat dissipation, and they are the hottest parts on a board. The thermal design is an important part of the board and system design, managing the heat extraction and device temperatures. A board, module, or chassis product is specified to operate reliably within a certain temperature range. For example, consumer units would have a 0C to +45C range, some data center products would have a -5C to +55C range, some aerospace units would have a -25C to +70C or -40C to +85C range. The same is true for silicon chips and all other components having a lower and upper temperature limit. For chips, the upper limit of potential damage is the maximum junction temperature (Tjmax). Limits on elevation above sea level can be also a part of the system specification. This depends on the product type, the market segment, and specific uses. At the low end of the temperature range electronics designs might experience intermittent startup failures, and at the high end they might experience long run-time overheating or thermal shutdown. The lower end requires resilient circuit design and extended range parts to be used, the higher end requires a cooling system design with heatsinks on the main ASICs and system fans. The cooling system is designed by mechanical engineering, but it has to be workable with the hardware design and board floorplan.

The four main types of cooling are passive air cooling, active air cooling with fans, conduction cooling, and liquid cooling. The most complex boards in data centers use active air cooling. Air is sucked or pushed through the chassis using chassis fans. Each main ASIC or hot device has its own passive heatsink, and the air may be guided to them by air baffles. Many active air-cooled consumer electronics use active fan-sinks and no chassis fan (just chassis perforations). The lower power and cheaper consumer units use passive air cooling, with just air vents on the top and bottom of their chassis, where the air moves through by being heated by the hot chips. In aerospace electronics conduction cooling (CC) is also common. In this case there is no air movement. This means that all the hot chips are touching the main board heat frame, which conducts heat sideways into the guide rails where wedge locks conduct the heat into the chassis. The CC chassis has very heavy and thick walls; they are not made of sheet metal, so they further conduct the heat to the mounting base. The CC chassis is mounted onto a vehicle's structural frame to complete the heat extraction. The vehicle, airplane, satellite, or truck design has to ensure the frame is suitable to absorb all the power/heat from the electronics chassis. This method has higher thermal resistance than air cooling, so it limits the maximum power dissipation of our chips—we cannot use 400W ASICs, but perhaps 40W. Liquid cooling seems to be the most effective way of cooling hot chips, although it is not very common due to impracticality in most situations. It pumps a liquid between the ASIC-attached small heat frame and a big fan-sink that is external to the chassis. All types of cooling solutions might unitize heat pipes or vapor chambers for conducting heat away from the hot chip sideways with minimal thermal resistivity. Large heatsinks might be too large and their far reaches might be ineffective without built-in heat pipes.

Many small components dissipate heat into the PCB through their center thermal solder pads; only devices above 1 to 2W require heat sinks. The main devices on a PCB dissipate most of the power, so they will have their own heatsink or will be attached to a shared whole-board heat frame in some form factors. The PCB acts as a big heatsink for most small chips, especially the VRM circuits. The goal of the thermal design is to ensure that all chips will remain below their maximum datasheet specified temperature, when the fans are running at 100% and the unit is operating at the high end of the specified range. Thermal design is assisted by thermal simulations. The thermal/mechanical engineers need data from the hardware engineers about device power dissipation and maximum junction temperatures. Any device with a soldered-down power pad is usually cooled through the PCB, up to 1–2W, so their dissipation adds to the overall distributed PCB power dissipation. All the VRMs on the board have an efficiency about 85%, so about 15% of the total power budget plus the power of any QFN non-VRM parts are dissipated through the PCB into the air.

The fan-control thermal algorithm written by software engineering that controls the fans ensures that the fans will only run at 100% speed when they really need too; otherwise, reduce power consumption and noise. The airflow can be pushed or pulled by fans—they can be bottom to top, top to bottom, front to back, back to front, or sideways. Chassis fans are often removable modules. In case one fan fails, the system should still remain operational until the system administrator replaces it. That means the system has to be designed for fan redundancy. For example, 2+1, 4+1, 8+2, similarly to the PSU module redundancy, described Chapter 4, "Power Supply Circuits". Fans also consume power. When selecting fans, we will likely end up with as much fan power as 5% to 20% of the system power dissipation. The fans and PSUs have right angle power/signal connectors, which can connect into our main board directly or into an adapter board that plugs into our main board. Fan modules (fan trays, Figure 8.3) and power supply modules (Figure 8.4) can be plugged into a chassis from the back. The images are snapshots from 3D mechanical models. The PSUs, having their own fans, might need to access air that is not pre-heated by the ASICs. The PSU fans and the system fans might work against each other if the chassis is not properly designed. The ASIC passive heatsinks have to catch as much of the air flow as possible, instead of letting the air go around them. All these can be handled by added air baffles in the mechanical design.

8.2 CONSUMER, INDUSTRIAL, SCIENTIFIC

Some consumer, industrial, or scientific electronics can be considered complex hardware, for example, computers, laptops, graphics cards, and data acquisition cards. Industrial computing is similar in complexity and signaling speeds to consumer computing, while they are designed to withstand

FIGURE 8.3 FAN module inside and outside.

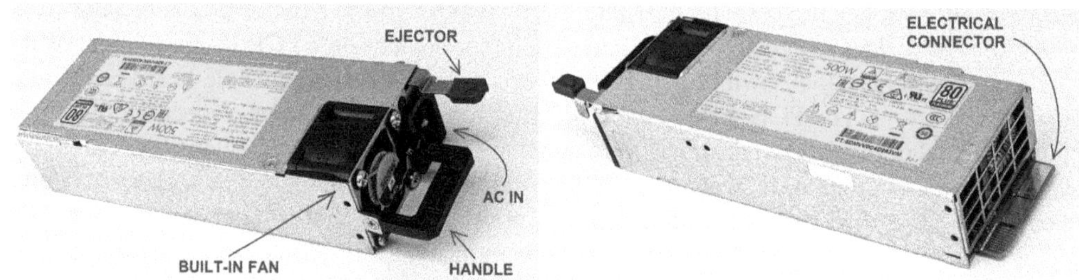

FIGURE 8.4 Power supply module outside and inside.

wider temperature range and high dust/humidity environments, and usually they have special interfaces to directly control industrial equipment, like robots, wending machines, or vehicle doors. Automotive computer boards are often rated to an even wider temperature range. Many consumer and industrial computing devices are in small boxes or hand-held. Usually they have an ARM processor or a "mobile" X86 processor meant for laptops, with 6 to 25W power dissipation. Newer cars with self-driving features and machine vision might contain a motherboard with medium size CPUs, AI ASICs, FPGAs, or GPUs.

Industrial computer form factors like Mini-ITX, Com-Express, ETX, and others are commonly produced by companies that specialize in them and are integrated by third-party companies into their systems. COM-express cards are very popular mezzanine cards, the smallest that can host a laptop class X86 processor. Companies design their functionality on a large board that also acts as a carrier to the mezzanine card. Figure 8.5 shows a custom industrial computer motherboard produced by Blue Chip Technology. This motherboard hosts an AMD Athlon-II Neo processor and its chipset, several video outputs, SODIMM memory modules, and a graphics card slot. Industrial computers have similar low-power processors as laptops have, but they have large robust external connectors, bigger heatsinks, and some connectors that would be considered obsolete in consumer electronics like DB-9 serial ports or PS/2 ports, and often GPIO signals.

At the open hardware repository website, we can see several board designs that were created to support scientific research in particle physics. One example is the DIOT System Board, which we can see in Figure 8.6, developed by CERN for their own internal scientific instrumentation. This card can be plugged into a custom chassis. Its purpose is to receive digitized signals from an FMC mezzanine card, then process it by the AMD (Xilinx) Zynq-Ultrascale FPGA, which has memory-down on the board.

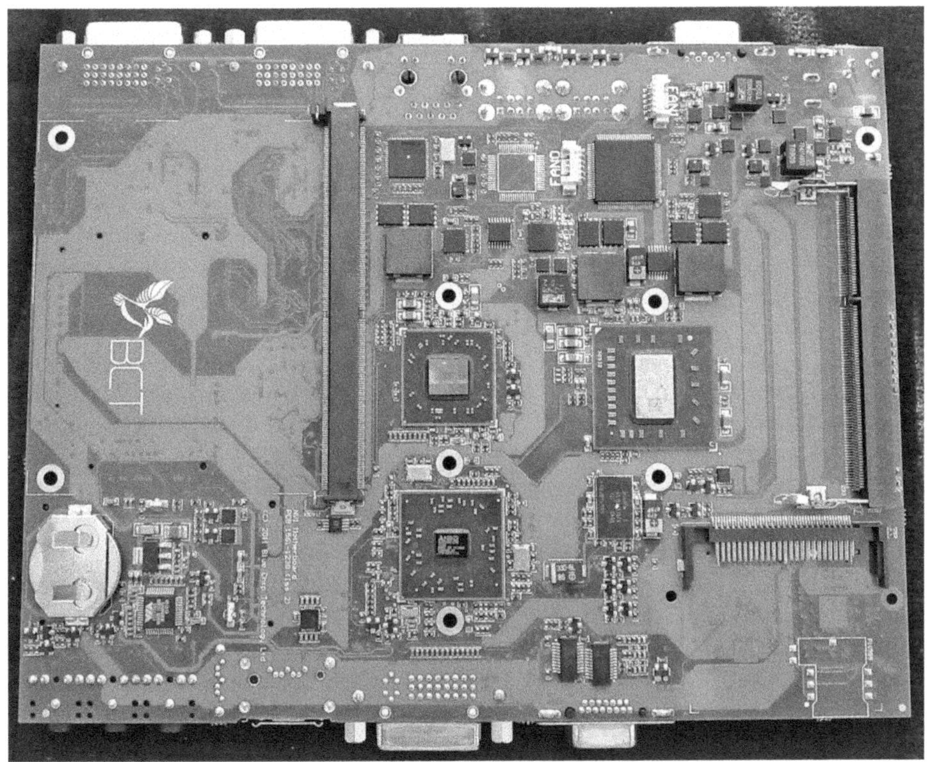

FIGURE 8.5 NV1 custom industrial PC motherboard. Photograph provided by Blue Chip Technology Ltd.

FIGURE 8.6 The DIOT System Board from CERN and ohwr.org. Copyright CERN 2022, licensed under CC-BY-SA.

Test equipment like high-speed oscilloscopes, vector network analyzers, spectrum analyzers, and communications analyzers can be also put into the industrial category. They include complex boards with processors, FPGAs, and high-speed A/D converters. They typically contain a laptop-grade processor and/or a single FPGA.

8.3 MILITARY/AEROSPACE HARDWARE

These systems are often made in the form of a chassis with cards plugged into a backplane. Most or all of the I/O connectivity of the main front cards go through the backplane. From the backplane the signals might go to other cards or to external rugged military style connectors. The cards are often CPU cards, FPGA cards, or various specialty logic cards. The aerospace CPU cards have similar low-power processors as laptops have, but the I/Os used are typically serial console and more than single-port Ethernet, USB, and PCIe. Aerospace hardware chassis are often called "mission computers". The cards are typically "Eurocard" 3RU or 6RU mechanical form factors, which describe the board size. 3RU is around 4x6", while 6RU is around 6x9" in size. The actual form factors like 3RU VPX define far more than just board size. Since around 2010 the VPX form factor defined by the VITA 46 standards has been the most popular, while before 2010 for at least a decade the Compact-PCI form factor defined by the PICMG2.0 standard was popular. The VME form factor (VITA 1 standard) mainly in 6RU format was popular before Compact-PCI, but they still design and sell new VME boards for upgrading existing equipment. The main difference between VPX, VME, and Compact-PCI is the backplane electrical interface and the connector. VPX uses the Tyco Electronics RT2 and RT3 series connectors. VPX allows up to 25Gbps differential signals on the RT3 type, or 10Gbps on the RT2 type. Compact-PCI and VME can support up to 66MHz parallel buses. The VXS form factor is basically a VME board with an extra high-speed connector for rear card SERDES connectivity. Several VITA standards describe different aspects of VPX, for example, Ethernet over backplane or mechanical requirements for space grade systems. There are VITA standards for implementing flyover backplane connectors for RF (VITA67) and optical (VITA66) connections in VPX systems. Several other standards govern rugged mil/aero systems and boards, for example, Open VPX, SOSA (Sensor Open Systems Architecture), FACE (Future Airborne Capability Environment), VICTORY (Vehicular Integration Interoperability), and CMOSS (Modular Open Suite of Standards). In VPX standards there is a long list of "slot profiles" that define cards of different functions. Military and aerospace designs are more heavily involved with form factor compliance than are other industries, and a lot of engineering work goes into it.

The 3RU Eurocard allows about maximum ~2000 components, while the 6RU would fit max ~3000 to 4000, assuming very high component density, with routing channels under components. Figure 8.7 shows an example 6U VPX card made for aerospace conduction-cooled applications, with an Intel Xeon-D processor, a DDR4 memory-down, and a Microsemi PolarFire FPGA. The card made by Extreme Engineering Solutions Inc. (X-ES) is normally covered with a heat frame from top and bottom and has wedge locks on the sides to allow heat conduction into the chassis and into an airplane frame. These are not shown on the photograph so as to allow us to see the board components and complexity. The card is a universal design. The customer (system integrator) can run their own software on the CPU and their own data or signal processing application on the FPGA. The VPX 3RU form factor connector set allows about 64 diffpairs max, if running at 25Gbps, that is, 0.8Tbps in each direction, limited by the number of pins in the standard VPX connectors. The 6RU size allows three times as much.

They normally have more stringent environmental standards than other types of products in terms of operating temperature range, mechanical shock, and vibration. Space-grade cards have even more stringent requirements, but the same 3RU/6RU VPX form factors are common. Some systems are air cooled, others are conduction cooled. Conduction-cooled means the mechanical design conducts heat through the board frame from hot chips to the card wedge-locks to the chassis walls to the aircraft's frame for final heat extraction, without fans or air flow. Figure 8.8 shows an example of a conduction-cooled chassis of a custom off-the-shelf (COTS) computer system, or sometimes called mission computer with X86 CPU cards, an Ethernet switch card, and payload FPGA cards. We can see that all the signal I/Os from any external cabling are connected to the internal electronics through the military-style rugged circular connectors. Air-cooled chassis are similar to hardware we find in other industries, with the main difference being the whole board is

FIGURE 8.7 XCalibur4840 6U-VPX card with an Intel Xeon-D processor and a Microsemi FPGA, photo courtesy of Extreme Engineering Solutions (X-ES).

FIGURE 8.8 XPand6240 3U-VPX conduction cooled COTS system. Photo courtesy of Extreme Engineering Solutions (X-ES).

covered with a single metal frame heatsink combo that attaches to all hot chips through thermal pads. The frame is similar to the conduction cooling frame, but without wedge locks and with fins covering the whole top surface. Using thermal pads can conduct heat from chips less than 50W, but aerospace hardware rarely uses higher-powered ASICs or processors. Above that dissipation level the use of thermal paste (thermal interface material, TIM) is common and requires individual device heatsinks due to flatness plane mismatch and the need for super thin layers of TIM.

Ruggedized electronics must work in a wider temperature range, in strong vibrations, and in high humidity environments. For this we avoid high-impedance circuits (like >100k resistors and bare crystals), use industrial temperature grade chips, and apply corner bonding of large BGAs and conformal coating of boards.

Aerospace hardware is designed to be more resilient in terms of radiation, and space hardware is even more resilient. SEU mitigation (for example non-programmable VRMs) and radiation hardened chips are common. There are a few radiation-hardened devices available, for example, 200MHz PowerPC processors from BAE systems and flash-based FPGAs in large packages from Microchip (Actel RTG4).

8.4 TELECOM EQUIPMENT

Telecommunications providers (carriers, mobile communications, broadband Internet service providers) use modulated cable or radio signals at the end user access, but they also have complex infrastructure to aggregate data traffic that relies on standard interfaces like fiber optic Ethernet and large chassis equipment. They have small regional data centers and base stations. Many of these are spread across in the country instead of all being in a few large data centers. The typical requirement for telecom-use computing and networking equipment is reliability, manageability, and compatibility with legacy technologies. Inside those there are processors, large FPGAs and ASICs for parsing and processing the data traffic and to process digitized analog waveforms to extract data from them. They can be digitized baseband radio signals as well as audio samples. The telecom industry also uses different types of large chassis with plug-in cards, often in the ATCA (Advanced Telecom Computing Architecture) form factor, defined by the PICMG3.x standards; others are custom form factors.

The ATCA boards, "blades", are much larger than VPX modules. They are 8RU height vertically inserted boards, in about 11x12.7 inches board size, and they can fit 7000 components and 400W of power. An ATCA chassis has two to four switch blades that distribute the data traffic to the two to 14 server processor blades, typically in a dual-star or dual-dual star topology, but full-mesh is also possible with processor blades talking to each other. The backplane data plane (fabric) communications can be through 10G-KR Ethernet (PICMG3.1), PCIe, InfiniBand, or SRIO. The backplane connectors (Zd, Zd+, HM-eZd+) have 120 diffpairs per blade, that is 60x25Gbps=1.5Tbps bandwidth each direction. There is also a 1Gbit Ethernet dual-star or dual-dual-star control plane called management Ethernet or base channel. The base channel is usually distributed by the switch blade, but the actual active host is the shelf manager card. Further, there is an I2C based IPMI subsystem for controlling board power up/down, blade insertion, and ejection, controlled by a small processor card (two cards in redundant configuration) called shelf manager. Boards receive power from the PSU modules at 48V, so each blade has to have a 48V-to -12V intermediate VRM module, as well as a dual source selector power switch. The back side of the chassis sometimes supports rear transition modules (RTMs) for additional external I/O or extra processing. They often process real-time communication data streams or modulated digitized waveforms using software running on regular server processors on the processing blades.

3G and 4G/LTE mobile phone networks are not discussed here in much detail, as no one will be designing them from now on. The baseband units (BBU) used in them were custom designed CPU/FPGA boards. Figure 8.9 shows a typical card used in these 4G-LTE BBUs. It has six main ASIC devices on a custom 15" x 11" form factor. It provides the interfaces to the cell tower and performs baseband RX/TX signal processing and data switching using its six main devices. Modern 5G mobile phone networks (RAN or Open-RAN radio access networks) have to route data packets just like Ethernet networks do between base stations and process the packet data in between. It heavily relies on software-defined radio (SDR), meaning radio waveforms are digitized and processed by CPUs and FPGAs. Since the waveforms are transferred into the digital domain, they can be handled like any regular data and sent over the Internet to remote servers for further waveform or data processing. The RAN is a layered structure like Ethernet with many of its layers implemented in software that are running on embedded CPU/FPGA cards, blades, or servers. Part of the network is over radio links to the subscribers; the other part is through an Ethernet/Internet network. The data passing through has to be identified for call line establishment and billing. The infrastructure

FIGURE 8.9 Chanel Element Module card from a Nokia 9926 BBUv2 4G-LTE base band unit.

hardware inside the base stations includes complex board designs for specialized routers and servers with FPGA, CPU, DSP, and NPU (network processor) based processing, and mixed RF/digital cards. Modern 5G networks are organized into three stages of equipment. The stage closer to the radio links directly interfacing the subscribers' cell phones is the RU (radio unit) inside the cell towers. These contain high-speed A/D converters and FPGAs to capture and packetize the waveforms into Ethernet data. This is where the concept of software-defined radio (SDR) translates the radio communication into wired digital communication. We can check out a Zynq FPGA-based cell tower radio unit design on the Open Compute Project (OCP) website under the project name Evenstar Dual-Band RRU. The next stage is the distributed unit (DU), and it is the farthest from the radio link is the central unit (CU). All these three stages communicate through fiber optic Ethernet cabling and the Internet. The DU is basically a low-cost server with FPGA or NPU-based accelerator cards. These cards are RAN or Telco accelerator cards with FPGAs or network processors for waveform (modulation, baseband) and data computing. The server processor performs the control plane and part of the data plane functions. It is still possible to make DU appliances with FPGAs and a CPU integrated on a single board, although it would cost more. A single-purpose CPU/FPGA combination rack-mount chassis is often called an "appliance". The CU is also a low-cost server with FPGA accelerator cards, but it focuses on higher protocol layer data packet processing instead of waveform processing.

8.5 DATA CENTER HARDWARE

8.5.1 What Is in a Data Center

"The Cloud" is the full set of all data centers providing one service like a search engine or a video streaming service. A data center is a large facility that contains tens of thousands of servers, thousands of network switches and routers, security appliances, and accelerator appliances. Whenever an Internet service is accessed by a consumer through smartphone, laptop, streaming device, or smart TV the data is located, accessed, and transmitted by the data center equipment to the Internet access point of the data center, then to the user over the Internet. This is shown in Figure 8.10. Edge

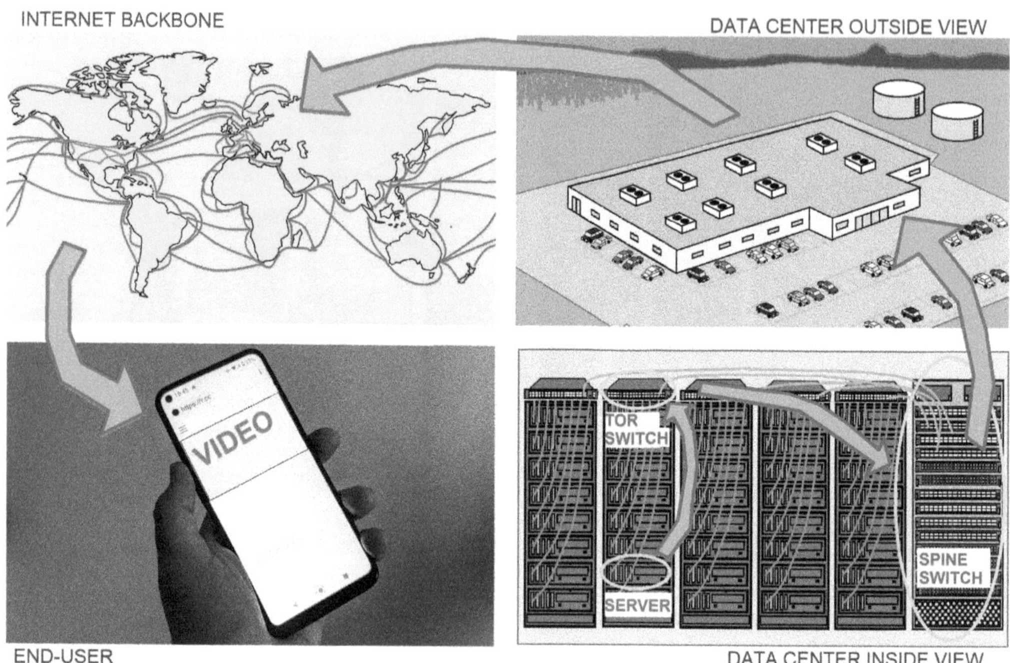

FIGURE 8.10 How data centers fetch data for the users (sketch).

computing is when the big (core) data center is broken down into a larger number of small regional data centers that are geographically closer to the customers. Edge routers are made to handle a lower amount of Ethernet traffic bandwidth than core routers.

The devices used in the data centers, especially the main network switches/routers, have very high bandwidth for data transmission and processing compared to consumer electronics, sometimes thousands of times. They utilize higher level technology than other parts of the wider electronics industry. Data centers utilize 19" wide (or wider) and 6ft tall racks to mount equipment into them. So all data center equipment are made in the form of rack mount style chassis. A data center chassis is a metal box with fixed or removable cards, power conversion (110V or 240V AC or DC, to 12V DC) modules, and chassis fans for cooling. Some chassis are 1 to 4 RU (rack unit, N*1.75") tall and typically 20" to 30" deep. These are typically used for individual servers, top-of-rack switches, and appliances (AI or network security). The other common form factor are the modular chassis with live-removable cards (blade servers, line cards, SSD modules, etc.). These are also 19" wide and 20" to 30" deep, but 1ft to 6ft tall—basically high-end electronics in the size of a family refrigerator. Some of the cards that go into them are industry standard form factors, like ATCA, but most data center chassis vendors develop their own form factors and card sizes. These cards are typically 12" to 20" in their longer dimension, fully packed with multiple large silicon devices, each device consuming hundreds of Watts.

In data centers we have servers, switches, and appliances. The connectivity between servers, and between servers and the outside Internet, is always Ethernet. The connectivity between servers and appliances can be PCIe, CXL, NVLINK and between servers and storage clusters it can be Fiber Channel or FCOE.

The Ethernet network within the data center have a hierarchy and a topology, as we can see in Figure 8.11. On the top of the hierarchy are the highest bandwidth switches and routers (core routers and spine switches), which are implemented as large chassis with removable blades. This will call for a tree or star topology to aggregate the traffic of all the tens of thousands of servers into the few external Internet connections. Modern data centers search and hand off data between servers too,

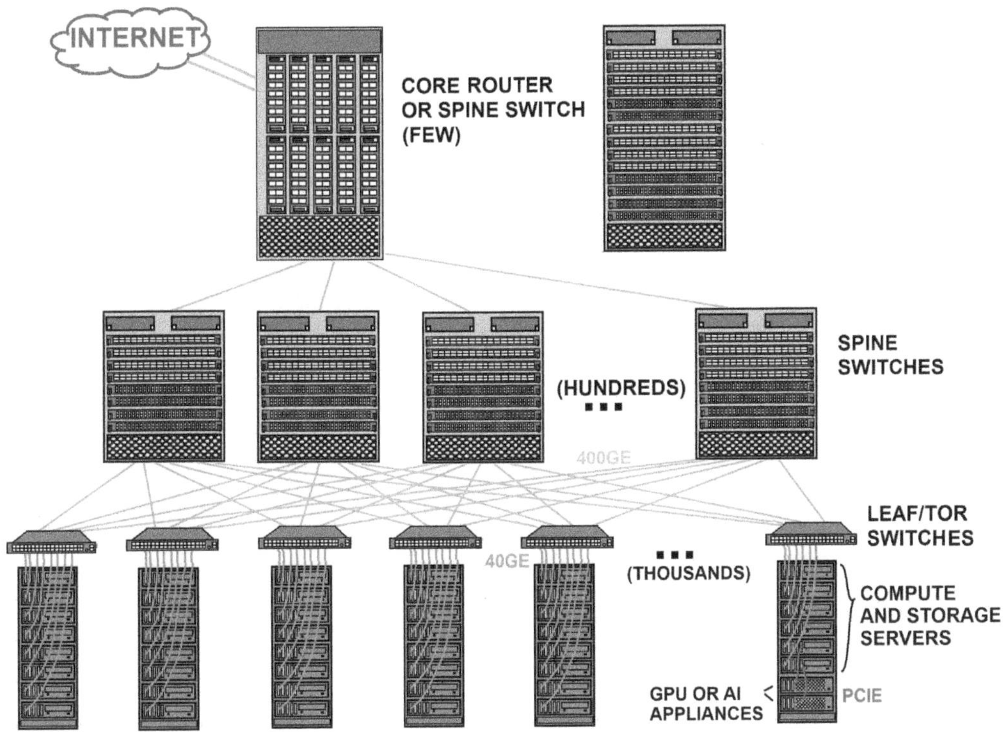

FIGURE 8.11 Data center network hierarchy.

so a large bandwidth connection is also provided horizontally through the spine switches in a mesh configuration through multiple paths. That is the leaf-spine architecture. This creates the need for much higher bandwidth Ethernet switches in the middle and lower parts of the hierarchy.

8.5.2 Servers

The role of serves is to provide data (pictures, movie streaming, bank account access page), to the user as a response to a request coming to the data center from the user's computer across the Internet. Tens of thousands of servers are housed in every data center in tall racks. Servers are implemented as rack servers either with their own single chassis or with multiple blade servers plugged into the same chassis. Chassis are placed into racks. These servers typically contain two or four server processors each on one motherboard and a single port of 10 to 100Gbps network connection to the top-of-rack (TOR) leaf switch over cables. The processors inside the server motherboard are connected together through a mesh of cache coherent SERDES buses like UPI or CCIX. The inter-CPU communication over the backplane inside large chassis blade servers is implemented either as UPI/CCIX (up to a certain number) or as regular communication links like Ethernet or InfiniBand, with or without switching cards. In applications that have to distribute many independent workloads to the many servers, regular Ethernet seems to be the most common, while in applications that require one large workload to be distributed to multiple processors a lower level software-less protocol is more efficient. Storage needs of each server might be provided for as disk drives inside each chassis or motherboard or through bulk SAN storage chassis with Fiber Channel/SAS switching hardware that is shared by multiple servers or motherboards. The server processors are usually in LGA sockets instead of BGA, and a two-socket motherboard design is the most common. On server motherboards the X86 or ARM processors are the data plane and control plane devices, and a board management microcontroller or server management processor (ARM processor with board-level

DRAM memory) is the management plane processor. This is almost always coupled with a small FPGA or CPLD for glue logic. The server boards usually implement ~100 diffpairs of 10-64Gbit signals, and have 50–400 Watt processors, 6–12 separate 3–5Gbps memory interfaces for each processor. Their layer count and board density are much lower than switches, routers, or appliances have, in the range of eight to 12 layers. Since service providers have to purchase tens of thousands of servers every few years, the motherboards and mechanical parts have to be very low cost. Server chassis usually have multiple wired Ethernet ports, optical and RJ45, serial console, USB ports, and sometimes HDMI display outputs too. Sometimes the Ethernet is integrated on the motherboard, other times they use NIC cards in PCIe slots.

Figure 8.12 shows a typical X86 rack server designed for high-density data centers and massive scale-out operations, by Meta and released into the Open Compute Project (OCP). The images are taken from 3D mechanical models and PCB layout files. Three separate node server assemblies are plugged into a subchassis. Multiples of these subchassis are mounted on a regular data center rack tower. The motherboard contains two CPUs, has an elongated shape, has some DIMM memory

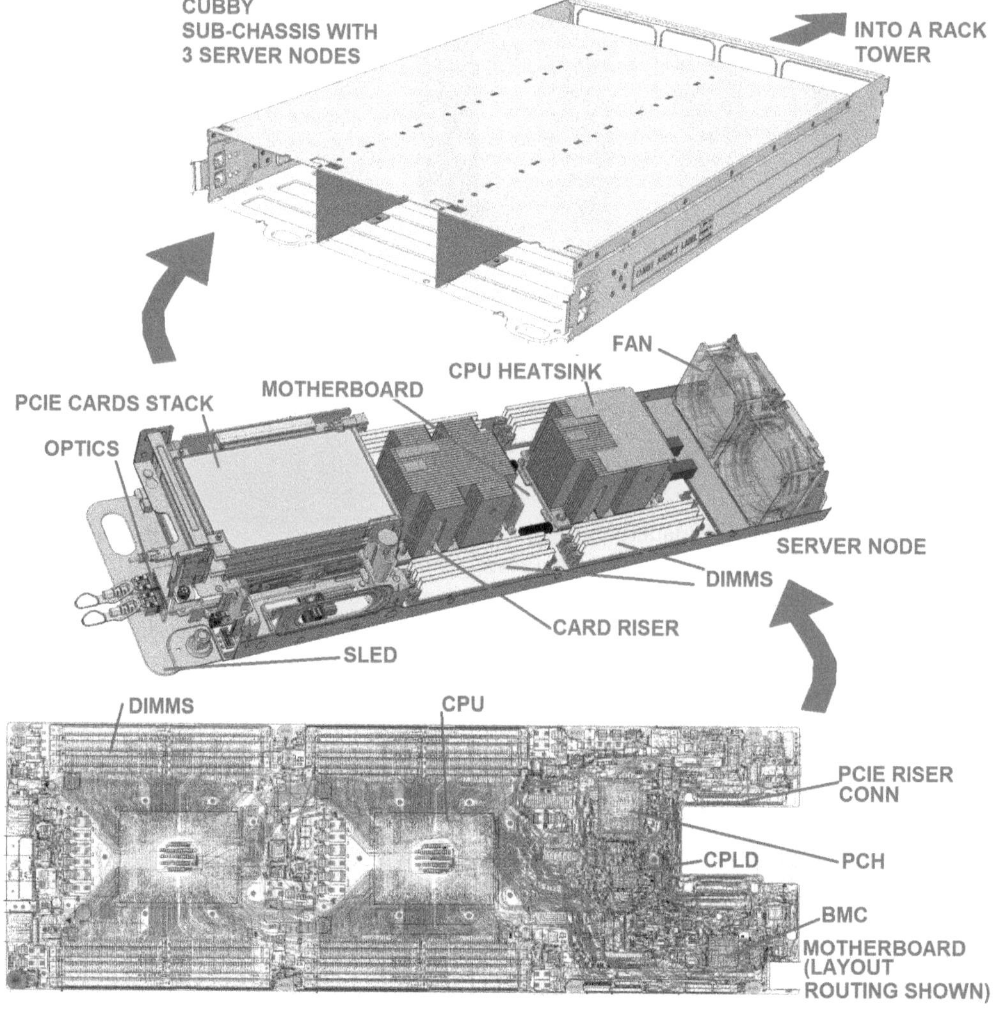

FIGURE 8.12 Tioga Pass node server triple rack and motherboard from the Open Compute Project, the layout and mechanical design images are used for illustration under the Open Web Foundation Final Specification Agreement ("OWFa 1.0") signed by Quanta Computer Inc.

modules, and minimum hardware, including a PCH chipset, server management BMC processor, a CPLD, and a riser subassembly with PCIE cards. The CPUs are connected through UPI links. The several cards can be a mix of external I/O cards with optics, accelerator cards, or storage cards. The external connectivity ports can be used as Ethernet going to a top-of-the-rack (TOR) switch or to an AI appliance. Since there can be at least two ports, both can be connected in the same time. The left side of each CPU is occupied by VRM circuits. The motherboard is compact, it has 14 layers and a 20" x 6.5" board size, while larger rack server motherboards would typically have eight to 12 layers and 17" x 17" size. Servers used for scientific computations require more system memory through a larger number of DIMM slots, making the boards larger and taking up a full rack width.

8.5.3 Accelerators and Appliances

Accelerators can be smaller PCIe cards plugged into a servers or they can be separate appliance chassis connected to the servers over external cables. The cables are many-lane twinax cable bundles, sometimes with QSFP-DD or mini-SAS standard connectors. The electrical interface is SERDES and can be PCIe, NVLINK, or CXL. The accelerator appliances are normally 19" wide, 1-4 RU height and 20" to 30" deep. The acceleration is based on GPU, FPGA, custom ASIC, or AI ASIC devices. Accelerator ASICs simply take data from a processor, process it, and then return the results. Usually switch chips are included in the base boards to distribute the external server processor's data flow. Additionally, direct ASIC-to-ASIC mesh connections are used as well to facilitate peer-to-peer communications within the same chassis through NVLINK or other SERDES interface. These ASICs each dissipate 10 to 400W each, and have x16 SERDES connectivity. A chassis might have four to eight such ASICs. The ASICs are usually not available on the open market, so they are either sold to select few customers or made by the same company that builds the chassis or the whole data center. Figure 8.13 shows an AI accelerator appliance or GPU server, called the Big Basin, designed by the Meta/Facebook hardware team and released into the Open Compute Project (OCP). The image is a snapshot from the 3D mechanical file. The really large base board

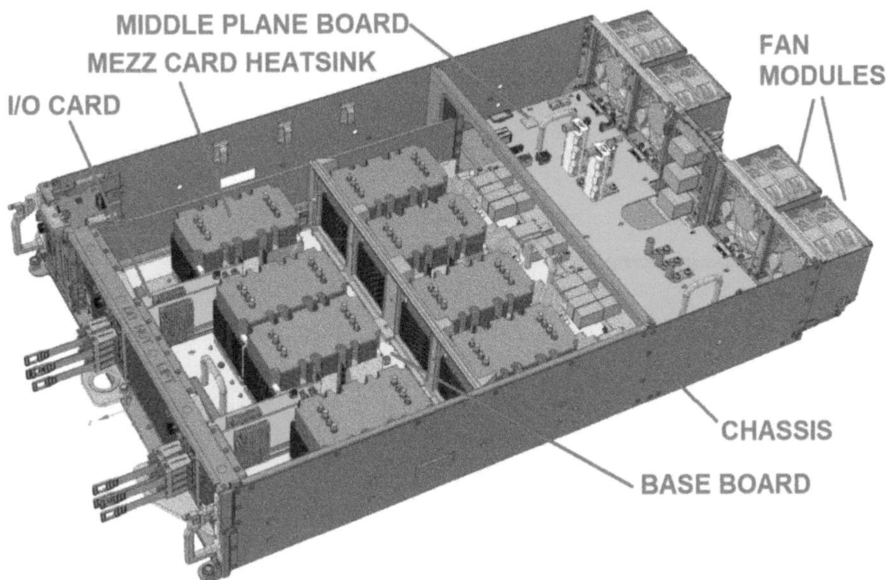

FIGURE 8.13 Meta Big Basin accelerator Appliance chassis from the Open Compute Project, the screenshot image from the mechanical design is used for illustration under the Open Compute Project Hardware License (Permissive) Version 1.0 (Open Compute ProjectHL-P) signed by Facebook, Inc. (Meta Platforms, Inc.)

that hosts eight 6.5" x 4" OCP Accelerator Module (OAM) mezzanine cards is mounted on a sheet metal "sled", which can be pulled out of the main chassis. Each mezzanine card was meant to host one GPU chip with its VRMs and memory or one AI ASIC. We can also see that the large base and mid-plane boards have handles attached to them, which serve the purpose only of system assembly of new units in the factory. The base board has a (dual) star connection from the cable-connected external server(s) through the four large PCIE switch chips to the eight mezzanine card slots and a mesh peer-to-peer connection between each ASIC mezzanine card slot. This distributes the data and control plane traffic to/from every ASIC. The board layout utilizes odd angle routing with loose bundles (appear as thick lines) of SERDES links on 18 layers, as we can see in Figure 8.14.

Network Security appliances are larger 1 to 4 RU Ethernet switches with built-in accelerator ASICs. These security appliances or firewalls guard and isolate traffic going through a corporation's external Internet connection. They are connected through Ethernet optical links rather than CXL/PCIe cables.

8.5.4 Network Switches

The top of the rack (TOR), or "leaf", switches allow all the servers in one rack to communicate with the aggregation larger (spine) switches, which allow connecting all racks to the Internet. A layer-2 switch works with MAC addresses only (within the same data center). A layer-3 switch or router can do all the work of a layer-2 switch and additional routing as well with IP addresses. A layer-3 switch is both a switch and a router or a router with lots of local Ethernet ports. Modern data center switches with large ASICs can handle layer-3 IP-address-based switching and routing. Many years ago, the most high-end systems were the router chassis, with multiple custom ASICs and CPUs computing traffic routing paths. Nowadays these functions are integrated on modern switch ASICs.

The Ethernet protocol was developed decades ago with a seven-layer model, called the OSI-Model. The physical layer SERDES and cabling are at layer-1. Ethernet packets, MAC, and IP

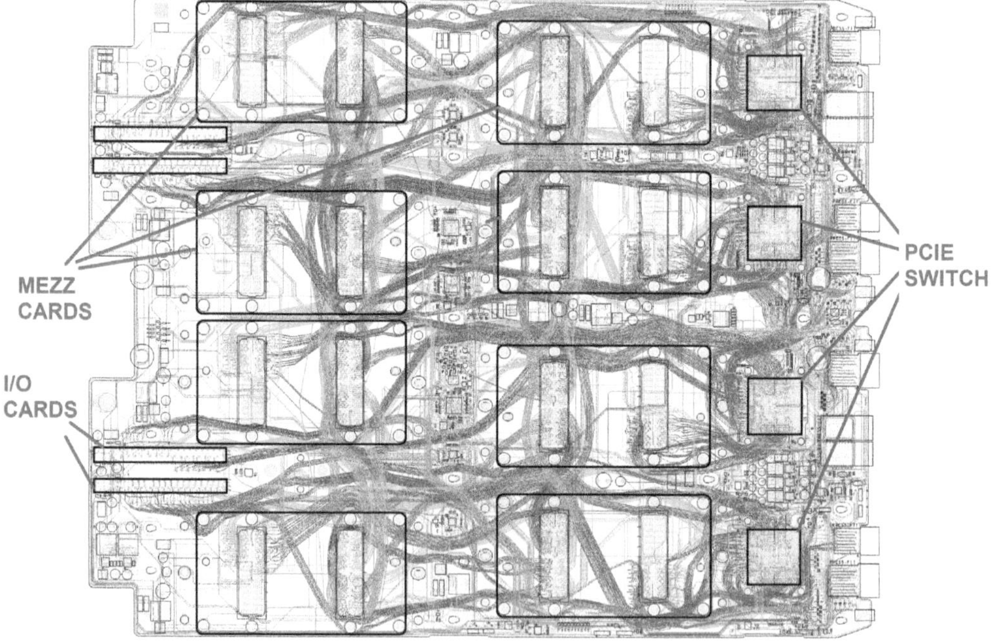

FIGURE 8.14 Meta Big Basin base board routing in the PCB layout from the Open Compute Project, the screenshot from the layout design is used for illustration under the Open Compute Project Hardware License (Permissive) Version 1.0 (Open Compute ProjectHL-P) signed by Facebook, Inc. (Meta Platforms, Inc.)

addresses are handled by the middle layers of the standards. IEEE standardized the lower/mid-layer implementations in various speed/type Ethernet standards, while silicon manufacturers produce ASIC chips that comply with them.

The ASICs used in the switches depend on the user's (system administrator's) needs, namely, about what type of network and security protocols to be supported. There are different TOR and spine switch devices available for different needs, equipped with different selection of ASICs inside. A large amount of software engineering goes into setting up the ASICs to the desired mode of operation. The software teams working on these products can have 10 to 100 times as many engineers as the hardware team has. These switches also contain a processor for initializing and managing the switching ASICs. Small consumer switches use an integrated ARM process inside the switch ASIC, while larger switches use a separate processor chip on board or a separate processor card in the chassis. Some of the traffic control and monitoring functions are integrated onto the main switch ASIC chips, others require separate ASICs or FPGAs. The largest switches have the switching function break out of using one switch ASIC into using multiple ASICs, and they split into a large chassis with multiple boards. Still each board is more complex than any board design in other industries. The front boards are called the line lards, the back-end boards are the fabric or switch cards. One card can have several of the largest ASICs and FPGAs on the market.

Very small consumer switch units are based on a single low-power switch ASIC and its on-die ARM processor. The same chips that are used in consumer switch boxes might be used on complex

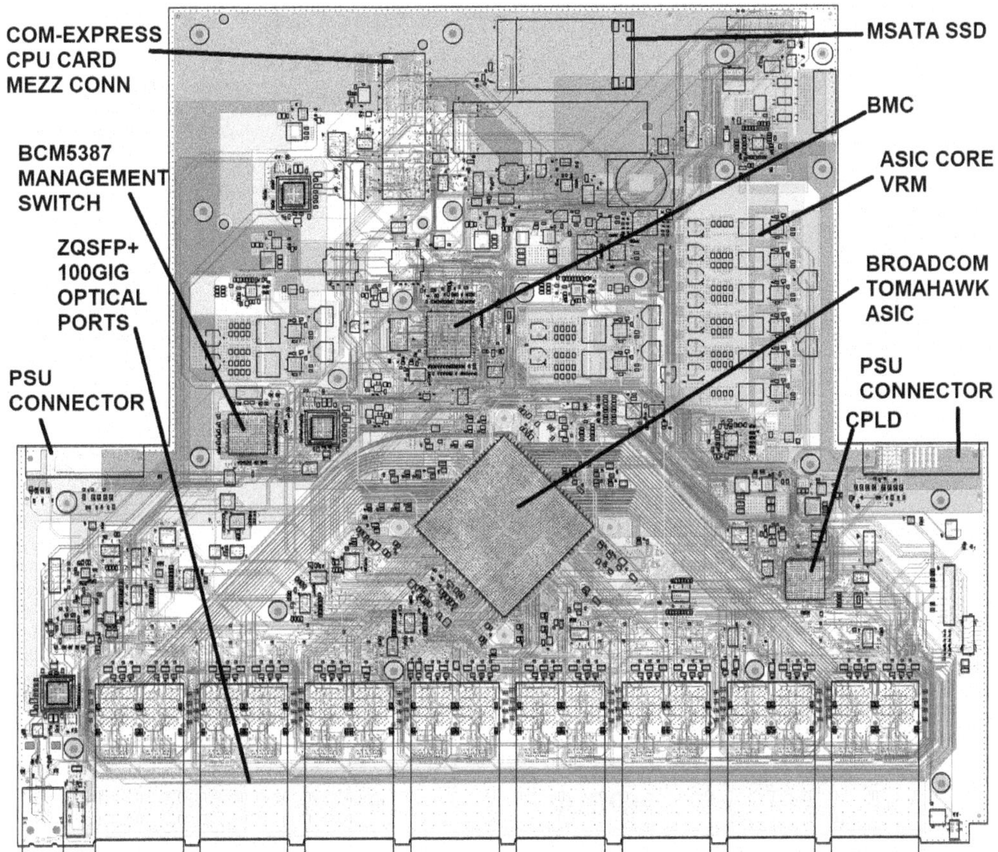

FIGURE 8.15 Wedge 100S single-ASIC leaf/TOR switch main board from the Open Compute Project, the screenshot from the layout design is used for illustration under the Open Compute Project Hardware License (Permissive) Version 1.0 (Open Compute ProjectHL-P) signed by Facebook, Inc. (Meta Platforms, Inc.)

boards as an additional minor feature, for example, in the management plane of large complex boards. The smallest switches in data centers are the top-of-the-rack (TOR), or "leaf", switches, each rack has one. A modern TOR switch has many 40Gig or 100Gig optical downstream ports to connect to the servers in the rack and a few 100Gig or 400Gig upstream ports to connect to the farther-located spine switches. They might also have several RJ45 1Gig downstream ports for the BMC management connectivity. Previous generations had lower speed ports, with 10Gig SFP+, and before that 1Gig RJ45 ports. These are still used by corporate data centers or single racks supporting an office or a lab. A typical TOR switch contains a main board with one or two main switching ASICs and a few PHY chips. Usually, a low-power X86 processor is also included in the box, either integrated on the switch board or on a separate card. The cheaper versions might rely on an on-chip ARM processor that most switching ASICs have. If the ARM processor is not used, it can be disabled and our X86 card attached instead.

Figure 8.15 shows the layout of a medium complexity networking board with a single Tomahawk ASIC used in a 1RU TOR switch called the Wedge 100S, released by Meta to the Open Compute

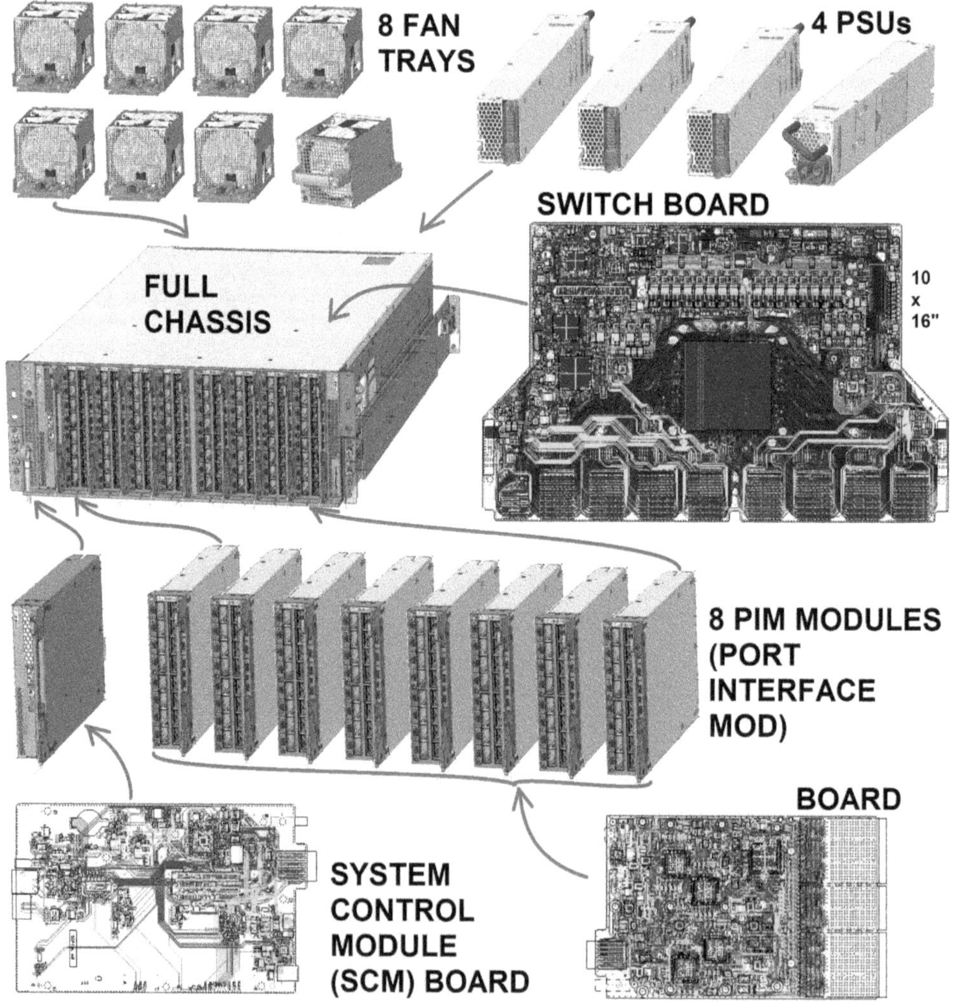

FIGURE 8.16 The Minipack2 spine switch system from the Open Compute Project, the images from the layout and mechanical design files are used for illustration under the Open Compute Project Hardware License (Permissive) Version 1.0 (Open Compute ProjectHL-P) signed by Meta Platforms, Inc.

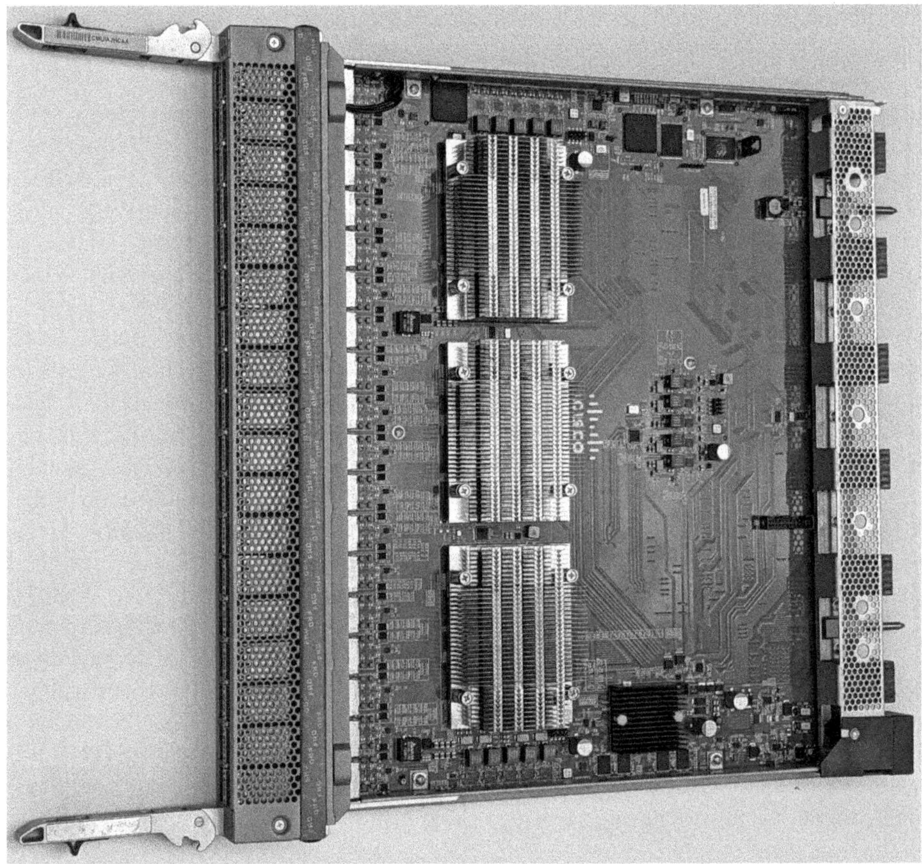

FIGURE 8.17 Cisco Systems N9K-X9636PQ line card.

Project (OCP). It has a few supporting devices, besides the main switch ASIC: a CPLD, a server BMC controller, a small 1Gig switch ASIC for the management subsystem, some PHY chips, and an SSD card slot for booting the operating system on the Com-Express CPU card. It allows two chassis PSU modules to be plugged in directly into the switch board. It has 3700 components and 22 layers on a 118mil thick stackup, at 16" x 12" board size.

TOR switches connect to spine switches in the data center, which are higher performance and only have high-bandwidth ports (400G/port in 2023). Spine switches provide data traffic up to the external Internet, as well as to other servers within the same data center. This is the mentioned leaf-spine architecture. Some spine switches are a 2 to 4RU height 19" wide and 20" to 30" deep fixed chassis, others are a few feet tall modular systems with four to 16 removable blades. They also have removable X86 processor or management cards, usually two for redundancy and system reliability. Smaller fixed spine-switch chassis (with non-removable cards) and the TOR switches just have one built-in processor card. Their front panels are fully stuffed with the highest speed optical Ethernet ports. Fixed chassis might have 24 to 72 such ports, modular systems might have hundreds. Different blades or line cards are available with different port type configurations (10 to 400GE, etc.). The modern routers have fewer but higher bandwidth ports to aggregate the internal Ethernet traffic to the external Internet traffic. The spine switches and routers utilize the highest bandwidth ASIC chips—5 to 50Tbps/chip as available in 2023. These switches also utilize high-end PCB manufacturing technologies and tight constraints, the latest SI analysis techniques and materials. The boards are large 16" to 20" in size, contain over a thousand 56Gig signals, with many thousands of components per board (sometimes over ten thousand). Data center switches and accelerator/security appliances are the leading edge of electronics, ~5 years ahead of the computer industry, that is another ~5 years ahead of the industrial, aerospace, and consumer electronics.

Figure 8.16 shows a smaller spine switch modular chassis, also from the Open Compute Project (OCP), called the Minipack 2. The images are from 3D mechanical models and PCB layout files. We can see the main parts being a main switch card built around a Tomahawk type ASIC, eight removable port interface modules with optical transceiver cage connectors and PHY chips, one management board in the form of a COM-Express processor card carrier, several fan and power supply modules. This spine switch has 128 ports of 100Gbps Ethernet, which puts it into a medium size.

Larger spine switch chassis have four to 16 replaceable line-cards with each providing 24 to 36 ports of 40 to 800 Gbps/port Ethernet, to a total of 192 to 576 ports. The back of the chassis can contain several removable fabric cards that provide packet switching and connectivity between the line cards. This allows the chassis to act as one big switch that can forward Ethernet packets from any port to any other port in a non-blocking fashion. Modern spine switches are equipped with ASICs that have layer-3 routing capabilities, so they may replace routers in the top of the data centers. One line card might host several such ASICs and FPGAs. Figure 8.17 shows a photograph of a N9K-X9636PQ line card that was made by Cisco Systems, with 36 QSFP+ ports on the front panel. It can be plugged into a Cisco Nexus 9500 modular switch chassis. An 8-slot version of the chassis when fully populated by this line card type acts as a single switch device that provides 288 ports, each running at 40Gbps bandwidth. The card hosts three switch ASICs for the data plane and other devices. Each ASIC handles 12 40Gig QSFP+ ports, a third of the total 36 front panel ports of the card, from which the Ethernet traffic is routed to the fabric card connectors. The card is about 15" x 16" in size. It was released around 2013. Newer line cards have higher speed SERDES links, larger total bandwidth, higher power ASICs, and more advanced technologies, although the design structure is similar, in terms of having a few data plane ASICs and a few FPGAs, with many optical ports on the front panel.

9 Hardware-Firmware Integration

Any CPUs we have in the system or on our board design will run software. We, the hardware engineers, must have a basic understanding of the parts of the software that directly exercises our hardware through registers, the parts that are involved in initializing our devices, and any test software specifically written for testing our hardware—mainly what these pieces do, where they are stored on the board, which one is which, when their development is completed, and what features they have or should have, not their source code itself. It is written by the software engineers, and most often they are run through the console by the software or test engineers for us in the lab. Compiled software code has a layered structure. Firmware is the type of low-level software that interacts with hardware chip registers and bus addresses, as opposed to regular user software that is at the higher application level only and is hardware independent. Regular software still relies of the existence of the main chips but treats them as simplified objects to extract the actual functionality of the system. User software often relies on the firmware downstream to it to complete a hardware access task, but that is not very interesting to us.

Most of the times we have to design our prototype board and system to work with existing or customized software. Completely new BIOS, device drivers, or operating systems will usually not be written for it, but some customization will take place to match the new hardware. The on-board devices and buses, their addresses, and their required initialization and operational sequences have to be explained to (and negotiated with) the firmware/software teams. This is finalized in documents that are reviewed by them, like the hardware specs or hardware-software ICDs (interface control documents). They contain explanations, subsystem block diagrams, and data tables. Tables are for bus/device numbers and addresses, I/O port parameters, pinouts, dependencies, and device programming information.

What "firmware" goes into a complex hardware project:

- BIOS for X86 processors, bootloader for ARM and DSPs. They need to be customized to work on new hardware. Especially the memory configuration and the display or console ports.
- Operating system, a customized console-Linux image, containing custom device drivers.
- Micro controller firmware image, for a management processor.
- Linux drivers for devices and custom circuits, sometimes customized standard drivers.
- Test (diagnostic) software for prototyping, some chip vendor provided, some open-source Linux, some custom written or customized, some purchased. Its purpose is to detect and exercise individual devices and ports and report back to the user as well as run full imitated functionality.
- Test software for manufacturing test, custom developed or customized for each design, runs on Linux usually. It is to find any PCB connectivity issues or dead devices.
- Device configuration images for USB bridges, PCIe switches, clock chips, and other supporting chips, sometimes stored in EEPROMs attached to the devices, other times stored in an internal flash or ROM memory.

9.1 BIOS

The BIOS is the firmware (software) that initializes the X86 chipset, initializes and calibrates the memory interfaces, checks for bootable drives, enumerates (bus by bus, port by port, device by

DOI: 10.1201/9781032702094-9

device, the discovery of) all PCI/PCIe devices and assigning memory-mapped address ranges to them. After the chipset reset de-assertion, the X86 processor starts executing at address FFFFF0h, which is where the SPI flash memory chip is mapped by the chipset silicon logic. The BIOS image is programmed into the SPI flash using a dongle by the engineers for prototyping or by technicians in production. After reset the BIOS code copies itself into the CPU-die cache memory and continues to run from there, then initializes all devices and the system memory, then copies itself into the system memory and continues to run from there, then it starts loading the operating system executable code from the larger SSD storage drive and copies that into the main system memory, and finally it executes a jump instruction to let the OS take control. Then the OS will perform additional boot tasks, like loading device drivers, and setting up a complex memory map of devices until it arrives into its final idle state or runs automated scripts endlessly.

The BIOS firmware has three main components:

- The legacy BIOS code used on earlier chipsets. This can be obtained from:
    - Purchased or licensed as source code from commercial vendors like Insyde or AMI (American Megatrends).
    - Open source, called CoreBoot. This one is usually lagging one to two years behind the commercial versions for each new chipset, so while working on freshly released silicon chips it is risky to rely on it (project delays and bugs).
- The new X86 chipset driver code released by the X86 chipset/CPU vendor.
- Customization, specific to the new prototype board. Port usage, memory configuration, GPIO connections.

The company that makes the motherboard (any complex board design with integrated X86 CPU) must have a BIOS engineer that can merge the three parts together, then edit and debug the third part. In some cases, a universal firmware engineer is employed who is somewhat experienced with BIOS too.

9.1.1 BIOS Customization

First, the hardware engineer generates a spreadsheet with differences between the reference board schematic and our new design schematic, focusing on the chipset and CPU pin connections. Then the BIOS firmware team will obtain any BIOS source code they need to re-use. It comes from our older projects, from the chipset vendor, and from commercial BIOS code vendors. Instead of purchasing a new vendor BIOS, we might re-use a BIOS code from our company's earlier projects, if we have a suitable one. The benefit of that is we can re-use any code already made and tested for custom logo display, security, or any re-used circuit modules. Then they will modify the BIOS source code based on board differences spreadsheet and then compile it into a binary. The spreadsheet may contain data about disabled or unused interfaces, port speed forcing or downgrading requirements, implement memory-down SPD (DIMM serial presence detect) data hard-coding, disable DIMM detection, enable/disable interrupt sources, implement board status register access, and hard code addresses to any LPC-bus FPGA registers. Then they also need to obtain any firmware image binary used for in-chipset management processors from the chipset vendor. This must match the chipset variant and part number. With a CPU vendor provided flash image tool they build a flash image. During this setup they have to set the soft strapping parameters, which have to match our schematic and/or the schematics differences spreadsheet. Soft strapping is simply dozens or hundreds of settings for the chipset, one bit per setting. For example, SPI bus selection, memory interface selection, etc. Sometimes some bits are not set by the tool, so we need to set them in a hex editor manually accordingly to the programming guide. Once the flash image is generated, then we program it into the SPI-flash memory on the prototype board, for example, with a DediProg100 SPI programmer. The code merging and building process is illustrated in Figure 9.1. Every time a new

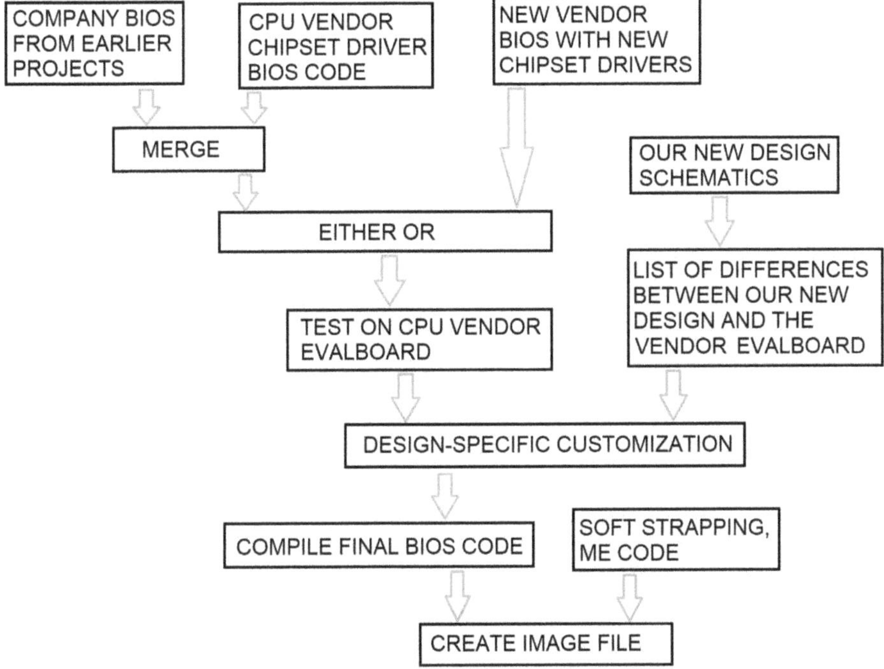

FIGURE 9.1 BIOS customization process.

X86 board is designed, a new BIOS image has to be created. The default or evaluation board image will not run on it, it will hang.

There are several silicon/software debugging options available on X86 chipsets. The BIOS source code can be enabled to produce a verbose serial console message log. This will list every phase of every step in the boot process, including any errors the BIOS encounters. It should also show the memory read leveling tuning results. Note that it will lengthen the BIOS boot time significantly, so we remove them for the production version. We can attach (a dongle) or design-in an (FPGA-based) LPC-bus "Port80" POST code decoder. This will display the two-digit hexadecimal POST (power on self-test) code on two digits of seven-segment LED displays or in a register that we can read out of our FPGA. The BIOS keeps writing to I/O address 80h and 81h a code at every step of the BIOS boot process. These codes should be provided by the BIOS vendor. BIOS engineers sometimes use a JTAG debugger (for example the American Arium JTAG tool) to access internal register content (to compare with the reference board's register content), set up break points or single step instructions. This is expensive and not used in every project. A debug mode can be enabled in the firmware to broadcast POST-codes over an I2C port. These are not BIOS POST codes. If the chipset will not boot, it might be because the internal management controller is preventing it. By connecting an I2C sniffer dongle to the I2C port and capturing its log file, then sending it to the chipset vendor we can determine what is causing the holdup.

9.1.2 ARM Bootloaders

ARM processors use a boot loader software or pre-boot firmware, which is similar to a BIOS but not based on the PCI(e) architecture. Sometimes there are two stages of bootloaders, each with a separate set of tasks. The most common ARM bootloader is the U-Boot open-source code, but it needs to be customized to match the hardware design. Especially the memory configuration has to be hard coded into it—DIMM versus memory-down, memory chip parameters, and number and types of chips. It works the same way as the X86 BIOS development. There is usually a bootloader and a Linux source code package from the chip vendor or from third parties. This package was likely optimized to work with the processor's memory and I/O connections designed on the evaluation board. So we document the new design schematic's deviations relative to the eval board schematic, then the same changes have to be made to the software source code to make it work on the new prototype. The software package has to be ready before prototype arrival. During the board hardware bring-up, after the VRM and power sequence debugging, we work full time on debugging the software boot process. First debugging the bootloader with the memory and I/O devices, then the OS and the drivers with the more complex hardware interfaces. This requires both the hardware and the software engineer in the lab. The same vendors who produced X86 BIOS codes for decades now also offer ARM bootloader firmware, mainly for the larger ARM-server and network processors.

9.2 CUSTOM OS IMAGE

Every embedded system, servers, data center switches and routers, automated systems, and aerospace mission computers run a customized Operating System (OS) with drivers and scripts initializing and operating the custom hardware in them. A script is a text file that contains Linux commands. This is typically your company's own Linux distribution, compiled from the open-source code of a common distribution like Debian and modified by the software engineering department, probably years ago. Almost always it is a text-only console-based variant without graphics drivers, and the console is accessed through an RS232 serial port (RJ45 Rollover cable) or Ethernet management port (Telnet). The software engineer will install this on the proto hardware from a USB flash drive or a micro-SD card, so we need a USB or micro-SD connector on the hardware design. These interfaces will likely be used only in development and manufacturing, but not by the end users. Usually ASIC vendors provide SDK's (software development kits) that need to be modified, compiled, and included in our OS image. In the case of an FPGA-based board design, it is fully written by your company's software team.

On complex hardware systems the OS usually runs scrips or user programs, while on consumer computers the OS waits for the user to decide what applications to start. The shipped complex product OS image version runs scripts and programs automatically after power on and infinitely, while the development lab version waits for the engineers to decide which scripts to run and when.

9.2.1 Device Drivers

Device drivers will be re-used, modified, or written from scratch. Re-used drivers made by chip companies might be available as source code or as executable binary files. In any case, the software team needs to know what drivers will be needed, with exact parameters. This is why the hardware designer needs to write a document that explains:

- All the devices that need any driver.
- Any device modes (list, tables) that need to be configured from software.
- PCIe bridge/switch devices that have burst/packet size restrictions.
- Data plane and control plane block diagrams, with device port numbers and / or pin numbers, speeds.
- Slow I2C, PMBUS, SPI, MDIO, UART buses, their tree or block diagrams, with device addresses and port numbers, any multiplexer port selection, any GPIOs needed for controlling the port selection.
- All the device ports that need a specific configuration or settings.
- All devices that need to be programmed by software running on embedded CPUs, instead of using dongle cables.

- The data that are supposed to go into a programming image to be created by software team.
- List of image files created in chip vendor GUI (sequencers, clock chips, CPLD) that will be prepared by the hardware team and where they go (bus, device address)
- Any FPGAs, DSPs, or accelerator ASICs that need to be loaded with a code image and re-loaded during regular OS operation.
- Any SERDES transceivers that will need to be tuned and tuning data.
- Any SERDES transceivers that will need to support console-based on-die eye capture from Linux, or JTAG eye capture.
- Interrupt routing and mapping, for both OS and BIOS engineering.
- GPIO routing and mapping, and what sequence they need to be controlled at, with flow charts if needed.
- DDR memory configuration for the BIOS team (or bootloader team) to support memory-down with hard-coded SPD data, and disable SPD scanning over SMBUS. Memory device part numbers, address bus width, number of ranks, latency parameters.
- Any LPC devices, and their intended uses and addresses, for BIOS engineering.
- Any settings that go into soft strapping in X86 BIOS or in ARM bootloader.

The OS-level software drivers initialize devices and manage their operation. For PCI(e) devices the base address register (BAR) is already initialized by the BIOS during the PCIe system enumeration, unless the device like an FPGA is loaded in run-time, which requires the OS and driver to enumerate it after that. Run-time enumeration is not in the standard Linux, but many embedded systems need it, so it needs to be developed in-house. A "rescan" is usually not sufficient. One possibility is to have memory-space and bus number resources pre-allocated to all root complex and switch downstream ports, so when the FPGA finally loads it will not shuffle the bus numbers and address spaces of the rest of the system. PCI(e) devices do have the standard PCI configuration header registers as well as the application or device specific configuration registers. The first type is written by the BIOS, while the second type is always initialized by the driver. Sometimes the device driver has to be customized to initialize other devices too that are being used to access the main device. For example, a VRM chip needs to be initialized over the I2C bus, and the I2C host (for example an USB/I2C bridge chip) has to be initialized (loading a third-party chip driver) before the VRM can be initialized, and maybe even an I2C multiplexer also has to be set to a correct port number before accessing our main device becomes possible. There might be a chain of devices leading to our main device, then the whole chain has to be initialized with different drivers combined to run together. All these drivers will have to auto load after startup in the correct sequence and included in our OS image.

Sometimes a device like an AI ASIC has to be fed data regularly, which is done through the driver layer in the software stack. So the application running on a processor talks to a driver, not to the ASIC device directly.

9.3 WORKING WITH A DATA PLANE FPGA TEAM

Data plane FPGA code is developed by teams of people, sometimes by a few individuals, other times by a large department. If it is a department, then there will be one contact person or an FPGA-lead for the hardware engineer to work with on a regular basis. The board hardware designer has to work out the board needs of the FPGA, such as I/O connections, memory devices, and clocking as well as the feasibility of their requirements. Data plane functionality is developed and decided by management, systems, software, and FPGA/ASIC engineering. The board designer has to provide the platform for that vision on a solid ground of hardware and SI excellence as well as point out and negotiate the limits of feasibility. We can be pro-active and do a floorplan and pinout analysis to determine how many lanes of what speed, how many channels of memory controllers we can fit into a new FPGA device and board form factor, and then propose that to the mentioned disciplines.

Different levels of speed is achievable on external memory interfaces, depending on pinout and channel width. For example, two channels of 64bit will likely have a lower top speed than four channels of 32bit. The FPGA engineering has to analyze how many processing pipelines they have and the bandwidth need of each. In some cases, the wider DDR4 channel will have combined two pipelines with no bandwidth benefit to each, in other cases a single pipeline needs a very high bandwidth that a 32bit channel could not produce. The top speed is also affected by the pinout design viewed on the die view, as explained in Chapter 6, "Main Chips".

The number of reference clocks that need to be provided to an FPGA depends on the FPGA's internal regional clock routing resources and the FPGA engineer's approach about utilizing them. Usually we provide an LVDS reference clock to each memory controller IP, a CML or LVPECL clock to each SERDES-based multi-lane interface, a clock to an embedded CPU, and one LVDS core clock. The frequency of the clocks depends on the FPGA logic design and silicon PLL limitations.

Which interface to be assigned to which transceiver tile is constrained by both board design (to avoid bus crossings and crowding some hard to reach areas) and FPGA logic design (packing different interfaces next to each other might prevent us from utilizing regional clock resources on chip that we need). The general I/O pin assignment is also constrained by both the board design (routing crossings drive the layer count up) and the FPGA design (maximizing I/O data rate, all signals of a matched group needs to be assigned to neighboring silicon die bumps and within a single clock region).

The amount of logic resources needed by the project has to be closely estimated at the beginning, for FPGA selection and for and power/clock supporting device selection and PCB floor planning. The preliminary code must be compiled without timing and placement violations before the layout design finishes for purposes of resource-fit and pin-out validation. This does not necessarily have to be a debugged and functional version, but with all the re-uses IPs in it and wired up. At that point the FPGA engineer might be able to generate a power (and load current) estimate from the FPGA tool, which is to validate the already created power tree with all the VRM current capabilities. Some FPGA vendors provide an Excel sheet for power estimation. If there is an issue, we might have to upgrade to bigger VRMs and adjust the board floorplan also. So we need to know as early as possible. If we use any parallel buses (other than DDR memory), then the FPGA team needs to generate timing parameters for a board level timing analysis too, to be performed by the board hardware engineer. These would be input and output setup and hold times, or in the constraints and timing report they might call it input delay and output delay. They can set a constraint, see if it passes, and then tell us that constraint as a guaranteed timing parameter.

Some features can be implemented with soft IP cores on an FPGA or as a hard chip connected to the FPGA. For example, an Ethernet PHY or a TCAM ASIC for looking up data at the line rate. Adding a chip costs money in terms of BOM cost and board space, but adding it to FPGA logic also costs money in terms of FPGA device size selection. The decision has to be based on FPGA chip and team resources. Then the implementation (interfaces, handshaking, clocking, initialization) has to be developed together between the FPGA and the hardware team.

9.4 TEST SOFTWARE

Test software is made to check if devices and connections on the board are functional or not. Some are used during prototyping with great manual control, others are used in production with great automation and scripting. We cannot test out a prototype hardware with only end-user software. We also need software specifically written for exercising and debugging hardware features. We also need the software team to add more debug software capabilities on demand as we go along with a prototype board bring-up. The custom drivers, high-level applications, and test software all have to be ready before the prototype arrives, and code alterations have to be made promptly to be able to test out and debug the hardware, otherwise the bring-up will take several months longer than planned. Hardware is not delivered by the hardware engineer like ordering online, it is delivered by the whole team. Usually, the software also has bugs in it, so we have to debug the new hardware with the new software together in the lab. Fully automated test software cannot be expected to run on new proto-1 boards, as they are debugged and developed on the prototypes. After the proto-1 board and the test software bring-up is complete, we can run automated test software on subsequent proto-1 units and later on proto-2 units and on production units. Even the manual test software (command bit bang, manual read/write) will need to be debugged on proto-1 units.

Since prototypes likely have design bugs and manufacturing defects. Some devices and interfaces will not work on them initially and so the hardware engineer has to find out which ones work and which do not to be able to focus the debugging effort on making circuit alterations on the non-working ones. Test software can help with identifying which programmable device works by trying to access them through the I/O interfaces and buses, trying to read and write registers inside them and show on the screen of the test computer or console log the result of the access attempt. If we get an error or a bus timeout, or we read back 0xFFFF from all registers, then it is likely the device or the bus is bad. The hardware engineer has to look up which register address is worth checking, and what the expected data pattern should be. This kind of test should be done without high-level drivers or end-user applications, rather using an address-space read/write access driver. This has to be made available or written from scratch by the software team. A few ready-made test commands exist, like the LSPCI and the LSUSB that works on PCIe and USB devices, but for other buses, like I2C or Ethernet, we need custom test scripts or software made by the software or diagnostics firmware team. At a later stage of the board bring-up we can use higher level device drivers and application software to test out whether the devices are set up correctly in the hardware to perform their main function. So first we check if the device is accessible or alive, then later we check if it fully functions. We cannot start by checking if it fully functions, we have to progress step by step, and we have to start at the beginning.

A weaker test software will only tell if the whole system is working, such as it runs traffic or executes the payload app or not. In an even worse case, if the whole board is powered down, and therefore none of the ports can work and the software reports that port-1 failed because port-1 is the first to report, that can mislead the debug effort and waste engineering resources. In both prototype bring-up and in manufacturing test we need to know more. If the board fails the test, we need to know which part of it failed so we can repair it or debug that part. Even if we can reduce the fault location to 1/4th of the board, it helps a lot with debugging, but the smaller proportion the better.

A good test software will initialize and run the different parts of the system one step at a time, and at each step report back if that step was successful or not. It will "walk" the device hierarchy based on the scientific process of "graph discovery" from "graph theory" in mathematics. Each step is related to one device or one port on a device. Instead of reporting "device 3 all 16 ports are up", the test software should report "device-3 port-0 up, device-3 port-1 up, device-3 port-2 up". It would be even better if it did not stop at the first failure because we need to know if it is just the first port that is bad or the whole thing, because the root cause would be very different. In simple test software all devices are loaded with the driver, then the test scrip checks for the status of external ports, which will not tell us much in case of a failure. It should report internal devices also. The addition needed is to check each chip in the chain and check them using a graph discovery algorithm. It would start at the host processor, then in each step downstream detect all devices at that branch and level. The control plane topology has to be scanned with device register access, then the data plane topology with interface links and ports.

Checking devices means after loading drivers we also do a configuration space read, ideally without a thick driver stack, rather using a simple memory-mapped read/write driver, and compare the results with expected values, for example, if we read FFFFh then it failed. We can read a device ID or any register with a known value. When a device is not accessible, then the low-level Linux driver usually returns FFFFh read data value or an error code.

Once we have a bad device identified, we can measure a few basic things with multimeter and oscilloscope, including VRM voltages and clocks that feed the device, any glue logic signals that show any boot or initialization process (like EEPROM signals), glue logic signals going to/from it with JTAG logic analyzer, and the main I/O interface in both RX/TX directions with a high-speed scope and a solder-on active probe for signal/no-signal check (dead chips do not talk).

External ports can be tested only by attaching an external active device over cabling or attaching test fixtures or loopbacks to them. Some interface types like Ethernet allow loopback testing, while others like USB require an active device. With loopback testing of an external port, we send let's say 1000 bytes of data, and we count the number of bytes received with a loopback test software. If it is zero, then the port is bad, if it is between 1 and 998 it is still bad with quality issue. For ports that require an active device, we test them the same way as on-board devices through a read/write access or packet transfer.

A device or port or interface is bad if it is not soldered correctly (one instance would be bad) or its circuits are not designed properly (all instances would be bad) and have design bugs. So we need the test program to tell if all are bad or just one. A particular device failure might be reported if the device itself is soldered badly, its support circuits are bad, its upstream interface is bad, or the one port on the upstream device is bad.

If some ports are partially working, then we need to detect that too through bit error count or an eye margining test. Partial failure can still be caused by individual pin manufacturing error or design mistakes. For each port we can check if the RX packet count matches the TX count, assuming loopback plugs are inserted by the test technician. A typical production issue is when one BGA pin is cold soldered, or one connector pin has a contact issue due to residue, airborne debris, or mechanical damage. This would disconnect one leg of a differential pair, which will cause the SERDES link to likely receive data but with an almost closed eye diagram and high bit error rate. If a large decoupling capacitor is tombstoned in soldering, it can also degrade signals seen by a receiver.

In summary, the test software needs to:

- Check each device as whether it is "dead or alive" by reading a register and compare with expected value.
- Check each interface if it is linked up or not, link status bit or send data.
- Check each SERDES interface quality with eye margin or BER test by running PRBS or traffic.
- Have a good quality graph walk through algorithm.
- The software has to continue on failure and report everything that works and everything that fails, a complete list of all devices and ports.

The block diagram topology affects how the test should run. If the design is so complex that it splits into separate data plane and control plane, then the topology of both needs to be scanned. Devices in parallel can be tested in any order, like FPGA1 and FPGA2 in Figure 9.2. But any devices in a series in a chain, or in a hierarchy, should be tested starting with the device that is most upstream, then the ones below, then the ones below that level. For example, FPGA1 first, then PHY1 after that. Both the control plane and the data plane have to be scanned to verify full functionality. For example, on the diagram PHY1 should not be tested before fully testing FPGA1. The diagram shows two FPGAs on one board, with each FPGA having four PHY chips connected to them (PHY1 to 8), and each PHY chip having one external port (P1 to 8). If we report only the port number test pass/fail status but not the FPGA and PHY test status first, then we have to be guessing about whether we cannot see Port1 because Port1 is bad, PHY1 is bad, or because FPGA1 is bad. But if we test FPGA1 to 2 first, then PHY1 to PHY8 then Port1 to 8, then we can tell which exact device failed in case of a board failure. There can be several valid paths for the graph walk through, as long as we follow the basic rule to only check device-N if we have already checked its upstream device. We have to display in

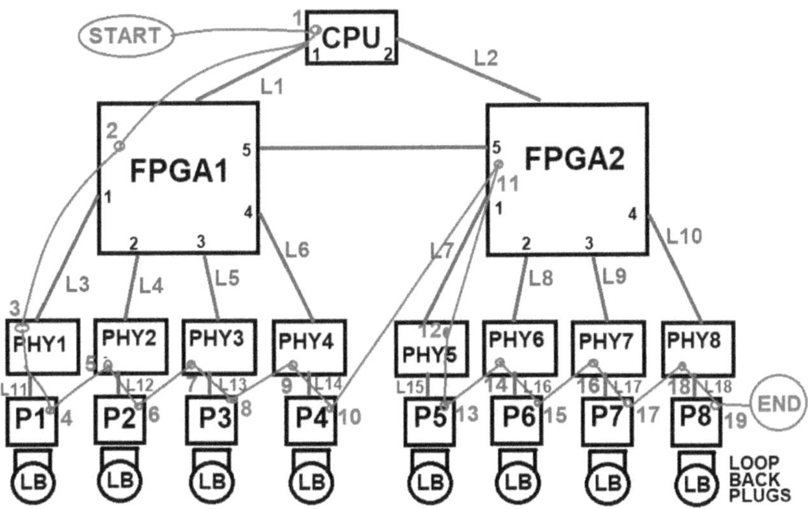

FIGURE 9.2 Example of a hierarchical board with graph discovery algorithm.

the log file at each step whether it was performed, then passed or failed, before moving onto the next device or port. Trying to run an end-user application as a test software results in an un-debug-able bone-pile in the production floor.

Let's see how this method reduces the issue. Let's say the VRM attached to PHY5 is missing a resistor. With a good test software, we would get a report file that shows that FPGA1 to 2 are good, PHY1 to 4 are good, PHY5 is bad, PHY6 to 7 are good, portsl to 4 are good, Port5 is bad, Port6 to 8 are good. In a real log file this would not be summarized; rather, each item would be listed in a separate line. Since PHY5 failed to respond to register reads, we can assume there is nothing wrong with anything downstream from it, which means we can ignore Port5 and Link15. We also know that since PHY6 works, PHY5 is likely not failing due to a common design problem, perhaps the individual module/port hook-up or a manufacturing issue. This would reduce the problem to: Either PHY5, Link7, or port-1 of FPGA2 is bad (FPGA2 partially bad). That is about 1.5/19=7.8% of the devices and 1/19=5.3% of the links to be inspected and probed in detail with hardware lab instruments. The amount of labor and luck required to debug this board is reduced by 92.2%, by using a good quality algorithm. It still requires an engineer to look at the block diagram and make a determination, for example, about ignoring port-5 and link-15.

This could perhaps be further automated with more software algorithms. But at least the hardware engineers can finish the prototype bring-up with this. In production, the test technicians might need assistance from hardware engineers, at least for the first few batches of production runs. But without an algorithm like this above, even the hardware designers would be sitting in the factory for months, so it is still a big improvement. The hardware engineer could create a causality table that either the test technician can read or the software engineer can implement in code, like the one in Figure 9.3. This would only work if the test script runs the above-described algorithm, otherwise the whole table would have to be painted orange, which would not be useful. The table on the figure shows all link, port, and main device combinations from the previous block diagram. If the test log shows that object-N failed, then the table will tell with orange cell color, which other objects might have caused it that need probing, inspecting, or debugging. For example, at Link3, the table shows that it might have failed the test due to FPGA1, PHY1, or Link3 itself being faulty. So the rest of the design can be ignored for debugging. The table and the test software should also decode object names like "PHY1" and "Link3" into actual reference designators and net names that can be found in the schematic. Any repair will require it; otherwise, the test technicians and the test engineers might have to spend hours in trying to decode it. It is really hard to associate object names between

	A	B	C	D	E	F	G	H	I	J	K	L	M	N	O	P	Q	R	S	T	U	V	W	X	Y	Z	AA	AB	AC	AD	AE	AF	AG	AH	AI	AJ	AK	AL
1			If this fails																																		
2			ASIC 1	ASIC 2	PHY 1	PHY 2	PHY 3	PHY 4	PHY 5	PHY 6	PHY 7	PHY 8	Port 1	Port 2	Port 3	Port 4	Port 5	Port 6	Port 7	Port 8	Link 1	Link 2	Link 3	Link 4	Link 5	Link 6	Link 7	Link 8	Link 9	Link 10	Link 11	Link 12	Link 13	Link 14	Link 15	Link 16	Link 17	Link 18
3		ASIC1																																				
4		ASIC2																																				
5		PHY1																																				
6		PHY2																																				
7		PHY3																																				
8		PHY4																																				
9		PHY5																																				
10		PHY6																																				
11		PHY7																																				
12		PHY8																																				
13		Port1																																				
14		Port2																																				
15		Port3																																				
16	Then	Port4																																				
17		Port5																																				
18	this	Port6																																				
19	might be	Port7																																				
20		Port8																																				
21	causing	Link1																																				
22	it	Link2																																				
23		Link3																																				
24		Link4																																				
25		Link5																																				
26		Link6																																				
27		Link7																																				
28		Link8																																				
29		Link9																																				
30		Link10																																				
31		Link11																																				
32		Link12																																				
33		Link13																																				
34		Link14																																				
35		Link15																																				
36		Link16																																				
37		Link17																																				
38		Link18																																				

FIGURE 9.3 A test failure causality table example.

Linux console, schematics drawing, and block diagrams. So some effort should be spent on documenting an association table up front or early during prototyping. Often the only way to determine the ID association is by attaching a device to one port at a time on the prototype and checking in console which device number reported a link event. By the look of it, we can call this table a "cat scratch diagram"; it is not a standard thing. The standard and most common solution is the "no-solution" with test logs that lead nowhere. This book tries to help with that.

9.5 SYSTEM MANAGEMENT FIRMWARE

System management firmware that runs on management microcontrollers and management CPU cards is developed by firmware engineers. Sometimes it is implemented as standard IPMI (Intelligent Platform Management Interface). IPMC, which is the on-board microcontroller used in an IPMI system, communicates with management cards in a larger multi-board chassis. On desktop, laptop and server motherboards they often use BMC (board management controller) chips, which possess the same kind of functionality as IPMI but for one standalone motherboard. BMCs can be remotely managed through the Ethernet network. The firmware image is programmed into the controller if it is a small device or into a flash chip.

The management firmware is responsible for the system and power management of a board or a whole chassis. The firmware engineers need to know the power and system management signals, GPIO tables, I2C trees, fan PWM settings, temperature sensor locations and alert thresholds, power sequence requirements, microcontroller pinouts, hot swapping schemes, and device list (bus, port, address) to be able to write the IPMI firmware. In most cases the majority of system glue logic signals are implemented by the hardware engineer on a small flash-based glue logic FPGA or CPLD, so only a few are left to be also connected to the controller (and documented). Developing the controller firmware is usually done by modifying the firmware written for a previous product to customize it to a new board. All the information needs to be communicated through the same document that is written for the OS/driver team. Power and system management signals need to be described through block diagrams, pinout tables, schematics, and flow charts. Their intended initialization sequence, hot swapping event sequence, and error (temperature and voltage out of limits) handling sequence need to be explained and clearly shown.

9.5.1 Temperature Thresholds Settings

System temperature is controlled by the management plane or subsystem by keeping track of all board and ASIC die temperatures. If the sensor that is already closest to its set limit gets even closer to its limit, then the IPMC needs to increase the fan speed (through PWM control) to cool everything down. If even one ASIC or board reaches its shutdown temperature limit, with the fans already running at 100% PWM, the board or system needs to shut down to prevent malfunction, damage, or fire. This should never happen in normal operation, even at the high end of the advertised temperature range, as long as the users use the product properly. But the hardware still must have the protection mechanism in place. It can still happen for example for cases of misuse, like blocked airflow or building air conditioning breakdown.

De facto industry standard temperature limits for fan control are upper non-recoverable (UNR, for immediate shutdown), upper critical (UC, when the fan speed must reach 100%), or upper non-critical (UNC, when the fan speed should start to increase from the minimum). Most electronic systems start up at 100% fan speed for a few seconds to make sure that during the time the processors are still booting and the sensor-based control loop is not active yet, the system will still not overheat. That could happen in a hot restart. Each sensor should have its own UC/UNR/UNC limits, hard-coded into the management controller's firmware as a table and provided by the hardware engineer to the software engineer. The IPMI management controller of the chassis monitors all sensors and increases the fan speed above the minimum if any one sensor crosses UNC. Similarly, it locks the fan speed to 100% if any sensor passes its UC limit. Finally, if any one sensor in the chassis crosses UNR the whole card that hosts that sensor or the whole system needs to power down immediately.

On a typical complex board, we have all the main ASICs die temperatures monitored by the local management controller through remote temperature sensors, and each board temperature is monitored through small temperature sensors. All of the sensors are I2C devices. The remote types have a two-wire analog connection to the thermal diode pins of each ASIC. All big ASICs have thermal diodes built-in, which are accessible on the ASIC's pins. The ASIC die is the hottest part of any system because that is where most of the heat is generated.

UNC for each sensor can be calculated by measuring the sensor value, when the ambient temperature is such that we do not want more than the minimum fan speed. For the NEBS environmental standard used on ATCA systems it is 27C ambient, as the standard requires the designers to ensure

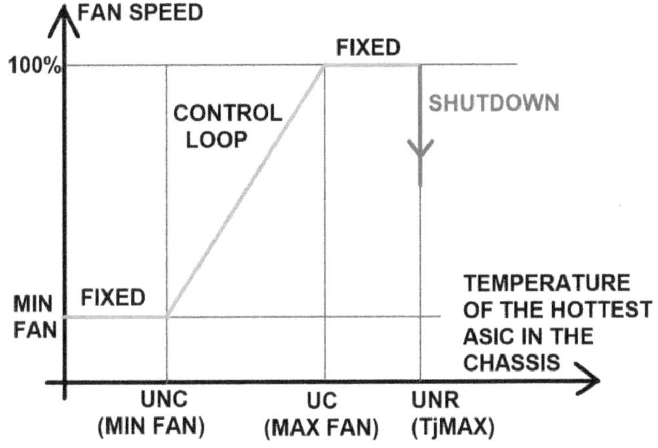

FIGURE 9.4 Fan speed algorithm.

that in normal conditions the systems will not produce too much fan noise. Large data center chassis can sound like jet engines. The fan control does not "servo" between 0% and 100% because at near zero percent it would have electrical problems, so a minimum level, around 30% is used. We can have zero if we turn the fan off completely, then jump to 30% when needed. UC can be calculated in many ways. One way is simply UNR-10C, but we should not run a system near the UNR too often because components will experience accelerated aging. UNR-20C might be better for prolonging component lifetime. A typical fan control algorithm is shown in Figure 9.4.

10 Timing Analysis

Timing analysis is concerned with the propagation delays of signals. It is important for traditional parallel and serial interfaces, like memory buses, SPI flash interfaces, and others. If the timing (trace lengths and delays) is not right, then the interface will not work reliably. It seems that technical books/papers rarely talk about timing, and, if they do, they just give brief introduction or they discuss a specific case in detail, without helping the readers to acquire an understanding of it. Another issue is they often use their own terminology, which is different from the terminology used for different interface standards. In this book a generalized terminology is used that can be applied to any type of interface.

There are two kinds of timing: dynamic (protocol) timing and static timing. This chapter focuses on static timing, but we need to consider the dynamic timing as well to be able to select the appropriate static timing equations. The dynamic timing is basically the sequence of signal assertions/values quantized at the data rate. Common dynamic timing parameters are data rate, number of clock cycles per transaction, and "latency", which describes a data packet being delayed when passing through the internal logic of a chip.

The static timing is more like an analog phenomenon—its purpose is to ensure that the signals will be captured correctly at the correct logic-value. The area dealing with this is Static Timing Analysis (STA). In STA, we take the available time for a signal to arrive and then we add or subtract other parameters from this (budget) to calculate a timing margin. A margin is simply the remainder. This margin has to be greater than zero, otherwise the interface will not operate reliably on every production unit and within the temperature range. A timing violation is when the timing margin is less than zero. With negative margins a few prototype units will likely function in the lab, but many production units will fail at the customer after hours of run-time. There are two sides of the static timing: the SETUP and the HOLD side. In the setup analysis we check if the signal arrives soon enough before the sampling edge, while in the hold analysis we check if the signal is still stable for a little while right after the sampling edge.

10.1 CHIP-LEVEL TIMING ANALYSIS

Board hardware design engineers rarely do chip-level timing analysis, perhaps only when we are designing our CPLD glue logic and need to compile it. When ASIC chips or FPGA logic projects are designed, we use the compiler tool's automatic static timing analyzer. It makes sure that the synthesized and mapped, placed, and routed logic will meet the setup and hold timing requirements on all signals and provide a detailed timing report to the user. The requirements are typed into a timing constraints file by the user. The report shows details about meeting or failing any defined timing constraints on each relevant logic path instance. Chip-level designs are always common clock synchronous systems. For a large design that is basically thousands of small elements like flip flops, combinatorial logic pieces, and routing elements between them. Timing constraint files (Xilinx UCF, or standard SDC formats) are text files listing timing constraints for the compiler and for the timing analyzer. The chip logic designer has to write it and include it among the project files to be used in compilation. The compilers can sometimes choose how to synthesize a high-level logic definition or how far to place them on the silicon die automatically for best timing. Compilation is mainly timing driven and automatic. Since all chip-level logic is common clock synchronous, the clock distribution with minimizing skew is very important, which is why all FPGA and ASIC chips contain low skew global clock networks that reach every flip-flop on the chip, driven by high power

DOI: 10.1201/9781032702094-10

driver buffers. The "skew" or mismatch between two or more traces is the trace length difference or how shorter or longer one is from the other(s).

Only the board-level chip-to-chip interface designs can use other than common clock synchronous interfaces. For them, the board and chip timing parameters have to be considered together. The chip or ASIC/FPGA designers have to design their I/O interfaces to be operational with realistic board designs. To achieve this, they create timing constraints (based on a timing analysis or just by taking numbers from standards), and they use I/O logic and I/O flip-flops close to the die pads on the silicon. The on-chip timing design is not presented here with many details since this book is aimed more at board-level designers.

If a signal's launch flip-flop is clocked by a different clock signal than the one clocking the capture flip-flop, then it is the case of the clock domain crossing. Chip designers invented different ways of handling it and of ensuring no data corruption. The common methods for the crossing problem are, for example, using double-flopping, handshaking, or dual-port FIFO memories. Different cases call for different solutions. Double flopping simply eliminates metastability, but the signal would still be off clock, although it does not matter for very slowly toggling individual signals. Handshaking means two devices or two state machines ensure each other will not get or provide corrupted data. For example, first putting the data out, then wait, then signal that the data is available, the other device waits, then takes it, then waits and signals back that it is taken. FIFOs are used to pass bus data at higher rates, with similar clock rates on the two sides.

10.1.1 Timing Constraints

Chip-level designs are made of logic elements and interconnects between them. The mapping of the instances in the RTL code design to the instances on the chip and the routing of the interconnects are automatic. The auto place and route software makes its decisions about locations and coordinates based on meeting or failing the timing requirements. We write a timing constraint file for the software to be able to make the right decisions. The most standard file format is the SDC format. The timing-driven P&R tool uses these constraints in action, but, once done, we also get a timing analysis report showing which constraints were met, which objects failed the constraints, and by how much. The most important constraint is the clock (domain) constraint, where we identify the signal name of the clock net, we specify its frequency. Signal paths have a propagation delay; they involve logic elements and interconnects. All flip-flops that are clocked by the defined clock, and all signal paths that go between them, will be applied with the clock constraint, so the tool will limit the delays on these paths. Similarly, a minimum hold time limit will be also applied as a minimum delay requirement. An example of clock constraint below makes the "CORECLK" signal to be treated as a clock by the timing analyzer and defines the clock period time in nanoseconds:

```
create_clock -period 100 "CORECLK"
```

Other constraints that can be used are the "multi-cycle path" and the "false-path". In better designs we can avoid using them because if we have to use them, then the burden is on the designer to identify and set up all possible instances. Multi-cycle paths can also exist on board-level I/O interfaces, for example, programmable asynchronous interfaces or 2T clocking on a DDR memory address bus. Clock domain crossing is a case when the launch flip-flop and the capture flip-flop are not driven by the same reference signal or clock. If we use a FIFO memory to handle the crossing then the path terminates at the FIFO pins. If we do not use a FIFO then the path cannot be analyzed, should be set up as a false path, and the signal should not be relied on without double flopping or handshaking protocols.

There are also timing constraints for I/O pins, which basically guarantee that the completed chip design will not have larger input setup and hold requirements than the constraints allow, and it will not have larger output setup/hold times (output delays) than we allow. Once the design is placed and routed and meets these I/O constraints, we can design our boards through board-level timing analysis, while using the chip-level I/O constraints as the new "datasheet parameters" describing the chip/FPGA. We do not directly enter the t_{ISU}, t_{IH}, t_{OSU}, or t_{OH} into the constraint file; rather, we enter the portion of the clock cycle that we want to leave for the board, so for example number=t_{CK}-t_{ISU}. An example of an I/O constraint:

```
set_input_delay -clock PCICLK -max 23 PCIAD
```

If we decide that we want to have a certain datasheet parameter, like t_ISU, similar to other chips on the market, then we can calculate the numbers for the constraints as:

```
t_InpDelay_max = t_bit - t_ISU
t_InpDelay_min = t_IH
t_OutpDelay_max = t_bit - t_OSU
t_OutpDelay_min = t_OH
```

Reset signals can also have constraints applied to them, called the "reset recovery" and the "reset removal" timing constraints. They work similarly to setup and hold around clocks. A signal should not change state close to when the clock rising edge happens, similarly a reset signal should not de-assert near the clock rising edge. The best recovery and removal times can be achieved if the reset de-assertion is synchronous to the clock, and it happens at the falling edge of the clock, then we do not necessarily have to set up timing constraints for the reset.

The constraint syntax depends on the FPGA/ASIC development tool, so we have to use their SDC constraint manuals to determine how to enter them.

10.2 BOARD-LEVEL TIMING ANALYSIS

We do two types of timing analysis calculations for board-level interfaces, pre-layout and post-layout types. In the pre-layout calculations, we investigate possibilities (maximum number of devices, maximum data rate, etc.) and we determine PCB-layout design trace-length constraints, which will ensure larger than zero timing margins. The PCB layout will have to be designed to meet these constraints. In post-layout timing analysis, we verify whether the finished board will work reliably (with positive timing margins) in all cases. We have to always take the possible worst-case combination of the timing parameters into account. By rearranging the equations, from the margins we can calculate, for example, the maximum data rate or the pulse width programming values for asynchronous interfaces. Most of the board hardware designers use the trace length constraints as magic numbers coming from some standard or datasheet, although we could calculate those ourselves as well using timing analysis.

Timing analysis requires the engineer to deal with hardware architecture, logic design, signal integrity simulations, and chip design as well as generate length/delay constraints for chip/package/PCB designs. High-speed digital board design requires the engineer to control the trace lengths on the board in a very detailed way, pin to pin on multipoint signal nets. To achieve this, we have to use proper design software that supports Pin-Pair-based trace length control and matching groups. In some cases, the design engineers can use standard trace length rules specified in the chip manufacturers' design guides, while at other times if they do not really fit our architecture, we have to calculate the length constraints ourselves from pre-layout timing analysis.

Bi-directional data paths or buses have to move data in two different directions where the driver/receiver parameters may be different in the two directions. The two directions are usually called read and write, although in some multi-master interfaces it is not straightforward which transaction is read or write. We need to do separate timing analysis for the two directions. Multi-point (or multi-drop, or fly-by) buses will require a separate timing analysis for each valid driver/receiver combination. The propagation delays are considered between two specific points (Pin-Pairs) on the nets, often not through all trace segments.

We have to do a "setup analysis" and a "hold analysis" separately for both read and write. So, on a bi-directional bus this means at least four different analyses (RD-SU, RD-H, WR-SU, WR-H), with their simulation and calculation portions. The setup analysis is related to the slowest signal case, and the hold analysis is related to the fastest signal case. If the setup analysis fails (setup violation, margin<0), then it means that the moment the capture flip-flop captures the signal on its input, it perhaps has not finished with the transition to the new logic level yet. If the hold analysis fails (hold violation), then it means that the moment the capture flip-flop captures the signal on its input, it might have already started to transition to the next logic value. In both cases, we might capture the previous or next bit but not the actual/correct bit.

10.2.1 Basic Synchronous Data Path

Every type of system is a derivative of the basic common clock synchronous data path (see Figure 10.1). This consists of delay elements between a launch flip-flop and a capture flip-flop. For board-level interfaces the two flip-flops are on two different chips, and the data and clock paths contain PCB interconnects as well as on-chip delays. Timing graphs can reveal the timing architecture, so we can find the launch and capture flip-flops and the delays between them, and to make sure we are using the correct equations for the particular case. A basic D-flip-flop (or sometimes called 1-bit "register") launches the data signal to the bus at the edge of the reference signal (the signal that is connected to its CK-pin, a clock or a strobe signal), another D-flip-flop captures/samples the data at the next rising or falling edge of the reference signal. We can see this on the timing diagram in Figure 10.2. On a bus, there are multiple signals, and their I/O buffers have some delay difference between each other (skew), so they do not transition in the exact same time. In these cases, the data is only valid when all signals are valid.

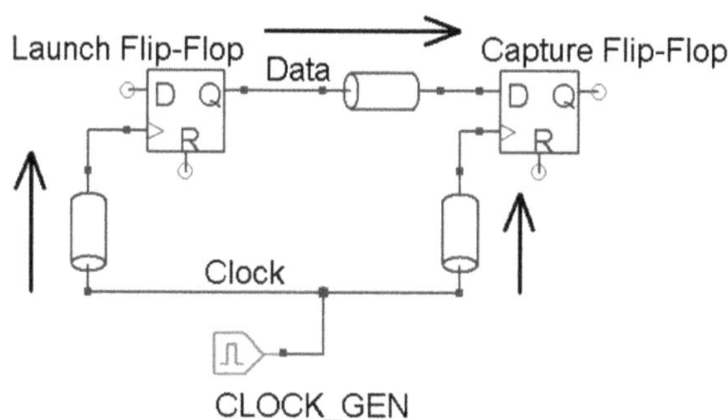

FIGURE 10.1 Simple synchronous data path.

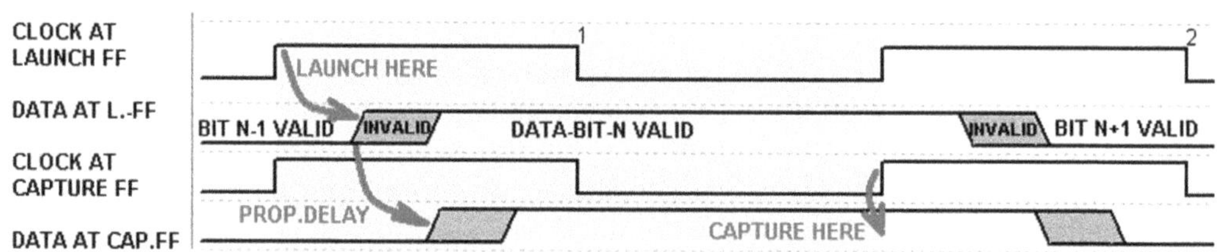

FIGURE 10.2 Signals at flip-flop pins.

The chip designers usually use I/O flip-flops that are close to the I/O pins on the silicon die. These I/O flip-flops usually act as gatekeepers between the core logic and the board-level signals to break up the static timing path, to help meeting the timing at the highest data rate. The edges of the reference signal will initiate data launch (at the output) and capture (at the input). There is always a reference signal (a clock or strobe) and a data signal (data, address or command…, here we just simply call it "data"). On a bi-directional interface, there is an I/O buffer and a launch and a capture flip-flop associated with the same chip pin. For a given bus transaction, only one of the two flip-flops in the same chip is used, the other one is inactive. Sometimes there is a flip-flop also for controlling the output enable pin of the I/O buffer (see Figure 10.3). In the timing graph diagrams in this book only one of these flip-flops will be shown, the one used in the particular transaction so as to make the explanations easier to understand.

A strobe signal has an edge only when it is needed (asserted and de-asserted by the controller), while a clock signal toggles all the time when the power is on. Both of them feed I/O flip-flop CK pins. Strobes are used in asynchronous and source-synchronous board-level interfaces. Digital chips need a clock signal for their internal operation, not only for their I/O flip-flops. The clock that is on a PCB trace and feeds I/O flip-flops is the I/O clock. The same clock signal can be used for both core and I/O flip-flops, while an I/O strobe cannot be used for clocking internal logic since it is not always toggling; we use separate free-running core reference clocks for that.

10.2.2 Timing Parameters

There are three categories of timing parameters for board-level interfaces. The first describes chip output pin capabilities, and input pin requirements against the arriving signals, found in datasheets. The second is the chip-level logic path and cell delays. They are included in the datasheet parameters for hard chips, but in the case of FPGAs the FPGA team has to ensure they are not too large by using I/O registers and constraints. Then the "datasheet" value comes from the FPGA timing report. The last category is the interconnect delays on the board.

10.2.2.1 Output Guaranteed Timing

The chip manufacturer or the FPGA engineer guarantees that their device will provide output signals with at least as good timing as the output guaranteed parameters they listed in their datasheet or timing report in case of an FPGA project. These are the worst-case late times until the signal

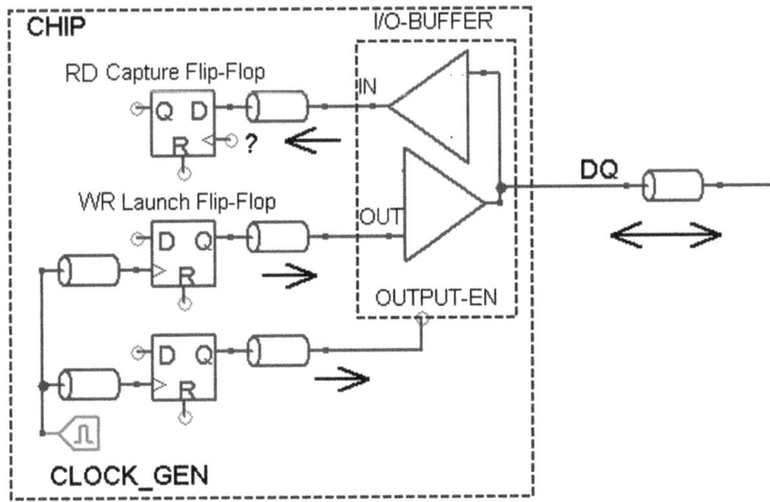

FIGURE 10.3 Bi-directional I/O Circuit.

becomes valid for setup or the worst-case early time to until it stay valid for hold. These are originally the parameters of the flip-flops generating the signals (between their CK and the Q pins), but there are on-chip delays between the flip-flop pins and the die/package pins and also between the clock generator and the flip-flop CK-pin. So these are combined together at the chip or die pin for the parameters listed in the datasheet. The D-type flip-flop generates the data on its Q output pin as the effect of the signal edge on its CK-pin. This takes time for the flip-flop to do, and this time is called clock-to-output delay (t_CK-Q).

The flip-flop output pin has to drive an interconnection on-board through a strong I/O buffer. It takes additional time until the output voltage reaches the new logic value—we can call it Transition Delay (TD) in this book. TD is related to rise time or fall time, measured from start until the signal crosses the new logic level the last time before stabilizing. TD is dependent on the output loading, so usually in the datasheet it is specified at a test/reference load condition, usually 50 Ohm and 50pF in parallel. The datasheet output timing t_OSU, and t_OH contains both the transition delay and the on-chip parameters (flip-flop's own t_OSU, t_OH, and on-chip propagation delays). Figure 10.4 shows these delay portions.

The Output Setup Time (t_OSU) is the longest worst-case clock-to-output-valid delay, guaranteed at the chip output. The signal is "valid" after it crosses the new logic level the last time before stabilizing. This parameter has different names in the different vendor datasheets: t_OSU, t_VAL_max, t_acc, etc. Figure 10.5 shows the three chip output parameter types.

The Output Hold Time (t_OH) is the minimum worst-case clock-to-output-invalid delay. It describes the longest time for the previous bit at the output pin to remain valid after the clock-edge, as well as the earliest time the data will start transitioning to the new value. This parameter has different names in the different vendor-datasheets: t_OH, t_VAL_min, etc.

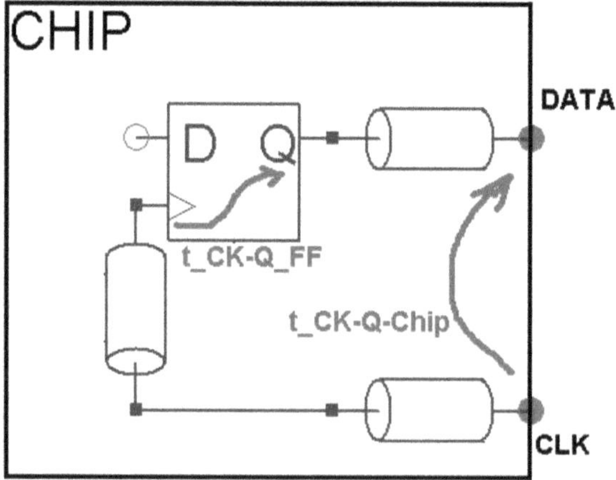

FIGURE 10.4 Flip-flop or chip output timing(t_CK-Q is either t_OSU or t_OH).

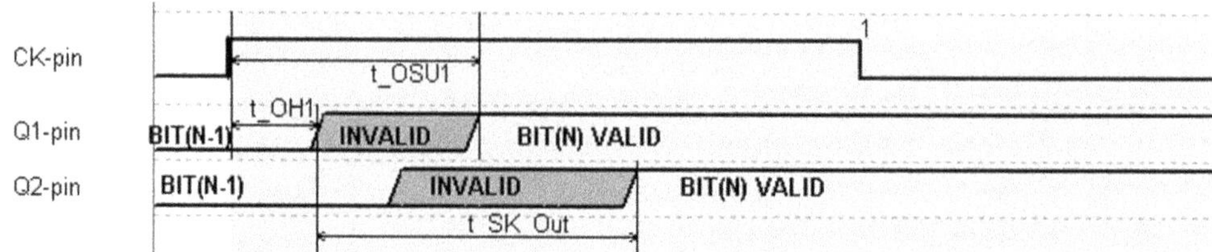

FIGURE 10.5 Output timings for two flip-flops.

The Output skew (t_SK_Out) is the maximum variation between the t_OSU (or t_OH) of two different output pins of a chip. The skew can be specified in different ways, including or excluding the t_OSU-t_OH difference. It can also be defined as a peak-to-peak value or as a min/max value as we can see in Figure 10.6, and in the equations below. The datasheet writers do not literally mean "maximum" and "minimum", but values measured from the minimum-delayed data or to the maximum-delayed data. Before using skew values from datasheets, we have to interpret them, and we might have to transform them to a format compatible with our calculations.

Peak-to-peak skew:

```
t_SK_Out = Max(t_OSU1, t_OSU2) - Min(t_OH1, t_OH2)
```

Min/Max skew:

```
t_SK_Min = t_OH_data - t_OSU_Ref
```

Which is usually negative, and

```
t_SK_Max = t_OSU_data - t_OH_Ref
```

In some cases, if the skew is specified between the reference signal and a data signal, they specify skew as:

```
t_SK_Out = |t_SK_Min| + |t_SK_Max| = (t_OSU_Ref - t_OH_Ref) +
(t_OSU_data - t_OH_data)
```

10.2.2.2 Input Requirements

The chip manufacturer or the FPGA engineer guarantees that their device will never require better timing at their input pins as the input parameters they listed in their datasheet or timing report in case of an FPGA project. The input requirements describe that the signal at the input pin must be at least this good, it has to become/stay valid, guaranteed by the system/board designer and the other chip driving the signal. This is demonstrated in Figure 10.7. These are originally the parameters of the D-type flip-flop capturing the data signal, but there are on-chip delays between the flip-flop pins and the die/package pins and also between the clock generator and the flip-flop CK-pin, similarly to the output timing. So, these are combined together at the chip/die pin, by the datasheet writers, as seen in Figure 10.8.

The Input Setup Requirement (t_ISU) is the time interval for the input signal to become stable at the new level, relative to the sampling moment (clock edge) that follows it. The signal must become

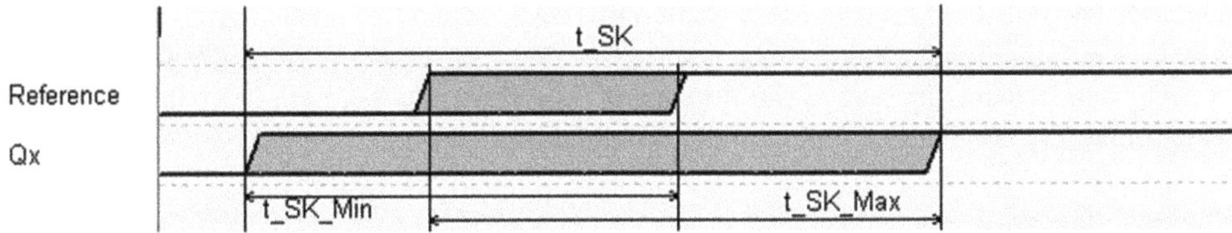

FIGURE 10.6 Examples for how they mean the skew on the datasheets.

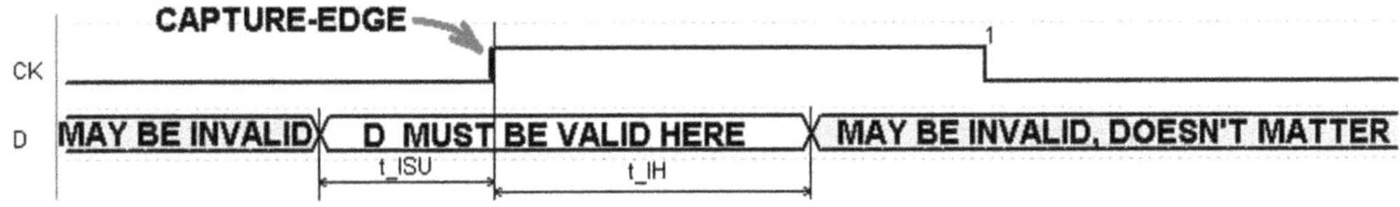

FIGURE 10.7 Input timing requirements.

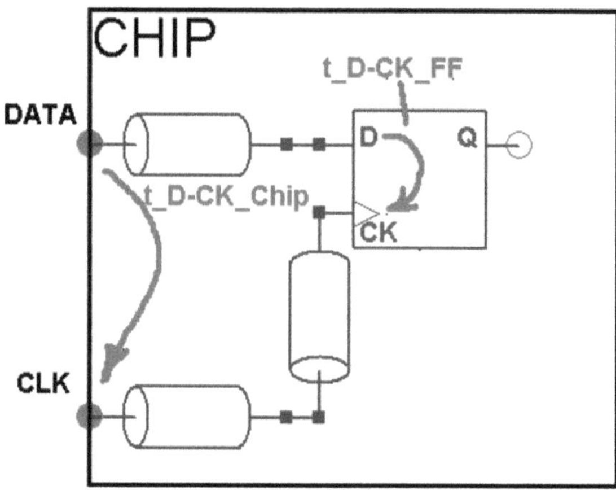

FIGURE 10.8 Flip-flop or chip input timing (t_D-CK is either t_ISU or t_IH).

stable earlier than this. This parameter has different names in the different vendor datasheets: t_ISU, t_SETUP, or t_DS. Very often this parameter is simply called "Setup Time". Confusingly some documents refer to something else by the same name. For example, the actual value of arrival time from the previous clock edge or the worst-case arrival time guaranteed by the board design. We cannot rely on the names of datasheet timing parameters to figure out what they mean, we have to look at the diagrams. If it is referenced from the previous clock edge instead of the capture clock edge, then we have to convert it, as T2=T_clk-T1

The Input Hold Requirement (t_IH) is the minimum time interval after the clock sampling edge until the input signal remaining stable at the old level. The signal must not start transitioning any earlier than this. This parameter has different names in the different vendor datasheets: t_IH, t_HOLD, t_DH. Very often this parameter is simply called "Hold Time". Sometimes it is measured from the previous (launch) clock edge and not from the capture reference edge.

The Input skew (t_SK_In): This specifies the maximum allowed skew/deviation between the arrival times of two input signals on two different pins of the same bus interface.

The input requirement (slew rate) derating is a process of altering the input requirements based on how fast the signal edge is transitioning. Some I/O standards like DDRx memory requires us to do that, they provide "derating tables" in the datasheets. The transistor inputs need a certain amount of charge to build up to make it switch to the new logic level. If our slew rate is different from the nominal, then the threshold level to cross will be different. Instead of recalculating the threshold, the JEDEC standards handle this by introducing the slew rate derating, basically modifying the input timing requirements instead of the thresholds. The slew rate is a parameter that we can get from signal integrity simulations. The best is to calculate the slew rate this way:

```
Slewrate = |V_th_new - V_th_old| / time_it_takes
```

10.2.2.3 Propagation Delay

The Propagation Delay (t_pd) describes the interconnect delay from a flip-flop output to a flip-flop input. The difference between the propagation delays of two signals (or their trace lengths) that are driven by the same chip is the trace delay skew. It can be between two data lines of the same bus or between two I/O-clock signals that go to two different devices from the same clock generator. The propagation delay is made of two parts, the Transition Delay (TD, rise/fall-time related), and the Flight Time (FT, PCB trace length-related). All the parts of propagation delay measurements are demonstrated in Figure 10.9. In some documents the worst-case slowest t_pd is referred to as "setup time" and the worst case fastest t_pd as "hold time".

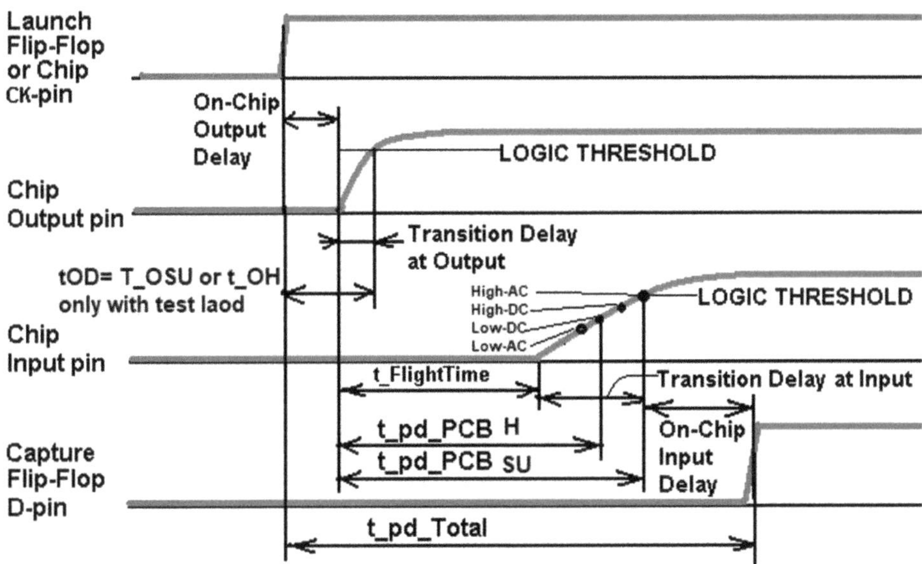

FIGURE 10.9 The delays from flip-flop to flip-flop.

The flight-time delay (FT) is the time it takes for a signal to travel through the interconnection. It is hard to separate it from the transition delay accurately because they have effects on each other. If the trace is longer (a lot longer) then the trace-capacitance is higher and so the buffer will not be able to make the signal to transition as fast, and the ringing will occur in a later position relative to the signal edge, affecting the time when it is able to cross and stay above the logic thresholds. For PCB design we need length constrains, which are directly proportional to flight time. We can convert between flight time and trace length easily:

```
FT = length * SQRT(DK) / 11.8 [ns, inch]
```

The Transition Delay is the time needed for the signal to reach the new logic value threshold and become stable and valid through a slowly rising waveform and ringing due to reflections. We can see this in Figure 10.10. It is similar to the "rise time" or "fall time", but those are measured between 20% and 80% voltage level crossings. We can separate TD from a simulated delay by subtracting a calculated FT:

```
TD = sim_delay - FT = sim_delay - length * SQRT(DK) / 11.8
```

The chip output delay (t_OD) is an important part of a timing analysis, and it needs to be extracted from the datasheet output guaranteed parameters. The chip datasheet output timing (t_OSU/t_OH) is usually a combination of the TD at the output pin at test-load condition and the on-chip delays (t_OD). This extraction can be done by doing a signal integrity simulation, where the chip output pin is connected to a 50pF+50Ohm reference load with no transmission line, with both fast and slow IBIS model settings, and both the rising and the falling waveforms, displayed on an eye diagram.

```
t_OD_max = tOSU - TD(SimTestLoad)
t_OD_min = tOH - TD(SimTestLoad)
```

In simulation we measure the combined delay=TD+FT, while the datasheet output parameters include TD as part of the t_OSU, as t_OSU=t_OD+TD. For our timing calculations we have to make sure we do not include TD twice, so we have to extract it either from the simulated delay or

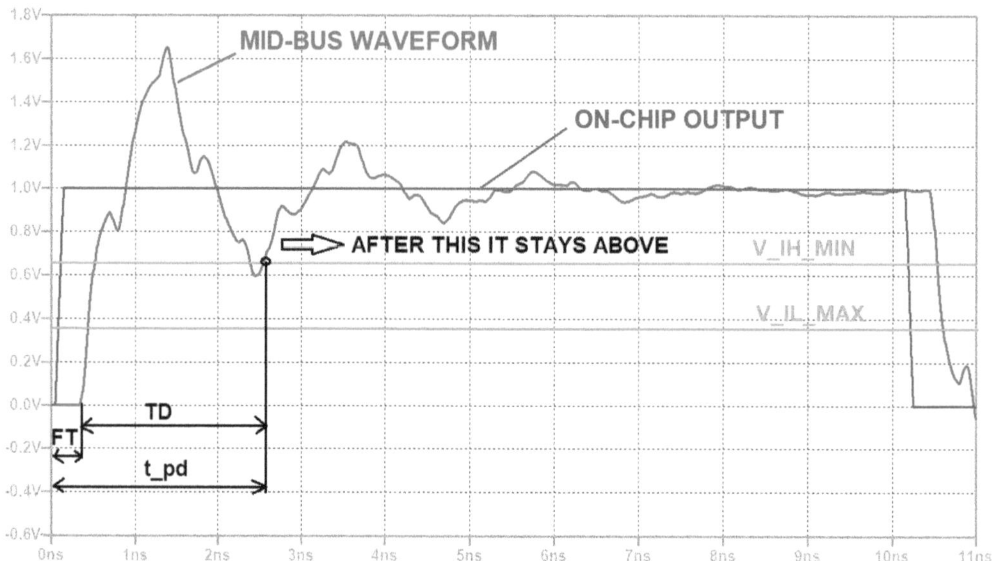

FIGURE 10.10 Transition delay in a choppy simulated waveform in Ltspice.

from the datasheet output timing. For example, we can use t_pd and t_OD where t_pd contains TD, or we can use FT and t_OSU where t_OSU contains TD. We cannot use t_pd and t_OSU in the same equation, unless we assume TD=0, which is what we can do when calculating PCB layout design constraints.

If we do a post-layout signal-integrity simulation, and display the waveform at the receiver chip-pin, then we are measuring the combined t_pd. For post-layout timing verification calculations, we need to obtain the shortest and the longest propagation delays from the SI simulations. We need to run it with both fast and slow IBIS model settings, and both the rising and the falling waveforms to be displayed on an eye diagram, then from the four combinations we can find the slowest one and the fastest ones, t_pd_max and t_pd_min, that are needed for the equations calculating timing margins. For the post-layout stage, we have to use all the parameters as described so far, then while filling these into the equations, we will calculate the margins:

```
t_pd = TD + t_flighttime
t_OD_max = tOSU - TD(SimTestLoad)
t_OD_min = tOH - TD(SimTestLoad)
```

A pre-layout feasibility analysis can be done like a post-layout analysis, but instead of extracting a PCB file we build a pre-layout style simulation model with parametrized transmission lines, then obtain the full t_pd_max and t_pd_min that are needed for the equations, calculating timing margins. This is like a pre/post-layout combo method.

For pre-layout constraint calculations we can make a few assumptions, then, filling these into the equations, we will calculate the min/max delays or trace lengths that satisfies zero margin. The assumptions:

```
t_pd = t_flighttime = 0
t_OD_max = tOSU
t_OD_min = tOH
```

10.2.2.4 Errors and Noises

There other parameters that have a random direction and degrade our margins, in this book we just call them "errors" and "noises", and their sum is denoted as t_err_X. All different types should be

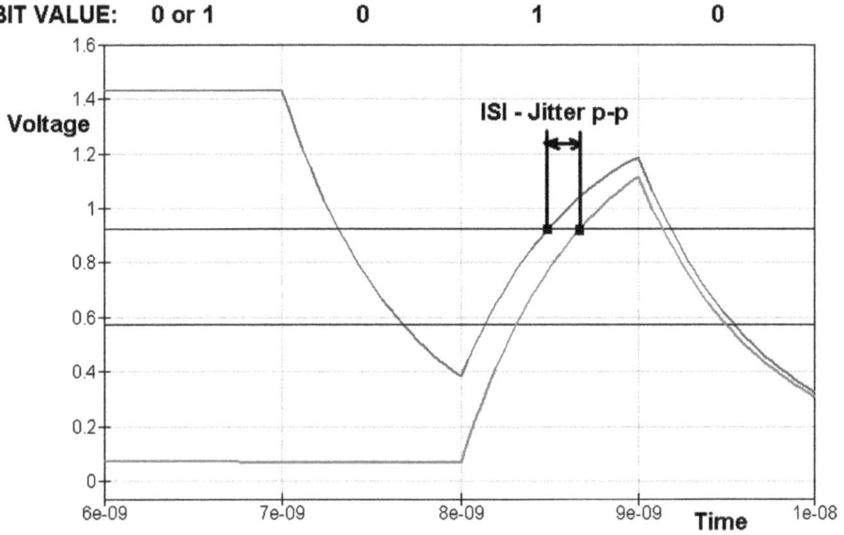

FIGURE 10.11 Inter Symbol Interference on a waveform with different starting values.

TABLE 10.1
Errors Table (ET)

<table>
<tr><th>Interface Type</th><th>Case</th><th>t_err</th></tr>
<tr><td rowspan="2">Synchronous</td><td>SETUP</td><td>Clock skew, DCD</td></tr>
<tr><td>HOLD</td><td>Clock skew</td></tr>
<tr><td rowspan="2">Asynchronous</td><td>SETUP</td><td>DCD</td></tr>
<tr><td>HOLD</td><td>0</td></tr>
<tr><td rowspan="2">Source Synch.</td><td>SETUP</td><td rowspan="6">Clock jitter, VRM noise, Vref noise, Cap/res mismatch, DCD</td></tr>
<tr><td>HOLD</td></tr>
<tr><td rowspan="2">Clock Forwarding</td><td>SETUP</td></tr>
<tr><td>HOLD</td></tr>
<tr><td rowspan="2">Unidir. Synch.</td><td>SETUP</td></tr>
<tr><td>HOLD</td></tr>
<tr><td rowspan="2">Embedded Clk</td><td>SETUP</td><td>Clock jitter, VRM noise</td></tr>
<tr><td>HOLD</td><td>Clock jitter, VRM noise</td></tr>
</table>

summed up as t_err. For all of these errors we have to take into account only half bit time of it, half the peak-to-peak value. Some of these are already included in the t_pd, for example, crosstalk, inter-symbol-interference (ISI), and reflection-related sources. The way ISI is causing an alteration to the TD is demonstrated in Figure 10.11. Others like clock jitter, duty cycle distortion (DCD), Vref noise, power supply ripple, simultaneous switching noise (SSN), interference from unrelated buses, and the altered TD caused by component value tolerance have to be accounted for under t_err. In most cases we can only guesstimate all these with a single number.

The types of errors and noises we use in a particular case depend on the interface type and the ratio between the error source and the bit time. For example, for a 10MHz bus with 100ns bit period we can safely ignore a 0.1ps jitter source. Table 10.1 summarizes which error types we include in which calculation, due to practicality.

Component tolerances can be categorized under capacitive load mismatch between pins and termination resistor value tolerance. It is likely about 0.1pF maximum and 1% for termination resistors. The timing error it may cause can be estimated as:

```
t_err_cap = delta_C * R
```

Or

```
t_err_res = C * delta_R
```

Simultaneous Switching Noise (SSN) is when multiple output buffers are switched in the same time, causing a higher amplitude power rail dip. This supply voltage noise shifts the output voltage and input threshold voltage levels for CMOS type I/O. Any noise on the reference voltage pin of an SSTL input buffer has the same effect, and it can be estimated as:

```
t_err_rail = Rail_noise_amplitude / slew_rate
```

Duty Cycle Distortion (DCD) is when the clock signal does not spend equal time at high and low levels. It is given as a percentage, but we can convert it to a time unit:

```
t_err_dcd = |Duty_Cycle-50%| * t_clk
```

10.2.2.5 Other Timing Parameters

Combinatorial logic circuits also cause delays. These can be on-chip logic or on-board, for example, if there is a CPLD used for slow bus multiplexing. If the logic code is designed in-house, then we can get the delay values from the on-chip STA report. Non-programmable logic and analog chips have a delay that can be obtained from their datasheets. Flip-flops or registers are NOT combinatorial; they break signal/timing paths, so the paths always have to be analyzed from one flip-flop to the next flip-flop. The timing path is not always chip-pin to chip-pin, but always flip-flop to flip-flop.

The Clock skew in a synchronous system is the propagation delay difference between the traces from the clock generator to two or more different chips. This only matters for I/O clocks, not for reference clocks. Usually the designer's goal is to minimize the clock skew to achieve better timing margins. For a bi-directional bus, if there is a clock skew, then it means, for example, that the read-setup-margin and the write-hold-margin are increased by the skew value, but the read-hold and write-setup margins are decreased by the same amount, which can cause a problem. If the sign or absolute value of the clock skew is unknown, then we have to assume the worst-case situation and subtract the maximum value from both the setup and the hold margins.

10.2.2.6 Datasheet Parameters

In datasheets from different chip manufacturers or in relation to different standards the same timing parameters can have totally different names, or different parameters can have the same name. In other cases, the way they measure the timing parameter can be different. It is common that one datasheet measures a parameter relative to the capture clock edge, while another measures it relative to the previous (launch) clock edge. For example, instead of saying the chip input setup requirement is 7ns, they say "setup time 26ns". What they mean is the signal has to be launched and arrive from the other end within 26ns. Basically, instead of specifying their own chip's limitations, they specify how the rest of the system has to perform. We have to convert them sometimes before using them in calculations:

```
t_x → (t_bit-t_x)
```

Sometimes the same name is used for different things: For example, the "Setup Time", in some documents is referred to as Input Setup Requirement, while some other documents refer to the output buffer and trace delays combined, and some others might refer to what we called Output Setup Time. In most of the datasheets the skew between two signals is specified as the deviation between them, while some other datasheets name a parameter as "skew", even though they are trying to describe the t_data_period-t_skew value, basically the skew-less region of a bit-time.

10.2.3 Signal Integrity Analysis

To obtain accurate propagation delays on the PCB trace interconnections for a timing verification of a design, including the effects of various disturbances (ISI jitter, crosstalk, reflections, bus capacitance, etc.), we have to do a signal integrity analysis, by using I/O buffer models (IBIS models). Figure 10.12 shows a post-layout simulation setup with buffer models and an S-parameter block that was extracted from a board design using an electromagnetic SI simulation tool. The results of this simulation (the t_pd) is a parameter we need to feed into the timing analysis calculations. To calculate timing driven layout constraints, we might not have to run SI simulations, but for a post-layout verification it is necessary. The result of the signal integrity simulation is a set of waveforms or waveform images. We have to measure times and voltages on these waveforms—this could be called "Geometric Waveform Analysis". In most cases we can place cursors or markers into the diagram in the simulation tool, which reads out time or voltage values, that we have to write down. Finally, we supply the timing information from this into a timing calculation to obtain the timing margins. We might also have to determine signal slew rates, for input requirement derating, if the chip/standard requires it. In case of multi-point buses, we have to simulate the complete bus with all valid driver/receiver Pin-Pairs and extract the waveforms at each valid receiver. For example, if we have one CPU talking to two DRAM chips, then the valid combinations are CPU-DRAM1 and CPU-DRAM2, while the DRAM1-DRAM2 combination is invalid as they never talk to each other. We will have to take the latest arriving waveform (seen from the unluckiest receiver input pin) for the setup analysis, and the earliest one for hold. The receiver that is closest to the transmitter might not be the one seeing the longest delay, as the closest one has to wait for a round trip delay of a reflected wave coming from the far end of the trace to push the waveform across the logic level threshold to complete the TD. So we have to look at all waveforms to find the slowest and fastest ones.

These signal integrity simulations and the IBIS I/O buffer models do not include on-chip and flip-flop timing parameters, only the interaction between traces and I/O buffers.

The IBIS models have a selector parameter: "Fast"/"Slow"/"Typical". These are the silicon manufacturing, supply voltage, and temperature-related speed parameters and corners. The IBIS models describe the I/O buffers as I(V) and V(t) curves. There is a set of curves for all of the three speed corners. The silicon manufacturing process cannot create chips to have exactly the same speed capabilities. The voltage and speed do not vary (statistically) much on the same chip; it varies a lot more between different production units. The slowest chip ever manufactured, running at the lowest temperature and voltage would behave like the "Slow" setting in the IBIS model, while the fastest ever made running warm and at slightly higher voltage would be as fast as the IBIS I/O buffer with the "Fast" setting. Silicon chips are supposed to get faster at cold temperatures, but many newer chips get slower due to a process called "temperature inversion". If the same chip is driving both the data and the reference signals, then we would expect the two buffers to be at the same speed corner, since the on-chip variation is much less than the variation between different chips and boards.

The times on the waveforms have to be measured between points where the signal crosses the logic threshold voltage levels, from the simulation start time (zero). The threshold levels can be different in voltage and different in nature for the different types of interfaces. The measurements can be done as absolute time measurements (t_pd from simulation time zero) or as relative time measurements (between the reference signal and the data signal). Some of the simulation tools extract the measurement automatically, but they produce an intermediate margin (t_X_MAR1). In

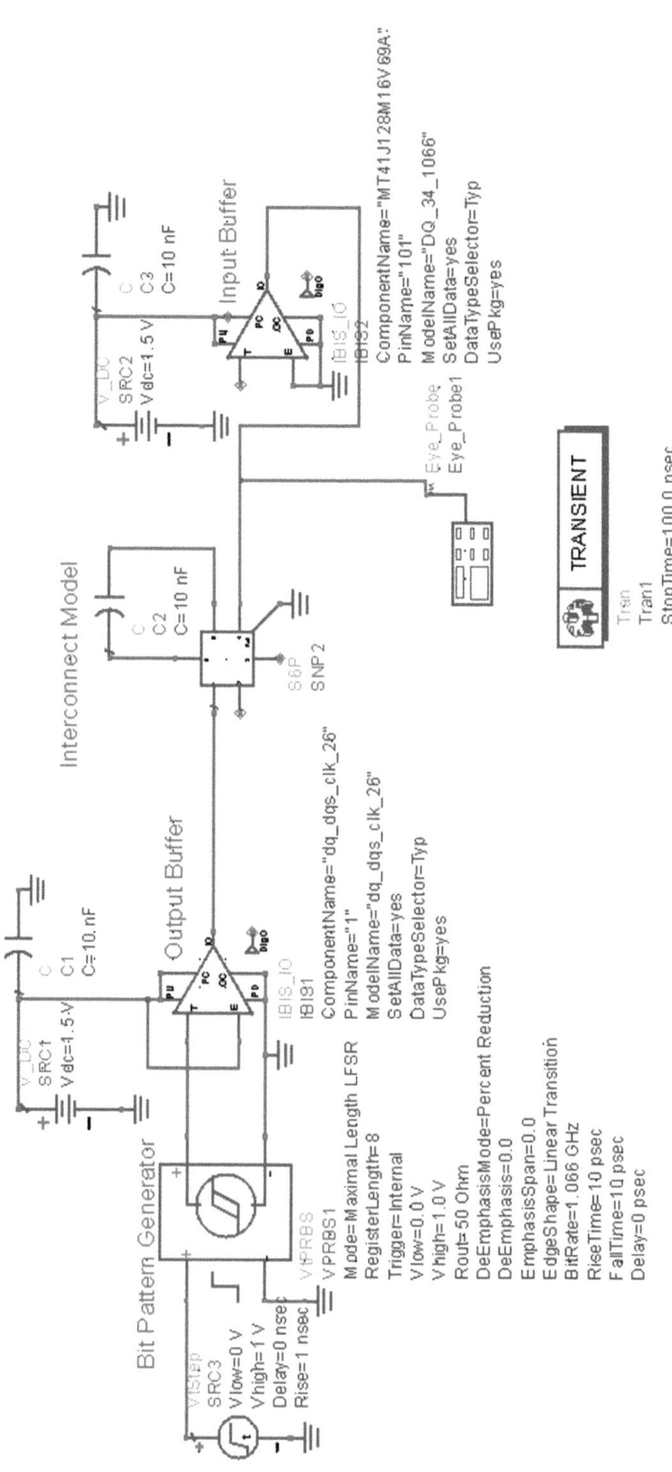

FIGURE 10.12 Post-layout simulation setup in Keysight ADS.

the timing calculations after the simulation, we still need to subtract other parameters (e.g., t_err, etc.) from this to get the final timing margins.

```
0 ≤ t_X_MAR = t_X_MAR1 - t_err
```

There are three main input voltage threshold decision types:

- Single-ended maximum low and minimum high, V_{IL_MAX}, V_{IH_MIN}. As a waveform starts rising from low to high, when it passes the low threshold it terminates the hold time, when it crosses the high threshold and stays above (after all ringing) it no longer incurs setup time. A falling waveform does similarly but the opposite direction. This can be seen in Figure 10.13.
- Single-ended AC and DC threshold-based. Similar to the above, but we now have four thresholds, V_{IL_AC}, V_{IL_DC}, V_{IH_AC}, V_{IH_DC}. As a waveform starts rising from low to high, when it passes the low-DC threshold it terminates the hold time, when it crosses the high-AC threshold and stays above (after all ringing) it no longer incurs setup time. This is common with DDR1 to 3 memory interfaces. This can be seen in Figure 10.14. The four thresholds are derived from a single reference voltage-based threshold to account for input pin transistor imperfections.
- Differential eye opening is checked against an eye-mask that is a combination of the thresholds and the input setup/hold requirements. We do not calculate timing for these; rather, we check for an eye mask width violation (the signal crosses through the mask area).

The data signal can be sampled in three different ways:

- SDR (Single Data Rate): The data is launched/captured at only one edge of the reference signal. Usually, it is the rising edge. Sometimes the capture edge is the rising edge and the launch edge is the falling edge, for example, on a slow shift register interface driven by fast FPGA chips using loose unmatched cables so as to avoid a hold violation.

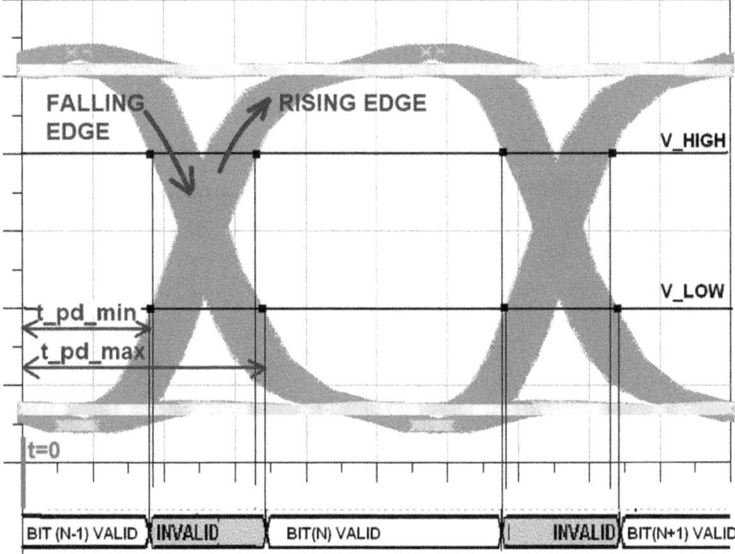

FIGURE 10.13 High/low threshold type input logic timing.

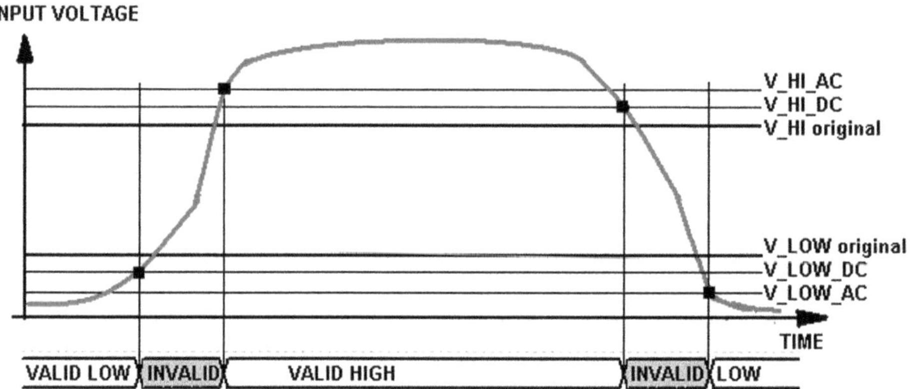

FIGURE 10.14 Input thresholds with AC/DC thresholds.

- DDR (Double Data Rate): The data is launched/captured at both rising and falling edges of the reference signal. Usually they use two different flip-flops for the two edges, or they use a DDR flip-flop. The DDR flip-flop has one DDR input and two SDR outputs, or two SDR inputs and a DDR output. With DDR the data and the reference signal have the same analog bandwidth.
- QDR (Quad Data Rate): The data signal is launched/captured at both edges of the reference signal but also half-way between the edges. This was common only with QDR SRAM memory chips attached to FPGAs, providing low latency SRAM.

The process of reading out timing parameters from waveform displays can be called Geometric Timing Measurements. The minimum propagation delay is measured from simulation time zero until the signal's previous bit value goes invalid (the earliest of the rising/falling edges). The maximum propagation delay is measured from simulation time zero until the signal actual bit value goes valid (the last of the rising/falling edges). Which moment and which threshold from which simulation needs to be used for each time measurement is listed in Table 10.2. Just to recap, we check both falling and rising edges and take the worst. Worst in hold analysis means fastest, worst in setup means slowest. We use minimum t_pd for hold, maximum for setup, and fast IBIS model setting for hold and slow for setup.

10.2.4 Generalized Timing Equations

This section explains the details of the timing calculations for our understanding, even though in most real-world cases we would use a spreadsheet template or a simulation tool. We have to understand how this works, otherwise we would misuse the tools and we end up in a "garbage-in/garbage-out" situation. Or we might want to make a new template. The same one generalized equation will be customized for all interface types and all transaction cases.

```
0 ≤ t_X_MAR = t_available + t_improving - t_degrading - t_err
```

This equation can be used for any type of interface. The "X" in the index can be read-setup, read-hold, write-setup, write-hold, or in the case of multi-point buses any driver-receiver pair. These can be calculated in a spreadsheet or just on paper with a calculator. t_X_MAR is the Timing Margin. t_available is the time available for the signal to arrive, depending on interface or architecture type. t_err is a sum of various signal integrity effects, and it always decreases the timing margins, but it is treated separately because of its nature—it is not a delay type parameter. Which delays are

TABLE 10.2
Simulation Cases for Timing Parameters

Simulate What	Number of Logic Thresholds	Case	Corner	Edge	Threshold	Use which
Real Board, to get t_pd and Transition Delay at input	1	SU	Slow	Rise	Vref	larger
				Fall	Vref	
		H	Fast	Rise	Vref	smaller
				Fall	Vref	
	2	SU	Slow	Rise	VIH_min	larger
				Fall	VIL_max	
		H	Fast	Rise	VIL_max	smaller
				Fall	VIH_min	
	4	SU	Slow	Rise	AC-H	larger
				Fall	AC-L	
		H	Fast	Rise	DC-L	smaller
				Fall	DC-H	
	4 with calibration	DVW	Slow	eye	AC left, DC right, eye mask fit	smaller
			Fast			
Test Load to get Transition Delay at output, for tOD calculation	1	n/a	Typ	Rise	Vref	larger
				Fall	Vref	
	2		Typ	Rise	VIH_min	larger
				Fall	VIL_max	
	4		typ	Rise	AC-H	larger
				Fall	AC-L	

improving and which ones are degrading the timing margin depends on the interface type or architecture, and they are listed in a table below. For improving parameters, we have to use their smallest value and for degrading ones their largest value.

In the case of some datasheets, it is hard to associate their parameter names to the ones described in this book. For them, engineering judgment is needed to decide if they would improve or degrade the margins, separately for setup and hold, read and write analysis. If a parameter improves the margins, then it is an "improving" parameter, otherwise it is a "degrading" parameter. Before putting any parameter into the calculations, we have to remove any negative sign if they have one, and we might have to transform them if they are referenced to a different clock edge than this book references it to. The generalized method cannot comply to most standards and parts, as different ones describe the same things differently. Instead, a method of forcing compliance by transformation is described. In very rare cases, a datasheet parameter's negative sign really means negative, so again engineering judgment is needed. For example, a chip datasheet may specify1ns Input Setup Requirement due to the on-chip delay arrangement, so that chip actually tolerates if the actual bit of valid data arrives 1ns after the sampling edge seen on the device pins.

When the data and the reference signal are going in opposite directions, like an asynchronous read, then in the setup analysis the data propagation delay is degrading and the reference signal propagation delay is also degrading, for the hold analysis the data is improving and the reference signal is also improving the margins. When they go in the same direction, then for setup the data is degrading and reference signal is improving, while for hold it is the other way around.

In a post-layout timing verification, if the simulation tool provides a timing margin (t_X_MAR), but we see that it did not include all parameters we would like, then we can calculate it further, for more accuracy:

```
0 ≤ t_X_MAR = t_X_MAR1 + t_improving - t_degrading - t_err
```

In all the different transaction cases and interface types, the parameter groups (like available time, degrading and improving parameters and errors) have to be looked up in the timing analysis parameter table (TAP), shown in Table 10.3. We have to fill in the input parameters, and then get the parameter strings for the generalized equation. White cells are the output parameters (from table to equation), blue cells are architecture selectors, pink cells are case selectors, green cells are the parameter names.

Note 1: Most of the synchronous systems have t_available_hold = 0, t_available_setup = T_clk_period, since the rising edge of the clock is used to both launch the output data and capture the input data. It is rare, but there are systems where we launch the output signal at the falling edge and capture input at the rising edge, so for those designs

```
t_available_setup = t_available_hold=T_clk_period/2
```

Note 2: If the clock is supplied by the master to the slave chip, then t_pd_clk is straightforward. If it is routed to both the master and the slave from a central clock generator, then we can substitute:

```
t_pd_clk = t_pd_to_slave - t_pd_to_master.
```

Note 3: If the data is driven to the bus before the strobe gets asserted, then we have more time than just the RD# or WR# strobe pulse width

```
t_available = RD_pulse_width + t_programmed_setup_time.
```

Note 4: All the parameters here are receiver-chip design internal delays, the board hardware designers never have to calculate it.

Note 5: The terminology here is taken from the DDR2-SDRAM standard (JESD79-2x). The output skew is specified in the datasheets, it is used instead of t_OD. We need to check the section about source-synchronous systems for more details on the parameters. The memory device output skew parameters have their own names as t_DQSQ and t_QHS. For propagation delays where the table mentions "t_pd_str - t_pd_data", we can use the skew value instead.

```
output_skew = t_OD _data - t_OD_str
```

10.2.4.1 Maximum Data Rate Calculation

In general, the maximum data rate or clock frequency is the frequency that if we put into the timing calculations, we get zero for one of the margins. This way we can calculate how fast our bus may run. We would have to run it below that, maybe by 10%, to allow some design margin. We have to calculate how much time we must have available, in the variable t_available_min first, for all four setup/hold and read/write combinations, then take the <u>largest</u> number. But we do only those calculations where the t_available is not specified as zero in the TAP table.

```
t_available_min = t_degrading - t_improving + t_err
```

Once we have calculated that, the minimum bit period or the maximum data rate can be calculated from t_available_min, depending on the actual system, as seen in Table 10.4.

10.2.4.2 Programming an Asynchronous Bus Interface

Microcontrollers and DSPs have a programmable parallel bus interface. The transaction bit timing protocol consists of several phases, each phase can be programmed to take a certain amount of time duration. The duration is in whole numbers of periods of the processor's internal clock. First, we have to look up all four sets of equation parameters from the timing analysis parameter (TAP) table, listed for the asynchronous RD/WR and SU/H cases. Then we have to put them into four equations for the "required time" below, instead of putting it into the original equation used for timing

TABLE 10.3
Timing Analysis Parameter Table (TAP)

Interface Type	Case	t_available	t_improving (List)	t_degrading (List)	Notes
Synchronous	RD-SU	T_clk	0	t_ISU_master + t_OD_max_slave + t_pd_data + t_pd_clk	1,2
	RD-HOLD	0	t_OD_min_slave + t_pd_data + t_pd_clk	t_IH_master	1,2
	WR-SU	T_clk	t_pd_clk	t_ISU_slave + t_OD_max_master + t_pd_data	1,2
	WR-HOLD	0	t_OD_min_master + t_pd_data	t_IH_slave + t_pd_clk	1,2
Asynchronous	RD-SU	RD# pulse-width	0	t_ISU_master + t_OD_max_slave + t_pd_data + t_pd_strobe	
	RD-HOLD	0	t_OD_min_slave +t_pd_data + t_pd_strobe	t_IH_master	
	WR-SU	WR# pulse-width	t_pd_strobe	t_ISU_slave + t_OD_max_master + t_pd_data	3
	WR-HOLD	0	t_OD_min_master + t_pd_data	t_IH_slave + t_pd_strobe	3
Source Synch.	RD-SU	T_bit/2	0	t_ISU_master + (t_pd_data-t_pd_str) + t_DQSQ_max	5
	RD-HOLD	T_bit/2	0	t_IH_master + (t_pd_str-t_pd_data) + t_QHS	5
	WR-SU	T_bit/2	0	t_ISU_slave + (t_pd_data-t_pd_str) + t_master_skew_max	5
	WR-HOLD	T_bit/2	0	t_IH_slave + (t_pd_str-t_pd_data) + (-1*t_master_skew_min)	5
Clock Forwarding	RD-SU	T_clk	t_pd_clk	t_ISU_master + t_OD_max_slave + t_pd_data	
	RD-HOLD	0	t_OD_min_slave + t_pd_data	t_IH_master + t_pd_clk	
	WR-SU	T_clk	t_pd_clk	t_ISU_slave + t_OD_max_master + t_pd_data	
	WR-HOLD	0	t_OD_min_master + t_pd_data	t_IH_slave + t_pd_clk	
Unidir. Synch.	WR-SU	T_clk	t_pd_clk	t_ISU_slave + t_OD_max_master + t_pd_data	
	WR-HOLD	0	t_OD_min_master + t_pd_data	t_IH_slave + t_pd_clk	
Embedded Clk (SERDES)	WR-SU	T_clk/2	unknown	unknown	4
	WR-HOLD	T_clk/2	unknown	unknown	4

TABLE 10.4

Maximum Data Rate Calculation Table (MDCT), Look Up the Interface Type → Get Equation for Max Data Rate

Interface Type	Case	t_available	Minimum bit time	Max data rate	Final max data rate
Synchronous	RD-SU	T_clk	t_avail_min	1/ t_avail_min	Take lowest max DR value
	RD-HOLD	0	n/a	n/a	
	WR-SU	T_clk	t_avail_min	1/ t_avail_min	
	WR-HOLD	0	n/a	n/a	
Asynchronous	RD-SU	RD# pulse-width	t_avail_min	1/ t_avail_min	Take lowest max DR value
	RD-HOLD	0	n/a	n/a	
	WR-SU	WR# pulse-width	t_avail_min	1/ t_avail_min	
	WR-HOLD	0	n/a	n/a	
Source Synch.	RD-SU	T_bit/2	2* t_avail_min	0.5/ t_avail_min	Take lowest max DR value
	RD-HOLD	T_bit/2	2* t_avail_min	0.5/ t_avail_min	
	WR-SU	T_bit/2	2* t_avail_min	0.5/ t_avail_min	
	WR-HOLD	T_bit/2	2* t_avail_min	0.5/ t_avail_min	
Clock Forwarding	RD-SU	T_clk	t_avail_min	1/ t_avail_min	Take lowest max DR value
	RD-HOLD	0	n/a	n/a	
	WR-SU	T_clk	t_avail_min	1/ t_avail_min	
	WR-HOLD	0	n/a	n/a	
Unidir. Synch.	WR-SU	T_clk	t_avail_min	1/ t_avail_min	Take lowest max DR value
	WR-HOLD	0	n/a	n/a	
Embedded Clk	WR-SU	T_clk/2	2* t_avail_min	0.5/ t_avail_min	Take lowest max DR value
	WR-HOLD	T_clk/2	2* t_avail_min	0.5/ t_avail_min	

margins. Then we have to calculate the actual programmable intervals. Finally, we have to determine the number of system clock cycles needed for each. The result will have to be programmed into the bus interface control registers, as part of the firmware code.

The programming value calculation is described step by step below:

1) Obtain the four sets of parameter sets from the TAP table, for asynchronous RD/WR and SU/H cases.
2) Calculate all four required times for the four cases, by filling parameters into this equation:
   t_required = t_degrading – t_improving + t_err
3) Calculate the Minimum Strobe Pulse Width, the larger of t_pulse_RD#, t_pulse_WR#:
   MSPW = MAX (t_required_RDSU, t_required_WRSU).
   N_clk_MSPW=round(t_required/t_clk_period)
4) Calculate the Programmable Hold Time:
   PHT = MAX (t_required _RDH, t_required _WRH).
   N_clk_PTH=round(t_required/t_clk_period)
5) Calculate the Address Setup Time:
   TASU = t_required _WRSU
   N_clk_TASU=round(t_required/t_clk_period)
6) Program the bus interface with the three numbers above, N_clk_MSPW, N_clk_PTH, and N_clk_TASU.
7) Calculate the Max Data Rate:
   DRMAX = 1 / (f_clk*(N_clk_MSPW+ N_clk_PTH+ N_clk_TASU))

10.2.5 Complete System, Timing Graphs

Timing graphs can help us understand the timing architecture of a particular design and also helps us writing up timing equations. An I/O timing calculation is always concerned with two signals: the data/information signal (data, address, command, and call it "data" here) and the reference signal (clock or strobe). The data signal always propagates from the launch flip-flop to the capture flip-flop. It is usually a group of signals, so the timing requirements have to be met for each one of them. The reference/clock signal always propagates from a clock generator to both the launch and the capture flip-flop. This creates two paths: the data-path and the reference-path. We can see this concept in Figure 10.15. The data path consists of trace segments both in the clock signal (from the clock generator to the launch flip-flop) and in the data signal traces. It is important to not mix up "signal" with "path". Both paths originate at the clock generator and end at the capture flip-flop's clock pin inside the receiver chip I/O circuits. They may propagate through multiple circuit nets. The flip-flop clock-to-output and input-setup and input-hold delays have to be included in the paths, this way both signals propagate between the same two points in the system. The start point is the clock generator, and the end point is the capture flip-flop CK pin. In some types of interfaces, the reference signal may propagate to a slave device through a second flip-flop—the strobe-generation flip-flop—instead of through basic buffering. We can treat the digital I/O circuit as a graph, as from graph theory in mathematics, and "walk" through it in two different paths, while measuring the delays in each step in each path. The difference between the sums of delays in the two paths will be the timing margin, minus the errors and noises.

The definition of the data path: the signal propagation path from the start point (on the diagram) to the capture flip-flop's CK pin through the capture flip-flop's D-pin. The reference path is from the start point to the capture flip-flop's CK pin without going through the D-pin. Both paths can be walked only in the direction of the signal propagation only. Both paths may include any number of flip-flops between the clock generator and the launch/capture flip-flop's CK pin. However, between the launch flip-flop and the capture flip-flop, no more flip-flops can be included since they would break the timing paths to separate paths. From the reference clock generator to the flip-flop's CK pin there are exactly two valid paths through the system. The one approaching through the D input pin of the capture flip-flop is the data path, the other one is the reference path. If we find a third path, then one of the existing ones is not valid.

We have to introduce a convention here to simplify the graph-based analysis. We have to use a negative value for the input hold requirement (t_IH → -1 * t_IH). This way we will get correct values during both the setup and the hold timing analysis, we can use the same end point and therefore the same graph for both setup and hold. Otherwise, the setup graph will end at the capture flip-flop's clock pin while the hold graph will end on the D pin. But with this "minus hold trick" both graphs end on the clock pin, so we can use the same single graph. This is needed only for the graphical

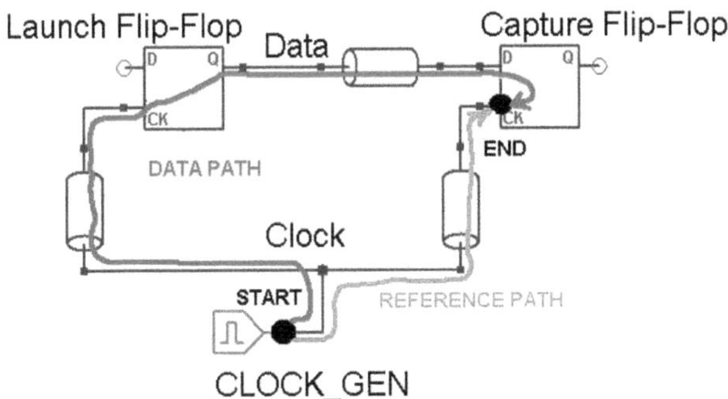

FIGURE 10.15 Timing graph on a simplified synchronous data path.

analysis with the graph; the calculations in the TAP table do not require it, and chip datasheets do not follow it either.

Ideally, to be able to perform the timing analysis with timing graphs, we need to know all the on-chip delays, which is usually not available. If the chip datasheet specifies a skew between the data and the reference signal, then we might transform it to on-chip delays. These delays might not be real, but they will give us a correct final result. For example, we can choose t_OD_ref=0 and then we can use t_OD_data=t_skew. If some of the delay elements in either of the two paths are identical, then they can also be eliminated in the analysis. This way we do not really need to know exact delays for everything in the system. Chip/board designers can take an advantage of this fact by using identical (matched with a tolerance) trace lengths and use identical I/O circuits on-chip for signals included in the two paths. Chip designers may improve or simplify the timing by copying a segment into one of the paths from the other path. For example, using drivers with similar I/O buffer characteristics for both the clock and the data, or introducing a flip-flop in the reference path (since the data path always has a flip-flop). A flip-flop in the reference path does not break (segregate) the path, which would happen only in the data path. The segment of both paths, which is from the clock generator until the point where the two paths split, can be ignored. The schematics diagrams in the examples are simplified views of the I/O circuits, but they contain enough details to let us perform the graph-based timing analysis.

Interface types that support timing calibration using delay-locked-loops (DLLs) can shift the data signal until both SU/H margins become positive. Without DLLs the chip designers can still delay data signals by whole clock periods using a flip-flop. If one of the margins (setup or hold) is negative, then we have to shift both of them by the same amount and opposite direction until both becomes positive, if possible.

To perform the analysis, we have to write a delay budget on both paths from the start until the end point, to get t_del_data and t_del_ref. This is basically a weighted graph, where we have to determine the weight of the two paths between the start and the end points, by summing up every delay element in the path. The error/noise parameters come from SI analysis, datasheets, or earlier projects. After this, we can calculate the remaining margins as:

```
0 ≤ t_SU_MAR = t_bit + t_del_ref - t_del_data - t_err
0 ≤ t_H_MAR = t_del_data - t_del_ref - t_err
```

The t_bit parameter is equal to the clock period for single-data-rate systems (SDR), and it is equal to half the clock period for dual-data-rate (DDR) interfaces. For single data rate synchronous systems, if the falling edge is used to launch the data and the rising edge is used for capturing, or the opposite combination, then it means that there is an inverter in the system, and maybe also an extra clock buffer/tree. Theoretically this would reduce the available time for setup by half a bit time, but increase the available time for hold from zero to also half a bit time.

Both paths will include PCB traces as well, and their signal integrity effects. As mentioned earlier, the propagation delay t_pd has two components, the flight time (FT) and the transition delay (TD). Further, the TD is dependent on exact logic thresholds crossings and might be different for rise and fall waveforms. We can run simulations with different model settings, the slow setting would be used for setup analysis, the fast setting for hold analysis.

10.3 TIMING ARCHITECTURES

The structure or architecture, which the PCB traces, flip-flops, PLLs, buffers and other parts are arranged into, has a strong effect on meeting timing margins, or pushing up the speed limitations. The bus speed is limited by many parameters, but even if we use the fastest chips and best materials, there is still an inherent speed limit in some interface types and timing architectures. This limitation of different architectures is illustrated in Figure 10.16. With real chips those limits are even

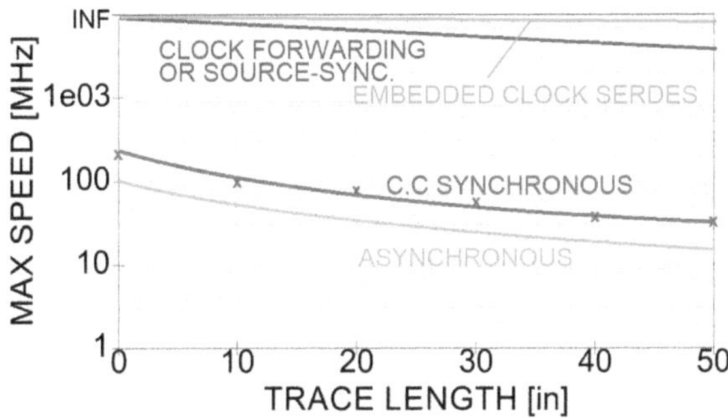

FIGURE 10.16 Rough estimate on speed capability versus trace length, for different timing.

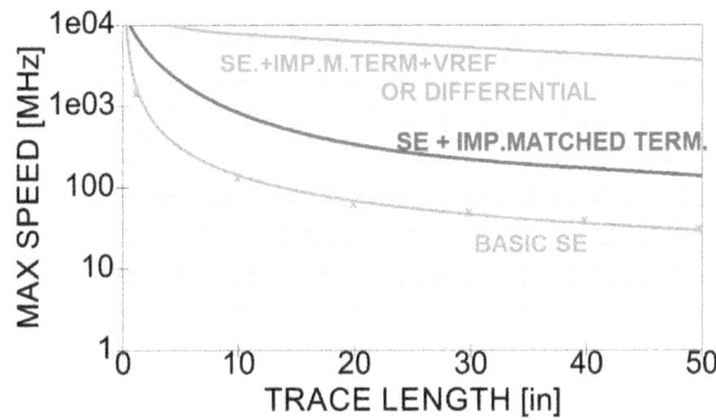

FIGURE 10.17 Rough estimate on speed capability versus trace length, for different signaling and termination schemes.

lower than on the diagram. Synchronous and asynchronous systems are limited by the round-trip delay through PCB traces and setup timing. Clock forwarding and source-synchronous interfaces are limited by signal-to-signal delay mismatch. Embedded clock (SERDES) interfaces are unlimited, except for skew, accumulated on PCBs. Even with rotation and dual ply spread glass prepregs 1ps/in skew is expected. With basic PCBs and no rotation, a several ps/in skew is accumulated on some traces on some random units in the worst case. The theoretical maximum speed depends on the architecture, the trace lengths, and the component capabilities.

Speed is also limited by the I/O buffer type, signal integrity (losses, reflections, crosstalk), and termination schemes, as we can see in Figure 10.17. The available solution space is under the curves, while above the curves it will fail. Without termination the reflection arrival time becomes such that it interferes with the signal in the middle of the bit time. Even with termination we get plateaus that can interfere with logic level detection, but using a single reference voltage threshold solves that. Using point-to-point links only, instead of multi-drop buses, eliminates the plateaus and we do not have to wait for a reflected wave, so we could achieve twice the maximum speed. Differential signaling also solves the threshold problems, but are still limited at higher rates by insertion loss and inter-symbol interference.

10.3.1 Design Elements to Control Timing

We (board hardware designer) can control delays on the board using trace length constraints in the PCB layout design. These can be absolute lengths or relative, both in a given range. The chip designers control delays in various complex ways too. We need to know what controls were in place, or what to request.

PCB trace length control with timing constraints is the most obvious way to control the signal arrival time to the capture flip-flop on a board-level interface. The delay on a trace is equal to the t_pd propagation delay. As discussed earlier, this delay is made of two main portions: the transition delay (TD), which is related to signal rise/fall times to the logic thresholds, and the flight-time (FT), which is proportional to the trace length. If the traces are longer then FT is proportionally longer, and it also depends on the stackup material dielectric constant. TD is also longer by a little amount, but not proportional and can be determined only from SI simulations. With zero length the TD is not zero—it depends on the silicon output buffer capability and the capacitive loading.

```
FT = TraceLength / (11.8 / SQRT(DK))
```

PCB constraints can be minimum absolute length (must route at least this long or longer) or maximum absolute length, but we can also use relative length or matching rules that define two or more signals.

The feedback clock is a great invention for common clock synchronous systems. All devices in synchronous systems use the same clock source to run their I/O and core flip-flops. For this, there is always one clock generator, and its output is distributed to every device on the same bus. If the bus is bi-directional, then the best way to balance the read/write setup/hold margins is to balance/match the propagation delays from the clock generator to all devices in the system. If there is a clock skew between two chips, then in one case (e.g., IC1 reads from IC2) the setup margin will increase by the skew amount and the hold margin decrease by the same amount, in the opposite case (e.g., IC1 writes to IC2) the margins increase/decrease the opposite way. For that reason, we always want to minimize the clock skew to be much less than the input setup and hold requirements by length matching the clocks within +/-5 to 40mils. In case when the "master" (e.g., CPU) generates and provides the I/O clock to the "slave" (e.g., SDRAM memory), the clock length from the generator to the master will be zero (since it is inside the master), and the clock length to the slave will be equal to the clock trace length on the board, so the length difference (clock skew) will be equal to the clock length from the master to the slave. The skew can be reduced by adding a delay to the clock signal from the generator to the master chip, without adding that to the slave device's clock signal. Some chips support a "feedback clock" input pin (like the PI7C9X130 PCIe/PCI bridge chip), where we can connect our delayed clock signal. We can delay it by routing it through a long, controlled trace on the board. The I/O circuits of the master chip, which contains the clock generator, is not directly clocked from its own internal clock generator; rather, it is clocked from the feedback clock pin. Figure 10.18 shows this concept. As we can see all three chips receive the clock signal through the length matched traces labeled as t_pd1 to 3.

The PLL (Phase-Locked Loop, a chip-level design element) can be used on continuously running clocks to introduce phase delays in degrees, negative delays, or frequency multiplication. The

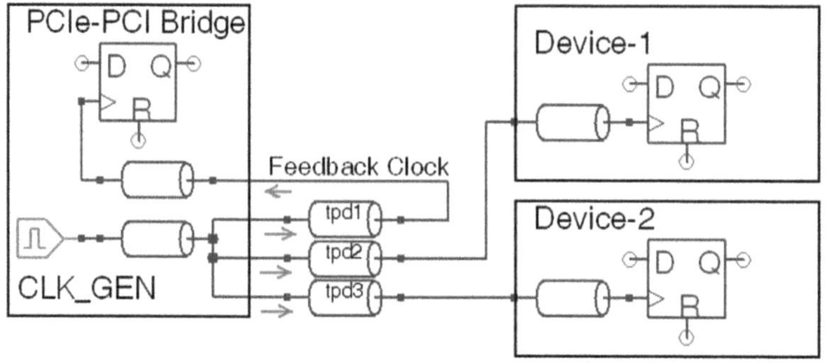

FIGURE 10.18 Using a feedback clock to eliminate clock skew.

PLL controls its output signal's phase to maintain zero phase difference between its two inputs (IN and FBin). PLLs usually contain some kind of a modifier element in their feedback loop, between the output and the FBin pin, as we can see in Figure 10.19. If this modifier element is a frequency divider (by M), then the PLL will generate an output clock that has a higher frequency at M*f_in. If the modifier is a delay element, then the FBin will be delayed from the output by the same amount, in picoseconds or degrees. An absolute delay K on a clock is identical to an absolute delay of Tclk-K since every period is identical. A whole number of clock cycles can be ignored. It is more useful to look at clock delays as a 0 to 360 degree phase delay. Since the two inputs are always in phase, an X-delay of the feedback loop would be an X delay on the FBIN input and on the IN input. This way the input is delayed relative to the output, which means the output is delayed by 360-X degrees, which is identical to a negative amount of -X degree delay. This is how PLLs achieve negative delay, set by a trace or delay element in the feedback loop. We can compensate for a positive delay already existing in the system by adding the same amount of negative delay using a PLL. Common examples of PLL phase delay tricks are the zero delay clock buffer chips, on-chip zero delay clock distribution networks, and providing negative delayed clocks to A/D converters. Some converters require us to provide a negative delayed clock. We can utilize PLLs in FPGA chips that we already have on the board or design in an FPGA just for using its PLL. The zero-delay clock buffer is a 1-in multi-out clock fanout buffer chip that has its input and output clock signals in phase. This is useful when we want to add one more clock signal to the board, without delaying the clock and ruining the timing. I/O interface controller blocks on FPGA designs should utilize PLLs to improve their "datasheet" timing parameters by feeding the IOB flip-flops from an on-chip PLL that is in a zero delay arrangement.

Board designers have to be aware of the on-chip clock distribution networks. All chip designs have common clock synchronous on-chip logic circuits. To maintain the best timing for all data paths, the chips contain clock buffers with delivery networks that follow a balanced tree topology, so the clock will arrive to each flip-flop on the chip with the same t_pd. The clock tree has a rather large delay between the source and the destinations. Normally there is an option to place a PLL before the clock buffer with the same delay but with a negative sign as the clock delivery network has to form a zero delay clock buffer. This is done by connecting one of the many end points to the FBin pin of the PLL. This is demonstrated in Figure 10.20. This way the combination of the PLL with the clock buffer and delivery tree will have zero phase delay. This is especially important when we are trying to run several flip-flops from a clock that arrives from another chip as part of a synchronous bus on the PCB. This will improve the FPGA design's input setup/hold requirements and the output setup times. By neutralizing the massive clock buffer delay, we can ensure that the I/O capture flip-flops will have the same phase relationship between the arriving clock and data as the chip pins see it.

We can feed a clock with a "negative delay" into a device. Figure 10.21 shows an example of the use of a negative delayed clock that is sent out to an A/D converter so when it sends the data to the FPGA it will arrive in sync with the internal clock inside the FPGA. The feedback clock trace is routed between two pins of the same device, but it is expected to be routed to a certain trace length t_pd3, which is twice as much as the ADC clock t_pd2 and the data t_pd1 lengths. This way the FPGA receives data with t_pd1+t_pd2 round-trip delay, while that round-trip delay starts with the same amount of negative delay, resulting in a zero delay between points G–A.

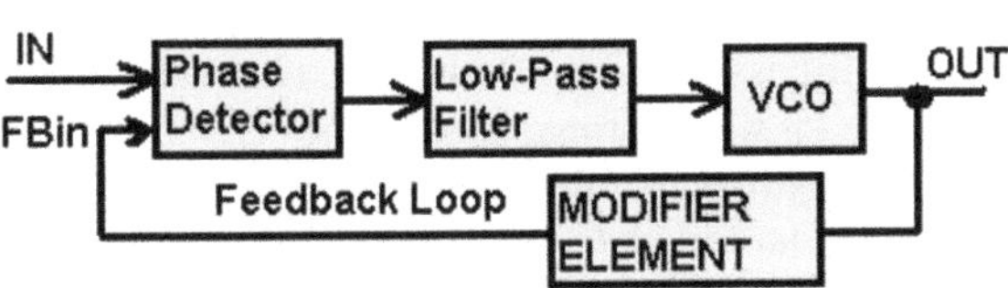

FIGURE 10.19 PLL.

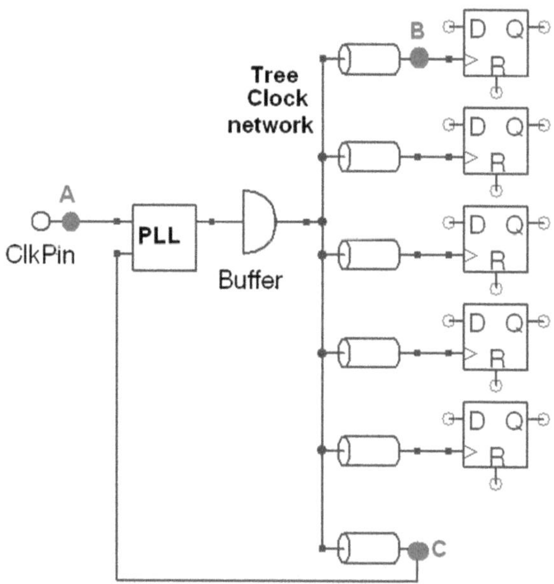

FIGURE 10.20 On-chip clock tree network with PLL. Delays A–B and A–C are balanced.

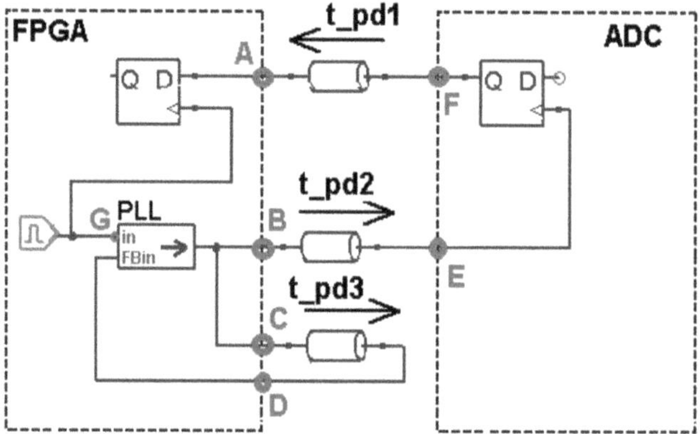

FIGURE 10.21 Using PLL to create a negative propagation delay.

The DLL (Delay Locked Loop, on-chip device) is a fixed or an adjustable delay element on-chip, usually programmable. It has "taps"; each tap has a unit delay value. It is used in many DDRx memory interfaces to adjust the strobe signal to the-data signal and to support timing calibration like "read leveling". The number of delay elements switched in our out of a chain determines the delay, and the switching circuits can be controlled from a programmable register.

Registers can be added to produce whole clock cycle delays. The static timing data path ends in a capture flip-flop. A data path with a certain delay in it can be divided into two separate paths by inserting a flip-flop into it. FPGA designers often refer to the flip-flops as "registers"—it is not the software read/write register we discussed earlier. Both of the two paths after a division by a register will have the same available time for signal propagation as the original path had, but with only some of the original delay. A part of it is included now in the first segment while the remaining part is included in the second segment. If the path delay is long for some reason (for example, long traces or long transition delays), then we can make the data path or interface to be more reliable by dividing it to two parts. Note that the data will arrive one bit time or one clock cycle later (latency) to the final capture flip-flop, but it will be captured with better static timing margins. This technique is usually used on high speed on-chip data processing, and also on registered DIMM (RDIMM) card designs. In registered DIMM memory cards, the address bus signals arrives from the CPU through the motherboard and incur some delay. On the DIMM card there is a long way to go through the long fly-by bus to reach every single DRAM chip. If it is a dual rank card, then driving two separate buses might be a good idea too. By designing in a register, this path is broken up into two. What motherboard designers can do, is to decide whether to use registered DIMMs or "un-buffered" DIMMs.

10.3.2 Topology Diagrams

On topology diagrams, we can easily visualize the delays between any two points on a multi-point bus/net, and they also tell us how the net has to be routed on the board. Some standards specify PCB design rules on topology diagrams, for example, DDR-SDRAM DIMM memory card designs (various JEDEC JESD21C documents) or chipset motherboard design guides. For layout design we define the topology as a diagram (graphical), plus Pin-Pair-based trace length constraints (numerical). The capable layout tool measures the length of trace segments connecting the given two pins but ignores trace segments that are leading to other components/pins. An already routed board net topology can be visualized by extracting a topology, for example, to Cadence Signal Explorer or HyperLynx LineSim. It will show pins as buffers and trace segments as transmission line schematic symbols.

An example of a topology applicable to DIMM memory modules and memory-down layouts can be seen in Figure 10.22. The JEDEC JESD21C standards specify a few different topologies for designing standard DIMM memory modules, and also the trace length rules for them.

Add-in cards have specific considerations for timing and trace lengths. If a signal or bus is routed through multiple boards, then the timing and length rules have to be correct for the whole system together, chip to chip. If the boards are designed by different people or different companies, then they have to agree in the way of dividing the timing or PCB length constraints between the boards. This is how some add-in card form-factor standards specify trace lengths. Usually, these lengths are related to a skew in a clock tree, or a data bus stub length (signal integrity related rule). In case of the clock tree, if we make sure that the add-in card clock trace length is the same for all cards, then the skew can be controlled by the motherboard design, as we can see in Figure 10.23. Because all of these clocks have similar drivers and trace lengths, the propagation delay and the transition delay will be also very similar, so we do not need to do signal integrity simulation for this, we can decide the propagation delay matching by the trace lengths. On the example the designers of the two add-in

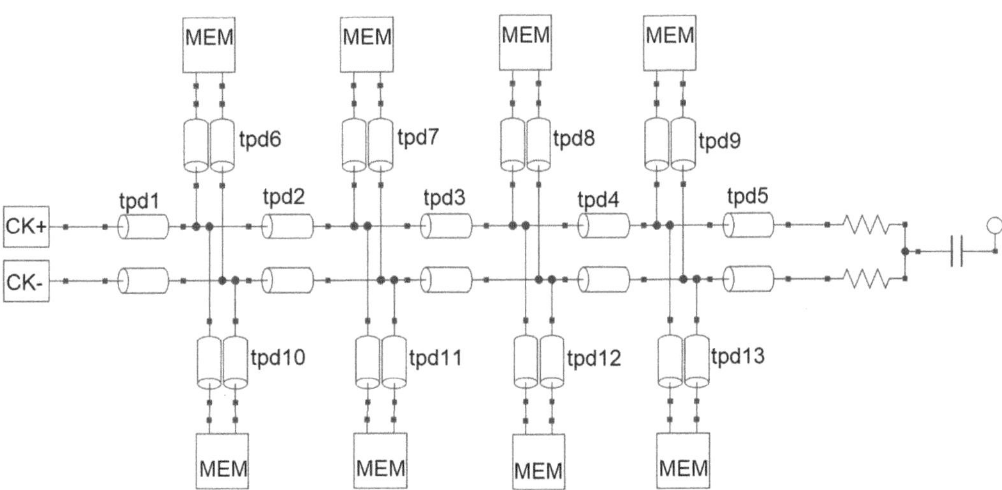

FIGURE 10.22 Clock net topology for DDR3 memory (sketch in QUCS).

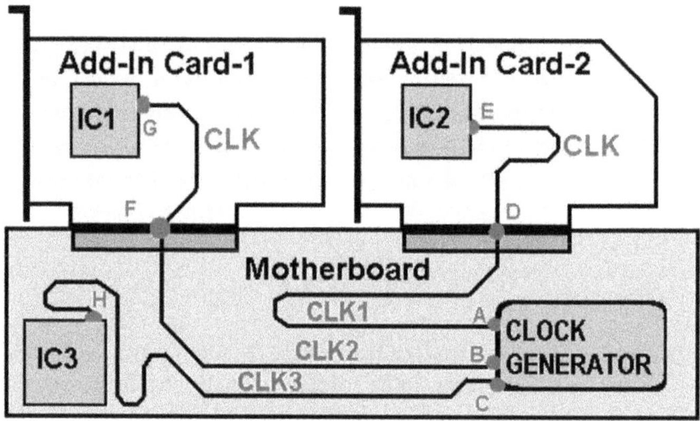

FIGURE 10.23 Add-in card clock matching example.

cards have to route the F-G and D-E traces to be a specific length within tight tolerance, for example 2.5"+/-0.04". Then the motherboard designer has to ensure that the three clock traces will be matched to each other within +/-0.04", while applying an offset of +2.5" to the CLK3 trace. We would set up a matched group in the Cadence Allegro Constraint Manager. All signals will have tolerance=0.04", the CLK1 and CLK2 signals will have a delta=0, but the CLK3 signal will have a delta=-2.5".

10.3.3 Main Interface Types

Chip-to-chip interfaces have to deal with board-level timing, and they are start/end in I/O pin flip-flops inside the chips. Often they contain additional logic to help the timing closure, and they require trace length constraints for board design. This can be implemented in several different ways, depending on cost, available technology, and need for speed. The different implementations are the different timing architectures or interface types, and they are chosen by the chip designers.

10.3.3.1 Common Clock Synchronous Interfaces

Previously we saw a simple example for a synchronous system. Other examples are Single-Data rate SDRAM, PCI-bus, SPI bus, etc. The main feature of the common clock synchronous systems is that all data launch and capture happen on the edge of the free-running clock (reference signal), which is routed to every device on the bus. This clock is always running, not only during bus transactions. The chip-level logic design is always synchronous.

In most cases the rising edge of the clock is used, although there are systems where they make use of both edges. In these cases, for example, they launch the data at the falling edge and capture at the rising edge. Then the full available time for both setup and hold is half the data period. This can be useful when the bus is slow, and there are potential hold violations, due to uncontrolled trace or cable lengths, so this arrangement balances the setup and hold margins. If only one edge is used, then the full available time for the setup side is equal to the date period (also equals to the clock period) and the full available time for hold equals to zero, relying on non-zero delays.

In synchronous interfaces all components on the board are clocked from the same clock generator. The clock propagation delay to each flip-flop in the system is preferred to be equal. This is why we match the clock trace lengths from the clock generator to every device, for example, in a PCI-based system. If they are not balanced, then either the setup or the hold margin is reduced by the difference for a read transaction, and the other margin has to be reduced for a write transaction. In many cases the master chip provides the clock to the slave (for example a processor to an SPI flash memory). This means the clock delivery is no longer balanced; the slave device will see the clock edge delayed by the clock trace propagation delay.

On an already laid-out board, if we increase the clock frequency, it will reduce the setup margins but leaves the hold margin unchanged. The clock frequency where the setup margins (read or write) reach zero is the maximum clock frequency at which the system can operate. We can help on setup violations by decreasing the clock frequency, but the hold violation can be fixed only by proper propagation delay arrangements through trace length constraints.

Figure 10.24 shows the read and write transactions on timing graphs, helping us see what delays are involved. If the two chips are too far from each other, then during a read transaction the data path might have too much delay, called a round-trip delay. This consists of the clock having to reach the slave device, and the data from it having to reach the master device. If the bus delay or the clock frequency exceeds a certain value, then it causes a setup violation (less than zero margin) during a read transaction. This manifests itself either as a maximum trace length rule at given data rate or as a maximum data rate at the given trace lengths. If we have routed the data with less propagation delay than the clock or the clock generator is external and has a lot of skew, then it may cause a hold violation during a write transaction. The length where the hold violation occurs is the minimum length for the synchronous data bus.

Usual PCB design rules:

- Maximum data trace length: If this is exceeded, then one of the setup margins (read or write) will be negative and the interface will not work reliably.
- Minimum data trace length: If it is shorter than this, then one of the hold margins will be negative. In most of the cases the minimum trace length is negative, so it is very easy

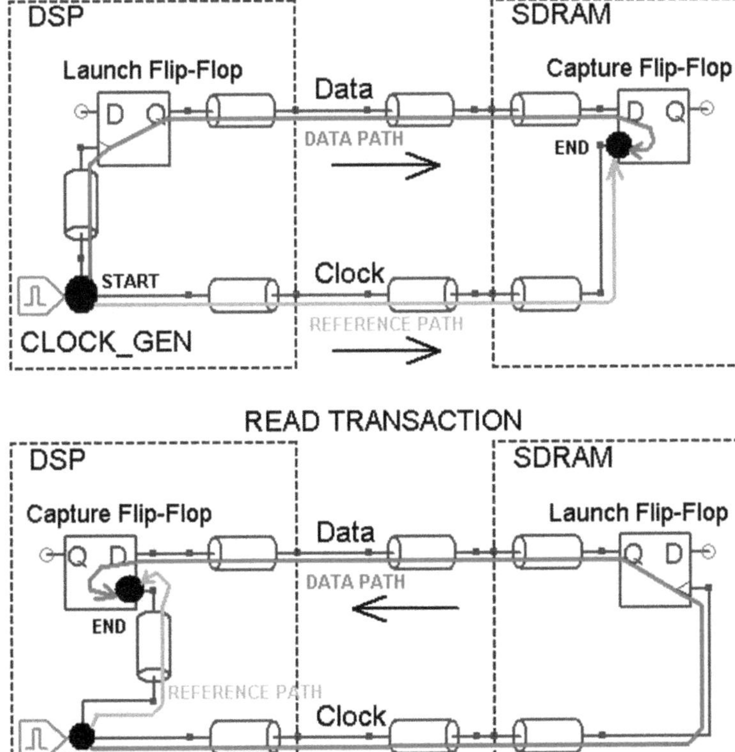

FIGURE 10.24 Synchronous SDRAM interface timing graphs.

to design a PCB where the traces are longer than this, although it is worth calculating it because this is not always the case. We can easily route a trace that is longer than minus 2 inches, even a 0.2" trace is longer than that.
- Maximum clock trace length (if there is no feedback clock) or maximum skew between clock traces (if there is): The value of this is always subtracted from the timing budget, and it may possibly violate write hold timing, so we need to keep it small.

10.3.3.2 Asynchronous Interfaces

Examples of asynchronous systems are the parallel peripheral buses of microcontrollers and DSPs, with separate read and write strobes, without a clock signal going to the slave devices. Sometimes there is an address-latch (ALE) strobe as well if the data and the address buses are multiplexed. The main feature of the asynchronous systems is that data launch happens on the falling edge of the strobe signal and capture happens on the rising edge of strobe signal. In some cases, the master can pre-launch the data to the bus before the WR# strobe assertion to improve on the write setup margin. These strobes are not always running—they assert and de-assert once per bus transaction. The master generates the strobes. The master's chip-level logic design is always a common clock synchronous system internally—it schedules the strobes based on its internal clock, with programmable intervals, called strobe pulse width. They usually have programmable "setup time" and programmable "hold time" as well. The software engineer has to program this into the master's bus interface control registers, but the hardware engineer calculates it. In this context the setup time means a programmable interval (number of internal clock cycles) when the slave is addressed/selected but the strobe is not asserted yet. The hold time here means that after a strobe de-assertion, the slave remains selected (for read or write) and the write data remain on the bus for a while, to improve on the hold margins. The input requirements are measured from/to the capture edge, which is usually the rising edge of the active low strobe, aka the de-assertion. Output guaranteed timing is measured from the launch edge, which is usually the falling edge or assertion of the strobe. Very often the output setup time of the slave is called "Access Time" (t_acc) because it includes the time it takes to access the data bits inside the slave device. The read data on the bus are de-asserted by the slave as the effect of the RD# strobe de-assertion, although they remain on the bus for t_OH. The data might be captured in a D-type flip-flop (inside the master) or by a transparent latch (inside the slave).

The chip timing parameters do not just come from the datasheets rather the chosen programmed intervals have to be also included. The t_available for setup is equal to the strobe pulse width (+ "programmable setup time" for writes); while for the hold it is equal to the programmable hold time.

Figure 10.25 shows the read and write transactions on timing graphs, helping us to see the delays that are involved. The timing diagrams for them can be seen in Figure 10.26 and in Figure 10.27.

Usual PCB design rules:

- Maximum data bus length: The same as for the synchronous interface type.
- Minimum data bus length: The same as for the synchronous interface type.

10.3.3.3 Source-Synchronous Interfaces

In SS interfaces, for every transaction type (read or write), the reference signal (strobe) is generated by the actual device that is driving the data signals at the time. The most common example of source-synchronous systems are the DDRx-SDRAM memory data buses.

For a usual synchronous system, the biggest length limitation is coming from the read setup timing budget due to round-trip delay. The source synchronous interfaces do not have this problem since they have the data and the reference signal propagating in the same direction for all bus transactions. The only length limitation for these systems comes from length mismatch between the data and the strobe, but that is easier to ensure and not sensitive to board size and floorplan. If the data is much longer than the strobe, then it can cause setup violations, if it is much shorter than the strobe then it can cause hold violations.

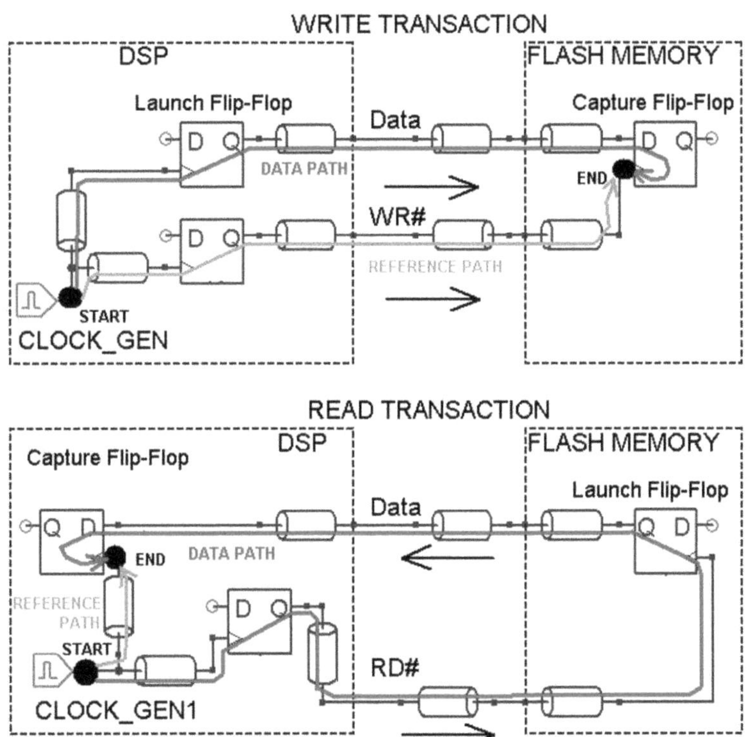

FIGURE 10.25 Timing graphs for a typical asynchronous DSP peripheral bus.

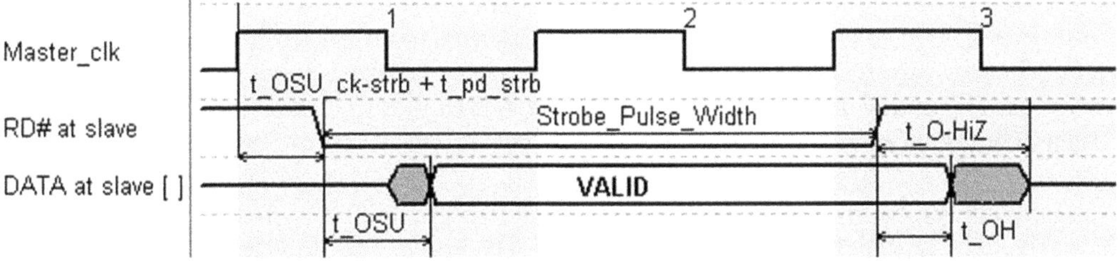

FIGURE 10.26 Asynchronous interface, read transaction timing.

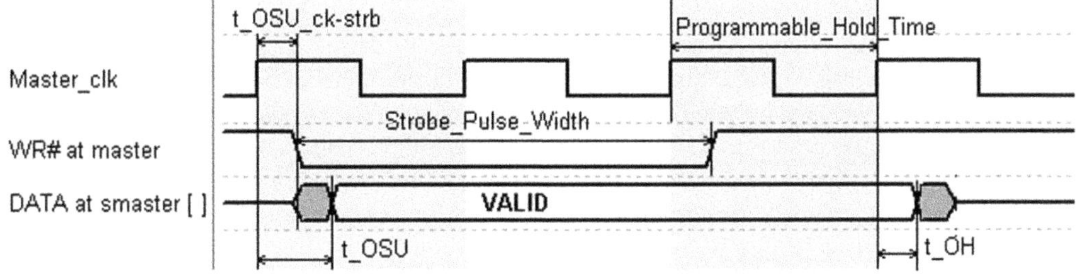

FIGURE 10.27 Asynchronous interface, write transaction timing.

The DDR-SDRAM memory strobe signals are generated by flip-flops clocked by the same clock as used for clocking the data flip-flops. The datasheets usually specify skew timing (delay difference) between the data and the strobe signals, so they do not specify the strobe and the data output delays separately. This way our timing calculations will be different—they will be based on relative timing or skew parameters.

DDRx memories use double data rate sampling, so their bit time is half a clock cycle, which means a half bit time delay is a 90-degree internal-clock phase delay. The SS interfaces are only source synchronous on the board; the chip I/O circuits convert the signals to the internal common clock synchronous domain. Because of the higher speeds, to maximize both the setup and hold margins, the architecture also balances them to be near equal. This requires the strobe to be delayed inside the controller, aligned into the middle of the bit time. Starting with DDR3, the 90-degree is not a fixed value, but calibrated, to fully balance the setup and hold timing, meaning aligning the strobe edge into the middle of the bit time (data valid window, horizontal eye opening). The delay is always done in the master, so for writes the strobe on the PCB is already 90-degree aligned to the data, while for reads the strobe is 0-degree aligned as it travels through the PCB, but receives the delay inside the controller input logic just before using it for sampling the data.

The PCB trace lengths can be derived from a c.c. synchronous system having only write transactions. If the reference (strobe) length is given, then we can calculate the minimum and the maximum trace lengths for the data. At speeds above 200MHz, we would find that the minimum data trace length is just a little bit less than the actual strobe trace length, and the maximum is just a little longer than the strobe length. We would also find that if the strobe trace is much longer, then the data also have to be much longer, but relative to the strobe the data will still be required to be no more than slightly shorter or longer. This realization gives the obvious idea of just matching the data to the strobe and ignoring the absolute length of each. As the bus speed increases, both the minimum and the maximum length values of the data signals get closer and closer to the length of the reference signal.

```
delta_length(+) < Max_Data_length - Strobe_length
delta_length(-) > Strobe_length - Min_Data_length
```

Figure 10.28 shows the read and write transactions on timing graphs, helping us see the delays that are involved. The timing diagrams for them can be seen in Figure 10.29 and in Figure 10.30.

Usual PCB design rules:

- Maximum strobe-to-data skew: We create a matched group of all signals, with the strobe labeled as "TARGET", all signals having zero delta and just 5mil tolerance. At 1GHz for DDR3 we already use 5mil as maximum mismatch, as it is easy to implement and still good at 5GHz for DDR5. Note that vias are a lot longer than this, so we have to route all signals of a matched group on the same layer.

10.3.3.4 Uni-directional Synchronous Interfaces

These are synchronous interfaces; however, the data is always driven by the same device, there are only write transactions. The analysis of these is exactly the same as the normal synchronous systems, except that we have only to do write setup and write hold analysis, no read setup or read hold, since there are no read transactions. Examples of uni-directional synchronous systems are ITUR-BT656 parallel digital video interface, or the DDRx-SDRAM memory address bus. It has the same advantages in high-speed timing as the source-synchronous interfaces have, and we can use the same PCB rules also.

Clock alignment: For higher speed interfaces, the transmitter can align the clock to a better position inside the data valid window to balance the setup and hold margins. This alignment can be done by a DLL (absolute delay) or a PLL (phase delay in degrees) circuit on-chip. Another way of clock alignment is to invert the clock that is transmitted to the slave, since it is equal to 180° phase

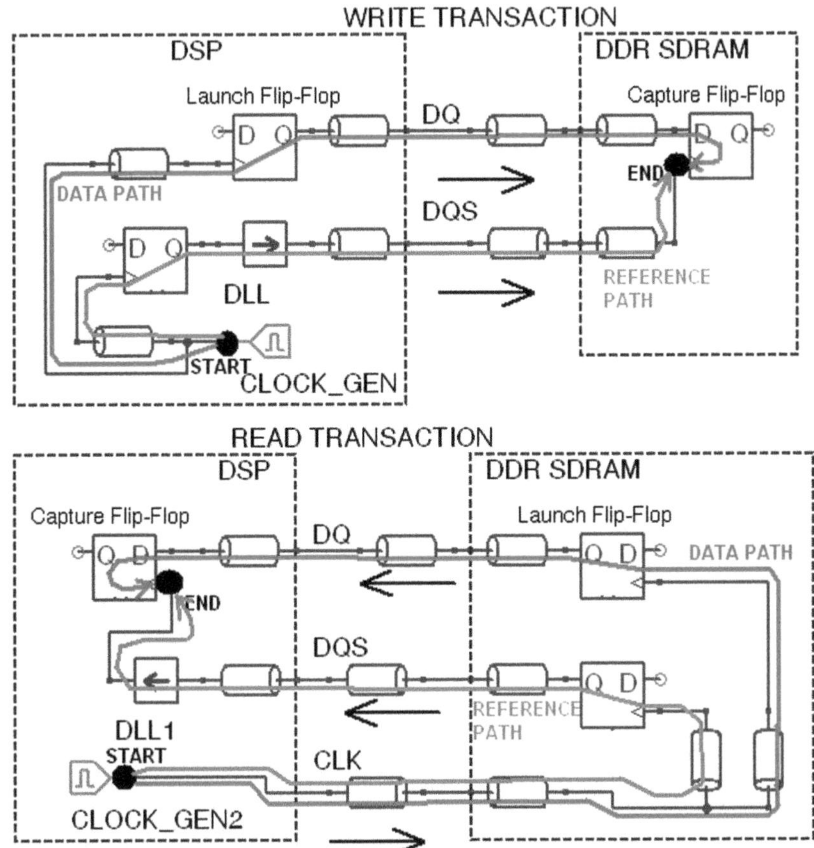

FIGURE 10.28 Timing graphs for a typical implementation of a source-synchronous DDR SDRAM interface.

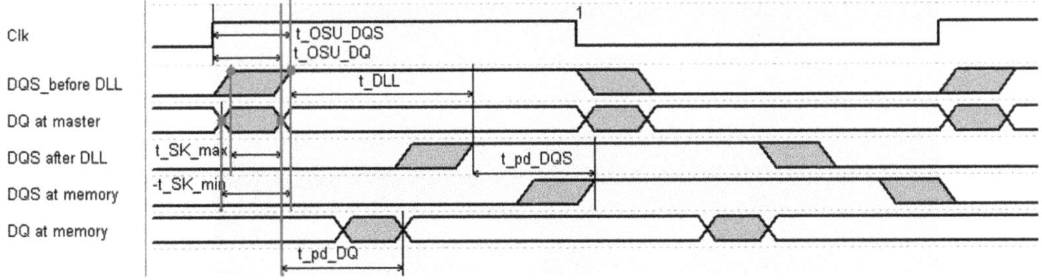

FIGURE 10.29 Source-synchronous interface, write timing.

shift, although that is not a solution to double-data-rate unidirectional-synchronous interfaces, like many medium-speed analog to digital converter chips (like the ADS5517) use. Figure 10.31 shows the transactions on timing graph, helping us see what delays are involved.

Usual PCB design rules:

- Maximum clock-to-data skew: The access on a uni-directional synchronous bus is always like a write access on a synchronous interface where the master supplies the clock to the slave device. If the reference length is given, then we can calculate a minimum and

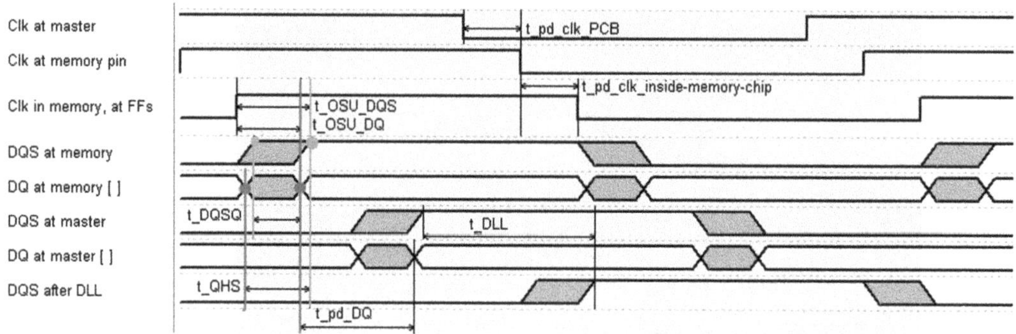

FIGURE 10.30 Source-synchronous interface, read timing.

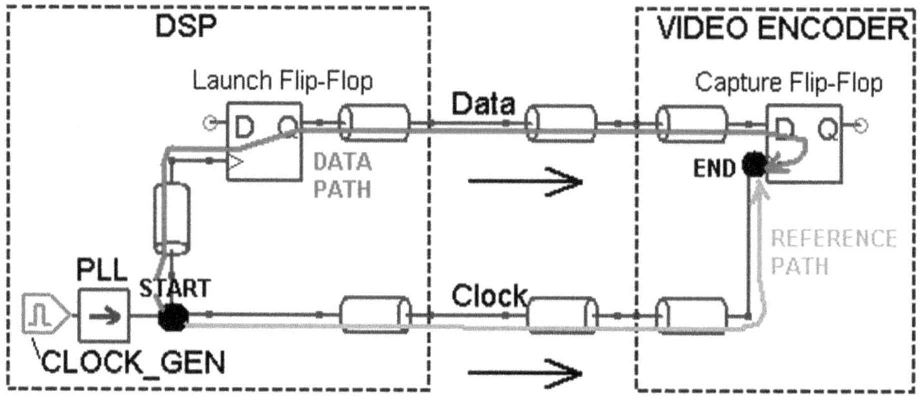

FIGURE 10.31 Timing graphs for a typical uni-directional synchronous interface.

a maximum data trace length. These can also be expressed in most (not all) cases as a relative length comparing to the reference signals' length, so it becomes a matching rule or maximum skew (t_pd difference) rule. As the bus speed increases, tighter matching is required.

10.3.3.5 Clock Forwarding (Source Clock) Interfaces

The clock-forwarding interfaces are basically two sets of uni-directional synchronous interfaces, one for read and one for write transactions. This includes a read data, a read clock, and a write data and write clock. The arriving data go through a clock domain crossing inside the chip, which is handled by using a FIFO buffer. A state machine in both devices has to reset the FIFO pointers after the PLL has locked to the arriving clock. If we want to simplify the chip design of one of the two devices, then we can use a loopback clock in that one device, which eliminates the clock domain crossing inside that device, basically feeding the write clock back as a read clock through the internal clock domain. We can see this scheme in Figure 10.32.

In some cases, the data bus might be multiplexed between read and write, while keeping separate read clock and write clock signals, to reduce the number of component pins required through bi-directional I/O buffers, as used on AMD's Hyper Transport 1.0 standard. The timing is not affected by this choice. We can see the timing graph for this architecture in Figure 10.33.

Usual PCB design rules:

- Maximum clock-to-data skew: The same rules apply as to the uni-directional synchronous buses.

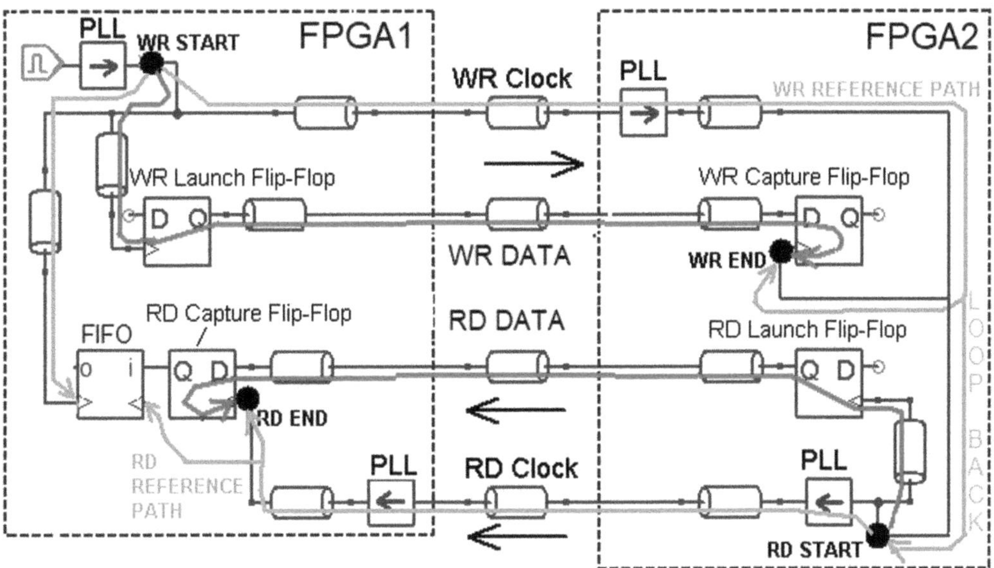

FIGURE 10.32 Timing graphs for a clock-forwarding interface with uni-directional data buses and clock loopback in one device.

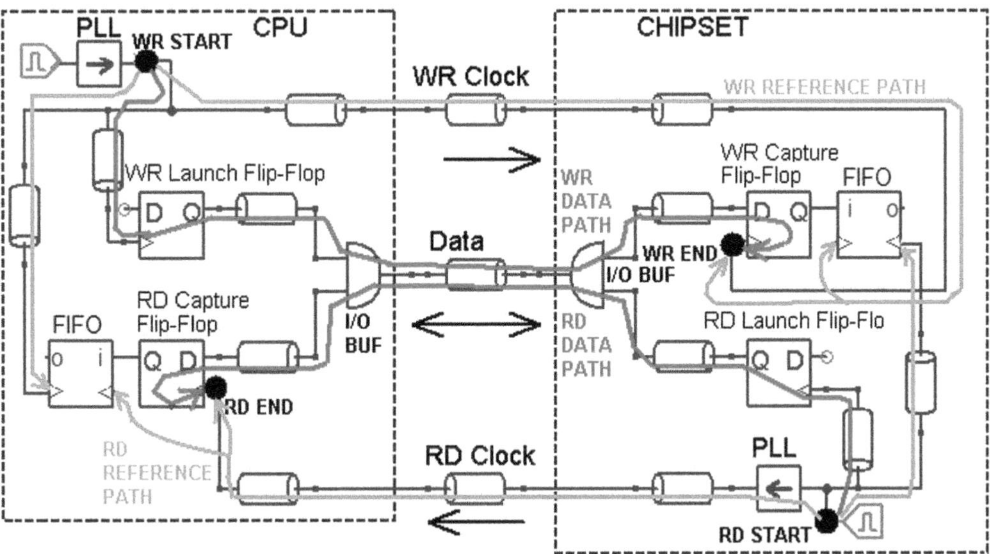

FIGURE 10.33 Timing graphs for a clock-forwarding interface with bi-directional data bus and separate reference clocks.

10.3.3.6 Embedded Clock Interfaces

These are also called high-speed SERDES transceivers, which are serial interfaces where the clocking information is embedded into the serialized data signal in the form of encoding and scrambling. They are implemented as differential pairs. There are no separate clock and data traces that would need length control or matching, but there are separate signals for read and for write transactions. The receiver device re-creates the clock signal from the data stream by using a clock-data recovery circuit and automatically aligns the clock into the center of the data eye.

We just have to make sure that the received eye is wide enough, as defined by the eye mask requirements. This is made of the input setup and hold requirements, although they publish only the total width of the mask in the datasheet. Examples are PCI-Express, SATA, and various types of Ethernet 10Gbps or above. The board designer does not have to deal with timing of these systems; although there are "trace length" related PCB design rules. The diffpair phase tolerance matching constraints reduce the P/N skew on the PCB, so only the Fiber Weave Effect skew remains. That can be further reduced by angled routing, using two-ply dielectrics in the stackup or panel rotation.

SERDES links are often multi-lane. This means there are several diffpairs in each direction. One RX pair and one TX pair together is one lane. Each diffpair has its own timing with their own embedded clocks, their own CDR circuits. Lane-to-lane matching requirements exist on some interfaces that do not have deep FIFOs on-chip, but usually very loose like +/-10". This is easy to meet and there is nothing to calculate for the board designer for timing analysis. The depth of the FIFO is a resource that is shared by several functions, like clock frequency difference compensation, clock domain crossing, and board skew compensation. The chip manufacturers specify how much skew they allow between different diffpairs.

Usual PCB design rules:

- Differential pair phase tolerance: matching the positive and negative leg of the pair, within 1 to 5mils.
- Board rotation or wavy routing, to reduce the skew caused by Fiber Weave Effect. Un-mitigated FWE can cause up to 50ps skew on long traces, which is more than the bit time at 25Gbps.
- Using two-ply spread glass prepregs in the stackup, to reduce the skew caused by Fiber Weave Effect.
- Maximum length rule, not from timing but from loss budget calculations. See the chapter about initial design.
- Lane-to-lane matching: The chip manufacturers specify how much skew they allow between different diffpairs, based on the internal design of the chip. If not specified then no requirement exists, but if we want to be safe we can use 2".

10.3.4 Custom Interfaces

In a real design we often use signal buffering, switching, deliberate delays, and multiple replaceable boards in a chassis, which makes the timing paths more complicated.

If we have any buffers and multiplexers in the signal path, they have to be included in the timing analysis. Lower speed buses (<50MHz) can be routed to different destinations in a programmable way through simple logic chips like buffers and analog multiplexers. Each buffer will divide a signal path into two independent channels in terms of signal integrity (transition delay), but maintain the same one single path for timing analysis, with an added buffer delay. Each analog multiplexer will maintain the same channel for both SI and timing and also adds a delay, so it can be modeled as a zero Ohm resistor or short in SI-simulation while we account for the internal chip delay in the timing calculation later. We will generate two separate t_pd numbers from two separate SI simulations, and then we add the buffer and multiplexer delays to calculate the total delay as:

```
t_pd_final = t_pd1 + t_pd2 + t_buf + t_mux
```

This is also demonstrated in Figure 10.34. Since multiplexers route to multiple possible devices, the SI and timing analysis both have to be done separately for all destinations or for all master-slave pairs. Buffer and multiplexer delays can be obtained from the chip datasheets.

Compact PCI is a form factor of processor and peripheral boards that we plug into a backplane/chassis, mainly used in the aerospace industry. Around 2010 they were more or less replaced with

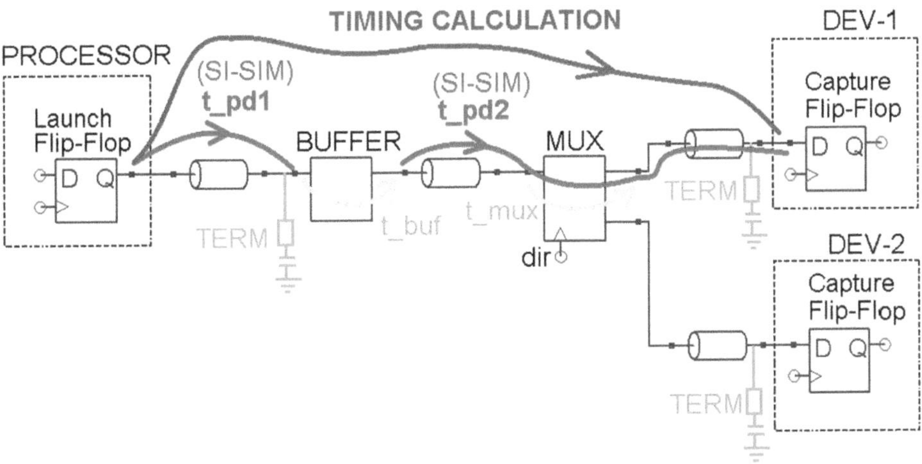

FIGURE 10.34 Slow bus with buffers and multiplexers.

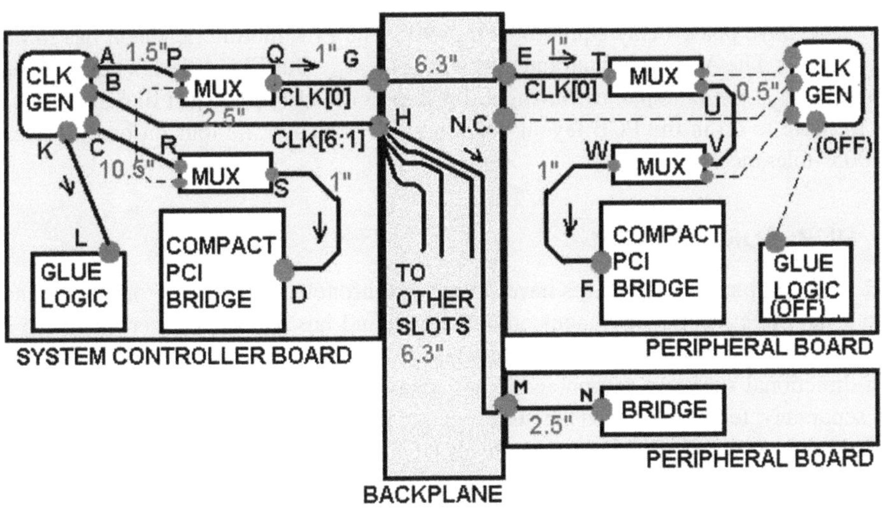

FIGURE 10.35 Compact PCI universal card clocking.

the VPX form factor, but it is educational to look at some of the timing solutions used in them. Processor cards can be plugged into host slots, where they have to provide PCI-bus I/O clock signals to the backplane, or they can be plugged into peripheral slots where they have to receive a clock form the backplane and use it in the bus bridge ASIC. The SYSCON signal from the backplane tells the card whether it is plugged into a host slot. This information is used by glue logic circuits to control backplane signal routing through multiplexers and ASIC device strapping. The PCI-bus I/O clocks have to be matched to +/-0.04" in all possible multiplexer routes, from the clock generator to each board's bridge ASIC. To help this implementation and promote card vendor compatibility, two rules are used: The backplane has 6.3+/-0.04" matched routes from the controller slot to every peripheral slot, and the peripheral cards have 2.5"+/-0.04" routes from the connector to the bridge ASIC. Figure 10.35 shows the clock nets and multiplexers. The hardware engineer has to ensure that the routes between E–F and M–N will be absolute 2.5"+/-0.04"; A-G will be matched to B–H, while C–D will be as long as 6.3"+2.5"+L_{A-G}. This will achieve the ultimate goal that is to match A–F to C–D within 0.04". It is heuristic, but we can iterate to a solution. We can for example allocate budgets to segments, route them to the defined length within +/-0.005", like the L_{QG}=1", the L_{AP}=1.5", then L_{BH}=2.5", the L_{SD}=1", which results in L_{AF}=L_{BN}=11.3", so we need L_{CR}=6.5+2.5+2.5-1=10.5" and L_{UV}=0.5". Note that L_{QG}=L_{ET}, and L_{SD}=L_{WF}, as those are the same traces on the same board design file but two different production units.

Some DAC chips require peculiar timing arrangements. The MB86065 digital-to-analog converter from Fujitsu receives the data as LVDS differential serialized signals from the host (e.g., an FPGA) and provides the I/O bit clock to the host. The DAC datasheet specifies the I/O timing as the data input and the clock output have to be in phase + 90°at the DAC chip pins. Because of the PCB propagation delays, they are completely out of phase at the FPGA pins, but the PCB and FPGA-logic designs have to provide correct timing measured at the DAC pins. The trick is to use a clock feedback net on the PCB with a length equal to the clock length plus the data length on the PCB. It is routed through the feedback pins of the DAC to achieve the same on-chip delays as the clock and data have on the DAC chip. This way we create a negative delay in the data path, the exact same amount but opposite sign as the clock and data signal routings have together. The PLL needs to have a 0° and a 90° output, the 0° will be used for the feedback loop; the 90° output will be used to clock the data out of the FPGA (output flip-flop or SERDES). This interface is a uni-directional synchronous interface, but the clock is provided by the receiver chip, which makes the clock delay to be negative comparing to a normal uni-directional synchronous interface. The delays are explained in Figure 10.36. The data path (AG) contains a segment DP inside the PLL which has a negative phase delay equal to -1*t_{QM}+90°. The PLL modifier element has to have the delay t_{QM}=t_{AD}+t_{PQ}. The ADC chip guarantees that t_{AB}+t_{FG}=t_{JK}. Our FPGA design has to ensure that t_{CD}=t_{LM} and t_{PE}=t_{QH}, for example, by having a flip-flop in the Q-H path, just like in the data path. Then all we have to do in the PCB layout constraints is to match the four on-board traces to be within 0.005" tolerance.

10.3.5 DDRx SDRAM Memory

The DDR-SDRAM memory interfaces have source-synchronous data buses grouped as lanes, and they have a uni-directional synchronous address/command bus. X is the generation, like DDR1, DDR2, etc. Timing only matters from chi to chip.

The bi-directional source-synchronous double data rate data bus timing has to be met in each byte lane separately; technically each lane is a separate bus. There are eight data signals and a data-mask signal in one lane, all sampled by the lane's DQS strobe signal, so all have to be matched to the DQS within 5mils.

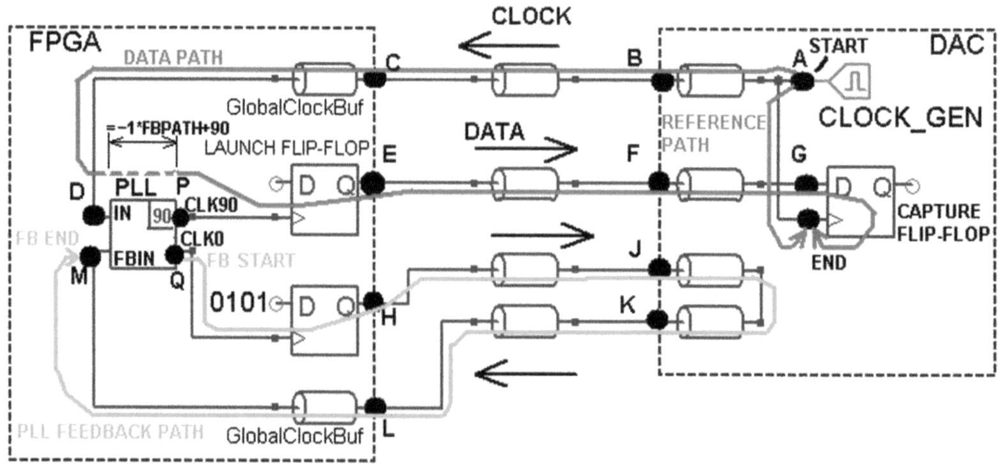

FIGURE 10.36 FPGA and MB86065 DAC interface timing graphs.

The uni-directional synchronous address/command/control (ACC) bus is sampled by the memory chips at the rising edges of the clock signal provided by the memory controller. Because of this the board designers have to match the ACC bus signals to the clock, in Pin-Pairs, between the controller and the first DRAM chip, and between the controller and the second… until the last one, which creates 8 to 16 matching groups with Pin-Pairs (not nets), depending on how many chips are in one channel. The ACC bus is routed to every memory chip in one memory channel in a multi-drop bus connection. For the old DDR1 and DDR2 standards the layout topology was a balanced-T (see Figure 10.37), while from DDR3 to 5 is it a fly-by topology (see Figure 10.38). If we design a motherboard with DIMM sockets on it, then we need only simple rules for the address bus, since the difficult part was implemented by the engineer who has designed the DIMM card. There can be one or two sets of chips attached to the same data bus, also called one or two ranks. Most medium to larger processors have 64-bit or 72-bit (8/9 lane) wide data buses with 4/8/16 memory chips in one rank depending on the data width per chip being 4/8/16-bits. All of the chips in all the ranks in one channel need the ACC bus to be connected to them. This is a very heavy load on the bus, with four to 96 chips. If the number of chips is above a certain value, then the system has to be designed

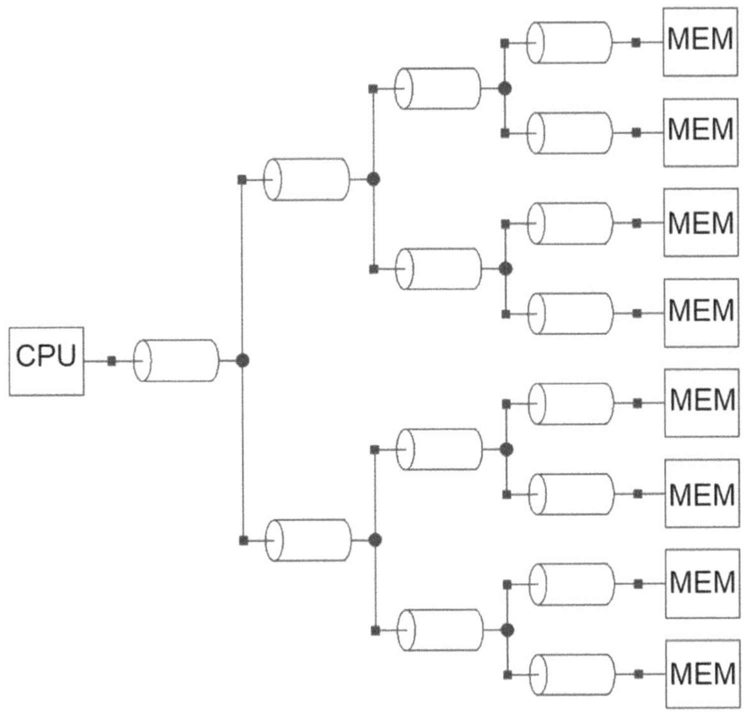

FIGURE 10.37 DDR-1/2 DIMM balanced tree clock/ACC topology.

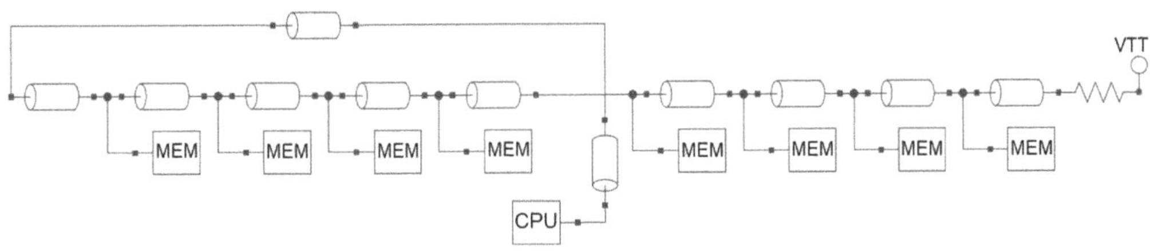

FIGURE 10.38 DDR3/4/5 DIMM fly-by clock/ACC topology.

with registered/buffered DIMM memories, so, for example, the controller has to drive only four loads, while the register chips on the DIMMs will drive up to 16 chips. On the balanced tree, the designer makes sure that the propagation delay from the DIMM card edge or the controller pins to every memory chip pin will be the same (matched with a tolerance). DIMM design trace lengths and topologies are defined in the JESD21-C documents, which we can also use for memory-down designs.

Write timing is about the relationship between eh data bus and the address bus. The DRAM memory chips will expect the first valid data bit and strobe to arrive a certain time after the memory chip has detected a write command (from the ACC bus, latched by the clock). The controller puts the first data bit to the bus with the right timing, but the board design has to make sure that this timing is still maintained when the signals (clock, command, strobe, and data) arrive to the memory chip from the controller. This requires a length matching between the clock and the strobe signals, but only to the first DRAM chip on the fly-by ACC bus. For this matching, there is an output guaranteed skew timing parameter from the controller datasheet and an input maximum skew parameter from the memory chip datasheet. This input parameter of the memory is the t_DQSS, between the rising edge of the clock and the rising edge of the DQS signal. They also specify another clk-rising to DQS-falling-edge input rule because the DQS should be stable when the clock has its rising edge. This is the t_DSS and the t_DSH parameters together. The DQS has to stabilize minimum t_DSS time before the clk rising edge, and the DQS has to be stable for minimum t_DSH time after the clock rising edge.

Read-data capture used to be difficult. Some of the simpler DDR1/2 controllers had a clock output to DQS input skew requirement, which is affected by the round-trip delay and the bus length. The memory controller had to pass the captured data from the DQS clock domain to the internal clock domain without FIFOs. The memory chip datasheet specifies the maximum skew between the input clock and the output DQS, as t_DQSCK. The controller datasheet specifies a maximum skew of the output clock and the input DQS on its pins, in vendor-specific terms. The issue and the concept are demonstrated in Figure 10.39. The primary timing loop ends at the capture flip-flop, but a secondary loop starts there and crosses a clock domain. No one designs DDR1 systems any longer, so it is not a common requirement. The equation to be met:

```
t_sk_in_max ≥ t_DQSCK + t_pd_clk + t_pd_DQS + t_err
```

Timing calibration is a great invention. The chip/FPGA-designers can include DLL delay circuits in either the data or the DQS paths. These delays can be fixed, or they can be adjusted by a hardware state machine or by software to achieve optimal timing. With timing calibration, we can adjust the

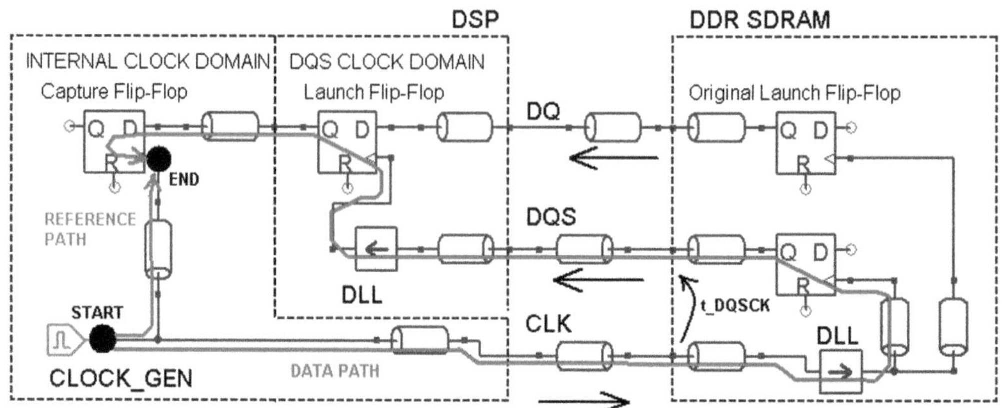

FIGURE 10.39 Read data capture secondary timing loop in DDR1.

already included delays to the right value. The board and chip delays are mostly static for a given manufactured board, although they vary between production units and over temperature. As a board heats up during use, re-calibration might be necessary. That is why we calibrate after power up; to check what values are most optimal on a specific unit. We can measure signal quality by adjusting DLL delays step by step, capturing the data and detecting the DLL value where the captured data is different from in the previous step. This way we can find the two edges of the valid timing windows (Data Valid Window, DVW). Then we can set the final delays in the middle of the valid region. The DDR3 to 5 interfaces have timing calibration features, called Write Levelling and Read Levelling, to balance setup and hold margins after power up and after some time intervals regularly.

The write leveling calibration process compensates for any clock-to-strobe matching issues. The controller puts the memory chips into write levelling mode. Then the memory will sample the CLK with using DQS edges then it sends the captured value to the controller on the DQ0 line. The controller increments the DLL delay register value on the DQS signal step by step, until it finds the two DLL values where the sampled value changes. Finally, the controller sets the DLL to be half-way between the two found values. In the DDR3 Fly-By topology, each memory chip has a different clock delay, so this calibration will result in a different DLL value for each byte lane.

The read-leveling calibration process balances the data bus read setup/hold margins by adjusting the DQS delay DLL value. We can achieve the maximum speed if both the setup and the hold sides have margin, and they have equal margin. If they are unbalanced, then one will run out of margin at a lower data rate than the other and lower than a balanced controller would. In read-levelling mode, all the data written into the memory will be stored in the General-Purpose Register (instead of using the memory array). The controller writes a fixed test pattern into it. Then the controller reads it back again and again, while incrementing the DLL delay register value on the DQS signal step by step. The controller state machine is looking for the minimum and maximum delays where it can still read the correct data. Then it sets the DQS-DLL into the middle between the two found values. The two found values represent the two edges of the data valid window, so the final DLL value will be at the safest position. It is basically a horizontal eye capture feature. Some DDR3 memory controllers or BIOS/bootloader software do not support this feature.

10.4 TIMING-DRIVEN PCB TRACE LENGTH CONSTRAINTS

This chapter explains how to design our boards to meet timing by calculating trace length constraints for the PCB design tool. These constraints can be calculated from the timing margins of the pre-layout timing analysis, with a few assumptions. Trace length constrains are specified to ensure certain propagation delays, more specifically flight times. If the traces have similar (order of magnitude) length, trace width, and loading, then we can simplify the propagation delay control to flight time control, which can be converted to trace length control. There are two types of length constraints: the absolute constraints where an object (net, XNET, Pin-Pair, net class) or multiple objects have to have a trace length within a range between a minimum and a maximum value, and the relative constraints where a group of objects have to have trace lengths no different from the other objects in the group, within tolerance.

Delays through traces have a meaning only between Pin-Pairs, for example between pin-5 on IC1 and pin-32 on IC2. Point-to-point nets have only pins on them, so we can use simple net name objects instead of having to define Pin-Pairs. Multi-point nets have more than two chip pins on them, so we need to define Pin-Pairs in the layout constraint manager and define trace lengths between them. Only the valid Pin-Pairs need to be defined, between driver-receiver pairs, not between receiver-receiver pairs. In Figure 10.40 we can see an example of a memory address signal routed from an FPGA (IC1) to a DRAM chip (IC2), and to a termination resistor (R35). We have to create Pin-Pair objects like "IC1.K6-IC2.N2" for all signals on the address bus and match those Pin-Pairs to each other. In the drawing we can see that a multi-point net can have many trace segments, but only some of them (the red highlighted ones) will be counted for the Pin-Pair. The blue segments

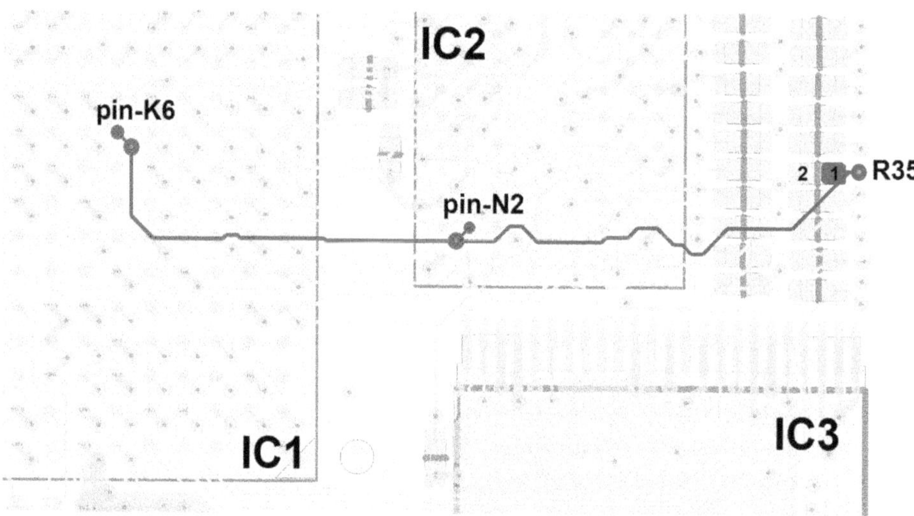

FIGURE 10.40 Net segments of a Pin-Pair in the layout (in red).

while still being on the same net will not be counted by the layout tool. If we matched nets instead of Pin-Pairs, then we would end up with all trace segments being counted for the total length, including the segments running from IC2 to R35, which has no meaning in the timing between IC1 and IC2.

Sometimes the signal travels through a series element, for example, a damping resistor or an AC coupling capacitor. The design program has to be able to measure the chip-pin to chip-pin lengths, even if the two chip pins are on the two separate sides of the series component. In these cases, the design tool should create an extended net (Xnet in the Cadence Allegro terminology) automatically for every net with series elements between two non-power nets. Non-power means any termination resistors touching VTT or GND would not be picked up for XNET creation. Not all the PCB design programs are capable of creating XNETs and Pin-Pair objects.

For the absolute data signal length calculations, we consider an already specified reference signal routing length (or propagation delay). These can be estimated from a floorplan, then we can add 20% to it and route the reference signal to that length (+/-5mil), and use that also in the calculation for the min/max data signal length. For relative length type buses, we don't need to calculate anything, we just route both the data and the reference signals as we can, leaving a little space around them for tuning. Then we add a little length to the reference signal to ensure it is not the shortest in the group. Then we lengthen any trace that is too short and shows a red tuning gauge bar.

Package Length Compensation has to be part of the constraints setup on most designs. For some chips in bigger packages, like X86 chipsets or large FPGAs, the chip manufacturer provides "package length" or "pin delay" information. This means that they provide a spreadsheet of routing lengths inside the package for every signal pin. Large chips are made of a silicon die soldered on a package substrate, which is like a small PCB with very fine pitch traces, that will be soldered onto our board. When we calculate or measure board routing lengths, the package lengths have to be included in the total length. For example, if our trace length has to be 2.5"+/-0.04", and the package length for the particular signal is 0.531", then our board routing length has to be length_rule - package_length which is 2.5"- 0.531"+/-0.04". The length rules apply from silicon-chip die-pad to silicon-chip die-pad where it is possible (if package lengths are provided); otherwise, we apply the length rules to/from package pins. The design software has to be able to handle it, but unfortunately many tools do not have any support for this. When we extract trace delay information from layout, we have to make sure we are using the type of report that includes package length. The concept is visualized in Figure 10.41.

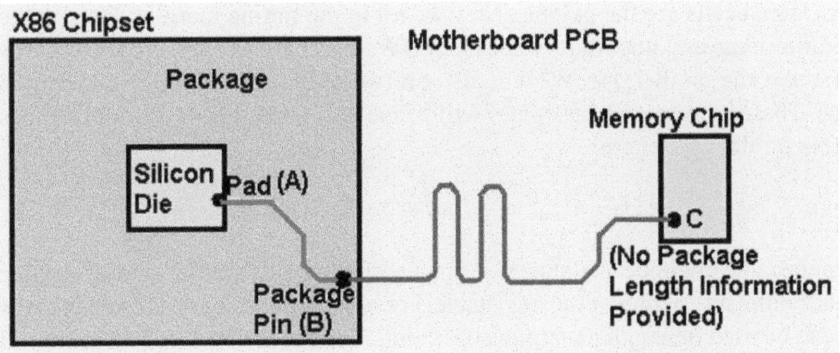

FIGURE 10.41 Package length in routing.

TABLE 10.5
Constraint Calculation Table (CCT)

Interface Type	t_pd_min (or delta t_pd min) =	t_pd_max (or delta t_pd max) =	Rule Type
Synchronous	- 1 * max(t_H_MAR_RD, t_H_MAR_WR)	min(t_SU_MAR_ RD, t_SU_MAR_ WR)	Absolute
Asynchronous			Absolute
Source Synchronous			Relative to strobe if they were taken into account with zero PCB skew. Absolute if the strobe delay was taken into account and data delay was zero.
Clock Forwarding			Relative to clock if they were taken into account with zero PCB skew. Absolute if the clock delay was taken into account and data delay was zero.
Unidirectional Synchronous	- 1 * t_H_MAR	t_SU_MAR	Relative to clock if they were taken into account with zero PCB skew. Absolute if the clock delay was taken into account and data delay was zero.
Embedded Clock	-	-	Lane-to-lane matching is relative.
Arbitrary, Timing Graph	- 1 * t_H_MAR	t_SU_MAR	Relative to the original t_pd_data if that was already taken into account in the timing graph, otherwise absolute.

10.4.1 The Length Calculations

We can calculate the PCB design trace length limits from the timing margins, which we can use for entering layout design constraints into the PCB tool. The maximum lengths are related to setup margins, the minimum lengths are related to hold margins. First, we have to make a few assumptions, such as T_pd=0, t_OD_max=t_OSU, and t_OD_min=t_OH. Then we have to look up the appropriate two or four equations with all their parameters relevant to the interface type from the timing analysis parameters table (TAP) mentioned earlier and write them down. Then substitute the assumed values for t_pd and t_OD, and substitute the chip datasheet parameters into the equations, and calculate the timing margins. Then we look up the appropriate two or four equations from the Constraint Calculation Table (CCT, Table 10.5). White cells are the input parameters, blue cells are case selectors, green cells are the outputs. Now we fill in the timing margins. Finally, we solve the equations for minimum and maximum trace delays. We will have two maximum delays; we have to take the worst one, the smaller one. We will also get two minimum delays; also take the worst one, the larger one. These margin or delay values will be the flight time limits for our PCB design. Then we have to convert them to length:

```
TraceLength = flight_time * 11.8 / SQRT(DK) [ns, inch]
```

The output of the table might be a relative rule or an absolute t_pd rule, depending on interface type, as noted in the comment column of the CCT table. For certain interface types we are getting relative lengths that can be used in length matching constraints, instead of absolute constraints. That means for example L_{MIN} is the amount the data traces can be shorter than the reference signal trace. If the maximum length is negative or the maximum length is smaller than the minimum length, then it means there is no way this interface will work at that data rate. If the minimum length is negative, then we can just use zero for the constraint in the layout tool.

We may apply some overdesign, so after the layout design is completed, we can still expect much greater than zero timing margins. This means tightening. Let's say we want a three times more tight range, so we apply an over-design factor of OVDF=3. This way we keep one-third of the margin for trace skew allowance, and two=thirds for PVT variation and noises. Then we can calculate the new constraints as:

```
Length_range = Length_max - Length_min
Length_min_new = Length_min + 0.5 * Length_range * (1 - 1/OVDF)
Length_max_new = Length_max - 0.5 * Length_range * (1 - 1/OVDF)
```

We can transform between absolute (min/max) and relative (delta and tolerance) trace length rules using simple algebra, if we need it for some unusual cases. For example, we might have to merge constraints coming from two chip manufacturers or two different standards if we want to copy/paste a JESD-21C DIMM design that has absolute rules into our motherboard and want to wire it to our processor that has matching rules. There are better ways of implementing memory down layouts using Pin-Pair constraints, as described earlier.

```
Delta = (lenght_min + lenght_max) /2
Tolerance = lenght_max - Delta
```

10.4.2 Architecture Specific Considerations

For synchronous interfaces, usually we handle the reference path and the data path separately. The I/O clock can be supplied to both chips from an on-board clock generator, or it can be supplied by a master chip to itself internally and to a slave chip on-board by the master. This is a design choice for the chip designers only; the board designer has to work with what the chip supports. We specify maximum clock skew (in case of a central clock source) or we estimate the clock net routing length from a floorplan, add 20% to it to be the clock routing length rule, then calculate min/max data length. If the master supplies the clock to the slave, then the read setup analysis will be the biggest limiting factor on the maximum data signal length, therefore on the complete bus length as well.

The design rules of the asynchronous interfaces are the same as the synchronous interfaces have, which is minimum/maximum trace lengths for the data signals based on predefined strobe trace lengths. In the calculations the available times are different. Note the reference signal is always driven by the master chip, never by an external clock chip.

The source synchronous systems are designed in a way to make sure that the reference signal (strobe) and the data signal paths have identical elements, so their delays are close to identical. This means that for a PCB designer the goal is to keep the data signal length within a +/-delta_length (tolerance in Allegro) window around the strobe trace length. This is the simplest to design, since we provide simple data for the design software and we are not restricted to guess a pre-defined reference length as with the synchronous and asynchronous interface designs.

For uni-directional synchronous interfaces only the write setup and write hold margins have to be considered. It works like a common clock synchronous bus, but we only calculate only write transaction related timing. Most designers use matching rules instead of absolute rules, as it is easier to implement in the layout tool. We can calculate absolute rules and then convert them, although the data delay range might not be centered around the clock length.

The layout design for clock forwarding interfaces works in the same way as the uni-directional synchronous type, but it supports both read and write operations with separate clock signals for them.

The only trace length rules for embedded clock SERDES links are the insertion loss based maximum (and sometimes minimum) lengths and, in some cases, lane-to-lane matching rules.

10.5 SUMMARY DESIGN FLOW

During the hardware design process, we select the main chips. Then we select the interface types we will use. In many cases the interface type is already given; sometimes we can craft a custom interface architecture when working with FPGAs. Then we can collect the datasheet parameters and go ahead and calculate the PCB trace length constraints, as well as estimate the maximum data rate. The steps for this are described in Table 10.6. We can do this based on datasheet parameters quickly or we can use signal integrity simulations to more accurately model the signal transition delays to see how soon the signal actually registers at a new value, using estimated trace lengths. Then we can go ahead and finish the schematic and layout design (with the constraints we calculated). Then with the exact trace lengths, PCB stackup, and other details we can run a post-layout SI simulation (PCB-extracted) to obtain transition delays, which we can feed into a timing analysis calculation to see if we have a positive margin, aka the verification passes. The steps for the post-layout analysis are listed in Table 10.7.

TABLE 10.6

Pre-layout Constraint Calculations

Step	Name	Parameters to calculate
1	Datasheet extract	Get input requirements and output guaranteed timing parameters
2	Substitute fixed values	T_pd=0, t_OD_max=t_OSU, t_OD_min=t_OH
3	TAP table lookup	Identify the relevant equations for the interface type, 2 or 4 RD/WR/SU/H cases, in the timing analysis parameter (TAP) table. Fill part parameters then get new parameters for the generalized equation.
4	Write out equations	Write out the 2 or 4 versions of the generalized equation, with parts filled from the TAP, for the 2 or 4 cases
5	Calculate margins	Solve the equations for margins; substitute both datasheet values and the fixed values.
6	CCT table lookup	Identify the relevant equations for the interface type, RD/WR case, in the constraint calculation (CCT) table. Fill in the margins then get propagation delay limits.
7	Write out equations	Write out 2 or 4 equations for t_pd_min and t_pd_max
8	Calculate trace length	Solve the equations with the margins from step-5; calculate min/max absolute/relative trace lengths.
9	Fill PCB Constraint Manager	Depending on PCB tool, fill the constraints.

TABLE 10.7
Post-layout Design Validation

Step	Name	Parameters to calculate
1	Datasheet extract	Get input requirements and output guaranteed timing parameters
2	Substitute values from SI-Sim	T_pd= simulated delay to threshold crossing, t_OD_max=t_OSU-TD(SimTestLoad), t_OD_min=t_OH-TD(SimTestLoad)
3	TAP table lookup	Identify the relevant equations for the interface type, 2 or 4 RD/WR/SU/H cases, in the timing analysis parameter (TAP) table. Fill part parameters then get new parameters for the generalized equation.
4	Write out equations	Write out the 2 or 4 versions of the generalized equation, with parts filled from the TAP, for the 2 or 4 cases
5	Calculate margins	Solve the equations for margins; substitute both datasheet values and the simulated values above. Margins must be larger than zero to pass the analysis.
6	Programming value calculations	For asynchronous buses calculate programming values

10.5.1 Example: Synchronous SPI interface

This example shows how to actually do all the steps discussed throughout this main chapter.

First we gather the datasheet parameters:

- Master PCIe switch
  - MISO input hold requirement tIH=0ns
  - MISO input setup requirement tISU=20ns
  - MOSI output setup time tOSU=10ns
  - MOSI output hold time tOH=10ns
- Slave SPI EEPROM
  - MISO input hold requirement tDVCH=tIH=2.3ns
  - MISO input setup requirement tCHDX=tISU=2.3ns
  - MOSI output setup time tCLQX=tOSU=7ns
  - MOSI output hold time tCLQV=tOH=1.5ns

Then we record any design assumptions and design details: In this case the master supplies the clock, so the clock skew will be zero and t_pd_clk will be the clock trace delay. Assume a 25MHz SPI bus I/O clock (40ns period), DK=4 for the PCB material, 3" long clock trace with 0.5ns delay, 20% duty cycle distortion that is 10ns.

We need to write down the main generalized equation four times:

```
t_X_MAR = t_available + t_improving - t_degrading - t_err
t_X_MAR = t_available + t_improving - t_degrading - t_err
t_X_MAR = t_available + t_improving - t_degrading - t_err
t_X_MAR = t_available + t_improving - t_degrading - t_err
```

Then we have to look up the four rows in the TAP table that are relevant to this interface type. The table provides three lists of parameters in each row that we have to use in the three main parts of the generalized timing analysis table. These lists or main parts are the t_available, t_improving, and t_degrading. We have to rename the outputs as T_su_mar_rd, T_h_mar_rd, T_su_mar_wr, and T_h_mar_wr. Then fill in the three main parts in each of the four equations, with variable names from the TAP table. The errors can be looked up in the errors table (ET).

```
T_su_mar_rd = T_clk + 0 - (t_ISU_master+t_OD_max_slave+t_pd_data+ t_pd_
clk) - (t_clk_skew+DCD)
T_h_mar_rd = 0 + (t_OD_min_slave+t_pd_data+t_pd_clk) - (t_IH_master)
- (t_clk_skew)
T_su_mar_wr = T_clk + (t_pd_clk) - (t_ISU_slave+t_OD_max_master+t_pd_
data) - (t_clk_skew+DCD)
T_h_mar_wr = 0 + (t_OD_min_master+t_pd_data) - (t_IH_slave+t_pd_clk)
- (t_clk_skew)
```

Layout constraints:
At this step we calculate all four margins to be used for the trace length calculations: By substituting t_pd=0, t_OD_max = t_OSU, t_OD_min = t_OH, and filling in the datasheet parameters and design assumptions too. The equations will be:

```
T_su_mar_rd = 40ns + 0 - (20ns+7ns+0+0.5ns) - (0+10ns) = 2.5ns
T_h_mar_rd = 0 + (1.5ns+0+0.5ns) - (0) - (0) = 2ns
T_su_mar_wr = 40ns + (0.5ns) - (2.3ns+10ns+0) - (0+10ns) = 18.2ns
T_h_mar_wr = 0 + (10ns+0) - (2.3ns+0.5ns) - (0) = 7.2ns
```

We have to look up the equations from the CCT table for the layout trace delay for our synchronous type of interface:

```
t_pd_min = - 1 * max(t_H_MAR_RD; t_H_MAR_WR)
t_pd_max = min(t_SU_MAR_RD; t_SU_MAR_WR)
```

Fill in the numbers and calculate:

```
T_pd_min = -1*min(2ns,7.19ns) = -2ns
T_pd_max = min(2.49ns,18.2ns) = 2.49ns
```

Calculate trace lengths from the delays:

```
Lmin = t_pd_min*11.8/SQRT(DK) = -11.8in, but practically Lmin ≥ 0″
Lmax = t_pd_max*11.8/SQRT(DK) < 14.7″
```

Verify the post-layout design:
Let's assume the bus is already routed in the board file and we have simulated it. From the SI simulation we got t_pd_data=0.8ns for both read and write, and we got TD=0.2ns with the test load in all cases. Remember we wanted to rout the clock to 3" that is 0.5ns, and then we calculated the constraints based on that, so we did route it at 3". First, we have to calculate the output delays so we will not double count the transition delay in both the t_pd and in the output delay.

```
t_OD_max = tOSU - TD(SimTestLoad)
t_OD_min = tOH - TD(SimTestLoad)
```

Fill it in:

```
t_OD_max_master = 10-0.2=9.8ns
t_OD_min_master = 10-0.2=9.8ns
t_OD_max_slave = 7-0.2=6.8ns
t_OD_min_slave = 1.5-0.2=1.3ns
```

We have to take the four filled generalized equations again, and fill in the datasheet parameters again, but this time for the t_pd we fill in the simulated delays, and for t_OD we use calculated output delays from above:

```
T_su_mar_rd = 40ns + 0 - (20ns+6.8ns+0.8+0.5ns) - (0+10ns)
```

= 1.9ns that is larger than 0 so it passes.

```
T_h_mar_rd = 0 + (1.3ns+0.8+0.5ns) - (0) - (0)
```

= 2.6ns that is larger than 0 so it passes.

```
T_su_mar_wr = 40ns + (0.5ns) - (2.3ns+9.8ns+0.8) - (0+10ns)
```

= 17.6ns that is larger than 0 so it passes.

```
T_h_mar_wr = 0 + (9.8ns+0.8) - (2.3ns+0.5ns) - (0)
```

= 7.8ns that is larger than 0 so it passes.

Calculate the maximum data rate:
At this point we write down the t_available equation:

```
t_available_min= t_degrading - t_improving + t_err
```

We have to look above to find which of the two setup margins was lower in the post-layout cases. In this case it is the read setup margin at 1.9ns, so we have to use the improving and degrading parameters from the read setup case. We fill the equation in from the post-layout read setup case:

```
t_available_min= (t_ISU_master+t_OD_max_slave+t_pd_data+ t_pd_clk) - 0 +
(t_clk_skew+DCD)
```

Calculate it:

```
(20ns+6.8ns+0.8+0.5ns) + 0 - (0+10ns) = 18.547ns
```

According to the MDCT table, the max data rate or bus frequency for synchronous systems is:
`F_max = 1 / t_avail_min = 1/18.547ns = 53.9MHz`

10.6 AUTOMATING THE TIMING CALCULATIONS

Writing up the series of equations, looking up parameters, and calculating all of them without mistakes is very complicated and time consuming, so it makes sense to automate it. There can be different automated calculation setups for different interface types. Some of the timing parameters come from signal integrity calculations. They require waveform parsing, and their results have to be fed into the calculations. Other parameters come from PCB layout files, like trace lengths, also to be entered or imported. The component parameters can come from datasheets or from standards. In real life most hardware engineers only have to use automated timing calculation methods, we rarely have to write up the equations ourselves, as in the previous sections. But it makes sense to study the rest of this chapter to understand what is going on and how our design decisions affect timing. Some chip vendors also provide Excel trace length calculators for their processors and FPGAs for verifying designs.

We can create an Excel calculator template that can be re-used in different projects. An example can be seen in Figure 10.42. It shows several tabs, each tab for a different timing architecture, separate tabs for pre-layout timing analysis that generates PCB design trace length constraints, and post-layout timing analysis that is for design validation. This template can also be downloaded from the link in the appendix.

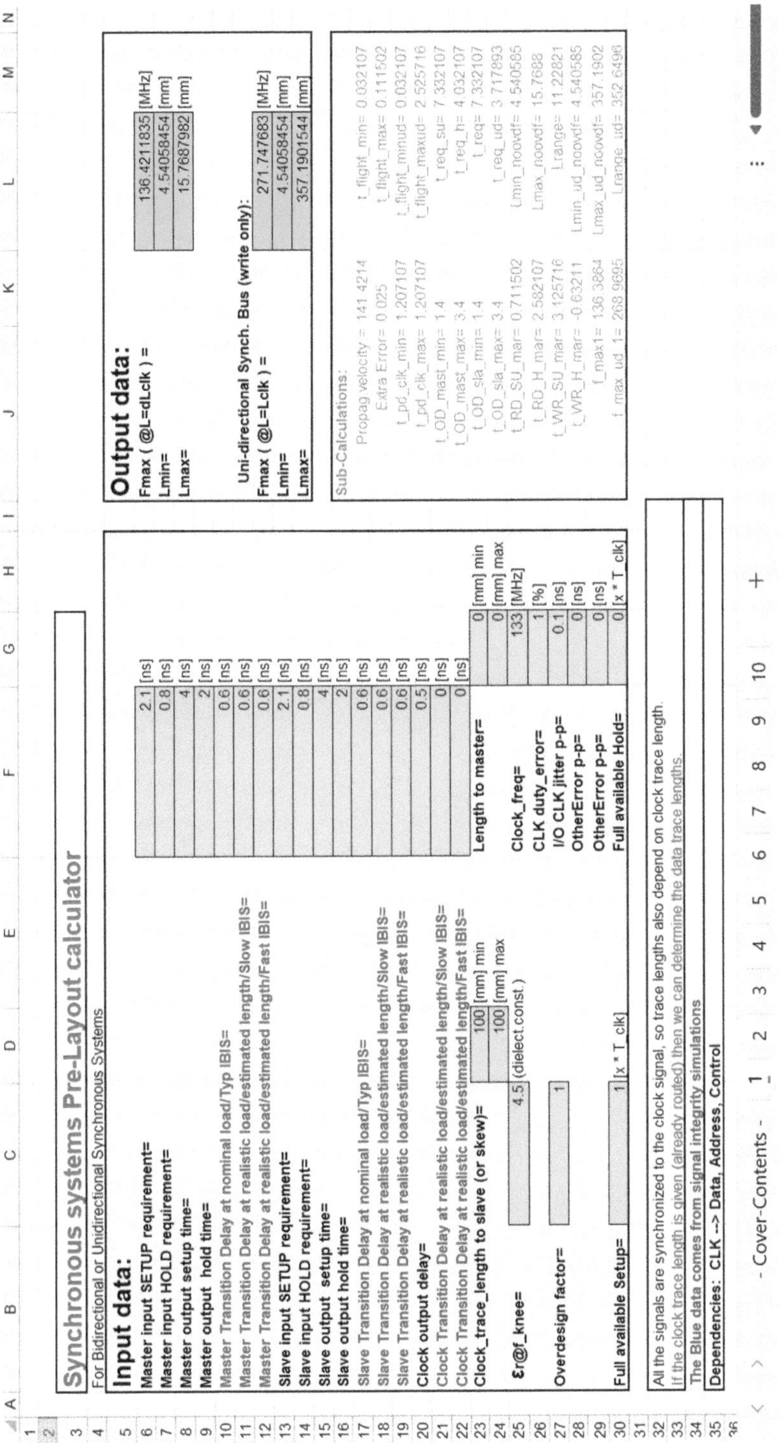

A B C D E F G H I J K L M N
Synchronous systems Pre-Layout calculator
For Bidirectional or Unidirectional Synchronous Systems
Input data:
Master input SETUP requirement= 2.1 [ns]
Master input HOLD requirement= 0.8 [ns]
Master output setup time= 4 [ns]
Master output hold time= 2 [ns]
Master Transition Delay at nominal load/Typ IBIS= 0.6 [ns]
Master Transition Delay at realistic load/estimated length/Slow IBIS= 0.6 [ns]
Master Transition Delay at realistic load/estimated length/Fast IBIS= 0.6 [ns]
Slave input SETUP requirement= 2.1 [ns]
Slave input HOLD requirement= 0.8 [ns]
Slave output setup time= 4 [ns]
Slave output hold time= 2 [ns]
Slave Transition Delay at nominal load/Typ IBIS= 0.6 [ns]
Slave Transition Delay at realistic load/estimated length/Slow IBIS= 0.6 [ns]
Slave Transition Delay at realistic load/estimated length/Fast IBIS= 0.6 [ns]
Clock output delay= 0.5 [ns]
Clock Transition Delay at realistic load/estimated length/Slow IBIS= 0 [ns]
Clock Transition Delay at realistic load/estimated length/Fast IBIS= 0 [ns]
Clock_trace_length to slave (or skew)= 100 [mm] min
100 [mm] max
Length to master= 0 [mm] min
0 [mm] max
Ɛr@f_knee= 4.5 (dielect.const.)
Clock_freq= 133 [MHz]
CLK duty_error= 1 [%]
Overdesign factor= 1
I/O CLK jitter p-p= 0.1 [ns]
OtherError p-p= 0 [ns]
OtherError p-p= 0 [ns]
Full available Setup= 1 [x * T_clk]
Full available Hold= 0 [x * T_clk]
Output data:
Fmax (@L=dLclk) = 136.4211835 [MHz]
Lmin= 4.54058454 [mm]
Lmax= 15.7687982 [mm]
Uni-directional Synch. Bus (write only):
Fmax (@L=Lclk) = 271.747683 [MHz]
Lmin= 4.54058454 [mm]
Lmax= 357.1901544 [mm]
Sub-Calculations:
Propag.velocity = 141.4214
Extra Error= 0.025
t_pd_clk_min= 1.207107
t_pd_clk_max= 1.207107
t_OD_mast_min= 1.4
t_OD_mast_max= 3.4
t_OD_sla_min= 1.4
t_OD_sla_max= 3.4
t_RD_SU_mar= 0.711502
t_RD_H_mar= 2.582107
t_WR_SU_mar= 3.125716
t_WR_H_mar= -0.63211
f_max1= 136.3864
f_max_ud_1= 268.9695
t_flight_min= 0.032107
t_flight_max= 0.111502
t_flight_minud= 0.032107
t_flight_maxud= 2.525716
t_req_su= 7.332107
t_req_h= 4.032107
t_req= 7.332107
t_req_ud= 3.717893
Lmin_noovdf= 4.540585
Lmax_noovdf= 15.7688
Lrange= 11.22821
Lmin_ud_noovdf= 4.540585
Lmax_ud_noovdf= 357.1902
Lrange_ud= 352.6496
All the signals are synchronized to the clock signal, so trace lengths also depend on clock trace length.
If the clock trace length is given (already routed) then we can determine the data trace lengths.
The Blue data comes from signal integrity simulations
Dependencies: CLK --> Data, Address, Control
- Cover-Contents - 1 2 3 4 5 6 7 8 9 10 +

FIGURE 10.42 A timing calculator spreadsheet template.

Post-layout timing analysis is automated for DDRx memory interfaces in a few commercial software. Signal integrity simulators like HyperLynx with its Batch DDR Wizard or Cadence Sigrity can analyze all waveforms on all signals of a complete DDRx memory interface and provide pass/fail information and timing margins for every signal in an auto-generated report document. It is called a batch simulation. This case we only have to import a fully PCB design file, provide IBIS buffer model files, and enter a few parameters like bus speed. The component timing parameters may be imported from a file, manually entered, or the JEDEC standard default values can be loaded automatically according to the component speed bin. JEDEC specifies data tables for every standard speed like 2133MT/s, 2400MT/s, etc. Compliant parts can be manufactured only by the chip vendors if their parameters are at least as good as the ones in the JEDEC standard speed bin. These DDR wizards also require IBIS models for the controller and the DRAM chips. If the controller is an FPGA, then we might have to generate a custom IBIS model file.

11 Signal Integrity

Signal integrity describes how much degradation a high-speed digital signal gets on its way from the transmitter chip to the receiver chip, and whether the digital data is still recoverable from the signal. If it is not recoverable then the signal or the design has bad signal integrity. There are clear standards to determine that. High-speed digital design is a method of physical structure design in printed circuit board layout to ensure good signal integrity. This involves stackups, traces, constraints, structures, vias, pads, planes, voids, component pins, and their electromagnetic interactions with each other. The main SI-related design and decision-making activities for hardware design engineers are the hardware architecture and components selection for signal paths, PCB layout high-speed design, and design confidence or validation through simulation and measurement.

The signal is a voltage/time waveform, theoretically measurable on an oscilloscope. Starting at few GHz and above we more often do frequency domain analysis of the physical channel using S-parameters, instead of time domain analysis of the signal waveform. The shift happened when we started using a few Gigabits per second signals. IEEE Ethernet and other standards also shifted their focus to S-parameters. At 10Gbps the eye diagram is usually closed on the board signal at the receiver, and opens up only after the RX DFE stage inside the chip. The PCB trace S-parameters can still be analyzed even at that speed and beyond. Analyzing the trace instead of the signals is an indirect approach, but it is more measurable and more predictable, with more precise scientific parameters. S-parameters can tell a lot more about why a SERDES interface is not working/reliable than a time domain waveform. The time domain waveforms just pile different channel pathologies on top of each other so we cannot tell which one is which, while in frequency domain the different sources of problems are usually separated to different frequencies, so we can focus on one problem at a time to resolve them. For example, a bad component pinout might cause issues (resonance or suckout) near 10GHz, while an AC-capacitor via structure might do it at 15GHz.

Time domain eye diagram simulations start and end from the chip die internal circuits (SERDES pre-FFE and post-DFE), so they do include chip I/O buffer and SERDES models as well as BGA package models. S-par simulations do not include buffer or package models, only the passive PCB plus connector channel. The board hardware designers have to design only this passive interconnect. Passive interconnect models do not rely on chip vendor provided models, so our analysis has to cover only our own work's quality. The chip pin is like a legal boundary—from the board up to the chip pin we are responsible for delivering a reliable solution, but past the chip pin the chip vendor is responsible.

Time domain tools are still available to provide additional insight, and they are also used for lower speed interfaces below 8Gbps. Most SI simulation tools support both types of analysis. We still use SPI buses, DDRx interfaces, and ONFI flash buses, which are more meaningful to simulate or measure in time domain.

The use of signal integrity in the old days was simply running post-layout SI simulations. On modern designs containing 10Gig and faster signals we need to do several additional new SI activities early on in the project, like loss budget calculations, impedance controlled via optimization, pre-layout simulations for component selection and architecture validation, and floorplanning. Actually, the main focus of SI activities, let's say 70%+ is at the proposal and pre-layout stages. At pre-layout we do "what-if" simulations, we do via impedance optimization, and we define constraints and 3D high-speed layout features/patterns to be used. See Chapter, 14, "Initial Design". After all these considerations, we still do post-layout signal integrity simulations sometimes but not for design verification, rather for increasing confidence in a design. The accuracy of post-layout simulations at 10G+ is far from perfect, unlike at lower speeds. Pre-layout sim before moving forward with

DOI: 10.1201/9781032702094-11

schematic design, post-layout sim before moving forward with manufacturing the prototype. All high-speed interfaces require some pre-layout SI work, but not always a simulation, more like a constraint or feasibility calculation. When we have a non-standard case, like having an extra connector in an SFP+ signal path, or having a very short channel, we should definitely simulate. In standard cases we usually just do a loss budget calculation. A standard case is what is explicitly described in standard documents like SFF and IEEE, for example, an QSFP-DD chip to module link with the exact number of connectors described (no extras) or a PCIe motherboard to add-in card channel. For parallel buses a timing analysis calculation for layout constraints and frequency limit is needed, with SI simulation for setup times (transition delay).

11.1 S-PARAMETERS

S-parameters have been used in radio frequency and microwave analog engineering for generations. Its mathematical and engineering methods were well developed, but mostly used on single-ended signals. A subset of those became the common way of describing and analyzing multi-Gigabit SERDES channels in digital board designs. At around 8Gbps or above, S-parameters (scattering parameters) became more useful than the traditional time domain waveform and eye diagram analysis for digital signals. S-parameters describe the passive interconnect (PCB traces, capacitors, resistors, connectors, vias), not the signals (voltage/time waveforms). A pass/fail criteria can be constructed using limit lines and curves, which the S-parameter curve must not cross and be on the right side at all times or frequencies (within a range of interest).

11.1.1 RF Techniques for High-Speed Digital

S-parameters have been in use by RF and microwave engineers for decades. This chapter gives a quick start guide on using S-parameters in digital designs. Note that RF engineers often deal with the so-called Smith Chart that we digital engineers never use; instead, we use regular rectangular or Cartesian plots. Another parameter that RF engineers commonly use is VSWR (voltage standing wave ratio), but instead we rely on return loss and TDR impedance plots that describe similar things.

A passive channel, made of PCB traces, vias, capacitors, and connectors, can be fully modeled by a set of scattering parameters (S-parameters, S-par). It is a matrix of S-parameters, covering all port combinations of an N-port network. A diffpair on a board is a 4-port S-parameter matrix or a 4-port network. With four ports we get 4x4=16 combinations that are 16 S-parameters. Each of these 16 S-parameters are measured or simulated at several frequency points and listed in an S-parameter file (Touchstone file). It is a text file that simply has data records, like [frequency1 S11 S12 S13 to S44], many of these. Several measurements take place, with each measurement having a signal generator applied to a port and measuring the outgoing signal on all ports, including the one with the generator. The "measurement" can be an actual measurement in the lab with a vector network analyzer (VNA) or in a frequency domain signal integrity (S-par) simulation. Measurements take place with every port used as a source, one by one, and then the VNA instrument or the simulator software combines all the measurements into one S-parameter set or file. The measurement port number combinations (source - probe) become the S-parameter matrix indexes. The parameter index is two numbers; the first is the port number where the signal comes out, the second one is where it goes in. The instrument or simulator uses a reference impedance value for the measurements. This can be set by the user for simulators, which can be useful with 85 Ohm or 93 Ohm signals, but lab instruments are always 50 Ohm single ended. It can be converted into another reference impedance system in post processing with a flexible simulator tool like ADS. Measuring or simulating a 93 Ohm system with a 50 Ohm reference impedance would make it seem like we have more return loss, but in the real prototype we will not have as much, so the conversion before final assessment makes a lot of sense. In a 4-port S-parameter file we have 16 (complex) numbers (each real and imaginary parts) at ~1000 frequency points, which is 32 thousand numbers. The number of frequency points is user selectable, simulation tools interpolate between them, and extrapolate above the highest one. Each of these S-parameter numbers is a complex number. Refer to EE College classes on complex numbers. They can also be represented as polar coordinate number pairs of gain (ratio) and phase (degrees), not just as real and imaginary complex numbers. The gain can be as a natural number or in decibels (dB). The set of these thousands of numbers act as a very accurate model of a passive channel, which can be compared against standard specifications, like the IEEE, SFF, OIF, or PCIe standard-defined limit lines. They can be displayed on normal rectangular graphs, S_xy versus frequency; usually we have more frequency points than the pixels on the screen trying to display the curve, and typical S-par display software interpolates between the points too. Each S-parameter number at a certain frequency describes how much signal passes through out of port x (reflected or transmitted wave) when we apply a full signal into port y (incident wave) and all ports are terminated at the reference impedance (usually 50 Ohms). It is a ratio of the reflected or transmitted wave and the incident wave. Return loss is signal transmission back into the same port. For a signal trace, we would want most of the signal energy to come out at the output port when we feed a signal into it at the input port, and we do not want much of the signal energy to exit on other unintended ports or to come back to the input port and interfere with the signal transmission. It always comes out a little bit on the wrong port. The goal of an SI analysis is to determine how much comes out on the wrong port and how much comes out on the right/intended port. The goal of the design process is to ensure that as much signal comes out of the right port as possible and to ensure that as little comes out on the wrong port as possible. This explanation is a little bit barefooted, compared to what we would find in an RF engineering book on S-parameters, but for us digital hardware designers this better fits the concepts of digital circuits. Figure 11.1 shows the concept of these measurements and the names of some of the parameters.

S-parameters have quality metrics. Sometimes the measurement error produces unrealistic S-parameters that cannot happen in a real physical device. Passivity and causality metrics help us evaluate how real the curves are. Some simulation tools can alter our S-parameter curves to "enforce" passivity and causality a little amount. Passivity means a PCB trace is not an amplifier and does not add energy to the signal. Causality means the signal will not jump ahead on the trace above the speed of light. If it does, then the model is inaccurate and unreal.

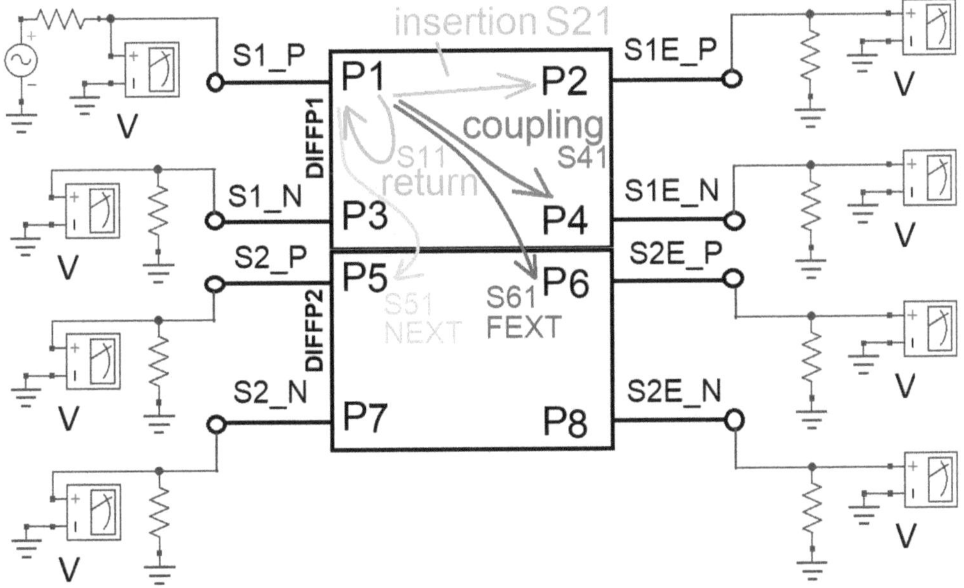

FIGURE 11.1 S-parameter measurements with VNA or a simulator on two diffpairs.

In some rare cases we work with Z-parameters, Y-parameters, or Transfer matrices instead of S-parameters. These can be converted back and forth using matrix computations.

Insertion loss (IL) is basically the attenuation of a signal seen at the far end of the line. For example, if the transmitter chip sends a signal with 1.0V amplitude, but the receiver sees a 0.4V amplitude signal, then the passive channel has attenuated the signal to 0.4 times the sent signal. The ratio "0.4x" can also be written up in decibels (dB) as LossdB=20*log(Vout/Vin), or -7.95dB for the 0.4V/1.0V ratio. Passive channels have a complex insertion loss versus frequency curve, because the loss varies at different frequencies. It is mostly sloping towards down+right, so we can fit a linear approximation to it, called fitted attenuation (FA), for certain types of simplified analysis. There are different algorithms to do this, with moving average computation, or with an algorithm published in IEEE802.3 Ethernet standards. Either way it will produce a mostly straight line that starts near 0dB at 0GHz and slopes towards the down and right direction. This means that if a sinusoid signal attenuates to 0.4x or -7.95dB at 20GHz, then we can approximate that it will attenuate about half as much dB at half as much frequency, so -3.98dB at 10GHz. We read out the fitted attenuation at half the baud rate or at a standard defined frequency (13GHz for 25Gbit Ethernet), as a number, to describe how lossy our channel is. For example, 1.2dB/in@13GHz. If there is too much loss or FA, then the signal attenuates too much. So one of the design goals is to make sure that there is not too much loss at half baud rate, through a loss budget calculation at the early stage of the project, and to select PCB materials and processes that will reduce the overall loss. Chapter 14, "Initial Design", explains it. It is important to point out that in engineer lingo there are three different meanings of the term "insertion loss", depending on context. They are the IL versus frequency curve (diagram), the loss number in dB@f0 of a specific trace, and a loss number in unit length in dB/in@f0 describing PCB materials. The IL versus frequency curve shows all the design-specific imperfections, and it can be checked against limit lines on a diagram, from the interface standard, that we can use for design verification. We can see various S-parameter curves with typical shapes in Figure 11.2. It also demonstrates limit lines for them (arbitrary example). The main design goal is to keep the curves away from the limit lines, and a secondary goal is to keep them as far as possible on the

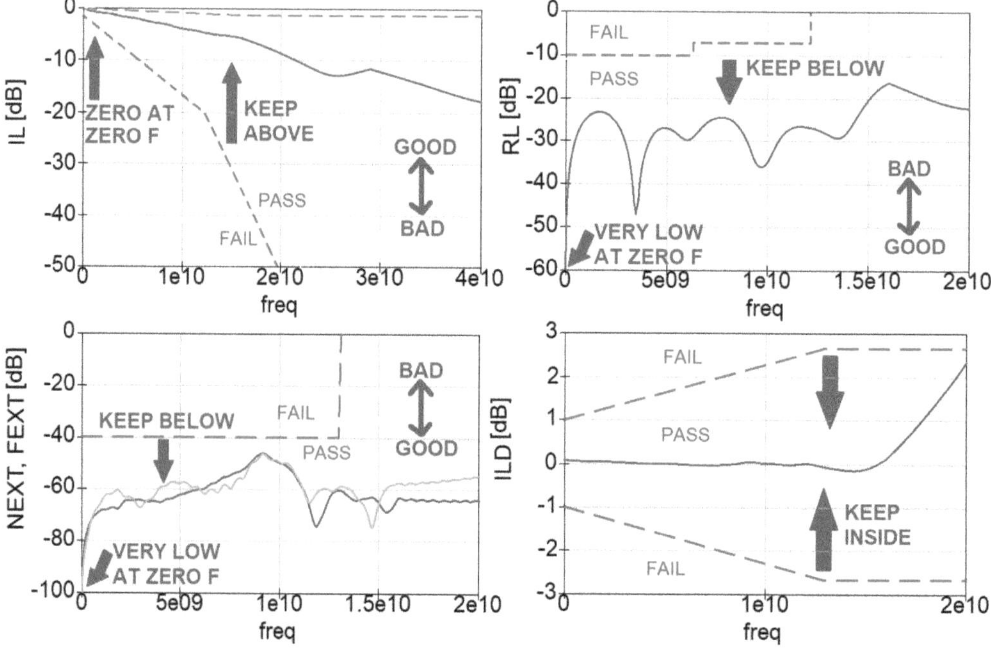

FIGURE 11.2 Signal trace S-parameter shapes, examples (blue) with limit lines (red).

correct side. Simulated or measured S-parameter curves do not fully represent all future production boards, they might vary a few dB. For this reason, we need a certain amount of margin between our curves and the limit lines.

A real insertion loss profile is not a completely straight line; rather, it has "suckouts", which are V-shaped depressions in the sloping line caused by resonances at certain frequencies. These resonances can be caused by reflections from impedance discontinuities, like unmatched via impedance, sharp trace bends, connectors, and fanout neck downs. Together with the loss slope, they define what the passive channel does to a signal, aka describe the channel quality. We also have to look at other S-parameters to qualify a passive channel's "performance", but really it is about reliability, not performance. Usually, S21 is the single-ended insertion loss, but not always—the port numbers might be mixed up by a simulator or the engineer performing the measurement, so we always have to make sure of the port mapping. For us digital engineers, we measure only passive channels; S21 will always be insertion loss, with a negative sign in dB. For RF engineers, S21 might go through a chain of amplifiers, and they might call it gain or something indicating signal boost.

Coupling happens between the two nets of the same differential pair. It is similar to crosstalk, as one single-ended leg of the diffpair affecting the other leg. Tight coupling means better immunity from common mode interference.

Return loss (RL) is the amount of signal that gets reflected back inside the channel from impedance discontinuities, and comes back out on the same port where we apply the input signal. So the two S-parameter indexes are the same, like S11 or S22. This is not just energy wasted, taken out of the energy arriving at the destination, but disturbs the transmitted waveform so that it degrades the eye diagram and causes bad signal integrity. The less RL the better. Since both S11 and S22 are imperfect on real board traces, the reflected disturbance will get reflected at the source too, and ping-pong back and forth, so it also arrives to the receiver and disturbs the received signal.

When we analyze multiple diffpairs, let's say three of them, then we have made a 12-port S-parameter model to describe the section of a board. Any signal energy that comes out on the ports of another diffpair is considered crosstalk. There can be far end crosstalk or FEXT and near end crosstalk NEXT, described in the next chapter.

11.1.2 Mixed-Mode S-Parameters

Single-ended S-parameter means we analyze the transmission of a single-ended input to a single-ended output. Mixed mode means we also analyze all four combinations of energy transfer amount between differential and common mode signals, known as mode conversion. These are the diff-to-diff transmission (SDD), diff-to-CM conversion (SDC), CM-to-diff conversion (SCD), and CM-to-CM transmission (SCC). The diff-to-CM results in energy loss from the received signal, and causing interference into other signals, not just crosstalk but interference to other unrelated buses too. The CM-to-diff describes the sensitivity to receive such interference. When a radiated interference arrives on our signal as a common mode noise, then it gets transformed into differential mode, that is how it degrades our signal. Conversion is caused by imperfections in the trace/via routing. CM-to-CM is not very interesting; while diff-to-diff is the main signal transmission we analyze to describe our channel performance. For the diffpairs we have differential insertion loss SDD21 and differential return loss SDD11. It is more useful to assess SERDES channels with using SDD21 and SDD11 than the single-ended original parameters.

Fixed feature-set software like HyperLynx or Cadence Clarity have built-in functions to produce some of the mixed-mode S-parameters, while in Keysight ADS or QUCS the user can implement custom equations for producing them. An equation will take a curve data set stored in a "vector" and produce a new curve data vector, wihch can be displayed like the original one. A 4-port single-ended S-parameter file with 16 complex numbers per frequency point can be converted to a 2-port mixed mode S-parameter file with 16 complex numbers per frequency point, as we can see in Figure 11.3.

$$\begin{bmatrix} S11 & S12 & S13 & S14 \\ S21 & S22 & S23 & S24 \\ S31 & S32 & S33 & S34 \\ S41 & S42 & S43 & S44 \end{bmatrix} \Rightarrow \begin{bmatrix} \begin{bmatrix} SDD11 & SDD12 \\ SDD21 & SDD22 \end{bmatrix} & \begin{bmatrix} SDC11 & SDC12 \\ SDC21 & SDC22 \end{bmatrix} \\ \begin{bmatrix} SCD11 & SCD12 \\ SCD21 & SCD22 \end{bmatrix} & \begin{bmatrix} SCC11 & SCC12 \\ SCC21 & SCC22 \end{bmatrix} \end{bmatrix}$$

FIGURE 11.3 Single-ended versus mixed-mode S-parameters.

These are computed as:

```
SDD11= 0.5*(S11-S13-S31+S33)
SDD21= 0.5*(S21-S23-S41+S43)
```

...And so on, all 16 of them... at every frequency point

With perfect localization of everything there would be no interference, but that is not achievable, there are limits to it, especially on complex high-density digital boards. With imperfect localization we have to minimize our signal's sensitivity to interference through reduced SCDxx and its tendency to emit interference through SDCxx. We have to really put some effort into designing our layout to have as little mode conversion as possible. Most SI simulations do not include unrelated buses, or a whole board, so we will not see the effect of a DDR4 bus interfering with the PCIe bus in terms of eye diagram reduction; we will see it only indirectly by looking at SCD and SDC curves. We can try to reduce mode conversion by using good layout techniques. For example, using less serpentine tuning, avoiding over-tuning and using twists at the via entry, increasing spacing to planes, or considering escape route directionality.

11.1.3 Derived S-Parameters

We can compute or derive further curves or S-parameters from the measured or simulated S-parameters. We can do this from single-ended or from differential (mixed-mode) S-parameters. IEEE has defined several of them in various Ethernet standards. They can help us to better understand the board's ability to deliver a good quality high-speed digital signal. All these computations can be done on curve vector data in ADS or QUCS.

A few IEEE-defined computed parameters:

- Insertion loss deviation (ILD) that describes how choppy our IL curve is, how much it deviates from FA. ILD(f)=IL(f) – FA(f). We also have pass/fail limit lines to ILD, usually a few dB around the 0dB line.
- We can calculate a Power Sum Crosstalk Noise (PSXT) as a combination of all FEXT and all NEXT from all aggressors, summed up. The sum calculation is done in the ratio domain, not in dB, so a conversion is necessary. Crosstalk, like insertion, reflection, and coupling, can be analyzed in frequency domain with S-parameters too. We typically display them in dB gain format, and we do not display the phase component from the gain-phase number pair. A Typical crosstalk limit for all types is -40dB up to half the baud rate.
- The Insertion Loss to Crosstalk Ratio (ICR) describes that the attenuated signal has to remain larger than the crosstalk noise. ICR(f) = –IL(f) + PSXT(f) in dB.
- Another metric is Integrated Crosstalk Noise (ICN). ICN in milli Volts is displayed not against frequency like the rest of them, but against the insertion loss, with a limit line.

We could just make our own S-parameters if it helps looking into a particular cause of system performance issues. This is not part of IEEE standards, but it makes sense to compute and display a

Combined Insertion and Return Loss (CIRL) curve, or attenuated reflection. This is not to replace the original standard curves and limit line checks. Many of us have noticed that on longer traces we can tolerate more reflections, and the shorter ones are more likely to fail from even small reflections. Often, we lengthen traces to help with reflections or set minimum trace lengths. So CIRL can be used as a combined curve from return (RL) and insertion (IL) loss, and the pass/fail limit line can be the original return loss limit (RLL). This CIRL limit is useful for analyzing designs as to whether they will work as well as for measurement accuracy of test boards when de-embedding computations are needed. The CIRL curve likely crosses the limit line at a certain frequency, above which designs might not be functional. If it happens above the half baud rate of the signal then it might be okay. To calculate the CIRL curve, we can compute this for every frequency point:

```
CIRL(f) = IL(f) + RL(f)   [dB]
```

All of these S-parameters are measurement sample sets or vectors, an S-par value set at each arbitrarily spaced frequency point, meaning they are functions of frequency (f). The equations are computed separately at each frequency point, by the tools, ADS or QUCS. Remember both IL and RL are negative numbers. For example, if RL= -20dB and IL= -1dB then we get CIRL= -21dB, which would be 89mV assuming the transmitter was sending a 1V signal. But if the channel is more lossy at -15dB, then we get CIRL=-35dB aka 18mV noise caused by reflection. Insertion loss works the same way, if we have a 1V TX signal and an IL= -15dB then the signal amplitude at the RX pin would be 178mV. We can compare this 178mV signal to the 18mV noise from above at every frequency point. Ideally we would use differential IL and RL, meaning SDD21 and SDD11. With 1V TX amplitude the decibel to Voltage conversion of any S-parameter is:

```
S_Volts = 10^(S_dB/20)
```

If we want to go even further, then we can combine all disturbances with the signal to get a single 2D curve that accounts for attenuation and noises like return loss, FEXT, and NEXT. Let's call it Signal to Noise Ratio (or SNR) but still display it against frequency as a curve. When we compute the combined disturbances, we have to do it with ratios or voltages, instead of dB, to get correct results. A ratio becomes a voltage level if it is relative to 1V. With a 1V transmitted signal, the received signal is equal to IL, for example, -20dB means 1/10th, or 0.1V. Usually the transmitter and the crosstalk aggressor transmit at the same voltage swing, so summing up ratios will be accurate even if the voltage swing is not 1V.

```
SNR = 20 * log10(Signal[V] / Noise[V])    [dB]
```

Where the input parameters to SNR are calculated in Volts, computed from RL, IL, FEXT, and NEXT that are in dB:

```
Signal = 10^(IL/20)    [V]
Noise = 10^(RL/20) + 10^(NEXT/20) +10^(FEXT/20) )    [V]
```

We should really use attenuated noises to get the SNR correct, like the above mentioned CIRL:

```
Noise = 10^(CIRL/20) + 10^(NEXT/20) +10^(FEXT/20)
=10^((IL+RL)/20) + 10^(NEXT/20) +10^(FEXT/20)    [V]
```

The NEXT is not attenuated, while the FEXT already contains attenuation. So, there is no need to add more loss to them. We only simulate crosstalk from every aggressor's TX pin to the victim's RX pin. In SERDES channels the IL, RL and the crosstalk are all differential. For IL we use SDD21, for RL we use SDD11, and we calculate crosstalk based on the coupling from the positive and negative legs:

```
FEXT_AGGRESSOR1 = S25+S47-S27-S45
```

We can define limit lines for the SNR just like we do for IL, RL, and other curves. A modern (10Gig+) TX/RX equalizer pair can account for ~10dB of insertion loss. FEC error correction can help another 5dB. It is usually already included in the insertion loss limit lines in the standards, but if we are calculating our own IL limit from eye opening voltages then we have to account for it in our calculations. Any noises from reflections and crosstalk degrade the SNR the same way as loss does, so the maximum allowed loss becomes the maximum allowed loss and noise. If we assume that the transmitter sends 1V signals, and the receiver needs minimum 0.1V input, then it is a 10x ratio or 20dB maximum loss, for NRZ signals up to half the baud rate. For PAM4 it has to be a three times higher ratio (9.55dB more) because in PAM4 the actual signal is three times smaller than the full TX amplitude aggressor crosstalk. Reflections and crosstalk may come from the largest level transition, while the signal might come from the smallest transition (in the worst-case). Our S-parameters are relative to the source amplitude. We have to also subtract any equalizer and FEC improvement from that SNR requirement before applying them as limit lines. This number as a limit line is to be displayed as a horizontal line on the same diagram with the SNR(f) curve, then end it or turn it downward at half baud rate. It is simply a linearly spaced vector with all the same values up to half the baud rate, then it continues at -1000dB with the graph not showing anything below -20dB, so it appears that the line becomes vertical and disappears. The way it all looks on actual curves is demonstrated in Figure 11.4. To compute the limit lines:

```
ILMAX = 20 * log10(Voutmax / Vinmin)
SNR_LIM_NRZ = ILMAX - EQ - FEC = 5  [dB]
SNR_LIM_PAM4 = ILMAX - EQ - FEC + 9.55dB = 14.55  [dB]
```

The regular SNR in RF and analog electronics, as well as in COM calculations, is calculated from actual voltage of the signal and the noise at the receiver. They do not depend on the source amplitudes. Here we are using source to destination ratios (S-parameters) for both the signal and the noise, instead of absolute voltages at the destination. So, our SNR here is really a ratio-ratio, so to be very precise it should be called SNRR or SRNRR (signal ratio to noise ratio ratio), but that would be cumbersome.

Another combined loss-with-noise metric is the Channel Operating Margin (COM) defined by IEEE for 25Gig. It is a single 1D number in dB from a time domain eye simulation, not a frequency dependent curve. It can be computed from time domain simulations. Later in this chapter COM will be further explained. The above CIRL(f) and SNR(f) would instead spread the effect in 2D, without any arbitrary tweaks, so we could potentially identify separate causes of channel quality issues. Since SNR(f) above uses a ratio of ratios while COM uses a ratio of absolute voltages, the behavior for PAM4 will be different. The SNR(f) formula is the same for NRZ and PAM4 on the same board,

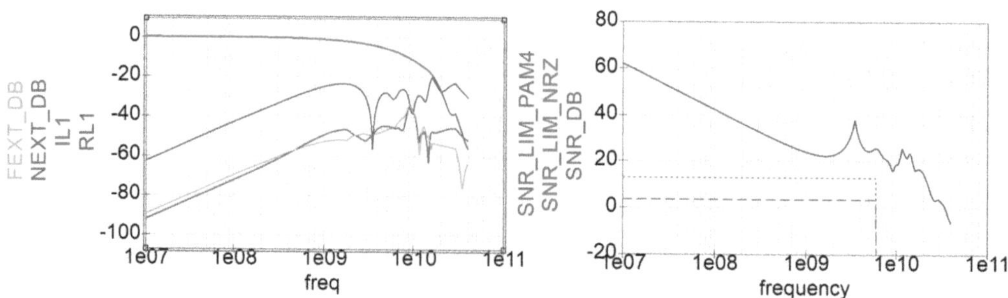

FIGURE 11.4 Computed SNR as an S-parameter and its sources.

but the SNR_LIM is different, while the COM calculation formula will be different for NRZ versus PAM4 on the same board and the COM limit will be the same.

11.1.4 Margins

We can compute a curve using an equation in ADS or QUCS, which shows the difference between the actual channel performance and the standard's limit line requirement; we can call this a margin curve. For example, the return loss margin from the return loss (RL) and the return loss limit (RLL) line is:

```
RL_MAR(f) = RLL(f) - RL(f)
```

We can also generate a single number from a margin curve with another equation by finding the smallest (minimum or worst-case) value on it or, in rare cases, reading it out at a specific frequency (at half the baud rate). This is the "minimum margin" number. A curve and a number are not the same. These numbers can be used to compare different design approaches or materials or components and present the comparison to coworkers from other departments who might not be familiar with recognizing S-parameter curve shapes and pathologies. We can also write down these numbers in any simulation reports or test reports. From a return loss curve, we can compute a return loss margin curve, and then find the minimum margin number. This will be the smallest worst-case gap between the RL curve and the RLL curve, regardless of what frequency point it occurs at.

Note that the simulation produces IL and RL curves and values at a certain parameter set point, but if we measured all production units, we would see a variance, about 10% for IL, and about 1 to 2dB for RL, due to manufacturing process tolerance (materials, PCB etching), temperature, and aging (months or years of use). When we simulate a design and want to assess the resulting margins, those margin requirements should incorporate the expected variance. For example, "the minimum margin number must be at least 2dB". We don't measure all production units, usually just a prototype for DVT, so the proto unit has to have enough margin for all effects. Each failed production unit when debugged needs to have at least 0dB margin (no crossing), or some partial margin for temperature and aging, without the need for process variance. Margin for variance is needed only for the full set of all units, relative to the prototype, not for one single unit.

Usually we look for these numbers:

- Fitted attenuation at half baud rate, for calculating loss per inch
- Minimum crosstalk margin: XT_MAR_MIN = |min(XTL-PSXT)|
- Minimum return loss margin: RL_MAR_MIN = |min(RLL-RL)|
- Minimum insertion loss margin: IL_MAR_MIN = |min(ILL-IL)|
- Insertion loss margin at half baud rate:
  `IL_MAR_HALFB = ILL(half_baud) - IL(half_baud)`
- Insertion loss to crosstalk ratio (space between PSXT and IL curves) at half baud rate:
  `ICR_MAR_HALFB = IL(half_baud) - PSXT(half_baud)`

11.1.5 The Touchstone File Format

This is a simple text file with a list of S-parameters at any number of frequency points. This file is used as a simulation model, as a simulation output, or as the output of a VNA measurement. When used as a model it may describe a board, a chip package, a connector, a via, or other design element. It has comment lines (anything after "!"), one line defining the data format (after"#"), and many data record or frequency point lines. The format can be "MA" as magnitude in absolute terms and phase in degrees, "DB" as magnitude in decibels and phase in degrees, "RI" as real and imaginary complex number pairs. The frequency format and measurement reference impedance are also listed.

Sometimes the numbers are separated by spaces, sometimes by tabs. Large port number files are sometimes one line per frequency point, sometimes they are broken down into four lines per frequency point. Simulation tools can read these files in with any format. We can even paste them into an Excel spreadsheet to process measured data, but that requires the use of the exact same format every time, fortunately we can format them in a text editor before use. It is worth studying the file format so we can alter the space/tab formatting when importing the files into basic tools that cannot recognize all formatting types.

An example of an S-parameter file:

```
! Data File Written: 08/23/2018 11:16:11
! Mapping: P1: SIGNAL_P, P2: SIGNAL_N, P3: SIGNALEX_P, P4: SIGNALEX_N
# MHZ S MA R 50
!freq      S11                S21                S12                S22
1.00000 0.6688 -132.1545 0.7413 -41.9828  0.7413 -41.9828 0.6688 -132.1545
10.0000 0.9935 -173.6918 0.1101 -83.5149  0.1101 -83.5149 0.9935 -173.6918
100.000 0.9998 -179.4951 0.0112 -89.3233  0.0112 -89.3233 0.9998 -179.49511
1000.00 0.9994  178.7346 0.0015  87.05724 0.0015  87.0572 0.9994  178.7346
```

11.2 SI BASICS

We can find complete book-sets on signal integrity. This book includes the "SI Basics" section for completeness and also to present this topic from the designer's point of view, not from the usual analyst's point of view.

11.2.1 Transmission Lines

Every trace or physical interconnection (PCB trace, via, cable) that is longer than the distance the signal would travel during its rise time acts as a transmission line that requires terminations and impedance control in order to recover meaningful data at the receiver. In digital signal transmission, there is always a transmitter and a (or multiple) receiver(s). A digital signal has to be confidently beyond one logic voltage threshold or the other at the time it is sampled on a clock edge by the receiver. It is the logic level that carries the information in a signal. It takes time for even a good signal to reach that logic level, but a badly terminated signal bounces around, pauses half-way on a plateau, or rings for a while, which takes even longer time to settle to a new logic level. For traditional (non-SERDES) interfaces we directly analyze rising and falling waveforms and feed the result into timing analysis calculations to determine if they will work reliably or not. SERDES receivers just have a small eye height opening requirement instead of the traditional logic thresholds. They are more effectively analyzed through S-parameters in the frequency domain. An imperfect or non-existing termination on high-speed lines creates reflections, which we can see as plateaus and ringing in time domain, and the return loss S-parameter curve approaching 0dB in the frequency domain. With lower speed interfaces the choice of using terminations or the type of terminations comes up, while SERDES interfaces always have a built-in differential termination at 85, 93, or 100 Ohm. The same return-loss issues we see with termination issues, also comes up on SERDES links when the signal path impedance has discontinuities. They appear only at higher frequencies, not noticeable by slow interfaces. The discontinuities can be caused by imperfections of PCB features like traces, vias, and planes, but also components like connectors and series components. All of which needs to be impedance controlled if they are individually longer than than the distance the signal would travel during its rise time.

Practical termination schemes are described in Chapter 2, "Digital Circuits". Incident wave is the first wave front that arrives to a receiver device, reflected wave is what travels backwards towards the transmitter, after the incident wave has already reached and bounced back from the far end of the transmission line. We try to eliminate the reflected wave in most cases by reducing discontinuities and improving terminations or, in the case of slow signals driven by FPGA, simply reducing the drive strength.

When the transmitter chip flips the output signal from 0 to 1 or vice versa, the signal will start rising or falling, transitioning to the new logic level voltage. It takes time to do that, due to trace and input pin capacitances. It can be so slow to rise that the signal does not even make a full swing within a bit time; this is called inter-symbol-interference (ISI). Differential signal receivers do not require a full swing, so they can tolerate it even when the signal only makes it 20% of the way through the transition. But if it slows further than that within a bit time, then the signal cannot be recovered. This is usually caused not just by capacitances, but by the insertion loss of the PCB material as well, which becomes dominant of the rise/fall slowdown at 5 to 10 Gigabits per second. Complicated SERDES DFE equalizers and FEC error correction engines help with it a little. We mitigate this mainly by controlling the PCB dielectric material, copper foil, and lamination process parameters in the stackup design and by requesting insertion-loss controlled boards. Another aspect of insertion loss control is the loss budget and maximum trace length calculation, so with given loss (dB/inch at half baud rate), we calculate how long we can route our traces. Either we control the loss or the trace length or both. This is described in a later chapter.

The signal transition might swing back through the logic level threshold due to reflections. In that case we can consider the transition complete once all the swinging remains beyond the new threshold. Because of this, instead of simply rise time, we can consider a transition delay (TD) as described in Chapter 10, "Timing Analysis". It will include anything and everything that causes a signal to delay the time it reaches and stays beyond the logic threshold. TD is also important for calculating timing analysis, both for design verification and for calculating trace length constraints on slower (up to few GHz) buses. There are two types of trace length constraints for PCB design: the loss-budget based and the timing based. For slower buses, the rise time is less than the bit time, but not negligible; actually we need to know how much it is exactly as it is part of the timing budget calculation. For high-speed SERDES links the timing really comes down to the width of the eye diagram, we do not have to calculate exact delays, just make sure the signal reaches the new level outside of the eye mask on the sides. The CDR inside the SERDES receiver still has input setup and hold requirements, but that is combined into an eye mask width requirement. In an S-par-based analysis we ensure this indirectly by complying with frequency domain limit lines.

11.2.2 Crosstalk

Crosstalk is when a digital input buffer receives the intended signal mixed with an attenuated version of nearby signals. It is undesired, so we try to minimize it through layout design techniques. We can analyze crosstalk in frequency domain as an S-parameter or in time domain as a noise voltage that is super-positioned on a signal analyzed in an eye diagram. We call the trace being analyzed for noise voltage "victim", and the other traces in the analysis that are causing the crosstalk "aggressors". In time domain simply the eye opening has to meet the eye mask inside the receiver or the transition delay has to meet the timing equations. Crosstalk is looked at as an absolute voltage on time domain eye diagrams, while it appears as a ratio between the source and destination voltages when using S-parameters. In frequency domain we would analyze an at-least 8-port S-parameter model of two differential pairs, where the single-ended S25 or S15 or a mixed-mode SDD13 or SDD23 parameter has to meet a typical -40dB limit up to half baud rate, meaning 1% amplitude. For CMOS signals we could have 5% crosstalk (one-third of the noise budget), but on SERDES links due to tight loss budgets, we can afford only a very small amount, maybe 1% or -40dB. Figure 11.5 shows the paths through which crosstalk can affect a signal.

Crosstalk can happen from trace to trace, via to via, via to trace, or trace to via. We can analyze complete traces, main routes, or component fanout regions (pin fields) for crosstalk. All types can be described as S-parameters.

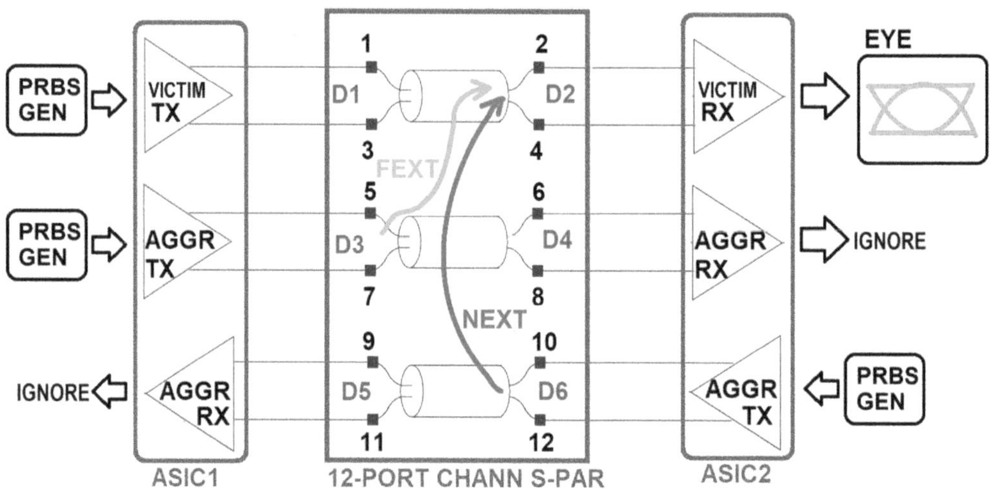

FIGURE 11.5 Crosstalk model.

When the crosstalk is taking place under one ASIC's pin field, between its own receive and transmit pins, we call it near-end crosstalk, aka NEXT. Basically, the aggressor transmit and the victim receive pins are in the same chip. When the crosstalk takes its effect through parallel lines in the same direction, between two TX lines or two RX lines, we call this the far-end crosstalk, or FEXT. In this case the aggressor transmit and the victim receive pins are in different chips. The total crosstalk PSXT to each victim is the complex sum of N NEXT and (N-1) FEXT sources in an N-lane interface. Crosstalk is typically analyzed between signals of the same bus, for example, between two or more lanes of the same PCIe link. The sum of multiple aggressors (PSXT) is the most useful metric, so we would simulate up to eight signals together, including both RX and TX traces. The crosstalk between different interfaces like DDR4 memory to PCIe are hard to simulate with current tools; instead, we can look at interference through mode conversion. Usually we leave larger gaps between different types of interfaces in a layout to avoid having to deal with interference. But if they are not sufficiently localized, then they will still affect each other. TX-to-RX NEXT at the same chip is reduced by ASIC chip companies, by leaving a gap row of ground pins (acting as a via fence) between TX and RX pins in the device pinout, but that can be ruined by board designers by not letting the GND vias to go all the way through the stackup or via sharing between ground pins.

Crosstalk and interference are caused by capacitive or inductive coupling or electromagnetic (EMI) radiation. Inductive coupling can be between vias and traces, between overlapping return current loops (to stitching vias), and between overlapping return current spread in the plane under the traces. The return current loops are described in Chapter 15, "PCB Layout Design". The plane return current spread is described under impedance discontinuities. The coupling is stronger at higher frequencies. If a digital signal's slew rate or rise time is faster, then it translates to a higher knee frequency by applying the famous formula: f_knee=0.35/t_rise. The data rate does not really matter; the rise time does, except for very fast SERDES signals where the rise time is expected to be more tied with the data rate. For SERDES signals we use half the baud rate instead of rise time as it is more readily available information. Crosstalk happens when the aggressor is having a transition. A faster transition results in stronger crosstalk. Low toggle rate signals might still have very fast rise times if the same chip uses similar buffers on its high-speed and low-speed pins. This happens typically with high-end chips like X86 processors or large FPGAs. The aggressor's current change causes a noise voltage in the victim trace; the aggressor's voltage change causes a current in the victim that drops a noise voltage on the trace impedance. Ground planes block electric fields, so they can help with capacitive coupling to other layers, but they also pull the field away from traces on the same layer. Magnetic coupling can be blocked by ferromagnetic materials like cobalt, which is not a PCB material, or by physical spacing. The noise voltage caused by crosstalk is larger if the traces are closer (smaller spacing); if the dielectric layer in the stackup is thicker, if the parallel segment is longer, or when the aggressor signal's slew rate is faster. This means slower signals that have slower edges can be routed closer on the board than high-speed signals. We can look at any crosstalk S-parameter profile and see the left side of the curve almost linearly rising with frequency, up to a certain limit at a few hundred Megahertz, then above that it goes up and down due to resonance.

To be sure, slow signals could be simulated, but based on experience, for example, up to 133MHz, we usually route the traces tightly packed in "4mil trace 4mil space" bundles or bunches. If we have a lot of board space then we can use 8mil spacing. Different simulator tools can vary hugely in their crosstalk levels in the S-parameter results at low frequencies, which are related to basic logic signals. They were not really created to simulate crosstalk on low-speed signals.

Free running clock signals need more spacing because they are more affected than data signals. Data signals are checked in the middle of the bit time, and they have to be within the bounds of a logic level. Clocks are checked on their edges, so their edge must be monotonic. For example, a 1V CMOS data signal can still be detected fine if have a 0.25V crosstalk noise super-positioned on it half-way in its bit period, while a clock receiving a 0.025V noise on its rising edge would cause some state machines to progress two states in one legal clock cycle while others only progress one. Some flip-flops will see an extra edge while others will not. A counter can jump the count as a result. On the other hand, data signals on the same bus will not change state during the time interval while the clock is transitioning, so that theoretical crosstalk can be ignored, which is guaranteed by the timing architecture. Data signals of other buses may change in that unfortunate interval, but not the ones of the same bus. Data signals of the same bus, if they are timing locked (e.g., synchronous buses), only disturb each other during their own transition interval, but not when they are sampled, so they are naturally immune to crosstalk to some extent. Different lanes of SERDES links or DDRx memory interfaces can disturb each other at any time, as they are not phase matched at every point or at all. Glue logic signals like PowerGood and resets only change state once in run-time, before any processing would even begin, so they will not disturb any data or clock signals. On the other hand, they are sensitive only when they are at the high level. Spacing rules can be applied to "everything" or we can waive it to signals based on their function, after we applied much critical thinking. When we write a layout constraint document, probably we should not expect everyone to know all that; thus, we can opt for "constraining everything" to keep it simple. But we can individually waive constraint items if there is no other way of completing the layout while trying to meet them. A smaller amount of crosstalk into a SERDES ref clock can increase jitter in it, even if the edge remains monotonic. SERDES transceivers require very low jitter levels in the hundred femto-second range.

11.2.3 Jitter

Jitter is the random deviation of the bit time from the average or from the previous bit time. This is usually analyzed on SERDES data lines and also on reference clock lines. For data lines we can see the eye closing horizontally, caused by ISI and jitter. ISI is the inter symbol interference, basically it means if the signal was low for several bit times, then it will take longer for it to rise to the logic high level, compared to a case when it was low for only one bit, as it did not settle that low. There are several types of jitter, such as random jitter (RJ), deterministic jitter (DJ like the one created by ISI), cycle-to-cycle jitter, and phase noise. They have different histograms that can be simulated or measured.

All SERDES interfaces of ASICs and FPGAs require an external reference clock, usually in the range of 100 to 622MHz, and differential LVPECL, LVDS, CML or HCSL. Usually, a group of SERDES shares one, so one ASIC may need one to eight identical clocks. These "refclock" inputs have maximum RMS phase noise jitter requirements, which the ASIC datasheets specify. Oscillator and buffer vendors also specify the worst case the jitter on their output. A 10Gbps SERDES usually tolerates 250 to 500fs jitter, but we have to rely on the ASIC datasheet for an exact number. Any fanout buffers add to the jitter, for example, if the input has 100fs jitter and it adds 50fs, then the output will have 150fs jitter on it. We typically measure the phase noise type of jitter with a signal analyzer and a splitter/combiner.

The jitter on a reference clock signal gets added, sometimes multiplied by the SERDES PLL, and ends up in the SERDES data line. So minimizing the refclock jitter minimizes the data line jitter and opens the eye horizontally. Power rail noise generated by the ASIC itself, by VRM ripple, and by other sections of the same ASIC also adds to the jitter in the transmitters and in the receivers. Even if the received signal is without too much jitter, the actually captured data might have excessive jitter due to power rail noise inside the RX SERDES. This is why it is important to provide a clean voltage rail to the SERDES power pins. Each SERDES has a refclock PLL that has its own power pins on the ASIC package. We usually supply these from an LDO (free of switching ripple) or from a separate small switching VRM set to have a low ripple current. Some ASIC vendors require each SERDES tile to have its own filtered voltage rail, through series ferrite beads, but that adds lots of components and plane cuts to the board design that has to be considered.

11.2.4 Stubs

A stub caused by incorrect multi-point bus trace routing or by vias will create reflections when the rise time is comparable or faster than the propagation delay through the stub length. In case of multi-point nets, we need to add terminations to both ends, for this we can have only two ends of a net route topology, by routing the trace on the PCB from one device to another, to another, etc., without branches or splits. A stub will create an additional trace end, but we cannot terminate nets at more than two points, as the splits will require the trace impedance to be halved in the branches passed the split and the drivers to provide current/power to feed the extra terminations.

Via stubs are a problem above 5Gbps typically, especially near the TX SERDES where the rise time is faster than it is at the RX SERDES. For example, a 0.75mm long via stub creates a 1.5mm reflected signal travel path, which means the reflection arrives with about 10ps propagation delay. The stub reflection path is explained in Figure 11.6. On a 25Gig signal, near the transmitter we can have 7ps short rise times. This via stub reflection time meets the $T_{pd} > T_{RISE}$ criteria and interferes with the signal. That criteria was first mentioned here for the need for impedance control and terminations of traces, but at a basic level it also applies to stubs, as the via stubs are always unterminated. But instead of trying to add terminations to the via stubs, we remove the stub or reduce its length. Even a 10Gbps signal would be interfered by via stubs, that is why 8 to 10Gbps and faster boards must have via stub elimination strategy for the fast signals.

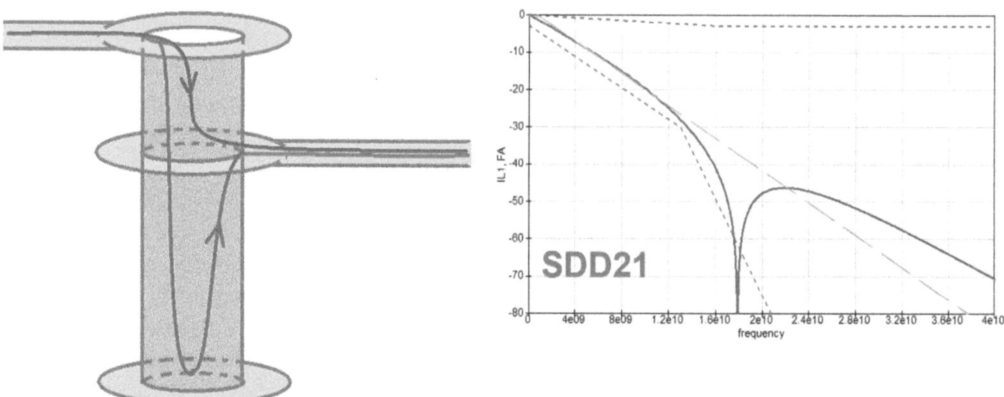

FIGURE 11.6 Via stub explanation.

We can determine the exact via length to frequency relation when via stubs become a problem. If we are assuming the rise time being equal to one-fourth of the bit time, and want to be safely away from the rise-time-versus-delay criteria by four times, then we can calculate the maximum acceptable via stub length as:

```
StubLength > 11.8 / (SQRT(DK)*baud_rate*4*4)   [inch and Gbps]
```

To be precise, via stubs are twice as long electrically than their mechanical length because the signal travels through twice. For all other discontinuities the length to electrical length ratio is 1:1. We could re-use the same formula for other discontinuities, for example, the wrong-impedance-via, but then it will be relaxed by two times. Via stubs can be eliminated by backdrilling, by using microvia stacks, or by only routing the high-speed signals on Layer-(N-2) then returning to layer-1 on both ends. During backdrilling, an already drilled and plated via is drilled again using a slightly larger diameter drill bit and applying a controlled depth technique until just before the routing layer. See Chapter 15, "PCB Layout Design".

In frequency domain, the extra reflection creates resonances as dips in the insertion loss curve and peaks in the return loss curve. If the via resonant frequency matches the half data rate, then the original signal and the stub-reflected delayed previous bit signal arrive to the receiver at the same time. If they are inverse level (1 versus 0), then they cause the signal to have a mixed level between 1 and 0, aka attenuate. If the stub is shorter, then the delay is shorter, and the inverse level alignment occurs at a higher frequency. The higher the better, if the resonant frequency is much higher than the signal's bandwidth (half data rate), then it will not interfere with the signal. Backdrilling reduces stub length from 20 to 160mils to 4 to 12mils. In a circuit simulator a via stub can be modeled with a transmission line ending in a 0.1 to 0.8pF capacitor connected to ground. The longer the stub, the longer the transmission line, the larger the capacitance and lower the resonant frequency, the higher the risk of interfering with the signal.

11.2.5 Return Path

A high-speed signal travels through a path in 3D, through traces, vias, and component pins in the form of an electrical current flow, from the transmitter chip pin to the receiver chip pin. Another current of the same magnitude flows in the opposite direction from the receiver to the transmitter through the ground or power nets (planes, pins, and vias), it is called the return current. The return current for a high-speed signal forced by the laws of physics tries to keep its travel path within the absolute closest proximity to the 3D path of the signal current, called the return path. This is demonstrated in the schematic view in Figure 11.7. We want the return currents to go into the ground planes (not power planes) because we design modern boards with ground-only referencing. Sometimes the return current goes through the chip power pin (instead of the ground pin) when driving a logic high output or Thevenin terminations receiving a signal. This creates the need for decoupling capacitors to route the return current from the power pin into the ground plane. This might not show up in an SI simulation if the simulator assumes ideal power sources. Even if it is not shown there, the design still has to take care of re-routing return currents into the ground planes through decoupling in the schematic and layout design.

The PCB design and connector pinouts have to ensure that the return path can be very close to the signal path. Some designers make trade-offs that result in the two paths separating to an unnecessary distance or, in some cases, diverted far away (even 100 times farther than necessary) through a detour, lacking ground stitching vias. This detour introduces series parasitic inductances into the signal path (causing increased ISI) and a mutual inductance between the return path loops of different signals (causing increased crosstalk). The return path must include the continuous planes adjacent to the routing layer and the well localized ground stitching vias at the component fanout that connect all the ground planes together. SERDES signals require at least one directly adjacent

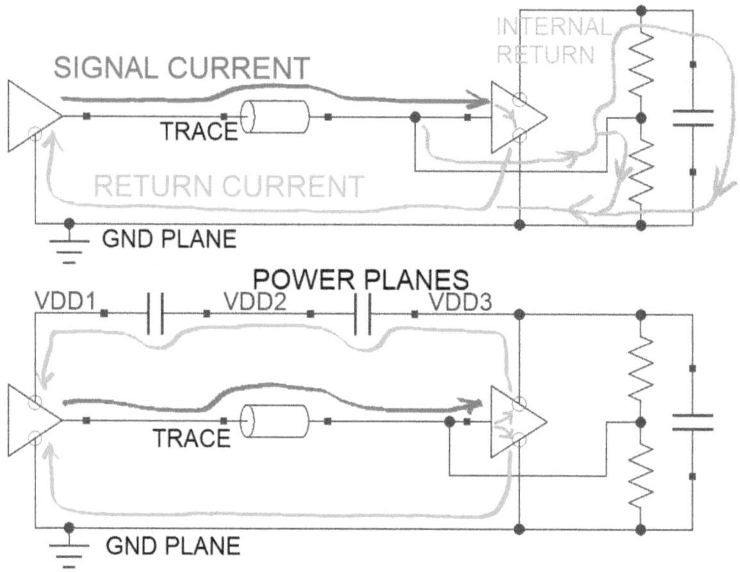

FIGURE 11.7 Return current path in I/O circuits.

ground via for each signal via at an exact small distance to also ensure proper via impedance. Memory interfaces are typically good when a few signals share one ground via. About 20 glue logic signals can share a ground via. Typical signs of return path issues can be seen on an insertion loss S-parameter profile as a big suckout resonance at a few Gigahertz, plus at its higher harmonic frequencies (2x, 3x, 4x, 5x...) also. If the ground via is there, but at a wrong location and forms a big impedance spike or dip, then it appears as a big suckout resonance at 10 to 30GHz.

In modern high-speed hardware we always create PCB layer stackups where the high-speed routing layers are sandwiched between two ground planes, not ground and power planes. This ensures that the return currents will low only through ground planes, not power planes. Power planes for return path are not preferred, as the power supply noise gets added to the signals seen by the receivers. Another issue is the power planes are usually not continuous, because we have multiple power nets, so providing a return path will be possible only through AC-coupling capacitors between the power nets. This creates much larger discontinuities than a fully ground-referenced design, it will work up only to about 100–200MHz. Termination resistors should be placed between the signal and its layout route reference net, be it ground or power, or to a VTT voltage rail. Thevenin terminations on ground-referenced nets require capacitor decoupling of the termination resistors.

11.2.6 Impedance Discontinuities

The trace impedance will be the same as the calculated value, only if the there is a continuous path provided in (both of) the reference plane(s) where the return current can flow. If we cut its way (plane splits), or there are large voids on the plane that the return current has to go around, then the return current is forced away from its natural path and the calculated impedance is no longer valid. It is just a simplification to say that the impedance is defined by the PCB cross-section geometry. In reality it is more defined by the shape of the distributed currents in both the trace and the reference planes and by the shape of the magnetic and electric fields. These shapes are just guided by the PCB copper object geometry.

For example, a 100um wide microstrip trace over a 100um dielectric has an impedance of 69.5 Ohms (FEMM simulation), but when the trace has to cross a plane split and go above the wrong plane in parallel to the split edge at a distance of 9mm, then the impedance will be as high as 158.9

Ohms. This is shown in Figure 11.8. Figure 11.9 shows the magnetic field lines in case of the split crossing from the previous figure.

We always need to provide a continuous ground return current path in both of the reference planes, since the return currents flow in both of them. An inner routing layer (stripline) is between two ground reference planes. Some people say that only the closer plane matters for return path and impedance, but as we can see the effect of both planes is significant. In an example FEMM simulation, with 3.3:1 dielectric thickness ratio, we find that 24% (not insignificant) of the current is flowing on the farther plane. Figure 11.10 shows the return current distribution inside the two ground planes at 1GHz.

Any small voids in the plane along the return path also modify the impedance for the short segment. When a trace passes through an area of several small undercuts, like in a connector pin field or under a BGA component, the undercuts are at equal distance. This is a periodicity in the geometry, and it will create a periodic discontinuity in the return path and the trace impedance. The

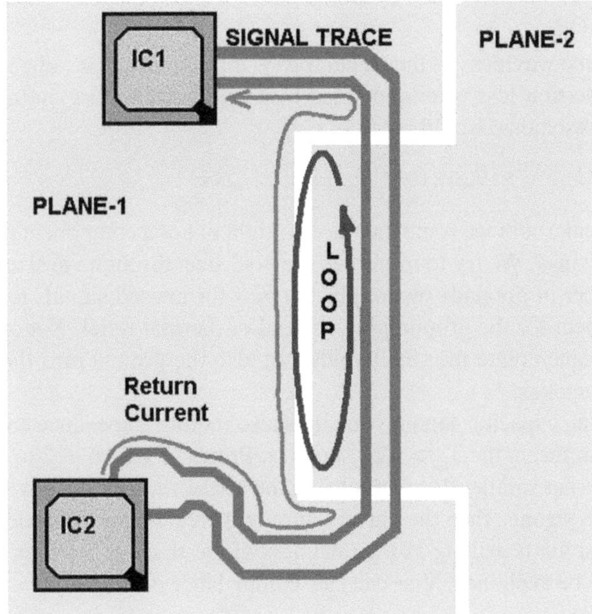

FIGURE 11.8 Routing two traces over the wrong split plane.

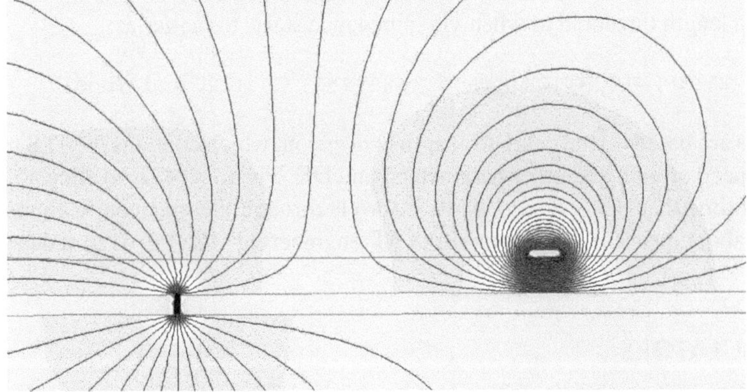

FIGURE 11.9 Magnetic field with plane split-crossing. FEMM simulation at 10GHz.

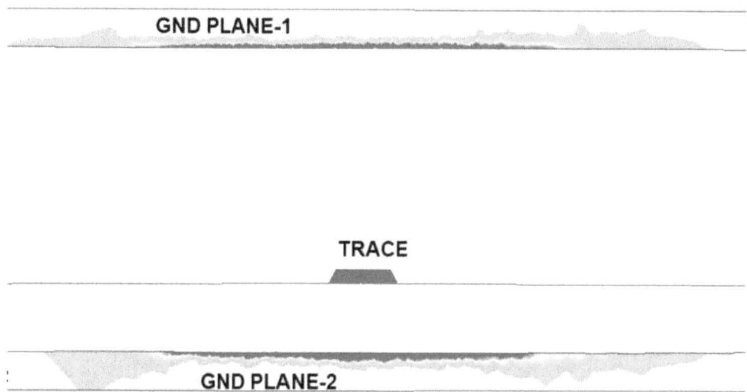

FIGURE 11.10 Return current distribution for a stripline cross-section, FEMM simulation at 10GHz.

TDR plot will show some waviness as the signal travels through. The periodic nature of this creates a resonance on the insertion loss profile, defined by the pin pitch representing propagation delay through one cell. The resonance would be at:

```
F_res = 11.8 / (pitch * SQRT(DK))  [inch, GHz]
```

What we can do is to make sure we route the trace straight out of a component pin field to minimize the number of void passings. We try to minimize the void size, through via size and clearances. We try to reduce the number of antipads by not placing vias for unused signals to break the periodicity. We use direct connect for the ground pins, instead of thermal relief. Not only the pins that are not connected to the plane create the small voids, but also the ground pins that are connected but through thermal relief spokes.

Vias and AC-coupling capacitor fanout structures also require impedance control if the propagation delay through them meets the $T_{pd} > T_{RISE}$ criteria. Practically even at 2 to 5x slower rise times it would create a somewhat smaller discontinuity. If the board was designed without via impedance control on the SERDES signals, then the via structure will create an impedance discontinuity in the signal path. The longest via is as long as the thickness of the stackup. Later in this chapter, the via impedance control will be explained. Vias can cause impedance discontinuities when their length is:

```
ViaLength > rise_time * 11.8 / SQRT(DK)  [inch and ns]
```

If we are assuming the rise time being equal to one-fourth of the bit time near the SERDES transmitter, and want to be safely away from the rise time versus delay criteria by four times, then we can calculate the via length threshold to when via impedance starts to matter as:

```
ViaLength > 11.8 / (SQRT(DK)*baud_rate*4*2)  [inch and Gbps]
```

These equations are based on the delay-to-length conversion, which contains the 11.8 magic number (derived from speed of light and other parameters) and DK. The first "4" is to allow the reflection to arrive half a bit time that is worst case, while it travels through the via once. It almost sounds like we are talking about quarter wavelengths from RF engineering. The "2" is to reduce the effect to a safer level.

11.3 SI SIMULATORS

With simulators we can get a close approximation several months in advance to how clean and usable the signal quality will be once we build the prototype. We need to understand how simulator programs work, what they do, and what they do not do. It is not trivial what we should or should not simulate, at what stage of the project, what data we need beforehand, and what conclusions we can make from the results. The unfortunately typical use case for SI simulators, known as the "garbage in garbage out", is not the best way to make use of this great resource. It is not enough to reach the last page on the setup wizard, based on a training, but we also have to understand what is happening. All the parameters have to be properly set up. If one uses a random, default, or wrongly assumed value, then the final results can be off by orders of magnitude. This means that we must be very thorough in setting up our simulators, and if we find a parameter we do not fully understand, then we have to study up on it. Even if we think we kind of understand it, still study up more. Also note that different tools will produce different results, especially on non-ideal boards, suggesting that none are infinitely accurate. Simulation results should not be considered hard proof for design quality. Simulations are inherently optimistic while measurements pessimistic.

The results have to be assessed for boundaries and corner cases by an experienced engineer. We have to do sanity check on the results, for example, comparing them against measured results from other projects. For example, when it shows that we are getting 10V reflected waves on a 1.5V signal, then maybe we should pause and double-check before presenting it on a team review meeting. Every time we simulate or measure something, we have to have expectations of a value range beforehand. If the results are far off from the expectation, then we have to go back to the setup. For example, if the noise value is expected to be around 10mV but we are getting 1V, then we have to go back most likely and not release statements about it yet, but if it is 30mV, then the design might actually be that bad. Beyond 5x deviation from expectation, it is most likely a setup error. The hard part is to know what the expectation should be. That comes from our own experience, or we can ask others.

We can do absolute simulations where we check a detailed design as to whether it meets standards or chip requirements. We can also do a comparative or "what if" analysis where just one design feature is simulated with two different options, like different trace impedances or via sizes, or different connector vendors, and decide which one produces relatively lower return loss than the other. The comparative analysis is less sensitive to simulation tool inaccuracies; it simply tells which option is better than the other. If we have a prototype test result already, from proto-1 or from a previous project, then the new design can be improved, and therefore its reliability can be improved. This is not an exact verification, and it is without guarantees. It would help improve the design by making a design change based on a comparative simulation, without having a full scientific explanation of all the un-simulated parameters. For example, if proto-1 fails to boot up 0.1% of the time, with our PCIe link having 3dB return loss margin in simulation (that should be good enough but it is somehow not), then by making changes to improve the apparent return loss margin to 6dB, maybe that 0.1% failure rate could be completely eliminated.

11.3.1 Simulation Basics

We use signal integrity simulator software for helping us decide on high-speed features and hardware architecture decisions before we start the detailed schematic design (pre-layout simulation) as well as for validating designs when the PCB layout is already completed (post-layout simulation). It is like a virtual prototyping lab where we can generate voltage/time waveforms like we would see on oscilloscopes in a real lab (time domain simulation involving ASIC pin buffers) or we can generate S-parameters like we would if we measured the bare board (frequency domain, without ASIC silicon) with a VNA in the lab. All that is done before building any prototypes. The purpose of these simulations is a pass/fail check under worst-case conditions. Fail means the design is bad or unreliable and needs to be changed, assuming the simulation was set up with the most accurate parameters. In-pre-layout we can adjust some parameters (within a limited design decision space) then do a pass/fail check. In post-layout there is nothing to adjust in the simulator (other than re-route the signal trace on the PCB) and it is only a binary pass-fail check. The same applies to power integrity simulations too. It is important to remember that a signal is a voltage/time waveform in time domain, while the passive channel is the metal+dielectric structures that conduct the signal to its destination. The passive channel is most often described with S-parameters in frequency domain. For non-SERDES interfaces we just analyze the signals in time domain. For SERDES interfaces we could do both time domain signal and frequency domain passive channel analysis, but we mostly rely on the latter. RF engineers analyze their signals in frequency domain as a spectrum; we (digital hardware engineers) analyze them only in time domain. In rare cases we may look at the passive channel in time domain, using a TDR test/sim, but most of the time we look at the passive channel in frequency domain with S-parameters.

A special case of simulation is the via structure optimization for impedance (SI) or inductance (PDN), which is used for generating design parameters or constraints, its output is not a pass/fail check but a set of design parameters to be implemented in the PCB layout.

Some simulations do not make sense to run, as they do not provide useful information about how the chips will see the signal. But all that really matters is how the chip sees the signal, not how a mid-bus waveform looks like with no active chips there. Simulating eye diagrams at connector pins instead of chip pins does not make sense. In most cases it makes sense only to simulate a complete channel that starts and ends with an active silicon ASIC pin. In some cases, there are S-parameter requirements on “partial channels” like an add-in card or base board, if we might have to plug third-party cards into it. Standard organizations like PCIe, Ethernet, and OIF focus on complete channel specs, while SFF, VITA, and PICMG focus on partial channel budget allocations. Often a chip-to-chip link involves multiple boards, so we have to simulate multiple boards together as one model.

Most companies don't simulate every interface type on every board design, only the ones that seem more critical or risky, for example due to being longer or faster. Simulating all would cost too much resource/time. A type is defined by interface standard (PCIe vs KR vs InfiniBand), and by on-board versus off-board ending. If we have many signals or lanes on an interface, then we usually just simulate one or a few signals. We rarely have a full coverage, for example using a DDR batch simulation, but in basic 2D mode. The RX and TX channels on SERDES links are usually differently laid out, so we need to extract at least one RX and one TX trace. On some designs we need to also extract the longest and shortest traces, or length-match them in the design to avoid it. While setting up each extraction, we could include two to 8 signals together into one larger S-par file to evaluate crosstalk effects. Half of them being RX and the other half TX can ensure that we capture the strong NEXT effect. Traditionally we only run simulations on the nominal trace impedance and nominal material loss model, while we vary the chip speed corners (slow/fast/typ in time domain only). To better predict the manufacturing tolerance of PCBs, we could extract the +/-10% low and high impedance versions of the same trace, with low and high insertion loss (in dB/in@f0 for SERDES links only). This quadruples the number of PCB to S-par model extractions required, from 2...4 to now 8...16 per type, or up to 48 per board. It is not reasonable to run that many, we usually keep it to 2...8 total per board. We could just extract the RX/TX from the layout, longest/shortest, that is four, and apply the imp/loss variations to the S-par models in a post processing tool to generate the remaining models quickly. With the multiple model files, we can run a batch-mode back-end simulation that substitutes all S-par model combinations, to run hundreds of simulation permutations (value combinations). This is mainly useful on multi-board SERDES channels where each board can vary independently, although not commonly done. In frequency domain this results in multi-curve diagrams, while in time domain a BER contour height/width or COM table. A simpler alternative is to just run one nominal simulation with a stricter limit line or extra margin requirement. Each PCB extraction costs one or more days to run, a model post-processing costs a minute, additional batch permutations a minute each. For space and other "mission critical" designs we might have to simulate every signal, or every type of signal, while for many basic products we usually don't simulate anything. If we have designed our SERDES links with only 3D-EM pre-optimized or fully re-used structures, then simulations might also be skipped.

The type of SI simulations we do depends on the interface type and speed. For SERDES links we usually do S-parameter simulations in frequency domain, sometimes eye-diagram, BER-contour, and COM simulations in time domain. Specifically, pre-layout simulations to aid architectural decisions and perhaps post-layout for increasing confidence (or to find layout mistakes). For all other types of interfaces, we sometimes do pre-layout simulations to determine transition delays (related to rise time) that we can use in timing analysis calculations for determining the trace length constraints. Then we can also do post-layout simulations to observe any issues with waveforms and to do a final timing analysis verification. For DDRx memory interfaces some tools have a DDR batch wizard that automates the SI/timing analysis on many signals all at once. For tools that do not support batch DDR, we can simulate waveforms, then we read out the timing (transition delay and propagation delay) information from the graphs, then feed that into our Excel timing calculator.

We often perform simulations to analyze design concepts, we do not just simulate every instance or every signal trace on every project. This requires the design to be implemented in a way of "replication", symmetries, and regular grids, instead of free-form routing and placement. Free form means each instance of similar items is different. Many layout engineers are accustomed to implementing free-form routing, consisting of zero strategy, and just incrementally building a design one step at a time in isolation from all other steps. That does not work well for modern high-speed designs. Exact distances between vias determine the impedance and S-parameters, which can be ensured only using copy/paste replication. With replication we can reduce the uncertainty, risk, and amount of required simulation work.

11.3.1.1 Speed Limits

Slow signals in the range of 10kHz to 150MHz are sometimes simulated because their bus drivers, timing architecture, and termination schemes are designed in a way that they can barely make it even at those speeds. We have to consider their rise times, rather than toggle rate, as the rise time is more related to signal integrity of non-SERDES signals. These can be SPI buses, JTAG, BroadSync, and other interfaces. Sometimes we have a tendency to say that we have 25Gig signals, so we do not care about any 10MHz signals on the board anymore, but that would be a mistake. On the other hand, we really do not simulate most low-speed signals, for example, I2C buses when we have no more than eight loads, 1-inch-long SPI buses, or 25MHz clocks when they do not go through any connectors—basically when they are used in low-risk configurations. Glue logic signals like power enables or thermal alerts are never simulated. Crosstalk is usually not a concern for signals below 150MHz because their rise times are so slow (few Nano seconds) that they do not induce much noise voltage through capacitive or inductive coupling. So their spacing can be in tight groups of 4mil trace and 4mil space and do not need simulating, except if their parallel segment is unusually long (like 10" or more). Crosstalk is dependent on spacing, dielectric thickness in the stackup, DK, and frequency. We can assume that a SERDES signal will have a rise time ~ 0.2*UI near the TX pins while ~2*UI near the RX pins. "UI" is the unit interval or bit time. Regular or non-SERDES signals usually have a rise time ~0.0001*UI to 0.5*UI. Glue logic will have a nanosecond. Slow clocks might need to be spaced out to 10mil from the 4/4mil (or 4/8) tight bundles to ensure smooth and monotonic edges. Signal transition delays need to be simulated for timing, on clock or strobe-based interface buses above 1MHz but not on any asynchronous glue logic signals. Asynchronous glue logic signals (not the same as asynchronous buses with strobes) do not have any timing relative to another signal. Layout extraction for any slow signals is done in 2D cross-section mode. Low-speed SI simulations are typically concerned with edge monotony of clocks, verifying that the signal reaches proper logic levels, measuring transition delays for timing analysis calculations, and with experimenting with different termination schemes. Terminations do not work below 10 Megahertz on PCB traces because trace impedance shoots way up below that frequency.

In some cases, the SI effects do not matter as much, in other cases they matter more. CMOS signals can take 5% crosstalk and only 5% loss, while SERDES signals can take 95% loss but only 1% crosstalk. To account for crosstalk properly, we usually extract up to seven aggressors and compute their sum as PSXT. Differential signals are analyzed in differential mode S-parameters. Timing-driven buses can take more crosstalk from other data signals on the same bus or lane, in the time interval while they are transitioning, because that time they are not being sampled yet. Glue logic signals like PowerGood and resets change state only before any processing even begins, so they will not disturb any other signal in real operation. A smaller amount of noise into a SERDES ref clock can increase jitter in it above the tight limits in the hundred femtoseconds range. A differential signal is less affected by crosstalk than a single-ended one.

We could try to quantify the speed limits. Above these limits high-speed design layout features, termination schemes, trace impedances, and SI analysis becomes important. The formulas give a speed limit, but even when we are approaching the limits the effects are becoming strong. Normally we would compare the signal's rise time to the propagation delay, but, in practice, we have to start paying attention when the rise time is comparable to eight times the propagation delay. This safety margin can be included in the calculation. Near the speed limit, we should already design the board with high-speed considerations, and the simulations also start showing any PCB effects. Table 11.1 shows speed limit estimations for different cases that tell when SI considerations become necessary. All the formulas have complex explanations, some are mentioned in other chapters, but they are simplified here to make it easier to use. Some of these scale linearly with rise time, noise allowance and trace length, but in a non-linear way with spacing (obtained from a field solver). We can run signals over this speed limit (except the stub), but we have to apply high-speed layout design rules, and we might have to run simulations if the solution is unusual or tight.

11.3.1.2 Correlation

Usually simulations are optimistic (they might give a false pass) and measurements are pessimistic (might give a false fail). Correlation eliminates both the optimism in simulation and the pessimism in measurement by pulling them both closer together. It also makes simulations more accurate. The simulation is useless if it would not match (correlate) with a measurement that can be done later on a prototype. To be specific, it is not about running a specific sim on a specific board, but the methodology has to correlate throughout multiple product cycles. For example, the insertion loss curve has a different steepness, the via resonances appear at very different frequency or do not

TABLE 11.1
Speed Limit Estimations

Issue	Signals	Formulas: when "true" then we are over the limit and need to simulate and apply proper layout techniques	Explanation
Trace Impedance and terminations	All	rise_time < 0.68* TraceLength * SQRT(DK)	When the round-trip propagation delay is in the same order of magnitude as the rise time. [inch, nanosecond]
Discontinuities	Single.e.	rise_time < 0.68 * TraceLength* SQRT(DK)	when the propagation delay through the discontinuity is comparable to the rise time: [inch, nanosecond]
	SERDES	baud_rate > 1.46/ (ViaLength* SQRT(DK))	
Via Stubs	Single.e.	rise_time < 1.35* ViaLength * SQRT(DK)	When the round-trip propagation delay through the stub is comparable to the rise time. [inch, nanosecond]
	SERDES	baud_rate > 0.74 / (ViaLength* SQRT(DK))	
Inter-symbol interference	SERDES	baud_rate > 87 / TraceLength basic fabrication baud_rate > 935 / TraceLength loss contr.+DFE	when the insertion loss gets near 10…25dB: [inch, Gbps]

appear at all, or the eye openings are much larger or smaller. So simulations have to be set up with such parameters, especially PCB material parameters, which already correlated well in a previous recent project. This is the measurement-simulation correlation. We have achieved "correlation" if we have set up both the simulation and the measurement parameters in a way that the results of the simulation and the measurement are similar. We tune simulation parameters to match the measured results. We only have that once we get the prototype. We typically want to simulate designs before the proto stage, so this tuning had to be done on the previous project. Correlation tuning cannot be done on the current project at an early stage. The correlation tuning work while being performed, it will benefit only future projects since we no longer need accurate simulations once we already have prototype boards.

We can measure traces on a prototype with a VNA or measure signals with oscilloscopes or with on-die eye capture, for proto validation, as well as to feed back into our simulation methodology for having a set of more accurate parameters for future simulations. For example, if a given software tool needs to use a different DK than the material actually has, in order to achieve good correlation, then the adjustment parameter of k=DKreal/DKused needs to be documented and used every time we simulate with that particular tool. Either the tool does not account for a parameter accurately or it does not account for another known or unknown effect at all, but we can pull-in the results if we alter some parameters before entering them into the SI simulation software. It can be DK, DF, roughness parameters, copper conductivity, trace width, via barrel diameter, or anything that needs to be adjusted. The adjustment should be always the same for a given tool, in terms of a ratio for a parameter, like 120% or something. See Chapter 12, "PCB Materials and Stackups".

11.3.2 A Multi-stage View

In the old days, there were "all-in-one" SI tools that took a board file and displayed a waveform. As designs became higher speed and more complex, the simulation software setup had to be divided into three main parts or stages and had allow user to access them separately:

1) Stage-1, Layout Extractor or electromagnetic simulator for the PCB traces and planes. A PCB trace will be extracted into a circuit model (S-par or Tline schematic). It allows selecting traces in a layout view or in a wizard window.
2) Stage-2, Back-end SPICE-like circuit simulator with additional features like convolution, S-parameter, and IBIS models. It is either run in time domain (transient) mode or in frequency domain (S-parameter) mode. If the user can access the model before running the simulation then it looks like a schematic drawing.
3) Stage-3, Waveform post-processing and display plots, together with standard limit lines.

Figure 11.11 shows the analysis and model flow in three stages. These stages pass data forward to the next one or generate a file that can be taken to another vendor's software tool. Stage 1 to 2 is an S-parameter file or an RLGC+Tline circuit; stage 2 to 3 is either a vendor specific waveform file or an S-parameter file. An S-parameter file describes a board trace sufficiently as a Black box model, suitable for SERDES links. Similarly, a circuit schematic model (containing transmission lines and passive parts) describes it in a way suitable for slower non-SERDES interconnects. It contains all information that the next stage would need. In one simulation run, we simulate one or a few signal traces. In a batch simulation we would run multiple single-net simulations one by one and display the combined results of them with assessed statistics or even generate a report file. With some tools batch means multiple nets will be simulated in one run, with other tools batch means we simulate the same net with a few user-defined parameters varied within a range. For example, in pre-layout simulation we can vary the trace length (to cover many traces in a complex system) and the trace impedance (to mimic manufacturing tolerance). This second type is sometimes called a parametric sweep simulation, or a Monte Carlo analysis if statistical variables are used.

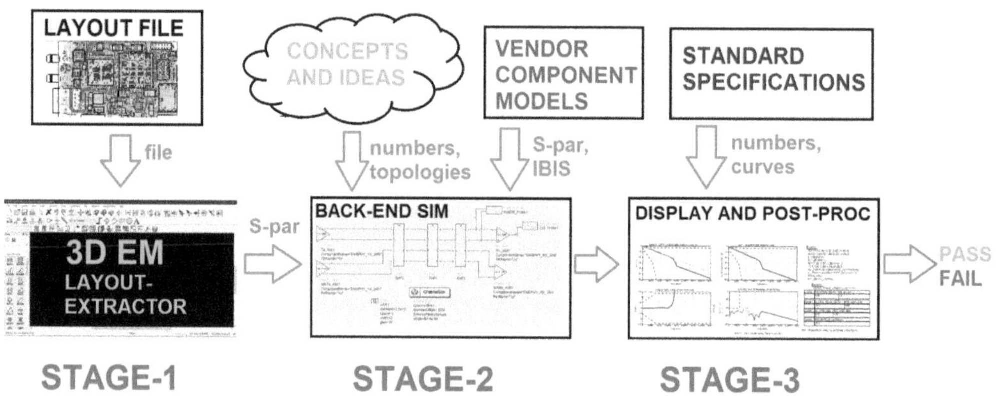

FIGURE 11.11 Simulator stages.

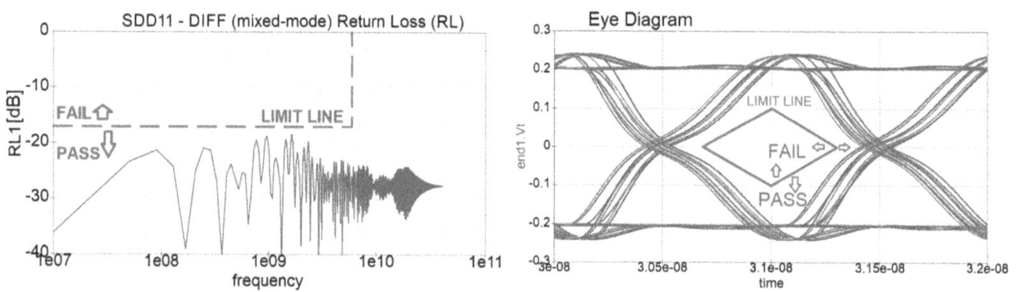

FIGURE 11.12 Limit lines (red) on stage-3 diagrams in QUCS, with dataset (blue).

Of course, there are still simulators that provide an all-in-one solution or an option to be used in the all-in-one mode, but then the users deprive themselves of the level of control they need for the accuracy needed for 10Gig and faster SERDES channels. All-in-one simulators simply hide the stage-2 circuit model from the user, and do not allow custom equations for waveform processing in stage-3; instead, they have ready-made equations for waveform processing and limit lines working in the background. Often in SI analysis we might want to analyze a phenomenon that is so new, just published in a conference paper, that no existing simulator program releases support it. That is when the 3-stage manual mode would help; as we can implement the analysis ourselves overnight.

Stage-3 displays the circuit simulation results from stage-2, and it might process (using equations) the resulting curve (a set of numbers in a sequence) into a new curve, and calculates and displays the “limit lines”. Limit lines tell the user whether the waveform is acceptable or not, for example, too much return loss at certain frequency range, or if the eye opening too small. Figure 11.12 shows both time and frequency domain limit lines. If the curve is on the wrong side or it has crossed the limit line, then the design has failed the simulation. On time domain eye diagrams, the closed limit line is an “eye mask”.

Most of these SI simulation programs can also be used for power integrity simulations, normally in frequency domain, but in the stage-2 circuit model we run an AC simulation instead of an S-parameter simulation.

In pre-layout simulations we do not perform stage-1 as the layout does not exist yet, so instead we manually place and connect parametrized lossy Tline models in a schematic-like drawing. Stage-2 and -3 are still used in pre-layout sim. This can be done in Keysight ADS, QUCS, HyperLynx LineSim, or Cadence Sigrity. Pre-layout simulations can help us to increase confidence in a system (multi-board chassis) concept. We know that the parametrized lossy Tline models are not super accurate representations of the traces on the board, but they will not have misplaced resonances, and the loss slope can be set according to recent loss coupons measurements. This can be a more accurate match with a prototype sometimes than a badly set up post-layout simulation.

In post-layout simulations we utilize all three stages, one after the another. Post-layout simulations can help us to increase confidence in a completed board design. It can also help us finding mistakes, so we can quickly fix our PCB layout before release. It is not a verification (meaning a pass/fail signoff official legal statement); it is only for increasing confidence for moving forward with a project. Project risks are not 0% versus 100%, so if we increase our confidence from 30% to 80% by running a simulation then we can move forward. The layout extraction simulations (stage-1) are often inaccurate, unless the user or team is in full mastery of all tool and material parameters. Before starting the stage-1 post-layout simulation, during the tool parameter setup phase we have to enter the stackup layer data exactly from the approved fab-vendor stackup document, otherwise the whole simulation will be pointless. If we have any correlation process in place, then we might skew these parameters accordingly to get more accurate results. Post-layout simulators or layout-extractors and simulation runs are very demanding on accuracy and precision. They also require large sum of computing resources. With the same amount of computing resources, we can achieve better accuracy when simulating just one via transition than we can when simulating a whole end-to-end channel. A complete channel with maximum via transition accuracy is usually run on remote servers with hundreds of Gigbytes of RAM. A more practical and coarse solution geared towards resources and speed can be run on a laptop in a day. Layout-extraction can be done with 2D simulators, 2.5D, or 3D simulators.

The 2D option simply utilizes a 2D field solver program to compute an impedance and crosstalk parameter from the trace cross-section (that is a two-dimensional vertical mesh), then scale that to the detected trace length. All vias and other elements will be modelled using estimated RLGC lumped element circuit models calculated from formulas. A 2.5D simulator creates a horizontal mesh on each layer of a "planar" model, assumes zero-layer thickness, and uses RLGC lumped element models for the vertical structures. 2.5D is most useful for power plane and RF-microwave circuit simulations. In a 3D simulation, a selected part of the board is analyzed as a 3D structure, using a 3D volume mesh. 2D sims are less computationally heavy; a 100 x 100 cell structure creates a 10k cells, while in 3D a 100 x 100 x 100 cell structure would require 1 million cells. Each adjacent cell-to-cell combination will be solved with a separate set of Maxwell's electromagnetic equations. Even among 3D solvers, there are at least two types, the quasi-static and the full wave. The former is faster but less accurate at higher frequencies, the latter is preferred for 10G+ via modelling.

To speed up 3D simulation while maintaining reasonable accuracy, "decomposition" was invented. The layout extraction process can be performed in three ways. As the whole board structure all at once, or it can be using a "cookie cutter" around the trace and its immediate surroundings, or it can be done using "Decomposition Analysis". This third type reduces the computation requirement so that a regular server or workstation computer in 2023 can complete the simulation in a day or less. It analyzes small structures in 3D, typically via-transitions; while the long interconnect traces are analyzed as 2D cross-sections. The simulation tool will stitch the 2D (Tline) and 3D (S-par) parts together into one channel and provide one final S-parameter model for the whole channel. The parts that are analyzed in 3D are the "3D Areas", they are either defined by the user (drawing a bounding box) or automatically defined by the tool. This method is accurate only if the layout features like via transitions are designed to be well "localized". Not only the features of the analyzed signal have to be localized, but all other signals on the board too. If everything is badly localized, then everything causes interference in everything else. See the Chapter 15, "PCB Layout Design". The user has to make sure to envelope ground stitching vias in at least three different directions near the bounds when drawing the box for a 3D area. Better quality designs are simulated more accurately. If a simulation is inaccurate, then it is usually optimistic. Bad designs might appear to perform better in simulation than on the prototype, giving a false pass. Note that simulations when inaccurate are optimistic, measurements are pessimistic. If the simulation and measurement correlate well, then we know they both were done accurately.

Multi-board simulations can be done simply by importing more than one board S-parameter model into the stage-2 back-end simulation circuit model and import the S-parameter models for any connectors we have in the path. There has been an effort for multi-board simulations, with boards represented by EBD models, but in recent years S-parameters have become more common, as their accuracy is better for SERDES links. We still have to export a full trace (or XNET) from each board into separate S-parameter model files. In common backplane-based systems, a full decomposition stage-1 trace extraction with 3D areas is performed on the first board, then on the backplane, and finally on the other board where the signal arrives to the receiving ASIC. Then it is stitched together with connector S-par models in the same or another vendor's stage-2 manual model simulator. We talked about two types of decomposition, one where one PCB trace is decomposed and automatically stitched together by a stage-1 simulator and the one where three separate boards have their S-par models that the engineer stitches together in a stage-2 simulator schematic view manually.

A time domain simulation that displays eye diagrams (or bathtub and COM) includes the PCB trace model, the BGA package model, the chip buffer model with internal SERDES DFE details, and any connector model. A frequency domain simulation that displays S-par curves will include only the PCB trace model and any connector model. Most channel standards specify S-parameter limits of board-level interconnects from ASIC package pin to ASIC package pin, not ASIC internal logic points. The board is designed and marketed by one company, the chip with the package as one unit is marketed by another company. The PCB and system is the board vendors "legal" responsibility, the chip and package is the chip vendor's responsibility. In both time and frequency domain simulations we usually chain multiple S-parameter models together to form a SERDES channel.

11.3.3 Eye and BER

Eye diagrams created in stage-3 of the simulation tool, in pre-layout sim, or in the last stage of the post-layout simulation are used less often for SERDES channels than they are on lower speed designs. At around 10Gig the simulated eye diagrams seem to be less accurate or less useful, as the eye usually closes at the receiver at 10Gig, and opens up only after the DFE stage inside the chip, which is harder to simulate and dependent on third-party model accuracy. So we rely on S-parameter direct assessment more. Simulating eye or BER makes sense only on an end-to-end complete channel; it is completely meaningless when simulating it on one of the module cards (in a chassis) alone. An eye diagram is a signal time domain waveform that is wrapped around itself at every bit period, by the stage-3 display waveform processing functions, as we can see in Figure 11.13. Eye diagrams are sometimes called eye density plots.

The bit error rate is simply BER=BE/RunTime, where BE is the number of error bits received. The bit error ratio (ratio instead of rate) is calculated as BER=BE/Nbits is a ratio of the bad received bits divided by the total number of bits sent. Both are labeled the same, "BER" confusingly. So the

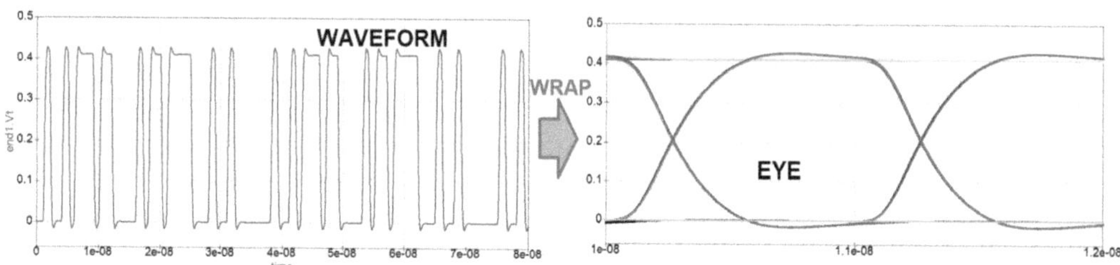

FIGURE 11.13 Eye diagram wrapping demonstration in QUCS.

BER as rate is in errors per second, but the BER as ratio is the portion of all bits that are bad. The latter is the most common one, and it is used in contour plots and bathtub curves. When BER=1 it means every bit is bad and nothing goes through, but when BER=0 then all bits are good. Most commonly 0<BER<<1, or a small fraction, but it can still cause big trouble.

The "Bathtub Curve" shows how much the bit error rate is if we alter the data sampling position within the simulation. There can be a horizontal alteration or scan, called the timing bathtub, and a vertical scan, called the voltage bathtub. The simulator runs N bits of a data stream and captures the waveform at hundreds of sample points in the same time. This will create a timing bathtub curve, at a certain voltage threshold level, that reaches down only to a bit error rate of 1/N. Below that it will show zero BER. Fortunately, these curves have a smooth expected shape without breaks, so they can be extrapolated beyond that. We have to simulate as many bits as it would pass the main curvature of the bathtub curve, so the extrapolated part will become more accurate, usually 1 to 10 million bits.

If we have to look at eye diagrams, then most often we look at a BER-contour plot instead of actual eye diagrams. In time domain simulation we usually run a few million bit-times of simulation, but our interconnects must be designed to run at le-12 BER (bit error ratio). The eye would look more closed if we run le-12 bits, but that would take thousands of years to run. So instead, the modern SI simulation tools create multiple timing bathtub curves at multiple voltage threshold levels, extrapolate each below 1E-12 to 16, then generate a 3D diagram from it, then take slices at specific user-choice BER levels from it and display that on a 2D plot called the "BER-contour plot". Each slice is an eye-shaped closed contour curve at a specific BER level. This shows all the voltage and timing offsets where the exact same BER is achieved. The 1E-12 contour shows the true eye opening that has to fit the standard eye mask, or the chip vendor's eye mask requirement. This is shown in Figure 11.14. So if we have to look at time domain diagrams, then we should look at these

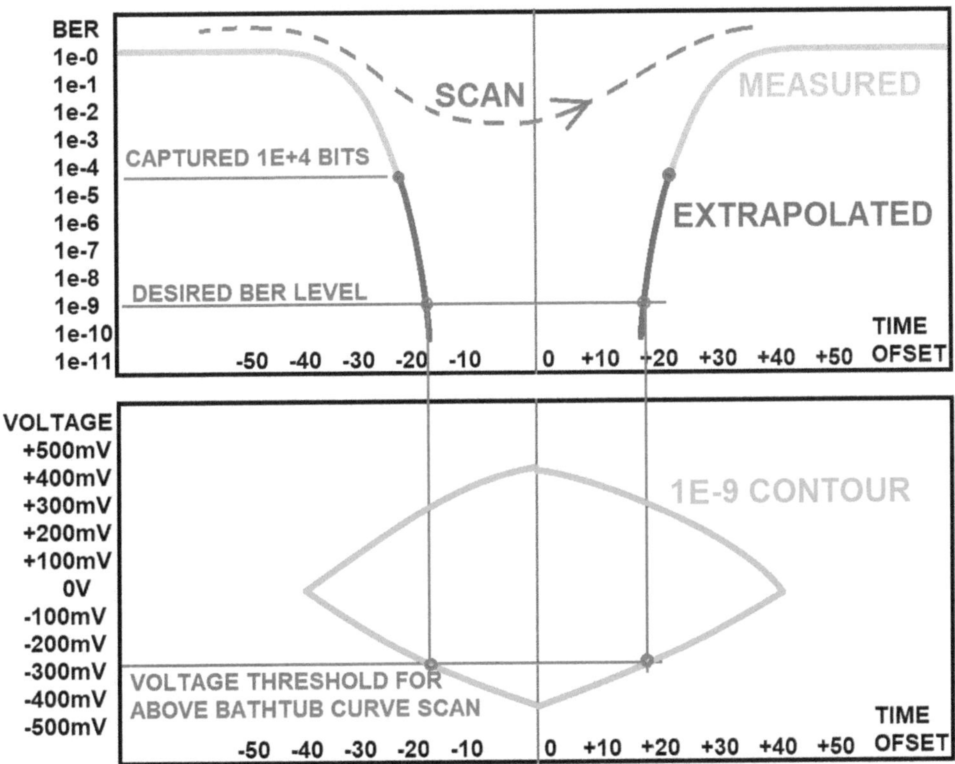

FIGURE 11.14 Bathtub curve and BER contour creation (sketch).

BER-contour plots instead, as they are more useful. The simulated BER contour plot looks similar to a BERT scan that is a result of a prototype test, as described in later chapters.

There are two types of time domain simulations, one is called "bit-by-bit", which is basically like a SPICE transient simulation, and the other type is the "statistical" simulation that is proprietary algorithm to reproduce the system behavior on trillions of bits in a short run time. Both can produce the same kind of waveforms and displays.

11.3.4 IBIS Models

For time domain eye diagram simulations in stage-2, the boards and connectors are usually represented by S-parameter models for SERDES channels and either S-parameter or Tline circuit models for non-SERDES channels. The transmitter chip output buffer and the receiver chip input buffer with relevant chip-level I/O circuit behavior are modeled using chip-vendor-supplied IBIS or IBIS-AMI model files. IBIS-AMI models are used for multi-gigabit SERDES transceivers, while regular IBIS models are used for slower (usually single-ended) non-SERDES interfaces. The regular IBIS model is just an *.ibs file, while the IBIS-AMI is a set of files like a *.ibs, *.ami, and *.dll files. Additionally, they may come with BGA package substrate trace models in S-parameter format.

The main purpose of IBIS models is to provide a circuit model that accurately represents the buffer voltage/current characteristics, using fine sampled curves. One model file contains multiple buffer types or pins that can be selected by the simulator user. Every IBIS model allows the user to select one of the three PVT (process/voltage/temperature) corners like fast/slow/typical. Silicon devices become faster at lower temperature, but, due to a secondary effect on modern devices, they become slower again. The fast corner contains the temperature effects, the highest power rail voltage, and the manufacturing tolerance (process) combination. The simulation has to represent all production units, any unit can be anywhere between the model's fast and the slow corners, so we have to simulate at both end corners. The slow corner will be affecting the setup timing more, and the fast corner the hold timing.

IBIS-AMI models are not just buffers; they contain the digital logic inside the SERDES transceivers, like encoding, equalization (DFE, FFE), and CDR. They allow the user to select equalizer tap values or to run simulations where the tap values are automatically optimized. They also provide RX post-DFE waveforms and eye diagrams for the simulators to display. Since a basic eye diagram is closed at the receiver chip pin at 10Gbps and above, we need to see the eye diagram behind the receiver equalizer. This is the purpose of the AMI models. The model files have to be obtained from the chip vendors, usually through secure websites.

11.3.5 SI Simulation Report

When we run simulations for a project, we should document what we did, why, how, what the passing criteria was, what the results were, and what we concluded based on it. This is good practice for project management. Via impedance optimization is a separate type of "simulation"; its reports would be different from the pre/post-layout simulations below; they will provide optimized dimensions and TDR impedance curves. The sections that should be in regular SI simulation report documents include:

- Design requirements and assumptions (speed, topology, system architecture, main components).
- Describe what is simulated and why.
- Any applicable standard documents (IEEE, SFF, PCI-SIG…), which section/page, the actual numbers from it, eye masks, and S-par limit curves that we need to comply to.
- Simulation setup details, such as which model files and selectors were used and how many points or bits were run.

- Simulation results as time domain eye diagrams, BER contour plots, height and width readout, if needed.
- Simulation results as frequency domain channel S-par plots against limit lines, for SERDES channels.
- Simulation results as TDR impedance plots, if needed.
- Compare numbers to requirements and standards, conclude about pass/fail, or any needs for design alteration. Re-simulate with design alteration, show new curves and new conclusion.

11.3.6 Layout Model Resolution

PCB discontinuities (like stubs, via structures, pinouts) can interfere with signals if their size is larger than 1/10th of the quarter wavelength. Figure 11.15 demonstrates why. Signals are made of combinations of sine waves. The signal's components are voltage/time sine-waves at a given point in space, but also voltage/dimension sine waves at a given point in time. The signal's "frequency" that we compare against discontinuities is the half baud rate for SERDES signals, the knee frequency (0.35/t_rise) or the fifth harmonic of the half baud rate for non-SERDES signals, and the 5th harmonic of the clock frequency for clock signals. A sine wave has its peak amplitude at the quarter wavelength. That peak amplitude has to be much larger than the noise amplitude, let's say by 20dB or 10x. This means the discontinuity on the PCB should have smaller dimensions than the 1/10th of the 1/4th wavelength, aka 1/40th the wavelength. Below 10GHz discontinuities are basically the return current loops. The discontinuity size is the loop size, not the via size or gap size.

This is also related to the SI simulator accuracy, it has to be able to have the spatial resolution of the size of any discontinuity that could interfere with our signal (1/40 wavelength), and even to resolve the tolerance on that dimension (1/10 of its size). Post-layout electromagnetic extractor software (SI simulation tool) accuracy depends on whether the tool is capable of resolving the feature size required by the signaling speed. Some simulation tools, while building a model, replace some PCB structures with ideal structures, for example, they use voidless infinite ground planes, the return current magically jumping layers without vias. They are not suitable for accurate SI simulations, if the size of their simplification is within the range described above. From 200MHz and up we need to model the return path through vias, with a feature size 1/10 inch and resolution 1/100 inch. From 8GHz and up we need to model the via impedance, which depends on feature (clearance gap) sizes of 1/200", with the resolution 1/2000". If a feature affects SI, then we need to be able to see that feature as well as see its size with a suitable mesh resolution like 10 samples through it. Figure 11.16 shows how this concept applies to common structures simulated, like a memory interface card, and a SERDES link's differential via structure. We know that the via impedance is

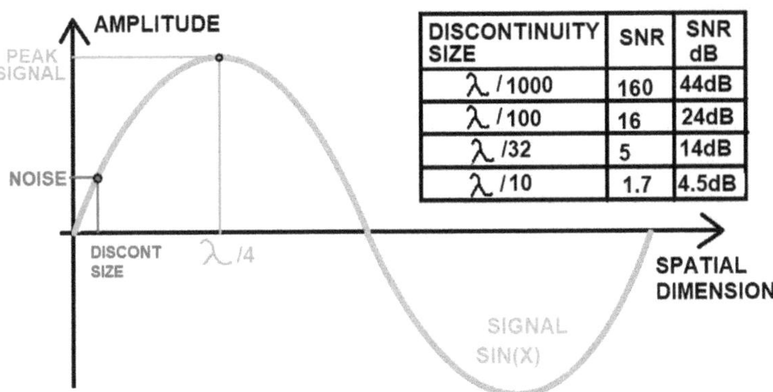

DISCONTINUITY SIZE	SNR	SNR dB
λ/1000	160	44dB
λ/100	16	24dB
λ/32	5	14dB
λ/10	1.7	4.5dB

FIGURE 11.15 Feature size and interference.

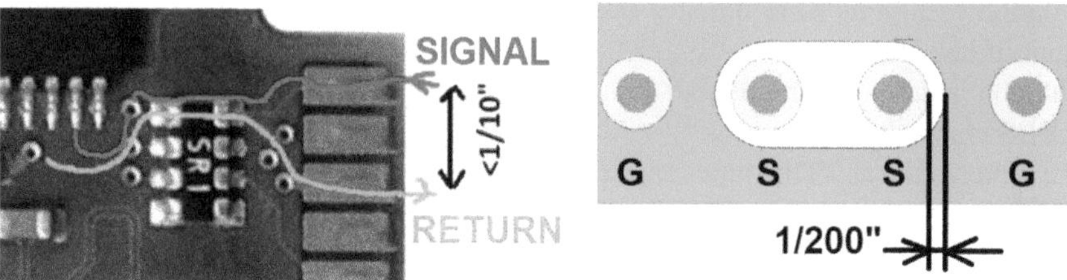

FIGURE 11.16 Feature sizes needed for analysis, memory interface left, via impedance right.

affected by, for example, the gap between the via pad and the plane void edge, that is ~4mils, so we need that 4mils to be accurately modeled and differentiated from a 5mil gap. Either the cell size should be 4mils and have additional numeric resolution, for example able to create a 4.4mil cell or a 3.6mil cell, or create 0.4mil cells and fit ~10 of them into the gap. If a tool does not model via structures accurately, then it can show only lower frequency discontinuities on the board but not the ones that can wreck 10Gig+ signals but passing 5Gig signals fine.

11.3.7 Examples of SI Simulators

A short list of simulator programs is provided below. It is not comprehensive for the whole SI tool market, but it includes enough software to cover most SI-related analysis tasks.

11.3.7.1 Keysight ADS

ADS (Advanced Design System or PathWave Advanced Design System) might be the most flexible SI simulation software out there. It allows full control to the user to build the stage-2 simulation circuit model, and any custom type of stage-3 waveform post-processing and display that they want. Basically, the user can add a new parameter or feature that the tool vendors have not thought of yet or focus on analyzing any unusual detail without having to wait a few years until hard features are released. Most hardware engineers might not prefer this much flexibility, for the convenience of easy setup, but those of us who do prefer flexibility this is very useful. We can set up one-off experiments or do data mining from our waveforms. Post-processing the S-parameter files that are the results of VNA measurements is also often performed in ADS. We can mix circuit components (often representing parasitic elements) with digital buffers, theoretical transmission lines, and S-parameter models. S-parameters can come from component vendors, measurements, or other simulations. We can chain together the models for multi-board signal paths for a decomposition analysis. ADS is a back-end simulation software, it performs stage-2 and stage-3 roles. Keysight also provides stage-1 layout extractors that also start from the main ADS window, but in this book we usually refer to the schematic modeler as "ADS".

ADS is not a board-to-waveform auto simulator; rather, everything has to be created here manually and requires a deep understanding of the tool and physics. High-end high-speed issues are sometimes complex, they require complex analysis and complex solutions. We can deal with sufficient complexity only if we have full control over the stage-2 model and the stage-3 waveform processing, which is provided in ADS. Usually it takes days to develop a good simulation model, so we might as well save it as a template and re-use it in the next project. There are two kinds of SI simulations: the regular everyday design checks and the complex problem solving. ADS supports both, but it really excels in the second type.

Keysight offers the Momentum and the EMPro packages to be used as stage-1 layout electromagnetic extractors, but many users use ADS in combination with other vendors' tools, like HFSS+ADS, HyperLynx+ADS, or Symbeor+ADS. There are also automated setups for SI and PI runs on imported layout files, with the SIPro and PIPro licenses.

The ADS software has these frequently used windows:

- The main window is where the project's files are listed. In one project we can have multiple simulations, called "cells". Within each cell we have schematics, data displays, and other files. A project is called a "workspace" here.
- The schematic window is where we draw the stage-2 schematic simulation model in the form of a schematic drawing, basically component models connected with wires and virtual probes. We even define the simulation type here by placing a simulation "component". An example simulation model schematic with a mix of different types of models is shown in Figure 11.17.
- The data display is where the simulation results can be post-processed using custom equations, and then displayed. The user has to place rectangular plots or tables to display multiple curves on the same page. An example user-customized display window with time domain plots and post processing is shown in Figure 11.18.
- Layout: This is used only when we want to perform a post-layout extraction with Keysight Momentum.

There are several simulations or simulation controllers in the ADS schematic model. We use the "Channelsim" for generating eye diagrams in time domain from a channel with SERDES IBIS-AMI models or to produce a COM (channel operating margin) number. It is similar to the SPICE simulators' transient simulator but with IBIS-AMI model, crosstalk, BER/bathtub, and statistical eye support. There is also an actual "transient simulation" controller that is also time domain, but it is used on lower speed interfaces with IBIS (non-AMI) models, like LVDS buses or DDRx memory. For both types of time domain simulations, we have to place "eye probes" into the schematic. The transient sim requires a PRBS generator source component driving the IBIS model, while in Channelsim the AMI models have the source built in. With the convolution-based simulator engine, we can stitch together time-domain buffer models with frequency-domain S-parameter models for a single simulation in time domain. We can also use transient simulations for computing a TDR (time domain reflectometry) impedance curve.

The S-parameter simulation is used to generate overall S-parameters of a complete physical channel (traces, connectors) and post-process them into derived curves and numbers. This type of simulation requires us to place numbered ports into the schematic, and the port numbers will become the S-parameter indexes.

To generate derived curves and waveforms, we need to type in custom equations or copy them from a re-used template. ADS can generate standard waveforms like eye diagrams (density plot), BER contour plots (in transient and channel simulation), and single-ended S-parameters (in S-par simulation). With equations we can create further derived custom waveforms, like mixed-mode S-parameters, ILD, PSXT, fitted attenuation, or even combination or difference curves. We can also use equations to derive numbers from curves, like minimum value, average, or a readout at a specific point (like FA@13GHz). Readout-number variables can be displayed in a table format. We can process waveforms through multiple equation stages, until the desired variable extraction becomes possible. We can create limit line waveforms using equations. We can perform measurement post-processing, like Delta-L coupon loss per inch number extraction or probe de-embedding.

We can run batch simulations with varying one or more parameters like a termination resistor value, or the IBIS PVT corner-selector stepped through, then at the end multiple curves will be displayed. This way we can find the worst-case waveforms with worst-case margins. For simulating memory interfaces, Keysight offers a separate license called Memory Designer, with additional features on top of ADS and Momentum for both pre- and post-layout parts. We can use ADS for pre-layout PDN analysis too—in this case we use the "AC simulation" controller. The possible applications for ADS are endless.

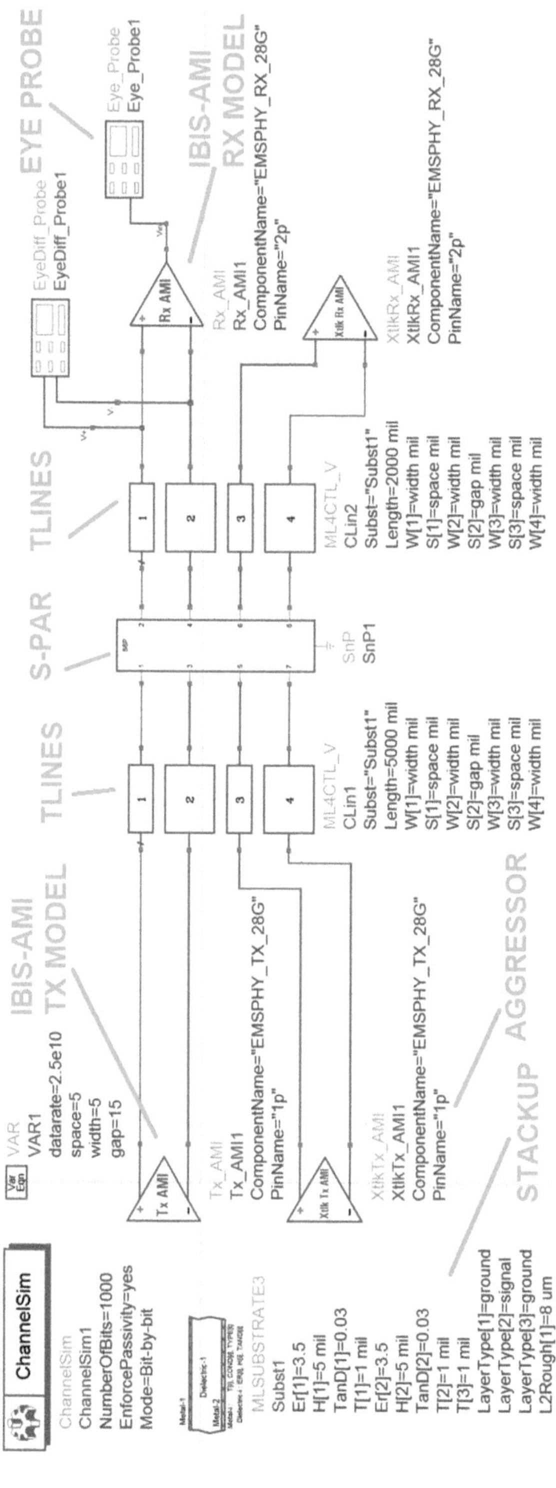

FIGURE 11.17 Example ADS stage-2 circuit model for time domain simulation with IBIS-AMI buffers and channel model.

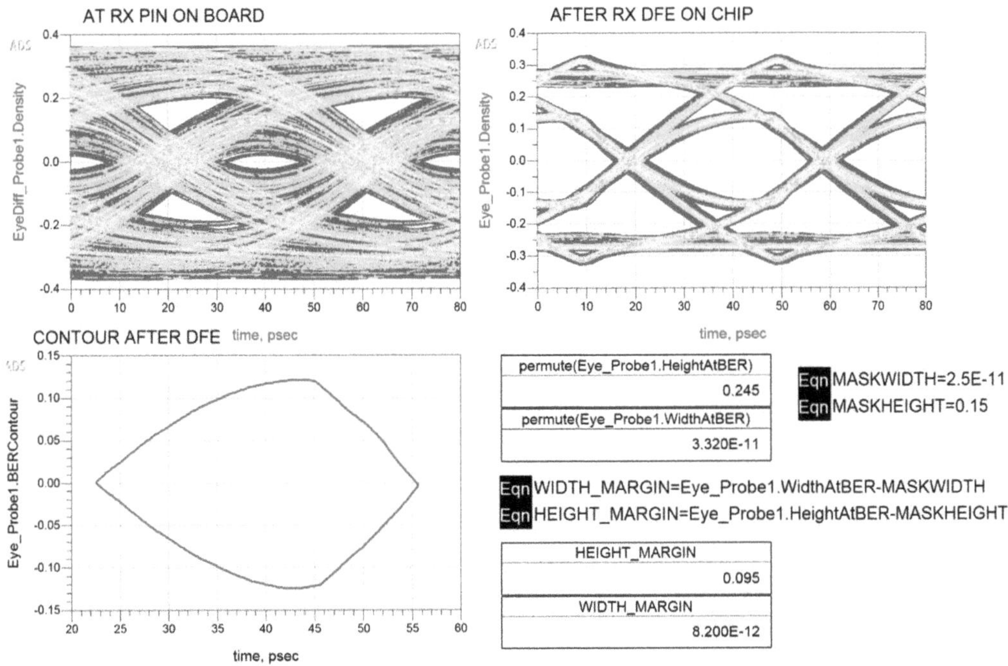

FIGURE 11.18 Example ADS stage-3 custom data display and post processing.

11.3.7.2 QUCS

The "Quite Universal Circuit Simulator", or QUCS, is a free program that works very similarly to Keysight ADS, but with many limitations and with a much smaller number of features. The main limitations are the lack of support for using the S-parameter models and Tlines in time domain simulations (they can only be used in AC-sim or S-par sim), meaning it has no "convolutional simulator engine", and the lack of support for IBIS and IBIS-AMI models. Even though lossy Tlines are not supported, we can make support for those using the equation-defined RF Device, such as the channel simulator template provided in the appendix. QUCS also has a few bugs, so we have to work around them. For example, Tlines work only in frequency domain or some equations produce error messages that makes us search for alternative equations. Whatever we can do in QUCS, we can do all that more accurately, and more, in ADS. The main uses for QUCS are frequency domain passive SERDES channel analysis with S-parameter processing, PDN impedance simulation with measured VRM and RLC capacitor models, Rogue wave computation for PDNs, Bode Plot analysis, SPICE circuit simulations, and for generating lots of demonstration waveforms for this book. Figure 11.19 shows a few example uses of QUCS.

11.3.7.3 Siemens (Formerly Mentor) HyperLynx

HyperLynx comes with a large set of simulators and features to cover a wide range of SI- and PI-related investigative and validation tasks. This includes electrical rule checking (HyperLynx DRC), 3D electromagnetic extraction (HyperLynx Advanced Solvers), DC and AC power analysis (HyperLynx PI), and signal integrity simulation (HyperLynx SI). The main advantage of HyperLynx is the time saving on analysis setup and resulting data extraction through automation. There are two avenues by which the tool achieves this. The first one is by the tool performing all three stages of the simulation task in succession, as explained at the beginning of this chapter, after an initial setup by the user. The second one is through batch simulations that allow many signals to be simulated in a single run and presenting the results in a report format, including data tables.

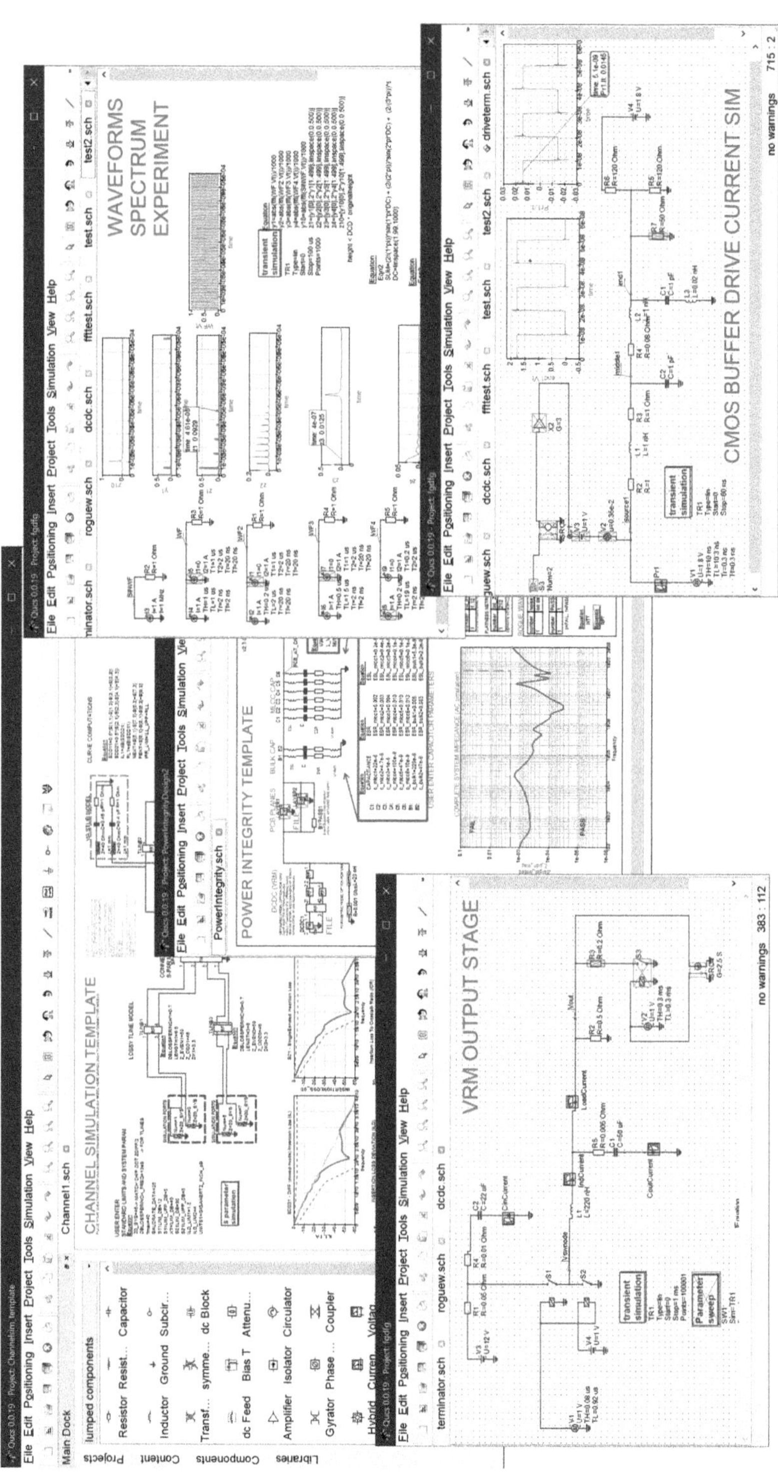

FIGURE 11.19 Various simulation examples in QUCS.

It provides complete, automated analysis flows for pre-layout design exploration (pre-layout analysis to develop rules for how the board should be placed and routed), design optimization, and post-layout design verification (post-layout analysis that determines if the board is ready for fab-out). The two main user interfaces are the LineSim and the BoardSim. Pre-layout analysis uses LineSim, a net topology-oriented schematic-based model editor that lets you define a layout topology and simulate it. Post-layout analysis uses BoardSim, which lets you read in a PCB database, select signals, and simulate them. Topology extraction and simulation from the PCB database is automatic, so you do not have to set up any circuit model drawings or waveform processing equations. BoardSim is a stage 1-2-3 all-in-one post-layout simulator, while the LineSim is a stage 2–3 all-in-one simulator. It is possible to perform "what-if" analysis on a post-layout circuit model by exporting the net to LineSim and then editing and simulating it from there. The HyperLynx DRC has a separate user interface that provides a report of SI-related layout design issues, like missing stitching vias. For accurate crosstalk we have to enter estimated signal rise times. It checks a layout file for high-speed design feature implementations without running an actual simulation. When we run simulations of SERDES channels in BoardSim, often we have to define and set up the 3D areas. This is opened from the BoardSim setup menus into a separate user interface called the Advanced Solvers. The 3D areas help with performing decomposition analysis, where only the vertical structures and discontinuities are analyzed in a 3D solver, while the long interconnections are analyzed by a much faster cross-section 2D solver, then stitched together automatically by the tool.

HyperLynx has a number of different analysis flows, depending on what you are simulating and what you want to accomplish. Power integrity flows include various types of DC and AC analysis. In the DC domain we can simulate a board design for voltage drop, local current density, and point-to-point resistance (DCR). In the AC domain we can perform a quick, lumped, and distributed inductance modeling to determine the impedance response of the PCB power delivery network at specific points of interest and to perform decoupling optimization. Signal integrity flows include protocol-specific (DDR3-5) memory interface simulation, serial link Protocol Compliance analysis, IBIS-AMI serial link simulation, crosstalk analysis, pulse response simulation, termination analysis, and general-purpose signal integrity simulation. HyperLynx divides signal integrity simulations into two modes – interactive and batch. Interactive simulations are meant for getting a quick assessment of how a design will behave and performing "what-if" experiments on a small set of signals. Batch analysis is meant for performing more exhaustive simulations on a larger set of signals or an entire interface. This is best suited for full-sweep design verification. Batch simulations generally produce HTML report documents showing simulation results at varying levels of detail. They also contain file links to other report documents showing more details on specific items, in a hierarchy. At the highest level, the reports list which signals passed their associated requirements and which signals failed and by how much. The reports then drill down into lower levels of details depending on the analysis performed and the simulation options used. In the report file, from the data tables we can also look up the actual eye diagrams of any signal by selecting one table entry, as we can see in Figure 11.20. Many parameters are automatically extracted from each signal, for example, eye openings, mask margins, and other timing- and voltage-related parameters.

HyperLynx is intended for hardware engineers who want to perform detailed simulations but who do not want to obtain and integrate a number of different modeling and analysis tools themselves. In fact, it is more suited for hardware engineers who are not full-time SI specialists, the main audience of this book. Because HyperLynx is a complete product family, the tools are already integrated with proven analysis workflows. It is more of a turnkey solution; the user will not have to spend time on developing methodology, templates, models, and low-level processing tasks.

11.3.7.4 Other Vendors

Cadence Sigrity, Cadence Clarity, Simberian's Simbeor, Ansys SiWave, Ansys HFSS, and SPISim are other SI simulation tools on the market currently. This list is not complete. Some of the standard organizations and chip vendors also provide tools, like the SeaSim statistical eye simulator from

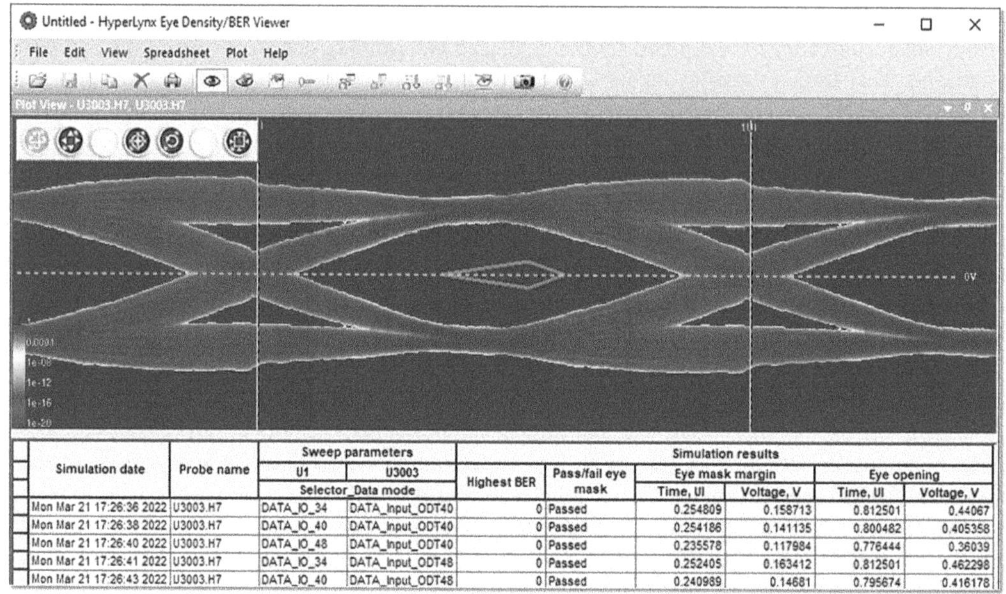

Simulation date	Probe name	Sweep parameters: U1 (Selector_Data mode)	Sweep parameters: U3003 (Selector_Data mode)	Highest BER	Pass/fail eye mask	Eye mask margin: Time, UI	Eye mask margin: Voltage, V	Eye opening: Time, UI	Eye opening: Voltage, V
Mon Mar 21 17:26:36 2022	U3003.H7	DATA_IO_34	DATA_Input_ODT40	0	Passed	0.254809	0.158713	0.812501	0.44067
Mon Mar 21 17:26:38 2022	U3003.H7	DATA_IO_40	DATA_Input_ODT40	0	Passed	0.254186	0.141135	0.800482	0.405358
Mon Mar 21 17:26:40 2022	U3003.H7	DATA_IO_48	DATA_Input_ODT40	0	Passed	0.235578	0.117984	0.776444	0.36039
Mon Mar 21 17:26:41 2022	U3003.H7	DATA_IO_34	DATA_Input_ODT48	0	Passed	0.252405	0.163412	0.812501	0.462298
Mon Mar 21 17:26:43 2022	U3003.H7	DATA_IO_40	DATA_Input_ODT48	0	Passed	0.240989	0.14681	0.795674	0.416178

FIGURE 11.20 HyperLynx DDR5 Batch Wizard results and eye diagram display.

PCI-SIG, which is a stage-2-3 fixed feature simulator for generating eye diagrams from IBIS-AMI and S-parameter models. PyBERT is a free and independent tool built on top of Python to generate BER estimations, eye diagrams, and bathtub curves. It is also a stage-2-3 simulator. We can use IBIS-AMI (RX and TX) and S-parameter (interconnects) models in the PyBERT setup or we can use parametric entry. It will also produce several other details, like pulse responses and DFE adaptation curves.

If someone can use only free tools, then the set of things that can be analyzed is significantly reduced, but there are still a few useful things that can be simulated. We can perform our pre-layout SERDES channel analysis with QUCS in frequency domain with S-parameters or with PyBERT in time domain with IBIS-AMI models. We can determine trace impedance from the TNT-MMTL field solver. The "S-View" tool in the Windows store can be used to look at S-parameters. LTspice is used for circuit simulation, but we can analyze pre-layout termination arrangements on low-speed signals. The setup time, feature limitations (like post layout trace extraction), and accuracy of some of these might induce us to buy the commercial tools.

11.4 VIA STRUCTURE IMPEDANCE OPTIMIZATION

Starting at around 8Gbps with SERDES links, the characteristic impedance of the via transitions begin to matter, and we have to design them to match the nominal impedance of the traces. It is not a single via barrel that has an impedance; rather, a "via structure" does, which consists of several PCB features and objects. The via structures carry differential pairs. These PCB objects are plane voids, P/N signal vias, ground vias, dog-bone traces, and stackup layers. Their dimensions and relative distances determine the impedance. Via impedance optimization is not a verification or analysis task; it is a design task for the purpose of generating layout constraints in a complex 3D format. Most layout constraints are just sets of numbers. A via structure with all its dimensions, optimized in a field-solver program, has to be exactly replicated in the layout design. It is a more complex kind of constraint. The tolerance from the nominal target impedance value is less and less with higher speeds—we might need 20% at 10Gig while 5% at 100Gig. A via structure consists of two signal vias as it is a differential pair, usually two or more ground vias, and the manually created oval or rectangular voids around the signal vias on all the plane layers. They together form an impedance. A single signal via does not have an impedance by itself, impedance is a relative measure between signal and ground objects. Sometimes in the BGA chip fanout area it might be two signal vias with four to 10 ground vias. If the BGA fanout is such that diffpairs are fenced away from each other, then we should include multiple ground vias nearby while still leaving out the neighboring signal vias. If we want to analyze the via field for crosstalk, then we need to also include the neighboring signal vias and traces in the model, but for TDR impedance analysis they do not add anything meaningful.

The process starts with first obtaining a vendor approved stackup for our board, then creating the via structure manually in a suitable 3D electromagnetic software tool like Ansys HFSS or Simberian Simbeor. We have to adjust/optimize its dimensions to achieve minimum return loss, then export an S-parameter file from it and analyze it in a TDR simulation to see the actual impedance. The return loss expectation is more stringent on single features (like a via structure) than on a whole channel, usually -17.5dB or 20dB if we can make it, and -40dB for crosstalk, both checked up to half the baud rate. In the EM software the port impedance should be set to the desired differential impedance (usually 85/2, 93/2 or sometimes 100/2 Ohm), otherwise we will get a false failure in the RL-limit check, even with a perfectly good design. We should use the most accurate setup with dielectric materials, copper foil and lamination process–related roughness parameters, manufactured cross-section effects (trace etching compensation trapezoid, via barrel imperfections),and anisotropic DK and DF.

If the extracted S-parameter model meets the impedance requirement on the TDR plot, then we can start exactly replicating the structure with all its dimensions in the layout design without any slight modification to it. We cannot "draw" it free form, only copy/paste. We treat it as a component footprint or sub-drawing. First, we manually replicate one instance, making sure it is an exact replica, and then copy/paste it into all other locations. Many layout engineers who are not used to it will think it is okay to put let's say one of the ground vias 10mils off the relative location prescribed in the optimization report or to override the plane void with a larger global clearance constraint. But it is not okay, and the hardware engineer has to make sure of it through daily layout reviews, as any alteration also alters the via impedance. After replicating it to all instances on a board design, and all traces routed to them, we have to start applying stub removal individually depending on routing layer. If we used regular drilled vias, then it means applying the backdrill symbols, with the correct must-no-cut layer designation. If we used offset multi-lam microvia structures, then instead of backdrilling we remove the parts of the structure that extend beyond the routing layer. In both cases we can remove the dual (oval) voids from any layer where the stub is removed because it will help in reducing the plane cuts affecting nearby signals.

Design reuse is an important part of hardware design. In the case of optimized via structures, we can re-use them as is (meaning we do not have to re-do the electromagnetic analysis), if the layer stackup is re-used exactly or the dielectric and copper sheets in the stackup are re-used. For example, if we have a 22-layer stackup with 2x1035-RC75% Tachyon prepregs and 1/2oz copper layers, then the via structure should be re-usable on another design with a 30-layer stackup that also uses 2x1035-RC75% Tachyon prepregs and 1/oz copper.

Sometimes we have to ask an RF engineer or SI engineer to perform the optimization and analysis for us, and then we have to ask them to provide return loss plots instead of VSWR and provide an S-parameter file so we can run a TDR simulation on it. If it is done by an SI engineer, then they are already prepared for providing those. Running a 3D field solver might require a specialist engineer instead of everyone running it for their own designs. We have to prepare our requirements and data—they will provide an optimization report document—then we can double check the impedances in our own TDR simulation on the S-par models they have provided.

The hardware engineer requests and reviews the analysis, but an RF or SI engineer performs the actual analysis and runs the tool, so a lot of data has to be clearly communicated between them. We have to define the via-constellation in a sketch diagram, with all important dimensions, and list which are fixed (like BGA pitch), which are adjustable, and at what range (like via drill 7mil to 10mil). We have to provide other data like stackup document, manufacturing-related copper clearances, and loss coupon information. The target requirements have to be specified, for example, what nominal impedance and impedance tolerance we expect, and how much worst-case (-17.5dB, up to half baud rate) differential return loss we expect. When the optimization and analysis come back, in the form of a report document and an S-parameter file, we have to review the dimensions as to whether they make sense and doable in the design, whether they still allow a diffpair routing channel between, the return loss is really below -17.5dB. Then we run a TDR simulation on the S-par file and verify that the impedance does not swing too much from the nominal impedance and its tolerance band.

Also note that for up to 5Gbits/sec signals we usually do not bother with via impedance optimization, as the rise time of the signal is slower than to notice the impedance of vias. A similar rule applies as with termination requirement on traces, if the propagation delay (through the via) is much less than the rise time of the signal then no matching or via optimization is required. That typically happens on 5Gbit or slower buses, although a close return path still has to be provided with 2 GND/signal via down to 1Gbit speed. If we assume the rise time near the transmitter being 1/4th the bit time, and we want to stay away from the "$T_{pd} > T_{RISE}$" limit by 4x, then we need via impedance control on designs where the vias are longer that this threshold:

```
ViaLength > 11.8 / (SQRT(DK)*baud_rate*4*2)   [inch and Gbps]
```

What can be adjusted to affect via impedance:

- Width of the dual void
- Length of the dual void
- Via center-to-center spacing, Sig-Sig, and Ground-Sig
- Via drill diameter
- Via pad diameter
- Using dog-bones versus via-in-pad
- DK of the dielectric material
- Thickness of dielectric and copper layers
- Anisotropic DK settings in the software
- Manufacturing artifacts or via barrel imperfections
- Non-Functional pads, whether they are removed by the fab or the layout designer or not.

In the example in Figure 11.21, we have simulated the return loss on the same via structure with several different plane void shapes and sizes (28mil and 30mil wide oblong, 30mil rectangle), as well as re-simulated all three cases with a larger via and pad diameter. We can either set up a few versions of the model with slightly different parameters (like we did in this example) or we can create just one model and set up a parameter sweep analysis that automatically creates simulations with the chosen dimension adjusted in steps (for example, antipad width in 1mil increments). On the results we can see all three antipad sizes failed the 17.5dB return loss limit due to high impedance, while after adjusting the via drill size all three meet the return loss requirements and the impedance got a lot closer to the target impedance of 92 Ohm differential. We analyze the odd-mode single-ended impedance that is exactly half of the differential mode impedance. A lLarger via drill diameter will result in lower via impedance, while a larger void results in higher via impedance. On low layer count boards, we usually have a thick core in the middle, so the signal via will not see nearby GND shapes on a long travel distance, resulting in high impedance, which means on low layer count boards we need larger via drill size for the same impedance. On high layer count boards with thin prepregs we see the opposite, the via impedance is very low and we need to increase it through making larger plane voids and smaller via drills and pads, or to lower the DK. If a design will use ground pour on signal layers, then it must be part of the 3D model too, as it will significantly lower the via impedance. Or alternatively, we can practice not using ground pour near SERDES signals.

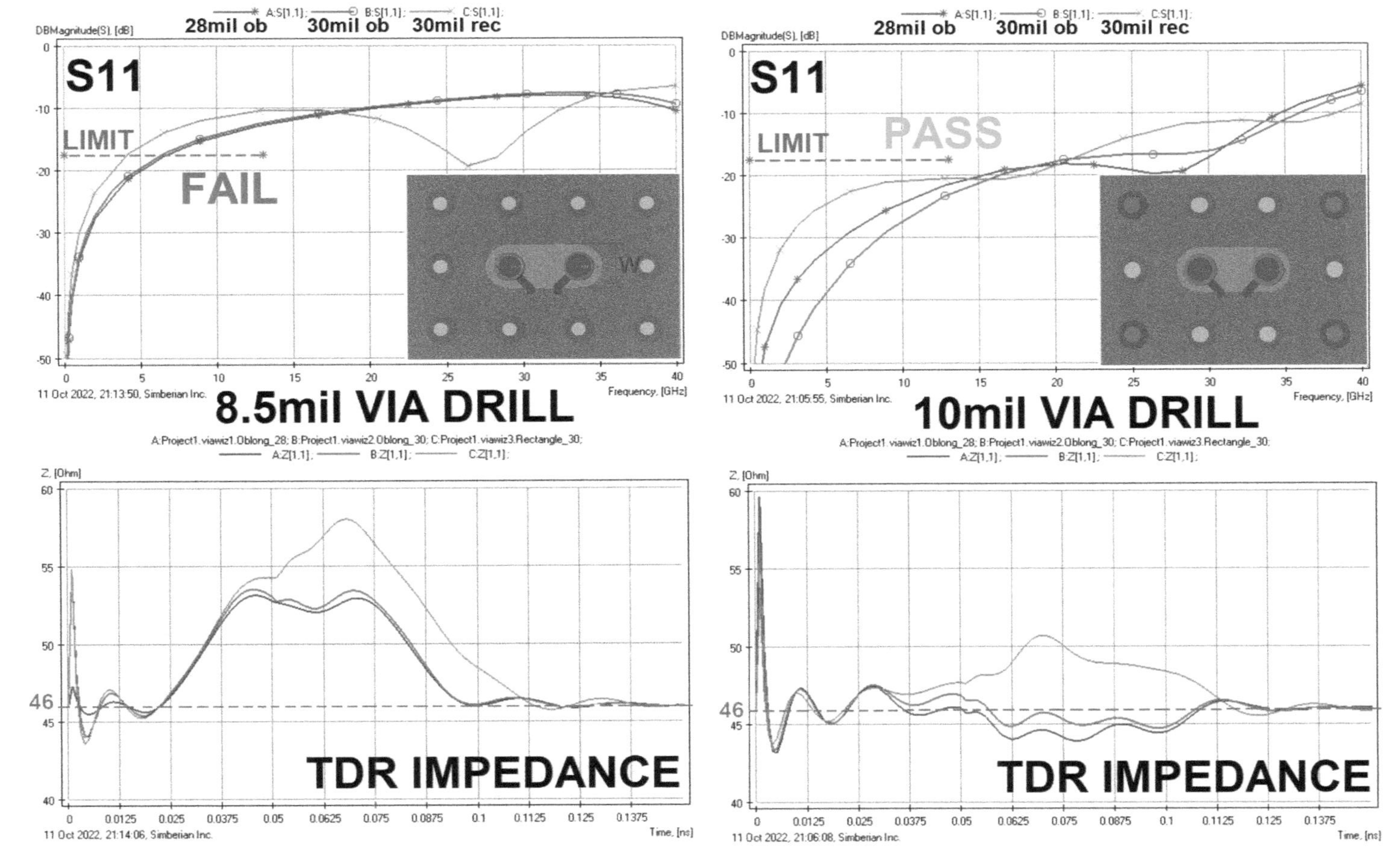

FIGURE 11.21 Example via optimization results in Simbeor.

In simulations we need to use via drill diameter, not finished (plated) inner diameter. For this to work we have to get the layout designer to also specify drill, not finished, diameter, at least for these small signal vias. If the via model contains non-functional pads (NFPs), then we cannot apply NFP removal in production, or vice versa if we have to use NFP removal in production then the 3D via model should be set up like that too. We need a lot of accurate data from fabrication before starting our via optimization. For high-reliability products a certain percentage of the NFPs have to remain on each via. Which layers remain or gets removed should not be chosen by the fabricator rather by the designers to make sure the simulated model will match the fabricated board.

This type of detailed single-feature analysis is sometimes also used to analyze other types of objects. For example, a fanout plus escape route area can be analyzed for the effects of plane antipad fields, or for via-to-trace crosstalk through voids. We can analyze a complete differential AC-coupling capacitor structure with the two capacitors and all the eight vias. We can also analyze the layer-2 plane void arrangement under large surface mount connector pads.

11.4.1 Manufacturing and Layout

The resulting impedance-optimized via structure contains the oval void dimensions. The void is where the planes do not contain copper around a via. They cannot be too big, otherwise they would block the diffpair routing channels between voids under a BGA. There has to be copper planes under the traces. The oval void we use should be at least as big as the backdrill antipad size, and the via-pad plus plane clearance, but sometimes larger as it is enlarged during the via impedance optimization. So the void opening is driven by three separate processes: the via-impedance optimization, the backdrill to copper clearance requirement (drilling related), and the pad-to-plane clearance requirement (etching related). The last two will be enforced and created automatically by the CAD tool if we set up the constraints correctly based on vendor capability. If the constraints are applied at a later stage of the layout design, then the voids might get unintentionally enlarged, which would eliminate our impedance-optimized manual void dimensions. So we have to verify the void dimensions before fab-out, against our optimized dimensions. We also have to verify the manufacturing constraints before we start our via optimization. The optimization result cannot contain a narrower void than the backdrill antipad size; otherwise, the manufacturing clearance constraints will override it. The backdrill antipad size can be obtained from the PCB fabricator, or calculated from the via drill diameter, backdrill oversize, and backdrill to copper trace clearance. The etching antipad size is simply the via pad size plus clearance requirement. The via pad size is the drill size plus the fabricator's annular ring requirement, which is related to the drill positioning tolerance. For via diameter in impedance analysis we use the outer diameter of the plated copper barrel that is equal to the drill bit diameter, not the finished hole size (used traditionally). We need a minimum of 11mil routing channel (RC), to fit 3.5mil wide traces and a 4mil gap, as a minimum manufacturable trace size. 12mil would be better. This has to fit between backdrills and also between via pads. Figure 11.22 shows where these dimensions interact in the escape route area under a grid component like a BGA package. We have to review the optimized via structure results whether it meets this route-ability requirement. If these equations below are satisfied, only then we have the needed routing channel width, and the board is also manufacturable.

```
BGA_pitch - BD - 2 * BDTCL - 11mil >= 0
BGA_pitch - Via_pad_inner - 2 * trace_clearance - 11mil >= 0
BGA_pitch - Via_pad_inner - 2 * plane_clearance - 11mil >= 0
```

Where:

```
BD = PD + BD_oversize
Via_pad_inner = PD + 2 * annular_ring
BD_antipad = PD + BD_oversize + 2 * BDTCL
Etching_antipad = Via_pad_inner + 2 * plane_clearance
```

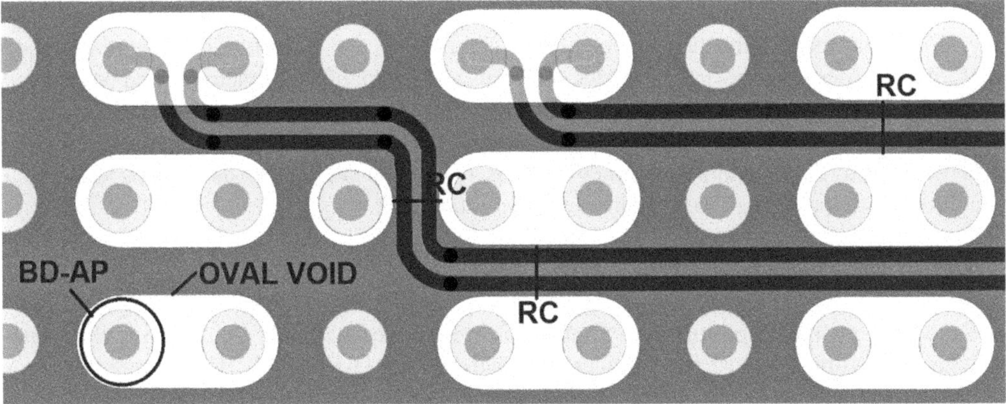

FIGURE 11.22 Routing channels (RC) between oval voids and backdrilled antipads (sketch).

The manual dual voids we place on diffpairs also have to be confined by backdrill and etching antipad sizes, as well as the BGA pitch and the 11mil routing channel width:

```
antipad =< void_width =< BGA_pitch - 11mil
antipad + BGA_pitch =< void_length =< 2 * BGA_pitch - 11mil
```

BD is the backdrill tool size, PD is the primary drill or via drill size, BDTCL is the backdrill tool to trace spacing in radius. Annular ring is the amount by which the via pad has to be larger than the drilled hole on each side. We pick some of the parameters, while the rest of them have to be calculated from them using the formulas above. If the calculated ones turn out to be non-manufacturable, then it means the ones we picked initially were the wrong ones. We have to work with our PCB fabricators to find out the best numbers to pick and to verify the manufacturability of the calculated ones. To implement this "diffpair routed between two backdrilled vias" structure, we will have to use the parameters from the advanced capability table of the best manufacturers. Basic manufacturers will not be able to manufacture them. A complete set of numbers together has to be verified with the chosen fabricator company. Some of our older parameters might have to be re-negotiated to allow a working complete set.

The via impedance on our manufactured board might be different than what we saw in our simulation, because the board features have geometric imperfections, and the fabricator might have modified our design data to benefit their yield expectations. We can find out about both tendencies, by cross-sectioning a board from each of our fab vendors, and taking measurements on them under a special microscope. The unauthorized changes will have to be discussed, while the side effects could just be fed back into our simulation models.

11.4.2 HFSS

The Ansys HFSS is the gold standard for 3D electromagnetic modeling. It has a full-wave 3D solver with anisotropic material properties and support for parametric sweep simulations for choosing structure dimensions for a design. The typical use case of HFSS is to analyze one 3D structure or small area from a PCB at a time. Although we can also import complete board files and simulate a whole signal path with it. Often we use HFSS to create an S-parameter file from a board structure and then use Keysight ADS to analyze the S-parameters or to chain multiple S-par models (areas and via/trace models) together into a complete signal path. It is called macro-modeling and decomposition. The typical problem size for HFSS model creation or import is one via structure (constellation), or a BGA breakout area with two to 10 signals and all surrounding GND vias, with all copper features between the signal pins and the outside of the ASIC/connector perimeter. There have been many correlation studies published between HFSS simulations, and VNA measurements with good results. Still the user has to set up the model, materials and simulation parameters based on detailed research, material test coupons, and recent in-house correlation projects. All this work is necessary to get an accurate simulation that takes several electromagnetic effects and every small PCB feature into consideration. The simulation accuracy depends a lot on the material model setup, so a detailed preparation is needed before the simulation can even start.

11.4.3 Simbeor

The Simberian company's product, the Simbeor, is a 3D electromagnetic simulation tool for analyzing layout features (via structures, traces, pin fields), in pre-layout (with 3D structure editor) or post-layout (design import) modes. It is normally used either in macro-modelling or in single feature optimization. The most useful use case for digital hardware engineers is the pre-layout modeling, simulation, and optimization of 3D structures, like BGA fanout via structures, component pin fields, and AC-coupling capacitor structures. Simbeor also supports complete signal path or multi-trace post-layout simulation with fiber-weave effect models in the dielectric layers. Simbeor allows a direct TDR plot to be generated from a simulation that helps us with via impedance modeling.

Each project has a material library, a stackup, any number of 3D structures (called "circuits"), Via Analyzer views, and Graphs Views. It also supports anisotropic material properties if we manually create a horizontal and a vertical dielectric. The user interface is shown in Figure 11.23.

Simbeor has an interesting feature, the "Via Analyzer". In this we can create a via structure with one or two signal vias and any number of ground vias, using dimension parameters, and a complex 3D structure drawing will be auto generated. The dimensions of the vias, pads, antipads, and relative distances can be set in a spreadsheet-like user interface. There are "transmission line" objects in the structure, which are simulator artifacts needed for simulation, but we need to change these "inputs" to a non-extended type or a via-port type (for the BGA pad) so it will not interfere with our

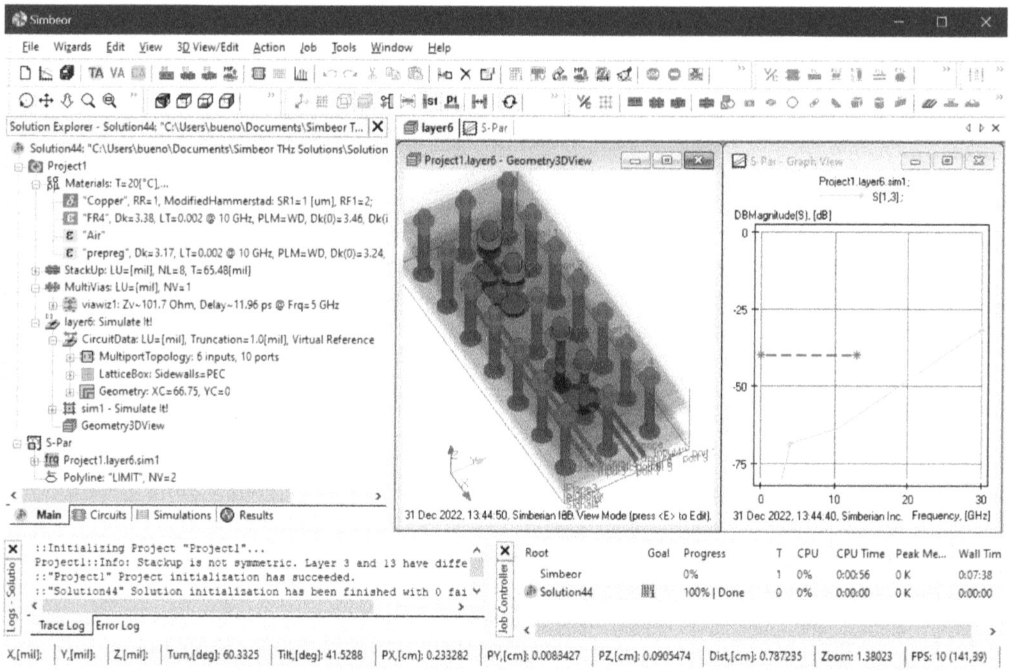

FIGURE 11.23 Simbeor user interface.

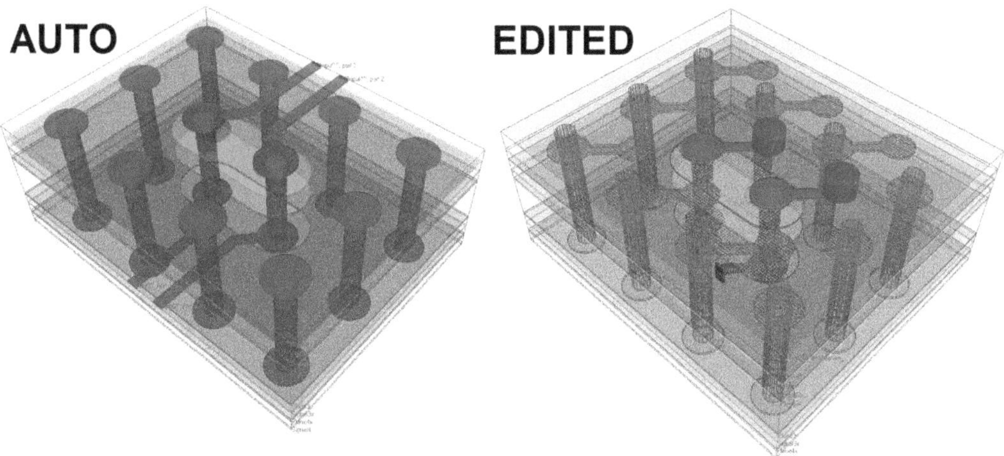

FIGURE 11.24 A generated and edited 3D via model of a 12-via constellation in Simbeor.

complex model. This can be seen in Figure 11.24. The tool then generates a 3D model and simulates it for S-parameters and TDR plots. From the ASIC datasheet pinout diagram and footprint view we will look up the pinout pattern and the signal/ground constellation, then set up a model of two signal vias (diffpair) and all immediately adjacent GND vias in the Via Wizard. For a quick analysis, we will set up the stackup, the aniso materials, the simulation-sweep, and the model, and then run the simulation; once done, it displays regular and mixed-mode S-parameter plots. We can also display TDR plots; just enable the compute TDR Response option in the simulation options first. For us digital hardware designers, the return loss and the TDR impedance versus time/distance plots are the interesting parameters, not so much the impedance versus frequency nor the voltage standing wave ratios that are default in most electromagnetic tools. The Via Analyzer does not contain BGA pads and dog-bone traces, only the vias. So for a real analysis we will have to edit the model in 3D view to add the BGA pads (ellipses and traces), then run the simulation from there. So from the via analyzer, we generate the 3D structure, then we find the Circuit Data item and start editing it, then simulate it and display or export the data. After a simulation, while creating a new Graph View, we can add the S-par or the TDR plot. We have to set the simulation port impedance to our target impedance; otherwise, we will see more reflections than there is in reality.

The via analyzer is an easy solution for boards that are made with through-drilled vias, like most data center hardware, but for boards with staggered microvia stacks we have to do a lot of manual editing. We can use the Via Analyzer editor to create a basic through structure, and then replace the vias with the microvia stack manually. This can be done by editing and copying the composite object's "cylindroids", pads and traces in the 3D editor (not in the Via Analyzer editor).

In all cases it makes sense to use the via analyzer to create the main elements of a model, then manually edit the 3D model to accommodate component pads, dog-bones, stubs, microvia stacks, and non-functional pads—it saves 90% of the labor. For BGA fanout crosstalk analysis we can copy paste the whole structure multiple times, then add traces to it. The simulation time is reasonable on a low power laptop for a 10-via structure, but for crosstalk analysis with 20 vias a remote server will be required.

11.4.4 Via Issues on S-Parameter Profiles

If we did not optimize the vias in a 3D field solver then we might end up with a very low impedance dip on the TDR profile, and some high bumps on the return loss profile. For a single feature (like a via, a connector), we usually set a 17.5dB or 20dB RL limit, unlike for a whole channel that is 4 to

12dB. On a whole channel there are several other contributors to the overall return loss, so we make sure that each component will not eat up much of the budget by itself. The two simulations in Figure 11.25 in QUCS contained a channel with a 4 inch- and a 15-inch lossy transmission line, and a via model (1.5mm long Tline model) between them. The via model was either 60 ohm unmatched or 94 Ohm matching the trace impedance. We can see the unmatched via impedance caused the return loss limit to be violated above 4.5GHz, while the matched via did not and it had more than 5dB margin.

Via stubs are basically unterminated transmission lines, they show up as a resonance suckout on the insertion loss profile, and a bump on the return loss profile. In a pre-layout simulation, we can model a via stub with a tap-on short transmission line that is terminated to ground with 0.3pF capacitors. A 1.5mm long via stub violated both the insertion and the return loss limits, seen in Figure 11.26.

If we backdrill the same via, then we will get a maximum of 12mil residual stub. That is 1/5th the length of the original one, so we can model it with a 1/5th long transmission line and 1/5th capacitance. This does not eliminate the resonance, but it pushes it up to a five times larger frequency, that is way above our signal's bandwidth so it will not affect it. There is no need to eliminate stubs to zero. As we can see in Figure 11.27, backdrilling makes the via acceptable. This also matches prototyping experience, on four channels of short 10Gbps SERDES links, one channel had missing backdrilling and that one had unreliable link with closed eye in the on-die eye capture, while the other channels that had the backdrilling in place were operating with a wide-open eye diagram. This behavior was matched on every prototype unit. After the board re-spin with fixed backdrilling, all four channels had wide-open eye diagrams on all boards.

11.5 SERDES LINK ANALYSIS

We have industry-wide best practices for the analysis of multi-gigabit (usually above 5Gbps) SERDES transceiver-based interface standards. The physical board features (traces, vias, pads) with passive components (AC-capacitors, connectors) together with the passive SERDES channel, which delivers the signal from the transmitter (TX) to the receiver (RX) ASIC. We can analyze the channel that we designed or we can analyze the signal that shows how the (third party) chip interacts with our board (channel). Analyzing the channel is always more accurate than analyzing the signal because we design the channel and we can measure its parts, while the signal simulation depends on the third-party chip performance and black box model accuracy. The chip pin is also a legal boundary—we ensure that the board meets objective standards and the chip company makes sure their chip will meet objective standards or document in their datasheet what they meet. Design verification of prototypes is best done with on-die time domain eye scan. All other methods can help in gaining confidence and understanding or aid in debugging, but they carry too many inaccuracies to be usable for pass/fail verification.

In case of multi-board SERDES links, what is analyzed and when is complicated but logical. An eye diagram or a BER test makes sense only on a complete channel chip to chip, sampled inside the receiver chip. Comparing S-parameters against full IEEE, PCI-SIG, or other channel specs only makes sense on full channels when we have chained together all boards' separately obtained S-par models in a simulation tool. We can only compare one board's S-par curves against limit lines if they were adjusted for budget allocations. Analysis in all other cases would just mislead our project/design decisions.

All the analysis described in this book are for board and system designers who use ASIC chips made by third-party chip companies. The boards have to be designed to meet standard and basic signal requirements. Board hardware designers and SI engineers at chip companies have additional tasks on these SERDES channels, for example, chip characterization, that can tell if the chip would work on a board that is designed to meet standards (like IEEE, PCI-SIG, and so on). The PCIe Base Gen-4 specs include several test board features to be designed and measured by chip companies, for example, the "calibration channel" and the "replica channel". It is a PCB trace of same length and kind as the one routed to the ASIC prototype chip to be able to measure what the channel

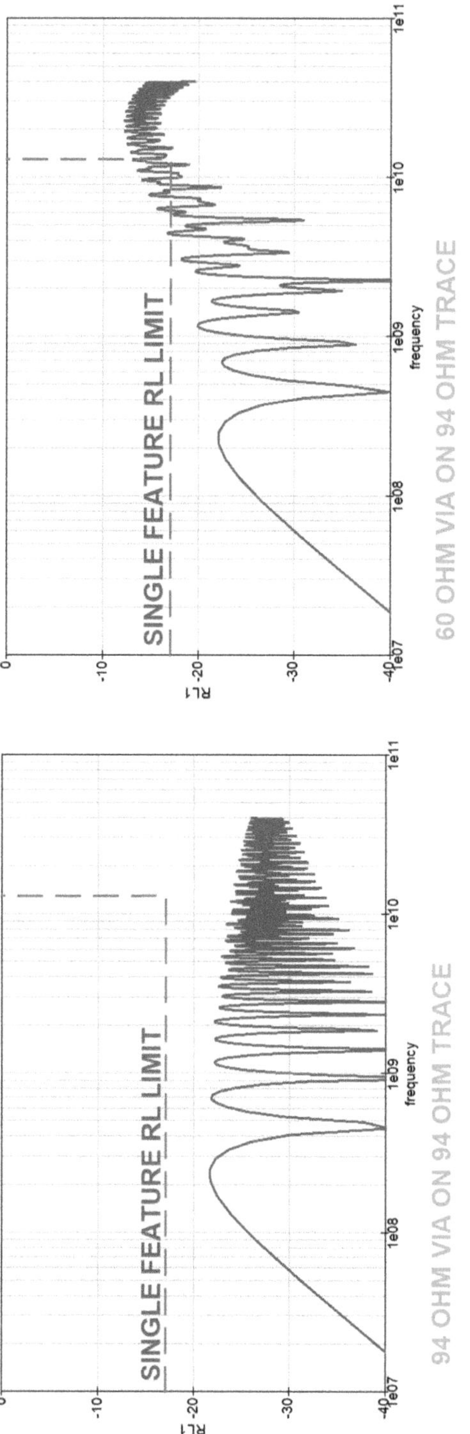

FIGURE 11.25 Return loss of trace and a via with matched and unmatched impedance.

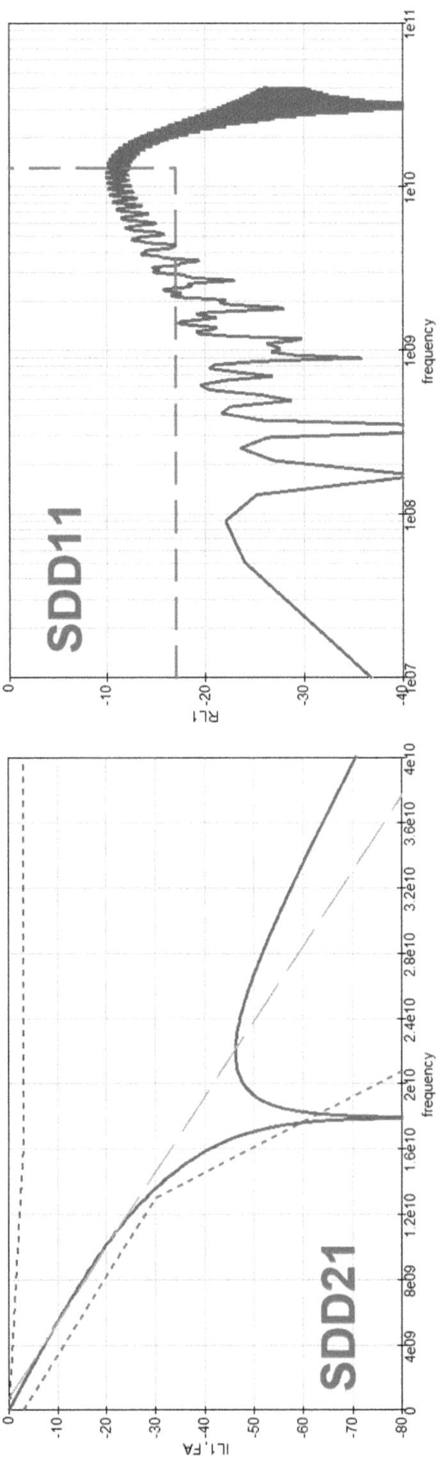

FIGURE 11.26 S-parameters of a via stub.

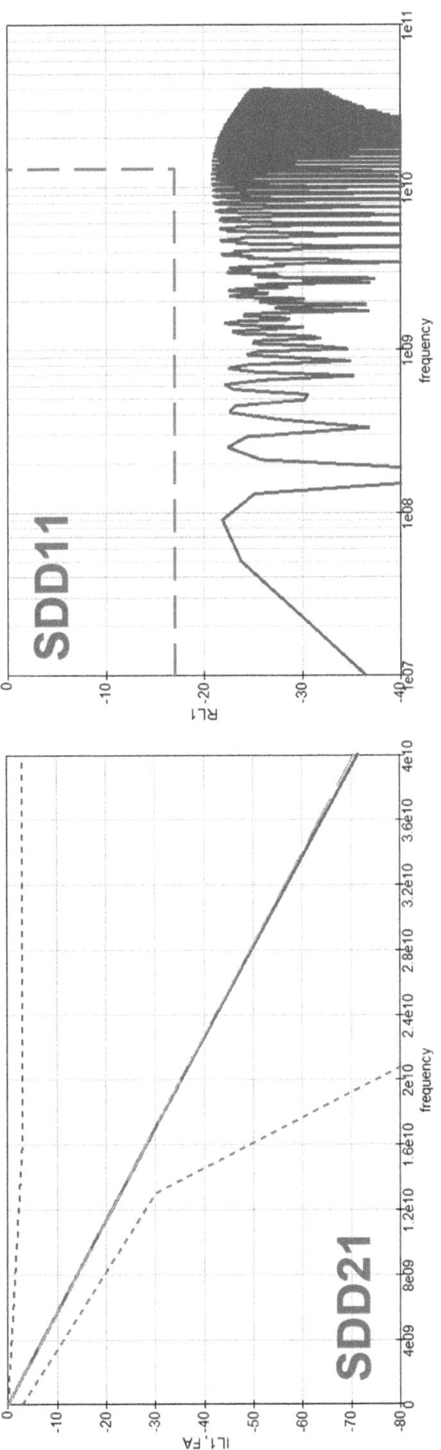

FIGURE 11.27 S-parameters of a via with a reduced 12mil residual stub after backdrilling.

(S-parameter) looks like on a signal path similar to the one leading to the chip on the same exact board and stackup, but with coax connectors. It also allows eye measurements to see what the signal would look like at the chip (at the end of the similar trace) without having to do tap-on measurements with double termination. Someone has to design these chip characterization SI test boards, which is part of the design tasks of board hardware engineers who are working at chip companies.

11.5.1 Analysis Domains

Either the passive physical channel or the signal can be analyzed and either can be checked in time domain or in frequency domain. Each combination has its use cases. The domains:

- Passive channel frequency domain analysis with S-parameters, it has to meet relevant standards (limit lines). This can be simulated or measured (with VNA) on the prototype.
- Passive channel time domain analysis with TDR plots, it should be smooth enough without too much impedance deviation. This can be simulated or measured (with a TDR-scope) on the prototype. This analyzes the physical channel only.
- Signal analysis in frequency domain is something digital hardware engineers just do not do, unlike RF engineers.
- Signal analysis in time domain (physical channel together with the driver and receiver active silicon devices).
  - Signal integrity simulation result as eye diagrams and BER contour plots, with few crosstalk aggressors and IBIS-AMI models, against input signal eye mask requirement after the RX equalizer point.
  - Eye measurement with oscilloscope. It also has to meet eye mask requirements, but the measured eye is degraded from probing artifacts.
  - Eye (BERT) scan on the prototype system with an on-die built-in eye scan feature. This is without any inaccuracy, but it shows the eye margin instead of the signal eye.
  - Bit error count and BER test. It can be done on the prototype system while the data can be read out from registers using custom software. It is simpler than an eye scan, as it produces a number instead of a diagram.

11.5.2 Channel Frequency Domain S-Parameters

For Backplane Ethernet interfaces various IEEE802.3xx standards provide frequency domain channel characteristics limits for chip-to-chip full channels. OIF-CEI (Optical Internetworking Forum, Common Electrical Interface) also defines similar full channel specs for any SERDES interface type in general. These limits are defined up to a certain frequency that is at or near half the baud rate, also called the "Nyquist frequency", or up to twice the baud rate. When we do the PCB extraction to S-parameters, we have to use a 3D Full-Wave simulator that properly accounts for the GND-plane discontinuities like via-antipads. We usually simulate or measure the longest and shortest of each SERDES link type (on-board, backplane, front panel).

A chassis with a multi-board channel requires macro-modelling (decomposition), where the S-par models of each board are manually stringed together for a stage-2 frequency-domain S-par simulation. This can be done manually in Keysight ADS, QUCS, or others. The result is either the curves to be displayed or a new single S-par file.

We run an S-par simulation on either a single S-par model file of a board, a chain of S-par models of connecting boards and connectors or a combination of board and connector S-par models with parametric Tline models. The simulation results are post-processed by the simulation tool to display standard and derived S-parameters against their standard limit lines. In ADS and QUCS we can use user-created templates for the post-processing, such as the one in Figure 11.28 that contains a large number of waveform processing equations.

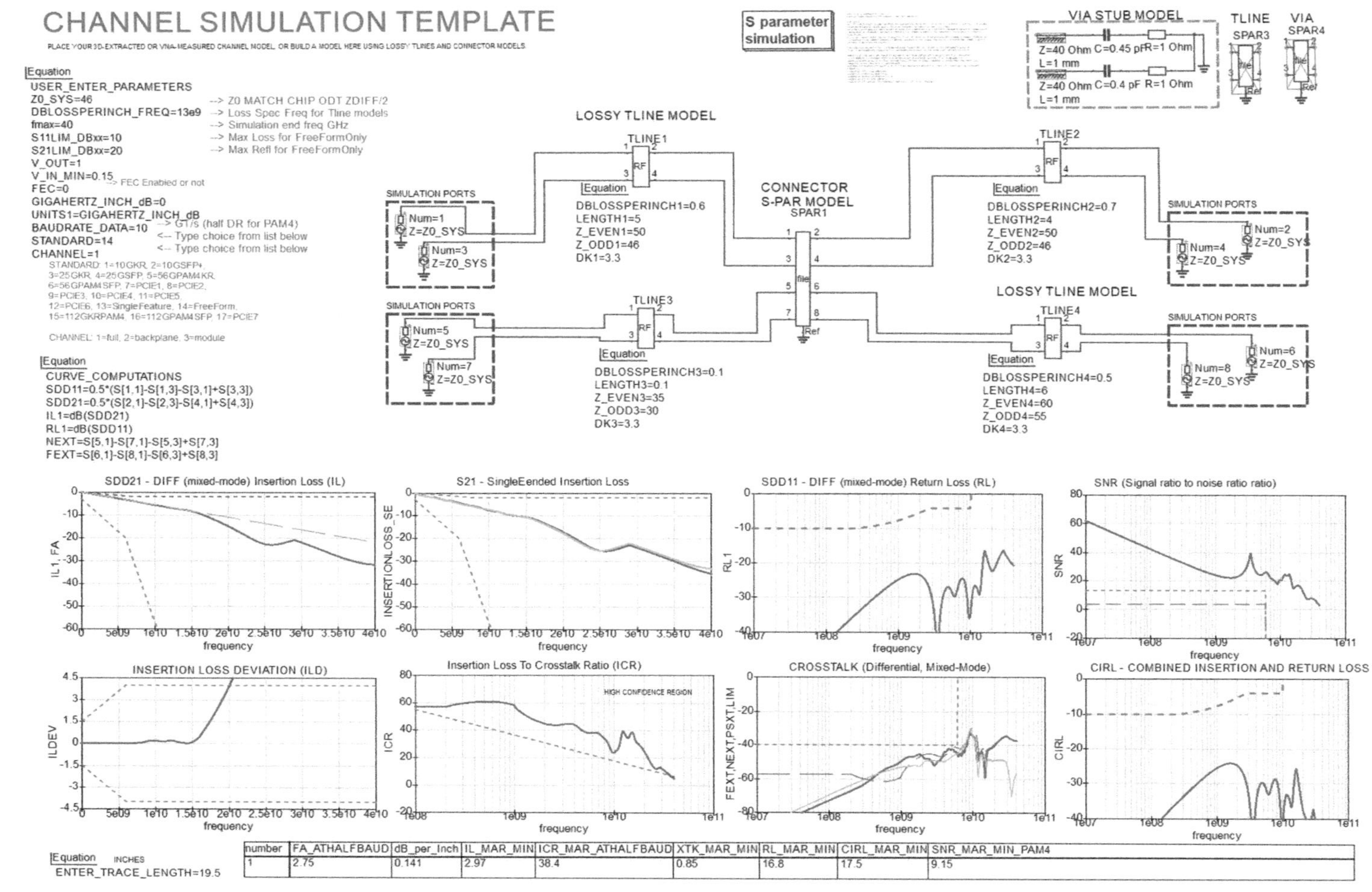

number	FA_ATHALFBAUD	dB_per_Inch	IL_MAR_MIN	ICR_MAR_ATHALFBAUD	XTK_MAR_MIN	RL_MAR_MIN	CIRL_MAR_MIN	SNR_MAR_MIN_PAM4
1	2.75	0.141	2.97	38.4	0.85	16.8	17.5	9.15

FIGURE 11.28 Channel simulation template in QUCS.

Most standards define only a maximum insertion loss limit line for the longest and lossy-est SERDES links. It is worth defining a minimum insertion loss for each board, especially if we have very short links in the range of 1" to 2". For example, as 10% of the maximum insertion loss curve, that helps with achieving RL limits, like the SFF-8418 does with its upper limit. Or simply we can define a minimum trace length (3") as a number.

11.5.2.1 S-Parameter Curve Pathologies

When the limit lines are violated on S-parameter curves, then the causes can often be identified and mitigations can be prescribed. Typical channel design issues, their causes, and the typical mitigation options used can be seen in Table 11.2.

What objects we can see on insertion loss profiles:

- There is a loss slope that can be extracted using fitted attenuation (FA) computation; we can extract a loss number if we read out FA at half baud rate. This is related to the insertion loss budget and max trace length calculations. It is demonstrated in Figure 11.29.
- There are resonances or suckouts caused by discontinuities. Everything resonates at their f0 base harmonic, and also at their 2xf0, 3xf0, 4xf0, etc. higher harmonics too.
  - Fiber Weave Effect, trace crossing the glass bundles periodically. With straight traces it can be as low as 4 to 20GHz. With 10degree traces f0>35GHz, with 20degree f0>70GHz.
  - Traces passing through an antipad field in the fanout area. f0 = c / (2*Pitch*SQRT(DK)).
  - Trace resonances, if the ends are not matched or terminated well (to chips, resistors, other traces or connectors). f0=c/(2*Length*SQRT(DK))
  - Trace segment resonances, the segment between the chip and the AC-cap, the AC-cap and the other chip/connector.
  - Trace segment resonances, segment between chip and via, or a via-and another chip/connector, if the via impedance is not well matched to trace impedance. Typical if the designer did not do via impedance optimization.
  - VIA stub resonances, depending on stub length, and anisotropic DK.

11.5.2.2 Complete Chip-to-Chip Channel Related Standards

These standards describe a whole chip-to-chip channel. The limit lines for S-parameter curve compliance come from standard documents. They present them sometimes on diagrams, or the end point coordinates of the limit lines in tables, or as formulas that we can use to compute the curves. Most S-par numbers are negative values, unless we flipped them before display. The list below shows some common standard document names and the numbers:

- The main IEEE802.3 standard is for Ethernet. There are link type designators like "25GBase-KR", and there are standard documents that refer to them like IEEE802.3bj. The chip-to-chip link type names in IEEE have a suffix as "-KR" for long backplane links, or "-C2C" for on-board only SERDES links. There are separate documents called "amendments" with a 2-letter post-fix in the name like IEEE802.3xy. Any IEEE amendment document might contain specifications for several different interface types in separate chapters or annex sections. For example, IEEE802.3ap-Annex69B is for 10GBase-KR backplanes, these are listed in tables in Chapter 3, "Major Interfaces". Our ASIC datasheets or even Wikipedia might also tell us which speed/type we are using. The IL limit line is near ~30dB at half the baud rate for most backplane links, but it varies a lot depending on which standard. Chip-to-chip (C2C) interfaces typically have around half as much IL budget as the backplane channels do. The standard documents with exact channel specs (formulas and numbers) can be purchased from IEEE.

TABLE 11.2
S-Parameter Pathologies

Symptom	Cause	Mitigation
Too Much IL (FA)	PCB stackup materials	Use lower loss dielectric and/or more smooth copper foil, or use retimers.
	PCB fabrication process	Work with a fabricator that can build better loss-controlled boards, or use retimers.
	Too long traces	Change floorplan, board size, backplane arrangement or system architecture, or use retimers. See loss budget analysis.
Too deep IL Suckouts	Return path and impedance discontinuities	< 5GHz: missing ground via >15GHz: via stubs or via impedance mismatch
	Same items as below with too much RL cases	Same as below
Too Much RL	Too short traces	Not enough IL. Lengthen traces to a minimum 2…4 inches
	Plane continuity	Eliminate thermal relief, reduce plane antipad size, escape route shortest path
	Via impedance	Need to optimize the via impedance in 3D-EM closer to the trace impedance
	Low speed connectors	Use better connectors, or use retimers.
	Big connector pads	Add voids underneath signal pads.
	Too many connectors	Insert retimers when having more than 2 connectors in a path.
	Fiber Weave Effect	Odd-angle or wavy routing, or board rotation
	Inadequate ground return at transitions	Every transition needs a GSSG pattern, at least 2 GND vias per diffpair, or more. The GND vias have to go all the way through the stackup.
	Too many layer transitions (too many vias)	Only use 2 vias per net, or 4 vias when AC-coupled.
	Over-tuning of phase tolerance matching	Change row/direction and use twists at pad entry, eliminate duplicate meander bumps.
	Fanout area does not have good G/S pattern	Use a chip from a different vendor with better pinout.
	Using random single-ended microvia fanout	Use differential impedance controlled fanout with dual void, use through vias.
	Too long uncoupled length	Keep signals together at pad entry, do not use split-row escape route, minimize tuning meanders
	Impedance mismatch	Choose board impedance to match connector and chip impedance.
Too much crosstalk	Fanout area does not have good G/S pattern	Use a chip from a different vendor with better pinout, or use retimers.
	Fanout area has merging dual voids	Follow regular pattern/direction, reduce plane clearance, and avoid merger
	Trace spacing is too small	Increase spacing, in regular clearance or running length clearance (max parallel segment).
	AC caps of different lanes are too close	Staggered AC cap placement
	Fanout layer usage	swap the layers used for RX and TX

- The OIF-CEI standard from the Optical Internetworking Forum is called Common Electrical Interface. New versions cumulatively include the old versions' data, the latest is version 5.0 for up to 112Gbps links. It is a protocol-independent general specification for chip-to-chip and chip-to-optical module links. It defines different categories of links (short, medium, long/backplane). An alternative to IEEE and SFF. It can be applied to any

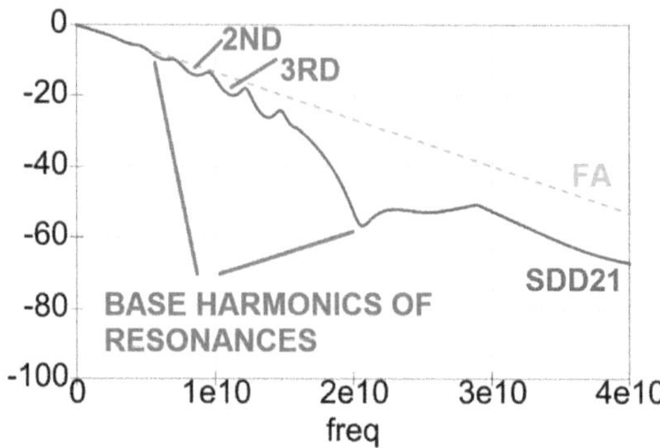

FIGURE 11.29 Objects on insertion loss profiles.

interface, even if it is used for Ethernet, PCIe, or other otherwise defined standards. Figure 11.30 shows an example channel spec for CEI-25G-LR.

- Both the PCIe Base and the CEM (Card Electromechanical, system board and add-in-card) specifications from PCI-SIG have different versions or generations from PCIe 1.0 to 7.0. Version-3.0 runs at 8Gbit, every new version doubles the baud rate, with PAM4 introduced at V5. In the PCIe BASE spec the board design RL limit lines are described clearly, while our design IL has to be derived from the calibration channel IL limits table, only using their maximum limits. Starting from V4, the table lists the limits for the current and all previous generations. The CEM spec contains detailed IL and RL specs, but only for connectors, and budget allocations for motherboard versus add-in card PCB designs. The exact numbers and curves can be found in the specification documents that can be purchased from PCI-SIG.
- JESD204B and JESD204C from JEDEC defines electrical channel characteristics for A/D converter to FPGA interfaces, with IL and RL limits adopted from IEEE and OIF-CEI specs. We are supposed to calculate the limit lines from IEEE formulas based on design-specific data rate. JESD204B allows speeds up to 12.5Gbps, JESD204C up to 32Gbps. JESD204C has two categories, and three classes each, for SERDES channels depending on length (short, medium, and long) and transceiver core type. Each has different S-par limits calculated.
- Some ASIC devices allow more or less insertion or return loss than the IEEE specs, depending on chip input sensitivity, as we can find on their datasheets.

11.5.2.3 Partial Channels

There are also standard documents describing partial channels that were made to guarantee inter-operability between boards designed by different companies. They describe channels from chip to connector. A few examples are below:

- VITA68.x standards for VPX backplane-based systems. They define RL and IL budget allocations between backplane and front boards for third-party inter-operability. For each card (front module or backplane), the RL limit is shifted vertically by a certain amount of dB from the original IEEE or PCI-SIG specs, while the IL is scaled by a certain percentage. When analyzing VPX boards we have to compute the new limit lines, with a suitable tool like ADS or QUCS. VITA specs can be purchased from VITA.com, for looking up the exact values.
- PICMG3.1 standard for the ATCA form factor. They define FA, IL, ILD, ICR, and mode conversion for the whole channel as well as budget allocations between backplane and front boards for third-party inter-operability.

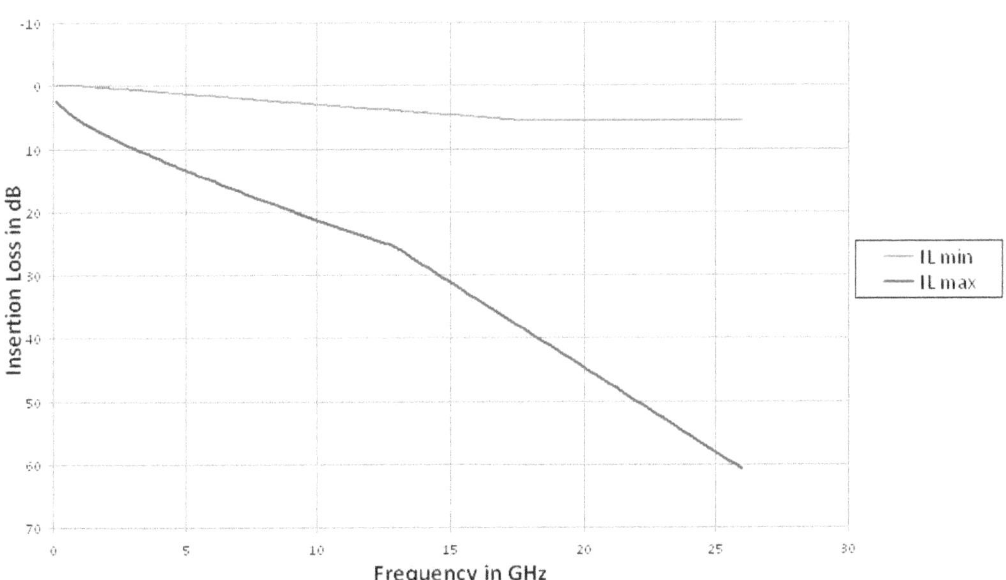

FIGURE 11.30 Channel insertion loss limit lines for long backplane channels running at 25Gig, from OIF-CEI5.0. © 2022 Optical Internetworking Forum. Copyright paragraph: This document and translations of it may be copied and furnished to others, and derivative works that comment on or otherwise explain it or assist in its implementation may be prepared, copied, published, and distributed, in whole or in part, without restriction other than the following, (1) the above copyright notice and this paragraph must be included on all such copies and derivative works, and (2) this document itself may not be modified in any way, such as by removing the copyright notice or references to the OIF, except as needed for the purpose of developing OIF implementation agreements.

- Various SFF, OSFP, and QSFP-DD standards define PCB trace channels between ASIC pins and optical cage connector pins. The SFF-8418 is for 10Gbps SFP+ optical modules, and it has minimum and maximum loss budgets. Some IEEE802.3xx amendment specs also define such electrical channels—they call them chip to optical module (C2M) links. If copper cables are used, then the channel continues into the cable, so the chip to module traces are even more partial channels, but they work only if the chip supports it. The SFF specs are available from snia.org.
- For a single board in a multi-board system, when no standard is available, we can use insertion loss budget allocation in percentages (scale the whole chip-to-chip IL curve) and a more stringent return loss limit line (offset the standard RL limits by 5 to 10dB).

11.5.2.4 Individual Design Elements (Single Features)

When we design a board, we also have to design the individual elements of the signal path. For example, a pin-field of a connector, a BGA escape route area, a via structure or an AC-capacitor structure. The S-parameter limits for design elements have to be more stringent, to prevent them from eating up the whole channel budget. We mainly check this for crosstalk and return loss:

- Crosstalk: NEXT and FEXT should be below -40dB up to half baud rate, which is a 1% amplitude.
- Return Loss: Practically RL should be below -17 to 20dB up to half baud rate.

11.5.3 Channel Time Domain TDR response

The TDR (Time Domain Reflectometry) response of the channel shows the impedance of the signal path as the signal travels through it. It is basically the step response. On this any impedance discontinuities show up as peaks and valleys. They can be identified by their time position, which is related to spatial location along the line, after converting time to distance and then measuring the distance from the test port on the PCB. The design goal is to optimize the PCB layout to reduce the impedance deviation to less than +/-10%. The negative valleys show low impedance points, often via transitions and breakout with high capacitance. The positive peaks show high impedance, for example, GND plane undercut by nearby antipads. All of the impedance discontinuities (peak/valley) directly cause reflections, indirectly IL suckouts, ILD, and crosstalk. Most of the time we analyze channels in frequency domain with S-parameters. If we see issues on our S-parameter profiles, then we can run the S-par model through a TDR simulation to see which location on the signal path deviates from the nominal impedance the most. The layout object at that location is likely responsible for the return loss or insertion loss limit line violations. Sometimes we notice that the whole TDR curve seems to tilt up/right, due the trace losses; it is normal.

How a TDR simulation works: In ADS, HyperLynx LineSim or other tools we can apply a step voltage source to the trace S-parameter model and run a transient simulation, then compute and display the impedance along the trace. The left side of the TDR plot shows the impedance at port-1 of the S-parameter file or at the TX pin on the channel. The circuit model setup can be seen in Figure 11.31, and an expected impedance/time curve in Figure 11.32. TDR uses a step waveform as a test signal with a very fast rising edge. As the test signal travels through the channel, the edge slows down gradually due to insertion loss. Objects near the TX location see the full fast waveform, while objects near the end see a slower rise time that might be too slow to accurately show the impedance of the object, so we get smeared or smoothed object shapes. Objects like vias, connectors, fanout neck-downs, and void-passing show as a sharp peak because sharp means short or small size. If the distance that the test signal travels during its rise time is longer than the object size, then the object appear smeared or completely invisible to the TDR. We can see the same channel with lossy traces in Figure 11.33 and with reduced trace dielectric loss in Figure 11.34. On the second plot the two connectors appear more similar, than on the first plot, while they have the same S-parameter model. The first plot completely fails to show the via at the receiver. If the real data signal travels the same direction as the test signal, then the via at the receiver is not visible in the test, but also not affecting the real data transmission too much. The lead-in and lead-out transmission lines in the simulation model are the only really horizontal parts and a big cliff at the end.

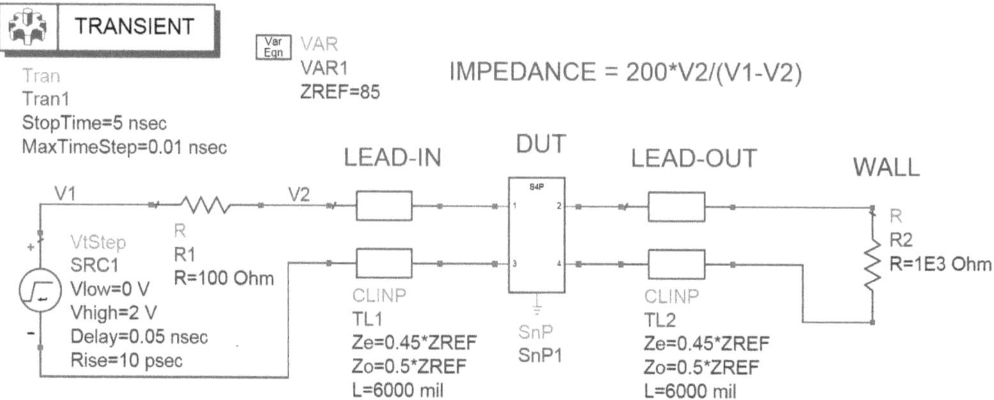

FIGURE 11.31 TDR simulation setup schematic in ADS.

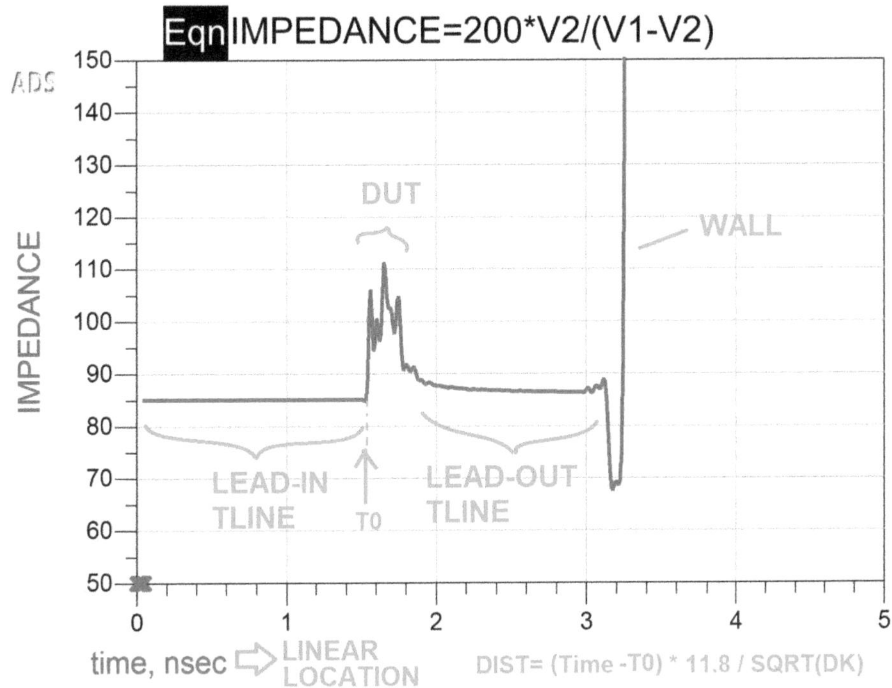

FIGURE 11.32 TDR simulation results assessment ADS.

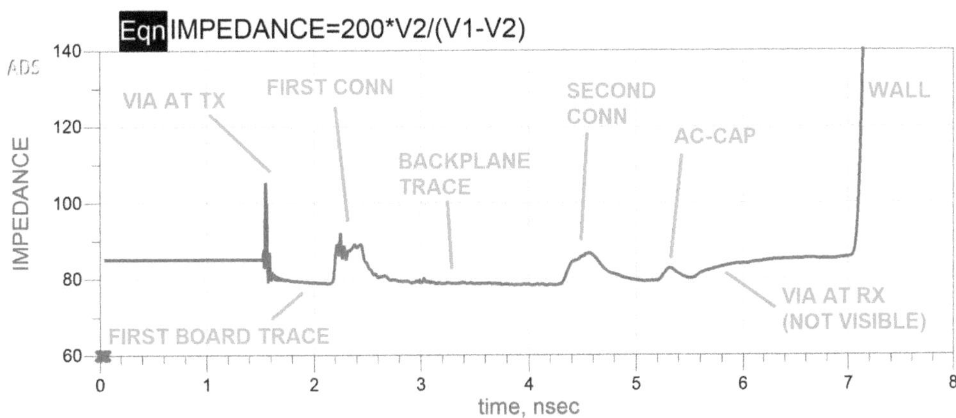

FIGURE 11.33 Complete lossy channel TDR plot object identification in ADS simulation.

The TDR response can also be measured with a TDR-capable oscilloscope on a prototype. On a TDR response we can observe elements of the design. A BGA fanout via is an impedance dip, a connector is a dual dip with a spike between (via on each board and the contact), a trace is a straight line but not horizontal, rather with a slight slope caused by insertion loss. The lead-in cable is the only really horizontal part and a big cliff at the end. The impedances of different boards in a multi-board arrangement might not line up due to manufacturing tolerances.

11.5.4 Signal Time Domain Eye Diagrams

The time domain eye diagram of the signal can be simulated, it can be measured with an oscilloscope, or it can be captured on-die. The simulation accuracy depends on the models and the material

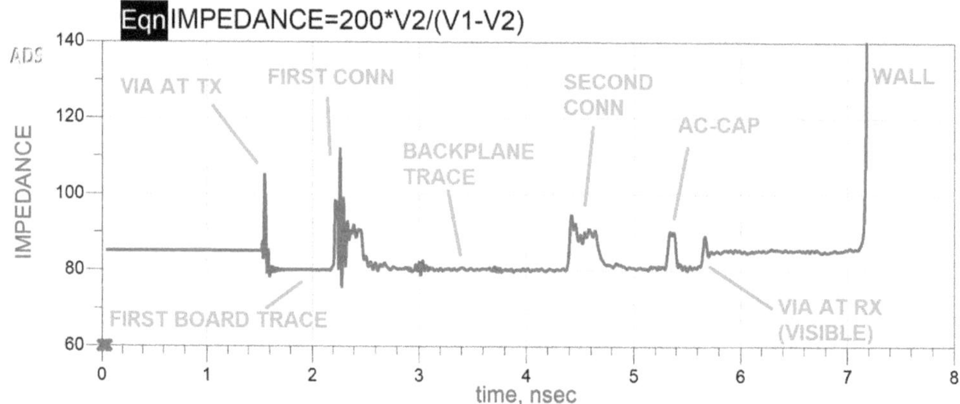

FIGURE 11.34 Complete reduced-loss channel TDR plot object identification in ADS simulation.

parameter setup. The oscilloscope measurement is severely limited by the probe bandwidth and the stub that is created by the probing and by the fact that it is not measuring the signal at the output of the RX equalizer, but at a location on the PCB. The on-die eye scan measures an eye margin diagram, instead of an eye diagram, and it measures it with 100% accuracy, as it is being done on the real hardware without any probing artifacts. In simulation we can display a regular eye or a BER contour, while the on-die eye scan looks similar to the BER contour plot but with margins. The eye opening has to meet the chip vendor's input eye mask requirement, but in case of the on-die eye scan we have a reduced mask-fit requirement. For all types of eye diagrams, we must run real data or PRBS pattern to capture a stressed eye, not just IDLE characters, otherwise the measurement might be too optimistic. The difference between stressed and IDLE eye is more pronounced when the signal path design quality is bad.

11.5.4.1 SI Simulation Eye Diagrams

This is done with IBIS-AMI models and passive channel S-parameter (or lossy Tline) models in a time domain simulation. The simulator has to support convolution to make use of S-par models in time domain. Usually we generate eye diagrams, bathtub curves, and BER contour curves. We can use any of the SI simulation software on the market, although each has a different accuracy. The eye diagram can be captured in simulation at the RX pin as well as at the on-die point after the RX-DFE equalizer, which is more useful. The eye width and height after the DFE (part of IBIS-AMI model) has to meet the receiver datasheet RX eye mask requirements if it exists. Regular eye diagrams are the least accurate representation of a SERDES channel design, especially when we are running less than a few billion bits. BER contour plots are better; they extrapolate to trillion bits when we run a time domain simulation on a few million bits. More details can be found in the previous section at "SI Simulators".

The accuracy of the silicon model (IBIS) is often lower than the accuracy of the physical channel model. Many times a model is not even available, so we might substitute with a model from a different but similar chip vendor, which results in even lower accuracy. Board and system manufacturers design/make the physical channel, so for "legal" reasons analyzing the physical channel only with S-par without the silicon would make more sense.

11.5.4.2 COM

Starting with 25Gbps, IEEE 802.3 Annex 93A defined the Channel Operating Margin (COM), and the complex equations and algorithms for computing it from simulation results. It is a measure of the received eye in time domain, the signal versus noise ratio (SNR), caused by effects in the passive channel. It is a single number that represents the passive channel with the active chip model or an ideal equalizer model, together with jitter, reflections, and noises. The signal amplitude and the combined noise amplitude have to be such that a DFE can open it up to become detectable by a standard eye mask at 1E-12 BER level. Equalization can be modeled only as part of the IBIS-AMI models, or ideal SERDES models, so we have to use those. In ADS the COM is generated in the time domain simulation called "Channelsim", which is the IBIS-AMI-based eye and BER contour simulation normally, but instead of "Statistical" or "bit-by-bit" modes we select the COM mode for result computation. The COM represents the passive channel in decibels [dB], as a ratio between the received signal and all noises combined, in milli-Volts. How the tools calculate COM from the post-equalizer received eye diagram is as follows:

```
COM = 20 * log(signal_amplitude / (noise_amplitude))   [dB]
```

The actual signal amplitude and noise amplitude are obtained from other complicated equations shown in IEEE standard documents but not listed here. COM just checks how much the noise voltage and how much the signal voltage is at the receiver relative to each other, regardless of how big the sources of those were. S-parameters are source versus received amplitude ratios, so an S-parameter-SNR would be a ratio of these ratios. COM>3dB is a typical requirement for all interface types. PAM4 has to detect a one-third size (9.55dB worse) signal voltage due to the four-level signaling, so it is more sensitive to noises caused by the full swing sources, so it can allow only a smaller noise voltage too. The standard equations that calculate the signal and noise amplitudes include the number of logic levels as a variable. They account for both the signal and the noise reduction in PAM4, so we end up with a lower COM number for a PAM4 versus NRZ signal on the same board/system, but the same 3dB COM limit requirement. To meet the same 3dB COM limit on a board, now used for 28G-baud PAM4 (56G data rate), previously used for 28G-baud NRZ, we would need to improve the FEXT and RL S-parameters. So the board layout design has to be improved. We need better S-parameters (input/output ratios) but the same COM (output SNR) for PAM4 versus NRZ at the same baud or symbol rate.

COM helps in corporate program decision making but hides the sources of issues, unlike S-parameters that can be used to identify channel pathologies. COM might also help with automated batch simulations or measurements of many signals in a system, where software can easily compute the pass/fail criteria, and technicians can assess the results. It is not a complete analysis or exact verification, but it aggregates so many details that it can be used for a good/bad assessment. We can even list a COM margin. The equations might be different for future standards.

The Effective Return Loss (ERL) is another single-number "figure of merit" that can be generated from the channel, in dB. The computation is complicated; it involves pulse responses, waveform-gating, weighting and statistical equations. Just like COM, it also considers equalization effects. The computation details of it are not listed in this book. If we can get an SI simulation tool with built in ERL computation, or an ADS template that does the same, we could use those.

11.5.4.3 Eye Measurement with an Oscilloscope

See Chapter 18, "Measurements". With oscilloscopes we can measure accurately only if the oscilloscope replaces the receiver chip, so the receiver chip is no longer connected to the channel, so we do not have two receivers. SERDES links are supposed to be point-to-point, not multi-drop. This can be done at external I/O connectors and at backplane connectors.

If we have a chip-to-chip link on a board, then we have to do a tap-on measurement using a soldered-on active probe. This creates a ~1" long stub and a double termination that makes the signal no longer impedance matched terminated. Scope active probe input impedance degrades from 100 kOhm to 100 to 500 Ohm above few GHz, or above 1/20th of the advertised probe bandwidth. The reflections a probe introduces cannot be eliminated by the scope software due to the law of preservation of entropy (second law of thermodynamics). All this causes the tap-on measurement to be very pessimistic and only suitable for debugging, not for verification. It cannot be used for pass/fail testing on SERDES links because we would fail completely good designs.

Connector fixture-based scope measurements can be used to meet standard eye opening at the legal boundary between our board and a third-party board/cable. These QSFP-to-coax, HDMI-to-coax, and similar fixtures can be purchased from various vendors.

11.5.4.4 On-Die Eye Scan

Also see the section about prototyping and transceiver tuning. Eye scan is done using the on-die (inside the chip) built-in eye diagram capture feature that is part of the SERDES transceiver tiles, for those chips that support it. It captures an eye-like image, which is actually a BERT-scan (bit error ratio test), or eye-margin scan, not a measured signal eye diagram. The chip uses the same on-die circuits for this capture as it uses to receive the data stream, like the CDR and the DFE, so it has the exact same limitations and signal eye opening requirements. This also means the signal is not distorted during the measurement. It can be read out using a JTAG dongle for some chip vendors, or an I2C dongle (Aardvark), or through I2C/PCIe/SPI to an embedded host processor with Linux console. Most large chip vendors provide software tools for extracting an on-die eye scan. Some are windows GUI-based that we would run on our laptop with a JTAG or I2C dongle, others are text console-based and run on the DUT's host processor under a Linux console. Note that some devices have a 1.8V I2C bus, and the Aardvark dongle is 3.3V, so we need to use an Aardvark Level Translator board in between the DUT and the dongle. Once connected, we need to use the Aardvark GUI to enable port power to enable the level translator circuits, then use the eye capture GUI to check port status (the link must be up) and capture the eye.

The BERT scan is created by the RX SERDES inside the chip by altering the SERDES CDR sample point of the incoming signal, in time offset and in voltage offset. It divides the 2D plot into about 100 to 1000 "pixels", it measures BER at each pixel and displays the BER value with a color code or a 1-digit number. Basically, each pixel is a result of a separate BER test. The CDR sampler circuit has a minimum RX eye opening requirement for it to correctly detect a signal, created by the input setup and hold requirement (Wmin=T_{ISU}+T_{IH}) and the comparator gain (Vmin=Noise+Vout/Gain), which are undocumented. This mini window that exists only in prototype testing, not in simulation, is shifted within the eye until it starts to overlap with the eye wall, and starts to receive lots of bad bits. We know if a bit is bad by running a PRBS test where a PRBS data sequence is computed by both the TX and the RX ASICs so the RX knows what data is supposed to come in. In some cases, we can rely on the CRC bit in data packets while running real data traffic, instead of PRBS. The PCI-express 4.0 standard has introduced the "lane margining" test, which is basically a horizontal BERT-scan with the results showing in PCI-SIG standard registers. A BERT scan really shows an eye margin outside of the center-located receiver minimum eye mask (Vmin and Tsu+Th), instead of an eye, so the "margining" name is actually accurate. Figure 11.35 shows the difference between an eye and an eye margin.

If we try to put a mask into a BERT-scan eye image, then it becomes an eye-margin mask, not an eye mask. How much margin do we want to have will determine the size of the eye-margin mask we would use, but it does not come from standards, we have to make them up (e.g., 20% to 80% of

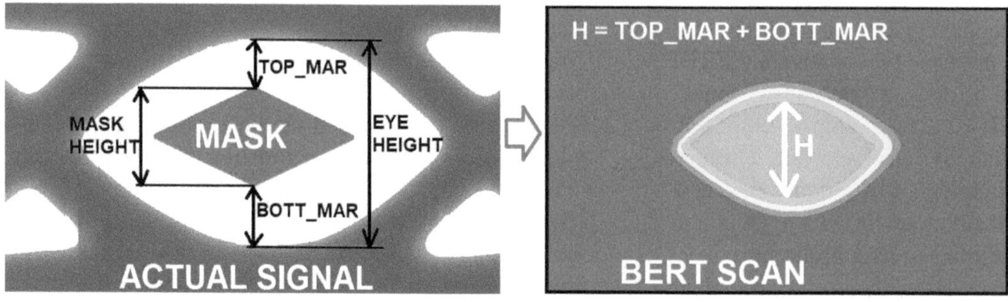

FIGURE 11.35 BERT scan concept for on-die eye capture (sketch).

the standard eye mask). A simulated BER contour is made with the assumption of a perfect receiver with 0V/0ps eye mask. The on-die captured BERT-scan shows how much margin we have on top of the receiver's minimum eye mask that the chip on the particular unit requires. The receiver requires a minimum eye mask that is smaller than the official standard RX eye mask specification, and it varies with process and temperature unit to unit. If we buy the same part number ASIC, quantity of 10, each chip will have slightly different minimum eye requirements, so each will show a different eye margin scan opening. So a BERT-scan will tell us the eye margin relative to the particular unit's capability. When the actual signal eye opening is less than the receiver's actual eye mask requirement, and/or the sample point is shifted horizontally or vertically, then it will detect many bit errors, so that pixel will be marked red…yellow. The chip manufacturers have to make their chips to not require more than the standard or their own datasheet-defined eye mask, and if the board manufacturer provides at least as big an eye as that then it will certainly work at the center sample point pixel but with no margin. If the receiver requires 100mV and 100ps minimum eye opening on the actual signal, and our BERT-scan shows 56mV and 78ps then it means the actual signal eye is 100+56=156mV and 100+78=178ps. Since we do not know the eye mask requirement of the unit or instance we are testing, the measured BERT-scan will only tell us how good signal arrives through our board, relative to the chip instance in the particular unit. This is not ideal for design verification, but it is more useful in production testing of every single unit.

If we want to use BERT-scan for design verification, then we would do it on multiple units in a temperature chamber and make our eye-margin mask large enough to cover the unit-to-unit variation of the input mask requirement, plus temperature variation. The total variation cannot be more than the standard specification eye mask (zero to max), so if we require the eye-margin mask to be as big as the eye mask from the standard, only then we can be sure that our BERT-scan validates our design, and it should work on all future production units. This means that if the particular chip unit requires 0.001% of the standard mask, and we apply the standard mask to the BERT-scan, and it passes, then we can be assured that any another unit that require 99.99% of the standard mask will also work on the same board design without even testing it. It appears that we are suggesting to use the standard eye mask on the on-die eye capture results, as an eye-margin mask, but it is more convoluted than that, as explained here. Requiring such a large 100% margin might be impossible to meet on many good designs, it can be considered overdesign, but it removes the ambiguity. It would be reasonable to assume that the actual device unit eye mask does not vary unit to unit more than 30% to 50% as much as the size of the specification eye mask. In that case we can use an eye-margin mask in the BERT-scan to be half the size compared to the eye mask in the specs. A 50% choice might cover device to device and temperature variation of the receiver eye mask requirement and the variation of the TX chip and PCB material. Basically, the suggestion is to use as big of an eye margin mask as the expected variation of the input mask requirements unit to unit, or half the eye mask. This variation is unknowable, but we can guess it will be no more than 50% of the standard eye mask size. Even using 50% suggests that some units can be twice as fast as others (50% versus 100%), or 3.5 times faster (20% versus 70%), which is very unlikely. If we measured how much the eye scan height varies unit to unit on a few prototypes, by comparing eye scan results it would likely result in a low number (<<50%) and it would not cover the variation between all units to be manufactured in the product's lifecycle. Instead, we could just use the 50% number. This also allows us to perform design verification on one or a few units only, as the margin will cover all other boards. Sometimes chip datasheet eye-opening requirements might be ambiguous. They might be simulated voltage waveform eye openings, in which case the 50% of it can be used in an eye margin scan/test. If their requirement is an eye scan opening, then 100% of that has to be used in an eye scan/test.

It is very useful to capture BER values on every link and every lane in production, but we cannot have an engineer with a JTAG dongle manually doing it. What could be done instead is to capture only 1 pixel, the BER at the 25% offset position in both voltage and timing, basically 45 degrees off the center in any direction. The 25% is not unit interval (UI); rather, it is 25% as much as the standard eye mask size from the center. It is 25% instead of 50%, as the 50% we talked about is in width, not each side. This way the captured BER value could be automatically compared with a threshold in a Linux script for pass/fail. Assuming the BER can be measured from registers through the host upstream interface (PCIe, I2C, or SPI), not having to use dongles. PCIe4.0 and newer versions have defined standard registers for this kind of test—they call it margining.

A few standards define how good of a signal eye opening is required to be provided by the board designers after the receiver chip's DFE, while other standards have only frequency domain specs. PCIe started out with a receive eye height requirement at Gen1, and it requires much less at Gen6. The actual numbers can be looked up in the standard documents that can be purchased from the organizations like IEEE and PCI-SIG. A post-EQ eye can only be simulated, while measurements after the EQ are only possible with on-die eye scan that measures margins, not signal eyes.

During the eye scan, the DUT can be in regular transfer mode where loopback is not necessary, but instead of just relying on IDLE characters, real data should be pushed through using a custom test program or script to "stress" the eye. We can send a large data file or keep reading a few registers in an infinite loop. It is best to use the PRBS (pseudo random binary sequence) generator/counter mode with external loopback plugs/boards, if the chip and I/O standard allows it because it will generate a worst-case pattern to stress the eye and allows easy error checking. Practically on most prototypes this is not possible, since ASICs from different vendors are connected together with SERDES links, but the real data–based test is always available. PRBS testing would either require a loopback connection or have ASICs from the same vendor and chip generation on the two ends of the same SERDES link. When testing with real data the receiver has no way of calculating every bit for correctness, so the applications have to rely on checking the CRC bit in large data packets. Or the interface IP core to have a FEC error count register. This will tell if any bit in a 100 to 1000 bit packet went bad, which is useful enough in most cases.

To cover 1E12 bits and directly measure down to 1E-12 BER (bit error ratio), we would need to send 1E12 that is 2^40 unique combinations, and use PRBS40. At 10Gbps that would take 100 seconds for each pixel on the eye scan. With 1000 pixels that is 27 hours. We run shorter tests usually, which takes only a few minutes. With PRBS31 we could send ~2B unique combinations to 1E-9 BER level that takes 1/5th of a second per pixel or three minutes for an image. Basically, we measure to a 1E-9 contour. In simulation we cannot send as many unique bits as we can in measurement, and usually 2 to 5M bits are enough to extrapolate bathtub curves to 1E-12 BER level, so we can use a PRBS21 pattern in simulation and PRBS31 in measurement.

We can display a 2D color plot, BER contour plot, or a text-based console plot, depending on what the chip vendor supports. The text-based plot, like the one shown in Figure 11.36 will have each pixel showing a BER value in X as 1E-X. A single digit with hexadecimal encoding can display 0 to 15 as 0 to F, where F would be a 1E-16 BER level. If the test is deliberately only up to 1E-9 BER using PRBS21, then the lower than 1E-9 pixels can be displayed as a space or dash. Or the tool might just display "x"-es at the open parts of the eye and dots at the closed parts. Most FPGAs and

```
>> eyescan

0000000000000000000000001112234321100000000000000000000000
0000000000000000000123456789987654321000000000000000000000
0000000000000000001234567899999987654321000000000000000000
000000000001122345678999-------99987654321110000000000000
0000001122345678999-----------------99987654321110000000000
00001122345678999----------------------9998765432111000000
0000112234567899------------------------999876543211100000
0000001122345678999-----------------9998765432111000000000
00000000001122345667899 9-------99987766543211100000000000
000000000000000111123456789--99987654321000000000000000000
0000000000000000000123456789987654321000000000000000000000
```

FIGURE 11.36 Text console based on-die eye capture (sketch).

PCIe switch devices use a graphical user interface (GUI) with color-coded images (like the one in Figure 11.37), while most Ethernet chips use a text console running on the embedded host processor. The color of a pixel or a single digit number represents the BER at each CDR-offset position. With some chips a complete image eye scan is not available, but a BER test (but error rate) or an error counter might be available.

For design validation, a BERT-scan using an on-die eye capture should be done on every single lane. Since it is an eye margin scan, it will show whether the design has sufficient margin on the few units that were tested. The purpose of having a margin is to ensure that boards that did not take part of the design validation will also work. They are similar, within a tolerance, not identical. As a last resort, we should also ensure signal integrity of each production unit. That does not have to be a full BERT-scan on all lanes, a single center point bit error ratio test, or even just counting the number of bit errors for a half an hour run would be sufficient in an ESS chamber. The production test only has to prove that the particular unit works, while design validation has to prove that all future builds will work also. Product aging might require each unit to have some margin. Cards that might be plugged in with third-party cards need to be production tested for a margin; in-house boards do not. This can also be simplified, not running a full BERT-scan eye diagram, just a single point (up and sideways a little from the center) margin scan. Single-point error ratio or error count tests can be done quickly and be interpreted by Linux or Python test scripts easily. On very large boards we might have a thousand lanes of SERDES, so we cannot wait 10 minutes on each lane to capture a diagram, the production test must be economical. If we use error count test, then the counter should really stay low, not in the millions by the end of the test. If it counts millions of errors, but the functional test passes, it is still a really low quality design with no margins. The production test script will have to check the single-point error count or ratio and decide if it is above (fail) or below (pass) a threshold.

11.5.5 Bit Error Counters and BER Tests

This is a numerical, not graphical analysis. Most SERDES interface IP cores contain registers (error counters) that show how many bit errors were detected. Our custom test software or some chip-vendor GUIs can read this out. While running a 10 Giga bits per second link for 10 minutes (600sec,

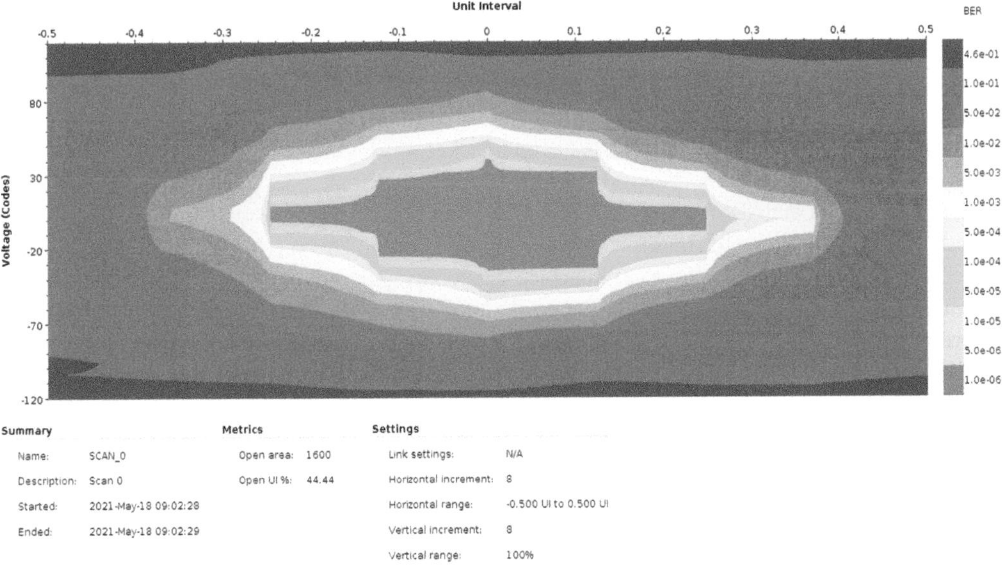

FIGURE 11.37 GUI-based on-die eye capture with Xilinx iBert in the DIOT system board project at ohwr.org and CERN. Copyright CERN 2022, licensed under CC-BY-SA.

6E12 bits) with a 1E-12 BER requirement, we should see less than six total errors in the error counter registers. If we see more, or a lot more than that, then our design is not reliable. The error count number can be displayed as a simple error count or as a bit error ratio (BER). When BER=1 then all bits are bad, when BER=0 then all bits are good. Typically, a low percentage of the bits are bad, meaning the BER is between 1E-2 and 1E-18, but it can still cause problems. BER can be calculated by software; by simply knowing how long the test was running at what speed, then calculate the number of bits that went through the link, then divide the error bit count with the total bit count. Simple Linux scripts can read this number and compare against a threshold number for a pass/fail test. The BER on the same link on another unit varies by manufacturing tolerance, and even on the same unit it varies over temperature and aging. This variation is not a few percent, but a few orders of magnitude. We should expect our test to have a margin of a few orders of magnitude for a pass/fail criteria to make our product reliable. We need to test BER on our prototypes as design verification (DVT), but it has to pass with a big margin (1000x) to cover unit-to-unit (process) tolerance. We should test all production units too, but they have to pass with only a small margin (10x) to cover the aging of the particular unit. All these tests should be done in temperature chambers and with voltage margining to account for those variations. To pass a test, we need to satisfy the equation:

```
ERROR_COUNT < DATA_RATE_BPS * TEST_TIME_SEC * BER_REQ / MARGIN
```

The main design goal on a SERDES link is to make the physical channel as good as possible. Despite our efforts, there will be bit errors seen in the receiver. This is why silicon SERDES IPs have bit error mitigation features. We cannot rely solely on BER mitigation in a design—we have to put sufficient effort into high-speed layout features first. The two main domains of BER-mitigation are the error correction (EC) and the error detection (ED). They also report the number of error bits they corrected or detected in real data traffic, without a PRBS test pattern. Error correction restores the correct data stream from a partially faulty data stream seamlessly. Two types of error correction are common: the Forward Error Correction (FEC), which runs on physical layer symbols, and the Error Correction Code (ECC), which runs on higher protocol layer complex data packets. Modern SERDES interfaces utilize 10 to 300 bit physical layer symbols and kilobyte sized higher layer data packets. FEC became common in 25 to 56Gig links, it is sometimes turned on or off by software. EC will catch and replace most error bits, but a few will escape. This way we can analyze a pre-FEC BER and a post-FEC BER. On 56Gig links it is often impossible to achieve 1E-12 BER, so we have to turn on the FEC and aim for a pre-FEC channel BER requirement of 1E-3 to 6. On a 10Gig link we still use the full 1E-12 requirement. Error detection is also done on higher layer packets like ECC is, but it cannot correct the bit errors; instead, it will tell the main state machines or software to send back a re-send request and discards the bad packet waiting for a new one. This uses a Cyclic Redundancy Check (CRC). The downside of ED (CRC) is that some packets have to be sent again, so some packets will arrive with more latency delay than other packets, and the total bandwidth is reduced due to having to send the same thing again and again. The variance on latency might be unacceptable on critical buses. External interface data coming through are checked by higher layer applications that expect latency variations and delays. Internal system buses (PCIe, DDR5) need to be more reliable than external, as their failure can wreck control systems, distort generated signals, or crash processors and operating systems. We have to design them with better signal integrity, and we have to allow more orders of magnitude (1000x versus 10x) margin on their pass/fail BER test.

With error detection (CRC), if every packet has one bit error, then every packet has to be re-sent an infinite number of times, resulting in zero bandwidth. With 1-bit error correction, the first bad bit in a symbol/packet can be corrected at the receiver, but additional bits cannot be, so they become uncorrectable bit errors. We can introduce the UCBER (uncorrectable bit error ratio) as a derived measure, basically post-FEC or post-ECC BER, seen by the higher level application. It shows how many bad bits were in a stream that were beyond repair, when the error correction capability was exhausted by previously received bad bits or clustered bad bits. Each of these uncorrectable bad

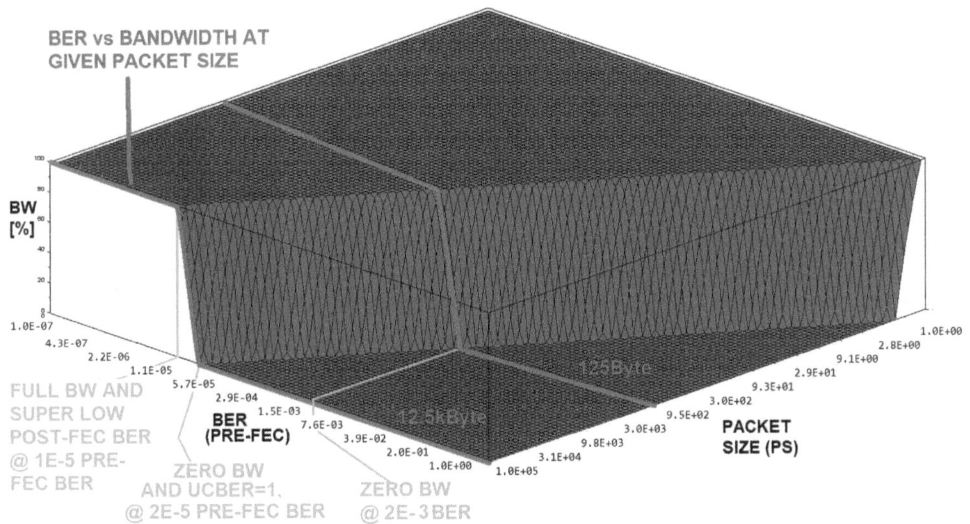

FIGURE 11.38 Channel bandwidth from bit error ratio with FEC, computed in Scilab.

bits will take down a whole symbol or packet, basically as many good bits as the packet size (PS). The PS can vary layer to layer in the protocol stack, so we have to use the one where the EC/ED is applied. This issue emerges from the higher layers of the digital hardware architecture; it is not purely signal integrity. BER and UCBER as bit error ratios max out at one. With 1-bit error correction, when every packet has a bad bit (when BER=1/PS), then we still see the full bandwidth and UCBER is zero—assuming even error bit distribution. When every packet has two bad bits (when BER=2/Ps), then the bandwidth drops to zero and UCBER is one. A small region of the BER to bandwidth curve is linear, between 1/PS and 2/PS, but it is so small that we rarely encounter it. It is the breakdown area. If we measure "bandwidth" instead of BER, then we cannot tell whether we are near this breakdown or not, whether we have a few orders of magnitude margin or not. UCBER reaches one when the pre-FEC BER is about 1E-3 to 1E-6, and the link breaks completely. With error detection only, we reach zero bandwidth at BER=1/PS. With 1-bit error correction we reach zero bandwidth at BER=2/PS. With N-bit error correction we reach zero bandwidth at BER=(N+1)/PS. But if the channel is better than the BER<(N+1)/PS limit then UCBER becomes theoretically zero, as the formula shows. In reality UCBER is not really zero in that region but very good, around 1E-12 to 1E-18. This also guarantees a uniform latency link by not having to re-send any random packets. The pre-FEC BER to post FEC BER curve would be non-linear, similar to the BER to bandwidth curve. Figure 11.38 shows how a small number of bad bits diminish the channel bandwidth. The diagram simply calculates the bandwidth from pre-FEC BER and PS variable combinations and creates a surface plot that shows a link-down condition in the lower flat portion. It is based on the equations below.

```
UCBER = max(0, min(1,(PS*BER-N)))
BW_EC = 100 * min(1, max(0,(1+N)-PS*BER))        [%]
BW_ED = 100 * min(1, max(0,1-PS*BER))            [%]
BW_Gbps = DataRate * BW_EC / 100                 [Gbps]
```

A larger packet size requires a stricter pre-FEC BER to achieve full bandwidth and avoid a link-down. In 400G Ethernet the smaller 257bit encoder-symbols are given a FEC error correction in the physical layer, so the symbol size replaces the packet size in the equation, making it a much better ratio, having a lower BER requirement. It allows the decoded post-FEC BER to be better than the 1E-12 requirement, even when the board signal's BER is as bad as 1E-3. When the FEC is turned off, the passive channel must be designed to perform with 1E-12 or better BER, according to IEEE. With FEC on, 1E-3 to 6 pre-FEC BER can produce sufficient 1E-12 to 16 post-FEC BER. The OIF-CEI-56G standard defines a channel requirement to be 1E-6 pre-FEC. When the pre-FEC BER is so bad that even the post-FEC BER is below 1E-12, then the link is totally unreliable.

If we do not comply to the standards and we do not have FEC, then we still need to meet practical BER limits. Without FEC our higher-layer packets might be 1000x larger than the symbols used for FEC, and we need to keep the packet retry events below a 1/1000x rate. Then we need a 1000*1000=1E6 times better BER than we would need (1E-3) if we had FEC. Then we need BER=1E-3/1E6=1E-9. But that does not allow the few orders of magnitude tolerance we need to cover PVT (process, voltage, temperature) tolerance, so adding another 1000x for that makes it to a 1E-12 requirement. So we end up complying to the standard anyway.

12 PCB Materials and Stackups

Digital printed circuit boards (PCBs) are made of dielectric and conducting layers laminated together into a stackup. Hardware designers have to keep very close attention to the materials and processes that go into the digital board's stackup because that determines signal integrity performance through trace impedance, insertion loss, via impedance, crosstalk, mode conversion, Fiber Weave Effect skew, and other things. It is important for us to accurately characterize these materials for SI simulations as well as for design and manufacturing documentation.

The initial stackup sketch is created by the hardware design engineer and then negotiated with the fab vendor to arrive to a final version, which is the "approved vendor stackup" document. This document must list all dielectric layers (with detailed glass style, resin content, thickness), copper layers (thickness, plating, foil type), drill types/depths, and impedance-controlled trace information (width, space, impedance). The glass style originally describes the glass-woven fabric yarn dimensions, but we use it for identification of a complete glass/resin combination item. It is a four-digit number like "2113". This stackup negotiation must take place before the layout design starts because the trace routing, the via impedance optimization, and SI simulations rely on the exact stackup data. The hardware designer must be included in the approval process; the stackup detail is part of the design and any SI analysis and via impedance optimization. Often old corporate processes include only purchasing departments or maybe layout engineers in the communication loop. They also used to allow the fabricators to choose the exact dielectric sheet and glass style, so they refrained from including it in their own design documentation. Starting at about 1GHz this cause several problems, so it became the industry trend to document the glass styles with the design.

Impedance identification in layout and Gerber files is another important topic. The fab vendor gives us a stackup document that also includes trace width and spacing for impedance control for all impedance/layer combinations in a table. We should use those trace width and spacing parameters when we route our board. If we did not for some reason, then we have to be able to tell the fab vendor during the ordering process which trace is which, so they can adjust the trace width on our Gerber files. For example, the approved stackup calls for 5/5/5mil for 93 Ohm diffpairs, but we routed it at 4/4/4, then we need to know that the 4/4/4 traces are the ones the vendor has to adjust post-Gerber to 5/5/5 to meet the 93 Ohm. The different impedances should always be routed with different width/space, otherwise the identification will become impossible, and the information will be lost. This free adjustment worked on 100MHz to 5GHz designs, but above that the designer and the fab vendor have to lock down the exact glass style and resin content to prevent variation in trace width from prototype to production, which would cause variation in other things also, such as crosstalk, insertion loss, and Fiber Weave Effect. That variation makes the design a different design. It is better to route with the vendor-provided width, which will ensure two things. There will be no variation later effecting SI and there will be no chance of ending up in a situation where the traces have to be widened but they cannot fit due to board density and objects.

Sometimes fab vendors define diffpair spacing; sometimes they define pitch (that is center-to-center distance instead of edge-to-edge spacing). Layout designers in some cases look at the stackup document, which prescribes 9mil pitch, then they route it with 9mil spacing instead. This is a mistake that has to be caught in layout reviews. So the hardware designers have to verify all routed diffpairs to match the width and space with the stackup document, and whether there was any space/pitch mix-up. We cannot simulate a board accurately that the vendor will later have to adjust for the space/pitch mix-up.

Similarly, to trace identification, via type identification is also required. If we use VIPPO vias, but not all vias need to be VIPPO, then the design has to allow easy identification of which to apply

DOI: 10.1201/9781032702094-12

the process to. For example, if our standard via has 8mil drill size, then we can use 8.1mil for the VIPPO vias, both will be drilled with 8mil drill, but the fabricator will be able to identify which to be filled as the NC drill file will have two separate groups of coordinates. On many designs we just use VIPPO on all, and then there is no need to spend time on identification.

12.1 DIELECTRIC MATERIALS

The dielectric materials are the prepreg and core (laminate) sheets, made of fiberglass fabrics embedded into resin. The materials have a part number (for example Isola IS410), but it does not specify the material exactly for an impedance calculation. An exact material specification contains a set of parameters, for example like this one: "Isola IS410 prepreg, 2116 glass style, 125um finished thickness, 67% resin content". The materials are available in a few certain thicknesses. Each different thickness variant has a different dielectric constant and loss tangent, so we need to know the exact DK and DF for the trace and via impedance and loss simulation. A common mistake is to use the DK and DF data from the one- or two-page material datasheet, which can have up to 20% difference to the value of the chosen thickness variant. PCB material vendors, not the PCB fab vendors, can provide a document with DK/DF tables on request. It is worth building a material library since it is hard to get those material DK and DF values for each thickness. An example screenshot of a material library can be seen in Figure 12.1.

Dielectric sheets are either "core" or "prepreg"; they are made by the material vendors, and they are used by the PCB vendors for making PCBs. The core (sometimes called "laminate") arrives already hardened and covered with copper foil on both sides, while the prepreg is by itself and not hardened yet. The heat and pressure in PCB lamination will harden it. Lamination is when the fabricator puts all the etched layer sheets together and, while applying heat and pressure, the layers fuse together into a hard multi-layered PCB. The DF is the parameter that contributes to the insertion loss, together with trace width, copper foil, and copper adhesion promotion process. DK contributes to the trace and via impedance. The DK/DF data is specific to one specific glass style and resin content percentage variant, so that has to be exactly listed in the stackup and its data used in our simulations. The glass style is important for two reasons: it exactly identifies a sheet as each sheet variant has a different DK, and it is also related to Fiber Weave Effect mitigation strategies, as described later in this chapter.

12.1.1 DK VERSUS FREQUENCY

The dielectric core and prepreg sheets' DK and DF vary over frequency, while the material vendors provide measured data that they measured at a certain frequency point. They often provide the data at a few measurement points. Both DK/DF are strongly changing over frequency, so we need to pick the

Manufacturer	Name/Brand	Core/Prep	Glass Style	Glas material	Spread Glass	Resin %	Fin.Thickn. [mm]	Fin.Thickn. [mil]	DK	DF	DK/DF FREQ.	Tg[°C]
Company X	Model name Y	Prepreg	1080	STD E-Glass	no	0.69	0.0932688	3.6654638	3.34	0.003	10GHz	170
Company X	Model name Y	Prepreg	1078	STD E-Glass	1D	0.63	0.0751332	2.9527348	3.49	0.003	10GHz	170
Company X	Model name Y	Prepreg	1067	STD E-Glass	1D	0.71	0.06477	2.545461	3.29	0.004	10GHz	170
Company X	Model name Y	Prepreg	1067	STD E-Glass	1D	0.75	0.0751332	2.9527348	3.19	0.004	10GHz	170
Company X	Model name Y	Prepreg	1037	STD E-Glass	1D	0.71	0.0492252	1.9345504	3.29	0.004	10GHz	170
Company X	Model name Y	Prepreg	1037	STD E-Glass	1D	0.75	0.0595884	2.3418241	3.19	0.004	10GHz	170
Company X	Model name Y	Prepreg	2113	STD E-Glass	1D	0.55	0.0984504	3.8691007	3.7	0.003	10GHz	170
Company X	Model name Y	Prepreg	3313	STD E-Glass	1D	0.59	0.116586	4.5818298	3.6	0.003	10GHz	170
Company X	Model name Y	Prepreg	7629	STD E-Glass	1D	0.45	0.2020824	7.9418383	3.94	0.003	10GHz	170
Company X	Model name Z	Core	106 ×1	NE-glass (low-DK)	no	73	0.05202	2.044386	3.09	0.003	10GHz	170
Company X	Model name Z	Core	1035X1	NE-glass (low-DK)	1D	70	0.05202	2.044386	3.12	0.003	10GHz	170
Company X	Model name Z	Core	1067X1	NE-glass (low-DK)	1D	70	0.05202	2.044386	3.12	0.003	10GHz	170
Company X	Model name Z	Core	1067 ×1	NE-glass (low-DK)	1D	73	0.06528	2.565504	3.09	0.003	10GHz	170
Company X	Model name Z	Core	1080 ×1	NE-glass (low-DK)	no	66.5	0.07752	3.046536	3.15	0.003	10GHz	170
Company X	Model name Z	Core	1078 ×1	NE-glass (low-DK)	1D	66.5	0.07752	3.046536	3.15	0.003	10GHz	170
Company X	Model name Z	Core	3313X1	NE-glass (low-DK)	1D	54.5	0.09078	3.567654	3.28	0.003	10GHz	170

FIGURE 12.1 DK and DF data from material library.

one near our signal's main frequency or derive their values on the signal's exact main frequency. This main frequency is the half baud rate for SERDES links, and either the same or the third harmonic for slower interfaces. Figure 12.2 shows the DK variation. Note that at very low frequencies below a few Megahertz the impedance is very high, but at those frequencies we do not need impedance control. It also starts rising in the Terahertz range, but now in 2023 we do not have to deal with that yet on digital boards. The slope of the DK curve depends on the DF value—higher DF leads to a bigger change in DK over frequency. We can re-calculate DK to a different frequency if DF and the measured frequency are known, basically if three numbers are known. This variation is described in the "wideband Debye model". For using any stackup design software or SI simulation software accurately, they must have an option to enter DK, DF, and the frequency point they were measured at, instead of just specifying it as a number. Different tools might have slightly different algorithms for the DK/DF frequency dependence, we just have to make sure to enable it manually, otherwise they will use flat DK by default. If DK0 and DF0 are given at f0 frequency, then we can calculate DK at any "f1" frequency:

```
DK(f1) = DK0 - (0.637*DK0*DF0) * ln(f1/f0)
```

Digital signals are wideband signals. However, most of the signal's energy is located in a not too wide frequency band. For 8b10b encoded and AC-coupled signals, like the PCI-express 2.0 and SATA, the frequency band has a lower limit, which is around one-tenth of the data rate, or the data rate divided by the encoder symbol length. We can see this in Figure 12.3. The highest significant frequency component depends on the interface type and speed. For lower data rate signals that usually have a longer bit period than their rise time, we use the knee frequency, but for multi-gigabit SERDES links the highest significant frequency is at half the baud rate.

12.2 FIBER WEAVE EFFECT

The PCB dielectric materials are not homogenous; they are made of glass fibers in a woven pattern (weave) and filled around with epoxy resin. These two components have very different dielectric

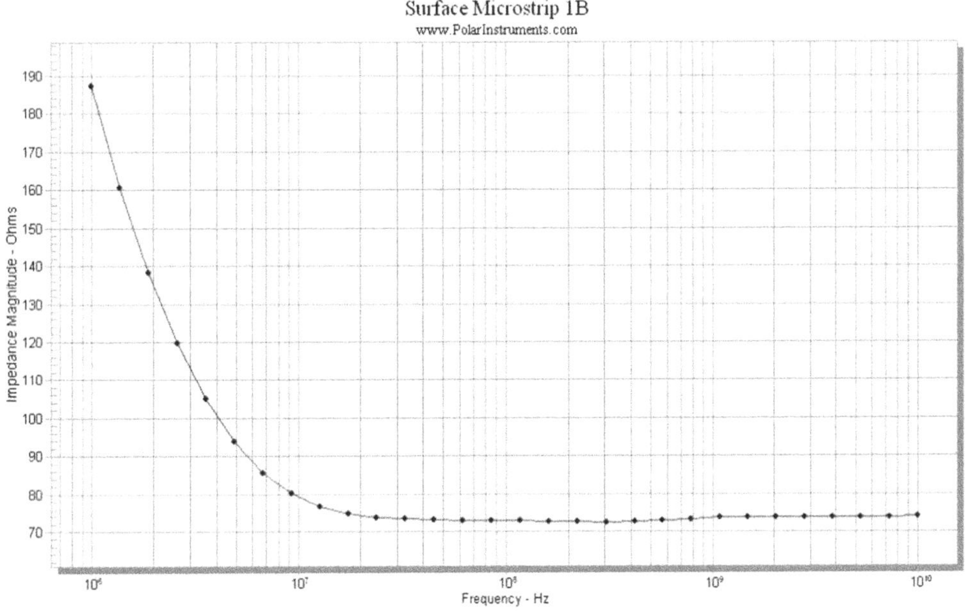

FIGURE 12.2 Impedance magnitude versus frequency for a 100um wide microstrip on a 100um thick dielectric. Polar Instruments Si9000 simulation.

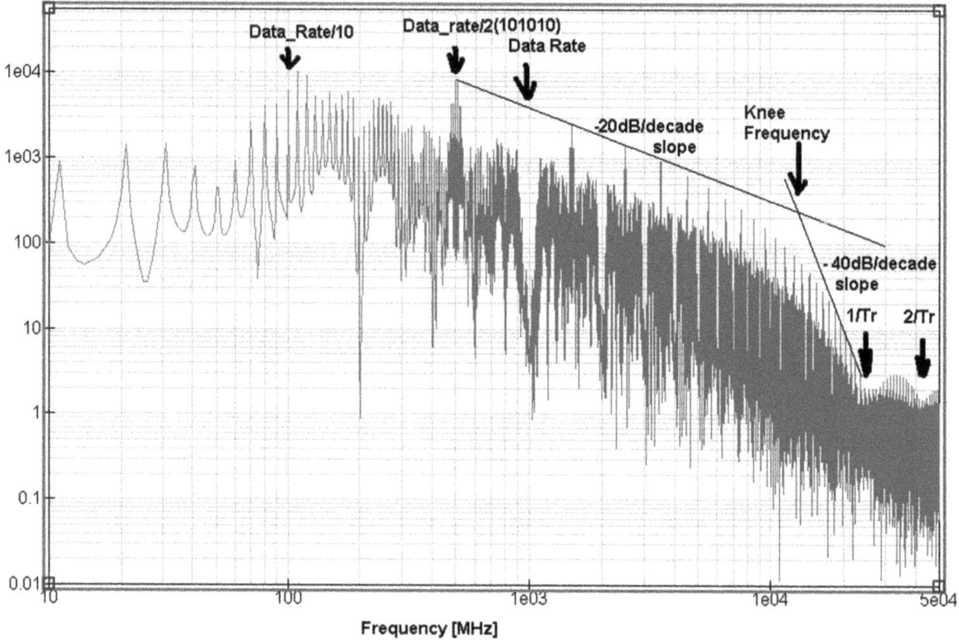

FIGURE 12.3 Frequency spectrum of an 8b10b encoded 1Gbps digital signal in a QUCS simulation.

constants (DK), the resin has typically ~3, and the glass has typically ~ 7. As an attempt to overcome this huge variation they invented "NE-glass" that has around ~5. The different glass styles have different yarn thickness and density, degree of yarn spread, shape, and structure. The woven pattern of the glass fabric causes different traces to experience different DK and propagation delay, creating a skew between them. The harsher the pattern the larger the skew. This skew might be too much for SERDES links and faster DDR5 memories near and above 5 to 10Gbps. The alignment is random across production units, causing a yield issue when the design already passed DVT.

For anything at 10Gig or above, we need to use spread glass styles like 1035, 1037, 1027, or 1078, and use two plies/sheets at once to further reduce the glass bundle versus resin area contrast. The double ply can reduce worst-case skew on straight traces several times, from the few picoseconds per inch to less than one. Different single plies vary a few times. Skew accumulates over the length of the trace, so time-per-inch is an appropriate way to describe it. The ones that look evenly distributed on the top-down glass photo (obtained from vendors) are the best. A few example glass style photos can be seen in Figure 12.4. Loose styles like 106 and 1080 are unsuitable for SERDES links. It is not enough for the fabric to look even from the top-down view, but they have to avoid the glass bundles waving up/down and touching the surface too much with too small a "butter coat" of resin over glass. That is why a 2116 fabric is not really good. It is one of the most spread seen from the top, but it has the biggest bumps seen from the cross-section. Some materials are available with regular glass yarns and with E-Glass yarns. The E-Glass has a DK closer to the resin's DK, which reduces the Fiber Weave Effect amplitude. For example, Panasonic Megtron-6 R-5775 versus Megtron-6 R-5775(N).

If a PCB trace is parallel to a glass fiber direction, then the location of the trace relative to the glass fiber determines the effective DK around the trace, this way the impedance and the propagation delay will also be dependent on the relative location. In case of a differential pair, if one leg of the pair sits on a glass bundle, while the other sits over a sparse path, this being the worst-case alignment, then the two legs will see different average DK and propagation delay, which is detectable as a delay skew. This is called the Fiber Weave Effect (FWE). It is demonstrated in Figure 12.5.

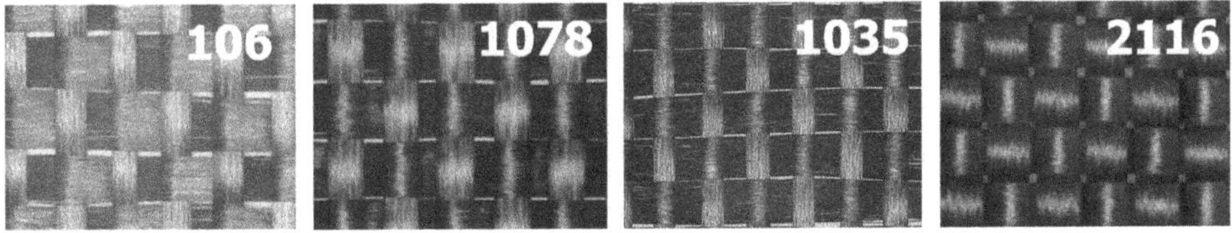

FIGURE 12.4 Example of glass style X-ray photographs, courtesy of Nanya Glass Fabrics.

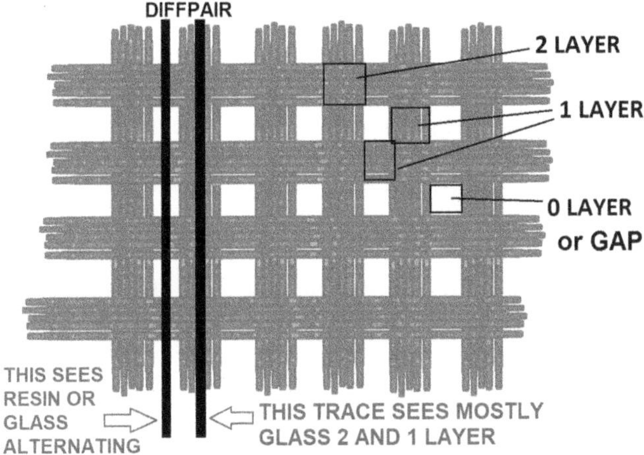

FIGURE 12.5 Fiber Weave Effect worst case alignment (sketch).

However, if the traces are in some angle to the glass thread direction, then the error appears as a periodicity over the length with a mean value around the nominal dielectric constant, which is the desired way, instead of accumulating into a large sum of skew. The larger the angle, the higher the periodicity length, translating to a higher frequency suckout on the insertion loss profile. Diffpairs in SERDES links and byte-lanes in DDR5+ memory interfaces can be severely affected. The time domain skew is seen as an insertion loss suckout in frequency domain.

Fiber Weave Effect (FWE) might split into two effects. Typically, we talk about Fiber Weave Effect to describe accumulated skew at the end of the diffpair, caused by fiber weave to trace parallelism, that creates a resonance (suckout) at 4 to 125GHz. Angled routing (or rotated boards) when crossing the weaves at low angles creates impedance waviness on the TDR plot, which creates suckouts above 30GHz. This is a second Fiber Weave Effect. To differentiate, we could call the first one "fiber weave skew effect" (FWSE) and the new one "fiber weave crossing effect" (FWCE). From measurements and research done, we know that we can significantly minimize FWSE by rotating at minimum six degrees or more. With 56G-PAM4 designs, FWCE does not interfere with the signal on a good stackup, as the signal's Nyquist frequency was still at 13GHz, while this effect is predicted to be around more than twice as much. 56Gig-NRZ and 112Gig-PAM4 would have a Nyquist frequency of 28GHz, which can potentially align with a ~30GHz resonance. Table 12.1 shows a few typical examples of skew and suckout frequencies that we obtain in different cases. The solution to that is to rotate by a larger angle so as to push this resonance further up.

Important points:

- We cannot allow suckouts on the IL curve near the "half baud rate"; otherwise, the eye diagram can get reduced by half.
- Any skew discussed was worst-case, observable on <10% of production boards that can become nonfunctional, a yield issue. This can easily escape design verification testing.

TABLE 12.1
Fiber Weave Effect Resonance Frequencies

Case		2x1035 dielectric (15mil pitch)		1x1078 dielectric (19mil pitch)	
		Straight (1ps/in, <4deg 0.2-5in period)	10 deg angle (2.3mm period)	Straight (7ps/in, <4deg 0.2-5in period)	10 deg angle (2.9mm period)
Macro: FWSE, Accumulated skew due to parallelism. F=0.5/skew	15" Long (backplane)	15ps, >33GHz	4ps residual, >125GHz	105ps, >4.7GHz	4ps residual, >125GHz
	4" Short (module)	4ps, >125GHz		28ps, >17GHz	
Micro: FWCE, Glass bundle crossings. F=0.5/periodicity	Low angle MCP	NA, 0.6-16GHz High variability	14ps, >35GHz	NA, 0.5-13GHz High variability	17ps, >29GHz
	Direct cross SCP	NA, 220GHz	NA	NA, 174GHz	NA

- A "straight" trace still has a -5 to +5deg angle to the glass fabric yarn, which also varies +/- 2deg along the trace in a given unit. This is why we need a larger than 5 degree angle.
- The angle can vary layer by layer too, so the average periodicity of the layer below and above the stripline trace will create the final suckout frequency.
- A diffpair's P/N legs can vary by 20% from each other in suckout frequency, causing asymmetry.
- FWE is seen in a VNA measurement, but not in a simulation.

12.2.1 Rotation or Angle

If traces are aligned with the weave, then the Fiber Weave Effect appears worst case. Most weaves are not straight, so some production units do align while others do not align. The glass yarns might not be perfectly in a horizontal or vertical direction, they might be up to 5 degrees off on some of the production units. A trace to board edge angle at more than 5 degrees has zero chance of alignment. To avoid parallelism, we have to have an angle larger than 5 degrees or use an angle 5 degrees more than we would otherwise use. We can apply rotation to a whole board on the production panel design, but that often costs more money due to a larger panel size requirement. We can also increase the trace to weave angle by doing odd-angle routing, and wavy routing. Figure 12.6 shows wavy routing, which is routed upward, then downward, then upward again, etc. to stay within a horizontal routing channel. This will increase the width of the routing channel requirement by 10% to 30%, which has to be considered while working on the floorplan of the board.

The FWE resonance should be much above our signal's Nyquist frequency, or even above the baud rate to be safer. The FR4 materials have the glass fiber threads in two directions, just like the yarns in a fabric, called fill and warp directions. We can get a pitch (yarn distance) measurement from the material vendors. We can calculate how much weave crossing periodicity we should have to avoid FWE issues from all the above considerations in GHz and inch:

```
Periodicity < 11.8 / (1.3 * BaudRate * 2 * SQRT(DK))
```

That requires an angle of:

```
Angle = Arcsine(GlassFabricPitch/Periodicity) + 5deg
```

Typically, 15 degree for 10 to 25G NRZ (and 56G PAM4), and 20 degree for 112G-PAM4.

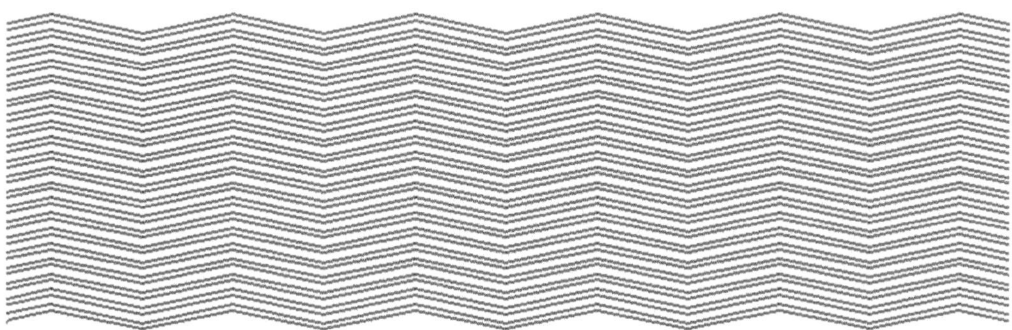

FIGURE 12.6 Wavy routing (sketch).

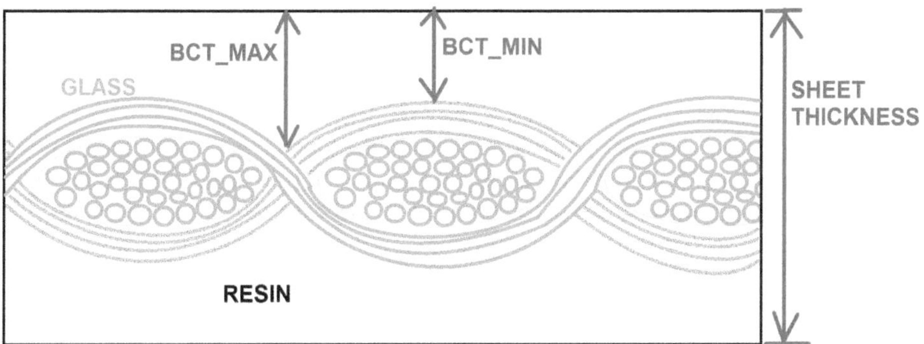

FIGURE 12.7 Butter coat measurements in a dielectric layer cross-section (sketch).

12.2.2 Butter Coat

The "Butter Coat" is the resin layer between the surface of the raw prepreg or core and the surface of the internal glass fabric yarns, as we can see in Figure 12.7. For traditional glass styles there were big open areas where the traces only saw resin. With more modern spread glass styles the resin openings are significantly reduced, so a secondary effect takes precedent for FWE causation. That is the butter coat variation in terms of ratio or percentage.

```
r=BCT_MAX/BCT_MIN
```

The larger the butter coat thickness (BCT) variation along the surface, the larger the dielectric constant variation and the larger the Fiber Weave Effect. With different glass styles, we get different results. On the glass styles where BCT_MIN approaches zero, we get the largest variation ratio, for example, on the 2116 glass style, even though from the top view the 2116 seemed to be the most promising in terms of spread glass. For this reason, we usually pick glass styles with high resin content, around 70% to 75%, thin sheets of moderately spread glass, and use two plies of them. Using two plies can reduce FWE skew five times, compared to a single ply of the same glass style.

12.2.3 Diffpair Asymmetry

After spending considerable effort on designing a nicely symmetrical-looking differential pair, then measuring it with a VNA on the prototype, we might notice with horror that the S21 and S43 curves (the single-ended insertion loss curves of the two legs of the diffpair) are not similar enough. But that happens to everybody. We should still try to design it to be even more symmetrical next time, but often asymmetry cannot be completely eliminated. The differential insertion loss is the one that really needs to comply with the standard limit lines since all our SERDES links use differential signaling.

The asymmetry can appear in suckout existence, depth, or frequency. For example, the P leg might have a resonance at 15GHz while the N leg does not, or it is less severe. Or the P leg has a resonance at 15GHz while the N has it at 17GHz. Skew causes resonances at a frequency of F=1/skew for first, and 3*F for the third harmonic also. Sources of diffpair skew are FWE (Fiber Weave Effect), via stub backdrilling asymmetry, phase tolerance matching meanders, and trace route bends. The trace-glass alignment can also be different between the P/N. FWE causes accumulated skew at the macro level and periodicity (glass bundles) at the micro level. Both improve with board design rotation or angled routing. The accumulated skew (FWSE) suckout can appear on the SDD21 curve usually around 4 to 120GHz. The periodicity (FWCE, Glass-bundle) suckout appears on both single-ended and differential modes around 30 to 120GHz.

12.3 TRACE IMPEDANCE CONTROL

PCB traces and connectors act as transmission lines at higher frequencies—they have a characteristic impedance, or just "impedance" in short. This is the ratio of the voltage and current of a wave propagating along the line when reflections are eliminated by design—often marked as Z0. High-speed signals require impedance control of the PCB traces. Impedance control simply means we take steps to ensure the traces in our layout design, in the stackup, and in manufacturing will conform to the desired impedance by controlling the geometry, the materials, and processes. The threshold where it becomes mandatory is where the signal's rise time becomes comparable to the propagation delay through the trace. It is not a sharp threshold; we have to already use impedance control when we are within the ballpark of this threshold. In addition, termination resistors will be required. If our signal meets the equation below, then the traces should have impedance control and terminations.

```
TraceLength > 11.8 / (SQRT(DK)*baud_rate*4*2)   [inch and Gbps]
```

Signals with low data rates below 50 to 200MHz are considered "slow signals", and we usually do not prescribe impedance control for them, except reference clocks. That is because usually they also have slow rise times. We can tell by experience which ones they are. But if they are driven by the same chip that can drive Gigabit speeds on the same buffer type then they will have fast edges and might also need impedance control, even if they toggle only once a day. In those cases we can replace the baud_rate with the knee frequency. On FPGAs they should be set to low current drive modes. The truly slow signals, like any power management signals or open drain buses or anything driven by low-end devices (flash chips, logic gates or microcontrollers), never require impedance control.

We need impedance control in the design-to-manufacturing pipeline, but we also need accurate impedance representation in SI simulation. For design we need accurate material and geometry data as well as accurate impedance calculation methods. For manufacturing, we need detailed documentation of all the parameters we used in our design, and we need to make sure they are followed and manufacturable. We also put our impedance requirements in a document for manufacturing. For SI simulation, we also need the accurate parameters and tools capable of handling them. Obtaining and handling the material data constitute a scientific process.

Signal traces on routing layers always "reference" to an adjacent plane layer for outer layer traces, or two in case or inner layers. Trace impedance is determined by a signal-ground structure, involving metal and dielectric. A microstrip trace is a trace routed on an outer layer like a top or bottom layer. Their impedance reference plane is the one on the next layer. A stripline is a trace routed on inner layer, referenced to inner ground planes above and below. Dual stripline means there are two stripline routing layers between the same two plane layers. On modern complex designs at/above 1Gbps we use only ground planes for impedance referencing and return path, not power planes. Embedded microstrip is rarely used, it is when we route on layer-2, referenced to layer-3, but layer-1 is open above the trace. Skip layer routing is when we have a stripline trace routed on layer-N, and the reference planes are on layer-N+2 and layer-N-2, meaning there is an opening on layer-N+1 and layer-N-1. Skip layer routing is the only way to achieve very wide 10-20mil wide traces that could achieve extremely low insertion loss needed on 200Gbps/lane designs, but it wastes a lot of layers and blocks routing for many other signals. Basically, a small number of such signals can be routed on a board, which is a solution for "high speed" but not really for a complex high-speed design.

Impedance control is about accuracy. We have to take lots of parameters into account to be able to do our calculations accurately. If one or two parameters are not carefully determined, we can lose the advantage of the more accurate parts of the process, for example, use of the expensive field solver programs. With simulators and calculators, we can determine the impedance from trace width or the trace width from the impedance requirement. This calculation is usually done by the PCB fab vendor during the stackup negotiation process. Before the negotiation starts, we can perform our own calculations and use that as a starting point. We can also use it for floorplan analysis, routing channel, and loss budget calculations. This chapter describes how the impedance control calculations work. Vias also have an impedance; their impedance control design methodologies are described in Chapter 11, "Signal Integrity", and Chapter 15, "PCB Layout Design".

10Gbit Ethernet designs, boards, connectors, and chip on-die terminations all follow the industry trend of 92–93 Ohm, instead of the IEEE standard 100 Ohm. Connector vendors tried to support both 85 Ohm PCIe and 100 Ohm (old) Ethernet with a single connector that is set half- way, meeting the 10% tolerance of both. On the most common PCB materials and technologies, with 1mm pitch BGA's and differential via fanouts, the via impedance was closer to 93 Ohms than to 100 Ohms. On most modern digital designs, we end up with 80-, 85-, 93- and 100-Ohm differential pairs for different interface standards. Most SERDES links will be 93 Ohm. Single-ended traces might be impedance controlled to 40/50/60 Ohm, mostly in memory interfaces. The trace impedance value that we should use in our layout is mainly driven by the main chips we use. On-chip SERDES transmitters and receivers, as well as memory interfaces, have on-die termination (ODT) resistors. We have to find out from the chip datasheet what value these ODT resistors have, so we can design our PCB traces to match the impedance value. Sometimes the information is hidden in a programmer's manual. Some chips are programmable and support two or three impedance values; others are fixed at one value. They are not scalable or tunable impedances; rather, they are a selection from a very short list of available values. These ODT values are usually calibrated at system startup using on-board 1% tolerance SMD resistors, while PCB traces can have 5% to 10% deviation from the nominal intended values.

On a complete chip-to-chip signal path we might have several boards and connectors. Each has an impedance. We are trying to avoid reflections created by impedance mismatch. The mismatch is between adjacent elements, not between one board and a standard document. Having the wrong impedance is only a problem if it is adjacent to an element with the "right" impedance and there is a mismatch, creating reflections. Above a few Gigabits per second speeds a connector's impedance will appear as a separate element in the signal path with its own impedance. If our connector is 93 Ohms, but we designed nice standard 100 Ohm traces, then we will get reflections at each side of each connector. At high frequency (above a few Gigahertz) the board-to-connector matching is important, at low frequency the board-to-board matching is important in order to improve the return loss. For 10Gig and faster systems we could design our boards to match the connector's impedance or get a different connector with different impedance, if available. The on-die termination impedance of some chips was also designed to be 93 Ohms like most connectors, while a few others support either 100 or 85 Ohm. We are really better off not trying to match to the standard but match the elements of the link to each other. Some elements have fixed impedance, others we can choose to match the fixed ones. This way the number of mismatched impedance transitions on the full path will be reduced. For example, a channel with 100 Ohm traces looks like this: chip-trace-conn-trace-conn-trace-chip being 93-100-93-100-93-100-93, that is six impedance mismatched transitions. But, if we route the backplane with 93 Ohms like this: 93-100-93-93-93-100-93, then it has only four transitions, so it should have an improved return loss. We can visualize this on a return loss profile that gets near the limit line on the left side of the curve (low frequency) if the boards are not matched to each other, while the right side of the curve (high frequency) gets near the limit line when the boards are not matched to the connector. A simplified design goal is to minimize the number of impedance transition points in the channel. In the quest to reduce overall return loss, the trace impedance only matters relatively, namely, between adjacent elements, not as an absolute requirement.

Single-ended traces just have a single impedance value. Differential pairs do have more parameters. The differential impedance can be calculated from the odd-mode and even-mode impedances that are the direct results from field solver programs like TNT-MMTL. Differential traces also have a single-ended impedance value and a common-mode impedance value that describes unwanted common mode interference signal propagation. For digital board designers the differential impedance is usually sufficient. Many tools display or calculate the odd-mode impedance, which is half of the differential impedance. The standard conversions for diffpairs:

$$Z_{DIFF} = 2 * Z_{ODD}$$
$$Z_{SE} = (Z_{ODD} + Z_{EVEN}) / 2$$
$$Z_{CM} = Z_{EVEN} / 2$$

12.3.1 Frequency Dependent Impedance

As the activity of impedance control, we calculate the trace width and differential-pair separation based on the impedance requirement and other parameters. Ideally, we would use a frequency-dependent impedance control process. This means we would re-calculate the dielectric constant to our signal's frequency or use a DK value measured at a frequency within the same order of magnitude. Then use that DK in the calculations. Simulator programs can handle the full frequency dependent DK if we enter the value set as DK, DF, and the frequency they were measured at. For NRZ-type SERDES link signals we should use the Nyquist frequency that is half the baud rate, and for PAM4 the Nyquist is quarter of the data rate that is also half of the baud rate. On slower interfaces like DDRx memory buses we would use the knee frequency calculated from the rise time, or the 5th harmonic of the half baud rate. For clocks it is the 5th harmonic of the clock frequency.

```
f_knee=0.35/t_rise.
```

Figure 12.8 shows all the parameters affecting trace impedance that are discussed in this chapter. The calculation could be done by using common formulas, but those can be extremely inaccurate. Instead, we have to use trace cross-section-based 2D electromagnetic field solder programs. The field solver program by itself is not enough, the accuracy depends on further parameters. The traces are formed in the PCB copper foil through etching, which undercuts the photoresist mask covering it. This requires width compensation before lithography, which is handled by the PCB fabricator contractor for us, but it is worth knowing about. The trace width we need to use is provided in the stackup document's impedance table. An official approved stackup document usually contains two main items: the actual stackup drawing or table and a trace impedance/width table. For diffpairs we have trace width and edge-to-edge-spacing or center-to-center pitch.

```
Space=pitch-width
```

We usually get approved stackup documents from two to four vendors for a project. We have to make sure (during the negotiation) that those are all compatible, having very similar width and

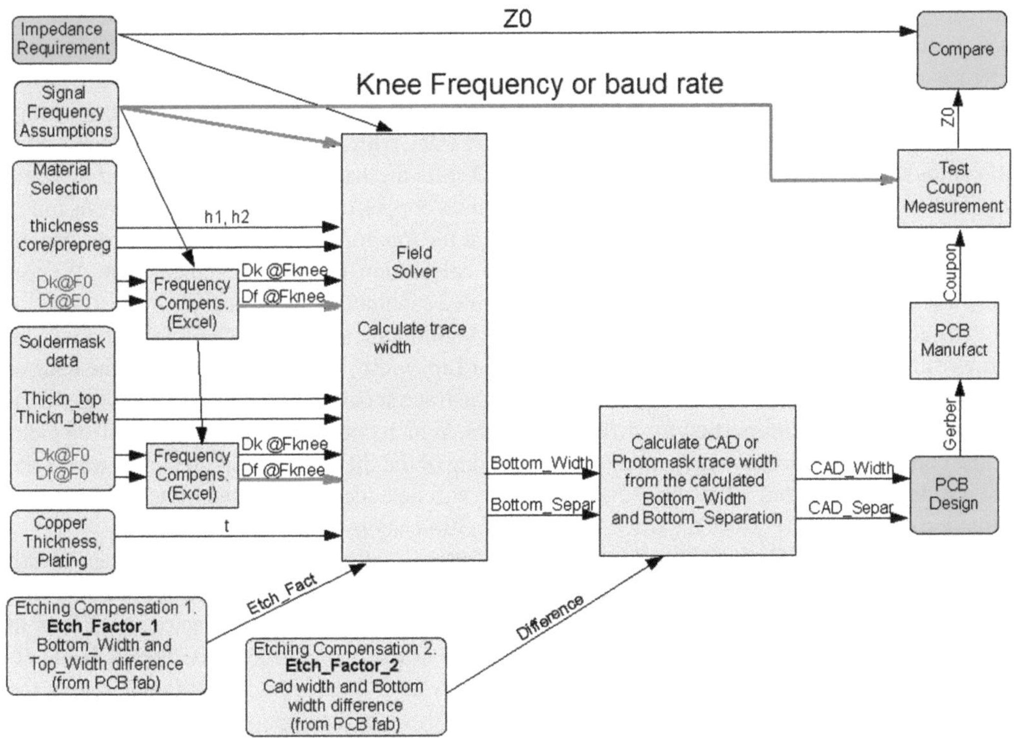

FIGURE 12.8 All parameters involved in impedance control.

spacing, and then we can select a trace width for our design constraints and PCB routing that is close to the trace width listed in all approved stackups and impedance/width tables. Then we also have to put an impedance table in our fab drawing or fab notes that lists the exact width/space we used in the layout/Gerber and match each to their impedance values. This way each fabricator can identify which traces to pick up for width alteration to achieve the impedances we agreed upon in the approved stackup documents. So our table will not contain the width/space from the approved stackup document, but it will contain the width/space used in our layout, even though the two have to be very close, often the same.

All parameters have tolerances, the calculation has tolerances, the manufacturing and the measurements also have tolerances. To get a reasonable accuracy, we need to minimize all of them, so they all together have to remain within the specification (usually 10% up to 56Gbps, then above that 5%) on a fabricated board. Even if we have few parameters with loose tolerances, we still need to keep tight tolerances on all the others. If we specify our nominal impedance with a loose tolerance (choosing 90 Ohms nominal for a 100 Ohms diffpair) and it will be manufactured at +/-10%, together they will result in a 90 Ohms +/-10% (81 to 99 Ohms) range, which is outside of our original specification (100+/-10% = 90 to 110 Ohms). The PCB manufacturer measures the test coupons on each panel, not each trace on each board. The dielectric and copper thicknesses are not perfectly equal everywhere on the panel, so the real traces will also have a small deviation from the test-coupon measurement results.

12.3.2 Geometry

The PCB cross-section around the traces is complex, and it is affected by manufacturing artifacts. These have to be also considered during impedance or trace width calculations.

Etching used for fabrication alters the trace width. The traces are formed in the PCB copper foil through etching, which under cuts the photoresist mask covering it. The CAD or Gerber design trace pattern is copied into a photoresist layer through lithography. This resist pattern will keep some parts of the foil from dissolving in acid. Figure 12.9 shows how the traces are made with etching. The acid will not etch away the copper under the film's trace pattern, except along the edges, and it will cut under the film pattern. The PCB design CAD software had the traces represented at a certain width, the film will have the same width, but the final copper trace will be narrower by as much as the under-etching. The trace will also be narrower at the top, forming a trapezoid or a mushroom shape. This has to be accounted for in the impedance calculation as etching compensation. We can model it with a trapezoid with most advanced impedance calculator/simulator tools.

Let's call the trace width in the design files CAD_width. During etching, the final trace will be narrower than the CAD_width, and the top side width (Top_width) will be narrower than the bottom side (Bottom_width). This has the opposite effect on the trace separation; the gap will be larger than the CAD_gap, which is important for differential pairs. Which one is the top/bottom? During etching, the copper foil is already stuck on the surface of one of the dielectric layers, which is where the trace will have its "bottom". The other dielectric layer will be added after the etching, during board lamination. Figure 12.10 shows the trace cross-section dimensions.

The difference between the Top_width and the Bottom_width, called the "Lower trace width etch factor" in the Polar Instruments terminology, but here we just call it the Etch_Factor_1. The difference between the Bottom_width and the CAD_width here is the Etch_Factor_2. This is in width, not each side. The value of both is about the same as the copper thickness. The PCB manufacturer handles both of these etch factors for us, and they alter the trace width before applying the lithography to end up with boards that have the trace width we agreed upon.

Plating affects the copper thickness. For outer copper layers, or to be more accurate for those copper layers where any drilled holes are ending, the manufacturer increases the copper thickness

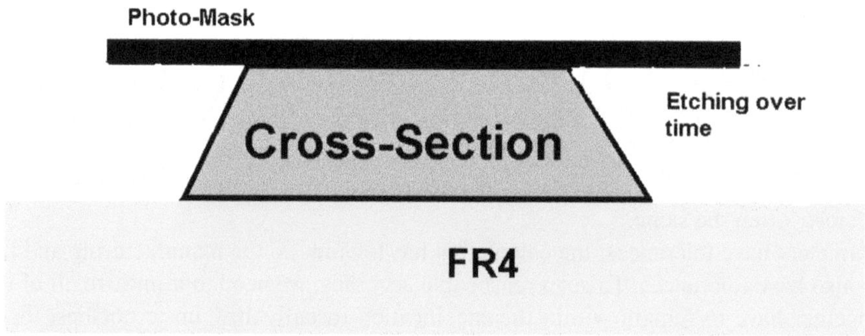

FIGURE 12.9 Etching over time (sketch).

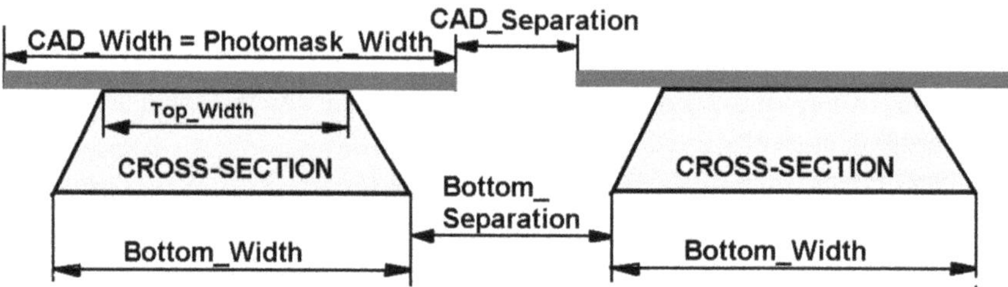

FIGURE 12.10 Trapezoid cross-section model (sketch).

with added copper plating to be able to create the plated through-holes. For example, making microvias, or blind/buried vias. This increases the thickness of those layers and must be taken into account for impedance calculations. This thickness measurement data can be requested from our PCB manufacturer. If we change the manufacturer in the product's lifetime, then the plating thicknesses might also change.

The build-up order affects the dielectric thicknesses. The copper layer is always between two dielectric layers (inner), or on the top of a dielectric layer (outer). For the inner layers, before etching, the copper foil is already on the surface of one of the dielectrics, which is hardened already (core, or "earlier" prepreg in a build-up multi-lam board). Then they do the etching, and then they put the other dielectric (prepreg) layer on it, which is soft until the layers will be laminated together, and then it becomes hard. The result is that the copper pattern is embedding into the second layer, which is the prepreg layer. This way the trace surface gets closer to the other side of the prepreg, while it maintains its distance to the other side of the core. So the effective thickness of the prepreg is really the prepreg sheet thickness minus a portion of the copper trace thickness. The effective thickness of the core remains as the original value. Impedance calculations have to use the effective thickness of the prepreg, that can be obtained from a negotiated vendor stackup or from a stackup tool, not from the material vendor's table. This can be seen in Figure 12.11. The wider part of the trace cross-section is on the surface of the hard layer (core or earlier prepreg). Being upper and lower dielectric in the structure view is not based on the board orientation or layer number but on the core-prepreg or build-up order.

The copper coverage is the ratio of the remaining copper and the removed copper on a given layer. It has an effect on the final effective thickness of the prepregs. When the copper trace gets embedded into the prepreg, then the area of the prepreg pushes its resin out sideway to fill the gaps between the traces. If there is a small area covered with copper, then the trace embeds almost as far as the copper trace thickness. On the other hand, if most of the layer area is filled with copper shapes or traces, then the embedding is not as deep, while the small gaps are filled with the flowing resin quickly. The prepreg's resin is flowing a little bit during the lamination process, and it fills in the gaps between the traces horizontally. The prepreg's glass fabric cannot flow or melt. The resin's DK is much lower than the prepreg's average DK, so the traces will see more resin sideways than vertically. The "finished thickness" in a material datasheet is the thickness of a prepreg layer when it is laminated between 100% fully covered copper layers, which is different from that in a real design. Software tools like the Polar Instruments Speedstack and the Z-Zero can calculate the effective thickness after lamination. In most cases we just rely on the fab vendor's negotiated stackup for the final thickness and for the impedance-to-width calculations.

The solder mask must be taken into account for outer layer microstrip impedance calculations. It has a dielectric constant (DK), a loss tangent (DF) data (on a given frequency) just like the other dielectrics in the stackup. These parameters can be obtained from the solder mask datasheet. We deal with multiple solder mask thicknesses and provide all of them to the field solver program. The thickness on the top of the copper traces and the thickness between the traces are different, and they vary a lot, making it harder to control impedance accurately. If conformal coating is used, then that is also part of the calculation.

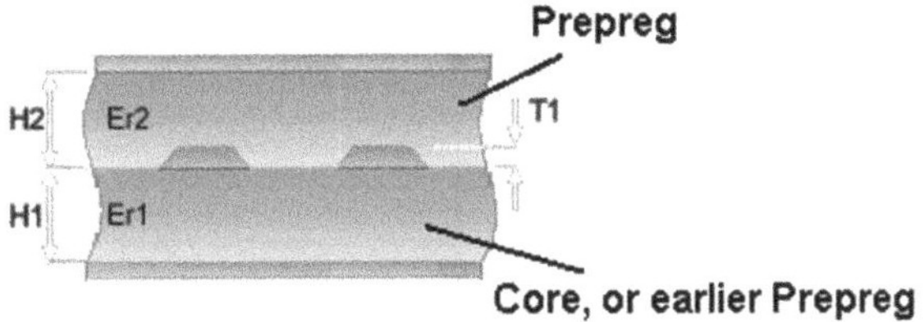

FIGURE 12.11 Copper embedding into a prepreg.

12.3.3 Impedance Measurements

PCB manufacturing validation testing for impedance is done by time domain reflectometry (TDR) measurements on test coupons. The test coupons are manufactured on the same panels with the real PCBs, and they contain the same controlled impedance trace width definitions as the real PCB has. It is easier to probe traces on a test coupon than on a dense digital board, especially with the exact probe landing patterns designed in. The TDR instruments generate a single very short pulse signal, then measure the reflected signal. Based on the TDR test result, that is a voltage-time waveform, the instrument calculates the impedance using post-processing. To achieve accurate frequency-dependent impedance measurements, we should set the TDR instrument to have the same rise time as the signal will have on the real PCB. This is not done in practice; it would be impractical to request it from the fabricators.

12.3.4 Impedance Calculator Software

There are simple impedance calculator programs based on analytical equations, but those are outside of the scope of this document since their calculation error can be as high as 50%. So we have to focus on the cross-section-–ased 2D "field solver" programs instead. The only inaccuracy they can have is inaccurate data provided by the user. The mesh density is high and it is set internally by the software developers. The exact trace width and impedance will be calculated for us designers by the fab vendors during the stackup negotiation, but we can calculate the trace width before we talk to them so we can avoid having too many iterations. This can also help us with our PCB floorplanning, routing channel calculations, and insertion loss budget calculations.

Field solver programs divide the cross-section geometry into a "mesh" of small cells or nodes, and then they solve the Maxwell's differential equations in all of them to get electric and magnetic fields and current distribution. From the field equations they determine the RLGC per-unit-length parameters, and then they finally calculate the impedance from those. R is the series resistance, L is the series inductance, G is the shunt conductivity to ground, and C is the shunt capacitance to the ground. Figure 12.12 shows the four different fields that are computed by field

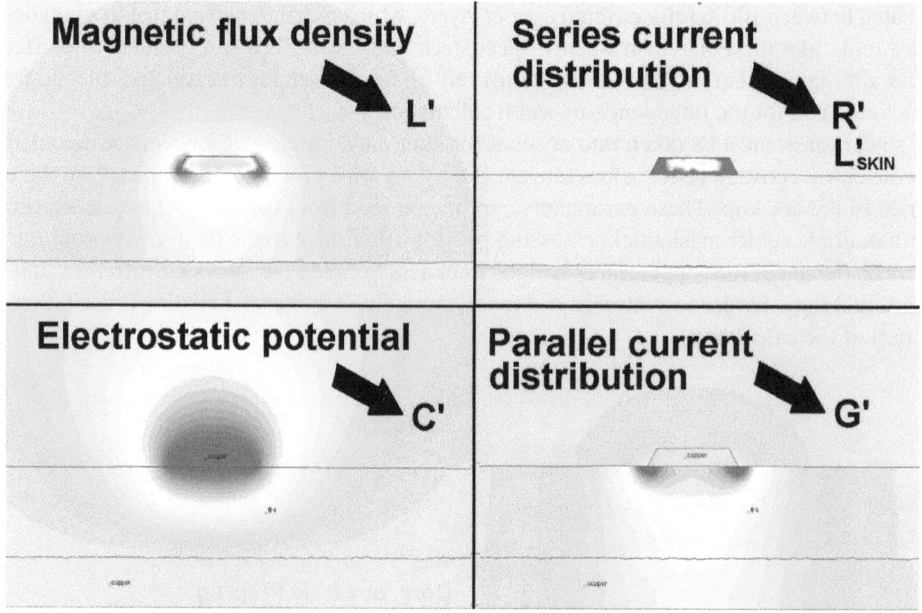

FIGURE 12.12 Field simulations in FEMM for obtaining RLGC parameters.

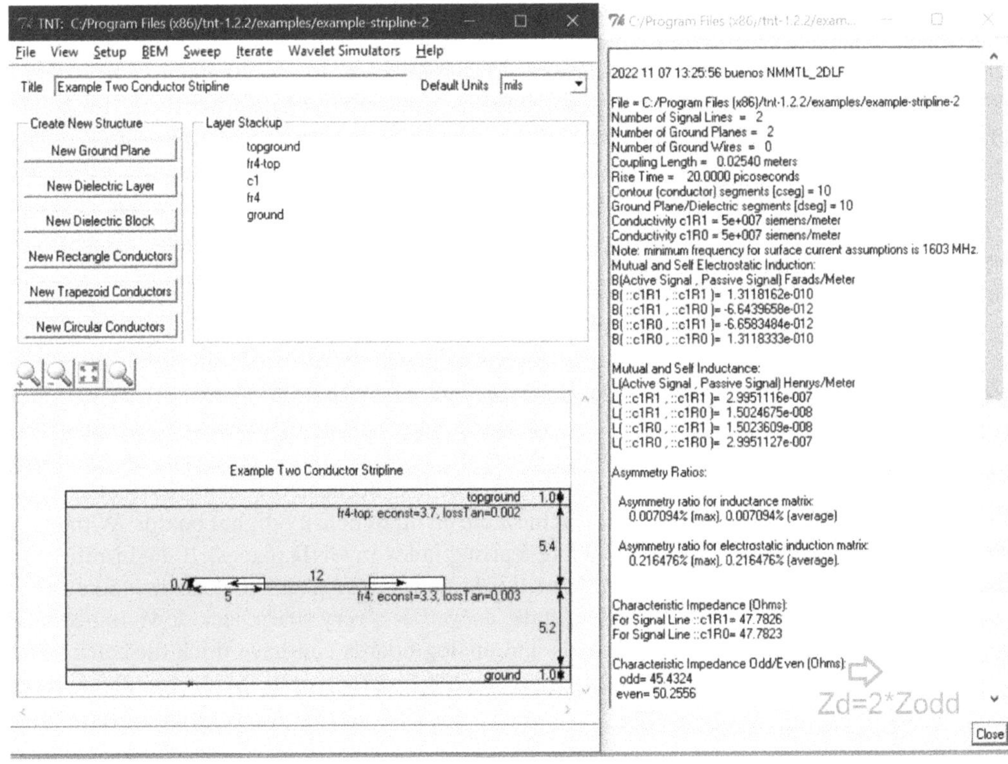

FIGURE 12.13 The TNT MMTL free impedance field solver.

solvers on a PCB trace cross-section. The characteristic impedance is defined in the well-known equation:

$$Z0(f) = \sqrt{\frac{R(f)' + j \cdot 2\Pi \cdot f \cdot L(f)'}{G(f)' + j \cdot 2\Pi \cdot f \cdot C(f)'}}$$

The Si8000 and SpeedStack tools from Polar Instruments are the industry standard impedance calculators. They can calculate in both directions between trace width and impedance. Si8000 is just a single impedance calculator; SpeedStack is a full stackup batch impedance calculator that also automatically adjusts thicknesses for copper embedding after lamination.

Z-Zero is a newer commercial tool, available from the website z-zero.com. It can be used to prepare stackup documentation, create re-useable library stackups and material libraries, and perform impedance and stackup building calculations. Fab vendors can receive our first stackup proposal in a Z-zero generated document before we start the approved stackup negotiation process.

TNT-MMTL is an open source tool made by the Special Purpose Processor Development Group at the Mayo Clinic and available at Sourceforge.com. Figure 12.13 shows the TNT setup and the result pages.

12.4 INSERTION LOSS CONTROL

The problem with loss is reach; it limits trace lengths, especially on large boards and chassis. Insertion loss (IL) has to be limited by design and manufacturing release documentation on most high-speed designs at 10Gbps or above. We need to know how much worst-case insertion loss we will get from a specific PCB fabrication supplier and design our boards and systems accordingly through floor planning and loss budget calculations. The insertion loss is measured in dB/inch@13GHz, or at half the baud rate's frequency. If we have too much loss, then the signal attenuates too much and the data cannot be recovered at the receiver. In this chapter we refer to the single loss number at the Nyquist (half baud rate) frequency as "loss", not the detailed S-par curve. The insertion loss curve of a trace has resonances, and those should not be allowed to affect the final number we are extracting. This is why a fitted or smoother version of the insertion loss curve, called the fitted attenuation (FA) curvc, is what we prepare before looking up a number from the curve at the frequency point of interest.

Losses are created by multiple effects in the same time; they contribute a different percentage to the total loss value, as we can see in Figure 12.14. At higher signal frequencies due to the skin-effect, the current in the trace cross-section flows closer to the surface and pushed towards the cross-section perimeter. The more they are pushed into the perimeter region, the more they are affected by copper roughness. Copper roughness is affected by the copper foil type used and by the manufacturing process. Wider traces have a larger cross-section perimeter (2*width+2*thickness), so they have a lower amount of loss because the signal current spreads wider—5 to 6mil wide traces are the widest achievable on high- density digital boards. With thick dielectric sheets or with skip-layer referencing (cutting holes in GND planes) 10 to 15-mil wide traces could be used, and we would get half or a third as much loss. Thick dielectrics would result in a bad height to space ratio and strong crosstalk, as well as a very sharp neck down impedance step in the BGA fanout. Low-density boards and analog boards can have thick dielectrics and wide traces without these problems, but complex digital boards cannot. Skip-layer referencing is only doable if only one or two of such traces are needed per board, not hundreds or thousands like on complex boards.

The dielectric sheet variants, as identified by their material vendor name, product name, glass style (4-digit number), and resin content percentage, will have a dielectric constant (DK) and a loss tangent (DF), measured at a certain frequency. The DF is the part of the dielectric that contributes to the losses.

A summary of all of the loss contributors:

- Trace width: Wider traces with larger cross-section perimeter have lower loss.
- Dielectric material loss tangent or DF. Larger DF has more loss. DF=0.002 to 0.003 is used for 25Gig, 0.005 to 0.008 for 10Gig.
- Copper surface roughness, measured as Rz in micro meters

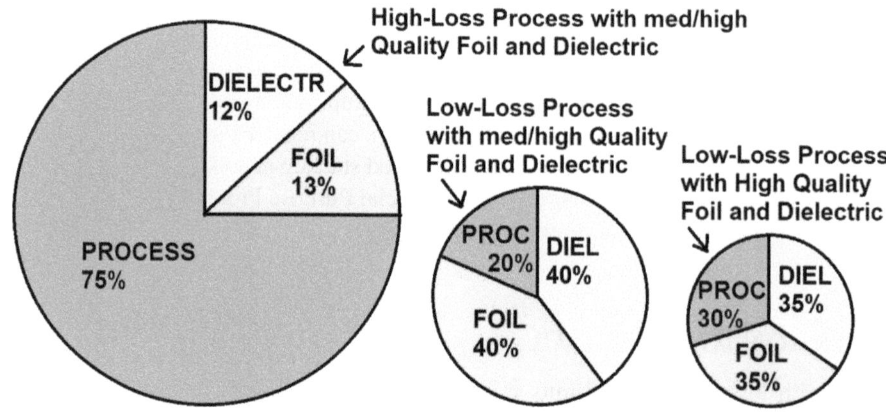

FIGURE 12.14 Loss contributors, area proportional to total insertion loss.

- Copper foil type
  - RTF (Rz=8 to 20um), up to 5Gbps
  - VLP (4um), for 5–10Gbps
  - HVLP (2.5um), for 10–25Gbps
  - HVLP2 (2um), for 25–112Gbps
  - ANP (1um), for 56–224Gbps
  - Other single-vendor foil brands or types
- Copper adhesion promotion chemical process and lamination
  - High loss, total >>1.5dB/in@13GHz on 4...6mil wide traces, even with good dielectric and good foil. This uses a traditional process, creating 8-20um Rz.
  - Low loss, <<1.5dB/in@13GHz on 4...6mil wide traces, only achievable when we also use good dielectric and good foil. This uses special HF chemicals, mostly preserving the foil's original Rz.

12.4.1 Copper Surface Roughness

At higher signal frequencies, the current in the trace cross section flows closer to the surface perimeter and is pulled out from the center. This way, the effective usable cross section decreases, which increases the resistance and the losses. This is called the skin effect. At signal frequencies where the skin depth from "skin effect" is comparable to the surface roughness, the losses are very pronounced.

The surface of the copper layers is not perfectly flat and smooth, but they have a surface roughness. It is displayed or measured in micrometers, and denoted as Rz. It is not measured on every board, maybe once a new foil is introduced. It can vary between 0.5...20um on modern boards. To estimate, a rule of thumb we could use is dB/in@13G=Rz/3, for example 3dB/in caused by 9um Rz.

In traditional cases, the copper Adhesion Promotion Process (APP) that is used for roughening copper surfaces before PCB lamination has a much larger contribution to the total loss than the other parameters combined. This means that using expensive dielectrics or very smooth copper foils will have very little benefit when used with traditional APP. Only when using a low loss process does the dielectric and foil selection have any measurable effect. If the fab company uses a special high-frequency (HF) type chemical, or uses medium rough chemicals at the lower-end of their usage parameters, then we get less process-related extra roughening, and the overall roughness will be dominated by the original foil's roughness. If that is a smooth foil, then we can get a lower amount of loss. Each chemical can create a roughness within a range, but which end of the range a particular board is at is determined by the fab company's process engineers. The ranges of high-frequency and medium range chemicals may overlap.

Lower roughness may or may not result in reduced peel strength, which can be a problem for applications that have high shock and vibration requirements. For some product types, we have to ensure both a low-enough loss and a high-enough peel-strength at the same time, both with appropriate separate testing.

If multi-level microvia build-up layers are required on the board (multiple lamination cycles), then the copper layers will receive additional plating while making the inner microvias; then they may receive additional roughening too. The result is they might have a very different roughness and insertion loss-per-inch than regular single-lam boards. This is dependent on the capability of the vendor-facility. Some vendors cannot provide microvias and loss control on the same board, or on the same layers. If we have to order from there, then we need a stackup that does not have microvia start layers being the same layers that need loss control. Basically, having only a few SERDES signals, filling up maybe two layers. Large data center networking boards need hundreds of loss-controlled signals, which require a dozen or more loss-controlled inner routing layers with via stub removal in place. Wherever loss control is needed, stub control is also needed, unless we can have all our signals on layer N-2; that is only possible if we have no more than 2…8 such SERDES signals. If microvias cannot be used due to the lack of loss control capability on multi-lam boards at a particular fabricator, then backdrilling will have to be used instead of microvias.

A small minority of fabricator facilities offer low loss APP in 2023. Usually, any one factory uses one type of APP on all boards, but they can tweak it. To select a low loss process is to select a vendor and a facility that uses it. Within one fab supplier company, there are several factories or facilities, identified by the name of the city they are in. Each facility has different capabilities. So, we have to remember the names of the company/town combination where we can get a low loss process, or we have to keep track how low loss we get from each factory. Before asking them about their low loss capabilities, we have to make sure to set some boundaries for the conversation, like dielectric brand and trace width range. Since they are not system designers, they might think extreme ratios are plausible for our designs, when they are not. For example, 20mil wide traces with 20mil dielectric layers can produce low loss traces with high loss process, but a complex digital board cannot fit 20mil wide traces in, only 4.6mil max.

In summary, the emerging industry standard is that we the designers pre-select the foil type based on roughness range and the dielectric sheets (with glass style) in the stackup document, but after that we only deal with combined dB/inch@f0 loss numbers measured on coupons, not a measured roughness in microns. We also restrict our supply chain to the few vendors/facilities we have verified to have suitable loss control capability. The foil type pre-selection will put the process in the right band, but within the band the fabricators will make adjustments.

12.4.2 Documentation

How the hardware designer can control what board they get: Even with the right factory, we have to define what we want. By relying on recent loss test board or test coupon data that shows the capability of the fab facility we want to use, adding 10% margin on top of it, and writing it down as a requirement for every purchase order. For example, if we have test data showing 1dB/in, then we need to specify 1*1.1=1.1dB/in as a requirement. When we release the board manufacturing files to fabricator companies, we provide notes about technology parameters we used in the layout as well as parameters we want them to use. These notes may be on the fab drawing layer in the board design and Gerbers, or in a fab notes document. Either way we have to add a note about loss control. It would explain that insertion loss has to be limited to XXX dB/in at 13 GHz on marked items in the trace impedance table, and tested on coupons. The trace impedance table in the stackup document and/or fab note should have a column for loss control, and the value field would be the required loss limit or n/a for each specific trace/impedance type. Not all impedance-controlled traces will need loss control, and we have to communicate that. The manufacturer will insert their own loss coupon into the production panel next to our board, and they will measure it to see if they have met the customer's requirement. If we tried to specify roughness or specific chemicals in our fab notes, instead of the final loss value, then it would prevent them from freely adjusting the necessary parameters. Additionally, we should also put our own VNA test coupon into our design, in the form of a short and a long diffpair with wafer probe landing pads, so we can spot-check our boards if they don't perform.

12.4.3 Loss Testing

Each fab facility needs to provide their best loss number (using 5–6mil wide traces) for multi-lam and single-lam cases. This is done through the hardware engineering department designing, ordering, and measuring loss test boards from different fabs. An example basic loss test board's concept can be seen in Figure 12.15. We have to design our loss test board with a "2X Thru" de-embedding structure (for a Delta-L process), mark the fab notes with desired loss specification, order them from different fab vendors, and then we measure it with a VNA to check how much loss they are

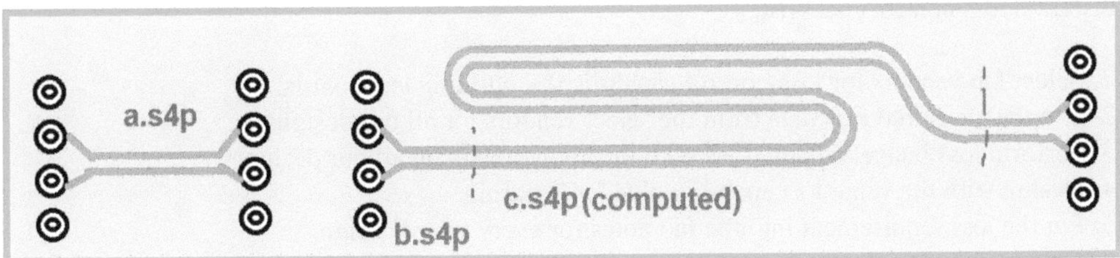

FIGURE 12.15 Loss test board concept (sketch).

really making. Basically, we have to guess how much loss they should produce through talking to them, put that into the fab notes as a requirement, and then see how much we are actually getting. This way we can evaluate the capabilities of individual fab facilities. Then we need to record that loss number, add 10% for tolerance, and use that for every design that is using the same dielectric material, copper foil, and PCB fab facility. The number will be specific to one facility of one fab company. Then we have to design our chassis and product boards through loss budget calculation to make sure we are not using longer traces than the calculation results would allow. This process is described in Chapter 14, "Initial Design". We might have to shop around multiple fab vendor facilities with building boards with each. Now in 2024, only a small subset of all fab facilities is able to produce loss-controlled boards.

There are simplified loss coupons with just a trace and a reference de-embedding structure (short trace) for production verification of each/any product unit. There are also loss test boards with multiple different types of traces for evaluating a particular vendor only once. In both cases the de-embedding trace is about five times shorter than the main trace, which allows de-embedding of the connector or probing discontinuities from the measurement results. We also have to make sure the short trace is at least two to three inches long to reduce reflections. Basically, we will perform two S-parameter measurements, and then we will use the instrument or a post-processing software on our computer, to subtract the short trace from the long one, together with the probing, that leaves a virtual middle section. Theoretically we could subtract whole S-parameter curve of the short trace from the long one, in a process called "2X-Thru" deembedding, but that often has a severely limited upper frequency limit due to reflections from the probing. Instead, we use the Delta-L method that computes the FA for both traces separately first (from their SDD21 diff-mode insertion loss), it reads out the loss numbers from both separately (at the standard's Nyquist frequency), then it subtracts only one loss number from another loss number. This will smooth the curves out before the subtraction, which would otherwise be sensitive to rough curves. We can use pre-layout simulation tools with equation/computation capabilities, for example, Keysight ADS or QUCS. We can create a template for this post-processing. The final loss value is:

```
LossPerInch = (|FA_long@F0| - |FA_short@F0|) / (Length_long
- Length_short)
```

The vendor evaluation test boards can be designed and measured by the hardware design team or it can be outsourced to SI consulting firms. In production the SET2DIL or SPP coupons were commonly used for loss measurement and pass/fail check. SET2DIL is a method of computing Differential Insertion Loss (SDD21) using a single-ended TDR measurement. It was developed by Intel. SPP is a similar time domain measurement with conversion. Many PCB vendors these days use frequency-domain VNA coupons instead, as they are more accurate for higher frequencies. For example, standard "Delta-L" or "FD" or custom coupons. The standard Delta-L method is basically the test coupon structure with the short and long trace described above but with several parameters, including the curve fitting standardized.

Insertion loss control checklist:

1. Select fab vendors for loss-control capability by building test boards.
2. Use the measured loss data from the select vendors for all our designs.
3. Perform loss budget calculations with the coupon data on all our designs.
4. Design with the vendor's capability plus 10% margin.
5. Put the loss requirement into the fab notes for every board design.
6. Design in our mini coupon into every board for later spot-checking.
7. Always verify in the stackups that the trace width will land in the 5 to 6mil range.
8. During the ordering, make sure the loss requirement and the trace width were not changed at the last minute to pass DFM.

12.5 STACKUP DESIGN

The layer stackup is the structure that defines what material sheets are sandwiched together into a multi-layer printed circuit board (PCB). For high-speed digital boards the hardware engineer needs to have full control over the PCB layer stackup, otherwise the board will most likely not perform the way it is supposed to. Traditionally stackups were handled by purchasing departments and later by layout departments, but in recent years it is done by the hardware department that also handles signal integrity. We design for signal integrity targets, and the main parameters that we can adjust are in the stackup. The dielectric material, the copper foils, copper process, and trace widths are all in the vendor stackup document, after a stackup negotiation process. So the process should work this way: The hardware design engineer defines what layers will be in the stackup, what material they should be made of in a sketch text or diagram or spreadsheet. This is given to the layout or manufacturing department to send out to the chosen PCB fab vendors. Fab vendors are chosen based on capability and prior deals. They respond with a more precise version of it, with trace width calculations for impedance control. Let's call it a "vendor stackup". Then the hardware designer, the layout engineer, and the manufacturing engineer all review it, discuss it, and, if needed, request modifications from each vendor. It goes on until it meets our SI and design requirements, and all vendors meet it the same way. Usually, we talk to two to three vendors to get a final stackup, a different document from each company, but we have to make sure they are similar enough. The last one they send us that we no longer need to modify can become the approved stackup, when the hardware engineer responds usually in an email with "This stackup is approved". Then it becomes a binding dataset document for layout design, SI analysis, and purchasing. Then we have to document it in our design or ordering document with our own format, twhich contains all the data needed and that does not contradict the vendor's approved document. We send out our format when ordering, so each vendor will not receive documents made by the other vendors. We file our own stackup document as well as each vendor's document in our design folders.

In a stackup document we have dielectric-copper-dielectric-copper alternating order. We can list in the stackup document which dielectric is core or prepreg, which copper layer came already attached to a core and which came as foil. The outer layers, top and bottom, are copper, with solder mask on it and surface finish on the exposed pads (solder mask openings). Components will be soldered on them.

"Surface finish" is the corrosion-resistant metallic plating applied on copper solder pads because bare copper would corrode very quickly preventing a good quality solder joint. Usually most boards use nickel-gold (Electroless nickel immersion gold, ENIG) finish on high-end boards, but organic finishes are also used. Low-tech boards sometimes receive tin; i form of hot air solder leveling (HASL). Any user contact areas like edge contacts on add-in cards receive "hard gold" plating that is thicker and resistant to being scratched off by edge connectors, like DIMM memory or PCIe cards.

PCB stackups are made of three types of sheets or layers:

- Core dielectric with copper foil on both sides added by the material vendor made of fiberglass reinforced resin and already hardened or cured. Also called double-sided core layers.
- Prepreg dielectric that is not hardened yet; it will flow to fill gaps between traces and the rough copper surface wrinkles. It is also made of fiberglass reinforced resin with no copper added yet.
- Copper foils, used on some stackups.

12.5.1 The Three Main Aspects of Stackup Design

(a) Functional (high-level) design

The number and types of layers have to be defined first, before getting into the materials. This is what hardware design engineers usually discuss with layout engineers in every project. We have to determine how may high-speed routing layers, how many low-speed layers, power planes, and ground planes are needed and in what order. We need to decide whether we want single stripline, dual-stripline, or microstrip routing. We can estimate high-speed routing layer count from floorplan, flowplan, and fanout analysis. A floorplan can tell if major buses need to cross and how wide the routing channels can be, affecting the required layer count. If two major high-speed buses cross, then the total routing layer count is at least the sum of the layer usage of both buses since we cannot change layers with those to get around each other, unlike with slow buses. The fanout analysis results in direct layer count need per bus at a component. We can also determine what type of vias and drilling structures we need for component fanout. For example, through-drilled, laser-drilled, or blind/buried.

(b) Manufacturing aspects

To avoid warpage, the stackup should be symmetrical and have an even number of layers, this is a hard rule. A total thickness is always calculated. Usually around 65mil for up to 14 to 16 layers, 65 to 200mils for many-layer data center boards. Copper thickness is measured in ounce per square feet (1oz=1.4mils=35um), we can have 2oz, 1oz, 0.5oz, or 3/8oz. Most signal layers use 0.5oz or 3/8oz. Power planes can be any thickness, thin for symmetrical stackup or 1oz to 2oz for high-powered ASICs. The thicker the copper, the larger the minimum width/clearance. The outer layers will be covered with solder (blocking) mask, except on the solder pads for component pins. These exposed pads will receive a surface finish, one of few types of metal plating, like nickel-gold, immersion silver, organic or other. Based on how many times lamination and plating cycles are applied to one board/panel, there are different construction types, as we can see in Figure 12.16 and in the text below.

In Single-lamination-cycle boards all sheets with etched patterns are put together, then all laminated together at once, then drilled and plated. They have two subtypes: the core construction and the foil construction. Core construction is when we etch separate thin double-sided cores with copper already attached on both sides, then put prepreg sheets between them for the lamination. Foil construction is when the outer copper layers do not come from double-sided cores, rather from a free roll of copper foil. This also means there will be an additional etching cycle after the lamination, and the outer layer will likely receive more roughening than the core-attached copper layers have. The core/prepreg order is reversed from the core construction. This is usually preferred.

Multiple lamination cycle boards (multi-lam), with buildup layers, are typically used with laser-drilled microvias, or blind/buried mechanically drilled vias. First, we start out from a laminated stack of cores, then one layer is laminated on the stack on each side, then etched and (laser) drilled, vias plated, then another one laminated on each side, etched and laser drilled. Similar to foil construction, but with more than two foil layers. With this we end up with blind and buried (BB) vias, in the form of mechanically or laser drilled. Laser-drilled microvias are only between adjacent layers. For

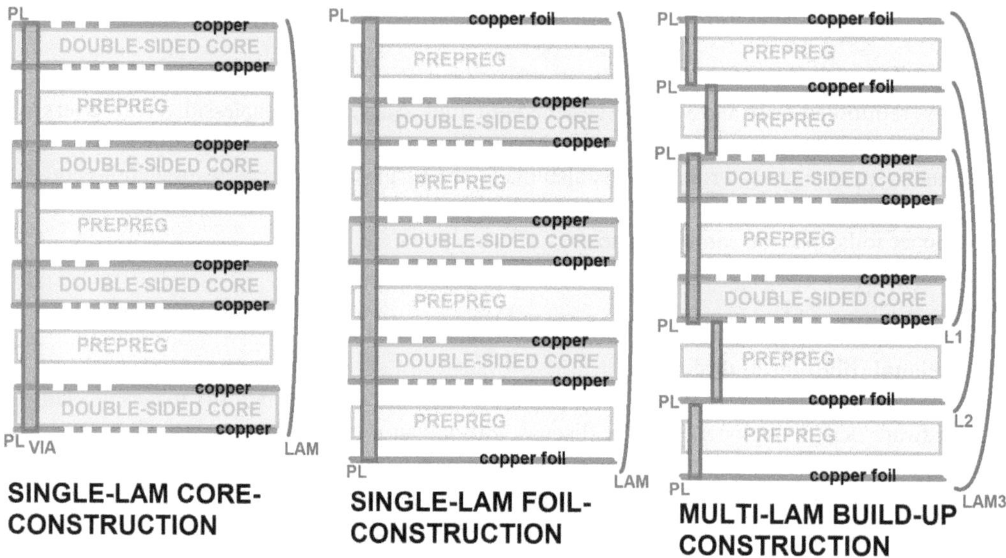

FIGURE 12.16 Stackup construction types (sketch).

every drilling cycle, a via-plating and layer-plating cycle is added. The plated layers get thicker and have a different roughness and texture. Thicker copper layers have increased clearance and increased minimum trace width requirements as well as higher insertion loss. Every copper foil layer might get roughened up more than core-attached copper layers. If microvias are used, then first we determine the largest microvia size (d, diameter) that we can fit between traces and pads, then the maximum dielectric thickness (t) will be determined by the aspect ratio of 1:0.75 or 1:1 typically:

$$t<d_{VIA}*0.75$$

(c) SI design (for multi-gig SERDES links)
This section focuses on the SI aspects of stackups and recent research into PCB materials. It is about the small details of the dielectric and the copper layers. Some of these details were traditionally ignored by hardware engineers, and stackup details were treated as simply manufacturing parameters. These aspects are all explained in other sections of this book. For signal integrity control we define these parameters for our board stackups:

- Exact dielectric sheet definition with glass style and copper sheet name: An issue related to documentation process. The glass style affects FWE directly, and crosstalk and impedance indirectly through exact thickness.
- Trace impedance control: Impedance depends on DK; exact DK depends on brand and glass style. Thicker dielectric or lower DK results in wider traces for the same impedance requirement.
- Via impedance control: Impedance depends on DK; exact DK depends on brand and glass style. Higher DK lowers the via impedance, or it makes it necessary to use larger voids or smaller via drill size that might not meet our design requirement.
- Insertion loss control: Loss depends on the DF of the dielectric layers, the roughness of the copper layers, and the trace width. The trace width depends on the dielectric thickness, due to impedance control. Exact DF depends on brand and glass style. Copper roughness depends on foil type and adhesion promotion process. Thinner dielectric or higher DK results in narrower traces for the same impedance requirement, but narrower traces have higher insertion loss.

- Crosstalk: Increasing the dielectric thickness while keeping the spacing between unrelated signals the same will increase crosstalk.
- Fiber Weave Effect mitigation: FWE depends on glass style. We usually try to use two-ply spread glass dielectric sheets and higher resin content.

12.5.2 Building the Layer Sequence

The number of routing layers is chosen from floorplan and fanout analysis. In a fanout analysis we determine how many layers it takes to fan out all (high-speed) signals from under a grid type (BGA chip or connector) component. From the floorplan we can tell whether major high-speed buses cross or not, the crossing adds up the layer count. Sometimes we add two more inner routing layers for glue logic and low-speed signals, near the top side, where press-fit connector minimum barrel lengths would create stubs for high-speed routes anyway. Usually, one diffpair can be routed between via columns, so if we have four rows of diffpairs (not rows of pins), then it takes four layers to fan out. Outer rows on BGAs can save a layer, but only for low-speed signals at 5Gbps or below because above that we need to use an extra ground row. If there is no extra ground pin row, then we have to add an extra ground via row to ensure the via structure impedance and low crosstalk. More on fanout analysis can be found in Chapter 14, "Initial Design", which also deals with floor planning.

Microstrip traces are top or bottom layer surface traces. Striplines are traces on inner layers. Single stripline means there is only one signal layer between two plane layers, while dual stripline is when two signal layers are between planes. For 3Gig and faster signals, we can use only single striplines. For those boards that only have slower signals we could use dual striplines or even microstrips, if we really have to but still not advised. If we have two dedicated glue logic and low-speed signal layers, then we can use a dual stripline for those in the center of the stack. Below 1Gig we can do power+ground referenced routing, above that we can use only ground-only referenced routing (layer above and below), so the power planes are separated from signal layers by additional ground planes. We cannot use layer-2 or layer-(N-1) for high-speed routing, because high-speed traces need a continuous plane both above and below them. Above layer-2 is layer-1, which is filled with component pads that make it non-continuous.

Once we have the number of signal routing layers, we can add two or four for power planes, and add ground planes to separate them. Modern high-speed designs use only complete ground plane layers, with no trace or power net shapes. For boards that carry 150 to 200W or larger chips, we typically use four power plane layers in the stackup of 1 to 2oz each, and use two planes plus one or two signal or outer layers to deliver the same voltage rail. Below 100W, two planes of 1oz each are unusually sufficient. When using chips only up to 15W, all layers 1/2oz is fine. Remember, if the VRM uses remote sense lines, then we can allow a two to four times larger DC voltage drop on the power planes than the ASIC's input tolerance. If we use 2oz power planes, then the cores they are attached to also carry ground planes, which need to be no more than 1oz thick to prevent having to use oversized antipads that undercut routing channels. Ground planes are used as return current reference, while power planes are not used for that, at least on SERDES-based boards. Sometimes we want to use a very thin dielectric, like 1 to 2 mils between power and ground planes, with high DK (like Dupont or FaradFlex) although that has high cost. The benefit is high frequency and wideband decoupling that cannot be achieved by discrete capacitors. The power planes are typically placed either in the middle of the stackup or near the top or near both the top and the bottom. Having it near the middle will provide balanced access from both the ASIC and the decoupling capacitors. Having it near the top helps the ASIC but increases the mounting inductance of the capacitors. Having it both near the top and near the bottom provides the best and worst of both worlds.

We have to decide how many via types (through, blind, buried, microvia, backdrill) are needed; it will go on the stackup document. It also has to be consistent with logical lamination cycles, for example, we cannot have two different buried vias with partially overlapping layers. Using <0.8mm pitch BGA components mandates microvia design, 0.8mm and above is the choice of the designer for the via type. The via list also determines how many laminating and plating cycles will be used, so the copper layers that receive additional plating should be listed. Any build-up layers can only be on prepregs with foils, not on cores. Thicker dielectrics require a larger microvia size due to the shallow aspect ratio. This way the via size affects the available layer thickness choices. A larger microvia stack used in a 3D controlled impedance structures might grow so big sideways that we cannot fit it under a BGA component while still wanting to route diffpairs between them. One microvia is rarely used by itself, it is used in a structure of multiple microvias, mini dog-bones, and core vias, in a staircase shape, which is what takes up so much space.

The trace width is calculated using 2D cross-section field solver programs, from dielectric thickness, impedance requirement, etching compensation, and diffpair separation. We can do a sketch calculation, but let the fab vendor do the final calculation for us accurately, based on their manufacturing process parameters. See the previous section on Trace Impedance Control. We choose layer thicknesses in order to achieve certain trace width targets. For example, if our main routes are long backplane Ethernet signals, then we might want to have them around 5 to 6mil wide to achieve low insertion loss. Then the dielectrics are chosen to achieve the 93 Ohm impedance with that chosen trace width. Or if we have lots of short memory-down interfaces and no long SERDES links, then we might want our 60 Ohm DDR4 data bus to be routed narrow at 4mil (manufacturability), so we chose the dielectrics to achieve 60 Ohm at 4mils width. Plated layers (due to microvia build-up) require larger minimum trace width and larger minimum clearances, including larger antipads. In any case, a 3.5mil trace width is the narrowest manufacturable on large boards, and the best yield and impedance accuracy is at 4mil or above. Having a wide range of impedance requirements on a single board design is often inconvenient because the high impedance traces will get very narrow near the manufacturability limit, and the lower impedance traces will get very wide and cause routing difficulties. So we might want to look into what on-die termination values are available in our devices to narrow our impedance range of the whole board design. Sometimes we compromise the highest and the lowest requirement intentionally by 5% to 10% if the interface is free of most other SI issues, for example, if the bus is very short, run at a lower speed, or we have no connectors in the path.

12.5.2.1 An Example Project

In our made-up example design we have a mezzanine connector with many SERDES signals. Our connector having four diffpair-rows when fully stuffed needs four inner high-speed routing layers. Our data plane ASIC connecting to it has two rows of 10Gbps diffpairs, so it needs two inner high-speed routing layers. That requires four as the super-set of two and four. The floorplan shows no major bus crossings, so we remain at four. We also need two power planes and two outer layers for components, that's eight so far. We need two more signal layers for routing the control plane and the slower glue logic signals, which will likely cross the high-speed buses in all directions, so we are at 10 layers. To isolate all that into single striplines and ground-only referencing we need to add eight ground planes, to a total 18 layers. The number of ground plane layers can be calculated as the number of power planes plus the number of inner signal layers, in the case of single striplines with ground plane referencing.

How we should order these layers: L1 and L18 would be component/signal/power mixed-use layers. The ones adjacent to them would be ground, so L2 and L17 are ground. From the six high speed inner signal layers, we put three from each side, with ground planes between them, so L3:8 would be sig-gnd-sig-gnd-sig-gnd, and L16:11 also sig-gnd-sig-gnd-sig-gnd. We will need thin double ply prepreg/core dielectrics between each to provide low FWE and 5mil wide traces. What is left is layers-9-10; they will be the two power planes. We normally use thicker copper on the power plane layers and also on the ground planes that are attached to the same core sheets as our thick power plane layers are attached to. Usually 1oz is used power planes, and all other layers (signal and ground) are 1/2oz or 3/8oz. We might use 2oz for very high-powered ASICs, but that might necessitate increasing the clearances that undercut traces with increased antipads in routing channels, unless we refrain from using 2oz for any of the ground planes.

Layers 3-5-7-12-14-16 are signal layers. We should route the SERDES signals on layers-7-12-14-16, as they can have the stubs removed at the connector, while layer-3-5 will be in the minimum barrel length (MBL) region of the connector. MBL is the connector datasheet requirement for minimum length of a copper barrel remaining after backdrilling. Layer-7 will also be in that region, but we can backdrill it partially to have a shorter stub.

For SI, let's select two-ply moderately spread 1075 glass styles for the dielectrics adjacent to the inner signal routing layers, which provides FWE mitigation, while also instructing the layout engineers to use wavy routing on the longer segments of the 10Gig routes. For the signal copper layers themselves, we will use smooth, but not the most advanced copper foils like HVLP. We could use HVLP on the ground planes adjacent to the routing layers, but often we end up with RTF on them. Skin effect also happens in planes, the return current is high speed too, but it spreads ~5 times wider in the open plane than in the narrow trace.

We should not end up with two ground planes adjacent unless it is in the center. Usually, the center layer is a thick core, calculated by summing up all other layers, then subtracting it from the desired total thickness. We can put this into a stackup sketch, as seen in Figure 12.17, and end it out for negotiating vendor stackups.

	A	B	C	D	E	F	G	H–R
1	Number	Type	Use	Thickness	Sheet	DK	Other notes	Drills
2	1	copper	component/sig/plane	0.5oz+pl	copper foil		plated	
3		dielectric	prepreg	5mil	2x1075-75%RC	3.8		MINIMUM
4	2	copper	ground	0.5oz	attached copper			BARREL
5		dielectric	core	5mil	2x1075-75%RC	3.8		LENGTH
6	3	copper	signal1	0.5oz	attached copper		HVLP	OF
7		dielectric	prepreg	5mil	2x1075-75%RC	3.8		CONNECTOR
8	4	copper	ground	0.5oz	attached copper			
9		dielectric	core	5mil	2x1075-75%RC	3.8		
10	5	copper	signal2	0.5oz	attached copper		HVLP	
11		dielectric	prepreg	5mil	2x1075-75%RC	3.8		
12	6	copper	ground	0.5oz	attached copper			
13		dielectric	core	5mil	2x1075-75%RC	3.8		
14	7	copper	signal3	0.5oz	attached copper		HVLP	mnc
15		dielectric	prepreg	5mil	2x1075-75%RC	3.8		
16	8	copper	ground	0.5oz	attached copper			
17		dielectric	core	5mil	2x1075-75%RC	3.8		
18	9	copper	power plane1	1oz	attached copper			
19		dielectric	prepreg	10mil	2x2116-56%RC	4.1	center	
20	10	copper	power plane2	1oz	attached copper			
21		dielectric	core	5mil	2x1075-75%RC	3.8		
22	11	copper	ground	0.5oz	attached copper			
23		dielectric	prepreg	5mil	2x1075-75%RC	3.8		
24	12	copper	signal4	0.5oz	attached copper		HVLP	mnc
25		dielectric	core	5mil	2x1075-75%RC	3.8		
26	13	copper	ground	0.5oz	attached copper			
27		dielectric	prepreg	5mil	2x1075-75%RC	3.8		
28	14	copper	signal5	0.5oz	attached copper		HVLP	mnc
29		dielectric	core	5mil	2x1075-75%RC	3.8		
30	15	copper	ground	0.5oz	attached copper			
31		dielectric	prepreg	5mil	2x1075-75%RC	3.8		
32	16	copper	signal6	0.5oz	attached copper		HVLP	mnc
33		dielectric	core	5mil	2x1075-75%RC	3.8		
34	17	copper	ground	0.5oz	attached copper			
35		dielectric	prepreg	5mil	2x1075-75%RC	3.8		
36	18	copper	component/sig/plane	0.5oz+pl	copper foil		plated	
37								VARIOUS BACKDRILLS VIA

FIGURE 12.17 An example of a stackup sketch.

12.5.3 Crosstalk versus Stackup

The crosstalk depends on the dielectric layer thickness, just like the impedance does. Actually, crosstalk depends on the space-to-thickness ratio, while impedance depends on the width-to-thickness ratio. Sometimes the fab vendors increase the layer thickness and then increase the trace width to maintain the impedance. This will cause the spacing between traces to decrease, but, more importantly, the ratio of horizontal trace spacing to thickness changes to be much worse for crosstalk. The thickness might change also when we go to another fab vendor and we did not lock down the layer thicknesses. To prevent these problems, a corporate stackup approval process is required, which also specifies the exact glass style sheet variants. This process has to obtain the approval of the hardware engineer or the SI engineer. It is necessary that the hardware and SI team fully understand how layer changes affect SI, including crosstalk, insertion loss, and Fiber Weave Effect.

Crosstalk can be traced back to mutual inductances and mutual capacitances between traces. Figure 12.18 shows the electrostatic fields in a simulation in the freeware FEMM, in two cases, while varying the dielectric thickness. Using the thicker dielectric, we see stronger fields between the traces than they have towards the ground plane, while with a thinner dielectric the stronger field is towards the plane. We want to reduce unrelated signals affecting each other through electric and magnetic fields. Figure 12.19 shows the actual crosstalk waveforms in a pre-layout simulation, showing the same conclusion, the thinner dielectric results in a smaller crosstalk amplitude.

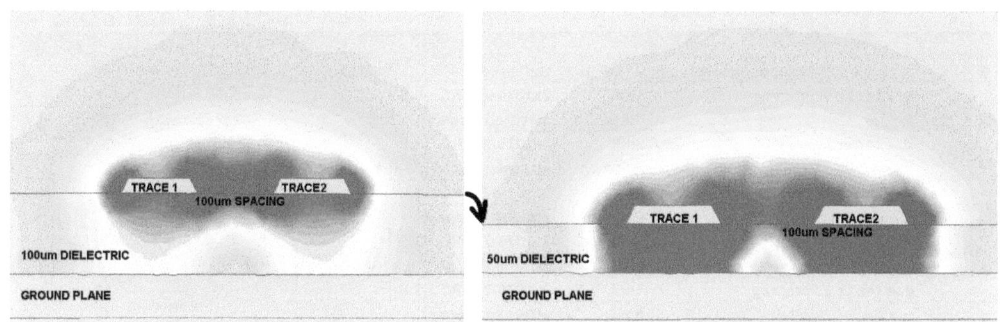

FIGURE 12.18 Electrostatic fields of two microstrips, simulated with FEMM.

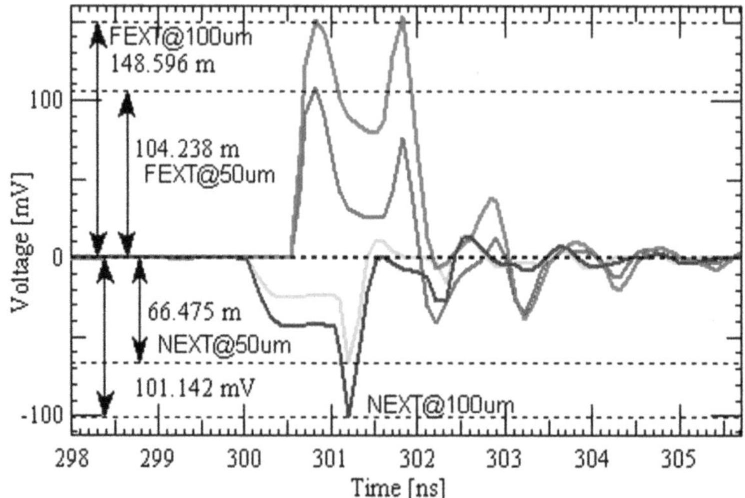

FIGURE 12.19 Simulating crosstalk as time-domain waveforms for the same structure, in the Cadence Signal Explorer.

12.6 ANISOTROPIC MATERIAL PROPERTIES

12.6.1 Anisotropic DK

The dielectric constant in the horizontal X/Y direction between the via barrel and plane antipad edge is higher than the DK in the vertical Z direction between trace and plane, due to its anisotropic nature. The z-direction affects the trace impedance, it is the more available data point. If we take DK in the Z direction from the material vendor's data tables, then we can calculate the X and Y direction by multiplying the Z direction value by a constant. This constant is a bit larger than one, and it varies based on glass fabrics. A 2024 DesignCon paper (in the references) by Bert Simonovich explains how to obtain it. We can enter these three DK numbers into some simulation tools. Those simulator programs that do not allow the user to enter aniso-DK and use basic uniform DK instead will show via resonances at a higher frequency than a measured prototype will have. That is an obvious inaccuracy that causes issues that are not obvious. If the signal's base (half the baud rate) and 3rd harmonics frequency components align with a resonance, then it can cause significant eye-opening degradation. But if the resonance is not aligned, then it causes a smaller amount. It might still be too much if the design was already without margins. So if a proto board has alignment, but the alignment does not show in simulation (due to missing aniso-DK feature of the simulator), then the simulation will show optimistic and unrealistic results, a false pass. If the board is bad but it seems good in simulation, or if the proto board is good but appears bad in simulation, then it reduces the usefulness of any such simulation tool. Some people might say "we haven't seen a problem on our board", that's fine, but they have not looked hard enough. It is like texting and driving, it usually works, except when it does not.

12.6.2 Anisotropic DF

The dissipation factor (DF), or loss tangent in horizontal x/y direction between the via barrel and plane antipad edge might be different from that in vertical Z direction between a trace and plane. The Z direction affects the trace insertion loss. To make the via resonance "V" as deep in simulation as it is in measurement, we need the via models to be much less lossy. The X/Y direction DF might be several times lower than the Z direction. The real number might depend on actual materials.

If the simulator software does not support aniso-DF, then it will optimistically show less deep than realistic resonances on the insertion loss profile. We have the same issue as with the lack of aniso-DK. Misplacing or underestimating resonances on the insertion loss S-parameter profile will fail to point out design flaws or falsely exaggerate less severe design flaws, which can mislead a design team before testing any prototypes. Figure 12.20 shows how the inaccuracy in DK and DF aniso modeling can alter the shape and location of via resonances on an insertion loss curve.

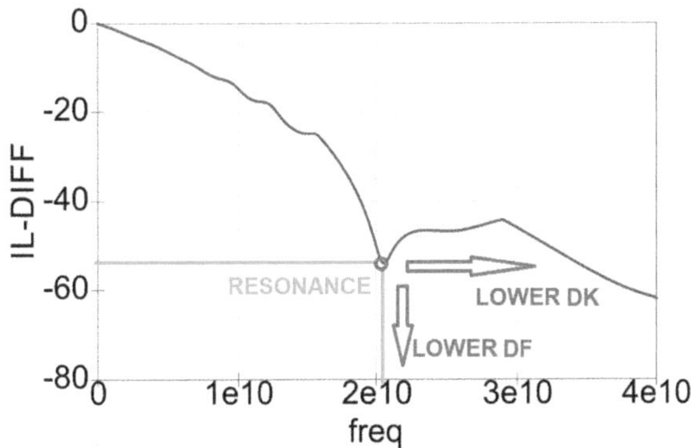

FIGURE 12.20 The dependence of resonance on (aniso) DK and DF.

Measured via resonance might be mode blunt, instead of a very pointy V-shape, due to multiple vias on the signal path having slightly different resonance frequencies, due to manufacturing tolerances and surroundings.

12.7 SIMULATION TO MEASUREMENT CORRELATION

Simulating or measuring the same trace should produce very similar results, meaning they should correlate. Often they fail to correlate enough. The purpose of a correlation study is to obtain more accurate simulation results in the next project by identifying PCB material parameters and settings in the simulation software and adjusting them to make the simulation and measurement results match in the current project. Basically, we measure and simulate the same board, then re-simulate it with adjusted parameters in experimentation until the simulation results fit the measured results. It helps us adjust our company simulation process. Then we write down the adjustments, so for any future projects we can apply them again and obtain more accurate results even before the prototypes are made. The parameter identification is done using frequency-domain S-parameters, as the different effects are separated in these curves while they are combined in eye diagrams. This adjustment experimentation is possible only when we are already prototyping the current project, so simulation accuracy for the current project is no longer useful. When we have a prototype, we can measure it—no need to simulate it. Before releasing a board to proto manufacturing, we might want to simulate it to see how bad it is, but we cannot tune our method to be accurate then as the tuning had to be done in the past on a previous completed project.

Once the proto arrives, we might take a solder sample board and measure the trace with a VNA and wafer probes in the lab, assuming it was designed to meet the DFT for wafer probing (GSSG pad pattern on both ends). We will find that the better the design quality, the better the maximum achievable measurement to simulation correlation. Many papers and articles about correlation studies, use SI-test boards as examples where the signals are very well localized. On any high-density digital product board, the correlation will be worse; the curves will not have the exact same shape. They are designed differently. A digital board cannot afford a large board area for a single transition, and it includes BGA breakouts and many other objects that SI test boards do not have. We need a correlation methodology that works on real product designs. How do we build a correlation study? We can either measure and simulate a complete signal trace end to end on a product board or we can build SI test boards with isolated features and 2X Thru de-embedding. The IEEE P370 standard helps with designing and testing SI test boards. A few SI consulting companies like Wild River Technology have ready-made SI test board designs and consulting service if we do not want to design our own.

We need to make adjustments to the material parameters (DK, DF, Rz) and the trace or via geometry (based on measured cross section) as well as to the tool settings (meshing, aniso, DK frequency dependency model). First, we should aim to obtain more accurate material data, but if that does not take us to a good correlation with a certain simulator, then we have to start altering the data to skew the results. The material data can come from datasheets or coupon measurements. If we used an X parameter from a material vendor, but by using k*X we get stronger correlation, then we need to remember the k adjustment parameter we discovered. Then for our next project, when we receive a Y for the same type of parameter, we will enter k*Y instead into the simulation tool. For example, if the accurate DK=3.0 does not work, but 3.3 works, then k=3.3/3.0=1.1 will be our adjustment number, so in the next project with a DK=4 material we will enter 1.1*4=4.4 into the simulation tool.

There are obstacles to correlation. The Fiber Weave Effect (FWE) can cause additional resonances and P/N asymmetry on a prototype board that will not show up in simulation, which will cause them to be uncorrelated. The only way around it is to use 15 to 25 degree angled routes. Traditionally a few PCB parameters were altered by the layout and procurement departments while ordering the prototypes, for example, via drill diameters. That process cannot be followed as the via diameter change would result in via impedance and via resonant frequency change. We have to manufacture the PCB that we designed, and we have to design the exact via structures that we optimized for impedance. If it is not manufacturable, then the issue is that we started the project with wrong assumptions about what via parameters we can get fabricated. If we change the via size, then we should re-optimize the via impedance with the correct manufacturable parameters and update the design. If we did it right, then we cannot also allow the supply chain to freely agree to change these parameters.

If our S-parameters are expected to be very close, then we can compare them using a difference-curve algorithm. For this to work we need all the resonances that exist on both the simulated and the measured curves, and they have to mostly overlap. The algorithmic comparison in ADS or QUCS will compute an S21diff=S21a-S21b difference value at every frequency point to create a new curve that we can assess visually, or we can go further and compute a single number form also using a definitive integral (sum). We can do this on multiple S-parameters, like the positive and negative leg single-ended IL, the differential SDD21, the single-ended and differential RL, the ILD, mode conversion, coupling, crosstalk, or any S-parameter. We can multiply the numbers we get from each to obtain a final-final number. We can call it a difference score. Then by adjusting the simulation and material parameters we will try to minimize this number to as small as possible. The smaller the number, the greater the correlation between the measurement and the simulation.

We can also visually compare the simulated and the measured curves, one detail at a time, then try to adjust the relevant simulation and material parameters until that one detail has a closer fit. The visual comparison will look for a few identifiable features on the insertion loss curve, as we can see in Figure 12.21 and in the list below:

a) Loss slope: We have to generate the FA@f0 number (fitted attenuation at half baud) for both the simulated and the measured versions, then compute their ratio that describes the un-correlation. We can improve correlation by adjusting DF and copper roughness parameters, in the loss-tuning process described later.
b) SDD21 shape similarity: The simulation and measurement need to have the same number of main resonances to be considered similar enough, while small wrinkles should be ignored.
c) Resonant frequencies: Each major resonance should occur at the same frequency in simulation and measurement. Aniso-DK affects via resonant frequency; regular DK affects both via and trace segment resonant frequency. These parameters have to be tuned. The FWE resonance does not appear in simulation at all.
d) Resonance depth: Each major resonance should have the same depth in dB in simulation and measurement. Aniso-DF affects the depth of the via resonance; regular DF affects the depths of both via and trace segment resonances. These parameters have to be tuned.

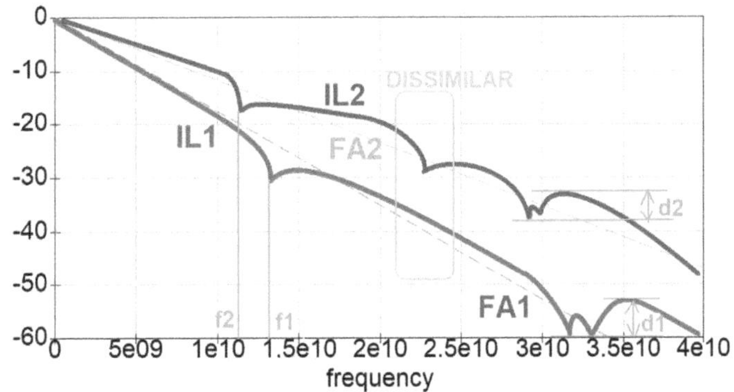

FIGURE 12.21 S-parameter (IL) similarity (sketch).

12.7.1 Loss Tuning for Correlation

Signal integrity simulator programs need to be calibrated to correctly model insertion loss, according to measured coupon data. This is to improve the correlation between measured and simulated S-parameters. Different simulator programs over-estimate or under-estimate losses and crosstalk, and they vary a lot. The default number in each simulation tool does not know about what loss coupon data we have. The loss from different PCB fabricator vendors vary, while default values in software tools do not vary with them. The copper surface is irregular, while the roughness model in the simulation tools uses simplified shapes. There is no good match between them that can be derived by microscopic measurements. Instead, we can treat the tool's shape size parameter as a black box number, then we adjust it until the overall loss in dB/inch@f0 matches our prototype or loss coupon's dB/inch@f0 data. Actually, it is a differential insertion loss curve computed into a fitted attenuation (FA) curve, which is read out at a certain f0 frequency point. The same point the coupon data was measured at, usually at or near half of the baud rate of our signal. First, we obtain the dielectric DF data as accurately as possible, and then we tune the Rz and DF data freely until the FA@f0 matches between the simulated and the coupon data. Basically, we will use a fictitious roughness parameter instead of trying to obtain the microscopic dimensions from optical measurements of the copper surface cross-section. We can also use a DF different from the one provided by the material vendor.

We have to use the loss data from our own SI test board VNA measurements, from previous prototype board measurements, or from a fab vendor provided loss coupon data. It is worth designing in a small loss coupon into every digital board for easy probing. We cannot use loss or Rz parameters we found on the Internet or what our friend used at his company as they use different vendors and other design parameters. Everyone obtains the loss-per-inch coupon data (L_coupon) by using the "Delta-L process" these days. This involves measuring a short and a long trace to produce S-parameter files that are post-processed. This is described later, but, in summary, it involves processing fitted attenuation curves for both traces, then reading them out at half the baud rate, subtracting them, then dividing the result by the trace length difference (short and long trace).

Before simulating any real board design, we will perform the "1-inch trace loss tuning process". This will be done in our SI simulation tool's pre-layout part or stage-2 modeler. First we have to configure a 1" long transmission line model, simulate it for S-parameters, extract the fitted attenuation at half the baud rate as a number, then calculate the "loss-per-inch" number L_sim from it. The loss on a one-inch long trace is equal to the loss-per-inch number, since it is divided by one. We obtain the measured loss-per-inch data L_coupon from the PCB fab vendor or our own coupon measurement. Then we have to calculate the correlation error as:

```
Correlation_error = (L_sim / L_coupon) - 1
```

Then we have to adjust any parameters of the Tline model (Rz and/or DF), and re-simulate, recalculate, until the error is within 1%. Then write down the new tuned Rz/DF data. Finally, we can simulate our real board design's post-layout model with the same exact Rz and DF parameters. Since it does not require our prototype, we can get accurate simulations early on in any project.

Unfortunately, there is a secondary phenomenon that affects an SI simulator's loss modeling accuracy. Basically, even after we have obtained a tuned Rz number and simulated our board design with it, there might still be some loss-slope correlation issues with the measured S-parameters. This is caused by the way the simulator handles the loss in high-density (HD) complex board designs versus in low-density very well localized SI test boards. The measured board will not have that issue, only the simulation. The issue is related to a tool's ability to handle issues in localization. Some tools do a better job with this than others. We can perform the "1-inch trace loss tuning process" based on the fab vendor's coupon data, then with the DF and Rz parameters we simulate our board. We also measure the board with a VNA. We can now calculate the measured loss number divided by the simulated loss number as a ratio (CF, correction factor). After this we have to redo the "1-inch trace loss tuning process", but not directly with the fab vendor's coupon data, rather with the coupon data multiplied by CF. Then if we redo the board simulation, it should correlate better. This CF number is tool specific, and it can be re-used in future projects. This method requires a prototype, so we can only benefit from the CF number in future projects.

13 Power Integrity

Power integrity (PI) is the scientific field of analyzing and designing the power distribution network (PDN) from VRMs to the ASICs. The main PI-related activity for hardware designers is the decoupling capacitor value/quantity selection for the schematic, PCB design (fanout, placement, planes, and stackups), VRM output impedance tuning, and design validation. The ASIC datasheets require the local voltage at the power pins at any moment to remain within a tight tolerance band relative to the nominal value. Due to design imperfections, this voltage tends to deviate and may go over the tolerance limits in a static or dynamic way. Our objective is to prevent that.

13.1 PI INTRODUCTION

A power disturbance budget has to be calculated. The ASIC chip power input pin tolerance from its datasheet is the budget, and parts of this budget are taken up by different effects. Usually, larger ASICs and FPGAs have a 1% to 3% tolerance on the voltage level of the core and SERDES power rails for all of these effects combined. Most other rails on a board have 3% or 5% tolerance. The list of voltage rail disturbances include the VRM DC voltage set tolerance, the power plane DC voltage drop (if no remote sensing is used), and the VRM's ripple noise amplitude and load transient spikes. The voltage fluctuation seen on the PDN impedance caused by the ASIC's load current variance may also be part of this budget. If we have worked only with low power devices, then we might be accustomed to sum up all disturbances and still meet the wide (3% to 5%) tolerance of the device, but this is not achievable with really large devices. Some higher-power ASICs allow us (if explicitly mentioned in the datasheet) to combine only a few disturbances for the budget, so the remaining effects can be on the top of the budget for a limited time interval. The Intel Load Line compatible VRM controllers allow the load transient spikes to be always excluded, but that is ensured by cleverly changing the DC set voltage depending on load current, so that spike will always be in the lucky side (swing in) of the voltage waveform. The load transient is actually measured together with the ripple on an oscilloscope, they are inseparable, so we should not measure them separately and add them up later. We can do a ripple noise measurement with full software/traffic load (stress test) or with a DC electronic load and a step load tester on a "power board" (ASIC depopulated) to ensure we are catching most of it. The VRM ripple is the one always present and easy to measure or simulate. It depends mostly on the output capacitor's ESR. The transient response needs to be measured on a prototype with a LoadSlammer or similar equipment. In the frequency-domain method a low slew rate (low frequency) load step is not considered to be summed up on top of a high-frequency noise like the one at the core clock frequency.

The power plane DC voltage drop only adds to the budget, if the VRM does not have differential remote voltage sense lines. If it does have sense lines, like most multi-phase VRMs, then the VRM controls the voltage to be constant at the ASIC pins through the sense lines, eliminating the drop. The only plane voltage drop that directly affects the ASIC is from the bulk capacitors to the ASIC pins, and that is only for very fast transients temporarily. This is because the VRM's control loop usually has a lower bandwidth than the bulk capacitor's resonant frequency. So when the load changes by several Amps, all that extra current drops extra voltage on the bulk-to-ASIC plane section until later when the VRM can correct it. This is why we supposed to place the bulk caps around the ASIC body outline, not near the VRM. In the main DC voltage drop simulation, we should really mark all of the bulk caps together as the voltage source, instead of the VRM. The VRM to ASIC plane path DC voltage drop still needs to be minimized to about two or five times the ASICs voltage tolerance, due to indirect effects like control loop imperfections. On smaller voltage rails

 DOI: 10.1201/9781032702094-13

without remote sense lines, the total DC voltage drop is directly affecting the ASIC power pin inputs so they need to be simulated in full, from VRM to ASIC and included in the input tolerance budget. The PDN impedance-related voltage noise is expected to be at higher frequencies or if it is at a low frequency then it is the load transient itself, so it should not be counted twice. This is explained in detail below.

We typically simulate or measure the shunt frequency-domain impedance profile of a whole PDN against a target impedance line at the ASIC's location on the board in frequency domain. We also simulate the series resistance number (DCR) between the source and the destination in a DC voltage drop simulation. The PDN's impedance is the AC voltage noise seen on the power rail divided by the ASIC's load excitation current, according to Ohm's law Z=V/I. This is analyzed at many independent frequency points, where the voltage and current values are sine waves, sitting on top of a nominal rail voltage DC level. The goal is to ensure that the ASIC will not see too much voltage fluctuation on its power pins, while the ASIC itself is acting as a noise excitation, simply by having its load supply current changing suddenly at different rates and repetition frequencies. Since the ASIC's internal processing is time dependent, for example, they execute different code after different code, or receive different sizes and types of data packets, their supply current demand also changes. We can call it a load transient (load step or load dump), but it can repeat/toggle up and down with a certain frequency also, at a software code– or data packet–related frequency. The load transient amount we assume for PDN analysis is usually a 20% to 80% step, meaning 60% of the maximum load current for most chips. For the largest ASICs above 100Watt it might just be 10%, otherwise we get unachievable low-target impedances. For most high-end PCB designs about 0.5 to 1 milli Ohm is the lowest we can achieve. The load current also has a periodic current spike at the internal core logic clock frequency, usually with an unknown amplitude, so we exclude it from the analysis. When it is analyzed on an I/O voltage rail of the ASIC, they call it simultaneous switching noise (SSN), as multiple I/O pins switch in the same time.

The design goal of a PDN is to minimize this fluctuation, so the voltage at the ASIC pin remains within the ASIC's tolerance limits. From the ASIC's datasheet we have to obtain a few numbers, the nominal voltage, the voltage tolerance requirement (like 3% or 0.03x), and the maximum load current. Some datasheets specify the target impedance too, then we do not have to calculate it. We assumed above that the largest load step would be at 60% (or 0.6x) of the maximum current for most ASICs from most vendors. From all this the target impedance requirement line can be calculated as:

$$Z_T = V_{DD} * Tolerance/(0.6 * I_{DDMAX})$$

This is according to the commonly used "Frequency-Domain Target Impedance Method". Figure 13.1 shows what a typical impedance profile and a target impedance requirement look like. It is in logarithmic scale in both axis. The requirement appears as a horizontal line on the impedance versus frequency graph, the PDN impedance profile must remain below this line with less impedance. We have to set an upper-frequency limit to our target impedance requirement to be realistic because the PDN impedance profile will reach infinite impedance at infinite frequency no matter what we do. Some chip vendors list a limit in their appnotes or datasheets, typically 20 to 50MHz for large BGA chips, but it might be as high as 100MHz for small QFN chips. It is very hard to decouple anything on a PCB above 20–50MHz, especially large BGA chips. The point where the chip package pin touches the board is kind of a legal boundary, each side takes care of their parameters. The board company guarantees impedance below Z_T, while the chip company guarantees that it will work on any board that meets Z_T.

The most successful way of designing PDNs involves pre-layout simulations for determining capacitor values and vetting the VRM solution using measured VRM models and later tuning the VRMs on the prototype while measuring the board PDN with a VNA. The flow chart for this PDN development method is shown in Figure 13.2. Often we perform only some of these steps due to limited resources.

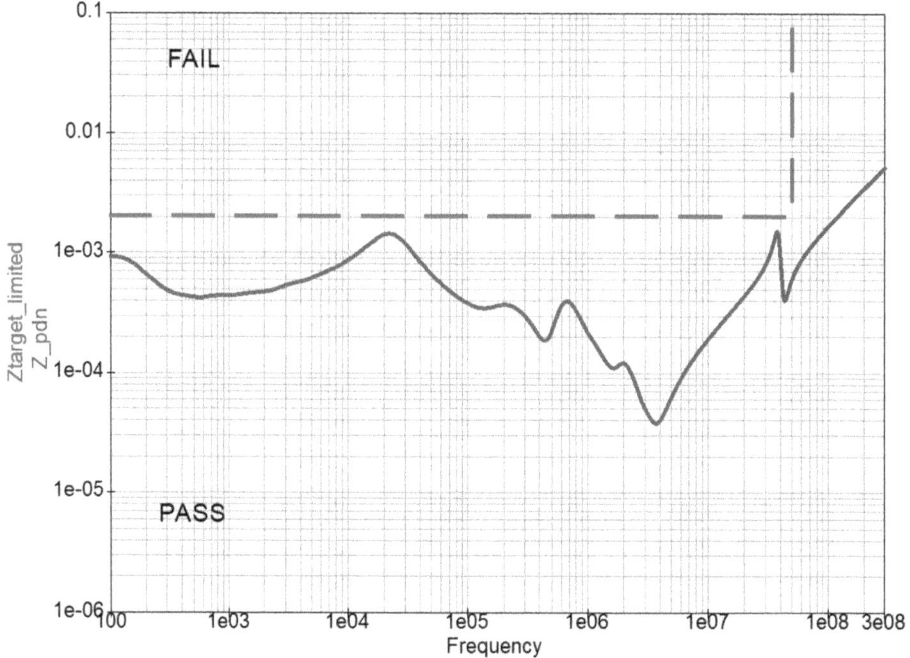

FIGURE 13.1 Example of an impedance profile and limited target impedance line.

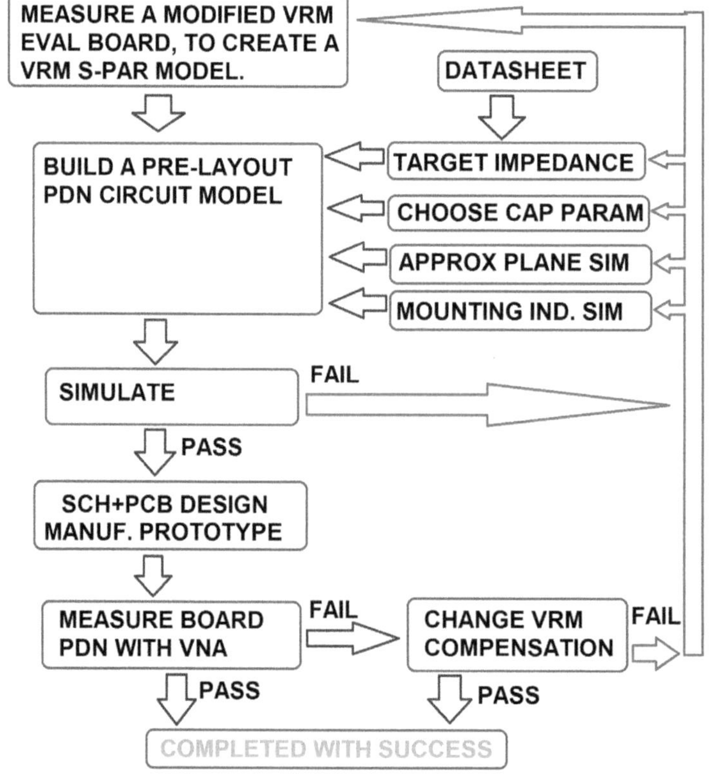

FIGURE 13.2 PDN design flow.

13.2 ELEMENTS OF PDN

The PCD is made of an electrical circuit combination of several common elements. Each of these elements has its own impedance profiles in frequency domain, but when combined together they create the one PDN impedance profile that is the result of our entire design. Each element can be modelled with an S-parameter file or with lumped passive components (resistors, capacitors, inductors). Figure 13.3 shows a typical PDN simulation model. A PDN is usually simulated using a circuit model that looks like a schematic in a stage-2 pre-layout style SI/PI or circuit simulator. It has series elements between the load and the VRM and shunt elements that are parallel to the load and the VRM. The shunt elements have an impedance profile between the power rail and the ground. All impedances should be minimized. The circuit model might be internally generated, such as in HyperLynx PI, or we have to draw it in an editor or re-used in a template in ADS or QUCS.

The PDN is made of the following elements:

- VRM, as a shunt impedance.
- Power and ground planes in series.
- Bulk decoupling capacitors, as a shunt impedance.
- Ceramic decoupling capacitors, as a shunt impedance.
- BGA fanout vias and dog-bone traces in series.
- ASIC internal parts, which we board designers usually omit from our analysis. For simulation purposes we connect a 1Amp AC current source at the point where the ASIC would connect.

13.2.1 VRMs

The VRM circuits and their operation are described in Chapter 4, "Power Supply Circuits". For the purpose of PDN analysis, the VRM is represented as a frequency-dependent shunt impedance that can be included in a simulation as an RLC lumped model or an S-parameter file. Lumped RLC and RL models were commonly used, but they do not represent control loop capabilities very well, especially high-performance high-power core voltage regulators. We can create an S-parameter model of a VRM from a measurement. This is done by requesting an evaluation board from the VRM chip vendor, measuring its output impedance with a low frequency VNA (Omicron Lab Bode-100 or Keysight Technology E5061B-3xx), save it into an S-parameter file, and then post-process the results with an Excel file to smooth it and cut off the high-frequency parts that represent the eval board PCB. The cutoff would replace the samples above the cut point with a 20dB/decade inductive slope, as it is implemented in an Excel template (S-Par Smoothie) in the appendix. When importing the measured data into the template, we can check where the main impedance peak of the VRM

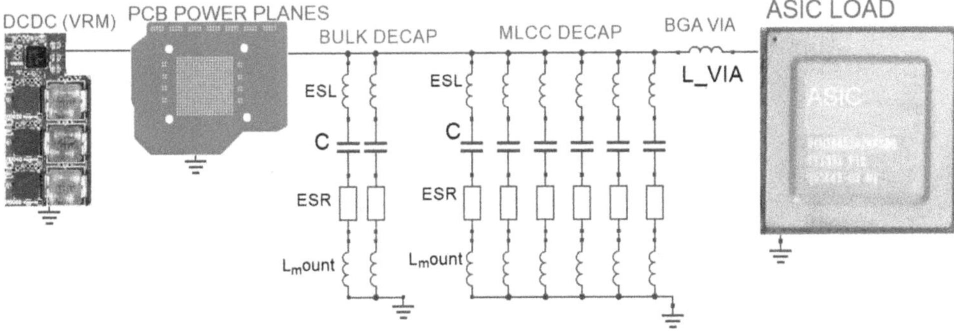

FIGURE 13.3 Elements of a PDN.

is (at the Bode cutoff frequency), after which the impedance goes low into a valley and increases again. That is the point where we should set the post-processing cutoff point. Figure 13.4 shows a measured impedance profile of a turned-on VRM, a post-processed smoothed and cut version, and a turned-off VRM. In some cases, we can convert a vendor-provided VRM Spice model into an S-parameter model, for example in HyperLynx LineSim.

13.2.2 Decoupling Capacitors

We place many capacitors between the power rail net and ground, usually at the ASIC's power pins or fanout vias. In the schematic they appear as many capacitors in parallel, connecting to a specific voltage rail and a group of power pins of the ASIC. Their values, types, and quantities are chosen by the hardware designer as the main exercise of the PDN design. Capacitors are usually modeled as RLC lumped models, both the bulk (usually polymer or tantalum), and the MLCC (multi-layer ceramic capacitor). It is a resistor (ESR, equivalent series resistance), an inductor (parasitic inductances, mounting and internal ESL), and a capacitor in series in the PDN simulation circuit model. Each of the RLC parameters has an effect on the capacitor's own impedance profile, as we can see in Figure 13.5. A "capacitor bank" in simulation is the set of capacitors that have the same value and package size in one rail's PDN. For example, if we have ceramic capacitors such as 500 pieces of 1uF/0402, 100 pieces of 22uF, then the 100 pieces of 1uF capacitors, these are three banks. A bank of N pieces of capacitors is modelled as a single capacitor in the simulator's circuit model, with N times larger capacitance, N times smaller inductance and N times smaller resistance than a single capacitor would have. The inductance is the sum of the package inductance from the vendor's datasheet (ESL, equivalent series L) and the mounting parasitic inductance we simulate from our board. The package size determines inductance, so for a given package size the right side of the V remains the same, but the left (capacitive) side gets shifted left/down with larger capacitance. Or with given capacitance, a smaller package having lower inductance has the right side of the V shifted right/down.

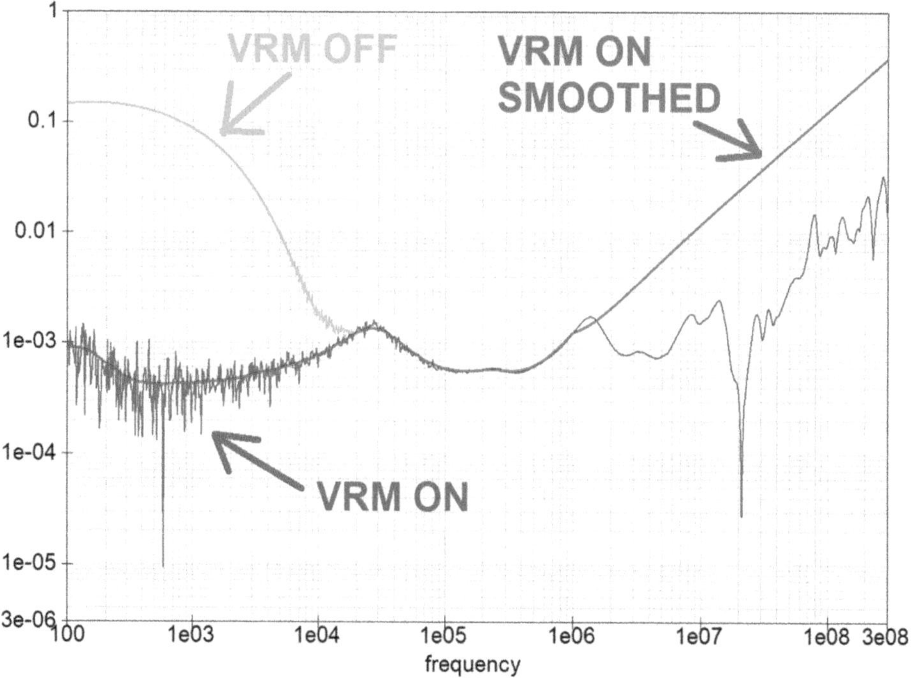

FIGURE 13.4 VRM output impedance.

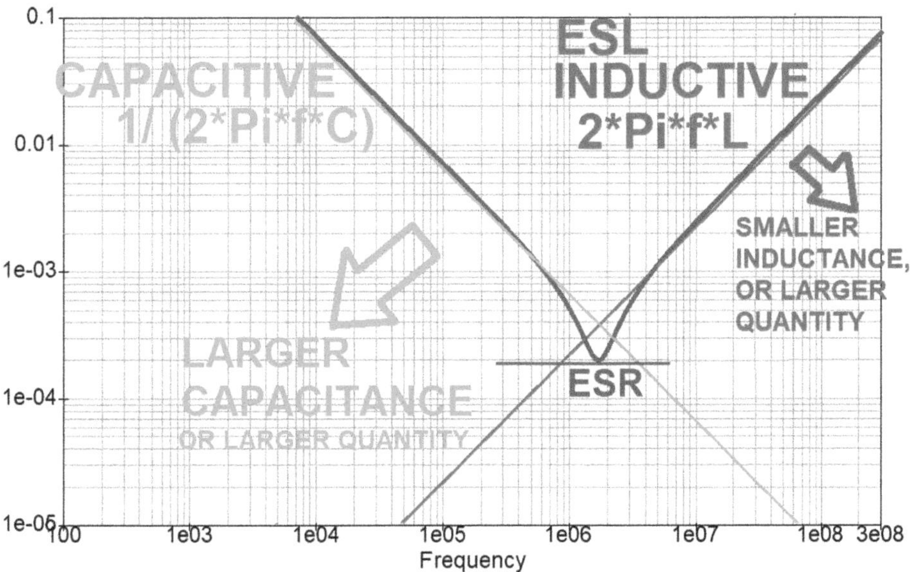

FIGURE 13.5 Capacitor bank impedance.

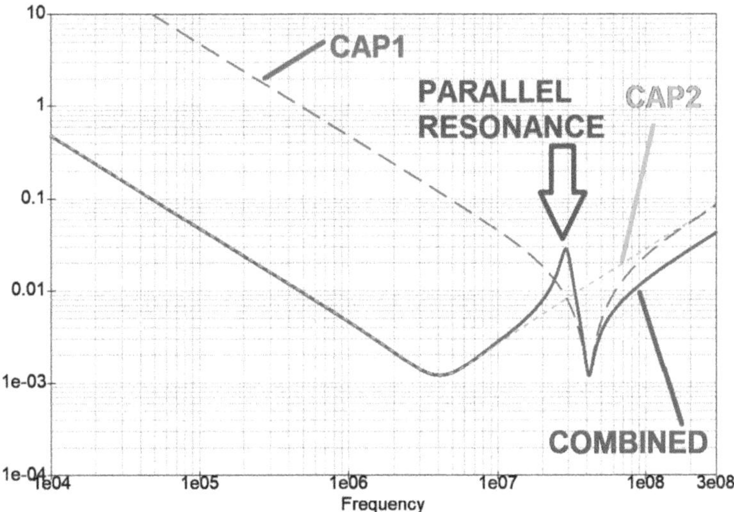

FIGURE 13.6 Parallel resonance between two capacitor banks.

There is a parallel resonance between two neighboring capacitor banks; this is shown in Figure 13.6. The PDN impedance at the parallel resonance can get much higher than the impedance of any individual capacitor bank on its own. This is true in any pair of elements of the PDN; a capacitor can have a parallel resonance with the power plane, for example. A parallel resonance has an "A" shape; a series (self) resonance has a "V" shape. Every shunt element has a series resonance by itself. Parallel resonances are between different elements. We have to avoid getting too sharp parallel resonances, as the system can resonate on this, making the ASIC fail, or if we have more than one sharp parallel resonances then we can get rogue waves, then the ASIC will more likely fail. These failures are typically intermittent. To avoid a parallel resonance, we usually avoid using very high-frequency capacitors that have a very sharp series resonance because it will also have a sharp parallel resonance with a nearby capacitor bank.

13.2.3 Power Planes

Power planes act as very low-resistance resistors or wires in series between the source and the load, and as a very small size but very low inductance capacitor in parallel (shunt), in the same time. The shunt impedance of the plane has a series V-dip resonance between 50 and 1000MHz, seen from the board. We can simulate a power plane with estimated main dimensions, free of fine details, in a 2D electromagnetic simulator program like Sonnet Lite or Ansys SiWave and create an S-parameter model for a PDN analysis. This would usually only include the shunt impedance because modeling the series impedance accurately requires 20+ digit numbers that are not always available in S-parameter files and in simulation tools. Instead, we model the series behavior separately in a DC voltage drop analysis, not part of the PDN frequency domain analysis. The DC drop analysis will tell us the amount of the voltage drop caused by the DC load current between the VRM and the load ASIC. High-current VRMs use remote sensing, so the voltage will be actually correct at the load ASIC, but at any load step event the VRM control loop has to account for the voltage drop step also.

Plane waves can/will occur on power planes. As the excitation load current (toggle, step) introduces the wave into the plane, it spreads away in every horizontal direction in a circle pattern, just like surface water waves when we drop a rock into a lake. In the case of digital circuits, it is more like dropping rocks with equal time intervals at the same spot in the lake, causing more and more waves. In the case of power planes, the wave reaches the edge of the plane and gets reflected back and travel back to the excitation source. This, of course, gets hugely damped by decoupling capacitors. If the wave arrives back to the ASIC (excitation) the same time it starts another wave, then the amplitudes pile up into a high amplitude noise or resonance. This arrival time depends on the major dimensions of the plane, not the finer details. The plane shape is similar to a rectangle, and the resonance can be modeled by a simple rectangle plane model that is easy to draw, for example in Sonnet Lite (frequency domain), MEFiSTo-2D (time domain), Keysight Momentum (frequency domain), or Ansys SiWave (time or frequency domain). Figure 13.7 shows an approximate plane model setup for simulation and S-parameter extraction in Sonnet Lite. The frequency that the power/ground plane

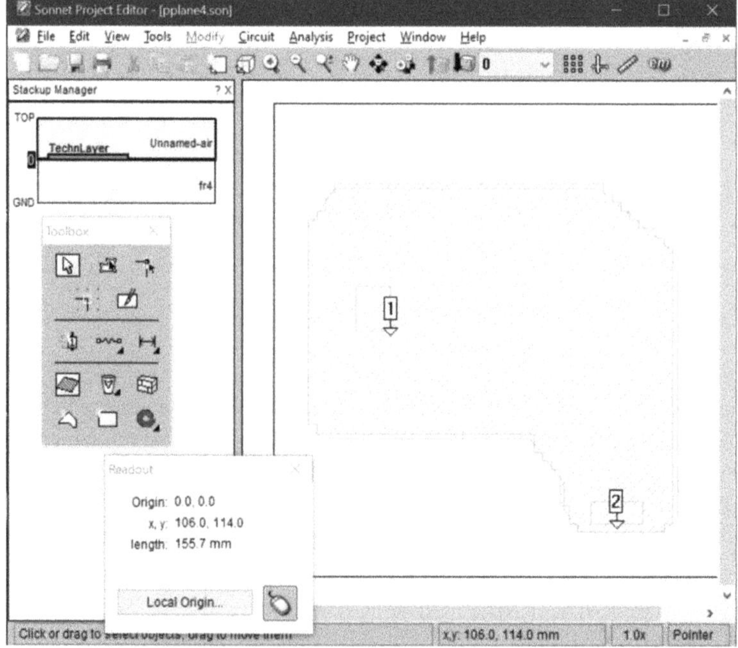

FIGURE 13.7 Power plane approximate model setup in Sonnet Lite.

pair resonates at corresponds to A-shaped impedance peaks seen on the impedance profile. This peak is usually way above the 50MHz we usually analyze our PDN impedance, but, in some cases, it can cause a problem. There can be multiple peaks from non-square shaped planes. Each dimension between parallel edges creates a new resonant frequency. For this reason, it makes sense to create a rectangle or basic hand-drawn plane model, simulate it, and use the results as an S-parameter model in our PDN circuit model simulation. Some simulators can take the S-parameter model as is, others require a conversion into an impedance element.

13.3 PARASITIC INDUCTANCES

All elements of the PDN, especially the fanout vias of the capacitors and BGA pins, have parasitic inductance in series and with them increasing their impedance at higher frequencies and reducing their effectiveness. We can study the parasitic inductance of the capacitor and BGA vias together because some of the effects are a result of their relative positions. In the old days we placed decoupling capacitors on the same side of the board where the processor/FPGA chips were, this created a very large spreading inductance. However, in recent decades everyone has been placing the smaller decoupling caps on the opposite side of the board, right on top of the BGA fanout via. To make this type of placement easier, we had to start using VIPPO vias, which means "via in pad plated over", where the via hole overlaps with the capacitors pad and is not visible. This has improved plane spreading impedance a lot. Spreading inductance is a property of a power and ground plane and via pair; it is the inductance of the loop area between the power and ground vias and planes, as we can see in Figure 13.8. The inductance is proportional to the cross-section area of the currents. We make sure with design that this area is as small as possible. We are not including the BGA ball and package inductances; we (hardware designers) design the boards for chips that are supposed to work on boards that meet the datasheet requirements. Large bulk capacitors are not placed on the BGA fanout vias as they do not fit; rather, they are placed around the perimeter of the BGA chips, usually with two to 12 vias in each pad to provide low enough inductance. Parasitic inductances (via, spreading) can be obtained from 3D full-wave electromagnetic simulations, or we can use "typical values" that were previously determined on a similar project.

We can determine parasitic inductances by simulating a simplified structure in a 3D field solder like HFSS, Simbeor, FastHenry, or Sonnet Lite into a 2-port S-parameter file, then converting it to Y-parameters and computing the inductance curve (in ADS or QUCS), then read out the inductance value a twice the resonant frequency of the capacitor, or at a suitably high-frequency where the inductance stabilizes (~ 200MHz). This will be the parasitic inductance of one instance, but because we have multiple capacitors in a bank, and multiple BGA vias, this will have to be divided by the quantity before entering it into the PDN simulation model.

Since we put the capacitors on the opposite side of the ASIC in modern designs, we can just simulate the decoupling capacitor's mounting inductance together with the spreading inductance as one. We can do this by creating a 3D model containing the capacitor pads, the two

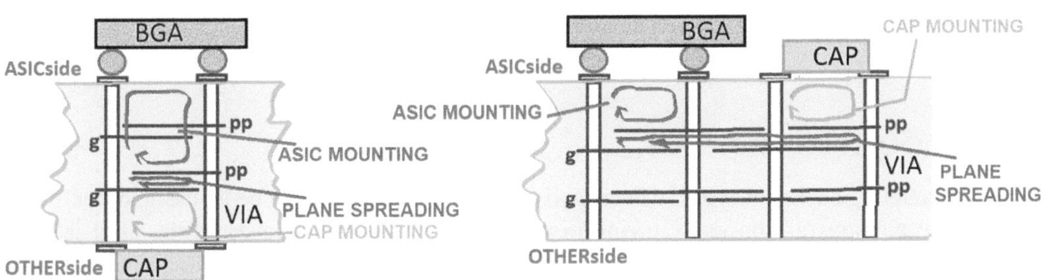

FIGURE 13.8 Parasitic inductances of capacitor and ASIC pins (sketch).

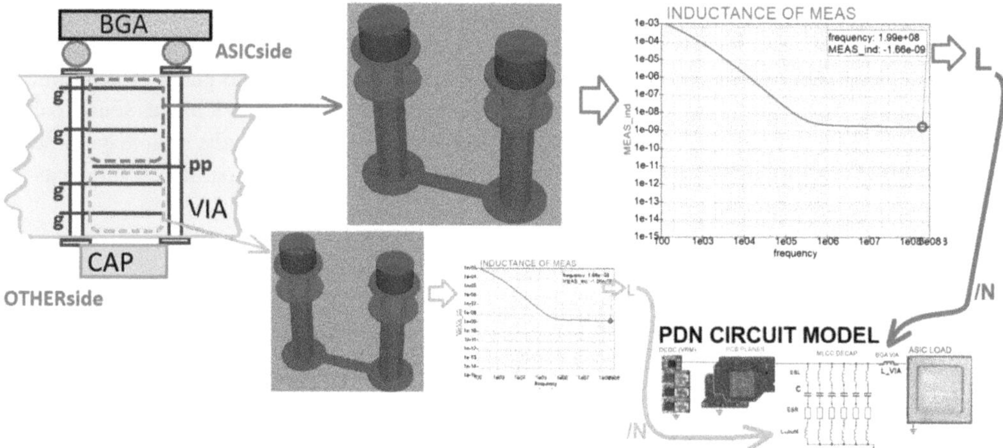

FIGURE 13.9 Parasitic inductance extraction of power vias in Simbeor and QUCS.

vias that are shorted with a trace on the farthest power plane. Then simulate the BGA fanout via similarly, with a model containing the BGA pads, dog-bone traces, the two vias that are shorted with a trace on the nearest power plane layer's position—near or far side is relative to the component. If we have multiple planes, then we can pick one GND/VDD plane pair. For this simulation we do not need a complex stackup in the 3D model, just the top layer, and a layer that will be at the position/depth of the VDD plane in the real stackup. We end up extracting S-parameters and the inductance value for the BGA and another one for the capacitor. In the PDN circuit model the capacitor's result will be an inductor in series with the capacitor's RLC model (Lmount), the BGA's result in series with the BGA load (current source). We can see the 3D loop simulation model and the results in Figure 13.9.

The inductance depends on metal structures, but not on dielectrics, so the model can be a lot simpler than the model we need for high-speed differential signal via analysis. We need only two layers and two vias. The only thing that needs to be accurate are the via length (outer layer to the power plane distance in the stackup), pin pitch of the BGA component, and via diameter. The rest of the model is component pads, and a fake trace shorting the two vias on the inner layer to create a loop. The simulation can be done in any suitable 3D EM tool. The model in Figure 13.10 was created in SonnetLite, with two ports at the model boundary, vias, pads, and traces. In Simbeor we can use the (differential signal) via wizard, then edit the 3D "circuit" to delete the output ports, then add a trace to short the two vias on the inner layer. After the EM simulation, we should get a 2-port S-parameter file that we need to post process in QUCS or ADS. The S-parameters will be converted to Y-parameters, and then the inductance will be extracted at a suitably high frequency (200MHz or 2e8) where we can accurately read out the inductance value, free from unrelated effects.

```
Inductance(f) = |(1/im(y11))/(6.28*frequency)|
Inductance = |(1/im(y11(2e8)))/(6.28*2e8)|
```

13.4 DECOUPLING METHODS

The way decoupling capacitor types, values, and quantities are chosen can be heuristic or methodical. Heuristic methods are basically trying to plug holes in the impedance profile, until it stays below the target impedance line. There are several well documented methodical options, resulting in different kinds of trade-offs. Another common "method" is to just use the capacitor values used on the ASIC reference design schematics and not conduct any analysis. It is very popular, although

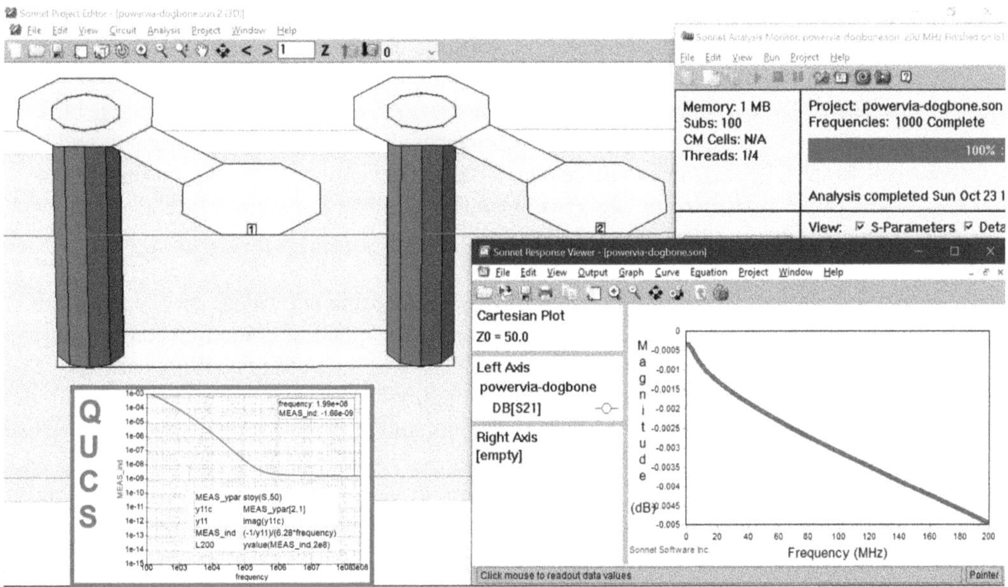

FIGURE 13.10 Sonnet lite power via model and QUCS post-processing.

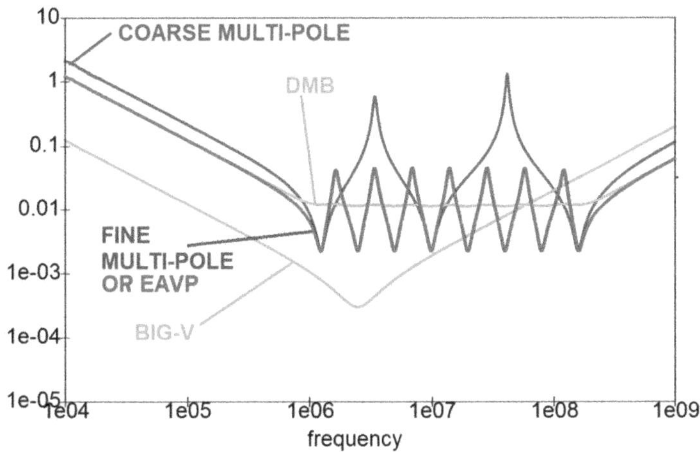

FIGURE 13.11 Decoupling methods impedance profile comparison in QUCS.

this book focuses on all other options instead. We can use the reference design as a starting point for an iterative design/analysis. Figure 13.11 shows the impedance profiles of several different methods.

The main methods for capacitor selection:

- Coarse multi-pole is when we select a few common capacitor values, like 1uF, 100nF, and 10nF, then adjust their quantities until the PDN impedance is below the target line.
- Fine-multipole is similar to the above; just we use more capacitor values, maybe 3 to 5 times as many. This sometimes helps with reducing the parallel peaks, other times makes it worse.
- EAVP, or extended adaptive voltage positioning is similar to the above, but we pick the capacitor values and package sizes (inductance, ESL) by calculations for capacitor bank pairs for reducing the parallel resonances. ESL1/ESR1=ESR2/ESL2.

- Distributed matched bypassing (DMB) is similar to the above, but with controlled-high-ESR capacitors, which would eliminate the waviness of the impedance profile, creating a flat one. These capacitors are not commonly available.
- Big-V is when only one value of ceramic capacitor is used, and one value of very large bulk capacitor. This eliminates all the parallel resonances. It is very easy to implement and it is smooth. Usually we are able to place one 0402 size decoupling capacitor on each of the power pins of the ASIC, so for Big-V we would pick the largest capacitance available in 0402 package size.

During decoupling design, we choose the capacitor types (capacitance value, package size, ESR) and the quantities of each type. But there is a hard limit on the quantities, and that comes from the ASIC BGA pinout. In almost all cases the high-end ASICs come in 1mm pitch BGA packages. The 1mm pitch BGA is well matched with 0402 size decoupling capacitors, fitting on its grid on the underside of the board, using VIPPO vias in the capacitor solder pads. The best possible capacitor attachment with lowest parasitic and spreading inductance is when we place the cap directly on a VDD/GND via pair, of the BGA fanout vias. So the number of power pins on the BGA footprint will end up being equal to the number of 0402 ceramic capacitors we use in the decoupling network. Then larger bulk capacitors in larger packages are typically placed outside of and around the BGA package perimeter, their number is not hard fixed to the BGA pinout. Typically, two or four sides of the ASIC are packed with bulk caps, whatever quantity fits. So the ceramic capacitor quantity can be guessed from the schematic symbol or the layout footprint, and the bulk capacitor quantity can be guessed from the layout placement. This quantity should be fed back into the PDN analysis, then choosing values for the given quantity. When choosing anything other than the Big-V method, we end up having different value capacitors on different VDD pins of the ASIC. The ASIC might not like that, it might perceive it as some pins are insufficiently decoupled. This is a strong motivation for using the Big-V method.

Sometimes we use a “flare-out” BGA fanout, towards the four corners, that creates a crosshair shaped channel under the BGA free of vias, that allows medium package–sized bulk capacitors to be placed under the BGA instead of the perimeter, which helps with providing low-inductance bulk decoupling near the load.

13.5 ROGUE WAVES

Rogue waves are basically the super positioning of the voltage responses to two different frequency excitations if only one excitation is present in any given moment, but the responses may overlap in time due to stored energy. By following the target impedance method for decoupling design, the voltage response should be below the maximum allowed noise voltage on the ASIC’s power rail, simply because the PDN’s impedance and impedance peaks are below the target impedance line. But what if a PDN has two parallel resonant peaks, and we apply a load toggling at the rate that is matching one of the peak’s frequency, then we change the frequency to match the other peak? The PDN will keep resonating at the first frequency for a while after the switchover. The result is two responses will be present in the same time until the first one decays, while only one excitation is present at any time. This is called a “rogue wave”, namely, the superposition of present and past responses. This is demonstrated in Figure 13.12 in a circuit simulation. First an AC simulation was done to determine the peaks, then a transient simulation was carried out with the toggle rates matching the resonances. We can see that right after the switchover the noise amplitude is larger than the amplitude before and far after the switch. It can be higher than the maximum allowed noise voltage, even though we designed the PDN to stay below the target impedance line that was calculated from the load current step and the noise voltage allowance.

If an Ethernet switch ASIC keeps receiving 1500Byte packets, then suddenly it starts receiving 64Byte packets on its 10Gbit/s ports, then it changes its core rail load current toggle rate from

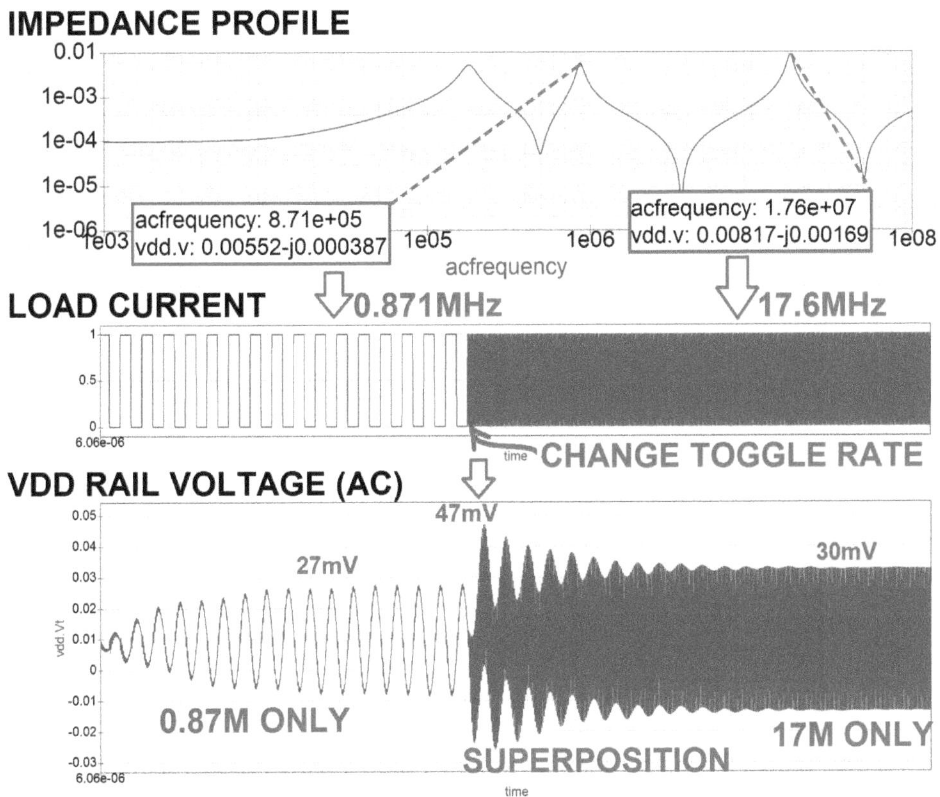

FIGURE 13.12 Rogue wave occurrence.

0.833MHz to 19.5MHz. If our PDN is so unlucky as to have parallel resonant peaks at these exact frequencies, then a rogue wave will form. During this toggle rate transition the voltage noise will be temporarily higher—it can have double amplitude, outside of the ASIC's VDD tolerance, and it can cause the ASIC to malfunction (hang, drop packets, report errors, reboot).

The industry has been evaluating different approaches in dealing with rogue waves (RW), for example, adjusting the target impedance and even lower or looking to flatten the impedance profile. If we expect three peaks to create a RW, then we need a three times lower target impedance. Achieving flat impedance profiles ($Q<0.5$) with different capacitor values on real digital designs is impractical—it would require non-existent high-resistance capacitors. The Big-V capacitor selection method also eliminates most of the sharp peaks, which can be implemented easily in practice. Flatness can be computed from the quality factor of the adjacent decoupling capacitor banks, which is not really about obtaining a straight line, just about having blunt resonances instead of sharp ones. Sharp ones resonate longer. There are also complex methods for estimating worst-case rogue wave amplitudes, which are more practical, described here. For a board hardware designer, a practical approach that can help with the initial capacitor selection during schematic design is needed. This would tell if we have a potential for a rogue wave over the voltage tolerance or not. Rogue wave amplitude estimating calculations are done in the QUCS template linked in the appendix.

Figure 13.13 shows four cases of impedance profile shapes and marks the susceptibility to rogue wave appearance. The first one does not meet the target impedance requirement, so that would fail (intermittently unreliable). The one with one peak that is under the line is acceptable, as RW's require two or more peaks. The one with three peaks under the line is the prime suspect for RW and intermittent product failure. The one with no peaks, is very smooth and an ideal solution if we can achieve it.

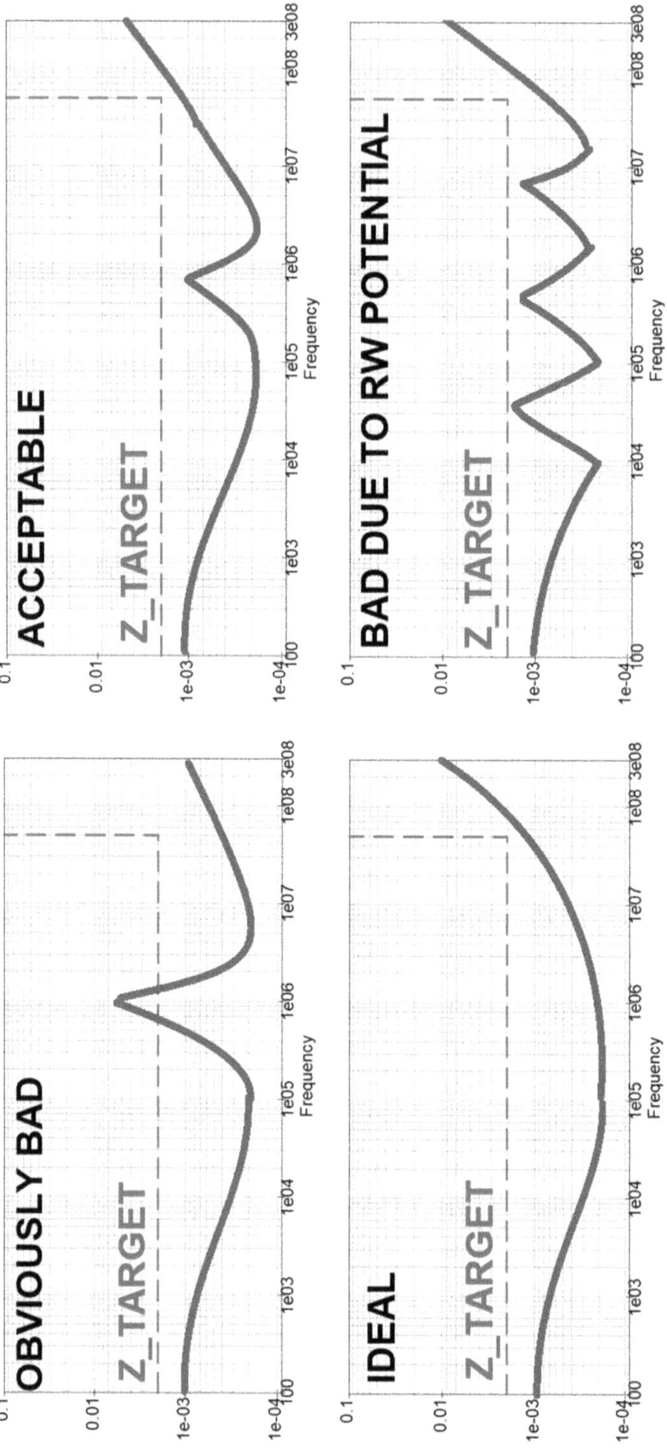

FIGURE 13.13 Rogue wave susceptibility cases (sketch).

13.5.1 Known Methods of Estimating a Maximum Rogue Wave

In addition to the target impedance crossing criteria, another criteria is needed for the designer, namely, to check whether the worst-case noise amplitude is larger than the maximum allowed noise voltage or not by using a crafted worst-case excitation waveform in simulation. We can do this new type of check by computing the required excitation from the simulated PDN impedance profile. Two methods are presented below: the RPT and the MTT. Both methods allow only the load current to change from min to max with a fast rise time, but the timing detail is different. The MTT finds the peaks, then it assumes that an ASIC will somehow apply toggle rates in the worst-case sequence. The RPT tries to create the actual sequence itself. The spectrum of the two excitation currents can be compared in Figure 13.14, where we can also see how their peaks align with peaks in the impedance profile.

The more common method for worst-case voltage response or rogue wave computation is the Reverse-Pulse Technique (RPT). It computes a wide band waveform consisting of a rectangular load step sequence with very specific timing detail. This requires FFT, IFFT, differential, integral, and time (vector) reversal computations that will be correct or accurate only when using linear sampling on both the frequency and the time domains. With logarithmic frequency sampling we

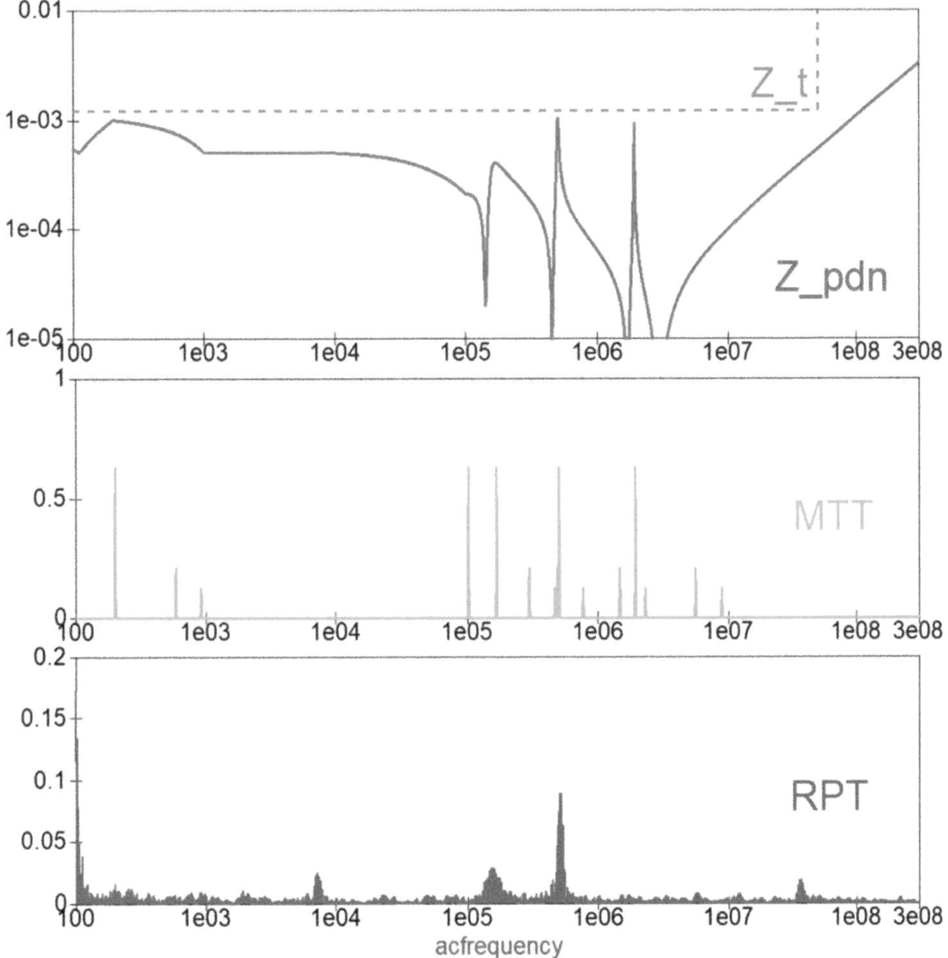

FIGURE 13.14 PDN impedance profile and two different RW excitations in QUCS.

expect large inaccuracy or distorted curves, but the spectrum of the excitation waveform still seems to align exactly with the peaks and high-impedance areas on the impedance profile, so perhaps it is not that bad. A linear scale RPT down to DC would require at least 100k or more likely millions of frequency points to have decent coverage of the lower frequency range that is prohibitive in most simulation tools and laptop computers. We can compute a very wide band RPT in log scale on only 1000 points; it will have enough samples at low frequencies, which can be easily processed on a laptop. The computation of RPT can be automated using post-simulation equations in Keysight ADS or in the open source QUCS. First, we have to simulate a PDN circuit model in an AC-simulation and then post-process the results with equations:

```
[AC-sim] → Z_pdn(f) → [BW-limit] → [symmetrize] → [IFFT] → Impulse
Response(t) → [Integral] → Step Response(t) → [Detect Voltage
Fluctuation] → [Create a binary toggling Waveform] → [Time Reversal] →
Excitation(t) → [FFT] → Excitation(f) → [Multiply by Z_pdn(f)] →
Noise(f) → [IFFT] → Noise(t) → [min/max] → Vpp
```

Another method, the Multi-Tone Technique (MTT) avoids the accuracy (in logarithmic scale) or computation resource (in linear scale) issues within the Reverse Pulse Technique (RPT) and provides a simple and fast way to a hardware design engineer to checking the design for worst-case rogue waves. MTT simply finds all the peaks (tones), sums their value up multiplied by the load step current automatically, then checks if the RW amplitude is larger (fail) or smaller (pass) than the max allowed noise from the datasheet. The MTT assumes that these "tones" will be applied in a worst-case sequence to the DUT, relying on stored energy, creating the rogue wave. Therefore, it is not really needed to compute a time domain waveform from it using IFFT, and the IFFT will be inaccurate due to the logarithmic sampling we used. Instead of manually reading the frequency values of the peaks from an impedance curve, we can automate all that with waveform processing equations while remaining in the frequency domain. That is the point of the MTT. This runs much faster even on a low-power laptop than the RPT does. The implementation of both the log-RPT and the log-MTT can be found in a QUCS template made for PDN analysis, linked in the appendix. We can observe that the computation results in narrow excitation peaks, which are constant toggle rates, right where the PDN impedance profile had its peaks. RPT uses random-looking pulse widths; MTT uses constant frequency and frequency switch. First, we have to simulate a PDN circuit model in an AC-simulation and then post-process the results with equations:

```
[AC-sim] → Z_pdn(f) → [BW-limit] → [Differential] → [Magnify] →
[signum] → [edge to pulse] → [crop] → [Filter Wrinkles] → Noise(f) →
[add harmonics] → Noise(f) →[Definitive Integral] → Vpp
```

13.5.2 Quality Factor

The Q, or "quality factor", describes how under-damped an oscillator or resonator is. It is the ratio of the energy stored in the resonator to the energy lost in one radian of the cycle of oscillation. The parallel peaks on a PDN act like oscillators or resonators. With higher Q peaks on the impedance profile the oscillations decay more slowly after the excitation is turned off (keeping constant load current). This means that it oscillates longer while the load switches the excitation to another resonant frequency that, in turn, increases the chances of creating a rogue wave. This is why often there is a focus on flattening the impedance profile to prevent the resonances from lasting too long. If we want 90% of the stored energy to be lost within a half period of the load toggling (3.14rad), then a limit on the quality factor is required:

```
Q<1/(1-(0.1^(1/pi)))=1.92
```

For 80% energy loss we would need a different limit:

```
Q<1/(1-(0.2^(1/pi)))=2.5
```

That is often achievable with 100nF or larger capacitors, while smaller capacitors have a higher quality factor. Ensuring 80% loss after half period is not a guarantee to zero rogue waves but an improvement. Our simulation template can check for Q factor between capacitor bank pairs analytically. Q does not compute the RW voltage amplitude; it just gives a vague measure for RW susceptibility.

```
Q12=sqrt((ESL1+Lmnt1)/C2)/(ESR1+ESR2)
```

13.5.3 Automated PDN Design through Optimization

With pass/fail variables for the rogue wave amplitudes and for the target impedance, we can create a simulation that automatically adjusts capacitor quantities to produce a design that meets all the requirements and simulates the PDN impedance profile with the new values. The mentioned QUCS template does all that automatically. A pass/fail variable in QUCS or ADS is simply using an If/Else function like "if V_MTT > X then pass=0, else pass=1". The results of this can be seen in Figure 13.15. The simulator adjusts capacitor quantities instead of values, as it is more practical, from a selection of a few different catalog parts we entered. The quantity to any capacitor type can end up being zero. This can be done using a simulation controller called "Optimization" that re-runs the AC simulation a hundred times with different pseudo-random component parameters (individual capacitor quantities) while looking to satisfy a set of user-entered "goals". Both the AC-sim and the OPT simulation controllers are placed in the QUCS (or ADS) model schematic. QUCS uses an optimizer simulator that is another separate open-source project called ASCO. While the individual capacitor quantities are controlled by the optimizer, the VRM S-par model would have to

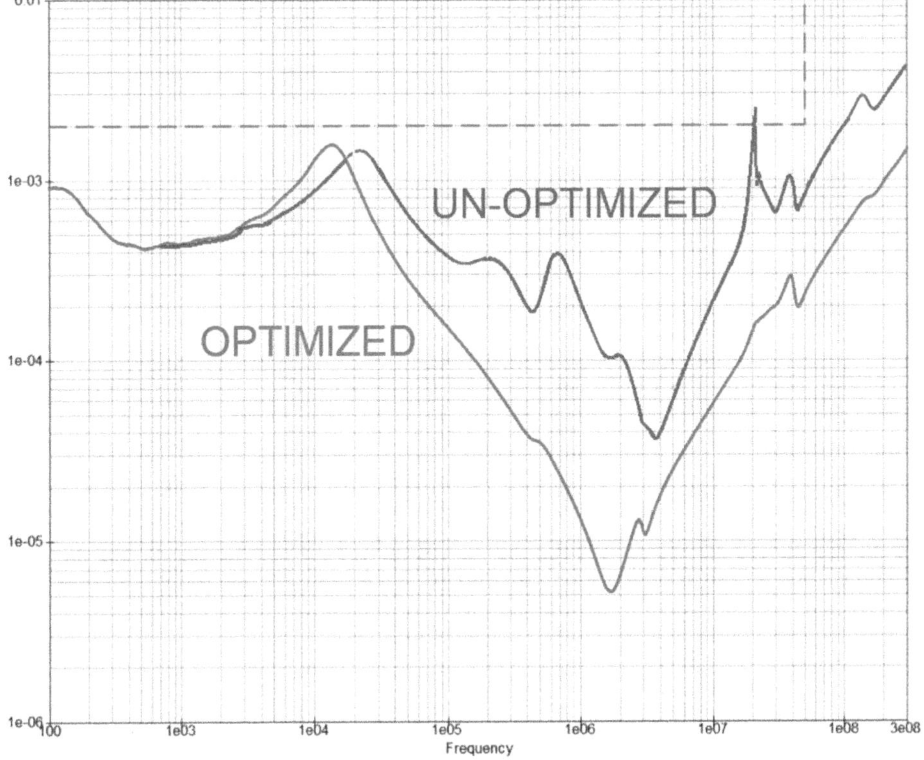

FIGURE 13.15 PDN auto-optimization in QUCS.

Name	Value
Zlow	min(Z_pdn[1])
Zhigh	(Z_pdn[1022])
Zhigh2	(Z_pdn[1021])
Zhigh_delta	Zhigh-Zhigh2
ZBOT_RANGE	Zlow*linspace(1,1,50)
ZTOP_RANGE	Zhigh+(Zhigh_delta*linspace(0,100,100))
Z_EXTENDED	[ZBOT_RANGE,Z_pdn,ZTOP_RANGE]
Z_FITTED	runavg(Z_EXTENDED,100)
Z_FITTED_lim	Z_FITTED[50:1072]
Z_dev	abs(Z_pdn)-abs(Z_FITTED)
Z_dev_rel	abs(Z_dev)/abs(Z_FITTED)
Z_dev_rel2	((Z_dev))/abs(Z_FITTED)
Z_dev_rel2_diff	diff((Z_dev_rel2+1)*acfrequency,acfrequency)-1
Z_dev_rel2_diffs	sign(Z_dev_rel2_diff*1e12)
Z_dev_rel2_diffsc	-1*((Z_dev_rel2_diffs[0:1022])-([Z_dev_rel2_diffs[0],Z_dev_rel2_diffs[0:1021]]))
int_Zdev_rel	integrate(bw_limit2*Z_dev_rel,1)
Z_dev_peaks_s	0.25*(-1*Z_dev_rel2_diffsc)*(1+sign(-1*Z_dev_rel2_diffsc))*abs(Z_dev_rel2)
Z_dev_peaks_p	0.25*(1*Z_dev_rel2_diffsc)*(1+sign(1*Z_dev_rel2_diffsc))*abs(Z_dev_rel2)
peak_all_p	((Z_dev_peaks_p)^(1))
peak_all_s	((Z_dev_peaks_s)^(1))
int_pr_pk	integrate(bw_limit2*peak_all_p,1)
int_sr_pk	integrate(bw_limit2*peak_all_s,1)
phase_all	phase(Z_pdn)
phase_all_diff	(diff((phase_all+1)*acfrequency,acfrequency,1)-1)
Q_all_p	abs(phase_all_diff*Z_dev_peaks_p)
Q_all_s	abs(phase_all_diff*Z_dev_peaks_s)
int_pr_Q	integrate(bw_limit2*Q_all_p,1)
int_sr_Q	integrate(bw_limit2*Q_all_s,1)
combined_flatness	20+log10(1/(int_Zdev_rel*int_pr_pk*int_pr_Q*int_sr_pk*int_sr_Q))

FIGURE 13.16 Flatness computations used in the example in QUCS.

be manually swapped out and re-run. The optimizer goals for a PDN design will be the pass/fail variables for Z_PDN(f)<Z_target and V_MTT<V_noise_max, the total MLCC cap quantity has to be equal to the number of power pins on the ASIC, the bulk capacitor quantity to be less than a user defined maximum, and even a flatness metric limit can be added to help with the other goals indirectly.

The template computes flatness in the following way. Flatness can be measured using several arbitrary metrics computed from the impedance profile, then combining them into a single number. A fitted impedance curve can be computed as a moving average to cut between the peaks. Then the deviation from it in relative terms is computed, and then several further variables also. It uses differential and integral calculations, signum comparator functions, computes peak heights for resonances, and sums up the peaks to create several different intermediate scores. These scores can be multiplied with each other to get a final flatness score. Figure 13.16 shows the equations used in the template.

13.6 PDN SIMULATION

13.6.1 Pre-Layout PDN Analysis

The pre-layout PDN analysis can be done either in Keysight ADS, HyperLynx LineSim, the freeware QUCS, or in other tools. We can also use Excel templates. Its main purpose is to help the hardware designer to select the right components (capacitors and VRM solutions) for the schematic design. We have to complete our complex board design schematic, with all parts on it, as good as we can make it, before moving on with layout and prototyping. The models in the pre-layout simulation circuit are pieced together in the schematic model view of the simulator, and then we run an AC analysis or an S-parameter analysis. The PDN simulation model schematic and the digital board design schematic are different things. The elements in the models are the measured VRM impedance in the form of an S-parameter file, simulated approximate power planes as S-parameter files, lumped RLC components for all decoupling capacitor types, and chip power vias as series impedance. The VRM model will be measured on a VRM eval board, re-worked to match the output caps on our design, then post-processed. The capacitor RLC parameters can be entered directly into the parts or through equations. The free QUCS PDN template seen in Figure 13.17 helps with all the model setup, plus it also does rogue waves estimation and optimization. See the download link in the Appendix.

13.6.2 Post-Layout PDN Analysis

Post-layout PDN analysis is very tool specific. It adds to the analysis the horizontal location information of the elements on the PCB. If a capacitor is closer to the ASIC pin, then its impedance V-dip is more pronounced as seen from the ASIC. Smaller capacitors that have a higher resonant frequency are more local—they are only effective right at the ASIC's power via—while very large bulk capacitors are effective even from a few inches. The effectiveness circle or effect distance depends on the capacitance and package size. A post-layout analysis can show this effect. Some tools display a circle around every capacitor. The PDN impedance profile would look slightly different at different locations on the board/plane. Multiple impedance profiles can be displayed with multiple selected locations. For example, center, corners, and half-way between.

Many years ago it was common to put decoupling capacitors on the same side of the board as the ASIC, therefore far away from the ASIC's power fanout via; this resulted in a much-decreased decoupling efficiency. These cases can be analyzed with the post-layout PDN analysis. But these days it is common practice to put the ceramic caps right under the BGA on the opposite side on the fanout via. HyperLynx, SiWave, and Sigrity have post-layout PDN simulation capabilities. They can show the PDN impedance seen from different locations as well as automatically draw effectiveness circle lines around capacitors. Some can show the noise voltage levels by location or plane waves in time domain or at specific frequency.

The pre-layout mode ignores spatial information, and it implies a uniform impedance requirement for each pin. This might be a problem if we used several different capacitor values at different pins because on a real board the ASIC will see a different impedance profile at different power pins. For example, the pins with 100nF caps will see a dip at 20MHz and high impedance elsewhere, while the pins with 1uF capacitors will see a dip at 6MHz and high impedance elsewhere. The distant capacitors will be seen from each pin as a shallow and blunt V dip. Some of the ASIC's I/O buffers or some regions of the die will be decoupled better than others, and that is a problem. The most reliable solution to this is to use the big-V method for capacitor value selection that provides uniform impedance at all of the power pins of the ASIC.

13.6.3 Post-Prototype PDN Analysis

It is a lab measurement. With this one, we measure the prototype's PDN impedance profile using a low-frequency power VNA, and compare it against the target impedance line in post-processing in a tool like ADS or QUCS. An example of a QUCS template for measurement post-processing can be seen in Figure 13.18. The measurement would be done on what we call a "power board", which is simply a prototype board with the main ASICs de-populated and the glue logic and VRMs wired to operate with the main ASICs not present. Some large chips communicate with VRMs, and they

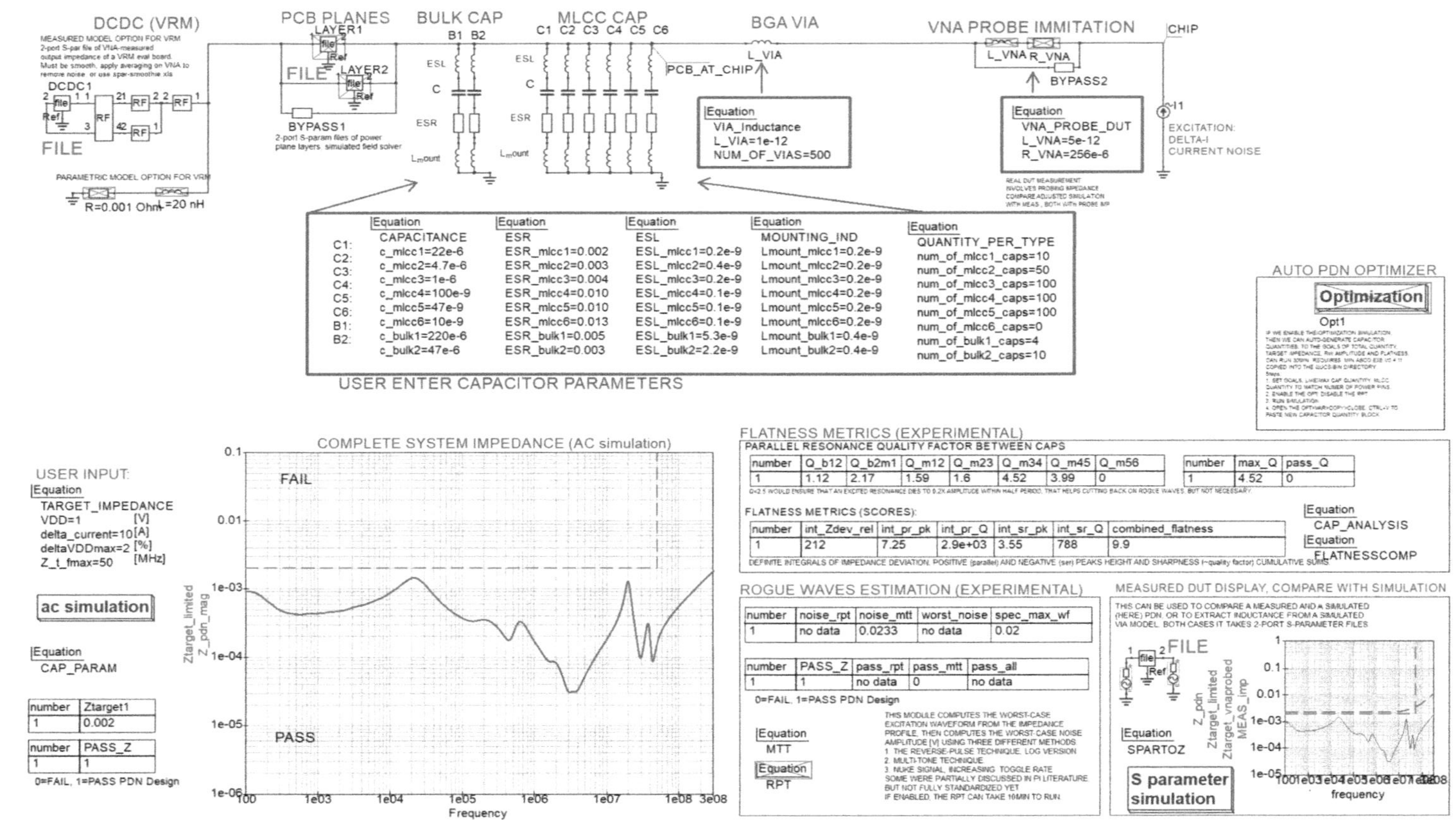

FIGURE 13.17 PDN template in QUCS.

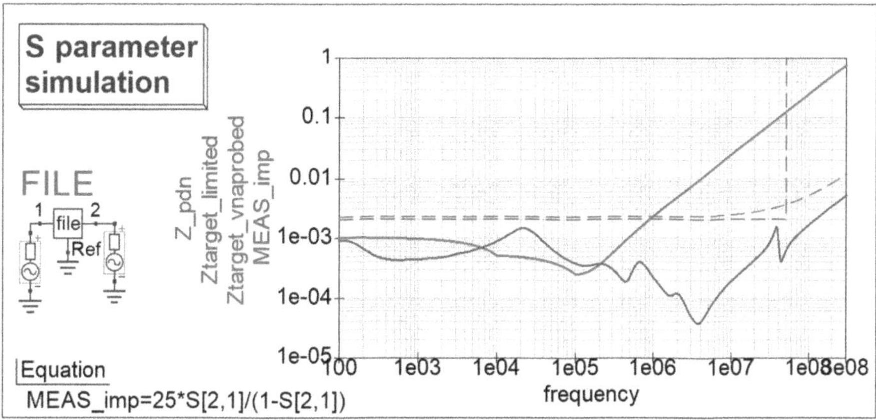

FIGURE 13.18 QUCS post-processing to display and compare measured data.

provide differential voltage sense lines. When the ASIC is not there the communication breaks unless we added debug options like catch resistors or debug mode jumpers. The use of the power board is needed to eliminate the ASIC's load current changes from interfering with the VNA measurement. The VNA sends a test signal to the board, so we do not want the ASIC to send a different signal in the same time. The measurement is described in Chapter 17, "Measurements".

13.6.4 DC Voltage Drop Analysis

We have to analyze the quality of the PCB power plane design (power delivery from source to load) in a 2D planar field solver program, using DC voltage drop or plane DCR (direct current resistance) simulation. This is a post-layout type simulation that can tell how much voltage drop we are getting through the PCB power planes while they are trying to deliver the load current from the VRM to the ASIC. Several commercial simulation tools are available and can be used easily, for example, Ansys SiWave, Siemens/Mentor HyperLynx, Keysight PathWave, Cadence Sigrity. One free tool is available called FEMM, although it is very hard to set it up and it is very time consuming. Figure 13.19 shows a plane voltage drop analysis in FEMM. The data display is in a voltage gradient color map mode with location-specific voltage, and it also shows the current flow directions with little arrows. A small window shows a line-integral as a single number voltage drop. Often, we deliver power to an ASIC through multiple layers, so it is best to use a simulator that automatically simulates all involved layers and vias together. FEMM cannot do that, but the mentioned commercial tools can. For debugging power plane designs, these tools can also display current density, so the designers can widen the plane shapes at the high current density areas to reduce voltage drop.

The big ASIC chips are usually supplied by VRMs that have remote voltage sense lines, so the voltage drop does not materialize at the load, but it can still cause issues with the control loop and power loss, so we still have to minimize it reasonably. On a 1V rail with 100A load current, typical ASIC datasheets call for 1% voltage tolerance. A 0.25 milli Ohm power plane causes 25mV drop that is 2.5%, or 2.5 times over the limit of what a chip could tolerate, but it is okay because with the remote sense feature it is reduced to zero at the load. Instead, the VRM control loop has to deal with the drop. As the load current changes (load step or load dump), the voltage drop changes. A load dump from 100A to 50A will cause the voltage drop to change from 25mV to 12.5mV. Before the drop the VRM outputs 1.025V, but after the load dump it now has to output only 1.0125V to maintain the 1V at the load. Basically, the VRM has to now output 12.5mV lower voltage than before. This simple formula applies:

```
V_load=V_source-V_drop
```

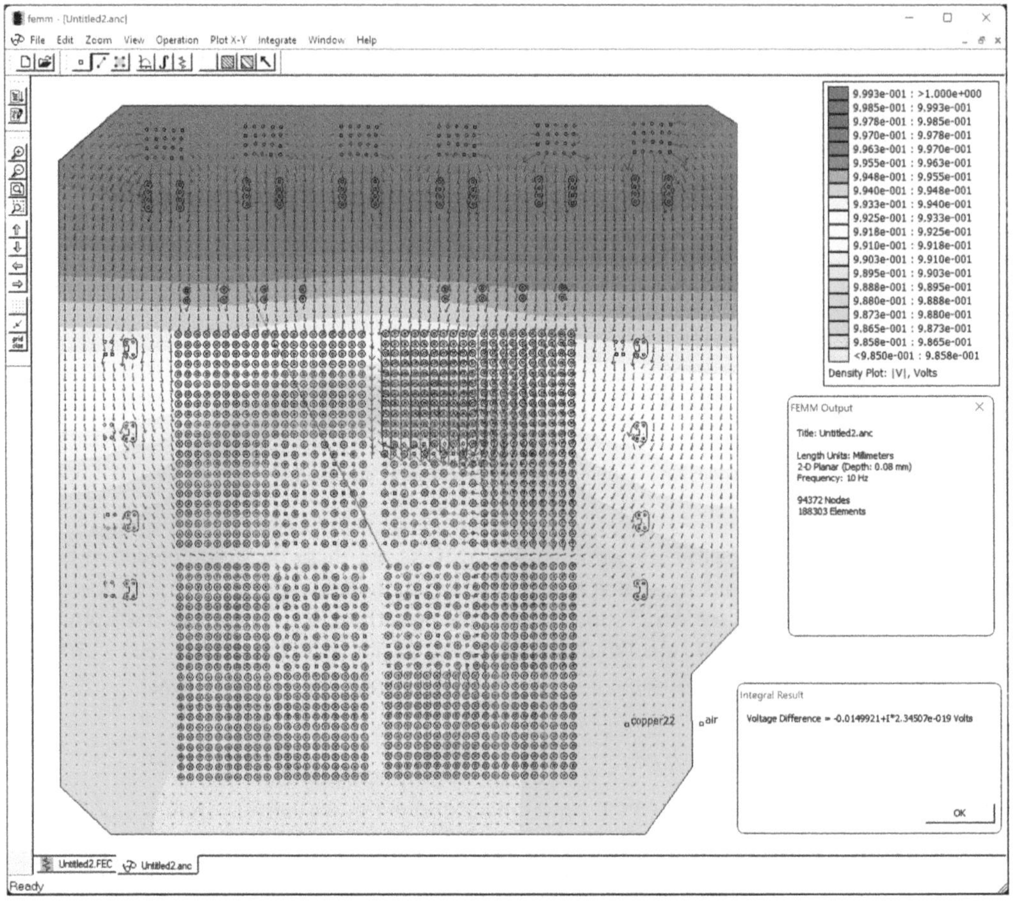

FIGURE 13.19 Voltage drop analysis in FEMM with a 100A load (sketch design).

As fast as the load current changes, the VRM has to change its output voltage too, as seen at the output inductor. VRM control loops are not perfect, they operate better when not stressed so much, which requires us to reduce the voltage drop (through reducing the plane resistance in layout design) to about two to five times the ASIC's tolerance. So ASIC core VRMs are not designed to hold a constant voltage on their outputs, but rather to hold a constant voltage at the load and respond quickly to transients. For this reason, the output inductor values on high-current cores are selected to allow a very high ripple current ratio. The holding of a voltage is required at the ASIC pins, so that is where the large bulk capacitance needs to be placed around the ASIC package. Rails with remote sense are more sensitive to the drop effect between the bulk capacitors and the ASIC power pins, although a fast (>100kHz) VRM control loop can still eliminate most of the DC voltage drop seen by the ASIC power pins. Smaller voltage rails usually exclude a remote voltage sense, so we simulate the VRM to ASIC drop to see whether they violate the ASIC's voltage tolerance. For remote-sensed rails having slower loops we would run two simulations: one from the VRM (source) to the ASIC (load) pins to see that we meet the 5x tolerance requirement for not stressing the control loop and then another one will be run from the bulk capacitors (source) to the ASIC pins to see if that is well within the ASICs tolerance, which will experience a temporary voltage drop during fast transients only. This drop can appear on the plane segment for a short amount of time until the VRM control loop reacts to the transient. The ASIC will see the full voltage drop if the VRMs does not have remote sense, it will see a temporary drop between the bulk caps and the ASIC if the VRM has remote sense but a slow loop, and it will see no drop if the VRM has remote sense and a fast loop. The VRM or the bulk cap will be the voltage source in the simulation, while all the ASIC power pins together will be one single current source having a negative value.

13.6.5 PDN-Related Simulators

We can do our pre-layout PDN analysis and capacitor selection while designing the schematic of our board using Keysight ADS, the freeware QUCS, HyperLynx LineSim, or the free Altera PDN Tool (excel calculator). Most of these support S-parameter models for VRMs and planes. We can verify our PDN solution at the post-layout stage to see how the placement of the components and the variation of the values affect the pre-layout PDN design. This can be done in commercial software like HyperLynx BoardSim and Cadence Sigrity. The Ansys SiWave can visualize time domain plane waves and find resonant frequencies. They all come out with new features on a regular basis. We can analyze DC voltage drop with HyperLynx BoardSim, Ansys SiWave, Cadence Sigrity, or the freeware FEMM. FEMM is very hard to use for plane simulations, but it is free. We can create an approximate power plane drawing or a power-via parasitic inductance model, then extract a S-parameter models that we can import into our pre-layout PDN analysis by doing the electromagnetic extraction in Ansys SiWave, in HyperLynx BoardSim, or in Sonnet Lite. This list is not comprehensive.

14 Initial Design

Before we go ahead to design the PCB layout, we have to perform initial hardware design tasks. This includes all the analysis, decisions, and documents produced for creating the system architecture and the board schematics. This is taken later into the physical implementation of the PCB layout and mechanical designs. Hardware designs are done differently by different companies and different individuals. The concept of "one guy one board" is workable even on the most complex designs, but only by very capable designers, usually self-activated type personalities. Some companies divide every board design between several designers or develop it in the "one team one board" approach, with one of the designers being the lead designer while all other members are responsible only for a well-defined hardware block, plus participate in debugging all blocks together. In all cases there is a wider R&D team assembled for every project, including cross-functional engineering disciplines like software, FPGA, mechanical systems, and power supply engineers. The hardware engineer(s) from the hardware team is assigned as a member of the project team. Some designers need a mentor, who is another designer at the company who can help answer questions and provide regular course corrections. Others do not need a mentor and are self-taught through the process of "individual research". This means figuring out what problems are there, figuring out what causes them, and determining what is the best approach to solving them, from literature, intuition, experience, and experimentation. Master's programs at universities require students to practice this method of engineering, which is more scientific than trade-like. In the "one guy one board" approach that one person has to figure out what needs to be done, including all activities, materials, tools, and arrangements required, and do it all until its done. In the team approach, the lead designer has to figure those things out and guide the other team members to implement it.

The hardware development process starts with a design requirement or a project proposal; it depends on the company which comes first. The proposal, written by the hardware engineer, describes what features the product will have and what challenges it will take to develop it. In a larger system with multiple boards the hardware engineer might write a small portion of the system proposal that belongs to the particular board. Then a design plan is written by the hardware engineer with many more details, while also performing trade studies and different kinds of analysis. A trade study, trade-off study, trade analysis, or feasibility study is the investigation of options and consequences in a written form for any major design decision or functional module. It can be a document or a chapter in a document. After this the hardware engineer designs the schematics drawings and defines the layout constraints. Then the layout engineer designs the layout with supervision and regular review by the hardware engineer. At small companies it is common that the hardware engineer is also the layout and the FPGA engineer as well. More analysis can be performed post-layout, then the prototypes are ordered, and again the hardware engineer performs the board bring-up together with software and FPGA engineers. There are several smaller steps that are not mentioned here but will be described in detail in this book.

14.1 PREPARATIONS

We have to create block diagrams, write a feasibility study (project proposal) and later a design plan (hardware design specification) before the schematic design can start. A proposal or feasibility study lists the proposed features, expected performance, design challenges, their proposed solutions, consequences of choosing particular options, costs and risks, and detailed project schedule. One might assume that we can come up with any type of system architecture concept and then "someone" will work out the details later. The problem is that some architecture concepts are not feasible, they will

DOI: 10.1201/9781032702094-14

never work, no matter how we want to tweak the details later after we have already driven our whole team into a corner with a bad concept. It is not one detail that is feasible or not; rather it is a set of features together in the same confined space that are feasible or not. Feasibility studies investigate this before it is too late. An architecture might not be feasible due to signal integrity, component limitations, board area fit, or any other unexpected detail. The study might include a decision tree flow chart. PCB materials and board dimensions have to be chosen before or during the feasibility study, as it affects the longest signal traces, which are limited by signal integrity (insertion loss budget).

A design plan simply captures all main chip selections and more details than the feasibility study will, for example, it contains subsystem diagrams and supporting chip selections as well as connector pinouts. Both the proposal and the plan with all details have to be reviewed by hardware peers, management, software engineers, FPGA/ASIC, and systems engineers. There will be peer and cross-functional reviews at several stages of a project, which is to reduce risk, ensure meeting the original goals, and assure design quality and reliability. The actual names of the documents and the activities listed in them have different names at different companies. Although in the data center hardware business the project proposal and the hardware specification are common naming conventions.

In high performance high-tech teams, the whole product development cycle is iterative with multiple feedback loops between different parallel processes, rather than being strictly sequential filling out the gaps months after decisions have been made. A (good quality) design is a discovery process, not just a simple implementation of orders. For example, we re-draw block diagrams a dozen times before finishing the design, not just before starting it. Still there is a logical time sequence to it, but expect several re-draws. These re-dos or re-draws are not failures of the project; rather they are a way of optimizing to get the best possible product at the end. A project is constantly optimized towards its completion. At each stage of a project, we just need to have "enough confidence" to move forward, rather than having everything exactly defined. Otherwise the project could take several times longer to complete, and we would not be satisfied with the end results. We have to do analysis at each stage to have the most optimal plans and parameters at that stage; however, a small percentage of it will still change later. The point is to make a move when reaching the point of diminishing returns of such an analysis. This requires common sense, talent, expertise, and experience with relevant technologies to execute a project this way. It will just not happen that halfway into the project we have to replace our two FPGAs with a CPU, but likely we might have to swap out our 2Gbit DRAM chips with 4Gbit DRAM on proto2, or we have to add an extra EEPROM or a connector when we have almost finished the schematic.

In government contracting, such as military and NASA projects, the main project stages are named after the gating reviews rather than the documents capturing the information. A "Basis of Estimate" (BOE) contains material and labor cost estimations as well as the technical documentation that this book describes as the proposal. A Preliminary Design Review (PDR) is an official milestone meeting/document to assess the program's readiness to proceed into detailed design, basically our design plan. A Critical Design Review (CDR) is another milestone to assess a program's readiness to proceed into manufacturing and system integration, basically reviewing the design files and drawings as well as calculations and more diagrams. These are required for all defense acquisition programs. Their purpose is to provide accountability and to authorize the release of funding. These stages demand more finalized parameters at intermediate review stages than the high-tech industry does. There are several other gating stages also, which mostly apply to the system level (like a complete aircraft) but their derivatives or a subset are also applied to subsystems and individual boards. Also the projects are called programs. Medical device projects also have a requirement for gating reviews and official documentation as set by the US Food and Drug Administration (FDA).

14.1.1 The Proposal

Before writing the proposal, the hardware engineer has to receive some kind of formal requirements list or a needs description from management, systems engineering, or marketing, depending on company and industry. In government contracting it is a long detailed list. This list has to be well developed, but it will never be complete until the design is done due to the iterative nature of the development process. A set of requirements is turned into an architecture concept by making dozens of choices. The elements in the architecture can have an effect on the other element selections through unintended effects and device limitations; thermal, electrical, mechanical, or supply chain effects; and support software or firmware development needs.

For example, if we choose the main ASIC from one vendor, we might need to develop some extra software, as compared to working with the other vendor's similar ASIC that comes with complete software libraries. In another made-up case our requirements call for having 20 lanes of 112Gig external I/O, having an accelerator ASIC with 10 lanes of 56Gig, and the main ASIC must support an internal feature XYZ. It might turn out that our main ASIC has only 24 lanes of SERDES. Then we will have to settle for 14 instead of 20 external I/Os, drop the accelerator, hook up the accelerator with half bandwidth, or use a different main ASIC that does not have feature XYZ but has 32 lanes of SERDES. These options have to be presented in the proposal, or we need to pick the most likely one and work it out in detail with diagrams. As we discover these cross-element effects, we have to make alterations to the architecture concept and re-check for more cross-element effects. This creates an iteration of the concept every time. The last iteration will be when we do not discover any deal breaker effects even after due diligence.

The first thing in writing up a project proposal for a board/chassis hardware project is to determine what will be on the data plane and how the main ASICs and boards will be connected. This includes drawing a data plane block diagram, selecting the main chips based on I/O bandwidth, and processing performance requirements using the latest ASICs. For example, if one FPGA can do 120GBytes/s of data processing, and our product requires 300GBytes/s, then we need 300/120=2.5 FPGAs, or round up to → 3 FPGAs in the chassis. We can design a big board with three FPGAs and I/O ASICs or design a base board with the ASICs and three identical FPGA cards will be plugged into it. This is the system partitioning, where the cross-functional team needs to find all meaningful and feasible options, make block diagrams and floorplans, and analyze them to select the best partition. When moving blocks from one board to another, in each iteration we have to verify several aspects on every board of the system. These are the component density, floorplan, power budgets, loss budgets, and connector signal counts. If any of the checks fail, that means the particular proposed architecture is not feasible and we have to change and re-check it until we get a feasible one. The hardware engineer can write up a few different options each with diagrams, so the team can debate them and choose. The best one is the one that is feasible for SI and thermal and has good marketable feature set and performance at a lower cost. This is a heuristic creative process, and it involves frequent discussions with management (sometimes top executives), marketing, mechanical and systems engineering, and FPGA/ASIC engineering.

In the official proposal we need to document all reasonable options, feasibility studies, and tradeoffs, explained with cost (layer count, materials, main parts, and extra components), performance, and risk of each solution. Part of the feasibility study for high-speed complex digital boards is the loss budget calculation and the floorplan analysis as well as the collection of component-driven manufacturing constraints that will be needed. For multi-board systems we have to check if the chosen connectors can provide a sufficient number of connections, if not then we need to change connectors or the board shapes/sizes might have to change or we might have to move main ASICs from one board to another to ease the connectivity requirement. Connectors have a bandwidth bottleneck, which does not exist on same-board interconnects. We might have to move ASICs between boards also when the board density will be too high or the high-speed via fanout design is compromised by using smaller size and finer pitch components. A floorplan analysis is important, not only for the physical fit in a given board size, but also to determine high-speed SERDES link PCB routing length/reach, which we need to use in a loss budget calculation. Similarly, we need routing length/reach information for timing analysis calculations on parallel buses. The loss budget reveals if the concept is feasible or if we have to change PCB materials, add retimer chips, reduce data rate, or completely change the architecture to reduce routing lengths. We might have to move ASICs from one board to another, which would reduce the routing length of a high-speed link at the expense of increasing the routing length of slower interfaces. We might have to redo all details and diagrams several times until we iterate to achieve a good solution that satisfies all seemingly conflicting requirements. These checks cannot wait until the detailed design phase; at that late stage we will not be able to make architectural changes. So the hardware architecture is checked against signal integrity; it is a two-way street until all sides are feasible and worth doing. SI is not some detail that is taken care of later, SI approval is needed for the architecture.

If we go into a lot more detail than traditionally considered, then we can avoid a situation later down the road where we have to make costly alterations to the system architecture to resolve contradictions. Some teams have panic meetings in a late stage, others do not. It looks like we are skipping ahead into the detailed design, but it is orders of magnitude less labor than the actual detailed design plan, although it takes some effort. Contradictions in the requirements cannot always be discovered simply by looking at a list of features; rather, they can be found by building a detailed concept. We could call this an "architecture simulation" (architecture study or an extremely detailed proposal), a kind of complex thought experiment. In this concept we propose details and, by reasoning, we find out how they fit with all the other details proposed. We usually end up re-drawing complete (not partial) block diagrams several times. For example: If they want four FPGAs, it is fine; if they want 32GB RAM for each, it is also fine; but if they also want it in X form factor, that could pose a problem. Let's make a floorplan, fit all that in, then we might find we can fit only three FPGAs with 32GB RAM or four FPGAs with 8GB RAM. Normally there are more than a dozen parameters to fit together, not just these two as in this example. There might be a certain interface type requiring eight PHY chips, but if we can settle on another interface type, then we could do it without the eight PHY chips, which is an obvious difference in board space and fit. Or if we can use a different input voltage range, then we could use a different VRM, that might have a feature (like telemetry, auto restart, or better efficiency), which is not available on the wider input range devices. We will not find that out from an Excel sheet. The level of detail we need for the architecture simulation, are detailed subsystem block diagrams, main and supporting device selection, device datasheets, power budget, signal count budget for connectors, FPGA utilization from IP cores, PCB floorplans, and SI feasibility. We have to check with each chip datasheet for which the connections we want in our block diagram are actually supported (e.g., 40G XLPPI instead of 40G XLAUI) or what limitations they have.

In a more convoluted and made-up example, we find two ASIC devices from two different vendors for our on-board data plane logic, from vendor-1 (V1) and vendor-2 (V2). In both cases the same control plane CPU can be used. V1 supports feature-A, but requires an additional off-loading ASIC for feature-B. V2 supports both feature-A and feature-B without extra ASICs (cost, board size, and power), but it has a bandwidth bottleneck when all ports are utilized. If our system never produces data on all ports in the same time, then this limitation is okay, but if our system sends critical data at full bandwidth on all ports in the same time, then we cannot use the ASIC from V2. Further, if the off-loading ASIC needed by the V1 main ASIC requires an unusual memory chip that is obsolete, then we are back to V2, and we have to have two of their ASICs to make up for the bottleneck and find a way to fit it into the board space. Further, if V2 can be cascaded only with a special firmware that was never released nor planned to be, then we are back to V1 and we have to add an FPGA that transforms a conventional DRAM into appearing as the special memory chip needed by V1 that was obsolete. Further, if the memory simulator logic for the extra FPGA would have too much latency for our software architecture, then we are back to V2, and we have to use a switch ASIC to cascade two of those V2 ASICs. This already needs a lot more board space for the three main chips than we thought we needed with only one ASIC from our initial block diagram. Further, it turns out that the only switch ASIC that supports the port type needed for cascading two V2 ASICs is huge and will increase our product cost and double its power dissipation, so we are back to V1. We have to drop the external memory buffer of the off-loading ASIC that is hanging off the V1 ASIC and use it with internal buffering only, but it turns out marketing did not really need that much buffering for this product, so we have a solution with a vendor-1 ASIC and one small off-loading ASIC at a reasonable size/power/price. This is all illustrated in Figure 14.1. We have to work out the concept in as much detail as possible to ensure that if there are any showstoppers then we will find them early. In the example, we were unlucky enough to run into several of these showstoppers, and then we had to go back to the drawing board to create a modified or new concept, and then worked out the details again. We need to keep doing this until we reach a solution that does not present any showstopper problems when we already worked out enough detail. We only find them out if we are making a sufficiently detailed concept or an architecture simulation at the beginning of the project. This is not how everyone develops hardware, but it definitely results in more successful projects.

In another made-up example we might have SI challenges conflicting with architecture. Let's say our block diagram calls for an ATCA processing blade with eight FPGAs and a PCIe switch ASIC to hook the 32Gig PCIe links up with the backplane. After preparing a floorplan, we find out that we cannot fit eight FPGAs on the board in the 1mm pitch package, only six of them, or we could fit eight of them in a 0.7mm pitch BGA package. If we analyze the manufacturing constraints together with the 0.7mm pitch, we find out the backdrilling would not be possible. Now we have two choices, eight small-package FPGAs and via stubs failing the PCI-SIG return loss limits or six regular-package FPGAs without via stubs and open eyes on a reliable product. If six are not enough to achieve a competitive system performance, then we might have to look into other solutions. For example, we could put six of them on the ATCA blade and two more on a big RTM card, which requires making our chassis four inches deeper. Or we could implement the same processing algorithm on two network processors plus two accelerator FPGAs that fit on the fixed board size, but it requires a software team to write most of the algorithm in multi-core software, instead of an FPGA team to write it in Verilog code. What each team can implement in reasonable time has to be determined by talking to them. The trade-offs can span across board layout, manufacturing, signal integrity, software and FPGA coding, and project team resource management.

A symmetrical split can be applied to a design concept, which would facilitate RnD and manufacturing cost reductions. If we have created a data plane block diagram that looks very arbitrary, we can make it more symmetrical by applying more resources, then we can split it to two or more identical cheaper boards. When two boards are identical, then we need to design and bring up only one, and we need to have only one in production at double quantity. Higher quantity has a lower cost per unit, and also helps us finding low probability intermittent failures. For example, if we need to have a medium and a larger FPGA, we could instead have two larger FPGAs and use them as single-FPGA plug-in or mezzanine cards, instead of designing-in the two different ones on the motherboard or having to design two different plug-in cards. Sometimes the extra cost will be very little and it produces the return on investment through development cost reduction. In another example we might have four FPGA boards, each with an ARM processor to manage them. Instead, we could

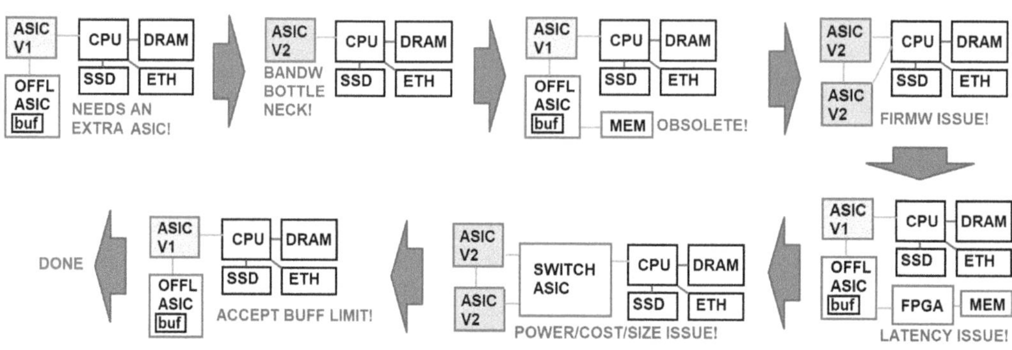

FIGURE 14.1 An example project architecture study.

have four FPGA cards without any ARM processors and have one card with the ARM processor only, managing the four FPGA cards. This results in the overall complexity of each FPGA card to be reduced; therefore, its cost will be reduced and yield will be increased. Or the other way around, if we need three FPGA cards with ARM processors and one without, then we just create one design with ARM processor included that will be held in reset on the last card. Sometimes we add complexity to a system or a board design, at other times we reduce the complexity to improve cost, yield, performance, and reliability. Cost comes as R&D cost for each board as well as manufacturing cost and BOM cost for each board and BOM cost for the whole system. Manufacturing cost includes NRE (non-recurring engineering) and per-unit cost as well as yield expectations.

Sometimes management or marketing demands an early official response from engineering about agreeing to a requirements list, and then they want to force engineering to implement it, no matter how costly it is to resolve the contradictions in it later. Having a "must have" and a "nice to have" feature requirement list is the simplest way to relax this constraint. Something called Royce's waterfall model was used by corporate management to divide R&D cycles between different departments and linear timelines. Contrary to that model, a really good design (better, faster, cheaper, and more reliable) is created when the different project phases overlap and have recursive feedback loops. For example, through having an architecture simulation early on, then closing in on the features, then start the detailed design, then do a smaller architecture simulation in parallel, then re-align the design, then finish the design. If we have to follow the waterfall model, then we can still start the next few tasks early, not waiting for the gating phases. Expert designers conduct problem framing and problem solving simultaneously so as to derive a "good" solution, rather than trying to just fulfill speculative assumptions as they are.

Just to recap, these items typically go into a proposal: the architecture of data, control, management planes, main devices, functional description, features, PCB floorplan, loss budget, SI challenges, pre-layout simulation, main port mappings, external ports, device limitations, thermal challenges, cost, and schedule.

14.1.2 The Plan

Once the proposal is discussed, altered several times, and finally accepted, the project is given a green light. Now we have to look into more details by filling in the gaps in the proposal. By expanding on the proposal with much more detail, we can write the design plan, preliminary design, or hardware design specification document, most often called the "Hardware Spec". We need to get the content of the document officially reviewed by peers, cross-functional team members, and management before the schematics design. At this point we have to create separate detailed exact block diagrams for all the different subsystems and functions. These include the control plane, power delivery map, clocking tree, power management logic diagram, management subsystem, thermal control, JTAG ports, I/O bank mapping, floorplans, all I2C bus maps, and all buses and device address tables. These diagrams have to contain exact information, based on the needs of the main ASICs. For example, what supply voltages each ASIC needs and the amount of current in each rail. These diagrams have to contain exact part numbers of supporting components, marking their port numbers and other details. Management processors and IPMI solutions have to be selected. If it is a system product, then every board in it needs to have the diagrams, port and GPIO tables, floorplan, and all details. To recap, first (at the proposal) we select the main data plane ASICs, then the main control plane devices, then (at the detailed plan) the supporting circuit chips for each data/control plane device, as well as their connections and parameters.

The feasibility study from the proposal is expanding at this stage to more detail and more areas of the system to study. From I/O bank assignments we go to detailed pin assignments, from number of connector pins to exact pinouts. We have to check what it looks like, and what further conflicts might arise when we have implemented all the required features and those that are nice to have. For example, if a feature that is nice to have requires adding another main ASIC for little benefit, then we may reconsider having that feature. During the proposal and the architecture simulation we should have discovered any conflicts of the data plane devices. At the detailed plan we will discover similar issues in the control, management planes, and finer details, sometimes even further conflicts on the data plane. We will probably discover that some required features would limit the implementation of other required features, and then we have to choose which is more important. For example, if we need a 2GHz processor, but we also need to operate up to 85C, it might not be possible, one of those two might need to be reduced to a 1.5GHz processor or to a 75C temperature range. In some cases, fitting one more main ASIC into a fixed board size might require us to use the smaller package option with finer pitch, which would, in turn, require smaller drill sizes and clearances that would force us to have a lower production yield or find new suppliers. We cannot leave that to the end of the layout design. Ideally we will discover it at the proposal stage or at least at the detailed planning stage.

Components have to be selected with consideration given as to availability. If the part was released several years ago (see date on datasheet or website), then it may be soon obsolete. If it is too new, it may take too long time to receive production chips. Also, there might be a shortage, long lead times, or too high minimum order quantities. Small chips can be checked for availability in online shops like Digikey and Mouser. If they are in stock there, then they can be purchased anywhere anytime and are safe to design-in. Main ASICs are not purchased in online shops; they are likely based on contract price from chip vendors or main distributors. Some ASICs are available to us under a contract price if a previous project has made the arrangement. This can be less than half the price compared to an off-market random part number. If our design needs eight ports, and the ASIC variants have either eight or 10, then we might conclude to use the one with eight as we can save a few dollars, but if the device with 10 ports is in a contract price arrangement, then we will save more than a few dollars and get free extra features.

The checklist for what to put into the design plan or hardware spec or into separate documents at the design planning stage:

- Description of main functionality and features of the board.
- Description of the chassis/system the board is going into.
- Main devices selection, features, performance, limitations, price.
- Block diagrams for all subsystems, including data plane, control plane, power tree, resets, clock tree, I2C, JTAG, MDIO, SPI, or at least one main combined diagram.
- Power rail spreadsheet and current/power calculations.
- FPGA power consumption and preliminary fit reports.
- System initialization sequence at power-up.
- Programming sequence of devices for production.
- Port and I/O-bank mapping tables of chips and connectors.
- Non-plug-and-play device access table, with bus/port numbers and device addresses.
- Glue logic and system manager features, signals, diagrams.
- Glue logic FPGA/CPLD programmable register descriptions.
- Software customization requirements, drivers, and settings.
- A table of differences from the main ASIC reference design, for the BIOS/OS driver customization needs.
- Power sequence requirements of devices and whole board.
- PCB floorplan analysis and flowplan.
- All SI work already done and planned to be done.
- May include VRM auto-generated circuits with part values.
- Loss budget calculation of SERDES links.
- Mechanical construction.
- Thermal analysis results.
- Stackup sketch.
- PCB manufacturability concerns or any leading-edge constraints.

14.1.3 Component Selection

First at the proposal stage we have to select the main parts, FPGAs, processors, ASICs, based on features, performance, and functionality that are specific to a project. Typically, we look for the newest devices (for years of availability and competitive performance), then we select based on performance, speed, power, price, and features. The block diagram we made for the data plane has connection lines marking various interfaces, the parts we select have to have interface ports supporting those types of interfaces, speed and number of links/lanes, which can be seen on chip product briefs and datasheets. The device core performance requirement (compute power or data flow bandwidth) has to be estimated with software and FPGA engineering. Then we select a device that can deliver that performance and some extra, if possible. To accurately assess the performance capability, as well as the supporting circuit needs, we have to actually read the full datasheets and design guides for all main chips before the schematic design starts. It is best to write notes about any important details or unusual requirements the main devices have. Some datasheets are behind secure access, so we have to have the accounts and FAE contacts lined up when the project starts. After the main block diagrams and main/supporting parts selection are agreed, we also have to request library parts from the CAD librarian department, so when we start the design the library parts will already exist and not cause delay.

Package sizes and pin pitch are important considerations for component selection. BGAs with less than 0.8mm pitch definitely require microvia and multi-lam PCB fabrication. For them, via impedance control is usually not achievable, the crosstalk is too high, due to the microvia structure (set of vias and dog-bone traces on each layer) being too big. BGAs between 0.8mm and 0.99mm pitch will likely conflict with drill, pad, and backdrill related manufacturability constraints and end up with layout solutions having bad signal integrity. The layout engineers will be pushed to cancel backdrilling to fit the diffpair escape routes, or split the diffpairs into adjacent columns, or use microvias that create a whole other set of problems. All of which are not suitable at 8Gbps or above, making the design fail standard S-par limit lines and be unreliable. With microvias the whole 3D via structure is larger than the through drilled one, and it often overlaps with adjacent diffpairs and cannot achieve acceptable via impedance and crosstalk control. If we can, then we should use 1mm pitch regular grid or 0.9mm row pitch (1mm diagonal) offset grid (hex) BGA packages and make the sacrifice with larger chips affecting floorplan and architecture. It is worth sticking to the 1mm BGAs for the SI benefit, even if we have to use larger boards or more slots in the chassis. Vias are not some detail for the layout engineer to take care of later—the main part selections must depend on them. This applies only to ASICs carrying >8Gig SERDES signals due to backdrilling clearances, while chips without SERDES links like memory or glue logic chips are fine with 0.8mm pitch. Below 0.8mm definitely microvias are required. If a single chip on the board requires microvia stacks, then the whole board becomes a microvia board, but whether it is worth it should be considered. Dual-row QFN chips cannot be inspected visually for the inner row pin soldering quality (open or short), while all QFNs are prone to opens and cold solder. This means we should use only dual-row QFN chips as a last resort or use them on small-size board form factors where the temperature distribution during reflow is more uniform.

Device pinouts are another important consideration. Some chips do not have sufficient ground pins forming GSSG patterns on their SERDES signals, and therefore the package itself poses a large discontinuity, eating away too much of the return loss budget needlessly. Some chips provide more ground via fencing between SERDES diffpair pins than other devices—the more the better. See Chapter 15, "PCB Layout Design", specifically the section about high-speed via design. If we can find an alternative device from another vendor that has better ground pin arrangements, it is better to choose that part.

14.1.3.1 Processor Selection

We do not want to put down a 200W server processor when a 25W mobile processor will do. How the software team estimates it is up to them, but they will likely build and run a skeleton software package on a different computer or evaluation board, or simply rely on a recent project and extrapolate the numbers inherited from it. For example, if our processor had to compute 2M pixels at 60Hz rate on the previous product and it took 50% (or ½) CPU load on a dual-core 15W processor, but now we need three displays at the same rate, then we will likely need a hex or octal core variant processor with 3/2 times higher power or benchmark rating plus 20% to 100% margin. So an eight core 60W processor will possibly be suitable. Processors also have the interfaces, pinouts, and packages that were mentioned earlier that have to be considered. Most larger processors have only a one- or two-year production schedule, while the ones in embedded programs can have five or ten. We have to check the number of years we will manufacture our new design. For smaller processors we have to check software package availability and the estimated software engineering resources that are needed.

14.1.3.2 ASIC Selection

This is done based on the ASIC vendor's roadmap, and on our project's required I/O count and speed and core bandwidth. Based on our planned product launch, and the ASIC vendor's planned launch date in their roadmap, we can choose the most modern device available. Newer devices usually dissipate much lower number of Watts per Gbps, so to remain competitive we have to choose the newest devices possible. After the ASIC selection we have to check any blocking limitations, for example if an ASIC has 100 lanes of 100Gig, that will mean 10Tbps bandwidth, but if the core is only capable of processing 8Tbps simultaneously, it's a blocking limitation, we just need to point that out in our proposal. Unless we are planning on not hooking up all lanes, or we don't expect data on all ports in the same time. The SERDES lanes are organized into tiles or "cores", with five to 16 lanes in each. After a device is selected, we need to do a SERDES tile assignment to see if the I/O needs are really met because we cannot have a half a tile running at a different line rate than the other half of it. Also, sometimes network switch ASICs are partitioned into two to eight parts (quadrants, slices, etc.) that each have a core bandwidth limitation below the total I/O lane bandwidth, so our assignment has to distribute different speed lanes around the device to mitigate and balance that.

14.1.3.3 FPGA Device Selection

Some designs are price sensitive where we have to choose the part that is a bit less performing than we wanted but much cheaper. Other designs have a fixed performance requirement, so we have to pick the device that can deliver that and later try to negotiate a contract price.

The main aspects for FPGA selection are I/O pins (speed, voltage, drive strength, ODT, number of pins of certain types available), SERDES tiles (maximum speed, number of lanes), any hard-IP needs (number of ARM processors, PCIe endpoints), and logic resources. For glue logic FPGAs the number of 3.3V capable pins are important. We might need one 3.3V I/O pin for every 10 to 50 components on the board. From our data plane block diagram in the proposal, we can determine the I/O and SERDES lane type and count requirements. We can also calculate the data bandwidth from the I/O speed that might have to also go through other interfaces like memory buffers. From reading IP core datasheets, or even better from doing a skeleton project compilation (only include re-used IP cores) we can determine the number of "logic cells" required for the project, add 50% to 100% on top of that and look for a device with that much logic cells or flip-flops of "gates". FPGAs have two types of I/O pins: the regular I/Os, which can do single-ended or differential signaling usually up to 200 to 1000MHz and SERDES pins, which are for multi-gig serial differential standards like PCIe or KR Ethernet. The SERDES lanes are organized into tiles or "cores" with five to 16 lanes in each. The advertised maximum speed is often not met on all the package types and speed grades, so we have to check the datasheet for these limitations.

After a device is selected, we need to do an I/O bank and SERDES tile assignment to see if the I/O needs are really met because we cannot have a half an I/O bank powered from one voltage rail and the other half from another, and sometimes other parameters like drive current capability or terminations are available only in a few banks. We have to count the number of signals of each type we want to put into each bank to see if that fits. Then we need to put this bank and tile assignment into the floorplan and see if we can still route the board without main bus crossings. If any of these checks fail, then we might have to select a different FPGA device. Before the board schematic design starts, we need to do a first-level pin assignment validation by using the FPGA tool GUI and assigning the pins there. When we are doing the detailed pin assignment and skeleton code compilation, this is the last chance to swap out the FPGA device to a different one if needed.

14.1.3.4 Supporting Device Selection

VRM selection is based on the main ASIC datasheet power rails and load currents. We write down the ASIC's needs into the board power budget calculator. We can go online to known VRM chip vendor websites to select a suitable device. Each different voltage or different type of rail below 3.3V needs a separate point-of-load VRM. Each main ASIC needs its own set of VRM chips—even for the same ASIC and same voltage we might need separate VRMs. For example, the 1.8V I/O bank voltage is separate from the 1.8V PLL voltage, but all 1V digital core related power pin groups (VCCINT, VCCBRAM, etc.) can be combined sourced from one VRM. We can also combine multiple devices on higher voltage rails like 3.3V or above if it does not interfere with power sequencing requirements. If it does, then we can add power switches to create separate 3.3V rails. SERDES blocks of the ASICs usually require two to four separate VRMs.

We select the VRM devices for the identified separate rails by voltage, load current, use, and features. The voltage and the load current are listed on the ASIC datasheet. We pick a VRM that can deliver 1.2 to 3.0 times as much current as the rail needs. The VRM has to be able to operate from a narrow range of the intended input voltage, about +/-20%, to maintain load transient response stability—usually 12V. We have to ensure our input power does not vary more through system design. Rails that are not shared between devices and that have to deliver 20 Amps or more need remote sense capability. Usually we need power enable and PowerGood pins. We need to ignore devices that have a fixed soft start below 1ms, we need adjustable at >1ms. Our output voltage has to be within the VRM chip's capability. If our management subsystem is meant to collect rail faults and currents, then select PMBUS capable smart devices, but if we are designing for aerospace or space then register-less devices might work more reliably in high-radiation environments.

Clock chip selection is based on the clock tree block diagram we made in the hardware spec, which was also based on the main ASIC or CPU datasheet. In the case of FPGAs, we have to provide SERDES and core and memory clocks, as described in Chapter 7, "Hardware Architecture". SERDES reference clocks do have a jitter specification in the ASIC datasheet, and we have to provide clocking sources that can meet that. Some clock chips are simple discrete devices with separate buffer chips or we can use programmable clocks. All other parts will be selected according to our block diagrams, ASIC datasheets, form factor standards, and heuristic ideas.

EEPROMs and flash memory chips have to be on the ASIC datasheet's supported device list. Their size is determined by the datasheet and our own firmware team. DRAM memory is selected for speed and total memory size (density). We have to ensure that the controller ASIC has enough address bits to support the memory chips and sizes and support the speed. We can use memory chips with higher speed capability than the controller but within the same DDRx generation, they will just be run slower than their maximum. Level translators and other small logic chips are selected on a heuristic basis, carefully considering I/O voltage standards and package types.

14.1.4 Project Schedule

A project schedule has to be written up together by the hardware designer and project manager to know how many resources (labor cost) and how long it will take to deliver a new product. It is created in a software tool, in a Gantt diagram editor, like in MS project, Open Project, or Gantt Project.

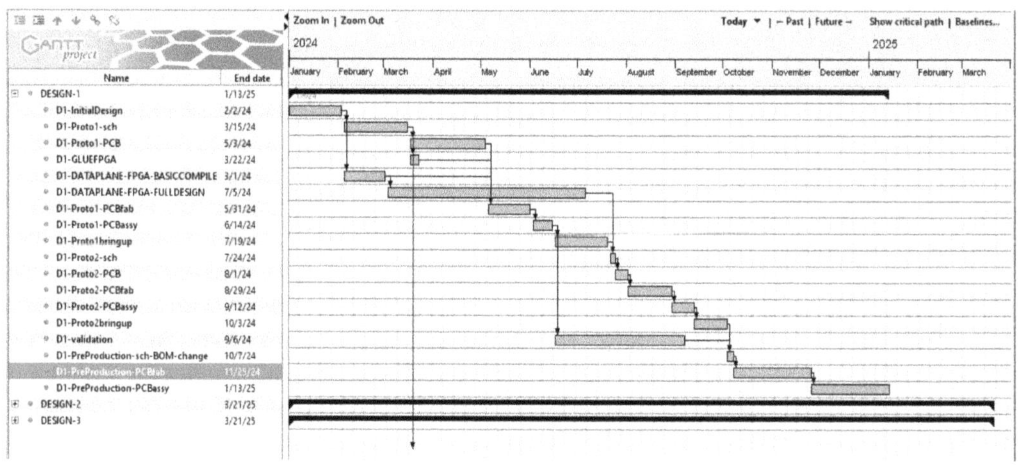

FIGURE 14.2 Example of a multi-project timeline.

Figure 14.2 shows an example mock-up project schedule. It shows each task or subtask, when they start and finish, and the dependency of tasks relative to other tasks. For example, the schematics must be completed for the layout to start, and a basic FPGA compilation must be completed before the Gerber files can be sent to the PCB fab or all design validation must be done before production. The initial design with proposal and hardware spec, floorplans, and so on might take a few weeks. The schematics design might take a month per 2000 components, the same for proto bring-up time, while the layout can take the same unless design partitioning speeds it up.

Some board/system companies release new products based on new chips released by the main chip company. For example, when the chip vendor releases its Nth generation processor, our company has to design different types of servers with that CPU and release them in close succession. In that case there will be a lead project to work out the chip to board integration details, and the several spin-off projects can start in a pipeline partly parallel, re-using some of the design to create new products. A very conservative company might wait until the lead design is in production before starting the spin-off projects, but then the spin-off designs will have little chance of selling on the market when the competition has flooded the market months ago. For this reason, a pipelined development of multiple designs makes sense, with the spin-offs waiting only for the schematics blocks of the lead design to be created. The project schedule will include multiple boards.

In most projects the first design cycle leads to a set of proto-1 prototype boards, maybe four to 20 units quantity. Then the board bring-up testing starts, where we test out all parts of the design and make alterations (re-work) to fix hardware bugs until all features work. With re-work the proto-1 should be fully functional. Then we apply the re-work items into schematic and layout design changes, this is the re-spin, then we build and test a set of proto-2 boards. Testing the proto-2 boards should take shorter time, and it should not require another re-spin, but perhaps a few components BOM-change, then we can release the drawings into series production. In some cases, with late discovered bugs due to insufficient test software coverage, we might have to do a proto-3 series.

At many stages of the project there will be gating reviews before the project can proceed. The purpose of these is to check for correctness, make choices, or approve details. These can be cross-functional reviews with different departments ensuring system level considerations or peer reviews with other hardware engineers focusing on the circuit correctness. The proposal, design plan, schematics, SI analysis results, layout placement and routing, as well as major decisions like choosing between two devices have their own review and decision-making meetings. A list of action items or a “meeting minutes” document is usually written up before, during, and after the meeting. A review comments document can also be used, as a shared MS-teams or Google Docs file that multiple people can edit in the same time.

In a project schedule we (hardware engineers) have to estimate how many workdays each phase or task of the project will take, including proposal research, writing the hardware spec, schematic design, layout design, SI analysis, PCB fabrication, PCB assembly, prototype functional bring-up, design verification, system and HW-FW integration, proto-2 schematic and layout design, proto-2 manufacturing, proto-2 bring-up, and preparing for reviews. The schematic, layout and bring-up should each take about 0.01...0.05 day/component, plus five to 70 days for each hard bug, there may be zero to three of such. An average time can be allocated for this in the schedule. The custom driver and test software have to be ready before the prototype arrives, and code alterations have to be made promptly during testing to be able to test out and debug the hardware, otherwise the bring-up will take several months longer than planned. While encountering prototype bugs, even if it is a software bug (like a register bit change), until it is found the hardware engineer is debugging it with the software engineer. It is important to estimate component count from the block diagram, based on experience from previous projects, so we can calculate board space/size and design time. High-density hardware designs can accommodate 100 components per square inch if they are not very routing intensive, but if they are (e.g., 1000+ SERDES diffpairs on a switch board) then the ceiling is around 30 to 90 components/sqin.

The component count has to be estimated for board density and fit feasibility checks as well as for project schedule. We can scan through the main block diagram for main ASICs in all three design architecture planes, then sum the component count from each ASIC’s support part group to get a total component count estimate. More details are provided in the section on floor planning.

Every board design project requires money to be invested into it. The most complex multi-ASIC board design project might cost a few million dollars, including the cost of manufacturing the prototypes, the labor of the hardware and the layout engineer, and the labor of the dozens of members of the cross-functional team (test, mechanical, software, firmware). Very complex hardware requires a lot of custom software and firmware engineering also done by a sizable team. Many companies have a 10:1 or 100:1 software to hardware team headcount ratio. An industrial PC motherboard development might cost ten times less with a 1:1 hardware to software team headcount ratio. A smaller single-FPGA card with some memory might cost a bit less than that. A single complex prototype board unit might cost $1k to 20k, while basic electronics can be as cheap as $100 per unit. Some main chips vary their pricing based on purchase volume, between $500 and $20k, affecting the total cost per board unit. Timewise, the largest board projects might take a year or two from concept until pre-production, while a smaller FPGA card will be a few months to a year. Before proposing or starting a project the cost has to be considered. Smaller companies might not be able to invest twice their annual budget into one large project. This is why the most complex hardware types are developed by medium- to larger-sized corporations.

14.2 PARADIGM SHIFT

A paradigm shift happened in the hardware development flow about the time 10Gbit interfaces became widely used. New activities were added; old activities were dropped or demoted. Figure 14.3 shows the changing development flow. Table 14.1 lists the detailed differences in the approach as well as the signal and noise parameters. The same new methodologies can also be used down to 8Gbps and beyond 112Gbps. Some of these rules should be used also on the reference clock signals that feed the 10G+ transceivers due to jitter and noise sensitivity. A few of these new activities are also useful for even 1 to 5Gbit designs with relaxed parameters and a few items waived. Note that 1 to 5Gig designs do not need 3D via optimization, for example, as it is very labor intensive, nor do they need rotation as the FWE skew is much smaller than the bit time.

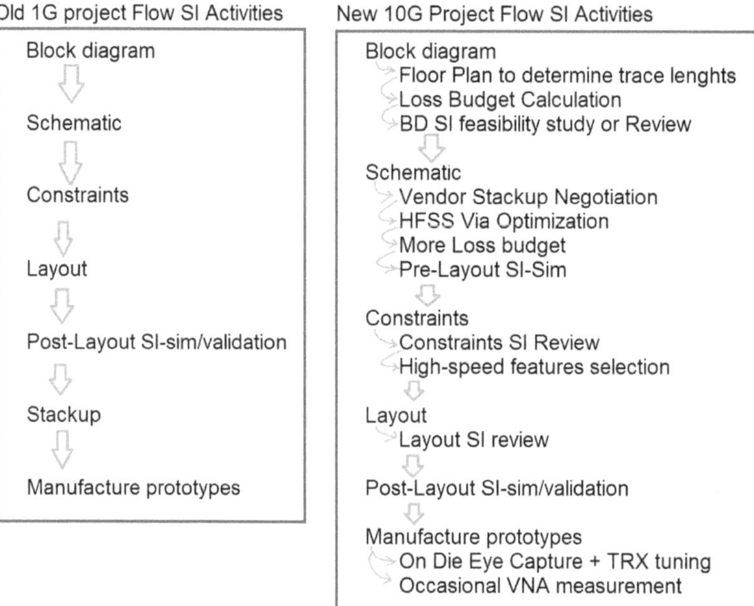

FIGURE 14.3 SI activities in project flow then and now.

14.3 TYPICAL PROJECT DOCUMENTATION

There is a general set of documentation that is common across industries, while companies have their own variations to the set. Most of them are prepared by the hardware design engineer. Some of the documents can be combined; they can have different names or a different focus. Each company has its own specific names for documents, their format, and what they would combine into one. These include written documents as well as design artifacts/drawings (schematic and PCB layout files, FPGA code) that are stored in various databases with official releases and sign-off. In some cases, it is just a shared folder on the network, in other cases it is some kind of a web-based interface like MS-Teams, SharePoint, or Google Docs. The most professional way to store design files is in databases like Agile or SAP or in version control systems like Perforce or Apache Subversion (SVN).

A list of typical documents:

- Design requirements: it details what features must be designed in. Usually created by marketing, management, or systems engineering. Ideally they do it before the design starts.
- Project proposal when the project starts.
- Design plan or hardware specification: every feature-related micro decision and how it will work, how it will be tested.
- Design notes to capture any decisions, part numbers, analysis, and findings.
- Design review comments and action items.
- Layout design guidelines and constraints: Instructions for the layout designer, from the hardware engineer, when the layout starts. It contains numerical constraints in tables, as well as text descriptions and rules, floorplan diagrams, and 3D via structure dimensions.
- Layout design communications file (layout tracker): A spreadsheet to capture all change requests and completion status, updated during the daily layout review. It can be an Excel file, but it should be a MS-Teams or Google doc so people can edit it in the same time. We can take screenshots in the PCB viewer, mark them up in MS Paint, and paste into the spreadsheet. Figure 14.4 shows an example.

TABLE 14.1
Focus Area Changes with Signal Speed

Design item	< 8 Gbit/s	>= 8 Gbit/s
Hardware architecture definition	Functionality and board density	Functionality and board density, loss budget and other SI aspects (max 2 conn)
ASIC selection	Functionality and board density	Functionality and board density, 1mm pitch BGA for SERDES backdrilled via structure
Connector selection	Number of pins, and ground pins	Number of pins, and ground pins, impedance, via fencing
Simulation focus	Post-layout validation	Pre-layout architectural decisions.
Simulation domain preference	Time domain eye diagram	Frequency domain S-parameters. Time domain simulated eye is information only (not for compliance).
Simulation result usage	Design validation	Increase confidence
Simulate what	Active devices with passive channel.	Passive interconnect quality only.
Measure	Signal Eye with Oscilloscope	Signal eye margin scan on-die, or measure passive channel with VNA.
Layout features	Manufacturing constraints-driven	Field-solver-optimized 2D/3D structures, SI-driven.
Layout Constraints	Mainly numbers	Numbers and 3D structures, design-tailored constraints.
Via design	Manufacturing constraints-driven	Field-solver-optimized 2D/3D structures, impedance-driven.
Via simulation method	Length and RLC model.	3D field solver with anisotropic dielectric material.
PWB Routing Strategy	Convenience	SI-driven
Plane connection	Thermal relief	Solid
Resonant Frequency of Discontinuities must be	>> Data Rate 5rd harmonic	>> Half baud rate, or 1x baud rate.
Clock Jitter, VRM noise, interference	<< 0.1 UI	> 0.1 UI
Skew introduced by bad Glass Style	<< 0.1 UI	> 0.1 UI
Insertion Loss @ DataRate/2	<< 10dB	> 20 dB
Copper Roughness Loss	<< Dielectric Loss	> Dielectric Loss

- Approved vendor stackup documents: During the stackup negotiation, the fab vendor will provide a stackup document with layer details, drills, impedance, and loss data.
- SI simulation reports: Any SI or PI simulations, timing analysis.
- Fab notes: PCB manufacturing-related constraints we used in the layout as well as parameters we want the fab to use—either as a layer in the Gerber files or as a separate PDF document.
- Fab vendor deviation requests prepared by the fab vendor if they cannot make our design as is.
- Manufacturing and test guidelines for assembly, programming, and functional test.
- Prototype bring-up plan: This lists all activities that need to take place immediately after prototype arrival.
- Prototype bring-up log: lists all tests and debug attempts done, results and symptoms observed in a sequential test file.
- Proto-1 bug list: A numbered list of bugs we found on the prototype design, with re-work instruction for proto-1 and design change instruction for proto-2.

	A	B	C	D	E	F
1	Item	Status	Req Date	Requester	Details	Response
2	1	Closed	1/15/2024	Peter	Move U12 to X456y789	Ok, done
3	2	Open	1/15/2024	Peter	Move U33to X123y456	
4	3	Question	1/21/2024	Paul	Re-route the net XYZ_123 under U36 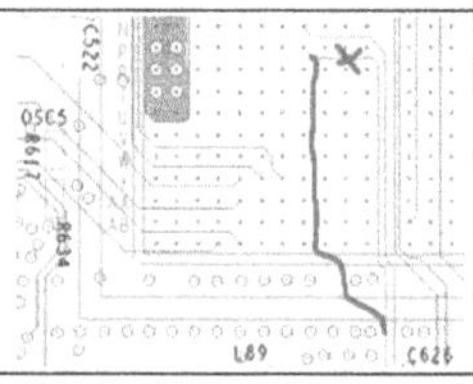	Shoud we also re-route the net ABC_456?
5	4	Closed	1/22/2024	Peter	Move the vias from under C45	Ok, done
6	5	Open	1/22/2024	Peter	Edit the shape edge near X741Y258 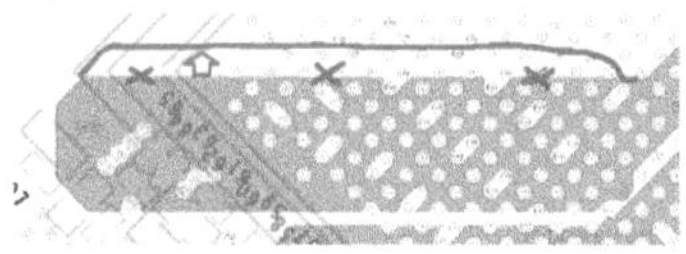	
7	6	Open	1/22/2024	Peter	add more GND vias near X963Y654	
8	7					

FIGURE 14.4 A mock-up layout tracker spreadsheet.

- Board tracker: Listing all prototype boards with serial number, and the numbered re-work items done, as well as known damage and bugs.
- Design validation test plan: The tests to be done to validate the design quality, expected results, conditions, and measured numbers to be captured in a Word or Excel document.

14.4 FLOOR PLANNING

Traditionally, floor Planning was done only later in a project, when the schematic was already done, just as a basic design step, not as an analysis. For modern complex and high-speed board designs, floor planning can be used as an early-stage analysis step to determine the feasibility of several design aspects, part selection, and other things. It is a feasibility check because if we cannot find a placement arrangement that results in trace lengths that meet the loss budgets, port mapping limitations, board size or other aspects, then the architecture is not feasible. Then the architecture, block diagrams, device selection, board sizes, or something else must be changed. The hardware architecture cannot be reviewed and approved until this check is completed. The floorplanning should happen when the project gets assigned and the proposal is being written. So we really create two floorplans: an early stage one using a graphical editor for analysis purposes and a late stage one in the layout tool as a design step. To differentiate, we can call the first one a "Floorplan Analysis", and the second one a "Layout Design Floorplan". The second one should replicate the first one in a different tool, with increased accuracy. This chapter focuses on the early-stage high-speed design floorplan analysis. The main goals of this are reducing or eliminating high-speed-on-high-speed crossings (layer count issue) that helps with reducing the stackup layer count and a fit/feasibility check with all main and medium/supporting parts in a given board size to obtain trace length information for insertion loss budget calculations on SERDES signals, to help mechanical engineering come up with a chassis and heatsinking concept sooner, and to perform efficient ASIC I/O bank/port assignments. We have to check if the trace lengths from the floorplan are within the range that we calculated from the loss budget.

Before making a floorplan drawing, a quick calculation can be used to verify whether all the parts from our block diagram will even fit in the chosen board size or form factor. If not, then we might have to split the design into multiple boards, give up some features, or change the board size. Changing to smaller package sizes for the ASICs usually compromises signal integrity at 10Gbps or above, so that is not a solution, and this is why component count is used instead. Typically, 30 to 100 components per square inch can fit. The low end is in case of I/O heavy designs like switch boards, the high end is with lower/medium power processing boards. We can estimate the number of components each main device requires in its subsystem by the pin count of the main device. For FPGAs it will be about 0.7 comps/pin, for large network ASICs it will be 0.5 comps/pin, for embedded ARM processors 1 comp/pin, for secondary ASICs (like PHY chips, SSDs, and PCIe switches) it is about 0.8 comp/pin. A laptop-type X86 processor and chipset without special peripherals will pull about 1500 components. Special glue logic requires 1comp/pin, I/O connector interfaces all together 0.25comp/pin. Any special circuits are counted separately. Global supporting glue logic, power, and management circuits usually take up about 10% of the total board component count. We add up the component counts from each subsystem block on the main data plane block diagram, not on the subsystem block diagrams, to get the total count. The board area can be calculated by multiplying the length and width. Component density is the component count divided by the board area.

Traditionally hardware engineers create only a basic floorplan in a diagram editor, with a big rectangle as the board outline and small rectangles as the main components. These simple diagrams are good for corporate documentation, but they do not give a high confidence fit check, neither do they allow us to estimate trace lengths for a loss budget. To solve these issues, we can create a detailed photographic floorplan instead. A similar accurate one can be created by using PCB layout viewer screenshots, edited in a graphics editor, where the traces and shapes are disabled from view and only show the components. Some people drop the main components into a skeleton schematic, export the netlist to layout, and place the parts in a layout editor; while this method is the most accurate, it takes up to 10 times longer to produce. The photographic and the screenshot-based options only take one to two hours.

It is easy to create a detailed photographic floorplan by creating a floorplan template first, then cut and paste parts of images together to create a new "fake" board photo, also called a montage or collage image. To create a template, like the one in Figure 14.5, we need to obtain some high-resolution photographs of complex boards with a top-down view. We can download pictures from the Internet if we know their board sizes. The web search engine "image search" option helps a lot, with keywords like "processor board". We can also take pictures of boards we have lying around in our lab. The actual third-party board images are omitted on this diagram here due to publishing, but when we are making a template for ourselves, these will be actual full board images. We also need to download or capture an image of an "inch+mm" ruler. We have to paste all these into a PNG

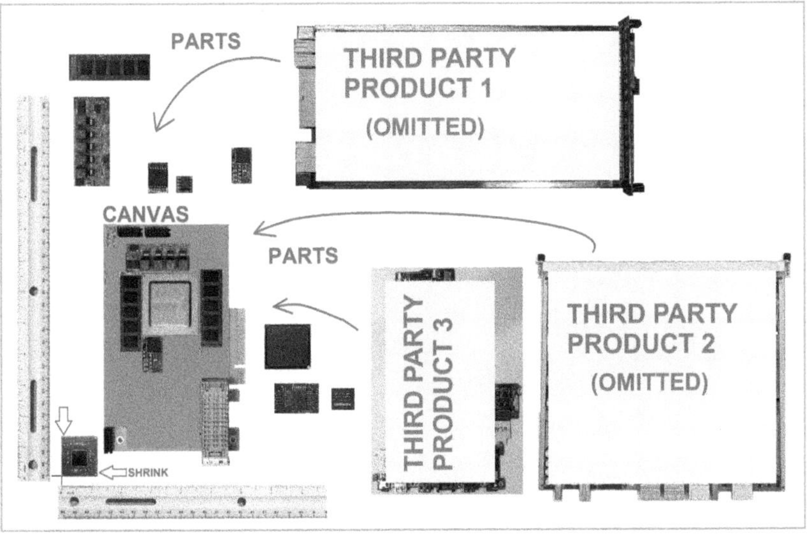

FIGURE 14.5 Floor planning template using stretched photographs.

or bitmap lossless image in an image editor like MS Paint. In the editor we can stretch all of these board images to match the scale of the ruler's picture. After that all board images will be to scale to each other too. After we have several boards stretched to size, we can start building our board. We can re-use a board image for our board outline, but we will need to clear all parts inside it and fill the space with green paint. Or we can draw a board outline at the ruler using basic lines, and then fill it with green. This will be our drawing canvas. Then we can start populating our board by selecting the pixel area containing a component or a component group (like a VRM or a memory-down) that looks similar to the ones on our block diagrams, press copy and then paste, and move them to the location on our board where we need them. The parts have to have the expected size we know from the datasheet. If not, then we have to stretch them to the correct size at the rulers. A photographic floorplan example can be seen in Figure 14.6.

The functional part of the floor planning is to know what location we want our parts from the block diagram. For this we need to know what kind of signals will come off the main parts and where they supposed to be routed. For example, a backplane bridge chip will be placed near the backplane connector, a PHY chip near the Ethernet connector, an Accelerator ASIC near the host ASIC and so on. We also have to fill the space efficiently, like in a Tetris video game or like when we are packing our suitcase for a vacation. High-speed signals will require wide routing channels free of high-density parts. The distance between their source and destination parts needs to be considered with signal integrity, while low-speed signals can be routed under components and to faraway destinations. Supporting parts like memory chips and VRMs are placed right next to the main ASICs.

Alternatively, we can also use a screenshot of a similar design's layout file in the PCB viewer program, with traces and vias hidden and silk screen and pins visible, then edit the screenshot image in MS Paint. We just use the keyboard's print screen button. One single big layout file could be used, and then no scaling or ruler is needed. A graphically edited layout screenshot-based floorplan example can be seen in Figure 14.7. In this case it is one made-up board transformed into another—we use only the components available on that one board, but we can place them in any way and multiply them too.

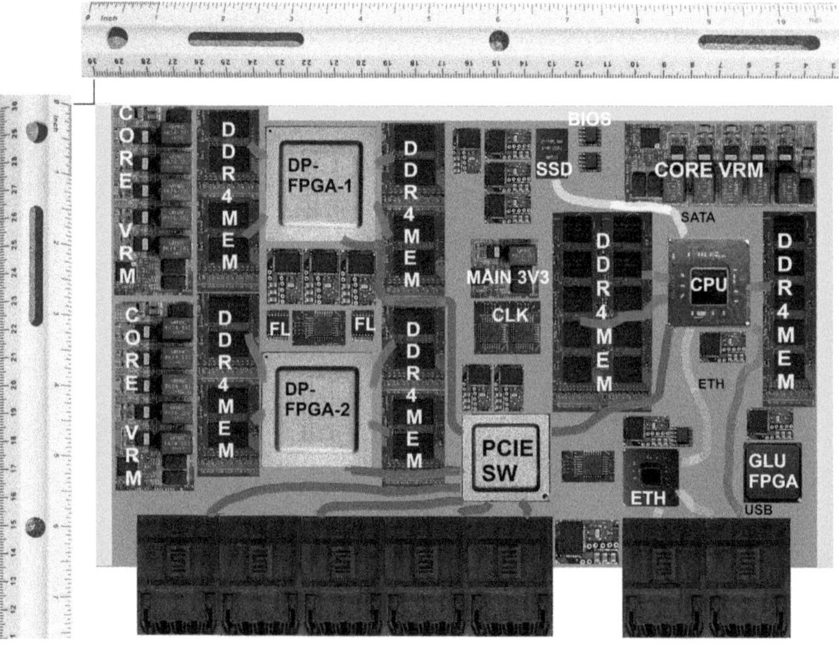

FIGURE 14.6 Result of photographic floor planning and flow planning.

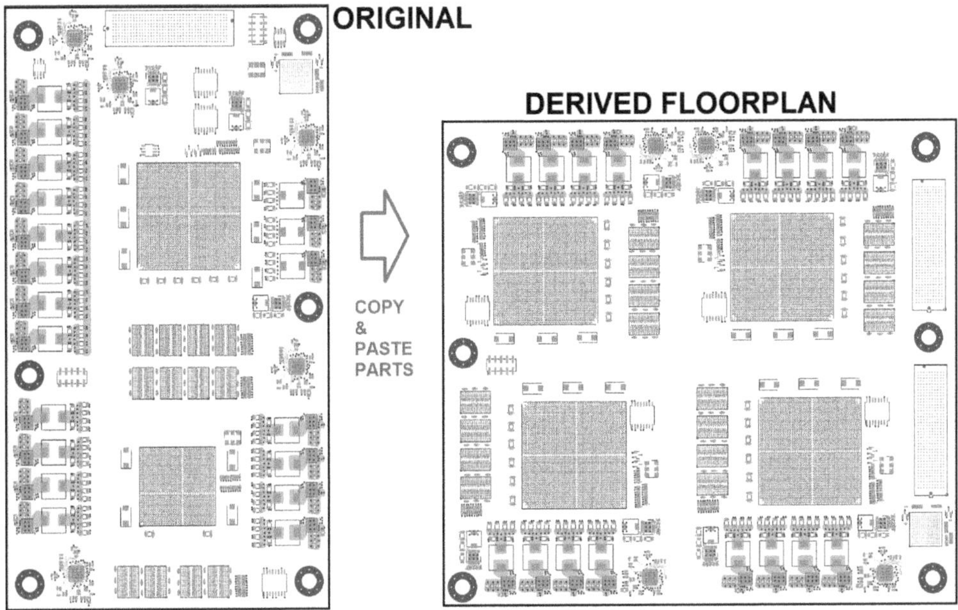

FIGURE 14.7 Results of PCB layout screenshot-based graphical floor planning from KiCAD.

We need to know what main components are in our block diagram, what supporting parts they need, and how they are supposed to look like on a board as well as what package sizes we need. At the early stage of the project, we need to select the exact part numbers and obtain the datasheets that will show the package sizes. For the main parts, we can estimate the supporting parts based on prior project experience. For this we have to know what the different circuits look like based on experience or from analyzing existing boards. Not just individual components can be copy/pasted, but subcircuits too, for example, a multi-phase VRM, a clock generator, a complete memory-down area, or a bridge chip with all its supporting parts. First, we copy the main ASICs and connectors, then the supporting circuits that go with each main ASIC and connectors, and finally the expected amount of global glue logic and clocking parts (small chips surrounded by lots of small passives). We also have to know what kind of supporting circuits each main ASIC will need, how many phases of VRMs, how many memory chips, how big the clocking chip, and so on, and what they look like. The detailed subsystem block diagrams we created, as well as chip vendor reference designs, should help with that. Once all is done, we fill the gaps with green color.

It also makes sense to mark up all the main parts and subcircuits with text labels so everyone can see what is what. Mark up all the different high-speed routes (flows) with different colored free-form lines to see how many crossings we have. With the route markup, it is now a "flowplan". Make sure to allow for sufficiently wide routing channels along the flow lines, either with no components or with low-density components (like large bulk capacitors, SOIC parts). The width of the routing channel can be calculated as:

$$\text{width} = N*(W+S)/M$$

Where N is the number of diffpairs, S is the pair to pair spacing used for crosstalk mitigation, W is the diffpair width (2x trace width + gap), and M is the number of layers we are planning to use in a given direction for this route. When using wavy routing, this channel width has to be increased by 10% to 30%. The flows or buses in the flow plan show where (start, destination, and route) the main high-speed signals are going. If two flow lines cross, it adds to the layer count, so we might need to reorder the part placement or the pin assignment to eliminate main bus crossings if possible. For example, if our main PCIe bus is routed on four layers, and it crosses with an InfiniBand bus that is routed on two layers, then we will need at least 4+2=6 inner high-speed routing layers. With the rulers, we can determine the length of these high-speed routes. If the lengths pass the loss budget or timing analysis calculation, then we are done; if not, then we might need to change the floorplan part placement, move chips between boards in the system, change stackup materials, or add retimer chips to the design.

For those who do not believe that these floorplans can be accurate, a preliminary schematic and layout can be created, with parts but without connection nets. It starts with a preliminary schematic with the main parts placed in the drawing, then the netlist files exported, and the mechanical engineer providing a DXF file with the board outline and main part locations. Both the netlist and the DXF will be imported into the layout design, and the main components in the layout tool are placed within the board outline boundary. Depending on how many "main parts" we want to place, it can take anywhere from a few hours to a few weeks. If we want to place all silicon devices, then it might take days, with all large passives also a week or two. We do not really need to place all small silicon chips or large passives; their space requirement can be estimated relative to the size of the main chips from experience. Since it is not a full layout and we do not have to use most features of the CAD tool, the hardware engineer should be able to make the floorplan in the PCB editor. A graphical one is usually accurate enough for a proposal or a design plan, and takes only one to three hours to make.

14.4.1 Fitting the Pinout into the Floorplan

For larger chips it makes sense to create a pinout drawing and substitute this instead of the chip photograph or overlay it. It should not contain all pin names; rather, it should contain a simplification with signal groups as well as start/end lane numbering. We need to see where the LSB and MSB bit or lane number is on each bus, which can help with placing components in a way to avoid lane reversal (15:0 to 0:15), crossing in the layout, or to identify pin swapping requirements for the schematic. We have to parse through the detailed pinout in the datasheet to recognize the approximate relative locations of the signal groups and mark those in our drawing. We can create a pinout diagram in MS Paint and paste it into the floorplan, such as in the example in Figure 14.8.

Some FPGA device datasheets provide I/O bank-color marked package drawings that we can re-use with print-screen and MS Paint pre-editing before pasting them into our floorplan. Some parts are heterogeneous and have different types of interfaces like a processor or an FPGA that already has the pinout from the FPGA team, or homogenous like a switch ASIC that has identical "cores" evenly distributed all around the package perimeter. This pin-marked floorplan will help

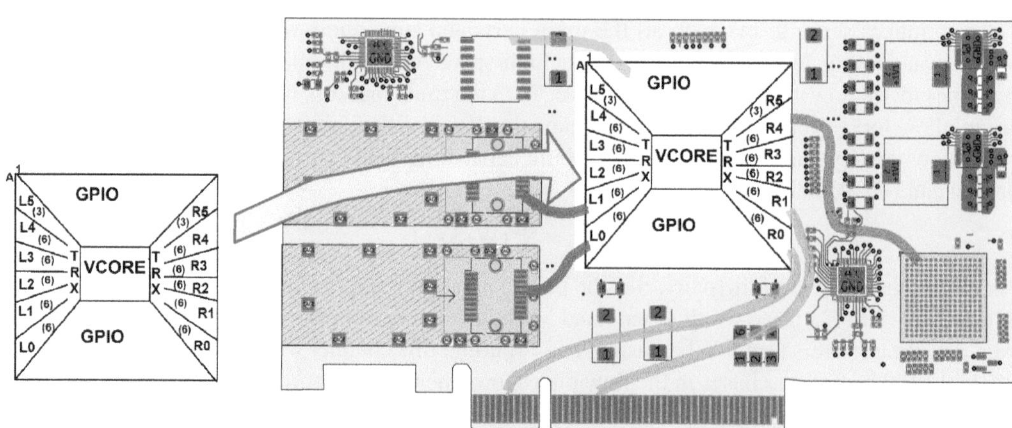

FIGURE 14.8 Floorplan and flowplan with chip pinout diagram.

with determining the need for any bus flow crossing on the flowplan diagram that would require additional stackup layers. For example, we can account for not only which type of interface has to enter the ASIC on which side, but also how many lanes can come out from a certain section. This also helps with connecting the right pins/ports in the schematic or swapping ports to avoid crossings.

We also have to determine what rotation each main device will need to have, so as to align the ports towards the routing direction and to balance the trace lengths (for loss budget or timing). For a 2-inch BGA package when rotated by 180 degrees, it can make some signal traces 4 inches longer (wrapping around the package) while making other signals 4 inches shorter (unwrap). We have to keep in mind the insertion loss budgets of each SERDES interface, so we can make the ones with tight budgets shorter at the expense of making the less demanding ones longer. Usually the off-board interfaces have tighter budgets because only a portion of the total standard budget is available to each board. Figure 14.9 shows what happens when we rotate an ASIC when one of the interfaces was a long connection already wrapped around a package while the other had a direct and short connection. It also shows that port/pin swapping can relieve bus crossings. For CPUs and ASICs, the swapping can be done only if they are identical ports of the same type, like PCIe with PCIe. On FPGAs we can even swap different types of ports, we just have to change the FPGA code and re-compile it. The only limitation on FPGAs is that we cannot swap SERDES ports with regular I/O ports (non-SERDES), also keeping in mind the I/O bank types. Some FPGAs have a few different types of I/O banks with different limitations, such as on a certain device family some of the banks support on-die terminations, while others do not. The use of SRDES tiles is flexible; any tile can be PCIe, Ethernet, Interlaken, InfiniBand, etc. The regular I/O can swap between DDR4, ONFI, MDIO, LVDS-LCD, SPI, PCI-X, etc. Swapping is done in the schematic by simply re-connecting schematic nets to different device pins.

Some devices have several instances of one or two types of pin groups (like FPGAs and ASICs); while other devices have several different types of pin groups (like processors). Pin group diagrams of both types of chips are shown in Figure 14.10. In a real project we do not have to color it, just add text and some lines that divide the sections. On some chip packages, such as X86 chipsets, there

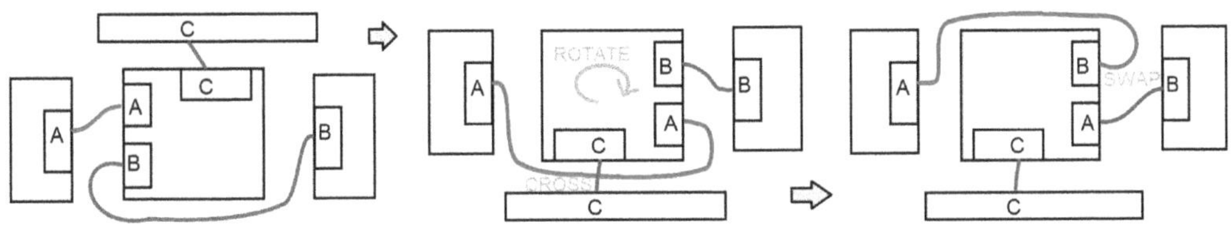

FIGURE 14.9 Device rotation and pin swapping.

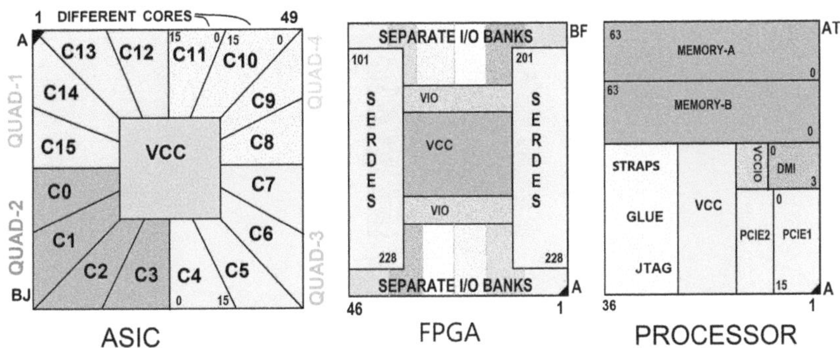

FIGURE 14.10 Example of package pin groups on sketch diagrams.

are so many different sections that we can omit even the divider lines. The ASIC chip on the left side of the image has its transceivers organized into cores (marked as C#), with a given number of lanes in each core. We can make a diagram of this chip pinout with signal group names of major buses instead of every signal name because there would be too much detail to fit on the diagram. Sometimes the chip vendor provides a similar drawing but mirrored, as viewed from the die top, but the silicon die is normally upside down in the BGA package (flip chip BGA, meaning flipped), so the pinout seen on the board will be the mirror image of the die view in those cases. Some ASICs also constrain the total bandwidth of each of its SERDES tile groups (half a chip or a quadrant) to be lower than the total bandwidth of its lanes summed up. So during floor planning we have to verify that we are not trying to get too much bandwidth from an already saturated section. If there is a bottleneck problem then we have to move some connections around to different cores or pins. Further rules define that all lanes within one core must be running at the same speed, so we have to arrange the different interfaces (1G, 10G, 25G) to avoid sharing cores. These rules are dependent on a particular chip part number; thus, we have to discover them from the datasheet.

On some board designs we need trace length balancing, to avoid violating minimum and maximum insertion loss limits. Although this will increase the layer count and cost, the min/max loss limits are hard constraints that must be met. Sometimes we can meet those length constraints only by trace length balancing, as we can see in Figure 14.11. The basic concept is to change the SERDES core or bank to connector pin assignment in a way that the cores farthest away from their destination will swap signals in the schematic with the cores that are closest to their destinations.

On the flow-plan diagram with inserted pinout drawings, we connect specific cores/ports of a main chip to specific connectors, chips or ports of chips. It is complete when all interfaces are connected, all unnecessary crossings are eliminated, necessary crossings are added, bandwidth bottlenecks resolved, and the final rotation (pin A1 position) is determined. This creates the final port mapping information that has to be listed in a table in the hardware spec or ICD, and must be fed back into block diagram and schematic updates too. Each connection line in the flow plan will have a net name range in the schematic, that we have to connect to the correct symbol pins on both

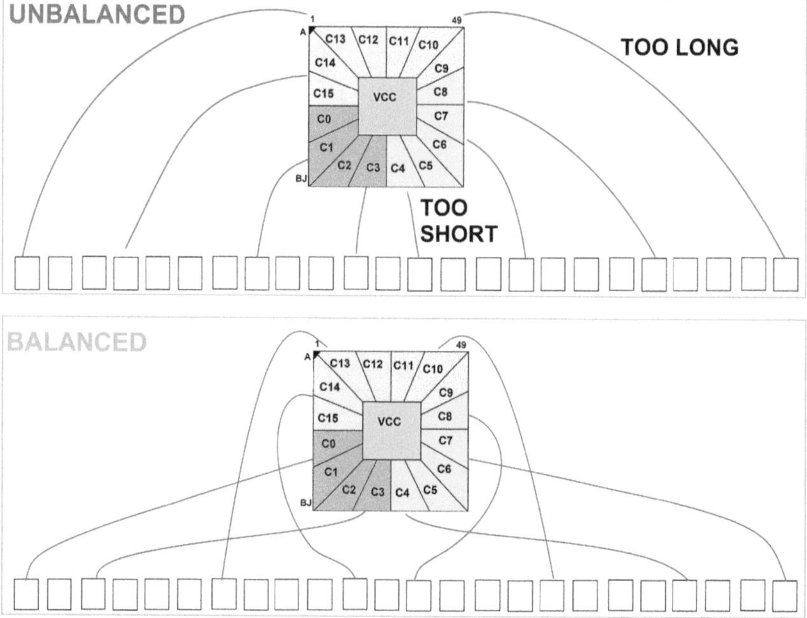

FIGURE 14.11 Length balancing with smart pin mapping (sketch).

ends. The software team also needs to know which ports are connecting to what. Glue logic FPGAs with hundreds of single-ended system control signals don't require flow-planning, we just assign signal functional groups (power control, backplane logic...) to different I/O banks in the schematic.

14.4.2 Fanout Analysis

A fanout analysis is done months before the layout designer starts drawing the actual fanout and escape routes because the hardware engineer has to plan ahead. A fanout analysis is needed as part of the flowplan. It will tell us how many high-speed routing layers it would require to escape route all signals of a certain bus from a certain grid-type component, like a BGA chip or a backplane connector. The escape routes continue to the main routes on the same layers without layer change, so it will use up the same number of layers. Extra layer changes would degrade signal integrity, especially on SERDES links. The results of this, together with any knowledge of bus crossings from the flowplan, tell us how many total high-speed routing layers we will need on the whole board, so we can start designing the stackup and negotiating it with the fab vendors. Any grid components can be measured in rows or columns of pins. The pin assignment includes signal and ground pins. We route out only the signals, while the ground vias connect straight to all the ground planes at the signal via. A row is along the package outline.

To start the analysis, we have to count the number of signal pins (exclude ground and power) from the component edge until the inner most signal pin before the center in one column. We also have to check how many signals can be routed between two vias, depending on pin pitch and other parameters. Usually we deal with diffpairs, so usually one diffpair or two single-ended traces can be routed between two vias so we can count how many diffpairs need escaping when counting from the edge until the innermost instance. This is dependent on design constraints (drill, backdrill, clearances). With old-style constraint values or with small-pitch BGA packages we cannot fit a diffpair or two SE traces in a column, only one SE trace, which will result in too many layers, thick boards, and high aspect ratio vias. A good quality high-speed design needs to fit two lines/columns in the fanout. Any SERDES links at/above 8Gbps must not split a diffpair into two columns to be able to pass the standard S-par limit lines. Figure 14.12 demonstrates both the single-ended and the differential signals escapes and their required layer counts. That number will be the number of routing layers required for that bus at that chip. If the chip at the other end requires more, then the larger number will be used in board routing.

On the flowplan diagram, every crossing of buses indicates a routing layer count requirement of M+N where one of the buses required M layers the other required N layers from their respective

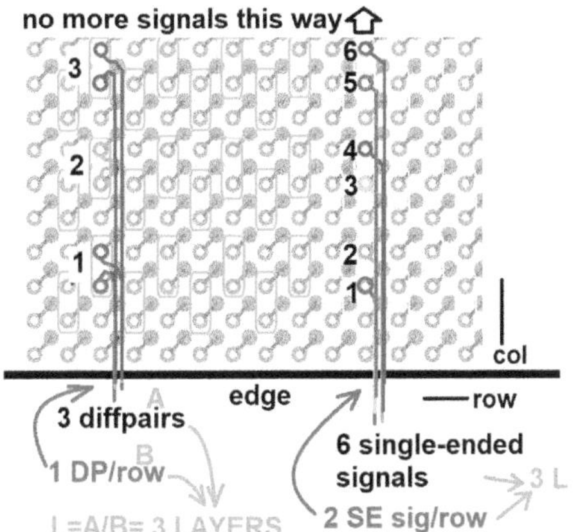

FIGURE 14.12 Fanout analysis examples (sketch).

fanout analysis. If a crossing can be avoided by well thought out placement and pinout assignments, then the M+N layer count requirement can be reduced to max(M, N), which is about half in most cases, resulting in a huge win for product cost and other considerations. With less layers we are less constrained by via aspect ratios, via lengths, and fitting thick boards into a chassis. It can easily happen that once we have failed to avoid a crossing and increased the layer count, we are now forced to increase the via diameter due to aspect ratio limits, and we will not be able to fit a diffpair within each via column, making our SI fail the IEEE or other specs.

14.4.3 Floorplan Investigation Example

Figure 14.13 shows a made-up project with three possible floorplans in which all seem to fit. The different interfaces have different insertion loss budgets and timing requirements at different frequencies, so we can calculate their maximum trace lengths from those. The budget calculation is described in the next chapter. Let's say we use a PCB material that gives us 3dB/in@13GHz loss. We can scale this to the different speeds of different interfaces, as 3dB/in@13G and 0.9dB/in@4GHz. From this we can write up a table of the maximum trace lengths for each interface, as seen on the bottom of the image. The memory has fixed maximum length of 5” from timing, the UART has no limits. The backplane interfaces have 30% of the full standard budget available for this board's portion of the channel. One might want to place the CPU next to the UART connector, but we should realize that the UART has no loss constraints, while other interfaces do. Once we have created three different floorplans and measured all bus (Manhattan) lengths, as marked on the diagram, we can analyze them to see which violates our loss budget constraints. Note that the connection lines are not just touching the devices at the closest convenience; rather, they have to connect at a certain section of the package, as explained earlier. Although the same type of ports can be swapped, different types cannot be. For example, a memory interface cannot be swapped with a PCIe interface as they have fixed pin group locations. This is why the diagram seems to show some buses wrapping around the devices, and this is why some devices are rotated to help the trace length of one interface at the

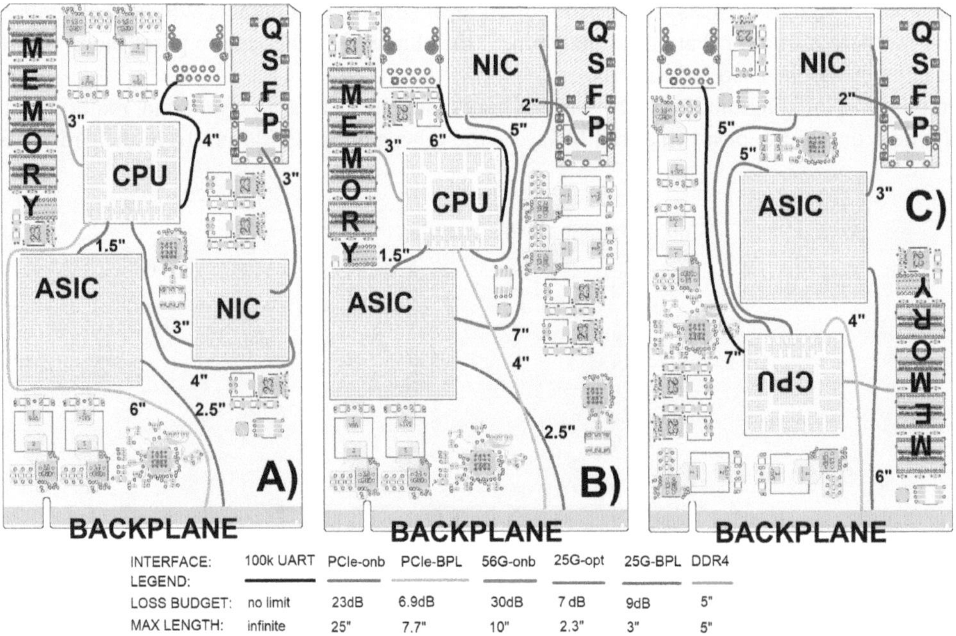

FIGURE 14.13 Three floorplan options for a made-up example board.

expense of another less demanding one. Rotating a 2" x 2" ASIC would redistribute as much as 4" of trace length. We can see that there are no main bus crossings on option-A, so we cheer for that one to meet the loss budgets. As we verify on each of the three floorplan options, most interfaces meet their loss budgets, except a few. On option-A the 25G-optical interface fails, and the backplane PCIe barely meets. On option-C we have three high-speed bus crossings, but the 25G backplane interface is twice the allowed length at 6". Option-B seems to pass all loss budgets. Even though it costs more layers due to crossings, option-B is the only one that would be functional or reliable. Of course, if we can get better PCB materials and or a better fabricator with lower loss, then we will find that all options meet their loss budgets in this particular example. Then we will choose option-A, as it requires less layers in the stackup due to the lack of high-speed bus crossings and due to its wider routing channels.

14.5 LOSS BUDGET CALCULATION

High-speed SERDES signals attenuate as they travel through the boards in the system. If they attenuate too much, then they cannot be recovered by the receiver. We can tell whether they attenuate too much by looking at their insertion loss profile or by performing a basic loss budget calculation. Limits to the losses were determined by standard organizations. The standards specify a limit line on the complete 2D insertion loss diagram (profile) that our S-parameters cannot cross at any point. It is a compliance analysis that was mentioned in the chapter about signal integrity. Meanwhile, this chapter treats something slightly different, a loss budget calculation at a single point instead of a 2D diagram. This single point is not simply read out of the diagram; rather, it has a complex process to compute it called Delta-L, already explained earlier. This number loss or loss number can be used in basic budget calculations. All the losses in our signal path added up are the loss budget that has to be below the limit that is based on the relevant standard. The loss budget at a certain frequency is related to the maximum trace lengths a design can have at a certain speed. If the interface has a higher speed but uses the same PCB materials/processes, then the maximum design trace length that allows the signal to be recoverable is reduced. If the speed is the same but the trace is longer, then the signal might not be recoverable.

The total allowed loss budget comes from the standard specifications, such as IEEE802.3xx for Ethernet, PCI Express Base Specification Revision x.x, SFFxxxx, and so on. The IEEE802.3bj document's section-93.9 describes the chip-to-chip backplane channel limits for 25Gbps NRZ signaling, the IEEE802.3ap Annex-69B is for 10G KR backplane Ethernet, while SFF standards define the channel limits between various optical cage connectors and the line ASICs. They usually define a limit line for the insertion loss curve that we can read out as a single number in dB at the Nyquist frequency. The Nyquist frequency is half of the baud rate or rounded up like 5.15 to 6GHz. The baud rate of a signal is the rate it changes state, which is equal to the data rate with NRZ signaling, but it is half the data rate for PAM4 signaling. The loss budget number read-out from a standard limit line is demonstrated in Figure 14.14. The standard limit lines might have a line break at the Nyquist frequency or they might not, it is not why we read out the value at that point, we just need the data at the Nyquist frequency.

Various backplane (long PCB link) Ethernet standards from IEEE allow in the ballpark of 30dB budget at the half baud rate rounded up to a whole Gigahertz number. It varies significantly based on speed, standard number, and whether FEC is enabled or not. Different PCIe generations have different maximum loss limits. The PCIe base specs list them under calibration channel IL limits for test boards that we can re-use for real designs. The channel loss specs for optical port to ASIC connections are defined by the various SFF, SNIA, QSFP-DD, or OSFP standards as well as IEEE standards (C2M types) and they are much stricter in the range of 6 to 13dB. On-board MAC-to-PHY (C2C type) Ethernet links usually allow about half as much loss as backplane links do, due to their simpler transceiver architecture in IEEE specs. The JESD204 A/D-converter to FPGA link standards allow user-defined custom speeds, so we have to calculate the loss budgets for those from

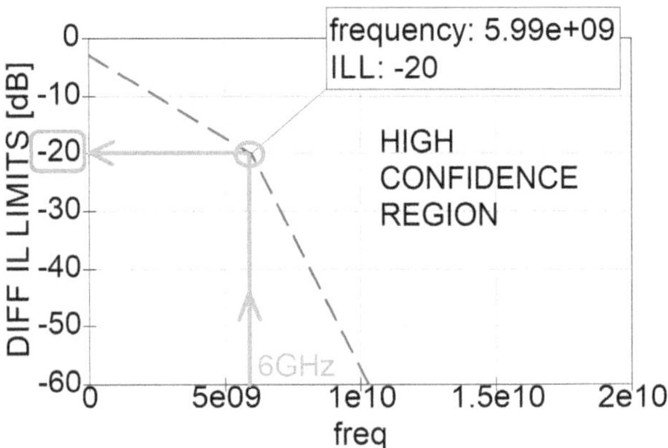

FIGURE 14.14 Getting loss budgets standards.

formulas in the specs. If an interface uses FEC, then it can tolerate more loss, about 5dB or more "coding gain" is achievable. FEC is the forward error correction coding logic. PAM-4 is more sensitive than NRZ, so at the same data rate they allow a few dB lower maximum loss. The PCIe CEM specs allocate portions of the full channel budgets into individual board budgets for motherboard and add-in card, while the VITA68.1 does the allocation for two front cards and a VPX backplane. To get the exact numbers, we need to purchase the relevant speed/type standard document from these organizations.

When we check our design's loss number after a measurement or a simulation to verify that we are within the budget, we really use the fitted attenuation (FA) computed from differential insertion loss (SDD21), which is computed from single ended insertion loss (S21). The real design's insertion loss profile contains resonances, which should be ignored while obtaining the loss number, and we need the differential mode. They are not ignored for an SI analysis, but here we are talking about a loss budget, so we ignore them here. The FA as described earlier is computed using a set of equations defined in IEEE Ethernet standards. It is a more or less straight line that is fit to match the choppy SDD21 curve. It represents the steepness of the slope of the SDD21 curve. The actual loss number read-out from an SDD21 curve is demonstrated in Figure 14.15.

The total loss number in our design has to be below the loss limit extracted from the standard, at the Nyquist frequency. This is the purpose of the loss budget. But between obtaining the budget and measuring the actual design's loss number, there are several design and analysis steps to be conducted. For example, we need to determine the maximum trace lengths we can have in the design to guarantee meeting that budget. It will become a PCB design constraint. The total insertion loss is proportional to the trace length. For this we need to know how much "loss-per-inch" we will get. This is normally specified in the format like 1.2dB/in@13GHz, denoting what frequency we want the number at. For this we need to know what kind of PCB stackup materials and which fabricator contractor will be available for our project. We also need to have completed loss test board projects or obtained coupon data from the same vendor. To recap, we have three ways of analyzing insertion loss: a 2D curve against a standard limit line, the single number obtained from the slope of the curve at a single frequency point, and the per-unit-length calculated value of the same.

It makes sense to create a minimum loss requirement as 1/10th of the maximum loss requirement. This is to ensure that reflections will be dampened by loss. This will result in a minimum trace length. Some standards require it, such as the various SFF standards use for optical transceiver module attachment to baseboards.

The loss budget calculation requires that we know how much loss-per-inch we will have worst case, on any production unit. To know that we have to have a vendor-approved stackup document

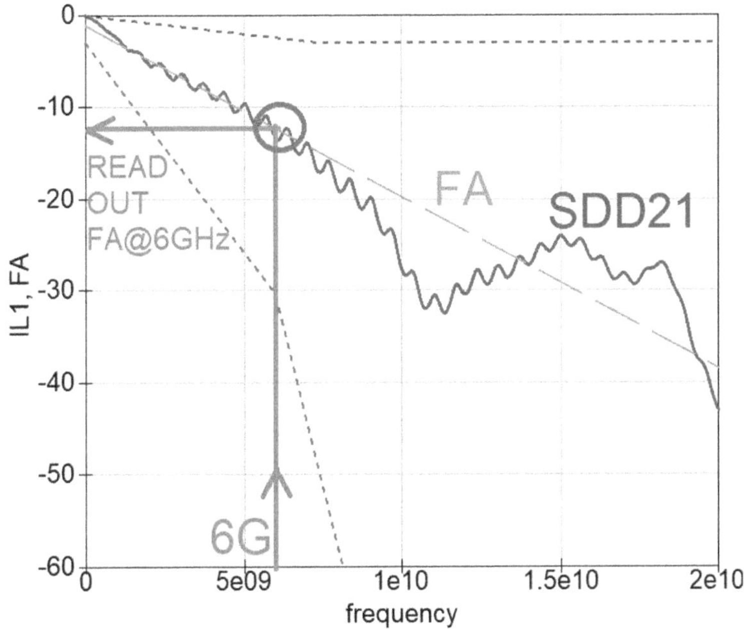

FIGURE 14.15 Getting fitted attenuation and number readout from simulated or measured IL curve.

with all the details (copper foil, dielectric, glass style, trace width, resin content) and a recently completed loss test board measurement by our department. We determine the loss control capabilities of individual fabricator facilities by designing, manufacturing, and measuring loss test boards, as described earlier. The result of that is a "dB/inch@frequency" number. We also need to have loss requirement fab notes in the manufacturing files to ensure that we will get what we expect to get. The parts of the stackup that are relevant to loss are the trace width, the dielectric, the copper foil, and the factory selection that is based on their capability. See Chapter 12, "PCB Materials and Stackups", which describes what manufacturing and material parameters affect insertion loss of a particular PCB construction.

We have to apply a design margin to cover PCB manufacturing tolerances and to allow a high-yield manufacturing setup. We can apply the margin to the previously received coupon data or in the loss budget. If we apply it at the coupon data, then it means, let's say we got 1dB/in@13GHz data from our SI test board, and then adding 10% margin would make it 1*1.1=1.1dB/in@13Ghz, which we would use in the budget calculation. The alternative method is to apply the margin at the budget, that is 30dB*0.9=27dB would be the total budget (if we had 30dB originally), but we would use the original 1dB/in@13GHz coupon data. Applying the margin at the coupon data has the benefit of allowing some slack for the BCB fab company, so they can produce the boards with better yield. This is the preferred method described here. In some cases, they may reject the purchase order or quote request if the requirement is right at their capability. Usually, we have at least two alternate PCB vendors lined up with tested capability for any design, so we can secure our supply chain. If one gives a "no bid", then it means we can still get the board made, but we eliminated our supply chain security. So, applying it at the coupon data is preferred. The margin can be 10% or 15% or 20%, but 20% would cut into our design capability, while anything less than 10% does not do much. When we specify our loss requirement on the fab notes, we have to use a value that is the capability plus the margin. For example, if the capability is 1dB/in, then we write down 1*1.1=1.1dB/in as requirement. The fab note also prescribes coupon testing for pass/fail based on the loss requirement.

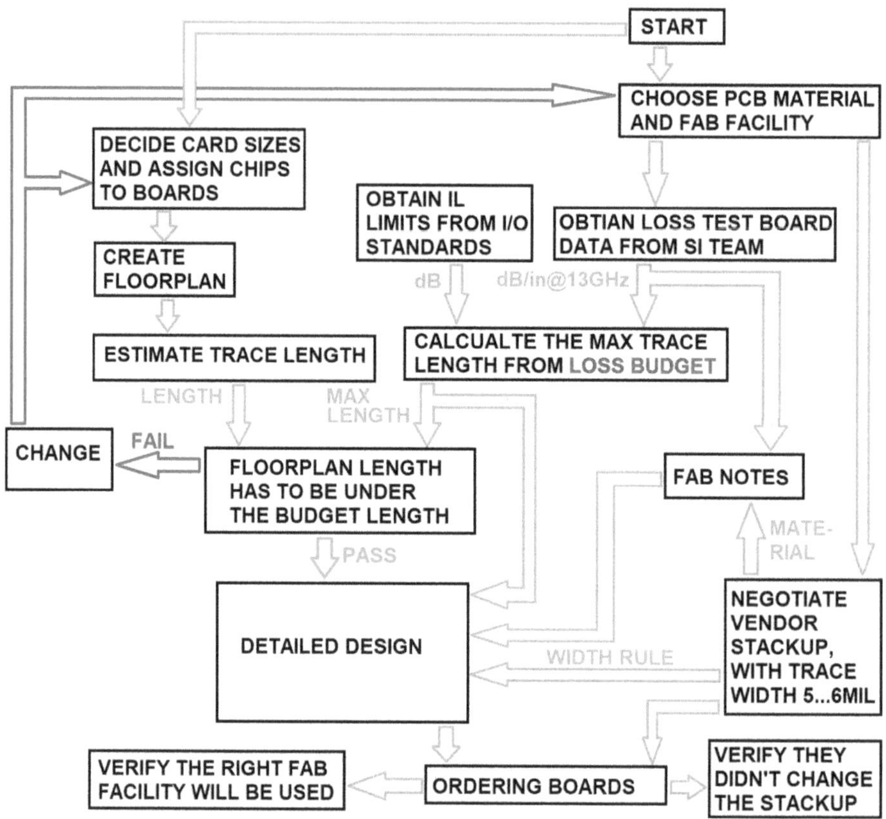

FIGURE 14.16 Design flow for insertion loss control.

All the steps we have been discussing so far can be compiled into a flow chart, as we can see in Figure 14.16, as well as into a step-by-step guide as can be seen below:

1. Obtain the loss budget data (IL limit, B at f1) from the standard. The frequency f1 is usually at half baud rate, or a rounded value. For example, B=20dB for XYZ interface, with a frequency of interest at f1=6GHz, that is 20dB@6GHz.
2. Take 1dB off for each connector in the path, and calculate a new total budget as B1=B-N*(1dB). In the example it is B1=20-2*1=18dB.
3. Obtain loss coupon or SI test board data (LC and measurement frequency f2) or capability data from the PCB fab or from our SI engineer. For example, LC=1dB/in@13GHz. It is for a combination of dielectric material, copper foil, process, trace width, and vendor (company-x, facility-y).
4. Apply the 10% design margin on the coupon data. LC1=LC*1.1. In this example LC1=1.1dB/in@13GHz.
5. Scale the loss data to our frequency of interest, that is our signal's Nyquist frequency, as well as the f1 from the standard. LC2=(f1/f2)*LC1. In our example we scale it to 6GHz by LC2 = (6GHz/13GHz) * 1.1 = 0.507dB/in@6GHz.
6. Calculate the max trace length constraint from the reduced budget and the margined-up coupon data: LMAX=B1/LC2. In the example LMAX=18dB/0.507=35.45". This LMAX is the total trace length allowed across multiple boards, if the signal travels through multiple boards and connectors and backplanes.

What does all this mean for system architecture? Before the loss budget analysis, we already had the material and the fabricator (with their process) picked, so we had a loss-per-inch number. After the loss budget calculation, we obtained a maximum trace length LMAX. Next, we have to check the feasibility of our board and chassis/system architecture and floorplan, whether we will violate this LMAX or not. If we violate it, then we have to pick either a new material or a new fabricator or change our floorplan or system architecture. In the case of an interface that starts and ends on the same board, we can set up a layout constraint for LMAX (total etch length), but that can leave us stranded with an un-routable design. It is more productive to analyze our placement in a floorplan diagram (that we have to create) and determine how long the routing length would likely be, and compare it with our LMAX. If it is longer than LMAX, then we have to either look into the new materials or re-arrange the floorplan until we no longer violate the LMAX from the loss budget. In the case of a multi-board system, we have to create the floorplans of all boards involved (TX module, backplane, and RX module) and add up the trace lengths. If the total length violates the LMAX from the loss budget, then we have to look into materials or re-arranging components on the floorplans of all three boards, or even add retimer chips to our block diagrams and schematic. On the module boards we might have to place the ASICs closer to the backplane connector, which might cause other issues that we need to resolve. For example, we have made the backplane interface shorter, but then we also made the external interface longer as a side effect, or we made the power delivery longer with more DCR. We have to come up with innovative ideas to satisfy all floorplan and routing requirements of all interfaces with the new position of the ASIC that is moved closer to the backplane connector. We might have to make the board form factor smaller/shorter so the ASIC can reach both the backplane connector on one end of the card and the other device or connector on the other end of the card, or we might have to add retimer or switch chips near the connector. A retimer is straightforward, while switch chips might provide additional benefits, such as extra ports or port modes or even bandwidth aggregation. On the backplane if the high-speed signal only has to go to a few other slots, then we can probably re-arrange the slot roles, so the slots/boards that talk to each other over the SERDES link will have to be next to each other—except if it causes thermal issues having high power boards in adjacent slots. If we need the SERDES link to reach all slots, then we need to place the card/slot that talks to all others into the middle slot so as to reduce the longest route. If nothing works then we might have to use retimer cards half-way in the route, distribute switching to more than one card, or ditch the backplane-based architecture and use orthogonal fabric cards with retimers or switch chips. We might have to change all the cards' form factors. Sometimes we can use larger cards so the ASICs that need to connect to each other can be on the same board and have much shorter routing length, and have only the slower signals go over the backplane. Alternatively, we could sometimes use smaller cards so the ASICs can reach the backplane connector through a shorter trace. If our total floorplan trace lengths do not violate the LMAX from the loss budget, then we just have validated our system architecture in terms of SI, and we can go on with designing the schematics and layouts for all the boards. Reflections might still be an issue from low-quality connectors, so changing to different connectors also has some effect on system architecture (but that is not the topic of this chapter).

If we have a multi-board SERDES link, but the different boards use different materials or different fabricator companies, we have to allocate loss budgets or length budgets to each board. Loss budget calculations have to consider all three cards' trace lengths and losses for a chip-to-chip loss budget. Losses only matter chip-to-chip really, as the signal is sent by a chip and received by another. For example, if our plug-in cards get 6dB each, and the backplane gets 18dB, that is a total 6+6+18=30dB budget. Then on the add-in cards with 1.5dB/in@6GHz materials we can afford to route as long as 4" traces, or with 3dB/in@6GHz materials we can route up only to 2" traces. In many typical cases the board with the longer traces (a backplane or motherboard) would be made with low loss material and then the cards having the short traces (plug-in cards) would be made with

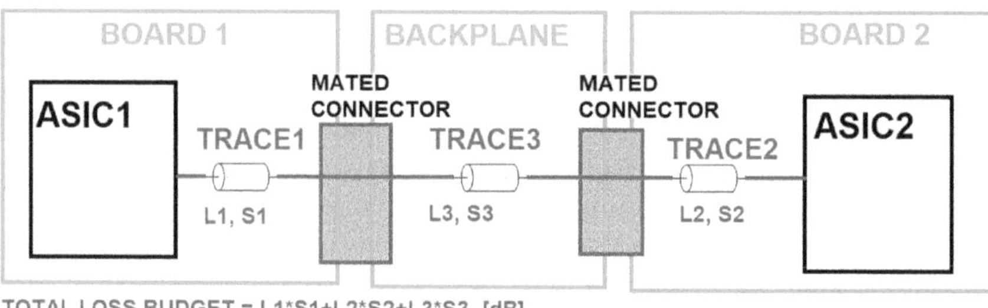

FIGURE 14.17 Losses in a backplane channel.

high loss factory/process. Figure 14.17 visualizes the loss budget division into separate card form factors.

14.6 DESIGN NOTES

During the detailed schematic design, we do small-scale (few minutes each) analysis and verifications to make decisions about low-level details of what we put into the schematic. Some of this can go into the design plan or hardware spec, but many small choices we make only while working on the detailed schematics design. These are things we look up in component datasheets before connecting one pin or before placing a supporting part or picking a resistor value. Any calculations will also be included if they result in component value choices. The very obvious ones or multiple instances do not need a written explanation, only the ones that can be ambiguous to our peers. We can create different format documents for each type of check or we can consolidate all of them into one document. The most basic option is to just put text comments into the schematic, so each part of it will be self-explanatory. At other times we have to take screenshots of tables from datasheets and mark them up with our choices or make diagrams (like connector orientation or pin direction tables or maps). In some cases where relevant, we can list drive strength requirements with load currents on some mixed digital/analog interfaces. Power domain crossing checks and port or boot mode selections can be listed with some text.

Logic compatibility analysis: For example, we have to see what kind of I/O standard or voltage level pin-5 of IC21 has, and what kind of I/O standard does pin-8 of IC22 require, if we want to connect them together. We have to make sure we are not driving a 1.8V CMOS input with a 3.3V TTL signal, or we are not driving a CML input with an LVPECL signal. It could belong to this topic of deciding whether AC coupling is required, if the input bias is unknown or different from the driver chip's output bias, in case of differential I/O standards. Checking the logic compatibility allows us a basic design verification as well as telling if we need level translating, AC-coupling or biasing circuits between the devices. This can be filled into a spreadsheet for all signals, but in most cases it is just a text in the schematic in the more ambiguous cases only.

Strapping table: Some ASICs have a few strapping (mode select) pins, so normally we put some text next to the strapping pin in the schematic about the choice of why we connected a pull-down instead of a pull-up resistor or what mode we selected (like Gen3 speed vs Gen2 speed). Larger parts, like X86 south bridge chips, might have dozens of such strap and GPIO uses, so we might have to create an Excel spreadsheet to collect all choices. This helps us to compare with reference designs as well as it helps software engineers to customize low-level BIOS or bootloader software to the custom hardware.

In hardware design we use Excel spreadsheets and basic text editors for formatting and analyzing data structures. This is needed when we are trying to move long lists between incompatible software, like schematic library editors, FPGA editors, layout editors, and simulation tools. For example, we can open an FPGA constraint file in a text editor, automatically replace all spaces with tabs, and then import it into Excel where we can further format it before importing it into a schematic library editor for symbol creation. We can remove irrelevant columns, and add columns for subpart index (large heterogenous symbols) or pin graphic name. Sometimes we have to format S-parameter files before using them in an Excel calculator template. Touchstone files can have different formats; our simple calculators might not support all. For example, one simulation tool might create an S-par file with spaces instead of tabs or spread one record in multiple lines. We also use spreadsheets for checking pin backplane mapping in multi-board systems, document constraints, pin strapping, pin swapping, ASIC port mapping, device addresses, pin delays, or just record data entries after measurements. Several complex engineering computations can be done in Excel templates that we can download from the Internet, like PDN analyzers and VRM component value calculators.

14.6.1 Connector Pinouts

We have to document the pinouts of board-to-board connectors, including the directions of each signal. We should also check whether there is any pin direction conflict by using a spreadsheet. Sometimes the connector pinouts are also listed in the hardware spec (plan), but without the direction checker, just the final version of the correct(ed) pinout. At some companies a separate document is written for documenting the final connector pinouts, this is called an interface control document (ICD). These are treated as official documents between hardware and software engineering and between the designers of different boards that are meant to operate together in the same chassis. We have to have documents with the connector pinouts of all boards. Sometimes we need a pinout translator spreadsheet as the mating connector's pin numbers might be different, for example, in the case of VPX connectors and orthogonal connectors.

When creating a pinout checker spreadsheet (or pin mapping analysis), we have to indicate which signal is an input to which board/chip and which is an output. Signal names are usually named after one of the two devices' pin name, and it can be confusing. Sometimes there is no indication which device was the origin of the signal's name. A good practice is to put a text into the schematic saying "pin names are based on U21" or similar. We have to trace all signals back to the silicon devices, we cannot just handle connector pin mapping based on schematic net names. This is demonstrated in Figure 14.18. A spreadsheet like this would be able to pinpoint if a transmit signal was routed to another transmit signal, creating a conflict. Any full duplex link like SERDES channels or even

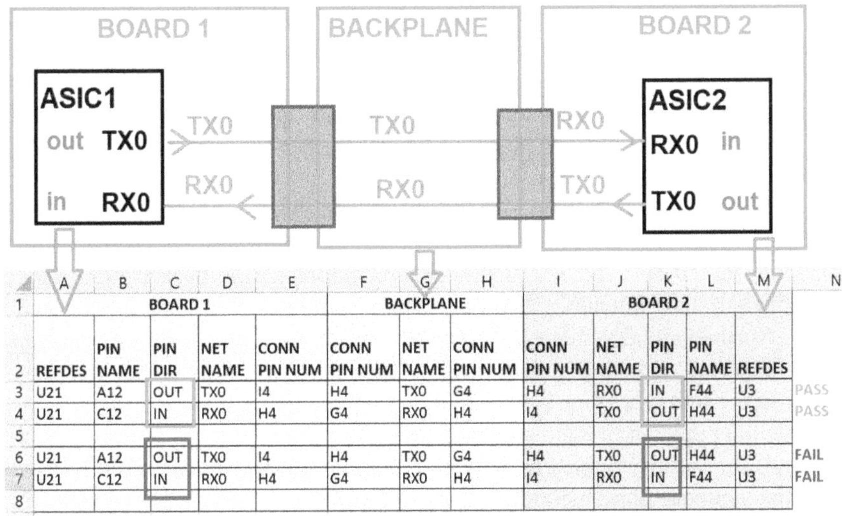

	A	B	C	D	E	F	G	H	I	J	K	L	M	N
1	BOARD 1					BACKPLANE			BOARD 2					
2	REFDES	PIN NAME	PIN DIR	NET NAME	CONN PIN NUM	CONN PIN NUM	NET NAME	CONN PIN NUM	CONN PIN NUM	NET NAME	PIN DIR	PIN NAME	REFDES	
3	U21	A12	OUT	TX0	I4	H4	TX0	G4	H4	RX0	IN	F44	U3	PASS
4	U21	C12	IN	RX0	H4	G4	RX0	H4	I4	TX0	OUT	H44	U3	PASS
5														
6	U21	A12	OUT	TX0	I4	H4	TX0	G4	H4	TX0	OUT	H44	U3	FAIL
7	U21	C12	IN	RX0	H4	G4	RX0	H4	I4	RX0	IN	F44	U3	FAIL
8														

FIGURE 14.18 Pin mapping analysis example.

RS232 requires a transmit and a receive pin on each device, and the transmit (output) pin of one device must be routed to the receive (input) pin of the other device for it to work. If the spreadsheet has two transmits (outputs) in one line, then that is a design mistake, and it must be marked as a failure.

Connectors for main interfaces have to be chosen early. We have to also define their pinouts and all signals we want to go through them early on in the project. This is a pinout analysis that tells us:

- Whether all the signals we wanted will fit in the chosen connector, or we have to get bigger connectors with more pins.
- Whether we have sufficient number of ground pins at important areas between signals or signal groups.
- Whether the connector is suitable for the signaling speed or not. Look at specs or simulate. We have to simulate with models of different connectors.
- Whether we get acceptable signal integrity through the assignment of ground and signal pins.
- Whether the RX and TX signals have such relative location assignments that keeps down the near-end crosstalk.
- The number of routing layers we will need to fan out our signals.
- It will help with pin assignment of the ASICs that are connecting many signals to the connector.

14.7 SCHEMATICS

We define the digital and analog circuits, all devices, and all connections in the schematics drawing in a graphical way. The component pins are connected to other component pins through nets. The schematics capture all functional details of one board. It is designed by hardware engineers. Some companies assign one board design project to a team of hardware engineers; others assign one board to one designer.

Before the schematics design even starts, we need to select any components that are new to our company and we want to use to have a schematic library symbol and a PCB footprint created. Resistors and basic parts were probably created by someone else years ago, so only the new parts, maybe two to 30 new parts have to be created. It helps to obtain spreadsheets with the pinouts of the larger ASICs from the ASIC vendor, so we (or the librarian) do not have to manually enter thousands of pin data. Then the pin list spreadsheets have to be imported into the library editor. For FPGA-based designs we often create a custom symbol. First, the FPGA engineer exports a pinout file that we transform using Excel into a format that the schematic tool can import. Each pin has a pin name like PCIE23_TX_P, and a pin number like numeric "15" or like alpha-numeric "B23" for grid/matrix components. Large parts have split symbols, so each sub part has 30 to 80 pins, placed on left and right sides.

The hardware engineer needs to read all pages of all datasheets (and design guides, ERRATA, appnotes, and other docs) that are relevant to the actual hardware design. Then we need to take notes of strappings, pin groups, and anything important before staring the schematics design so as to avoid designing based on potentially false assumptions and avoid missing any unusual requirements or details. Normally it takes 40 to 120 hours of work for an X86 platform. Some chip vendors provide a public datasheet and a non-public under-NDA version of the datasheet. We cannot design hardware based on the first type; they leave out important details.

The schematic drawing can be flat or hierarchical. On a flat schematic project, we simply add and fill pages until we capture everything we want. Signals connect to several other pages through off-page connector symbols. Basic hierarchical schematics just have a main page where all subpages are instantiated and wired to each other. In case of design re-use, we can create hierarchical schematics referencing existing design modules. Certain design blocks (like one ASIC and all its support circuits) are created as a separate design, then we reference that block using a hierarchical block symbol (with file path), and wire up its "ports" to the main schematic's flat nets. Inside the block the port symbols are floating on the page. Hierarchical designs can be heterogeneous with all blocks unique (see Figure 14.19) or homogenous with repeating identical parts. When very complex blocks repeat multiple times (like we use four identical FPGA blocks, each with multiple memory channels and so on), then we can reduce design mistakes and labor by using hierarchy. We can also save time on the layout design, as the re-used schematic block often comes with a re-used layout block file. The signals or nets change name at the port boundary. In OrCAD capture, when designing the module schematics, the reference designators and net names are "instance" properties, while in the final top-level design netlist they are re-assigned as "occurrence" properties to avoid repeating identical refdes-es. It is important that when we instantiate multiple copies of the same module, the reference designators and net names get re-mapped to the top level. For example, R1 inside the module becomes R456 in the first occurrence, and it (R1) becomes R789 in the second occurrence. If we have more than two levels of hierarchy, then it becomes very confusing and labor intensive trying to track down where any of the signals go and what names they change into multiple times. Still, most of the world uses flat schematics, as they are simpler to handle, net names are not ambiguous, and

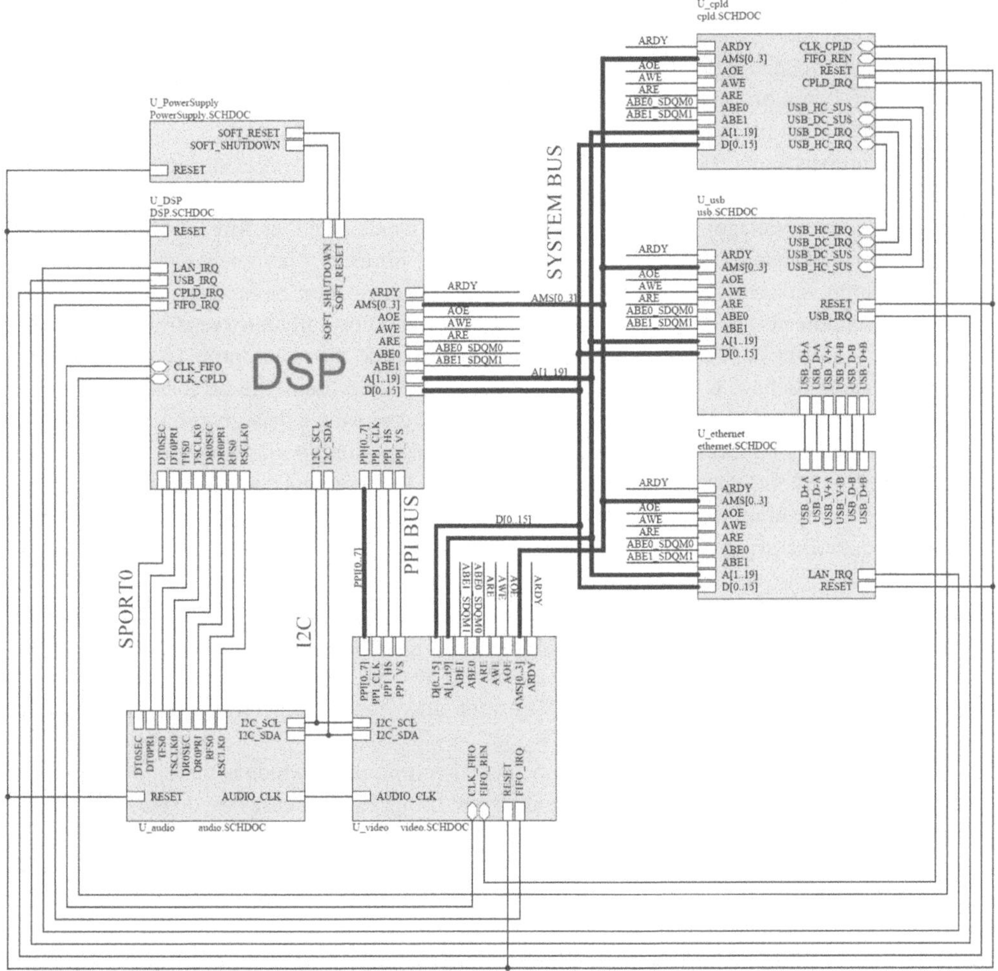

FIGURE 14.19 Top level schematic page of a heterogenous hierarchical design, from an old DSP board in Altium.

good layout teams have methods of quick layout replication on flat schematics. On flat schematic designs the signals go from any page to any other page without any structure—this might be what some people do not like. These page-to-page signal transitions go through off-page symbols, which get a page number text added to them. These numbers help us to detect any signals that go nowhere, with no number, aka not handled by the designer yet.

Large ASICs usually split into three to 30 schematic symbols, which are placed on one to 20 schematic pages. We can usually put one to four VRM circuits on one page, except multiple phase core regulators that split to a few pages. The design is broken down into many pages; each functional block from the main block diagram might split into multiple pages. Some designers use smaller sheets and lots of white spaces around components, but in that case the overall page count and the page count per functional block increases, which makes it harder to follow the functionality. If we use large sheets and some compacting, then we can fit, for example, one retimer chip on one page instead of two or three.

The major schematics tools are Cadence OrCAD, Cadence Concept HDL, Mentor DX Designer, and Altium Designer. KiCad is a free tool that allows some length tuning of traces in the PCB layout, which are used by hobbyists, academia and researchers on low to medium complexity designs.

Schematics design techniques like placing library parts, off-sheet connector ports, wires/nets, buses, component properties, net names, assigning reference designators (annotation), and generating netlists are considered basic electrical engineering, and they are not discussed here. They are also very tool specific, and it is better to attend a training hosted by a CAD tool vendor.

What is more common on complex digital boards than on simple boards is the heavy use of zero-ohm (design insurance) resistors and the company standard (whichever company you work at) component property sets. Properties are attached to every component to store information like part number, manufacturer name, footprint name association, descriptive text, electrical parameters (resistance, max voltage), or production related comments like "lead-free". Most companies maintain their own schematic symbol and layout footprint libraries where new parts are officially reviewed and approved. Only very small companies use downloaded or random library symbols. Value-driven components (like resistors, capacitors, inductors) normally have separate library parts for each value/footprint combination; we do not just overwrite the value property from 10nF to 47nF. Even resistors do have a part number; overwriting it would break the database link between the property set and the purchasable part numbers. At some companies they give some leeway to the contract manufacturers (CMs) by not specifying themselves or simply allowing the CM to replace any part that matches the description, but only for basic components like resistors and ceramic capacitors. Most companies create a component instance, based on part number in the CAD library as well as the manufacturing release database, like Oracle Agile or SAP. The part number can be our own part number or we can use the manufacturers' part number, it depends on the company. Resistors are really defined by resistance, tolerance, and footprint. Ceramic capacitors are defined by capacitance, voltage, material (X5R, X7R, NPO), and footprint. Tantalum and polymer capacitors, as well as power inductors, are defined by exact part number on our high-performance complex digital boards designs, due to tight ESR, RMS-current, and other parameters the vendors compete on. All other parts are by part number only.

We often use the "do not populate" option on several components, which is there for the purpose of design insurance—not assurance, which is a different thing. In most cases we do this to zero ohm 0402 resistors for routing signals or pull up/down resistors. We can remove a pulldown and solder down a pullup to change the PCIe speed of a device through strapping pins, for example, as we can see in Figure 14.20. This is often marked as DNP, DNI (do not insert), NF (no-fit), or NOPOP, depending on the company. We can alter the circuit behavior on the prototype by removing resistors and soldering-on parts that were originally marked DNP. We rely on these a lot to debug and make our proto-1 boards work. Depending on company and design tool the parts are marked differently. For example, attaching a "populate" property to them and setting the value to yes or no, or attaching a DNP property to only those we want to mark or typing "DNP" into the component value field or

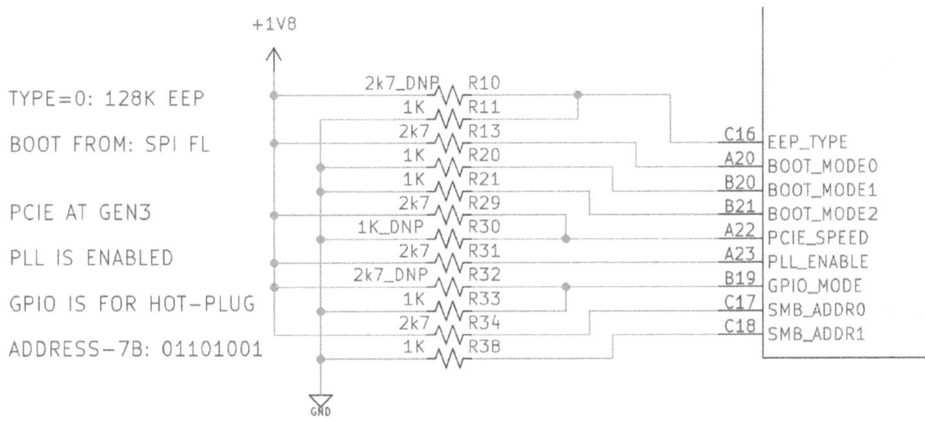

FIGURE 14.20 Device strapping with DNP resistor configurability in made-up schematic in KiCAD.

in some cases a checkbox can be assigned in the design software. The DNP component will end up being removed from the BOM, so the manufacturer will not solder it on the board. Although sometimes we have to check on the proto whether they really left it out or not.

When we start the schematic drawing, we create a sufficient number of pages for each main function from the block diagram, then during the design we add extra pages if needed. We also have to have pages for glue logic and power management, sensors, and management plane devices. We place the main parts from the library into the drawing, and then we try to hook up all of their pins. A few NC pins remain but each group has to be explained with text comment. As we make the local net/wire connections, we have to add supporting parts, memory chips, oscillators, strapping and pullup resistors, level translators, and transistors. We have to create pages for all the voltage regulators to produce all the rails from the power tree. We have to add and calculate the decoupling networks for all the ASICs, then place the caps into the schematic. We have to add pages for all required off-board I/O connectors, and add the nets to them and any support logic. On all pages we have to keep adding off-sheet connectors to any signal that has to go to other pages. We have to copy these off-sheet connectors on each page and paste them to their intended destination pages. If we manually type them instead of copying, then a few signals will go nowhere due to typos. We can go page by page, or we can start with the data plan and finish with the glue logic signals. We have to check all subsystem block diagrams to see if all minor functions are implemented with components and connected with schematic nets. We have to add programming and debug headers, and probe points and lots of SMD LEDs (showing boot up, power up, link up). We have to connect up all the new pasted off-page connectors on every page. There might be net name conflicts with existing ones that need resolving. This will establish the long connections through the design. The connections have to match the subsystem block diagrams we created, but the diagrams can be updated if we find extra signals or parts that need adding or removing. We have to make sure we do not connect a TX pin to a TX pin on another device. Signal names are not sufficient in determining the signal's direction; we have to trace all of them to the chip symbol pins, similarly to the connector pinout design. Every pin (except intentionally left out pins) of every component has to be hooked up or text noted why they are left out. If we scan the schematic for unconnected pins then we can see what is still to be taken care of. This way the schematic drawing acts as a self-checking checklist. We will find several glue logic signals and minor buses that need connecting and updating on the connector pinouts documents and block diagrams. We have to let the other board designers, FPGA, and firmware engineers about these changes through an updated hardware spec document. We have to cross check with the FPGA engineer whether their pinout still matches ours; correct any missing pins on both sides of the aisle (FPGA pin editor and board schematic). Some of the connections will require power domain crossing logic, terminations, pullups, isolating analog multiplexers, buffers, bus expansion logic (like I2C multiplexers), magnetics modules, transceiver or retimer chips, or level translation circuits. We pick them all from the library, place them, and wire them up. We have to verify that the glue logic will still work after any changes, to avoid chicken and egg situations when a board cannot start up.

At the end of the schematics design we run an "annotation" to automatically assign reference designators to each component, which uniquely identify them, and populate the off-sheet connector page index. We have to check if any off-sheet connector has no number assigned, that indicates the signal is not going anywhere. We have to go back into the design and fix the missing connections. Then we can run error checks, DRC, or third-party automated checks looking for unconnected pins, shorted nets, capacitor voltage ratings, and other drawing mistakes. Some schematics check tools can tell if any wire was assigned a net name but not connected to anything. We then generate the bill of materials or BOM, which can be uploaded into our manufacturing release database. The parts in the design have the part number property that matches with a purchasing database entry for the component, so they get linked after import. For each board design a database contains several files (schematic and layout drawings, system mechanical drawings, Gerber files), and BOM tables (for board, sub-assembly, and system). The purchasing departments purchase components and boards, order SMT services from CMs based on project files and BOMs in the database. Then we generate a netlist for the layout engineer and a PDF schematic drawing for the hardware peers and for ourselves. After this the schematic drawing is usually peer reviewed by multiple members of the hardware department (peers), who provide sometimes more than 100 comments in a spreadsheet, which all have to be considered. Most of them are implemented while the ones that are not implemented need to be explained in writing before the schematic final netlist is generated for layout design.

Schematics can contain several types of irregular parts, including the non-BOM parts like mounting holes, the non-layout parts like programming files, the non-electrical parts like stickers. Some companies place these into the schematic drawing; others place it only in the database version of the BOM. Non-BOM parts can be like mounting holes and frame attachment areas. Non-layout parts might be like programming files and heatsinks, screws, thermal paste, and spacers. Non-electrical parts might be like daughter card outlines and stickers.

Typically, there are multiple BOM levels in the company manufacturing database (Oracle Agile, SAP, etc.). One level is for the soldered board (PCA, CCA), one module-level subassembly is for the board with heatsinks and mechanical parts, one is for the chassis it goes into. Mechanical engineering deals with the BOM levels above the PCA BOM.

We also have to compare our schematic with any main ASIC reference designs, and investigate any differences, to see if the deviation will cause any malfunction or software incompatibility. Ideally we create a spreadsheet of functions, pins, and connections, showing how we connected it, how the reference design connected it, and how the datasheet wants us to connect it. I/O voltage, external PU/PD requirements, power domain, and other parameters can also be shown. This is for the software engineering to make the necessary changes to the re-sed software code. We almost always use reference design schematics that the chip vendors provide. All main ASICs have it; often we can get it for supporting devices also. This is usually the schematic drawing of the evaluation board that we can purchase. So we (our software engineer) can test the eval board with our software, and we can review the schematic of the eval board hardware that we tested. Often we copy the reference schematic pages into our design, manually part by part, while we are altering the parts we want differently. For example, we use a different EEPROM chip vendor for the ASIC config storage, or we connect MDIO signals differently. Any short connections between the main ASIC and its supporting circuits are usually closely followed, while the long connections of the data/control/management planes are specific to our new design. Usually we design-in several supporting chips that are different from those the eval board has, due to purchasing, our own library, as well as BOM consolidation. For example, if we use three different ASICs from three different vendors on our new board design, each specifying a config EEPROM from different vendors, but we will just pick one

EEPROM type and use that for all three ASICs. Often, we want to use a different boot method for a processor and a different memory size or type (memory-down versus DIMM), and these are all legitimate deviations from the reference design. The decoupling capacitors are sometimes copied, at other times we optimize them in our PDN simulation before drawing the schematic.

14.7.1 Schematics Readability

If we design the schematics in a way that is more readable and understandable, then anyone having to deal with it will save time when they have to look up connections and features. Hardware peers, test engineers, and FPGA and software engineers have to look things up on our schematics, so we do not just design it for ourselves. They usually use a PDF version, not the one in the design tool. In some cases, we can reduce the feature search time from one hour to less than a minute by using good design or drawing techniques. If we have to look up 20 features to find out what is going on, then 20 x 1min is much better than 20 x 1hr. It is not only time reduction, but also reduction in error proneness during the design process; we can make it easier for ourselves to spot mistakes before we Gerber out if details are more trackable. Many functions work through two to five details on different pages. By the time we looked up the fifth after five hours, we might be misremembering the parameter on the first one.

We should use flat or two-level hierarchical designs. Signals change names at hierarchy level, making it time consuming to follow all paths if three or more levels are used. If we keep each block on as few pages as possible, and we use densely packed large, then the functionality is easier to understand by looking at one page—try looking at a box of puzzle versus a magazine or a poster.

We need to put comments in the schematics about every non-trivial detail or decision. With these we can be assured that we will not get mistaken or confused about a detail while designing it, we can make sure that we have checked every detail, we will be able to debug and fix the prototype quickly and efficiently, and other people will be able to read the functionality out of the schematics. The schematics must document itself without having to look up lots of stuff in other documents (datasheets, product specs, meeting minutes, etc.). This way the design acts as a self-checking checklist and a complete drawing. We need to put large text titles on each page and each subcircuit block, so they will be readable when the PDF schematics is viewed in full-page view, without having to zoom in on each page while scanning through the document. Adding text comments at every feature group, all off-page connector or hierarchical port groups, describing where the signal is going, which device is input and which is output for that signal helps the reader to understand what is what. During schematics design we have to continuously cross-check different pages, and the comments help us to quickly understand what we are connecting the new subcircuit to, so we can avoid mistakes. Adding text at every strapping pin to explain the choice and any counter-intuitive detail helps in catching design errors and in understanding what mode the ASIC is supposed to be operating in. If it takes 30 minutes to understand a detail, then we do not want to re-do that 30 minutes research every time we look it, so a small text comment in the schematic can preserve that understanding and reduce it to a 15 second check. Adding text about I2C addresses of each device helps us avoid an address conflict. If we put down some text about the firmware part number next to programmable devices, it helps us track programming files. Later it is hard to tell which file goes to which device, even with reference designators. At each voltage regulator output, we can add text about the total capacitive load, the voltage, and the maximum load current.

A table of contents should be placed on the first page of the schematics to help the reader jump straight to the detail they are looking for. Block diagrams of every subsystem can be placed on the first or second page of the schematics. These are power tree, power control/management, resets, I2C busses, PCI/PCIe tree, control and data plane I/O connections, clocks, and JTAG chains. Other objects we often put on the top page are mounting holes, labels, test coupons, or heatsinks.

We should really use net names that are suggesting what they are and use one type of naming convention within one design. For example, instead of "P525ACTYXV_N", use "PCIE_5_TYXV_N".

The interface type and the functional group are clearly separated in the net name with under-scores, the signal type and port number are clearly mentioned. All power nets should have the same naming convention, which also allows easy net name filtering in the layout tool, for example, start with "+" or "-" or "P" and a number for positive nets like "P1.8V" or to avoid dots in net names use "P1V8".

The purpose of some of these suggestions is to maximize confidence in design details, minimize mistakes, minimize peer review time, minimize bringup/debug time, increase re-usability, and improve teamwork efficiency, for the price of a little upfront effort. Leaving these out may save time initially, but it will not save time in the whole product development process for the cross-functional team members. Typing in some text in 30 seconds can save multiple times 30 minutes having to figure out the detail every time.

Once the schematic design is complete, several automated checks should be run on it. Most tools have an electrical tool checker that finds shorted nets, unconnected pins, single-pin nets, and so on. There are design validation services available from a few vendors. We can write scripts or programs that parse netlists for automatic reading of schematic information. Main chip vendors provide their customers with schematic design checklists. These have many items; sometimes they give additional insight into where we should have connected that ambiguous strapping pin.

14.8 DESIGN FOR MANUFACTURING (DFM)

Manufacturing might run into problems that cannot easily be resolved by manufacturers alone if the designer did not anticipate and prevent these. They might run into chicken and egg problems, for example, device-A has to be programmed in order to access device-B for programming, but device-B controls the power to device-A, being unprogrammed it does not power up device-A, so device-A cannot be programmed, so device-B cannot be accessed for programming. The programming and power up sequences have to be designed together, and the schematic has to comply with these sequences. The hardware engineers have to actively resolve conflicting requirements and provide accessibility to hardware features for tools, probes, and software. Basically, the design has to be manufacturable by meeting DFM considerations. There are several areas where this has to be considered:

- PCB fabrication: We need to use feature sizes in the layout design that meets the fabricator facility's constraints.
- SMT assembly: Component locations have to be accessible by the pick and place machine. Fiducials to be placed strategically at board corners and at large part corners. Solder stencil thickness and patterns, as well as solder mask patterns, have to be such that the SMT assembly will produce good yield, free of shorts and opens (cold solder). The footprint designs have to serve solderability as well as signal/power integrity needs at the same time. Manufacturing engineering is often involved in reviewing footprints and layouts for these aspects.
- Re-work: Component-to-component clearance is provided so as to be able to remove a part without damaging others. This extra clearance might not be applied to every design, based on a cost/benefit analysis. For example, increasing the re-workability at the expense of signal integrity degradation would not be worth it.
- Through hole assembly requires clearance areas around the components for custom mechanical fixtures, otherwise the parts cannot be press-fitted or wave soldered into the board.
- Device programming headers: All devices that require programming or debug-access need a programming header, and it needs to be accessible even with the mechanical frames in place. Any device that needs programming cannot be dependent on another device that is disabled at the time. For example, a JTAG chain used for programming the power sequencer chip cannot run through devices that are unpowered at the time the sequencer

is not yet programmed. We have to have the ability to detach unpowered devices using standby-domain multiplexer chips designed-in. All JTAG capable devices require a test heeder on the board, dedicated or shared. Some devices do not need their own header if they can be programmed through another device. For example, FPGA config flash chips can be programmed through the FPGA JTAG port, while X86 BIOS flash chips cannot be programmed through the chipset's JTAG. Some devices can share a programming port, for example, smart VRMs from the same vendor sharing a PMBUS header. JTAG devices should be on a separate chain if they are made by different chip vendors, but we can combine them temporarily for a test. The headers or connectors might be chip vendor standard size and pinout, or we might use combined fine pitch headers and programming adapter fixtures.

- Mechanical assembly (heatsinks, frames) require a way to assemble them without breaking any parts on the board.
- Basic functional tests have to be easy to run to exercise most parts of the hardware.
- Chips and programming headers need a large pin-1 marking in the silkscreen, which helps us in the lab, preventing human errors with incorrect orientation of soldered parts and plug-in programming cables. Other information is also placed on the silkscreen, such as connector use names and serial numbers.

This requires a lot of common sense, thought experiments, cross-functional experience, and working with other departments. For any part of the design that is affected by one of the manufacturing stages above, the hardware designer has to think while implementing it "how will this be programmed/assembled/tested…"—during the design, not just after the design is done. The device programming and the mechanical assembly also require a programming sequence and an assembly sequence written down in a document and reviewed by relevant departments before the detailed design starts/completes. Ideally it will be mentioned in the design plan. All devices have to be programmable in circuit when some other devices are not programmed yet. This requires some glue logic to be designed in, for example for JTAG or SPI bus multiplexing. We do not want to be in a situation where we have to remove a BGA processor on every board in order to program an EEPROM memory.

14.9 DESIGN FOR TEST (DFT)

The hardware has to be designed in a way that we will be able to run functional tests in a logical sequence as well as probe signals or take measurements. This may separate into DFT for production and into DFT for engineering validation. We have to be aware early on, before the schematics start, which signals we will need to measure. Then we have to design them in a way that they will have pads able to be probed (for example, GSSG land pattern for VNA), probe access for live signals will not be blocked by heatsinks or other objects, test points will be on the side of the board that is more accessible. Sometimes we have to design in some glue logic that puts devices into test modes. For example, a dip switch that is altering a processor's or FPGA's boot modes, or a jumper driving a signal telling a glue logic FPGA to ignore power faults. We can force a power sequencer to ignore rail failures and keep turning on everything and remain on, so we can probe the failing rails on a broken board for debugging. We have to provide debug headers to access devices over JTAG or I2C or SPI; sometimes they require analog multiplexers to temporarily detach host devices from memory chips to be able to control them from a header. Sometimes we implement complex JTAG chains with buffers and multiplexers to allow both combining and separating devices from a shared JTAG chain. This is for both in-factory ICT boundary scan testing as well as for proto debugging through the same JTAG ports. For debugging we usually want to access one device at a time, in boundary scan factory testing we like to have as many devices in one chain as possible, so our glue logic can allow switching between these modes using jumpers.

Test points are small SMT or through-hole pads (1-pin component) on a surface layer with soldermask removed but no solder paste applied. They are used for probing signals with oscilloscopes or multimeters up to <<1GHz. We can manually place test points in the schematic and have a footprint for them. There are also the ICT test points that are not placed in the schematic, are much smaller, have a high number of them used in a design, and are intended for bed of nails (ICT) test bed spring-contact landing. An ICT test fixture might be developed for our board if we plan a medium to high volume production, which probes many signals automatically, to determine if a production unit is good or bad, and it may even program devices.

On many high-end designs we also allow the programming of all programmable devices either from headers or from the local host processor or from both. Assuming the processor can run with these devices unprogrammed. We can design in a simple VNA test coupon (2 diffpairs with 2X Thru De-embedding) so we can gather insertion loss data from any board when needed. For example, if one production batch has many units failing to link up on a SERDES interface, we can ship one such unit to the R&D lab to measure it to see if the loss was out of spec or not.

14.10 DESIGN FOR DEBUGGING (DFD)

DFT and DFM focus on the part of the project after the development cycle has completed. The prototype board bring-up cycle is typically done heuristically and with a lot of random probing of signals on the boards. This way the time it takes from concept until production is less deterministic than it could be. Certain hardware design bugs can be found faster, without wasting many peoples time, or without unnecessary delays in product launch. Most engineers have some kind of debugging hooks in their designs, but it is typically a few JTAG and I2C headers and that is it. Some signals can be probed on component pins with oscilloscopes or multimeters, but there is a cost to this in terms of a lot of time spent on looking up those pins in the schematic and layout. By designing in the following features we can improve signal visibility, and we can also make it fast and easy to alter/correct the circuit behavior:

- Using lots of DNP and zero-ohm resistors: Re-working one resistor takes a lot less time than re-spinning the board design. This way we can have confirmations about the effectiveness of design corrections right away.
- Fault-logging: When an intermittent failure happens, it is useful to know which event happened first. With black box or fault-logging features on glue logic FPGAs, microcontrollers, and other devices, the first failed signal's identifier can be logged into an EEPROM or an FRAM memory, so later we can read out the log.
- We usually provide a bus-access header to any device that can report information through its registers or capture an eye diagram if they have low-speed I2C, SPI, or JTAG ports. These ports can be accessed through USB-based dongles. We need a lot of information for debugging prototype boards.
- We should separate the devices made by different vendors to independent I2C busses: This will save the time of fingerpointing when some devices are inaccessible, have failed data transfers, or a vendor GUI misbehaves.
- For glue logic FPGAs and microcontrollers, we often use DIP-switch components or header jumpers to put our device into certain states. We might want our power sequencer to be in a smart-VRM programming mode that requires the enable signals to be driven a certain way. We might need a power sequencer debug mode for prototype or production failure debugging, by telling the sequencer state machine to not shut down all rails at a failure but remain partially on. We might want a board to power up without a processor. Sometimes we have a JTAG chain with a multiplexer to attach/detach devices. We might want our main device to have different boot modes available for factory programming or debugging. We might want to tell our FPGA or CPU which system it is placed in or what mode our

system should run on. A DIP switch or a jumper simply drives a signal constant high or low that goes to an FPGA or CPU pin to control its behavior. The FPGA/MCU simply reads this pin, and then its internal state machine or software decides what to do based on the signal state. A DIP switch is a small SOIC (1.27mm pitch) package with multiple switches that either conducts between two pins or not. A jumper is a pin header that we can short. In either case the "signal" is pulled up, then the switch can short it to ground or not short it.

- Eliminate discrete glue logic and use a small flash FPGA instead: This can help applying (soft) bug fixes without having to do excessive wiring re-work or having to wait for a design re-spin. The sooner we can confirm the final schematics in the development cycle, the better.
- Since the glue logic FPGA pins can be scanned with a JTAG logic analyzer, the more system control and status signals are going through the FPGA pins the more visibility we can have into the system's internal operation. We can monitor hundreds of signals on a timing diagram, whereas using oscilloscopes we can probe only up to four at a time. We can discover signal dependencies that can help identify root causes. For example, a clock chip's PLL_LOCK signal went down, and it happened right when its power rail's VRM's PowerGood signal went down, which saves us some debugging time.
- We design hardware in a way such that different parts and signals can be separated and tested separately; this way we can more easily debug them in the proto-lab and the factory. For example, we turn on one VRM at a time in a sequence, we feed all VRMs from 12V instead of from each other, or we create several I2C buses instead of having many devices on the same bus. It is exponentially harder and longer to debug an issue if the potential causes are more numerous.
- We can have alternate paths by implementing multiple selectable boot modes, multiple console access points (serial and Ethernet), multiple independent backplane Ethernet links, or multiple memory channels. We often hook up an I2C slave port in addition to the main PCIe endpoint interface to an ASIC, or design in a flash interface (can be depopulated) for the ASIC's internal ARM CPU even though we intend to initialize it over PCIe. Having an alternate interface, we can determine whether the interface or the device was bad. We can also test out other parts of the design without being completely held up. For example, we can switch to another KR link and start loading data to test devices behind the link while in parallel debugging the cause of the first link's failure.

15 PCB Layout Design

All the design choices that affected the functionality and reliability of low-speed digital boards of the 1980s could be designed by hardware engineers entirely in the logic design or schematic domain. Then the actual physical implementation was like the necessary plumbing. In more modern PCBs the traces and other 3D geometry structures start to interact with the functionality and reliability of higher-speed digital circuits. This is why the person responsible for functionality and reliability—the hardware engineer—has to closely control the PCB layout (physical) implementation. Layout for complex digital boards can be designed by the hardware engineer at smaller companies, but in most cases in corporate environments it is done by specialist layout engineers. The layout engineer might be part of an in-house layout team, a layout house that is an outsourcing service company, or they might be parts of large JDM or ODM manufacturing contractor companies. The schematic is designed by the hardware engineer. While the layout is being designed by layout engineers, the hardware design engineers have a leading and very involved role in it too. We have to create, document, and understand the constraints, draw the floorplan, and define the high-speed layout copper features that the layout engineer has to implement. Layout features are, for example, impedance-optimized via structures, power shapes, fanout patterns, wavy route sections, backdrills, manual plane voids, or stitching vias. We hardware designers have to know what to implement, while the layout engineers know how to implement it. We have to guide the layout engineers into implementing what we want, often by making sketch drawings that we provide in a layout tracker spreadsheet or by email. We use a layout viewer version of the PCB design tool to be able to see what was implemented so far and how, but sometimes we have to open the actual editor version to experiment with component fanouts and placement. While the layout is being designed, we have to perform a quick daily review of the daily drop of the layout file and write up a quick feedback. Our feedback would include issues we spotted and instructions about how to fix them; it usually takes less than an hour. It is not sufficient to just have one big review when all is done. This way hardware design engineers must have expertise in what goes into the layout, even if we do not know all the layout tool menus and tricks. On the other hand, it would not hurt to get a little practice as layout tool users, by occasionally designing a few adapter boards or SI test boards ourselves. Sometimes we have to delve into the complex board layout and implement an idea ourselves on a single instance, as it is not always possible to achieve it through verbal instruction to the layout engineer only. After we create the first instance, the layout engineer can replicate all other instances, while we keep reviewing whether the replication was similar enough concerning our important parameters. For example, if a via structure that was optimized in the 3D field solver has to be replicated in the layout, in some instances one of the ground vias might be missing, or they are shifted by 10mils so the relative distance is not as it should be, or the manual voids might be missing on some layers. We have to check all parameters, spot the outliers, and request change through our tracker document.

15.1 MAJOR CAD TOOLS

Complex and high-speed digital boards require a constraint-driven PCB layout editor. The constraints are not only for manufacturing clearances, but also for high-speed design to achieve good signal integrity. There are a few major computer-aided design (CAD) tools that are suitable for this:

- Cadence Allegro PCB Editor, with OrCAD or Concept schematic. This is the gold standard for constraint-driven complex hardware design. The spreadsheet-like Allegro Constraint Manager is the great innovation created many years ago that enabled the development

DOI: 10.1201/9781032702094-15

of timing analysis-driven board design, and basically it enabled the creation of modern computer motherboards. It supports all the design objects described in the next section. Hardware design engineers have to be able to review constraints directly in the constraint manager to see if they were entered in a way that conveys our design intent and signal integrity strategy.

- Mentor Expedition PCB editor and DX Designer schematic. It has a constraint manager that works by similar object types and concepts as does the Allegro Constraint Manager.
- Altium Designer, with built-in PCB and schematic editor. It has the most user-friendly GUI. The constraints are called "Design Rules" in the "Design Rules Editor" window. After creating the rules, we have to add objects (nets, net classes) to the rules. The high-speed diffpair support has existed for a long time, but the trace segment length (like Allegro Pin-Pairs) rule was recently updated. Until around 2020 the "FromTo" objects were meant to be used for memory-down timing, but later the "X-Signals" have been introduced that work better. Even a wizard to set up many X-Signals at once has been introduced. In the most recent version, a spreadsheet-based constraint manager was also introduced as an option.
- KiCAD is a free CAD tool. The layout high-speed support is very limited—it can do diffpairs and (total etch) trace length tuning but no segment length tuning constraints. It is usable for low to medium complexity designs and is typically used by academia and hobbyists.

15.2 PCB BASICS

The easiest way to learn basic PCB design and the use of a particular CAD tool is through a corporate training provided by the CAD tool vendor, but some of us can learn it on our own. This chapter on basics explains a few concepts, but it is not comprehensive. Engineers who have been designing medium complexity boards and who are just starting on complex boards might already know all the things cited in this section. Some of the layout design features can be used in a "wrong way" that might seem fine for low complexity and low-speed boards but would not work on high-end boards, so it might be necessary to re-learn them. The latter part of this chapter deals with high-speed features and rules, and it is more comprehensive, as that is the main focus of this book, namely the intersection of complex with high speed.

We need to have "footprints" for all component package types in our PCB library that contain the component outline and the solder pads for all pins. The footprint name is linked to the schematic symbol, so when we export a netlist from the schematic to the layout tool, it can place the right footprints for each part. The footprints reference to padstack files for each of their pins. The padstacks define the copper pads for each layer, the drilling, the solder paste stencil opening, and the solder mask opening. The solder mask prevents shorting pins to traces during soldering. The stencil defines where the solder paste will be applied to the board, where exactly on the pads. Often the pad shape and the paste mask shape do not match intentionally so as to improve production yield.

When the PCB design starts, the netlist that was exported from the schematic is now imported into the PCB editor. A 2D or 3D file created by mechanical engineering needs to be imported too, which defines the exact locations of mounting holes, large ASICs, connectors, and the board outline as well as areas with component height restrictions. Then the components are placed on the board by the layout design engineer, one by one. Then the traces are routed, tuned, the design rule violations (DRC) eliminated, and finally the manufacturing output files are prepared. The two main parts of the layout job are the placement and the routing. First, all the components are placed, and in the same the fanouts (kind of routing, with short traces and vias) are created, after that the power (shapes) are drawn and the signal nets (traces) are routed. A "via" is a small diameter hole drilled through a board, then its sidewalls are plated with copper in order to provide vertical connections between traces or power shapes on different layers. A via is a noun in hardware engineering language, not a preposition as in standard English. On the most complex boards we might have tens of thousands of vias. Horizontal connections are "traces" etched into a copper foil.

The layout design file has many layers. Some of them are stackup copper layers, others are manufacturing-related drawing planes, and some are design control related "mechanical" layers. Copper layers include outer top and bottom mixed (signal/plane/footprint) layers as well as inner signal and inner power/ground plane layers. Manufacturing-related layers are solder mask and solder paste, as well as layers for drill symbols and board outline (for cutting the board out from the fabrication panel). Mechanical layers are, for example, heatsink outlines, main part positioning, and fab drawing lines/text (fabrication instructions). Solder mask is applied on the outer surface of the board to prevent solder tin from sticking to traces and vias. The solder mask has openings only for the component solder pads and any edge connector pins. These exposed copper areas receive a "surface finish" in the form of nickel-gold, organic or HASL metallic material. The solder mask opening is slightly larger than the copper pad. The solder paste will be dispensed through a stencil (thin metal plate with etched or laser-cut openings for pads) onto the pads. The stencil opening might be as wide as the pad, or smaller, or it might have several openings for larger pads. The solder mask and the paste (Stencil) are all layout design layers, one set for the top side of the board, one set for the bottom side. The openings are defined as part of the component library footprints and padstacks. There are also "silk screen" layers in the layout design for top and bottom sides, which are white lines and text, to show component and heatsink boundaries as well as component reference designators (refdes). Some of those are parts of library footprints; others are drawn by the designer.

15.2.1 Placement

A basic placement rule is to start with the main ASICs following the floorplan, create the fanout of them, then place the passive parts (decoupling first, strapping later) that belong to the ASIC directly, then place the supporting chips and their passives—like big cities, suburbs, and small towns on a map. The houses of one town are a lot closer to each other than any house to another house from another town. The same applies to PCB placement; we have to pack each subcircuit as tight as possible and avoid overlapping subcircuits. This helps to keep the noise down. It is very important to place the smaller 0402 decoupling capacitors directly on the power vias of the ASICs on the other side and the larger ones as close to the ASIC package perimeter as possible. This is why creating the ASIC fanout vias before placing the small passives is important. A design that overlaps a BGA ASIC with other circuits (like another BGA) on the other side of the board deprives the ASIC from having its decoupling capacitors directly on its power vias. This cannot be justified as it will not meet any PDN design requirement. Slow signal pullups can be placed farther from the fanout via than high-speed calibration resistors, for example (that also needs impedance-controlled traces). We cannot place everything right on the ASIC pin, so we have to prioritize. The main devices (ASICs, CPUs, FPGAs) are placed away from the board edge, and they are surrounded by their support circuit components. Programming headers are placed near the board edge in areas that are accessible by hand. Connectors, with the exception of mezzanines and internal-cable connectors, are placed at the board edge. All hot components are usually placed on the same side of the board, called top side, with their pins on the top layer of the stackup.

The "ratsnest" is a thin straight connection line between pins that are connected together by a schematic net. They visually aid the designer to see which component pairs will require trace routing between, so they are either placed in close proximity to reduce trace length or show us the main routes that will have to be routed across the board. Figure 15.1 shows how they look. During placement we also have to place the refdes objects (reference designator), which are the unique identifiers for each component, namely a letter plus number text like "R523". Some designs let the refdes to be on the silkscreen layer, but higher density designs will hide it on the manufactured board to free up space for components.

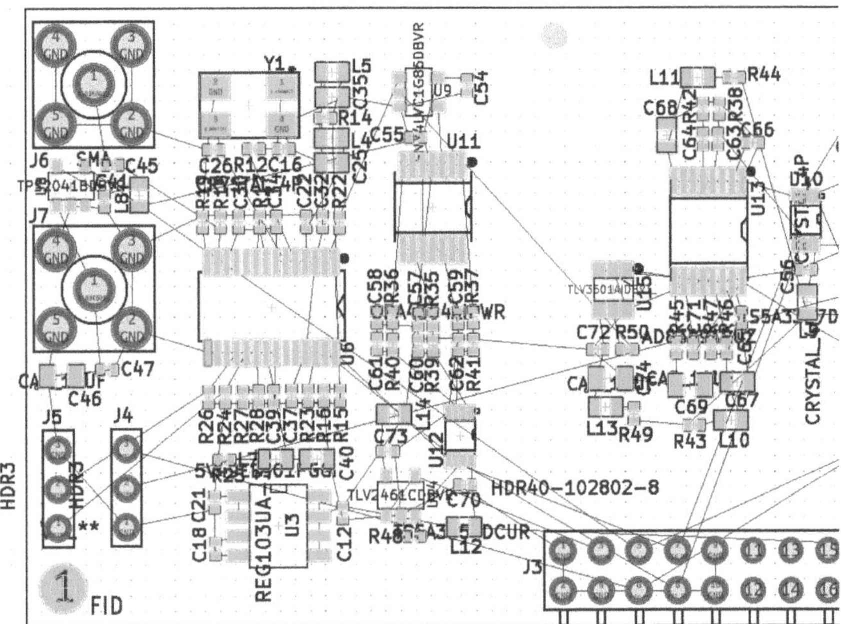

FIGURE 15.1 Placed but unrouted board with ratsnests showing in KiCad.

15.2.2 Fanout

The outer layer component pins will connect to vias, which will connect inside the stackup to inner layer traces, or they will connect to power shapes on power or ground plane layers if they are on power nets. The fanout via is connected to the component pin/pad through a very short outer layer trace. The fanout design has to start during placement to ensure that we have allowed sufficient space for the vias without interfering with other components so the signals can access other layers. All fanout should be completed before the long routing starts to ensure that we do not have to re-route everything once all fanout vias are in place. Normally we place the main components first, then we create their fanouts, then we place the small supporting components, and then we place their fanouts, and finally we implement the planes and the routing. The fanout is simply the process of connecting each pin of a silicon chip to a via through a short trace (called the dog-bone trace) on the outer layer where the component solder pad is located. The dog-bone trace has to be narrow (4 to mil) for signal nets and wide (5 to 10mil) for power nets. BGA fanouts can be automated in layout tools, to place one via and one dog-bone trace to each of the thousands of pins of large ASIC chips. This follows a pattern, either all dog-bones point in the same direction or it follows a "flare-out" pattern where the chip package is divided into four quadrants, associated with the four corners of the package, and the dog-bones are pointing outward in the directions from the center towards the corners. In PCB design we often describe directions like on a map, with north, south, west, and east, instead of left right or up and down. Up and down should mean one layer up or down in the stackup, while the top layer is layer-1 and the bottom layer is layer-N.

After the fanout we implement the escape route that takes place on the inner layers when we are routing the board (placement already done) by routing the traces out of the jungle, from under the component's pin grid to the open area. Figure 15.2 shows both stages, the basic fanout and the escape route. The difficulty is that the many vias already in place are creating narrow routing channels that allow only one diffpair or two single-ended traces to escape the area. Often, we have to use narrower traces in this area to fit between the vias, called a neck-down, usually driven by an area-constraint that overrides the trace width rule. The impedance of the trace will likely be higher

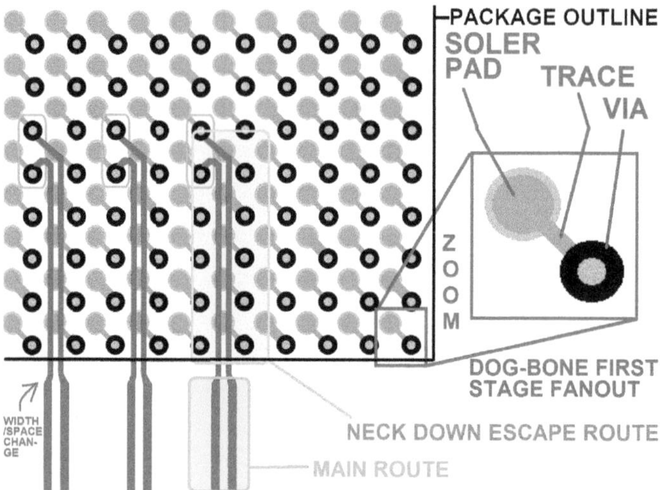

FIGURE 15.2 Fanout, escape route, and main route (sketch).

in the neck-down area, so minimizing the length of it, and creating a stackup where they are not much narrower than the main route, are the design goals. As we reach the package area boundary, the trace width will switch to being the main constraint driven width. The shorter the escape route the better; we have to route outwards from the center of the chip, instead of zig-zag-ing under the chip to find a way out. In the neck down controlled area we can mitigate the impedance a little bit by using alternating width, tab routing, or on offset-grid BGAs we can use a snake-fanout, as we can see later in this chapter. Non-grid component packages like QFN or SSOP do not have this issue of neck down, their fanouts do not have to pass through a tightly spaced via grid. We should not place dog-bone vias under QFN packages near the power pad as they will likely short to the power pad.

15.2.3 Routing

The routing starts with direct low-density routes for high-speed signals according to our flow plan, utilizing lots of high-speed constraints, then finished up with random routes with no constraints on low-speed signals. Most of the layout features and rules in this chapter describe the high-speed signal nets handling. Traces, pins, and vias have to follow high-speed pre-defined structures as well as length constraints. Many complex trace length–related and spacing constraints apply to the high-speed trace routes. High-speed signals can have vias only at the start and at the end, except in cases with an extremely large number of SERDES links. Low-speed signals are allowed to have several vias, with a ground via within a half inch to the signal via.

Power net routing utilizes the very few power plane layers we have in smart ways to allow several different power nets on the same layer while not compromising DC voltage drop on high current rails. Core rails have a square-ish shape; while low current rails utilize elongated get-around power shapes. Any leftover board areas on signal layers are often utilized for power delivery shapes also, but mostly for the lower current rails like PLL rails or clock chip core rails. A 400W ASIC will utilize two power planes plus two signal layers for its core rail, having four power plane layers in the stackup overall. Any ASICs below 100W will utilize half as many plane layers. The same signal layers outside of the area can still be utilized for signal nets. We draw the planes either as positive layers (like the signal layers) or as negative layers with only drawing the divider/split lines and voids. The places are also pulled back 20 to 60mils from the board edge to prevent any copper being cut and shorted between layers. Each power plane layer is divided into several regions or split planes, as explained later in this chapter at the power delivery section.

In modern high-speed digital boards, we use many differential pairs. All the multi-gigabit SERDES links are routed with differential pairs and take up two pins on the ASIC package for one "signal". The two nets that belong to one diffpair are routed together with the same mouse strokes, the two traces are automatically glued together while routing with a specified gap or spacing. That is the gap that participates in creating the differential impedance. The length of the two legs/nets has to be matched and tuned to be equal, within a tight tolerance, typically 1 to 10mil. This is called "phase tolerance matching". Not all diffpairs need phase tolerance matching and impedance control. VRM voltage sense lines and thermal diode connections to the ASIC die from a remote sensor are differential but not high-speed signals, so they do not need it. The matching is a high-speed feature, it is neither a "mandatory decoration" nor performative—engineering does not work that way.

15.2.4 Tool Features

Both the schematics components and the layout footprints (package symbols) are created and stored in a curated and controlled company library on a network drive. The basic CAD tool features used on every design are the editing filter controls, the visibility controls, netlist import, object find, coloring and highlighting, placement of netlist parts from footprint library, routing, and report generation. The editing filters help us to avoid messing up objects we did not intend to edit, when so many different things might overlap at the same location. For example, if we are working with traces, we do not want the components, text, or shapes to be moved or deleted. Visibility controls for layers help us enable one or more user selected layers for view, while all other layers are invisible and untouched. If everything is visible in the same time, then nothing is recognizable or properly visible. We can also make object types like pins, parts, shapes, vias, and traces visible or invisible. We can make some ratsnests visible. This can be all, except the currently dealt with net hidden, when we are working on one subcircuit, and we want to see clearly without too much unrelated information. We can also display or hide them by component association, such as all rats of U34 shown and all others hidden. Highlighting or coloring helps us when we want to see one long routed net or power plane, distinguished from all other objects, for review or for avoiding accidentally editing a different trace than the one we wanted to edit. We can also color several objects, each with different colors to review their relative positions. We can generate a design rule check report (DRC), net length reports, Pin-Pair–based length report (for SI analysis), completeness reports, and many more. The DRC tells the designer which objects violate which constraints. By the end of the design when we have fixed everything the list should be empty. Sometimes we end up with a non-empty list, but then we manually waive the ones we want to allow to pass.

Cadence allegro categorizes every object into classes and subclasses—kind of "layers" for the editor. It also helps us to decide which are visible/editable in the moment. For example, etch as a class is for traces and shapes, while each stackup copper layer's etch is a separate subclass. The same goes for pins (component pads), via pads, different types of keepout regions, refdes, board geometry, and package geometry. For some of these classes, the subclasses are not the real board copper layers, but silkscreen, paste (Stencil), and design guiding "mechanical layers" too.

The main high-speed design features in CAD tools are the constraints entry with live DRC enforcement, differential-pair routing (with enforced spacing), padstack editor (to set via dimensions), backdrilling, Pin-Pair net length support for multi-point topologies like memory-down, and the length-tuning gauge. In length tuning we add extra trace length to the signals that are shorter than desired. This is done semi-automatically by the tool replacing short trace segments with half-loop traces that are much longer, when the design uses the tuning mode with the mouse cursor. For example, if we have to match eight signals, then we have to lengthen the seven shortest ones until they are as long as the longest one, within the defined tolerance. The "skew" or mismatch between two or more traces is the trace length difference, or how shorter or longer one trace is from the other(s). Matching might be applied as the longest and shortest of the group cannot differ by more than the entered tolerance, or as no signal in the group can differ from a main trace marked

"TARGET" by more than the tolerance. The maximum allowed skew is called "tolerance", while sometimes we might also specify a "delta" to allow the length range center to deviate from the TARGET in a defined amount and direction. Positive delta means the trace range center is longer than the TARGET trace. We have two types of trace length constraints, the absolute and the relative (matching) types. The absolute length rules come from (minimum or maximum) loss budgets of SERDES links or timing analysis on basic synchronous or asynchronous buses that have a "round trip delay". The relative (matching, max skew) constraints come from the timing analysis of source synchronous and clock forwarding buses and from differential pair phase tolerance (netname_P to netname_N) matching. The net names for the two nets of a differential pair have to end with _P and _N. Shortening is usually not possible due to distance of components unless we re-do the component placement. Adding trace length is possible by using the length tuning feature of the layout tool, it adds meandered trace segments to a straight line, while it displays a "gauge" info pop-up window with the current trace length, the desired length, and whether we meet the constraint or not. Figure 15.3 shows how a gauge and the added meander traces look like in KiCad.

We do not always need to "match" lengths relative to other traces, sometimes simply there is a minimum absolute length constraint, for example, for insertion loss control (minimum loss to mitigate reflections) or to ensure static hold timing. The shape and spacing of the meanders is automatic and it can be set up using a few parameters. We can use rectangular bumps, rounded bumps, or trapezoid. The spacing between the bumps should follow same net crosstalk rules to avoid the signal from shortcutting (coupling or crosstalk) and to produce a less accurate delay than expected. We can also re-route our signal on a detour path, instead of adding meanders, then slide the edges to tune, which is preferred for SERDES signals. Diffpairs are made of two traces, which need their length matched. We can add one or two meander bumps on one leg of the pair or we can twist the via pad entry as described later. Sometimes single-ended nets are tuned, other times diffpairs are tuned. The routing mode has to be se to SE or diff. Modern SERDES interfaces made of diffpairs usually have a very loose pair-to-pair matching requirement of within tens of inches that makes it unnecessary to apply any tuning. A few rare diffpair-buses need tight tuning, for example, clock-forwarding types like the old Hyper Transport 1.0 bus or LVDS A/D converter interfaces. On memory-interfaces we match several single-ended data signals to a differential strobe signal very tightly within 5mils, and we might have to lengthen either type to match the longest member of the bus with all other members. Meanders and detours will take up a lot of extra board space, so when doing the initial routing we have to leave large gaps between the signals and components to allow it.

For any trace length control, we have to also include the "package length" or "pin delay", that is the trace length inside the BGA package substrate between the silicon die bumps and the BGA to board balls. CAD tools have to have a way to import this information into the constraint editor. In the Cadence Allegro Constraint Manager, it is entered in the Component "Pin Properties" group under Properties. Silicon chips are not soldered on motherboards directly, they are supplied soldered onto a "package substrate", that is a small fine-line PCB with an array of solder balls. The traces in this package substrate have a trace length. ASIC vendors have to provide a spreadsheet

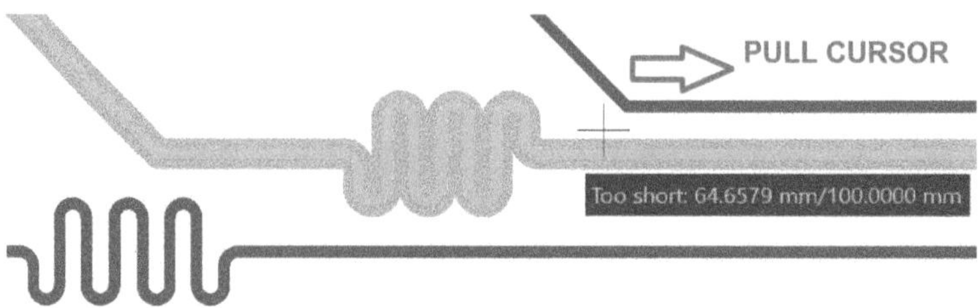

FIGURE 15.3 Length tuning in KiCad layout.

with package lengths listed for each pin. They provide it in the form of either a length in mils or a delay in picoseconds. We might have to convert it to match the format used in our layout tool. We can convert ps delay to mils length:

```
Length = Delay * 11.8 / SQRT(DK)
Delay = Length / ( 11.8 / SQRT(DK))
```

This formula is usable for inner layer routes (stripline traces). Outer layer (microstrip) traces will be surrounded partly by PCB material and partly by soldermask and air, resulting in a different (lower) effective DK than the prepreg material's DK. For BGA packages we have to assume a 3.5 DK as it is unknown. Most high-speed designs are done on inner layer only, with the exception of short outer layer fanout dog-bone traces. When the layout tool measures the net length in the gauge and in DRC, it has to display the sum of the board trace length plus the package length plus via length. This is demonstrated in Figure 15.4. On any design with ASICs in large BGA packages, we should really not use a PCB tool that does not support package length because traces within packages might have as much as over an inch of trace length and a half an inch mismatch, which is much more than the matching constraint we want to use in many cases.

Cadence allegro measures net lengths in different ways. It measures traces-only when we display a net property also known as "Total Etch Length", or it measures traces together with via lengths and package lengths when displaying Pin-Pairs in the Constraint Manager. Point-to-point nets really have one Pin-Pair, we usually refrain from creating it, but their length measurement is different, so it is worth using Pin-Pairs when we have a package length in our net. Pin-Pairs are also used for multi-drop nets when controlling the propagation delay between two specific components, ignoring the other parts that can have their own separate Pin-Pair-based constraints. Both the constraint entry and the length gauge display can show the Pin-Pair and topology-based length measurements together with via and package length. The Constraint Manager can populate measurements from a large number of objects in the spreadsheet view when we use the "Analyze" command.

Another important trace length–related feature that tools should have is the XNET or extended/electrical net, which is created by the tool on signals that are broken up into two separate nets by a series component, an AC-coupling capacitor, or a series damping resistor. It is done by the CAD tool automatically if a signal model is attached to the series component. In many cases series terminated nets have to be matched. Lacking this feature in some tools has a workaround, we just have to match the before and after segments of the signal paths, basically we do the matching work twice.

When the board routing and tuning are done, the layout engineer will do a design rules check (DRC) and fix any rule and constraint violation. The DRC is live enforced by the tool by forcing objects, and it also displays markers at the violating objects. A compiled full list of all violations is listed in a DRC report file.

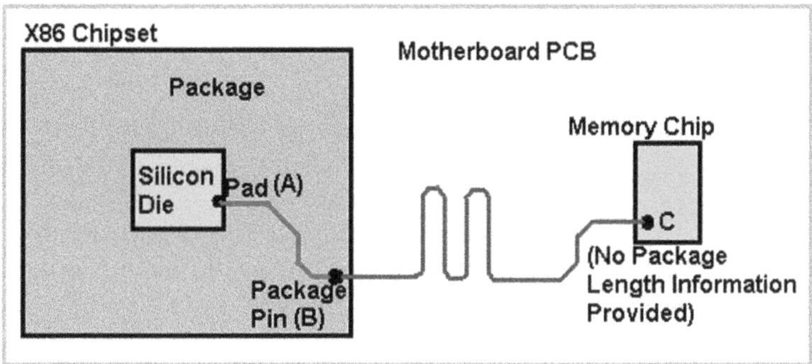

FIGURE 15.4 Package length concept (sketch).

A mechanical file will be exported for the mechanical engineer to check if the board shape and components still match the mechanical design (mounting hole locations, component height restrictions). Several official drawings files (usually in Adobe PDF) might get created, like fab drawing for fabricator instructions and assembly drawing for soldering and rework. Review meetings will be held, and manufacturing output files will be generated, like Gerber and NC drill files or ODB+ format. Then engineering will release the files into the company database, and a purchasing process will be initiated. This is the fab-out process.

Layout design for one board can be done by one layout engineer by the same hardware engineer who designs the schematic (at small companies) or by a layout team. In the team design approach, the one single board is divided into sections through "design partitioning", and different layout engineers work on the different sections in parallel. Some design tools support design partitioning by easily splitting and merging layout files. Another approach is to have two or three work shifts, so in a 24hr day 16 hours of work gets done by two people. Scripting is a feature of some layout tools, which allows companies to develop design automation features added to the tool. For example, replication of placement and routing in the layout of similar schematic sections that would be done in 80% less time than doing all of them manually one by one. This can even work when the replicated circuit is not 100% the same.

15.3 DENSITY AND ROUTING CHANNELS

We design large boards at the same density as the smaller form factor boards, due to signal and power integrity considerations and space saving. The larger boards will just have a lot more components on them, 4000 to 16000 parts versus 600 to 2000 parts. The density on complex boards is typically in the range of 40 to 100 components per square inch. I/O heavy boards that need hundreds or over a thousand high speed diffpairs will be at the lower end of the density range as the routing channels take up a lot of board space too. We typically pack one subcircuit (like a clock generator or a memory bank) into as small an area as possible, then fit these subcircuits together close up on the board, allowing routing space around and between them where needed. Where it is needed can be seen on the flow plan that we created while doing the graphical floorplan analysis. After putting the component blocks into the floorplan and marking up the long high-speed routes, we can see where the components have to be moved a little to make space for the routing channels. The shapes of the subcircuit areas have to be chosen so they will fit together with the other subcircuits without leaving large unusable areas. This is a Tetris game. The side effect of this is that a layout or a hardware engineer might pack a smaller suitcase for vacation more efficiently than regular folks do, after all that practice.

For really wide high-speed buses (like a 16-lane PCIe) we need to leave board space for a "routing channel". It is not enough to have space to cover the board with components. The width of the routing channel can be calculated from N number of diffpairs on M layers, S pair-to-pair spacing for crosstalk, and given width of each diffpair W.

```
ChannelWidth = N * (W+S) / M
```

For the spacing between pairs used for crosstalk mitigation, we can use 15 to 25mils up to 7Gbps, or 25 to 50mils at 8Gig or above. The width of the diffpair (W) is made of the trace width times two plus the gap between them (W_trace+Gap+W_trace), usually around 12 to 20mil.

If we apply wavy routing instead of whole-board rotation at 10 to 20 degrees then it widens the routing channel by 10 to 30%. For signaling rates at 10 to 25Gig a 10-degree angle should push the fiber weave resonance above the signal's bandwidth. At 56Gig or above we need to use 20 degrees. If our board is very tight and we cannot afford wavy routing, then it must be rotated in the panel. The extra channel width (W_EXTRA) required for wavy routing will be determined by the length of the segments and the angle (alpha).

```
W_EXTRA = sin(alpha)*SegmentLength
ChannelWidth = (N * (W+S) / M) + sin(alpha) * SegmentLength
```

In practice we just add a 25% overhead estimate:

```
Channel width = 1.25*N*(W+S)/M.
```

The channel can be 1.68 inch wide on x16 PCIe4.0 using two routing layers. We need to allow space for routing channels where the initial floor plan and flow plan indicated the main bus flows. For low-speed signals we do not need extra board area or specific routing channels due to the use of basic 4mil spacing and no wavy routing, and they can also go under higher density circuits and change layers many times.

There can be components in this routing channel, as long as they are low-density and low-speed circuits with minimal vias, and their fanout is arranged in-line to minimize route blocking, for example an SPI flash chip or some bulk decoupling capacitors. Basically, we can have a routing channel through empty areas or thorough low density (LD) areas, but not through high density (HD) areas. An HD circuit can have 0.5 to 1.5 vias/mm2, while an LD circuit might only have 0.02 to 0.25 vias/mm2. The LD areas have to be made super low density in one direction, by orientating the components and the fanout vias in lines that are parallel with the routing direction. Figure 15.5 demonstrates this. For example, a half square inch area might contain a clocking circuit with a 48pin QFN chip and lots of termination resistors, having 80 vias, or the same board area can be populated by four bulk capacitors having 16 vias. 16 vias is a lot less obstruction for a wide high-speed bus than 80 vias are, and the slower signals usually do not produce high-frequency interference. Another possibility arises in the fanout area of grid components like BGAs or high-density connectors. We can use long dog-bone traces for the fanout of slow signals to align their vias in a line out of the way from high-speed routes. If we use a large BGA chip, but we do not need to use all of its pins of ports, then we should assign the pins near the center, so the outer areas of the via field will be sparse, with many non-connected pins having no fanout vias. This would create a sparse routing channel under a main component.

Some boards must be designed in a larger board size to allow large component-free areas for routing channels, like we can see on the board in Figure 15.6. On the boards that require overall very high density due to board size restrictions, we cannot have completely empty areas for routing channels, we have to opt for creating low-density routing channels. An initial layout design placement might have components placed by proximity, which can have an even density distribution across the board. We have to rearrange them by moving low-frequency and

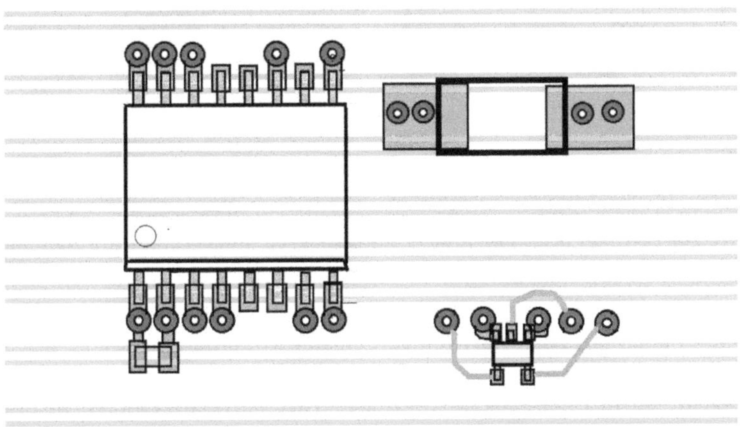

FIGURE 15.5 Routing channel creation with smart fanout (sketch).

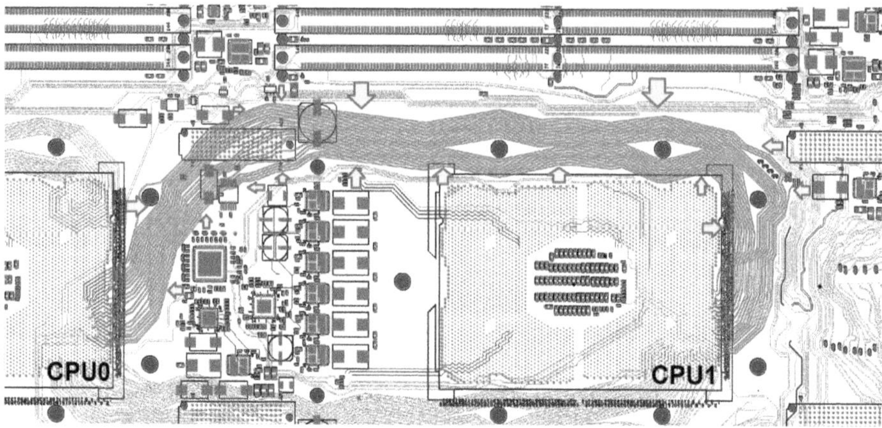

FIGURE 15.6 A signal layer with a QPI bus highlighted in a free routing channel on the Tioga Pass server motherboard from the Open Computer Project, the image from the layout design file is used for illustration under the Open Web Foundation Final Specification Agreement ("OWFa 1.0") signed by Quanta Computer Inc.

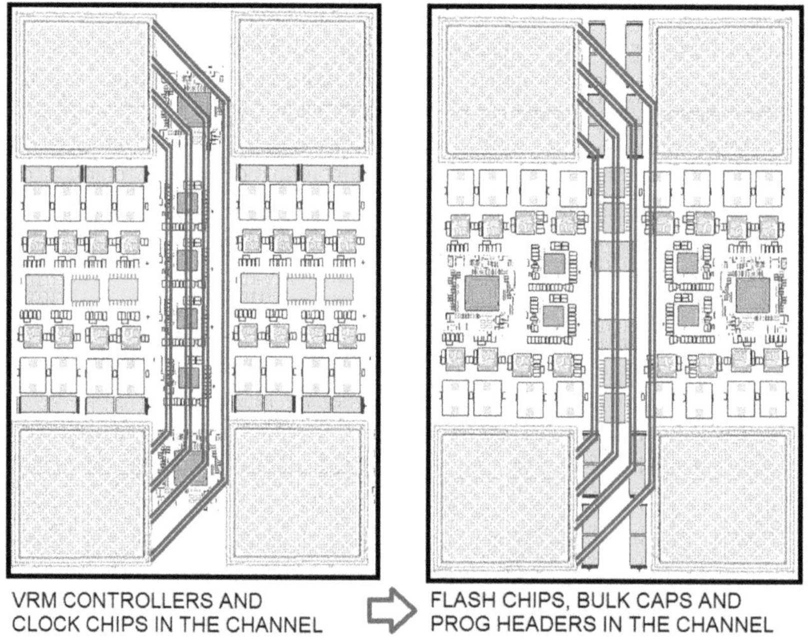

FIGURE 15.7 Rearranging components to create a low-density routing channel (sketch).

low-density parts (SPI EEPROMs, DC power MOSFET switches, and bulk decoupling caps) to form a long cluster of LD circuits along the routing channel. They can always be moved by up to an inch from their original location, as they are low frequency parts. The HD high-density (QFN, BGA, SSOP) and high-frequency (clock chips, VRMs) parts can take the original location of the moved LD circuits/parts. An example design alteration and forming of a LD routing channel is demonstrated in Figure 15.7. The low-density parts are colored in light green, the high-density parts in pink. By rearranging the low-density and high-density components we created a LD routing channel.

15.4 CONSTRAINTS

We want certain signals to not be longer or shorter than a certain number to meet our timing or loss budget; we want planes, traces, and vias to be at a certain distance away from each other to be manufacturable, and so on. There might be hundreds of types of such needs and thousands of instances of each type in one board design. When they are entered into a spreadsheet in a standard format for a design tool, then they are the constraints. We cannot manually recheck all of them every time something is changed in the layout. This is why the high-end PCB tools have constraints and DRC-check (Design Rule Check). The constraints sometimes force objects to comply with our requirements automatically (like plane voids pull back) or they help the tool to display the relevant compliance metric while we are editing an object (tuning gauge), and they drive an overall whole-design non-compliance list (DRC violations report) with details and locations. The DRC check is a one-time run to display the violations list; the online DRC is the enforcer of certain types of automatic rules.

The layout constraints have to be prepared by the hardware engineer before the layout can start. Entering the constraints into the CAD tool can be done by the hardware engineer or the layout engineer. Most often hardware engineers prepare the constraints in a document, and then the layout engineer enters them into the CAD tool. With constraints we define what we allow and what we do not allow in the finished layout design, for example, minimum and maximum values of various features' dimensions and sizes (width, length, and diameter). We can enter these in the Cadence Allegro Constraint Manager, the Mentor Expedition Constraint Manager, or the Altium Designer's Design Rules Editor in a spreadsheet form. During trace manipulations (routing, tuning, sliding), the software will display a graphical aid—the tuning gauge—to show the user whether the currently manipulated net meets the entered length constraints, by showing a red or green bar. We can enable the "online DRC" option that will display a visible marker on any object that does not meet any of the constraints to get a complete visual feedback on our constraint implementation. The online DRC also applies force to keep objects in positions meeting the spacing constraints. The online DRC makes the GUI slower. If we disable it, then we can still run a DRC report later that will list all of the constrained objects with a pass/fail designation.

Constraints are applied on objects. Some objects are natural, like nets and XNETs. Others are constructed manually by the designer as groups of natural objects, for example, diffpairs, net classes, Pin-Pairs, and matched groups. Pin-Pairs are a user selected pair of pins that reside on the same multi-point net to control propagation delay from one specific chip to another. Matched groups are a user defined group of Pin-Pairs, for the purpose of applying length matching constraints. Constraints are often written into constraint sets (design rules) that are applied to multiple objects that all need to be controlled by the same parameters. In the Cadence Allegro Constraints Manager, they are called constraint sets. In the Constraint Manager we have several categories of constraint sets, the electrical for high-speed rules (ECSETs), the physical for trace widths, the spacing for copper feature clearances, and the same net spacing for tuned trace meander sizing. Within each type we usually have two or three main categories. The CSET category for rule creation, the "Net" category where we can apply the CSETs or type in rules manually for objects in a list, and the "region" category where rules can be applied locally (like neck-down spacing). Within the electrical ECSETs, the subcategories are the wiring (max parallel or running length gap definitions), vias, total etch length (min or max trace length), diffpairs (define diffpairs, static and dynamic phase tolerance, primary width and gap, max uncoupled length), relative propagation delay (matching the trace lengths of group objects like "matched groups").

Where constraints come from:

- Manufacturability, including via parameters (minimum annular ring, aspect ratio, and drill sizes), clearances (minimum space between pair-combinations of vias, pads, traces, drills, shapes, etc.) and minimum trace width.

- Timing Analysis. It will define minimum and maximum trace lengths, or relative trace length matching between signals, used on non-SERDES interfaces. The differential pair phase tolerance match also belongs in this category. These are very exact rules and often tight tolerances. The length is related to flight time that is a linear function of length, in picoseconds/inch.
- Loss Budget Analysis. This also produces min/max trace length rules but not matching rules. They are not very exact and precise down to mils, more like inches. The insertion loss is proportional to the trace length, and it can be calculated from the length and the per-unit-length loss number.
- Impedance control through trace width and diffpair spacing.
- Signal Integrity, like crosstalk control through separation.

Constraint object types:

- Nets: They are obvious, schematic nets.
- XNETs: extended net on AC-coupled or series-terminated signals.
- Pin-Pairs: These are related to net topology, when more than two components or pins are on the same net, for example, one processor and eight memory chips. The Pin-Pair is the sum total of trace segments that are between two specific parts/pins, ignoring other segments on the same net that are not in the shortest path between the two selected parts. Mostly used with memory interfaces.
- Differential Pairs: One positive and one negative net or XNET that form one diffpair. The net names of the two nets are the same, except the last two characters that are either _P or _N. The diffpair object can be auto-generated for all nets that can be found with _P/_N ending.
- Matched groups that are simply lists of objects to be matched in length. We create a group as a new object manually, so the matching constraint can be applied on it. The objects within a group can be nets, XNETs, Pin-Pairs, or diffpairs, for example, one byte-lane of a memory interface.
- Net Classes: any list of nets can be added to a named class, so we only have to apply a constraint set to a class/group of nets once, not one by one. Typically used for point-to-point nets with length constraints or for any nets with trace width and clearance rules.
- Non-signal objects, like pads, vias, and shapes.

Types of Constraints:

- Minimum or maximum trace length (total Etch Length in Allegro). It is useful for timing-driven buses and insertion loss controlled SERDES links.
- Relative trace length or length matching. Mostly used for source-synchronous or uni-directional synchronous parallel buses.
- Diffpair rules, like phase tolerance matching between the positive and negative net, P/N trace spacing, max uncoupled length.
- Minimum Clearance, between specific nets, or object type combinations.
- Running length (max parallel segment) clearance or spacing, which is a clearance that applies only when the traces run parallel too long.

For SERDES links we just use the diffpair rules, maximum trace length, maximum running length (max parallel length), regions for neck down and clearances. They do not require lane-to-lane matching due to the on-chip de-skew circuits made with FIFOs. Early multi-gigabit interfaces did not have good de-skew circuits so we have to match the lanes of multi-lane diffpair-based buses.

What a "topology" is: In some cases, we need to control the signal propagation delay from one chip, like the CPU, to one other chip, like DRAM1. And also from CPU to DRAM2 separately. We create Pin-Pairs on nets, as ADD0 net's CPU-pin and DRAM1-pin together are one Pin-Pair,

ADD1 net's CPU-pin and DRAM1-pin together is another. We put all these Pin-Pairs between CPU and DRAM1 on the ADD0:7 nets into one matched group. Then we match/tune the trace lengths of these in the layout design. We again create Pin-Pairs on nets as ADD0 net's CPU-pin and DRAM2-pin together are one Pin-Pair, ADD1 net's CPU-pin and DRAM2-pin together is another. We put all these Pin-Pairs between CPU and DRAM2 on the ADD0:7 nets into another matched group. Then we match/tune the trace lengths of these in the layout design. What we have done is making sure that these ADD0:7 signals all arrive to the DRAM1 from the CPU within a small time window, then all arrive to DRAM2 within another small time window. It is for serving static timing requirements, controlling signal arrival time from one chip to another. We can see a simple topology diagram in Figure 15.8 that shows what is matched to what. One color is one matched group. Basically, the L1 length is matched to the L2 length, and then L3 matched to L4. Most topology diagrams just show one net, implying the other nets in the group have the same topology, and they will also have the same diagram. This diagram here shows two nets to demonstrate how that works. On a DDR4 memory address bus all the address signals with the clock have to arrive from the CPU to one DRAM chip in a certain time frame, then to another DRAM chip all signals in another time frame. It is meaningless to control propagation from DRAM1 to DRAM2, as DRAM1 will never send data to DRAM2. The hardware functionality needs to be understood for proper constraint setup, which is the hardware engineer's job not the layout engineer's job.

What hardware engineers have to document as high-level constraints in a Word or Excel document and provide to the layout engineers:

- Detailed vendor stackup.
- Numbers/tables for trace impedance calculation results like trace width and spacing for each impedance for each layer.
- Numbers/tables for trace width/space for basic low-speed traces.
- Numbers/tables for minimum clearance between different object types, listed for different layers.
- A floorplan and flow plan diagram.
- Placement instructions in plain text, which part on which side of the board, height restricted areas.
- 3D via structures that have to be replicated on SERDES links. Diagrams and dimension numbers/tables.
- Numbers/tables for trace length rules, some are calculated from loss budget, others from timing analysis. Min/max and matching.
- Power delivery plane layer usage. Hand-drawn markup diagrams.
- VRM power shapes for power stage parts in a diagram.
- Numbers/tables for any crosstalk and interference based (running length, max parallel) spacing requirements.
- Via dimensions, and use.
- Any specific high-speed rule that applies to the project.

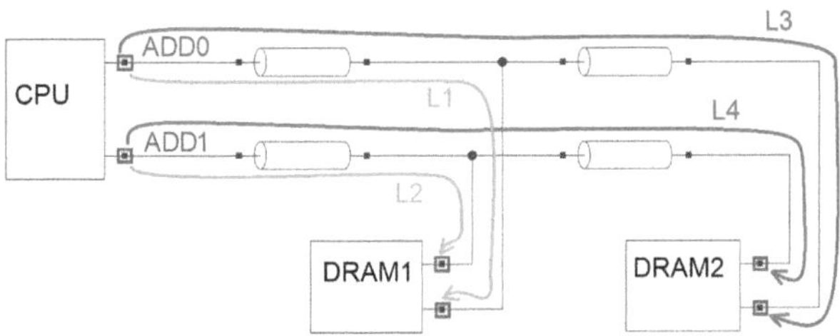

FIGURE 15.8 Pin-Pair objects on a memory address bus topology.

- Mechanical drawing from the mechanical engineer with board outline, height restricted areas, mounting holes, exact locations for connectors, metal touching surface areas, fixture areas for press-fit, wave solder or system assembly.

15.5 PCB MANUFACTURABILITY

Any randomly chosen object size on a PCB cannot be manufactured; there are value ranges that can be used. The main concerns with board manufacturability involve minimum object sizes, clearances, and via types. Their minimum size capability is listed in tables by each PCB manufacturer facility. They usually list a standard capability table (preferred with very good yield) and an advanced capability table, but really both are in large-scale production. They can make the objects larger but not smaller. In the case of some fabricator companies the listed minimum size is provided with low yield and it is experimental, while other companies make it every day with good yield in mass production. It depends on the self-reporting of different companies—some are reporting conservatively, others report it with overstatements. We have to assess their capability by building boards or test boards with them. Minimum object sizes include via drill diameters, trace widths, solder mask bridge width, via pad annular ring, and several others. Most high-tech boards can go down to 3.5 trace width and 4mil space, but for insertion-loss-controlled boards we try to use wider traces. Clearances include minimum distance requirements defined between object types as a matrix, between traces, via pads, component solder pads, drilled holes, planes, backdrill holes. The minimum copper pattern clearance requirement also depends on the copper layer thickness, be it half ounce, one ounce, and so on. Power plane layers and plated layers are thicker, so they require larger clearances. Outer layers are always plated, inner layers are plated on boards that contain microvias and blind/buried vias. We have to ensure that after putting in the fabricator's constraints into the design (constraint manager), the board still delivers the electrical high-speed design requirements, and vice versa. These two requirements might be in conflict, which requires us to deal with them in the same time up front when the project starts.

It is required for PCB fabrication to have a balanced copper pattern on every layer to improve the yield of the copper etching process on each layer and make all layers similarly dense to reduce board twisting. For example, it would be harder to manufacture it with a dense pattern in one area, while a single thin line goes across a big emptiness in another area. Balancing also makes the dielectric thickness and impedances more uniform. To achieve the balancing on plane layers, we have to expand any power shapes into all available space. If they stretch too far, then we have to add extra shapes attached to the GND net with many vias, or use thieving. On signal layers we often would end up with large empty areas that we have to fill. We can fill them with shapes connected to the GND net, while also making sure that many vias will stitch them to the ground plane layers at every quarter inch at least. We can also fill them with automatically placed small rectangles called "Thieving". Thieving creates floating metal objects that might be an issue in some applications. In both cases we need to make sure that the shape or the thieving rectangles stays far away from our high-speed traces as to not interfere with their impedance, typically by 50mils.

Boards are made on production panels at the PCB fab companies. Each fab facility has its own panel size list, while some sizes are standard. We can ask them before we start our design. Especially for larger boards we have to consider the panel size, as PCB price depends on the panel size not the board size. If our board design is larger by a small amount than one panel size, then we might want to reduce the design size to fit on a smaller panel, so it is cheaper, and the number of fab companies that can make it will not be limited that much. For smaller boards we can fit multiple instances on the same panel. If we request board rotation to mitigate fiber weave effect, then it will require more space on the panel or require a larger panel, or less instances per panel. The board outline in the design tool that defines the board shape and size can be just a simple closed line, or it can define the way the board is taken out of the fabrication panel. Sometimes the board comes in a handling strip that is used by the SMT soldering production line to hold the board without touching the useful design/component area. The board is broken out of the handling strips or out of the panel. It is routed around with a milling machine by the fabricator, with the exception of a few spokes that hold the board in the panel. These spokes will be broken by hand later to get the board out, after assembly at the SMT build contractor. The spokes might have scoring, chamfer, or lots of holes to make the breaking easier.

One of the design goals is to reduce the technology heaviness by using as little number of advanced constraints as really needed. At the same time, we cannot reduce our technology down to a level that prohibits high-speed feature implementation, resulting in bad signal integrity. Some advanced parameters are needed on some design, like smaller clearances, while not needed on others. For example, if we have only two SERDES signals, then we can route them on Layer-(N-2) and eliminate the need for backdrilling, assuming both end components are on the top side of the board. There is no real reason to route those two signals on layer-(N-6), or if we have some weak reason of convenience then that can be renegotiated. But if we have 512 SERDES diffpairs, we cannot expect all of them to be routed on layer-(N-2), so they will utilize most inner routing layers and they will need those backdrilling parameters.

15.5.1 VIA Usage

The vias are the vertical structures in PCBs, in contrast to traces and planes that are for horizontal signal or power propagation. Vias allow signals to go from layers to other layers. Via types include mechanically drilled and laser-drilled microvias. The mechanically drilled types can be regular through the whole stackup (through via) or blind or buried (BB) vias starting or ending on inner layers. Blind and buried vias are mechanically drilled, but they require multiple lamination cycles. A blind via starts on a surface layer but does not end on the other side. A buried via is not visible from the surface, it is between two inner layers. If we use microvias, then we also use buried vias to get signals through the center of the stackup, it is called a "core via". This case on an N-layer stackup, layers 1 to 7 and N…(N-7) might have microvias, and the center located inner layers have the buried core vias. The microvia boards are created through multiple (not one) lamination cycles. Basically, they drill with a laser down to the copper pad on the next layer, plate, fill, then laminate one prepreg and a foil layer on the top of it, and then drill/plate/fill/laminate again until the stackup is complete. Boards with multiple lamination cycles, which are needed for microvias and BB vias, are much more expensive than single-laminated boards with through-vias only, and they have longer fabrication lead times. Microvias cannot be stacked on top of each other, so we use staggered arrangements with mini dog-bone traces between them. Each microvia on the next layer, being offset from the previous one, creates enlarged oval antipads (for the mini-dog-bones) with shifted locations. These are different than the oval voids used for diffpairs. They often overlap with voids of nearby signals, which increases crosstalk and return loss and undercuts the return path for nearby traces.

The via hole is a copper barrel that connects to horizontal circular pads. The smallest possible via pad sizes come from the fabricator's "annular ring" requirements. It is the sliver of copper left between the via hole and the pad edge. The inner layer IAR and the outer layer OAR are treated separately as separate capabilities. For SI analysis we use the drill tool size. For annular ring and pad size calculators some companies use the finished and plated hole size, others use the drill tool size. We have to check with the vendor which one they use. The drilled hole wall receives a ~1mil thick copper plating that varies vendor to vendor and by hole size. With 1mil wall thickness, a 7.9mil via drill will have a 5.9mil finished hole size.

Microvias are necessary when we have smaller than 0.8mm pitch BGA chips, which are extremely rare on data center, telecom, aerospace, and industrial products. Cell phones and tablet computers have these 0.5mm pitch ARM processors in them; they are the typical driver for microvia technology. Powerful ASICs that are used in data center boards are intentionally made with 1mm pitch regular grid, or with 0.9mm pitch offset grid, for the purpose of avoiding microvias and allowing backdrills under them. Microvias can help with creating higher density designs, but that is debatable. Microvias have the downside of increased board cost (up to 10x) and fabrication lead time (2 to 5x); they reduce signal integrity due to the staggered mini dog-bone structure, which is a vertical zig-zag path. Most large data center boards do not have any microvias. There are a few large ASICs available with 0.8mm pitch BGA packages, but they create the problems mentioned. We will either be forced to use microvia stacks, have to compromise our manufacturability clearance constraints, or the common high-speed structures needed for 10G+ SERDES links cannot be implemented. We will end up with routing strategies (like diffpairs split to adjacent columns) and design practices that were meant to be used on <8Gbps designs only. The 1mm pitch regular grid and the 0.9mm row pitch (1mm diagonal) offset grid (hex) BGAs provide best SI results using through drilled (and backdrilled) vias. This is because they allow backdrilling and diffpair escape under them using reasonable clearance values. Even this can only be manufactured by a small subset of the fabricator companies. Boards with 0.9mm BGAs are harder to manufacture. Using 0.8mm pitch BGAs with smaller clearances, we may or may not be able to find any fabricator that can do it.

Through drilled via diameters used for SERDES links should be defined by the drill (outer) diameter, not the finished (inner) diameter after plating. Back in the day when we used to use many soldered through-hole components, the finished hole diameter mattered, as we had to be able to plug component pins into the plated holes. On newer designs, with via impedance control the outside diameter that is equal to the drill bit diameter is more important because via impedance depends on the outside diameter. The design clearances on high-density boards are also dependent on the outer diameter. The inner diameter, the finished hole size is about 0.5 to 3mil smaller. Vias are drilled into the dielectric and copper, then they apply electroless copper plating to the whole board surface, including the hole surfaces. That will short any pads together through the hole, creating the desired connection. The plating reduces the inner hole diameter.

Via aspect ratio is a typical fabricator constraint, for example "maximum 16:1", a ratio between via length (equal to the stackup total board thickness) and drill diameter. Each fabricator has a standard and an advanced capability table. All high-speed complex hardware requires the advanced capability. After building a stackup, the aspect ratio will define our minimum via drill diameter. For example, a 100mil thick board and a 1:10 AR fab capability will result in a d_min=100mil/10=10mil minimum drill diameter, rounded to the next standard drill size (ask the vendor), as our smallest vias we can use. Using large ASICs with many SERDES links the via diameter is critical for fitting impedance controlled structures under the BGA grid, and allowing diffpair or two-trace escape routes between them. The via pad diameter can be calculated from drill diameter plus 2x IAR for inner layers, or drill diameter plus 2x OAR for outer layers. Through-drilled via dimensions are explained in Figure 15.9, and microvias are explained in Figure 15.10. Vias should not overlap with component solder pads, unless the vias are filled and plated over flat, aka VIPPO types. The via pad size must be smaller than the component size, otherwise it causes soldering issues on the enlarged pads. Microvias cannot overlap with buried through-drilled vias or even with other microvias. This creates the need for offsetting the microvia used between layer-N and N+1, from the microvia used between layer-N+1 and N+2. Basically, each net will have two microvias on each layer, connected through a mini dog-bone trace. These requirements further result in the microvia structure taking up a lot more board space than a single microvia would imply, and larger than a through drill would take.

On plane layers where a via is not connecting to the plane, there is a clearance requirement between them that creates an antipad automatically in the CAD tool. The clearance is larger on plated layers, meaning any inner layers using microvias. On through drilled boards only the outer layers are plated, so only their outer layers need extra clearance, but that is not an issue for high-speed signals as we route them on inner-only. Antipad sizes are important for controlled impedance via design, and also for making sure the neighboring antipads do not fuse together and cut up the plane for return current or power current flow. In some designs some pins or vias are connected to planes using a thermal relief (spokes); in other cases we use direct connect. Thermal relief helps with soldering component through-hole pins, as ground planes can cool a pin so much that the solder does not melt. Press-fit connectors do not require that, only the soldered ones. For high-speed

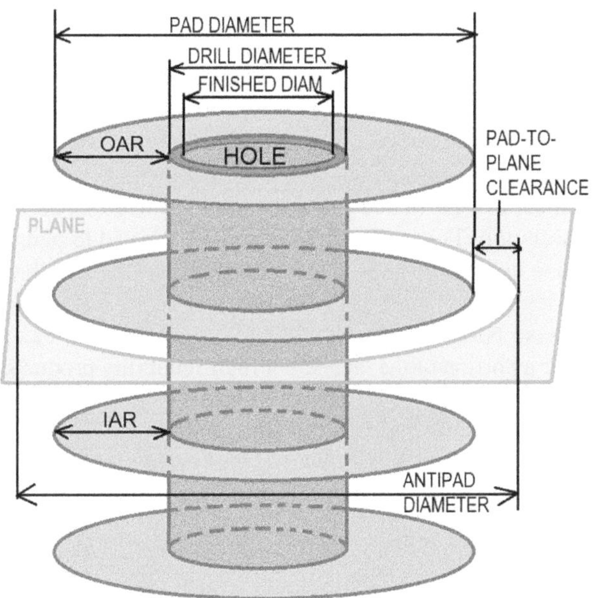

FIGURE 15.9 Through drilled via dimensions.

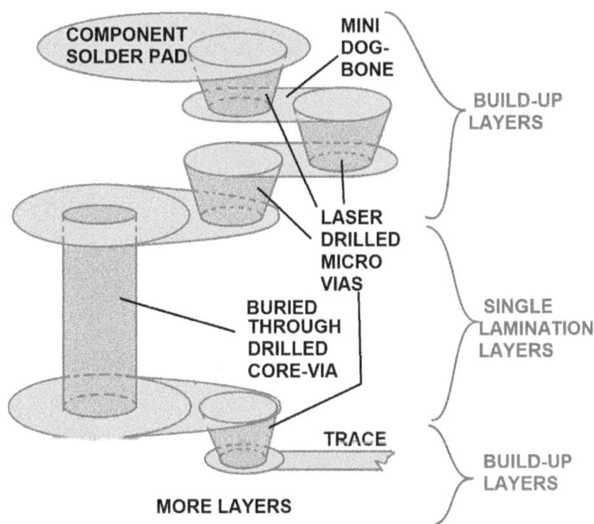

FIGURE 15.10 Offset microvia stack structure.

signal integrity, we have to use direct connect wherever we can and avoid wave soldered through hole parts. Outer layer SMT BGA pin to plane connections are usually with thermal relief. QFN power components are supposed to use direct connect to minimize parasitic inductances, and the solderability degradation has to be handled by stencil design tricks and thermal profile adjustments. Most holes are plated, but in a few cases connector manufacturers require a few un-plated positioning holes too.

A via would normally have pads on every single layer. But only two of those layers really need it. The via pad on all other layers is called the Non-Functional Pad (NFP). Sometimes we apply the "NFP removal" process when the design is ready for fab-out, which improves the production yield through the yield of backdrilling. With backdrilling we remove the portion of the via that is a stub, as explained later. NFP makes the via impedance higher, which can help when we otherwise have a too low impedance. The choice of whether we apply NFP removal or not has to be applied to both the via impedance optimization model and the manufacturing files identically. Otherwise, we are not modeling the actual board that we are getting. When vias carrying power nets connect to plane layers, they are supposed to be in the direct-connect mode, so there will not be an actual via pad. The vias that do not connect to a particular plane layer do not need a pad there, so we can apply NFP removal to plane layers too. This will help us eliminate the pad to plane clearance constraint and reduce the antipad size, making the plane less of a Swiss cheese. At that point only the drill-to-copper clearance will determine the antipad size. Often we use thick copper on plane layers that require a larger clearance, so NFP removal can help. NFP removal can be applied to all possible layers, to specific layers, or a portion of the layers. For high-reliability products a certain percentage of the NFPs have to remain on each via. The choice of layers of which the NFP removal is applied to should be determined by the design, not by the fabricator later; otherwise, we lose control and our simulations will not match.

15.5.2 VIPPO VIAs

VIPPO means via in-pad plated over. The via is placed inside the component solder pad, as they overlap. To prevent the solder to flow off the pad and into the hole, the via is filled and plated over. This technique basically eliminates the visible hole we see in vias on surface layers. They are made by filling the regular vias after they are plated, then plating them again to cover the filling material semi-flat. The point of doing this is to improve board density and signal integrity by eliminating the dog-bone trace. We still see a small dimple on the via pads. In some cases, we allow BGAs to be soldered on them, but we always allow capacitors to be soldered on them. In most cases a via pad is larger than the BGA solder pad, so making it VIPPO would require a solder mask defined pad, which has other issues. It is best to avoid that and use dog-bone for BGA pads, while using VIPPO on larger rectangular pads. A BGA fanout area uses either VIPPO vias or regular ones, but the regular ones cannot overlap with component solder pads so they require a dog-bone trace to connect to the pads. Figure 15.11 explains three cases of VIPPO versus dog-bone uses.

15.5.3 Through-Hole Parts

Decades ago all parts were through hole and their pins were soldered into plated holes. SMD (surface mount) components became common near the end of the 20th century but some parts were still

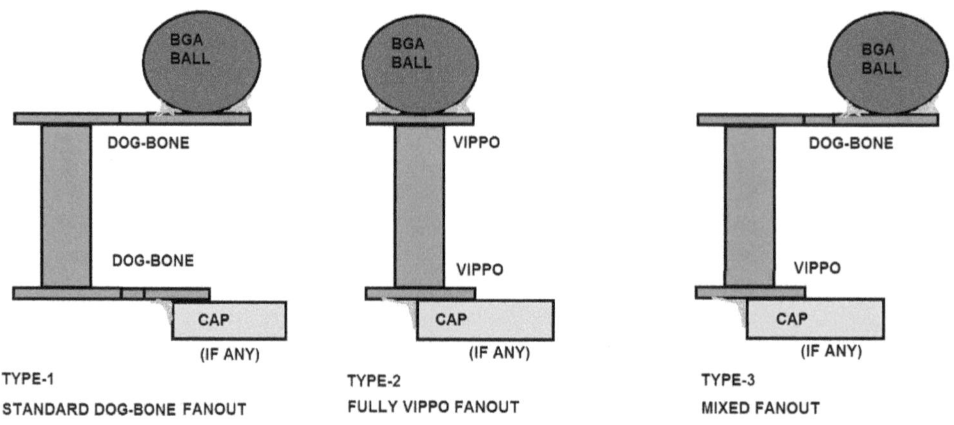

FIGURE 15.11 VIPPO versus dog-bone options.

through hole, like most connectors. In recent years many connectors transitioned to be SMD too, and the ones that are still through hole are press-fit types and are not soldered. They use a press fit tool with very high pressure to push the connector pins into the pin holes in the board. This usually requires a component keepout area around the press fit connectors on the opposite side of the board for a press fit fixture to be touching the board during the process. Soldered through-hole requires a similar keepout area. It is a rectangle enveloping all ins, and about 3mm larger on each side. We cannot have small SMD components in this area. The press fit test fixture provides pressure to the board against the force of the component being pressed in from the other side. We have to ask mechanical or manufacturing engineering or the factory contact person about the exact design constraint. It is a good design practice to not have any components in our design that is through-hole soldered. They would demand all kinds of compromises. They can be soldered in three ways: Manually by technicians (low production volume), using wave soldering, or using selective wave soldering. Selective wave soldering has several methods, the pallet method when a custom test fixture is attached to the board while it is passing a solder wave with openings only at the solderable pins, the fountain method when a custom test fixture is attached to the solder wave machine to create an up-flowing solder-fountain, and the CNC robot soldering that solders one pin at a time while moving a mini fountain to the board pins.

15.5.4 Solder Mask Expansion

Solder mask expansion is the distance from the copper component pad edge to the edge of the solder mask opening. This has to be at least as big as the solder mask positioning tolerance, which is 2mils typically. When two pads are near each other, each with expanded solder mask openings, there will be a remaining solder mask bridge between them. This has to be at least as big as the other two numbers, the SM expansion and the SM positioning accuracy. In fine pitch footprints (SSOP, TSOP) usually there is no solder mask between pads because the bridge would be too small. When a trace is passing by a solder pad, we have to ensure that the trace will never be exposed from under the SM, so when the pad is being soldered, it will not be shorted to the trace. For this purpose, the trace to pad clearance has to be at least as much as the SM expansion plus the SM positioning accuracy, or just twice the SM expansion value. So, if the positioning accuracy is 2mil, then we can set the SM expansion to 2mil and pad to trace clearance twice as much being >4mil. This would be good with parallel lines, but in corners the SQRT(2) times the SM-expansion value can be observed. To resolve that we have four choices: (a) Manually check/fix every corner of every pad by shifting traces away, (b) make all pads rounded, (c) set pad to trace clearance to be 2.5 times the positioning accuracy instead of 2 times, (d) or let the PCB fab company clip the pad corners where there is a conflict. All SM expansion issues are demonstrated in Figure 15.12.

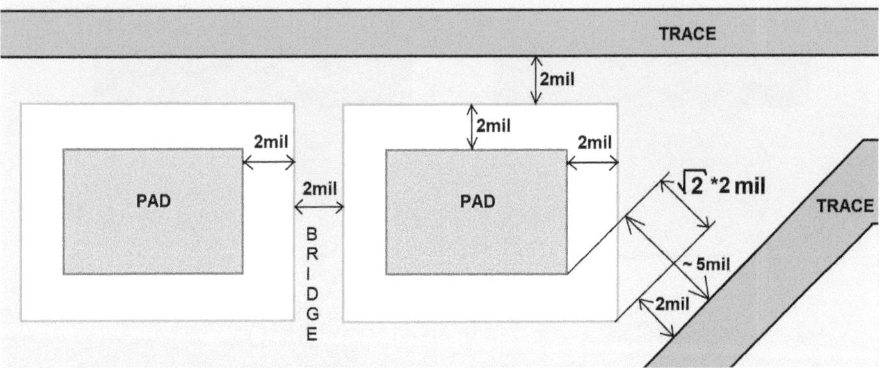

FIGURE 15.12 Solder mask clearance at pads (sketch).

Component pins or solder pads always have an opening on the solder mask layers (top and bottom), but vias have "tenting" options. VIPPO vias can be fully covered by solder mask (no opening) on both sides of the board. Non-VIPPO vias require "tenting", or solder mask coverage, to prevent solder from being sucked into the via hole, and from getting a solder bridge between component pads and via pads under BGA components. A non-VIPPO via cannot be fully tented on both sides of the board because we need to allow the via hole to have an exit hole for out-gassing. Typically, one side is fully tented; the other side is tented partially, covering most of the pad but not the hole. For example, if the BGA part is on the top side, then we must use via tenting on the top side, or use VIPPO.

According to the old saying: "solder mask is not an insulator". This means we cannot rely on the solder mask to keep metal parts from shorting to surface layer copper traces and power shapes. Any trace that is routed under a component that might have metal parts touching the board should be routed on an inner layer, and vias should not be placed under connector footprints. Many connectors and inductors have such metal shielding parts. It is best to look at photographs of these parts instead of drawings, or just assume they are all metal underneath.

15.5.5 Soldering in General

From bad quality design or bad quality manufacturing we can get soldering issues. These are either opens (cold solder) or shorts (short circuits). An open means one signal fails to pass through, a short means a signals shorted to another or to a power net. Both can be constant or intermittent (random or temperature dependent) on a particular unit. Soldering quality can be improved from the design stage by better footprint design and stencil design. The stencil simply follows the solder paste layer on the layout design, driven by the library footprint, although the contract manufacturer can modify the stencil drawing to improve yields. Stencils are thin metal plates with holes on them to allow solder paste to be dispensed on the component pad surfaces. This printing happens just before the board receives the components, placed by the pick and place machine, before going through the reflow soldering oven. The reflow oven melts the microscopic solder balls in the paste, and at the other end it will solidify into one piece. Stencils can also have stepped thickness to apply more paste in areas where more is needed. The center pads on QFN parts can have a full opening or they can have a very specific pattern developed in-house. Different patterns can be analyzed to improve both shorts and opens. While soldering these parts we have to prevent gasses from being trapped under the thermal pad, so the footprint shape (copper, solder mask, paste) has to allow their escape.

BGA chip solder pads on the board can be one of two types, either solder mask–defined pads (SMD) or non-solder mask–defined pads (NSMD). Figure 15.13 shows the difference between the two. Let's not confuse this with surface mount devices, same S.M.D. acronym, but different meaning. We almost always use NSMD, except with a few components with special requirements. To

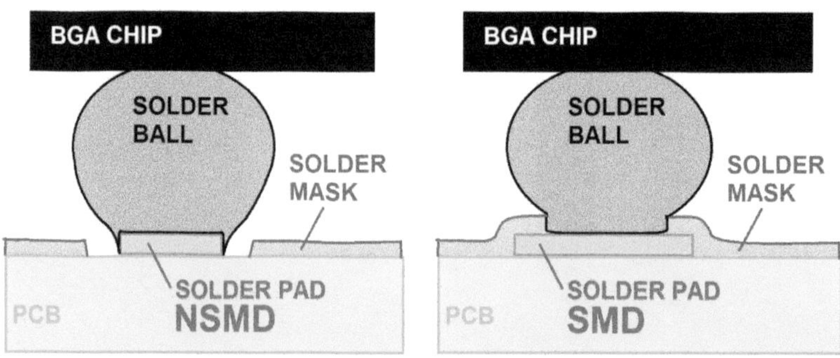

FIGURE 15.13 Non-solder mask–defined and solder mask–defined pads.

avoid having to use SMD, we should not use large VIPPO vias for BGA pins; rather, we should use dog-bone fanout. This is because a via pad is usually larger than the BGA solder pad, and we would have to use SMD to reduce the area to the diameter required by BGA ball soldering. A microvia might fit inside the solder pad, so it would not require SMD. We can use VIPPO on the decoupling capacitor pads that are much larger than the BGA pads.

Power components in QFN packages like VRM power stage chips require the power shapes to envelope the solder pads to achieve the lowest possible parasitic inductance. Due to solder mask expansion rules, these fine pitch (0.4 to 0.65mm) pin fields will just have one big solder mask opening in the pin rows. When the plane envelops multiple pins, and the SM has one big wide opening to multiple pins, we will end up with the solder flowing unevenly between the pins, causing insufficient solder between the component pin and the PCB pad, aka cold solder. This can be prevented by using SMD pads for the plane-connected power pins and NSMD pads for the trace-connected signal pins. This will ensure having solder mask between the power pins but not between the signal pins, which also allows gas escape in the signal pin area.

The "surface finish" is a chemical metal plating on top of the copper surface of outer layers. Any copper area that is not covered with solder mask will be plated with surface finish. This is most commonly nickel-gold (NiAu), or organic finish, or on low-cost consumer boards it can be HASL. They preserve the easy solderability of pads and prevent the underlying copper from corrosion.

15.5.6 Fiducials

Fiducials are positioning reference markers on the PCB, which are automatically checked by the SMT pick and place machine's camera, to determine the 0/0 coordinate. All part coordinates from the pick and place files are relative to a fiducial's position on the board. These are unsoldered exposed gold-plated copper pads with big solder mask opening and a recognizable shape like a circle, cross, or square. We have one to three global fiducials near the board's corners, but for large BGA components we often place additional fiducials near the package corners. Some companies like to also place corner marks as parts of BGA chip footprints. A corner mark is an L-shaped exposed unsoldered NiAu-plated copper shape, at two of the chip's corners, aligned with the package body outline. A component outline is usually printed on the silkscreen layer too, but that is just a visual aid for manual handling. Accurate pick and place or even rework placement require the positioning features to be in copper, not in silkscreen, as they are more accurately manufactured and have sharper and more accurate edges.

15.5.7 IPC Class 2 and 3

IPC is a standard organization that is concerned with PCB manufacturing. It has defined PCB classes for different industries and reliability classes, with different manufacturability layout design constraints. IPC class-2 is for regular industrial and data center boards. IPC class-3 is boards with enhanced robustness and oversized features, mainly for military/aerospace use. This can pose a problem while we are trying to implement impedance controlled via structures and other high-speed layout features that are required for 10Gig and above. Some of these features are tightly packed and their size might become too large to fit under a fixed grid component, when using increased feature sizes. One common solution is to design for a "class-3 with exception", that allows some objects, at limited quantity or within limited small areas to violate the class-3 dimensions, marked in the documentation and approved by all parties. We would mark the SERDES section of the main chip as an exception area for the clearance rule DRC.

The exact class-3 oversized constraints should be obtained from the fab vendor. Class-3 requires both design features (larger objects) as well as manufacturing parameters that the fabricator applies that are not in the CAD layout files or Gerber files (other than the fab notes). Several parameters are oversized for class-3. For example, the annular rings on vias are oversized, which also increases the via pad size. It is to allow the via hole drill to not cut through the edge of the pad but to be fully contained, even with bad drill tolerance. If the drill hole touches the pad boundary, it is called "tangency", or if it wanders through that boundary then it is a "breakout". Teardrops (fillets) on vias and pads are often added to further improve the via pad breakout prevention. Other spacing parameters and drill sizes can also be oversized.

15.6 HIGH-SPEED RULES

High-speed SERDES signal paths, especially at 8Gbps or above, have to be designed with more advanced and more complex considerations than even the few Gig signals had to. The constraints are tighter, there are more constraints, and the addition or replication of pre-designed 3D structures (visual, instead of spreadsheet based) becomes more common. This is because on medium to longer 10Gbps links the eye closes at the receiver pin, and only opens up after the on-die DFE. The effect is already strong at 8Gbps, but at 10Gbps it is overwhelming. At 25Gbps the via impedance control is very critical, but even at 10Gbps we need to use them to largely improve margins. The regular constraints are represented as numbers in a spreadsheet, the 3D ones are graphically communicated with drawings. A simplified view of how more constraints are needed at higher speeds to maintain the same product reliability that we are used to, is shown in Figure 15.14. We mainly focus on the 8Gig+ signals, but any digital signals between 20MHz and 8GHz also require a subset of the design considerations—the higher the speed, the more requirements.

On any board design that contains 8Gig or faster signals, we also have to design some of the lower speed signals with more advanced layout features and strategies. This is to avoid all other parts of the board from disturbing the delicate high-speed signals and reference clocks through bad localization and EMI interference. Only those features of the low-speed signals need improvement that would create interference into high-speed signals and SERDES reference clocks. The way low speed signals on high-speed boards disturb other low-speed signals does not create any increased concern, when compared to low-speed only designs. For example, ground stitching vias have to be added at the layer transitions to avoid large return loops radiating. Figure 15.15 shows a board with some 56Gig signals and some slow glue logic signals on the same board. The 56Gig signals are spaced out much more in their routing channel, having odd angles and rounded corners, compared to the slow signals routed in tighter bundles and straight lines. Spacing to sensitive signals has to be driven by the sensitive signal's needs, but spacing between two low-speed signals can remain tight. In fact, it was a common design practice to route them with "4-mil trace 4-mil space", like we can observe on old Pentium-II computer motherboards containing 100MHz buses. On high-speed boards we often route the low-speed signals on tight bundles (1:1 or 1:2 width to space ratio) to take up less space and less layers, while the high-speed signals are spaced-out at 30 to 50mils and use up most of the signal layers. When the signal's rise time is faster, above a threshold, then the reflected

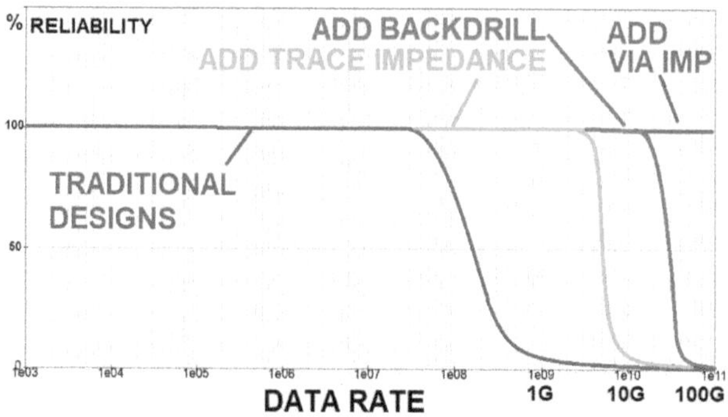

FIGURE 15.14 Addition of more constraints at higher speed designs (sketch).

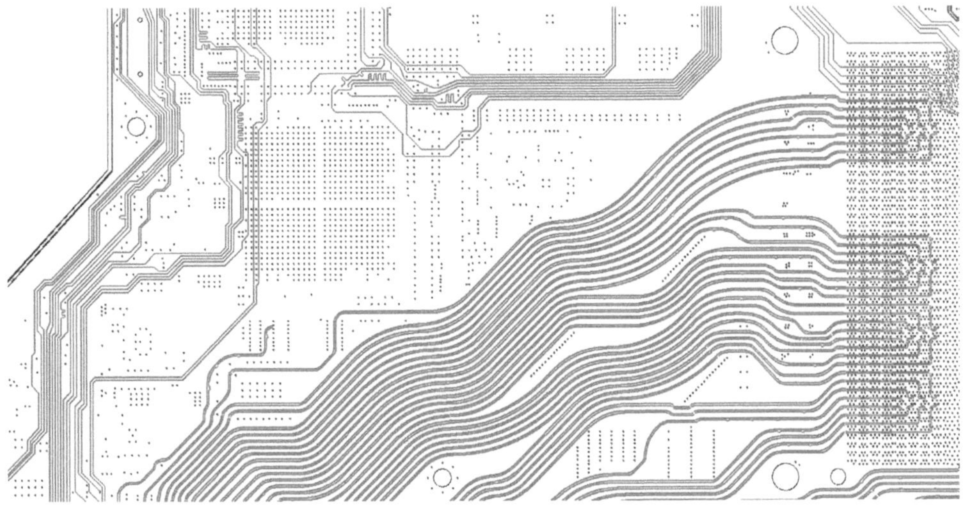

FIGURE 15.15 kHz/MHz signals (blue) and GHz SERDES signals (red) having different spacing and routing on the Minipack 2 SMB switch card from the Open Computer Project, the image from the layout design file is used for illustration under the Open Computer Project Hardware License (Permissive) Version 1.0 (Open Computer ProjectHL-P) signed by Meta Platforms, Inc.

wave arrival timing will be comparable to the signal's timing. A different threshold exists for the crosstalk, as faster rise times (slew rates) increase the crosstalk noise voltage through capacitive and inductive coupling. When the reflected wave ringing arrives in the middle of a bit period it can interfere with sampling the data. When the reflected wave arrives while the signal is still changing state, it is not even noticeable. Beyond these limits we need to use more high-speed constraints and terminations, and might have to simulate too.

Table 15.1 shows the suggested layout design rules and features, marked with speed bins. For the slow signals we are assuming that they are on boards that are also containing faster SERDES signals.

15.6.1 Summary for SERDES Links

Multi-gigabit SERDES trace routing has requirements different from basic low-speed signal traces have. They are more sensitive to skew, crosstalk, return loss, and insertion loss spec violations. We need to apply certain constraint types, insertion loss control and impedance control in the fab notes, need to use impedance-optimized via structure designs, symmetrical via/trace designs, via stub control (backdrilling), angled/wavy routing or rotation for FWE mitigation, over-tuning avoidance, phase mismatch consideration in route directionality, only using ground-referenced single-stripline routing, minimizing voids near the route, eliminate all voids directly in the path, adding manual voids under large SMT pads, and limit the number of layer transitions to the start and end points plus at any AC-cap locations. We should not allow mid-route layer transitions, unless the vias are backdrilled from both sides and there is no way to make a floorplan that allows crossing-free flow. These are described in detail throughout the PCB Layout Design chapter, some having their own sub-chapters.

The main layout constraint that we use for SERDES links is the differential pair object creation, the diffpair ECSET (electrical constraint set) creation, and applying that ECSET on the created diffpairs. "Differential Pair" rules are under the Electrical and Routing rule category in Allegro. This ECSET contains diffpair phase tolerance matching (1 to 5mil), trace width and spacing (from the stackup's impedance table) same-net spacing for dispersion, uncoupled length and parallel running

TABLE 15.1
Typical High-Speed Layout Constraints versus Signal Speed

#	Rule or feature	>= 16G	8-15G	1-7G	100-900M	< 100M
1	Length match diffpairs to 1mil, never more than 5mil.	must	must	must	must	must
2	Min and max trace length rules come from pre-layout simulation or loss budget calculation.	must	must	don't	don't	don't
3	Trace length rules come from timing analysis calculation.	don't	don't	must	must	must
4	Main route trace-to-trace max parallel segments clearance (spacing, running length, max parallel): 25 to 50mil. If running length is <1mm, a small 5mil clearance is okay.	must, 25…50mil	must, 25…50mil	15…25mil diff, 10mil SE	4…15mil depen on speed	4…8 mil, except clocks 10mil
5	Main route trace-to-shape long parallel segments clearance (running length): 40…50mil. If running length is <1mm, a small 5mil clearance is okay. See Figure 15.16.					
6	Additional spacing is required wherever there is available board area. After routing signals with the above constraints, we need to manually slide traces to fill all area available adjacent to them, to dissolve bundles, except low-speed signals. See Figure 15.17.	40… 100 mil	40… 100 mil	40… 100 mil	25… 100 mil	don't
7	Keep pad-to-shape clearance small enough to not override manually placed oval voids used on differential vias. Or remove NFPs.	must	must	nice	don't	don't
8	No mid-route Layer Changes should be used. If we have to, then need backdrill from both sides with impedance controlled GSSG via structures.	must	must	nice	don't	don't
9	Use GND stitching vias at layer changes. They must go to all layers with through drill, not shallow stacks of microvias.	must	must	must	must	must
10	No void crossings allowed; even small oval voids should not be crossed with high speed diffpairs.	must	must	must	must	nice
11	No thermal relief on GND pins of grid connectors and BGAs, because it would cause too much impedance discontinuity.	must	must	nice	nice	don't
12	Minimize the number of serpentine bumps used for phase tolerance matching of diffpairs, match at via with twist, or use fanout. directionality. The bumps need 5x width space. Avoid over-tuning (needlessly compensating back and forth). See Figure 15.18.	must	must	must	nice	don't
13	If teardrops are used, then they have to be identical on the p/n legs of the diffpairs and have to be small.	must	must	must	must	nice
14	Single ended or split fanout of diffpairs not allowed.	must	must	nice	don't	don't
15	The VRM power-stage and the inductor must be on the same layer, to avoid inner layer radiation and interference from power vias.	must	must	must	must	nice

(*Continued*)

TABLE 15.1 (CONTINUED)
Typical High-Speed Layout Constraints versus Signal Speed

#	Rule or feature	>= 16G	8-15G	1-7G	100-900M	< 100M
16	No dual-stripline layers. Must have 2 dedicated GND planes around any high-speed routing layer, aka using single striplines, and GND referencing only. Even though dual striplines should not be used, if using them anyway then at least don't put any copper GND pour on them.	must	must	must	nice	don't
17	Avoid layer transitions mid route. If you must, then it has to be backdrilled from both sides, and 2 GND vias to be provided.	must	must	no bd, 2 via	no bd, 1 via	no bd, 1 via
18	No outer layer routing. Their impedance accuracy is lower than inner layers, and they are affected by EMI too much.	must	must	nice	don't	don't
19	Negotiate vendor stackup with trace widths, and have it officially approved before the layout design starts. Use those to route.	must	must	must	must	nice
20	Dynamic length matching, with 3" segment length. It might not be sufficient that the diffpair is matched on the whole route; we might need to also match within small running-segments, to reduce mode conversion. Anything smaller than 3" is not practical.	nice	nice	don't	don't	don't
21	VIA aspect ratio 15:1 often required, to have small enough vias for impedance and allowing routing channels.	must	must	must	nice	nice
22	To reduce small resonances caused by sharp trace turns, use curvy corners.	must	nice	don't	don't	don't
23	FWE mitigation with 10degree odd-angle or wavy routing is cheaper than panel/board rotation. The trace will be kept at an angle to the fibers, while overall heading straight. The cost of this is the routing channel will be 15%–25% wider. Odd angle routing saves on both FWE and trace length. See Figure 15.19.	must	must	nice	don't	don't
24	Via nonfunctional pad (NFP) removal to help the backdrill tool longevity, but our via-optimization has to account for it.	nice	nice	nice	don't	don't
25	Thieving or GND fill must be 50-70 mils away from traces.	must	must	must	40mil	30mil
26	Differential signal vias (2 signal vias in one oval hole) require 2 GND vias, to complete the g-s-s-g structure. Only this 4-via GSSG structure has a definable via impedance. Just the 2 signal vias don't have an impedance. 3 single-ended vias can share one GND via.	must	must	must	1/dp, 8 se share	1/dp, 15 se share
27	Even clocks that run much lower than 1GHz need the same GSSG via structure as the 10G signals have, due to jitter, and additionally provide 30mil clearance from clock vias to 12V planes using manual voids.	must	must	must	must	nice

(Continued)

TABLE 15.1 (CONTINUED)
Typical High-Speed Layout Constraints versus Signal Speed

#	Rule or feature	>= 16G	8-15G	1-7G	100-900M	< 100M
28	Vias need differential impedance optimized in a field solver; they also need stub removal through backdrilling or microvia stacks, need differential structures to reduce crosstalk.	must	must	don't	don't	don't
29	Large surface mount (no-hole) connector pads and AC-capacitor bodies on layer-1 might need a small rectangle void on the layer-2 plane. Possibly also on layer-3 and layer-4. A field solver and TDR analysis can tell whether it is needed and how big. Small round BGA pads usually don't need it. Any layer-3 signals shouldn't cross it, but go around. See Figure 15.20.	nice	nice	nice	don't	don't
30	Top to bottom direct via does not need backdrill. Top to N-2 layer does not need it either when routing on N-3.	apply	apply	N/A	N/A	N/A
31	Backdrill parameters like via diameter, BD tool diameter, BD-to-copper clearance, antipad size have to be calculated and negotiated with the fab vendor to allow an 11-12mil routing channel (that fits a diffpair) between backdrilled BGA fanout vias on a 1mm grid.	must	must	N/A	N/A	N/A
32	Press fit connector pins are backdrilled up to "minimum barrel length". So, we should be utilizing upper routing layers for low-speed signals, as they cannot be backdrilled, so we can have lower routing layers for high-speed signals. The connector needs a certain depth of copper barrel remaining so it can make contact inside it.	must	must	N/A	N/A	N/A
33	AC caps need 2 diff via structures, each dual-cap should be placed staggered from other dual-caps if the traces are long or go over connectors. They can be in a tight row if no other sources of crosstalk expected, for example from connectors	must	must	nice	N/A	N/A
34	Define production acceptance tests in fab drawing in layout design mechanical layer. SET2DIL coupons for impedance test, SPP or VNA coupons for loss verification.	must	must	must, no loss	must, no loss	must, no loss
35	If low loss is needed, then calculate a loss budget, compare with floorplan, then define the dielectric material, glass style, copper foil type and loss testing dB/in@13GHz requirement in the fab drawing.	must	must	don't	don't	don't
36	Trace impedance control.	must	must	must	often	rarely
37	Same net spacing, for length tuning meanders, to prevent shortcut propagation. Usually, 3x width.	must	must	must	must	don't

("Don't" means no need to follow; "nice" means nice to have or prefer to follow; "must" means must follow the rule)

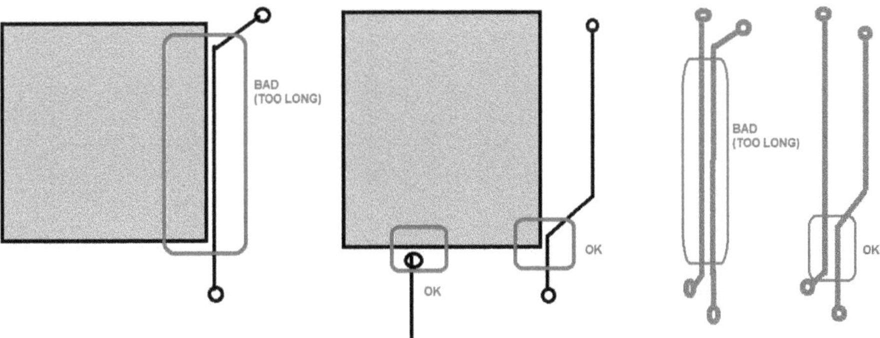

FIGURE 15.16 Running length based spacing (sketch).

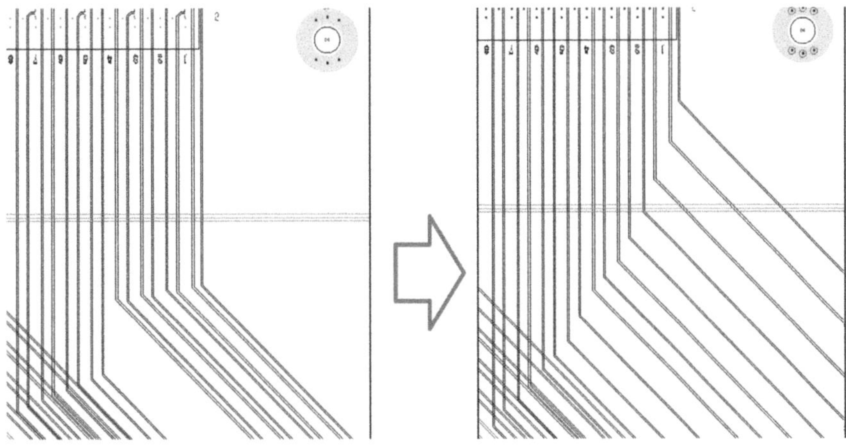

FIGURE 15.17 Spacing-out signal bundles in Altium.

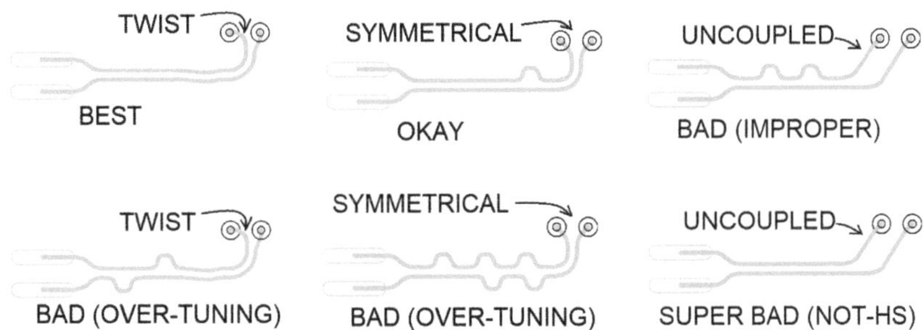

FIGURE 15.18 Tuning versus over-tuning (sketch).

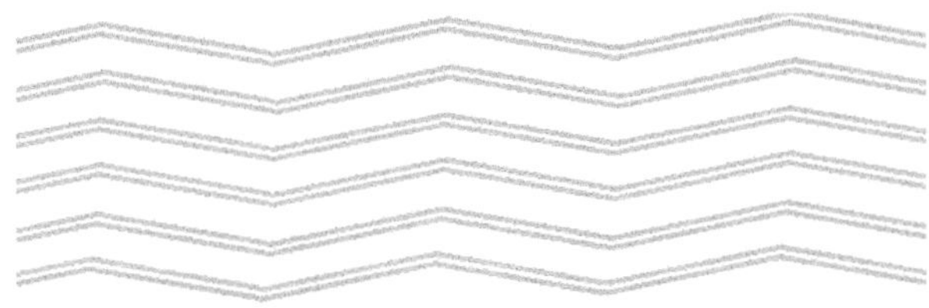

FIGURE 15.19 Wavy route concept (sketch).

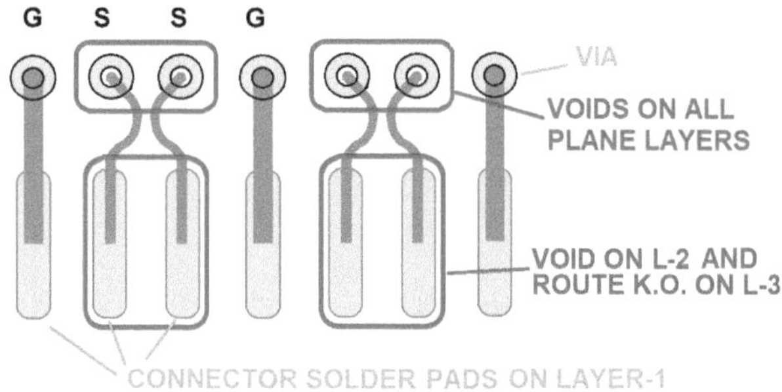

FIGURE 15.20 Plane voids under large SMT connector pads (sketch).

length (spacing for crosstalk) parameters. We can use "Total Etch Length" rules, where the maximum length to is limit insertion loss, and the minimum length is to mitigate return loss. Of course, we also set up all the manufacturability constraints with spacing and via parameters, which also have to match our plans with the dense BGA fanout via-structure designs. Special fab-notes are required to maintain low insertion loss manufacturing and tight trace impedance control. Tight lane-to-lane length matching is rarely required, due to FIFOs and protocol encoding. We should not confuse multi-lane SERDES links with simple clock-forwarding interfaces that do require tight lane-to-lane matching.

When we add length to a SERDES link, for example, for increasing insertion loss (dampening return loss), we should not use tight tuning meanders; rather we use detour routing with curved corners. Curves improve return loss a little and might just be what we need to pass the limit lines. Detour just means manually rerouting the long way, and sliding segments while looking at the tuning gauge, if we have set up a min/max etch length constraint.

15.6.2 Summary for Non-SERDES Signals

Individual (non-bus) slow system and glue logic signals are asynchronous and do not require any high-speed constraints. They are CMOS signals with 30% noise margin. Very slow interfaces below 1MHz like I2C and UART also do not require them. We might want to ensure their localization and ground return vias, just to prevent them from disturbing other, higher speed signals through large return loops. Non-SERDES interfaces/buses often require length control of groups of signals, based on timing analysis, sometimes on a topology basis, depending on timing architecture. We use timing-driven trace length constraints for them, in the Electrical and Routing constraint category in the Allegro Constraint Manager. Many such signals contain a series resistor, which necessitates using XNETs instead of nets that are created by applying an SI model to the series components. For any diffpairs, the diffpair objects have to be created in the Constraint Manager, for any signal net pair that match the front of the net name but differ with _P or _N suffixes at the end. The package length or pin delay for large chips is entered into the Constraint Manager in the Component "Pin Properties" group under Properties. For signals that are not part of any bus, or operate below 10MHz, we usually do not set up any trace length or impedance constraints. Any impedance controlled signals require a constraint set with trace width (from the stackup's impedance table). For single-ended nets it is in a Physical Constraint Set under Physical category, for diffpairs in an Electrical Constraint Set under Electrical and Routing category, then applied to all of the relevant nets.

For synchronous, asynchronous, unidirectional synchronous, and clock forwarding interfaces, we can determine the routing trace length rules in two ways. The most accurate one is when we route the whole bus first, then measure the clock trace length, feed it into a timing analysis calculator, and determine the min/max trace lengths for all other signals. Then we route and tune those. In the other method that is more suitable for corporate design projects, we determine all the constraints first, then we route all traces.

For synchronous and asynchronous types, the rules for the clock signals depend on the clocking architecture. If the master chip supplies the clock and has no feedback clock, then we estimate the clock trace length from the floorplan, plus add 10% on top of it. If there is a central clock generator or a feedback clock scheme then we match all clocks within 25mils and use zero clock length for the timing analysis. For the clocks we set up a "Relative Propagation Delay" constraint in the Electrical/Routing category. Then we can calculate the data/address bus length constraints as min/max absolute lengths from timing analysis. This will be entered into the Allegro Constraint manager as an ECSET under "Toal Etch Length" (under the Electrical/Routing category). Many of such buses have more than one device on them, so we have to create sets of Pin-Pair objects, one set is from the controller chip to a peripheral chip, another set of Pin-Pairs is from the controller to another peripheral chip. Pin-Pairs are based on chip reference designators. Multiple Pin-Pairs can be created on one net. Then we can apply the total etch length ECSETs on all of these Pin-Pairs. If we have just one master and one slave chip, then we do not need to create Pin-Pairs, and we can apply the ECSET on the natural net, net-class or XNET objects.

Source-synchronous, unidirectional synchronous (like DDR4 address bus) and clock-forwarding buses require length matching with a complex set of Pin-Pair objects and matched groups. DDRx memories require trace impedance control, while most other types of parallel buses do not. The data bus lanes on DDRx memory interfaces use basic matching rules with zero delta and a tight tolerance, as the strobe to data centering is aided by on-chip DLL (Delay Locked Loop) elements. These are implemented as "matched groups" in the "Relative Propagation Delay" under Electrical/Routing category, and applied on Net/Xnet or Pin-Pair objects. For the design tool to pick up the package trace lengths and the via lengths, the Pin-Pair is the better option (rather than using nets). Complete DDRx-memory interfaces use a complex set of matching rules, some are topology-based Pin-Pairs, and it is described in the subchapter about memory interfaces. The clock forwarding interfaces might use a matching rule or an absolute (min/max total etch length) rule, all others use absolute (min/max) rules.

Slower non-SERDES signals generate lower amplitude crosstalk than SERDES links do, but it is still a concern. So, their spacing rules are relaxed to 1 to 2x width up to 200MHz, and 3 to 4x between 200MHz and 5GHz.

Differential pairs used from tens of Megahertz to a Gigahertz require most of the same considerations as SERDES links, except via impedance, angled/curved routing, pad-voids and insertion loss control. Clocks are more sensitive to crosstalk and interference than data signals are, so their spacing, ground stitching, and void separation are important. Non-clocks below 200MHz are usually routed single-ended and close together, with 1...2x spacing, no impedance control, and with minimal ground stitching vias. Differential sense lines used for VRM voltage sense or thermal diodes are routed with diffpair rules, but with no impedance control.

15.7 GROUND RETURN PATH

As the signal current travels in a trace towards the receiver (chip input), a return current travels towards the transmitter through the ground planes, in tight proximity, but in the opposite direction. A measure of the design quality is how tight we can get the two currents together through the whole path. As signal-vias conduct the signal current in a layer transition, the "ground stitching vias" conduct the return current, and they must be placed by the designer in the layout. Horizontally, the ground return current travels in both adjacent plane layers for stripline traces. The ground stitching vias and component fanout ground vias have to reach both of those planes. A stitching via is simply a via on the ground net, shorting all the multiple ground plane layers together and provides a return path from layer to layer, typically placed in very close proximity to signal vias. If microvias are used, then the ground current still needs the shortest path, by using through vias for ground or a full stack of microvias all the way down. A layer transition diagram like the one seen in Figure 15.21 can help visualize the return path and the need for stitching vias. The trace impedance is created by the exact distance between the signal current and the return current. If the return current is meant to flow in a plane at a given distance (dielectric layer thickness), but some objects like voids and plane splits force it away from its natural path, then it will not maintain distance and therefore not maintain trace impedance. It might have 20 to 300 Ohm impedance within the diverted return path areas. It will go in a detour, creating a loop, degrading localization. This loop formed by the signal current and the return current is a "discontinuity"; its size has to be less than 1/40th of the wavelength of the signal's frequency to avoid impedance issues. The signal's "frequency" that we compare against discontinuities is the half baud rate for SERDES signals, the knee frequency (0.35/t_rise) or the fifth harmonic of the half baud rate for slower non-SERDES signals, and the 5th harmonic of the clock frequency for clock signals. A detour loop of one signal overlapping with the detour loop of another signal is like a single turn coil transformer, with coupling—in this case it causes crosstalk and interference.

With our trace routing we should not cross voids and plane splits, even small ones, with any signal at a few Megahertz rate and above. This is why on modern board designs having SERDES links and DDRx memory buses, we use only complete solid ground planes. Lower-speed designs used cut-up split planes, or even continuous power planes, but none of these are suitable above 50 to 200MHz. All other layers can be multi-purpose signal/power layers, but the ground planes are ground only, with no traces and no small shape carve-outs for power nets. We make sure it is clear on the stackup document, and the layout review has to verify it too. It is hard to implement it, but not that hard. Often people complain that it is impossible to get their job relaxed, as not everyone is interested in doing a good job. Dual voids created for differential pair vias seem small, but if another diffpair crosses them then the return current will have to go around the void, creating a localization issue with reflections and crosstalk starting at few Gigabits per second and up. So signal routes have to go around them. It can get even worse if nearby voids merge, regardless whether created manually or automatically through clearance DRC. The return current path is demonstrated in Figure 15.22. We have to make sure that the plane clearance constraint is small enough; the vias are small and spaced out so that the voids will not merge into one giant blob that the signals would have to go around. The merger might also happen due to using too large voids (from via impedance optimization or from manufacturing constraints) or due to irregular fanout via placement. There is a reason why we prefer symmetrical and orderly fanouts instead of random free-form fanouts. A discipline should be followed rather than convenience.

Pins and vias connecting to the GND planes under grid components (BGAs and connectors) require solid GND plane via connections instead of thermal relief types. This way we can reduce

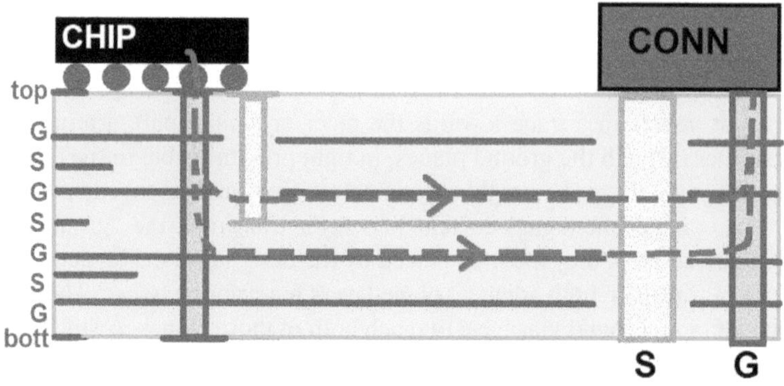

FIGURE 15.21 Return current in both planes on a layer transition diagram.

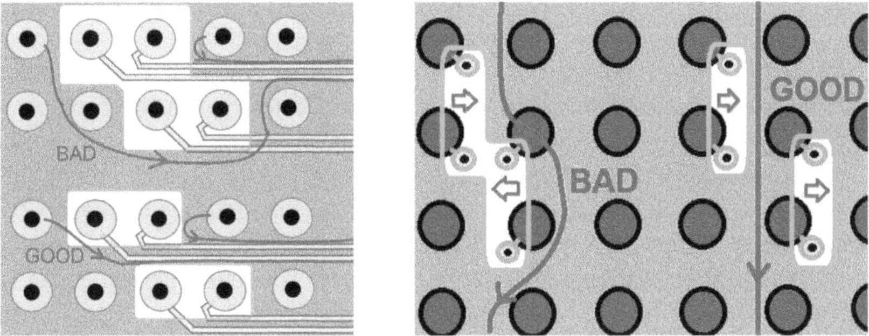

FIGURE 15.22 Return current around merged voids. Left void size issue, right fanout direction issue with microvias (sketch).

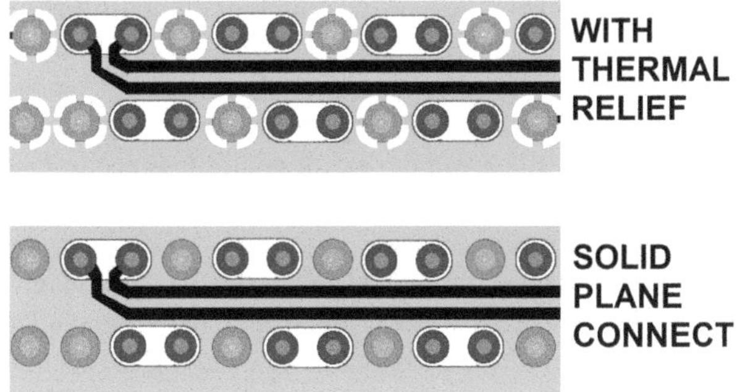

FIGURE 15.23 Plane connect options (sketch).

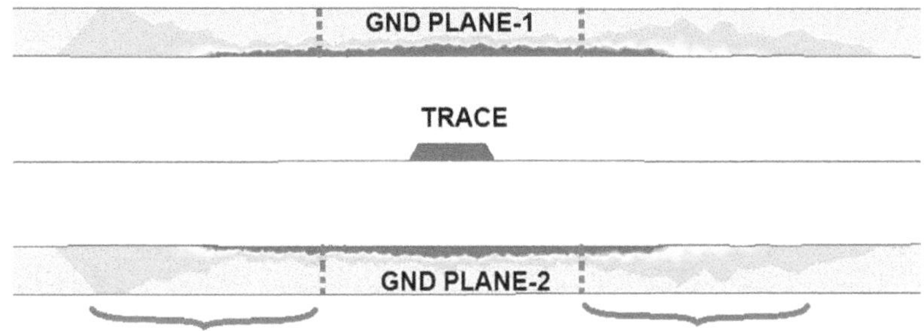

FIGURE 15.24 Return path undercut by voids on a current density plot in FEMM.

the periodic loading and impedance discontinuities that passing-by traces experience from a cut-up GND plane. With thermal relief there is not much GND left for the return current to form the intended impedance. It would zig-zag from the signal trace, each forced segment has a higher impedance. If the current is forced into a different shape than its natural shape, then it results in a different impedance. The intended impedance dies by a thousand cuts, as we can see the many plane under-cuts in Figure 15.23. The reason is the return current spreads in the ground plane sideways, and if we cut off the sides, then the return current cross-section shape will not be as intended, therefore the impedance will not be as intended. Impedance is formed by signal and ground metal shapes and the currents flowing in them. Altering the shape alters the current and the impedance. The portion of the current marked on the sides will be forced into the center section, as we can see in Figure 15.24.

15.7.1 Localization

Localization describes how well one circuit feature avoids interacting with its surroundings— how well separated they are. If it is well localized, then it is less affected by nearby objects, and it is less likely to affect other nearby objects. Bad localization can cause crosstalk (between similar signals) or interference (between unrelated circuits). Localization can be improved by adding GND stitching vias, improving impedance match, increasing clearance, reducing mode conversion terms in diffpairs, and avoiding sharing of GND return vias/pins. Bad localization is caused by shared GND return points (via sharing) or overlapping GND return areas. The return path with the signal path creates a current loop area. This loop is not shown in the design software, so some people cannot see them. This books helps with seeing them. With shared ground vias, the current loop areas of the different signals overlap, like two coils of a transformer. Figure 15.25 shows two diffpairs changing layers with one ground via; Figure 15.26 shows the area overlap acting as a transformer.

If a feature is not well localized, then other discontinuities in the signal path might affect the feature more severely. So localization helps to reduce the effects of other discontinuities too. Analyzing a badly localized signal by itself, then analyzing the other nearby discontinuity by itself will result in two separately clean-looking simulation results. But all at once is exponentially worse. This means that macro-modeling (decomposition analysis) works only on nice clean designs. A good design simulates more accurately, while a bad design simulates less accurately (too optimistically) but appears as a fake good design. Most simulation tools in 2022 do not have a good grip on localization, so their results are very optimistic.

Most of the time we cannot simulate different interfaces together. While relying on basic simulations we cannot see the interaction between a clock signal, a PCIe bus, and a DDR4 interface in one run, so we never see how bad it is until the prototype arrives and it is much worse than the simulations. Even if we pick two nets for crosstalk simulation, we might not find all the combinations that can disturb each other, especially the via-to-trace crosstalk cases. On a good board everything is well localized, aka everything is "bubble wrapped", made to be more resilient as well as not to disturb others.

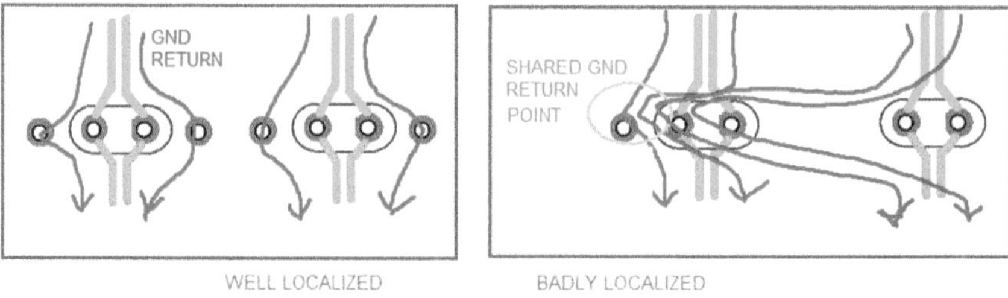

FIGURE 15.25 Localization with two diffpairs changing layers (sketch).

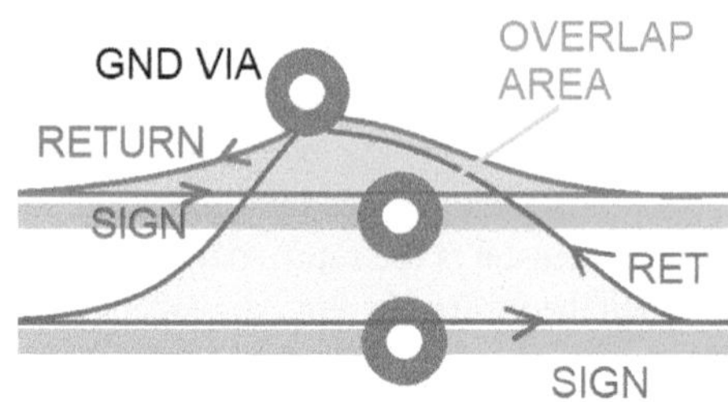

FIGURE 15.26 Localization: two signals and their return path at the layer transition with a shared via (sketch).

15.8 HIGH-SPEED ESCAPE ROUTE

The fanout and the escape route are parts of PCB routing where we get all signals routed out from under a grid-like part (BGA or LGA chip, backplane, or mezzanine connector). The first step of the fanout is to create the vias at each pin, which can be either a "dog-bone" or VIPPO. A dog-bone is a component pad connected to a via pad using a small piece of a trace, and the vias are 0.5x0.5y offset grid relative to the pin grid. This is often done using a "flare-out" pattern, where the dog-bone traces point 45 degrees off the horizontal line. This creates a cross-shaped channel in the middle for routing or placing more passive parts on the other side. There is also a narrow channel between every via column where most of the escape routes will go. When implementing the escape route, we have to make decisions about how to connect the traces to the vias, and which column or direction the signals or signal groups will try to escape. These decisions can have strong effects on signal integrity at 8Gbps or higher speeds. The considerations for these strategies are discussed on the following pages.

Main considerations:

- A via or pin row is a line of vias in parallel with the package outline. A column is a line of vias perpendicular to the package outline and directed towards the center of the package. So any straight and short escape routes go in columns.
- Board designs with SERDES links cannot set via parameters only based on manufacturing constraints. Instead, we have to plan for a fanout strategy and a pattern. Each high-speed diffpair will have an identical replica of the same impedance-controlled via structure. The replication will result in a two-dimensional repeating symmetrical pattern. A typical ASIC package has sections for different kinds of interfaces, so the repeating pattern will be visible within each section. If we place vias randomly, they will reduce the signal integrity of signals passing by.
- Diffpairs need to have differential vias, with oval or rectangle antipads. This increases coupling within a diffpair and decreases coupling between diffpairs.
- With SERDES signals we have to route outwards in columns from the package center on the shortest path to escape the BGA, which reduces the number of antipads on the route that causes periodic impedance discontinuities. This means neither sideways in rows nor across to the other side of the package.
- Single-ended (split column) fanout should not be used on 8Gig and faster signals. This is when one leg of a diffpair is routed in one column, but its pair is routed in the next column. With 1mm pitch BGA packages we can keep the P/N together, as long as we are using proper constraints. It is worthwhile to select a chip that comes in a 1mm pitch rather than a 0.8mm pitch package. We can enforce it by setting the diffpair uncoupled length constraint to no more than the BGA grid size.
- The via drill size, pad size, backdrill, and clearances have to be chosen so that it allows diffpair routing between two backdrilled vias on a 1mm pitch BGA grid. This is the case of "Backdrill under BGA". The constraints to be suitable, they need to leave 11–12mil gap between the antipads created by the backdrill to copper clearance.
- If teardrops (fillets) are used, then they must be identical shape/size on the P and N legs of the same diffpair. If it is too much work, then eliminate teardrops completely. Some boards require them for meeting IPC class-3 specs. They are small copper shapes that extend the via pad-to-trace connection to be gradual, which can help with bad tolerance drilling, preventing the drill from cutting off the via pad-to-trace connection. In most designs they are not needed.
- All vias should be on the same grid to allow via-structure replication, clean routing channels, and crosstalk mitigation.
- Phase tolerance of diffpairs should be mitigated first at the trace end by a twist (see Figure 15.27), then consider swapping the escape route to the other column and add meanders only if there is still mismatch.

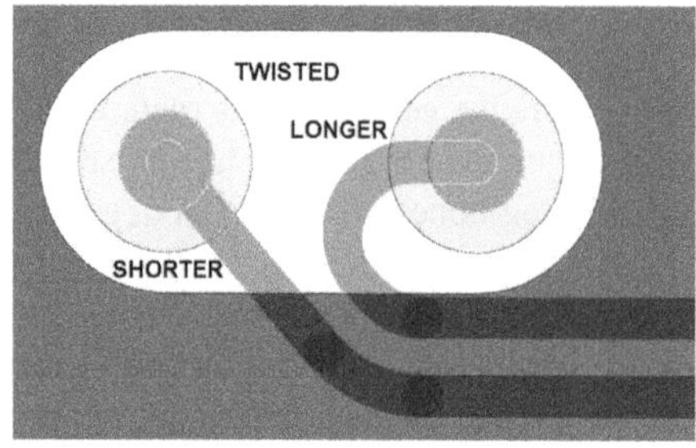

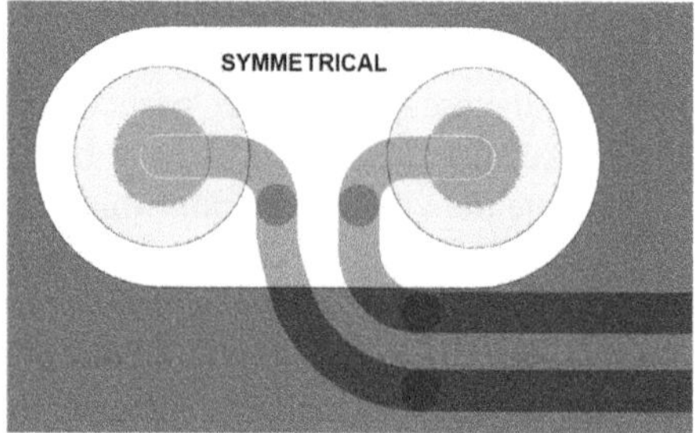

FIGURE 15.27 Differential escape route and via pad entry with/without a twist for length matching (sketch).

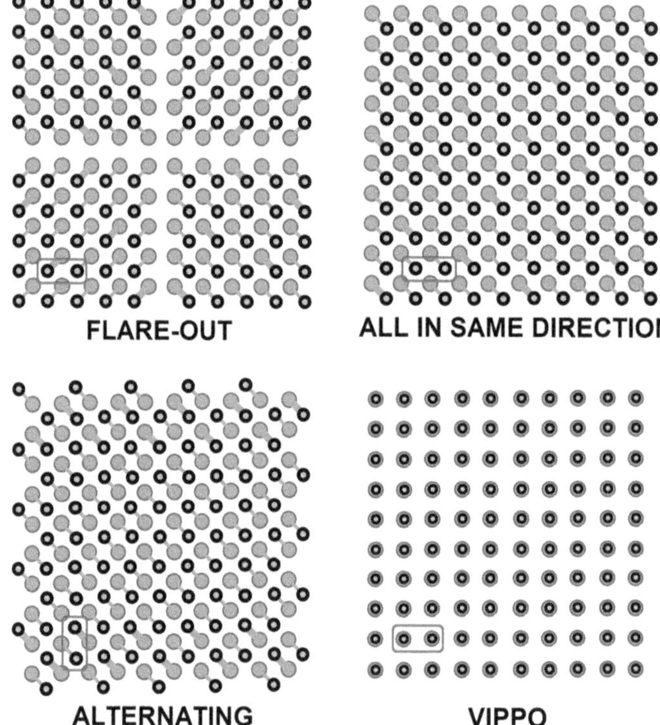

FIGURE 15.28 Fanout patterns (sketch).

15.8.1 Escape Artistry

There are several tricks that can help with keeping tight control over the layer usage, high-speed signaling, and other aspects at the same time while implementing the escape route from under a grid component. This section lists several of these.

15.8.1.1 Diffpair Rotation

If we alternate the neighboring pin fanout directions, then we can basically rotate the diffpair ovals by 90 degrees. As we go along a pin row, we add a dog-bone via up/left, then the next one down/right, then the next one up/right, etc. Figure 15.28 shows four types of fanout patterns, the third one is the alternating one. All four types have a diffpair marked up in red, so we can see the alternating one actually rotates it. This can help with chip pinouts that would otherwise block good high-speed fanout routing. This should be used only as a last resort or if we have to work with a chip pinout that was not made with considerations for high-speed escape routing.

15.8.1.2 Periodic Neck Down

Normally the trace impedance we originally wanted would result in wider traces, which cannot fit under the BGA package. So we use a neck-down escape route typically. This means that we use narrower traces in the area, driven by an area constraint. As the layout engineer continues to route the trace outward, when reaching the area boundary the tool will switch the trace width to the regular constraint-driven width. This narrower neck-down trace has a higher impedance and a higher amount of insertion loss.

In the escape route area, instead of providing a full neck-down with very high impedance, we can alternate the normal route impedance and the narrower traces that get around the backdrill antipad of the vias. This allows reducing trace losses and averaging a lower overall impedance in the fanout area. It would be very labor intensive to route these traces like this, so we can route one, and copy/paste the trace segments for all other signals. There will be two impedances alternating, but with a small difference between them, about 2% to 5%. The periodicity is 1mm as the package pitch, with a resonant frequency of ~160GHz, and a very shallow dip at that. This is shown in Figure 15.29.

15.8.1.3 Snake Escape Route on Offset-Grid Pin Fields

Some chip packages have a pin pattern where every other row is shifted by a half pitch, which we can call an offset-grid package—usually BGA or LGA format. It is the ASIC vendor's decision whether to use offset or regular grid, while at the board design stage we do not have a choice. This avoids the problem of the neckdown and allows us to do the escape route without having to reduce the trace width or backdrilling parameters. It also allows us to use smaller pitch BGA or LGA packages with the same trace and via dimensions. A smaller package can better fit in high-density boards. It requires us to use a snake-like route under the ASIC, as we can see in Figure 15.30. The half-grid shift creates a routing channel in a snake shape, which has a wider width at the same grid size, measured in a 45-degree line. It requires a snake route instead of a straight route in the package

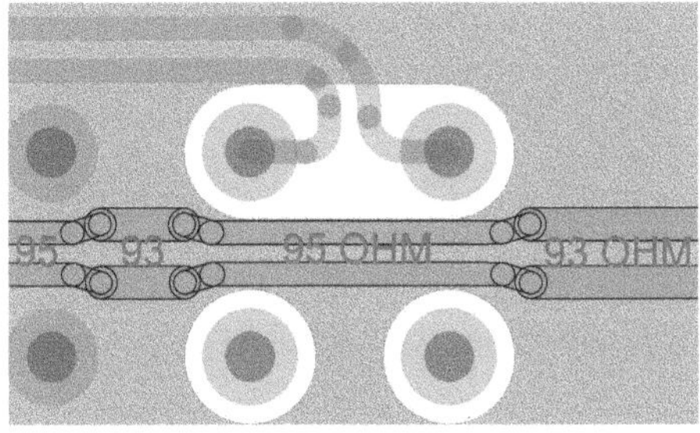

FIGURE 15.29 Periodic escape route neck-down, (sketch).

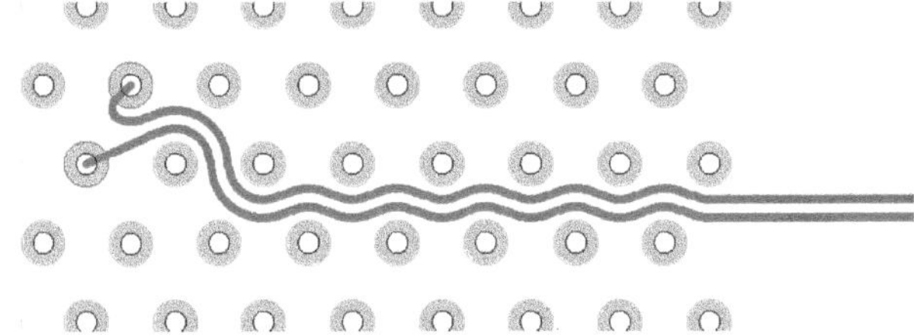

FIGURE 15.30 Snake escape route on offset grid (sketch).

escape area. The new via-to-via pitch is 1.118 times the original pitch, in the case of a 0.9mm pitch BGA that is 1.0062mm, which allows using constraints made for 1mm pitch regular grid BGAs. We can use the same trace width and clearance constraints on a 0.9mm offset grid (1mm diagonal hex) escape route as we can on a 1mm regular grid.

```
New_pitch = SQRT(pitch² + (pitch/2)²) = 1.118*pitch
```

15.8.1.4 Diffpair Length Compensation

When we are tuning the trace lengths to comply with the diffpair phase tolerance matching constraint, we have a tendency to just put more and more pumps in. Before any tuning, we should twist the trace at the pad entry to reduce the number of bumps we have to put in later, which will create a much larger uncoupled area. It is an SI-driven design goal to reduce the number of bumps on a SERDES diffpair. Each of these bumps is an impedance discontinuity. Usually no more than one bump should be in an area, or no more than two to three on the whole trace. Figure 15.31 shows how a bump was eliminated by adding a twist at the via entry.

Sometimes designers add bumps a few days later—as traces were moved they have to add more bumps and more, several bumps to both legs of the diffpair. This is called over-tuning; it should be eliminated until there are only a few bumps left that are only on one of the legs of the diffpair.

15.8.1.5 Tabbed-Lines on Single-Ended Memory Escape Routes

Intel has introduced the "tabbed-lines routing" for single-ended memory interface signals, where little copper fillets are attached to the traces as they pass through a pin grid area to help with crosstalk and impedance. An example layout with tabs is shown in Figure 15.32. The tabs lower the trace impedance, which helps with wide traces having to neck down under the pin grid area. It is similar to the periodic neck down but implemented with copper shapes instead of traces. Usually in the neck-down escape route area in the BGA pin field the traces are much narrower than the main route so their impedance is much higher, above the intended controlled impedance. Tabs can help lower them back to the impedance target.

15.8.1.6 Phase Tolerance Mitigation through Directionality

Route turns accumulate phase mismatch of diffpairs, while left turns and right turns cancel each other out. The goal is to try to match the number of left and right turns, so most will be canceled out.

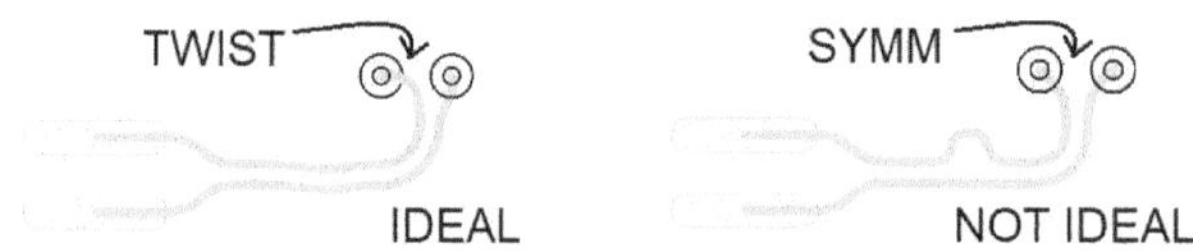

FIGURE 15.31 Phase tolerance at fanout, (sketch).

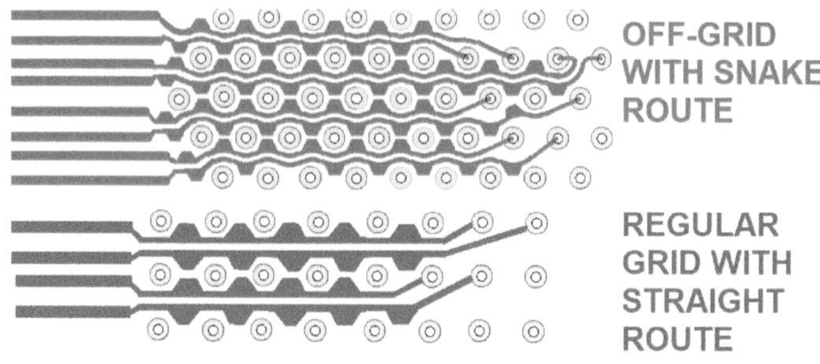

FIGURE 15.32 Tab routing (sketch).

We can swap the whole trace around at both ends if we escape-route in the adjacent column under the BGA. Each diffpair can be routed in one column, or in the adjacent column by exiting the dual void on the other side. The dual void has two sides. We can also go back to the schematic and pin swap the signals on one end, but it requires software engineering support, and the chip must have the capability to allow it. Figure 15.33 shows three cases of routing the same board, with three very different amounts of phase mismatch accumulation. The first has three times as much mismatch as the other two designs have, which will require the layout engineer to put three times as many bumps in the traces. Actually, the ones with reduced mismatch might just use the twist at the via entry with no bumps at all, while the one with more mismatch will need several bumps. As mentioned earlier, every bump is an impedance discontinuity, which is detectable on 8Gig and faster SERDES links. The turns should be looked at like when we are driving a car on the road on the map, through the path of the trace and not whether the turn looks left or right relative to this page or the screen. For example, when the signal is going south from IC1 towards IC2, then a left turn is towards the right of the page.

15.8.2 Layer Usage

There can be different layer assignment strategies for fanout escape routes. Normally one diffpair or two single-ended signals fit in one channel between the via columns, using the common 1mm pitch BGA chips. The simplest escape route strategy is when the signals that belong to one row of pins are routed on one layer, then the next row on another layer, then the next row on another layer again. A row is along the package outline.

Another strategy is to route a functional signal group on one layer, another group on another layer. Often a group is in one to four columns of pins. So the escape strategy is to route these columns on one layer, another set of columns on another layer. Then the traces will cross through the area of neighboring groups, but they are on other layers. Another group that is not adjacent, or far enough can be routed on the same layer. This allows signal groups to be routed on the same layer to have equal via length. For this we need to know or document which pins or nets are in a group. These two strategies can be seen in Figure 15.34.

We also have to consider RX and TX pins to reduce near-end crosstalk. For this we cannot route RX and TX signals on the same layers. For memory interfaces, it is important to route all signals of

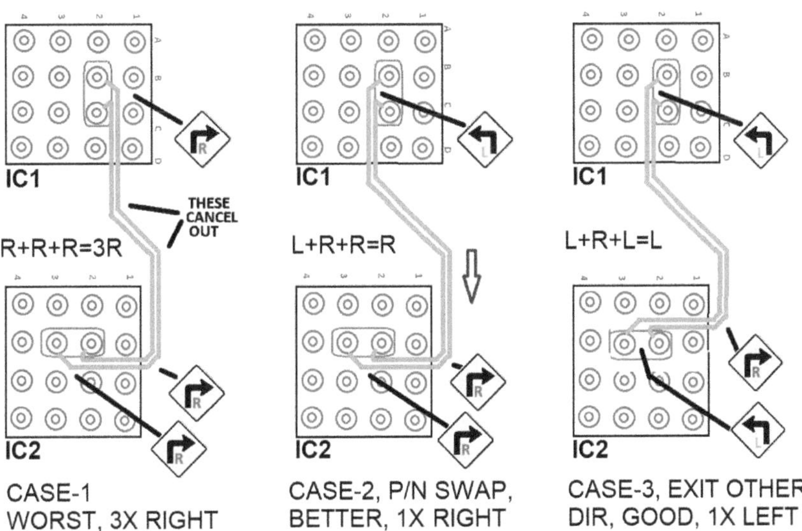

FIGURE 15.33 Escape route directionality.

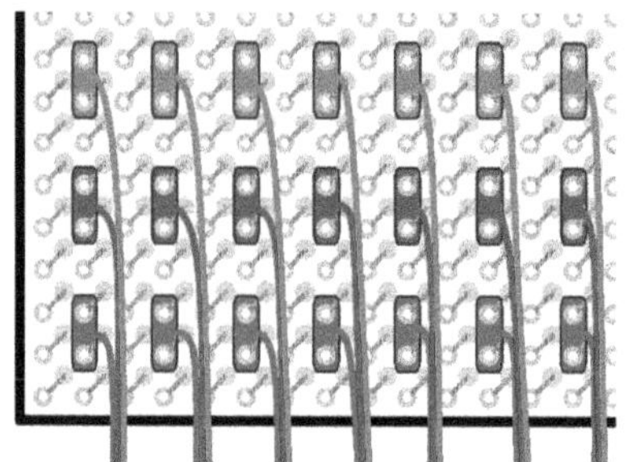

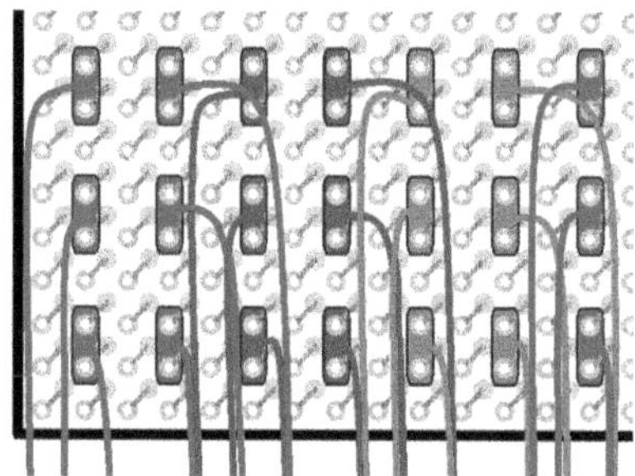

FIGURE 15.34 Escape routes, left row by row, right in functional groups (sketch).

one byte lane on one layer, otherwise some signals will have different delay through different length vias. During the fanout analysis we have to determine how signals will be grouped and how many layers will be needed, as described in Chapter 14.

The escape route strategy and the pattern also depend on the chip type, how dense the pinout is, the length matching requirements, the signal-ground pinout pattern, the BGA pitch, the signal speed, and the number and type of signals that need to escape the package. For example, a switch ASIC will have 32 to 1024 differential pairs in impedance-controlled differential via structures and a handful of glue logic signals. A processor will have two-thirds or more single-ended memory signals. A PHY or retimer chip or PCIe switch will have 8 to 200 diffpairs and a few glue logic signals. A glue logic FPGA will have only slow single-ended signals at random pattern and high density with less ground pins.

15.8.3 Escape Route and Backdrilling

High-speed boards with SERDES links will likely have backdrilling applied to the fanout vias. Traces from other rows will have to pass by these backdrilled vias in the routing channel. The diffpair vias are enveloped into a dual void. Nearby signals can pass by these voids, but they are not allowed to cross them in the middle between the P and N legs. We have to design the vias and void parameters such that it will allow an 11 to 12mil routing channel between via columns under the grid component, including required clearances. We have to check with the PCB fab how small the backdrill tool size is and the clearances can be in mass production. There are several as to backdrill parameters that are explained in the section about high-speed via design. If their numbers result in a smaller than 11mil routing channel, then we have to look for another vendor. The backdrill settings and pad-to-plane clearance settings will force the plane layers to create a circular antipad (void) around the vias. This will be larger than the antipad created by the basic via drill to copper clearance because the backdrill tool is larger than the via drill tool size. The design software has to have the backdrill parameters to interact with the online DRC. This antipad indicates the area that any trace cannot cross or hang over because the same clearance applies to the traces as to the planes. If a trace is routed through the circle antipads, then they might get drilled through, but more likely they will be picked up by the post-Gerber review by the fab company. We also manually place dual (oval or rectangle) voids to envelope one diffpair. This might be larger than the backdrill clearance-driven antipad. Our routing should not go over the edge of either the dual void or the backdrill antipad. The dual antipads in the ground planes have a wide area between the two vias. We should never route any trace across it. An important part of the daily layout review is to check for these mistakes. If the dual voids are oriented in an inconvenient way, then we can do an alternating via fanout that rotates all dual antipads by 90 degrees.

Backdrilling removes a portion of the via barrel, the stub that is not needed to make the connection. The dual void is needed on the layers where the signal via barrel remains, while the single circle backdrill antipad is needed on layers where the via is (back)drilled away. Sometimes we keep both types on all layers to avoid mistakenly selecting the wrong layers and to keep our work from getting over-complicated. The size of the dual oval void comes from via impedance optimization in an electromagnetic simulation tool like HFSS or Simbeor. The size of the single BD antipad circle comes from manufacturability parameters like primary drill size, drill-to-backdrill oversize, and drill-to-copper clearance.

This trace-to-void pass-by creates two issues, namely, with impedance and crosstalk. Traces have to pass by the larger dual voids that create stronger periodic impedance bumps than the single circle antipads do. Dual voids are really needed only on the layers where the via barrel remains. To reduce the periodic impedance discontinuity, we should assign escape route layers in such a way as to escape the innermost row on the lowermost layer, as is shown in Figure 15.35. This ensures that the inner row signals, while escaping, will not pass by any dual voids, assuming we removed the dual voids from those layers. If we routed the outer row on the lowest layer, then all the signals will experience unnecessary degradation. It is not fatal, but every little piece of SI margin we can get counts. The second issue is that crosstalk is created between the traces passing by vias of other signals. It is a trace-to-via crosstalk. Often it is a TX to RX crosstalk, which is the strongest and worst. While a trace is passing by a dual void, it is interacting with the signal that uses that void, causing more crosstalk than it would if the via did not have the big oval void at that layer. It helps if the via is backdrilled away at the pass-by layer, but it does not fully eliminate the crosstalk. Having the outer row pins escaping on the higher layer, having their vias backdrilled, and having the ovals eliminated below the routing layer is the maximum crosstalk reduction we can achieve. An SI simulation's 3D area must include both the aggressor and the victim signals' fanout vias and the board area between them.

In a special case of chip-to-chip links between identical chips, this strategy will not be possible, as we can see in Figure 15.36. Let's say the chips have RX on inner row pins and TX on outer row pins, then the RX of one chip has to connect to the TX of the other chip. In other words, the inner rows of one chip will be routed to the outer row of the other chip. This causes correct fanout at one chip but reversed layer ordering on the other chip. Unfortunately, there is nothing that we board hardware designers can do about it. Some chipsets are designed in a way to avoid this issue, by having RX on the outer row on one chip and TX on the outer row on the other chip. A chipset is two or more chips made by the same chip vendor, intended to be used together.

If we have to use a large backdrill tool size, or have a small pitch BGA chip that violates backdrill clearances, then whatever was good/bad above swaps. We can see this in Figure 15.37, comparing it to the previous figure. Now the new goal is to avoid having to backdrill through layers that have diffpair routing channels flying by. It is done by escape routing the outermost row on the lowest layer. This will have the issues we were trying to avoid above, the via to trace crosstalk and the larger periodic impedance, drop. But it will have the benefit of our being able to complete the design. If the BGA chip has less than 1mm pitch, this can help us out. If we are using 1mm pitch BGA but still running into this issue, then it is on us, we should have used a fab vendor that can deliver smaller backdrill parameters with reliable yield.

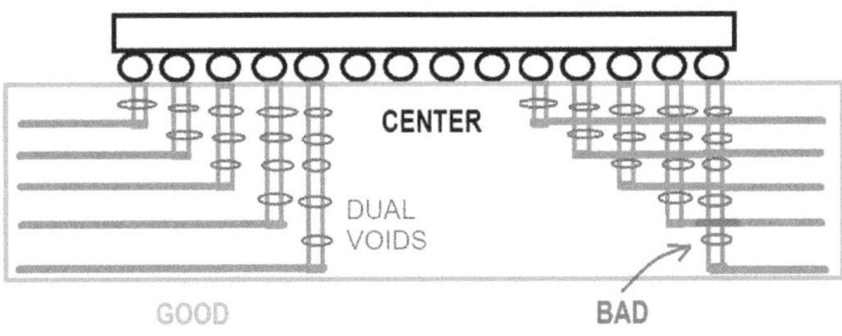

FIGURE 15.35 Backdrill and layer usage in general.

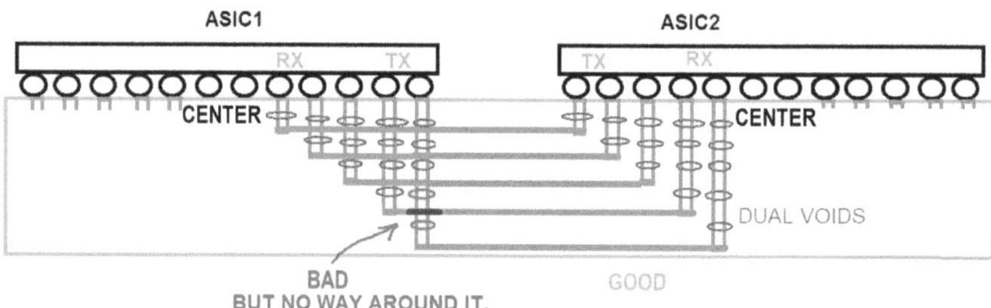

FIGURE 15.36 Backdrill and layer usage with two chips.

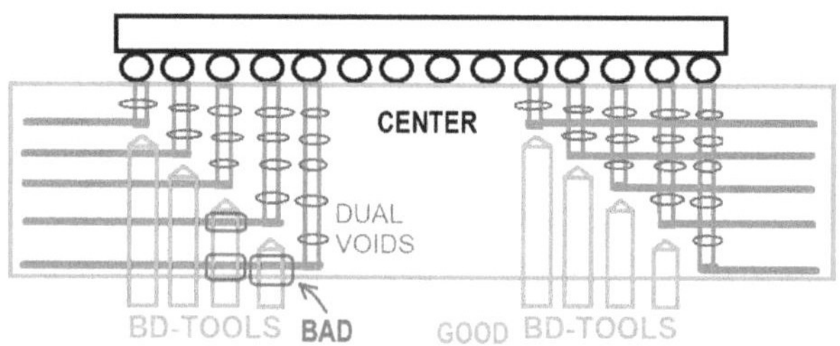

FIGURE 15.37 Backdrill and layer usage with large BD tool size.

15.9 HIGH-SPEED VIA DESIGN

Vias used for high speed 8Gig and above SERDES links are not just simple individual vias. They are complex 3D structures and differential. This is the only way to ensure that the impedance, the return loss, and the crosstalk will be within acceptable limits. Vias are electrically long enough at 8–10Gbps to be concerned with their impedance, especially near the transmit pins where the rise time and the propagation delay through a via are comparable time intervals. Without impedance match between the vias and traces, we get massive reflections on the return loss plot and deep suck-outs on the insertion loss plot. Most of the crosstalk we get on an 8Gig+ board is from the via fields in the component fanout areas, mainly as vertical via-to-via and via-to-trace crosstalk. We design and optimize these structures in a 3D full-wave electromagnetic field solver (like HFSS or Simbeor) with all their elements, then replicate them exactly in the board layout at multiple locations. They can be re-used in another design, if their stackup layers, like copper and dielectric sheets, are identical, but not necessarily with the same number of layers. A via structure consists of two signal vias, two ground vias, and a dual void on all layers. The dual void should exist at least on the layers the via barrel is not backdrilled away. It is a four element G-S-S-G (ground-signal-signal-ground) structure. Some of the more advanced BGA chip pinouts have their signal pins fully surrounded by ground vias from all sides, sometimes by 10 ground vias if it is a regular grid or by 8 ground vias if it is a half-pitch alternating grid. In that case it is a 2S+10G or 12 via structure that is to be analyzed in the 3D field solver. In all cases the exact number and exact relative position of the signal and ground vias is what defines the 3D via structure as one design unit or feature, and it is determined by the chip vendor. If the diffpair (two signals) has less than two ground vias around them, then the structure's impedance is not definable and will depend on surrounding circuits, aka having bad localization. The ground vias must reach all the ground planes, not only the near planes, and that might be a problem when using microvias or blind vias— at least the plane past the routing layer, but ideally farther down to all planes to act as ground shielding, reducing crosstalk through the voids.

Differential signals used for 0.1 to 1Gbit/s speed need one ground stitching via per signal pair and no dual voids and no impedance control is required. But for 1 to 10Gbit differential data signals, and the (100 to 300MHz) reference clocks used by the 10Gig+ devices, we should use the same

GSSG via structure described below without the 3D field solver optimization for impedance. The reference clock that feeds the SERDES must be kept super clean from interference that will cause jitter in the SERDES lines. If a board only has 1Gig signals, then the rules can be relaxed, but if the board contains both 1Gig and 10Gig signals then the 1Gig signals have to be designed to be less noisy. Memory interfaces even though running up to 5Gbps, usually have their single-ended signal vias sharing the ground vias in groups at a ratio of ~5:1. Any 8Gig+ differential signals used in SERDES links need to follow the controlled impedance via design below. Differential 3D via structures fulfill these roles, described on the pages below.

15.9.1 Differential Design

Vias have to be designed in a symmetrical differential structure for noise immunity and for reducing mode conversion (single ended interference into diff noise). Visually it means that the P an N signals are routed with a mirror-symmetry, and the ground plane antipads are overridden by a manually placed void in an oval or rectangle shape So, a hard symmetry is required, as we can see in Figure 15.38. The manual voids are also separated from other voids created by other differential pairs to reduce crosstalk. This separation has to be at least 1 to 12mils wide to provide a routing channel between them. If our design fails to achieve a clear separation on all layers, then it will fail the crosstalk S-parameter limit line compliance. In the case of microvias, which can be offset on adjacent layers, the voids could become offset too and overlap with neighboring voids, which will also fail compliance. We have to check for accidental void mergers and eliminate them. We have to make sure that the manufacturability clearances will not enlarge the manually placed voids, otherwise the via impedance we optimized will be way off. Of course, we should never route a diffpair through another diffpair's void so as to avoid a very strong via-to-trace crosstalk. For AC caps, the two ingress vias are in one void, and the two egress vias are in another void. One oval is for one differential pair, not for one component. The voids are replicated on all plane layers or on the layers where the via barrel remains after backdrilling, as described earlier about trace-to-void pass-by. If we use microvias, then we must use a folded-in structure where the P/N mini dog-bones are alternating in and out towards the center point, not alternating sideways, in order to keep the 3D structure small and compact and maintain the mentioned separation. For microvias the structure on the diagram does not just apply separately on each layer but through the whole offset microvia stack. All of microvias and mini-dog-bones must be enveloped in a small void that is identical on all layers. Most of the via descriptions in this book are about through drilled vias that are backdrilled because they are more compact and provide better signal integrity than microvia stacks, and they are the industry standard way of achieving good signal integrity at/above 8Gbps. A common mistake is to

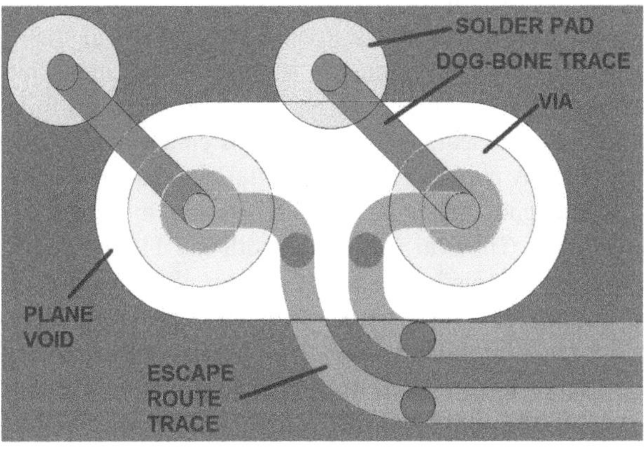

FIGURE 15.38 Differential fanout (sketch).

provide only ground microvias from layer-1 to layer-2, which cuts off the return path for the signal that is going deeper in the stack. Two through ground vias complementing the two signal microvias might work.

15.9.2 Stub Removal

When signals change layer in the board, they go through vias. The standard through drilled vias are made from the top to bottom layer. We rarely transition from top to bottom with high-speed SERDES signals, rather from outer layer (top or bottom component pad) to an inner routing layer. The portion of the via that is between the routing layer and the other side outer layer is the stub. As explained earlier, the stub creates resonances and signal integrity degradations, so they have to be removed during manufacturing. Stub removal becomes a required feature around 8Gbps, and all 10Gbps (per lane) designs, and especially the ones with short traces need it. It is usually done using backdrilling, but in some cases it is done by using stacked offset microvia structures. Backdrilling is simply a process of controlled depth drilling on an already plated via with a larger diameter drill bit to remove the plated copper from a portion of the hole. This will still leave a small residual stub because we cannot aim for zero, due to manufacturing tolerances. The microvia stack ends at the routing layer, the other side of the stack simply does not exist (deleted by the designer), this way eliminating a stub without backdrilling. So via stub removal can be done with either backdrilling (of through drilled vias) or microvia stacks. PCBs can be made as single-laminated boards containing only through-drilled vias or they can have multiple levels of microvias (to reach deep layers) created using multiple lamination cycles. The latter is more expensive.

With microvias we have to use multiple plating and lamination cycles, and extra copper surface roughening that can increase insertion loss on the traces. For most signal transitions we have to use multiple microvias, since they are only between adjacent layers. Most PCB fabricators do not want to put microvias on top of each other, so the next layer transition has to be at an offset location connected through a mini-dog-bone trace, so it is called an offset microvia stack. It is a zig-zag path vertically. All of the microvias, mini dog-bones, and the different voids on the different layers of both legs of the diffpair and ground together is one "microvia structure". This structure can either overlap with it is neighbors randomly on adjacent layers or it can be folded into a small compact area. If we allow the overlap then it violates several high-speed design considerations in tight BGA fanout areas and cannot have via-impedance control. If we fold it, then the structure is larger than a through-drilled via structure. Two offset microvias that are needed to transition two layers down, take up more board space than a single through drilled via does. The larger structure might block escape routes that can be a problem with large devices having many SERDES lanes.

With backdrilling a small portion of the stub remains, usually less than 12mil. This will have a much higher resonant frequency than the original 30 to 150mil stub had, so it will not interfere with our signal. The goal is not to have zero stub but to have a short enough stub. Around 100Gbps the common backdrill residual stub resonant frequency is closer to the signal frequency, so it requires an even smaller residual stub with more precise backdrilling. We need to keep traces and plane edges away from the drill bit by a clearance amount. This creates a circular antipad in the plane layers. The oval void we manually place for the differential via structures has to be at least as big as the backdrill antipad size, but sometimes it has to be larger as it might get enlarged during the via impedance optimization process. The oval void has a width and a length parameter. The width cannot be smaller than the backdrill antipad, otherwise the plane clearance will automatically override and enlarge it, resulting in a different via impedance than we optimized for.

The backdrill dimensions and clearances have to be chosen so that it will allow diffpair routing between two backdrilled vias on a 1mm pitch BGA grid. Let's call it "Backdrill under BGA". This is our main goal. A diffpair can be routed between if there is an at least 11mil wide channel so as to fit the smallest trace and gap. In 2023 most fabricators on the market are not offering boards with such tight backdrills, but several companies do, which allows the hardware industry to exist. The main parameters of a backdrilled via are the primary drill diameter (PD), the backdrill tool diameter (BD), the PD-to-BD diameter difference or "backdrill oversize" parameter, and the backdrill to trace clearance (BDTCL) on each side. The BD oversize is simply a rule about how much larger does the backdrill bit needs to be relative to the via drill bit to achieve guaranteed via barrel removal with good yield. The via drill size is mainly driven by the max via aspect ratio manufacturability constraint, from via diameter to via length (aka board thickness). We want the via drill diameter to be as small as possible. To be able to use this structure in BGA fanout areas, we need to use high aspect ratio primary drills. The backdrill to trace clearance creates the final clearance circle, which is a route keepout and also a plane antipad (automatically created circular void using DRC). The fixed BGA pitch and the required 11mil routing channel results in the maximum allowed clearance area (backdrill antipad) size. We can run the numbers about how big parameters need to be; they are all constrained by each other and by the BGA pitch. Once we have the numbers, we have to check which PCB fabricator vendor is able to manufacture boards with that number set with good yield. Many cannot, so the fab selection is restricted. These boards running 10Gig+ SERDES cannot be manufactured in random fab houses. Figure 15.39 shows the parameters from the cross-section view, while Figure 15.40 shows the same from the top view. All of our parameters must meet the equations below, to guarantee manufacturability and to allow a differential pair routing channel and good signal integrity in the same time. If the equations are not met, like we get "larger than" instead of "less than", then our number set and fab vendor is not usable.

```
BGA_pitch - BD - 2 * BDTCL - 11mil >= 0
BD = PD + BD_oversize
```

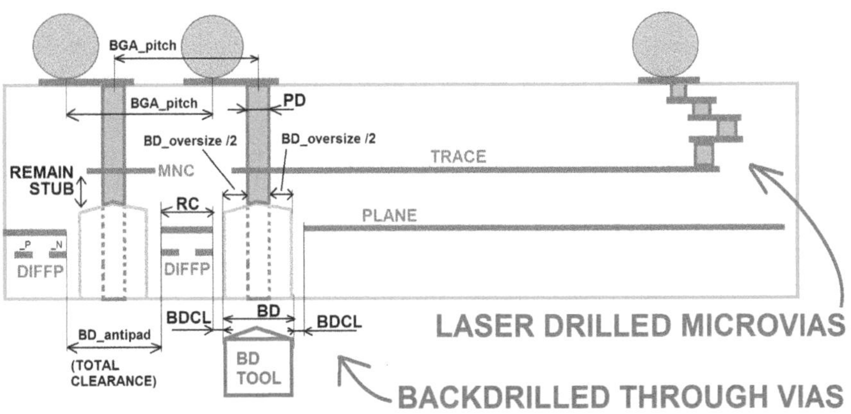

FIGURE 15.39 Via stub removal with backdrill or microvia.

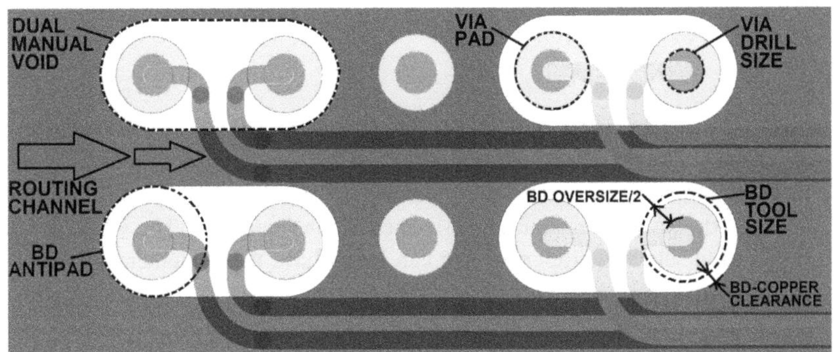

FIGURE 15.40 Backdrill dimensions relating to routing channels (sketch).

The manual dual voids we place on diffpairs also have to conform to:

```
BD_antipad = BD + 2 * BDTCL
BD_antipad =< void_width =< BGA_pitch - 11mil
BD_antipad + BGA_pitch =< void_length =< 2 * BGA_pitch - 11mil
```

To meet the equations above, we must have certain values for the input parameters. Everyone or every company has to come up with these numbers, while working with our favorite fabricators. Maybe we need new ones. If we chose the first few parameters in a way that the last few parameters are calculated to be in a non-manufacturable range, then it means that we chose the first few parameters wrong. This is true even if we have used those parameters for years. Some of our old parameters we thought we must use might turn out to be negotiable. Most of these numbers will land in the advanced capability range of the best fabricators, and low-end fabs will not be able to make it. Once we have a good set of numbers, we can re-use them in multiple projects. The BD oversize and the BDTCL are manufacturer (fab company and facility) specific parameters. By using random or low-end parameters we will not be able to fit diffpair routing between backdrilled vias on a 1mm BGA grid. The 1mm is given by the ASIC device manufacturer. Basically, we will not be able to implement the escape route. Note that with 8Gig+ signals we should not use split-column fanout, so both legs of the diffpair must fit in the same BGA column. We need to evaluate the capabilities of the fabs we want to work with. Our via impedance optimization from the 3D field solver provides the void's width and length, those have to meet the equations above too.

The manual void also has to satisfy similar equations for basic manufacturing requirements. These are the etching-related via-pad-to-plane clearance and the drill tolerance-related via pad annular ring requirements. These two create an antipad even on non-backdrilled boards. The annular ring defines the minimum via pad size based on the via primary drill size or the finished hole size. We have to check with the fab, which one (primary drill size versus finished hole size) the annular ring was measured to. We need to be concerned only with the inner layer annular ring, the IAR. The via pad diameter on inner signal layers (Via_pad_inner) has to be small enough to allow a diffpair pass-through between two via pads. So we subtract the 11mil routing channel with 4mil copper-to-copper clearances on each side of it, from the fixed BGA pitch, then what is left is the maximum pad size. The minimum clearance also depends on the copper thickness. The clearance is larger on plated layers, like in microvia boards. All of our via pad parameters must meet the equations below to guarantee manufacturability and diffpair routing between:

```
BGA_pitch - Via_pad_inner - 2 * trace_clearance - 11mil >= 0
BGA_pitch - Via_pad_inner - 2 * plane_clearance - 11mil >= 0
```

Where:

```
Via_pad_inner = PD + 2 * IAR
Etching_antipad = Via_pad_inner + 2 * plane_clearance =< BGA_pitch
- 11mil
```

Many designers simply do not specify in their fab notes the backdrill tool size, oversize, and BD-to-trace clearance; instead, they write an instruction to the fab vendor that they have to select those parameters in a way to avoid cutting into the traces. Although the designers still must ensure that they did not route any diffpair wider than 11mil in the escape route area. The fab note will say that the vendor is required to select the tool size. We can either have this statement or, instead, we can define the actual parameters.

Sometimes they define a radius difference "each side", or a diameter difference "both sides together", or just an added-up total diameter. It can be confusing, and it should be clarified with diagrams. They might call it spacing, or clearance, or oversize, or reduction. It helps if we do not just refer to the parameters by a single word or a number but also add "both sides combined" or "each side separately", or "in diameter" or "in radius". These variable names used in the formulas above might not apply to most fab vendors, but they are used in this book to help with clarity. Fab companies like to use diameters (hole and tool sizes) of everything and to distinguish between tool sizes, instead of coordinate-to-coordinate distances like we are used to seeing on mechanical drawings and in science.

"Backdrill under BGA with diffpair routing between" is easily doable using 1mm pitch regular grid and 0.9mm pitch offset-grid BGA packages, and it has been commonly used in the data center hardware industry by dozens of companies for many years, although not every single PCB fab is capable of making it. With 0.8mm pitch BGAs the differential pairs in the escape route split into separate columns, which is bad for via impedance control and return loss at 8 to 10Gbps or higher. This is an important consideration for component selection—to stick to the 1mm pitch package options if we can, or chose another vendor that has a 1mm pitch option.

Backdrilling is done from the opposite side of the board from the component and ends before the layer the signal is routed away from the fanout via. The "must not cut layer" or MNC for a backdrill instance is that inner routing layer. On any design there will be multiple different backdrill depths, which will be marked with different drill symbols. For each via instance the hardware engineer has to visually check that the correct backdrill MNC and symbol was assigned, based on which layer is used to route the trace away from the fanout via. There is a drill table on the fab drawing that lists each backdrill symbol, their diameter, and MNC layer as well as the stub length with tolerance. We cannot aim for zero stub; rather, we have to have some allowance, as big as needed to ensure manufacturability. The common residual stub of <12mil works very well up to 56Gbps. For 112Gbps a somewhat reduced stub might be needed. Stub length is specified as nominal plus/minus tolerance. On an N-layer board we cannot backdrill to routes on layer-(N-2) from the bottom. That means, for example, on a 30-layer stackup the routes on layer-28 will not be backdrilled; rather, they will have a via stub about 7 to 10mil, being the combined thickness of the layers, which is fine. If we have a design with only two to four high-speed traces, then we can route them all on layer-(N-2), and then the board will not require any backdrilling or microvias, but both end components must be on the top layer. Or we could route on layer-3 with both parts on the bottom side.

Press-fit through-hole connector pins have a backdrilling limitation called "minimum barrel length" (MBL). The connector pin is pushed into a plated through hole (like a via but larger) in the PCB. The metal pin requires a minimum amount (length) of the vertical area of hole metal plating (barrel), so the pin can retain contact inside it. The portion of the via barrel that remains after backdrilling has to be at least as long as the MBL parameter, which is defined in the connector datasheet. Typically, 0.8 to ..1.5mm long. So if we have a 3mm thick PCB, we can remove only about 2mm from it with the backdrill tool. We should use routing layers that are not within this MBL region, so the stub can be properly removed. If the connector is on the top (L1) then the first one to two inner routing layers can be used for low-speed signals. During layout design we have to revise the BD symbols, not to have any drill depths defined that are violating the MBL requirement.

15.9.3 Via Impedance Control

Vias are vertical transmission lines. As with any transmission line, they require impedance control when the signal's rise time is within the same ballpark with the propagation delay through it. This happens at around 8Gbps. If we assume the rise time near the transmitter to be 1/4th the bit time, and we want to stay away from the "$T_{pd} > T_{RISE}$" limit by 4x to eliminate any large impedance dip, then we will need via impedance control when we reach this threshold with our signal speed and via length:

```
ViaLength > 11.8 / (SQRT(DK)*baud_rate*4*2)   [inch and Gbps]
```

Someone might conclude from an equation like this, namely, that we need to only use vias that are shorter than this. That is not practical on complex designs; instead, we optimize the via structure to have a proper impedance and grounding. The differential pair requires a differential impedance, which has to be maintained, and it has to match the trace impedance, via impedance, and any connector impedance. A complete 4-via G-S-S-G pattern has an impedance, while one signal via by itself does not have a well-defined impedance. Typically, the trace impedance is 93 Ohm for Ethernet and 85 Ohm for PCIe, which has to match the via impedance also. The main goal of the electromagnetic via optimization is to ensure that the via will have a matching impedance to the trace impedance. All the horizontal dimensions within the via structure together will result in a vertical via impedance. For example, via barrel diameter, via pad diameter, antipad length and width, signal-to-signal pitch, and signal-to-ground pitch, as shown in Figure 15.41. For 8Gig, sometimes we might just use "reduced capacitance" vias, that look like the impedance controlled, with the dual voids and symmetry, but without optimization performed in a 3D field solver. Once a via model is optimized in a 3D electromagnetic simulator, we can export an S-parameter model of it, which can be put into a TDR simulation in ADS to see how good the impedance control was. During optimization we can adjust some of the dimensions, within manufacturability limits; we can also change the stackup to alter the material's DK. Figure 15.42 shows the TDR results from Simbeor. We can see how much the impedance is at every point on the path, as the signal travels through the via-structure.

There are also single-ended interfaces with impedance control requirement, for example DDRx memory buses, but they have random signal to ground via arrangements, that does not allow for via impedance control. They will have controlled impedance traces, but no controlled impedance vias. The best we can do in that case is to have the vias as short as possible, that reduces the length of the impedance discontinuity on the signal, for example by routing it all on the upper layers, closer to the ASIC's side of the board.

If we have a design with only a few SERDES signals, and they are all routed on layer-3, then they might be short enough (~10mil) to avoid being affected by the "$T_{pd} > T_{RISE}$" limit, so they could work without via impedance control up one or two technology nodes. A design with layer-3 routing only would be made with a stack of only two microvias or regular vias with backdrilling. Any connector would have a longer MBL than that. If we try to use the same techniques (of no impedance control) on another design that has a larger number of signals, that require more routing layers, and longer vias, then we will not get so lucky. For example, a 10mil long via to layer-3 would have an 80Gbps limit, a full stack 100mil long via would have an 8Gbps speed limit, above which the via impedance starts to be important. The speed limit is not a sharp brick wall type limit, rather gradual. As we get closer to it, without via impedance control the reflections get worse, then much worse.

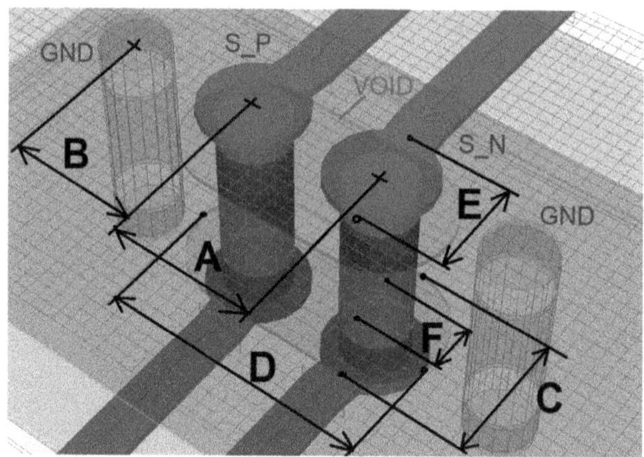

FIGURE 15.41 Via impedance control through structure dimension.

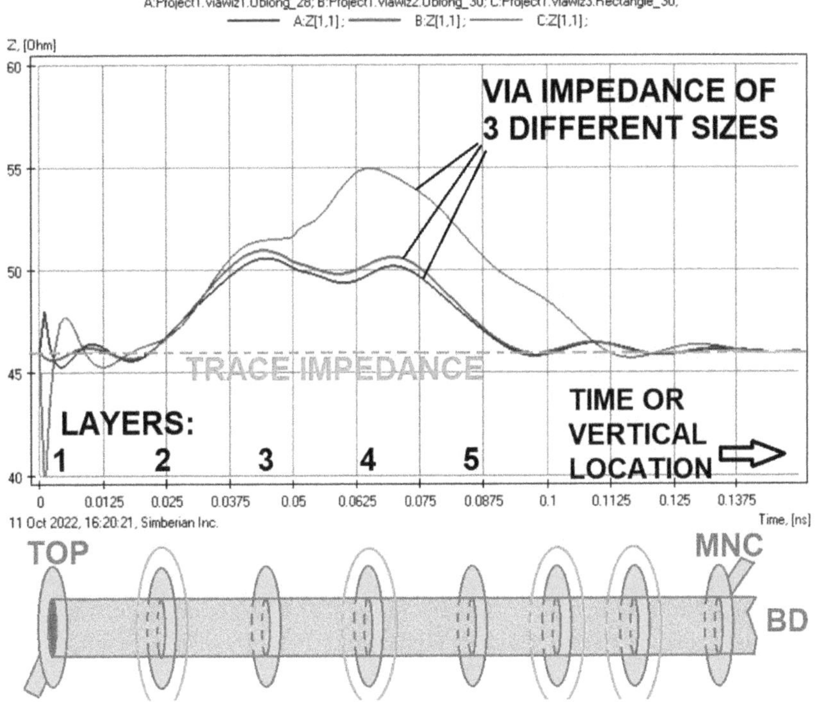

FIGURE 15.42 Odd mode (half of Zdiff) TDR impedance plot of a via model.

For the impedance optimization we have to use the via-drill bit diameter, not the finished hole size. Impedance depends on the outer dimensions of the via barrel. And vice versa, we also have to ensure that the layout will be designed with and the board will be fabricated with the exact drill bit diameter that we used for the optimization. All three must match. Sometimes during the fab-out process they negotiate a different via size. We cannot allow that with impedance controlled vias, so we have to make sure to obtain the drill size we can use from manufacturing engineering before the design starts. This depends on the stackup and the fab vendor. A hardware project has to start with full understanding, not randomly hacked all the way until its done.

15.9.4 Crosstalk Reduction

The oval-shaped differential via structures must be separated from neighboring instances by sufficient grounding as planes and ground vias. We cannot allow the oval voids of diffpairs to merge or even overlap with other diffpairs' oval voids; otherwise, there will be no ground shielding left between the signals, resulting in strong crosstalk. This can be caused by the use of too large clearances, too large backdrills, or a free-form fanout. Even if we have achieved a definite void separation, there are still different levels of separation that can be achieved, depending on how compact our structure is and in what pattern the chip vendor assigned the ground pins to the package. All that can still be ruined by missing ground vias, forcing the return currents to overlap. A smaller pin hole or via diameter also helps to reduce crosstalk.

We need to put two ground vias for each diffpair signal to complete the GSSG 4-via pattern. Ideally, we would have ground vias between the adjacent diffpairs, and the ground vias must go straight down to all layers, even below the routing layer. BGA and connector pinout patterns provide different crosstalk mitigation, depending on whether the different diffpairs are parallel, staggered, or separate by being boxed in by ground vias. The number of ground vias and their relative positions used in the ASIC pinout have a huge effect on via impedance and crosstalk. This pattern is chip vendor and device dependent; the board designer has no control over it—unless we work on the ASIC company's board hardware team and are helping the ASIC team to finalize the ASIC package design pinout. What we (board designers) can always do is to select a different chip for our design, one with a better pinout.

If we design a BGA fanout with randomly placed microvias, having no regular grid structure, then the via impedance, the return loss, and the crosstalk will become uncontrolled and likely fail the interface standard specs at 8Gig or above. Instead of randomness, we have to use symmetry and regular repeating patterns, using replications, copy/paste, or just designer's discipline. Microvia designs are usually spread out like a staircase, causing overlap (crosstalk) on a tight pin grid, and the large voids are crossed by traces, causing return loss. The repeating subset of the regular pattern of one diffpair with its immediate ground pins, which we model for via impedance, could be called a "Constellation". Figure 15.43 shows both the pattern and the constellation options. The "pattern" is the relative location of several constellation instances. All the rectangles together on each image form the patterns. Each cell in the pattern is a constellation. The picture shows six different patterns and constellations, depending on how many ground vias are shielding the signal vias from each other and providing return path and impedance. The signal and ground metal shapes and the shape of the space between them define the via impedance. The number and positions of the ground vias around each diffpair define the crosstalk mitigation performance of the pinout pattern. The larger the ground via count for each diffpair signal, the better the crosstalk and return loss will be. For 56Gig-PAM4 designs anything less than an 8-GND constellation will not leave much margin for any PCB discontinuities and possibly will not work reliably on anything other than a small and simple board. The 8-GND constellation requires an offset-grid BGA/LGA package, so if we have a regular grid then the equivalent performance requires the 10-GND constellation for being fully boxed in. In most complex boards 4-GND might work at 25Gig-NRZ with reduced margin, but 6-GND is better for project risk mitigation. Any chip package with 2-GND constellations could work up to 8Gbps. When we are selecting a chip for our board design, we should always check what

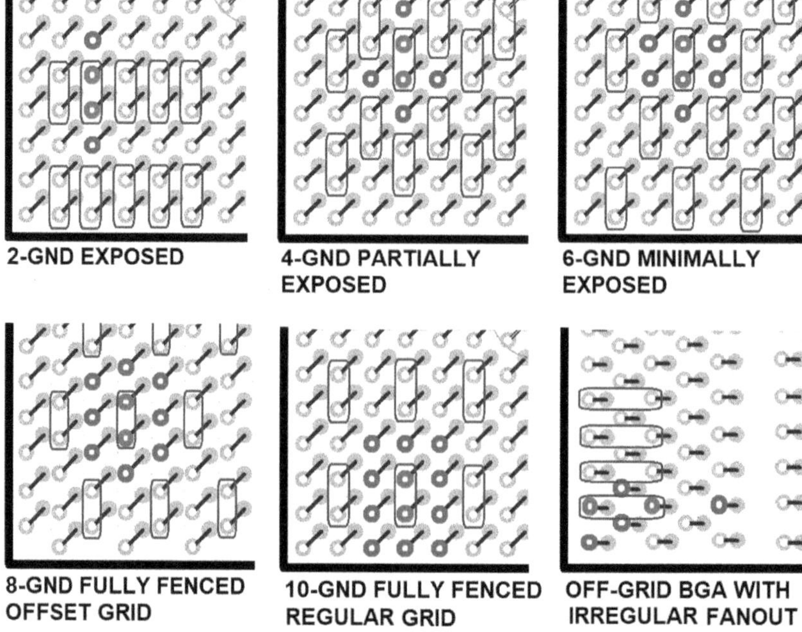

FIGURE 15.43 Via crosstalk mitigation options using common BGA diffpair pinout patterns (purple rectangles) and constellations (red signal, blue ground).

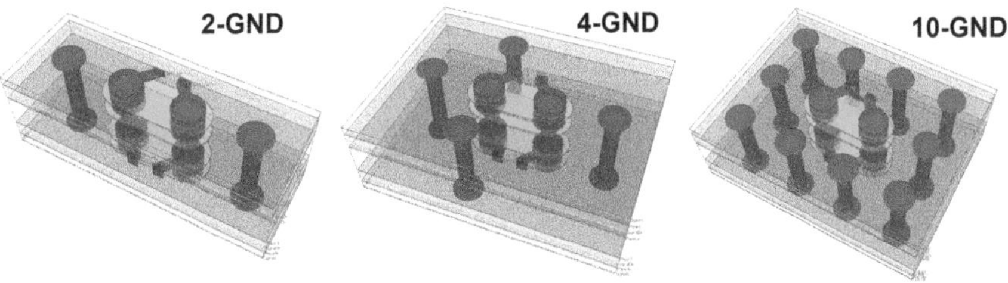

FIGURE 15.44 Different through-drilled via constellations in the Simbeor 3D editor.

FIGURE 15.45 Different via design types in KiCAD.

kind of pattern and constellation the ASIC package pinout has. Figure 15.44 shows how the constellations look when being analyzed in Simbeor.

On microvia-based multiple-laminated boards, the mini-dog-bones of the microvias have to be folded into the same oval shape as the through signal via would have, while for the ground pins we need through vias to maintain crosstalk, return path, and impedance at the same time. If the microvia mini-dog-bones all point in different directions (like in low-effort layout design lacking any strategy), then a meaningful pattern cannot be established. The voids will overlap or merge, then we lose impedance and crosstalk control. Basically, the ASIC package patterns and constellations have to be continued down through the PCB stackup all the way to the other side of the board; otherwise, its benefit is lost. That vertical continuation happens only with straight through-drilled vias or with properly folded microvia stacks. Figure 15.45 shows the three main via structure options. The free-form microvia structure on the left is the largest horizontally and may be suitable up to <3Gbps. The folded-in microvia structure is compact and would fit in a small void that is identical on all layers, making it suitable for higher speeds more than the previous one. The through-drilled option when applied with backdrilling is also compact, it is the one used by most of the industry at 100Gig. Compactness is required for keeping space from nearby signals, and to avoid overlapping with them to reduce crosstalk. The ground vias should really be through-drilled to provide the shortest return current path, and to reach past the routing layer. We might find innovative fanout patterns and routing strategies using larger object sizes and clearances, or at a lower technology level, but that only works if our design contains no more than one to four such high speed diffpairs. Many data center boards contain hundreds of such signals, so they can only be implemented with good SI if we use compact structures and small object and clearance sizes. Note that microvias are not "small", since they come in an offset structure.

On any PCB design we have four types of crosstalk: the trace-to-trace, trace-to-via, via-to-trace, and via-to-via crosstalk. Most of the board layout is mainly affected by the first type that is more prevalent on the main route, and the other three types are more prevalent in the BGA fanout and escape route area. The patterns and constellations resulting in different escape routes will have different amounts of crosstalk in those cases. The via/trace crosstalk types are most severe as NEXT between RX and TX pins. The 2 to 8-GND constellations require traces to be routed directly adjacent to the vias of other signals in the same or next row, while only the 10-GND constellation allows an extra column of separation to improve trace/via crosstalk to the best/lowest level. Backdrilling has a positive side effect of helping with via/trace crosstalk if the inner BGA rows are routed on lower layers. The 2-GND constellation has a lot of via-to-via crosstalk, the 4-GND has some but somewhat improved.

15.9.5 Via Design and Replication Summary

To achieve the via impedance and crosstalk control, we have to follow a several step process, starting from the requirement to the implemented layout, involving different departments.

- The hardware engineer has to document the via optimization parameters to make a request, including layout and manufacturing constraints, component pin constellation, impedance, stackup, and BGA pitch. This request with the data is to be given to an RF or SI engineer.
- The RF, SI, or hardware engineer will complete the via structure dimension optimization in a 3D field solver tool. It will be optimized to achieve the lowest possible differential return loss. The results are a set of dimensions and an S-parameter file. It is re-usable if the stackup was also re-used from a previous project.
- The hardware engineer needs to review the dimensions as to whether they still meet the constraints and fit under the component grid, and whether it allows the differential escape route channel. We also need to assess the S-parameter model in a TDR simulation in ADS to verify whether the impedance dip is within the 10% (for 10–25 or 5% for 100G-NRZ) tolerance and the return loss to be below -17.5dB up to half data rate.
- The layout engineer or the hardware engineer needs to draw one instance (one signal) manually in layout, exactly matching the 3D field-solver-optimized structure dimensions and positions. Some people might assume it is okay to replicate a "similar" one, for example, elements like the dual voids missing, or they move around dog-bone vias freely when it is not allowed. It has to be exact, for example, 64mils is not 61mils. This is the first replication.
- The layout engineer will have to replicate the first instance into all SERDES signal fanout via locations, using copy and paste. The hardware engineer has to review it to ensure all replicated instances will be identical and match the 3D field solver model. The replication cannot be drawn manually; only exact copy/paste is allowed, to ensure they all match the optimized model.
- The layout engineer will implement the escape route, then the long routes, and tune any traces if needed.
- Finally, the layout engineer will apply stub removal, and the hardware engineer will verify that the correct MNC layer was used on each instance. In the case of backdrilling, the layout engineer applies BD symbols. The hardware engineer needs to check with each BD symbol layer that the correct routing layer goes to them. With microvias the leftover part of the via stack will be deleted by the layout engineer, and the hardware engineer will review to make sure it was correct.

15.9.6 Connector Pin Field Guard Vias

If the connector has a wide column to column spacing, >>12mil, then we may put extra GND vias in between the columns for crosstalk reduction. A lot of the crosstalk is generated in backplane connector pin fields, column to column. This is usually mitigated when using 56Gig connectors using shadow or guard via columns. Usually, the connector vendor recommends this in their documentation. Figure 15.46 shows an example of implementation.

15.10 AC-COUPLING CAPACITORS

The series AC-coupling capacitors (AC caps) that we use on many high-speed differential signals for bias voltage isolation require special considerations. At 8Gig or higher we cannot have AC cap structures with less than 4 GND vias. An AC cap has an ingress and an egress differential pair, each would be a 4-via G-S-S-G impedance-controlled structure. Some 25Gig ASICs include on-die AC caps, so for board design with those an on-board capacitor is not required. We have to check in the ASIC datasheets of the two chips at each end of the link whether it is integrated or not.

The design and analysis of these goes the same way as the via structures. We can include all the eight vias and the component bodies in the 3D model. We optimize the shape and dimensions in a 3D solver, then replicate them in the layout without any modification to them. A capacitor structure has two capacitors, four signal vias, four ground vias, and two oval voids. One oval void is for the ingress signal vias, another one for the egress vias. The two ingress vias and the two nearby GND vias create a four-via impedance-controlled structure. The four egress vias also create another. They do not have to be exactly in line, the GND vias can be in an angle. Often we also make a void on layer-2 only under each capacitor body and the capacitor pad, merging with the two oval voids. Usually, we use VIPPO (via in-pad plated over) vias in capacitors. Sometimes the ingress and egress voids merge into one; that is fine if the optimization shows a low overall reflection and a low overall impedance dip. Figure 15.47 shows the typical AC cap structure.

If we expect reflections and crosstalk from connectors, then we should place the AC caps of different lanes staggered, so they will avoid creating additional reflection and crosstalk. If we have a chip-to-chip link on-board, without much additional crosstalk and reflections, then we can pack them closely tight and share the GND vias between. Both concepts are shown in Figure 15.48.

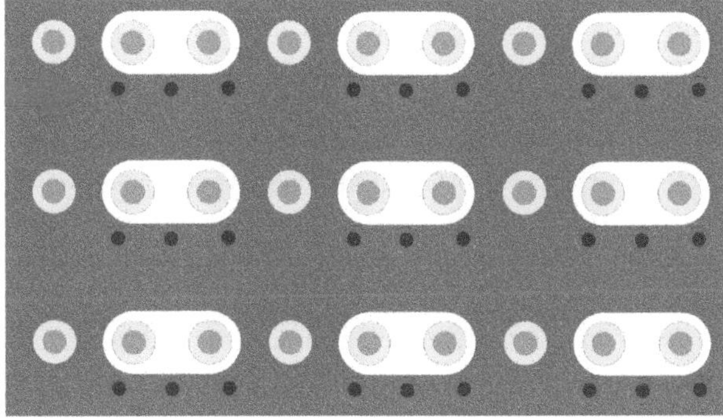

FIGURE 15.46 Shadow guard vias under connector (sketch).

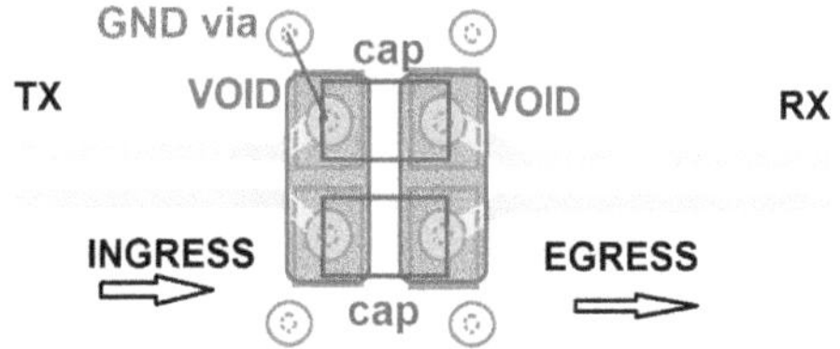

FIGURE 15.47 AC-cap layout (sketch).

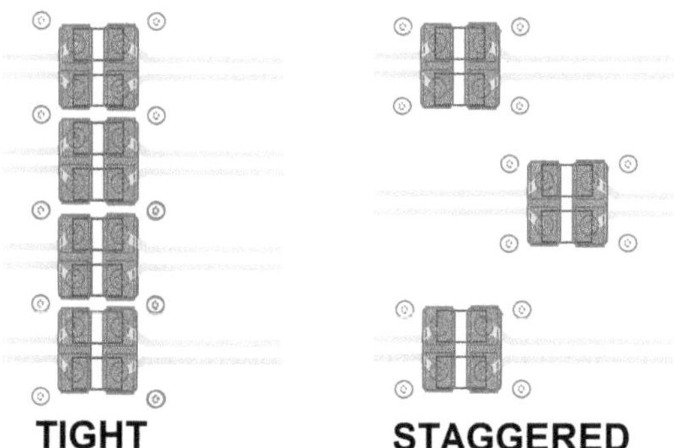

FIGURE 15.48 Multiple AC caps in layout (sketch).

15.11 MEMORY INTERFACES

While we are designing a processor board, FPGA, or ASIC board, we usually have to attach external DRAM memory devices to the main chips. This can be done in two ways: with DIMM memory sockets or a with memory-down layout. With DIMM the memory cards are plugged into the motherboard; these cards contain the memory chips. In a memory-down design we have the memory chips soldered down the motherboard.

Modern memory interfaces, since the release of DDR1, require a lot of group-based trace length matching. Memory-down requires more complicated constraints than dim-based motherboards do. The memory chips and buses are defined by JEDEC standards, specifically the JESD79-xx documents (79-5x is for DDR5, 79-4x is for DDR4). The memory DIMM card designs are standard form factors defined by JEDEC in the JESD21C documents. Most digital designers never have to design a DIMM card, but we can look at the JESD21C documents and JEDEC memory card reference design board files to get ideas about how we can implement our memory-down motherboard designs. All of these are downloadable from their website. Some require payment, others are free.

The DDRx memory interfaces require impedance controlled trace routing, each signal group with its own impedance. Via impedance control is not needed, and not even possible. The device acting as input has on-die termination (ODT or DCI) enabled for the transaction on the data bus. The address bus requires on-board or on-DIMM terminations for DDR1 to 4, while DDR5 uses on-die termination inside the last chip. The JEDEC standard is to route DQ signals at 60 Ohm single-ended impedance, DQS at 120 or 80 Ohm differential, ACC at 40 Ohm single-ended with 39 Ohm termination resistors to VTT, and the clock at 80 Ohm differential. On some embedded designs, to optimize our stackup we may route all traces at 50 Ohm. This way the data bus will be 20% off, but that might be okay on a very short bus if it looks good in simulation. Having a wide range of impedance requirements on a single board design is often inconvenient, because the high impedance traces will get very narrow, near the manufacturability limit, and the lower impedance traces will get very wide and cause routing difficulties. Another possibility is to route the DQ at 55 Ohm and the ACC at 45 Ohm, both being 10% off from the ODT values, but again, short buses and simulations might tell that it is okay. Memory-down, especially with a clam-shell configuration, can have really short traces, which allow more wiggle room for the impedance than does a long bus on a server motherboard.

Processors usually have two to 16 channels of memory, each are 72bit or 64bit wide (9 or 8 lanes), one channel is a full set of a memory interface. FPGAs and ASICs can have any number of channels at any width, from 8 to 72bit wide.

15.11.1 DIMM Memory

There are a few standard DIMM form factors. The SODIMMs are narrow and mainly used in consumer laptops and industrial computer modules, with four to nine memory chips, each chip being

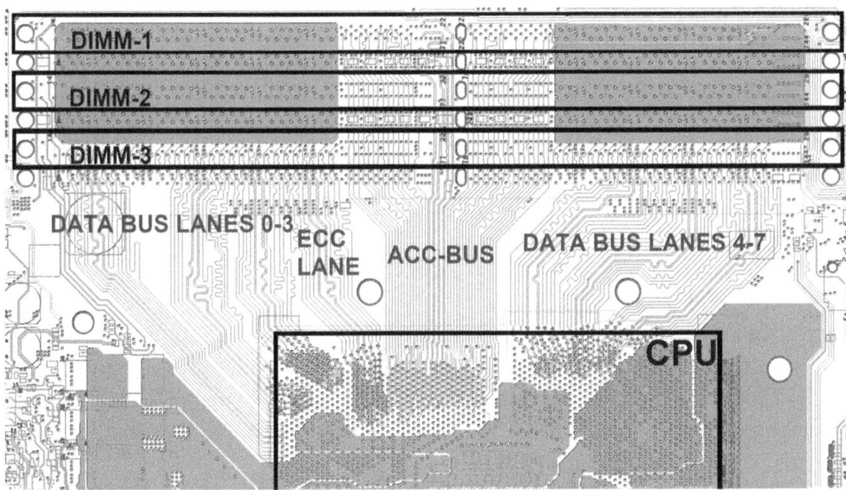

FIGURE 15.49 DDR4 memory interface routing on the Tioga Pass server motherboard from the Open Compute Project, the image from the layout design file is used for illustration under the Open Web Foundation Final Specification Agreement ("OWFa 1.0") signed by Quanta Computer Inc.

8-or-16 bit wide. The UDIMM and RDIMM cards have eight to 18 chips, each 4-or-8bit wide. They are used in desktop, workstation, and server motherboards. The 4-bit chips are only used with server processors that provide one DQS pair for each 4 bits of the data bus. SODIMM sockets are usually SMT; DIMM sockets are through-hole press-fit or soldered. The routing of a DIMM-based motherboard design is point to point, between the CPU/FPGA/ASIC and the DIMM connector, as we can see in Figure 15.49. We can also see that memory interface traces have lots of length tuning meanders due to the byte lane matching requirements. We have to place components and route traces to allow a lot of space for creating these meanders. Basically, the initial routing is done very sparsely. Sometimes there are two DIMM sockets on one memory channel to create a dual rank configuration. In this case we have to use Pin-Pair based constraints, and do the length matching between CPU-to-DIMMA and again between CPU-to-DIMMB. For one-socket/channel motherboards we might still need Pin-Pairs to be created in the Constraints Manager instead of just using nets if the design tool does not account for the CPU package lengths in net-applied matched groups.

The typical trace length constraints needed for a single-DIMM channel:

- Objects creation
  - Differential pairs for 1 to 2 CLK and 8 to 18 DQS signals (Electrical/Routing)
  - 1 to 18 matched groups on the source-synchronous data bus ("Relative Propagation Delay" under Electrical/Routing). One group for each byte-lane (point to point nets). One group includes 8 DQ nets (or 4 in case of server memory), 1 DM net and 1 DQS_P. Based on channel width, 64bit channels have 8 (if desktop) or 16 (if server) lanes, 72bit channels have 9 or 18. Dual rank/socket designs need double number of matched groups, based on Pin-Pairs. delta=0mil and tolerance=5mil, DQS_P is "TARGET".
  - One matched group, on the ACC/CLK bus (Address/Command/Control and Clock signals) as simple nets, with all DQS_P signals too ("Relative Propagation Delay" under Electrical/Routing). delta=5mil and tolerance=5mil, CLK_P is "TARGET". Being a uni-directional synchronous bus, the signals should never be shorter than the clock to avoid hold violations.
- Constraint Sets (xCSETs)
  - Diffpair routing ECSET with trace width/space (from the stackup's impedance table, 80 or 120 Ohm) for DQS, and with 5mil phase tolerance.

- Diffpair routing ECSET with trace width/space (from impedance table, 80 or 120 Ohm) for CLK, and with 5mil phase tolerance.
- Single-ended routing for DQ with trace width (from impedance table, 50 to 60 Ohm). It is a Physical Constraint Set under Physical category, applied to all of the relevant nets.
- Single-ended routing for ACC with trace width (from impedance table, 40 to 50 Ohm). It is a physical constraint set under physical category, applied to all of the relevant nets.
- All DDRx nets spacing at 2 to 4x width, same net spacing 2x width. Spacing CSET.

- Constraints
  - Apply diffpair ECSETs on CLK and DQS.
  - Apply the DQ PCSET on DQ nets.
  - Apply the ACC PCSET on ACC nets.
  - Fill out the tolerance column for all matched groups (in "Relative Propagation Delay" under Electrical/Routing), with tolerance value equal to a string "TARGET" for DQS in data matched groups, and CLK in ACC matched groups. Tolerance for all other signals is 10mils within their groups.

15.11.2 Memory-Down

An alternative to plugging memory DIMM cards into our board is to design in the memory chips. That is called a "memory-down" layout. The advantage is that it will take less volume within the chassis, less board space, and elimination of the connector allows design of low-profile boards without tall components, and it also improves shock and vibration resistance. In high-end embedded systems we typically use memory-down, except on server motherboards. If only one or two channels of memory are used then memory-down takes up less space. Server processors use up to 12 channels of memory, UDIMMs or RDIMMs with x4 chips. This would take too many layers to implement as memory-down, and too much board space, and it would require too many BGA chips to be soldered on the motherboard, causing production yield issues. With 18 chips per DIMM and 12 DIMMs that is 216 BGA memory chips. X86 processors and ARM-server CPUs have two or more 64-bit or 72-bit memory channels. Embedded ARM processors usually have a single channel at 16-bit or 32-bit width, sometimes 64-bit. FPGAs often have multiple independent smaller 16 to 32bit memory channels. Less than 64-bit wide channels can only be implemented with memory-down. In a typical embedded system with memory-down we have smaller processors with two to 32 memory chips total per CPU/FPGA in one or two channels. A 64bit (non-ECC) memory channel requires eight chips if they are x8 width each, or four chips if they are x16 width. A channel with ECC needs an extra memory chip, so nine chips of x8. 32-bit channels can be implemented with two x16 chips or four x8 chips. Processor to DIMM-socket routing is simple point to point, while memory-down routing requires complex constraints and more layers. They require a constraint-driven design flow that is available only in a few design tools, like Cadence Allegro and Siemens (Mentor) Expedition. The address bus has to cross itself or the data bus on memory-down designs, depending on how we arrange the chips and how many chips we use. We can see this on a JEDEC memory reference design layout in Figure 15.50, which is similar to some of the memory-down implementations. The picture shows an example with four x16 chips to provide clarity. The more common design with nine 8-bit wide chips has the address bus going around in a circle, and some of the data bus lanes overlap, so it would be harder to see its structure. Memory-down is usually implemented on rugged aerospace processor boards, telco boards, and data center FPGA boards. Usually, these applications are high reliability and require ECC (Error correction) by using 9 byte-lanes and 9 DRAM chips (8bit devices) per channel, instead of 8 byte-lanes as is common in consumer laptops.

Most memory layouts usually have a remaining trace stub in the PCB layout when the same signal has to reach two chip die pads. This in not ideal, but this enables us designing high-density boards. Either the data signals on dual-rank designs or the address signals on any design end up

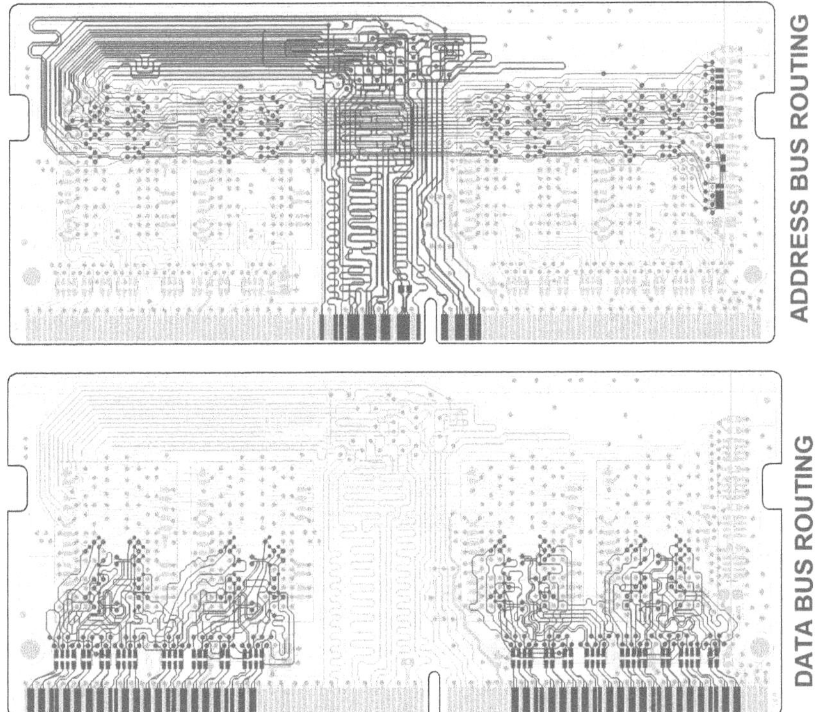

FIGURE 15.50 DDR4 SODIMM memory module routing highlighted. This figure is reproduced, with permission, from JEDEC PC4-SODIMM Raw Card C0 memory module design file registration. JEDEC standards and publications are copyrighted by the JEDEC Solid State Technology Association. All rights reserved.

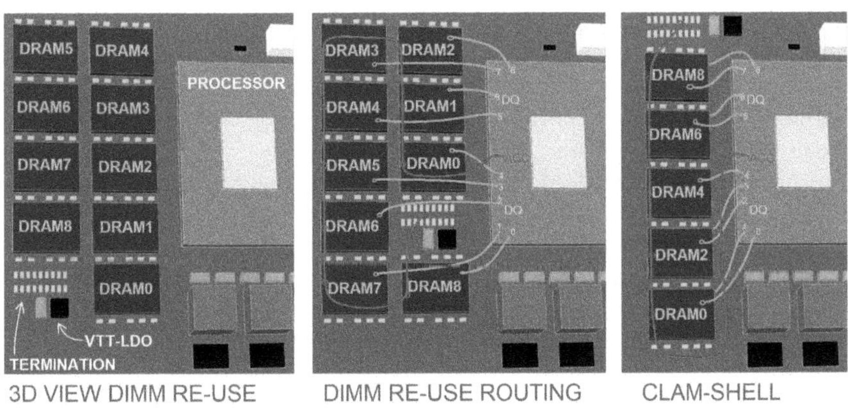

FIGURE 15.51 A 72-bit memory-down motherboard layout on a 3D board model with three placement options, and routing paths.

with stubs. Single-rank low-density layouts often have a stub by tapping on routing channels with very long dog-bone fanout traces. Dual-die (stacked) chips/packages have a less than 1/16" stub, dual-rank and clam-shell boards have less than 1/4", while motherboards with two DIMM sockets can have 1" to 2" stubs. Still all of these configurations are in use.

Figure 15.51 shows a few example board 3D models for a processor with nine memory chips. The numbering shows how the chips are tapping on the fly-by address bus, which may or may not match the lane numbers of the processor pins. The fly-by does not have to pass through the exact 0→9 byte-order, which helps with implementing more efficient memory-down layouts. Most memory-down layouts go in a circle, so they are not so wide, then we end up with a fly-by like 0-8-1-7-2-6-3-5-4, or with a shorter ACC bus we would have something like 8-7-6-5-0-4-1-3-2. To route all the traces, we often end up with byte swapping as well as bit swapping, which is described in a later section.

The DRAM chip packages are standardized, as far as the pin pattern goes, but not the package outline. Because of this we often design motherboards that support DRAM chips of different sizes (called densities, in Gigabits) and from different vendors. To allow that we need to use footprints that have multiple package outlines to help placement and assembly. If we use gold plated copper corner marks then they also have to accommodate at least two or three different outlines. The most likely ones, based on what is currently available on the market and what will be available in the near future. The outlines differ a little bit, for example 11mm and 10mm widths.

Note that BIOS firmware design for memory-down boards require the SPD EEPROM data to be incorporated into the BIOS source code, and the I2C SPD loading to be disabled by the BIOS firmware engineer. DIMM-based designs utilize the CPU SMBUS connected to the DIMM slots to read out the SPD data from the EERPROM located on the DIMM card. Memory-down does not have an SPD EERPROM.

Any memory-down implementation also requires a termination island. The DDR3/4 fly-by address bus is end terminated to a VTT voltage rail. Each of the ACC bus signals has a termination resistor, usually 39 or 49 Ohm, between the signal line and the VTT rail. The clock signal usually has a center tapped differential termination. For every few resistors we also place a decoupling capacitor from VTT to ground. To reduce the parasitic inductance of the termination resistors, we create an outer layer power shape directly fed by the VTT VRM (LDO or switcher), and the resistors are directly attached to the shape. These can also be seen on the diagram. Sometimes we use 4x resistor packs to save on the board area, like we can see on most DIMMs. DDR5 supports on-die termination inside the last memory chip on the fly-by bus, so it does not require a termination island.

For memory-down we have to implement the fanout first, which can be very complicated because a good routing depends on a good fanout. The fanout traces are routed on outer layers between the DRAM chip pins and the vias, using dog-bones that can be 1/4 inch long. DDRx chips require a very special fanout pattern. The address bus signal vias are placed in the center region of the package, while the data bus vias and power vias are right next to the pins. This is helped by the special BGA package that has a large gap free of pins in the center of the package. Then we implement the long routes to access the fanout vias on inner layers.

In most high-end hardware we need the maximum memory buffer size that is available on the market. So typically we pick the highest density (Gbits total) chips in x8 format. On designs that do not require large memory size, we could use x16 chips or x32 chips, then we would need less quantity per board that can be implemented in a much smaller board area right next to the ASIC.

A simple methodology for memory-down design was common, where a JEDEC DDRx layout file (downloadable JESD21C reference designs) was copy/paste-ed into the motherboard design, then they used simple processor-to-DIMM routing constraints to wire it up to the trace stubs at the (removed) edge connector-footprint. This can provide a 72bit interface on a 1.2x2.7" board area, with reduced design effort, and contains the long routes within the memory area. For high-density boards, we often need memory in a smaller board area. To achieve that, instead of copying the complete reference designs, we either design the memory channel from scratch, or re-use portions of the reference design and modify them. Re-using parts of the fanout can help us create a very efficient design. In both cases we will have to use several trace segment length constraints that are more complex.

We can implement a "clam-shell" layout with fully overlapped placement using special fanout patterns, where the even numbered memory chips are on the top side of the board; the odd numbered ones are on the bottom side. The top and bottom chips will be in a clam-shell arrangement, and they will share the power and address vias to access inner layers. The address pins are routed on the outer layers from both chips into three columns of vias in the package center, using very long dog-bone fanout traces. The data pin connections are separate and they don't share vias with the other side chip, having short dog-bone traces. The two chips are on different byte-lanes. The power vias will be shared between the top and bottom chip, and also have short dog-bone vias. If we use 9 chips, then we will end up with 5 chips visible on the top side, and 4 on the bottom, that takes 5/9th as much board space than a flat one-sided DIMM-copy layout. We can re-use the fanout traces and vias from a JEDEC reference design, if we modify it first. Some of the JEDEC designs contain a clam-shell dual rank fanout, where the two chips share both the data and the address buses. We don't need to modify the whole DIMM design, only one position that has a top and a bottom side DRAM chip, then re-use and rubber stamp that for a total of four instances in our design. The dual rank reference design has eight instances of top and bottom chip pairs, while ours will have four, that will be single-rank. A clam-shell memory-down layout is naturally single rank, unless we use dual-die DRAM packages. We need to add separate vias and fanout traces to the bottom chip's data bus pins, this is the hardest part but it can be done. After this we can copy/paste the outer layer traces and vias into our motherboard for the first chip-pair instance, then from there copy/paste it into the other three chip pairs to form an 8-chip 64-bit memory channel.

We can also implement a partial overlap layout where both the address and data pins are fanned out into a 3-via-column center area. Every odd numbered chip will be on the top and the even ones on the bottom like the previous example, but this time they only overlap about 1/3rd of the chip package area, not like a clam-shell that 100% overlaps. The power pins will share vias between the top and bottom chip, or the capacitors will overlap with the memory chips using VIPPO. What we see from the top is a chip, then three columns of vias, then another chip, then another three columns of vias…until the last one. This layout is easier to implement, but requires a larger board space than the clam-shell version. We can also start this from a JEDEC reference design, but we have to rip up all the data bus vias and fan them out into the center section. Then replicate the first modified instance seven more times.

All three fanouts or memory-down layout types are demonstrated on Figure 15.52 and Figure 15.53. Note that the clam-shell and partial overlap options require a higher layer count stackup for the main routing than the DIMM-based motherboard used, but that is usually available on embedded boards. The memory routing is usually confined in a small area and does not cross with other interfaces. The partial overlap layout takes up a larger board space than the clam shell does, when using x8 chips. The absolute smallest 64-bit memory-down layout using mass-produced memory chips would be using four chips of x16 width each in a partial overlap or clam-shell arrangement. Similar layout size can be achieved using two x32 chips side by side with short fanout, or using a single x64 device. The x32 and x64 DRAM chips are actually multi-chip module (MCM) or multi-die module packages, and not mass-produced. The eight and sixteen bit wide memory chips have a center gap that helps with the clam-shell fanout, but also helps with using larger through drilled vias on the 0.8mm pitch standard BGA size. Thanks to having only three BGA ball columns in one block, we can fan out easily even with that 0.8mm pitch. The 32 and 64 bit devices have full grid 0.8mm pitch BGA packages, that might be harder to wire up, need tighter clearance constraints or require more layers.

The main reason for choosing larger board size options with a larger number of chips is to achieve a larger total system memory size. For example, if this year the largest DRAM chip has an N Gbit density, then the x8 and x16 version chips all come in the same N Gbit total size. If we use an 8-chip x8 layout, then we can have 8*N Gbit total system memory, but if we choose the 4-chip x16 variant then we can have only 4*N Gbit total system memory. If we choose to use the JEDEC dual-rank SODIMM layout copy with x8 chips, then it will have 16 chips in it, it will take up a lot of board space, but we can have 16*N Gbit total system memory. In many embedded applications that is usually not needed, so we can choose smaller layouts. Some memory devices come with two silicon dies inside one BGA package. We can double the memory size if we use dual die x8 or x16 chips, which need two chip select signals, but we cannot have two sets of dual die chips on one

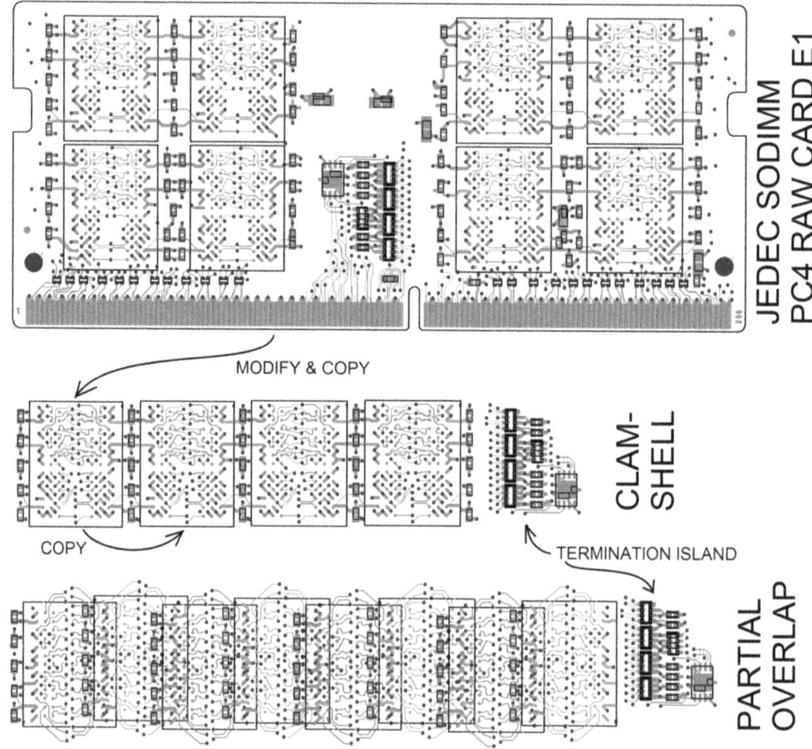

FIGURE 15.52 Comparison of 8-chip DDR4 memory-down fanouts, based on a JEDEC reference design. This figure is reproduced, with permission, from JEDEC PC4-SODIMM Raw Card E1 memory module design file registration. JEDEC standards and publications are copyrighted by the JEDEC Solid State Technology Association. All rights reserved.

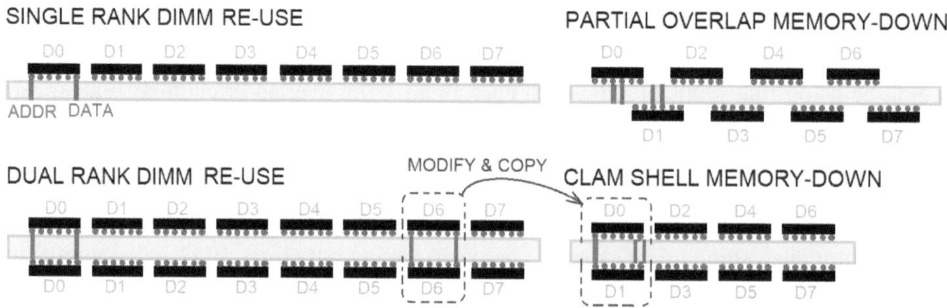

FIGURE 15.53 Cross-section comparison of 8-chip DDRx memory-down component placements.

channel. Either we have to use two sets of single die or one set of dual die. To recap, we modify the fanout traces and vias of one memory chip (one top and one bottom) from the DIMM reference design, copy it to our board, then copy to all other instances, and then we can do the main long routing from the CPU/FPGA to the DRAM fanout vias we just copied, then finally we tune the trace lengths according to the constraints.

For DDR3 interfaces both of the high-density memory-down layouts rely on creating a 3-via-column center cavity fanout for the ACC bus shared between the top and the bottom chip. The partial overlap layout also requires a center cavity 3-via-column for the data bus. DDR4 allows some partial address bit swapping through something called "address mirroring". Some DDR3 controllers supported it too, but it became common with DDR4. Some of the ACC pins on the opposite sides of the package can be swapped, like BA0/BA1, BG0/BG1, A3/A4, A5/A6, A7/A8, and A13/A11. The rest of the ACC bus is still fanned out into a center 2 or 3-via-column, but it is less effort. It only works if we swap all at once, we use a separate chip select signal for the top and the bottom side DRAM chips within the same rank, and the controller device supports address mirroring. This helps with creating more efficient top/bottom DRAM clam-shell designs where these pins will overlap as well as share vias. In the schematic we swap the schematic net/pin connections for the chips that are going to the bottom side. For DDR3 all the ACC bus bits had to go to the 3-via-columns in the center cavity of the DRAM package to the shared vias through very long fanout traces. For DDR4 most ACC bus bits still go to a center cavity with 2 or 3-via-columns and long fanout traces, but the mentioned signals are fanned out with short dog-bones in place. The JEDEC DDR4 DIMM reference designs all seem to utilize this technique. If the mentioned limitations about the DDR4 swapping are an issue, then we can still implement a similar fanout on a DDR4 clam-shell layout as we used on DDR3 layouts, where the address bits are not swapped, and they all get fanned out into the 3-via center cavity column through long top/bottom layer traces. The goal of both methods is to have the top and the bottom DRAM chip share the ACC bus fanout vias. In all cases the data bus pins will not share fanout vias between the top and the bottom DRAM chips, so the data pin portion of the package will have more vias to accommodate two byte-lanes of the clam-shell reduced layout in one small area. This is the harder part in transforming a dual rank clam-shell reference design where the top/bottom chips are on the same data byte lane into a single rank clam-shell reduced layout where the top/bottom chips are on separate data byte lanes, aka not share any data bus vias.

The required trace length constraints for a memory-down layout on a single channel:

- Objects creation
    - Differential pairs for 1 to 2 CLK and 1 to 18 DQS signals (in Electrical/Routing)
    - 1 to 18 sets of Pin-Pairs on the ACC/CLK bus (Address/Command/Control and Clock signals). One set of Pin-Pairs per each DRAM chip. The total number of Pin-Pairs equals the number of DRAM chips times the number of ACC signals. One set from CPU to DRAM0, one set from CPU to DRAM1, … one set for CPU to DRAM8. Pin-Pairs are based on the CPU and DRAM chip refdes.
    - 1 to 18 matched groups, on the ACC/CLK Pin-Pairs we just created (in "Relative Propagation Delay" under Electrical/Routing). One matched group per each DRAM chip. One group for the Pin-Pairs that are defined between CPU to DRAM0, one group for Pin-Pairs between CPU to DRAM1 … and one group for CPU to DRAM8. delta=5mil and tolerance=5mil, CLK_P is "TARGET". Being a uni-directional synchronous bus, the signals should never be shorter than the clock to avoid hold violations.
    - 1 to 18 matched groups on the source-synchronous data bus nets (in "Relative Propagation Delay" under Electrical/Routing). One group for each byte-lane (point to point nets). One group includes 8 DQ nets (or 4 in case of server memory), 1 DM net and 1 DQS_P. Based on channel width, 32bit channels have 4 lanes, 64bit channels have 8 or 16 lanes, 72bit channels have 9 or 18. Dual-rank designs need double number of matched groups, based on Pin-Pairs. delta=0mil and tolerance=5mil, DQS_P is "TARGET".
    - Sometimes required, depending on CPU, one matched group of DQS0 and the CLK Pin-Pair between CPU and DRAM0, ("Relative Propagation Delay" under Electrical/Routing). Some controllers require the DQS to be always shorter than CLK, that require delta=-5mil and tolerance=5mil, CLK_P is "TARGET".
- Constraint Sets (xCSETs)
    - Diffpair routing ECSET with trace width/space (from the stackup's impedance table, 80 or 120 Ohm) for DQS, and with 5mil phase tolerance.

- Diffpair routing ECSET with trace width/space (from impedance table, 80 or 120 Ohm) for CLK, and with 5mil phase tolerance.
- Single-ended routing for DQ with trace width (from impedance table, 50 to 60 Ohm). It is a physical constraint set under physical category, applied to all of the relevant nets.
- Single-ended routing for ACC with trace width (from impedance table, 40 to 50 Ohm). It is a Physical Constraint Set under Physical category, applied to all of the relevant nets.
- All DDRx nets spacing at 2 to 4x width, same net spacing 2x width. Spacing CSET.

- Constraints
  - Apply diffpair ECSETs on CLK and DQS.
  - Apply the DQ PCSET on DQ nets.
  - Apply the ACC PCSET on ACC nets.
  - Fill out the tolerance column for all matched groups (in "Relative Propagation Delay" under Electrical/Routing), with tolerance value equal to a string "TARGET" for DQS in data matched groups, and CLK in ACC matched groups. Tolerance for all other signals is 10mils within their groups.
  - Route VREF as a 20mil wide trace, VTT as a long power shape.

15.12 VRM LAYOUT

A good switching VRM layout has short direct power shape connections between elements of the power stage and it is overall compact. The switch node net from the power stage to the inductor is usually a simple rectangle shape on the outer layer without any vias. The inductor to output cap connection that is on the output net is also usually a direct connection on the same layer. We try to place all/most output caps on the same side of the board as the inductor to avoid injecting the ripple current EMI interference between the planes that can disturb high-speed signals and clocks. Unfortunately, it is often not possible on many high-density boards, so we end up with output caps under the inductor on the other side. The input capacitors of the VRM are also right at the chip pins on the same layer. Any vias between them would add power pin inductance, interfering with the top MOSFET's operation. Figure 15.54 shows a medium power VRM layout with all parts on the top layer. The ground connection of the lower MOSFET inside the power stage chip is through the center power pad and a few pins. The output and input caps need to have low impedance ground connections through many vias and no thermal spokes. Any inductance there would generate voltage

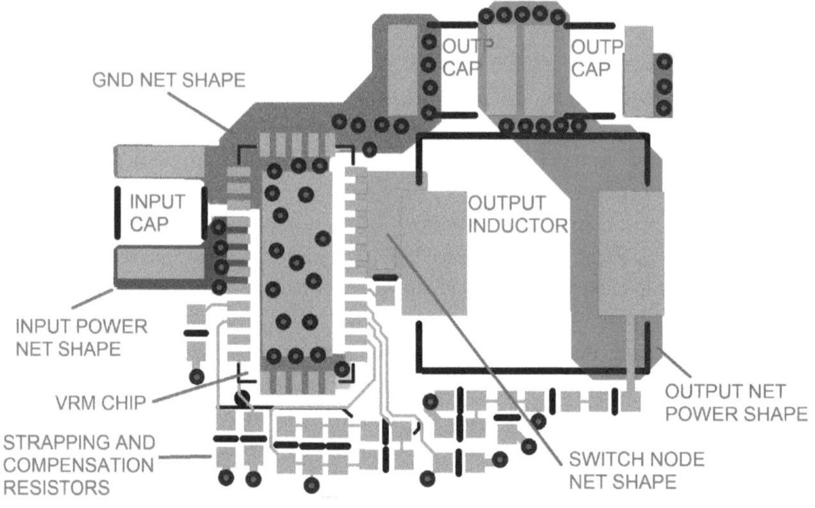

FIGURE 15.54 VRM Layout for a 6 Amp converter.

noise from the ripple current to the output voltage through the capacitor. Ideally the ground pins of the input caps, the output caps, and the power stage would also be connected together through a top (outer) layer power shape, in addition to each having vias to the inner ground planes. Similarly, the switch node and the inductor are directly connected to each other using a super-short and wide surface layer power shape to avoid injecting noise between the inner layers. Power part pins (QFN packaged power stage chip, inductor, and capacitors) have to connect to outer layer copper shapes with direct connection, instead of thermal spokes, to avoid adding extra inductance and resistance to the high-performance circuit. This is especially important at higher switching frequencies (0.5MHz and above) and higher currents (10A/phase or above). The direct connect creates difficulties with soldering, which has to be solved with proper footprint and stencil design helped by manufacturing engineers. Thermal relief or spoke connection together with insufficient number of vias can increase the noise at the output through parasitic inductance. Modern VRM chips have reduced parasitic inductance inside the package by using copper clips instead of bond wires, so the board inductances make a big difference. The power pins of the VRM chips have to be flooded with the power shapes on the PCB, while the signal pins are connected to traces only where it is not an issue. It is often the case that the solder amount is insufficient on the QFN pins, as the solder flows away from the pins. Flow-away needs to be prevented by either solder mask bridges between pins or copper separation. QFN chips have multiple adjacent pins on the same power net, and, when flooded, there is no copper separation between them. We can provide solder mask bridges between them by using zero SM expansion, which requires "solder mask defined pads" for the power pins in the PCB footprint. The signal pins can use regular SM expansion rules, which will cause the SM layer having one big opening for a row of adjacent signal pins due to the fine pitch, which is okay.

Sometimes VRM chips use a separate power ground and a signal ground, which are shorted through a single point. This is to avoid any power circuit currents from affecting the ground paths of the small signal control loop circuits. In many applications we do not need to worry about this because most VRM chips have their power pins on one side of the package and the small signal circuits on the other side. The power parts and signal compensation parts are placed on the board near the chip-pins they need to connect to. This way the power and signal circuits will end up being naturally away from each other.

QFN chips have a center pad that is grounded. We place a grid of vias into this center pad. This serves a dual purpose, a low inductance electrical connection and a low thermal resistance thermal connection. We sometimes call them "thermal vias" because they are the main path of colling these components through the multiple internal ground planes, instead of using external heatsinks, up to 1 to 2W. They should be VIPPO type so they will not suck the solder away from the pad. Many years ago it was common to have a signal ground and a switch node "power ground" net in VRM circuits and reference designs. The actual implementation required a lot of compromise and did not deliver most of the intended result. It became common to just have one ground net for a VRM that is the main ground plane net of the PCB.

When designing the VRM circuits, we have to be considerate of the sensitive high-speed and reference clocks signals on the board. Those signals, and even the low-speed signals, need to be kept away from VRMs, their components, copper traces/shapes, and vias. Unrelated signals should not be routed under the switch node area, near (>100mils) the power vias, near switch node net vias, or near ground vias of the power stage components. These components are the input capacitors, output capacitors, the inductor, and the power stage chip. Any fanout vias used for these parts are rough noise sources. On the surface layer we should also keep these components away (>100mils) from components that belong to high-speed signals or reference clocks.

15.13 POWER DELIVERY

Power is delivered to the ASICs and other circuits form the VRM using power planes. The power net delivery to voltage sense inputs of the management controller, as well as to reference voltage inputs of I/O buffers can be done using a 10mil wide trace instead of a plane. Modern ASICs have a core voltage rail, a few transceiver RX rails, transceiver TX rails, regular I/O bank voltage rails, PLL rails, and others. The ASIC core rail typically consumes 80% of the power, and requires 10 to 500 Amps to be delivered from a regulator. The core VRM is usually a multi-phase circuit above 20A/rail, utilizing 20 to 30A per phase, with up to 14 phases. The transceiver rails typically are implemented with one to three phases and require 1 to 100 Amps. One power net can be delivered on one or more layers, some of which being power planes, others signal layers. The parallel planes are stitched together to balance the currents. Low current power nets might change the layer on the route, using many stitching vias. If it looks like a patchwork, then we are close to finishing the design. Between 10 and 30A we would use one plane layer plus a partial signal layer, between 30 and 150A we would use two plane layers and two partial signal layers to deliver the power. The power has to be conducted from outer layer components to inner layer planes using vias. These vias can be larger "power vias" or preferably they can be the same small via size we use for the signals but a large number of them. For example, one capacitor pad might have 12 vias, or a power switch might have 40 vias. One small via can carry about one Amp of current. Before the power net enters the inner layer, we might have to distribute it a little wider on the outer layer with a small power shape, which can capture the larger number of vias. Smaller vias sometimes get thicker wall plating, which we can take advantage of by using a large number of small vias.

A DC voltage drop simulation needs to be done on the post-layout design. It can be done quickly to come up with instructions to the layout engineer for changes. The voltage tolerance on ASIC power pins is typically 1% to 3% on rails below 1.8V, then 3% for rails between 1.8 and3V, then 5% for voltage rails above 3V. The ASIC datasheet tells exactly how much it is. When using basic VRMs that have no remote sense lines, our voltage drop has to be less than the tolerance. When using VRMs that do have remote sense lines, we can allow a larger voltage drop than the tolerance between the VRM and the ASIC. The VRM will compensate out the voltage drop, but we it still affects the control loop, so we still have to minimize it to about 2% to .5% of the rail voltage, or to about 2 to 5 times the ASICs tolerance. Another analysis should also be run, between the bulk decoupling capacitors and the ASIC power pins, with similar tolerance as the ASIC power input has. The bulk caps need to be placed around the ASIC package on all four sides, to minimize drop from them. We can see on the simulation results the areas where the color gradient is strong, that is where the most voltage drop happens. We can improve that by widening the planes in those areas, enveloping objects, at the expense of neighboring power shapes. All these are instructions from the hardware engineer to the layout engineer. Sometimes we have to involve more layers in the power delivery of the particular power net or change the copper layer thickness. So we often end up with simulation to layout change to simulation to layout change cycles. We can also re-arrange fanout vias (except BGA) to avoid groupings and in-line arrangements of antipads to allow a better current flow through.

The core rail power planes (power shapes on the plane layer) for ASICs under 20 to 150 Watts usually enter the device along one edge of the package, while for ASICs above that the power shapes envelop the device completely. This is to allow currents to flow to the center of the package from all directions, with reduced voltage drop. We can see both cases on Figure 15.55. Delivering power under the BGA goes through a very cut up plane having higher resistance, compared to the outside area. With "enveloping" the supply current only has to travel from the four edges to the center, not from one edge to the opposite edge, that would be twice the resistance.

SERDES rails that exist on most modern devices also have similar considerations. The SERDES rails are even more sensitive than the core, so they also need wide spreading planes. The SERDES rail usually consumes 15% as much power/current as the core rail does on devices that mostly rely on SERDES transceivers rather than parallel I/O (like memory buses). This can still require a multi-phase VRM on a 500W ASIC. On less SERDES-heavy devices we might just need 1% to 10% as much. The SERDES transceivers usually have a TX and an RX rail and a

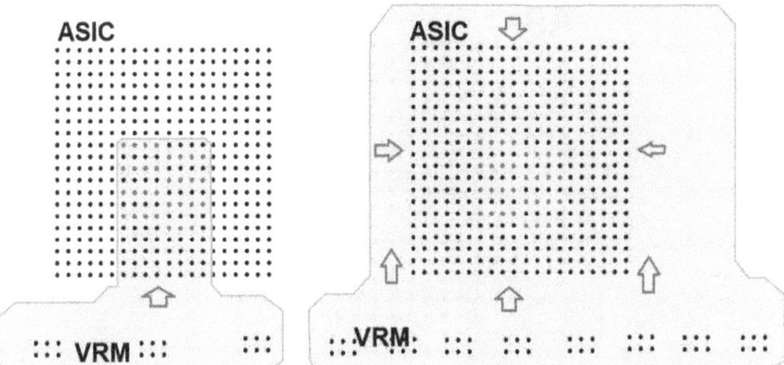

FIGURE 15.55 Core rail power plane shape concepts (sketch). Left image is for ASICs below 50W, the right image is for ASICs above 50W.

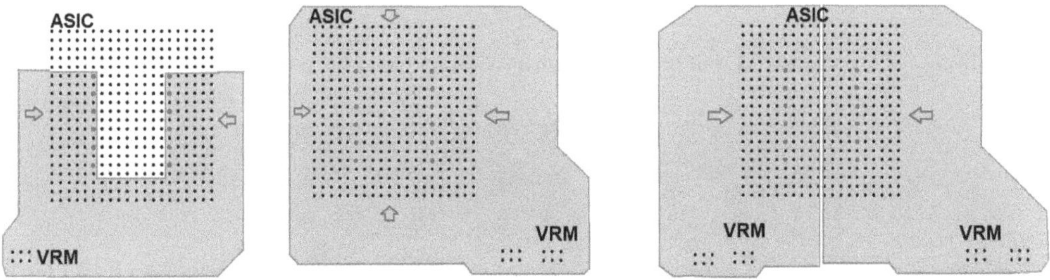

FIGURE 15.56 SERDES rail power plane shape concepts (sketch). Left to right, lower to higher powered ASICs.

PLL rail, or they have some other similar division. The PLL rail is usually narrow with low current. The other two SERDES rails go around the package on lower performance devices, while they have to envelop the package on higher performance devices just like the core power shapes need to. When the power shape envelops a device, then they have a square or octagon-like shape rather than an elongated rectangle or anything concave. The largest ASICs might have a division in place by having a separate rail for half or quarter of the transceiver power pins. Figure 15.56 shows SERDES rail power plane options, Figure 15.57 shows PLL and I/O bank power plane shapes.

Low current or wide tolerance power rails like the 3.3V, the standby rails, and the main 12V power delivery usually have a 1:10 width to length ratio and go around the board perimeter. With these narrow planes we have to be careful to avoid high resistance bottlenecks. During the daily layout review the hardware engineer has to spot these areas or sometimes quantify the issue with a DC voltage drop simulation. The simulators can display the areas that have a high current density, which are the bottlenecks responsible for a big part of the voltage drop. We can see examples of several types of power shapes used on plane layers, including low current main rails, core rails, I/O rails and SERDES rails in Figure 15.58. The low-current higher voltage rails wrap around the board perimeter, as described earlier. The core rail is concentrated near the inside of the board around the large ASIC, with more robust shapes, as described earlier. The power plane layers are usually set up as negative film layers, so we have to draw only the non-copper areas (anti-etch), which are basically the divider lines between the different power deliver net areas and the pad to plane clearance gap circles. If we used positive planes, then the layout files can become very large and slow down our computer. On positive planes we have to draw the shape objects for each split plane or net. Ground planes are usually not divided up into multiple nets, so they need to contain only the clearance gaps around the via-and component-pin pads. We also need a 20mil wide clearance gap around the board outline, so when the board is cut out of the production panel,

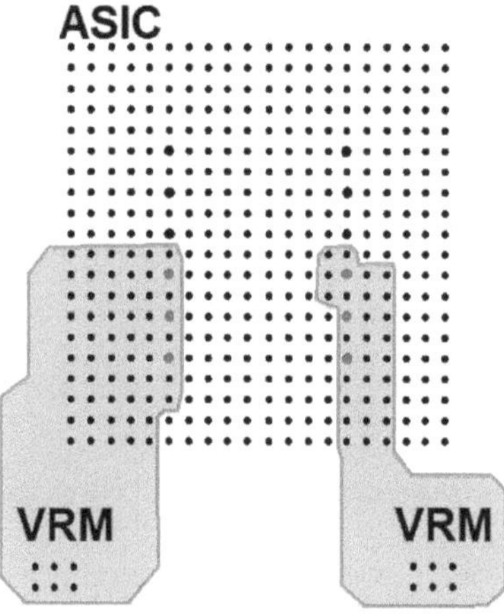

FIGURE 15.57 IO bank and PLL rail power plane shape concepts (sketch).

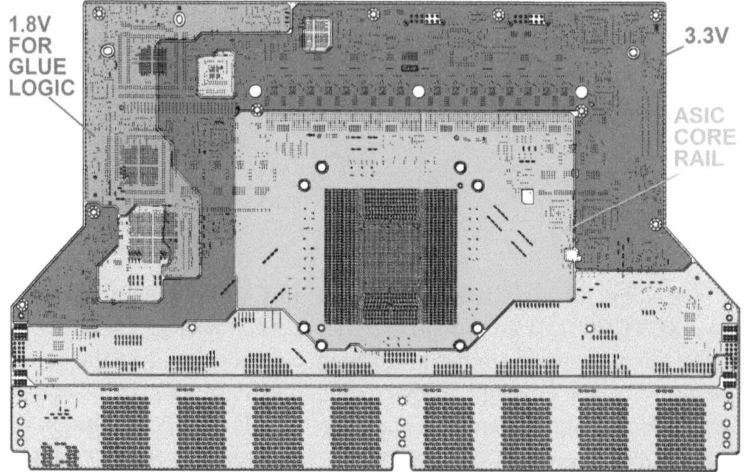

FIGURE 15.58 One of the power plane layers of the Minipack 2 SMB switch card from the Open Computer Project, the image from the layout design file is used for illustration under the Open Computer Project Hardware License (Permissive) Version 1.0 (Open Computer ProjectHL-P) signed by Meta Platforms, Inc.

the cutting tools will not have to touch copper, which would cause scrap metal shorting multiple planes together.

The way we determine what shapes we need to draw of the split areas on power plane layers starts with making use of net coloring. We need to have all fanout vias placed before we start partitioning the planes. We assign different colors to different power nets, and then we make only one layer visible. The vias appear on all layers, so they will show with their colors which power net they want to be connected to. Then we can create smart shapes to envelop the same colored vias in one area, then vias with another color into another area, and so on. The divider lines on the plane layers should be as wide as the clearance requirement on plane layers, or a little bit more, usually 5 to 10mil. So we partition the whole board area into areas of different power nets, then we assign those nets to the areas, then the vias will automatically make contact with the surrounding split plane area. We have to use solid contact option between vias and internal planes instead of thermal relief; otherwise, we cannot meet the power delivery voltage drop requirements of large ASICs.

15.13.1 Filtered Rails

Some ASIC datasheets divide their transceiver power rails into dozens of segments, for example, every N lanes of SERDES will have their own power rail, and expect the board designer to isolate them by ferrite beads. This is done in the schematic by creating several new power nets from the main power rail using series ferrite beads and capacitor on both sides. One 1 to 3 phase VRM will provide the power, but near the BGA package perimeter they split into several rails with a ring of ferrite beads around the ASIC. This creates a need for many narrow power delivery planes from the ferrite beads to the ASIC power pins. Figure 15.59 shows a section of an ASIC area in the layout with a few elongated power shapes on an inner layer, which are the filtered rails starting at the ferrites. The issue is the clearance gap between the narrow planes cannot be utilized for current delivery, so we get higher DCR, and the large high-current ferrites take up a lot of board space—with some chips they are not required or optional. There are not that many PLL rails and we should keep those filtered.

15.13.2 Voltage Sense Line Resistor Placement

The high-power voltage rails are generated by advanced voltage regulators that use remote sense lines to regulate the voltage not at the VRM output cap, but on the load ASIC die. The remote sense lines usually connect to the ASIC's VCCSENSE and VSSSENSE pins. In some cases the ASIC does not have such pins, or it does not have it on all high-current rails. In that case we have to connect the sense lines to the VCC and GND planes near the ASIC through zero Ohm resistors. The sense lines are routed as a differential pair with no impedance defined. If we use a set of two zero Ohm resistors, then we have to place them strategically in the layout. The zero Ohm resistors simply force the location of the sense-line-to-plane connection attachment point. Note that the concept of the sense line resistor is different from the "sense resistor", which is a large size part used for current sensing the VRM inductor on older VRM chips. A component location can be exactly defined by coordinates, while a via location might get overwritten by automatic loop removal or accidental re-routing. A via cannot be identified in documentation, they do not have a refdes but a component with a refdes can be unambiguously identified. We cannot place these sense line resistors under the ASIC center in most cases, but

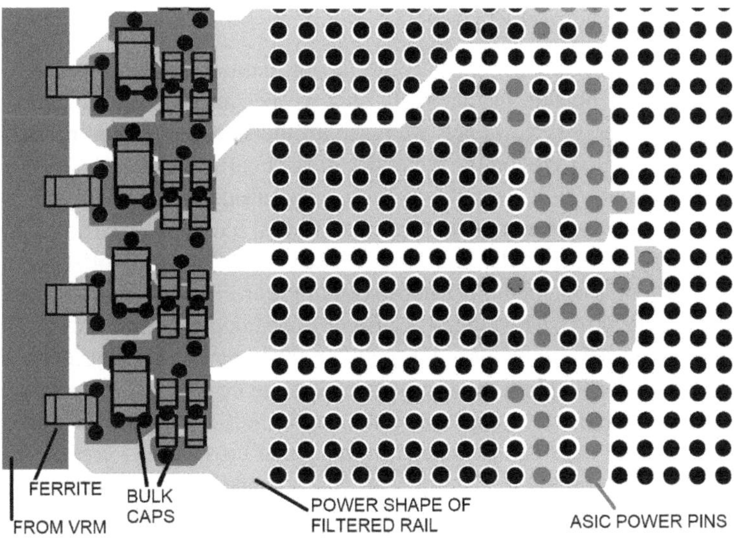

FIGURE 15.59 Filtered power rails under ASIC (sketch).

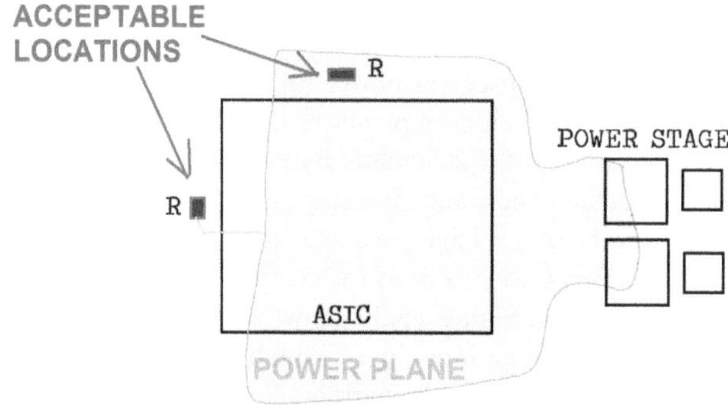

FIGURE 15.60 Sense line 0R resistor placement (sketch).

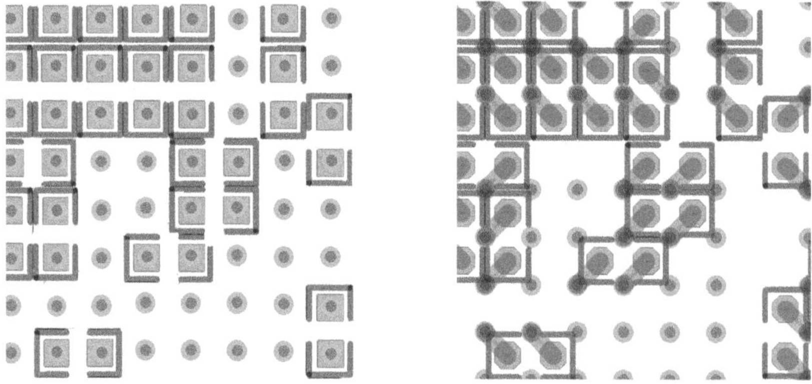

FIGURE 15.61 Decoupling capacitor placement with and without VIPPO (sketch).

we can place them on the far side of the plane at locations past the big voltage drop area. This is shown in Figure 15.60.

15.13.3 Decoupling Capacitor Placement

The way we place decoupling capacitors into the layout matters. In the old days we sometimes placed all decoupling caps outside of the ASIC package perimeter. With chips that run at only 25MHz this might have worked. Nowadays we place all the smaller decoupling capacitors on the ASIC fanout power and ground vias on the other side of the board, and those vias should be VIPPO type. We could do it without VIPPO technology with octagon shaped capacitor pads but that results in tight clearances and increased parasitic inductance. We will have to use partial solder mask cover on the vias that are very close to solder pads. The capacitors are half-grid offset from the via grid in case of dog-bone fanout. Both methods can be seen in Figure 15.61. Usually the ASIC's core rail power pins are in the center area, while the SERDES or I/O bank power pins are in a ring around the core. The decoupling caps have to be placed directly on those power and adjacent ground vias. An example of a large ASIC's decoupling capacitor placement can be seen in Figure 15.62. The ASIC is on the top side of the board, while the caps are on the bottom side underneath and within the boundary. Medium-sized ceramic caps can be placed in the center cross that is created by the flare-out fanout pattern. Large bulk caps and ferrite filters are placed outside of the ASIC package perimeter. The core rail power pins are usually near the center of the grid package, while the I/O and SERDES rails are on a ring around the core area near or mixed with the I/O pins. Next to the power pins usually we find ground pins to allow decoupling capacitors to have a small parasitic inductance.

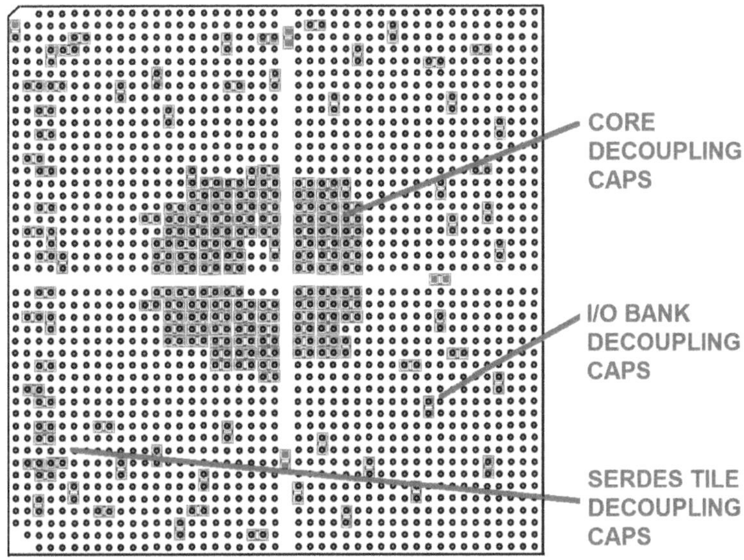

FIGURE 15.62 Decoupling cap area under an FPGA in KiCAD.

15.14 SIGNAL SWAPPING

With parallel buses we often end up with signals of the same bus wanting to cross over in ways that would require too many layers or mid-route vias to route. In some cases, if the chips allow it (within certain rules), we can swap signals with other signals connecting to pins to straighten the bus out. We can swap different lanes of SERDES links within the same port or transceiver block, depending on what is allowed in the ASIC datasheet or reference design. These vendor documents have to be studied very carefully. If unsure, then we should not do the swapping, or do only the obvious ones (like a complete port with another port). Some chips allow RX and TX lane numbers to be swapped independently, others only allow a whole port lane-order reversal (0:3→3:0), while some chips do not allow any swapping. Some chips allow only swapping lanes within four lanes of an eight-lane port. P/N swapping of the same differential pair is allowed by some chips but not by others. A complete port with all of its lanes can always be swapped with another complete port. Swapping some lanes of a complete multi-lane link to different refdes/component is never allowed (lane-2 going to QSFP3 instead of QSFP4 connector), but swapping a complete port to a different refdes is sometimes allowed depending on the data plane topology. For example, lane-0:3 goes to external port-1 and lane-4:7 goes to external port-2, while after the swapping lane-0:3 will go to external port-2.

Swapping is typically implemented by the layout engineer trying to route the initial design, then end the route from both directions at an area, observe the ratsnests (un-routed connection marker lines) crossings, then running an Allegro script or manually create a swap list. The ratsnests before and after will look like what we can see in Figure 15.63. This list has to be checked against the datasheet by the hardware engineer, then implemented as much as allowed in schematics, and then a new netlist for layout is generated. The new netlist will resolve the lane crossings. In schematics we might just edit the net wire names connecting to components or create a separate page for lane swapping using a schematic "ALIAS" feature to connect one net to another net. Each signal will have two net names, and which two net names we pair at one alias symbol will determine what is connected to what. They can be moved around to swap nets. It looks like this:

```
CPU_ETH0_P ------ALIAS------CONN_ETH1_P
CPU_ETH0_N ------ALIAS------CONN_ETH1_N
CPU_ETH1_P ------ALIAS------CONN_ETH0_P
CPU_ETH1_N ------ALIAS------CONN_ETH0_N
```

FIGURE 15.63 Ratsnests in layout before and after lane swapping (sketch).

All names of signals have a number, for example "ABCD_TX_P_96". Those numbers are grouped into 4's or 8's like 0–3, 4–7, 8–11, ... 76–79, ... 188–191; this is how we can identify the swapping boundaries. We cannot swap outside of these boundaries or groups. The hardware engineer might have to write a detailed swapping table with lane numbers for the layout engineers, so the rules are translated to exact net names by the hardware engineer, not by the layout engineer. The functionality is the hardware engineer's job. If the starting point of the swapping was already swapped (second attempt of swapping), then we have to look at the pin names on the ASIC chip to identify the groups of four or eight nets, not the schematic wire signal names nor the connector pin names. We can make a swapping table for rule checking in Excel.

With DDRx memory interfaces sometimes we need to swap the bits or bytes in the schematic to allow easier/shorter PCB routing on less layers or to allow a convenient memory-down chip placement. On embedded desktop and laptop DDRx interfaces we can swap bits within the same 8-bit byte lane, or within the same nibble (4-bit group) on server motherboards. We cannot swap bit-0 of any DRAM chip with other bits because bit-0 is used as a return signal during write leveling. One complete byte lane can be swapped with another complete byte lane, called byte swapping. We cannot swap one bit between two different byte lanes while keeping the rest of them as is. If all the bits, a complete byte lane is swapped with another, then the DM and the DQS strobe has to go with them to the new place. Signals on the address/control/command bus cannot be swapped. These restrictions can be eliminated only in FPGA-based designs, where we will do the swapping on the FPGA schematic symbol (instead of the DRAM schematic symbol), then we also do it in the FPGA logic design and pin-assignment editor, assuming we are using a soft memory controller IP not a hard-IP. For memory interfaces we rarely use alias pages in the schematic; rather, we just change the net names connecting the DRAM or the controller schematic symbols.

DDR4 memory interfaces allow some partial address bus swapping, through "address mirroring". Some of the ACC pins on the opposite sides of the package can be swapped, such as BA0/BA1, BG0/BG1, A3/A4, A5/A6, A7/A8, and A13/A11. But all must be swapped if we do any. This helps to create more efficient top/bottom DRAM clam-shell designs where these pins will overlap as well as share vias. The DRAM chips that go on the bottom side of the PCB will have these pins swapped at the schematic pin/net connections. It only works if we use a separate chip select signal for the top and the bottom side DRAM chips within the same rank, and the controller device supports address mirroring.

15.15 PCB LAYOUT REVIEW

When the hardware engineer works with the layout engineer implementing the PCB layout, the hardware engineer has to check the layout for correctness. The checking goes daily or bi-daily, it involves checking on the progress, issues, and change requests reported in the tracking sheet or communication file, and the responses and the statuses of each change request item updated when reviewed. It is not sufficient for the hardware engineer to just ask the layout engineer or have a meeting, the HW engineer has to open the layout file in the layout viewer program and take a detail look every day. At the end of the layout design, we need to re-check all the features in the layout as well as all the items in the checklist have to be completed and turned green. Only after this is done can we have an official layout peer review with other hardware engineers and cross-functional team members. For review, we often use the object highlight or coloring in the PCB editor or in the viewer version of the tools to select or identify an object to be reviewed. Then highlight another and review it, and so on. We can select one or few object(s) to be displayed with a bright color, while keeping all other objects in a darker dull color to help us review one design element at a time, be it traces, components, or planes/shapes. The signals will be identified based on net names from the schematic; components will be identified by their reference designators (refdes).

There are several categories of design elements and issues that the hardware engineer has to look for, review and if necessary, request to be changed:

15.15.1 General component placement

1) Verify footprints against datasheet, pad sizes, relative pin locations, corner mark. This is usually done when requesting the new library part, but we might have to re-visit during the layout design if it does not cooperate with our constraints.
2) Check the placement and part orientation against floorplan, mechanical design, and routing directions.
3) Ask for top/bottom side placement of certain components.
4) Check the placement of VRMs relative to input power plane and load ASIC location.
5) Check if there are sufficient routing channels based on flowplan. Ask to swap high-density and low-density parts to swap location if needed for creating routing channels.
6) Check the point of load VRM placement to be closest to load on the correct side.
7) Check the VRM power stage part placement for low inductance. Also keep these parts away from clocking-related components.
8) Check the placement of thermal sensors relative to air flow.
9) Check the placement of termination and pull resistors relative to bus routing path.
10) Check the placement of test points/connectors.
11) Check the placement of bussed devices for topology, like DDR chips.
12) Check the backplane connector location based on refdes.
13) Check the clock chip placement relative to ASIC.
14) Ensure the compacting of modules, like VRM phases.
15) Height check, with or without height keepout areas.
16) AC cap placement relative to ASIC or connector pins, their spacing to other AC caps.
17) Check the power switch placement to optimize the planes used in the power tree.

15.15.2 High Speed

18) Check the neckdown area for impedance and antipad interference.
19) Field-solver-optimized 3D via structure replication. Implement or check the first replication, then verify each instance replication. Look for missing voids on some layers, missing ground vias, shifted elements breaking the exact structure.
20) Look for over-tuning. Ask to implement twists at the via entry or route on other columns.
21) Check the pad entry for teardrops (fillets) being symmetrical if used.
22) In some rare cases, request to add plane voids under AC caps and SMD pins on Layer-2.
23) Check backdrilling: which vias need it, check whether the correct layers is used; check dimensions (via, BD and antipad).
24) At the end of the layout design, re-check backdrilling, if buses were moved on different layers, then the BD symbol needs change too.

25) Check the high-speed net spacing and manually space out.
26) Check the diffpair to power via spacing, manually slide them away.
27) Check high-speed layer usage. Some layers are better than others with shorter vias, routes on L(N-2) does not need backdrilling (if both parts are on the top side).
28) Check missing reference planes, or void crossing of high-speed signals.
29) Re-arrange some fanout vias (like large cap fanout) to help create low density routing channels.
30) Re-arrange some components to help create low density routing channels.
31) Check the constraint manager for constraint coverage and correctness. Verify trace width and space from stackup document. Verify the diffpair pitch/space was not mixed up.
32) Check the constraint manager for constraints check, to be all green.
33) Check the Pin-Pair or etch length report, for longest/shortest channels, to be used in SI analysis.
34) Lengthen any SERDES lanes that are too short (even by swapping ports) to balance loss versus reflection.
35) Check the routing topology of timing-driven buses like DDRx.
36) In some cases, ask for dynamic phase tolerance matching rules.
37) If there is a request to swap lanes, then implement swapping in schematics; make sure the swap list complies to chip rules on ASIC pin number basis (not connector pins or net names).
38) Check the termination resistor placement locations on all externally terminated interfaces and clocks.
39) Check or ask for the implementation of wavy or angled routing for 10G+ signals.
40) Check the stitching via placement at signal transitions. Their numbers, their layer reach and their relative distance has to be sufficient.

15.15.3 Plane Related

41) Check the clock vias to 12V plane spacing and add voids around.
42) Check the power planes for wideness and layer use, do DC voltage drop simulations, make sketch drawings for the layout engineer for re-drawing the boundaries.
43) Check the power plane stitching via count, when transitioning a power net from one layer to another layer.
44) Check the global plane (like 12V delivery to multiple VRMs) implementations for maximum width. Usually, a 1:10 width to length ratio without bottlenecks is good.
45) Check and instruct 0 Ohm sense-line resistor placement relative to power planes and ASIC body outline.
46) Update the dynamic shapes, and re-check them all, especially in overlapping areas.
47) Check the power planes for bottlenecks with too many antipads.
48) Check if the dual voids used for high speed vias are still there at the end of the layout design. Both power and ground planes.

15.15.4 Mechanical

49) The mechanical engineer's exported file to be imported by the layout engineer. This contains board outline, and main part locations. At the end of the design, a similar file to be exported for the mechanical engineer. This contains board outline, and ALL part locations and heights.
50) Check the heatsinks screws and mounting areas, keepouts with mechanical engineer.
51) Check the exact locations of connectors (power, IO, programming headers), LEDs, dip switches, and heatsink-related components with mechanical engineer.

52) Check any electrical part interference with mechanical parts, if there is a conflict then ask for moving components in layout or in mechanical design.
53) Check and clear standoff slide or positioning zones, by moving parts out of the way, to prevent damage during assembly.

15.15.5 General

54) Check the DRC reports.
55) Check the manufacturability DRC reports.
56) Check the solder mask expansion to be 2mil (maybe 3mil), on each component pin, defined by footprints.
57) Check the switching node to be avoided by sensitive signals.
58) Check the VIPPO via identification based on odd-number diameter, or use all vias VIPPO. Discuss with manufacturing engineering which option to choose.
59) Remove signal vias from under metal connectors or connector shield edges to avoid intermittent shorting when connectors are touched. Solder mask is not an insulator.
60) Provide a special fanout to the layout engineer for critical components like clam-shell DDR, main ASIC or connectors.
61) QFN center pad vias check, VIPPO/non-VIPPO, pattern.
62) Check all local-component and global fiducials.
63) Check the fab drawing for calling out PCB materials, prepreg glass styles, copper foils, impedance to trace width mapping, backdrill and drill tables, and insertion loss control notes.
64) At the end we send out the board file to the fab, and the pre-DFM checks start with a separate communication file between layout and hardware engineering and the PCB fab. Usually use the document format of the fab company. They ask for changes, waivers, clarifications.

16 Prototyping

We do not just design circuits to be shipped to customers, we do "prototyping" first. The prototype is the first version of the design, which likely has bugs, so its purpose is to find and eliminate those bugs. We call it a proto, proto-1, spin-1, version-1, or revision-1, depending on company. Testing the first prototype is called the "bring-up". After prototyping we update the design files and get the updated design manufactured that likely becomes the final version going to series production. We call this one a proto-2, spin-2, version-2, revision-2, pre-production, or production board design. Often proto-2 works well in the quick proto-2 bring-up test, with or without a few component value changes in the BOM, so we make more units, and we call it pre-production. Rarely a proto-3 is needed to fix a bug that was discovered late. This might be due to hardware bugs preventing us from testing out other circuits that have other hardware bugs or the lack of test software coverage at the time of ordering the proto-2 boards. If we have to get a proto-4, then something is wrong with career choices or project staffing.

The purpose of the prototype testing or "board bring-up" is to determine the list of design changes (bug fixes) required for a clean product manufacturing free of manual wiring rework. The full list of changes can be determined only from building/testing the proto, not from paperwork, meetings, or simulations. These are "random functional bugs", like missing net connections, wrong signal going to wrong pin, or wrong value of component used. Design reviews help to reduce, but not to eliminate, these issues completely. SI issues, on the other hand, have to be discovered from simulations, but more commonly they have to be prevented by using "best practices", which really mean correct PCB layout high-speed 3D features. Proto-1 will likely work after the bring-up with manual modifications (rework, wires, or mods) applied to it; but this is not a shippable product. A prototype is an engineering artifact.

Once the hardware and the layout design are done, and we have ordered the manufacturing of the prototypes from our fab and assembly vendors, we will receive a smaller set of prototype boards. We have to start testing it, and we have to make it work because they normally do not work out of the box, 99% of the cases. The main task of the hardware design phase is not only to implement the required features, but also to minimize mistakes in it. In previous chapters we discussed techniques about minimizing mistakes and how to take control of more parameters in the design. Even with all that, there will still be some mistakes in it, which is not a failure of engineering. An engineering failure would be if the mistakes were so big that we could not make them work by small hand-modifications of the prototype boards. The "board bring-up" of the prototype boards includes testing all the subcircuits of the board and debugging and modifying them if necessary until we achieve full functionality and full test coverage of all product features.

Hardware debugging involves experimentation, which requires using the on-board devices and some custom software as diagnostic instruments. Many times we have to make changes to the software or the FPGA code to exercise the hardware in a different way than originally intended to see if the board reacts differently, then make conclusions from possible causes of malfunction. Only writing the production software is not sufficient for a hardware project, the software and firmware teams also have a duty to participate in hardware bring-up and debugging. A new hardware is not "delivered" to the software and firmware teams, such as ordering something online, because a prototype is not a product. Hardware is not fully observable, even with the best instruments. We do not always know for certain what is wrong with the prototype, so we have to guess (logical hypothesis), then apply the fix to the guessed cause, and see if it worked. Coming up with several good hypothesis requires very strong logical reasoning skills in both deduction and induction. We might have to try several of these experiments until one hardware or glue logic FPGA bug is fixed.

DOI: 10.1201/9781032702094-16

This is because often we just cannot extract fully clear information from a partially dead board, and we cannot probe signals inside of the chips. The "root cause analysis" often demanded by "model based system engineering" is usually not feasible in the case of prototype board bugs. The experiments that did not work were not a waste of time since they helped us to gain a better understanding through the process of elimination of potential root causes. That saves time by not having to theorize with already eliminated causes. We also often need multiple experimental firmware versions before a bug is fixed. Inexperienced firmware engineers might not like having to implement firmware changes that are not guaranteed up front, or any changes without solid proof of a root cause, or any code that might not be deliverable to the customer. Management escalation might be required, although if they demand "proof", then we cannot provide that, logically. The proof will be available only after the experiment was performed. When we try multiple hardware rework "mods" on our own, no one will complain; rather, only when we need firmware changes. Sometimes the bug might turn out to be caused by a hardware design bug, at other times a firmware bug. It is not as obvious as some might think. It is often assumed that the hardware has to be fully fixed before anyone looks at debugging software, but that is nonsense. In the case of glue logic FPGA bugs, we can come up with maybe five experiments (code change, recompile, retest) a day, and with a 20% success rate we can still detect and fix one glue logic bug per day, instead of a month. Refusing to experiment will reduce the project team performance multiple times. Instead of saving time, it means wasting a lot more time. We might save effort (laziness), not time; sitting idle for months is still a project delay and cost.

All features and parts of the design have to be systematically checked out and tested, then documented. During the bring-up, every hardware bug (failure) we find and their identified solutions are documented. We need to identify two solutions for each, one that can be applied as a manual "rework" modification we can do on the same day on the prototype board and one we intend to apply to the design change for the "re-spin" or re-design that we will do later to generate the proto-2 schematics and layout. Both fixes will be listed for each numbered bug item, on the proto-1 rework list and in the proto-1-to-proto-2 design change list. Once all features are working on proto-1, we apply the changes to the schematic for re-spin, and we release the proto-2 schematics, then the proto-2 layout and manufacturing files. The proto-2 bring-up is usually much easier and takes a lot less time, usually fully working without modifications, or working with a few component value changes but without any cuts or wires in a day. During the later stage of prototyping, we capture in a document all DVT (design verification test) measurements, both hardware-bug resolutions (rework and design change), rework level and damage level per board serial number tables, functional test pass/failure status of each feature on each unit, and a lab testing log text. Hardware bugs causing observable "failures" can be one of two types, the always dead type and the "intermittent" type. Intermittent failures occur only in rare occasions but in our product they should never occur. So we have to put some effort into "reproducing" them through hundreds of trials, so we can properly observe, fix, and, later, prove that it was fixed.

Typical prototype functional hardware bugs are usually related to glue logic or system signals or low-speed interfaces having incorrect connections (wrong source, destination, or wrong voltage) or pull resistors. It is very common that a few of the VRMs do not work due to incorrect parameter-set resistors. Depending on contractor, we might have to look for soldering issues too. Most of these can be re-worked. A longer list of common mistakes is provided later.

Some issues might be caused by the firmware exercising the hardware wrong, for example, a pin is set as output when it should be input, a port is set in the wrong mode or speed, an internal feature is not enabled, power sequence timing causes a device to become unstable (might need to add delays or re-order), FPGA code IP has bugs, BIOS or bootloader trying to initialize the memory as a different type than we have on the board, the firmware is looking for a device that does not exist in the design, a too strong or too weak drive strength set on FPGA output causing SI issues, the console is directed to the wrong ports/pins, wrong initialization sequence (device-A must be loaded before talking to device-B), wrong programming sequence, wrong parameters expected on the input data, etc.

It is very common during prototyping that we cannot apply a proper fix to a hardware design bug, but we might be able to implement a "workaround". These workarounds will achieve the intended final functionality but in a more twisted way than intended. If we forgot to connect a system signal to a glue logic FPGA pin, then we might re-work that signal with a wire to the FPGA through some circuits that were originally intended for something less important. For example, a status LED output might be repurposed as an interrupt input. Sometimes we have to implement a hardware workaround for a software problem. For example, our processor has two similar low-speed ports that are not identical but similar enough for our needs, and for one of them the chip vendor never implemented a software driver, the one we connected in our hardware. That case we have to cut the fanout trace and wire our signal to the other port that has the proper software driver. This works only up to <<1GHz signals. Sometimes we have to implement a software workaround for a hardware problem. For example, if we connected an interrupt signal to our processor's GPIO interface, and it turns out it cannot generate an interrupt. Then the software has to implement polling and call a software subroutine when the signal is asserted, instead of using an interrupt subroutine.

During prototype bring-up we spend most of our time debugging and testing the slow CMOS system glue logic signals, not really the high-speed buses. And most of that is spent on the initialization sequence. This is a set of different sequences related to different major parts and subsystems of the hardware architecture. When we design the block diagrams and schematics, we also design the initialization sequences for all devices, so we have to know which signal has to toggle after which one and when. Then during prototype board bring-up if the hardware does not behave the way we expect, for example, no console messages appear, then we start probing signals with our scope. If the scope shows that a signal is in a different state (low versus high) at a given stage of the init sequence, then the device that should assert it failed to do so, so we know which device we have to look into more closely. We usually use a basic oscilloscope (200MHz analog bandwidth) to probe glue logic signals and slow buses (I2C, SPI), but we often also probe high-speed buses with Gigahertz bandwidth active probes. The purpose of probing high-speed buses during debugging is not to decode their bits, or even to check their signal integrity, but rather to see whether they are toggling or not, which can tell us that the chip on one end is alive and well to send complex data packets. An example of signal sequence debugging is when our CPLD toggles the power button signal to the CPU/chipset twice, then we expect the chipset to drive the SLP_S3# main power enable signal high. If the power button signal was toggled correctly, but the SLP_S3# fails to assert high within a second, then it means the chipset was unable to act. Then we can look into what could possibly make the chipset to act dead. For example, the standby reset signal is held low (instead of high) by our CPLD, or the standby rail PowerGood signal was not asserted high (stuck low), or the 32kHz crystal is not oscillating (no toggling square wave seen). In another example we probe the SPI flash interface of an ARM processor, then we probe the ACC bus of the SDRAM memory interface. We notice (on the scope screen) that right after reset the SPI bus keeps toggling for a few seconds, then it stops, then the memory ACC bus never toggles (flat line on the scope). What happens in this case is the CPU seems to execute code, is able to load program code form the flash memory, but never initializes the SDRAM memory. This case we have to ask the software engineer to tell us what steps the bootloader takes before even first time accessing the SDRAM memory, and what those states require (e.g., a display to be connected, a thermal sensor on I2C bus-3 at address-53 to be connected, etc.). To narrow down we might need the software team to add debug console messages or LED toggling through a GPIO pin into the code. Then we verify whether we have these device/port connections correctly in our design, the devices are alive, or ask the software engineer to change the code to not expect these devices. All these signals can be probed, and we can verify their state to find the one that is different than expected. Either a design issue (wrong/missing schematic connection, voltage, resistor value) or a manufacturing fault is keeping the signal from being in the expected state. We have to find that and re-work it, then re-test.

We can follow a board init sequence in the following made-up example. When the standby power appears, the standby VRM ramps up, then the POR circuit of the glue logic FPGA de-asserts, then the FPGA turns on the 12V and sequences all other VRMs up, enables the clock generator, then releases the reset to the multi-core CPU, the first CPU core type boots its bootloader code from flash, then releases the reset to the second CPU type as well as the ASICs, the second CPU core loads its bootloader then its OS, then the PCIe links up to the primary ASIC and gets negotiated down to 5Gig, then the OS drivers to the primary ASIC get loaded to initialize its registers, then through that the secondary ASIC gets loaded over I2C, then the Interlaken links up between the two ASICs.

Sometimes the board's init sequence or later its continuous operation might fail due to SERDES link issues. They have two types of failures: the completely dead link and the intermittent type (link up failure, surprise link down). The first type in some cases can be debugged with oscilloscopes, built-in LEDs, or console-driven manual register read commands. The second type is most often caused by signal integrity design issues. Every device monitors all of its SERDES ports and have information about the link being up or down. The information is available as a minimum as a bit in a status register that we can read out through a control plane interface and sometimes as a dedicated "Link_Up" pin. If the pin is driven high by the ASIC, it means the corresponding SERDES port/link is up and both link partners are healthy. The pin is usually connected on the board to an LED (sometimes through a transistor) or a test point. If an ASIC has an alternative control plane interface, for example, an I2C slave in addition to the PCIe endpoint, then we should have it in the design so we can access those registers even with the SERDES link down. The registers can also tell if it passed load detect but not link training, or which lanes are bad. In case of FPGAs, we have to ask the FPGA team to route the link up status bit to a pin. Either way we can read out pin states with live system boundary scan or probe with an oscilloscope or multimeter if accessible. There are protocol decode software available to be purchased and installed for high-speed oscilloscopes, which show what type of transactions are happening on the interface in the form of a list of recent packet codes. With PCIe we can see a list of physical layer packets or "ordered sets". By looking at the standard document we can decode them. If we see TS1/TS2 ordered sets repeatedly being sent, it means the devices are trying to link up but failing. If we see mostly idle characters but no TS1/TS2, then it means the link is firmly established. SERDES link well-being and device well-being are closely related. The debugging usually starts when a peripheral device is not detected in PCI-scan, in BIOS device list, or by the operating system software. Then there are two possibilities: either the device is dead or the SERDES link to it is not up. We have to look into both possibilities by probing the SERDES link (not for SI, just toggle versus flatline check) and by probing the supporting parts/signals (power, clock, EEPROMs) of the device. SI measurements are really taken through register read to display on-die captured eye diagrams or the values form the bit error counters. In cases with failing short links, putting the SERDES core into "low swing mode" through registers might help, in other cases transceiver tuning might help. To eliminate SI as a cause of a device failure, we can sometimes strap it into a lower speed mode. If it still fails it might be a device issue, if not then likely an SI issue. In the case of PCIe links we can look for further clues. If a device detects an electrical load representing the link partner device, then it will send out packets on the TX pins. If it does not receive similar packets on its RX pins, meaning the other device was present but did not respond, then it gives up trying to link up, and instead it will switch to "compliance mode" and keeps sending a compliance test pattern in an endless loop. A high-speed scope with the PCIe software can show the compliance pattern code.

Sometimes we find that chips or parts of chips (like an I/O port or an IP core) behave differently than expected. In this case we have to read the relevant parts in the datasheet again because maybe we misunderstood something when we read it before the schematic design. If we find that there is no misunderstanding, then maybe the section of the datasheet is misleading, then we have to contact our FAE or the tech support website of the chip company to find out what we missed or what they missed. Once we fully understand how the chip behaves and why, we might have to alter our prototype board to work with the correct operation. Sometimes we also measure signals on eval boards (sold by the chip vendor) and compare the waveforms and timing/protocol with what we see on our board.

One peculiar problem keeps coming up many times in various projects. Some design feature is discovered to have been designed incorrectly, but it somehow still works most of the time, and only fails intermittently sometimes (some units, some temperatures, some external mating boards, some data packets). The less correct question is why it fails in those specific cases. It is actually irrelevant, a misunderstanding of statistics. The more correct question is how to make the design compliant to specs and to which specs, so none of the units will ever fail.

16.1 BRING-UP SEQUENCE

The whole prototype bring-up usually takes weeks to months, depending on complexity, and whether we encounter any stubborn hardware bugs. This is usually related to one particular component not behaving as expected from our understanding of the chip datasheet. We have to write a bring-up plan document, before the prototype arrives, just to make sure we do not waste time figuring out what to do under stress. We also have to obtain all necessary equipment beforehand. Power supplies, dongles, instruments, soldering equipment. The plan also includes all steps to take until all functions are tested and programmed, and a daily log text as well describing all the issues that came up and the efforts made to resolve them.

We have to find creative ways of inventing test setups that can verify if one subcircuit if working or not, regardless whether other subcircuits are working or not. Most subcircuits rely on other subcircuits, so they cannot be tested out by themselves, but there are a few that can be. We have to start our bring-up process with these independently testable parts, then continue with other parts that rely on them but do not rely on parts we have not tested yet. After a few steps we can test out subcircuits that rely on multiple other parts of the board, but by that time we should already have tested and debugged those. The bring-up test plan includes the identification of the sequence of independency we just described here. Figure 16.1 shows an example made up hardware block diagram and a sequence that will achieve our goal. It checks the global power circuits and glue logic before checking VRMs that are controlled by them. It checks VRMs before checking clocking devices and ASICs that are fed by them. It checks all VRMs in succession as they are part of a power sequence. It checks the host processor before checking data plane ASICs. It checks non-volatile memory to allow software boot before the volatile memory can be checked by software.

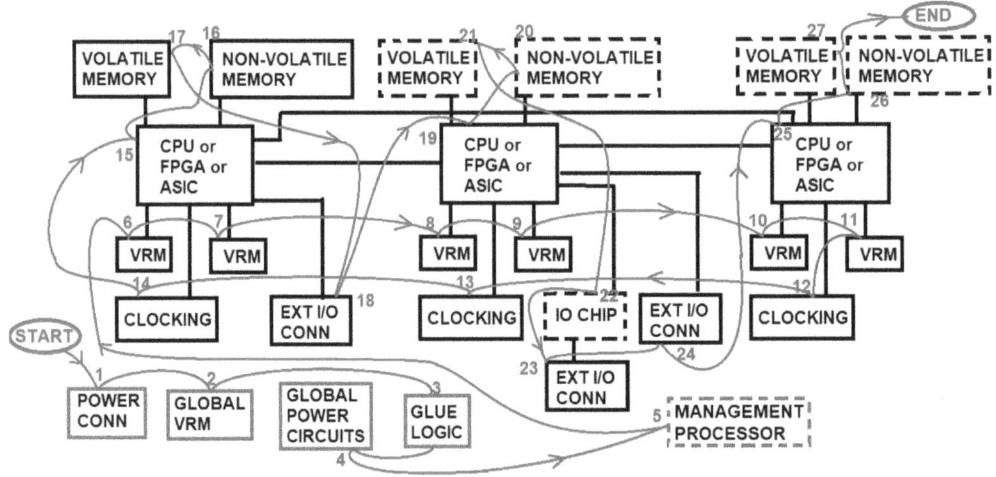

FIGURE 16.1 Example of a graph discovery path for board bring-up.

Some of these tests are initiated from the processor's console, while others are done with dongles and instruments like multimeters, oscilloscopes, and logic analyzers. Programmable devices can be partially tested by trying to program them from a local host or from a JTAG or I2C dongle and a laptop. This is an important "dead or alive test" for these devices. The programmer GUI tells the user if a device was found on the port or not. Later in the production test we will do automated tests only from the console scrips, but on prototypes we actually involve a lot of physical probing and developing test software on the fly as needs arise. Both cases can be described and developed by using graph theory and identifying a graph discovery path. The diagrams identify which device is looked at after which. It does not mention how each is tested. Based on how each device works, we have to figure out how they have to be tested. We should do this during the schematic design phase to ensure we provide access to those devices. Part of testing out a programmable device includes testing out the interface through which it is connected to the host processor. Usually we do not make a diagram like this; instead, we just write a list of test items while visualizing the walk path in our head. That would be the bring-up plan, and it will also include equipment or software to be used and a description of how each on-board device is tested. Some devices need to be programmed when we begin testing the particular device. So the bring-up plan is intertwined with a programming sequence also.

Based on the specific hardware architecture, the hardware designer has to write down a bring-up plan, in steps, before the design is fabbed out. The steps have to be "possible", given that the previous steps were executed. That means we cannot test an I/O port until the device is programmed, JTAG access of devices cannot be done until they are powered, and that cannot be powered until the sequencer is programmed, and so on. It is very logical. If a logical sequence breaks with a "chicken and egg" situation then the design has to be modified to resolve that and make it possible for one of the two steps to be performed before the other. For example, include analog multiplexers to divert a JTAG chain from devices that we know are unpowered at the time we need to program the first device in the chain. These issues should be discovered at the end of the schematics design, not when trying to program/test the prototype in the lab.

First-round prototypes of complex digital boards usually do not work out of the box at all, they will not turn on or they do not boot up. During the many step bring-up process we will likely run into "failures" when a device or an interface is not working. The board has probably rapidly progressed through several steps and failed at one, but we do not know which one yet. The failure happens because a few of the devices are set up incorrectly in the design and those devices are dead, until we resurrect them one by one through debugging and re-work. Turning on and booting up a board involves event sequences, such as power on sequence, programming sequence, reset release sequence, or boot sequence. Since it is so serialized, we can go through these step by step and see where in the sequence the board fails to execute the next step. The device that is supposed to perform at that step is one that is dead. Depending on what kind of device it is, often we can tell if it is not working, but it is harder to figure out what is causing it. For example, a chip has 20 strapping pins, 5 analog pins, and 4 interfaces. Any of these can cause the device to fail. We can check our hardware spec and datasheets about these sequences and verify the particular steps that the board has already completed before being stuck. We can also verify which step is the last one to confirm that the whole sequence and the whole board initialization are completed successfully. The sequences are really fast for direct human observation, so we use instruments that capture all events for later observation. For example, they can be observed from console log, oscilloscope screens with proper trigger, live-system boundary scan- timing diagrams, PORT80 dongles, I2C sniffer dongles, or any instrument. If we can halt a failing sequence, then we can also probe current states with instruments. Some of the checks are through probing on the PCB, others with a laptop using a dongle or a serial console. Sometimes we can try to access devices in their failing states using register access. So we look at our design documentation and check what is the first step and whether it completed or not by measuring relevant signals or looking at register bits. Then then next one and the next one. Analyzing a signal can tell us about the health of a device or vice versa. We should have a designed-in debug jumper that tells the glue logic to not restart in case of failure, so we can observe the crime scene.

In functional tests we are informed about the failure on the console log. There might be error messages or there might be a message we are supposed to see but fails to appear. After extensive testing and hundreds of runs, we might collect a few different failure signatures (a signal/device deviates from its expected state) or error messages. Most of them might be misleading, making us think of a pin or circuit that is actually not causing the failure, as we later find out. We have to discover all possible sources and probe signals/devices/pins at those sources. We can also drive/exercise output pins from the software console. Some chips allow us to monitor their digital or analog (voltage sense) input signals through a GUI on our laptop. The dongle and GUI setup can, in some cases, check device registers, which reflect an interface link state, device state, or received data value.

Once we have found the failing device, we have to debug and re-work it, verify it was fixed, then re-test the whole board and the init sequence again. We have to probe signals coming into the failed device and compare them against their datasheet input requirements. We have to probe signals coming out of the device and compare against their datasheet guaranteed output waveforms. Signals can be probed for voltage logic levels, signal integrity, protocol, and "toggling" (dead/alive). If the input signal is bad, then we have to debug the other device sending the signal to it, perhaps it is the wrong type of device or it is set in the wrong mode or it is dead.

Most of the proto hardware debugging is concerned with VRM analog circuits and slow glue logic or system signals. They are confusing and arbitrary. Even high-speed buses and digital chips can malfunction due to these low-speed circuits. These can be usually fixed with re-work, sometimes with creative software workarounds or functionality changes. A slightly different or altered management plane can still support the same data plane. High-speed and SERDES signals will not function with manually attached re-work wires, as these are low-frequency physical structures. SERDES and other buses have much simpler on-board circuits, their main complexity is on-chip, and they are well defined in standards. If they are screwed up anyway, then it requires a board re-spin. The main thing is to avoid a TX/RX swap in the schematic, but we do spreadsheet analysis for those. Transceiver tuning can help with mild SI issues but only re-spin can fix their strong SI issues and incorrect circuit/pin connections.

We have to read the relevant parts of the datasheets again, and we have to review the relevant part in our schematics again, focusing on the one device and its supporting components, looking for design versus datasheet (or reference design or firmware setting) discrepancies. Maybe we connected a signal to the wrong pin number or we used the wrong strapping resistors or signal pullups are missing. If the device input needs a 3.3V signal but our board is feeding it a 1.8V signal then the design is bad, and we have to change or rewire something under the microscope and solder station. We have to replace parts with different models/values and solder wires on or cut traces. Larger chips can be replaced in outside labs that have big BGA re-work stations; small 2-pin parts can be replaced in our solder station. Sometimes we add extra parts and wire them into a cut trace using 38-gauge re-work wires. Only small parts like resistors, capacitors, or small chips up to 10 pins can be added this way. Often we solder a pullup resistor to a chip pin, then solder a small wire between the resistor and a nearby power pin. Maybe we can wire in a voltage divider to help with the logic level incompatibility or cut the fanout trace and wire in a similar signal from another chip. Maybe we need to wire in an extra system signal for the glue logic FPGA so it can make the right decisions. If no signals toggle on our device on any of its outputs, then the internal operation is likely halted due to basic inputs like resets or power. If there are signals but the wrong data, then it is more of a high-level protocol problem. If there are signals coming out for a while and then they stop, then the device likely stopped because it did not receive the right signals on its inputs at the right time, such as their supporting part did not respond. SERDES links between two alive chips keep toggling even when no data is transmitted to keep the CDR running—we can tap on it to see. We have to understand the device internal operations and the interface standard bit-level and higher-level protocols to debug these issues.

With a JTAG logic analyzer we can sometimes visualize the sequence of all signals in a few seconds long test, which would otherwise take days of manual measurements. This applies only to slow system and glue logic signals (there are many), not high-speed buses. The one step where the signals do not look right points to a subcircuit or component driving that signal. It is especially useful for VRM and power sequence debugging. For example, at one of the VRMs the enable signal is high but the PowerGood signal is low, which clearly indicates that the VRM circuit is not functional, it has failed to turn on. Then we need to take more measurements and fix that particular VRM by applying part changes and wires, then if it works continue in the sequence debugging.

We should design-in a few debugging modes into our glue logic. For example, in normal mode if a power sequence fails halfway the glue logic shuts down all rails, but in debug mode if one rail fails the glue logic will keep all signals at the last state so we can probe the circuits with JTAG/multimeter/oscilloscope. The debug mode can be enabled using a jumper or DIP switch and some glue logic code/circuits that alter the rest of the glue logic behavior based on the jumper or DIP-switch signal. For higher-level functions that are tested through software, we can have a test version of the software that is "verbose" and displays every little detailed step. We can also have a test version of the device drivers that ignores errors and continues, so we can enable and access a partially working device. We should also design in several status LEDs, which turn on when an init step is completed (like all VRMs are up, FPGA configuration done, PCIe lanes linked up, etc.) or keep blinking when data is transferred (like a SATA or Ethernet activity LED).

X86 processor board prototypes should have a way of reading out post codes. POST means power on self-test. Post codes are sent on the LPC bus (I/O writes to address 80h) or an I2C bus by the BIOS, it sends one 8bit code after completing each initialization step in the BIOS init sequence. So we need our board to have headers on these buses. The code sequence information will come from the BIOS vendor or firmware engineering. If the code sequence display stops at a number that is not the intended last number, then the one where it stops (or the one before or after it) failed. A BIOS boot failure can be caused by the BIOS expecting something to be connected the way it was on the processor eval board that is different in our design or by a component not working (e.g., DDR memory Vref is noisy and cannot initialize the memory). So either a BIOS code change or board fix is needed before continuing with the BIOS boot sequence. We apply the fix and re-test and see which post code it reaches now. We can have an LPC-bus header and purchase an LPC dongle on eBay or route the signals to the glue logic FPGA that would decode it into something we can probe, read, or display. If the post code is driven to an I2C bus, then we can use an I2C-slave sniffer dongle or an oscilloscope that has I2C decode software on it. The I2C or LPC choice depends on the BIOS code—we can find out from the BIOS vendor or BIOS engineer.

Some of the board features we test are more electrical, like VRMs and clocks, while others are functional, whichare tested through the host processor's console. These are either features inside the processor, peripherals, and programmable control plane devices or data plane ASICs/FPGAs and the attached peripherals of the data plane ASICs. Most of this is done through a Linux console with the help of software/firmware engineering. We do dead/alive checks, functional checks and quality checks on every device and interface. This is done differently in every single project and for every different chip. The set of devices and the main behaviors of the main devices are different on different categories of board designs. A few of these differences are detailed in the list below:

Bring-up sequence differences between hardware types:

- X86 processor motherboard bring-up involves BIOS debugging for the first boot, the BIOS code having to match the features on the custom hardware. The BIOS first exercises the system hardware like memory interfaces, storage, and console. We often use Port-80 POST code displays to see how far the BIOS got. After BIOS boot, we debug any issues related to OS boot and peripheral chip driver loading. There is always a console, either serial or display+keyboard based.

- ARM processor board bring-up involves debugging the first boot with any bootloader code having to match the devices on our custom hardware and first exercising system hardware like memory interfaces, storage, and console.
- FPGA board bring-up involves JTAG device detection, then making sure that our bit file is in a format that can be successfully loaded. It often involves PCIe device detection from a host processor. Then each interface needs to be checked to see if any data passes through or the I/O state machines hang. We often debug internal state machines for not getting to the right state given expected input signals.
- Network ASIC-based board bring-up involves first the initialization over PCIe to complete successfully (or from local flash), then checking if each port came up in the right mode, if each port was able to link up with loopbacks or devices in the right mode and whether we are able to run traffic.

An example bring-up plan for a made-up case of a CPU-based design:

1. Start with a "power board" that has most digital parts depopulated. At each step if re-work is needed, the document in a re-work list with separate item drawings.
2. Visual check under a microscope for soldering and SMT placement/orientation errors, solder shorts, and opens.
3. Inspect the DNP/DNI no load components, if they follow the design choice, if not, then manually remove the DNP parts in the re-work station.
4. Measure resistance between voltage rails and ground while the board is off. High-current rails usually have a few Ohms, others a few kilo Ohms. If it is much less than one ohm, then there might be a short circuit that we need to locate with a milli Ohm meter or visual check.
5. Attach input power from a lab power supply in current limited mode, enable the output, look at the current (if in limiting then turn off), then measure the standby rail output voltages on the board with a multimeter. If they do not turn on or have wrong voltage then debug/re-work, with the help of a power supply engineer or FAE.
6. Power cycle. Device detection (dead/alive) and then programming of the power sequencing and management devices (FPGAs, EEPROMs, sequencers, micro controllers, etc.) and all the smart VRMs. The programming sequence (which device first) depends on our design and standby rail usage. This requires chip vendor–provided (JTAG, I2C, or UART) programming dongles, and chip vendor GUI software running on our lab laptop. The GUI should show if the device with the part number (and I2C address) we used was detected or not. If they are not detected, then debug/re-work the related circuits.
7. Debugging of the power sequence (order/timing) and management glue logic and VRMs for correct operation and features. If we used a sequencer chip with analog inputs in the design then we can monitor all voltage rails through it and its dongle/GUI. If we used an FPGA/CPLD then we can use TopJTAG probe to monitor all power enable and PowerGood signals on our laptop screen. The rail that has enable high but PowerGood low has failed. Also need to measure the DC voltages for correctness. The sequencer should be in a "keep on" mode, instead of "re-sequence" or "shut down at failure/timeout", which is more useful for the production version. The goal is to get the board powered up and remain powered up, at least several times in a row. If any VRM do not turn on or have wrong voltage, then debug/re-work with the help of a power supply engineer or FAE.
8. Tune the voltage regulators for bode, ripple, and load transient response. If issues found, then debug/re-work with the help of a power supply engineer or FAE.
9. Check if the clock signals are running with a basic oscilloscope, and have basic SI.

10. Switch over to using the fully populated board, apply the same re-work items from the documented list and drawings (ask a technician), and redo the previous test steps. Keep updating the re-work list with new items when they are discovered.
11. Program the BIOS, configuration, or bootloader flash with an image file received from the firmware/software team, using a dongle (SPI for X86, JTAG for other devices). Followed by the BIOS boot, after BIOS modifications by a firmware engineer, then test and debug the BIOS customization to see whether it works with the board design and whether the board is able to boot it through devices and interfaces. It also involves testing and using the serial port console, or USB and any display outputs. Most display output ports produce only a signal if a display was connected at startup.
12. OS Boot, installing customized OS from external (USB-stick, uSD card, network share) drive to the on-board flash/SSD drive and debugging the OS and the hardware to fit the custom board design and the board to be able to boot it. First, we can try to boot a live image instead of installation, which avoids using the on-board drive. Windows does not boot from USB stick, but it can be installed from it. There are several live Linux distros for free on the Internet. A full installation might hang with driver incompatibility with the new hardware, but the live versions usually slide through those issues. If our DUT has a graphics output, then any live Linux distro will work, a bootable DOS USB disk works too. We can create a DOS USB disk using free apps. DOS will not exercise the advanced graphics, only the basic one, which also helps debugging a proto. If we do not have graphics but only serial console (headless), then we will use a console-only Linux distro, but software engineering might have to create it. In most cases we use only the company's custom Linux package for all tests. Debug/re-work if some devices or ports crash the boot process.
13. Data plane FPGA bring-up and debugging. It starts with trying to access the devices over JTAG (FPGA chip vendor–provided dongle and GUI on our laptop). The JTAG tool GUI tells us whether anything (our device part number or device ID) on the JTAG chain was detected or not. We have to try to load the FPGA code and monitor CONF_DONE and any user defined status LEDs or interfaces. Debug/re-work if needed.
14. Peripheral device detection, debug/re-work circuits if a device does not respond:
    - In Linux, type "lspci" to see PCI/PCIe devices whether they are alive or not.
    - In Linux, type "lsusb" to see USB devices whether they are alive or not, for example, USB to UART bridges, USB hubs, and storage devices.
    - Use an I2C bit-banging driver to try a read access to every single I2C device. The same for SPI devices.
15. Data plane ASIC bring-up and debugging. It starts with trying to access the devices over PCIe. We have to try to load the ASIC SDK and monitor registers and console feedback.
16. Test all on-board devices and ports/buses on the data plane, control plane, and management plane through manual register read/write "bit-banging" commands, then also with their customized drivers. Debug/re-work if needed. Software team needs to provide the manual access drivers. Some interfaces can be tested with "bit-banging" commands or with I2C and SPI dongles if headers are designed-in. Plug and play device addresses can be obtained from lspci/lsusb scans, other devices require discovering their addresses from "base+offset" calculations or manual probing and known address strappings.
17. Test all external port types. If we have N ports of USB and M ports of Ethernet, then test and debug the first instance of each. Once working test all other instances too. The design is supposed to be identical for the same type ports.
18. Test and debug glue logic circuits, like I2C buses with level translation, thermal shutdown, sensors, interrupts, analog multiplexers, software control, IPMI board/system power control., etc.
19. Capture eye diagrams to see how bad they are.

20. Stress testing, like power dissipation test (TDP tool, Linux Memtest or benchmark software) for a processor or running "traffic" for ASICs/FPGAs, which is multi-device or multi-board functional test with full power loading. Debug/re-work failing/unreliable circuits.
21. Power cycle testing (thousands of runs, or over-weekend test, must power up every time)
22. Temperature chamber functional and power cycle testing.
23. Complete all required measurements and DVT.
24. Incorporate all re-work-based and other identified design changes and re-spin the design.

16.1.1 Test Software

We use a lot of test software for hardware prototyping. Some software is custom developed by the in-house software or firmware team, other software are ready made by third parties or by the chip companies. Many programmable chips have a vendor GUI available to program them from our laptop or to control them. For example, FPGA programming tools like Vivado Lab Tools, Quartus Lab Edition, Libero Flash Pro, as well as other device programming tools for power management and clocking chips from the chip vendors. FPGA vendors offer a JTAG-based eye capture GUI running on our Windows laptop, PCIe switch vendors offer Windows GUIs running also on our laptop for eye capture, Ethernet switch and retimer switch chip vendors offer Linux and text console-based eye capture applications running directly on the DUT. The Intel LanConf app running on the DUT under Linux, Windows, or DOS allows us to monitor Ethernet ports for packet error counts, to program PHY-EEPROMs, or to put the ports into loopback modes for DVT or factory testing. Some processor vendors offer a "TDP Tool" for driving their processors to dissipate a lot of heat, while running it on the DUT, for prototype motherboard stress testing.

There is also generic test software that can run on any hardware, for example, the freeware "RW-Everything", which allows us to read or write into any memory mapped register as long as we run a Windows 7 or older on the DUT. We can also run a memory test for hours or days on both Linux-based and Windows-based prototypes that will stress test the DDR memory subsystem and tell us if there was any read error caused by bus signal integrity, power integrity, or a bad silicon chip. If our DUT runs Linux then we can run the built-in LSPCI command for a PCI(e) device scan or on Windows or DOS we can run a PCI32 free app. Similarly, we can check if the USB chips are functional or the USB ports are working with externally connected USB devices using the LSUSB command under Linux or the device manager in Windows. We can wake our sleeping DUT over the local Ethernet network using a WOL-commander app. I2C and SPI dongles come with Windows GUIs for programming devices, manipulating registers or they can be used as listening bus analyzers.

See Chapter 9, "Hardware-Firmware Integration". It describes how the software team, firmware team, or diagnostics team can develop or provide custom test software that is tailored for the particular design or the particular company's product architecture. When dealing with low to medium complexity hardware, usually off-the-shelf or open-source tools are sufficient, but when dealing with complex hardware with data plane and control plane ASICs, even for lower volume production, a lot of custom test software needs to be developed or tailored for every new design. Most of the time our main test software will be Linux-based command line tools, running on the company version of Linux and provided as a single programming image with the OS. Basically, we will need to install new and newer OS images on the hardware whenever new test software or drivers are developed. Our hardware must provide ports for these, usually USB, Ethernet, or micro-SD. Some of the device programming will only be possible through custom test software, for example, to test the CvP loading of FPGAs by the host processor. Some systems flash program FPGAs over CvP, other systems use CvP every time for the startup time loading of the FPGAs to avoid any data plane code from being stored in flash memories.

Most of our embedded designs will boot Linux, which we commandeer through the serial cable and a text console. The console app like "Putty" runs on our laptop. They need only commands during testing, while in real deployment they run automated programs after startup. Some Linux commands are used for testing out prototype hardware (boards and FPGA logic). There are a few basic commands that come up while using them. After the unit has booted up, it will ask for a username and password to log in, so we type these in and press enter. Our software engineers can tell what the username and password is for the Linux image they created. The "root" is the main user with all access privileges on any Linux system. We (hardware engineers) often run lspci and lsusb commands to check whether any plug-and-play devices are alive or not. When we have an FPGA reloaded through CvP or over JTAG in the lab, we need to get it enumerated into the PCIe tree and the system memory map. This can be done with a command if we have some custom Linux kernel drivers that support it or with a warm reboot. A rescan command will likely not achieve that. There will be custom commands made by the software team for checking I2C, SPI, and other bus-connected devices. Complex functions like eye capture also have their custom commands, and our software engineers can tell us. Just type the command and press enter. If it is a script with multiple commands in it, then we might have to browse to its folder location using the cd command ("cd .." goes up, "cd /foldername" goes into a subfolder), then type the command and enter. The console prompt text shows our username (root) and our currently opened directory/folder like "root:/folder1/folder2$". Once we are done testing the prototype, we shut down the unit with the shutdown command. Commands usually have a help text that we can display by typing "XYZ –help" then enter, where XYZ is the particular command we want to inquire about. For example, "shutdown –help". This will also tell what the command does and what "switches" or modifiers are available. For example, "shutdown -P now" will power off the system and keeps it off through the SLP_S3# signal being driven low, but only after the Linux has unmounted the file system and ended all processes. The "reboot" will not drive SLP_S3# low; rather, it keeps it up and only pulses the PLTRST# main reset signal and restart the system in a warm reboot. The "shutdown -P -r now" will drive SLP_S3# low for a few seconds, for a cold reboot (also called power-cycle reset). A cold reboot also causes any FPGAs not in standby domain to reload. If we loaded an FPGA over JTAG, we might want to issue only warm reboots to get it detected by a hard CPU. The shutdown and reboot commands write into the X86 chipset's reset control register at address CF9h. ARM processors might not have a power control logic built in, so they might only do warm reboot or shutdown-to-halt from the command line. Some of the commands work only if we logged in as "root", but if we logged in with another username then those commands might need "sudo" to be typed at the beginning of the command. Linux has a numbering for external interface ports, like usb0, usb1... eth0, eth1... We can test an Ethernet port using pinging a known IP address (of a device on our local network), like "ping -I eth0 192.168.0.5". A Linux console can be accessed not only over the serial cable but also over the local Ethernet network using a telnet app running on our laptop if we know the prototype board's local (not Internet) IP address. Some of these Linux commands do not work the way we expect on some Linux distributions or on some computers/chips. Most of the time we hardware engineers sit in the lab together with the firmware/software engineers and ask them to type the commands into the console and run the tests for us, not just develop/compile the code. For example, we ask the software engineer to send data on the 5th I2C bus so we can probe it with an oscilloscope for a signal quality measurement.

16.1.2 PCI Scan

We can check a full list of what devices exist and are alive (without hardware bugs) in the system using the Linux LSPCI command, which lists the results of a previously (at boot or at rescan) completed PCI scan. An example lspci command response is shown in Figure 16.2. It lists all PCI compatible devices in the system. The first number is the bus number, followed by the device number and then the function number. The first few dozen devices are IP cores inside the X86 chipset. Any PCI-capable chips we designed in are listed after those. The way a PCIe switch appears is each port appears as a separate device, a virtual PCI-to-PCI bridge. The one with the lowest bus number

```
>>lspci
...                   ← many devices integrated inside the chipset, not listed here
00:1d.0 USB controller: Intel Corporation ...  ← device inside the x86 chipset
00:1f.0 ISA bridge: Intel Corporation ...      ← device inside the x86 chipset
00:1f.2 SATA controller: Intel Corporation ... ← device inside the x86 chipset
00:1f.3 SMBus: Intel Corporation ...           ← device inside the x86 chipset
01:...                              ← any chip or plug in card
02:...                              ← any chip or plug in card
03:00.0 PCI bridge: PLX Technology ...       ← PCIe switch upstream port
04:01.0 PCI bridge: PLX Technology ...       ← PCIe switch downstream port
04:02.0 PCI bridge: PLX Technology ...       ← PCIe switch downstream port
04:03.0 PCI bridge: PLX Technology ...       ← PCIe switch downstream port
04:04.0 PCI bridge: PLX Technology ...       ← PCIe switch downstream port
05:00.0 Memory Controller: Xilinx Corporation ... ← FPGA downstream from PCIe sw
...                          ← possibly more devices, not listed here.
```

FIGURE 16.2 Example of a PCI scan console results (truncated and commented).

is the upstream port, then several devices at the next bus number. It will decode vendor IDs into a company name string, but if not, then we can look them up in VID search on the PCI-SIG website.

Using "lspci -vvv" will list all devices with all details. For example, we can use text search for "LinkSta" in the saved console log and find what speed the device linked up to and what width. This can be used to verify connectivity and link reliability on our PCIe traces and FPGA implementation. It will list the base address, so our prototype FPGA device logic can be manually tested by reading and writing to that address we found in lspci. Sometimes our Linux has a too high payload size or burst length set, causing system instability. We can check all devices what they can handle (find the string "MaxReadReq") and set our system to the lowest common denominator device's value.

Any FPGA device will show up under the vendor ID that we put into the FPGA source code, and the device description (like "memory controller" or "peripheral bridge") will also reflect what device ID we put into the FPGA code. Some device IDs are standard (like peripheral bridge), but we can put a part of our system part/model number or product name into this field in the FPGA code. We can put our system/board company's vendor ID (if we have one) or just put the FPGA vendor's ID. These vendor and device IDs are 4-digit hexadecimal numbers.

There are third-party free programs for PCI scan to be used under MS-DOS and Windows that can be downloaded from the Internet. MS-DOS is still used for X86 prototype hardware debugging due to its lack of reliance on too many system components.

16.1.3 Ethernet Ports

All Ethernet controllers and ports need to be programmed (likely into an EEPROM chip) with a valid and unique MAC address before testing them. They might also need LED modes and other parameters too. The device itself can be tested through its upstream interface, PCIe, or other. The ports have to be tested functionally by connecting something to them and sending data over to see if they arrive. The very first functional test we do is to see whether it links up (register or LED status), then whether it can obtain/provide an IP address (when connected to a switch), then whether we can receive data packets through it, and then whether it can keep doing it for hours/days without many errors. They also have to be tested for signal integrity using eye capture on ports that run at/above 10Gbps. Functional tests run with regular Ethernet packets, while eye measurements can run with regular packets or with PRBS test patterns if both ends are put into PRBS mode by the test software. The PRBS mode is better for measuring worst-case bit error rates accurately. On-die eye capture works with counting bit errors in "pixels" created by sweeping through different offsets in the clock/data recovery circuit. Both the packet-based traffic test and the PRBS-based test requires special chip vendor specific test software or drivers that might be graphical- or text console–based. We can test internal Ethernet ports by setting up both of the two chips at the two ends of the link for test modes. External ports have more testing options since we can decide what to connect to them.

For Ethernet and any other bi-directional peer-to-peer type interfaces and external or internal ports we need to do two types of checks: connectivity (functional) and quality (signal integrity). The connectivity check ensures that the design and manufacturing was correct with signals going to the right pins that are soldered properly and the devices are in the correct modes (schematic nets and strapping) and are alive (support circuit pins soldered properly, initialized properly). The quality check ensures that the signal arrives in good condition and will be reliable. Prototype board bring-up requires the connectivity check, and, if that fails, then we try to do a quality check too. During DVT testing we need to do only a quality check. In the manufacturing test of each unit, we mainly do a connectivity check, and sometimes a limited quality check if it is easy and cost-effective to set up, for example, with automatically parsed on-die eye scans and loopback plugs.

The simplest (and cheapest) SI qualification for DVT is with an optical self-loopback to check the SI of the RX traces with an on-die eye scan, and then with a copper self-loopback to check the SI of the TX+RX traces together, although the latter is pessimistic. In a production test usually a copper self-loopback is sufficient. Any tests suggested here with optical cables applies only to optical ports like SFP+, while the Base-T type Ethernet ports can do only copper cables and loopbacks.

External port test connections options:

- A high-speed oscilloscope for precise TX-only eye measurement. This does a connectivity check on the TX path only and a quality check on the TX traces only. DVT tests only.
- An external Ethernet switch over a cable and optical transceiver. This does a connectivity check on the RX and TX paths and a quality check on the RX traces only. Proto or DVT.
- A traffic generator instrument (Keysight/Ixia) over a cable and optical transceiver. This does a connectivity check on the RX and TX paths and a quality check on the RX traces only. Proto or DVT.
- Port-to-port copper loopback, with a copper cable between two ports. This does a connectivity check on the RX and TX paths and a quality check on the TX and RX traces and the cable in series. Proto or DVT.
- Port-to-port optical loopback, with an optical cable with transceiver modules between two ports. This does a connectivity check on the RX and TX paths and a quality check on the RX traces only. Proto or DVT.
- A copper self-loopback plug. This does a connectivity check on the RX and TX paths and a quality check on the TX and RX traces in series. Self-loopback plugs are also used in manufacturing in large numbers and can be purchased anywhere. There are RJ45, SFP, QSFP-DD, and other types available. Proto, DVT, or production.
- An optical self-loopback cable plugged into an optical module. This does a connectivity check on the RX and TX paths and a quality check on the RX traces only. Proto, DVT, or production.

16.1.4 Example of Prototype Bugs

A list of typical hardware bugs that we might find on our prototypes is below. In real life most hardware bugs are very convoluted and tricky, and they have something to do with ambiguous aspects of the device operations or interface circuits. Another issue is the cascading failures, where after fixing the first bug, several other circuits are no longer working as they were damaged by the badly set up first circuit. Some bugs can mask other bugs, when they prevent a function from starting so it never produces errors, until the first bug is fixed. SI and timing issues can rarely be fixed on a proto as all we can do is slow the signaling speed down or tune the transceivers. Hardware failures can be caused by software, PCB manufacturing, and schematic design mistakes.

General small part issues:

- Soldering issues, part orientation, wrong/missing part, open/short, they can cause any kind of symptoms.
- DNP parts were mistakenly populated, causes the circuit to behave differently.
- Connector pin mapping mismatch between two sides, causes system init failure and link down connectivity issues, worst case shorts and power issues.
- Connector contact issues with dirt/debris or bent pins causing link down and device detection issues.
- Missing I/O pullup resistors on all/any sides of buffers, level translators, or multiplexers.
- Missing I/O pullup resistors on open drain signals.
- Too weak or too strong pullup or pull down.
- The chip input termination scheme does not match the incoming signal expectation.
- Wrong or missing strapping resistor combination, driving a wrong chip operating mode.
- Missing strapping resistors on dual purpose I/O and strapping pins.
- Multi-device address strap conflict on a bus.
- Missing or unnecessary AC coupling caps on SERDES or clock signals.
- Missing inductive pullup on C2C Base-T Ethernet lines.
- Missing power connection on a Base-T Ethernet transformer center tap causes link down.
- Missing catch resistor on VRM circuits when tested on a power board, causing them to fail to start up.
- Backplane input control signals missing a weak pull, causing a float when bench testing.
- PCB drawing mistake with missing backdrills, causing excessing return loss on SERDES link.
- Mismatched strap or port configuration relative to reference design.

Analog issues:

- Wrong value parts around VRMs or transistors, causing wrong voltage or instability.
- Too much stress (RMS current, voltage derating) on components, they might die while testing.
- VRM circuit connection issues and wrong connections, need re-wiring.
- VRM is set with too low overcurrent limit. Even if it is considerably above our max load current, it can still trip on noises.
- VRM parameter issues, causing false overcurrent shutdown, wrong voltage (ASIC damage), instability with dip or shutdown.
- Too fast turn on time, wrong soft start resistor, or lack of soft start capability of a VRM chip might cause upstream rail instability, rippling down to other VRM startup failure.
- Too much VRM ripple noise causes digital chip malfunction.
- Impossibility to sequence rails in certain order due to upstream rail being supplied by downstream rail.
- Power sequence fails due to one VRM failing to assert its PowerGood signal.
- Power sequence fails due to sequencer pin connection issues on the Enable and PowerGood pins.
- The whole board shuts down unexpectedly in run time, due to one VRM de-asserting its PowerGood signal caused by instability, prompting the sequencer to turn all off.
- Sensitive VRM components (feedback filter) too close to switch nodes, causing random VRM shutdown.
- Missing, too small (high ESR), or unnecessary power filter ferrite bead inductors, causing ASIC SERDES or PLL to malfunction intermittently.
- Crystal load capacitor values might prevent oscillation.

- LED or transistor is distorting the logic level on an open drain signal that also goes to a CMOS input.
- Too much capacitance on the input of a hot-swap controller, crashing at hot insertion.
- Power net is routed as a trace, with too much DCR, causing voltage fluctuation, and intermittent digital chip or interface failure.
- Too much power plane DC resistance, causing out of range voltage and fluctuation, causing intermittent ASIC crash.
- Missing bode resistor prevents us from tuning a VRM.
- MOSFET is driven with insufficient gate voltage, not opening properly.

Chip power pin issues:

- Chip power output (decoupling-only) versus power input pin mixed up, shorting two power rails at the pin.
- Wrong voltage rail is connected to the ASIC's system-signal bank VIO pin.
- Chip is in wrong power domain, cannot act on or produce signals when needed during system startup.
- Unconnected power or ground pin of a chip (schematic error), causing heat-up.
- Programming header missing some power pins, so dongle cannot work.
- Programming header input (meant to power the board) vs output (powering the dongle) power role mix up.
- Invisible power pins of a chip in schematic gets default connected to wrong voltage rail in netlist.
- If a device controls its own power, then a new board in an un-programmed state cannot power up or be programmed either.

Chip signal pin issues:

- P/N swap, RX/TX swap (two TX pins driving the same net), or lane swap issue.
- Signal connected to wrong pin of a chip, needs trace cutting and a wire rework, only below 1GHz.
- Half a diffpair connection issue (P or N on connector or soldering), causing link up with bad eye.
- Unconnected inputs, causing random signal detection.
- Unconnected system signal input pin on a chip, causing a failure of initialization or intermittent down.
- Typo in net label, causing missing connection on the board.
- Multi-drop system signal is driven by an unintended device in the wrong time.
- Signal not driven at startup for a limited time interval, and a receiver acts on noise.
- Cold solder on chip pins, causing signal float or intermittent drive.
- Signal stuck low or high with no one driving it due to design issue or cold solder.
- The pin is really an output not an input on one chip, causing double drive and crash or damage.
- The pin is really an input not output on one chip, causing the signal to float as no one is driving it.
- A chip drives its output low while initializing, which confuses another chip. Has to gate inputs with status sig.
- An input pin is driven as an output by default during initialization.
- Some pins marked as NC on the datasheet are actually strapping/system logic pins on the reference design.
- I/O standard (voltage level and termination scheme) incompatibility between two chips.

- Power domain crossing issues, causing a signal to be shorted to ground or VCC by an input or float by an output temporarily during startup.
- Some control signal pins need disconnecting from glue logic and use a fixed PU/PD in the right power domain.
- Missing or unneeded level translator on RS232 or I2C or glue logic signal.
- Output with too weak drive capability used to drive multiple load chips.
- Open drain versus full drive signaling mix up, causing data corruption in one direction.
- Slow edges due to open drain signaling at higher data rate, causing data corruption.
- The FPGA compiler has eliminated some input pins and now driving them as default output low.
- Signal rise too slow, causing metastability at device input.
- Clock rising edge is non-monotonic, causing double clocking and chips to go to indeterministic states.
- Missing connection on reference voltage or calibration pin of an FPGA, causing I/O standard issues.

Circuit issues:

- JTAG chain issues, wrong connections, too long chain with no buffering.
- JTAG chains blocked by unprogrammed or unpowered devices.
- Thermal alert signals glitching or shorted low during startup, needs ignoring at startup.
- Optical port control signal missing control line or strapped wrong.
- Weak LED drive or wrong voltage causes LED to be never on.
- Missing system signals for glue logic or management controller, unable to do its role.
- CPLD/FPGA glue logic VHDL code issues, with state machines and protocols.
- Device needs dongle-programming but a header is missing for that.
- Missing programming mode or debug mode jumper.
- Missing debug/programming ports or headers.
- Missing one or two signals from headers.
- Impossibility of programming some devices, due to chicken and egg situations, with one chip's power on or programmed status blocking access to another chip.
- Missing config EEPROMs, causing the main ASICs not to be able to initialize or retain parameters.
- Bus running faster than one of the devices can handle.

Functional issues:

- Firmware issues, expecting wrong connections on wrong ports.
- An active high output is driving an active low input.
- Chip hangs because the design is missing an input signal that is expected by firmware at a certain time.
- Chip hangs because the design is missing a device that is expected by firmware at a certain port/address.
- Wrong reset timing for some late devices in the startup sequence, causing enumeration/detection issues.
- Device powers up too late for host to detect/initialize it.
- Intermittent device detection or enumeration failure caused by race condition between independently initializing devices.
- Clock enabled too early (damaging an unpowered device) or too late (hang).
- Write protect signal asserted on device, making programming unsuccessful.
- Board-level signal was designed to be impedance-terminated inside the ASIC's input, but the firmware is not enabling the termination, or vice versa.

- A signal is not strong enough without buffering, causing degraded levels.
- Interrupt-driven peripheral with no interrupt signal connected, does not work properly.
- Thermal alert is asserted at default temperature threshold before sensor is programmed.
- Missing a programming-mode type control signal going to the ASIC strapping pins, should be at the programming header or dip switch.
- Backplane signals with too much capacitance or missing weak pulls, crashing the system when a card is hot inserted.
- Backplane power nets at hot-swap controller input with too much capacitance, crashing the system when a card is hot inserted.
- Insufficient flash memory size and lack of multi-outline footprint to support replacement to larger device.
- Missing reset signal in the design to a chip input.
- Device expecting a protocol or system signal to toggle, but nothing is driving it.
- Device expecting a reset rising edge, but it is just pulled up.
- Wrong sequence due to carry over signal missing between cascaded devices in both directions.
- A bad power up sequence might cause intermittent startup issues.
- A bad power down sequence might cause intermittent startup issues next time.
- Power management signal timing/schedule needs to be changed to work with a device, like an X86 chipset and domain PowerGood inputs.
- If a strapping pin tells a device to use an I/O port that is not connected, it might hang.
- Bad UART baud rate, causing communications error due to wrong main oscillator frequency selection.
- Multiplexers directed wrong by glue logic, firmware, or resistor straps.
- Signal connector contact issues, causing link down and device detection failures.
- I2C device incompatibility with lack of support for clock-stretching, or protocol.
- Multi-lane bus link training issue when separate/split retimers are used.
- Wrong retimer chip used without correct protocol support, or without FEC support.
- Some or all ports of an ASIC are lacking support for the interface mode/speed we intended to use it for.
- ASIC does not have enough logical MAC ports internally, as a limitation not considered.
- Some devices require certain control signals to come in a specific sequence, but we hardwired them.
- Failed SERDES linkup caused by a host running in SSC mode while not providing a reference clock to the downstream device.
- EEPROM data corruption, caused by the design not ensuring a power holdup circuit for finishing any erase/write cycles during shutdown.
- Any design connections out of the ordinary can cause the management engine in an X86 CPU to refuse to boot.
- BIOS boot hang due to using a memory down scheme, when the BIOS is looking for a DIMM SPD-EEPROM.
- BIOS boot hang due to using a memory down scheme, when the wrong DRAM parameters are hardcoded in the BIOS source code.
- The main chip is dead, due to support circuit issues, such as wrong voltage, the clock not running, wrong boot strapping option, or cannot communicate with a boot flash chip or system memory.

16.2 DONGLES

A hardware engineer's toolbox mainly consists of a screwdriver and a bunch of programming and debugging dongles. Figure 16.3 shows a few examples of dongles. They are small plastic boxes that

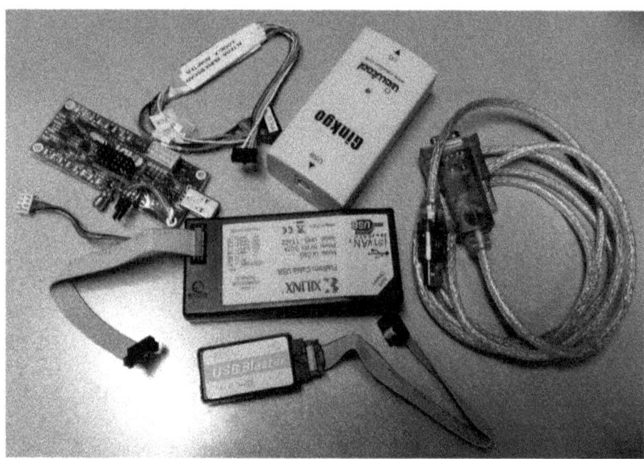

FIGURE 16.3 A bunch of dongles from a hardware engineer's toolbox.

convert a computer's USB port into a chip vendor–specific JTAG port, I2C, MDIO, UART, or SPI port. They are also supplied with a GUI program to control/monitor the dongle operation. They are typically used for device programming or for extracting data from the on-board devices, for example, on-die eye diagram capture, voltage rail sensing, I2C bus traffic monitoring, or a JTAG-based logic analyzer displayed on a laptop screen. Most prototype probing on modern digital boards happens through dongles and cables (serial console and Ethernet), less so through oscilloscopes multimeters or logic analyzers. To keep physically poking the board as in the old days is not as common. All smart-device chip vendors provide dongles and GUI programs to hardware designers, some for free and others can be purchased online. They operate over standard interfaces, but they often utilize non-standard additional features of the interface to access vendor-specific core logic. There are dongles available from third party vendors to operate with any chip over standard interfaces like JTAG (in standard non-vendor-specific modes), I2C or SPI. TotalPhase produces the popular Aardvark dongle that can act as I2C or SPI master and talk to any device on a prototype. We can initiate simple read and write accesses to devices from the Aardvark GUI or we can use the Aardvark dongle with a chip vendor GUI to talk to their devices. DediProg SF100 is another popular SPI dongle, often used for directly (through a multiplexer chip) programming flash memory chips that store BIOS firmware. There are also I2C sniffer dongles that do not initiate transactions, but monitor and display all I2C communications going on the I2C bus. With SPI dongles like the TotalPhase Aardvark or the DediProg SF100, we can talk to SPI-based devices like retimer chips or we can program SPI flash chips. Some chips send out a boot data log over an I2C bus, which can be logged with a sniffer dongle. The board has to be designed to detach the host processor from the SPI bus and connect the programming header to the SPI flash chip during programming, which can be done using an analog multiplexer chip that has rail-to-rail I/O voltage support. In some cases, we can program the flash memory and EEPROM chips through the JTAG port of the host device that the flash chip is attached to, although it can take a long time. The dongles interface with our board through debug headers we have designed into our board. They must have the size, pitch, pinout, and sometimes part number that the chip vendor has defined. It is very important to make sure that the I/O voltage range of all the dongles we intend to use are compatible with the ASIC chip port I/O voltage. If not, then we might have to design in some level translators next to the debug connectors, or connect the ASIC IO power pins in the schematic to a different rail if possible.

Chip vendors who produce smart VRM controllers, clock chips, or power sequencers also make their own I2C dongles. Usually they give it to the hardware engineers for free. These are used for device programming or to run telemetry (measurement read out) on their chips. VRMs and sequencers can report back rail voltages without us having to probe with a multimeter or oscilloscope. Multimeter or scope probing requires minutes to hours of layout lookup for each probing attempt, which can be replaced with easy computer screen–based quick probing through on-board smart devices. In most cases we program smart devices with dongles, but many of them can be programmed from an embedded host too, but only if we have designed our system in a way that it has a processor already powered up and running while these devices are not yet programmed. In-system automated programming can be enabled by appropriate power management and power sequence design.

With JTAG dongles we can program devices like flash-FPGAs or the attached configuration flash chips of the SRAM-FPGAs using the chip vendor's GUI. In some cases, we want to program an EEPROM device that is attached to a JTAG-capable major chip, which can be done through third-party GUIs like the TopJTAG Flash Programmer that uses the chip's IO pins to bit bang into an SPI protocol and handle the flash chip through it. This is slow because the tool has to load hundreds of JTAG register bits for each bit transition on the SPI bus, creating an access speed of 5MHz/200=25kHz. Some FPGA vendors have a method for their tool to load a flash memory image that de-serializes a stream and acts as bus master, instead of bit-banging, which can be much faster. Every JTAG capable device can be instructed through standard IEEE1149 JTAG protocol, in several JTAG modes. In EXTEST mode we can use them for flash device programming or for PCB open/short connectivity testing or in SAMPLE/PRELOAD mode to use as a live system logic analyzer application. The device programming is through non-standard, vendor-specific JTAG instructions.

16.3 TEST FIXTURES

For functional testing of external interfaces, we have to use test cables or loopback plugs. Master-slave type interfaces, like USB and PCIe, cannot be tested with loopbacks. Peer-to-peer type interfaces, like Ethernet, CXL, or Interlaken, can be. For a production test we will rely more on loopbacks when possible, but for a prototype functional test we test them with both. The loopback is a simple device that plugs into a standard external I/O connector and connects the port's transmit signals to the receive signals for testing purposes only. Cables connect our prototype board to external devices to see if our design and firmware are set up in a way that it will be able to communicate with third-party standard devices. Optical Ethernet ports can be tested first with "copper" cables then with optical transceivers too. In this two-step approach we test the data plane (SERDES signals on the SFP) without control signals (like TXEN), first, to isolate potential faults or bugs, and then all together. USB ports are usually tested with USB flash drives, video outputs are tested with consumer type displays.

Interfaces that go to a board-to-board connector or backplane connector need to be tested with an existing compatible product (like an off-the-shelf add-in card or chassis/backplane) or with a custom-designed test fixture board. On these test fixture boards we can have basic devices for the purpose of being detected or route signals to external ports with standard connectors. Peer-to-peer type ports can be tested with loopback traces on the fixture board. Master-slave type interfaces, like PCIe, I2C and SPI, require a peripheral chip or an add-in card socket to be designed onto the fixture board. For PCIe and USB instead of designing in a chip, we can have a connector that is suitable for plugging in consumer devices like USB sticks or SSD cards. We might need an IPMI or management processor to be on the test fixture board or we can design in a CPLD to emulate a management processor or connect a PC to act as a host processor. Many of the prototype tests need to be done only once on one single unit, such as those verifying protocol compatibility. Some fixtures are for functional checks, others are for SI measurements. Fixtures can be designed to route backplane or external interfaces to 2.92mm coax connectors, which can be hooked up with a high-speed oscilloscope or a VNA for SI measurements.

Device programming might require test fixtures or custom split cables to be made. Often we have multiple programmable devices on one board, but, due to board space shortage, we connect all JTAG and I2C/SPI programming ports to one single high-density header (0.5 to 1mm pitch), instead of providing chip-vendor dongle-compatible low density IDC headers that are typically 10 to 14 pins at 2 to

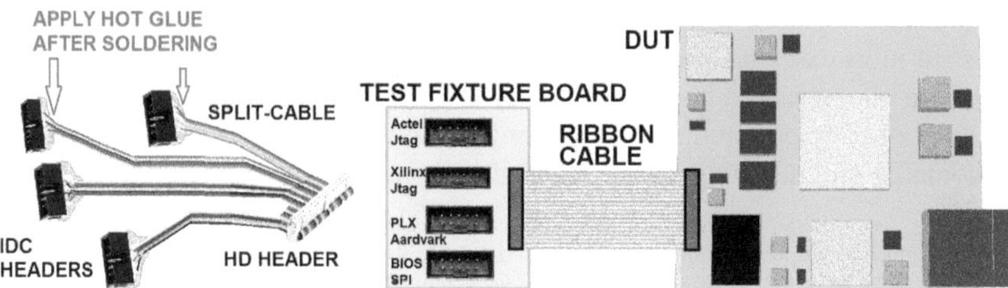

FIGURE 16.4 Programming cable adapters (sketch).

FIGURE 16.5 Home-made lateral fan assemblies.

2.54mm pitch. This requires making either a split cable or a fanout board. We can see both in Figure 16.4. The split cable simply has the wide header sockets manually soldered to a ribbon cable, which is crimped to the high-density header plug. A fanout board will use a standard flat ribbon cable with the high-density header and a custom PCB to split the signals into vendor-specific low-density headers. Then the vendor provided JTAG/I2C/SPI dongles can be directly plugged into the test fixture board or the split cable's IDC headers. These might have to be made for every board design, but, in some limited cases, we might re-use them from project to project. Some large or lower density board designs can afford to design in the vendor headers directly, then we not need these adapters.

Often we test prototype boards without a full chassis, especially during the early board bring-up, so the intended cooling solution and power delivery features are not available. Cards that are designed to plug into backplanes will need a mini power-backplane board to be designed and manufactured, which contains the normal backplane's power connector only and some banana sockets that we can use to connect it to a lab power supply. For cooling, we can use smaller heatsinks than the final one, with double-sided thermal adhesive sheet. They can be removed later by heating and twisting. The heatsinks on larger ASICs usually cover a larger board area, preventing us from probing signals, but the ones we will use in early prototyping will cover only the ASIC's outline, although we can use much taller ones. During the early bring-up we will not (should not) run them at full software or traffic load, so they will not dissipate that much heat. The lack of chassis fans and airflow can be substituted by using a cheap table fan or by making a lateral fan assembly that we can put next to the board on the lab bench. This will be made of a few standard fans, zip ties, some cut cardboard, and a 12V laptop charger. When the board is upside down on the bench, the lateral fan module can blow air under it through the heatsinks. When the heatsink is on the top, we might still need lateral air, as many heatsinks have a closed top and a regular fan will not blow through it. Figure 16.5 shows examples of this.

16.4 LIVE SYSTEM BOUNDARY SCAN

We can turn any complex device into a logic analyzer because they all have standard JTAG ports. With that, we can observe the behavior of the device itself, and everything that is connected to it through its pins. A glue logic FPGA or CPLD typically has all the glue logic and system signals of all the major chips (processors, ASICs, data plane FPGAs) connected to it. Every pin of the FPGA becomes an oscilloscope probe at the same time—except the SERDES pins. So a single FPGA can be used to spy on the whole system's behavior by looking at a live timing diagram in the third-party JTAG software tool's user interface.

This is the most useful prototype board debug feature we have, but it requires that all important system signals (power management, reset, and system status) be connected to the pins of a JTAG capable device, ideally a device that is in the standby domain like a small glue logic FPGA or CPLD. This means that we should design our board with an FPGA-based glue logic instead of using lots of discrete chips. We can also spy on a limited set of signals through the JTAG port of a data plane FPGA/ASIC. Data plane ASICs do not connect their system signals to everything on the board. On a server motherboard we might spy on the system through the JTAG port of the BMC or server management processor. This spying through device pins scheme works by simply connecting a USB-JTAG dongle to the chip's JTAG port and using a program that was made for this kind of test. The glue logic FPGA always has a JTAG connector, while control and data plane devices do not. We can add headers to them in our schematic design or chain them together in a big JTAG chain. Although the most useful one is the glue logic FPGA's JTAG access.

The "TopJTAG Probe" is a low-cost software tool that can perform this JTAG logic analyzer testing. It can be purchased from a website. Figure 16.6 shows the user interface of TopJtag Probe. It works well with the Intel/Altera USB Blaster JTAG dongle. If we have a chip from any other vendor, we can still connect to it with the TopJtag probe and use the USB Blaster cable, but we have to

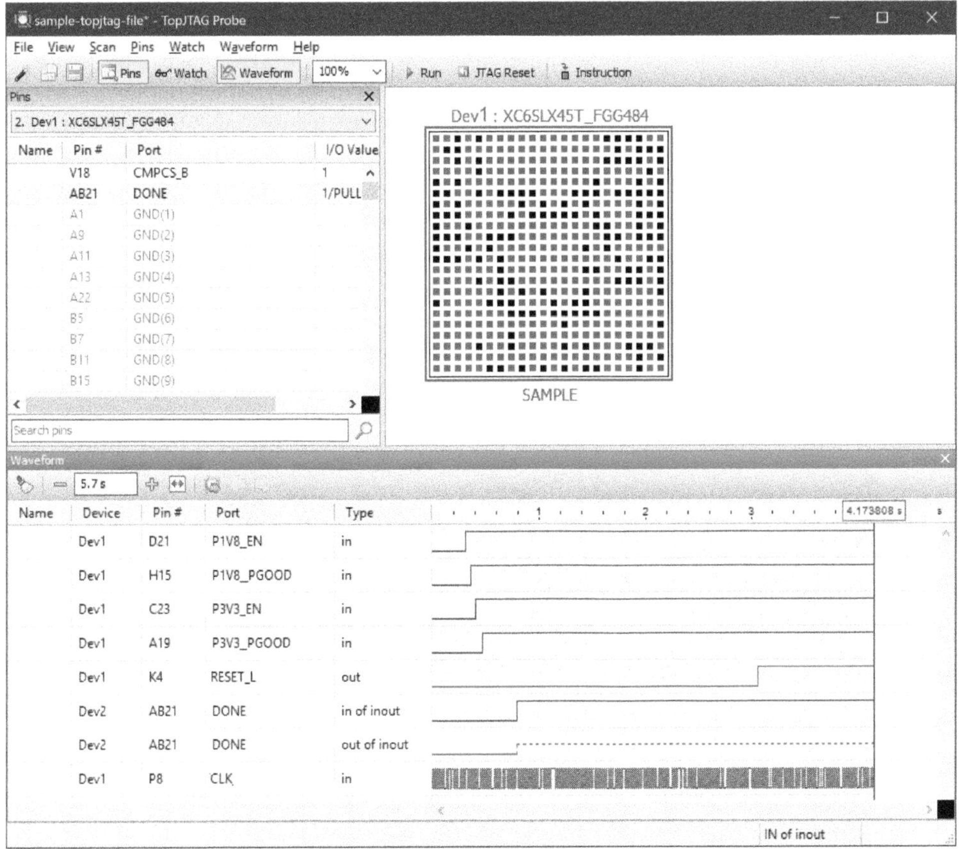

FIGURE 16.6 TopJtag probe logic analyzer GUI.

make a cable adapter to swap the pinout. Yes, an Altera JTAG dongle works with a Xilinx FPGA, in standard IEEE 1149.1 boundary scan modes but not in FPGA programming mode. The tool will put the device into "Sample/Preload" mode, which allows the normal operation of the chip to continue, while snooping on all its pins. The better-known uses of boundary scan, especially in production, put the devices into "EXTEST" mode, where the device stops normal operation and drives out a test vector defined by the boundary scan tool. That is different from live system boundary scan. One is passively listening; the other is actively controlling the pins. The scanning can be started once the device has powered up, and then we can display any of its pin signals in a timing diagram in real time. We can have a JTAG chain of multiple devices, and then we can monitor all the pins of all the devices at the same time on the same diagram. With this method, we can inspect, for example, a system initialization sequence. We can also debug intermittent system failures by simply probing all signals at the same time and, when the unit fails, we check which one signal changed state first. No oscilloscope has hundreds of inputs and hours of memory, but this thing has. The time resolution is in the milliseconds range, so any fast bus protocols cannot be analyzed with it, but it is perfect for analyzing power and system management signals and events. Most of the board bring-up activity is concerned with system signals like resets, power enables, thermal alerts, config done, port link-up status, and so on. We can also look at buses that are faster than the 300Hz update rate, but instead of decoding them, we just check if they are toggling or not, which is a simple dead or alive check.

Note that the same software company also has a TopJtag Flash Programmer software to access JTAG-capable devices in EXTEST mode and drive their flash interface buses in bit-banging mode to program those attached flash or EEPROM chips.

16.5 RE-WORK

When we are debugging our prototype, we might find some small mistakes that can be resolved by soldering on or removing a resistor or capacitor, cutting a trace with a medical scalpel, or adding a small wire. Figure 16.7 shows a typical re-worked board. Typically, we use 38 to 40-gauge (AWG) enamel-coated transformer wires. We can also strip a regular power cable that has a multi-thread tinned copper core and take one thread out of it. Some wires do not stick to solder too well, so we need to find a better one. The fix with all the parts and wires for one functional bug is considered one re-work item. About 1one to 40 of these re-work items should be enough to achieve full functionality on proto-1, depending on board complexity. Some boards might have over 10k components. It might contain multiple parts or have multiple instances, and still one item. Complex hardware design is one of the hardest professions in the world, and it costs employers considerable sums of money. A complex board project can cost anywhere from $50k to $10M, plus millions in lost

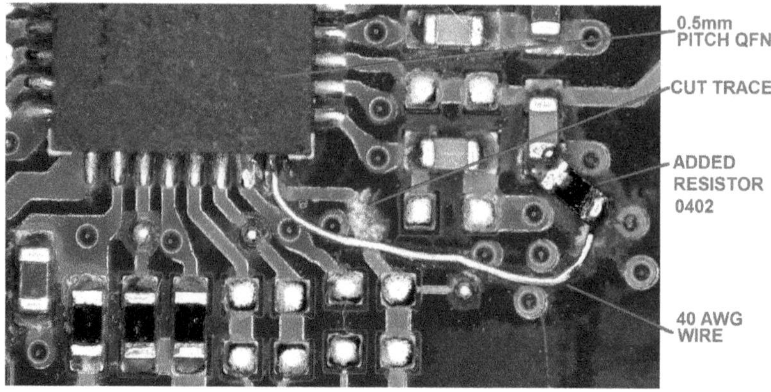

FIGURE 16.7 Re-work demonstration on a laptop motherboard.

business opportunities from delays. It requires a lot of talent and expertise and requires several peer reviews to bring down the number of bug items to two to 40, with good quality initial design, but we will still have to do re-work and debugging on the prototype. Think of a hardware design team like an Olympic athlete team, not a random office job. Re-work is for random functional bugs only. SI, PI, and timing issues can be fully prevented by proper design and analysis techniques, as they cannot be fixed on a prototype board. Adjusting transceiver equalizer settings, which we can do on a proto, or slowing down a bus is not a fix for SI issues; rather, they are meant to improve design margins not to be relied on to make the system barely work. Note that high-speed (>1GHz) signals cannot be re-worked or rewired on a prototype. Transceiver tuning is the only prototype alteration that can be done for SI, but that was meant for improving margins, not for making marginal designs.

Typically, we document the re-work items in re-work drawings or re-work instructions for technicians. The drawing has to be readable by trained technicians, and it should not require an engineer to figure it out. We cannot ask "to look up where R45 is and replace it with a stronger one". Rather, very specifically say "replace R45 as shown on the diagram with a 2.7k Ohm 0402 resistor", then an arrow points to it. Even for the first instance it is worth creating a drawing, but it definitely helps with subsequent boards. We usually get a half dozen or more proto-1 units manufactured, so the first instance of the re-work may be done by the hardware engineer or by the technician, but any subsequent ones are done by a technician. An example of a re-work drawing with sufficient detail can be seen in Figure 16.8. Often hardware designers implement new re-work items to quickly check if it resolves an issue, and later ask the technician to replicate it on the other board units.

The re-work is typically performed with a dual solder iron station, under a binocular optical microscope that has a 20x to 40x magnification. Removing 2-pin parts requires two solder irons. Putting a new one in requires one. The microscope has to be able to focus on objects on the desk (not on a metal base) at several inches away from the lens (working distance) to allow for tall components nearby and hand tool access. A PCB does not fit flat on the small metal base used in biological microscopes, so it is placed on the desk, while the microscope is leaning over it with its "boom stand". Other equipment needed are 0402 resistor (at 1% or E96) and capacitor (E12) kits, a tantalum/polymer capacitor kit (E6), 38 AWG wires, solder-wicking wires, Q-tips, alcohol in a top dispenser, flux, Kapton tape, pointy tweezers, medical scalpels, and thin solder wires. ESD protection is also needed, either through a heel-strap or through a wrist strap.

Sometimes we need a QFN or a BGA chip to be removed or replaced, which cannot be done at a re-work station. In that case we have to send the board out to an internal facility or to an external contractor that has an infrared BGA rework station.

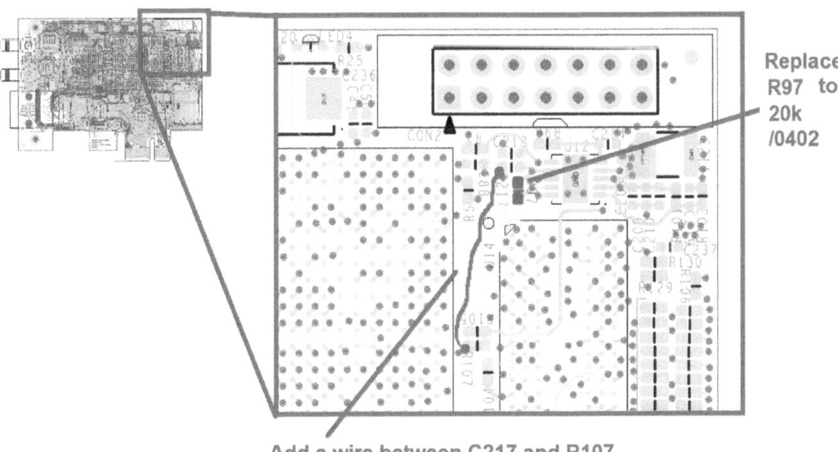

FIGURE 16.8 Example re-work instruction.

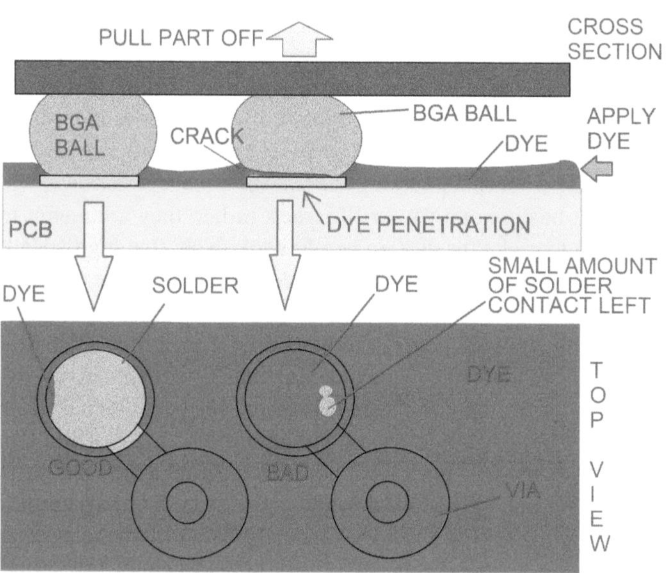

FIGURE 16.9 Dye and pry test concept.

Sometimes we can ask the re-work facility to take X-ray images of the BGA components before removal, while we are looking for solder shorts or opens (cold solder). A top-down X-ray image cannot show cold solder at all, a "5D X-ray" image may or may not show it either. 5D X-ray is mostly used when looking for solder shorts or via fabrication issues. The most reliable way of proving that there is an open circuit between a BGA ball and a board pad is by using the "die and pry" test. This will destroy the board on purpose. It is usually done by outside contractors or contract manufacturers. In this test they inject a special ink under the BGA, which seeps into the gaps between a cold-soldered BGA ball and a pad. Then they rip the BGA chip off the board with excessive force. After this they take a photograph of the board area. Wherever we find ink coverage on the torn BGA balls, those pads were cold-soldered. The sketch in Figure 16.9 shows what the dye and pry test result looks like on a badly manufactured board that had cold soldered or cracked BGA balls shown with red dye penetration. Another method of detecting a cold solder is by requesting the chip to be replaced with a new one. If it works after that, then likely it was a cold solder but with a low probability the silicon chip might have been bad.

16.6 VRM VALIDATION

All voltage regulator modules on proto-1 boards need to be tested and tuned. This should be done before any digital functional testing of the ASICs starts because unstable or noisy voltage rails can cause digital chip malfunction. Almost all designs have several VRMs that produce too much noise to pass the ASIC's input specs initially on the prototype, until they are all tuned. No calculation or simulation can fully prevent it, only manual adjustments/rework and trials on the proto board can. During the test the rail voltage deviates from the nominal value by a ripple voltage (under load) and by the load transient response voltage bounce. The test is done on the bench usually at room temperature. Any voltage fluctuation resulting from the test must be within the digital load ASIC's tolerance limits, as listed on its datasheet. VRM ripple measurements on oscilloscopes can be done with two types of probing; with a soldered-down micro coax cable or with an active (SE or differential) probe. In most cases the ripple should be practically <1%, while the ripple plus load transient <2%. For some 100W+ ASIC cores it needs to be lower since the whole budget might be only 1%.

There are four main possible VRM issues that we need to reduce: having too much ripple, too stark load transient response (LTR), too high output impedance (measured together with the whole board PDN), or an unstable control loop Bode plot. Any of these can cause digital ASIC or software code malfunction. Ideally we would test every VRM on the board for all four aspects. The tests for the LTR, the Bode plot and the PDN impedance provide similar verification and tuning for the overall stability of the VRM's control loop. The ripple always must be measured. Most of the time the output impedance is measured only on the core rails, and the Bode plot might not be accessible on some board designs or with some VRM chips.

The VRM control loop tuning process takes clues from load step and Bode plot testing. During this the power supply engineer replaces components (resistors or capacitors to different values) and re-tests the board in iterations until an acceptable response is achieved. Smart VRMs can be re-programmed over PMBUS with a dongle instead of manually re-working passive parts. The VRM control loops must be tuned in the context of the specific digital board design (capacitive load conditions) to improve stability and margins and to reduce ripple and the step response voltage noise. This is typically done by a VRM chip company FAE (field applications engineer), an in-house VRM engineer, or the hardware designer. Tuning on a VRM eval board or in a simulator is not sufficient. The end result of this process is a set of component value changes for the VRM circuits or a new programming file for the smart VRMs. The component changes have to be applied to the proto-1 boards through re-work and also incorporated into the proto-2 design changes list.

In normal operation feeding the digital chips, a VRM might shut down under certain load conditions or randomly after hours of system stress testing run, if the loop is unstable. A VRM can fail and shut down or it can have one single big voltage dip (load transient) after several hours that we cannot catch in lab testing. The VRM might recover and no one notices it was down for a few milliseconds. This can mislead us during prototype functional bring-up and debugging, thinking that our digital logic is bad. A VRM might power cycle itself, but the sequencer should detect that and power cycle the whole board and log the failure source in non-volatile memory (to help debugging later). "Should" means the board to be designed that way. If the whole board power cycles or shuts down, which is a common symptom, it is usually caused by a single failed VRM that prompted the sequencer to take down the whole board. That is actually better because then we will definitely notice the power issue. Before we get into debugging digital payload circuits, we need to get the voltages to be solid.

We could find VRM issues on functioning boards, but we cannot easily quantify the issues on them. This is why all of the VRM quality tests should be performed on a "power board" that has the main CPU/FPGA/ASICs removed. This way we can eliminate the ASIC's changing load current from interfering with our precise VRM analysis. The power board also has to be hardwired to stay powered without them. Often we implement a debug mode jumper to our power management glue logic that allows us to force the power sequencer to continue on or stop without restarting, even if a few rails fail. During the testing the VRM might fail, and untuned rails may fail at the start, but we want them to remain enabled to not interfere with the VRM analog test. Every VRM chip has an enable input pin to serve power sequencing needs. We can test only enabled VRMs.

The control loop Bode plot has to be measured against bandwidth and phase margin requirements. This is done through a Bode tester, like the Bode-100 instrument, with the help of "injection transformers". A test signal is injected into the control loop through the transformer near the voltage feedback or sense inputs on a small series resistor that we design in for this one purpose. A tuned Bode plot can help with meting the ripple and transient response requirements, but it also helps with stability to prevent accidental shutting down. Some modern VRMs have a non-linear control loop that cannot be accurately tested with a Bode plot.

The typical VRM measurements:

- We measure the ripple noise voltage under user application load or artificial DC load (Chroma 6300). We can use a ground spring–loaded probe, an active probe, or a solder-on micro coax cable with an SMA connector. Then the VRM output voltage waveform is displayed on an oscilloscope to determine if it is more than our limit.

FIGURE 16.10 Load tester concept (sketch).

- We measure the load transient response (from 20% to 80% of max load current, within a 0.5us rise time) with artificial load testers. The artificial load is soldered with short wires to the power pads of the bulk capacitors near the removed ASIC footprint. The wire needs to be no more than a few inches long for producing fast load transients on modern POL-VRMs and very thick to allow high currents with low drop. The 20% DC load will be provided by a programmable electronic load instrument like the Chroma 63xx series. The 60%=80-20 step load will be provided by a "Mini-Slammer" or a "Load Slammer", which are small solder-down dongles that are usually controlled over USB. A chroma instrument can be used by itself if a slower transient is sufficient. The concept is demonstrated on a sketch 3D diagram in Figure 16.10. We can probe the output waveform through a soldered-down micro coax cable and display it on an oscilloscope to see how much the voltage fluctuates during load step and load dump. This has to be less than the limit defined by the digital load ASIC chip datasheet.
- A Bode plot analyzer (a type of VNA) can be used to directly measure the control loop stability in frequency domain. Using a low frequency VNA or a Bode box and an injection transformer. A low value "injection resistor" needs to be designed into our schematic, where the test signal is being applied, in series with the sense input (at the feedback resistor or remote sense line).
- Part of the PDN verification on the prototype is to measure the whole PDN impedance profile. Anything below 1MHz is dominated by the VRM, so if the impedance is above the target impedance line below 1MHz, then the VRM control loop has to be tuned and re-tested until it goes below. This measurement is done by the hardware engineer, while the VRM engineer or FAE has to make the control loop adjustments. It is described in detail in Chapter 17, "Measurements".

16.7 TRANSCEIVER TUNING

The high-speed SERDES interfaces utilize transceiver blocks or IP cores. These transceivers have standard features, like transmitter FFE (feed-forward equalizer, in a simple form it is called pre-emphasis), receiver DFE (decision feedback equalizer), and receiver analog filter. They enlarge the eye diagram we see on an oscilloscope or eye scan if we apply the most optimal parameters. We can determine these parameters using simulation results, and mathematics or through a process called "transceiver tuning" performed on a prototype board.

For chip-to-chip links we utilize on-die eye capture to measure the eye opening after each parameter change. We can write into the registers of the SERDES cores to control their parameters through the control plane interface from the host processor (PCIe, MDIO, I2C, SPI) or from a side-band interface and a dongle (I2C, SPI, JTAG) connected through a debug header. The same interface is used for eye capture and register access. The on-die eye scan always captures an eye margin, instead of an actual eye diagram. See Chapter 11, “Signal Integrity”, which deals with SERDES link analysis for the theory behind the eye scan operation. For external ports we use an oscilloscope and a test fixture (for example SFP to SMA). In the end we settle with the parameter set that produces the best eye. On-die eye capture is available on many digital chips, ASICs, FPGAs, and retimer chips. Usually when the embedded host interface is utilized for the access, then we typically get a text console-based eye diagram. Sideband interfaces typically used with a laptop computer running the chip vendor’s eye capture GUI.

We must run real data or use PRBS mode, not just rely on IDLE characters; otherwise the measurement might be too optimistic. SERDES links when not sending data are not turned off but automatically keep sending IDLE characters infinitely. For eye opening measurements we need a stressed eye, which is achieved by real data or PRBS characters, not with IDLE. Some devices can be put into PRBS test mode. If the device is wired to a loopback plug through an external connector, then it will send and receive/check the PRBS code. If the ASIC is wired to another ASIC, then both need to be in PRBS test mode and compatible with each other. If that is not possible due to incompatibility, then we need to stress the eye by sending user data packets. We can send dummy files or keep reading a few registers in an infinite loop using a Linux script (with help from software engineering). We tune transceivers for maximizing the vertical eye opening, decreasing the amplitude (to avoid stressing the circuits and improve signal to noise ratio) and decreasing the jitter (increase horizontal eye opening). Actual amplitude measurement is not available in eye scan tools, only in oscilloscope-based tests of external ports. They can measure the inner eye opening. Figure 16.11 shows the three main eye parameters that we will see on an oscilloscope.

In many cases we have a short chip-to-chip link with very little loss, which makes the reflections caused by PCB vias too harsh. These cases we typically set the transmitter into something called “low swing mode”, where all TX equalizations are turned off, then we check with the eye scan if it solves the issues. We might have to turn off link training, override it, or put the port into a different mode (Base-X instead of Base-KR).

There are two types of reasons for doing this tuning. The first is when the link is already unreliable on the prototype, and it can be made barely reliable during the test in the lab through tuning. The issue with this reasoning is that even if it works in the lab on one unit, we do not have any design margin, and some of the production units will be unreliable while operated by the customer. We cannot assume that our proto unit represents the worst-case production unit. The second reason is to improve the margins (by enlarging the eye opening) on a design that already works in the lab. Improving margins helps our chances of getting good eye opening on all of our production units in the whole temperature range and over several years of aging also. Actually, this is the main motivation behind this exercise.

There are 5 to 20 RX parameters and about 1 to 5 TX parameters, each with a granularity of 10 to 100 values. That can be 100^25 that is 1E50 value combinations. Even if we automate the trials and

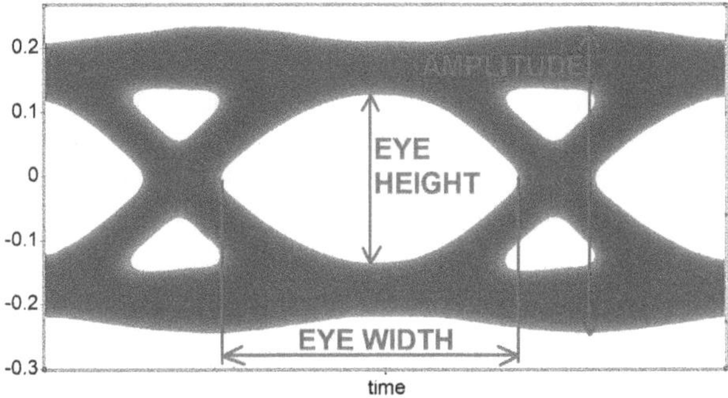

FIGURE 16.11 Eye dimensions (sketch).

eye scans, each eye scan may take a minute—it will take billions of years to try all combinations. We can reduce this task by not trying all combinations, but only 2 to 4 values for each parameter, and only adjust the four major parameters, then it would take 2^4=16 combinations and 16 minutes to scan the whole solution space. Then we will pick the combination that has the best eye opening and hardcode that into the firmware, so every time the system starts up, the transceivers get initialized to those values.

The digital equalizer part of the parameters, the RX-DFE and the TX-FFE together act as a digital discrete-time domain filter. The filter is supposed to match the inverse of the passive interconnect channel's impulse response, quantized at the data rate. The impulse response is the inverse Fourier transformed result of the insertion-loss profile (S-parameter). In practice it would be very hard to generate that data, so we most often resort to scanning through the solution space instead.

Sometimes we see one of the signals or lanes showing an almost closed eye diagram but only on one unit. This is likely caused by connectivity issues, a connector pin contact surface has either caught some debris or residue or is bent or broken off, or it is caused by a component (BGA) pin cold solder. Basically, only half a diffpair is transmitting a signal, and it appears as a false SI issue. It can usually link up and pass some data at room temperature, but it has no SI margin and catches bit errors. Re-seating cards, replacing connectors, reflowing, or replacing BGA chips can help with that.

16.8 EMI TEST

All chassis products are tested to see whether they emit too much electromagnetic radiation compared to official FCC (Federal Communications Commission) standards. This is done either by the EMI engineers or by the hardware engineer. Usually the test is done at a third-party external lab company that can issue certificates. EMI radiation is usually blocked by metal mesh on the air ventilation openings and conducting soft EMI gaskets in the gaps between connectors and the metal front panel. The opening size on the mesh has to be determined based on the frequency we are trying to block. A clue to what it will be is the half baud rate of the main buses will likely show up in the RF radiation measurement. These air vent mesh sheets are usually thick solid honeycomb (hexagon pattern) types, which allow better airflow and better shielding than a woven mesh. Many third-party vendors provide honeycomb vent screens. Most system/board companies have EMI engineers who take care of this, but in some cases the hardware designer might end up in the EMI lab. The lab engineer conducts the actual RF measurements, we just have to set up our proto hardware in the lab and run it, and, if it fails, then we have to make quick alterations on the spot, using EMI blocking materials. We can pre-scan our design in our own hardware lab with a handheld mini-loop near-field EMI probe (for example Tektronix TekBox TBPS01) that can be attached to a spectrum analyzer or oscilloscope, and we can move it near different components and areas of the front panel to find EMI leaks or radiation sources.

16.9 DESIGN VERIFICATION TESTING (DVT)

Every new design has to be thoroughly tested in a design verification test (DVT), sometimes called EDVT or electrical design verification testing. The prototype boards and systems get functionally tested, and major signals are measured and documented. All of the signals, interfaces, or devices get functionally tested or measured one at a time, and then all together in a stress test scenario also. Some signals always run, such as clocks or memory buses, others require manual test commands to exercise them. A functional test consists of initializing, detecting, and accessing every single device and interface link either by using manual Linux commands or by running a complete test software or user/production software on them. We also make sure they are able to perform complete and complex tasks as intended by the application. In a stress test we blast data and processing tasks everywhere all at once to create conditions with the highest potential for VRM current, device thermal overloads, and signal crosstalk. This is ideally done in an (thermal) environmental chamber, similarly to the ESS (Environmental Stress Screening) used on production units of high-reliability products. We would ideally also apply voltage margining to take care of two of the PVT (process, voltage, temperature) corners of the silicon devices on our boards. The last one, "process" can be tested only by running tests on multiple units. A full process sweep is only possible in production, as it tests all units. The measurements are done using multimeters (DC voltages, voltage rail DC resistance to ground), oscilloscopes (<1GHz internal signals or external signals at any speed at a connector), on-die eye capture (>1GHz SERDES signals), and signal analyzers (reference clock jitter). We have to capture all measurements, as numbers and scope shots into a document, spreadsheet, or other document. We also have to document all the modifications (mods, re-work items) that we had to make to allow the proto board to be working and what changes we have to make to the schematics for proto-2. Some of the functional tests we perform together with firmware and FPGA engineers in the lab, the stress test is sometimes run by dedicated test engineers, while the VRM circuit validation is usually performed by power supply engineers.

We also have to power cycle the units thousands of times, making sure it starts up and initializes correctly every single time. A power-cycle test consists of remotely controlling the main power source to turn it on, then wait for the console boot messages to conclude, then turn the power off, then turn it on again, in many cycles. We need at least a thousand consecutive successful cycles to determine a test pass condition.

We have to "run traffic" or run applications that stress the interfaces and processing elements to make them consume and dissipate full-power level. For processors, a "TDP tool" might be available, X86 systems that have graphics outputs can run third-party "3D benchmark" software, while most embedded hardware can run custom Linux software. In Linux we can use either the production test program, a diagnostic software, or manual commands typed into a Linux command line. Any RAM type memory interfaces need to run a memory test (read/write in varying patterns), which is deemed a success if it runs for 48 consecutive hours without errors. The memtest checks for board signal integrity issues and DRAM chip fabrication issues.

If any item on the design validation test fails, we have to make alterations to the proto board and retest, making sure it is fixed. Measurements have to be captured in tables, and the value and the pass/fail condition have to be indicated. Lab testing at room temperature on a single unit are suitable only for functional testing, for example, to see if the unit loads the right operating system, or whether it produces the right sequence of events under ideal conditions. To check design reliability, which includes interface signal integrity, we have to test multiple units in temperature extremes and with margining for many hours. Margining is done for the VRM output voltages as well as utilizing on-die eye scan on SERDES links (that is basically an eye margin scan). The reliability test should reach into the combined ten thousand hours of run-time, when multiplying the units tested with the hours each run at temperature extremes. In most cases this is achieved only at the end of the pre-production run.

A design works if it works statistically. A single unit passing 99% of the data through a SERDES interface at room temperature is not a design validation. Some units will likely fail intermittently while the customer is using it, unless we tested several units in temperature chambers with margining and they all passed, with a margin. A margin is required to cover production unit variation and aging. The SERDES links have to pass not at 99% bandwidth but with a 10e-12 BER. That is 99.99999999990%. In some cases, we might be okay to pass it with 10E-8 or with 1E-4 when FEC is used, on every unit in the full temperature range, but anything lower is an unreliable product. The PVT variation with aging can vary the BER from unit to unit and over time by three orders of magnitude. For SERDES link DVT this test and this passing criteria should be included.

Test items:

- Access every device manually (dead/alive test), document each.
- Initialize every device.

- Initialize every port and run traffic (full function test).
- Run the system with the top-level application or in stress-test mode, utilizing multiple modules and interfaces, force to dissipate power. Measure thermals (I2C temperature sensors logged by Linux app, and thermocouples logged with laptop app), first on the bench, then in an environmental chamber. Thermocouples need to be attached to several board locations as well as into ASIC heatsinks through drilled holes touching the ASIC lid.
- Run the factory test and programming script, see if it can run on it.
- Measurements:
  - Every voltage rail (off) resistance to GND with multimeter.
  - Every voltage rail (on) voltage measurement with multimeter.
  - Every voltage rail needs measuring load transient response, and ripple noise under load, after tuning, and Bode plot phase margin. These measurements and the tuning will likely be done by a VRM engineer or FAE on a "power board".
  - Measure clocks for level and monotony.
  - Measure SERDES clocks for phase noise RMS jitter.
  - Measure the level and rise time on slow I2C and SPI buses.
  - On-die eye scan width/height results for chip-to-chip links and external ports. If the eye is bad, then we have to tune the transceivers through software.
  - External connector TX port signal eye measurement through test fixture to oscilloscope. If the eye is bad, then we have to tune the transceivers through software.
  - PDN impedance profile measurement with low-frequency VNA. If the impedance profile does not meet the target impedance line, then we have to make adjustments. If the issue is at low frequency, then we have to work with the VRM engineer to tune the VRM, then re-measure. If it is a bulk decoupling issue, then we can solder on extras. If it is a higher frequency issue, then it is likely design change with MLCC capacitors but the proto will likely work enough to do functional tests on the bench.
  - Trace losses per inch, on loss coupon with VNA, or collect loss data from PCB fab vendor.

16.10 MECHANICAL TESTING

Shock and vibration testing is where we check if anything moves inside the unit that can cause it to stop functioning. This is performed by test engineers or mechanical engineers, usually in an external test facility or contractor. The test setup is extremely noisy, and it is not hosted in an office building. There is also the packaging testing, which means the product is placed in shipping boxes that are tested by dropping them repeatedly. These shipping boxes are custom designed for each product, using cardboard and foam materials, in complex 3D shapes.

17 Measurements

We perform measurements during the prototype board bring-up phase for diagnosing bugs, during the design validation to collect data, during transceiver tuning as a feedback, and sometimes in production for debugging failing units. We also measure SI test boards to obtain material data that we can use in later design projects. With oscilloscopes (scopes) we measure signals as voltage versus time diagrams, with vector network analyzers (VNAs) we measure PCB traces as frequency-domain S-parameters, with signal analyzers we measure derived properties of periodic signals as numbers. Scopes can also extract numbers from the diagrams. The result of a scope or analyzer measurement is a screen image, the result of a VNA measurement is a screen image and an S-parameter model file. The prototype board is referred to as the device under test (DUT). Most of this chapter is about high-frequency measurements.

Most high-end measurements involve impedance-controlled 50 Ohm coaxial cables and connectors. Up to a few hundred megahertz we use BNC connectors. Below 18GHz we usually use 3.5mm standard coax or 3.5mm "SMA" connectors. The ones that are done up to 40 Gigahertz use 2.92mm coax connectors, where the inside diameter of the shield is 2.92mm. The 2.4mm connectors are used up to 50GHz, 1.8mm connectors up to 65GHz, 1mm to 110GHz. All of these coaxial connectors have the same outside diameter and hex nut size, but they should never be mated together to avoid damaging them. They have to be tightened with torque wrenches, which ensures that we apply sufficient force, but not too much force. Cables used for VNA and high-speed oscilloscope measurements are special high-frequency coax cables with accurate impedance control, excellent shielding, and low DCR, usually costing hundreds to a few thousand dollars apiece.

Often we use probes, fixtures, and adapters between the instrument and the DUT, which distorts our measurement. We use them to provide access to the signals, while maintaining better fidelity than we would get without them. Internal signals are accessed through probes, external signals are accessed through fixtures for high-speed or through probes for low speed. For oscilloscopes we use passive or active (buffered) probes, soldered-down micro coax cables, or cabled passive fixtures. The probes are well known, but also explained later. The passive cabled fixture used for external signals has a standard connector (like QSFP or HDMI or backplane) that connects to the DUT and fans out the signals through thin coax cables into coax connectors, which we can connect through a thick coax cable to the oscilloscope. Oscilloscope measurements cannot remove the fixture or probe effects from the measurement results with any software processing, while VNAs can to an extent. With power VNAs we normally use injection transformers, wide-band amplifiers, and soldered-down micro coax cables. We can calibrate out their main cabling and amplifiers, but we often fail to remove the effects of the soldered-on micro coax cables above ~50MHz; this we have to live with. With signal VNAs we either use wafer probes, native coax connectors of the DUT, or rigid test fixtures. A rigid fixture has a PCB instead of a cable, which is designed with RF microwave techniques. It connects to the main cable through coax connectors. A rigid test fixture is needed for VNA measurements because a flex-cabled fixture will have too severe discontinuities. For signal VNAs the main coax cable is calibrated away with an eCAL, a wafer probe with the main cable might be calibrated away with a passive cal substrate, and the rigid fixture can be de-embedded from the measurement with proper processing software. SI test boards contain their own de-embedding structures, which we use to remove the connector launch effects up to the main coax connector.

The measurement bandwidth is limited by the probing loop by any parasitic capacitances or inductances and by any waveform post-processing algorithms. High-frequency probes keep the signal and ground wiring very close to each other consistently. In the end, the ultimate limit is the design's signal-ground pin pitch. The same physical PCB structure will have a higher data pass

DOI: 10.1201/9781032702094-17

through bandwidth than a measurement bandwidth because for measurements being "analog" we need better accuracy than for passing digital signals. For low-speed digital signals we typically need a test setup bandwidth of at least 2.5 times the data rate to be able to see fast edges produced by the 5th harmonic of the Nyquist (half baud rate). For SERDES links the standards usually do not even specify the frequency-domain channel requirements above the baud rate (or half baud rate), for our VNA measurements. When capturing SERDES eye diagrams in time domain with an oscilloscope, we still need the 3rd or 5th harmonic of the Nyquist to pass through the setup. For time domain signals the bandwidth limitation of the test setup means any higher frequency components are shown as lower amplitude than they really are, distorting the waveform. For frequency domain, the test setup bandwidth means the right-side portion of the curve above the bandwidth limit is erroneous and should be ignored—not the whole curve, only the upper portion goes bad. If post-processing algorithms are also applied on the measurement, like VNA fixture de-embedding, then the bandwidth might get even lower than the one caused by the probing arrangement. Our unique test setup's bandwidth is usually lower than the instrument's advertised bandwidth. All measurement results have to be assessed while keeping the likely bandwidth in mind.

A sanity check is an important part of any measurement and test setup. Once we set up the instrument, we have to check it by itself or by using a known good source or test fixture, whether it shows a realistic baseline. For example, if a power VNA setup shows a 2 milli Ohm impedance floor, then we proceed to measure our prototype that is expected to operate below 0.5 milli Ohm, then after the measurement we would erroneously report that our board has a high 2 milli Ohm PDN impedance. Similarly other measured variables or waveforms like voltages, amplitudes, impedances, return loss, and insertion loss curves have expected baseline (floor) values. The baseline must have room for imperfections of our prototype DUT. When disconnected, a power VNA setup has to have a less than 100 micro-ohm impedance floor, a signal VNA should show less than -20dB return loss using a through-cal unit, an oscilloscope should have less than 1/10th as much noise as the signal we are expecting. The frequency range where it is true is our bandwidth. Then if the instrument is showing that it is not producing garbage by itself, we can start probing our prototype DUT. After that, again we have to do another sanity check to see if the measured results make sense because something might be blocking our signal or the level is scaled or parasitics are distorting it. For example, if someone asks me about what the time is, then I look at my watch that displays 79PM, then before I would tell the other person that "it is seventy-nine PM in the afternoon", I have to pause and realize my watch is broken, it should only show between 0 and 12PM, then try to fix it or report back that I cannot provide the time yet. The same goes for oscilloscopes, VNAs, and other instruments that might provide hard to understand types of parameters. This is why the person performing the setup/calibration and the measurement has to check at each step if the numbers make sense. This requires expertise, not an untrained intern.

17.1 CLOCK MEASUREMENTS

Basic CMOS/TTL clock signals need to be measured with a regular 200MHz+ oscilloscope and an active probe or ground spring. We have to verify that they reach proper logic levels and their edges are monotonic. If the clock's rising edge is not monotonic while the voltage is rising, then it can cause some register bits in digital chips to step twice, while other bits will step forward once, driving the device into an undefined state.

The differential reference clock signals (typically 50 to 600 MHz) that feed memory controllers and SERDES transceivers need to be verified for more parameters besides level and monotony. Even the level and monotony require the use of an active probe and an oscilloscope that has over a Gigahertz analog bandwidth. The probing location has to be close to the receiver die pin, which is unattainable with most large BGA chips that have 1 to 2 inches of package trace lengths, as we can probe on the board only at the BGA fanout via. Due to this package length, we will see an edge

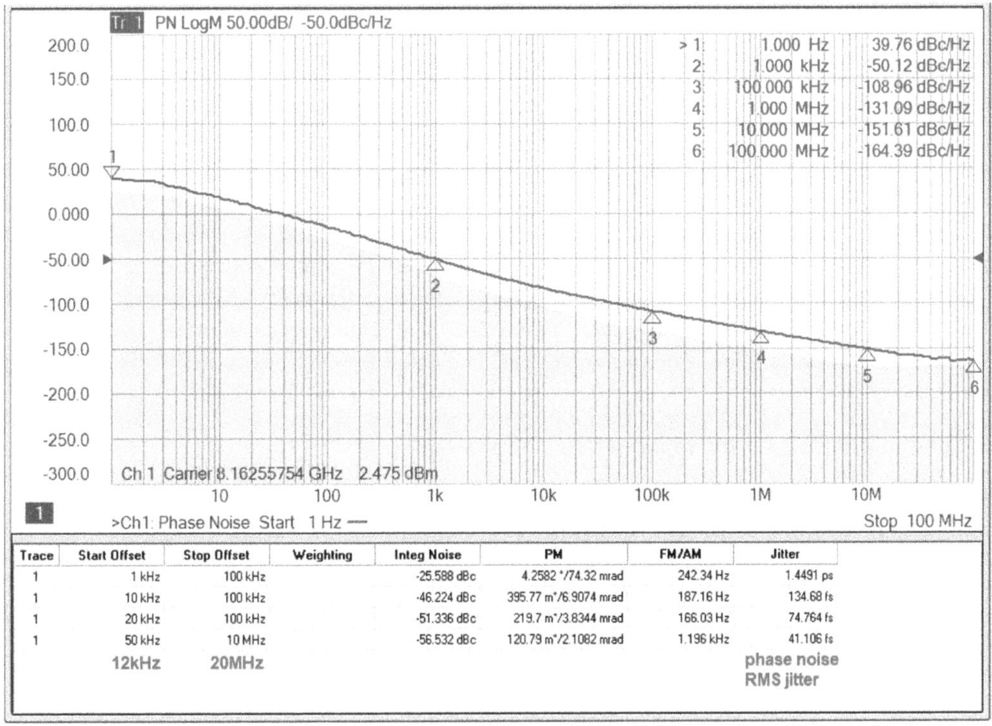

FIGURE 17.1 Signal analyzer (Keysight E5052B) measuring RMS jitter.

monotony issue that is only an artifact of the measurement and not real at the die input, so to be ignored.

For 10G+ transceivers we have to verify that the reference clock jitter is within the ASIC/FPGA chip's specification. This can be done using a "Signal Analyzer". It shows the frequency spectrum of a signal, an amplitude versus frequency curve. It can also compute and extract information (numbers) from it, like center frequency or jitter. We have to connect a 3-SMA-terminal (2-way) "180 degree hybrid coupler" module (also known as combiner, splitter/combiner, S/C, or 180 degree hybrid) between the DUT cabling and the analyzer. Two micro coax/SMA cables will be soldered on the DUT for the diffpair's two legs. We have to use a "power board" prototype, which has the man ASIC depopulated, to avoid double termination with the analyzer's 50-Ohm input. The combiner will convert the two legs of the differential clock signal into a single-ended signal, which can be cabled into the signal analyzer using a good coax cable having SMA or 2.92mm connectors/adapters. It has to support a bandwidth from a few Megahertz to a Gigahertz, have good port isolation, and be equipped with three SMA connectors. It is a small metal box device (module). On the signal analyzer we need to select the "Phase Noise" mode where it computes the "RMS Jitter" using a definitive integral measurement within a frequency band like 12kHz to 20MHz (or whatever the ASIC datasheet requires) on the phase noise curve. The instrument has to display either a text that says "==Noise==" or a table with start/stop offset and jitter values. Figure 17.1 shows an example clock measurement on a signal analyzer.

17.2 ON-DIE EYE SCAN

The only accurate eye-opening measurement of on-board chip-to-chip (not external) SERDES links is the on-die eye scan (capture). Although it is an eye margin scan, instead of an eye scan. For some devices it is done through the host processor and its text Linux serial console; for others it is done using a chip vendor dongle/GUI combination. The dongle accesses the chip through a pin header we designed onto the board, having an I2C, JTAG, or similar interface. In both cases it will appear on our laptop screen, so we can take screenshots for our DVT documentation. For a pass/fail check we can use a reduced eye mask, since it is an eye margin scan, or simply assess whether it is clearly open or not.

Most DDRx memory controllers support read leveling, which is basically a one-dimensional eye on-die capture or eye margin capture, that adjusts the DQS delay in small increments until it scans through the whole bit time to find the two edges of the data valid (eye) window. This can be extracted and displayed in a text console if we enable the BIOS or bootloader software to boot in verbose mode. DDR4 and onwards allows the programmable adjustment of the reference voltage, that we can use to create a full 2D eye scan. This is the most accurate measurement we can do on a DDRx interface because there is no probing effect. The result for DDR3 would look like this:

```
0000001111111111111111110000000000000011 →good
0000000000001111110000000000000000000000 →bad
```

17.3 OSCILLOSCOPE MEASUREMENTS

Recent graduates in electrical engineering must be familiar with the basic use of "Scopes". Oscilloscopes show time domain waveforms and eye diagrams (wrapped waveforms) on a given physical location (probing) on our circuit board. These are voltage versus time curves or rectangular plots. They show the voltage at each time sample and how the voltage changes over time, sample to sample. We can observe signals and voltage rails on our prototype boards with it. Sometimes we need to see the exact bit-timing protocol of a bus in a snapshot, which is a small time duration (like a few nanoseconds) stretched to the full screen width. In other cases we can find it useful to see that the device or an interface port "is doing something" and it is alive, not dead. We can apply automatic measurements to the waveforms, that will read out in number format any voltage levels and relative timing information on a signal or between two signals. The trigger is an important feature of oscilloscopes that allows the capture of a fast event and freeze it on the screen for human observation. In continuous trigger mode we can see a periodic signal constantly realigned on the screen and slowly animate if it changes characteristics like a data pattern. In one-shot or single-event trigger mode we can capture an event that only happens once and fast. Without trigger a periodic signal will be "running" on the screen, and a one-off event (like a startup sequence) will quickly disappear after showing up for a moment. The oscilloscope keeps filling up and overwriting its FIFO memory buffer with waveform samples until the trigger event (a signal crosses a threshold) occurs, then it puts the buffer data on the screen as a waveform plot. Zoom is a useful feature; it helps us save a lot of time in the lab. Scopes with zoom can capture many times the number of samples that would fit on the screen. After the trigger event, we can browse through several level transitions in a zoomed-out mode to find the one relevant to our analysis, then zoom-into that to analyze it in detail. When there is no basic trigger-level differentiation between the events that we want to see and the ones we do not care about, we capture enough transitions to include a large enough number of events. For example, on an I2C bus we want to see when the master accesses a particular device, for investigating issues with that one device, while ignoring when it accesses the other devices.

We can use basic 200MHz oscilloscopes to measure, debug, and verify (design verification, DVT) any low-speed signals like I2C, SPI, UART, or voltage ripple and load transient response of VRMs. We usually verify the signal quality, like edge monotony, signal levels, edge rise times, and ripple amplitudes. Sometimes we check if there is activity on a bus or not; other times we want to decode what communication was going on the bus by displaying one or more bit-times. The zoom and large memory feature can help with this. We capture the whole sequence in zoom-out mode, then once the screen is frozen we can zoom into the specific bits to decode them to 1/0 data from the screen waveform scanning through. Sometimes we want to verify power sequencing timing relations between two or more voltage rails by triggering on one of the rail voltages in a single-shot mode. Sometimes an oscilloscope measurement is picking up a 50Hz or 60Hz AC ground noise. The only way to eliminate that is by using a non-grounded power cable for either the DUT or the scope, but that might not be allowed.

There are different grades of waveform display quality available with different types of probing arrangements. Passive probes that are simply metal and plastic parts put together produce lower accuracy and more distorted waveforms than active probing does. Different types of passive probes also have different grades for accuracy and waveform distortion. The lowest grade is the cheap probes with ground wires and crocodile clips. The next step up is with spring-shaped ground contacts. This reduces the signal-ground loop area from ~10 square inches to about 0.25 square inch. The highest grade is when we solder a micro-coax cable to the DUT, which has an SMA connector on the dangling cable. The soldered part of the cable has an even smaller loop than the spring contact has. The loop area is proportional to self-inductance as well as featuring mutual inductance. Reducing the areas and therefore the inductances is beneficial for accurate measurements. The probe loop inductance distorts the signal, while the mutual inductance induces crosstalk noise into our displayed signal from other signals. This can come from another probe nearby or from any discontinuity that other signals have on the board. Active probes are expensive, they have an amplifier built into the probe head, so the signal source does not have to maintain the signal quality through the long cable to the scope, only up to the amplifier. The signal having to travel and reflect back from the other end of the long cable (that happens with passive probes) is eliminated with this arrangement. Short paths have smaller reflection time constants than long cables have; therefore, they have a higher frequency bandwidth. The active probes maintain a high input impedance that degrades with frequency to near the trace impedance and creates a double-termination with the receiver chip's termination. At the end all probes have an upper usable frequency limit, caused by probing loops, stubs, and amplifier input impedances. For low-speed signals we use high-impedance or un-terminated mode on the oscilloscope inputs. High-speed signals need a high-impedance (at the signal's 5th harmonic) tap-on active probe or a terminated direct coax connection to the oscilloscope with the original load chip/board removed.

Any impedance-terminated on-board high-speed signals should be measured only at the load chip near the end termination using a high-impedance probe and scope input, or with a 50 Ohm terminated input with the original receiver ASIC depopulated (called a "power board"). This kind of measurement typically happens while measuring 50 to 600 MHz clock signals for DVT. When a reference clock is measured for jitter on a signal analyzer we use the power board, but when we measure other clock parameters we do it on a fully populated and initialized board. It is very important to measure them only on a fully initialized board, with already configured FPGAs and booted OS-drivers because the firmware usually alters the termination arrangements to the final intended scheme, so without the firmware the termination might be incorrect. Signals above a few Gbps should be measured only inside the load chip with on-die eye capture.

We do three types of scope measurements; quantitative measurements, digital bit or level decoding, and "dead or alive" checks. The quantitative measurements require accurate -enough probing to be used. For voltage rail ripple, this would be a soldered-down micro coax cable. We often measure switching ripple and load transient response on voltage rails. For chip-driven digital signals it would be usually active probes touching down near the receiver chip's pins, but in a few exceptions we can use passive probing. If the signal is slow and not terminated, then we can use passive probes or soldered-down micro coax cables, while the scope input is set to high-impedance mode. If the signal is terminated, but runs at no more than a few hundred Megahertz and the load chip is depopulated, then we can also use soldered micro coax cables (at the receiver chip's pins), while the scope input is set to 50 Ohm terminated. In some cases, a zero ohm series resistor or a parallel termination resistor can be removed to eliminate double termination and make the cabled passive probing usable. Accuracy is needed when we want to determine signal quality. For example, exactly how much overshoot we have, how much time it takes for the signal to cross the logic threshold (transition delay), to capture eye diagrams, or to see whether the clock edge is monotonic or not. For SERDES signals, the accuracy of the active probes is limited, they cannot be used for design verification in tap-on arrangements above 1/10th of the listed frequency range due to input impedance degradation and double termination. With directly connecting signals from special I/O connector to coaxial test fixtures to the oscilloscope's internal terminated receiver, we can measure accurately up to the instrument's listed full frequency range. For digital data decoding we can afford to have extra distortions as long as they do not completely move the middle of the bit time to the other logic level. We can decode digital bits up to 100MHz with any type of probing. Faster buses and SERDES links can be probed for bit decoding with active probes up to the probe's listed full frequency range. Dead/alive checks can be done with ground-lead probes up to a few hundred Megahertz, with spring contacts up to 1GHz, with tap-on active probes up to the probe's listed full frequency range. Dead or alive checks are often very useful when debugging a prototype. For example, if we want to know whether a chip is working internally, we can look at its outputs and see whether it sends any digital signals out on any of its output interfaces. Sometimes we have a particular port or link not detecting a link from software, so the first thing we check is which link partner is sending or not sending anything out. If it is toggling then it is alive. It acts as digital, GHz-speed heartbeat signal, that tells whether the "patient" is alive.

With oscilloscopes we want to see the waveforms as they really look, so we need the scope to have an A/D converter sample rate at least 10 times the baud rate of the signal and an analog bandwidth at least five times the half baud rate (5th harmonic, 2.5x the baud rate). We display high-speed SERDES and even DDR memory signals as eye diagrams, disregarding each bit's unique look—we are just looking for the worst case on overlapping bits. High-speed scopes should have a serial data wizard software or similar for setting up the capture and display of eye diagrams. Sometimes protocol specific wizards are used, like PCIe or SATA. The scope needs to know the data rate by the user entering it. During these measurements the scope is acting as a SERDES receiver with its own clock/data recovery (CDR) circuit, that is the only way to align the eye diagram edges of degraded high-speed signals and to know the exact data rate that is affected by clock generator tolerance. CDR is used instead of level trigger on these high-speed eye diagrams. The recovered clock goes through a PLL inside the scope to stabilize it and to be able to measure and display the input signal's deviation from the averaged clock rate, called jitter.

We can use high-speed (20-50GHz analog BW) oscilloscopes for rough debugging, to decode bus protocols, or to see if the transceiver tuning attempt from software had any effect or not. For example, on a PCIe bus we can monitor the TS1 ordered sets to see the link training status. This is called a qualitative measurement, not quantitative with signal quality like in DVT. We can also use these high-speed scopes for quantitative measurements of SERDES links, but only on external connectors like HDMI or QSFP ports. This is done using a breakout adapter fixture, like the one in Figure 17.2. We plug the fixture into the external I/O connector instead of the intended external device. In this measurement the scope and its termination replace the RX chip completely,

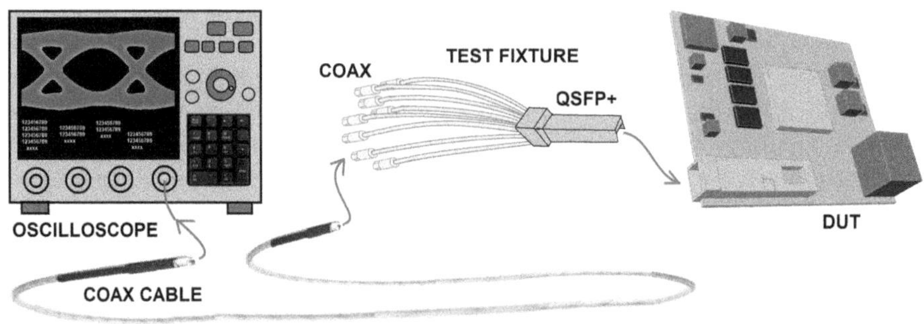

FIGURE 17.2 External port compliance test with an oscilloscope and a QSFP+ fixture (sketch).

preventing a double termination and splitting of a transmission line—this way we get a compliant channel. During this measurement we can verify whether our board provides standard compliant output signal at the attachment point (a "legal" line at the connector for compliance test) or we can tune our TX FFE or pre-emphasis to meet the requirements or to maximize margins. We have to put the SERDES into PRBS mode so it keeps sending stressed signals without a link partner present.

17.3.1 Tap-On Measurements

It is called a tap-on measurement when we have an active chip to chip SERDES link and we are attaching a probe to tap on the signal. This is demonstrated on the sketch diagram in Figure 17.3. These measurements are done using high-speed scopes and active differential probes (with built-in unity gain amplifier/buffer) and usually with solder-down tips to reduce stubs and provide access to small fine pitch components like AC-caps. The alternative is using "browsing probes", but they can introduce additional noise as the contact is unstable, unless they are held by solid probe holders and not by hand. The solder-down tips are on a very small adapter with a tiny wire (1/4 inch long) soldered on the proto board (DUT), usually on top of a pair of AC-capacitors or fanout vias. We cannot probe under the BGA in most cases because it is usually backdrilled. Clocks are usually not backdrilled, and Layer-(N-2) routes are also not backdrilled in case both end parts are on the top side. These probes are supposed to have high impedance to avoid creating a double termination. Unfortunately, at Gigahertz frequencies this input impedance diminishes into the hundreds of Ohms, which creates a strong double termination together with the receiver chip in our design. The double termination limits usable measurements to 1/10th of the advertised bandwidth of the probe, while we can perform data decoding or dead/alive measurements up to the full bandwidth. The 1/10th bandwidth has to be larger than the 5th harmonic of the half baud rate, or in other words we can measure signals that have a baud rate no more than 1/25th of the probe's advertised bandwidth. This will still have more than 10% inaccuracy. The soldered-on probe also adds a 0.25- to 0.5-inch-long stub by splitting the signal path or transmission line. Both of these effects distort the signal on the board so much that the measurement is usually not suitable for design verification (DVT) but only for debugging or qualitative (not quantitative) checks. We can check if a device is dead or alive (sending data or flat lined), we can decode the low-level protocol (like PCIe TS1 ordered sets) to see what state the link training is stuck at and why, or we can check whether the software engineer's attempt to change TX equalizer settings take any effect on the signal or not. Sometimes there is another register somewhere that needs to be enabled to allow the equalizer alteration.

17.3.2 TDR Measurements

Time domain reflectometry (TDR) can show how the channel's (PCB traces, connectors, vias, AC-caps) impedance changes as the test signal travels through the channel or how far (propagation delay or distance) the path ends. It is an impedance versus time plot. TDR is a built-in feature of some high-speed oscilloscopes. We can perform single-ended or differential TDR measurements,

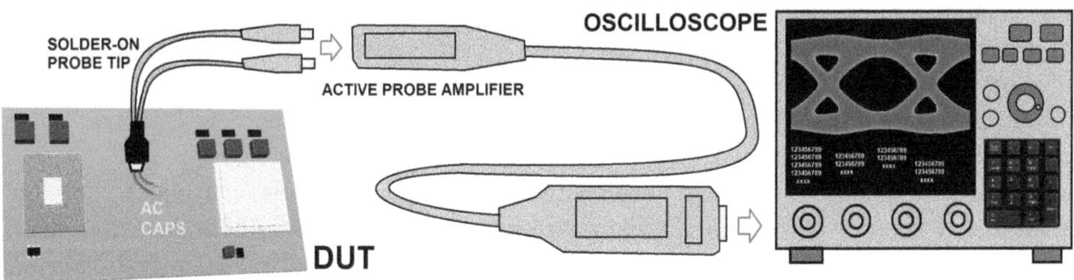

FIGURE 17.3 Oscilloscope used in a tap-on arrangement for debugging (sketch).

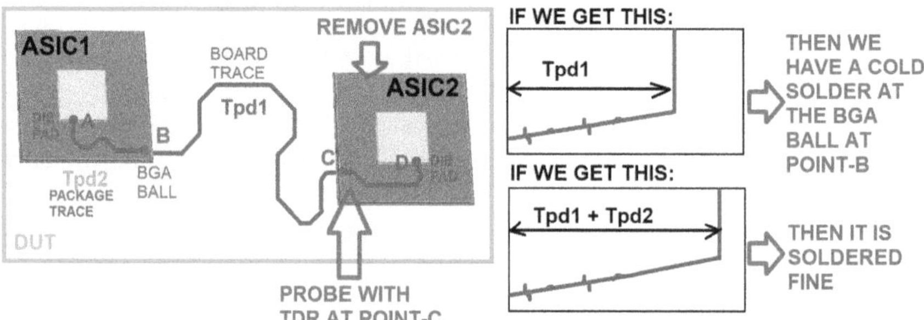

FIGURE 17.4 Using TDR for debugging cold solder (sketch).

using passive well-grounded probes, in a one-port setup. The results are similar to what was described in Chapter 11, "Signal Integrity". We normally perform TDR testing for two reasons, and on most projects this is never done. The first reason is to validate the design quality, to see how much the impedance deviates from the nominal value caused by vias, connectors, fanout structures, and discontinuities. The second reason is to find where the open circuit is located on a faulty board, which is not a design validation but more of a repair debug task. During prototyping we often get badly soldered boards, and we have to provide some proof to the manufacturing engineers about which component and which pin was not soldered properly so they can adjust the stencil design and the thermal profile next time. If the signal cannot pass through a certain point, then it gets reflected back and we get a "wall" on the TDR curve—either at the very end or somewhere closer. We can calculate the length or distance to that wall based on the propagation delay. From the layout viewer we can determine the trace lengths. Let's say our trace has a 6" route (meaning 1ns delay) to an AC-cap, then another 3" (or 0.5ns) route to the end. If we see the wall is at 1ns, then we know the signal did not pass through the AC cap, but if we see the wall at 1+0.5=1.5ns then we know it has reached the end.

In a more practical case, with large BGA chips, if the SERDES channel has failed a functional test, then we remove one of the ASICs, then TDR the trace from its pins towards the other ASIC that is still on the board. This is demonstrated in Figure 17.4. Then let's say we have a 6" trace to the ASIC1, and the ASIC1 BGA has a 1" package length trace (1/6ns=0.17ns). The same principle applies, if we see the wall at 1ns then the signal is stuck at the BGA package pin, meaning the BGA pin has a cold solder; on the other hand, if we see the wall at the 1+0.17ns=1.17ns mark then it means that the TDR signal has reached the silicon die and the BGA pin is soldered fine. If it is fine, then it means we should have removed ASIC1 and not the ASIC2, but it is too late for this unit to find the root cause.

17.4 SIGNAL VNA MEASUREMENTS

Vector network analyzers (VNAs) are used for frequency domain measurements of passive channels (used for SERDES links), like PCB traces, or even for power distribution networks (PDNs) by some digital hardware engineers. RF engineers use VNAs for other purposes that are not discussed here. In any case, the result of the measurement is a set of S-parameter curves saved into a Touchstone file. S-parameters were discussed in Chapter 11, "Signal Integrity", being input-to-output voltage-ratio versus frequency curves in 2D.

To measure the quality of our high-speed SERDES link traces, we use a 4-port VNA with an upper frequency limit of 40 to 70GHz. The instrument bandwidth has to be higher than the half baud rate, ideally higher than the baud rate. The frequency range where the third and fifth harmonic of the signal would pass through is usually not needed for SERDES channels, as it was commonly done on lower speed signals or even oscilloscope measurements. For 56Gbps PAM4 signals the baud rate is 28GHz, half that is 13GHz, a 40GHz VNA setup can handle that well. For 112Gbps PAM4 the half baud rate is 28GHz, a 40GHz VNA can still handle that but not exactly up to the full 1x baud rate.

Signal VNAs are used with either wafer probes or with compression coax connectors designed into the DUT. The wafer probes can be used on SI test boards or on product design boards if they meet the DFT having GSSG landing patterns. Wafer probing 1mm BGA pads work only up to ~35GHz. Above that we can still measure SI test boards designed for material characterization or for design strategy characterization. We could modify our product design by removing the ASIC footprints and instead design in some 2.4mm, 1.8mm or 1mm compression coax connectors and manufacture a VNA-version of our prototype with no components soldered down.

17.4.1 Test Setup and Measurement

We have to calibrate every VNA every time before taking measurements. This is to eliminate the effects of the non-ideal characteristics of the VNA's circuits and the cabling, which also changes with aging and temperature. If the VNA was turned off, then we have to calibrate again after startup. Calibration methods are described in the section dealing with Power VNAs. For signal VNAs we often use an eCal module, or maybe a passive SOLT cal-kit (calibration substrate). The eCal module is a small plastic box with coax and USB connectors. It will allow us to calibrate the VNA up to the long coax cable end. That means the coax cable's end becomes the "calibration plane". Anything after that, for example fixtures or probe connectors are not calibrated out; rather, they will be part of the measured model data. We can de-embed them using a probe-vendor-provided S-parameter file after the measurement, or we can have the instrument perform the de-embedding of them in some cases. We can also use a SOLT PCB/substrate cal-kit instead of eCal and deembedding, to move the calibration plane to the wafer probe tip. A "TRL" cal kit can also be used with wafer probes, which contains a through, an open (reflect), and a "line" that is a PCB-trace. We can buy the eCal or a coax cal-kit from the same company that makes the VNA, or a TRL or SOLT PCB substrate cal-kit from the probe vendor.

Another equipment we need is a probe station with differential wafer probes, a microscope, and some high-quality VNA coax cables. These coax cables are precision high-quality pieces, usually costing thousands of dollars each. Two differential wafer probes will have to touch the differential pair signal on our board, one at each end. The boards we design usually have 0.8mm to 1mm pitch BGA components on them, the wafer probes for this large pitch are frequency limited to about 35GHz. We need "micro positioners" (knob-adjustable probe tip holders) in the probe station to attach the wafer probes to, which allows moving the probes with very fine detail. We also need a microscope to be able to see the probe movements relative to the pads and observe a probe touch-down without destroying the probes and the DUT. A slightly wrong move can destroy these wafer probes. The micro positioner is either attached to an expensive sliding-rail probe station (like the GigaTest Labs GTL4060 seen in Figure 17.5) or they can be attached with a magnetic base to a steel plate. The board we measure needs to be securely tied down with a vacuum pump–powered board-holder, or with MagJig tie downs to a large steel plate. All this together is the custom probe station we need to build. Figure 17.6 shows a ready-made probe station from GigaTest Labs. For any magnets to work we need at least a ¼ thick steel plate.

To perform a measurement, we need to secure the board down, then move the micro positioners near the probing locations. The next step is to set up the VNA for the correct frequency sweep, then calibrate the VNA with the eCal module. We have to attach the coax cables in order given by the calibration wizard using the torque wrench. After this we put the wafer probes on the micro positioners, then connect the coax cables to the probes using the wrench. If we choose to use a cal substrate, then we can calibrate the wafer probes to that, then swap it out for the DUT. We can now start making a touchdown attempt using the knobs on the micro positioners while looking with the microscope. When the probe tip appears to move sideways or slide on the pad surface, we are

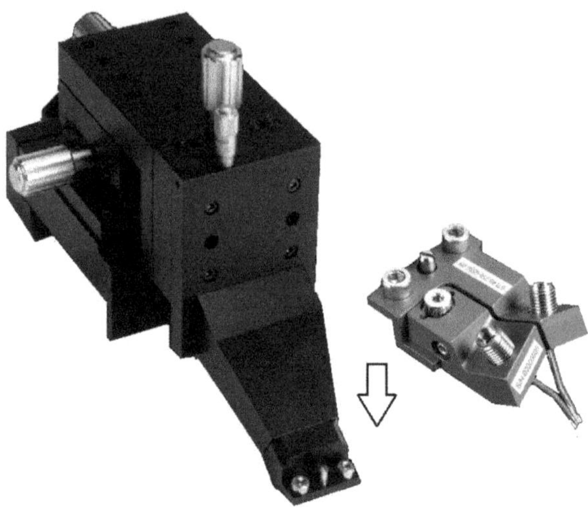

FIGURE 17.5 Micro positioner and differential wafer probe, photo courtesy of GigaTest Labs.

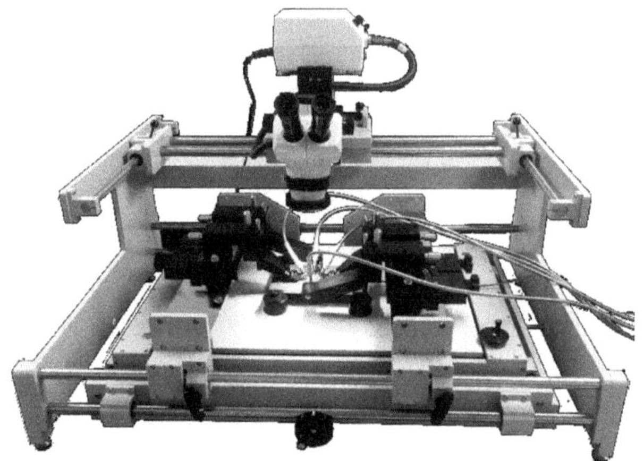

FIGURE 17.6 GTL4040 Probe station, photo courtesy of GigaTest Labs.

supposed to have made contact with the DUT. Then we have to sanity check and debug the touchdown attempt and the measurement to detect any probe landing contact issues and fix them. Then we save the measured data into a 4-port S-parameter file. We sanity check again to see whether the probe dislodged or not. We should redo the touchdown, debugging and measurement one or two more times to make sure we had at least one good measurement. We also have to de-embed the probes from the measured data, either as post-processing for example in ADS or on the VNA instrument itself. We should not leave the probes in touchdown position for more than few minutes as they can be destroyed by vibrations when someone walks by or someone accidentally touches the cables or the bench. Never attempt to attach or detach the coax cables from the probes while the probes are still touching the DUT, otherwise the probes will likely get destroyed. When we are done, we have to lift up the micro positioners, remove the cables with the wrench, remove the probes with the screwdriver, and then finally put the wafer probes away into their boxes safely.

The result of the measurement is an S-parameter file. We have to post-process this on a computer, usually with a custom ADS template. Sometimes we perform probe de-embedding, comparison against standard (IEEE, PCI-SIG, SFF, etc.) limit lines or extract various numbers from them like loss number or any custom data. The S-parameter curves are not very useful by themselves, so we display them with the limit lines to observe compliance and margins, as described in Chapter 11, "Signal Integrity".

17.4.2 Preparation and Design Requirements

To be able to perform VNA measurements of signal traces on our board, we need to design it in such a way that it allows probe landing on both ends. This is a "design for test", or DFT, requirement. We do these measurements for multi-gig SERDES links that are routed as differential pairs. The probing area has to provide a GND-SIG-SIG-GND aka GSSG pad pattern. Sometimes ASIC chip pinouts have diffpairs on their outer row that do not complete the 4-pin pattern because the last ground is missing. In that case we can add an extra row of GND vias in the layout design. For via structure impedance control the extra GND via will be in line with the other vias not with the pads, so we will have to design in an extra fake pad or copper shape with exposed copper that lines up with the BGA solder pads for the probe. The extra via is needed anyway for the impedance, and the extra pad is for probing. Figure 17.7 shows how the extra via and pad looks on one diffpair. Once we are in the lab, it's too late to add extra vias, so some boards cannot be probed. Many chips have irregular constellations in their pinout, basically having a power pin or glue logic pin instead of a ground. These signals cannot be probed, we need to find signals in the layout viewer that have a correct GSSG pattern.

Even if it was designed with DFT considerations, we still have to prepare the prototype board. We have to use a board with no components, which is called a solder sample board. AC caps might need to be soldered on by hand. We should create a probing plan drawing from a layout screenshot before going to the lab so as to be able to find the correct pins while we are in the lab. An example is shown in Figure 17.8.

In some cases, we have a "G-S-S-Nothing" pattern, but we have a GND poor next to it. In that case we have to scratch the GND pour at the 4th probe pin location (like in Figure 17.9), apply flux, add solder, then cut off the top of the soldered bump with a medical scalpel horizontally with a single stroke. We have to repeat this on the actual pins also to make sure all four landing pads have similar material and height. This also applies to probing on through-hole connector footprint pins that have a hole. If we have a through hole footprint like a press-fit connector, then we can prepare it by adding solder into the plated pin hole and on the pad, and cutting the top off, to create hole-free

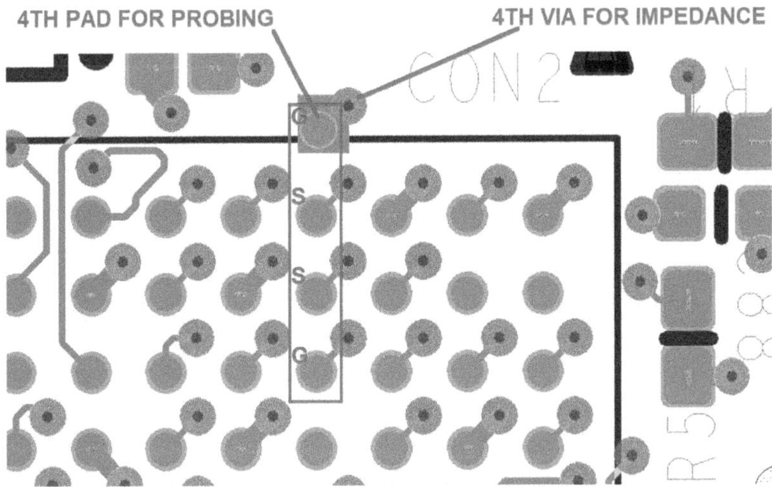

FIGURE 17.7 GSSG landing pattern with added 4th pad (sketch).

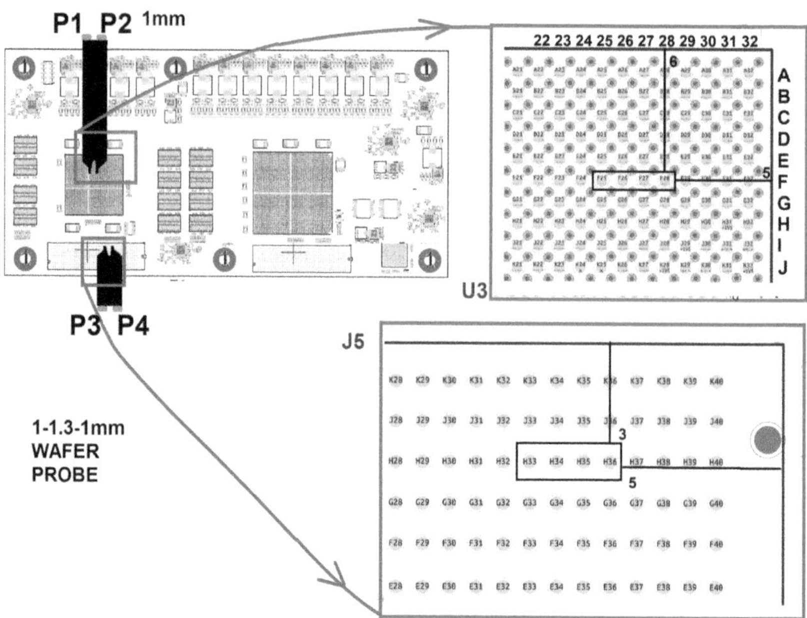

FIGURE 17.8 Probing plan drawing from a made-up floorplan board.

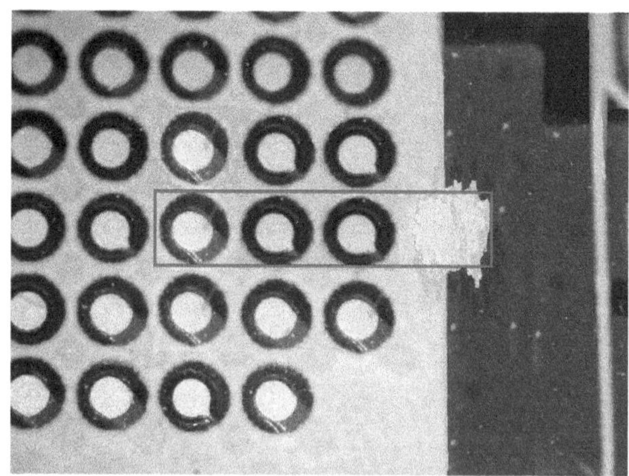

FIGURE 17.9 Extended GSSG pattern using a scratched plane (sketch).

landing pads for the probe landing. Cut-solder pads can be probed a few times, until we start getting deep scratches. Then if we want to probe it again, we have to re-apply the solder to prevent probe damage.

The signal VNA is used for two main things: for verifying traces on prototype boards and for obtaining material or design effect parameters from SI test boards. The DFT for prototypes was described above. The DFT for SI test boards is more stringent. Some SI test boards can use wafer probing pads if the data we expect from them can be processed in a way to eliminate the effects of reflections and noises. For example, when all we need is a single loss number, we can use the Delta-L method with suitable curve fitting. On SI test boards where we are investigating frequency dependent discontinuities, we have to use compression coax connectors (2.92 or 2.4mm) and design our boards with super quality "launches". Basically, where the VNA cables are launching the signal into/from the test board, the transitions have to have super low return loss. This can be achieved by using a high (>10:1) gnd:sig via count ratio. The Fiber Weave Effect has to be eliminated by designing all test traces with an angle. The angle should be at least 20 degrees to push the FWE resonances way above our measurement range. The IEEE P370 standard gives detailed recommendations.

17.4.3 Fixture De-embedding

When we are measuring a board (DUT) with a 4-port VNA, we are really measuring a probe+DUT+probe combination. The purpose of the measurement is to characterize the differential signal path on the DUT only and save it into an S-parameter model file. To get "DUT" from "probe+DUT+probe", we have to remove the left-side probe and the right-side probe from the measured S-parameter. It can be a probe, a test fixture, or some test cables. This can be done by performing the calibration to the probe tip using a calibration substrate kit, instead of calibrating to the coax cable end with an eCal module. It can also be done as a post-processing task on the saved S-par file, which is called de-embedding or fixture removal.

De-embedding is a complex mathematical process, using matrix algebra, performed by a software simulation tool. There are software tools available to do this. They take a measured DUT S-parameter file, the probe or fixture S-parameter files (captured by us, or received from the probe vendor) and create a DUT-only S-parameter file. It can be done on our computer using an SI simulation software tool or in some cases on the VNA itself if the VNA de-embedding software was purchased. The simulator would run an S-par simulation with the DUT and probe files as de-embedding blocks connected in a schematic style model, then it creates a new S-par file. If the instrument does the de-embedding, then it will produce a de-embedded S-par file as the result of the measurement. There are three cases of de-embedding.

In simple regular probe de-embedding, each probe pin is provided with a de-embedding S-par file by the probe vendor. A differential probe has two signal pins and two files. ADS and HyperLynx can handle this, and if we have software on the VNA that can do it too. Figure 17.10 shows how the simulation setup will look.

In reflection-only or open-only de-embedding, when a complex fixture has to be attached to the board, such as a backplane plug-in SMA fixture or an OSFP-to-coax fixture. We have to take a measurement with the fixtures attached to the VNA, but the DUT is not attached to the fixture. Then we save the results into the de-embedding software, then connect the fixture to the DUT and take the real measurement. The VNA will automatically de-embed the first measurement from the second one if the software is available. The concept is shown in Figure 17.11.

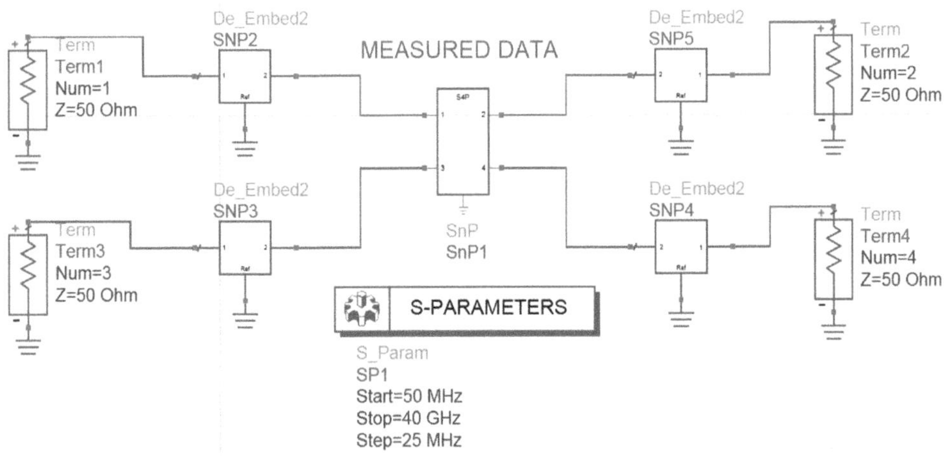

FIGURE 17.10 Regular post-measurement de-embedding in ADS.

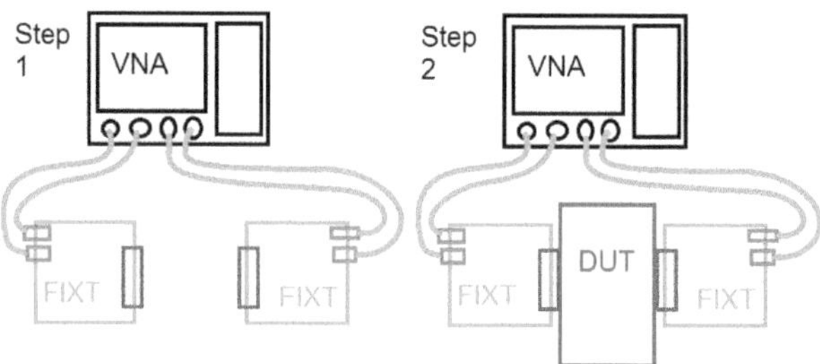

FIGURE 17.11 Reflection-only de-embedding.

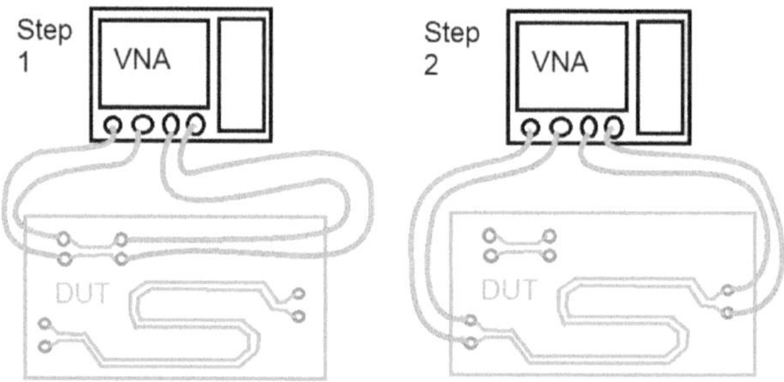

FIGURE 17.12: 2X Thru de-embedding.

In "2X Thru" de-embedding, on SI test boards and loss coupons, a short trace and a much longer trace are provided on the board design with identical coax or wafer-probe-landing connections. The long trace is the one we are analyzing. We have to take a measurement on the short trace first, and we save the results into the de-embedding software. In the second step we measure the long trace, then the VNA will automatically de-embed the first measurement from the second one to provide the S-parameters of the trace section between the two launches if the software is available. The concept is shown in Figure 17.12.

All de-embedding methods have accuracy and bandwidth limitations due to matrix computations with a mix of very large and very small numbers and due to any dissimilarity between the fixture and the fixture model. The de-embedded S-par model's bandwidth will be lower than the raw measurement's bandwidth. The accuracy of both measurements and computations degrades more when our DUT and our fixture have poorer return loss than they should have. It also degrades even more when the fixture model is not similar enough to the real physical probe or the launch pad/trace on the DUT. Instead of loading a vendor file on an eCal-calibrated VNA, we might try to calibrate to the probe tip using a PCB SOLT cal kit. The 2X-Thru is very sensitive to Fiber Weave Effect. We really need the whole SI test board to be rotated or the traces to be routed in odd angles to avoid that. A wafer probe has much poorer return loss than a coax connector, and a digital board has much poorer return loss than an SI or RF test board has. A bad digital design also has much poorer return loss than a good quality design has, which uses high-speed features like impedance controlled vias and reduced over-tuning. The worse the design, the worse the measurement bandwidth, and much worse the de-embedded model's bandwidth.

When we measure the short trace ("thru" or reference) and de-embed it from itself using a 2X Thru computation algorithm, then we should see a flat horizontal S21 insertion loss line. This is how we can check whether our settings and design were correct or not. It is possible that the IL line will be horizontal up to a certain frequency, then it becomes noisy and choppy above that. We can do similar checks on other types of de-embedded measurements too. Above a certain frequency the RL often gets closer to the zero line than the IL does (they cross), then it is another sign of inaccuracy. Above a certain frequency either the IL or the RL might become positive (>0dB), and therefore non-passive. We cannot rely on the portion of the curve above that frequency. This is how we can check the accuracy and the bandwidth of our setup and our de-embedding algorithm. We have to write it down, and any S-par files from DUT measurements have to be ignored above that bandwidth in our reports. With poor setups and poor board designs this frequency might be several times lower than the probe's bandwidth. This might only improve if we choose not to employ any type of de-embedding, then our results will have better bandwidth but a higher uncertainty over the whole frequency range.

If we only need to extract a loss-per-inch data at a certain frequency point above our measurement bandwidth, then we might be better off using a simpler "Delta-L" method that does not require de-embedding. The fitted attenuation (FA) computation might also need to be using more modern algorithms in presence of more return loss. There are several different methods in existence, some are published in IEEE802.3xx standards. The newer ones differ in their ability of overcoming reflections caused by fixture discontinuities. The Delta-L test is done by measuring the short and the long traces separately, computing the SDD21 curves separately, then computing the FA separately, extracting the loss number at our frequency of interest separately, then subtracting the number of the short trace from the number of the long trace. Basically, the application of curve fitting before subtraction ensures that our results will be insensitive to measurement inaccuracies. We can create an ADS or QUCS template for a simple Delta-L computation post-measurement, that takes two S-parameter files and produces our final loss-per-inch number, such as the example in Figure 17.13.

Real digital board measurements with wafer probes usually have worse return loss than SI test boards have that use compression coax connectors. Even the SI test boards have to be excessively over-designed. The best way to achieve accuracy at high bandwidth in both measurement and post-processing algorithms is by following the IEEE370P guidelines for designing the test board. In this case the short trace of a 2XT structure will be at least a few inches long, all traces will be routed in an angle to the fiber weave, the "launches" will be using compression connectors instead of wafer probes and any via transitions will be over-designed with >10:1 ground to signal via count ratio. SI test boards require a lot more purity with much smoother TDR impedance profiles than a digital board channel requires, since they have to pass through precision measurements instead of just a 1-or-0. This can be verified by using electromagnetic field solver programs to optimize the

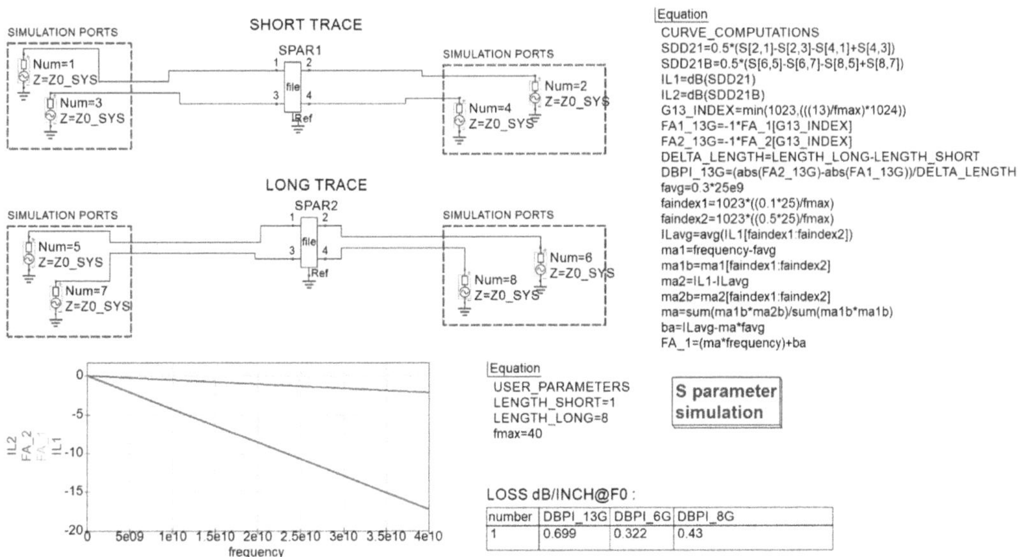

FIGURE 17.13 Delta-L loss extraction in QUCS.

structures, traces, and connector-to-trace "launches". Digital I/O standards often have 5 to 10dB RL requirements at the high frequency end, so SI test boards have to be at least 10dB better than that. We can design SI test boards and measure them ourselves or we can hire a consulting company like Wild River Technology to do it for us. Either way we need to have some understanding on the scope and difficulties of this kind of work. SI test boards might be created for characterizing PCB dielectric materials or copper treatment processes to see how much insertion loss we get per unit length or we might create them for measurement/simulation correlation studies on various isolated single features like vias, connector pinouts, and so on.

17.4.4 Probe Landing Issues

While probing a board with a probe station and wafer probes, we often run into the problem of some of the probe pins not making contact. This happens in most of the cases. This prevents us from conducting a successful measurement. So during the VNA measurement we have to verify whether we have a successful touchdown or whether we have probe landing issues, and we have to fix them before saving the S-par file. We might be spending hours on setting up and conducting the measurement, so we do not want to go back from the lab with faulty data.

In a 4-port S-parameter matrix there are "Insertion" (I), "Reflection" (R), and "Coupling" (C) terms, a total of 16 terms. Their index numbers in the matrix depend on the port mapping, as we can see in Figure 17.14.

We have to verify that the S-parameter curves have the expected shapes, as seen in Figure 17.15 and Figure 17.16. If they do not, then it indicates a probe contact issue. If the shapes of Insertion/Reflection seem swapped, then there is a signal probe pin contact issue. The wafer probe is broken or dirty or one of the coax nuts is not tight. The correct or expected S-parameter values: IL@ Fmin~0dB, RL@Fmin<<-20dB. With contact issue: IL@Fmin<-20dB, RL@Fmin~0dB. First we

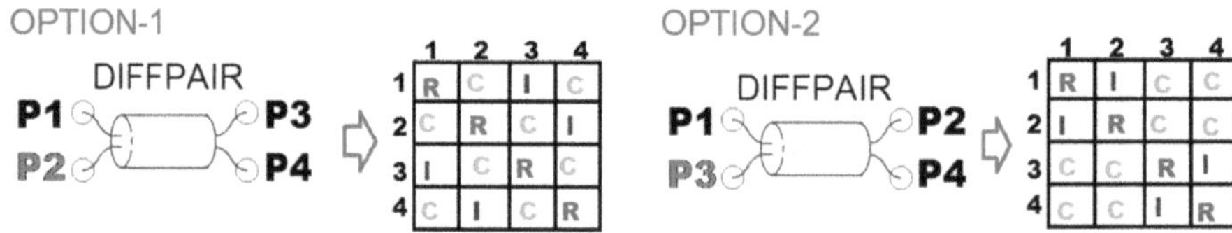

FIGURE 17.14 S-parameter port mapping options.

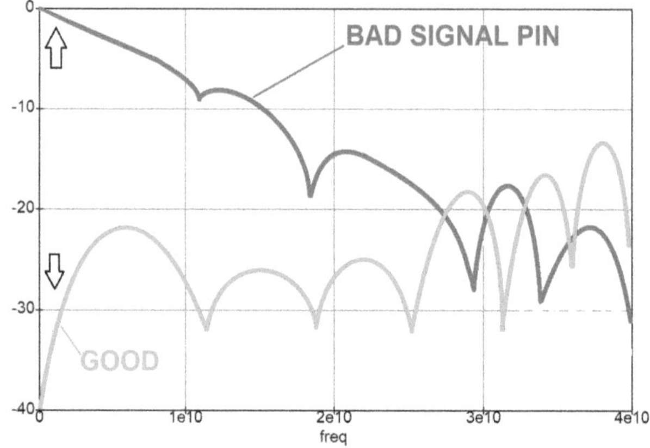

FIGURE 17.15 How RL should look like (sketch).

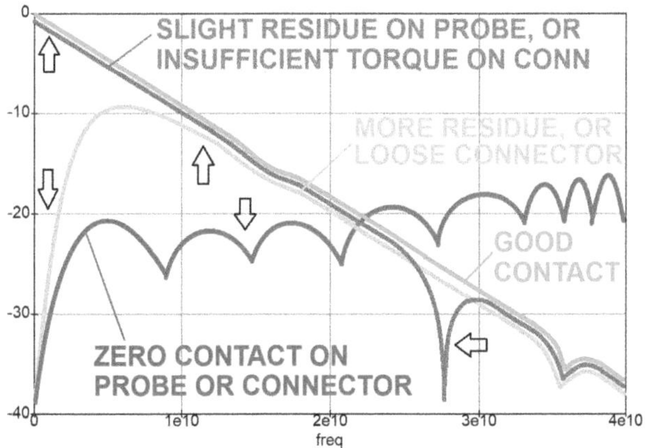

FIGURE 17.16 How IL should look (sketch).

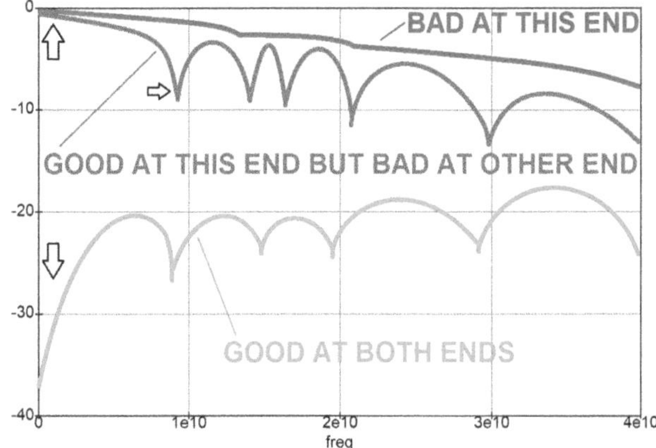

FIGURE 17.17 Signal pin debugging on RL profile (sketch).

check whether we have any issues or not by looking at the four R terms. Basically, all four must have <<-20dB on the left side of the curve. If one does not, then we have any number of contact faults. Look at these curves one by one by hiding the rest of them on the screen.

If we have contact issues, as our curves do not match with the expected shapes and values, then we have to start debugging the test setup and find out which pin has the contact issue. Then we can take action by inspecting probes, cleaning them, cleaning the board pad surface, or tightening the coax nuts. We might have to inspect the probe or the pads under a microscope or re-apply solder on the pads if we used any. We need to clean the probe pin with Q-tips and alcohol, bend it back with a tweezer, or buy a replacement. By touching the probe stem with a pen, it may make contact, changing the curve shape on the display, suggesting a bent pin. We can follow a debugging process step by step as systematic elimination of possible causes.

First, we check if we have any signal pin connection issues or not, using the reflection terms: Keep both probes down, touching the board. Check if Port-1 makes good contact or not with its signal pin by selecting S11 on the VNA. It would tell if port-1 is touching properly or whether the other end of the line is touching properly, depending on which line in Figure 17.17 it is more similar to. If it is similar to the red line, then port-1 failed to make contact. If it is similar to the brown line, then port-1 has good contact, but the port/probe at the other end of the PCB trace is lacking good contact. The green is obviously good. We have to repeat this on the other three ports. This time use S22 for port-2, S33 for port-3, S44 for port-4.

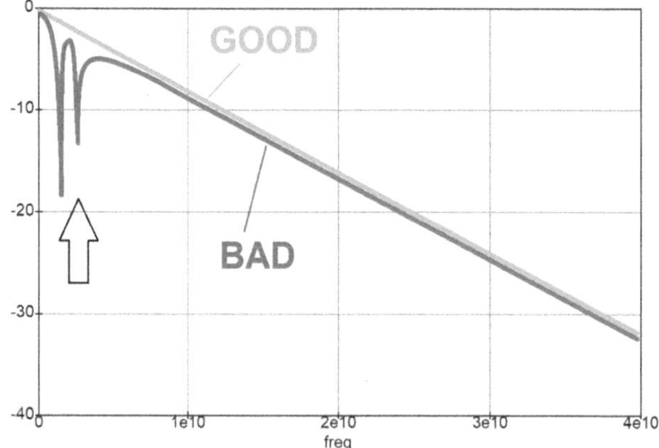

FIGURE 17.18 Ground pin debugging on IL profile (sketch).

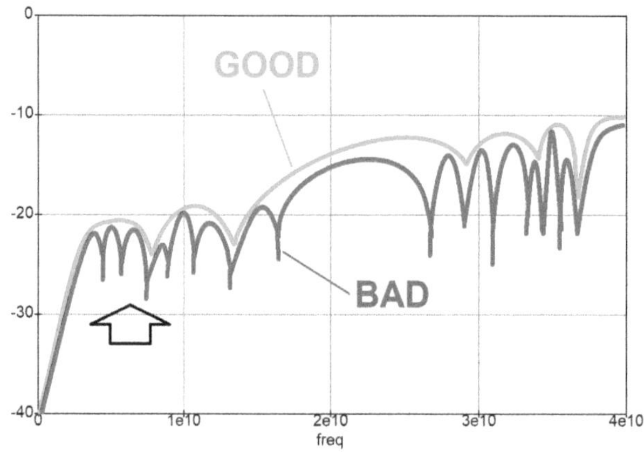

FIGURE 17.19 Ground pin debugging on RL profile (sketch).

Second, we check if we have any ground pin connection issues or not: Keep both probes down, touching the board. On the VNA select the first Insertion term Sxy. The curve should NOT have any big sharp suckouts below 4GHz, as we can see in Figure 17.18. If it does, then port-x or port-y failed to make contact on its ground pin, and we have to check which one. For this we have to look at the two corresponding reflection curves Sxx and Syy and compare them. The one that looks to have higher swinging noise is the one with the ground contact issue, as we can see in Figure 17.19. For example, S33 indicates port-3. We need to redo this check for the other three insertion terms too.

We basically browse through the individual S-parameter views on the VNA, looking for issues, before saving the final measurement S-par file. Start with all the four RL curves, then two of the insertion curves. For this context S21 will show the same issues as S12, with the same two port indexes. In case of the option-2 port numbering we quickly check 11, 22, 33, 44, 12, and 34. If we find any contact issue, then we have to move lift up the probe, move it by X and Y, then touch-down again. If that does not work then try cleaning it and touch down again.

17.5 POWER VNA MEASUREMENTS

We sometimes take power integrity or impedance profile measurements of a PDN with a low-frequency 2-port VNA. The impedance magnitude versus frequency diagram is captured or an

S-parameter file that represents it. These instruments have their lower end of their range into the few Hertz range. It is not that they only do 100M-3GHz instead of 100M to 10GHz; rather, the lower end of the range is lower, for example 5Hz to 1GHz instead of 100M to 1GHz. They also contain software that can display impedance and even allow impedance calibration. We also need a special amplifier or a common-mode transformer.

17.5.1 The Purpose of the Measurement

We can either measure our prototype board to validate that its impedance profile meets the target impedance requirements or we can measure a VRM evaluation board to create a VRM S-parameter model that we can use in a pre-layout PDN simulation (and capacitor selection).

In both cases we have to solder down two micro coax cables near the center of the load ASIC. These cables are originally made for Wi-Fi-antennas with a U.FL connector on one end and an SMA on the other end. They are only about 1.5mm thick. We cut off the U.FL connector and strip the cable under a microscope. With a sharp tweezer, we can separate the shielding wire threads from the core, and cut off about two-thirds of the shield threads, otherwise it would be too thick. Then twist and tin both the core and the shield wires with a solder iron. We can solder the cable end on the smaller capacitor pads or capacitors. In most cases we solder to 0402 capacitors to reduce the probing effect. The cables must be tied down with tape first to prevent movement. These small pads or parts can easily break off and damage the board if the cable is not secured with a Kapton or clear tape first. This should be done under a stereo microscope with a 20 to 40x magnification. Figure 17.20 shows an example digital board with soldered-down micro coax. Figure 17.21 is a similar soldered-on arrangement but for VRM model generation from an eval board. This allows a measurement bandwidth of about 50MHz. The coax cable center conductor retains a ~3mm insulator, so the soldered-down cable will have a loop area of about 4mm2, which has about 5pH parasitic probing inductance. Both cables are connected to the same nets, the center conductor to the VDD pin of the capacitor, and the shield to the ground pin of the capacitor. The two cables are not soldered on the same capacitor but rather two nearby capacitors so as to avoid the test signal bypassing most of the PDN. This is the shunt-through arrangement, where the input and output ports are in parallel with each other and the DUT voltage rail, seen in a schematic diagram. If we used wafer probes on a microscope-based probe station, then we could achieve a much higher bandwidth, although any well-designed board is effective only up to about 10 to 50MHz, and the wafer probe station is harder and slower to use. For prototype measurement, the main ASIC or FPGA/CPU has to be depopulated at the factory or removed; we call this a "power board". The

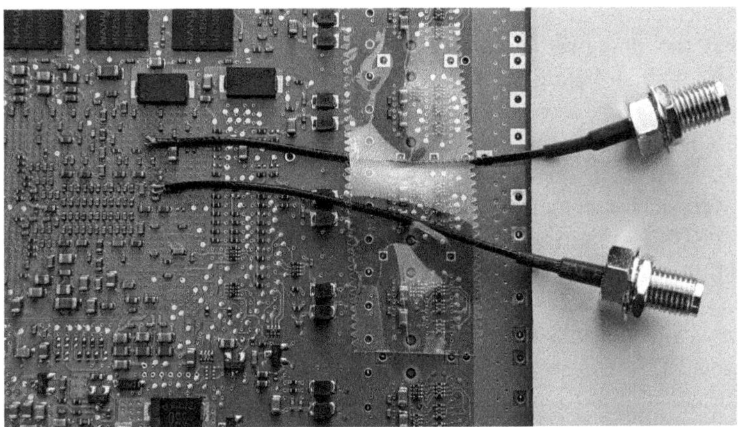

FIGURE 17.20 Digital board prepared for power VNA measurement using micro coax cables.

FIGURE 17.21 Intersil ISL68137 VRM eval board prepared for power VNA measurement using micro coax cables.

board has to be designed in such a way that it will power up without the main digital chip present in normal or in a debug mode.

17.5.2 Test Setup

We can use a Keysight Technology E5061B-3xx or an Omicron Lab Bode-100 low-frequency VNA. There might be other suitable instruments too. In this context "low frequency" means the low end of the range being lower than most VNA's have, below 100Hz. Most VNAs do not go below many Megahertz, so they are not suitable for PDN measurements. For the higher end of the range, the Bode-100 only goes up to 50MHz, the other one to 500MHz. We need to also use a wide-band low-frequency amplifier, like the Picotest J2113A to achieve a low, flat, and smooth impedance/noise floor in our measurement range. Note that the probe connections have a bandwidth up to 30 to 100MHz, so the DUT impedance profile portion above this limit will sit on top of an inductive slope, created by the loop inductance of the solder point and the mutual inductance between the two soldered-on micro coax cables. That is not too bad because our board's decoupling network also does not work effectively above 20 to 100MHz. It is very important to set a logarithmic frequency sampling sweep; otherwise, the lower decades will be averaged out. Usually we set it from 100Hz to 50MHz with a 30Hz bandwidth. The ideal coax cables for this measurement are equipped with 3.5mm SMA, and they have very high-quality thick shielding and low DCR.

We do impedance profile measurements in a 2-port shunt-through mode. The output port provides a test signal, the input port measures the signal amplitude coming through. We need to use a PicoTest J2113A amplifier before the port-2 input to lower the impedance/noise floor. The instrument and cabling setup can be seen with a Bode-100 in Figure 17.22. First, we set up the parameters, then we need to calibrate the instrument using a coax "through" calibration module called a "bullet" for the Bode-100, or an "eCal" module for the E5061B. Then we should do a sanity check by measuring a very low resistance shunt resistor module to see if the VNA displays what we expect. Then we can connect the DUT's micro coax cables to the long coax cables and measure. If the voltage rail is 1.8V or higher, then we need to have the Picotest low-frequency DC-blocks (P2130A) attached between the micro-c ax and the long coax cables. We do the measurement with the DUT powered up, then save the results into an S-parameter file.

In the pre-layout PDN analysis that we do for selecting decoupling capacitors for our schematic, we will use a measured S-par model to represent the VRM. When making VRM S-par models from eval boards, we have to smooth the measured S-parameter from the excessive noise as well as replace the upper frequency range with an ideal inductor's Z(f) slope because above 0.5 to 5MHz

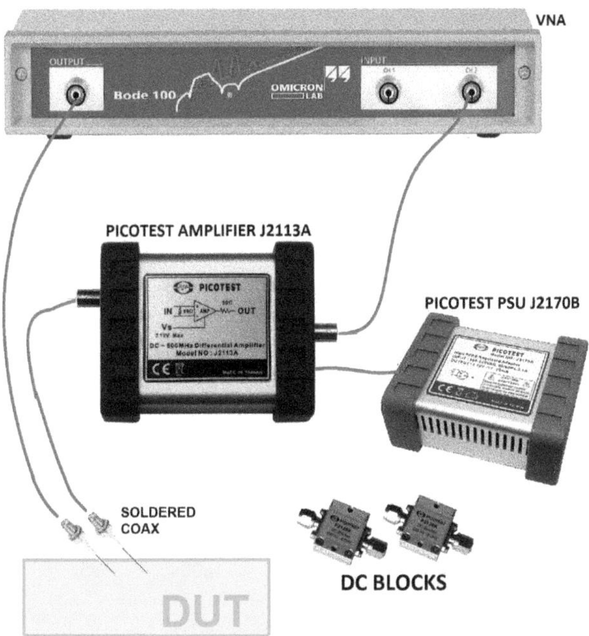

FIGURE 17.22 Power VNA test setup using a Bode-100 and Picotest J2113A (sketch).

the VRM eval board contains elements like power planes and small capacitors that we don't want to carry over into our pre-layout PDN analysis. These artifacts will interact with our capacitor banks in our simulation, creating resonances that will not be present on our custom hardware prototype, leading us to select non-optimal capacitors. The resulting S-parameters are usually very noisy because with very low impedance PDN measurements down to 10 uOhm, we get into the very high dynamic range of 90 to 110dB, where the noise floor of the measurement amplifier is located. All these post-processing operations can be done in the "spar-smoothie" free Excel calculators' package; see the download link in the appendix. An example measured VRM eval board impedance profile and its smoothed version are both demonstrated in Figure 17.23.

17.5.3 Power VNA Calibration

We have to calibrate every VNA every time before taking measurements. If the VNA was turned off, then we have to calibrate after startup. If it was running all night, but it was calibrated yesterday, then we still have to calibrate it again. There are different types of calibration modes and different types of calibration devices. We either use an eCal device or a set of passive modules called a "calibration kit". The kit can be a set of coax modules or PCB modules for wafer probing. Whether we calibrated to the coax cable ends or the probe ends determines where our "calibration plane" is located. Any discontinuity up to that "plane" is compensated away by the VNA instrument. Figure 17.24 shows all the calibration and sanity check options. Signal VNAs can use either the SOLT (short-open-load-through) kit or the eCal. Power VNAs can use the SOLT kit, Impedance-cal kit, or the eCal. For power VNAs sometimes we do not use a whole kit, just a through "bullet" coax module. The easiest is to use an eCal (electronics calibration module), it is a small box that is controlled by the VNA over a USB cable. Sometimes our fixtures and probes are of such bad quality that the calibration attempt might fail, in which case we have to calibrate to the main coax cable end—that always works. Even the thin and flexible micro coax cable attachments can be too challenging for calibration algorithms. After calibration, we can do a "sanity check" to see if the calibrated instrument is able to perform a valid measurement by attaching a sanity check module to the cable, and

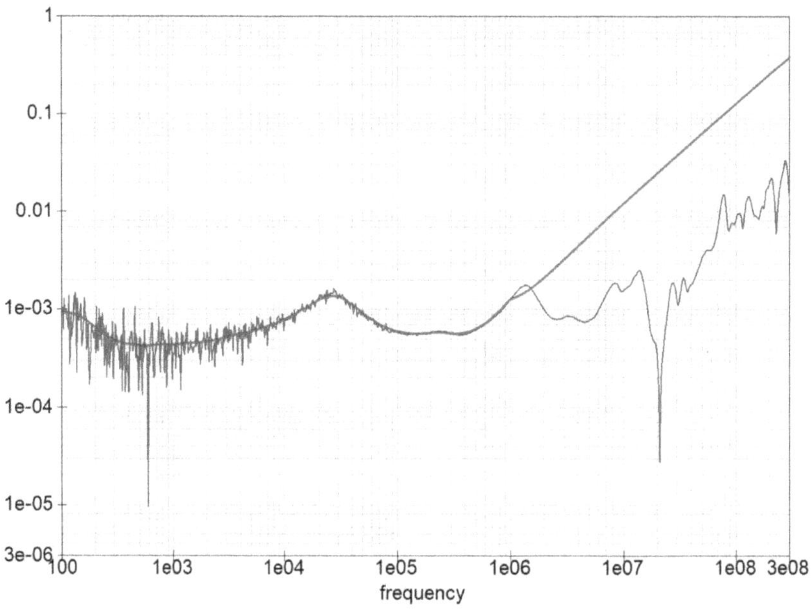

FIGURE 17.23 Measured (blue) and post-processed (red) PDN impedance profiles from a VRM eval board.

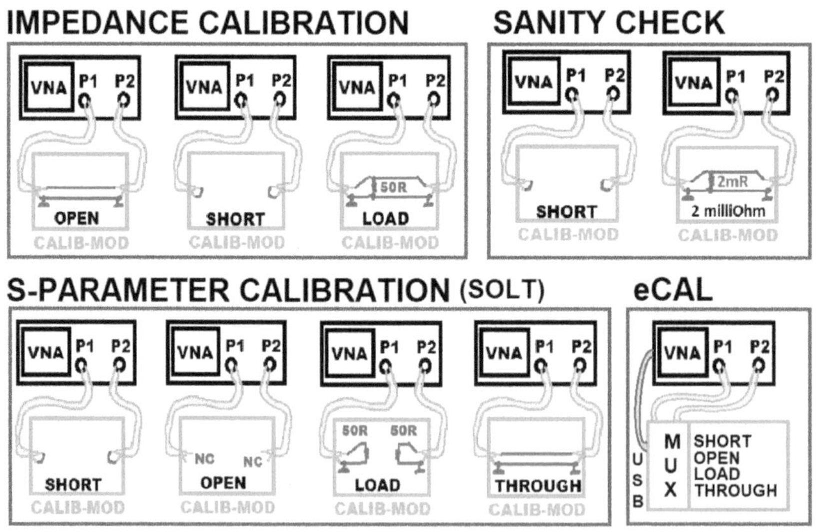

FIGURE 17.24 Calibration modules and modes.

observing the measured impedance profile. If it is all good, then we can perform our DUT measurement and save its results into an S-parameter file for later processing or display on our computer. We can make a simple sanity check module by having two SMA connectors soldered together with a 2 milli Ohm shunt resistor soldered between the center conductor and the shield. This should show a flat 2 milli Ohm resistance more or less up to a few hundred Kilohertz.

17.5.4 Probing Inductance

The probing attachment we use during a PDN VNA measurement has a mutual inductance and a self-inductance. The stripped coax cable with the two solder points creates a loop that has a self-inductance. The two stripped cables next to each other create two loops, which together have a mutual inductance. Even the cable bodies have mutual inductance, depending on shielding quality. Mutual inductance transfers energy, signals, and noise. Both limit the upper frequency range of the measurement by forcing the impedance floor higher on the right side of the curve and suppressing any detail in the upper frequency range. When a short circuit is attached to the VNA cables, then the shunt impedance should be zero, but it displays something larger than zero, that is the measurement limitation known as the impedance floor. We can check this floor in the whole frequency range. It is typically, 10 to 500 micro-Ohms, we need below 100 for high-end digital board measurements. The inductance appears as a rising straight line on the impedance floor going towards the upper right corner at 20dB/decade. Anything under that curve is lost from observation. The goal of the probing is to reduce the inductance by using as small of a solder loop as possible and as dense shielded cables (lowest mutual inductance) as possible. Reduced inductance means the straight line that is limiting our observation is shifted down towards lower impedances, allowing us to see more details on the impedance profile of the DUT.

In an experiment to determine that inductance, partly created by cable shield and partly by the attachment loop, two micro coax cables with a shorted loop at the end were moved around. The cable end was stripped and the center conductor with the ground shield was shorted into a small loop to mimic a DUT attachment. When the two cables were closer, the mutual inductance increased, and the right-side inductive slope shifted upward. Shielding deficiency causes an inductive slope, limiting the measurement bandwidth. Different cable brands have different levels of mutual inductance. We need to test different brands and pick the one with the lowest mutual inductance seen on the VNA check and the lowest DCR of both the shielding and the core conductor as seen on a multimeter.

If we design in some kind of small coax connector (for example U.FL) into the board, then likely we get much worse probing inductance than the soldered one. This is because the connector can be placed only outside of the BGA perimeter, while the solder-on is done near the center of the BGA grid. With outside-perimeter U.FL connectors we get 30 to 100pH, which is much higher than the soldered 5pH. How these options would appear on the VNA are demonstrated on the sketch drawing in Figure 17.25.

17.5.5 VNA Attachments

Depending on the setup arrangements, we get different instrument bandwidth and noise/impedance floor. The impedance floor, or the lowest impedance we can measure, can be checked by measuring

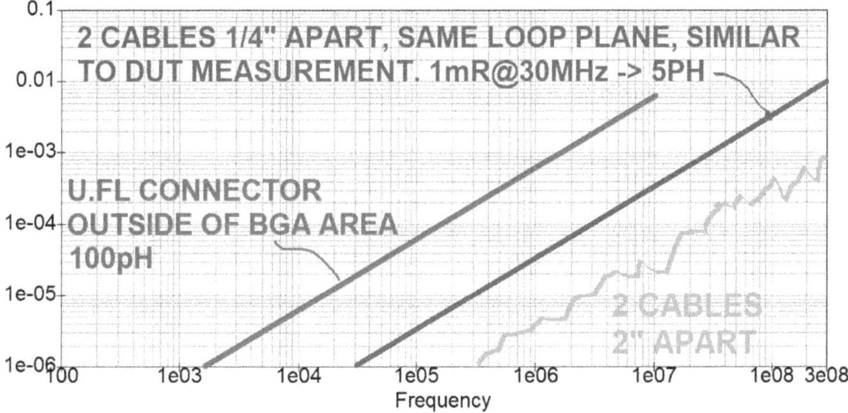

FIGURE 17.25 Micro coax cable mutual inductance (sketch).

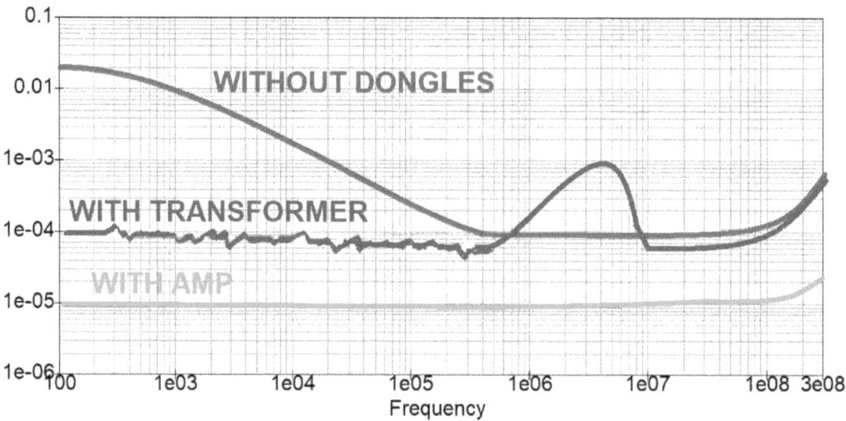

FIGURE 17.26 Impedance floor with different dongles (sketch).

a short. The sketch drawing in Figure 17.26 demonstrates the achievable impedance floor curves with different attachments. With no attachments, by using only the VNA and the cables, we get higher impedance below 1MHz, which prevents us from measuring milli-Ohm range impedances in that frequency range, like VRM effects. If we connect a PicoTest common mode transformer between the DUT and the VNA input, it helps with the low frequency, but we have a bump around 1 to 10MHz. If we connect a PicoTest J2113A amplifier between the DUT and the VNA input, then we get a nice smooth and flat impedance floor way below 100 micro-Ohm in the whole frequency range. The power level also helps lowering the impedance floor and calibration helps removing a noisy right side inductive slope.

18 Manufacturing

The whole point of hardware development is that someday it will be manufactured in larger quantities that our company can sell and deliver to the customers. Even the prototype has to be manufactured in factories. Manufacturing concerns are not only for manufacturing engineers. Hardware design engineers have to understand and interact with the manufacturing process. A design is not an abstract diagram, it is a physical object that is dependent on how it was made. We have to design our boards to be made easily, and we also have to "design" the manufacturing process of every new board design.

18.1 MANUFACTURABILITY

The concept of "manufacturability" and design for manufacturability (DFM) were discussed earlier. The PCB fabrication, board assembly/soldering, device programming/testing, and the system or mechanical assembly all require board design considerations. All of these design aspects require the hardware engineer to work with mechanical engineers, PCB technologists, applications engineers, SMT engineers, and firmware engineers. We present our schematic and layout designs for manufacturability review, and we also prepare documentation in a way that points out potential risk areas. We have to design our boards using the planned manufacturing parameters, and we sometimes have to negotiate them. We have to design our boards to be manufacturable to the extent that it will still produce good signal integrity (product reliability) and marketable feature sets.

The PCB fabricator companies have their capability parameter tables, describing the smallest object sizes they can make. The smallest objects in our design should not be smaller than those. These parameters are, for example, drill sizes, trace width and spacing, drill aspect ratios, drill to copper clearances, annular ring, solder mask expansion, etc.

The assembly of the bare boards with components in SMT soldering, wave soldering, and press-fit has to produce fully assembled boards with a good yield. Yield loss can be caused by open or short circuits (on component pins) and damaged components. We have to design our boards in such a way as to minimize the chances of these issues occurring. The typical assembly-related DFM considerations are in the area of footprint, solder mask, and stencil designs. These are heuristic design ideas implemented differently by different design companies. We also have to design in keepout areas that the wave soldering (if used) and press-fit fixtures will need. We often try to eliminate all parts from the design that would need hand soldering or wave soldering.

The board logic design should be done in such a way that devices can be programmed sequentially, without any catch-22 situations. Every programmable device needs programming port access connected to headers, unless we try to program them from the host device's programming header indirectly. The JTAG chains, power domains, and device dependencies cannot block the programming of blank devices in the factory. We should also allow a good boundary scan test coverage by providing switchable JTAG chains or separate JTAG headers accessing several devices.

Component height limitations by area, mounting hole locations, slide-areas, and clearance areas (frame, spacer) have to be designed into the layout to allow damage-free and short-circuit-free system assembly. The system assembly sequence is designed by the mechanical engineers, but it will inform hardware and board designers about these areas that require implementing area constraints.

DOI: 10.1201/9781032702094-18

18.2 MANUFACTURING RELEASE

We have to get the prototypes manufactured in a small series, and later we will have to prepare the design for larger scale production. Both of them are concerned with the same board files, but production will have tasks to be performed by the manufacturing company rather than the design engineer. The design engineer has to develop procedures for the manufacturing teams and monitor the production setup progress.

The first stage is the PCB fabrication of the bare board. We release the "fab-out files" in our own database and then send them to the vendor with a purchase order, which consists of Gerber files (layer plots) and NC drill files (vias, pins, backdrills), or alternatively ODB+ files. These are generated in the PCB layout tool once the design is done and reviewed. We prepare the "fab notes", either as some Gerber layers or as a separate document, which is a list of technology parameters (object sizes, materials, tools, etc.). These are parameters that we used in the design, and the ones we want the fab company to use for making the board. The fab notes also contain object identification tables. For example, trace width to impedance association, which shows, for example, that any trace found in Gerber plots at 4.1mil width belongs to 100 Ohm impedance control that the fabricator will adjust to let's say 4.2mils to actually meet the impedance requirement. There are also dill size charts and backdrill charts or tables and insertion loss control parameters, all of which are used similarly. Trace impedance and backdrill are layer dependent, so the tables will have different rows per layer. What is fabricated is not exactly what is in the Gerber trace data; rather, it is slightly off, and the association to which is found in these tables. Before we release the Gerbers, we make sure it meets the vendor's or our own DFM guidelines and constraint tables. This is partly done by using the layout tool's DRC feature, and finally it is done by a Valor tool. Then we release our files internally in our database, and the purchasing department sends the data to the vendor with a purchase order. After this the vendor might find capability-related issues and sends us some documentation to clarify or request to change a list of items in our design. This should be checked or implemented quickly by the hardware, layout, and manufacturing engineers. PCB fabrication is almost always performed by a contract manufacturer, called the PCB fabricator company.

The second stage is the PCB assembly (PCA, PCBA, CCA), which consists of soldering and press-fitting of components on the bare boards. The PCBA factory also needs some files generated by the layout tool, these are the pick and place files (with refdes and coordinate for each part), the assembly drawing, and the BOM (bill of materials). The SMD/SMT components will be soldered on the board in a conveyor-belt style SMT production line. This line starts with the bare boards fed in on one end, then the solder paste gets printed on the board through a stencil, then the pick and place machine places all the components on the board from a series of feeders, then finally the boards go through an infrared reflow soldering oven. The part feeders are either large rolls containing a few thousand small parts called "tape and reel" or plastic trays containing a few dozen larger parts. The stencil is an etched or laser cut sheet metal plate, manufactured based on the Gerber files and custom made for each board design. It has small openings to allow the cold solder paste to pass through the openings at the component pad locations. The paste is made of 20 to 50um solder balls mixed with sticky flux. The reflow oven melts the solder balls and when it cools down on the way out they solidify into one piece on each pad. With the exception of very basic boards, we have components on both sides, so the board has to go through the line twice, or go through a second line after it is flipped over. Some parts might be glued down. Any through-hole soldered parts will be soldered on by wave soldering or by solder iron. Any press-fit through-hole components, usually connectors, will be pressed into the board. The pins will be forced into the pin holes using a press-fit fixture and a pressing machine. Soldered boards have to be washed to remove any solder flux residue, then tested using AOI (automatic optical inspection). Component purchasing through the supply chain usually belongs here. PCBA is sometimes performed within the product design/owner company, but usually it is done by contract manufacturers.

The third stage is the system assembly, when the boards are fitted with heatsinks, frames, front panels and other mechanical parts, then placed inside a chassis with other boards and internal cabling. For line replaceable cards or modules, they would be inserted inside a test chassis. This has to be done in such a way so as to avoid damaging components on the board. The board design is supposed to have small keepout areas near mounting holes, so when the assembly worker is trying to position the mechanical parts into their intended location, and it wobbles a little the screws and metal parts will not touch any soldered components. The assembly workers have to minimize the wobble so it stays within the allowed keepout areas. Some chassis types require sliding the board into position, so they have oval slide areas around the mounting holes. The hardware and mechanical engineers are heavily involved in setting up the mechanical assembly stations, together with the factory engineers.

The fourth stage is the functional tests and device programming. This is done at the same company that did the SMT and mechanical assembly, but usually at a different designated area of the factory floor or a separate building. The final high-level tests like ESS and burn-in might be done by the system design company in some cases. Every programmable flash-based chip will have to be programmed. This can be done through bed-of-nails ICT fixtures, through dongles/cables, or through running custom software on the DUT's own processor. Devices that need programming are typically EERPROMs, flash memories, FPGAs, sequencer chips, smart VRMs, and clock generators. The test software and test/debug documents are also released to the contractors.

There are several test fixtures and custom cables that are designed for the purpose of manufacturing and testing. The fixtures might be designed by the product/design company or the manufacturing contractor, and their drawings are released in the same database as where the board manufacturing files are. The ICT bed-of-nails test fixture is made for some projects, for automated probing and programming, custom designed for the DUT. It has a high cost, so it is used only in medium to larger scale production. Press-fit connector assembly requires a mechanical fixture, custom designed for the DUT. This touches the board surface on the opposite side from the connector and applies a large amount of (counter)force while the connector is being pressed in. Wave soldering fixtures (pallet or fountain) are made if through-hole soldered parts are used in the design. Functional test fixture boards are sometimes designed by the hardware engineer, which the DUT can be plugged into or vice versa that provide system imitation circuits and standard programming headers to test out the DUT's low level interfaces. Programming adapter cables or boards are also often made custom for each design, which fan out a high-density header into several different vendor-standard programming headers. Off-the-shelf loopback plugs are purchased and used on external port testing.

Once the layout design is completed and reviewed (and corrected), it can be released in the product design company's manufacturing database. Often it is Oracle Agile, or SAP, or another similar system that has a web interface and a database server, or a GUI program. The release has company specific steps, usually involving official document creation and signing (ECO, engineering change order), then uploading the fab-out files. Then the program management or procurement can place the orders for manufacturing, from the PCB fabricator and the PCBA vendor, as well as any cable or fixture vendors.

18.2.1 Components and BOM

The components of the board are listed with part number and quantity in the BOM (bill of materials) that is also released in the same manufacturing database where the fab-out files are released to. The BOM has column headers like quantity of each type, manufacturer part number or our company part number, refdes list, populate/DNP, and description. Some design/owner companies include manufacturer part numbers in the design BOM, others have their own part numbers that link to a list of approved manufacturer parts to help the supply chain with multi sourcing. This mainly benefits parametric components like passive parts. The BOM should really be released as preliminary, as soon as the schematics are done, to give extra time for purchasing all of the parts. Components have a lead time, sometimes it takes months to get them in. This means the vendor guarantees that it will be shipped no later than the order date plus lead time. Some are manufactured after the orders come in, or a pool of orders come in, while others ship from stock. In-stock items have much shorter lead times. It is worth designing in parts that are in stock at online stores to ease the prototyping procurement. It is common practice that the product design/owner company purchases the main ASICs from the chip company, as there may be a lower price negotiated in an arrangement. Then the rest or all of the parts are purchased by the PCBA company. Contract manufacturers also keep stock of basic passive parts, which we can rely on, but only if we have a system in place that allows the contractor to use them instead of our defined exact part numbers. Chips and special components (like high-speed connectors, optical transceivers) are usually purchased from distributors, not directly from the chip companies. When an ASIC is new and has not yet hit the market, we can purchase samples or "engineering samples" (ES parts), so by the deadline of the chip company's release date we can be ready with a tested board/system prototype. It is usually not allowed to ship products to customers containing ES parts. Often the ES parts are prototype chips that have bugs that will be fixed for the production release chips. Some chips can be obtained in very limited quantity as free samples, but for complex hardware prototyping we usually try to purchase them in larger quantity. We usually build 5 to 20 boards for protol series, and 5 to 50 for proto-2 and pre-production. That requires a lot of chips. For example, 36 memory chips per board on a series of 20 boards is 720. The BOM usually changes no more than a few percent from proto-1 to proto-2, so the major parts can be purchased up front for the whole proto and pre-prod board quantities. Buying potentially unneeded parts is a smaller risk than being stranded for a 10-month lead time with parts.

Some components cannot be purchased by smaller system design companies, as they may have MOQ (minimum order quantity) in the tens of thousands, such as some GPUs or AI ASICs. Some chips are developed by systems companies for their own use, so those cannot be purchased by third parties at all. Chip design-in support and datasheet availability for board companies are often refused if they cannot meet the high ~100k MOQ. Some expensive components are sold with ~1000 MOQ, which is usually too high for prototype builds, so we might select parts that are available with MOQ ~ 1 to 100. Unless it is a $0.01 resistor, which would only cost $10.

It is a good practice to only design in components that are easily obtainable, not likely to get obsolete soon, have short lead time (manufacturer's promise to ship within timeframe after order), or basic vendors have large quantities of it in stock. A quick search on Mouser, Digikey, or Farnell can help finding these. Some components have a fixed life cycle, like X86 processors. They release CPUs into different product ranges with different life spans, meaning they will manufacture a certain part number for fixed number of years. It is one year for consumer laptop processors, five years for embedded, seven or ten years for network infrastructure CPUs.

18.2.2 Factory Selection

Boards and systems can be manufactured domestically or off shore. In most cases the design/owner companies have abandoned manufacturing their own products themselves, so they pay contract manufacturers to do it for them, aka outsourcing. Assembly (soldering the parts onto the bare boards) is sometimes done in-house at the system design company, at other times, depending on the company, it is outsourced. Bare board PCB fabrication is almost always outsourced. So two vendors are involved in producing every board, the fab and the assembly company. In some industries outsourcing includes contractors that are based in foreign countries, most commonly Taiwan and China. In other industries only domestic companies can be considered.

If only the (assembly) manufacturing is outsourced, then it is a contract manufacturer, or CM, working for us their customer. In that case our design/owner company is the OEM, or original equipment manufacturer. The CM manufactures the OEM's design. At this point OEMs should be called OEDs as original equipment design, or just referred to as M as marketing instead of manufacturing, it would make more sense but that is not the common naming convention today. If part of the development (like layout and validation testing) is also outsourced to the CM, then it is a JDM (joint development manufacturing) arrangement and a JDM vendor. Some companies offer both CM and JDM services. If we just write the product requirement document, but let the vendor do the detailed design, then it is called ODM, or original design manufacturing, and then the contractor is the ODM vendor.

Prototypes can be made at small-scale manufacturing CM companies, then we can do the mass production at larger companies. This might save time and money up front, but it can prove costly later. It will definitely require the fine tuning of the production process (thermal profiles, stencil designs, etc.) twice, which can cost time and money. It is also a schedule risk. This is why many companies build their proto boards at the same large-scale CM where they will also build the production. It costs more, but the process is smoother and offers better quality control and more reliable products. The selection of the plant or CM that is used for assembly (soldering components on the bare board) is part of the ongoing evaluation that upper management and program management does.

The bare board fabricator (company and facility/location) selection, especially for high-speed boards, cannot be done just by management; rather, it involves the hardware engineer as well as the manufacturing-engineering department at the OEM. High-speed board designs require special PCB features like tight backdrilling, insertion loss control, special copper foil types and processes, and specific sets of small object parameters. These cannot be manufactured by every single fabricator company, so the ordering of boards cannot be done from random suppliers. High-speed boards are designed to a specific vendor's capability. To be fair, we pick two or three vendors that can make the parameters we want, and we design for the lowest common denominator of their parameters—not the lowest common denominator of all fabricator companies in existence. The fabricator company and facility location selection is a make-or-break decision for the product. When bare boards (of high-speed designs) are ordered, they cannot be ordered from random or cheap fabricators. Our test adapter board or power backplane or the little LED board can be ordered from the basic vendors, but the high-speed complex hardware boards cannot be.

We also cannot swap fabricators randomly as they will manufacture the board with a totally different stackup, different in terms of signal integrity. The Fiber Weave Effect, crosstalk, insertion loss, and via impedance will be different. Instead, we negotiate stackups with two to three fabricators early on during the design, then it is locked in for the rest of the product lifecycle. A common mistake is when purchasing or management asking an intern to just approve a new stackup from the new vendor, not knowing what the SI-architecture intent was in the original stackup, while the main designer is on vacation, then they end up producing unreliable boards.

18.3 PRODUCTION TESTING

Every single unit that is manufactured also has to be programmed and tested before shipment to customers. They are shipped to customers in custom-designed shock-absorbing boxes. Depending on the product type, removable boards are tested/programmed by themselves, others can be tested only inside the product chassis with other boards. There are several common tests being done on most products.

The most important tests are the visual inspection and the automated visual testing, called AOI (automated optical inspection). The inspection machine looks for misaligned or badly soldered components at the end of the SMT production line. Sometimes a component is wrongly oriented by 90 or 180 degrees or a wrong part is used that looks different due to the marking code being different. Very small parts do not have a full part number printed on the top of the package; rather, they have a "top marking" code, with a few characters, that helps with visual or AOI inspections. For example, a chip in a SC-70-6 package cannot fit more than three characters.

Coupon testing is done for bare board fabrication. The fabricator puts small coupon designs next to our board on the production panel, which they use for measuring SI parameters. Some coupons are used for verifying trace impedance control, others are used for insertion loss testing or mechanical tests. Mechanical tests can be done to verify the strength of via barrels.

Flying probe testing is sometimes used on bare PCBs for the purpose of a connectivity check for open/short. The PCB fab may do it for us before shipping.

Boundary scan testing is sometimes done on assembled and programmed boards. This uses the JTAG ports of devices on board to drive and sample many on-board signals for a connectivity (open, short) check. It is automated, usually with a custom test vector. It uses the "EXTEST" mode of the JTAG ports found on many devices.

A bed of nails test, also called ICT (in-circuit test), can be done on fully assembled boards. A custom bed of nails fixture is developed for a specific board design. It usually costs 10 to 20 times the cost of a fully assembled board, so it is only justified in medium to higher volume production. It can do a connectivity check, device programming, and a JTAG boundary scan, and it can read voltages and low-speed signals on a functional board. It might involve testing a system boot and device initialization from flash memory chips. The tests are low-level circuit related, as the main ASICs will not be fully cooled as in the final chassis.

Bench-top device programming and functional testing (ESS and burn-in) are also done on every unit. These are usually automated using scripts that run either on the DUT or on a test computer that controls the DUT. These are described in the following sections.

18.3.1 Device Programming

When the board is being manufactured, after the SMT and AOI, several devices need to be programmed. During this process a stored image file gets loaded into each device. Several device types need programming, like flash-based devices (microcontrollers and small FPGAs), smart devices (smart VRMs, clock chips, power sequencers), and non-volatile memory chips (Flash, EEPROM). The smart devices get configured to work in the specific board design, the flash memories get loaded with already compiled software or user data, the EERPROMs get small pieces of information about Ethernet port MAC addresses and other device operating mode parameters, board serial numbers, and other things. There are three main device programming methods: cable-dongle-based programming (JTAG, SPI, I2C), offline programming before SMT assembly, and being programmed by an in-system host processor. Some devices can be programmed in multiple different ways, which also depends on the board hardware architecture. Most programming can be done through chip vendor–provided software and dongle, through the programming headers we have designed in. Flash memory chips are usually attached to a host ASIC. Flash chips that are attached to JTAG-capable host devices can be programmed through a third-party boundary scan flash programmer software by bit-banging the ASIC's pins at a few hundred Hertz rate. Some host devices support the programming of attached flash memories through the chip vendor's JTAG GUI, which is faster than standard boundary scan-based bit-banging programming. Many flash chips have an SPI or I2C interface to their host, which can be isolated with a multiplexer chip in our design, and then an SPI or I2C dongle can hijack the bus as a new master and write into the memory chip.

In some cases they run a script that automates all of this, at other times a factory technician (user) has to click/type through the apps. Medium to larger companies invest into automating this. Some programmable devices might be purchased pre-programmed with custom part numbers from the chip vendor (like some clock chips), others get pre-programmed at a distributor with the image file we send them (like EEPROMs). Pre-programmed devices often receive a marking in the form of a dot with a certain color, documented in a specification document.

Usually, the devices on a new board have to be programmed in a logical sequence because some devices are inaccessible or unpowered when some other devices (like the power sequencer FPGA) are not programmed yet. So the hardware designer must design the board with a valid programming sequence being designed in the same time and then tested on the prototype. It passes the test only when we run a whole sequence on a fully blank (erased) board. This has to be thought through very carefully to avoid a chicken and egg situation when we cannot program a device because it relies on another devices that is unprogrammed at the time, but that one cannot be programmed either because the first device is unprogrammed. The programming sequence is part of the hardware design. This is "design-for manufacturing", or DFM. A test PC is used for handling all the programmer dongles, console access to the DUT (device under test), and control of the board's power source in order to power cycle it when needed between programming steps. There are power switch devices on the market that are remote controllable over the Ethernet network.

Some boards can be designed with the "dongles" being designed into the board so the factory worker does not have to connect any cables to them. This can be a function inside a glue logic or control plane FPGA, or it can be done by bit-banging a GPIO using software running on a processor inside the product. Then the workers simply plug in power and console, or they plug the DUT into a backplane, log into the unit's console, and issue the programming command. A hybrid method can also be developed, where we use a dongle to program one device, then that device programs all other devices. Most complex designs require some devices being JTAG programmed, while other devices (like ASIC-attached EEPROMs) are programmed through the DUT software. Often the programming and testing steps are interleaved, for example detect device1, detect device 2, program device2, detect device3, etc.

There are two types of smart VRMs, one with resistor strapping for voltage and overcurrent settings and one with all parameters being set by PMBUS programming. This second type probably requires its enable pin to be held low (not sequenced) before and during the first factory programming to avoid damaging any digital load ASICs. The board glue logic must be designed in a way to allow this programming mode.

18.3.2 Functional Tests

Immediately after the device programming, the production facility performs several steps of functional tests. The two main and most common functional tests used in complex hardware manufacturing are the ESS and the burn-in. Both of them are needed to validate that each new production unit is functional and reliable. Both tests look for failures, like boot failures, unintended reboot, inaccessible devices, unreliable devices, bad ports, and link down or dropped packets. The units must be fitted with heatsinks and airflow during this test. The names of the test stages might be company specific.

"ESS" means environmental stress screening, with the temperature going up/down and power cycling. This is done inside an environmental chamber that can control the temperature to any level, and it is able to linearly ramp it up or down. With voltage margining turned on, environmental chamber temperature cycling and the fact that we test every production unit, we get a full coverage on all PVT corners to ensure the reliability of every unit shipped. We cannot just run the user application; we have to run a manufacturing software in stress test mode.

"Burn-in" means constant temperature testing for long hours on each unit with maximum power. It drives all processing elements to compute heavy load benchmark software as well as communication to ASICs to process packets at full bandwidth (traffic test). This causes them to consume and dissipate maximum power; it drives the VRMs to near their limits with increased ripple noise.

These tests are usually automated, a test script or software runs either on the DUT's (device under test) processor or on a test PC. They might be written by the software or diagnostics team at the OEM or by the firmware engineers at the CM. The OEM's level of control over manufacturing test varies by company and by each product. The main goal is to discover all programmable chips in the system, initialize them, then "run traffic" or workload, aka exercise all I/O buses and processing elements while monitoring whether they produce a correct output. The test script has to report back to the user in a log file whether all devices and ports were discovered and initialized, and how many bits or other units of data/processing were sent through different parts of the system total. These log files have to be stored in an accessible place for debugging. They have to report failure signatures, such as "FPGA3 reported 474654 bit-errors at 10.08.2023-09:15:21". The test software or script can be designed to stop at the first sign of trouble or to continue discovering more parts of the unit and report all passes and all failures. The latter helps more with debugging the failed units. The operation and designing of these diagnostic software is described in Chapter 9, "Hardware-Firmware Integration".

Some kind of automated minimal signal integrity test should be included in the manufacturing test, at least on any memory buses and off-board SERDES interfaces. It is still not very common to do that on every unit, but it could prevent field failures and RMAs. This will be a simplified version of the tests being done in design validation. For example, a single-point bit error ratio or bit error count test can be used, instead of an eye scan. Then the result being a number instead of a diagram can be parsed by a script. A design validation test is used to estimate margins to cover manufacturing tolerance of all future units. In production we need less margin to cover only future aging of the devices, not to cover process tolerance since every unit is tested. This simplified test will be done in ESS to apply temperature corners, together with VRM margining to apply voltage corners and on all units to apply process corners—all PVT corners. A Linux or Python script or test software can easily initiate and assess the results by writing and reading the control and status registers of the interface controller blocks of each port in each device. Then the script can assess whether the resulting number is too high or not to pass/fail the test. External ports could be tested with loopbacks in PRBS mode. Same-vendor ASIC links can also be tested with PRBS, and other chip-to-chip links can be tested with packet CRC or FEC error counters.

Those boards, systems, or units that failed will get transferred into the production debug area within the factory, where trained technicians will try to manually test, debug, and repair them. This involves running the production test software with real-time supervision, typing in commands for manual access, manual probing with multimeters and other instruments, and performing visual checks. It requires a trained person as "debugging" is usually not trivial, at least until we have already manufactured hundreds of units and collected a list of common failure signatures. The common failure list is design specific. It makes sense for the hardware engineer to write a document like this, to help the production technicians to decide what steps to follow in different debugging situations. We spend some time in the factory to discover the design-specific most common failures list.

18.3.3 Manufacturing Test/Debug Guidelines Document

The manufacturing team needs guidance from design engineering about two things: the standard programming and testing procedure as well as the situation-specific debugging of failed boards. Both of these could be written into one document. This might be written together between the hardware and the test software engineers. It would include a sequence of activities to be performed on each production unit, from the blank state of mechanically assembled modules to the fully programmed and tested units. To help the technicians with debugging and to help them understand how the product works, we can provide information about hardware architecture with subsystem block diagrams, device addresses, and port numbers. The most useful is a list of common symptoms and probable causes and solutions. We need to detail the manual debugging steps to be done for diagnosing test failures. We could include dependency diagram or test failure causality tables too. An example symptom item might look like this:

```
If the console message says "Eth-24 link-up failure", then issue command
"READ 0x1234 0x4567". If the result says "data=0x9632" then inspect U36
and surrounding components visually, probe the related voltages VCC34
(expected 3.3V+/-10%) and VCC56 (expected 1.2V+/-3%). If the result says
"data=0x1478" then inspect U51 and surrounding components visually, probe
the related voltages VCC12 (expected 3.3V+/-10%) and VCC13 (expected
1.8V+/-3%). In case of any voltage regulator outputting the wrong
voltage, touch up the pins with solder-iron then re-test, if the issue
persists then replace the VRM chip.
```

A test engineer has to spend a lot of time writing the above port name to refdes translation. It is labor intensive, so it is not done in most cases, except maybe at high-volume production.

Typically we include these items in the test/debug document:

- Hardware architecture, a simple introduction to ports, main chips, boot modes, with subsystem block diagrams.
- List of all programming and debug headers and locations.
- List of programming cables and other equipment.
- Mechanical assembly order with part numbers.
- Production test and programing sequence.
- Manual test commands and expected console responses.
- Image file part numbers, device addresses, reference designators.
- Debug modes, dip switches.
- Mapping tables from software console device IDs to schematic reference designators.
- Mapping tables from software console signal name to schematics signal name and refdes + pin number.
- A dependency diagram or test failure causality table, that shows if any device failure symptom might be caused by a list of devices.
- Rail voltages.

18.3.4 Automation of Test and Programming

Most complex hardware are automated boxes that can be also controlled and configured over a text console. For Linux scripting–based testing and programming, there are two options. In all cases a manufacturing test PC is connected to the DUT over a serial cable, usually a “Rollover” RJ45 cable. This establishes a serial connection to issue commands to the Linux console on the DUT. A “script” is a text file that contains console commands with parameters to execute in a list of several commands. A “log” is simply a capture of all commands and responses that have accumulated in a text-based console interface, into a text file on the test PC, or on a server.

In the first option, a simple script runs on the test PC and a detailed script runs on the DUT. The Linux console of the DUT’s processor is running the complex test script that is included with the OS image booted from its internal storage drive or from a USB stick that is plugged in for the duration of production test. The simple script running on the test PC sends a single command over serial cable to the DUT to start the whole test sequence, calling the script, during the test the PC receives every command response and saves them into the log file. This will contain all test results and programming status, and it might have a final statement such as “all passed”.

In the second option a detailed script runs on the test PC and the DUT just has the regular command interpreter of the Linux console. The DUT has only the main production version of the OS, but it can also execute individual complex commands. The test PC runs the complex test script that sends individual commands for each test item over serial cable to the DUT, which responds to each command by running a single test and produces a response text string. Then the test PC script checks the response, whether it is as expected. For example, if it is looking for a string saying “EEPROM 3 programming passed”, instead of “EEPROM 3 programming failed”. Then the test PC script aggregates all results into an overall pass/fail condition of the DUT and saves a complete log file.

The test script on the test PC might be a python script, LabView GUI, Windows GUI, Linux script, or custom C++ program. Scripts running on the DUT can be Linux or DOS. Each production unit has a unique serial number. At the end of the test the PC has to report by serial number an overall pass/fail result and a test log file saved into a shred area or server. The serial number is either entered on a keyboard or scanned from a bar code label by the factory technician during test, then stored in an EEPROM on the board. If we have to insert several power cycles into the process due to device programming, or startup testing, then the second option makes more sense, so the script can continue. If we are manufacturing a peripheral card, then the console cable is not plugged into the DUT but into any processor card that will be part of the test chassis setup.

The test PC might be a rack server type computer, so dozens of them can be placed in the production floor on a 19" rack, and many DUTs can be tested at the same time. Connecting all (many) test PCs on a factory floor to the network and to a remote server helps managing the production floor better. This way the test engineers can access statuses and logs from anywhere instead of having to find and physically access the particular test PC that was used to test a particular unit. Figure 18.1 shows such a factory floor arrangement.

In rare cases when the DUT has its own display output, a test PC might not be needed, but then a technician has to start up each unit, using a keyboard to start the test script on the DUT. The test station will include a display and a keyboard as well as a USB stick to boot the test OS, which is plugged into every production unit one after another.

An example test log could look like this:

```
OS boot logs...omitted
Login:
admin
>> baseboard_test
detecting PCIe switch 1 device ..passed
programming PCIe switch 1 EEPROM ..passed
detecting PCIe switch device 2 ..passed
programming PCIe switch 2 EEPROM ..passed
detecting ASIC 1 device ..passed
initialize ASIC 1 ..passed
detecting PHY 1 device ..passed
detecting PHY 2 device ..passed
detecting PHY 3 device ..passed
detecting PHY 4 device ..passed
link detection on Ethernet port 1 ..passed
running traffic on Ethernet port 1 with <10 bit errors ..passed
link detection on Ethernet port 2 ..passed
running traffic on Ethernet port 2 with <10 bit errors ..passed
link detection on Ethernet port 3 ..passed
running traffic on Ethernet port 3 with <10 bit errors ..passed
link detection on Ethernet port 4 ..passed
running traffic on Ethernet port 4 with <10 bit errors ..passed
detecting FPGA1 device ..passed
detecting FPGA2 device ..passed
all passed ..exiting
>>_
```

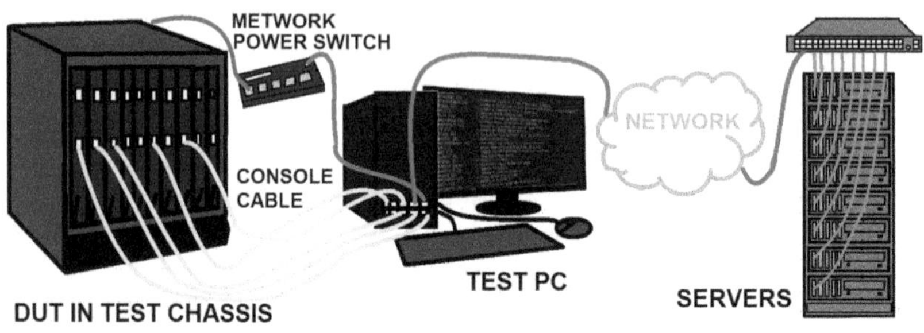

FIGURE 18.1 Common automated manufacturing test setup (sketch).

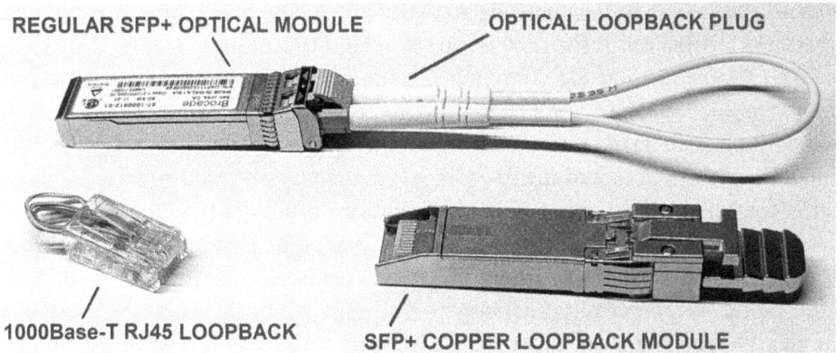

FIGURE 18.2 Ethernet loopback plugs.

A real log file would be much longer, often with more verbose test parameter detail and many more ports and devices, sometimes hundreds of pages long. Often the actual test commands with device or file path or raw data (like a full PCI scan device list) is included in the console log. Usually there is an overall automatically generated "all passed" statement at the end. If there is not (it failed), then the technicians have to search the log for details using the text search. We have to use text search for strings like "error" or "failed" or "FPGA 2" to find the parts we are debugging or trying to verify. If the technicians cannot figure out what is wrong with the failed boards, especially during the pre-production run, they will contact the hardware design engineering department for guidance. Hardware engineers might have to travel to the factory for a week during pre-production.

During functional tests we use many loopback plugs instead of connecting the DUT to outside devices over cables. The serial console, USB ports, and external PCIe ports are always connected to other devices, but all Ethernet ports are tested with loopbacks. Typically, Ethernet ports are either RJ45 for lower speed or optical cages for pluggable transceiver modules (SFP+, QSFP-DD, OSFP) for higher sped ports. Usually self-loopback plugs are used, instead of connecting one port to another, to help fault isolation. Not all digital interfaces work with self-loopbacks, only the ones that do not require a single master device in a logical tree hierarchy (like PCIe or USB). Figure 18.2 shows what common loopback plugs look like.

18.4 PRODUCTION ISSUES

In production some units just do not work, and they will have to be debugged. If all boards have the same problem, then it is likely an SMT programming issue or the wrong orientation of a component. The issues that do not seem to affect all boards are caused by either soldering errors or design reliability. Soldering issues usually occur around a few weak spots of the board. Soldering issues might be caused by (footprint) design issues or by the manufacturing setup, like stencils and thermal profiles. The two types are mixed in as unknowns at the beginning. Both have to be discovered and debugged. This is why we usually call the first larger (20-100 units) batch of manufacturing the "pre-production". The designers have to keep a close eye on the pre-prod failures. Once we start making larger quantities of boards and systems, we will discover more problems with the design that could not be detected during DVT. This is due to low probability reliability issues and the process tolerance of the parts and circuits. This will usually result in a half-dozen common failure types.

Pre-prod boards will be fully tested and brought up by the factory technicians according to the production documents and test procedures. Test logs (from programming or ESS scripts) are made available to RnD engineering. The CM's factory will report any typical problem types they run into. The hardware engineering department, often including the designer, needs to develop debugging steps and fixes for these common failure types and document them so the technicians later can easily repeat them. We can also start building statistics about how many units of each type of failure occurred to better prioritize our efforts. This can be added to a manufacturing test document later as an update. We can include console commands, screenshots, diagrams, board layout screenshots (showing component locations), re-work drawings, and explanations.

Failed units will be transferred into the "debug area" within the factory, where technicians will try to manually exercise boards and do basic measurements with multimeters, oscilloscopes and dongles. Boards for which they cannot find easy solutions often get transferred to a corner of the building for temporary storage, we call this the "bone pile". The CM or our own engineers should make all unit's test logs available so our engineers can check and figure out all the failure types. With this information we can develop debugging and repair guidelines so the production technicians have to identify only failures as pre-defined failure types and follow our documentation for fixing them. Production debugging performed by technicians should not be a heuristic creative process on most failed units.

Some boards might not work even after several debugging attempts. These will require an exponentially larger amount of RnD work to determine the failure type and a suitable fix. But if the quantity of units with this type of failure is very low, like 1%, then management might allow RnD to abandon it temporarily. Often hardware design engineers have to spend a few days on the factory floor with the manufacturing test engineers and technicians when the very first proto-2 and pre-prod units are transferred from SMT to system test/assembly. The factory floor at any CM is usually divided between different customers, so all their units will be assembled, tested, and debugged in designated areas separate from other customers' hardware. No peeking!

Typical causes of issues we may run into on random failed boards:

- PCB fabrication issues, like via fracture, trace or plane short, bad backdrill, or wrong material or copper APP used.
- A component is placed by the pick&place machine with wrong orientation or wrong part number.
- Open circuit (cold solder) caused by insufficient, splashed, or unmelted solder on some component pins in a certain board area. Manufacturing or process engineers have to mitigate it, working with the hardware design engineer. Opens under BGAs can be confirmed only by using the die and pry test that destroys the unit. Sometimes a reflow (heat it up locally in a BGA re-work station but not replace it) can fix it.
- Short circuit caused by solder bridges between pins, usually under QFN, SSOP, or fine pitch SMT parts. We can catch it with visual inspection and fix with a solder iron unless it is under a BGA (then replacement needed). Shorts under BGAs can be detected with 5DX-Ray.
- Connector contact issues of one pin, in optical cages and backplane connectors. It is caused by flying debris, residue or mechanical damage on one connector pin. It causes a SERDES differential pair to transmit only through one leg, which causes an almost closed eye diagram, it usually passes a basic functional test but it will produce many error bits in ESS or burn-in. Sometimes it can be seen with a pen microscope. We can attempt to clean it or replace the connector.
- BGA warpage: Large 50mm+ BGA packages might warp during the reflow cycle, for example, two opposite corners warp up during heat-up and then warp down during cooldown. It flaps like a bird. This creates cold solder joints at the BGA corner area, and bad or unreliable electrical connections. We can detect it with a dye and pry test.
- Some functions of a board might not work on some units as planned. This might be caused by the design not working across component and process tolerances, and it may require design change. Usually requires passive part BOM change. In this case the design is to be updated, re-work instruction drawing to be produced by the hardware designer, and all pre-prod boards to be re-worked. Transceiver tuning in firmware might work in some cases.

18.5 RMAS

There might be production unit failures with an even lower percentage (<<1%) that only get detected after the customer has been using the units for months. The OEM has to replace these units to the customer for free, while sending the failed units to a tech support or an RMA (return merchandise authorization) department, or sometimes to RnD to figure out what caused the failure and prepare corrective action (design or BOM change for future builds, usually without a recall). These failures can be caused by low probability random failures (like SI or PI) or premature component aging. Over-aging is either caused by a bad component as a product that does not meet its datasheet specification (needs to design it out), the design applied over the limit voltage/current or temperature conditions, or the user was using it inappropriately (for example, blocking system fan airflow and running hot). RMA return statistics are tracked by the OEM, but if several units are returned with the same symptoms, RnD hardware engineers might get involved in it. After an investigation and debugging a design change (usually an ECO for a BOM change) might become necessary.

18.6 RELIABILITY

Reliability is the study of when, how, and why electronics might fail. The failures are analyzed by design engineers so they can make their current and future designs more robust by eliminating the root causes. There are other techniques used on the top of design fixes, not instead of them, like redundancy, line replaceable units (modularity), and fault tolerance. Redundancy usually means two or more instances of a subsystem are contained within the system and, if one fails, then the other(s) can continue supporting the system. The system has to be able to detect the failure events and remain (partially) operational and switch resources over to the operational one. The most common scheme is the "2+1" redundancy of power supply modules in a chassis, where the chassis could run from two PSUs, but it runs from three, until one fails, then the administrators have hours or days to replace the failed units until one more PSU will fail. At the failure only the redundancy is lost, not the whole system functionality. Modularity can help with quick replacement of modules in the field, although in most cases the system has to be powered down, except in hot-swappable distributed systems. Any single point of failure (like the backplane) cannot be replaced in a live system. Fault tolerance means that something has failed but it is still partially operational, for example, an airplane can still be landed safely.

18.6.1 Product Failures

Components, subcircuits, boards, and complete systems might fail. The failure can be permanent or intermittent. Permanent means a defect, it breaks and dies, or it has never worked. Intermittent means it works most of the time, but sometimes fails, then later works again after a restart. A failure being intermittent might mean one of two different things. It can be about continuous operation; a unit works for several hours and then it fails. It can also mean power-cycling, the unit can be started up most of the time except on a few occasions when it fails to start up. So either a startup failure or a run-time failure can be intermittent. The unit might fail even at the first test in the factory and never work reliably, or it works for months and then it stops working. The ones that never worked will not be shipped to customers, as each unit is tested in the factory, but the question comes up about manufacturing quality or design margins across component tolerances.

A design has to work with all components being at any value within their tolerance bands. For passive components a Monte-Carlo simulation can be performed, for SERDES interfaces a simulation with both fast and slow corners can help, or an eye margining test can be performed on the prototype. A permanent failure of any component is expected, but only after hundreds of thousands of operating hours. Intermittent failures are expected on certain interfaces that have mitigation strategies designed in, like packet re-sending or FEC, but they have a limit on how often the failure can occur due to their limited ability to correct it. It is usually listed as bit error rate. On certain products like aerospace boards certain failure types can never be allowed to occur, like a random reboot. Depending on where the failure occurs and where or how it can be detected, the overall cost of a failure to the company can be very different. If the failure occurs or can be detected in the factory, then the cost is a low percentage yield issue. If the failure occurs after customer delivery, then the failure can cost lives, or millions of times the unit cost.

The root cause of a failure can be related to design (insufficient margins), manufacturing (opens, shorts), external damage (opens, shorts, faulty components), or component lifetime (they all die at the end). Note that an open or short can be permanent or intermittent, as the incorrect solder material shape might make contact as the temperature increases and then loose contact again a few degrees above. The intermediate cause can be a timing violation, SI, PI, VRM ripple/stability, power sequencing, or a missing circuit connection. A second-level intermediate cause of a system failure can be a subsystem not functioning and another subsystem detecting it as an error. For example, if the factory did not solder a capacitor properly, it might cause a differential signal to pass through only one leg of the pair that means severe eye closure and an SI issue, then an ASIC chip will not pass all data through and the processor will keep receiving ASIC error messages. The cause of any failure can have multiple levels of abstraction, as we can see in Table 18.1. For any debug or repair, we need to be able to dig down to the root cause, not only to the intermediate causes.

Most of the time when "reliability" is discussed, it deals with a board's or a system's mean time between failures (MTBF), which is caused by components reaching their lifetimes and dying permanently. Boards, systems, and components have an MTBF in the range of 100k to 10M operating hours. This is sometimes provided in product datasheets or the component engineer can obtain it or extrapolate it from similar components/boards. There are software tools and methods of calculating a board's MTBF from the MTBF data of all components (imported as a BOM).

The component MTBF numbers are assumed with using them at moderate temperatures and no stress. If we are running our devices closer to their maximum junction temperatures all the time, or closer to their maximum voltage, or their input buffers see overshoot voltages from unhandled reflections, their MFBF will be reduced. We can call it accelerated aging. Part of the design activity is to avoid accelerated aging, by applying margins and component derating. We should keep tens of degrees of thermal margins most of the time (at average environmental temperature), a few degrees at the high end of the temperature range, and have double or triple voltage rating on passive parts. Some components experience not just reduced lifetime, but also reduced performance at high temperatures, for example, ASICs consume more power, eye diagrams might be more closed, and capacitors have reduced capacitance.

TABLE 18.1
Typical Multi-level Causes of Failures

Root Cause	Secondary Cause	Third Order Cause	Symptom
FAB open/short	Timing Violation	Link Training failure	Power-up or boot failure
PCBA open/short	VRM ripple	Random link down and recover	Random reboot
Design Margin	VRM stability	Excessive BER	Error messages
Ext Damage	VRM wrong voltage	BER suddenly changes	Function not available
Comp Lifetime	PDN impedance	Enumeration failure	Loss of control
Functional design bugs (prototype only)	SI Eye closure	Device stops responding	Loss of input or output
	Loss of connection	Reboot or hang	System reacts to phantom events
	Power sequence	FPGA re-loads	
	Signal stuck	Erroneous glue logic signal states	Incorrect status display

The concept of MTBF can also be applied to intermittent recoverable failures, but that is not commonly discussed. It is acceptable for most consumer products to randomly stop working, as long as the user can recover it by restarting it. But it should not occur too often. Recovering a system while in use might not be an option at all for some products, like aerospace or military systems. Other industries might allow recovery but it must be fast so as to prevent financial loss that can be millions of dollars per second. In the latter cases the design has to be optimized to increase the intermittent MTBF to be larger than the planned lifetime of the product, at least for hi-rel products. We have to manage and or eliminate these failures by design changes, process changes, and feedback to RnD for future projects. IEEE and other standards define S-parameter limit lines that indirectly ensure a reliable operation on SERDES interfaces. A circuit board has to work statistically, not just the one unit working now. It has to work under all conditions every time and across all production units. When we have lots of bit errors or return loss, then it is a sign that we do not have a design margin. Without a design margin some units of a larger production batch will likely fail over a longer period of time.

Design, PCB fabrication, and PCBA (soldering, assembly) all can cause intermittent as well as "always dead" type failures. The always dead type is caught in a factory, easily reproducible, measurable, and can be fixed easily by any engineer, so we are not focusing on those. The bigger problem with the intermittent types of failures is when the probability is so low that we cannot reproduce it with reasonable resources. If we can never see the signs of the failure, then we can only theorize what it is and what is causing it.

For high-availability systems it is important to put a combined (tens of) thousands of hours of stress or burn-in testing and thousands of successful consecutive power cycles before the product can be launched into mass production. This verifies design margins and is supposed to catch most intermittent failure types. For startup type failures the MTBF can be referred to as the "number of startups", instead of hours. We can design our boards to support margining, for example, voltage levels adjusted to the limit and test the system that way or adjust the SERDES receiver CDR to a timing or voltage offset.

We should also design our systems and boards to detect and self-diagnose failures, since we might have to wait another month running 100 units to see the failure again. Self-diagnosis can be in the form of log files saved on an SSD drive or fault logs saved in EEPROMs or FRAM memory chips. For example, if on a large board with 50 voltage rails one VRM shuts down for a few milliseconds and then recovers, then the power manager (glue logic or IPMI uC) has to write the rail number that went down into the non-volatile memory so later the engineer can look at that one rail, stress test it in the lab, or simulate/measure it or tune it for more optimal operating margins. Many management and IPMI subsystems constantly monitor all voltage rails on a board and log or report even a glitch outside of the set tolerance.

Some industries require an analysis to be completed on the schematics design. This means basically filling out spreadsheets with parameters for every important component and important unique net type. We can get the object lists from netlists, BOMs, and other design tool reports, but we have to add the parameters we are checking manually. The parameters involve the micro decisions that were made during the schematic design, based on datasheet parameters. I/O (net/pin) and component stress are checked for every instance. Stress can damage parts in the long term, it is when they are operating beyond their rated limits or operating below but with insufficient margin. I/O interface issues are, for example, when a chip pin is connected to another through a net, but they cannot reliably operate together due to voltage (thresholds, bias) and current (drive, load, pull) parameters. Basic components are checked against their parameters, like decoupling capacitors (voltage plus derating), VRM components (voltages and currents), resistors (power dissipation), and diodes/transistors (voltages and currents). This assures the elimination of certain designer mistakes. Any finding (fail) requires a design change. This is mainly used for project milestones and reliability assurance or as contract documentation. The aerospace industry has formalized standards for some of these analysis in the RTCA DO-254 Design Assurance Guidance for Airborne Electronic Hardware.

18.6.1.1 Intermittent MTBF from SI Bit Errors

Signal integrity failures can be mild, when one bit is received incorrectly, or severe, when a link goes down as it cannot finish link training without most packets being plagued with error bits or even no signal is received at all. SERDES links and memory interfaces can have packet-resending, CRC error bit detection, or FEC correction. The interface standards specify a certain amount of bit errors that are acceptable to a production unit, typically 1e-9 to 1e-16 of bit error ratio (BER), and the system will not crash from a bad bit received in a sequence of 1000 billion good bits due to design features that are able to handle a low rate of error bits. With these rates, a failure would likely occur every few seconds, but the system remains fully operational. A low-level system would perform a routine error recovery without the high-level functions having to notice it. These interfaces are tested in design validation by measuring the BER level and any margin (eye capture or margining).

Larger SI issues that cause a loss of connection or generating system errors must be eliminated in the design, and they cannot occur during the system's planned lifetime. Design validation with tens of thousands of hours and thousands of power cycles can test for that. A product might be used one million hours in its component decay-driven lifetime, but we cannot test the design that long, only 1% to 10% of that. The testing can involve multiple units, so the total tested time can be the number of units multiplied by the number of hours each unit tested. This is needed to get anywhere near within an order of magnitude to the planned unit lifetime.

The same applies to PI issues, timing violations, VRM stability issues, and power sequencing issues (incorrect order causes intermittent startup failures). SI issues do not affect every single unit the same, so it often translates to a yield or RMA issue. In most cases 90% of the units will never fail, but we do not know which ones, as it is statistical. Inexperienced engineers might want to look for a specific cause that exists only the failed unit, while in reality the cause of failure exists in all units— it just does not cause a failure in all units due to tolerances.

18.6.2 Design Margins

It is all statistical. If we do not have any margins, then the system will still likely work right now. To release a design to production, "likely" is not good enough. It has to guarantee to work, every unit, every time. Consumer products might allow a low rate of failures, like crashing once a month, but high-reliability data center products as well as military, aerospace, or medical electronics cannot allow failures. They have to be designed with high reliability, which costs more in R&D and in BOM material. This means that no intermittent failures are allowed, except run-time correctible bit errors at a low amount meeting the standards. That is what the design margins are for. When a designer encounters intermittent failures (it failed only once, last Tuesday, but it is running now), it seems bad, and when it does not fail again some people feel the inclination to relax. Actually, the real problem for a (good) designer is the case when it is not failing at the moment, because it is harder to track down the cause of previously observed failures. So the wrong argument is why it fails 1% of the time, what is wrong with that 1% of cases or units? Actually nothing is wrong, it is just unlucky. Furthermore, the other 99% of cases when it does not fail it is still a bad design with no margins. It fails 1% of test cases, because it is a bad design in 100% of the cases. A "case" might refer to a specific startup run or a specific production unit. A design or test engineer must have the observation ability beyond the simple "I ran it in the lab yesterday". For a test setup or a test engineer, the "never failed" is not something to be proud of. It is not so much a proof of a good design; rather, it is a question of its not being pushed to its limits and of having no idea where those limits are. For a test engineer a failure is a success and vice versa. Most intermittent issues can be found in thousands of power cycles or in thousands of combined hours of run-time testing to confidently say "we didn't see failures". If less testing was done, then all we can say is "we don't know". If we did not look, and did not see, it does not mean it is not there. We can use pre-production and early

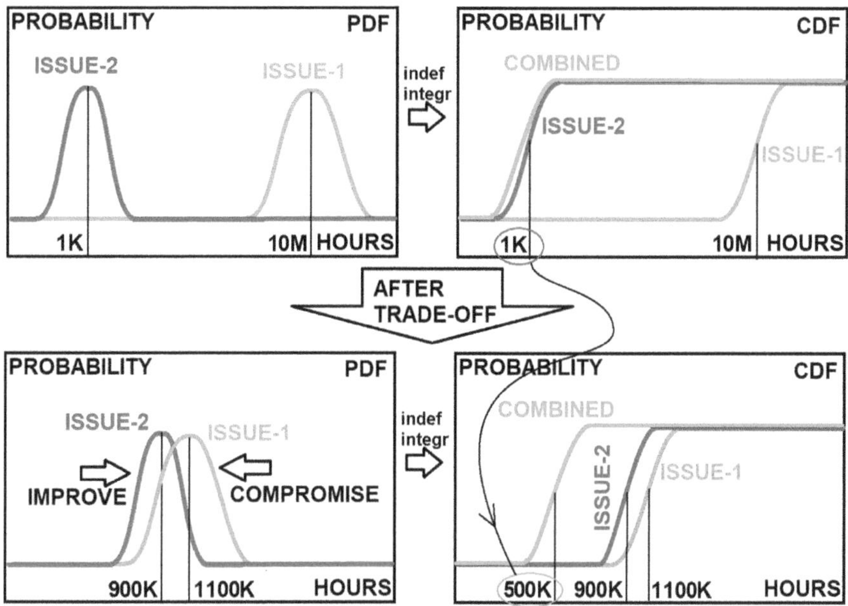

FIGURE 18.3 Combining PDF and CDF, before and after fixing SI design issues (sketch).

production runs, when we have more quantity and more total test hours, to feed back to a last-ditch effort for improvement of design reliability.

18.6.3 Statistics

Most of us probably studied statistics at college, but here it is again. The probability density function, or PDF, is usually a Gaussian/bell curve but not always. It shows the probabilities of something happening at different values of a variable. For example, the chance of raining exactly at 2 p.m., at 3 p.m., at 4 p.m. The cumulative distribution function, or CDF, is an indefinite integral function of the PDF. It shows the probability of something happening "up to" a certain value of a variable. For example, the chance of rain today happening by 2 p.m., by 3 p.m., by 4 p.m. The standard deviation shows the degree of spread of a Gaussian PDF curve.

Each failure type would have a PDF and a CDF curve to it. In most cases it is a bell-shaped curve (Gaussian or normal distribution). Certain type of failures, like a permanent damage, have a bell-curve statistical distribution across only the whole production quantity, while they have a Dirac Delta (always fail) distribution within each failed unit and a flat line zero on all other units. Other types of failures are Gaussian on each production unit. For example, via-plating issues will make the failed units always fail, which can be detected in the factory. Other issues related to SI, timing, PI, and power sequencing have a normal distribution within each unit.

18.6.3.1 Combining Two Sources of Failures

When two or more design parameters affect reliability, each parameter has its own PDF curve. The two Gaussian distributions seem like two independent objects, but looking at the CDF of the combined PDF we can see how one or the other source can dominate the expected time to failure. This combined PDF analysis can help in focusing company resources on the more severe issues. For example, we have issue-1 causing a likely failure after 10M hours, and issue-2 causing a likely failure after 1k hours, then investing into improving issue-1 does not have much return on investment, as issue-2 makes the system fail way before issue-1 could kick in. In some cases, the only way to improve issue-2 is by degrading issue-1 a little bit. It is necessary to focus on a better overall (combined CDF) system reliability. Basically, sometimes we just have to make a trade-off. For example, issue-2 might be a power integrity related to chip lockup failure, and issue-1 might be a component aging issue, while the trade-off is using a different component that allows lower ESR and lower voltage ripple. As technology evolves, for example, power circuits are getting smaller and hotter, a different trade-off might be necessary at a new technology node. For example, decades ago issue-1 and issue-2 might have been both in the 10M hours range, but now issue-2 is in the range of 1k due to faster load transients produced by newer digital chips. In a case like this the issue-2 load transient response can be improved to the 1M hours range with lower ESR capacitors that have a shorter lifetime. The designer trade-off in this case is to compromise the reliability of issue-1 from 10M to 1M at the benefit of improving issue-2 from 1k to 1M, resulting in a system reliability of 500k instead of 1k, which is a huge improvement. The combining of probability distributions is demonstrated in Figure 18.3. If the two issues are "owned" by different departments, then management has to make the decision, as the owners of issue-1 might not want to compromise, if they are evaluated only on their own work and not on the result of the whole team's work. Another common trade-off is when issue-1 is a factory yield issue and does not have an intermittent field failure MTBF. Then changing some constraints that will compromise issue-1 from a 0.00000001% yield loss to a 0.001% yield loss might allow issue-2 to be improved from 1k hours to 1M hours. The cost of a 0.001% yield loss is basically "cheap".

References

Examples of design files, simulation files, documents, and products used or mentioned in this book:

CHAPTER 2:

I2C bus specifications: https://www.i2c-bus.org/specification/
SMBUS specifications: http://smbus.org/specs/
PMBUS specifications: https://pmbus.org/specification-archives/
UART interface description on Wikipedia: https://en.wikipedia.org/wiki/Universal_asynchronous_receiver-transmitter
SPI interface description on Wikipedia: https://en.wikipedia.org/wiki/Serial_Peripheral_Interface
LPC interface specifications: https://www.intel.com/content/dam/www/program/design/us/en/documents/low-pin-count-interface-specification.pdf
JTAG standard for purchase: https://standards.ieee.org/ieee/1149.1/4484/
External parallel memory interface of Texas Instruments DSPs: https://www.ti.com/lit/ug/sprufo8a/sprufo8a.pdf
High-Speed Serdes Devices and Applications, by David Robert Stauffer et al., Springer 2009 (ISBN 978-1441946416): https://link.springer.com/book/10.1007/978-0-387-79834-9
Xilinx/AMD resources on transceivers: https://www.xilinx.com/support/documentation-navigation/design-hubs/dh0086-ultrascale-gth-tabbed-hub.html
Xilinx/AMD 56Gig Virtex UltraScale+ FPGAs GTM Transceivers User Guide (UG581): https://docs.xilinx.com/v/u/en-US/ug581-ultrascale-gtm-transceivers

CHAPTER 3:

IEEE802.3 Ethernet standards and amendments (802.3XY) for purchase: https://standards.ieee.org/ieee/802.3/7071/
Traditional optical interfaces (SFFxxxx): https://www.snia.org/technology-communities/sff/specifications
The OSFP optical interface standard organization website: https://osfpmsa.org/
PCI and PCI-Express specifications for purchase from PCI-SIG: https://pcisig.com/specifications
SATA interface specifications: https://sata-io.org/developers/purchase-specification
USB specifications: https://www.usb.org/documents
HDMI video port organization and specifications: https://www.hdmi.org/spec/hdmi2_1
JESD204 Serial Interface for Data Converters: https://www.jedec.org/standards-documents/docs/jesd-204a
Key Features of Intel Cascade Lake scalable Xeon Processor: https://www.intel.com/content/www/us/en/products/platforms/details/cascade-lake.html
CXL Interface specifications: https://www.computeexpresslink.org/download-the-specification
An introduction to CCIX interface: https://www.ccixconsortium.com/wp-content/uploads/2019/11/CCIX-White-Paper-Rev111219.pdf

CHAPTER 4:

Power Supply Cookbook (EDN Series for Design Engineers) 2nd Edition by Marty Brown, Newnes 2001, ISBN 978-0750673297
High-Speed Digital Design, A Handbook of Black Magic by Howard Johnson and Martin Graham, Prentice Hall 1993, ISBN 978-0133957242
QUCS free circuit/RF simulator: http://qucs.sourceforge.net/download.html
LTspice free circuit simulator: https://www.analog.com/en/design-center/design-tools-and-calculators/ltspice-simulator.html

CHAPTER 5:

Intel I210 Ethernet Controller datasheet: https://www.intel.com/content/www/us/en/content-details/333016/intel-ethernet-controller-i210-datasheet.html
Broadcom (acquired PLX) PCIe devices: https://www.broadcom.com/products/pcie-switches-bridges
Microchip PCIe switch chips: https://www.microchip.com/en-us/products/interface-and-connectivity/pcie-switches#
Diodes Inc (acquired Pericom) PCIe devices: https://www.diodes.com/products/connectivity-and-timing/pcie-packet-switchbridges/
Texas Instruments ADC12DJ5200RF A/D converter product page: https://www.ti.com/product/ADC12DJ5200RF
Examax connector product brief from Samtec: https://suddendocs.samtec.com/ebrochures/samtec-examax-high-speed-backplane-ebrochure.pdf
The QSFP-DD standard organization website: http://www.qsfp-dd.com/
Dynatron website heatsinks page: https://www.dynatron.co/product-page/b4a
Samtec Flyover cable website product page: https://www.samtec.com/solutions/flyover/
JEDEC memory chip standards: https://www.jedec.org/category/technology-focus-area/main-memory-ddr3-ddr4-sdram
JEDEC DIMM memory design standards: https://www.jedec.org/category/technology-focus-area/memory-configurations-jesd21-c
JEDEC DRAM DIMM design files: https://www.jedec.org/category/technology-focus-area/memory-module-design-file-registrations

CHAPTER 6:

Broadcom StrataGX BCM5871X series communications processors product page: https://www.broadcom.com/products/embedded-and-networking-processors/communications/bcm58712
Bluechip Technology RM3 module: https://www.bluechiptechnology.com/products/rm3/
Texas Instruments AM69 processor datasheet: https://www.ti.com/lit/gpn/am69a
Ampere Altra ARM server processors product page: https://amperecomputing.com/processors/ampere-altra
Marvell Octeon TX2 NPU product brief: https://www.marvell.com/content/dam/marvell/en/public-collateral/embedded-processors/marvell-infrastructure-processors-octeon-tx2-cn92xx-cn96xx-cn98xx-product-brief-2020-02.pdf
Texas Instruments DSP main page: https://www.ti.com/microcontrollers-mcus-processors/digital-signal-processors/overview.html
Analog Devices DSP main page: https://www.analog.com/en/product-category/processors-dsp.html
PowerPC history on Wikipedia: https://en.wikipedia.org/wiki/PowerPC
RISC-V soft processor specifications and ecosystem: https://riscv.org/
Intel® Xeon® and Intel® Core™ Processors For Communications Infrastructure Datasheet, Gladden CPU public datasheet from Intel website, Document #324803: https://www.intel.com/content/dam/www/public/us/en/documents/datasheets/xeon-core-communication-infrastructure-datasheet-vol-1.pdf
Intel® Communications Chipset 89xx Series Datasheet, PCH chipset public datasheet from intel website, Order Number 327879-005US: https://cdrdv2.intel.com/v1/dl/getContent/600584?fileName=intel-communications-chipset-89xx-series-datasheet.pdf
Xilinx/AMD FPGA devices and documentations: https://www.xilinx.com/products/silicon-devices/fpga.html
Altera/Intel FPGA devices and documentations: https://www.intel.com/content/www/us/en/products/details/fpga.html
Actel/Microchip FPGA devices and documentations: https://www.microchip.com/en-us/products/fpgas-and-plds
Achronix FPGA devices and documentations: https://www.achronix.com/products
Lattice FPGA devices and documentations: https://www.latticesemi.com/en/FPGA
Advanced FPGA design by Steve Kilts, Wiley-IEEE Press 2007, ISBN 978-0470054376
Broadcom StrataDNX™ Switch ASIC family product page: https://www.broadcom.com/products/ethernet-connectivity/switching/stratadnx
BCM56980 12.8 Tb/s Multilayer Switch (Tomahawk3 ASIC) datasheet: https://docs.broadcom.com/docs/56980-DS
Microchip VSC7558 switch ASIC product page: https://www.microchip.com/en-us/product/VSC7558

Marvell® Teralynx®8 Data Center Ethernet Switch, ASIC chip product brief: https://www.marvell.com/content/dam/marvell/en/public-collateral/switching/marvell-teralynx-8-product-brief.pdf
NVIDIA SPECTRUM-4 51.2 Tb/s Ethernet Switch ASIC DATASHEET or product brief: https://resources.nvidia.com/en-us-accelerated-networking-resource-library/ethernet-switches-pr?lx=LbHvpR&topic=Networking%20-%20Cloud#page=1
Intel/Barefoot Tofino switch ASIC product page: https://www.intel.com/content/www/us/en/products/network-io/programmable-ethernet-switch.html
Nvidia Tesla V100 GPU product page: https://www.nvidia.com/en-us/data-center/v100/
Article about the Microsoft Corsica compression accelerator ASIC: https://azure.microsoft.com/en-us/blog/improved-cloud-service-performance-through-asic-acceleration/
Broadcom BCM16K Knowledge-Based processor datasheet: https://docs.broadcom.com/doc/16000-DS1-PUB

CHAPTER 7:

OpenCores, the open-source FPGA IP core sharing website: https://opencores.org/
ACPI power management specification: https://uefi.org/sites/default/files/resources/ACPI_6_3_final_Jan30.pdf
Intel IPMI management specification: https://www.intel.com/content/dam/www/public/us/en/documents/product-briefs/ipmi-second-gen-interface-spec-v2-rev1-1.pdf
ASPEED Motherboard Management Processors: https://www.aspeedtech.com/server/
IEEE1588 time synchronization protocol standard: https://standards.ieee.org/ieee/1588/4355/
The Open Compute (OCP) website design file contributions section: https://www.opencompute.org/contributions
Open Compute Project Hardware License (Permissive) Version 1.0 (OCPHL-P): https://www.opencompute.org/documents/ocphl-permissive-v10
Open Web Foundation Final Specification Agreement ("OWFa 1.0"): https://www.opencompute.org/documents/owfa10-final-specification-agreement-fsa-as-of-august-2021
VXS DSP FMC Carrier card from CERN and Open Hardware: https://ohwr.org/project/vxs-dsp-fmc-carrier/wikis/home

CHAPTER 8:

PICMG standard form factors: https://www.picmg.org/openstandards/
VITA standard form factors: https://www.vita.com/
PCI-SIG standard form factors: https://pcisig.com/specifications
Bluechip Technology website: https://www.bluechiptechnology.com/
DIOT System Board at Open Hardware Repository: https://ohwr.org/project/diot-sb-zu/wikis/home
X-ES Inc. company website, Xpedite7674 card product page: https://www.xes-inc.com/products/end-of-life-sbcs/xpedite7674/
An article about radio access networks (RAN): https://www.5gtechnologyworld.com/open-ran-functional-splits-explained/
Open Compute Big Basin Accelerator Appliance Design Files: https://www.opencompute.org/documents/designfiles-zip

CHAPTER 10:

Generalized Timing Analysis Article in the PCDandF magazine October 2010: http://publish-it-online.com/publication/?i=49146 and http://publish-it-online.com/publication/?i=50463
Timing Analysis Calculator Excel Template: http://www.buenos.extra.hu/iromanyok/PCB_Timing_analysis.xls

CHAPTER 11:

Network Scattering Parameters by R Mavaddat, World Scientific Publishing Company 1996, ISBN 978-9810223052

Keysight ADS SI Simulator product page: https://www.keysight.com/us/en/products/software/pathwave-design-software/pathwave-advanced-design-system/pathwave-ads-high-speed-digital-design.html

Mentor/Siemens HyperLynx SI Simulator product page: https://eda.sw.siemens.com/en-US/pcb/hyperlynx/

Cadence SI Simulators product page: https://www.cadence.com/en_US/home/tools/system-analysis/signal-and-power-integrity.html

Ansys HFSS SI Simulator product page: https://www.ansys.com/products/electronics/ansys-hfss

Simbeor SI Simulator product page: https://www.simberian.com/

OIF-CEI channel standards: https://www.oiforum.com/technical-work/implementation-agreements-ias/#Electrical

Channel Analysis Template for QUCS: http://www.buenos.extra.hu/download/Channelsim_template_prj.zip

CHAPTER 12:

Understanding Glass Fabric, by ISOLA group: https://www.isola-group.com/wp-content/uploads/Understanding-Glass-Fabric.pdf

Accurate Impedance Control, PCDandF magazine article November 2009, Istvan Nagy

Via Stubs – Are They all Bad?, Signal Integrity Journal March 2017, Bert Simonovich (anisotropic material properties), https://www.signalintegrityjournal.com/blogs/7-voice-of-the-experts-signal-integrity/post/355-via-stubs-are-they-all-bad

A Heuristic Approach to Assess Anisotropic Properties of Glass-reinforced PCB Substrates, Bert Simonovich, DesignCon 2024

Panel – How to Avoid getting Totally Skewed, DesignCon 2018

Polar Instruments Si8000 impedance simulator software: https://www.polarinstruments.com/products/cits/Si8000.html

TNT MMTL free impedance simulator software: https://mmtl.sourceforge.net/

Z-Zero impedance simulator software: https://www.z-zero.com/

FEMM general 2D field solver: https://www.femm.info/wiki/HomePage

CHAPTER 13:

Power Distribution Network Design Methodologies by Istvan Novak IEC 2008, ISBN 978-1931695657

Frequency Domain Target Impedance Method for Bypass Capacitor Selection for Power Distribution Systems, Larry D Smith, DesignCon 2006: http://pdnpowerintegrity.com/wp-content/uploads/2018/05/DesCon_2006-Frequency-Domain-Target-Impedance-Method-for-Caps.pdf

SonnetLite simulation software: https://www.sonnetsoftware.com/products/lite/download.html

Rogue Wave Estimation in PDNs using the Multi-Tone Technique, PCDandF magazine, March 2022, Istvan Nagy: https://digital.pcea.net/issue/march-2022/

Electrical and Thermal Consequences of Non-Flat Impedance Profiles, DesignCon 2016, Jae Young Choi, Ethan Koether, Istvan Novak

ASCO optimizer for QUCS: https://asco.sourceforge.net/

Power Integrity Template for QUCS: http://www.buenos.extra.hu/download/PowerIntegrityDesign2_prj.zip

S-Par Smoothie, S-parameter filtering and manipulation Excel Template for PDN measurements: http://www.buenos.extra.hu/download/spar_smoothie.zip

Altera/Intel PDN Tool: https://www.intel.com/content/www/us/en/docs/programmable/683073/current/pdn-design-tool.html

CHAPTER 14:

Gantt Project, a free project management software: https://www.ganttproject.biz/

CHAPTER 15:

Cadence Allegro PCB layout design software: https://www.cadence.com/en_US/home/tools/pcb-design-and-analysis/pcb-layout/allegro-pcb-designer.html

Cadence Allegro Viewer, a free PCB layout Viewer software: https://www.cadence.com/en_US/home/tools/pcb-design-and-analysis/allegro-downloads-start.html

Altium PCB layout design software: https://www.altium.com/
Mentor Expedition PCB layout design software: https://eda.sw.siemens.com/en-US/pcb/xpedition-enterprise/
KiCad free PCB layout design software: https://www.kicad.org/
"Life beyond 10 Gbps: Localize or Fail!", article about localization by Yuriy Shlepnev at Simberian Inc. https://www.simberian.com/AppNotes/InterconnectLocalization.pdf

CHAPTER 16:

DediProg SF100 SPI programmer: https://www.dediprog.com/product/SF100
TotalPhase Aardvark SPI debugger: https://www.totalphase.com/products/aardvark-i2cspi/
TopJTAG Probe JTAG logic analyzer software: http://www.topjtag.com/probe/
LoadSlammer tester dongle: https://loadslammer.com/product/lsp200/
Dye and Pry testing at Process Sciences Inc.: https://process-sciences.com/Dye_and_Pry_Test_Service

CHAPTER 17:

Mini-Circuits splitter/combiner devices: https://www.minicircuits.com/WebStore/Splitters.html
Keysight E5052B Signal Source Analyzer: https://www.keysight.com/us/en/product/E5052B/signal-source-analyzer-ssa.html
Wilder-Tech QSFPDD-TPA2.92-HCB-P test fixture: https://shop.wilder-tech.com/product_p/640-0899-021.htm
GigaTest Labs differential wafer probes: https://gigatest.com/probes/
GigaTest Labs GTL 4060 VNA probing station: https://gigatest.com/probe-stations/
Delta-L QUCS template with fitted attenuation: http://www.buenos.extra.hu/download/Delta_L_prj.zip
Omicron Lab Bode-100 VNA for PDN measurements: https://www.omicron-lab.com/products/vector-network-analysis/bode-100
Picotest J2113A amplifier: https://www.picotest.com/products_J2113A.html

Index

Taylor & Francis eBooks

www.taylorfrancis.com

A single destination for eBooks from Taylor & Francis with increased functionality and an improved user experience to meet the needs of our customers.

90,000+ eBooks of award-winning academic content in Humanities, Social Science, Science, Technology, Engineering, and Medical written by a global network of editors and authors.

TAYLOR & FRANCIS EBOOKS OFFERS:

A streamlined experience for our library customers

A single point of discovery for all of our eBook content

Improved search and discovery of content at both book and chapter level

REQUEST A FREE TRIAL

support@taylorfrancis.com

Milton Keynes UK
Ingram Content Group UK Ltd.
UKHW020837141024
449570UK00003B/10